P9-BZG-033

TJ6B-RNPZ-53G1-CR2A-5I53

IMPORTANT

HERE IS YOUR REGISTRATION CODE TO ACCESS MCGRAW-HILL PREMIUM CONTENT AND MCGRAW-HILL ONLINE RESOURCES

For key premium online resources you need THIS CODE to gain access. Once the code is entered, you will be able to use the web resources for the length of your course.

Access is provided only if you have purchased a new book.

If the registration code is missing from this book, the registration screen on our website, and within your WebCT or Blackboard course will tell you how to obtain your new code. Your registration code can be used only once to establish access. It is not transferable

To gain access to these online resources

1. USE your web browser to go to: **www.mhhe.com/noe5e**

2. CLICK on "First Time User"

3. ENTER the Registration Code printed on the tear-off bookmark on the right

4. After you have entered your registration code, click on "Register"

5. FOLLOW the instructions to setup your personal UserID and Password

6. WRITE your UserID and Password down for future reference. Keep it in a safe place.

If your course is using WebCT or Blackboard, you'll be able to use this code to access the McGraw-Hill content within your instructor's online course.

To gain access to the McGraw-Hill content in your instructor's WebCT or Blackboard course simply log into the course with the user ID and Password provided by your instructor. Enter the registration code exactly as it appears to the right when prompted by the system. You will only need to use this code the first time you click on McGraw-Hill content.

These instructions are specifically for student access. Instructors are not required to register via the above instructions.

The McGraw·Hill Companies

Mc Graw Hill McGraw-Hill Irwin

Thank you, and welcome to your McGraw-Hill/Irwin Online Resources.

Noe
Human Resource Management, 5/E
0-07-310049-8

REGISTRATION CODE
REGISTRATION CODE

The McGraw-Hill Companies

Mc Graw Hill McGraw-Hill Irwin

Human Resource Management

GAINING A
COMPETITIVE
ADVANTAGE

Human Resource Management

GAINING A COMPETITIVE ADVANTAGE

Fifth Edition

RAYMOND A. NOE
The Ohio State University

JOHN R. HOLLENBECK
Michigan State University

BARRY GERHART
University of Wisconsin–Madison

PATRICK M. WRIGHT
Cornell University

Boston   Burr Ridge, IL   Dubuque, IA   Madison, WI   New York   San Francisco   St. Louis
Bangkok   Bogotá   Caracas   Kuala Lumpur   Lisbon   London   Madrid   Mexico City
Milan   Montreal   New Delhi   Santiago   Seoul   Singapore   Sydney   Taipei   Toronto

McGraw-Hill
Irwin

HUMAN RESOURCE MANAGEMENT: GAINING A COMPETITIVE ADVANTAGE

Published by McGraw-Hill/Irwin, a business unit of The McGraw-Hill Companies, Inc., 1221 Avenue of the Americas, New York, NY, 10020. Copyright © 2006, 2003, 2000, 1997, 1994 by The McGraw-Hill Companies, Inc. All rights reserved. No part of this publication may be reproduced or distributed in any form or by any means, or stored in a database or retrieval system, without the prior written consent of The McGraw-Hill Companies, Inc., including, but not limited to, in any network or other electronic storage or transmission, or broadcast for distance learning.

Some ancillaries, including electronic and print components, may not be available to customers outside the United States.

This book is printed on acid-free paper.

2 3 4 5 6 7 8 9 0 DOW/DOW 0 9 8 7 6 5

ISBN 0-07-111628-1

www.mhhe.com

In tribute to the life and ways of my dad
Raymond J. Noe
— R. A. N.

To my parents, Harold and Elizabeth, my wife, Patty,
and my children, Jennifer, Marie, Timothy, and Jeffrey
— J. R. H.

To my parents, Robert and Shirley, my wife, Heather,
and my children, Chris and Annie
— B. G.

To my parents, Patricia and Paul, my wife, Mary, and
my sons, Michael and Matthew
— P. M. W.

About the Authors

Raymond A. Noe is the Robert and Anne Hoyt Professor of Management at The Ohio State University. He was previously a professor in the Department of Management at Michigan State University and the Industrial Relations Center of the Carlson School of Management, University of Minnesota. He received his BS in psychology from The Ohio State University and his MA and PhD in psychology from Michigan State University. Professor Noe conducts research and teaches undergraduate as well as MBA and PhD students in human resource management, managerial skills, quantitative methods, human resource information systems, training, employee development, and organizational behavior. He has published articles in the *Academy of Management Journal, Academy of Management Review, Journal of Applied Psychology, Journal of Vocational Behavior,* and *Personnel Psychology.* Professor Noe is currently on the editorial boards of several journals including *Personnel Psychology, Journal of Applied Psychology,* and *Journal of Organizational Behavior.* Professor Noe has received awards for his teaching and research excellence, including the Herbert G. Heneman Distinguished Teaching Award in 1991 and the Ernest J. McCormick Award for Distinguished Early Career Contribution from the Society for Industrial and Organizational Psychology in 1993. He is also a fellow of the Society for Industrial and Organizational Psychology.

John R. Hollenbeck received his PhD in Management from New York University in 1984, and he is currently the Eli Broad Professor of Management at the Eli Broad Graduate School of Business Administration at Michigan State University. Dr. Hollenbeck served as the acting editor at *Organizational Behavior and Human Decision Processes* in 1995, the editor of *Personnel Psychology* from 1996 to 2002, and currently serves as the associate editor of *Decision Sciences.* Prior to serving as editor, he served on the editorial board of these journals, as well as the boards of the *Academy of Management Journal, Academy of Management Review, Journal of Applied Psychology,* and the *Journal of Management.* Dr. Hollenbeck has published over 60 articles and book chapters on the topics of team decision-making and work motivation, much of which was funded by the Office of Naval Research and the Air Force Office of Scientific Research. According to the Institute for Scientific Research this body of work has been cited over 1,000 times. Dr. Hollenbeck was the first recipient of the Ernest J. McCormick Award for Early Contributions to the field of Industrial and Organizational Psychology in 1992 and is a Fellow of the American Psychological Association.

Barry Gerhart is the Bruce R. Ellig Distinguished Chair in Pay and Organizational Effectiveness and Director of the Strategic Human Resources Program at the University of Wisconsin–Madison. He was previously the Frances Hampton Currey Chair in Organizational Studies at the Owen School of Management at Vanderbilt University and Associate Professor and Chairman of the Department of Human Resource Studies, School of Industrial and Labor Relations at Cornell University. He received his BS in psychology from Bowling Green State University in 1979 and his PhD in industrial relations from the University of Wisconsin–Madison in 1985. His research is in the areas of compensation/ rewards, staffing, and employee attitudes. Professor Gerhart has worked with a variety of organizations, including TRW, Corning, and Bausch & Lomb. His work has appeared in the *Academy of Management Journal, Industrial Relations, Industrial and Labor Relations Review, Journal of Applied Psychology, Personnel Psychology,* and *Handbook of Industrial and Organizational Psychology,* and he has served on the editorial boards of the *Academy of Management Journal, Industrial and Labor Relations Review,* and the *Journal of Applied Psychology.* He was a corecipient of the 1991 Scholarly Achievement Award, Human Resources Division, Academy of Management.

Patrick M. Wright is Professor of Human Resource Studies and Director of the Center for Advanced Human Resource Studies in the School of Industrial and Labor Relations at Cornell University. He was formerly Associate Professor of Management and Coordinator of the Master of Science in Human Resource Management program in the College of Business Administration and Graduate School of Business at Texas A&M University. He holds a BA in psychology from Wheaton College and an MBA and a PhD in organizational behavior/human resource management from Michigan State University. He teaches, conducts research, and consults in the areas of personnel selection, employee motivation, and strategic human resource management. His research articles have appeared in journals such as the *Academy of Management Journal, Journal of Applied Psychology, Organizational Behavior and Human Decision Processes, Journal of Management,* and *Human Resource Management Review.* He has served on the editorial boards of *Journal of Applied Psychology* and *Journal of Management* and also serves as an ad hoc reviewer for *Organizational Behavior and Human Decision Processes, Academy of Management Journal,* and *Academy of Management Review.* In addition, he has consulted for a number of organizations, including Whirlpool Corporation, Amoco Oil Company, and the North Carolina State government.

Preface

If you have watched television or read any newspapers or magazines, you have undoubtedly come across reports dealing with ethics and legal challenges to business practices (such as the discrimination lawsuits against Wal-Mart), offshoring and outsourcing of jobs (such as IBM plans to send 5,000 jobs to India), and changes in benefits and pension plans (consider Whole Foods' health care plan, which has a large deductible of $1,500 but allows employees to decide how to use the monies the company deposits in their health care account). Also, companies such as J. M. Smucker (the jam and jelly company), the Container Store (the storage and organization store), and Edward Jones (financial services firm) give employees a chance to make a difference at work and as a result have received positive media attention for being included on *Fortune* magazine's list of "The 100 Best Companies to Work For." These media reports highlight how choices that companies have made about human resource management practices influence employees, managers, shareholders, the community, and ultimately, the success of the company.

Companies are continuing to reexamine their business priorities and find ways to provide more value to customers, shareholders, and employees. Traditionally, the concept of value has been considered to be the primary concern of finance and accounting. However, we believe that how human resources are managed is crucial to the long-term value of a company and ultimately to its survival. Our definition of value includes not only profits but also employee growth and satisfaction, additional employment opportunities, protection of the environment, and contributions to community programs. Managers must make decisions about how to allocate resources across the different organization functions, including marketing, production, finance, accounting, information systems, and human resources, and how to ensure that they contribute to achievement of the company's goals and strategies. All company functions are being scrutinized for the value they add.

We believe that all aspects of human resource management—including how companies interact with the environment; acquire, prepare, develop, and compensate employees; and design and evaluate work—can help companies meet their competitive challenges and create value. Meeting challenges is necessary to create value and to gain a competitive advantage.

The Competitive Challenges

The challenges that organizations face today can be grouped into three categories:

- **The sustainability challenge.** Sustainability refers to the ability of a company to survive and exceed in a dynamic competitive environment. Sustainability depends on how well a company meets the needs of those who have an interest in seeing that the company succeeds. Challenges to sustainability include the ability to deal with economic and social changes, engage in responsible and ethical business practices, provide high quality products and services, and develop methods and measures (also known as metrics) to determine if the company is meeting stakeholder needs. Companies in today's economy use mergers and acquisitions, growth, and downsizing to successfully compete. Companies rely on skilled workers to be productive, creative, and innovative and to provide high quality customer service, and their work is demanding and companies cannot guarantee job security. One issue is how to attract and retain a committed, productive workforce in turbulent economic conditions that offer opportunity for financial success, but can also turn sour, making every employee expendable. Forward-looking businesses are capitalizing on the strengths of a diverse workforce. The examples of Enron and World-Com provide a vivid example of how sustainability depends on ethical and responsible business practices, including the management of human resources. Another important issue is how to meet financial objectives through meeting both customer and employee needs. To meet the sustainability challenge companies must engage in human resource management practices that address short-term needs but help to ensure the long-term success of the firm. The development and choice of human resource management practices should support business goals and strategy.

- **The global challenge.** Companies must be prepared to compete with companies from around the world either in the United States or abroad. Companies must both defend their domestic markets from foreign competitors and broaden their scope to encompass global markets. Recent threats to and successes of U.S. businesses (consider the semiconductor and steel industries) have proven that globalization is a continuing challenge

- **The technology challenge.** Using new technologies such as computer-aided manufacturing, virtual reality, expert systems, and the Internet can give companies an edge. New technologies can result in employees "working smarter" as well as providing higher-quality products and more efficient services to customers. Companies that have realized the greatest gains from new technology have human resource management practices that support the use of technology to create what is known as high-performance work systems. Work, training, programs, and reward systems often need to be reconfigured to support employees' use of new technology. The three important aspects of high performance work systems are (1) human resources and their capabilities, (2) new technology and its opportunities, and (3) efficient work structures and policies that allow employees and technology to interact. Companies are also using e-HRM (electronic HRM) applications to give employees more ownership of the employment relationship through the ability to enroll in and participate in training programs, change benefits, communicate with coworkers and customers online, and work "virtually" with peers in geographically different locations.

We believe that organizations must successfully deal with these challenges to create and maintain value, and the key to facing these challenges is a motivated, well-trained, and committed workforce.

The Changing Role of the Human Resource Management Function

The human resource management (HRM) profession and practices have undergone substantial change and redefinition. Many articles written in both the academic and practitioner literature have been critical of the traditional HRM function. Unfortunately, in many organizations HRM services are not providing value but instead are mired down in managing trivial administrative tasks. Where this is true, HRM departments can be replaced with new technology or outsourced to a vendor who can provide higher-quality services at a lower cost. Although this recommendation is indeed somewhat extreme (and threatening to both HRM practitioners and those who teach human resource management!), it does demonstrate that companies need to ensure that their HRM functions are creating value for the firm.

Technology should be used where appropriate to automate routine activities, and managers should concentrate on HRM activities that can add substantial value to the company. Consider employee benefits: Technology is available to automate the process by which employees enroll in benefits programs and to keep detailed records of benefits usage. This use of technology frees up time for the manager to focus on activities that can create value for the firm (such as how to control health care costs and reduce workers' compensation claims).

Although the importance of some HRM departments is being debated, everyone agrees on the need to successfully manage human resources for a company to maximize its competitiveness. Three themes emerge from our conversations with managers and our review of research on HRM practices. First, in today's flatter organizations, managers themselves are becoming more responsible for HRM practices. Second, most managers believe that their HRM departments are not well respected because of a perceived lack of competence, business sense, and contact with operations. Third, many managers believe that for HRM practices to be effective they need to be related to the strategic direction of the business. This text emphasizes how HRM practices can and should contribute to business goals and help to improve product and service quality and effectiveness.

Our intent is to provide students with the background to be successful HRM professionals, to manage human resources effectively, and to be knowledgeable consumers of HRM products. Managers must be able to identify effective HRM practices to purchase these services from a consultant, to work with the HRM department, or to design and implement them personally. The text emphasizes how a manager can more effectively manage human resources and highlights important issues in current HRM practice.

We think this book represents a valuable approach to teaching human resource management for several reasons:

- The text draws from the diverse research, teaching, and consulting experiences of four authors. They have taught human resource management to undergraduates, traditional day MBA students as a required and elective course, and more experienced managers and professional employees in weekend and evening MBA programs. The teamwork approach gives a depth and breadth to the coverage that is not found in other texts.
- Human resource management is viewed as critical to the success of a business. The text emphasizes how the HRM function, as well as the management of human resources, can help companies gain a competitive advantage.
- The book discusses current issues such as e-HRM, finding and keeping talented employees, diversity, and offshoring, all of which have a major impact on business and HRM practice.
- Strategic human resource management is introduced early in the book and integrated throughout the text.
- Examples of how new technologies are being used to improve the efficiency and effectiveness of HRM practices are provided throughout the text.

Organization

Human Resource Management: Gaining a Competitive Advantage includes an introductory chapter (Chapter 1) and five parts.

Chapter 1 provides a detailed discussion of the global, new economy, stakeholder, and work system challenges that influence companies' abilities to successfully meet the needs of shareholders, customers, employees, and other stakeholders. We discuss how the management of human resources can help companies meet the competitive challenges.

Part 1 includes a discussion of the environmental forces that companies face in attempting to capitalize on their human resources as a means to gain competitive advantage. The environmental forces include the strategic direction of the business, the legal environment, and the type of work performed, and physical arrangement of the work.

A key focus of the strategic human resource management chapter is highlighting the role that staffing, performance management, training and development, and compensation play in different types of business strategies. A key focus of the legal chapter is enhancing managers' understanding of laws related to sexual harassment, affirmative action, and accommodations for disabled employees. The various types of discrimination and ways they have been interpreted by the courts are discussed. The chapter on analysis and design of work emphasizes how work systems can improve company competitiveness by alleviating job stress and by improving employees' motivation and satisfaction with their jobs.

Part 2 deals with the acquisition and preparation of human resources, including human resource planning and recruitment, selection, and training. The human resource planning chapter illustrates the process of developing a human resource plan. Also, the strengths and weaknesses of staffing options such as outsourcing, use of contingent workers, and downsizing are discussed. Strategies for recruiting talented employees are emphasized. The selection chapter emphasizes ways to minimize errors in employee selection and placement to improve the company's competitive position. Selection method standards such as validity and reliability are discussed in easily understandable terms without compromising the technical complexity of these issues. The chapter discusses selection methods such as interviews and various types of tests (including personality, honesty, and drug tests) and compares them on measures of validity, reliability, utility, and legality.

We discuss the components of effective training systems and the manager's role in determining employees' readiness for training, creating a positive learning environment, and ensuring that training is used on the job. The advantages and disadvantages of different training methods are described, such as e-learning.

Part 3 explores how companies can determine the value of employees and capitalize on their talents through retention and development strategies. The performance management chapter examines the strengths and weaknesses of performance management methods that use ratings, objectives, or behaviors. The employee development chapter introduces the student to how assessment, job experiences, formal courses, and mentoring relationships are used to develop employees. The chapter on retention and separation discusses how managers can maximize employee productivity and satisfaction to avoid absenteeism and turnover. The use of employee surveys to monitor job and organizational characteristics that affect satisfaction and subsequently retention is emphasized.

Part 4 covers rewarding and compensating human resources, including designing pay structures, recognizing individual contributions, and providing benefits. Here we explore how managers should decide the pay rate for different jobs, given the company's compensation strategy and the worth of jobs. The advantages and disadvantages of merit pay, gainsharing, and skill-based pay are discussed. The benefits chapter highlights the different types of employer-provided benefits and discusses how benefit costs can be contained. International comparisons of compensation and benefit practices are provided.

Part 5 covers special topics in human resource management, including labor–management relations, international HRM, and managing the HRM function. The collective bargaining and labor relations chapter focuses on traditional issues in labor–management relations, such as union structure and membership, the organizing process, and contract negotiations; it also discusses new union agendas and less adversarial approaches to labor–management relations. Social and political changes, such as introduction of the euro currency in the European Community, are discussed in the chapter on global human resource management. Selecting, preparing, and rewarding employees for foreign assignments are also discussed. The text concludes with a chapter that emphasizes how HRM practices should be aligned to help the company meet its business objectives. The chapter emphasizes that the HRM function needs to have a customer focus to be effective.

Video cases at the end of the book integrate the concepts presented. These cases are intended to give students practice dealing with real HRM issues that companies are facing.

Acknowledgments

As this book enters its fifth edition, it is important to acknowledge those who started it all. The first edition of this book would not have been possible if not for the entrepreneurial spirit of two individuals. Bill Schoof, president of Austen Press, gave us the resources and had the confidence that four unproven textbook writers could provide a new perspective for teaching human resource management. John Weimeister, our editor, provided us with valuable marketing information, helped us in making major decisions regarding the book, and made writing this book an enjoyable process. We continue to enjoy John's friendship and hospitality at national meetings. We were fortunate to have the opportunity in the fifth edition to work with John again. Sarah Reed continued on our team as developmental editor. Sarah's suggestions, patience, gentle prodding, and organizational ability kept the author team focused and allowed us to meet publication deadlines. Many thanks to Marlena Pechan, project manager, for her careful review of the revised manuscript. Amit Shah of Frostburg State University wrote a first-class Instructor's Manual, PowerPoint presentation, and Test Bank, and he developed important content and study material for the OLC. Also, many thanks go to Interactive Learning LLC for their help with content for the OLC.

We would also like to thank the professors who gave of their time to review the text to help craft this fifth edition. Their helpful comments and suggestions during manuscript reviews have greatly helped to enhance this edition:

Kathleen Barnes
University of Wisconsin, Superior

Chris Berger
Purdue University

James Browne
University of Southern Colorado

Nancy Bereman
Wichita State University

Carol Bibly
Triton College

Gerald Calvasina
Southern Utah University

Martin Carrigan
University of Findlay

Donna Cooke
Florida Atlantic University, Davis

Craig Cowles
Bridgewater State College

Shannon Davis
North Carolina State University

Roger Dean
Washington & Lee University

Jennifer Dose
Messiah College

Angela Farrar
University of Nevada, Las Vegas

Art Fischer
Pittsburgh State University

Bonnie Fox Garrity
D'Youville College

Sonia Goltz
Michigan Technological University

Ken Gross
University of Oklahoma, Norman

Alan Heffner
James Monroe Center

Gary Hensel
McHenry County College

Kim Hester
Arkansas State University

Nancy Higgins
Montgomery College, Rockville

Fred Hughes
Faulkner University

Sanford Jacoby
University of California, Los Angeles

Frank Jeffries
University of Alaska, Anchorage

Vonda Laughlin
Carson-Newman College

Helen LaVan
DePaul University

Patricia Martina
University of Texas, San Antonio

Lisa McConnell
Oklahoma State University

Stuart Milne
Georgia Institute of Technology

Jim Morgan
California State University, Chico

Gary Murray
Rose State College

Teresa Palmer
Illinois State University

Mary Ellen Rosetti
Hudson Valley Community College

Miyako Schanely
Jefferson Community College

Robert Schappe
University of Michigan, Dearborn

Mark Smith
Mississippi Gulf Coast Community College, Gulfport

Tom Timmerman
Tennessee Technology University

George Tompson
University of Tampa

K. J. Tullis
University of Central Oklahoma

Kim Wade
Washington State University

Daniel Yazak
Montana State University, Billings

We would also like to thank the reviewers and focus group participants who made important suggestions for previous editions of this text. Their comments have helped to develop the book from edition to edition:

Alison Barber
Michigan State University

Robert Figler
University of Akron

Walter Coleman
Florida Southern College

Bob Graham
Sacred Heart University

John Hannon
SUNY—Buffalo

Fred Heidrich
Black Hills State University

Ken Kovach
George Mason University

Nick Mathys
DePaul University

Mark Roehling
Michigan State University

Mary Ellen Rosetti
Hudson Valley Community College

Cynthia Sutton
Indiana University, South Bend

Steve Thomas
Southwest Missouri State University

Dan Turban
University of Missouri, Columbia

Richard Arvey
University of Minnesota

Ron Beaulieu
Central Michigan University

Chris Berger
Purdue University

Sarah Bowman
Idaho State University

Charles Braun
University of Kentucky

Georgia Chao
Michigan State University

Michael Crant
University of Notre Dame

John Delery
University of Arkansas

Tom Dougherty
University of Missouri

Cynthia Fukami
University of Denver

Dan Gallagher
James Madison University

Donald G. Gardner
University of Colorado at Colorado Springs

Terri Griffith
Washington University

Bob Hatfield
Indiana University

Rob Heneman
Ohio State University

Wayne Hockwater
Florida State University

Denise Tanguay Hoyer
Eastern Michigan University

Natalie J. Hunter
Portland State University

Gwen Jones
Fairleigh Dickinson University

Marianne Koch
University of Oregon

Tom Kolenko
Kennesaw State College

Larry Mainstone
Valparaiso University

Nicholas Mathys
DePaul University

Cheri Ostroff
Teachers College Columbia University

Robert Paul
Kansas State University

Sam Rabinowitz
Rutgers University

Katherine Ready
University of Wisconsin

Mike Ritchie
University of South Carolina

Josh Schwarz
Miami University, Ohio

Christina Shalley
Georgia Tech

Richard Simpson
University of Utah

Scott Snell
Cornell University

Charles Vance
Loyola Marymount University

Raymond A. Noe
John R. Hollenbeck
Barry Gerhart
Patrick M. Wright
October 2004

A Guided Tour

The Fifth Edition of Human Resource Management: Gaining a Competitive Advantage was developed to teach students how to face and meet a variety of challenges within their organizations and how to gain a competitive advantage for their companies.

Throughout this text, the pedagogy focuses on HRM practices and strategies companies can employ to be competitive. These boxes, cases, and applications are found in every chapter and provide excellent real-business examples to underscore key concepts throughout the text.

Please take a moment to learn about this new edition and its exciting enhancements by paging through this visual guide outlining the text's new features.

"Competing through Sustainability" boxes discuss how companies succeed in a competitive environment considering aspects of social responsibility like environmental and employment issues.

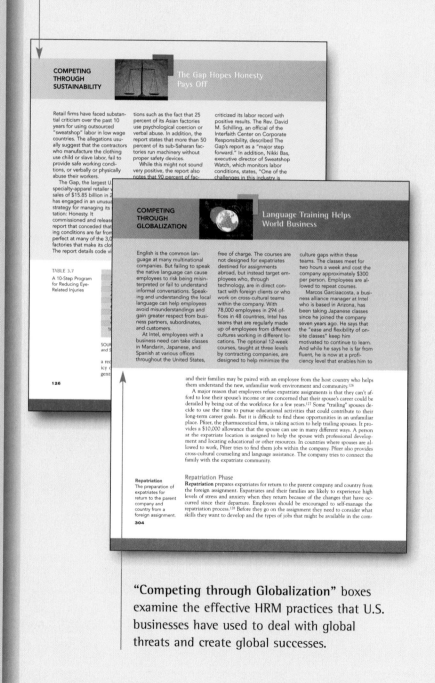

"Competing through Globalization" boxes examine the effective HRM practices that U.S. businesses have used to deal with global threats and create global successes.

The ability to use content validation in small sample settings makes it generally more applicable than criterion-related validation. However, content validation has two limitations.[8] First, one assumption behind content validation is that the person who is to be hired must have the knowledge, skills, or abilities at the time she is hired. Thus it is not appropriate to use content validation in settings where the applicant is expected to learn the job in a formal training program conducted after selection.

Second, because subjective judgment plays such a large role in content validation, it is critical to minimize the amount of inference involved on the part of judges. Thus the judges' ratings need to be made with respect to relatively concrete and observable behaviors (for example, "applicant detects common construction errors" or "arranges optimal subcontractor schedules"). Content validation would be inappropriate for assessing more abstract characteristics such as intelligence, leadership capacity, and integrity.

Generalizability

Generalizability
The degree to which the validity of a selection method established in one context extends to other contexts.

Generalizability is defined as the degree to which the validity of a selection method established in one context extends to other contexts. There are three primary "contexts" over which we might like to generalize: different situations (jobs or organizations), different samples of people, and different time periods. Just as reliability is necessary but not sufficient for validity, validity is necessary but not sufficient for generalizability.

Strategic Use of HRM

A good example of how strategic differences translate into different hiring policies can be seen in the different approaches taken by two of the country's largest booksellers, Barnes and Noble versus Borders. Although selling books would seem to be a pretty set task, in fact, there are major differences between these two franchises in philosophy and strategy. In a very real sense, the differences between these two organizations is manifested most clearly in hiring practices, which in turn influence customer service. Barnes and Noble is the more traditional retailer and focuses on stocking the most popular books at the lowest prices. The goal for employees is to get the right book into the customer's hand, and then execute the financial transaction as quickly as possible. Mitchell Klipper, CEO, notes that "our booksellers are nice, educated people. They wear collared shirts and have a cleaner look, as opposed to tattoos and T-shirts."

In contrast, Julie Johnson, manager of the Borders Michigan Avenue store in Chicago, notes, "We want our people to be comfortable and to show their personality. We pride ourselves on diversity." As a consequence, Borders employees dress much less formally, and are almost famous for their tattoos, piercings, and wide-ranging fashion sense. This diversity is then reinforced by the kinds of books stocked, in the sense that unlike Barnes and Noble, where the stock is almost the same for all stores, roughly 50 percent of the stock at any one Borders store is unique to that store. Store holdings are idiosyncratic and based upon the input of employees, who are just as likely to shape the customers' preferences as respond to them. Although these are radically different recipes for the same dish, in their own way each is a viable business model, and to some extent, this limits the direct competition each faces in the labor market. In fact, as one Borders manager notes, "It's surprising how few people we hire from Barnes and Noble; their environment is very different from ours."

SOURCE: J. A. Trachtenberg, "Investors Brace for a Plot Twist from Barnes and Noble," *The Wall Street Journal* (May 27, 2004), p. A1; S. F. Gale, "The Bookstore Battle," *Workforce*, January 2003, pp. 51–53.

NEW

"The Strategic Use of HRM" sections within the chapters highlight examples of how real companies have developed or executed competitive HR strategies to create value.

"Competing through Technology" boxes discuss how companies and employees work smarter by using new technologies and e-HRM applications.

COMPETING THROUGH TECHNOLOGY

Technology Makes Training an Easy Sale at Cisco Systems

Cisco Systems of San Jose, California, is a leading company that develops networking for the Internet. Cisco Systems grew from nothing in 1986 to a peak of 46,000 employees worldwide. However, Cisco fell on hard times during the 2001 economic downturn as the company's value fell by $430 billion and the company had to lay off more than 4,000 employees. Despite the downturn, Cisco did not cut back on its commitment to employee learning. CEO John Chambers believed that e-learning was an important force for helping Cisco recover from its economic woes, for creating strong ties with information technology, and for demonstrating real business results. It doesn't hurt that the more e-learning that companies use, the more demand there will be for the video, voice, and data network products that Cisco provides! Cisco believes that the future of the Internet is the convergence of voice, video, and data (telephone, television, computer) networks into one common network.

Through a partnership with the company's Internet Learning Solutions Group, the Information Technology Unit, and Chambers, the Cisco Media Network was developed. This collaboration was necessary to ensure a match between the company's tools and technology infrastructure, its business purpose, and effective learning principles. The Cisco Media Network is a large, private broadcasting network linked via satellite to a worldwide grid of servers. The network serves about 1,000 users. The content comes from business units, technology groups, and product marketing groups. The network broadcasts include the company's annual meeting, video briefings by executives, and learning portals for employees and customers. The Media Network allows Cisco to broadcast high-quality

learning approach. *Blended learning* combines online learning, face-to-face instruction, and other methods for distributing learning content and instruction. CAN, a Chicago-based company with employees across the United States and Canada, developed a blended learning approach.[90] Live seminars kick off a class and conclude it. But in between are online case studies, question-and-answer sessions, and simulations. Trainees work in teams of 10 people. They communicate with each other through chat rooms, threaded discussions, and virtual meetings. For example, employees might be assigned to come up with 10 questions. The instructor answers the questions, and the trainees discuss them. Trainees may be asked to put ideas into practice, using message rooms to provide updates and ask questions. Coaches or mentors may guide the trainees to additional reference materials. To be certified that they have completed training, trainees must complete an accountability plan. The plan summarizes actions that the trainees will take to prove to their managers that they have achieved proficiency.

Learning Portals. Learning portals are websites or online learning centers that provide, via e-commerce transactions, access to training courses, services, and online learning communities from many sources.[91] Learning portals provide not only one-stop shopping for a variety of training programs from different vendors but also access to online classes. Learning portals may also offer services to track employees' enroll-

Human Resource Planning and Recruitment

Objectives After reading this chapter, you should be able to:

1. Discuss how to align a company's strategic direction with its human resource planning.

2. Determine the labor demand for workers in various job categories.

3. Discuss the advantages and disadvantages of various ways of eliminating a labor surplus and avoiding a labor shortage.

4. Describe the various recruitment policies that organizations adopt to make job vacancies more attractive.

5. List the various sources from which job applicants can be drawn, their relative advantages and disadvantages, and the methods for evaluating them.

6. Explain the recruiter's role in the recruitment process, the limits the recruiter faces, and the opportunities available.

Bill's To-Do List

Gates keeps a tally of the top 50 tech initiatives he is responsible for pursuing throughout the company. Here are his clients on what is known at Microsoft as simply "The List."

SEARCH Look out, Google. Microsoft plans to put search technology into the operating system. And it will let people search the Web and their PCs all at once.

SECURITY Spam and viruses and worms, oh my. Windows draws attacks like no other, and the company has drawn fire for not doing enough to plug security holes. Gates vows to do better.

TELEPHONY Forget old-fashioned phone calls. Gates wants to bring computer innovation to telecom. Think video voice mails. Or instant messaging with talk, not text.

VOICE RECOGNITION Who wants to type? Microsoft is developing voice recognition so you won't have to. It's also developing software to read you your e-mails or Word documents.

FILE SYSTEM Finding things on a PC is too cumbersome. New software will let you find not just digital photos but, for example, e-mails from the people in them.

DIGITAL-RIGHTS MANAGEMENT Photos, music, and video are going digital. Microsoft is developing software to let people use that content without violating intellectual-property rights.

Restructuring the nature of work within a company can increase its efficiency and effectiveness. How did this decentralization of Microsoft's structure allow groups to work more responsibly and competitively?

Enter the World of Business

Structural Realignment at Microsoft: Opening New Windows of Opportunity

Throughout the 1990s, revenue growth at Microsoft averaged over 30 percent per year, making it one of the most successful business organizations in the world. However, with success comes new challenges, and both external and internal pressures have created problems that have cut into Microsoft's dominance. In fact, over the last five years, growth has been in the single digits. In terms of external pressures, Linux stands as a free, open source code that directly challenges Microsoft's operating system. IBM is also challenging Microsoft with its emphasis on customer service and system integration that allows clients to bypass Microsoft's bundles of integrated products.

Internally, as the organization increased in size and scope, the decision-making process at Microsoft was slowing to a crawl, with some suggesting that the new operating system known as "Longhorn" should be renamed "Long Wait." Also, Microsoft experienced turnover among key personnel, many of whom became millionaires as the company grew, but whose intrinsic motivation was low because they did not feel that they had enough autonomy in their jobs. As

one manager noted, "In the past, the system was optimized for people to get stuff done. Now, everybody is always preparing for a meeting."

In order to turn this situation around, CEO Bill Ballmer took unprecedented steps in strategically restructuring the organization to respond to these new competitive pressures. The question guiding this reorganization was how best to divvy up the 55,000 Microsoft employees and define their jobs so that innovation and productivity could be maximized, while turnover and bureaucratic impediments could be minimized. Turning first to the organization's structure, it was clear that Microsoft was too centralized given its current size, and that too much decision-making authority rested with the CEO and its founder, Bill Gates.

Ballmer wanted to decentralize the organization and create a large number of semiautonomous business divisions (e.g., a Personal Computer Division, a Server Division, a Gaming Division) that had responsibility for their own profit and loss figures. Gates initially resisted this move, however, because he felt that all Microsoft products had to work seamlessly together, and independent divisions would not provide for effective coordination and collaboration across units. Ballmer realized, "We'd have to come up with a structure unlike anything out there, to simultaneously give divisions enough autonomy to manage

---

Learning objectives at the beginning of each chapter inform students about the key concepts they should understand after reading through the chapter.

The chapter-opening stories present a real business problem or issue that provides background for the issues discussed in the chapter.

"Finding and Keeping the Best Employees" information appears throughout the text, showing the various strategies through which companies hire and retain talent.

---

with close to 30,000 employees, was organized into 28 separate regional centers, each with its own Human Resource Department. Each department operated independently, and thus they all had different technologies, different services, and different forms and procedures for all sorts of HR activities including recruiting. This precluded any form of coordinated activity across regions and also created huge redundancies and inefficiencies. In 2002, the organization restructured its Human Resource Department and went from being a decentralized and divisional structure to a more centralized and functional structure (see Chapter 4 for a discussion of these different dimensions of structure). Job descriptions and recruiting practices were standardized, and all existing employee's skill sets were entered into a central database to promote internal movement within the organization. One year later, the time it took to fill a vacancy went from 30 days to 20 days, and the cost per hire dropped from $1,100 to $900. Much of this was attributed to the more efficient utilization of internal applicants.[66]

Finding and Keeping the Best Employees

The value of a strong internal hiring system can also be seen in the experience of Whirlpool. In 2001, it was difficult for someone inside the company to know what jobs were or were not available within the huge manufacturing conglomerate. The job posting system was a paper and pencil process that was antiquated technologically and organized regionally, making it difficult and time consuming to obtain information about positions out of state. In order to rectify this situation, the company created a new Web-based system that allowed managers to enter open positions using a standardized format and employees to enter résumés in a standardized format, so that matches were identified instantly via an established search algorithm. In 2003, Whirlpool staffed over 50 percent of their new open positions with internal hires, saving the organization over $1 million in recruiting and training costs. The system also created a high degree of satisfaction among employees who could use it as a long-term career-planning tool. Indeed, relative to comparable manufacturers, where the average turnover rate is in the 10–15 percent range, the average turnover rate at Whirlpool in 2003 was less than 5 percent.

SOURCE: L. G. Klaff, "New Internal Hiring Systems Reduce Cost and Boost Morale," *Workforce*, March 2004, pp. 76–78.

With all these advantages, you might ask why any organization would ever employ external recruiting methods. There are several good reasons why organizations might decide to recruit externally.[67] First, for entry-level positions and perhaps even for some specialized upper-level positions, there may not be any internal recruits from which to draw. Second, bringing in outsiders may expose the organization to new ideas or new ways of doing business. Using only internal recruitment can result in a workforce whose members all think alike and who therefore may be poorly suited to innovation.[68]

Direct Applicants and Referrals

Direct applicants are people who apply for a vacancy without prompting from the organization. **Referrals** are people who are prompted to apply by someone within the organization. These two sources of recruits share some characteristics that make them excellent sources from which to draw.

First, many direct applicants are to some extent already "sold" on the organization. Most of them have done some homework and concluded that there is enough fit be-

Direct applicants
People who apply for a job vacancy without prompting from the organization.

Referrals
People who are prompted to apply for a job by someone within the organization.

need to be aware of these different approaches, understand the costs and benefits associated with each, and balance them appropriately to give the organization a competitive advantage.

A Look Back

The chapter opening about Microsoft showed how drastically restructuring the nature of work could increase both the effectiveness and efficiency of operations. The specific changes in how work was designed created a better fit between the organization and its environment, as well as between the organization and its internal strategy.

Questions

1. Based on this chapter, how would you characterize the changes that were made in terms of the degree of centralization and departmentalization?
2. What would be some characteristics of the environments or internal strategy that might force a different firm to move in the opposite structural direction?
3. How would each of these changes in structure "trickle down" and affect the jobs of individual workers?

Summary

The analysis and design of work is one of the most important components to developing and maintaining a competitive advantage. Strategy implementation is virtually impossible without thorough attention devoted to workflow analysis, job analysis, and job design. Managers need to understand the entire work-flow process in their work unit to ensure that the process maximizes efficiency and effectiveness. To understand this process, managers also must have clear, detailed information about the jobs that

exist in the work unit, and the way to gain this information is through job analysis. Equipped with an understanding of the work-flow process and the existing job, managers can redesign jobs to ensure that the work unit is able to achieve its goals while individuals within the unit benefit on the various work outcome dimensions such as motivation, satisfaction, safety, health, and achievement. This is one key to competitive advantage.

Discussion Questions

1. Assume you are the manager of a fast food restaurant. What are the outputs of your work unit? What are the activities required to produce those outputs? What are the inputs?
2. Based on Question 1, consider the cashier's job. What are the outputs, activities, and inputs for that job?
3. Consider the "job" of college student. Perform a job analysis on this job. What are the tasks required in the job? What are the knowledge, skills, and abilities necessary to perform those tasks? What environmental trends or shocks (like computers) might change the job, and how would that change the skill requirements?
4. Discuss how the following trends are changing the skill requirements for managerial jobs in the United States: (a) increasing use of computers, (b) increasing

international competition, (c) increasing work–family conflicts.
5. Why is it important for a manager to be able to conduct a job analysis? What are the negative outcomes that would result from not understanding the jobs of those reporting to the manager?
6. What are the trade-offs between the different approaches to job design? Which approach do you think should be weighted most heavily when designing jobs?
7. For the cashier job in Question 2, which approach to job design was most influential in designing that job? In the context of the total work-flow process of the restaurant, how would you redesign the job to more heavily emphasize each of the other approaches?

The end-of-chapter segment, **"A Look Back,"** encourages students to recall the chapter's opening story and apply it to what they have just learned.

---

or agents of the employer can be imprisoned. Criminal charges can also be brought against anyone who falsifies records that are subject to OSHA inspection or anyone who gives advance notice of an OSHA inspection without permission from the Department of Labor.

The Effect of OSHA

OSHA has been unquestionably successful in raising the level of awareness of occupational safety. Yet legislation alone cannot solve all the problems of work site safety. Indeed, the number of occupational illnesses increased fivefold between 1985 and 1990, according to a survey by the Bureau of Labor Statistics.[43] Many industrial accidents are a product of unsafe behaviors, not unsafe working conditions. Because the act does not directly regulate employee behavior, little behavior change can be expected unless employees are convinced of the standards' importance.[44] This has been recognized by labor leaders. For example, Lynn Williams, president of the United Steelworkers of America, has noted, "We can't count on government. We can't count on employers. We must rely on ourselves to bring about the safety and health of our workers."[45]

Because conforming to the statute alone does not necessarily guarantee safety, many employers go beyond the letter of the law. In the next section we examine various kinds of employer-initiated safety awareness programs that comply with OSHA requirements and, in some cases, exceed them.

Safety Awareness Programs

Safety awareness programs
Employer programs that attempt to instill symbolic and substantive changes in the organization's emphasis on safety.

Safety awareness programs go beyond compliance with OSHA and attempt to instill symbolic and substantive changes in the organization's emphasis on safety. These programs typically focus either on specific jobs and job elements or on specific types of injuries or disabilities. There are three primary components to a safety awareness program: identifying and communicating hazards, reinforcing safe practices, and promoting safety internationally.

Identifying and Communicating Job Hazards

Job hazard analysis technique
A breakdown of each job into basic elements, each of which is rated for its potential for harm or injury.

Employees, supervisors, and other knowledgeable sources need to sit down and discuss potential problems related to safety. The **job hazard analysis technique** is one means of accomplishing this.[46] With this technique, each job is broken down into basic elements, and each of these is rated for its potential for harm or injury. If there is consensus that some job element has high hazard potential, this element is isolated and potential technological or behavioral changes are considered.

Technic of operations review (TOR)
Method of determining safety problems via an analysis of past accidents.

Another means of isolating unsafe job elements is to study past accidents. The **technic of operations review (TOR)** is an analysis methodology that helps managers determine which specific element of a job led to a past accident.[47] The first step in a TOR analysis is to establish the facts surrounding the incident. To accomplish this, all members of the work group involved in the accident give their initial impressions of what happened. The group must then, through group discussion, reach a consensus on the single, systematic failure that most contributed to the incident as well as two or three major secondary factors that contributed to it.

An analysis of jobs at Burger King, for example, revealed that certain jobs required employees to walk across wet or slippery surfaces, which led to many falls. Specific

---

Key terms are highlighted and defined in the margin in order to help students learn the language of HRM.

Questions

1. Based on this chapter, what are the best methods of obtaining information about job applicants?
2. What are the best characteristics to look for in applicants, and how does this depend on the nature of the job?
3. If you could use only two of the methods described in this chapter and could assess only two of the characteristics discussed, which would you choose, and why?

Summary

In this chapter we examined the five critical standards with which all personnel selection methods should conform: reliability, validity, generalizability, utility, and legality. We also looked at nine different selection methods currently used in organizations and evaluated each with respect to these five standards. Table 6.5, on page 245, summarizes these selection methods and can be used as a guide in deciding which test to use for a specific purpose. Although we discussed each type of test individually, it is

important to note in closing that there is no need to use only one type of test for any one job. Indeed, managerial assessment centers use many different forms of tests over a two- or three-day period to learn as much as possible about candidates for important executive positions. As a result, highly accurate predictions are often made, and the validity associated with the judicious use of multiple tests is higher than for tests used in isolation.

Discussion Questions

1. We examined nine different types of selection methods in this chapter. Assume that you were just rejected for a job based on one of these methods. Obviously, you might be disappointed and angry regardless of what method was used to make this decision, but can you think of two or three methods that might leave you most distressed? In general, why might the acceptability of the test to applicants be an important standard to add to the five we discussed in this chapter?
2. Videotaping applicants in interviews is becoming an increasingly popular means of getting multiple assessments of that individual from different perspectives. Can you think of some reasons why videotaping interviews might also be useful in evaluating the interviewer? What would you look for in an interviewer if you were evaluating one on videotape?

3. Distinguish between concurrent and predictive validation designs, discussing why the latter is preferred over the former. Examine each of the nine selection methods discussed in this chapter and determine which of these would have their validity most and least affected by the type of validation design employed.
4. Some have speculated that in addition to increasing the validity of decisions, employing rigorous selection methods has symbolic value for organizations. What message is sent to applicants about the organization through hiring practices, and how might this message be reinforced by recruitment programs that occur before selection and training programs that occur after selection?

Self-Assessment Exercise

Reviews of research about personality have identified five common aspects of personality, referred to as the Big Five personality traits. Find out which are your most prominent traits. Read each of the following statements, marking "Yes" if it describes you and "No" if it does not.

1. In conversations I tend to do most of the talking.
2. Often people look to me to make decisions.
3. I am a very active person.
4. I usually seem to be in a hurry.
5. I am dominant, forceful, and assertive.

Discussion questions at the end of each chapter help students learn the concepts presented in the chapter and understand potential applications of the chapter material.

BusinessWeek cases look at incidents and real companies as reported by the nation's number one business weekly, and encourage students to critically evaluate each problem and apply the chapter concepts.

Video cases and accompanying questions challenge students to view HRM issues and problems from multiple perspectives. The video cases appear at the end of the text and are referenced at the end of applicable chapters.

agencies for top-level executives, notes that of the 70 background checks it did in the year 2000, 39 percent turned up problems such as fraud, bankruptcy, and SEC violations that were serious enough to nix the employment offers being considered.

One reason for the lack of "due diligence" on the part of employers is that in a labor shortage, too many are in a rush to secure top talent. For example, when the firm Christian and Timbers narrowed the search for the new CEO of Pinpoint Networks Inc. down to six candidates, rather than let the firm finish its work, the young founders of this company were so infatuated with the résumé of one applicant that they immediately took over and closed the search. Unfortunately, when it became clear 13 weeks later that the new CEO, Anthony J. Blake, was not who he claimed to be, it was too late. Without a seasoned CEO, Pinpoint blew the opportunity to attract venture capital when it was still available. When the technology sector tanked later that year, Pinpoint was forced to lay off over a third of its workforce.

Experiences such as these are prompting other employers to slow down the hiring process so that they have a much better idea of exactly whom they are asking to join their organizational family. Some firms do not only background checks but also extensive psychological testing to ensure that a person is who he or she claims to be and also fits the culture of the organization. You never know what

these kinds of investigations will uncover—unless, of course, you fail to perform them.

Questions

1. People applying for jobs are always motivated to display themselves in the best light, and as a result, this can sometimes lead to inaccurate portrayals of abilities, skills, experiences, and personality. Based upon what you have read in this chapter, how should you approach a job applicant's written application and résumé if your goal is to make sure that they accurately reflect the person's past experiences and accomplishments?

2. In the face-to-face interview process, what steps can be taken to ensure that the applicant is being frank and honest with you, and what steps should you take if you feel that he or she is portraying an inaccurate picture of himself or herself?

3. Beyond the traditional approaches of going over the application and conducting face-to-face interviews, what other steps can you as an employer take to ensure that the person who is being hired for the job has the right abilities, skills, past experiences and personality?

SOURCE: O. David, "You Just Hired Him: Should You Have Known Better," *Fortune* (October 29, 2001), pp. 205–6; D. Foust, "When the CEO Is Too Good to Be True," *BusinessWeek* (July 16, 2001), pp. 62–63; C. Daniels, "Does This Man Need a Shrink?" *Fortune* (February 5, 2001).

Managing People: From the Pages of *BusinessWeek*

Coming Out in Corporate America

One chilly fall day last year, Gary Osifchin trooped into a mandatory training session at S.C. Johnson & Son Inc. The privately held company, located in Racine, Wis., which was voted 2003's "all-American city" by the National Civic League, manufactures Raid insecticide and Glade air fresheners. It's the kind of place where factory workers ride to the assembly line on Harley-Davidsons, dine on local bratwurst, and chase it down with Milwaukee beer.

About 20 plant managers were seated in a circle in a drab conference room. Osifchin, an S.C. Johnson marketing exec, walked into the center and started telling stories—about his boyfriend, his romantic life, and his experiences as a homosexual. He told co-workers, for instance, that one constant source of stress was having to come out anew every time he sat down with a new supervisor or switched units. "Somebody might see a picture of a guy on my desk, and that just sparks conversation," he said.

The frank talk was the kickoff of Gay 201, the upper-level course in gay sensitivity training offered at S.C.

Johnson. It's available only to graduates of Gay 101, an introductory seminar that debunks stereotypes. The classes at Johnson are hardly anomalous. Eastman Kodak Co. offers similar sessions. Lucent Technologies, Microsoft, Southern California Edison, and dozens of others, meanwhile, send executives to weeklong training courses for gay managers at the University of California at Los Angeles' Anderson School of Management.

The programs are just one small piece of a growing gay, lesbian, bisexual, and transgender (GLBT) rights movement in Corporate America. Following in the footsteps of African Americans, women, and other traditionally marginalized groups, corporate gays are increasingly standing up for their rights. Defense contractors such as Raytheon Co. and Lockheed Martin Corp. now sponsor gay support groups. American Express Co. and Lehman Brothers Inc. promote their gay financial advisers in GLBT publications. Even culturally conservative Wal-Mart Stores Inc., which bans racy magazines and compact discs with offensive lyrics, this year adopted a nondiscrimination policy toward gays.

VIDEO CASE

Doing Unto Others— Abbott Laboratories

Why should a company establish ethical standards? For Abbott Laboratories, the answer is: "Because it is the right thing to do." It's also important for business reasons because a pharmaceutical company needs to establish trust with all its stakeholders: employees, customers, regulators, shareholders, and so on.

Abbott has been in business for over a hundred years. It now employs some 70,000 people around the world and operates in 130 countries. The company makes and distributes pharmaceuticals, medical devices, and nutritional aids. You can imagine the challenge the company has in meeting the legal, moral, and ethical codes of so many different countries. This is especially true in the pharmaceutical industry that is plagued by many ethical issues, like kickbacks, overpricing, and unethical promotions. Only an effort by top management is enough to address such major issues.

Abbott has had a compliance-based ethics code for many years. But it's one thing to talk about establishing a strong ethics program; it is quite another to implement one. That's why the company appointed Charlie Brock as Abbott's Chief Ethics and Compliance Officer. Each division has an ethics staff and Brock is the coordinator of them all.

One of Brock's first steps in implementing Abbott's ethics program

was to let everyone in the company know what the firm's ethical standards are. But the company did not stop with employees; suppliers, distributors, and customers also needed to know that Abbott has such standards and intends to apply them rigorously. That meant establishing a program based on specific standards that are communicated clearly and are enforced with penalties for noncompliance. Abbott uses the latest in technology to train employees in ethical standards. Interactive software developed by California-based company LRN presents difficult ethical cases and teaches employees what to do when hard ethical issues arise.

Abbott goes beyond just compliance-based ethics to integrity-based ethics. That is, it has a broad program of "global citizenship" that covers everything from how the company reports information to stockholders to how it treats its employees, from how it manufactures goods to how it tries to minimize environmental effects. The company has been very generous to many nonprofit groups, but takes special pride in its efforts to conquer AIDS in the world, including developing products to treat and maybe cure the disease. This effort also means teaching people in developing countries how to test for HIV in order to prevent spreading AIDS to their

children. All told, Abbott will spend over $100 million on such efforts over the next five years. That includes building partnerships with other firms to make a difference in the world.

Abbott is truly a company to be admired for its corporate citizenship and its active involvement in self-regulation. Not only has the company established an ethics office and set clear ethics codes, it vigorously applies those codes. Its community outreach, including a strong commitment to ending the AIDS crisis, sets a model for other companies to benchmark. Most important, the company does it all for the right reason. It is the morally right thing to do!

THINKING IT OVER

1. Do you believe Abbott's employee training contributes to its high ethical standards? Explain.

2. In your opinion, how does a company, facing such diversity in its working environments and employees, benefit from providing extensive training to the myriad of workers?

3. Discuss how ethical business behavior creates a competitive advantage for organizations like Abbott.

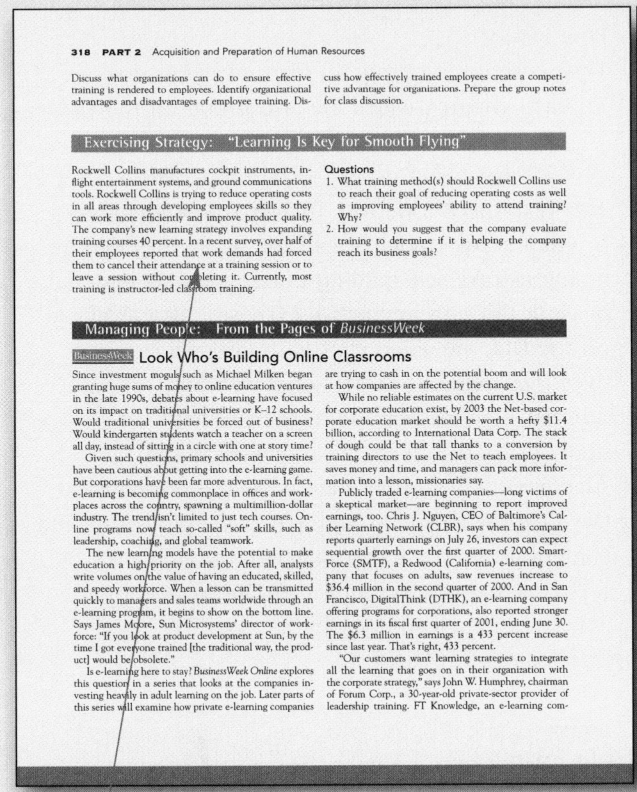

318 PART 2 Acquisition and Preparation of Human Resources

Discuss what organizations can do to ensure effective training is rendered to employees. Identify organizational advantages and disadvantages of employee training. Discuss how effectively trained employees create a competitive advantage for organizations. Prepare the group notes for class discussion.

Exercising Strategy: "Learning Is Key for Smooth Flying"

Rockwell Collins manufactures cockpit instruments, in-flight entertainment systems, and ground communications tools. Rockwell Collins is trying to reduce operating costs in all areas through developing employees skills so they can work more efficiently and improve product quality. The company's new learning strategy involves expanding training courses 40 percent. In a recent survey, over half of their employees reported that work demands had forced them to cancel their attendance at a training session or to leave a session without completing it. Currently, most training is instructor-led classroom training.

Questions

1. What training method(s) should Rockwell Collins use to reach their goal of reducing operating costs as well as improving employees' ability to attend training? Why?
2. How would you suggest that the company evaluate training to determine if it is helping the company reach its business goals?

Managing People: From the Pages of *BusinessWeek*

BusinessWeek **Look Who's Building Online Classrooms**

Since investment moguls such as Michael Milken began granting huge sums of money to online education ventures in the late 1990s, debates about e-learning have focused on its impact on traditional universities or K–12 schools. Would traditional universities be forced out of business? Would kindergarten students watch a teacher on a screen all day, instead of sitting in a circle with one at story time?

Given such questions, primary schools and universities have been cautious about getting into the e-learning game. But corporations have been far more adventurous. In fact, e-learning is becoming commonplace in offices and workplaces across the country, spawning a multimillion-dollar industry. The trend isn't limited to just tech courses. Online programs now teach so-called "soft" skills, such as leadership, coaching, and global teamwork.

The new learning models have the potential to make education a high priority on the job. After all, analysts write volumes on the value of having an educated, skilled, and speedy workforce. When a lesson can be transmitted quickly to managers and sales teams worldwide through an e-learning program, it begins to show on the bottom line. Says James Moore, Sun Microsystems' director of workforce: "If you look at product development at Sun, by the time I got everyone trained [the traditional way, the product] would be obsolete."

Is e-learning here to stay? *BusinessWeek Online* explores this question in a series that looks at the companies investing heavily in adult learning on the job. Later parts of this series will examine how private e-learning companies are trying to cash in on the potential boom and will look at how companies are affected by the change.

While no reliable estimates on the current U.S. market for corporate education exist, by 2003 the Net-based corporate education market should be worth a hefty $11.4 billion, according to International Data Corp. The stack of dough could be that tall thanks to a conversion by training directors to use the Net to teach employees. It saves money and time, and managers can pack more information into a lesson, missionaries say.

Publicly traded e-learning companies—long victims of a skeptical market—are beginning to report improved earnings, too. Chris J. Nguyen, CEO of Baltimore's Caliber Learning Network (CLBR), says when his company reports quarterly earnings on July 26, investors can expect sequential growth over the first quarter of 2000. SmartForce (SMTF), a Redwood (California) e-learning company that focuses on adults, saw revenues increase to $36.4 million in the second quarter of 2000. And in San Francisco, DigitalThink (DTHK), an e-learning company offering programs for corporations, also reported stronger earnings in its fiscal first quarter of 2001, ending June 30. The $6.3 million in earnings is a 433 percent increase since last year. That's right, 433 percent.

"Our customers want learning strategies to integrate all the learning that goes on in their organization with the corporate strategy," says John W. Humphrey, chairman of Forum Corp., a 30-year-old private-sector provider of leadership training. FT Knowledge, an e-learning com-

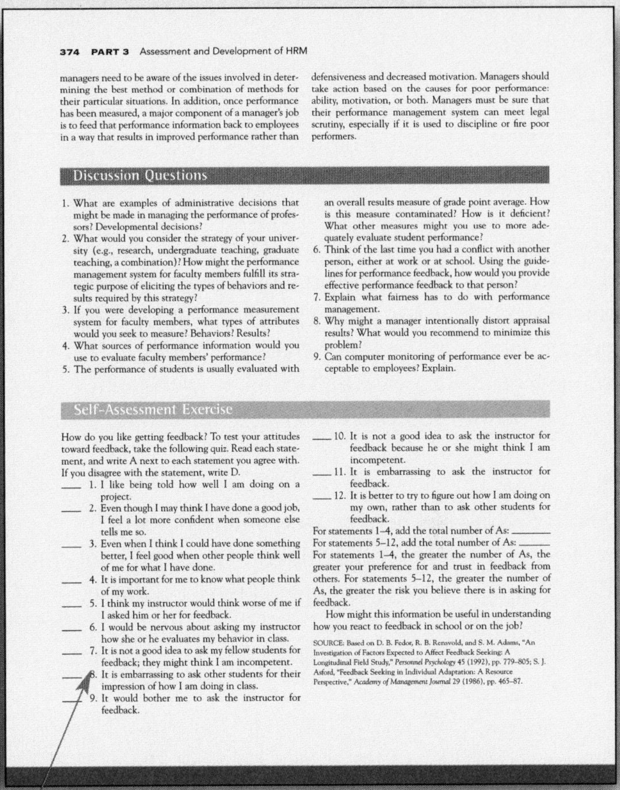

374 PART 3 Assessment and Development of HRM

managers need to be aware of the issues involved in determining the best method or combination of methods for their particular situations. In addition, once performance has been measured, a major component of a manager's job is to feed that performance information back to employees in a way that results in improved performance rather than defensiveness and decreased motivation. Managers should take action based on the causes for poor performance: ability, motivation, or both. Managers must be sure that their performance management system can meet legal scrutiny, especially if it is used to discipline or fire poor performers.

Discussion Questions

1. What are examples of administrative decisions that might be made in managing the performance of professors? Developmental decisions?
2. What would you consider the strategy of your university (e.g., research, undergraduate teaching, graduate teaching, a combination)? How might the performance management system for faculty members fulfill its strategic purpose of eliciting the types of behaviors and results required by this strategy?
3. If you were developing a performance measurement system for faculty members, what types of attributes would you seek to measure? Behaviors? Results?
4. What sources of performance information would you use to evaluate faculty members' performance?
5. The performance of students is usually evaluated with an overall results measure of grade point average. How is this measure contaminated? How is it deficient? What other measures might you use to more adequately evaluate student performance?
6. Think of the last time you had a conflict with another person, either at work or at school. Using the guidelines for performance feedback, how would you provide effective performance feedback to that person?
7. Explain what fairness has to do with performance management.
8. Why might a manager intentionally distort appraisal results? What would you recommend to minimize this problem?
9. Can computer monitoring of performance ever be acceptable to employees? Explain.

Self-Assessment Exercise

How do you like getting feedback? To test your attitudes toward feedback, take the following quiz. Read each statement, and write A next to each statement you agree with. If you disagree with the statement, write D.

____ 1. I like being told how well I am doing on a project.
____ 2. Even though I may think I have done a good job, I feel a lot more confident when someone else tells me so.
____ 3. Even when I think I could have done something better, I feel good when other people think well of me for what I have done.
____ 4. It is important for me to know what people think of my work.
____ 5. I think my instructor would think worse of me if I asked him or her for feedback.
____ 6. I would be nervous about asking my instructor how she or he evaluates my behavior in class.
____ 7. It is not a good idea to ask my fellow students for feedback; they might think I am incompetent.
____ 8. It is embarrassing to ask other students for their impression of how I am doing in class.
____ 9. It would bother me to ask the instructor for feedback.
____ 10. It is not a good idea to ask the instructor for feedback because he or she might think I am incompetent.
____ 11. It is embarrassing to ask the instructor for feedback.
____ 12. It is better to try to figure out how I am doing on my own, rather than to ask other students for feedback.

For statements 1–4, add the total number of As: ______
For statements 5–12, add the total number of As: ______
For statements 1–4, the greater the number of As, the greater your preference for and trust in feedback from others. For statements 5–12, the greater the number of As, the greater the risk you believe there is in asking for feedback.

How might this information be useful in understanding how you react to feedback in school or on the job?

SOURCE: Based on D. B. Fedor, R. B. Rensvold, and S. M. Adams, "An Investigation of Factors Expected to Affect Feedback Seeking: A Longitudinal Field Study," *Personnel Psychology* 45 (1992), pp. 779–805; S. J. Asford, "Feedback Seeking in Individual Adaptation: A Resource Perspective," *Academy of Management Journal* 29 (1986), pp. 465–87.

NEW

Exercising Strategy cases at the end of each chapter provide additional cases with discussion questions. These examples pose strategic questions based on real-life practices.

NEW

Self-Assessment Exercises at the end of chapters provide a brief exercise for students to complete and evaluate their own skills.

NEW

Manager's Hot Seat Exercises are included at the end of most chapters. If you have chosen to use the Manager's Hot Seat DVD with this text, these exercises include group and individual activities that relate to the Hot Seat segments. The segments help students develop skills that are critical to HR success.

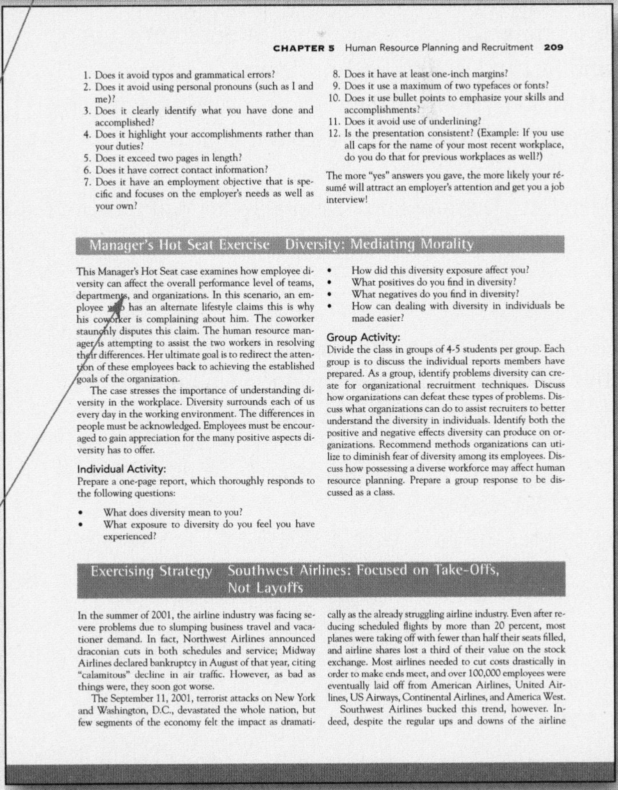

CHAPTER 5 Human Resource Planning and Recruitment **209**

1. Does it avoid typos and grammatical errors?
2. Does it avoid using personal pronouns (such as I and me)?
3. Does it clearly identify what you have done and accomplished?
4. Does it highlight your accomplishments rather than your duties?
5. Does it exceed two pages in length?
6. Does it have correct contact information?
7. Does it have an employment objective that is specific and focuses on the employer's needs as well as your own?
8. Does it have at least one-inch margins?
9. Does it use a maximum of two typefaces or fonts?
10. Does it use bullet points to emphasize your skills and accomplishments?
11. Does it avoid use of underlining?
12. Is the presentation consistent? (Example: If you use all caps for the name of your most recent workplace, do you do that for previous workplaces as well?)

The more "yes" answers you gave, the more likely your résumé will attract an employer's attention and get you a job interview!

Manager's Hot Seat Exercise Diversity: Mediating Morality

This Manager's Hot Seat case examines how employee diversity can affect the overall performance level of teams, departments, and organizations. In this scenario, an employee who has an alternate lifestyle claims this is why his coworker is complaining about him. The coworker staunchly disputes this claim. The human resource manager is attempting to assist the two workers in resolving their differences. Her ultimate goal is to redirect the attention of these employees back to achieving the established goals of the organization.

The case stresses the importance of understanding diversity in the workplace. Diversity surrounds each of us every day in the working environment. The differences in people must be acknowledged. Employees must be encouraged to gain appreciation for the many positive aspects diversity has to offer.

Individual Activity:
Prepare a one-page report, which thoroughly responds to the following questions:

- What does diversity mean to you?
- What exposure to diversity do you feel you have experienced?
- How did this diversity exposure affect you?
- What positives do you find in diversity?
- What negatives do you find in diversity?
- How can dealing with diversity in individuals be made easier?

Group Activity:
Divide the class in groups of 4-5 students per group. Each group is to discuss the individual reports members have prepared. As a group, identify problems diversity can create for organizational recruitment techniques. Discuss how organizations can defeat these types of problems. Discuss what organizations can do to assist recruiters to better understand the diversity in individuals. Identify both the positive and negative effects diversity can produce on organizations. Recommend methods organizations can utilize to diminish fear of diversity among its employees. Discuss how possessing a diverse workforce may affect human resource planning. Prepare a group response to be discussed as a class.

Exercising Strategy Southwest Airlines: Focused on Take-Offs, Not Layoffs

In the summer of 2001, the airline industry was facing severe problems due to slumping business travel and vacationer demand. In fact, Northwest Airlines announced draconian cuts in both schedules and service; Midway Airlines declared bankruptcy in August of that year, citing "calamitous" decline in air traffic. However, as bad as things were, they soon got worse.

The September 11, 2001, terrorist attacks on New York and Washington, D.C., devastated the whole nation, but few segments of the economy felt the impact as dramatically as the already struggling airline industry. Even after reducing scheduled flights by more than 20 percent, most planes were taking off with fewer than half their seats filled, and airline shares lost a third of their value on the stock exchange. Most airlines needed to cut costs drastically in order to make ends meet, and over 100,000 employees were eventually laid off from American Airlines, United Airlines, US Airways, Continental Airlines, and America West.

Southwest Airlines bucked this trend, however. Indeed, despite the regular ups and downs of the airline

Supplements for Students and Instructors

Instructor's Resource CD

This multimedia CD-Rom includes the instructor's manual, test bank, computerized test bank, and PowerPoint. These individual supplements are available in print-on-demand only.

Instructor's Manual

The Instructor's Manual contains a lecture outline and notes, answers to the discussion questions, additional questions and exercises, teaching suggestions, video case notes and answers, and answers to the end-of-chapter case questions.

Test Bank

The test bank has been revised and updated to reflect the content of the 5th edition of the book. Each chapter includes multiple choice, true/false, and essay questions.

EZ Test

McGraw-Hill's EZ Test is a flexible and easy-to-use electronic testing program. The program allows instructors to create tests from book specific items. It accommodates a wide range of question types and instructors may add their own questions. Multiple versions of the test can be created and any test can be exported for use with course management systems such as WebCT, BlackBoard or PageOut. The program is available for Windows and Macintosh environments.

Videos

Twelve new videos on HRM issues are available with this edition. The accompanying video cases are included in the text at the end of the book.

PowerPoint

This presentation program features detailed slides for each chapter, which are also found on the OLC.

Online Learning Center (www.mhhe.com/noe5e)

This text-specific website follows the text chapter by chapter. As students read the book, they can go online to take self-grading quizzes, review material, or work through interactive exercises. Also available on the OLC are video clips with discussion questions, relevant professional web links, additional Internet activities, and current news with daily updates. Professors can also download the supplements here (these are password protected). OLCs can be delivered multiple ways—professors and students can access them directly through the textbook website, through PageOut, or within a course management system (i.e., WebCT, Blackboard, TopClass).

Manager's Hot Seat DVD

This DVD is an optional package with the text. It includes 15 interactive segments with actors in situations with real-life managers—and the managers have to react live and unscripted. Segments include topics like interviewing, office romance, personal disclosure, and diversity.

Brief Contents

Contents

Human Resource Management

GAINING A
COMPETITIVE
ADVANTAGE

1

Chapter

Human Resource Management: Gaining a Competitive Advantage

Objectives After reading this chapter, you should be able to:

1. Discuss the roles and activities of a company's human resource management function.

2. Discuss the implications of the economy, the makeup of the labor force, and ethics for company sustainability.

3. Discuss how human resource management affects a company's balanced scorecard.

4. Discuss what companies should do to compete in the global marketplace.

5. Identify the characteristics of the workforce and how they influence human resource management.

6. Discuss human resource management practices that support high-performance work systems.

7. Provide a brief description of human resource management practices.

Human resources plays a key role in determining the competitiveness of a business. At Xerox, HR makes sure employees understand the company and how to achieve success there through its training and development programs.

Enter the World of Business

At Xerox, Human Resource Management Excellence Helps Company Rebound

Anne M. Mulcahy, Xerox Chairman and CEO, explains, "At Xerox, our digital strategy is committed to world-class products and services for our customers, and a world-class work environment for our employees. . . . That means, we must attract and retain world-class people. Our new Employment Brand trademark, *eXpress yourself*, distinguishes Xerox as a place where the passion, diversity, ideas and contributions of every member of the Xerox family define our capability for bold innovation and a leading edge work environment. It's hard to believe that just a few years ago human resource management initiatives like employee branding were not at the forefront of Xerox human resource management initiatives, but company survival was!"

In 2000, Xerox was $17 billion in debt, and by 2001 the company's stock price had dropped from a high of $63 to about $4. Xerox suffered seven straight losing quarters. The company also faced an accounting investigation by the Securities and Exchange Commission into the way it accounted for customer leases on copiers.

Today the company has shifted its main business from small copiers to desktop copiers for offices and high-quality printers for publishers. Xerox has experienced a remarkable comeback. Fourth quarter net income for 2003 rose to $222 million or 22 cents a share from $19 million or 1 cent a share in 2002. Recent stock prices have been in the $15 range and are expected to go higher. The company's operations are guided by customer-focused and employee-centered core values such as social responsibility, diversity, and quality and a passion for innovation, speed, and adaptability. How did the company save itself? Among the steps taken by the CEO included sales of international operations and business units, early retirements, attrition, layoffs—and the strategic involvement of human resource management.

Since 1993 Xerox has been one of the innovators in using technology for HR functions such as employee and manager self-service, benefits enrollment, and other employee transactional processes. The HR function is a shared services organization in which pay, bonuses, staffing, recruiting, benefits, diversity, learning, and HR systems are all part of corporate HR. When business became difficult in 1999, HR came through with several alignment workshops and retention incentives to help the company. The single biggest cost-savings opportunity was the consolidation and expansion of the HR Service Center. The center started with transactional work (e.g., address and employment change information), web-based processes were added, and the center now provides research and analysis to HR professionals working in Xerox operating units and handles employee relations issues for most U.S. employees. This has enabled HR to reduce its staff without reducing the level of service it provides to managers and employees.

HR has also provided support for the business strategy as it evolved to help the company survive. HR played a key role in helping the company conduct workforce reductions and sell off businesses, which resulted in losing 30,000 employees. HR helped treat employees with dignity throughout the downsizing process. Xerox's separation package offered up to one year of salary, with full benefit coverage for employees with 30 or more years of service. The company also allowed employees close to retirement age up to a year of inactive, unpaid status to reach the required age or service needed for retirement. Despite the layoffs, Xerox continued with its yearly employee attitude surveys and focus groups designed to determine if employees understood the company's direction and their willingness to support the company. Results indicated that the employees understood the direction but they weren't willing to commit to it. Another key HR issue that Xerox faced was how to keep the most talented employees from leaving. The HR department created a series of strategies which included a "we really care" message communicated using town meetings, audio, and video. Another strategy was to offer a solid cash-bonus compensation package to employees who stayed.

Today, HR continues to ensure that talented employees get the right experiences, job assignments, visibility, and learning opportunities including international experience and general management positions to prepare them for leadership positions in the company. Internal training and development at Xerox includes a reliance on virtual learning and technology to increase the number of employees who have access to training, while reducing training time. For example, Xerox's new management development program is a two-month program that uses e-learning, virtual learning programs, coaching, and one week of classroom training. Another important role that HR plays is to ensure that employees understand the "new" Xerox and how to achieve success. HR has focused on building three key initiatives: an employee value proposition, building a high performance culture, and developing a pipeline of three candidates for every position within the business. The employee value proposition represents both the expectations that the employee has of the company and what the company can expect in return. According to the vice president of human resources, "Everyone says we want the best talent. We want to keep them. We want to motivate them. But how do you do that? It all comes down to the point of inclusion, and I mean inclusion in the broadest sense of the word, one that allows an employee to bring his or her uniqueness to the table and allows [him or her] to make a difference. All practices, policies, and initiatives must put forth those value propositions—if not we'll be in trouble."

Source: T. Starner, "Processing a Turnaround," *Human Resource Executive* (May 16, 2004), pp. 1, 16–24, www.xerox.com.

Introduction

Competitiveness
A company's ability to maintain and gain market share in its industry.

Xerox illustrates the key role that human resource management (HRM) plays in determining the survival, effectiveness, and competitiveness of U.S. businesses. **Competitiveness** refers to a company's ability to maintain and gain market share in its industry. Xerox's human resource management practices have helped support the company's business strategy and provide services the customer values. The value of a product or service is determined by its quality and how closely the product fits customer needs.

Competitiveness is related to company effectiveness, which is determined by whether the company satisfies the needs of stakeholders (groups affected by business practices). Important stakeholders include stockholders, who want a return on their investment; customers, who want a high-quality product or service; and employees, who desire interesting work and reasonable compensation for their services. The community, which wants the company to contribute to activities and projects and minimize pollution of the environment, is also an important stakeholder. Companies that do not meet stakeholders' needs are unlikely to have a competitive advantage over other firms in their industry.

Human resource management (HRM) refers to the policies, practices, and systems that influence employees' behavior, attitudes, and performance. Many companies refer to HRM as involving "people practices." Figure 1.1 emphasizes that there are several important HRM practices. The strategy underlying these practices needs to be considered to maximize their influence on company performance. As the figure shows, HRM practices include analyzing and designing work, determining human resource needs (HR planning), attracting potential employees (recruiting), choosing employees (selection), teaching employees how to perform their jobs and preparing them for the future (training and development), rewarding employees (compensation), evaluating their performance (performance management), and creating a positive work environment (employee relations). The HRM practices discussed in this chapter's opening highlighted how effective HRM practices support business goals and objectives. That is, effective HRM practices are strategic! Effective HRM has been shown to enhance company performance by contributing to employee and customer satisfaction, innovation, productivity, and development of a favorable reputation in the firm's community.[1] The potential role of HRM in company performance has only recently been recognized.

We begin by discussing the roles and skills that a human resource management department and/or managers need for any company to be competitive. The second section of the chapter identifies the competitive challenges that U.S. companies currently face, which influence their ability to meet the needs of shareholders, customers,

Human resource management (HRM)
Policies, practices, and systems that influence employees' behavior, attitudes, and performance.

FIGURE 1.1

Human Resource Management Practices

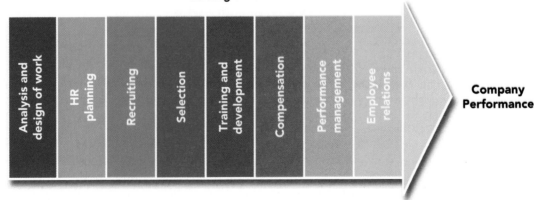

Strategic HRM

Analysis and design of work | HR planning | Recruiting | Selection | Training and development | Compensation | Performance management | Employee relations → **Company Performance**

employees, and other stakeholders. We discuss how these competitive challenges are influencing HRM. The chapter concludes by highlighting the HRM practices covered in this book and the ways they help companies compete.

What Responsibilities and Roles Do HR Departments Perform?

Only recently have companies looked at HRM as a means to contribute to profitability, quality, and other business goals through enhancing and supporting business operations.

Table 1.1 shows the responsibilities of human resource departments. The average ratio of HR department staff to total number of employees has been 1.0 for every 100 employees served by the department.[2] The median HR department expenditure per employee was $813, with wholesale and retail trade organizations spending the least ($282) and finance, insurance, real estate, advanced manufacturing, and communications and information companies the most ($1,300). As with other business functions, HR expenditures relative to operating costs have been fairly stable over the past few years.

The HR department is solely responsible for outplacement, labor law compliance, record keeping, testing, unemployment compensation, and some aspects of benefits administration. The HR department is most likely to collaborate with other company functions on employment interviewing, performance management and discipline, and efforts to improve quality and productivity. Large companies are more likely than small ones to employ HR specialists, with benefits specialists being the most prevalent. Other common specializations include recruitment, compensation, and training and development.[3]

Many different roles and responsibilities can be performed by the HR department depending on the size of the company, the characteristics of the workforce, the industry, and the value system of company management. The HR department may take full responsibility for human resource activities in some companies, whereas in others it

TABLE 1.1

Responsibilities of HR Departments

Employment and recruiting	Interviewing, recruiting, testing, temporary labor coordination
Training and development	Orientation, performance management skills training, productivity enhancement
Compensation	Wage and salary administration, job descriptions, executive compensation, incentive pay, job evaluation
Benefits	Insurance, vacation leave administration, retirement plans, profit sharing, stock plans
Employee services	Employee assistance programs, relocation services, outplacement services
Employee and community relations	Attitude surveys, labor relations, publications, labor law compliance, discipline
Personnel records	Information systems, records
Health and safety	Safety inspection, drug testing, health, wellness
Strategic planning	International human resources, forecasting, planning, mergers and acquisitions

SOURCE: Based on SHRM-BNA Survey No. 66, "Policy and Practice Forum: Human Resource Activities, Budgets, and Staffs, 2000–2001," Bulletin to Management, Bureau of National Affairs Policy and Practice Series, June 28, 2001. Washington, DC: Bureau of National Affairs.

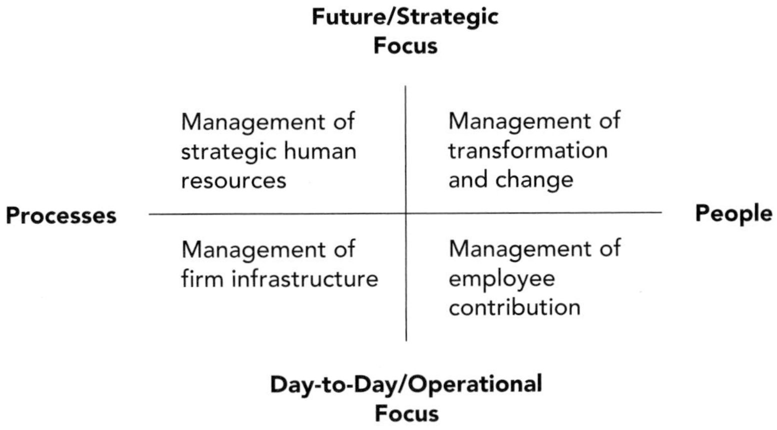

FIGURE 1.2

HR Roles in Building
a Competitive
Organization

**Future/Strategic
Focus**

Management of strategic human resources	Management of transformation and change
Management of firm infrastructure	Management of employee contribution

Processes — — — — — — — — — — — — — — **People**

**Day-to-Day/Operational
Focus**

SOURCE: Reprinted with permission of Harvard Business School Press. From
Human Resource Champions, by D. Ulrich. Boston, MA, 1998, p. 24. Copyright
© 1998 by the President and Fellows of Harvard College. All rights reserved.

may share the roles and responsibilities with managers of other departments such as
finance, operations, or information technology. In some companies the HR department advises top-level management; in others the HR department may make decisions regarding staffing, training, and compensation after top managers have decided
relevant business issues.

The roles and responsibilities of the HR department are summarized in Figure 1.2.
The vertical dimension represents the *focus* of a future or strategic orientation versus
a day-to-day operational orientation. The *activities* are shown as people versus process
along the horizontal dimension.[4] The figure shows that the HR function can play
roles in the management of strategic human resources (strategic partner), the management of company infrastructure (administrative expert), the management of
transformation and change (change agent), and the management of employee contribution (employee advocate). These roles are discussed next.

The role of HRM has evolved over time. As we saw in the opening story, it has
now reached a crossroads. Although it began as a purely administrative function,
most HRM executives now see the function's major role as much more strategic.
However, this evolution has resulted in a misalignment between the skills and capabilities of members of the function and the new requirements placed on it. Virtually
every HRM function in top companies is going through a transformation process to
play this new strategic role while successfully fulfilling its other roles.

Strategic Partner. One of the most important roles that HRM can play today is that
of a strategic partner. Aligning HRM strategies to business strategies is important to
help the company execute its business strategy.[5]

Administrative Expert. Playing the role of administrative expert requires designing
and delivering efficient and effective HRM systems, processes, and practices.[6] These include systems for selection, training, developing, appraising, and rewarding employees.

Employee Advocate. The employee advocate role entails managing the commitment
and contributions of employees.[7] No matter how skilled workers may be, if they are
alienated or angry, they will not contribute their efforts to the firm's success, nor will
they stay with the firm for long. Thus the role of employee advocate is of great importance for firms seeking to gain competitive advantage through people.

Change Agent. The final role, change agent, requires that HRM help transform organizations to meet the new competitive conditions. In today's fast-changing competitive world, firms need to both constantly change and develop a capacity for change. HR managers must help identify and manage processes for change.[8]

For example, the first person that Robert Nardelli hired after joining Home Depot as president was Dennis Donovan, a new vice president of human resources.[9] Nardelli wanted to bring order to the company, which had grown rapidly. Every function including human resources was decentralized with many of the company divisions operating as separate companies. The vice president attends all of the company's strategy review sessions and spends several weeks at the beginning of the year conducting human resource reviews of the top-level managers at all levels of the company. He also chooses human resource managers to oversee hiring and other human resource management functions at each Home Depot store. Within a few months of joining the company, Donovan and his team planned many human resource initiatives which have already been achieved including replacing 157 performance evaluation processes with one, creating learning institutes focusing on leadership, six sigma, and customer service, deploying a Web-based learning platform to deliver basic selling and product knowledge to store-level employees, and implementing a profit sharing plan for employees who are not eligible for bonuses. To get new ideas and perspectives, a new store leadership program hires from outside. Many of the selected candidates are junior military officers and graduates of military academies. With every initiative Donovan and his team first consults with the company's division presidents, regional managers, and store managers to get their acceptance and involvement. One of the things division presidents told Donovan was that because of the way previous HR projects were talked about but not executed, they were skeptical of the HR department's ability to actually deliver what was promised. To reduce the skepticism, HR staff are now required to submit detailed plans for each project and to document their progress each month.

What Skills Do HRM Professionals Need?

Figure 1.3 shows the competencies that HRM professionals need to be successful. These competencies are organized according to the four roles (strategic partner, administrative expert, employee advocate, and change agent). These competencies include the ability to consider current and future business goals and how HRM can contribute, as well as being able to analyze turnover, retention, productivity, and customer service problems to recommend potential HRM solutions (strategic partner). They also include overcoming resistance to new HRM policies and procedures, technology, and work designs (change agent); coaching and counseling employees and representing their views to management (employee advocate); and designing and delivering effective HRM systems and understanding how technology can make HRM systems more efficient and less costly (administrative expert).[10]

How Is the HRM Function Changing?

The amount of time that the HRM function devotes to administrative tasks is decreasing, and its roles as a strategic business partner, change agent, and employee advocate are increasing.[11] HR managers face two important challenges: shifting their focus from current operations to strategies for the future[12] and preparing non-HR

FIGURE 1.3
Human Resource
Roles and
Competencies

SOURCE: Adapted from "The Changing Human Resource Function," *The Conference Board*, 1990 (New York: The Conference Board Inc.), p. 11.

managers to develop and implement human resource practices (recall the role of HR in Xerox's turnaround from the chapter opening story).

The role of HRM in administration is decreasing as technology is used for many administrative purposes, such as managing employee records and allowing employees to get information about and enroll in training, benefits, and other programs. Advances in technology such as the Internet have decreased the HRM role in maintaining records and providing self-service to employees.[13] **Self-service** refers to giving employees online access to information about HR issues such as training, benefits, compensation, and contracts; enrolling online in programs and services; and completing online attitude surveys. For example, General Motors (GM) goal for its e-HR investment was to create an employee-friendly one-stop shop for employees to enroll in benefits, review their HR data, and get certificates for employee car discounts.[14] The portal, known as "mySocrates," is the place employees go for information about GM. Managers use the system for performance reviews. HR uses it for communications of benefits, training programs, and other programs, which saves time as well as printing and distribution costs. Annual benefits enrollment used to take several days. Now it takes a few minutes.

Outsourcing of the administrative role has also occurred. **Outsourcing** refers to the practice of having another company (a vendor, third-party provider, or consultant) provide services. One study suggests that 80 percent of companies now outsource at least one HR activity.[15] Outsource providers such as Exult, Accenture HR Services, Convergys, and Hewitt provide payroll services as well as recruiting, training, record managements, and expatriation. For example, in 1999 BP (used to be British Petroleum) contracted with Exult to take over all of the company's transactional HR activities. The only in-house function that remains is BP's learning and development program in the United States. Outsourcing is becoming more popular because in many cases external vendors can provide more efficient and cost-effective HR services than an internal department. For example, BP found that payroll is processed in

Self-service
Giving employees online access to HR information.

Outsourcing
The practice of having another company provide services.

a more timely and accurate manner, employees get benefits questions answered sooner, and HR processes are standardized across the company. Core HR staff has been reduced from 100 to 35 people.

Traditionally, the HRM department (also known as "Personnel" or "Employee Relations") was primarily an administrative expert and employee advocate. The department took care of employee problems, made sure employees were paid correctly, administered labor contracts, and avoided legal problems. The HRM department ensured that employee-related issues did not interfere with the manufacturing or sales of products or services. Human resource management was primarily reactive; that is, human resource issues were a concern only if they directly affected the business. Although that still remains the case in many companies that have yet to recognize the competitive value of human resource management, other companies believe that HRM is important for business success and therefore have expanded the role of HRM as a change agent and strategic partner.

Other roles such as practice development and strategic business partnering have increased. One of the most comprehensive studies ever conducted regarding HRM concluded that "human resources is being transformed from a specialized, stand-alone function to a broad corporate competency in which human resources and line managers build partnerships to gain competitive advantage and achieve overall business goals."[16] HR managers are increasingly included on high-level committees that are shaping the strategic direction of the company. These managers report directly to the CEO, president, or board of directors and propose solutions to business problems.

Consider the role of HR at retail closeout chain Big Lots which sells clothes, computers, and even cookies at 70 percent off retail prices.[17] At Big Lots the vice president of human resources and the chief financial officer sit on the operating review committee. The HR VP provides information regarding labor costs, theft, and employee and customer attitudes. HR is responsible for risk management and loss prevention, which are traditionally handled by finance. This was an opportunity for HR to tie more strategically to the business because it helps make business units more profitable. The reduction of theft and dishonesty can save the company millions of dollars. At Big Lots, the executive team includes the chief executive officer, chief financial officer, chief administrative officer, vice president of human resources, and the executive vice president of store operations. All members of the team contribute to sales, operations, or human resource issues. When the executive team determined that the company had to become more customer centered, the vice president of human resources proposed a project to measure the relationship between employee and customer attitudes and business outcomes including sales, profitability, inventory shrinkage, and customer satisfaction at every store.

Table 1.2 provides several questions that managers can use to determine if HRM is playing a strategic role in the business. If these questions have not been considered, it is highly unlikely that (1) the company is prepared to deal with competitive challenges or (2) human resources are being used to help a company gain a competitive advantage! We will discuss strategic human resource management in more detail in Chapter 2.

Why have HRM roles changed? Managers see HRM as the most important lever for companies to gain a competitive advantage over both domestic and foreign competitors. We believe this is because HRM practices are directly related to companies' success in meeting competitive challenges. In the next section we discuss these challenges and their implications for HRM.

TABLE 1.2

Questions Used to
Determine if Human
Resources Are
Playing a Strategic
Role in the Business

1. What is HR doing to provide value-added services to internal clients?
2. What can the HR department add to the bottom line?
3. How are you measuring the effectiveness of HR?
4. How can we reinvest in employees?
5. What HR strategy will we use to get the business from point A to point B?
6. What makes an employee want to stay at our company?
7. How are we going to invest in HR so that we have a better HR department than our competitors?
8. From an HR perspective, what should we be doing to improve our marketplace position?
9. What's the best change we can make to prepare for the future?

SOURCE: Data from A. Halcrow, "Survey Shows HR in Transition," *Workforce*, June 1988, p. 74.

The HRM Profession

There are many different types of jobs in the HRM profession. Table 1.3 shows various HRM positions and their salaries. The salaries vary depending on education and experience as well as the type of industry. As you can see from Table 1.3, some positions involve work in specialized areas of HRM like recruiting, training, or labor and industrial relations. HR generalists usually make between $60,000 and $80,000 depending on their experience and education level. Generalists usually perform the full range of HRM activities including recruiting, training, compensation, and employee relations.

A college degree is held by the vast majority of HRM professionals, many of whom also have completed postgraduate work. Business typically is the field of study (human resources or industrial relations), although some HRM professionals have degrees in the social sciences (economics or psychology), the humanities, or law. Those who have completed graduate work have master's degrees in HR management, business management, or a similar field. Professional certification in HRM is less common than membership in professional associations. A well-rounded educational background will likely serve a person well in an HRM position. As one HR professional noted, "One of the biggest misconceptions is that it is all warm and fuzzy communications with the workers. Or that it is creative and involved in making a more congenial

POSITION	SALARY
Top HR management executive	$204,900
HR directors	124,400
OD/training manager	102,800
Compensation manager	97,800
Employment & recruiting manager	87,500
Senior HR generalist	71,800
Human resource information system specialist	53,500

TABLE 1.3

Median Salaries for
HRM Positions

SOURCE: Based on Society for Human Resource Management—Mercer Survey 2003 as reported in J. Vocino, "On the Rise," *HR Magazine*, November 2003, pp. 75–84; F. Hansen, "2003 Data Bank Annual," *Workforce Management* 82 (13) (2003), p. 88.

atmosphere for people at work. Actually it is both of those some of the time, but most of the time it is a big mountain of paperwork which calls on a myriad of skills besides the 'people' type. It is law, accounting, philosophy, and logic as well as psychology, spirituality, tolerance, and humility."[18]

Many top-level managers and HR professionals believe that the best way to develop the future effective professionals needed in HR is to take employees with a business point of view and train them. At companies like General Electric, Citigroup, and Baxter Health Care training programs are used to develop HR professionals' skills. Also, HR professionals often rotate through job assignments in non-HR functions to help them learn about the business and become more strategic business partners.[19] For example, just several years ago for the first time in company history at General Motors, an HR person reported directly to the company CEO.[20] Many of the transactional activities are being outsourced or performed with the use of technology. GM is trying to develop HR people so that they can take on the role of internal consultants. The company has a global HR curriculum that helps HR employees understand what the goals of HR are, what the changes in HR at GM mean to them, and what the plans are for the HR function. The courses focus on helping HR employees gain business knowledge such as finance, change management skills, and the ability to develop relationships across the company. GM hopes that in the near future HR employees will be able to work with business units to diagnose problems. At the same time HR employees are being trained, top HR managers are working with line managers to help them understand that HR is available to help them with strategy, not transactional work. Line managers are now taking responsibility for some HR activities. For example, GM recently introduced a new compensation plan for employees that was implemented by line managers without any help from HR.

The primary professional organization for HRM is the Society for Human Resource Management (SHRM). SHRM is the world's largest human resource management association with more than 160,000 professional and student members throughout the world. SHRM provides education and information services, conferences and seminars, government and media representation, and online services and publications (such as *HR Magazine*). You can visit SHRM's website to see their services at **www.shrm.org**.

Competitive Challenges Influencing Human Resource Management

Three competitive challenges that companies now face will increase the importance of human resource management practices: the challenge of sustainability, the global challenge, the technology challenge. These challenges are shown in Figure 1.4.

THE SUSTAINABILITY CHALLENGE

Traditionally, sustainability has been viewed as one aspect of corporate social responsibility related to the impact of the business on the environment.[21] However, we take a broader view of sustainability. For our purposes, **sustainability** refers to the ability of a company to survive and succeed in a dynamic competitive environment. Company success is based on how well the company meets the needs of its stakeholders. **Stakeholders** refers to shareholders, the community, customers, employees, and all of the other parties that have an interest in seeing that the company succeeds. Sustainabil-

Sustainability
The ability of a company to survive in a dynamic competitive environment. Based on an approach to organizational decision making that considers the long term impact of strategies on stakeholders (e.g., employees, shareholders, suppliers, community).

Stakeholders
The various interest groups who have relationships with, and consequently, whose interests are tied to the organization (e.g., employees, suppliers, customers, shareholders, community).

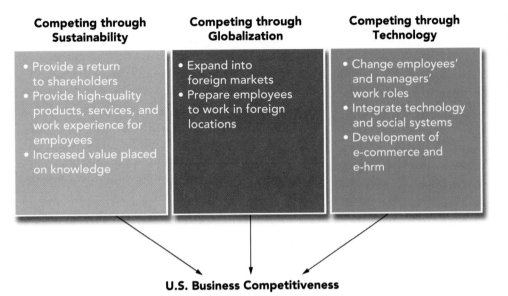

FIGURE 1.4

Competitive Challenges Influencing U.S. Companies

ity includes the ability to deal with economic and social changes, engage in responsible and ethical business practices, provide high quality products and services, and put in place methods to determine if the company is meeting stakeholders' needs.

Several changes in the economy have important implications for human resource management. Some key statistics about the economy and the workforce are shown in Table 1.4. These include the changing structure of the economy, the development of e-business, and more growth in professional and service occupations. Growth in these occupations means that skill demands for jobs have changed, with knowledge becoming more valuable. Not only have skill demands changed, but remaining competitive in a global economy requires demanding work hours and changes in traditional employment patterns. The creation of new jobs, aging employees leaving the workforce, slow population growth, and a lack of employees who have the skills

TABLE 1.4

Summary of Key Labor Statistics Influencing HRM

- The economy is expected to add 21 million new jobs.
- Professional specialty and service occupations will grow the fastest and add the most jobs from 2002 to 2012.
- More job openings are expected from the need to replace workers (35 million) than from employment growth in the economy.
- More than 25% of the workers will reach retirement age by 2010, resulting in a potential worker shortage of 10 million.
- The projected median age of the labor force by 2012 is 41, the highest ever recorded.
- Rising trends in immigration levels will add approximately 1 million persons through 2012.

SOURCE: Based on U.S. Bureau of Labor Statistics website http://stats.bls.gov; D. Hecker, "Occupational Projections to 2012," *Monthly Labor Review* 127 (2004), pp. 80–105; M. Harrigan, "Employment Projections to 2012: Concepts and Context," *Monthly Labor Review* 127 (2004), pp. 3–22.

needed to perform the jobs in greatest demand means that demand for employees will exceed supply. This has created a "war for talent" that has increased the attention companies pay to attracting and retaining human resources.

Economic Changes

In 2000 the economic picture was positive for the United States.[22] The Dow Jones index hit an all-time record high of 11,722. Unemployment was at under 4 percent nationally. The federal government had a record $236 billion surplus and was considering options for putting the money back into the private sector for investment. There was a shortage of talented employees for all jobs. Employers were importing thousands of workers from overseas to fill shortages in computer science, engineering, systems analysis, and computer programming.

Then came September 11, 2001. The loss of lives in the World Trade Center and Pentagon buildings was horrific, and the economic consequences of the attack were devastating. There were billions of dollars lost (e.g., human life, property damage, emergency response, cleanup, personal income, business profits). During September 2001, the Dow had dropped to 8,235, and between September 2001 and 2002 the Federal Reserve Board had cut interest rates 11 times, to their lowest rates in 40 years. The federal government account had a projected deficit of $157 billion for 2002. The events of 9/11 and the dot-com bust were major factors that triggered an economic recession. The unemployment rate increased from less than 4 percent to 5.8 percent in 2002. Between September 2000 and September 2002, manufacturing, retail, hotel, airline, and technology businesses combined to lay off close to 2 million employees.

The events of 9/11 combined with an economic recession put companies into a more uncertain economic period. The implications of this new economic period (which some are calling the "Next Economy") for human resource management are far-reaching. For example, HR programs and the HR function have increased pressure to relate to the business strategy and show a return on investment. Customer focus needs to be included in all HRM practices. New technology combined with economic uncertainty will mean that administrative and transactional HR activities will be delivered via technology creating less need for HR professionals to provide these activities. The aging workforce combined with reduced immigration because of security concerns may lead employers to focus more on retraining employees or encouraging older, skilled workers to delay retirement or work part-time. Some suggest that the weak economy and the effects of 9/11 may change the ways employees view work. Employees may not want to travel as much, may spend more time with friends and family, and may be more interested in training and development activities related to personal growth.[23]

Structure of the Economy. The competition for labor is affected by the growth and decline of industries, jobs, and occupations. Competition for labor is also influenced by the number and skills of persons available for full-time work. Fifteen of the 30 fastest growing occupations are health related (e.g., medical assistants, dental hygienists), seven are computer-related occupations (e.g., computer software engineers—applications and systems software, computer and information systems managers), three are teaching related (e.g., preschool teachers, postsecondary school teachers), and three are environment related (e.g, hazardous materials removal workers).[24] Occupations that are considered to be fastest growing are those that are projected to grow faster than the national average for all occupations which is 14.8 percent. The growth of occupational groups is determined by industry growth. Professional occupations and

FIGURE 1.5

Employment by Major Occupational Groups, 2012

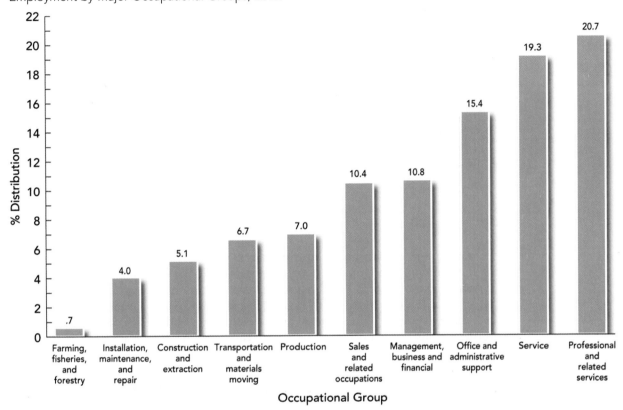

Based on D. Hecker, "Occupational Employment Projections to 2012," *Monthly Labor Review*, 127 (2004), p. 81.

service occupations are expected to grow the fastest because they are in fast-growing industries such as health care and social assistance. Although the major occupational groups growth rates will change by 2012, the relative ranking of the groups by employment size is not expected to change. Figure 1.5 shows that percent distribution of employment expected in 2012. Employment in professional and related occupations will remain the largest and farming, fisheries and forestry the smallest. The continued dominance of professional and service occupations has important implications for HRM. Research shows that employee perceptions of HRM practices are positively related to customer's evaluation of service quality. To maximize, customer service, companies need to provide a positive experience for the customer and progressive HRM practices.

Table 1.5 shows occupations with the largest job growth and decline. Twenty-one of the 30 fastest growing occupations require completion of post–high school education (either a vocational, associate, or college degree). The factors responsible for jobs in decline include advances in technology such as more automated processes (electrical equipment assemblers), advances in computer and voice recognition technologies (word processors, stock clerks), increased level of imports (sewing machine operators), and market pressures causing consolidation (farmers).

Another way to look at occupational growth is to consider the pay related to the occupation. That is, occupations that are fastest growing provide high pay (average

TABLE 1.5

Occupations with
Largest Job Growth
and Decline
2002–2012

LARGEST JOB GROWTH	LARGEST JOB DECLINE
Registered nurses	Farmers and ranchers
Postsecondary teachers	Sewing machine operators
Retail salespersons	Word processing and typists
Customer service representatives	Stock clerks and order filers
Food preparation and serving workers	Administrative assistants (excluding legal, medical and executive)
Cashiers	Electrical and electronic equipment assemblers
Janitors and cleaners	
General and operations managers	Computer operators
Waiters and waitresses	Telephone operators
Nursing aides, orderlies, and attendants	Postal service mail sorters, processors, and processing machine operator
	Loan interviewers and clerks

earnings are in the top half of distribution of earnings of all occupations). Examples of these occupations include network systems and data communications analysts, database administrators, physician assistants, software engineers, graphic designers, and structural iron and steel workers.[25] It is important to notice that the fastest growing and highest paid occupations are not exclusively limited to health or computer-related occupations or occupations which require a college degree. However, employers have a preference for hiring individuals with skills associated with higher levels of education. This also translates into higher earnings for employees. In 2000, full-time wage and salary earners with a bachelor's degree or more education had earnings that were about two times those of high school graduates.

Intellectual capital
Creativity, productivity, and service provided by employees.

Increased Value Placed on Knowledge. By one estimate, up to 75 percent of the source of value in a company is intangible **intellectual capital,** which refers to the creativity, productivity, and service provided by employees.[26] Effective management of people is key to boosting the value of intellectual capital. This includes understanding what the company is about, what it does, the expectations for performance, how and why performance will be rewarded, and how employee talents will be developed. Today more companies are interested in developing intellectual capital to gain an advantage over competitors. As a result, companies are trying to attract, develop, and retain knowledge workers. **Knowledge workers** are employees who contribute to the company not through manual labor, but through what they know about customers or a specialized body of knowledge. Employees cannot simply be ordered to perform tasks; they must share knowledge and collaborate on solutions. Knowledge workers contribute specialized knowledge that their managers may not have, such as information about customers. Managers depend on them to share information. Knowledge workers have many job opportunities. If they choose, they can leave a company and take their knowledge to a competitor. Knowledge workers are in demand because of the growth of jobs requiring them. Service-producing industries will account for much of the job growth to 2010.[27] Health services, business services, social services, and engineering, management, and related services are expected to account for almost one of every two nonfarm wage-and-salary jobs added to the economy.

Knowledge workers
Employees who own the intellectual means of producing a product or service.

Empowering
Giving employees responsibility and authority to make decisions.

To completely benefit from employees' knowledge requires a management style that focuses on developing and empowering employees. **Empowering** means giving employees responsibility and authority to make decisions regarding all aspects of product development or customer service.[28] Employees are then held accountable for products and services; in return, they share the rewards and losses of the results. For empowerment to be successful, managers must be trained to link employees to resources within and outside the company (people, websites, etc.), help employees interact with their fellow employees and managers throughout the company, and ensure that employees are updated on important issues and cooperate with each other. Employees must also be trained to understand how to use the Web, e-mail, and other tools for communicating, collecting, and sharing information.

As more companies become knowledge-based, it's important that they promote and capture learning at the employee, team, and company levels. Buckman Laboratories is known for its knowledge management practices.[29] Buckman Laboratories develops and markets specialty chemicals. Buckman's CEO, Robert Buckman, has developed an organizational culture, the technology, and the work processes that encourage the sharing of knowledge. Employees have laptop computers so they can share information anywhere and anytime using the Internet. The company rewards innovation and knowledge creation and exchange by including the sales of new products as part of employees' performance evaluations. Buckman also changed the focus of the company's information systems department, renaming it knowledge transfer department to better match the service it is supposed to provide.

In addition to acquiring and retaining knowledge workers, companies need to be able to adapt to change. *Change* refers to the adoption of a new idea or behavior by a company. Technological advances, changes in the workforce or government regulations, globalization, and new competitors are among the many factors that require companies to change. Change is inevitable in companies as products, companies, and entire industries experience shorter life cycles.[30] For example, Samsung Electronics cut one-third of the payroll, replaced half of its senior managers, sold off $1.9 billion in assets, and introduced new products to save itself from bankruptcy.

A changing environment means that all employees must embrace a philosophy of learning. A **learning organization** embraces a culture of lifelong learning, enabling all employees to continually acquire and share knowledge. Improvements in product or service quality do not stop when formal training is completed.[31] Employees need to have the financial, time, and content resources (courses, experiences, development opportunities) available to increase their knowledge. Managers take an active role in identifying training needs and helping to ensure that employees use training in their work. Also, employees should be actively encouraged to share knowledge with colleagues and other work groups across the company using e-mail and the Internet.[32] For a learning organization to be successful requires that teams of employees collaborate to meet customer needs. Managers need to empower employees to share knowledge, identify problems, and make decisions. This allows the company to continuously experiment and improve.

Learning organization
Employees are continually trying to learn new things.

Skill Requirements. The largest number of job openings will be in occupations requiring a bachelor's degree and on-the-job training. Two-thirds of projected openings require only on-the-job training—but these jobs typically offer low pay and benefits. Seventy percent of the fastest growing occupations require postsecondary education and training. Although companies will need employees with all levels of education and training, those with the most education usually will have more options in the job market and better chances of obtaining higher-paying jobs. As the occupational structure of the U.S. economy has shifted to emphasize knowledge and service work, skill requirements have changed.[33] The demand for specific skills is being replaced by a need for cognitive skills—mathematical and verbal reasoning ability—and interpersonal skills related to being able to work in teams or to interact with customers in a service economy (such as patients, students, vendors, and suppliers). Many jobs, especially those in which the use of the Internet is common, require employees to have technology-related skills (like using the Internet, spreadsheets, and statistical software packages). Cognitive and interpersonal skills are important because in the service-oriented economy employees must take responsibility for the final product or service. Variety and customization requires employees who are creative and good problem solvers. Continuous innovation requires the ability to learn, especially as technology changes jobs. To add novelty and entertainment value for customers, workers must be creative.

Most companies relate these skills to educational attainment, using a college degree as a standard to screen prospective new employees. However, some companies who are unable to find qualified employees rely on training to correct basic skill deficiencies after hiring.[34] Other companies team up with universities, community colleges, and high schools to design and teach courses ranging from basic reading to design blueprint reading. The skills gap has decreased competitiveness because it makes it difficult for companies to upgrade technology, reorganize work, and empower employees, which are key elements in high-performance work systems.

Psychological contract
Expectations of employee contributions and what the company will provide in return.

Changes in the Employment Relationship. Economic downturns will continue to occur, resulting in layoffs in all industries. Also companies that grow through mergers and acquisitions often have two sets of employees performing similar jobs. To eliminate this redundancy, employees are laid off and downsized. Layoffs and bankruptcies have played a major role in changing the employment relationship. The **psychological contract** describes what an employee expects to contribute and what the company will provide to the employee for these contributions.[35] Unlike a sales contract, a psychological contract is not written. Traditionally, companies expected employees to contribute time, effort, skills, abilities, and loyalty. In return, companies would provide job security and opportunities for promotion. However, in the new economy a new type of psychological contract is emerging.[36] The competitive business environment demands frequent changes in the quality, innovation, creativeness, and timeliness of employee contributions and the skills needed to provide them. This has led to company restructuring, mergers and acquisitions, layoffs, and longer hours for many employees. Companies demand excellent customer service and high productivity levels. Employees are expected to take more responsibility for their own careers, from seeking training to balancing work and family. In exchange for top performance and working longer hours without job security, employees want companies to provide flexible work schedules, comfortable working conditions, more autonomy in accomplishing work, training and development opportunities, and financial incentives based on how the company performs. Employees realize that companies cannot provide employment security, so they want employability—that is, they want their company to provide training and job experiences to help ensure that employees can find other employment opportunities. The human resource management challenge is how to build a committed, productive workforce in turbulent economic conditions that offer opportunity for financial success but can also quickly turn sour, making every employee expendable (consider Xerox's situation in the chapter opener).

Companies are concerned about employee satisfaction or morale and involvement in work because research shows it relates to motivation, productivity, customer service, and turnover (we will discuss morale in Chapter 5).[37] A survey of 35,000 employees across a wide range of companies found that only 53 percent reported that the company provided challenging work, 34 percent reported having excellent career opportunities, and 50 percent reported that the company inspired them to do their best work![38] Recognizing the importance of employee attitudes, several companies have taken steps to improve morale, satisfaction, and involvement. For example, Coca-Cola's new chairman and chief executive officer in a move to boost sagging morale is assuming direct oversight over the company's human resource function and making workforce development a major business priority.[39] Coke has had problems with poor morale and talented employees leaving, following a series of cost-cutting layoffs. J. M. Smucker Company, of jam and jelly fame, tries to rotate jobs and offer employees challenging work.[40] Nationwide, the insurance and financial service company, introduced a career planning website which provides information on job opportunities, career development, and mentoring. Nationwide also offered opportunities to move within the firm's seven other companies. One-third of the employees took advantage of this opportunity.

Besides having a greater concern for employee morale, companies are also using more alternative work arrangements. **Alternative work arrangements** include independent contractors, on-call workers, temporary workers, and contract company workers. The Bureau of Labor Statistics estimates that there are 12.2 million "nontraditional workers," including 8.2 million independent contractors, 2 million on-call workers, 1.2 million temporary workers, and approximately 800,000 contract company workers (workers employed by a company that provides them to other companies under a contract). One estimate is that workers with alternative work arrangements make up 28 percent of the total workforce.[41]

More workers in alternative employment relationships are choosing these arrangements. Alternative work arrangements can benefit both individuals and employers. More and more individuals don't want to be attached to any one company. They want the flexibility to work when and where they choose. They may want to work fewer hours to effectively balance work and family responsibilities. Also, individuals who have been downsized may choose alternative work arrangements while they are seeking full-time employment. From the company perspective, it is easier to add temporary employees when they are needed and easier to terminate their employment when they are not needed. Part-time workers can be a valuable source of skills that current employees may not have and are needed for a specific project that has a set completion date. Employees who may elect alternative work arrangements include those with a wide range and level of skills including professional employees (e.g., teachers, engineers, managers), employees in administrative and clerical support jobs (e.g., administrative assistants), health-care workers such as nurses, and employees in service occupations (e.g., bank tellers).

Alternative work arrangements
Independent contractors, on-call workers, temporary workers, and contract company workers who are not employed full-time by the company.

Strategic Use of HRM

FedEx Ground, a subsidiary of Federal Express Corporation, is a 43,000-employee company.[42] FedEx Ground is dependent on its team of 14,300 independent contractors who work as either pickup and delivery contractors or as long-haul contractors. During peak delivery season the company will add up to 2,800 temporary drivers and up to 2,000 part-time package handlers to work in facilities. All of the employees are trained so that they can contribute to the company mission, which is to be the best small-package carrier in the business with a focus on the customer. To make sure employees know what is happening with the day-to-day business operations a variety of communications techniques are used including intranet sites, posted weekly updates, monthly newsletters sent home, as well as formal presentations and contractor roundtables. FedEx Ground believes the use of independent contractors adds to the company mission and strategy by serving their customers and helping their customers grow their business.

Demanding Work, but with More Flexibility. The globalization of the world economy and the development of e-commerce have made the notion of a 40-hour work week obsolete. As a result, companies need to be staffed 24 hours a day, seven days a week. Employees in manufacturing environments and service call centers are being asked to move from 8- to 12-hour days or to work afternoon or midnight shifts. Similarly, professional employees face long hours and and work demands that spill over into their personal lives. E-mail, pagers, and cell phones bombard employees with information and work demands. In the car, on vacation, on planes, and even in the bathroom, employees can be interrupted by work demands. More demanding work results in greater employee stress, less satisfied employees, loss of productivity, and higher turnover—all of which are costly for companies.

Many companies are taking steps to provide more flexible work schedules, protect employees' free time, and more productively use employees' work time. Workers consider flexible schedules a valuable way to ease the pressures and conflicts of trying to balance work and nonwork activities. Employers are using flexible schedules to recruit and retain employees and to increase satisfaction and productivity. For example, at Deloitte & Touche employees who request a flexible work arrangement are not asked to state their marital or family status or explain why they are making the request.[43] Employees need only prove they can meet the job requirements. Deloitte & Touche believes that a flexible work environment that helps employees deal with their personal and professional responsibilities is a sound business practice. Flexible arrangements are provided to all employees provided that they continue to meet the service needs of the clients and the arrangement makes business sense. At Household International, the company's Complete Reward benefit package allows employees to pick and choose programs that meet their needs, lifestyle, and stage of life. The package includes flexible hours, training opportunities, subsidized dependent-care accounts, tuition reimbursement, and discounts for services. A Life Balance program provides phone consultation on a variety of benefits, as well as personalized referrals for child/ elder care resources and information on how to get the best deal on a car. At Intel, an employee who had a passion for painting and was most creative in the morning was able to arrange his schedule to arrive at work a few hours later. In response to the loss of talented computer service employees who were forced to answer calls late at night and on weekends, Hewlett-Packard redesigned work schedules to allow employees to volunteer to work either during the week or on weekends. As a result, turnover rates decreased and customer response times improved.[44]

Finding and Keeping the Best Employees

Several companies have taken steps to deal with actual or anticipated shortages of skilled employees.[45] Freddie Mac, the McLean, Virginia–based mortgage company, faced employee shortages in the technical areas but also in finance, accounting, and risk management. As a result, Freddie Mac hired 20 recent college graduates to attend a three-month training program that would convert them to entry-level information system professionals. None of the students had majored in technology although each had earned a liberal arts degree. Few of them were knowledgeable about basic computer operations. To qualify for the program, the students had to pass an assessment test and have strong communications, organizational, and project skills. During the training they received benefits and a salary equivalent to that of an entry-level information technology employee such as a Web-development programmer. Following the class all of the trainees were offered jobs and remain employed. Baptist Health Care, which employs approximately 5,400 people in five hospitals in Florida and Alabama, faced a similar problem due to the nursing shortage. Baptist Health Care recently created a nurse reentry program that invites registered nurses, such as those who may have resigned to raise a family, back to work with different responsibilities. They complete paperwork such as charting so that other nurses can spend more time interacting with patients.

Meeting Stakeholder Needs. As we mentioned earlier, company effectiveness and competitiveness are determined by whether the company satisfies the needs of stakeholders. Stakeholders include stockholders (who want a return on their investment), customers (who want a high-quality product or service), and employees (who desire interesting work and reasonable compensation for their services). The community, which wants the company to contribute to activities and projects and minimize pollution of the environment, is also an important stakeholder.

The Balanced Scorecard: Measuring Performance to Stakeholders

The **balanced scorecard** gives managers an indication of the performance of a company based on the degree to which stakeholder needs are satisfied; it depicts the company from the perspective of internal and external customers, employees, and shareholders.[46] The balanced scorecard is important because it brings together most of the features that a company needs to focus on to be competitive. These include being customer-focused, improving quality, emphasizing teamwork, reducing new product and service development times, and managing for the long term.

The balanced scorecard differs from traditional measures of company performance by emphasizing that the critical indicators chosen are based on the company's business strategy and competitive demands. Companies need to customize their balanced scorecards based on different market situations, products, and competitive environments.

Using the Balanced Scorecard to Manage Human Resources. Communicating the scorecard to employees gives them a framework that helps them see the goals and strategies of the company, how these goals and strategies are measured, and how they influence the critical indicators. For example, Chase Manhattan Bank used the balanced scorecard to change the behavior of customer service representatives.[47] Before the company implemented the scorecard, if a customer requested a change in a banking service, the representative would have simply met the customer's need. Based on knowledge of the scorecard, the customer service representative might now ask if the customer is interested in the bank's other services such as financial planning, mortgages, loans, or insurance.

The balanced scorecard should be used to (1) link human resource management activities to the company's business strategy and (2) evaluate the extent to which the HRM function is helping the company meet its strategic objectives. Measures of HRM practices primarily relate to productivity, people, and process.[48] Productivity measures involve determining output per employee (such as revenue per employee). Measuring people includes assessing employees' behavior, attitudes, or knowledge.

Balanced scorecard
A means of performance measurement that gives managers a chance to look at their company from the perspectives of internal and external customers, employees, and shareholders.

A Long-Term View Pays Dividends for Vanguard Group

For many companies sustainability is based on a business model that emphasizes commitment and loyalty to employees as well as high performance. Consider the Vanguard Group, the money-management and no-load mutual fund company based in Valley Forge, Pennsylvania. Vanguard regularly appears on *Fortune* magazine's 100 Best Companies to Work For list. Vanguard's ability to take a long-term view is reinforced by the business model in which customers, investors in Vanguard-managed funds, are also its shareholders. Because the customers are owners they don't have competing needs. The company has one client so it is easier to align the culture with the customer.

Vanguard's human resource management focus has changed over the 28 years it has been in business. At different times, Vanguard has been concerned with work/life programs, career management, and leadership programs. Today, the focus is on how employees are feeling about the company. The company is facing difficult times due to scandals in the mutual fund industry which have undermined investor confidence, and a decline in the economy. As a result, Vanguard has avoided layoffs because the company believes that a long-term approach to retaining and motivating employees is at the root of the company's success. While Vanguard does not have a no-layoff policy, the company has a "do what is right for the crew" policy. Vanguard believes that showing commitment to its crew (how the company refers to its employees) in tough times goes a long way to attract, motivate, and retain employees. For example, the company redeployed staff where they could be most useful while the company adjusted to new investment trends. Fundamental to Vanguard's approach is that the company grows from within. That is, when Vanguard hires someone they don't hire for a position but for a career. As a result, funds for training do not get cut during tough economic times. About 60 percent of Vanguard's 250 human resource staff are involved in training activities. Although employees appear to be satisfied with the company's "do the right thing" philosophy based on turnover rates which are half the industry average, they are concerned about what they can do to prepare themselves for the next opportunity within Vanguard. To stay in touch with employees, managers and executives have increased the frequency of face-to-face employee meetings. The company also has a tradition of monthly CEO breakfasts with employees to express their concerns.

Vanguard does not pretend to believe that employees are not concerned with money. The company's managing director of human resources says, "People always want to be paid at a competitive rate. You have to be clear that you'll be very competitive on pay and benefits. But at the end of the day, people come to organizations not because of money. They stay because of the culture and a career opportunity. Because of the people they work with." She recognizes that sustainability is not based on a program but a value system and actions based on the values that meet employee and customer needs. She says, "If you continue to stick to your value system and do the right thing for the shareholders and crew, whatever comes your way you're better able to deal with it." As a result, Vanguard Group is well positioned to deal with whatever economic and staffing challenges it may face in the future.

SOURCE: R. Stolz, "Keeping the Crew," *Human Resource Executive,* December 2003, pp. 20–26.

PERSPECTIVE	QUESTIONS ANSWERED	EXAMPLES OF CRITICAL INDICATORS
Customer	How do customers see us?	Time, quality, performance, service, cost
Internal	What must we excel at?	Processes that influence customer satisfaction, availability of information on service and/or manufacturing processes
Innovation and learning	Can we continue to improve and create value?	Improve operating efficiency, launch new products, continuous improvement, empowering of workforce, employee satisfaction
Financial	How do we look to shareholders?	Profitability, growth, shareholder value

TABLE 1.6

The Balanced Scorecard

Process measures focus on assessing employees' satisfaction with people systems within the company. People systems can include the performance management system, the compensation and benefits system, and the development system. The "Competing through Sustainability" box shows how people systems can contribute to competitive advantage. For HRM activities to contribute to a company's competitive advantage, managers need to consider the questions shown in Table 1.6 and be able to answer them!

For example, at Tellabs, a company that provides communication service products (such as optical networking) around the world, key results tracked on the balanced scorecard include revenue growth, customer satisfaction, time to market for new products, and employee satisfaction.[49] Every employee has a bonus plan; bonuses are tied to performance as measured by the scorecard. The performance appraisal process measures employee performance according to departmental objectives that support the scorecard. At quarterly meetings, how employee performance is evaluated according to the scorecard is shared with every employee, and the information is also available on the company intranet website.

Customer Service and Quality Emphasis

Companies' customers judge quality and performance. As a result, customer excellence requires attention to product and service features as well as to interactions with customers. Customer-driven excellence includes understanding what the customer wants and anticipating future needs. Customer-driven excellence includes reducing defects and errors, meeting specifications, and reducing complaints. How the company recovers from defects and errors is also important for retaining and attracting customers.

Due to increased availability of knowledge and competition, consumers are very knowledgeable and expect excellent service. This presents a challenge for employees who interact with customers. The way in which clerks, sales staff, front-desk personnel, and service providers interact with customers influences a company's reputation and financial performance. Employees need product knowledge and service skills, and they need to be clear about the types of decisions they can make when dealing with customers.

To compete in today's economy, whether on a local or global level, companies need to provide a quality product or service. If companies do not adhere to quality standards, their ability to sell their product or service to vendors, suppliers, or customers

Total quality management (TQM)
A cooperative form of doing business that relies on the talents and capabilities of both labor and management to continually improve quality and productivity.

will be restricted. Some countries even have quality standards that companies must meet to conduct business there. **Total Quality Management (TQM)** is a company-wide effort to continuously improve the ways people, machines, and systems accomplish work.[50] Core values of TQM include the following:[51]

- Methods and processes are designed to meet the needs of internal and external customers.
- Every employee in the company receives training in quality.
- Quality is designed into a product or service so that errors are prevented from occurring rather than being detected and corrected.
- The company promotes cooperation with vendors, suppliers, and customers to improve quality and hold down costs.
- Managers measure progress with feedback based on data.

There is no universal definition of quality. The major differences in its various definitions relate to whether customer, product, or manufacturing process is emphasized. For example, quality expert W. Edwards Deming emphasized how well a product or service meets customer needs. Phillip Crosby's approach emphasizes how well the service or manufacturing process meets engineering standards.

Malcolm Baldrige National Quality Award
An award established in 1987 to promote quality awareness, to recognize quality achievements of U.S. companies, and to publicize successful quality strategies.

The emphasis on quality is seen in the establishment of the **Malcolm Baldrige National Quality Award** and the **ISO 9000:2000** quality standards. The Baldrige award, created by public law, is the highest level of national recognition for quality that a U.S. company can receive. To become eligible for the Baldrige, a company must complete a detailed application that consists of basic information about the firm as well as an in-depth presentation of how it addresses specific criteria related to quality improvement. The categories and point values for the Baldrige award are found in Table 1.7. The award is not given for specific products or services. Three awards may be given annually in each of these categories: manufacturing, service, small business, education, and health care. All applicants for the Baldrige Award undergo a rigorous examination process that takes from 300 to 1,000 hours. Applications are reviewed by an independent board of about 400 examiners who come primarily from the private sector. Each applicant receives a report citing strengths and opportunities for improvement.

ISO 9000:2000
Quality standards adopted worldwide.

Pal's Sudden Service is a 2001 Baldrige Award winner, the first business in the restaurant industry to receive the award.[52] Pal's Sudden Service is a quick-service restaurant chain that serves drive-through customers within 60 miles of Kingsport, Tennessee. The restaurant has 465 employees; most are in production and service roles. The restaurants sell hamburgers, hot dogs, chipped ham, chicken, French fries, and breakfast biscuits with ham, sausage, and gravy. The company distinguishes itself from fast-food competitors by offering high-quality food quickly delivered in a cheerful manner and without error. Nothing that it does is done without a good understanding of how it impacts on customer satisfaction. Customer, employee, and supplier feedback is critical to all processes and is gathered both formally and informally. Pal's owners must spend a part of every working day listening to employees' and customers' views on how the restaurant is performing and on ideas for improvement. The company's training and development processes support the business. Managers use a four-step model for staff training: show, do it, evaluate, and perform. Employees must demonstrate 100 percent competence before they are allowed to work at a work station. Initial training for all employees includes intensive instruction on effective listening skills, health and safety, and organizational culture. Computer-based training, flash cards, and one-on-one coaching are used for training. Cross-training is required of all store-level staff to ensure that they understand all production and service fea-

Leadership The way senior executives create and sustain corporate citizenship, customer focus, clear values, and expectations and promote quality and performance excellence	120
Measurement, Analysis, and Knowledge Management The way the company selects, gathers, analyzes, manages, and improves its data, information, and knowledge assets	90
Strategic Planning The way the company sets strategic direction, how it determines plan requirements, and how plan requirements relate to performance management	85
Human Resource Focus Company's efforts to develop and utilize the work force and to maintain an environment conducive to full participation, continuous improvement, and personal and organizational growth	85
Process Management Process design and control, including customer-focused design, product and service delivery, support services, and supply management	85
Business Results Company's performance and improvement in key business areas (product, service, and supply quality; productivity; and operational effectiveness and related financial indicators)	450
Customer and Market Focus Company's knowledge of the customer, customer service systems, responsiveness to customer, customer satisfaction	85
Total Points	1,000

TABLE 1.7

Categories and Point Values for the Malcolm Baldrige National Quality Award Examination

SOURCE: Based on 2003 Baldrige National Quality Program Criteria for Performance Excellence from the website for the National Institute of Standards and Technology, www.quality.nist.gov.

tures and quality standards. Pal's believes it has the responsibility to help its employees (who are mainly in their first jobs) to develop knowledge and skills they can use in future jobs. As a result, turnover rates are less than half that of the best competitor, and sales per hour improved by about six dollars per hour since 1998. Customer satisfaction is high, speed of filling orders has improved, and errors are rare.

The ISO 9000:2000 standards were developed by the International Organization for Standardization (ISO) in Geneva, Switzerland.[53] ISO 9000 is the name of a family of standards (ISO 9000, 9001, 9004 and 10011) that include requirements for dealing with issues such as how to establish quality standards and document work processes to help companies understand quality system requirements. ISO 9000:2000 has been adopted as a quality standard in nearly 100 countries including Austria, Switzerland, Norway, Australia, and Japan. The ISO 9000:2000 standards apply to companies in many different industries—for example, manufacturing, processing, servicing, printing, forestry, electronics, steel, computing, legal services, and financial services. ISO 9001 is the most comprehensive standard because it covers product or service design and development, manufacturing, installation, and customer service. It includes the actual specification for a quality management system. ISO 9004 provides a guide for companies that want to improve.

Why are standards useful? Customers may want to check that the product they ordered from a supplier meets the purpose for which it is required. One of the most efficient ways to do this is when the specifications of the product have been defined in an International Standard. That way, both supplier and customer are on the same wavelength, even if they are based in different countries, because they are both using the same references. Today many products require testing for conformance with specifications or compliance with safety or other regulations before they can be put on many markets. Even simpler products may require supporting technical documentation that includes test data. With so much trade taking place across borders, it may just not be practical for these activities to be carried out by suppliers and customers, but rather by specialized third parties. In addition, national legislation may require such testing to be carried out by independent bodies, particularly when the products concerned have health or environmental implications. One example of an ISO standard is on the back cover of this book and nearly every other book. On the back cover is something called an ISBN number. ISBN stands for International Standard Book Number. Publishers and booksellers are very familiar with ISBN numbers, since they are the method through which books are ordered and bought. Try buying a book on the Internet, and you will soon learn the value of the ISBN number—there is a unique number for the book you want! And it is based on an ISO standard.

In addition to competing for quality awards and seeking ISO certification, many companies are using the Six Sigma process. The **Six Sigma process** refers to a process of measuring, analyzing, improving, and then controlling processes once they have been brought within the narrow Six Sigma quality tolerances or standards. The objective of Six Sigma is to create a total business focus on serving the customer, that is, to deliver what customers really want when they want it. For example, at General Electric introducing the Six Sigma quality initiative meant going from approximately 35,000 defects per million operations—which is average for most companies, including GE—to fewer than 4 defects per million in every element of every process GE businesses perform—from manufacturing a locomotive part to servicing a credit card account to processing a mortgage application to answering a phone.[54] Training is an important component of the process. Six Sigma involves highly trained employees known as Champions, Master Black Belts, Black Belts, and Green Belts who lead and teach teams that are focusing on an ever-growing number of quality projects. The quality projects focus on improving efficiency and reducing errors in products and services. Today GE has over 100,000 employees trained in Six Sigma. Employees are working on more than 6,000 quality projects. Since 1996, when the Six Sigma quality initiative was started, it has produced more than $2 billion in benefits for GE.

Table 1.8 contrasts the HRM practices in companies recognized for successfully implementing TQM with traditional management practices.

Six Sigma process
System of measuring, analyzing, improving, and controlling processes once they meet quality standards.

Changing Demographics and Diversity of the Workforce

Company performance on the balanced scorecard is influenced by the characteristics of its labor force. The labor force of current employees is often referred to as the **internal labor force.** Employers identify and select new employees from the external labor market through recruiting and selection. The **external labor market** includes persons actively seeking employment. As a result, the skills and motivation of a company's internal labor force are influenced by the composition of the available labor market (the external labor market). The skills and motivation of a company's internal labor force determine the need for training and development practices and the effectiveness of the company's compensation and reward systems.

Internal labor force
Labor force of current employees.

External labor market
Persons outside the firm who are actively seeking employment.

TABLE 1.8

HRM Practices in Total Quality Companies

In companies that successfully implemented TQM, the corporate climate emphasized collective and cross-functional work, coaching and enabling employees, customer satisfaction, and quality, rather than the traditional emphasis on individualism, hierarchy, and profit.

HUMAN RESOURCE MANAGEMENT CHARACTERISTICS	TRADITIONAL MODEL	TOTAL QUALITY MODEL
Communications	Top-down	Top-down Horizontal, lateral, Multidirectional
Voice and involvement	Employment at will Suggestion systems	Due process Quality circles Attitude surveys
Job design	Efficiency Productivity Standard procedures Narrow span of control Specific job descriptions	Quality Customization Innovation Wide span of control Autonomous work teams Empowerment
Training	Job-related skills Functional, technical	Broad range of skills Cross-functional Diagnostic, problem solving
Performance measurement and evaluation	Productivity Individual goals Supervisory review Emphasize financial performance	Productivity and quality Team goals Customer, peer, and supervisory review Emphasize quality and service
Rewards	Competition for individual merit increases and benefits	Team- and group-based rewards Financial rewards, financial and nonfinancial recognition
Health and safety	Treat problems	Prevent problems Safety programs Wellness programs Employee assistance programs
Selection and promotion	Selection by manager	Selection by peers
Career development	Narrow job skills Promotion based on individual accomplishment Linear career path	Problem-solving skills Promotion based on group facilitation Horizontal career path

SOURCE: *Academy of Management Executive,* by R. Blackburn and B. Rosen. Copyright © 1993 by Academy of Management. Reproduced with permission of Academy of Management via Copyright Clearance Center.

The Bureau of Labor Statistics, a part of the U.S. Department of Labor, tracks changes in the composition of the U.S. labor force and projects employment trends.[55] Over the 2002–2012 period, the labor force is projected to increase by 15 million from 128 million to 163 million workers. The composition of the labor force will change because of shifts in the U.S. population. The labor force aged 55 and older will grow faster than any other age group as the baby boom generation (born from 1946 to 1964) continues to age. One of the most important issues affecting the availability of workers is the impending retirement of employees in the baby-boomer generation. Baby-boomers are individuals who were born between 1946 and 1964. By 2010, when baby-boomers will be 46 to 64 years old, the number of 55- to 65-year-olds will grow by more than 11 million compared with 2000, an increase of 46 percent![56] Will the retirement of baby-boomers cause a labor shortage?[57] That is not an easy question to answer because companies can use different strategies to manage their human resource requirements. The loss of the baby-boomers may be offset by gains in employees resulting from immigration and outsourcing. Also, the use of technology to replace production and service processes performed by employees, mandatory overtime, use of self-employed contractors and contingent employees, and flexible hours of work and place of work may be used by companies to help deal with loss of employees due to retirement. An aging workforce means that employers will increasingly face HRM issues such as career plateauing, retirement planning, and retraining older workers to avoid skill obsolescence.[58] Companies will struggle with how to control the rising costs of benefits and health care. Companies face competing challenges with older workers. Companies will have to ensure that older workers are not discriminated against in hiring, training, and workforce reduction decisions. At the same time companies will want to encourage retirement and make it financially and psychologically acceptable.

As Figure 1.6 shows, the U.S. workforce is becoming increasingly diverse. It is projected that by 2012 the workforce will be 80 percent white, 12 percent black, 14 percent Hispanic, and 6 percent Asian. Labor force participation of women in all age groups is expected to increase, while men's participation rates are expected to continue to decline for all age groups. Asians are expected to be the fastest growing segment of the workforce. By 2012 the size of the Hispanic labor force is expected to exceed that of the black labor force because of higher birth rates, immigration, and more Hispanic women in the workforce.

Immigration is an important factor contributing to the diversity of the workforce. Immigrants will likely account for an additional 1 million persons in the workforce each year through 2012.[59] About 70 percent of these new workers will be Hispanics and Asians. Immigrants within the last five years have a greater likelihood than the population of U.S. workers to be employed in food preparation and serving and related occupations, production occupations, construction trades, or computer and mathematical occupations. There is considerable disagreement regarding the impact of immigration on employment prospects for U.S.-born workers and the U.S. economy. The U.S. economy has benefited by acquiring talented, intelligent workers from other countries, but it is unclear whether an influx of skilled workers from other coun-

FIGURE 1.6

Changes in the U.S. Workforce, 2012

SOURCE: Based on M. Toossi, "Labor Force Projections to 2012: The Graying of the U.S. Workforce," *Monthly Labor Review* 127 (2004), pp. 37–57.

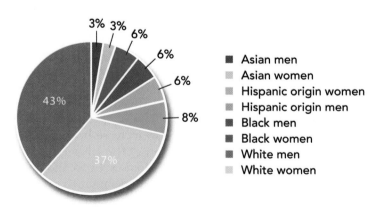

tries lowers wages or increases unemployment for U.S.-born employees. Immigrants who enter the United States illegally tend to have less education and depend more on the welfare system than those who enter legally.[60]

Besides women and minorities another source of diversity in the workforce is disabled workers. Disabled workers can also be a source of competitive advantage. To find enough precision machinists who operate lathes and milling equipment IBM has recruited from the National Technical Institute for the Deaf.[61] The Institute is the world's largest technological college for students who are unable to hear and offers a degree in computer integrated machining technologies. Without finding employees with these skills IBM would have to send jobs to outside vendors, slowing job turn-around time and raising costs. Hiring disabled workers gives IBM access to a much larger talent pool and exposes the company to new ideas, providing an important point of view for a company that makes and sells technology for the disabled. At IBM, hiring disabled workers is not just a nice thing to do, it's the right thing to do for the business. IBM has also developed outreach programs to attract disabled students and interest them in careers in technology.

The heterogeneous composition of the workforce challenges companies to create HRM practices that ensure that the talents, skills, and values of all employees are fully utilized to help deliver high-quality products and services.

Because the workforce is predicted to become more diverse in terms of age, ethnicity, and racial background, it is unlikely that one set of values will characterize all employees.[62] For example, Generation Yers (born between 1976 and 1995) begin their career with the assumption they will frequently change jobs. They place a high value on money as well as on helping others. "Baby busters" (employees born between 1965 and 1975) value unexpected rewards for work accomplishments, opportunities to learn new things, praise, recognition, and time with the manager. "Traditionalists," employees born between 1925 and 1945, tend to be uncomfortable challenging the status quo and authority. They value income and employment security.

Most employees, however, value several aspects of work regardless of their background. Employees view work as a means to self-fulfillment—that is, a means to more fully use their skills and abilities, meet their interests, and allow them to live a desirable life-style.[63] One report indicated that employees who are given opportunities to fully use and develop their skills, receive greater job responsibilities, believe the promotion system is fair, and have a trustworthy manager who represents the employee's best interests are more committed to their companies.[64] Fostering these values requires companies to develop HRM practices that provide more opportunity for individual contribution and entrepreneurship.[65] Because many employees place more value on the quality of nonwork activities and family life than on pay and production, employees will demand more flexible work policies that allow them to choose work hours and locations where work is performed.

The implications of the changing labor market for managing human resources are far-reaching. Because labor market growth will be primarily in female and minority populations, U.S. companies will have to ensure that employees and human resource management systems are free of bias to capitalize on the perspectives and values that women and minorities can contribute to improving product quality, customer service, product development, and market share. Managing cultural diversity involves many different activities, including creating an organizational culture that values diversity, ensuring that HRM systems are bias-free, facilitating higher career involvement of women, promoting knowledge and acceptance of cultural differences, ensuring involvement in education both within and outside the company, and dealing with

TABLE 1.9

How Managing Cultural Diversity Can Provide Competitive Advantage

1.	Cost argument	As organizations become more diverse, the cost of a poor job in integrating workers will increase. Those who handle this well will thus create cost advantages over those who don't.
2.	Resource acquisition argument	Companies develop reputations on favorability as prospective employers for women and ethnic minorities. Those with the best reputations for managing diversity will win the competition for the best personnel. As the labor pool shrinks and changes composition, this edge will become increasingly important.
3.	Marketing argument	For multinational organizations, the insight and cultural sensitivity that members with roots in other countries bring to the marketing effort should improve these efforts in important ways. The same rationale applies to marketing to subpopulations within domestic operations.
4.	Creativity argument	Diversity of perspectives and less emphasis on conformity to norms of the past (which characterize the modern approach to management of diversity) should improve the level of creativity.
5.	Problem-solving argument	Heterogeneity in decisions and problem-solving groups potentially produces better decisions through a wider range of perspectives and more thorough critical analysis of issues.
6.	System flexibility argument	An implication of the multicultural model for managing diversity is that the system will become less determinate, less standardized, and therefore more fluid. The increased fluidity should create greater flexibility to react to environmental changes (i.e., reactions should be faster and cost less).

SOURCE: *Academy of Management Executive*, by T. H. Cox and S. Blake. Copyright © 1991 by Academy of Management. Reproduced with permission of Academy of Management via Copyright Clearance Center.

employees' resistance to diversity.[66] Table 1.9 presents ways that managing cultural diversity can provide a competitive advantage. Traditionally, in many U.S. companies the costs of poorly managing cultural diversity were viewed mainly as increased legal fees associated with discrimination cases. However, as Table 1.9 illustrates, the implications of successfully managing a diverse workforce go beyond legal concerns. How diversity issues are managed has implications for creativity, problem solving, retaining good employees, and developing markets for the firm's products and services. To successfully manage a diverse workforce, managers must develop a new set of skills, including

1. Communicating effectively with employees from a wide variety of cultural backgrounds.
2. Coaching and developing employees of different ages, educational backgrounds, ethnicity, physical ability, and race.
3. Providing performance feedback that is based on objective outcomes rather than values and stereotypes that work against women, minorities, and handicapped persons by prejudging these persons' abilities and talents.
4. Creating a work environment that makes it comfortable for employees of all backgrounds to be creative and innovative.[67]

Many companies are realizing the competitive advantages that are shown in Table 1.9.[68] Ryder Systems Inc, a logistics, supply chain, and transportation company, found that its diversity program resulted in fewer litigation costs. Ryder Systems tracks the progress of its diversity program by analyzing the number of women and minority group members hired and promoted in key jobs throughout the company. The company also uses a scorecard for each business unit that includes a diversity component with specific targets for hiring and promoting women and minorities. Senior manager bonuses are linked to meeting these hiring and promotion targets. Cendant, a real estate company, includes its diversity program as part of a larger initiative to make the company an employer of choice for prospective employees. The company has used diversity training and has a vice president for diversity. The value of diversity is measured by the number of hires, the volume of services provided by minority suppliers, the volume of business generated by multicultural initiatives, and the number of minority franchisees. PricewaterhouseCoopers, the world's largest accounting firm, has found that diversity is very important for marketing and securing new business. Clients are demanding that the company's staff and partners involved in obtaining new business and delivering the work reflect the diversity within the client organization.

The bottom line is that to gain a competitive advantage in the next decade, companies must harness the power of the diverse workforce. These practices are needed not only to meet employee needs but to reduce turnover costs and ensure that customers receive the best service possible. The implication of diversity for HRM practices will be highlighted throughout this book. For example, from a staffing perspective, it is important to ensure that tests used to select employees are not biased against minority groups. From a work design perspective, employees need flexible schedules that allow them to meet nonwork needs. From a training perspective, it is clear that all employees need to be made aware of the potential damaging effects of stereotypes. From a compensation perspective, new benefits such as elder care and day care need to be included in reward systems to accommodate the needs of a diverse workforce.

Legal and Ethical Issues

Five main areas of the legal environment have influenced human resource management over the past 25 years.[69] These areas include equal employment opportunity legislation, employee safety and health, employee pay and benefits, employee privacy, and job security. There likely will continue to be continued attention paid to age, race, and religious discrimination, and discrimination against physically challenged employees.

There is also likely to be continued discussion about legislation to prohibit discrimination by employers and health insurers against employees based on their genetic makeup. Advances in medicine and genetics allow scientists to predict from DNA samples a person's likelihood of contracting certain diseases. To reduce health care costs, companies may want to use this information to screen out job candidates or reassign current employees who have a genetic predisposition to a disease that is triggered by exposure to certain working conditions. Legislation is being debated that permits genetic testing only to monitor the adverse effects of exposure to hazardous workplace exposures (such as chemicals) and prohibits the requirement to provide or request predictive genetic information.

Although women and minorities are advancing into top management ranks, "glass ceilings" are still keeping women and minorities from getting the experiences necessary to move to top management positions.[70] A recent survey showed that women held only 10 percent of all of the corporate officer positions in the *Fortune* top 50 companies.[71] We are likely to see more challenges to sex and race discrimination focusing on lack of access to training and development opportunities that are needed to be considered for top management positions.

An area of litigation that will continue to have a major influence on HRM practices involves job security. As companies are forced to close plants and lay off employees because of restructuring, technology changes, or financial crisis, cases dealing with the illegal discharge of employees have increased. The issue of what constitutes employment at will—that is, employment that can be terminated at any time without notice—will be debated. As the age of the workforce increases, the number of cases dealing with age discrimination in layoffs, promotions, and benefits will likely rise. Employers' work rules, recruitment practices, and performance evaluation systems will need to be revised to ensure that these systems do not falsely communicate employment agreements the company does not intend to honor (such as lifetime employment) or discriminate on the basis of age.

Many decisions related to managing human resources are characterized by uncertainty. Ethics can be considered the fundamental principles by which employees and companies interact.[72] These principles should be considered in making business decisions and interacting with clients and customers. As a result of corporate scandals at Enron, Arthur Andersen, Tyco International, and WorldCom Inc., current interests in ethics focuses on transparency and honesty in accounting systems as well as criminal behavior.

Ethical, successful companies can be characterized by four principles.[73] First, in their relationships with customers, vendors, and clients, these companies emphasize mutual benefits. Second, employees assume responsibility for the actions of the company. Third, such companies have a sense of purpose or vision the employees value and use in their day-to-day work. Finally, they emphasize fairness; that is, another person's interests count as much as their own.

Sarbanes-Oxley Act of 2002
A congressional act passed in response to illegal and unethical behavior by managers and executives. The Act sets stricter rules for business especially accounting practices including requiring more open and consistent disclosure of financial data, CEO's assurance that the data is completely accurate, and provisions that affect the employee-employer relationship (e.g., development of a code of conduct for senior financial officers).

Corporate scandals such as those at Enron and WorldCom have increased attention on preventing illegal and unethical behavior by managers and executives. The **Sarbanes-Oxley Act of 2002** sets strict rules for corporate behavior and sets heavy fines and prison terms for noncompliance. For example, a CEO or CFO who falsely represents company finances may be fined up to $1 million and/or imprisoned for up to 10 years. The penalty for willful violations is up to $5 million and/or 20 years imprisonment. The law requires CEOs and CFOs to certify corporate financial reports, prohibits personal loans to officers and directors, and prohibits insider trading during pension fund blackout periods.[74] A "blackout" is any period of more than three consecutive business days during which the company temporarily stops 50 percent or more of company plan participants or beneficiaries from acquiring, selling, or transferring an interest in any of the company's equity securities in the pension plan. The law also requires retention of all documents relevant to a government investigation.

The law also has a number of provisions that directly affect the employer–employee relationship.[75] For example, the act prohibits retaliation against whistleblowers (individuals who have turned in the company or one of its officers for an illegal act) and government informants. To comply with the act, every employer will need to issue new policies. For example, the act requires all public companies to develop a code of ethics for senior financial officers. HR professionals will need to document the fact that employees have received these policies and have attended training to ensure their compliance with the act. Because of the potential liability for retaliation in the context of discrimination and harassment, policies should include assurances that an employee will not be retaliated against for making a complaint or for serving as a witness. Executive compensation programs will need to be reviewed and modified to ensure that the program is in compliance with the no personal loans and no sales of pension funds during blackout periods provisions.

Nationwide Insurance has an ethics office that reports to the general legal counsel.[76] The biggest ongoing interface between the three-person ethics staff and the much larger HR staff at Nationwide comes from dealing with the confidential telephone "help line" for employees. As is typical for most such help lines, about two-thirds of the calls concern issues squarely in HR's bailiwick—conflicts with co-workers, for example, or treatment by supervisors or sexual harassment. The reason, says Pat Hendey, director of associate relations, is that "a lot of times employees don't know who to call, but they always seem to be able to find the ethics hotline. What they like is that they can do it anonymously."

HR investigates many concerns, including employee allegations of internal conflicts of interest. The rest of the help-line cases are delegated to internal security, legal, and other departments for investigation. The ethics staff itself handles the legwork for only about 5 percent of the cases that come in via the help line. HR relies on ethics officers to look into issues such as potential conflicts of interest. For example, the ethics officers have checked out employees who would like to run a business or who want to go out and teach a particular course with a competitor. What brings HR and ethics into even closer quarters at Nationwide than at other companies, is that Nationwide has moved beyond a compliance-based stance on ethics toward a "value-based" approach where expectations and transmission of ethical behavior become integral to the company culture. To promote an ethical culture, HR and the ethics office collaborate on activities such as the ethics office's periodic communications blitzes.

United Parcel Service (UPS) takes several steps to ensure that ethics is not only championed by the human resource function, but it is something that every employee is responsible for.[77] Support for ethics starts at the very top of the UPS management team. UPS's chairman and CEO makes it clear that there is a strong business rationale for "leading with integrity." He emphasizes that employees who get results at the cost of violations of laws or other unwise business dealings do more than violate standards—they undermine UPS's ability to grow the business and they have a negative impact on UPS's reputation. This impacts customers and affects the company's reputation as an attractive employer. The chief operating officer is also the chief compliance officer. A set of formal processes and procedures including a Code of Business Conduct is read and agreed upon by all new employees. The booklet describes expected behaviors covering a variety of situations and issues affecting employees, customers, shareholders, and the communities served by UPS. UPS uses a vendor to manage a hotline service to respond to ethical breaches. All information is forwarded to UPS's compliance department where it is evaluated, investigated and monitored. Summaries of the results are given to unit managers whose own performance is judged by how they address the ethical issues. On an annual basis, managers complete a code of conduct profile in which they describe employee and business relationships and record keeping issues and answer questions about ethical problems they may have encountered.

Human resource managers must satisfy three basic standards for their practices to be considered ethical.[78] First, HRM practices must result in the greatest good for the largest number of people. Second, employment practices must respect basic human rights of privacy, due process, consent, and free speech. Third, managers must treat employees and customers equitably and fairly. Throughout the book we will highlight ethical dilemmas in human resource management practices.

THE GLOBAL CHALLENGE

Companies are finding that to survive they must compete in international markets as well as fend off foreign corporations' attempts to gain ground in the United States. To meet these challenges, U.S. businesses must develop global markets, use their practices to improve global competitiveness, and better prepare employees for global assignments.

Every business must be prepared to deal with the global economy. Global business expansion has been made easier by technology. The Internet allows data and information to be instantly accessible and sent around the world. The Internet, e-mail, and video conferencing enable business deals to be completed between companies thousands of miles apart.

Globalization has affected not just businesses with international operations. Companies without international operations may buy or use goods that have been produced overseas, hire employees with diverse backgrounds, or compete with foreign-owned companies operating within the United States. To succeed in the global marketplace the challenge for all businesses is to understand cultural differences and invest in human resources.

Many companies are entering international markets by exporting their products overseas, building manufacturing facilities in other countries, entering into alliances with foreign companies, and engaging in e-commerce. The "Competing through Globalization" box shows how PricewaterhouseCoopers tries to build a common company culture across multinational business. Developing nations such as Taiwan, Indonesia, and China may account for over 60 percent of the world economy by 2020.[79] Globalization is not limited to a particular sector of the economy or product market. For example, Procter and Gamble is targeting feminine hygiene products to new markets such as Brazil. The demand for steel in China, India, and Brazil is expected to grow at three times the U.S. rate. Starbucks Coffee recently expanded into Beijing, China.[80] Competition for local managers exceeds the available supply. As a result, companies have to take steps to attract and retain managers. Starbucks researched the motivation and needs of the potential local management workforce. The company found that managers were moving from one local Western company to another for several reasons. In the traditional Chinese-owned companies, rules and regulations allow little creativity and autonomy. Also, in many joint U.S.–China ventures, local managers were not trusted. To avoid local management turnover, in its recruiting efforts Starbucks emphasized its casual culture and opportunities for development. Starbucks also spent considerable time in training. New managers were sent to Tacoma, Washington, to learn the corporate culture as well as the secrets of brewing flavorful coffee.

Besides training and developing local employees and managers, many companies are sending U.S. employees and managers to work in international locations. Cross-cultural training is important to prepare employees and their families for overseas assignments. Cross-cultural training prepares employees and their families (1) to understand the culture and norms of the country they are being relocated to and (2) to return to the United States after their assignment.

Cross-cultural training has become even more important since 9/11. Since 9/11 U.S. companies doing business overseas have recognized that many parts of the world have the potential to become dangerous.[81] Before 9/11 many U.S. employees working abroad had lived normal lives without any security concerns. But recent attacks and threats on American interests have shattered that sense of security. Overseas assignments are now considered more risky by many employees. Also, companies with a global workforce must manage across boundaries that are more nationalistic. Whereas

Building a Common Company Culture in a Global Company

PricewaterhouseCoopers is a global organization that provides assurance, tax, and advisory services. The company has more than 120,000 employees worldwide with 25,000 located in the United States. The company developed a global leadership training program, known as Genesis Park, to encourage development of innovative ideas and relationships between future company leaders. Participants include employees from both the company's assurance practice and advisory services. The five-month program program held in Washington, DC, is designed to rid any cultural biases that participants may have about teamwork and creative thinking and build them into an effective multinational team who can help solve in-house or client problems. The unique learning environment exposes the participants, who work in 22 different countries, to goals that are universal throughout the company including establishing effective communications and mentoring.

The program helps them develop skills in many areas including strategic thinking, global networking, and coaching, which includes offering feedback, listening, and understanding personality differences. The program gets the participants actively involved in learning. For example, throughout the program participants work on projects and interact with the company leaders to better understand their values and challenges. In sessions with the company leaders they brainstorm about various topics such as how the company should be structured in the future and what its objectives should be. Participants make their recommendations based on research they uncover about how corporate reporting and internal audits will change. One exercise during a class conducted during the Enron scandal of 2002 had participants analyze their own company's audit practices and suggest changes.

What's really special about Genesis Park is the learning that comes from individuals from different countries and cultures interacting with each other. In the projects and exercises that the participants complete no one is boss. To come up with the best values, everyone's ideas must be heard. Participants must influence each other through their leadership abilities instead of their titles or based on the acceptance of their ideas by other participants. For some participants, learning to work in a nonhierarchical structure is a challenge. Participants from Asia, Singapore, Malaysia, and China often struggle because their cultures encourage deference based on title or position. Also, small clients from small countries are challenged by different business issues than clients from large countries such as the United States. However, the leadership skills that participants learn in the program are effective across countries and cultures.

The company has found that the program is valuable for several reasons. Besides the value of the program content, program graduates expand their personal networks. They frequently contact other graduates from different countries to ask for help on audits or other projects that are under way in their countries. Interviews with program graduates suggest that they have many desirable characteristics of future leaders such as improved confidence, inquisitiveness, and willingness to challenge the status quo. Most important, Genesis Park is helping to shape the future leaders and culture of the company. PricewaterhouseCoopers desires to be a company in which ownership and professional development are part of the core culture.

SOURCE: Based on C. Patton, "The Genesis of Talent," *Human Resource Executive*, February 2004, pp. 34–38.

most U.S. citizens have felt united in actions, such as the invasion of Iraq, that they believe are justified as a valid response to hostile intentions, citizens of some countries consider the U.S. military response an act of aggression.

Globalization also means that employees working in the United States will come from other countries. The United States takes more than 1 million immigrants, some who are illegal. Immigrants provide scientific talent as well as fill low-wage jobs. Immigrants will likely account for an additional million persons in the workforce through 2006.[82] The impact of immigration will be especially large in certain areas of the United States, including the states on the Pacific Coast where 70 percent of new entrants to the workforce are immigrants. Many of these immigrants will have to be trained to understand the U.S. culture. U.S. employees will need skills to improve their ability to communicate with employees from different cultures. The terrorist attacks of 9/11 have not changed the use of immigrants but have raised security issues, resulting in more deliberate approval of visas (and longer waits for hiring to be approved).

Offshoring
Exporting jobs from developed to less developed countries.

Globalization also means that U.S. companies may move jobs overseas. **Offshoring** refers to the exporting of jobs from developed countries, such as the United States, to countries where labor and other costs are lower. India, Canada, China, Russia, Ireland, Mexico, Brazil, and the Philippines are some of the destination countries for offshored jobs. Why are jobs offshored?[83] The main reason is labor costs. Workers in other countries earn a fraction of the wages of American workers performing the same job. For example, Indian computer programmers receive about $10 an hour compared to $60 per hour earned by U.S. programmers. Other reasons include the availability of a highly skilled and motivated workforce. Both India and China have high numbers of engineering and science graduates. Finally, cheap global telecommunications costs allow companies with engineers 6,000 miles away to complete design work and interact with other engineers as if they were located in the office down the hall.

Initially, offshoring involved low-skilled manufacturing jobs with repeatable tasks and specific guidelines for how the work was to be completed. Offshoring now includes high-skilled manufacturing jobs and is also prevalent in the service and information technology sectors, for example, telephone call center, accounting bookkeeping and payroll, legal research, software engineers, architecture, and design.

Although companies may be attracted to offshoring because of potential lower labor costs, several other issues have emerged that are also important. First, can employees in the offshored locations provide the same or higher level of customer service as customers receive from U.S. operations? Second, would offshoring demoralize U.S. employees such that the gains from offshoring would be negated by lower motivation, lower satisfaction, and higher turnover? Third, are local managers adequately trained to motivate and retain offshore employees? Fourth, what is the potential effect, if any, of political unrest in the countries in which operations are offshored? Fifth, what effect would offshoring have on the public image of the company? Would customers or potential customers avoid purchasing products or services because they believe offshoring costs U.S. employees their jobs? Would offshoring have an adverse effect on recruiting new employees? Dell recently opened a call center in Twins Falls, Idaho, after closing one in India because of customer complaints. US Bank considered opening a call center in India but decided against it because of the bad publicity that would have resulted. US Bank chose instead to put the call center in Coeur d'Alene, Idaho, where the 500 new jobs would reduce the area's unemployment rate and make a difference in the quality of life in the community.[84]

There is considerable debate whether offshoring results in loss of jobs for Americans or actually creates new jobs. Smaller entrepreneurial companies are finding that

From Hiring to Dispatching, Technology Makes a Difference

Many companies are finding that technology can make work more efficient, change what, when, and how employees work, and result in considerable benefits for a company's "bottom line." Boston Coach uses a wireless network to track limos and combine customer bookings to manage its fleet. No more walkie-talkie chatter between the driver and the dispatcher. The drivers hit a button on a wireless phone to let dispatchers know their location. At the control center dispatchers track the drivers. One monitor shows the driver's location, the other shows who needs to be picked up, where, and when. Software for mapping and matching tells dispatchers which car is best for picking up customers. The system has resulted in 20 percent more rides out of the limos adding $10 million to the company's sales. Yellow Corporation, a trucking com-

pany, uses a computer program to determine how many drivers it will need during the four shifts at every one of its terminals. Every day the company receives 60,000 orders over the Internet or at its call centers. Employees who are not needed are told via the company intranet to take the day off. This has helped save Yellow $100 million per year in payroll costs.

Technology allows individuals to do valuable paid work yet still balance work and life. Willow, based in Miramar, Florida, is a provider of home-based call center agents known as CyberAgents. Willow contracts with businesses such as Office Depot whose call centers need to be staffed at certain hours, and recruits and trains people to work out of their homes. The CyberAgents sign up for their shifts on a website. They take their calls at home, using the same software applications and equipment as the agents at the

clients' call centers. The agents are monitored and their calls recorded as if they were in a traditional call center. Cyber-Agents can get help in an online chat room. One of the keys to making the Cyber-Agents effective is that expectations are set for their performance. They are told what they will be evaluated on, such as speed and call length, and are given tools and training to meet the performance expectations. Unlike traditional call centers whose turnover rate is 25 percent or more, Willow's rate is just 8 percent. The company has about 1,000 people waiting for positions. If agents move from the area they ask to be notified if new opportunities become available.

SOURCE: Based on F. Arner, "Boston Coach," *BusinessWeek* (November 24, 2003), p. 101; M. Arndt, "Yellow," *BusinessWeek* (November 24, 2003), p. 100; H. Dolezalek "Virtual Agent Nation," *Training*, June 2004, p. 12.

Working in Teams. Through technology, the information needed to improve customer service and product quality becomes more accessible to employees. This means that employees are expected to take more responsibility for satisfying the customer and determining how they perform their jobs. One of the most popular methods for increasing employee responsibility and control is work teams. *Work teams* involve employees with various skills who interact to assemble a product or provide a service. Work teams may assume many of the activities usually reserved for managers, including selecting new team members, scheduling work, and coordinating activities with customers and other units in the company. To give teams maximum flexibility, cross training of team members occurs. *Cross training* refers to training employees in a wide range of skills so they can fill any of the roles needed to be performed on the team.

Use of new technology and work designs such as work teams needs to be supported by specific human resource management practices. These practices include the following actions:

- Employees choose or select new employees or team members.
- Employees receive formal performance feedback and are involved in the performance improvement process.
- Ongoing training is emphasized and rewarded.
- Rewards and compensation are linked to company performance.
- Equipment and work processes encourage maximum flexibility and interaction between employees.
- Employees participate in planning changes in equipment, layout, and work methods.
- Employees understand how their jobs contribute to the finished product or service.

Changes in skill requirements. High performance work systems have implications for employee selection and training. Employees need job-specific knowledge and basic skills to work with the equipment created with the new technology. Because technology is often used as a means to achieve product diversification and customization, employees must have the ability to listen and communicate with customers. Interpersonal skills, such as negotiation and conflict management, and problem-solving skills are more important than physical strength, coordination, and fine-motor skills—previous job requirements for many manufacturing and service jobs. Although technological advances have made it possible for employees to improve products and services, managers must empower employees to make changes.

Working in Partnerships. Besides changing the way that products are built or services are provided within companies, technology has allowed companies to form partnerships with one or more other companies. **Virtual teams** refer to teams that are separated by time, geographic distance, culture, and/or organizational boundaries and that rely almost exclusively on technology (e-mail, Internet, video conferencing) to interact and complete their projects. Virtual teams can be formed within one company whose facilities are scattered throughout the country or the world. A company may also use virtual teams in partnerships with suppliers or competitors to pull together the necessary talent to complete a project or speed the delivery of a product to the marketplace. For example, the Technology One Alliance was created between BankOne, AT&T Solutions, and IBM Global Services. The success of virtual teams requires a clear mission, good communications skills, trust between members that they will meet deadlines and complete assignments, and understanding of cultural differences (if the teams have global members).

VeriFone, an equipment supplier for credit card verification and automated payments, uses virtual teams in every aspect of its business.[98] Teams of facilities managers work together to determine how to reduce toxins in the office. Marketing and development groups brainstorm new products. Some teams include only VeriFone employees, though others include employees of customers or partners. Virtual teams have distinct training needs. For example, VeriFone makes sure that virtual team members are trained to understand when and how to use communications technology. Guidelines stipulate that for keeping in contact remotely, teams use beepers, cell phones, and voice mail; for disseminating information, they use faxes, e-mail, and application sharing over the network. For brainstorming, discussion, and decision making, teams use e-mail, conference calls, and videoconferencing. VeriFone also emphasizes the psychological problems of virtual communications. Subtleties of meaning are lost

Virtual teams

Teams that are separated by time, geographic distance, culture and/or organizational boundaries and rely exclusively on technology for interaction between team members.

and, moreover, misunderstandings and conflict are more common than when teams work face to face. If virtual teams are global, lack of face-to-face contact can worsen cultural differences. Training related to understanding cultural differences in written and verbal communication is important for virtual teams.

Employees must be trained in principles of employee selection, quality, and customer service. They need to understand financial data so they can see the link between their performance and company performance.

Changes in Company Structure and Reporting Relationships. The traditional design of U.S. companies emphasizes efficiency, decision making by managers, and dissemination of information from the top of the company to lower levels. However, this structure will not be effective in the current work environment, in which personal computers give employees immediate access to information needed to complete customer orders or modify product lines. In the adaptive organizational structure, employees are in a constant state of learning and performance improvement. Employees are free to move wherever they are needed in the company. The adaptive organization is characterized by a core set of values or a vital vision that drives all organizational efforts.[99] Previously established boundaries between managers and employees, employees and customers, employees and vendors, and the various functions within the company are abandoned. Employees, managers, vendors, customers, and suppliers work together to improve service and product quality and to create new products and services. Line employees are trained in multiple jobs, communicate directly with suppliers and customers, and interact frequently with engineers, quality experts, and employees from other functions.

Increased Availability of Human Resource Management Databases and e-HRM. Improvements in technology related to computers and software have also had a major impact on the use of information for managing human resources. Large quantities of employee data (including training records, skills, compensation rates, and benefits usage and cost) can be easily stored on personal computers and manipulated using user-friendly spreadsheets or statistical software packages. A **human resource information system (HRIS)** is a system used to acquire, store, manipulate, analyze, retrieve, and distribute information related to the company's human resources.[100] Some of the most popular HRIS systems include PeopleSoft and SAP. From the manager's perspective, an HRIS can be used to support strategic decision making, to avoid litigation, to evaluate programs or policies, or to support daily operating concerns.

Performance management, succession planning, and training and employee-development applications are becoming increasingly important. For example, projections of the level of skills that will be available in the future workforce suggest that math and reading competencies will be below the level required by new jobs. Changing technology can easily make the skills of technical employees obsolete. These trends demand that employees' skills and competencies be monitored carefully. Complicating this need for information is the fact that many employees are geographically dispersed across several locations within the same city or country, or across countries. In response to these needs companies have implemented global human resource management systems. Northern Telecom Limited (a Canadian telecommunications company that has facilities in 90 countries, including the United Kingdom, China, and the United States) needed access to information about employees located worldwide. The company has created a central database built on a common set of core elements. Anyone with authorization can view employee records from around the globe. Head count, salary, and recruiting data are continually updated as changes are made around

Human resource information system (HRIS)
A system used to acquire, store, manipulate, analyze, retrieve, and distribute HR information.

TABLE 1.10

Implications of
e-HRM for HRM
Practices

HRM PRACTICE	IMPLICATIONS OF e-HRM
Analysis and design of work	Employees in geographically dispersed locations can work together in virtual teams using video, e-mail, and the Internet.
Recruiting	Post job openings online; candidates can apply for jobs online.
Training	Online learning can bring training to employees anywhere, anytime.
Selection	Online simulations, including tests, videos, and e-mail, can measure job candidates' ability to deal with real-life business challenges.
Compensation and benefits	Employees can review salary and bonus information and seek information about and enroll in benefit plans.

Electronic human resource management (e-HRM)
The processing and transmission of digitized information used in HRM.

the world. Although the system is customized to specific country needs, several common data fields and elements are used globally. Northern Telecom's system has enabled managers around the world to obtain up-to-date employee data to meet customer needs and address internal staffing issues.[101]

Electronic human resource management (e-HRM) refers to the processing and transmission of digitized information used in HRM, including text, sound, and visual images, from one computer or electronic device to another. e-HRM has the potential to change all traditional human resource management functions. Table 1.10 shows the implications of e-HRM. For example, employees do not have to be in the same geographic area to work together. Use of the Internet lets companies search for talent without geographic limitations. Recruiting can include online job postings, applications, and candidate screening from the company's website or the websites of companies that specialize in online recruiting, such as Monster.com or HotJobs.com. Employees from different geographical locations can all receive the same training over the company's intranet. Because the globalization of business requires employees to be located throughout the world, to meet customer demands employees need to work in teams with members who have different functional skills and are in different places. This global reach allows companies to reduce travel and lodging costs associated with having to find and identify potential recruits or bring geographically dispersed employees to one location for meetings and training. It also can increase the speed with which employees can bring a product to market by facilitating communications between employees on virtual teams using Internet discussion forums, video- and audioconferencing, and global scheduling. For example, at Procter and Gamble a team of employees from two different divisions, paper and cleaning agents, developed the Swiffer, a "broom" containing disposable cloths, in just 10 months—half the usual time. The team used the Internet to analyze markets, demographics, and cost information; it also had the ability and authority to access any of the company's engineers, who are located in 23 sites around the world.[102]

Competitiveness in High-Performance Work Systems. Unfortunately, many managers have tended to consider technological and structural innovations independent of each other. That is, because of immediate demands for productivity, service, and short-term profitability, many managers implement a new technology (such as a networked computer system) or a new work design (like service teams organized by product) without considering how a new technology might influence the efficiency or

TABLE 1.11

How HRM Practices
Support High-
Performance Work
Systems

Staffing	• Employees participate in selecting new employees, e.g., peer interviews.
Work Design	• Employees understand how their jobs contribute to the finished product or service. • Employees participate in planning changes in equipment, layout, and work methods. • Work may be organized in teams. • Job rotation used to develop skills. • Equipment and work processes are structured and technology is used to encourage flexibility and interaction between employees. • Work design allows employees to use a variety of skills.
Training	• Ongoing training emphasized and rewarded. • Training in finance and quality control methods.
Compensation	• Team-based performance pay. • Part of compensation may be based on company or division financial performance.
Performance Management	• Employees receive performance feedback and are actively involved in the performance improvement process.

SOURCE: Based on S. Way, "High Performance Work Systems and Intermediate Indicators of Performance within the U.S. Small Business Sector." *Journal of Management* 28 (2002), pp. 765–85; J. A. Neal and C. L. Tromley, "From Incremental Change to Retrofit: Creating High-Performance Work Systems," *Academy of Management Executive* 9 (1995), pp. 42–54; M. A. Huselid, "The Impact of Human Resource Management Practices on Turnover, Productivity, and Corporate Financial Performance," *Academy of Management Journal* 38 (1995), pp. 635–72.

effectiveness of the way work is organized.[103] Without integrating technology and structure, a company cannot maximize production and service.

Human resource management practices that support high-performance work systems are shown in Table 1.11. The HRM practices involved include employee selection, performance management, training, work design, and compensation. These practices are designed to give employees skills, incentives, knowledge, and autonomy. Research studies suggest that high-performance work practices are usually associated with increases in productivity and long-term financial performance.[104] Research also suggests that it is more effective to improve HRM practices as a whole, rather than focus on one or two isolated practices (such as the pay system or selection system).[105] There may be a best HRM system, but whatever the company does, the practices must be aligned with each other and be consistent with the system if they are to positively affect company performance.[106] We will discuss this alignment in more detail in Chapters 2 and 16.

GE Fanuc Automation North America is a good example of the holistic approach needed for high-performance work practices to be effective. This joint venture between General Electric Company and FANUC Ltd. of Japan has developed a high-involvement workforce. Based in Charlottesville, Virginia, the joint venture employs 1,500 people. Recognition of the company's commitment to quality is reflected in its being one of the first U.S. firms to become a certified ISO 9000 manufacturer.

GE Fanuc Automation achieved its reputation and recognition for quality as a result of the use of high-performance work practices. Central to its practices is the idea that employees closest to the work have the best improvement ideas. As a result, employees must be encouraged to voice their opinions and make changes.

How does the company use high-performance work practices? The facility has three layers of management, and over 40 work teams set their own goals and measure success factors based on the overall business goals. Each team spends at least one hour per week measuring the goals and discussing new ways to be effective. To ensure team effectiveness, all employees receive more than 100 hours of training. Employees are also guaranteed that they will never lose their jobs due to an idea developed by the teams. Managers (known as coaches) are evaluated based on their support of the teams. Each functional team within the business has a dedicated HR manager who helps the team develop its strategies, accompanies the team on sales calls, and does whatever she can to help the team.[107]

Meeting Competitive Challenges through HRM Practices

We have discussed the global, stakeholder, new economy, and high-performance work system challenges U.S. companies are facing. We have emphasized that management of human resources plays a critical role in determining companies' success in meeting these challenges. HRM practices have not traditionally been seen as providing economic value to the company. Economic value is usually associated with equipment, technology, and facilities. However, HRM practices have been shown to be valuable. Compensation, staffing, training and development, performance management, and other HRM practices are investments that directly affect employees' motivation and ability to provide products and services that are valued by customers. Research has shown that companies that attempt to increase their competitiveness by investing in new technology and becoming involved in the quality movement also invest in state-of-the-art staffing, training, and compensation practices.[108] Figure 1.7 shows examples of human resource management practices that help companies deal with the three challenges. For example, to meet the sustainability challenge, companies need to identify through their selection processes whether prospective employees value customer relations and have the levels of interpersonal skills necessary to work with fellow employees in teams. To meet all three challenges, companies need to capitalize on the diversity of values, abilities, and perspectives that employees bring to the workplace.

HRM practices that help companies deal with the competitive challenges can be grouped into the four dimensions shown in Figure 1.8. These dimensions include the human resource environment, acquiring and preparing human resources, assessment and development of human resources, and compensating human resources. In addition, some companies have special issues related to labor–management relations, international human resource management, and managing the human resource function.

Managing the Human Resource Environment
Managing internal and external environmental factors allows employees to make the greatest possible contribution to company productivity and competitiveness. Creating a positive environment for human resources involves

- Linking HRM practices to the company's business objectives—that is, strategic human resource management.
- Ensuring that HRM practices comply with federal, state, and local laws.
- Designing work that motivates and satisfies the employee as well as maximizes customer service, quality, and productivity.

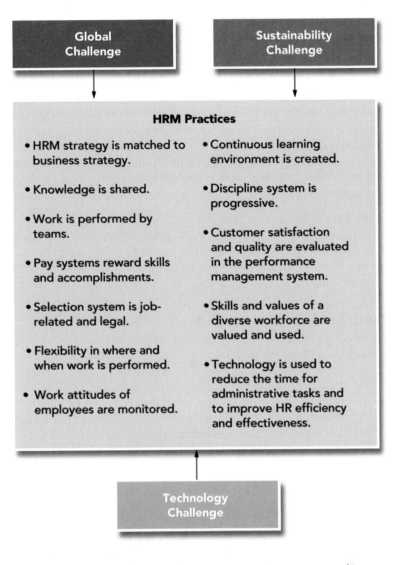

FIGURE 1.7

Examples of How HRM Practices Can Help Companies Meet Competitive Challenges

HRM Practices

- HRM strategy is matched to business strategy.
- Knowledge is shared.
- Work is performed by teams.
- Pay systems reward skills and accomplishments.
- Selection system is job-related and legal.
- Flexibility in where and when work is performed.
- Work attitudes of employees are monitored.
- Continuous learning environment is created.
- Discipline system is progressive.
- Customer satisfaction and quality are evaluated in the performance management system.
- Skills and values of a diverse workforce are valued and used.
- Technology is used to reduce the time for administrative tasks and to improve HR efficiency and effectiveness.

Global Challenge

Sustainability Challenge

Technology Challenge

FIGURE 1.8

Major Dimensions of HRM Practices Contributing to Company Competitiveness

Dimensions of HRM Practices

| Managing the human resource environment | Acquiring and preparing human resources | Assessment and development of human resources | Compensating human resources |

Competitiveness

Acquiring and Preparing Human Resources

Customer needs for new products or services influence the number and type of employees businesses need to be successful. Terminations, promotions, and retirements also influence human resource requirements. Managers need to predict the number and type of employees who are needed to meet customer demands for products and services. Managers must also identify current or potential employees who can successfully deliver products and services. This area of human resource management deals with

- Identifying human resource requirements—that is, human resource planning, recruiting employees, and selecting employees.
- Training employees to have the skills needed to perform their jobs.

Assessment and Development of Human Resources

Managers need to ensure that employees have the necessary skills to perform current and future jobs. As we discussed earlier, because of new technology and the quality movement, many companies are redesigning work so that it is performed by teams. As a result, managers and employees may need to develop new skills to succeed in a team environment. Companies need to create a work environment that supports employees' work and nonwork activities. This area of human resource management addresses

- Measuring employees' performance.
- Preparing employees for future work roles and identifying employees' work interests, goals, values, and other career issues.
- Creating an employment relationship and work environment that benefits both the company and the employee.

Compensating Human Resources

Besides interesting work, pay and benefits are the most important incentives that companies can offer employees in exchange for contributing to productivity, quality, and customer service. Also, pay and benefits are used to reward employees' membership in the company and attract new employees. The positive influence of new work designs, new technology, and the quality movement on productivity can be damaged if employees are not satisfied with the level of pay and benefits or believe pay and benefits are unfairly distributed. This area of human resource management includes

- Creating pay systems.
- Rewarding employee contributions.
- Providing employees with benefits.

Special Issues

In some companies, employees are represented by a labor union. Managing human resources in a union environment requires knowledge of specific laws, contract administration, and the collective bargaining process.

Many companies are globally expanding their business through joint ventures, mergers, acquisitions, and establishing new operations. Successful global expansion depends on the extent to which HRM practices are aligned with cultural factors as well as management of employees sent to work in another country. Human resource management practices must contribute to organizational effectiveness.

Human resource management practices of both managers and the human resource function must be aligned and contribute to the company's strategic goals. The final chapter of the book explains how to effectively integrate human resource management practices.

Organization of This Book

The topics in this book are organized according to the four areas of human resource management and special issues. Table 1.12 lists the chapters covered in the book.

TABLE 1.12

Topics Covered in This Book

The content of each chapter is based on academic research and examples of effective company practices. Each chapter includes examples of how the human resource management practice covered in the chapter helps a company gain a competitive advantage by addressing sustainability, global, and technological challenges. Each chapter also includes examples of how HRM helped a company find and keep the best employees and strategic human resource management practices.

A Look Back

The chapter opening story illustrated how managing human resources contributed to helping save Xerox.

Questions

1. Consider the HRM practices shown in Figure 1.8. For each dimension describe the role it can play in helping a company in a downsizing situation such as Xerox faced. What might be different if the company was prosperous and growing?
2. What role should line managers play in helping support Xerox's HR practices? That is, what should they do? Explain.

Discussion Questions

1. Traditionally, human resource management practices were developed and administered by the company's human resource department. Line managers are now playing a major role in developing and implementing HRM practices. Why do you think non-HR managers are becoming more involved in developing and implementing HRM practices?

2. Staffing, training, compensation, and performance management are important HRM functions. How can each of these functions help companies succeed

in meeting the global challenge, the challenge of using new technology, and the sustainability challenge?
3. This book covers four human resource management practice areas: managing the human resource environment, acquiring and preparing human resources, assessment and development of human resources, and compensating human resources. Which area do you believe contributes most to helping a company gain a competitive advantage? Which area do you believe contributes the least? Why?
4. What is the balanced scorecard? Identify the four perspectives included in the balanced scorecard. How can HRM practices influence the four perspectives?
5. Is HRM becoming more strategic? Explain your answer.
6. Explain the implications of each of the following labor force trends for HRM: (1) aging workforce, (2) diverse workforce, (3) skill deficiencies.
7. What role do HRM practices play in a business decision to expand internationally?
8. Is business emphasis on quality a fad? Why or why not? What might a quality goal and high-performance work systems have in common in terms of HRM practices?
9. What disadvantages might result from outsourcing HRM practices? From employee self-service? From increased line manager involvement in designing and using HR practices?
10. What factors should a company consider before offshoring? What are the advantages and disadvantages of offshoring?

Self-Assessment Exercise: Do You Have What It Takes to Work in HR?

Instructions: Read each statement and circle *yes* or *no*.

Yes   No   1. I have leadership and management skills I have developed through prior job experiences, extracurricular activities, community service, or other noncourse activities.

Yes   No   2. I have excellent communications, dispute resolution, and interpersonal skills.

Yes   No   3. I can demonstrate an understanding of the fundamentals of running a business and making a profit.

Yes   No   4. I can use spreadsheets and the World Wide Web, and I am familiar with information systems technology.

Yes   No   5. I can work effectively with people of different cultural backgrounds.

Yes   No   6. I have expertise in more than one area of human resource management.

Scoring: The greater the number of yes answers, the better prepared you are to work in an HR department. For questions you answered *no*, you should seek courses and experiences to change your answer to *yes*—and better prepare yourself for a career in HR!

SOURCE: Based on B. E. Kaufman, "What Companies Want from HR Graduates," *HR Magazine*, September 1994.

Manager's Hot Seat Exercise: Ethics: Let's Make a 4th Quarter Deal

This case explores the issue of conducting business in an ethical manner within an organization. As the scenario unfolds, a financial opportunity has manifested itself to one manager. This manager is determined to see the deal come to fruition for a variety of reasons—including personal recognition and gain. A major flaw in the plan for concluding the deal is that it would have to be signed without first gaining the approval of the company's shareholders. This is a significant breach of organizational protocol at this company! The manager seeks the alliance and support of her friend and fellow manager to help bring the deal to reality. However, this second manager has no desire to conduct business without first having the approval of the organization's stakeholders. He has no desire to sign off on the deal without being able to adhere to the established guidelines of the company's protocol.

The case depicts how unethical business behavior can lead to internal organizational stress and disruption. It in-

dicates the unethical tactics some individuals may utilize, such as threats, coercion, and accusations in order to sway others to act unethically along with them. It displays the turmoil that can ensue when unethical behavior takes a lead role in conducting business.

Group Activity:

Have the class divided in groups of 4–5 students. Discuss the topic of ethical business behavior. As the group begins its discussion, particular attention should be paid to the following issues/questions:

• Identify what ethical business behavior means to each individual in the group.

• Discuss where each student would draw the line for what is or is not ethical business conduct based on the case (such as gaining vast monetary savings for the organization by not replacing hazardous ma-

chinery versus the safety of employees utilizing faulty, outdated manufacturing equipment).
- Identify prominent reasons for conducting business in an ethical manner.
- Identify prominent reasons for conducting business in an unethical manner.
- Identify potential gains/problems for organizations that act ethically.
- Identify potential gains/problems from conducting business unethically.

- Discuss practices that can be employed by organizations to ward off unethical business behavior such as those exhibited in the case.
- Discuss the advantages of utilizing an ethics officer at the organization.

Once the group responses are prepared, the class can discuss the above issues as a whole to develop more comprehensive answers.

Exercising Strategy: Container Store Does Great HRM

The Container Store, a retailer of boxes, bags, racks, and shelves that organize everything from spices to shoes, is respected for its commitment to employees. The Dallas-based company has 2,000 employees in 11 states. The company has been ranked as one of the best companies to work for by *Fortune* magazine and has received awards for its people management strategies. The company's success is attributed to its low turnover rate (15–20 percent in an industry where 100 percent is common) and a strong customer service philosophy that allows employees to take ownership and make decisions they believe will benefit the customer. The company invests more than 235 hours of training in first-year employees, far above the industry average of seven hours per year. Employees are paid 50–100 percent above the industry average, financial information is shared with employees, and benefits are offered to both full- and part-time employees. Until recently managers were responsible for many traditional human resource management functions such as attracting, motivating, and retaining employees. This is based on the philosophy that because managers are closest to employees they best understand what human resource management practices are necessary. The company now has a semiformal human resource management structure with recruiting, training, payroll, and benefits departments. HR managers are given responsibilities for other areas such as store operations and are required to take store-level positions so

they can better understand the company's purpose. Most HRM employees begin with the company as salespeople. Despite the new HRM structure, managers take the lead in recruiting and evaluating potential employees as well as in employee training.

SOURCE: Based on R. Laglow, "Container Store Does Great HRM: Even without an HR Department," *HR Executive*, August 2001, p. 23; J. Labbs, "Thinking outside the Box at The Container Store," *Workforce*, March 2001, pp. 34–38. Visit The Container Store's website at www.containerstore.com.

Questions
1. As the Container Store continues to expand and grow (the company has grown at an annual rate of 20–25 percent), do you think the manager's role in human resource management should grow, shrink, or remain the same? Explain. Indicate what HRM practices managers should be responsible for and what practices should be the responsibility of human resource management staff?
2. Consider our discussion in this chapter of HR roles and competencies. What are the advantages and disadvantages for successfully performing these roles by having human resource management staff come from store-level positions?
3. Should Container Store consider outsourcing any HRM practices? Which ones? How might they determine which ones?

Managing People: From the Pages of *BusinessWeek*

BusinessWeek The Future of Work

Flexible, creative, and good with people? You should do fine in tomorrow's job market No low-wage worker in Shanghai, New Delhi, or Dublin will ever take Mark Ryan's job. No software will ever do what he does, either. That's because Ryan, 48, manages people—specifically, 100 technicians who serve half a million customers of Verizon Communications Inc. out of an office in Santa Fe Springs, California. A telephone lineman before

moving up the corporate ladder, Ryan is earning a master's degree at Verizon's expense in organizational management, where he's studying topics like conflict resolution.

That's heady stuff for a guy who used to climb poles. "The technical side of the business is important," says Ryan, "but managing people and rewarding and recognizing the people who do an outstanding job is how we are going to succeed."

Sab Maglione, 44, is more vulnerable. The computer programmer from Somerville, N.J., was hired by an insurance company as an independent contractor in 2000 for good money but soon found himself training the representatives of Tata Consulting who would eventually move his work to India. His next contract in New York City paid half as much—but even that soon ended when he found himself out of work the day after Christmas last year. Maglione, who has an associate's degree in computer science, is studying hard and remains optimistic about getting a job but says he's been stymied by the "barrelful" of recent experience in the latest programming languages prospective employers demand. "If you don't have it, they say, 'Let's outsource it.'"

Ryan the happy manager and Maglione the worried programmer exemplify two powerful crosscurrents in the American job market. Changes in the economy in recent years have made some people more valuable and secure than ever, while pushing others—even those with skills that were recently regarded as highly valuable—to the margins.

What makes the difference? New research by economists at Massachusetts Institute of Technology and Harvard University concludes that the key factor is whether a job can be "routinized," or broken down into repeatable steps that vary little from day to day. Such a job is easier to replace with a clever piece of software or to hand over to a lower-paid worker outside the U.S. By comparison, the jobs that will pay well in the future will be ones that are hard to reduce to a recipe. These attractive jobs—from factory floor management to sales to teaching to the professions—require flexibility, creativity, and lifelong learning. They generally also require subtle and frequent interactions with other people, often face to face.

The good news is that a substantial majority of the jobs in the U.S. economy are nonroutine. And when you think about it, that has to be the case. In the relentless pursuit of productivity, the U.S. has already demolished millions of routine jobs in manufacturing, clerical work, programming, and other fields. So it stands to reason that the people who have survived are doing things that the downsizing experts—try as they might—haven't figured out how to reduce to software or ship abroad.

The Survivors Nor do you need an advanced degree to have a nonroutine job. You just need to do something that can't be boiled down to a repeatable procedure or that requires a lot of human interaction. The surviving secretaries, for example, have moved up from typing and answering phones to planning meetings, keeping books, and other more complex tasks. Bank tellers now spend more time handling special requests, while ATMs have taken over much of the job of taking deposits and dispensing cash. The factory workers most likely to keep their jobs

will be those who make themselves experts on a variety of computer-controlled machines, or who excel at quick turnaround of custom orders. Those jobs aren't going away.

As the economy evolves, two kinds of jobs will remain impossible to routinize, according to Frank Levy of MIT and Richard J. Murnane of Harvard, in a forthcoming book called *The New Division of Labor: How Computers Are Creating the Next Job Market*. One kind involves complex pattern recognition. Such skills as spotting business opportunities or repairing a complicated machine fall into this category. The other relies on complex communication skills, such as those required to manage people, devise advertising campaigns, or sell big-ticket items such as cars. Says Levy: "If you can really write the whole job down on paper, then someone else can do it."

Viewed through the lens of routine versus nonroutine work, the debate over job growth and the future of jobs takes on a new hue. It suggests that Americans looking for good jobs would do well to bet on such constantly varying occupations as manager, entrepreneur, or artist, as well as jobs such as teaching, lending, and sales jobs that require lots of people skills.

At the same time, some jobs that are highly compensated today could soon be routinized. Powerful computers, advanced software, and speedy communications have vastly increased the vulnerability of routine work. Well-paid legal researchers, tax preparers, and accountants, for example, are seeing their jobs outsourced abroad. The jobs require intelligence and technical knowledge, of course, but because the procedures are highly standardized, they can be done at a distance by well-educated workers willing to do the job for far less. Likewise, stock traders could eventually be replaced by automated trading systems. Computer programming is a routine job that used to pay well because few people could do it. Now, part of the work has been taken over by clever software, and part has been exported to lower-wage nations connected by fiber-optic networks.

The people displaced from those jobs are shifting into jobs that can't be so easily standardized. And clearly, the growing importance of nonroutine work increases the value of education. College graduates have steadily broadened their lead over the less-educated in earnings. College grads also have more stable employment. Yes, there are pockets of high unemployment, such as in computer and math professions. But the unemployment rate for all people with a bachelor's degree or better was just 2.9% in February, vs. 8.5% for people with less than a high school diploma. "Fear of outsourcing is absolutely a key factor in driving our enrollment," says Todd S. Nelson, CEO of Apollo Group Inc., parent of the University of Phoenix, which caters to working adults across the country through campuses in 30 states and online courses. The university's enrollment soared nearly a third last year to 186,000.

As valuable as education is, technical knowledge alone won't cut it, because workers in other countries read the same textbooks. For many good jobs, in fact, education isn't as useful as specialized local knowledge. Lin Stiles, a headhunter in New London, N.H., says that demand is hot for plant managers who can improve a factory's efficiency. A fancy degree isn't necessary. Says Stiles: "We frequently do not have college requirements even for a vice president for operations."

While the debate over the future of work pervades the whole economy, information technology is where it's most pointed now. That's because the IT sector is being split in two. More routine tech jobs, such as the programming done by Sab Maglione, are vulnerable to automation or outsourcing. In contrast, there's still plenty of demand in the U.S. for people who combine technical skills with industry-specific knowledge and people skills. That's certainly true at UNUMProvident Corp., the disability insurer. Says Robert O. Best, the chief information officer: "You used to be able to get away with being a technical nerd five years ago. Those days are over." Now, he says, "We're looking for softer skills," like the ability to work with others, change direction quickly, and understand the business.

SOURCE: Peter Coy, with William C. Symonds in Boston, Stephen Baker in New York, Michael Arndt in Chicago, Robert D. Hof in San Mateo, Calif., and bureau reports, *BusinessWeek*, March 22, 2004, pp. 50–52

Questions

1. What can companies in their human resource management practices do to ensure that employees are flexible, creative, and provide good customer service?

2. Many companies have recognized the value of educating their workforce and as a result offer training programs and provide tuition reimbursement for employees seeking high school, college, or advanced degrees. Many companies are concerned that they will not get a return on their investment in education. That is, once employees finish their degree they will leave the company. What should companies do to ensure that they get a return on the money they invest in education and training?

3. Provide an example of a job that you believe will soon be replaced by technology or become so highly routinized that it will demand employees with low levels of skill who receive low pay. Describe the job and discuss your reasons for choosing it.

 Please see the video case at the end of the book that corresponds to this chapter: HotJobs.com.

Notes

1. A. S. Tsui and L. R. Gomez-Mejia, "Evaluating Human Resource Effectiveness," in *Human Resource Management: Evolving Rules and Responsibilities*, ed. L. Dyer (Washington, DC: BNA Books, 1988), pp. 1187–227; M. A. Hitt, B. W. Keats, and S. M. DeMarie, "Navigating in the New Competitive Landscape: Building Strategic Flexibility and Competitive Advantage in the 21st Century," *Academy of Management Executive* 12, no. 4 (1998), pp. 22–42; J. T. Delaney and M. A. Huselid, "The Impact of Human Resource Management Practices on Perceptions of Organizational Performance," *Academy of Management Journal* 39 (1996), pp. 949–69.

2. F. Hansen, "2003 Data Bank Annual," *Workforce Management* 82 (13) (2003), p. 87.

3. SHRM-BNA Survey No. 66, "Policy and Practice Forum: Human Resources Activities, Budgets, and Staffs: 2000–2001." Bulletin to Management, Bureau of National Affairs Policy and Practice Series, June 28, 2001 (Washington, DC: Bureau of National Affairs).

4. D. Ulrich, *Human Resource Champions* (Boston: Harvard Business School Press, 1998).

5. D. Ulrich and N. Smallwood, "Capitalizing on Capabilities," *Harvard Business Review*, June 2004, pp. 119–27.

6. Ulrich, *Human Resource Champions*.

7. Ibid.

8. Ibid.

9. K. Maher, "Human Resource Directors Are Assuming Strategic Roles," *The Wall Street Journal* (June 17, 2003), p. B8; A. McIlvaine, "Retooling HR," *Human Resource Management Executive* (October 2, 2003), pp. 1, 18–26.

10. Ulrich, *Human Resource Champions*.

11. A. Halcrow, "Survey Shows HRM in Transition," *Workforce*, June 1998, pp. 73–80: J. Laabs, "Why HR Can't Win Today," *Workforce*, May 1998, pp. 62–74; C. Cole. "Kodak Snapshots," *Workforce*, June 2000, pp. 65–72.

12. Towers Perrin, *Priorities for Competitive Advantage: An IBM Study Conducted by Towers Perrin*, 1992.

13. S. Greengard, "Building a Self-Service Culture That Works," *Workforce*, July 1998, pp. 60–64.

14. G. Yohe, "Building Your Case," *Human Resource Executive* (March 2, 2003), pp. 22–26.

15. S. Caudron, "HR Is Dead Long Live HR," *Workforce*, January 2003, pp. 26–29.

16. Towers Perrin, *Priorities for Competitive Advantage*.

17. F. Hansen, "The CFO Connection," *Workforce Management*, July 2003, pp. 50–54.

18. J. Wiscombe, "Your Wonderful, Terrible HR Life," *Workforce*, June 2001, pp. 32–38.

19. R. Grossman, "Putting HR in Rotation," *HR Magazine*, March 2003, pp. 50–57.

20. Caudron, "HR Is Dead Long Live HR"; S. Bates, "Business Partners," *HR Magazine*, September 2003, pp. 45–49.

21. A. Jones, "Evolutionary Science, Work/Life Integration, and Corporate Responsibility," *Organizational Dynamics* 32 (2002), pp. 17–31.

22. C. Thompson, E. Koon, W. Woodwell, Jr., and J. Beauvais, "Training for the Next Economy: An ASTD State of the Industry Report on Trends in Employer-Provided Training in the United States" (Alexandria, VA: ASTD, 2002).

23. "Workplace Visions," *Society for Human Resource Management* 4 (2002).

24. D. Hecker, "Occupational Employment Projections to 2012," *Monthly Labor Review* 127 (2004), pp. 80–105.

25. M. Horrigan, "Employment Projections to 2012: Concepts and Context," *Monthly Labor Review* 127 (2004), pp. 3–22.

26. L. Weatherly, *Human Capital—The Elusive Asset* (Alexandria, VA: Society for Human Resource Management, 2003); E. Zimmerman, "What Are Employees Worth?" *Workforce*, February 2001, pp. 32–36.

27. "BLS Releases 2000–2010 Employment Projections." From U.S. Bureau of Labor Statistics website, http://stats.bls.gov.

28. T. J. Atchison, "The Employment Relationship: Untied or Re-Tied," *Academy of Management Executive* 5 (1991), pp. 52–62.

29. "CIO Panel: Knowledge-Sharing Roundtable," *Information Week Online*, News in Review, April 26, 1999 (from *Information Week* website, www.informationweek.com); Buckman Laboratories website, www.buckman.com.

30. P. Drucker, *Management Challenges for the 21st Century* (New York: Harper Business, 1999); Howard N. Fullerton Jr., "Labor Force Projections to 2008: Steady Growth and Changing Composition," *Monthly Labor Review*, November 1999, pp. 19–32.

31. D. Senge, "The Learning Organization Made Plain and Simple," *Training and Development Journal*, October 1991, pp. 37–44.

32. L. Thornburg, "Accounting for Knowledge," *HR Magazine*, October 1994, pp. 51–56.

33. A. Carnevale and D. Desrochers, "Training in the Dilbert Economy," *Training & Development*, December 1999, pp. 32–36.

34. "Industry Report 2002," *Training*, October 2002, p. 51.

35. D. M. Rousseau, "Psychological and Implied Contracts in Organizations," *Employee Rights and Responsibilities Journal* 2 (1989), pp. 121–29.

36. D. Rousseau, "Changing the Deal While Keeping the People," *Academy of Management Executive* 11 (1996), pp. 50–61; M. A. Cavanaugh and R. Noe, "Antecedents and Consequences of the New Psychological Contract," *Journal of Organizational Behavior* 20 (1999), pp. 323–40.

37. J. Harter, F. Schmidt, and T. Hayes, "Business Unit Relationships between Employee Satisfaction, Employee Engagement and Business Outcomes: A Meta-Analysis, *Journal of Applied Psychology* 87 (2002), pp. 268–79.

38. "Employee Attitudes" and "Engagement Indicators," 2003 Data Bank Annual, *Workforce Management* 82 (13) (2003), p. 90.

39. "New Coca-Cola CEO Seeks to Boost Morale," *The Wall Street Journal* (June 3, 2004), p. B5.

40. D. Koeppel, "The New Cost of Keeping Workers Happy," *New York Times* (March 7, 2004), p. 11.

41. Table of "Free Agent Workforce," in Data Bank Annual, *Workforce Management* 82 (13) (2003), p. 96.

42. A. Freedman, "Staffing Up," *Human Resource Executive*, January 2004, pp. 24–31.

43. M. Hammers, "Family-Friendly Benefits Prompt Non-Parent Backlash," *Workforce Management* 82 (8) (2003), pp. 77–79.

44. C. Johnson, "Don't Forget Your Shift Workers," *HR Magazine*, February 1999, pp. 80–84.

45. C. Patton, "Future Shock," *Human Resource Executive* (March 16, 2003), pp. 16–22.

46. R. S. Kaplan and D. P. Norton, "The Balanced Scorecard—Measures That Drive Performance," *Harvard Business Review*, January–February 1992, pp. 71–79; R. S. Kaplan and D. P. Norton, "Putting the Balanced Scorecard to Work," *Harvard Business Review*, September–October 1993, pp. 134–47.

47. M. Gendron, "Using the Balanced Scorecard," *Harvard Business Review*, October 1997, pp. 3–5.

48. S. Bates, "The Metrics Maze," *HR Magazine*, December 2003, pp. 50–55; D. Ulrich, "Measuring Human Resources: An Overview of Practice and a Prescription for Results," *Human Resource Management* 36 (1997), pp. 303–20.

49. E. Raimy, "A Plan for All Seasons," *Human Resource Executive*, April 2001, pp. 34–38.

50. J. R. Jablonski, *Implementing Total Quality Management: An Overview* (San Diego: Pfeiffer, 1991).

51. R. Hodgetts, F. Luthans, and S. Lee, "New Paradigm Organizations: From Total Quality to Learning World-Class," *Organizational Dynamics* (Winter 1994), pp. 5–19.

52. "Malcolm Baldrige National Quality Award 2001 Award Recipient, Small Business Category, Pal's Sudden Service." From Baldrige Award Recipient Profile at www.nist.gov, the website for the National Institute of Standards and Technology.

53. S. L. Jackson, "What You Should Know about ISO 9000," *Training*, May 1992, pp. 48–52; Bureau of Best Practices, *Profile of ISO 9000* (Boston: Allyn and Bacon, 1992); "ISO 9000 International Standards for Quality Assurance," *Design Matters*, July 1995, http://www.best.com/ISO 9000/att/ISONet.html/. See www.iso9000y2k.com, a website containing ISO 9000:2000 documentation.

54. General Electric 1999 Annual Report, www.ge.com/annual99.

55. H. N. Fullerton, "Labor Force 2006: Slowing Down and Changing Composition," *Monthly Labor Review*, November 1997, pp. 23–28. Also see the Bureau of Labor Statistics employment projections on the Web at www.bls.gov/news.release/ecopro.nws.htm.

56. U.S. Census Bureau.

57. N. Lockwood, *The Aging Workforce* (Alexandria, VA: Society for Human Resource Management Research, 2003).

58. M. Horrigan, "Employment Projections to 2012: Concepts and Context," *Monthly Labor Review* 127 (2), pp. 3–22.

59. Ibid.

60. M. Mandel, "It's Really Two Immigrant Economies," *BusinessWeek* (June 20, 1994), pp. 74–78.

61. J. Mullich, "Hiring without Limits," *Workforce Management* 83 (6) (2004), pp. 53–58.

62. C. M. Solomon, "Managing the Baby Busters," *Personnel Journal*, March 1992, pp. 52–59; J. Wallace, "After X Comes Y," *HR Magazine* (April 2001), p. 192; C. Solomon, "Ready or Not, Here Comes the Net Kids," *Workforce*, February 2000, pp. 62–68.

63. B. Wooldridge and J. Wester, "The Turbulent Environment of Public Personnel Administration: Responding to the Chal-

lenge of the Changing Workplace of the Twenty-first Century," *Public Personnel Management* 20 (1991), pp. 207–24; J. Laabs, "The New Loyalty: Grasp It. Earn It. Keep It," *Workforce,* November 1998, pp. 34–39.

64. "Employee Dissatisfaction on Rise in Last 10 Years, New Report Says," *Employee Relations Weekly* (Washington, DC: Bureau of National Affairs, 1986).

65. D. T. Hall and J. Richter, "Career Gridlock: Baby Boomers Hit the Wall," *The Executive* 4 (1990), pp. 7–22.

66. T. H. Cox and S. Blake, "Managing Cultural Diversity: Implications for Organizational Competitiveness," *The Executive* 5 (1991), pp. 45–56.

67. M. Loden and J. B. Rosener, *Workforce America!* (Homewood, IL: Business One Irwin, 1991).

68. F. Hansen, "Diversity's Business Case Doesn't Add Up," *Workforce* 82 (4) (2003), pp. 28–32.

69. J. Ledvinka and V. G. Scarpello, *Federal Regulation of Personnel and Human Resource Management,* 2nd ed. (Boston: PWS-Kent, 1991).

70. N. Lockwood, *The Glass Ceiling: Domestic and International Perspectives* (Alexandria, VA: Society for Human Resource Management, 2004).

71. *Women in U.S. Corporate Leadership: 2003* (New York: Catalyst, 2003).

72. M. Pastin, *The Hard Problems of Management: Gaining the Ethics Edge* (San Francisco: Jossey-Bass, 1986). T. Thomas, J. Schermerhorn, Jr., & J. Dienhart, "Strategic Leadership of Ethical Behavior in Business," Academy of Management Executive 18 (2004), pp. 56–66.

73. Ibid.

74. J. Segal, "The 'Joy' of Uncooking," *HR Magazine* 47 (11) (2002).

75. D. Buss, "Corporate Compasses," *HR Magazine* 49 (6) (2004), pp. 126–32.

76. D. Buss, "Working It Out," *HRMagazine online,* www.shrm.org/hrmagazine/04June.

77. R. Stolz, "What HR Will Stand For," *Human Resource Executive,* January 2003, pp. 20–28.

78. G. F. Cavanaugh, D. Moberg, and M. Velasquez, "The Ethics of Organizational Politics," *Academy of Management Review* 6 (1981), pp. 363–74.

79. C. Hill, *Informational Business* (Burr Ridge, IL: Irwin/McGraw-Hill, 1997).

80. J. Lee Young, "Starbucks Expansion into China Is Slated," *The Wall Street Journal* (October 5, 1998), p. B13C.

81. E. Tahmincioglu, "Opportunities Mingle with Fear Overseas," *The New York Times* (October 24, 2001), p. G1.

82. M. Cohen, *Labor Shortages as America Approaches the Twenty-First Century* (Ann Arbor: University of Michigan Press, 1995); H. Fullerton, "Another Look at the Labor Force," *Monthly Labor Review,* November 1993, pp. 31–40.

83. J. Schramm, "Offshoring," *Workplace Visions* 2 (Alexandria, VA: Society for Human Resource Management, 2004); P. Babcock, "America's Newest Export: White Collar Jobs," *HR Magazine* 49 (4) (2004), pp. 50–57.

84. R. Chittum, "Call Centers Phone Home," *The Wall Street Journal* (June 9, 2004), pp. B1, B8.

85. J. Kahn, "Small Firms Find That Outsourcing Cuts Both Ways," *Fortune* (April 28, 2004), at www.fortune.com.

86. M. Kripalani and P. Engardio, "The Rise of India," *BusinessWeek* (December 8, 2003), pp. 66–76.

87. "Two-Thirds of Americans Online," *CyberAtlas* (May 10, 2000), http://cyberatlas.internet.com.

88. Ibid.

89. B. Manville, "Organizing Enterprise-Wide E-learning and Human Capital Management," *Chief Learning Officer,* May 2003, pp. 50–55.

90. A. Weintraub, "High Tech's Future Is in the Toy Chest," *BusinessWeek* (August 26, 2002), pp. 124–26.

91. *2002 Benefits Survey* (Alexandria, VA: Society of Human Resource Management Foundation, 2002).

92. C. Johnson, "Don't Forget Your Shift Workers," *HR Magazine,* February 1999, pp. 80–84.

93. J. Cook, "Keeping Work at Work," *Human Resource Executive,* July 2001, pp. 68–71.

94. P. Choate and P. Linger, *The High-Flex Society* (New York: Knopf, 1986); P. B. Doeringer, *Turbulence in the American Workplace* (New York: Oxford University Press, 1991).

95. J. A. Neal and C. L. Tromley, "From Incremental Change to Retrofit: Creating High-Performance Work Systems," *Academy of Management Executive* 9 (1995), pp. 42–54.

96. K. A. Miller, *Retraining the American Workforce* (Reading, MA: Addison-Wesley, 1989).

97. D. Welch, "How Nissan Laps Detroit," *BusinessWeek,* December 2003, pp. 58–60.

98. W. Pape, "Group Insurance," *Inc. Technology* 2 (1997), pp. 29, 31.

99. T. Peters, "Restoring American Competitiveness: Looking for New Models of Organizations," *The Executive* 2 (1988), pp. 103–10.

100. M. J. Kavanaugh, H. G. Guetal, and S. I. Tannenbaum, *Human Resource Information Systems: Development and Application* (Boston: PWS-Kent, 1990).

101. S. Greengard, "When HRMS Goes Global: Managing the Data Highway," *Personnel Journal,* June 1995, pp. 91–106.

102. M. Stepanek, "Using the Net for Brainstorming," *BusinessWeek e.biz* (December 13, 1999).

103. R. N. Ashkenas, "Beyond the Fads: How Leaders Drive Change with Results," *Human Resource Planning* 17 (1994), pp. 25–44.

104. M. A. Huselid, "The Impact of Human Resource Management Practices on Turnover, Productivity, and Corporate Financial Performance," *Academy of Management Journal* 38 (1995), pp. 635–72; U.S. Dept. of Labor, *High-Performance Work Practices and Firm Performance* (Washington, DC: U.S. Government Printing Office, 1993).

105. B. Becker and M. A. Huselid, "High-Performance Work Systems and Firm Performance: A Synthesis of Research and Managerial Implications," in *Research in Personnel and Human Resource Management* 16, ed. G. R. Ferris (Stamford, CT: JAI Press, 1998), pp. 53–101.

106. B. Becker and B. Gerhart, "The Impact of Human Resource Management on Organizational Performance: Progress and Prospects," *Academy of Management Journal* 39 (1996), pp. 779–801.

107. G. Flynn, "HR Leaders Stay Close to the Line," *Workforce,* February 1997, p. 53; GE Fanuc Corporate Profile, "World Class Excellence," www.ge.com/gemis/gefanuc.

108. S. A. Snell and J. W. Dean, "Integrated Manufacturing and Human Resource Management: A Human Capital Perspective," *Academy of Management Journal* 35 (1992), pp. 467–504; M. A. Youndt, S. Snell, J. W. Dean Jr., and D. P. Lepak, "Human Resource Management, Manufacturing Strategy, and Firm Performance," *Academy of Management Journal* 39 (1996), pp. 836–66.

1 Part

The Human Resource Environment

2
Chapter

Strategic Human Resource Management

Objectives After reading this chapter, you should be able to:

1. Describe the differences between strategy formulation and strategy implementation.

2. List the components of the strategic management process.

3. Discuss the role of the HRM function in strategy formulation.

4. Describe the linkages between HRM and strategy formulation.

5. Discuss the more popular typologies of generic strategies and the various HRM practices associated with each.

6. Describe the different HRM issues and practices associated with various directional strategies.

7. List the competencies the HRM executive needs to become a strategic partner in the company.

JetBlue promises low fares, friendly employees, and quality service (including free in-flight Direct TV). What are some of the strategies this airline can employ to make sure they remain distinctive, but maintain their growth?

Enter the World of Business

Flying High at JetBlue

In an industry that has lost money for the past 25 years, JetBlue Airways seems to be bucking the trend. Founded in 1999 and flying since 2000, JetBlue has earned profits for 12 consecutive quarters, even following the tragedy of September 11, 2001. It is among the industry leaders in operating margins, percentage of seats filled, and on-time arrivals. Founder and CEO David Neeleman has ambitious plans: to vault from a newcomer with 57 planes and 6,000 employees into the ranks of the major airlines with 290 planes and 25,000 employees within seven years.

The challenge JetBlue faces is that other airlines have had these plans before, and failed miserably. JetBlue has built its distinctiveness through the enthusiasm of its employees, its tremendous customer focus, and a slightly countercultural image, but these characteristics are much easier to build and maintain when a firm is small, than when it is big. And when small firms grow quickly, maintaining these characteristics becomes even more problematic.

For instance, in the early 1980s a new airline emerged shortly after deregulation, People Express. People Express similarly built its reputation on energetic and committed employees delivering a good product at a lower than average cost. That airline built a billion dollars in annual sales in less than five years, but then in an effort to expand quickly, it stretched too far. With systems unable to handle rapidly increasing volume, the people became overworked and were unable to sustain the customer service that had led to their success. Within a year, the airline had folded.

What are the specific challenges that JetBlue faces? For one, part of the low cost stems from flying an almost completely new fleet of planes, but as these planes age, maintenance costs will certainly rise. In addition, the employees all started at the introductory pay rates, but again, their wages will rise as the airline grows older and larger. In addition, as the airline grows it will need to standardize processes and tools to drive consistency throughout the organization, and much of this will entail building an extensive information technology system. As JetBlue handles these challenges, it must continue to preserve its personal touch.

Source: C. Slater, "And Now the Hard Part," *FastCompany,* May 2004, p. 67; pf.fastcompany.com/magazine/82/jetblue.html.

Introduction

As the JetBlue example just illustrated, business organizations exist in an environment of competition. They can use a number of resources to compete with other companies. These resources are physical (such as plant, equipment, technology, and geographic location), organizational (the structure, planning, controlling, and coordinating systems, and group relations), and human (the experience, skill, and intelligence of employees). It is these resources under the control of the company that provide competitive advantage.[1]

The goal of strategic management in an organization is to deploy and allocate resources in a way that gives it a competitive advantage. As you can see, two of the three classes of resources (organizational and human) are directly tied to the human resource management function. As Chapter 1 pointed out, the role of human resource management is to ensure that a company's human resources provide a competitive advantage. Chapter 1 also pointed out some of the major competitive challenges that companies face today. These challenges require companies to take a proactive, strategic approach in the marketplace.

To be maximally effective, the HRM function must be integrally involved in the company's strategic management process.[2] This means that human resource managers should (1) have input into the strategic plan, both in terms of people-related issues and in terms of the ability of the human resource pool to implement particular strategic alternatives; (2) have specific knowledge of the organization's strategic goals; (3) know what types of employee skills, behaviors, and attitudes are needed to support the strategic plan; and (4) develop programs to ensure that employees have those skills, behaviors, and attitudes.

We begin this chapter by discussing the concept of strategy and by depicting the strategic management process. Then we discuss the levels of integration between the HRM function and the strategic management process in strategy formulation. Next we review some of the more common strategic models and, within the context of these models, discuss the various types of employee skills, behaviors, and attitudes, and the ways HRM practices aid in implementing the strategic plan. Finally, we discuss the new competencies needed by HRM executives to fulfill the strategic role of HRM.

What Is Strategic Management?

Many authors have noted that in today's competitive market, organizations must engage in strategic planning to survive and prosper. *Strategy* comes from the Greek word *strategos*, which has its roots in military language. It refers to a general's grand design behind a war or battle. In fact, *Webster's New American Dictionary* defines *strategy* as the "skillful employment and coordination of tactics" and as "artful planning and management."

Strategic management is a process, an approach to addressing the competitive challenges an organization faces. It can be thought of as managing the "pattern or plan that integrates an organization's major goals, policies, and action sequences into a cohesive whole."[3] These strategies can be either the generic approach to competing or the specific adjustments and actions taken to deal with a particular situation.

First, business organizations engage in generic strategies that often fit into some strategic type. One example is "cost, differentiation, or focus."[4] Another is "defender, analyzer, prospector, or reactor."[5] Different organizations within the same industry often have different generic strategies. These generic strategy types describe the consistent way the company attempts to position itself relative to competitors.

However, a generic strategy is only a small part of strategic management. The second aspect of strategic management is the process of developing strategies for achieving the company's goals in light of its current environment. Thus, business organizations engage in generic strategies, but they also make choices about such things as how to scare off competitors, how to keep competitors weaker, how to react to and influence pending legislation, how to deal with various stakeholders and special interest groups, how to lower production costs, how to raise revenues, what technology to implement, and how many and what types of people to employ. Each of these decisions may present competitive challenges that have to be considered.

Strategic management is more than a collection of strategic types. It is a process for analyzing a company's competitive situation, developing the company's strategic goals, and devising a plan of action and allocation of resources (human, organizational, and physical) that will increase the likelihood of achieving those goals. This kind of strategic approach should be emphasized in human resource management. HR managers should be trained to identify the competitive issues the company faces with regard to human resources and think strategically about how to respond.

Strategic human resource management (SHRM) can be thought of as "the pattern of planned human resource deployments and activities intended to enable an organization to achieve its goals."[6] For example, many firms have developed integrated manufacturing systems such as advanced manufacturing technology, just-in-time inventory control, and total quality management in an effort to increase their competitive position. However, these systems must be run by people. SHRM in these cases entails assessing the employee skills required to run these systems and engaging in HRM practices, such as selection and training, that develop these skills in employees.[7] To take a strategic approach to HRM, we must first understand the role of HRM in the strategic management process.

Components of the Strategic Management Process

The strategic management process has two distinct yet interdependent phases: strategy formulation and strategy implementation. During **strategy formulation** the strategic planning groups decide on a strategic direction by defining the company's mission and goals, its external opportunities and threats, and its internal strengths and weaknesses. They then generate various strategic alternatives and compare those alternatives' ability to achieve the company's mission and goals. During **strategy implementation,** the organization follows through on the chosen strategy. This consists of structuring the organization, allocating resources, ensuring that the firm has skilled employees in place, and developing reward systems that align employee behavior with the organization's strategic goals. Both of these strategic management phases must be performed effectively. It is important to note that this process does not happen sequentially. As we will discuss later with regard to emergent strategies, this process entails a constant cycling of information and decision making. Figure 2.1 presents the strategic management process.

In recent years organizations have recognized that the success of the strategic management process depends largely on the extent to which the HRM function is involved.[8]

Strategic human resource management (SHRM)
A pattern of planned human resource deployments and activities intended to enable an organization to achieve its goals.

Strategy formulation
The process of deciding on a strategic direction by defining a company's mission and goals, its external opportunities and threats, and its internal strengths and weaknesses.

Strategy implementation
The process of devising structures and allocating resources to enact the strategy a company has chosen.

FIGURE 2.1
A Model of the Strategic Management Process

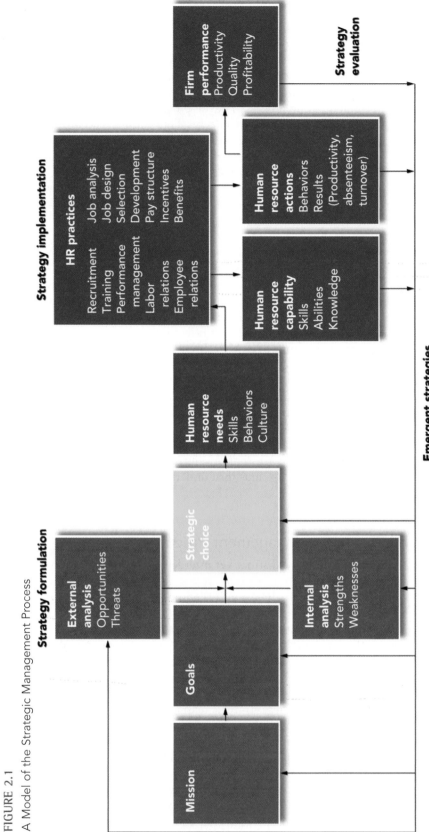

Strategy formulation

Mission

Goals

External analysis
Opportunities
Threats

Internal analysis
Strengths
Weaknesses

Strategic choice

Human resource needs
Skills
Behaviors
Culture

Strategy implementation

HR practices
Recruitment
Training
Performance management
Labor relations
Employee relations
Job analysis
Job design
Selection
Development
Pay structure
Incentives
Benefits

Human resource capability
Skills
Abilities
Knowledge

Human resource actions
Behaviors
Results (Productivity, absenteeism, turnover)

Firm performance
Productivity
Quality
Profitability

Strategy evaluation

Emergent strategies

1. Where to compete?
   In what market or markets (industries, products, etc.) will we compete?
2. How to compete?
   On what criterion or differentiating characteristic(s) will we compete? Cost?
   Quality? Reliability? Delivery?
3. With what will we compete?
   What resources will allow us to beat our competition?
   How will we acquire, develop, and deploy those resources to compete?

FIGURE 2.2

Strategy—Decisions about Competition

Linkage between HRM and the Strategic Management Process

The strategic choice really consists of answering questions about competition—that is, how the firm will compete to achieve its missions and goals. These decisions consist of addressing the issues of where to compete, how to compete, and with what to compete, which are described in Figure 2.2. Although these decisions are all important, strategic decision makers often pay less attention to the "with what will we compete" issue, resulting in poor strategic decisions. For example, PepsiCo in the 1980s acquired the fast food chains of Kentucky Fried Chicken, Taco Bell, and Pizza Hut ("where to compete" decisions) in an effort to increase its customer base. However, it failed to adequately recognize the differences between its existing workforce (mostly professionals) and that of the fast food industry (lower-skilled people and high schoolers) as well as its ability to manage such a workforce. This was one reason that Pepsi-Co, in 1998, spun off the fast food chains. In essence, it had made a decision about where to compete without fully understanding what resources it would take to compete in that market.

Boeing illustrates how failing to address the "with what" issue resulted in problems in its "how to compete" decisions. When the aerospace firm's consumer products division entered into a price war with Airbus Industrie, it was forced to move away from its traditional customer service strategy toward emphasizing cost reduction.[9] The strategy was a success on the sales end as Boeing received large numbers of orders for aircraft from firms such as Delta, Continental, Southwest, and Singapore Airlines. However, it had recently gone through a large workforce reduction (thus, it didn't have enough people to fill the orders) and did not have the production technology to enable the necessary increase in productivity. The result of this failure to address "with what will we compete" in making a decision about how to compete resulted in the firm's inability to meet delivery deadlines and the ensuing penalties it had to pay to its customers. The end result is that after all the travails, for the first time in the history of the industry, Airbus sold more planes than Boeing in 2003 and the gap is expected to widen over the next few years.

Role of HRM in Strategy Formulation

As the preceding examples illustrate, often the "with what will we compete" questions present ideal avenues for HRM to influence the strategic management process. This might be through either limiting strategic options or forcing thoughtfulness among the executive team regarding how and at what cost the firm might gain or develop the human resources (people) necessary for such a strategy to be successful.

FIGURE 2.3

Linkages of
Strategic Planning
and HRM

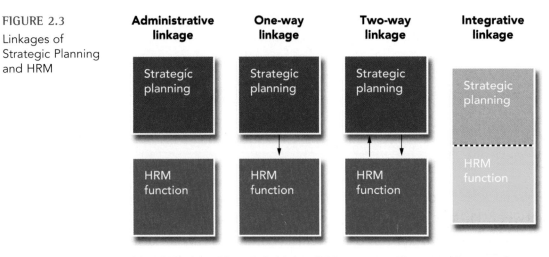

SOURCE: Adapted from K. Golden and V. Ramanujam, "Between a Dream and a
Nightmare: On the Integration of the Human Resource Function and the Strategic
Business Planning Process," *Human Resource Management* 24 (1985), pp. 429–51.

For example, HRM executives at PepsiCo could have noted that the firm had no
expertise in managing the workforce of fast food restaurants. The limiting role would
have been for these executives to argue against the acquisition because of this lack of
resources. On the other hand, they might have influenced the decision by educating
top executives as to the costs (of hiring, training, and so on) associated with gaining
people who had the right skills to manage such a workforce.

A firm's strategic management decision-making process usually takes place at its
top levels, with a strategic planning group consisting of the chief executive officer, the
chief financial officer, the president, and various vice presidents. However, each component of the process involves people-related business issues. Therefore, the HRM
function needs to be involved in each of those components. One recent study of 115
strategic business units within Fortune 500 corporations found that between 49 and
69 percent of the companies had some link between HRM and the strategic planning
process.[10] However, the level of linkage varied, and it is important to understand
these different levels.

Four levels of integration seem to exist between the HRM function and the strategic management function: administrative linkage, one-way linkage, two-way linkage,
and integrative linkage.[11] These levels of linkage will be discussed in relation to the different components of strategic management. The linkages are illustrated in Figure 2.3.

Administrative Linkage

In administrative linkage (the lowest level of integration), the HRM function's attention is focused on day-to-day activities. The HRM executive has no time or opportunity to take a strategic outlook toward HRM issues. The company's strategic business
planning function exists without any input from the HRM department. Thus, in this
level of integration, the HRM department is completely divorced from any component of the strategic management process in both strategy formulation and strategy
implementation. The department simply engages in administrative work unrelated to
the company's core business needs.

One-Way Linkage

In one-way linkage, the firm's strategic business planning function develops the strategic plan and then informs the HRM function of the plan. Many believe this level of integration constitutes strategic HRM—that is, the role of the HRM function is to design systems and/or programs that implement the strategic plan. Although one-way linkage does recognize the importance of human resources in implementing the strategic plan, it precludes the company from considering human resource issues while formulating the strategic plan. This level of integration often leads to strategic plans that the company cannot successfully implement.

Two-Way Linkage

Two-way linkage allows for consideration of human resource issues during the strategy formulation process. This integration occurs in three sequential steps. First, the strategic planning team informs the HRM function of the various strategies the company is considering. Then HRM executives analyze the human resource implications of the various strategies, presenting the results of this analysis to the strategic planning team. Finally, after the strategic decision has been made, the strategic plan is passed on to the HRM executive, who develops programs to implement it. The strategic planning function and the HRM function are interdependent in two-way linkage.

Integrative Linkage

Integrative linkage is dynamic and multifaceted, based on continuing rather than sequential interaction. In most cases the HRM executive is an integral member of the senior management team. Rather than an iterative process of information exchange, companies with integrative linkage have their HRM functions built right into the strategy formulation and implementation processes. It is this role that we will discuss throughout the rest of this chapter.

Thus, in strategic HRM, the HRM function is involved in both strategy formulation and strategy implementation. The HRM executive gives strategic planners information about the company's human resource capabilities, and these capabilities are usually a direct function of the HRM practices.[12] This information about human resource capabilities helps top managers choose the best strategy because they can consider how well each strategic alternative would be implemented. Once the strategic choice has been determined, the role of HRM changes to the development and alignment of HRM practices that will give the company employees having the necessary skills to implement the strategy.[13] In addition, HRM practices must be designed to elicit actions from employees in the company.[14] In the next two sections of this chapter we show how HRM can provide a competitive advantage in the strategic management process.

Strategy Formulation

Five major components of the strategic management process are relevant to strategy formulation.[15] These components are depicted in Figure 2.4. The first component is the organization's mission. The mission is a statement of the organization's reason for being; it usually specifies the customers served, the needs satisfied and/or the values received by the customers, and the technology used. The mission statement is often

FIGURE 2.4

Strategy
Formulation

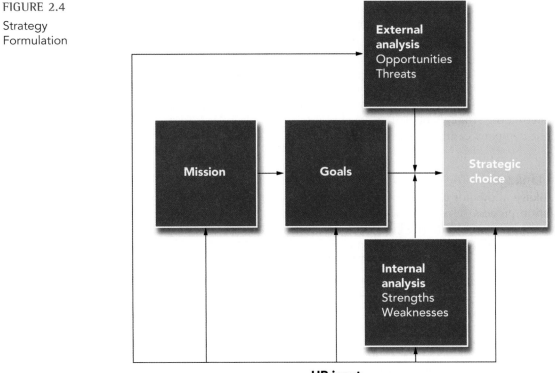

HR input

SOURCE: Adapted from K. Golden and V. Ramanujam, "Between a Dream and a Nightmare," Human Resource Management 24 (1985), pp. 429–451.

Goals
What an organization hopes to achieve in the medium- to long-term future.

External analysis
Examining the organization's operating environment to identify strategic opportunities and threats.

Internal analysis
The process of examining an organization's strengths and weaknesses.

accompanied by a statement of a company's vision and/or values. For example, Table 2.1 illustrates the mission and values of Merck & Co., Inc.

An organization's **goals** are what it hopes to achieve in the medium- to long-term future; they reflect how the mission will be operationalized. The overarching goal of most profit-making companies in the United States is to maximize stockholder wealth. But companies have to set other long-term goals in order to maximize stockholder wealth.

External analysis consists of examining the organization's operating environment to identify the strategic opportunities and threats. Examples of opportunities are customer markets that are not being served, technological advances that can aid the company, and labor pools that have not been tapped. Threats include potential labor shortages, new competitors entering the market, pending legislation that might adversely affect the company, and competitors' technological innovations.

Internal analysis attempts to identify the organization's strengths and weaknesses. It focuses on the quantity and quality of resources available to the organization—financial, capital, technological, and human resources. Organizations have to honestly and accurately assess each resource to decide whether it is a strength or a weakness.

External analysis and internal analysis combined constitute what has come to be called the *SWOT* (strengths, weaknesses, opportunities, threats) *analysis*. After going through the SWOT analysis, the strategic planning team has all the information it needs to generate a number of strategic alternatives. The strategic managers compare

MISSION STATEMENT

Merck & Co., Inc. is a leading research-driven pharmaceutical products and services company. Merck discovers, develops, manufactures and markets a broad range of innovative products to improve human and animal health. The Merck-Medco Managed Care Division manages pharmacy benefits for more than 40 million Americans, encouraging the appropriate use of medicines and providing disease management programs.

Our Mission

The mission of Merck is to provide society with superior products and services—innovations and solutions that improve the quality of life and satisfy customer needs—to provide employees with meaningful work and advancement opportunities and investors with a superior rate of return.

Our Values

1. **Our business is preserving and improving human life.** All of our actions must be measured by our success in achieving this goal. We value above all our ability to serve everyone who can benefit from the appropriate use of our products and services, thereby providing lasting consumer satisfaction.

2. **We are committed to the highest standards of ethics and integrity.** We are responsible to our customers, to Merck employees and their families, to the environments we inhabit, and to the societies we serve worldwide. In discharging our responsibilities, we do not take professional or ethical shortcuts. Our interactions with all segments of society must reflect the high standards we profess.

3. **We are dedicated to the highest level of scientific excellence and commit our research to improving human and animal health and the quality of life.** We strive to identify the most critical needs of consumers and customers; we devote our resources to meeting those needs.

4. **We expect profits, but only from work that satisfies customer needs and benefits humanity.** Our ability to meet our responsibilities depends on maintaining a financial position that invites investment in leading-edge research and that makes possible effective delivery of research results.

5. **We recognize that the ability to excel—to most competitively meet society's and customers' needs—depends on the integrity, knowledge, imagination, skill, diversity, and teamwork of employees, and we value these qualities most highly.** To this end, we strive to create an environment of mutual respect, encouragement, and teamwork—a working environment that rewards commitment and performance and is responsive to the needs of employees and their families.

SOURCE: www.merck.com/about/mission.html.

TABLE 2.1

Merck & Co.'s Mission and Values

these alternatives' ability to attain the organization's strategic goals; then they make their **strategic choice.** The strategic choice is the organization's strategy; it describes the ways the organization will attempt to fulfill its mission and achieve its long-term goals.

Many of the opportunities and threats in the external environment are people-related. With fewer and fewer highly qualified individuals entering the labor market, organizations compete not just for customers but for employees. It is HRM's role to

Strategic choice
The organization's strategy; the ways an organization will attempt to fulfill its mission and achieve its long-term goals.

keep close tabs on the external environment for human resource–related opportunities and threats, especially those directly related to the HRM function: potential labor shortages, competitor wage rates, government regulations affecting employment, and so on. For example, as discussed in Chapter 1, U.S. companies are finding that more and more high school graduates lack the basic skills needed to work, which is one source of the "human capital shortage."[16] However, not recognizing this environmental threat, many companies have encouraged the exit of older, more skilled workers while hiring less skilled younger workers who require basic skills training.[17]

An analysis of a company's internal strengths and weaknesses also requires input from the HRM function. Today companies are increasingly realizing that their human resources are one of their most important assets. In fact, one estimate is that over one-third of the total growth in U.S. GNP between 1943 and 1990 was the result of increases in human capital. A company's failure to consider the strengths and weaknesses of its workforce may result in its choosing strategies it is not capable of pursuing.[18] However, some research has demonstrated that few companies have achieved this level of linkage.[19] For example, one company chose a strategy of cost reduction through technological improvements. It built a plant designed around a computer-integrated manufacturing system with statistical process controls. Though this choice may seem like a good one, the company soon learned otherwise. It discovered that its employees could not operate the new equipment because 25 percent of the workforce was functionally illiterate.[20]

Thus, with an integrative linkage, strategic planners consider all the people-related business issues before making a strategic choice. These issues are identified with regard to the mission, goals, opportunities, threats, strengths, and weaknesses, leading the strategic planning team to make a more intelligent strategic choice. Although this process does not guarantee success, companies that address these issues are more likely to make choices that will ultimately succeed. The "Competing through Technology" box illustrates how Nissan's mismatch between its strategy and its human resources have led to quality problems that may result in a competitive disadvantage.

Recent research has supported the need to have HRM executives integrally involved in strategy formulation. One study of U.S. petrochemical refineries found that the level of HRM involvement was positively related to the refinery manager's evaluation of the effectiveness of the HRM function.[21] A second study of manufacturing firms found that HRM involvement was highest when top managers viewed employees as a strategic asset and associated with reduced turnover.[22] However, both studies found that HRM involvement was unrelated to operating unit financial performance.

Research has indicated that few companies have fully integrated HRM into the strategy formulation process.[23] As we've mentioned before, companies are beginning to recognize that in an intensely competitive environment, managing human resources strategically can provide a competitive advantage. Thus companies at the administrative linkage level will either become more integrated or face extinction. In addition, companies will move toward becoming integratively linked in an effort to manage human resources strategically.

It is of utmost importance that all people-related business issues be considered during strategy formulation. These issues are identified in the HRM function. Mechanisms or structures for integrating the HRM function into strategy formulation may help the strategic planning team make the most effective strategic choice. Once that strategic choice is determined, HRM must take an active role in implementing it. This role will be discussed in the next section.

After the Turnaround, Quality Problems Creep Up at Nissan

Nissan Motor Company's fantastic financial turnaround has been lauded by many in the business world. CEO Carlos Ghosn kicked off an outstanding comeback beginning in 1999 through unleashing a half-dozen hot-selling vehicles in the U.S. market and generating solid profits after years of losses. However, Nissan now feels considerable growing pains as quality problems on the Armada, Quest Minivan, and Titan full-sized pickup dragged down its quality rankings. According to J. D. Power and Associates' annual initial quality survey which reflects flaws discovered in the first 90 days, Nissan dropped to 11th place in 2003 from 2002's 6th place finish. The 147 problems per 100 vehicles trail the industry average of 119.

Many of the problems stem from its Mississippi factory where consumers complained of poor workmanship. The problems include typical squeaks, rattles, and vibrations, but also have resulted in two recalls of the Quest minivan. The source of these problems seems to be Nissan's "pedal to the metal" mentality since 1999. Since then, Nissan has launched 13 new vehicles in the United States. While Nissan executives knew this would be a challenge, since quality seemed fine they thought they could pull off the launches with little difficulty. However, what quickly became apparent was that Nissan lacked the engineering resources to check thoroughly for defects before cranking up the assembly lines. In addition, in an effort to wring out costs from its suppliers, Nissan began using cheaper materials, often at the expense of manufacturing precision. Because parts aren't made to fit together as precisely as they should, assembly line workers had to find ways to make them fit snuggly together. The problem was exacerbated by the fact that many workers had never worked at a car plant before.

The lack of sufficient engineering talent and inexperience of the assembly line workers represents a mismatch between the strategy and human resources of Nissan which may cost it in the long run. "These things tend to persist," suggests Joe Ivers, executive director for quality and customer satisfaction at J. D. Power. "If things are this extreme, it will probably wind up costing them in warranty costs."

SOURCE: D. Welch, "Nissan: The Squeaks Get Louder," *BusinessWeek* (May 17, 2004), p. 44.

Strategy Implementation

After an organization has chosen its strategy, it has to execute that strategy—make it come to life in its day-to-day workings. The strategy a company pursues dictates certain HR needs. For a company to have a good strategy foundation, certain tasks must be accomplished in pursuit of the company's goals, individuals must possess certain skills to perform those tasks, and these individuals must be motivated to perform their skills effectively.

The basic premise behind strategy implementation is that "an organization has a variety of structural forms and organizational processes to choose from when implementing a given strategy," and these choices make an economic difference.[24] Five important variables determine success in strategy implementation: organizational

FIGURE 2.5

Variables to Be
Considered in
Strategy
Implementation

structure; task design; the selection, training, and development of people; reward systems; and types of information and information systems.

As we see in Figure 2.5, HRM has primary responsibility for three of these five implementation variables: task, people, and reward systems. In addition, HRM can also directly affect the two remaining variables: structure and information and decision processes. First, for the strategy to be successfully implemented, the tasks must be designed and grouped into jobs in a way that is efficient and effective.[25] In Chapter 4 we will examine how this can be done through the processes of job analysis and job design. Second, the HRM function must ensure that the organization is staffed with people who have the necessary knowledge, skill, and ability to perform their part in implementing the strategy. This goal is achieved primarily through recruitment, selection and placement, training, development, and career management—topics covered in Chapters 5, 6, 7, and 9. In addition, the HRM function must develop performance management and reward systems that lead employees to work for and support the strategic plan. The specific types of performance management systems are covered in Chapter 8, and the many issues involved in developing reward systems are discussed in Chapters 11 through 13. In other words, the role of the HRM function becomes one of (1) ensuring that the company has the proper number of employees with the levels and types of skills required by the strategic plan[26] and (2) developing "control" systems that ensure that those employees are acting in ways that promote the achievement of the goals specified in the strategic plan.[27]

How does the HRM function do this? As Figure 2.6 shows, it is through administering HRM practices: job analysis/design, recruitment, selection systems, training and development programs, performance management systems, reward systems, and labor relations programs. The details of each of these HRM practices are the focus of the rest of this book. However, at this point it is important to present a general overview of the HRM practices and their role in strategy implementation. We will then discuss the various strategies companies pursue and the types of HRM systems congruent with those strategies. First we focus on how the strategic types are implemented; then we discuss the HRM practices associated with various directional strategies.

FIGURE 2.6

Strategy Implementation

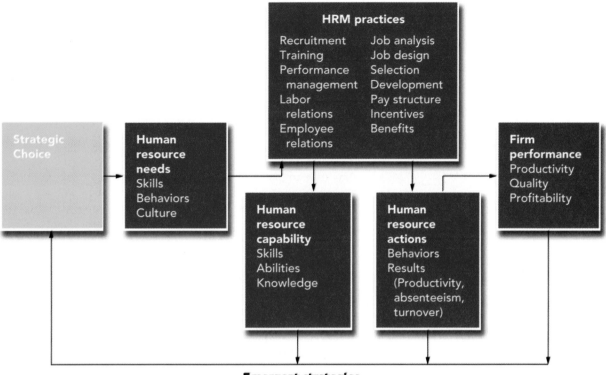

HRM practices

Recruitment   Job analysis
Training   Job design
Performance   Selection
  management   Development
Labor   Pay structure
  relations   Incentives
Employee   Benefits
  relations

Strategic Choice

Human resource needs
Skills
Behaviors
Culture

Human resource capability
Skills
Abilities
Knowledge

Human resource actions
Behaviors
Results
  (Productivity,
  absenteeism,
  turnover)

Firm performance
Productivity
Quality
Profitability

Emergent strategies

HRM Practices

The HRM function can be thought of as having six menus of HRM practices, from which companies can choose the ones most appropriate to implementing their strategy. Each of these menus refers to a particular functional area of HRM: job analysis/design, recruitment/selection, training and development, performance management, pay structure/incentives/benefits, and labor/employee relations.[28] These menus are presented in Table 2.2.

Job Analysis and Design

Companies produce a given product or service (or set of products or services), and the manufacture of these products requires that a number of tasks be performed. These tasks are grouped together to form jobs. **Job analysis** is the process of getting detailed information about jobs. **Job design** addresses what tasks should be grouped into a particular job. The way that jobs are designed should have an important tie to the strategy of an organization because the strategy requires either new and different tasks or different ways of performing the same tasks. In addition, because many strategies entail the introduction of new technologies, this impacts the way that work is performed.[29]

In general, jobs can vary from having a narrow range of tasks (most of which are simplified and require a limited range of skills) to having a broad array of complex tasks requiring multiple skills. In the past, the narrow design of jobs has been used to

Job analysis
The process of getting detailed information about jobs.

Job design
The process of defining the way work will be performed and the tasks that will be required in a given job.

TABLE 2.2

Menu of HRM
Practice Options

Job Analysis and Design		
Few tasks	↔	Many tasks
Simple tasks	↔	Complex tasks
Few skills required	↔	Many skills required
Specific job descriptions	↔	General job descriptions
Recruitment and Selection		
External sources	↔	Internal sources
Limited socialization	↔	Extensive socialization
Assessment of specific skills	↔	Assessment of general skills
Narrow career paths	↔	Broad career paths
Training and Development		
Focus on current job skills	↔	Focus on future job skills
Individual orientation	↔	Group orientation
Train few employees	↔	Train all employees
Spontaneous, unplanned	↔	Planned, systematic
Performance Management		
Behavioral criteria	↔	Results criteria
Developmental orientation	↔	Administrative orientation
Short-term criteria	↔	Long-term criteria
Individual orientation	↔	Group orientation
Pay Structure, Incentives, and Benefits		
Pay weighted toward salary and benefits	↔	Pay weighted toward incentives
Short-term incentives	↔	Long-term incentives
Emphasis on internal equity	↔	Emphasis on external equity
Individual incentives	↔	Group incentives
Labor and Employee Relations		
Collective bargaining	↔	Individual bargaining
Top-down decision making	↔	Participation in decision making
Formal due process	↔	No due process
View employees as expense	↔	View employees as assets

SOURCE: Adapted from R. S. Schuler and S. F. Jackson, "Linking Competitive Strategies with Human Resource Management Practices," *Academy of Management Executive* 1 (1987), pp. 207–19; and C. Fisher, L. Schoenfeldt, and B. Shaw, *Human Resource Management,* 2nd ed. (Boston: Houghton Mifflin, 1992).

Recruitment
The process of seeking applicants for potential employment.

Selection
The process by which an organization attempts to identify applicants with the necessary knowledge, skills, abilities, and other characteristics that will help it achieve its goals.

increase efficiency, while the broad design of jobs has been associated with efforts to increase innovation. However, with the advent of total quality management methods and a variety of employee involvement programs such as quality circles, many jobs are moving toward the broader end of the spectrum.[30]

Employee Recruitment and Selection

Recruitment is the process through which the organization seeks applicants for potential employment. **Selection** refers to the process by which it attempts to identify applicants with the necessary knowledge, skills, abilities, and other characteristics that will help the company achieve its goals. Companies engaging in different strategies need different types and numbers of employees. Thus the strategy a company is pursuing will have a direct impact on the types of employees that it seeks to recruit and select.[31]

Employee Training and Development

A number of skills are instilled in employees through training and development. **Training** refers to a planned effort to facilitate the learning of job-related knowledge, skills, and behavior by employees. **Development** involves acquiring knowledge, skills, and behavior that improve employees' ability to meet the challenges of a variety of existing jobs or jobs that do not yet exist. Changes in strategies often require changes in the types, levels, and mixes of skills. Thus the acquisition of strategy-related skills is an essential element of the implementation of strategy. For example, many companies have recently emphasized quality in their products, engaging in total quality management programs. These programs require extensive training of all employees in the TQM philosophy, methods, and often other skills that ensure quality.[32]

Through recruitment, selection, training, and development, companies can obtain a pool of human resources capable of implementing a given strategy.[33]

Performance Management

Performance management is used to ensure that employees' activities and outcomes are congruent with the organization's objectives. It entails specifying those activities and outcomes that will result in the firm's successfully implementing the strategy. For example, companies that are "steady state" (not diversified) tend to have evaluation systems that call for subjective performance assessments of managers. This stems from the fact that those above the first-level managers in the hierarchy have extensive knowledge about how the work should be performed. On the other hand, diversified companies are more likely to use quantitative measures of performance to evaluate managers because top managers have less knowledge about how work should be performed by those below them in the hierarchy.[34]

Similarly, executives who have extensive knowledge of the behaviors that lead to effective performance use performance management systems that focus on the behaviors of their subordinate managers. However, when executives are unclear about the specific behaviors that lead to effective performance, they tend to focus on evaluating the objective performance results of their subordinate managers.[35]

Pay Structure, Incentives, and Benefits

The pay system has an important role in implementing strategies. First, a high level of pay and/or benefits relative to that of competitors can ensure that the company attracts and retains high-quality employees, but this might have a negative impact on the company's overall labor costs.[36] Second, by tying pay to performance, the company can elicit specific activities and levels of performance from employees.

In a study of how compensation practices are tied to strategies, researchers examined 33 high-tech and 72 traditional companies. They classified them by whether they were in a growth stage (greater than 20 percent inflation-adjusted increases in annual sales) or a maturity stage. They found that high-tech companies in the growth stage used compensation systems that were highly geared toward incentive pay, with a lower percentage of total pay devoted to salary and benefits. On the other hand, compensation systems among mature companies (both high-tech and traditional) devoted a lower percentage of total pay to incentives and a high percentage to benefits.[37]

Training
A planned effort to facilitate the learning of job-related knowledge, skills, and behavior by employees.

Development
The acquisition of knowledge, skills, and behaviors that improve an employee's ability to meet changes in job requirements and in client and customer demands.

Performance management
The means through which managers ensure that employees' activities and outputs are congruent with the organization's goals.

Labor and Employee Relations

Whether companies are unionized or not, the general approach to relations with employees can strongly affect their potential for gaining competitive advantage. In the late 1970s Chrysler Corporation was faced with bankruptcy. Lee Iacocca, the new president of Chrysler, asked the union for wage and work-rule concessions in an effort to turn the company around. The union agreed to the concessions, in return receiving profit sharing and a representative on the board. Within only a few years, the relationship with and support from the union allowed Chrysler to pull itself out of bankruptcy and record profitability.[38]

Companies can choose to treat employees as an asset that requires investment of resources or as an expense to be minimized.[39] They have to make choices about how much employees can and should participate in decision making, what rights employees have, and what the company's responsibility is to them. The approach a company takes in making these decisions can result in it either successfully achieving its short- and long-term goals or ceasing to exist.

Recent research has begun to examine how companies develop sets of HRM practices that maximize performance and productivity. For example, one study of automobile assembly plants around the world found that plants that exhibited both high productivity and high quality used "HRM best practices," such as heavy emphasis on recruitment and hiring, compensation tied to performance, low levels of status differentiation, high levels of training for both new and experienced employees, and employee participation through structures such as work teams and problem-solving groups.[40] Another study found that HRM systems composed of selection testing, training, contingent pay, performance appraisal, attitude surveys, employee participation, and information sharing resulted in higher levels of productivity and corporate financial performance, as well as lower employee turnover.[41] Finally, a recent study found that companies identified as some of the "Best Places to Work" had higher financial performances than a set of matched companies that did not make the list.[42] Similar results have also been observed in a number of other studies.[43]

Strategic Types

As we previously discussed, companies can be classified by the generic strategies they pursue. It is important to note that these generic "strategies" are not what we mean by a strategic plan. They are merely similarities in the ways companies seek to compete in their industries. Various typologies have been offered, but we will focus on the two generic strategies proposed by Porter: cost and differentiation.[44]

According to Michael Porter of Harvard, competitive advantage stems from a company's being able to create value in its production process. Value can be created in one of two ways. First, value can be created by reducing costs. Second, value can be created by differentiating a product or service in such a way that it allows the company to charge a premium price relative to its competitors. This leads to two basic strategies. According to Porter, the "overall cost leadership" strategy focuses on becoming the lowest-cost producer in an industry. This strategy is achieved by constructing efficient large-scale facilities, by reducing costs through capitalizing on the experience curve, and by controlling overhead costs and costs in such areas as research and development, service, sales force, and advertising. This strategy provides above-average returns within an industry, and it tends to bar other firms' entry into the industry because the firm can lower its prices below competitors' costs. For example, IBM-clone computer manufacturers like Dell and Compaq have captured an increased share of the personal computer market by offering personal computers at lower cost than IBM and Apple.

The "differentiation" strategy, according to Porter, attempts to create the impression that the company's product or service is different from that of others in the industry. The perceived differentiation can come from creating a brand image, from technology, from offering unique features, or from unique customer service. If a company succeeds in differentiating its product, it will achieve above-average returns, and the differentiation may protect it from price sensitivity. For example, IBM has consistently emphasized its brand image and its reputation for superior service while charging a higher price for its computers.

HRM Needs in Strategic Types

While all of the strategic types require competent people in a generic sense, each of the strategies also requires different types of employees with different types of behaviors and attitudes. As we noted earlier in Figure 2.1, different strategies require employees with specific skills and also require these employees to exhibit different "role behaviors."[45] **Role behaviors** are the behaviors required of an individual in his or her role as a job holder in a social work environment. These role behaviors vary on a number of dimensions. Additionally, different role behaviors are required by the different strategies. For example, companies engaged in a cost strategy require employees to have a high concern for quantity and a short-term focus, to be comfortable with stability, and to be risk averse. These employees are expected to exhibit role behaviors that are relatively repetitive and performed independently or autonomously.

Thus companies engaged in cost strategies, because of the focus on efficient production, tend to specifically define the skills they require and invest in training employees in these skill areas. They also rely on behavioral performance management systems with a large performance-based compensation component. These companies promote internally and develop internally consistent pay systems with high pay differentials between superiors and subordinates. They seek efficiency through worker participation, soliciting employees' ideas on how to achieve more efficient production.

On the other hand, employees in companies with a differentiation strategy need to be highly creative and cooperative; to have only a moderate concern for quantity, a long-term focus, and a tolerance for ambiguity; and to be risk takers. Employees in these companies are expected to exhibit role behaviors that include cooperating with others, developing new ideas, and taking a balanced approach to process and results.

Thus differentiation companies will seek to generate more creativity through broadly defined jobs with general job descriptions. They may recruit more from outside, engage in limited socialization of newcomers, and provide broader career paths. Training and development activities focus on cooperation. The compensation system is geared toward external equity, as it is heavily driven by recruiting needs. These companies develop results-based performance management system and divisional–corporate performance evaluations to encourage risk taking on the part of managers.[46]

A recent study of HRM among steel minimills in the United States found that mills pursuing different strategies used different systems of HRM. Mills seeking cost leadership tended to use control-oriented HRM systems that were characterized by high centralization, low participation, low training, low wages, low benefits, and highly contingent pay, whereas differentiator mills used "commitment" HRM systems, characterized as the opposite on each of those dimensions.[47] A later study from the same sample revealed that the mills with the commitment systems had higher

Role behaviors
Behaviors that are required of an individual in his or her role as a jobholder in a social work environment.

productivity, lower scrap rates, and lower employee turnover than those with the control systems.

Directional Strategies

As discussed earlier in this chapter, strategic typologies are useful for classifying the ways different organizations seek to compete within an industry. However, it is also necessary to understand how increasing size (growth) or decreasing it (downsizing) affects the HRM function. For example, the top management team might decide that they need to invest more in product development or to diversify as a means for growth. With these types of strategies, it is more useful for the HRM function to aid in evaluating the feasibility of the various alternatives and to develop programs that support the strategic choice.

Companies have used five possible categories of directional strategies to meet objectives.[48] Strategies emphasizing market share or operating costs are considered "concentration" strategies. With this type of strategy, a company attempts to focus on what it does best within its established markets and can be thought of as "sticking to its knitting." Strategies focusing on market development, product development, innovation, or joint ventures make up the "internal growth" strategy. Companies with an internal growth strategy channel their resources toward building on existing strengths. Those attempting to integrate vertically or horizontally or to diversify are exhibiting an **"external growth" strategy,** usually through mergers or acquisitions. This strategy attempts to expand a company's resources or to strengthen its market position through acquiring or creating new businesses. Finally, a "divestment," or downsizing, strategy is one made up of retrenchment, divestitures, or liquidation. These strategies are observed among companies facing serious economic difficulties and seeking to pare down their operations. The human resource implications of each of these strategies are quite different.

Concentration Strategies

Concentration strategies require that the company maintain the current skills that exist in the organization. This requires that training programs provide a means of keeping those skills sharp among people in the organization and that compensation programs focus on retaining people who have those skills. Appraisals in this strategy tend to be more behavioral because the environment is more certain, and the behaviors necessary for effective performance tend to be established through extensive experience.

Internal Growth Strategies

Internal growth strategies present unique staffing problems. Growth requires that a company constantly hire, transfer, and promote individuals, and expansion into different markets may change the necessary skills that prospective employees must have. In addition, appraisals often consist of a combination of behaviors and results. The behavioral appraisal emphasis stems from the knowledge of effective behaviors in a particular product market, and the results appraisals focus on achieving growth goals. Compensation packages are heavily weighted toward incentives for achieving growth goals. Training needs differ depending on the way the company attempts to grow internally. For example, if the organization seeks to expand its markets, training will fo-

External growth strategy
An emphasis on acquiring vendors and suppliers or buying businesses that allow a company to expand into new markets.

Concentration strategy
A strategy focusing on increasing market share, reducing costs, or creating and maintaining a market niche for products and services.

Internal growth strategy
A focus on new market and product development, innovation, and joint ventures.

Questioning the Value of Global Megamergers

It seems to have become accepted wisdom that it's *good* to become bigger in a globalizing economy. Recent mergers such as Exxon and Mobil, BP and Amoco, Daimler-Benz and Chrysler, and even the failed attempt to merge GE and Honeywell were based on the logic that globalization will result in industries becoming more concentrated. The big winners will be the big companies, so the lesson is to get big fast, and global megamergers such as those noted are the quickest way to do so.

However, recent work seems to question the value of these megamergers. In addition to all the obstacles that face any merger, the logic itself may be flawed. First, evidence does not lead to the conclusion that industries are becoming more concentrated. In fact, industries such as oil and automobiles, those characterized by huge mergers, have become significantly *less* concentrated over the past 50 years. Second, industry concentration can actually destroy value rather than create it. Value can be created if the mergers reduce production costs, reduce risk, or increase volume, but these goals are seldom attained in any way that offsets the costs of the mergers.

Interestingly, one reason that these global megamergers have increased has a significant human resource component. As shareholders require top-line (revenue) growth of 10–15 percent per year, firms in industries seeing only 2–3 percent growth can achieve growth only through mergers and acquisitions. When virtually all the organizational rewards (bonuses, promotions, stock option values, and so on) are tied to revenue growth, it is not surprising that top managers will engage in such activity, even though it may not create true value for shareholders.

SOURCE: P. Ghemawat and F. Ghadar, "The Dubious Logic of Global Megamergers," *Harvard Business Review*, July–August 2000.

cus on knowledge of each market, particularly when the company is expanding into international markets. On the other hand, when the company is seeking innovation or product development, training will be of a more technical nature, as well as focusing on interpersonal skills such as team building. Joint ventures require extensive training in conflict resolution techniques because of the problems associated with combining people from two distinct organizational cultures.

Mergers and Acquisitions

Increasingly we see both consolidation within industries and mergers across industries. For example, British Petroleum's recent agreement to acquire Amoco Oil represents a consolidation, or reduction in number of firms within the industry. On the other hand, Citicorp's merger with Traveller's Group to form Citigroup represents firms from different industries (pure financial services and insurance) combining to change the dynamics within both. Whatever the type, one thing is for sure—mergers and acquisitions are on the increase, and HRM needs to be involved.[49] In addition, these mergers more frequently consist of global megamergers, in spite of some warnings that these might not be effective (see the "Competing through Globalization" box).

According to a report by the Conference Board, "people issues" may be one of the major reasons that mergers do not always live up to expectations. Some companies now heavily weigh firm cultures before embarking on a merger or acquisition. For example, prior to acquiring ValueRx, executives at Express Scripts, Inc., interviewed senior executives and middle managers at the potential target firm in order to get a sense of its culture.[50] In spite of this, fewer than one-third of the HRM executives surveyed said that they had a major influence in how mergers are planned, yet 80 percent of them said that people issues have a significant impact after the deals are finalized.[51]

In addition to the desirability of HRM playing a role in evaluating a merger opportunity, HRM certainly has a role in the actual implementation of a merger or acquisition. Training in conflict resolution is also necessary when companies engage in an external growth strategy. All the options for external growth consist of acquiring or developing new businesses, and these businesses often have distinct cultures. Thus many HRM programs face problems in integrating and standardizing practices across the company's businesses. The relative value of standardizing practices across businesses must be weighed against the unique environmental requirements of each business and the extent of desired integration of the two firms. For example, with regard to pay practices, a company may desire a consistent internal wage structure to maintain employee perceptions of equity in the larger organization. In a recent new business developed by IBM, the employees pressured the company to maintain the same wage structure as IBM's main operation. However, some businesses may function in environments where pay practices are driven heavily by market forces. Requiring these businesses to adhere to pay practices in other environments may result in an ineffective wage structure.

Finding and Keeping the Best Employees

Cisco Systems recognizes that when it acquires a new company, in large part, it is acquiring the human assets of that company. If the key people in the acquired company leave, then the acquisition was a tremendous failure. Thus Cisco first aims to screen potential acquisitions to ensure that the vision of the leader in that company and the company's direction are similar to Cisco's. In the acquisition discussion, it tries to make clear to the employees to be acquired that there will be massive change into the Cisco way of doing things. This is to ensure that employees are not surprised once they become part of Cisco. Third, during the integration, Cisco emphasizes that only one culture will survive and that it will be Cisco's. Fourth, it finds significant roles for the top executives and the top technical talent in order to give them challenging opportunities. By giving such people a major role, Cisco is much better than most firms at being able to retain the top talent after an acquisition.

SOURCE: C. O'Reilly, J. Pfeffer, *Hidden Value: How Great Companies Achieve Extraordinary Results with Ordinary People* (Cambridge, MA: HBS Press, 2000).

Downsizing
The planned elimination of large numbers of personnel, designed to enhance organizational effectiveness.

Downsizing

Of increasing importance to organizations in today's competitive environment is HRM's role in **downsizing** or "rightsizing." The number of organizations undergoing downsizing has increased significantly. In fact, from 1988 to 1993, 1.4 million executives, managers, and administrators were laid off during downsizing, compared with only 782,000 from 1976 to 1981.[52]

One would have great difficulty ignoring the massive "war for talent" that went on during the late 1990s, particularly with the notable dot-com craze. Firms during this time sought to become "employers of choice," to establish "employment brands," and to develop "employee value propositions" as ways to ensure that they would be able to attract and retain talented employees. However, what few probably noticed was that in spite of the hiring craze, this was also a time of massive layoffs. In fact, 1998, the height of the war for talent, also saw the largest number of layoffs in the decade.

This new trend seems to represent a "churn" of employees, in which firms lay off those with outdated skills or cut whole businesses that are in declining markets while simultaneously building businesses and employee bases in newer, high-growth markets. For example, IBM cut 69,256 people and increased its workforce by 16,000 in 1996.

The important question facing firms is, How can we develop a reputation as an employer of choice, and engage employees to the goals of the firm, while constantly laying off a significant portion of our workforce? How firms answer this question will determine how they can compete by meeting the stakeholder needs of their employees.

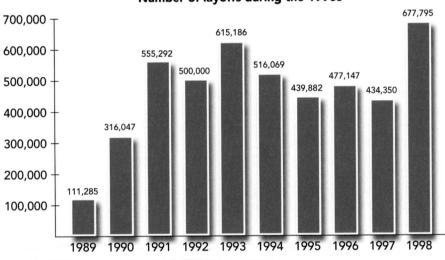

Number of layoffs during the 1990s

SOURCE: Challenger, Gray, and Christmas, 1998.

In spite of the increasing frequency of downsizing, research reveals that it is far from universally successful for achieving the goals of increased productivity and increased profitability. For example, Table 2.3 illustrates the results of a survey conducted by the American Management Association indicating that only about one-third of the companies that went through downsizings actually achieved their goal of increased productivity. Another survey by the AMA found that over two-thirds of the companies that downsize repeat the effort a year later.[53] Also, research by the consulting firm Mitchell & Company found that companies that downsized during the 1980s lagged the industry average stock price in 1991.[54] Thus it is important to understand the best ways of managing downsizings, particularly from the standpoint of HRM.

Downsizing presents a number of challenges and opportunities for HRM.[55] In terms of challenges, the HRM function must "surgically" reduce the workforce by

TABLE 2.3

Effects of Downsizing on Desired Outcomes

DESIRED OUTCOME	PERCENTAGE THAT ACHIEVED DESIRED RESULT
Reduced expenses	46%
Increased profits	32
Improved cash flow	24
Increased productivity	22
Increased return on investment	21
Increased competitive advantage	19
Reduced bureaucracy	17
Improved decision making	14
Increased customer satisfaction	14
Increased sales	13
Increased market share	12
Improved product quality	9
Technological advances	9
Increased innovation	7
Avoidance of a takeover	6

SOURCE: From *The Wall Street Journal*, Eastern Edition June 6, 1991. Copyright © 1991 by Dow Jones & Co. Inc. Reproduced with permission of Dow Jones & Co., Inc. via Copyright Clearance Center.

cutting only the workers who are less valuable in their performance. Achieving this is difficult because the best workers are most able (and often willing) to find alternative employment and may leave voluntarily prior to any layoff. For example, in 1992 General Motors and the United Auto Workers agreed to an early retirement program for individuals between the ages of 51 and 65 who have been employed for 10 or more years. The program provided those who agreed to retire their full pension benefits, even if they obtained employment elsewhere, and as much as $13,000 toward the purchase of a GM car.[56]

Early retirement programs, although humane, essentially reduce the workforce with a "grenade" approach. This type of reduction does not distinguish between good and poor performers but rather eliminates an entire group of employees. In fact, recent research indicates that when companies downsize by offering early retirement programs, they usually end up rehiring to replace essential talent within a year. Often the company does not achieve its cost-cutting goals because it spends 50 to 150 percent of the departing employee's salary in hiring and retraining new workers.[57]

Another HRM challenge is to boost the morale of employees who remain after the reduction; this is discussed in greater detail in Chapter 5. Survivors may feel guilt over keeping their jobs when their friends have been laid off, or they may envy their friends who have retired with attractive severance and pension benefits. Their reduced satisfaction with and commitment to the organization may interfere with work performance. Thus the HRM function must maintain open communication with remaining employees to build their trust and commitment rather than withholding information.[58] All employees should be informed of the purpose of the downsizing, the costs to be cut, the duration of the downsizing, and the strategies to be pursued. In addition, companies going through downsizing often develop compensation programs that tie the individual's compensation to the company's success. Employee ownership programs often result from downsizing, and gainsharing plans such as the Scanlon plan (discussed in Chapter 12) originated in companies facing economic difficulties.

Offshoring and the Future of Work

The topic of offshoring has become a sensitive one. Numerous U.S. manufacturing jobs were sent overseas to lower wage countries such as Thailand, Malaysia, and China during the 1980s and 90s. However, advances in telecommunications and information technology have resulted in more "white-collar" jobs being sent overseas as well. It began with call centers, and quickly evolved into software engineers and other information technology jobs moving primarily to India (because of high levels of both technical and English language skills there). With the economy exhibiting a sluggish rebound in 2004 and more and more firms sending white-collar work overseas, the issue has become quite political.

Critics of offshoring suggest that moving jobs overseas will result in a net loss of jobs in the United States, will depress U.S. wages, and will undermine the employment base. However, advocates argue that multinational companies can take advantage of high skills and lower wages (usually between 50 percent and 80 percent lower than in the United States) to reduce their cost base while maintaining or even improving the quality of the work. Global companies such as IBM maintain steadfastly that over 50 percent of their sales are from outside the United States, so they are merely globally sourcing their talent to mirror their customer base. Other companies have used outsourced suppliers such as Wipro or Infosys, both located in India, to perform the work on a contract basis. In addition, advocates argue that if one criticizes U.S.-based companies for moving work outside the United States, then one must also criticize companies such as Sony, ABB, Philips, BMW, and Toyota for locating manufacturing or service centers in the United States (referred to as reverse offshoring).

Given these cost advantages and the increasingly global nature of organizations, the trend will continue. Forrester Research estimated that the United States could offshore 3.3 million jobs by 2015. Another recent study looked at the types of occupations that are most at risk of being offshored. These researchers estimated that the maximum figure of offshored jobs would be 14 million, or 11 percent of the workforce, and while they acknowledge that this is the maximum, they believe the 3.3 million figure is an underestimate.

SOURCE: J. Schramm, *Workplace Visions—Offshoring* (Arlington, VA: Society for Human Resource Management, 2004).

In spite of these challenges, downsizing provides opportunities for HRM. First, it often allows the company to "get rid of dead wood" and make way for fresh ideas. In addition, downsizing is often a unique opportunity to change an organization's culture. In firms characterized by antagonistic labor–management relations, downsizing can force the parties to cooperate and to develop new, positive relationships.[59] Finally, downsizing can demonstrate to top-management decision makers the value of the company's human resources to its ultimate success. The role of HRM is to effectively manage the process in a way that makes this value undeniable. We discuss the implications of downsizing as a labor force management strategy in Chapter 5.

A topic related to downsizing is the new trend toward offshoring, which often entails laying off workers in the home country in order to capitalize on lower labor costs in a different country. The "Competing through Globalization" box describes some of the issues and trends.

[handwritten: Advantages to Downsizing]

Strategy Evaluation and Control

A final component to the strategic management process is that of strategy evaluation and control. Thus far we have focused on the planning and implementation of strategy. However, it is extremely important for the firm to constantly monitor the effectiveness of both the strategy and the implementation process. This monitoring makes it possible for the company to identify problem areas and either revise existing structures and strategies or devise new ones. In this process we see emergent strategies appear as well as the critical nature of human resources in competitive advantage.

The Role of Human Resources in Providing Strategic Competitive Advantage

Thus far we have presented the strategic management process as including a step-by-step procedure by which HRM issues are raised prior to deciding on a strategy and then HRM practices are developed to implement that strategy. However, we must note that human resources can provide a strategic competitive advantage in two additional ways: through emergent strategies and through enhancing competitiveness.

Emergent Strategies

Having discussed the process of strategic management, we also must distinguish between intended strategies and emergent strategies. Most people think of strategies as being proactive, rational decisions aimed toward some predetermined goal. The view of strategy we have presented thus far in the chapter focuses on intended strategies. *Intended strategies* are the result of the rational decision-making process used by top managers as they develop a strategic plan. This is consistent with the definition of *strategy* as "the pattern or plan that integrates an organization's major goals, policies, and action sequences into a cohesive whole."[60] The idea of emergent strategies is evidenced by the feedback loop in Figure 2.1.

Most strategies that companies espouse are intended strategies. For example, when Compaq was founded, the company had its strategy summarized in its name, an amalgam of the words *computer, compact,* and *quality.* Thus the intended strategy was to build compact portable computers that were completely free of any defect, and all of the company's efforts were directed toward implementing that strategy. Following that strategy allowed Compaq to become one of the fastest-growing companies in the world, commanding 20 percent of the world market in 1991. In 1992 Compaq's performance began to falter again, sparking new CEO Eckhard Pfieffer to change Compaq's strategy to one focused on being a low-cost producer. This strategic change resulted in Compaq becoming the leading PC maker in the world in 1994.[61] More recently, Compaq merged with Hewlett-Packard to create an integrated information technology company that could compete with IBM.

Emergent strategies, on the other hand, consist of the strategies that evolve from the grass roots of the organization and can be thought of as what organizations actually do, as opposed to what they intend to do. Strategy can also be thought of as "a pattern in a stream of decisions or actions."[62] For example, when Honda Motor Company first entered the U.S. market with its 250 cc and 305 cc motorcycles in 1959, it believed that no market existed for its smaller 50 cc bike. However, the sales on the larger motorcycles were sluggish, and Japanese executives running errands around Los Angeles on Honda 50s attracted a lot of attention, including that of a buyer with

Sears, Roebuck. Honda found a previously undiscovered market as well as a new distribution outlet (general retailers) that it had not planned on. This emergent strategy gave Honda a 50 percent market share by 1964.[63]

The distinction between intended and emergent strategies has important implications for human resource management.[64] The new focus on strategic HRM has tended to focus primarily on intended strategies. Thus HRM's role has been seen as identifying for top management the people-related business issues relevant to strategy formulation and then developing HRM systems that aid in the implementation of the strategic plan.

However, most emergent strategies are identified by those lower in the organizational hierarchy. It is often the rank-and-file employees who provide ideas for new markets, new products, and new strategies. HRM plays an important role in facilitating communication throughout the organization, and it is this communication that allows for effective emergent strategies to make their way up to top management. This fact led Philip Caldwell, Ford's chairman in the early 1980s, to state, "It's stupid to deny yourself the intellectual capability and constructive attitude of tens of thousands of workers."[65]

Enhancing Firm Competitiveness

A related way in which human resources can be a source of competitive advantage is through developing a human capital pool that gives the company the unique ability to adapt to an ever-changing environment. Recently managers have become interested in the idea of a "learning organization," in which people continually expand their capacity to achieve the results they desire.[66] This requires the company to be in a constant state of learning through monitoring the environment, assimilating information, making decisions, and flexibly restructuring to compete in that environment. Companies that develop such learning capability have a competitive advantage. Although certain organizational information-processing systems can be an aid, ultimately the people (human capital) who make up the company provide the raw materials in a learning organization.[67]

Thus the role of human resources in competitive advantage should continue to increase because of the fast-paced change characterizing today's business environment. It is becoming increasingly clear that even as U.S. automakers have increased the quality of their cars to compete with the Japanese, these competitors have developed such flexible and adaptable manufacturing systems that they can respond to customer needs more quickly.[68] This flexibility of the manufacturing process allows the emergent strategy to come directly from the marketplace by determining and responding to the exact mix of customer desires. It requires, however, that the company have people in place who have the skills to similarly adapt quickly.[69] As George Walker, president of Delta Wire, stated, "Anyone can come in and buy machines like I have. The difference is the knowledge of your workers."[70] This statement exemplifies the increasing importance of human resources in developing and maintaining competitive advantage.[71]

Strategic Human Resource Executives

For a reader who is just getting a first glimpse of the HRM function, it is impossible to portray what a vastly different role HRM must play today compared to 20 or even 10 years ago. As noted earlier, HRM has traditionally played a largely administrative role—simply processing paperwork plus developing and administering hiring, training, appraisal, compensation, and benefits systems—and all of this has been unrelated to the strategic direction of the firm. In the early 1980s HRM took on more of a one-way linkage role, helping to implement strategy. Now strategic decision makers are realizing the importance of people issues and so are calling for HRM to become the "source of people expertise" in the firm.[72] This requires that HR managers possess and use knowledge of how people can and do play a role in competitive advantage as well as the policies, programs, and practices that can leverage the firm's people as a source of competitive advantage. This leads to an entirely new set of competencies for today's strategic HR executive.[73]

In the future, HR professionals will need four basic competencies to become partners in the strategic management process.[74] (See Figure 2.7.) First, they will need "business competence"—knowing the company's business and understanding its economic financial capabilities. This calls for making logical decisions that support the company's strategic plan based on the most accurate information possible. Because in almost all companies the effectiveness of decisions must be evaluated in terms of dollar values, the HR executive must be able to calculate the costs and benefits of each alternative in terms of its dollar impact.[75] In addition, it requires that the nonmonetary impact be considered. The HR executive must be fully capable of identifying the social and ethical issues attached to HRM practices.

Second, HR professionals will need "professional–technical knowledge" of state-of-the-art HRM practices in areas such as staffing, development, rewards, organizational design, and communication. New selection techniques, performance appraisal methods, training programs, and incentive plans are constantly being developed. Some of these programs can provide value, whereas others may be no more than the products of today's HRM equivalent of snake oil. HR executives must be able to critically evaluate the new techniques offered as state-of-the-art HRM programs and use only those that will benefit the company.

Third, they must be skilled in the "management of change processes," such as diagnosing problems, implementing organizational changes, and evaluating results.

FIGURE 2.7

Human Resource
Competencies

Every time a company changes its strategy in even a minor way, the entire company has to change. These changes result in conflict, resistance, and confusion among the people who must implement the new plans or programs. The HR executive must have the skills to oversee the change in a way that ensures its success. In fact, one survey of Fortune 500 companies found that 87 percent of the companies had their organization development/change function as part of the HR department.[76]

Finally, these professionals must also have "integration competence," meaning the ability to integrate the three other competencies to increase the company's value. This requires that, although specialist knowledge is necessary, a generalist perspective must be taken in making decisions. This entails seeing how all the functions within the HRM area fit together to be effective and recognizing that changes in any one part of the HRM package are likely to require changes in other parts of the package. For example, a health care company in central Texas was attempting to fill a position in the X-ray department. It was able to identify qualified candidates for the position, but none of the candidates accepted the offer. It was not until the company examined its total package (pay, benefits, promotion opportunities, and so on) and changed the composition of the package that it was able to fill the position.

The new strategic role for HRM presents both opportunities and challenges. HRM has the chance to profoundly impact the way organizations compete through people. On the other hand, with this opportunity come serious responsibility and accountability.[77] HRM functions of the future must consist of individuals who view themselves as businesspeople who happen to work in an HRM function, rather than HRM people who happen to work in a business.

A Look Back

HANDLING THE CHALLENGES AT JETBLUE

In order to avoid the sad fate of People Express, JetBlue has a strategy in place to fuel its growth while maintaining its distinctiveness. First, it has built a tool called an "operational recovery system" which allows it to handle disruptions efficiently. For instance, if the goal is to eliminate cancelled flights or delays beyond three hours, the software can produce a solution and calculate its cost. One example of an effort to standardize processes is that JetBlue has developed a checklist for all the things that must happen as it enters a new market. This checklist will enable it to more efficiently enter new markets in the future.

However, all the processes in the world will not make a difference if the culture dies, and Neeleman focuses much of his attention on growing it. He flies with 8–12 crewmembers each week, working the jobs that they do. He states, "I want them to know that I value what they do. I value it so much that I'm not too good to do it." In addition, while he says he is not anti-union, he focuses on building a company where a union is not necessary. He believes that if management and crewmembers have mutual trust, and people feel they are fairly compensated (such as last year's 17 percent profit-sharing payment), there will be no need for a third party.

Neeleman teaches new employees how the company makes money and how each employee contributes to the bottom line during the first day of orientation. He says, "I always talk about the tripod—low costs, a great product, and capitalization. If everyone here understands how important it is to maintain each leg, you've got a very stable business model." By combining business literacy and the profit sharing, they have created employees who are passionate about the company's success.

Finally, in the face of internal employee climate survey results indicating that one-third of employees voiced unhappiness about their supervisors, JetBlue built a five-day "Principles of Leadership" (POL) course. The course teaches supervisors and managers to practice the five primary principles: "Treat your people right," "Communicate with your team," "Inspire greatness in others," "Encourage initiative and innovation," and "Do the right thing." The goal is that the graduates of the program become "anointed proprietors of the culture," so that instead of 25 officers, there are 800 people in leadership positions throughout the company who believe in the culture.

SOURCE: C. Slater, "And Now the Hard Part," *FastCompany*, May 2004, p. 67; pf.fastcompany.com/magazine/82/jetblue.html.

Questions

1. How successful do you think JetBlue will be in maintaining its culture while it quadruples in size over the next few years?
2. What must JetBlue do with regard to aligning its strategy and its people that it does not already seem to be doing?

Summary

A strategic approach to human resource management seeks to proactively provide a competitive advantage through the company's most important asset: its human resources. The HRM function needs to be integrally involved in the formulation of strategy to identify the people-related business issues the company faces. Once the strategy has been determined, HRM has a profound impact on the implementation of the plan by developing and aligning HRM practices that ensure that the company has motivated employees with the necessary skills. Finally, the emerging strategic role of the HRM function requires that HR professionals in the future develop business, professional–technical, change management, and integration competencies. As you will see more clearly in later chapters, this strategic approach requires more than simply developing a valid selection procedure or state-of-the-art performance management systems. Only through these competencies can the HR professional take a strategic approach to human resource management.

Discussion Questions

1. Pick one of your university's major sports teams (like football or basketball). How would you characterize that team's generic strategy? How does the composition of the team members (in terms of size, speed, ability, and so on) relate to that strategy? What are the strengths and weaknesses of the team? How do those dictate the team's generic strategy and its approach to a particular game?
2. Do you think that it is easier to tie human resources to the strategic management process in large or in small organizations? Why?
3. Consider one of the organizations you have been affiliated with. What are some examples of human resource practices that were consistent with that organization's strategy? What are examples of practices that were inconsistent with its strategy?
4. How can strategic management within the HRM department ensure that HRM plays an effective role in the company's strategic management process?
5. What types of specific skills (such as knowledge of financial accounting methods) do you think HR professionals will need to have the business, professional–technical, change management, and integrative competencies necessary in the future? Where can you develop each of these skills?
6. What are some of the key environmental variables that you see changing in the business world today? What impact will those changes have on the HRM function in organizations?

Self-Assessment Exercise

Think of a company you have worked for, or find an annual report for a company you are interested in working for. (Many companies post their annual reports online at their website.) Then answer the following questions.

1. How has the company been affected by the trends discussed in this chapter?

2. Does the company use the HR practices recommended in this chapter?
3. What else should the company do to deal with the challenges posed by the trends discussed in this chapter?

Manager's Hot Seat Exercise: Privacy: Burned by the Firewall

This case explores issues surrounding human resource management decision making. The scenario opens with a department manager attempting to defend one of her employees who has been suspended from his job with the company. The allegations against this employee are that he has inappropriately utilized company time and resources for personal endeavors. The manager has been away on vacation and was not informed of the organization's intentions to release the employee. She questions why such a decision was made in her absence and seeks reinstatement for her valued worker.

As the scenario progresses, the company's human resource manager responds to the department manager's questions. The HR manager staunchly contends that investigation of company records revealed the employee's actions were in violation of established organizational policy. She states that record evaluation has been conducted on several employees to see if they have remained within the organization's level of tolerance for policy infractions—even to the point of reviewing the records of the department manager and finding some blemishes on it. The HR manager affirms that the employee's suspension decision was made to rectify the misuse of company time and resources and the department manager had no need to be advised of the ongoing investigation. The HR manager explains the decision was made with the best interests of the company in mind.

The video stresses how important it is for managers to be aware of their own actions and realize that they are establishing a guiding example to each employee. Managers must adhere to the established corporate policies if they desire their employees to do the same. The video also indicates the importance of effective utilization of clear communication techniques in conveying organizational policies and expectations to every employee.

Group Activity:

Have the class divided in groups of 4–5 students. The groups are to discuss the possible impact human resource management decisions may have on organizations. This should be done from an organizational strategic viewpoint—such as establishing strategic organizational goals, developing an organizational strategy, and identifying how effective HR can contribute to them. The group discussion should address responses to such questions as: (do not limit the discussion to solely answering these questions as they are presented only as a guide).

- Why should organizations be concerned with satisfying their employees?
- How vital is effective and clear organizational communication?
- How can organizations better meet strategic goals through satisfying employees?
- Why are strategic goals important to organizations?
- How can an organization facilitate employees to better assist it in meeting its goals?
- What role behaviors were gleaned from the case study?
- What purpose do employee role behaviors play to organizational strategy?
- What other choices may have been available to the organization to rectify this situation?

Prepare a group position response on the above issues to be presented to the class.

Exercising Strategy: Strategy and HRM at Delta Air Lines

In 1994 top executives at Delta Air Lines faced a crucial strategic decision. Delta, which had established an unrivaled reputation within the industry for having highly committed employees who delivered the highest-quality customer service, had lost over $10 per share for two straight years. A large portion of its financial trouble was due to the $491 million acquisition of Pan Am in 1991, which was followed by the Gulf War (driving up fuel costs) and the early 1990s recession (causing people to fly less). Its cost per available seat mile (what it costs to fly one passenger one mile) was 9.26 cents, among the highest in the industry. In addition, it was threatened by new discount competitors with significantly lower costs—in particular, Valujet, which flew out of Delta's Atlanta hub. How could Delta survive and thrive in such an environment? Determining the strategy for doing so was the top executives' challenge.

Chairman and Chief Executive Officer Ron Allen embarked upon the "Leadership 7.5" strategy, whose goal was to reduce the cost per available seat mile to 7.5 cents, comparable with Southwest Airlines. Implementing this strategy required a significant downsizing over the following three years, trimming 11,458 people from its 69,555-employee workforce (the latter number representing an 8 percent reduction from two years earlier). Many experienced customer service representatives were laid off and replaced with lower-paid, inexperienced, part-time workers. Cleaning service of planes as well as baggage handling were outsourced, resulting in layoffs of long-term Delta employees. The numbers of maintenance workers and flight attendants were reduced substantially.

The results of the strategy were mixed as financial performance improved but operational performance plummeted. Since it began its cost cutting, its stock price more than doubled in just over two years and its debt was upgraded. On the other hand, customer complaints about dirty airplanes rose from 219 in 1993 to 358 in 1994 and 634 in 1995. On-time performance was so bad that passengers joked that Delta stands for "Doesn't Ever Leave The Airport." Delta slipped from fourth to seventh among the top 10 carriers in baggage handling. Employee morale hit an all-time low, and unions were beginning to make headway toward organizing some of Delta's employee groups. In 1996 CEO Allen was quoted as saying, "This has tested our people. There have been some morale problems. But so be it. You go back to the question of survival, and it makes the decision very easy."

Shortly after, employees began donning cynical "so be it" buttons. Delta's board saw union organizers stirring blue-collar discontent, employee morale destroyed, the customer service reputation in near shambles, and senior managers exiting the company in droves. Less than one year later, Allen was fired despite Delta's financial turn-around. His firing was "not because the company was going broke, but because its spirit was broken."

Delta's Leadership 7.5 strategy destroyed the firm's core competence of a highly experienced, highly skilled, and highly committed workforce that delivered the highest quality customer service in the industry. HRM might have affected the strategy to point out the negative impact that this strategy would have on the firm. Given the strategy and competitive environment, Delta might have sought to implement the cost cutting differently to reduce the cost structure but preserve its source of differentiation.

The present state of Delta provides further support to these conclusions. With the family atmosphere dissolved and the bond between management and rank-and-file employees broken, employees have begun to seek other ways to gain voice and security. By Fall 2001 Delta had two union organizing drives under way with both the flight attendants and the mechanics. In addition, labor costs have been driven up as a result of the union activity. The pilots signed a lucrative five-year contract that will place them at the highest pay in the industry. In an effort to head off the organizing drive, the mechanics were recently given raises to similarly put them at the industry top. Now the flight attendants are seeking industry-leading pay irrespective of but certainly encouraged by the union drive.[78]

The Delta Air Lines story provides a perfect example of the perils that can await firms that fail to adequately address human resource issues in the formulation and implementation of strategy.

SOURCE: M. Brannigan and E. De Lisser, "Cost Cutting at Delta Raises the Stock Price but Lowers the Service," *The Wall Street Journal* (June 20, 1996), pp. A1, A8; M. Brannigan and J. White, "So Be It: Why Delta Air Lines Decided It Was Time for CEO to Take Off," *The Wall Street Journal* (May 30, 1997), p. A1.

Questions

1. How does the experience of Delta Air Lines illustrate the interdependence between strategic decisions of "how to compete" and "with what to compete"? Consider this with regard to both strategy formulation and strategy implementation.

2. If you were in charge of HRM for Delta Air Lines now, what would be your major priorities?

Managing People: From the Pages of *BusinessWeek*

BusinessWeek Reprogramming Amazon

Sure, it still sells loads of books and CDs; but it's fast morphing into a tech company It's crunch time for retailers, and Amazon.com Inc. is no exception. At its nine massive distribution centers from Fernley, Nev., to Bar Hersfeld, Germany, workers scurry around the clock to fill up to 1.7 million orders a day—picking and packing merchandise, routing it onto conveyors, and shipping the boxes to every corner of the world. Like any retail warehouse running manpower and machinery at full holiday throttle, it's an impressive display. But utterly misleading. The kind of work that will truly determine Amazon's fate is happening in places like the tiny, darkened meeting room at its Seattle headquarters where, one recent afternoon, five intent faces gazed at a projection screen.

Jeffrey A. Wilke, a compact, intense senior vice president who runs Amazon's worldwide operations and customer service, and an engineering team were trying out a "beta" or test version of new software they wrote. When the buying automation program is ready for prime time in mid-2004, Amazon's merchandise buyers will be able to chuck reams of spreadsheets for graphics-rich applications that crunch data for them, so they can more quickly and accurately forecast product demand, find the best suppliers, and more. The effort is one of scores of technology projects under way at Amazon that ultimately may change the entire experience of shopping online—and Amazon itself.

Just as most folks have come to view Amazon as a retailer that happens to sell online, guess what? It's morphing into something new. In ways few people realize, Amazon is becoming more of a technology company—as much Microsoft Corp. and Wal-Mart Stores Inc. "What gets us up in the morning and keeps us here late at night is technology," says founder and Chief Executive Officer Jeffrey P. Bezos. "From where we sit, advanced technology is everything."

No, Amazon isn't selling its own shrink-wrapped software or leaving the retail business behind. But developing technology is becoming at least as important as selling Harry Potter books or The Strokes CDs. Indeed, some analysts say it's possible that in a few years so many other retailers will be using Amazon's tech expertise to sell on its site that they could account for more than half the products sold on Amazon.com. Says Bezos: "Amazon Services could be our most important business."

Already, Amazon's technological efforts have helped it reduce costs and boost sales so much that revenues are expected to surge 32% this year, to $5.2 billion. As a result, by the time the glittering ball descends in Times Square on New Year's Eve, Amazon may well reach a milestone some never thought it could: its first full-year profit. No wonder its stock has rocketed 152% this year, to $49.34 a share.

But all that is just the start. Building on a raft of tech initiatives, from an ever-richer Web site to new search technology, Bezos aims to reprogram the company into something even more potent. The notion is to create a technology-driven nexus for e-commerce that's as pervasive and powerful as Microsoft's Windows operating software is in computing. That's right: Bezos hopes to create a Windows for e-commerce.

Self-Reinforcing Cycle

Far-fetched? Not necessarily. After all, the Amazon.com Web site is already essentially a giant application that people simply use over the Web rather than in their personal computers. And bit by bit, just as its Washington neighbor did two decades ago,

Amazon is building what techies from Silicon Valley to Redmond call a platform: a stack of software on which thousands or millions of others can build businesses that in turn will bolster the platform in a self-reinforcing cycle.

Since last year, Amazon has been steadily turning innovations it developed for its own retail site into services available online. Using these so-called Amazon Web Services, reached via a browser, merchants who want to sell more can use its patented one-click purchasing system, for instance, or tap quickly into sales data for particular products. Even independent programmers are getting interested: In just 18 months, up to 35,000 programmers have downloaded software that enables them to pick and choose Amazon services and, much as they do with Windows, write new applications based on them.

Amazon doesn't make money directly from the Web services. Merchants and developers can get free access to the services and can use them to sell from any outpost on the Web. Still, many of the merchants who use applications spawned by Web services end up selling their wares to the 37 million customers assembled at Amazon.com. When that happens, Amazon takes a commission of about 15%, and these revenues have much higher margins than Amazon's own retail business. Already, 22% of Amazon's unit sales are by other merchants—and the Web-services push hasn't had a significant impact yet.

Busting Out

While Amazon isn't exiting retailing, its tech initiatives could, to some extent, set it free. By beefing up its technology and distributing it more freely, Amazon could bust out of the conceptual prison of stores and the virtual confines of a single Web site.

If Bezos' new plans work, Amazon could become not just a Web site but a service that would allow anyone, anywhere, to find whatever they want to buy—and to sell whatever they want almost as easily. For Amazon, that means its finances could look considerably better than traditional retailers'. Already it turns over inventory 19 times a year, nearly double Costco Wholesale Corp.'s 11 and almost triple Wal-Mart's 7. Yet unlike most retailers, it hasn't had to trade asset efficiency for profits. Its 25% gross margin is nearly double Costco's and three points higher than Wal-Mart's.

How much Amazon can expand the narrow margins of retail remains to be seen. But if even the conservative forecasts of analysts are correct, Amazon has a lot of upside in coming years. Shawn Milne of SoundView Technology Group Inc. sees sales continuing to rise no less than 15% a year through 2008, to $11.3 billion, with operating margins steadily marching up from 7% this year to 11.6% in five years.

Impossible Dream?

Bezos' vision won't be easy to fulfill. Trying to be a world-class retailer, a leading software developer, and a service provider simultaneously strikes some observers as a nearly impossible endeavor. Even some Amazon partners report shortcomings in merchandising and technical support. Others worry about Amazon's inherent conflict in playing both retailer and mall owner. "They're biting off a lot," says Forrester Research Inc. analyst Carrie A. Johnson. "That's their biggest risk."

Still, Bezos' bet on technology has paid off so far. Consider what has happened in its much-criticized distribution centers, which Amazon spent $300 million to build. Back in 2000, they were eating up at least 15% of sales, partly because processes to pick and pack different items such as books, toys, and CD players weren't very efficient. Chutes holding pending orders got backed up when products didn't arrive on time. Rampant mistakes required expensive manual fixes. Software was primitive, too: Workers had to enter data into the system using arcane Unix software commands.

Now, by most accounts, the warehouses hum more like Dell Inc.'s build-to-order factories. With a menu-driven software console, workers can anticipate where bottlenecks are likely to occur and move people around to avoid them. Another program rolled out this year sets priorities, based on current customer demand, for which products should be placed at the front of supply lines, further speeding the flow.

The result: Amazon's distribution centers can handle triple the volume of four years ago and cost half as much to operate relative to revenue, just 7% of sales. Wilke believes further software improvements can boost productivity by up to 10% a year.

All that has kicked off the virtuous cycle that's now propelling Amazon toward more consistent profits. Lower costs have enabled it to offer more product discounts and free shipping on most orders over $25. Those moves are credited with recharging sales—and with operating costs up only 5% this year, the benefits have dropped right to the bottom line.

Even so, Bezos isn't resting easy. While Amazon's spending on technology likely will remain fairly steady next year at about $216 million, thanks to declining tech prices, Chief Technology Officer Al Vermeulen says he will hire hundreds more software engineers and computer scientists in the next year to slake Bezos' thirst for tech. "Jeff is a very big driver of the technology," says Amazon director Tom Alberg, managing director of Seattle-based Madrona Venture Group.

For one, Bezos believes there's still plenty of room for improvement on the Web site itself. To that end, he hired last year what likely is a first for Corporate America: a chief algorithms officer, Udi Manber. His mission: to develop better versions of algorithms, the complex mathematical recipes that get software to do its magic. In particular, he's creating improved algorithms for Amazon's newest tech push: search. On Oct. 23, Amazon launched Search Inside the Book, a feature that allows visitors to find any word or phrase on 35 million pages in 120,000 books—and let them read entire pages around those keywords. In the week following, average sales growth for those books was nine percentage points higher than for books not in that database.

Manber has bigger plans yet. He now heads Amazon's first Silicon Valley outpost, a subsidiary called A9 that's charged with coming up with cutting-edge search technology. It's not just a defensive shot at search phenom Google, which is testing a shopping search engine it calls Froogle. "We need to help people get everything they need, not just a Web page," says Manber. And whatever he and his team come up with—he's mum now—it won't be confined to Amazon.com. A9 plans to offer search services it creates to other e-commerce sites as well.

Technologies like that, in which Amazon is reaching out beyond its own site, offer the most intriguing new opportunities—and challenges. Consider Amazon's Merchant.com business, which takes over the entire e-commerce operations of other retailers. By all appearances, it's a success. In Toys 'R' Us' most recent quarter, in which results were dismal, the one bright spot was a 15% jump in sales at Toyrus.com, run by Amazon. Other retailers seem happy, too. "Amazon is the most sophisticated technology provider and service partner on the Internet," says Target Vice Chairman Gerald L. Storch.

But how much that business will grow is debatable. As both retailer and mall operator, Amazon has divided loyalties. "Some companies worry about creating the next Wal-Mart that's going to take their business away down the road," says Dave Fry, CEO of Ann Arbor (Mich.)–based e-commerce consultant Fry Inc., which has helped several retailers sell on Amazon. As a result, many are going with rivals such as GSI Commerce Inc., which runs online operations for 51 retailers, from Linens 'n Things to The Sports Authority. Says Forrester's Johnson: "Ultimately, Amazon will be most successful selling their own and other retailers' products on their platform."

"An Ecosystem"   That's why Web services, unfettered by logistical challenges or business model conflicts, may offer the most expansive potential of all Amazon's tech initiatives. Nowhere is the potential more apparent than among the small merchants and independent programmers who are flocking to Amazon Web Services. "It's like an ecosystem," says Bezos. "People are doing things that surprise us."

People like Cleveland Wilson, a former tech recruiter who started selling books on Amazon in early 2002. Until this year, he didn't even think it would be enough to pay his rent in Berkeley, Calif. But he discovered a program called ScoutPal that uses Amazon Web services to let booksellers type or scan in a book's ISBN number to a laptop or wireless Web device and instantly see what it's selling for on Amazon. So when he visits thrift stores and garage sales, he can buy books he knows will be profitable to resell. For example, he paid $8 for *Suicide and Attempted Suicide: Methods and Consequences* and sold it for $275. From $100,000 in sales this year, he expects to do $250,000 next year because he has cut the time it takes to buy and sell books by two-thirds. "Without Amazon Web services, I wouldn't be in this business," he says.

That's not all. Now, he's starting a company to develop his own software using Amazon Web services that will help other sellers improve their businesses. It's still early, but it's possible that Amazon has latched onto one of tech's juiciest dynamics—a self-reinforcing community of supporters. Indeed, it seems to be harnessing the same "viral" nature of the open-source movement that made Linux a contender to Windows. Says Whit Andrews, an analyst at Gartner Inc.: "It creates an enormous community of people interested in making Amazon a success."

Even Microsoft. In Office 2003, people can click on a word or name in any document and be whisked off to Amazon.com so they can buy a related book or other product. Says Gytis Barzdukas, director of Microsoft's Of-fice product management group: "It gives Amazon the ability to market to a whole new set of customers and to become a part of people's work processes."

Amazon, the next Microsoft? Not so fast. For all the promise, building a broad platform is about as tough as a goal gets in the tech business—as nearly every competitor to Microsoft can attest. And unlike most tech companies, Amazon also has to contend not just with bits and bytes but also with the bricks and mortar of warehouses and the fickle fingers of Web shoppers. But for now, at least, Amazon's pursuit of cutting-edge technology has given it time to figure out what comes next.

SOURCE: Robert D. Hof (in Seattle), "Reprogramming Amazon," *BusinessWeek* (December 22, 2003), pp. 82–86.

Questions

1. Is the strategy described in this article a change in strategy for Amazon? Is it a change in where to compete, how to compete, or with what to compete?
2. What are the HR implications for Amazon's transformation to a technology company?

Please see the video case at the end of the book that corresponds to this chapter: JetBlue

Notes

1. J. Barney, "Firm Resources and Sustained Competitive Advantage," *Journal of Management* 17 (1991), pp. 99–120.
2. L. Dyer, "Strategic Human Resource Management and Planning," in *Research in Personnel and Human Resources Management,* ed. K. Rowland and G. Ferris (Greenwich, CT: JAI Press, 1985), pp. 1–30.
3. J. Quinn, *Strategies for Change: Logical Incrementalism* (Homewood, IL: Richard D. Irwin, 1980).
4. M. Porter, *Competitive Strategy: Techniques for Analyzing Industries and Competitors* (New York: Free Press, 1980).
5. R. Miles and C. Snow, *Organizational Strategy, Structure, and Process* (New York: McGraw-Hill, 1978).
6. P. Wright and G. McMahan, "Theoretical Perspectives for Strategic Human Resource Management," *Journal of Management* 18 (1992), pp. 295–320.
7. D. Guest, "Human Resource Management, Corporate Performance and Employee Well-Being: Building the Worker into HRM," *Journal of Industrial Relations* 44 (2002), pp. 335–58; B. Becker, M. Huselid, P. Pinckus, and M. Spratt, "HR as a Source of Shareholder Value: Research and Recommendations, *Human Resource Management* 36 (1997), pp. 39–47.
8. P. Boxall and J. Purcell, *Strategy and Human Resource Management* (Basingstoke, Hants, U.K.: Palgrave MacMillan, 2003).
9. F. Biddle and J. Helyar, "Behind Boeing's Woes: Chunky Assembly Line, Price War with Airbus," *The Wall Street Journal* (April 24, 1998), pp. A1, A16.
10. K. Martell and S. Carroll, "How Strategic Is HRM?" *Human Resource Management* 34 (1995), pp. 253–67.
11. K. Golden and V. Ramanujam, "Between a Dream and a Nightmare: On the Integration of the Human Resource Function and the Strategic Business Planning Process," *Human Resource Management* 24 (1985), pp. 429–51.
12. P. Wright, B. Dunford, and S. Snell, "Contributions of the Resource-Based View of the Firm to the Field of Strategic HRM: Convergence of Two Fields," *Journal of Management* 27 (2001), pp. 701–21.
13. J. Purcell, N. Kinnie, S. Hutchinson, B. Rayton, and J. Swart, *Understanding the People and Performance Link: Unlocking the Black Box* (London: CIPD, 2003).
14. P. M. Wright, T. Gardner, and L. Moynihan, "The Impact of Human Resource Practices on Business Unit Operating and Financial Performance," *Human Resource Management Journal* (2003), vol. 13, no. 3, pp. 21–36.
15. C. Hill and G. Jones, *Strategic Management Theory: An Integrated Approach* (Boston: Houghton Mifflin, 1989).
16. W. Johnston and A. Packer, *Workforce 2000: Work and Workers for the Twenty-first Century* (Indianapolis, IN: Hudson Institute, 1987).
17. "Labor Letter," *The Wall Street Journal* (December 15, 1992), p. A1.
18. P. Wright, G. McMahan, and A. McWilliams, "Human Resources and Sustained Competitive Advantage: A Resource-Based Perspective," *International Journal of Human Resource Management* 5 (1994), pp. 301–26.
19. P. Buller, "Successful Partnerships: HR and Strategic Planning at Eight Top Firms," *Organizational Dynamics* 17 (1988), pp. 27–42.

20. M. Hitt, R. Hoskisson, and J. Harrison, "Strategic Competitiveness in the 1990s: Challenges and Opportunities for U.S. Executives," *The Executive* 5 (May 1991), pp. 7–22.

21. P. Wright, G. McMahan, B. McCormick, and S. Sherman, *Strategy, Core Competence, and HR Involvement as Determinants of HR Effectiveness and Refinery Performance.* Paper presented at the 1996 International Federation of Scholarly Associations in Management, Paris, France.

22. N. Bennett, D. Ketchen, and E. Schultz, *Antecedents and Consequences of Human Resource Integration with Strategic Decision Making.* Paper presented at the 1995 Academy of Management Meeting, Vancouver, BC, Canada.

23. Golden and Ramanujam, "Between a Dream and a Nightmare."

24. J. Galbraith and R. Kazanjian, *Strategy Implementation: Structure, Systems, and Process* (St. Paul, MN: West, 1986).

25. B. Schneider and A. Konz, "Strategic Job Analysis," *Human Resource Management* 27 (1989), pp. 51–64.

26. P. Wright and S. Snell, "Toward an Integrative View of Strategic Human Resource Management," *Human Resource Management Review* 1 (1991), pp. 203–25.

27. S. Snell, "Control Theory in Strategic Human Resource Management: The Mediating Effect of Administrative Information," *Academy of Management Journal* 35 (1992), pp. 292–327.

28. R. Schuler, "Personnel and Human Resource Management Choices and Organizational Strategy," in *Readings in Personnel and Human Resource Management*, 3rd ed., ed. R. Schuler, S. Youngblood, and V. Huber (St. Paul, MN: West, 1988).

29. J. Dean and S. Snell, "Integrated Manufacturing and Job Design: Moderating Effects of Organizational Inertia," *Academy of Management Journal* 34 (1991), pp. 776–804.

30. E. Lawler, *The Ultimate Advantage: Creating the High Involvement Organization* (San Francisco: Jossey-Bass, 1992).

31. J. Olian and S. Rynes, "Organizational Staffing: Integrating Practice with Strategy," *Industrial Relations* 23 (1984), pp. 170–83.

32. G. Smith, "Quality: Small and Midsize Companies Seize the Challenge—Not a Moment Too Soon," *BusinessWeek* (November 30, 1992), pp. 66–75.

33. J. Kerr and E. Jackofsky, "Aligning Managers with Strategies: Management Development versus Selection," *Strategic Management Journal* 10 (1989), pp. 157–70.

34. J. Kerr, "Strategic Control through Performance Appraisal and Rewards," *Human Resource Planning* 11 (1988), pp. 215–23.

35. S. Snell, "Control Theory in Strategic Human Resource Management."

36. B. Gerhart and G. Milkovich, "Employee Compensation: Research and Practice," in *Handbook of Industrial and Organizational Psychology*, 2nd ed., ed. M. Dunnette and L. Hough (Palo Alto, CA: Consulting Psychologists Press, 1992), pp. 481–569.

37. D. Balkin and L. Gomez-Mejia, "Toward a Contingency Theory of Compensation Strategy," *Strategic Management Journal* 8 (1987), pp. 169–82.

38. A. Taylor, "U.S. Cars Come Back," *Fortune* (November 16, 1992), pp. 52, 85.

39. S. Cronshaw and R. Alexander, "One Answer to the Demand for Accountability: Selection Utility as an Investment Decision," *Organizational Behavior and Human Decision Processes* 35 (1986), pp. 102–18.

40. P. MacDuffie, "Human Resource Bundles and Manufacturing Performance: Organizational Logic and Flexible Production Systems in the World Auto Industry," *Industrial and Labor Relations Review* 48 (1995), pp. 197–221; P. McGraw, "A Hard Drive to the Top," *U.S. News and World Report* 118 (1995), pp. 43–44.

41. M. Huselid, "The Impact of Human Resource Management Practices on Turnover, Productivity, and Corporate Financial Performance," *Academy of Management Journal* 38 (1995), pp. 635–72.

42. B. Fulmer, B. Gerhart, and K. Scott, "Are the 100 Best Better? An Empirical Investigation of the Relationship between Being a 'Great Place to Work' and Firm Performance," *Personnel Psychology* 56 (2003), pp. 965–93.

43. J. E. Delery and D. H. Doty, "Modes of Theorizing in Strategic Human Resource Management: Tests of Universalistic, Contingency and Configurational Performance Predictions," *Academy of Management Journal* 39 (1996), pp. 802–83; D. Guest, J. Michie, N. Conway, and M. Sheehan, "Human Resource Management and Corporate Performance in the UK," *British Journal of Industrial Relations* 41 (2003), pp. 291–314; J. Guthrie, "High Involvement Work Practices, Turnover, and Productivity: Evidence from New Zealand," *Academy of Management Journal* 44 (2001), pp. 180–192; J. Harter, F. Schmidt, and T. Hayes, "Business-Unit-Level Relationship between Employee Satisfaction, Employee Engagement, and Business Outcomes: A Meta-analysis," *Journal of Applied Psychology* 87 (2002), pp. 268–79; Watson Wyatt, *Human Capital Index®: Human Capital as a Lead Indicator of Shareholder Value* (2002).

44. M. Porter, *Competitive Advantage* (New York: Free Press, 1985).

45. R. Schuler and S. Jackson, "Linking Competitive Strategies with Human Resource Management Practices," *Academy of Management Executive* 1 (1987), pp. 207–19.

46. R. Miles and C. Snow, "Designing Strategic Human Resource Management Systems," *Organizational Dynamics* 13, no. 1 (1984), pp. 36–52.

47. J. Arthur, "The Link between Business Strategy and Industrial Relations Systems in American Steel Mini-Mills," *Industrial and Labor Relations Review* 45 (1992), pp. 488–506.

48. A. Thompson and A. Strickland, *Strategy Formulation and Implementation: Tasks of the General Manager*, 3rd ed. (Plano, TX: BPI, 1986).

49. J. Schmidt, *Making Mergers Work: The Strategic Importance of People* (Arlington, VA: SHRM Foundation, 2003).

50. G. Fairclough, "Business Bulletin," *The Wall Street Journal* (March 5, 1998), p. A1.

51. P. Sebastian, "Business Bulletin," *The Wall Street Journal* (October 2, 1997), p. A1.

52. J. S. Champy, *Reengineering Management: The Mandate for New Leadership* (New York: Harper Business, 1995).

53. S. Pearlstein, "Corporate Cutback Yet to Pay Off," *Washington Post* (January 4, 1994), p. B6.

54. K. Cameron, "Guest Editor's Note: Investigating Organizational Downsizing—Fundamental Issues," *Human Resource Management* 33 (1994), pp. 183–88.

55. W. Cascio, *Responsible Restructuring: Creative and Profitable Alternatives to Layoffs* (San Francisco: Berrett-Koehler, 2002).

56. N. Templin, "UAW to Unveil Pact on Slashing GM's Payroll," *The Wall Street Journal* (December 15, 1992), p. A3.

57. J. Lopez, "Managing: Early-Retirement Offers Lead to Renewed Hiring," *The Wall Street Journal* (January 26, 1993), p. B1.

58. A. Church, "Organizational Downsizing: What Is the Role of the Practitioner?" *The Industrial–Organizational Psychologist* 33, no. 1 (1995), pp. 63–74.

59. N. Templin, "A Decisive Response to Crisis Brought Ford Enhanced Productivity," *The Wall Street Journal* (December 15, 1992), p. A1.

60. Quinn, *Strategies for Change.*

61. H. Mintzberg, "Patterns in Strategy Formulation," *Management Science* 24 (1978), pp. 934–48.

62. R. Pascale, "Perspectives on Strategy: The Real Story behind

Honda's Success," *California Management Review* 26 (1984), pp. 47–72.

63. Templin, "A Decisive Response to Crisis."
64. P. Wright and S. Snell, "Toward a Unifying Framework for Exploring Fit and Flexibility in Strategic Human Resource Management," *Academy of Management Review* 23 (4) (1998), pp. 756–72.
65. P. Senge, *The Fifth Discipline* (New York: Doubleday, 1990).
66. T. Stewart, "Brace for Japan's Hot New Strategy," *Fortune* (September 21, 1992), pp. 62–76.
67. Dunford, Wright, and Snell, "Contributions of the Resource-Based View," pp. 701–21.
68. C. Snow and S. Snell, *Staffing as Strategy*, vol. 4 of *Personnel Selection* (San Francisco: Jossey-Bass, 1992).
69. T. Batten, "Education Key to Prosperity—Report," *Houston Chronicle* (September 7, 1992), p. 1B.
70. P. Wright, "Human Resources as a Competitive Weapon," *Applied Advances in Strategic Management* 2 (1991), pp. 91–122.
71. G. McMahan, University of Texas at Arlington, personal communications.
72. G. McMahan and R. Woodman, "The Current Practice of Organization Development within the Firm: A Survey of Large Industrial Corporations," *Group and Organization Studies* 17 (1992), pp. 117–34.
73. B. Becker, M. Huselid, and D. Ulrich, *The HR Scorecard: Linking People, Strategy, and Performance* (Cambridge, MA: HBS Press, 2001).
74. D. Ulrich and A. Yeung, "A Shared Mindset," *Personnel Administrator*, March 1989, pp. 38–45.
75. G. Jones and P. Wright, "An Economic Approach to Conceptualizing the Utility of Human Resource Management Practices," *Research in Personnel/Human Resources* 10 (1992), pp. 271–99.
76. R. Schuler and J. Walker, "Human Resources Strategy: Focusing on Issues and Actions," *Organizational Dynamics*, Summer 1990, pp. 5–19.
77. J. Paauwe, *Human Resource Management and Performance: Unique Approaches for Achieving Long-Term Viability* (Oxford: Oxford University Press, 2004).
78. M. Brannigan, "Delta Lifts Mechanics' Pay to Top of Industry Amid Push by Union, *Wall Street Journal Interactive* (August 16, 2001); M. Adams, "Delta May See Second Big Union, *USA Today* (August 27, 2001), p. 1B.

3
Chapter

The Legal Environment: Equal Employment Opportunity and Safety

Objectives After reading this chapter, you should be able to:

1. Identify the three branches of government and the role each plays in influencing the legal environment of human resource management.

2. List the major federal laws that require equal employment opportunity and the protections provided by each of these laws.

3. Discuss the roles, responsibilities, and requirements of the federal agencies responsible for enforcing equal employment opportunity laws.

4. Identify the four theories of discrimination under Title VII of the Civil Rights Act and apply these theories to different discrimination situations.

5. Identify behavior that constitutes sexual harassment and list things that an organization can do to eliminate or minimize it.

6. Discuss the legal issues involved with preferential treatment programs.

7. Identify the major provisions of the Occupational Safety and Health Act (1970) and the rights of employees that are guaranteed by this act.

Legal issues, such as the class action lawsuit at Boeing, can cause serious problems for companies. As you read the chapter, try to determine what Boeing's side of the story may be.

Enter the World of Business

Problems at Boeing

Boeing, the global aerospace company best known for its 737 and 747 aircraft, has faced a number of problems over the past few years. As discussed in Chapter 2, their competition with Airbus placed them in a difficult position in the marketplace. However, a number of their problems have been internal as well.

In addition to being embroiled in several ethics scandals on its defense contracting side of the business, Boeing has faced a number of discrimination complaints as well. For example, 38 female manufacturing engineers filed a sex-discrimination case against the company in 2000. While the company denied the charges, some internal documents obtained by *BusinessWeek* may tell a completely different story. In 1997 Boeing created an internal Diversity Salary Assessment team tasked with examining its compensation and promotion practices. One presentation concluded that "females . . . are paid less" and "gender differences in starting salaries generally continue and often increase as a result of salary planning decisions." According to *BusinessWeek* these documents "seem to tell the story of a company that underpaid women, knew it, and yet bitterly contested both the sex-discrimination case and a 1998 Labor Dept. audit into the same issues."

The documents suggest that Boeing knew of the pay disparities as far back as 1994. A salary analysis project from 1999 showed that Boeing needed to allocate $30 million to eliminate the gender-based pay differences, but allocated only $10 million. Boeing HR executive Erika Lochow testified that she and her colleagues were shocked at just how big the pay disparity was. The company treated the studies with utmost confidentiality, keeping them in a "secured office location" not even janitors had access to, using special e-mail encryption software so that outside counsel and executives could exchange data in a "secure and safe" manner, and forbidding executives from taking any notes at meetings where the salary data were discussed.

The class action lawsuit facing Boeing includes 28,000 potential plaintiffs, and a potential liability exceeding $1 billion including compensatory damages, punitive damages, and attorneys' fees. As part of its settlement with the OFCCP in 1999, Boeing agreed to settle for $4.5 million, but their potential liability could have been over $120 million. In addition, Marcella Fleming, then Boeing's director of employee relations and one of Boeing's key dealmakers as part of the settlement, stated at a meeting following the settlement, "The fact that our compensation comes up . . . negative, negative, negative would suggest that there's something generally not right about the way we're doing it."

Source: S. Holmes, "A New Black Eye for Boeing?" *BusinessWeek* (April 26, 2004), pp. 90–91.

Introduction

In the opening chapter we discussed the environment of the HRM function, and we noted that several environmental factors affect an organization's HRM function. One is the legal environment, particularly the laws affecting the management of people. As the troubles at Boeing indicate, legal issues can cause serious problems for a company's success and survival. In this chapter we first present an overview of the U.S. legal system, noting the different legislative bodies, regulatory agencies, and judicial bodies that determine the legality of certain HRM practices. We then discuss the major laws and executive orders that govern these practices.

One point to make clear at the outset is that managers often want a list of "dos and don'ts" that will keep them out of legal trouble. They rely on rules such as "Don't ever ask a female applicant if she is married" without understanding the "why" behind these rules. Clearly, certain practices are illegal or inadvisable, and this chapter will provide some valuable tips for avoiding discrimination lawsuits. However, such lists are not compatible with a strategic approach to HRM and are certainly not the route to developing a competitive advantage. They are simply mechanical reactions to the situations. Our goal is to provide an understanding of how the legislative, regulatory, and judicial systems work to define equal employment opportunity law. Armed with this understanding, a manager is better prepared to manage people within the limits imposed by the legal system. Doing so effectively is a source of competitive advantage. Doing so ineffectively results in competitive disadvantage. Rather than viewing the legal system as a constraint, firms that embrace the concept of diversity can often find that they are able to leverage the differences among people as a tremendous competitive tool. "Competing through Globalization" illustrates how one company used blind employees as the basis of their business model.

The Legal System in the United States

The foundation for the U.S. legal system is set forth in the U.S. Constitution, which affects HRM in two ways. First, it delineates a citizen's constitutional rights, on which the government cannot impinge.[1] Most individuals are aware of the Bill of Rights, the first 10 amendments to the Constitution; but other amendments, such as the Fourteenth Amendment, also influence HRM practices. The Fourteenth Amendment, called the *equal protection clause*, states that all individuals are entitled to equal protection under the law.

Second, the Constitution established three major governing bodies: the legislative, executive, and judicial branches. The Constitution explicitly defines the roles and responsibilities of each of these branches. Each branch has its own areas of authority, but these areas have often overlapped, and the borders between the branches are often blurred.

Legislative Branch

The legislative branch of the federal government consists of the House of Representatives and the Senate. These bodies develop laws that govern many HRM activities. Most of the laws stem from a perceived societal need. For example, during the civil rights movement of the early 1960s, the legislative branch moved to ensure that various minority groups received equal opportunities in many areas of life. One of these areas was employment, and thus Congress enacted Title VII of the Civil Rights Act.

Blind Feeding the Blind

Many teachers use an exercise where students must walk around blindfolded for a few hours to help appreciate the situation of those who truly are blind. However, until recently, nobody actually made a business out of this.

At the Blind Cow restaurant in Zurich, Switzerland, nothing looks good to eat. The reason is not that the food is bad, but because patrons dine in total darkness. Rev. Jorge Spielman, a 37-year-old blind pastor, came up with the idea while tending bar at a public exhibit in Zurich. The exhibit required sighted people to grope their way through various dark rooms to experience what it is like to be blind. He and four blind colleagues decided to create a restaurant that would help sighted people appreciate the situation of the blind while providing jobs for the blind and visually impaired.

A blind waitress leads diners to their tables, asking one guest to place both hands on her shoulders, and other guests to do likewise to the guest in front of them. She explains the rules: no flashlights, no iridescent watches, and no wandering. Waitresses and waiters should be called by shouting, and guests who need to use the restrooms must be led by a waitress. The staff all wear bells to allow them to avoid colliding with one another while carrying hot plates of food.

The restaurant has been an unarguable success. Although Rev. Spielman worried that the novelty would wear off after a few months, a year after its opening the restaurant was still booked solid for the following three months. In addition, the breakage of dishes and glasses is no different from other restaurants because guests are extremely careful. In fact, the business has been such a success that the owners are now considering expanding into big U.S. cities like New York and Los Angeles.

Such expansion could succeed because the atmosphere provides for a variety of novel experiences. For instance, a group of three couples dined there, and when the ladies went to the restroom, the men changed places. When they returned, the men planted kisses on their "new" dates; not all the women noticed that the lips kissing them were unfamiliar ones. In addition, the restaurant was the site for a "blind date." The lady arrived early and sipped a drink until the man was led to her table. Unfortunately, according to the staff, they departed separately. Finally, Rev. Spielman has some ideas to keep the restaurant fresh. He plans to make Monday night "date night," bringing in guest speakers to discuss sex and relationships. He explains, "People can ask all kinds of questions in the dark."

SOURCE: J. Costello, "Swiss Eatery Operated by the Blind Keeps Diners Completely in the Dark," *The Wall Street Journal* (November 28, 2001), p. 1.

Similar perceived societal needs have brought about labor laws such as the Occupational Safety and Health Act, the Employee Retirement Income Security Act, the Age Discrimination in Employment Act, and, more recently, the Americans with Disabilities Act of 1990 and the Civil Rights Act of 1991.

Executive Branch

The executive branch consists of the president of the United States and the many regulatory agencies the president oversees. Although the legislative branch passes the laws, the executive branch affects these laws in many ways. First, the president can propose bills to Congress that, if passed, would become laws. Second, the president has the power to veto any law passed by Congress, thus ensuring that few laws are passed without presidential approval—which allows the president to influence how laws are written.

Third, the regulatory agencies, under the authority of the president, have responsibility for enforcing the laws. Thus a president can influence what types of violations are pursued. For example, many laws affecting employment discrimination are enforced by the Equal Employment Opportunity Commission under the Department of Justice. During President Jimmy Carter's administration, the Department of Justice brought a lawsuit against Birmingham, Alabama's, fire department for not having enough black firefighters. This suit resulted in a consent decree that required blacks to receive preferential treatment in hiring and promotion decisions. Two years later, during Ronald Reagan's administration, the Department of Justice sided with white firefighters in a lawsuit against the city of Birmingham, alleging that the preferential treatment required by the consent decree discriminated against white firefighters.[2]

Fourth, the president can issue executive orders, which sometimes regulate the activities of organizations that have contracts with the federal government. For example, Executive Order 11246, signed by President Lyndon Johnson, required all federal contractors and subcontractors to engage in affirmative action programs designed to hire and promote women and minorities within their organizations. Fifth, the president can influence the Supreme Court to interpret laws in certain ways. When particularly sensitive cases come before the Court, the attorney general, representing the executive branch, argues for certain preferred outcomes. For example, one recent court case involved a white female schoolteacher who was laid off from her job in favor of retaining a black schoolteacher with equal seniority and performance with the reason given as "diversity." The white woman filed a lawsuit in federal court and the (first) Bush administration filed a brief on her behalf, arguing that diversity was not a legitimate reason to use race in decision making. She won in federal court, and the school district appealed. The Clinton administration, having been elected in the meantime, filed a brief on behalf of the school district, arguing that diversity was a legitimate defense.

Finally, the president appoints all the judges in the federal judicial system, subject to approval from the legislative branch. This affects the interpretation of many laws.

Judicial Branch

The judicial branch consists of the federal court system, which is made up of three levels. The first level consists of the U.S. District Courts and quasi-judicial administrative agencies. The district courts hear cases involving alleged violations of federal laws. The quasi-judicial agencies, such as the National Labor Relations Board (or NLRB, which is actually an arm of the executive branch, but serves a judicial function), hear cases regarding their particular jurisdictions (in the NLRB's case, disputes between unions and management). If neither party to a suit is satisfied with the decision of the court at this level, the parties can appeal the decision to the U.S. Courts of Appeals. These courts were originally set up to ease the Supreme Court's caseload, so appeals generally go from the federal trial level to one of the 13 appellate courts before they can be heard by the highest level, the Supreme Court. The Supreme Court must grant certiorari before hearing an appealed case. However, this is not usually granted unless two appellate courts have come to differing decisions on the same point of law or if the case deals with an important interpretation of constitutional law.

The Supreme Court serves as the court of final appeal. Decisions made by the Supreme Court are binding; they can be overturned only through legislation. For example, Congress, dissatisfied with the Supreme Court's decisions in certain cases such as *Wards Cove Packing v. Atonio*, overturned those decisions through the Civil Rights Act of 1991.[3]

Having described the legal system that affects the management of HR, we now explore some laws that regulate HRM activities, particularly equal employment opportunity laws. We first discuss the major laws that mandate equal employment opportunity in the United States. Then we examine the agencies involved in enforcing these laws. This leads us into an examination of the four theories of discrimination, with a discussion of some relevant court cases. Finally, we explore some equal employment opportunity issues facing today's managers.

Equal Employment Opportunity

Equal employment opportunity (EEO) refers to the government's attempt to ensure that all individuals have an equal chance for employment, regardless of race, color, religion, sex, age, disability, or national origin. To accomplish this, the federal government has used constitutional amendments, legislation, and executive orders, as well as the court decisions that interpret these laws. (However, equal employment laws are not the same in all countries.) The major EEO laws we discuss are summarized in Table 3.1.

Equal employment opportunity (EEO)
The government's attempt to ensure that all individuals have an equal opportunity for employment, regardless of race, color, religion, sex, age, disability, or national origin.

Constitutional Amendments

Thirteenth Amendment
The Thirteenth Amendment of the Constitution abolished slavery in the United States. Though one might be hard-pressed to cite an example of race-based slavery in the United States today, the Thirteenth Amendment has been applied in cases where the discrimination involved the "badges" (symbols) and "incidents" of slavery.

Fourteenth Amendment
The Fourteenth Amendment forbids the states from taking life, liberty, or property without due process of law and prevents the states from denying equal protection of the laws. Passed immediately after the Civil War, this amendment originally applied only to discrimination against blacks. It was soon broadened to protect other groups such as aliens and Asian-Americans, and more recently it has been applied to the protection of whites in allegations of reverse discrimination. In *Bakke v. California Board of Regents*, Alan Bakke alleged that he had been discriminated against in the selection of entrants to the University of California at Davis medical school.[4] The university had set aside 16 of the available 100 places for "disadvantaged" applicants who were members of racial minority groups. Under this quota system, Bakke was able to compete for only 84 positions, whereas a minority applicant was able to compete for all 100. The court ruled in favor of Bakke, noting that this quota system had violated white individuals' right to equal protection under the law.

One important point regarding the Fourteenth Amendment is that it is applicable only to "state actions." This means that only the decisions or actions of the government or of private groups whose activities are deemed state actions can be construed

TABLE 3.1

Summary of Major EEO Laws and Regulations

ACT	REQUIREMENTS	COVERS	ENFORCEMENT AGENCY
Thirteenth Amendment	Abolished slavery	All individuals	Court system
Fourteenth Amendment	Provides equal protection for all citizens and requires due process in state action	State actions (e.g., decisions of government organizations)	Court system
Civil Rights Acts (CRAs) of 1866 and 1871 (as amended)	Grants all citizens the right to make, perform, modify, and terminate contracts and enjoy all benefits, terms, and conditions of the contractual relationship	All individuals	Court system
Equal Pay Act of 1963	Requires that men and women performing equal jobs receive equal pay	Employers engaged in interstate commerce	EEOC
Title VII of CRA	Forbids discrimination based on race, color, religion, sex, or national origin	Employers with 15 or more employees working 20 or more weeks per year; labor unions; and employment agencies	EEOC
Age Discrimination in Employment Act of 1967	Prohibits discrimination in employment against individuals 40 years of age and older	Employers with 15 or more employees working 20 or more weeks per year; labor unions; employment agencies; federal government	EEOC
Rehabilitation Act of 1973	Requires affirmative action in the employment of individuals with disabilities	Government agencies; federal contractors and subcontractors with contracts greater than $2,500	OFCCP
Americans with Disabilities Act of 1990	Prohibits discrimination against individuals with disabilities	Employers with more than 15 employees	EEOC
Executive Order 11246	Requires affirmative action in hiring women and minorities	Federal contractors and subcontractors with contracts greater than $10,000	OFCCP
Civil Rights Act of 1991	Prohibits discrimination (same as Title VII)	Same as Title VII, plus applies Section 1981 to employment discrimination cases	EEOC

gender = set

as violations of the Fourteenth Amendment. Thus, one could file a claim under the Fourteenth Amendment if one were fired from a state university (a government organization) but not if one were fired by a private employer.

Congressional Legislation

The Reconstruction Civil Rights Acts (1866 and 1871)

The Thirteenth Amendment eradicated slavery in the United States, and the Reconstruction Civil Rights Acts were attempts to further this goal. The Civil Rights Act passed in 1866 was later broken into two statutes. Section 1982 granted all persons the same property rights as white citizens. Section 1981 granted other rights, including the right to enter into and enforce contracts. Courts have interpreted Section 1981 as granting individuals the right to make and enforce employment contracts. The Civil Rights Act of 1871 granted all citizens the right to sue in federal court if they felt they had been deprived of some civil right. Although these laws might seem outdated, they are still used because they allow the plaintiff to recover both compensatory and punitive damages.

In fact, these laws came to the forefront in a Supreme Court case: *Patterson v. McClean Credit Union.*[5] The plaintiff had filed a discrimination complaint under Section 1981 for racial harassment. After being hired by McClean Credit Union, Patterson failed to receive any promotions or pay raises while she was employed there. She was also told that "blacks work slower than whites." Thus she had grounds to prove discrimination and filed suit under Section 1981, arguing that she had been discriminated against in the making and enforcement of an employment contract. The Supreme Court ruled that this situation did not fall under Section 1981 because it did not involve the making and enforcement of contracts. However, the Civil Rights Act of 1991 amended this act to include the making, performance, modification, and termination of contracts, as well as all benefits, privileges, terms, and conditions of the contractual relationship.

The Equal Pay Act of 1963

The Equal Pay Act, an amendment to the Fair Labor Standards Act, requires that men and women in the same organization who are doing equal work must be paid equally. The act defines *equal* in terms of skill, effort, responsibility, and working conditions. However, the act allows for reasons why men and women performing the same job might be paid differently. If the pay differences are the result of differences in seniority, merit, quantity or quality of production, or any factor other than sex (such as shift differentials or training programs), then differences are legally allowable.

Title VII of the Civil Rights Act of 1964

This is the major legislation regulating equal employment opportunity in the United States. It was a direct result of the civil rights movement of the early 1960s, led by such individuals as Dr. Martin Luther King, Jr. It was Dr. King's philosophy that people should "not be judged by the color of their skin but by the content of their character." To ensure that employment opportunities would be based on character or ability rather than on race, Congress wrote and passed Title VII, which President Lyndon Johnson signed into law.

Title VII states that it is illegal for an employer to "(1) fail or refuse to hire or discharge any individual, or otherwise discriminate against any individual with respect to his compensation, terms, conditions, or privileges of employment because of such individual's race, color, religion, sex, or national origin, or (2) to limit, segregate, or classify his employees or applicants for employment in any way that would deprive or tend to deprive any individual of employment opportunities or otherwise adversely affect his status as an employee because of such individual's race, color, religion, sex, or national origin." The act applies to organizations with 15 or more employees working 20 or more weeks a year that are involved in interstate commerce, as well as state and local governments, employment agencies, and labor organizations.

Age Discrimination in Employment Act (ADEA)

Passed in 1967 and amended in 1986, this act prohibits discrimination against employees over the age of 40. The act almost exactly mirrors Title VII in terms of its substantive provisions and the procedures to be followed in pursuing a case.[6] As with Title VII, the EEOC is responsible for enforcing this act.

The ADEA was designed to protect older employees when a firm reduces its workforce through layoffs. By targeting older employees, who tend to have higher pay, a firm can substantially cut labor costs. Recently, firms have often offered early retirement incentives, a possible violation of the act because of the focus on older employees. Early retirement incentives require employees to sign an agreement waiving their rights to sue under the ADEA. Courts have tended to uphold the use of early retirement incentives and waivers as long as the individuals were not coerced into signing the agreements, the agreements were presented in a way that the employees could understand, and the employees were given enough time to make a decision.[7]

However, age discrimination complaints make up a large percentage of the complaints filed with the Equal Employment Opportunity Commission, and the number of complaints continues to grow whenever the economy is slow. For example, as we see in Figure 3.1, the cases increased during the early 1990s when many firms were downsizing, but the number of cases decreased as the economy expanded. The number of charges increased again as the economy began slowing again in 2000. This of-

FIGURE 3.1

Age Discrimination Complaints, 1991–2003

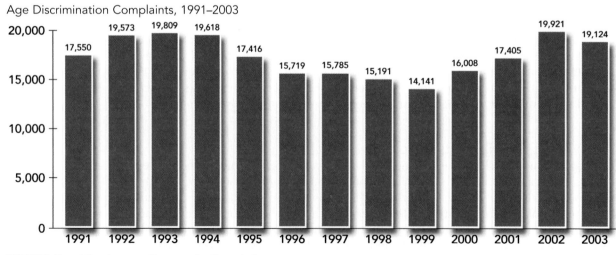

SOURCE: Equal Employment Opportunity Commission.

ten stems from firms seeking to lay off older (and thus higher-paid) employees when they are downsizing. These cases can be costly; most cases are settled out of court, but such settlements run from $50,000 to $400,000 per employee.[8] In one recent case Schering-Plough fired 35-year employee Fred Maiorino after he twice failed to accept an early retirement offer made to all sales representatives. After hearing testimony that Maiorino's boss had plastered his file with negative paperwork aimed at firing him, rather than trying to help him improve his performance, the jurors unanimously decided he had been discriminated against because of his age. They awarded him $435,000 in compensatory damages and $8 million in punitive damages.[9]

Finding and Keeping the Best Employees

In today's environment where firms are seeking talented individuals to execute their business models, older employees can be a tremendous pool of potential resources. In 1996 Bonne Bell, the maker of a number of cosmetics popular among teenage girls, faced a tight labor market and a strong growth in demand for its products in Canada. Jess Bell, the president and son of the founder, had an epiphany. Being 76 years old himself, he increasingly felt that working with younger people made him feel self-conscious about his own ability to keep pace. So he created an entire production department of older workers.

He figured that having a line of entirely older workers would allow them to compete at their own level, rather than against those much younger and more energetic. He also thought older workers would not necessarily want to listen to either the conversations or the music of 20-year-olds. Juliana Carlton, 65, supervises eight employees on the line and notes, "I raised my kids. It's my turn to be with people my own age group. We can talk to each other. We don't have to compete."

The experiment began with taking three older packaging machines and two conveyors out of storage so as not to invest much in new equipment in case the idea did not work. The senior workers tend to have more flexible hours to adapt to many of the aches and pains that accompany growing old. The employees listen to oldies like Frank Sinatra while they work. The department began with 16 people but has now grown to 50 workers on each shift. Pay starts at $7.50 an hour and moves to $8 after a year. The workers get 72 hours of paid time off but no health care coverage, which helps keep costs down. The average age of the assembly line workers is 70, and the oldest just turned 90.

Each worker has his or her own reasons for working. Some workers need the extra $600 a month to pay bills. Some need the money to help take care of their parents. But for others, working provides a sense of connection and self-esteem. Many are mothers who are not as integral to their grown children's lives as they once were. Mrs. Carlton states, "Instead of sitting around, I wanted to do something with my life."

So far, this experiment has been a success. The group has saved the company more than $1 million since it was launched while meeting shipment goals and experiencing almost zero turnover.

SOURCE: C. Ansberry, "Bonne Bell Retires Stereotypes with Seniors-Only Department," *The Wall Street Journal* (February 5, 2001), p. 1.

The Vocational Rehabilitation Act of 1973

This act covers executive agencies and contractors and subcontractors that receive more than $2,500 annually from the federal government. It requires them to engage in affirmative action for individuals with disabilities. Congress designed this act to encourage employers to actively recruit qualified individuals with disabilities and to make reasonable accommodations to allow them to become active members of the labor market. The Employment Standards Administration of the Department of Labor enforces this act.

Vietnam Era Veteran's Readjustment Act of 1974

Similar to the Rehabilitation Act, this act requires federal contractors and subcontractors to take affirmative action toward employing Vietnam veterans (those serving between August 5, 1964, and May 7, 1975). The Office of Federal Contract Compliance Procedures, discussed later in this chapter, has authority to enforce this act.

Civil Rights Act of 1991

The Civil Rights Act of 1991 (CRA 1991) amends Title VII of the Civil Rights Act of 1964, Section 1981 of the Civil Rights Act of 1866, the Americans with Disabilities Act, and the Age Discrimination in Employment Act of 1967. One major change in EEO law under CRA 1991 has been the addition of compensatory and punitive damages in cases of discrimination under Title VII and the Americans with Disabilities Act. Before CRA 1991, Title VII limited damage claims to equitable relief such as back pay, lost benefits, front pay in some cases, and attorney's fees and costs. CRA 1991 allows compensatory and punitive damages when intentional or reckless discrimination is proven. Compensatory damages include such things as future pecuniary loss, emotional pain, suffering, and loss of enjoyment of life. Punitive damages are meant to discourage employers from discriminating by providing for payments to the plaintiff beyond the actual damages suffered.

Recognizing that one or a few discrimination cases could put an organization out of business, thus adversely affecting many innocent employees, Congress has put limits on the amount of punitive damages. Table 3.2 depicts these limits. As can be seen, damages range from $50,000 to $300,000 per violation, depending on the size of the organization. Punitive damages are available only if the employer intentionally discriminated against the plaintiff(s) or if the employer discriminated with malice or reckless indifference to the employee's federally protected rights. These damages are excluded for an employment practice held to be unlawful because of its disparate impact.[10]

The addition of damages to CRA 1991 has had two immediate effects. First, by increasing the potential payoff for a successful discrimination suit, it has increased the number of suits filed against businesses. Second, organizations are now more likely to grant all employees an equal opportunity for employment, regardless of their race, gender, religion, or national origin. Many organizations have felt the need to make the composition of their workforce mirror the general population to avoid costly lawsuits. This act adds a financial incentive for doing so.

TABLE 3.2

Maximum Punitive Damages Allowed under the Civil Rights Act of 1991

EMPLOYER SIZE	DAMAGE LIMIT
14 to 100 employees	$ 50,000
101 to 200 employees	100,000
201 to 500 employees	200,000
More than 500 employees	300,000

Americans with Disabilities Act (ADA) of 1990

One of the most far-reaching acts concerning the management of human resources is the Americans with Disabilities Act. This act protects individuals with disabilities from being discriminated against in the workplace. It prohibits discrimination based on disability in all employment practices such as job application procedures, hiring, firing, promotions, compensation, and training—in addition to other employment activities such as advertising, recruitment, tenure, layoff, leave, and fringe benefits. Because this act is so new, we will cover its various stipulations individually.

The ADA defines a disability as a physical or mental impairment that substantially limits one or more major life activities, a record of having such an impairment, or being regarded as having such an impairment. The first part of the definition refers to individuals who have serious disabilities—such as epilepsy, blindness, deafness, or paralysis—that affect their ability to perform major life activities such as walking, seeing, performing manual tasks, learning, caring for oneself, and working. The second part refers to individuals who have a history of disability, such as someone who has had cancer but is currently in remission, someone with a history of mental illness, and someone with a history of heart disease. The third part of the definition, "being regarded as having a disability," refers, for example, to an individual who is severely disfigured and is denied employment because an employer fears negative reactions from others.[11]

Thus the ADA covers specific physiological disabilities such as cosmetic disfigurement and anatomical loss affecting the neurological, musculoskeletal, sensory, respiratory, cardiovascular, reproductive, digestive, genitourinary, hemic, or lymphatic systems. In addition, it covers mental and psychological disorders such as mental retardation, organic brain syndrome, emotional or mental illness, and learning disabilities. However, conditions such as obesity, substance abuse, eye and hair color, and lefthandedness are not covered.[12]

> **Americans with Disabilities Act (ADA) of 1990**
> A 1990 act prohibiting individuals with disabilities from being discriminated against in the workplace.

Executive Orders

Executive orders are directives issued and amended unilaterally by the president. These orders do not require congressional approval, yet they have the force of law. Two executive orders directly affect HRM.

Executive Order 11246

President Johnson issued this executive order, which prohibits discrimination based on race, color, religion, sex, and national origin. Unlike Title VII, this order applies only to federal contractors and subcontractors. Employers receiving more than $10,000 from the federal government must take affirmative action to ensure against discrimination, and those with contracts greater than $50,000 must develop a written affirmative action plan for each of their establishments within 120 days of the beginning of the contract. The Office of Federal Contract Compliance Procedures enforces this executive order.

Executive Order 11478

President Richard M. Nixon issued this order, which requires the federal government to base all its employment policies on merit and fitness, and specifies that race, color, sex, religion, and national origin should not be considered. (The U.S. Office of

Personnel Management is in charge of this.) The order also extends to all contractors and subcontractors doing $10,000 worth of business with the federal government. (The relevant government agencies have the responsibility to ensure that the contractors and subcontractors comply with the order.)

Enforcement of Equal Employment Opportunity

As discussed previously, the executive branch of the federal government bears most of the responsibility for enforcing all EEO laws passed by the legislative branch. In addition, the executive branch must enforce the executive orders issued by the president. The two agencies responsible for the enforcement of these laws and executive orders are the Equal Employment Opportunity Commission and the Office of Federal Contract Compliance Programs, respectively.

Equal Employment Opportunity Commission (EEOC)
The government commission to ensure that all individuals have an equal opportunity for employment, regardless of race, color, religion, sex, age, disability, or national origin.

Equal Employment Opportunity Commission (EEOC)

An independent federal agency, the EEOC is responsible for enforcing most of the EEO laws, such as Title VII, the Equal Pay Act, and the Americans with Disabilities Act. The EEOC has three major responsibilities: investigating and resolving discrimination complaints, gathering information, and issuing guidelines.

Investigation and Resolution

Individuals who feel they have been discriminated against must file a complaint with the EEOC or a similar state agency within 180 days of the incident. Failure to file a complaint within the 180 days results in the case's being dismissed immediately, with certain exceptions, such as the enactment of a seniority system that has an intentionally discriminatory purpose.

Once the complaint is filed, the EEOC takes responsibility for investigating the claim of discrimination. The complainant must give the EEOC 60 days to investigate the complaint. If the EEOC either does not believe the complaint to be valid or fails to complete the investigation, the complainant may sue in federal court. If the EEOC determines that discrimination has taken place, its representatives will attempt to provide a reconciliation between the two parties without burdening the court system with a lawsuit. Sometimes the EEOC enters into a consent decree with the discriminating organization. This decree is an agreement between the agency and the organization that the organization will cease certain discriminatory practices and possibly institute additional affirmative action practices to rectify its history of discrimination.

If the EEOC cannot come to an agreement with the organization, there are two options. First, it can issue a "right to sue" letter to the alleged victim, which certifies that the agency has investigated and found validity in the victim's allegations. Second, although less likely, the agency may aid the alleged victim in bringing suit in federal court.

Information Gathering

The EEOC also plays a role in monitoring the hiring practices of organizations. Each year organizations with 100 or more employees must file a report (EEO-1) with the EEOC that provides the number of women and minorities employed in nine different job categories. The EEOC computer analyzes these reports to identify patterns of discrimination that can then be attacked through class-action suits.

Issuance of Guidelines

A third responsibility of the EEOC is to issue guidelines that help employers determine when their decisions are violations of the laws enforced by the EEOC. These guidelines are not laws themselves, but the courts give great deference to them when hearing employment discrimination cases.

For example, the *Uniform Guidelines on Employee Selection Procedures* is a set of guidelines issued by the EEOC, the Department of Labor, the Department of Justice, and the U.S. Civil Service Commission.[13] This document provides guidance on the ways an organization should develop and administer selection systems so as not to violate Title VII. The courts often refer to the *Uniform Guidelines* to determine whether a company has engaged in discriminatory conduct or to determine the validity of the procedures it used to validate a selection system. Another example: Since the passage of the ADA, employers have been somewhat confused about the act's implications for their hiring procedures. Therefore, the EEOC issued guidelines in the *Federal Register* that provided more detailed information regarding what the agency will consider legal and illegal employment practices concerning disabled individuals. Although companies are well advised to follow these guidelines, it is possible that courts will interpret the ADA differently from the EEOC. Thus, through the issuance of guidelines the EEOC gives employers directions for making employment decisions that do not conflict with existing laws.

Office of Federal Contract Compliance Programs (OFCCP)

The OFCCP is the agency responsible for enforcing the executive orders that cover companies doing business with the federal government. Businesses with contracts for more than $50,000 cannot discriminate in employment based on race, color, religion, national origin, or sex, and they must have a written affirmative action plan on file.

These plans have three basic components.[14] First, the **utilization analysis** compares the race, sex, and ethnic composition of the employer's workforce with that of the available labor supply. For each job group, the employer must identify the percentage of its workforce with that characteristic (female, for example) and identify the percentage of workers in the relevant labor market with that characteristic. If the percentage in the employer's workforce is much less than the percentage in the comparison group, then that minority group is considered to be "underutilized."

Second, the employer must develop specific **goals and timetables** for achieving balance in the workforce concerning these characteristics (particularly where underutilization exists). Goals and timetables specify the percentage of women and minorities that the employer seeks to have in each job group and the date by which that percentage is to be attained. These are not to be viewed as *quotas*, which entail setting aside a specific number of positions to be filled only by members of the protected class. Goals and timetables are much more flexible, requiring only that the employer have specific goals and take steps to achieve those goals. In fact, one study that examined companies with the goal of increasing black employment found that only 10 percent of them actually achieved their goals. Although this may sound discouragingly low, it is important to note that these companies increased their black employment more than companies that set no such goals.[15]

Third, employers with federal contracts must develop a list of **action steps** they will take toward attaining their goals to reduce underutilization. The company's CEO must make it clear to the entire organization that the company is committed to reducing underutilization, and all management levels must be involved in the planning process. For example, organizations can communicate job openings to women and

Utilization analysis
A comparison of the race, sex, and ethnic composition of an employer's workforce with that of the available labor supply.

Goals and timetables
The part of a written affirmative action plan that specifies the percentage of women and minorities that an employer seeks to have in each job group and the date by which that percentage is to be attained.

Action steps
The written affirmative plan that specifies what an employer plans to do to reduce underutilization of protected groups.

minorities through publishing the company's affirmative action policy, recruiting at predominantly female or minority schools, participating in programs designed to increase employment opportunities for underemployed groups, and removing unnecessary barriers to employment. Organizations must also take affirmative steps toward hiring Vietnam veterans and individuals with disabilities.

The OFCCP annually audits government contractors to ensure that they actively pursue the goals in their plans. These audits consist of (1) examining the company's affirmative action plan and (2) conducting on-site visits to examine how individual employees perceive the company's affirmative action policies. If the OFCCP finds that the contractors or subcontractors are not complying with the executive order, then its representatives may notify the EEOC (if there is evidence that Title VII has been violated), advise the Department of Justice to institute criminal proceedings, request that the Secretary of Labor cancel or suspend any current contracts, and forbid the firm from bidding on future contracts. This last penalty, called *debarment*, is the OFCCP's most potent weapon.

Having discussed the major laws defining equal employment opportunity and the agencies that enforce these laws, we now address the various types of discrimination and the ways these forms of discrimination have been interpreted by the courts in a number of cases.

Types of Discrimination

How would you know if you had been discriminated against? Assume that you have applied for a job and were not hired. How do you know if the organization decided not to hire you because you are unqualified, because you are less qualified than the individual ultimately hired, or simply because the person in charge of the hiring decision "didn't like your type"? Discrimination is a multifaceted issue. It is often not easy to determine the extent to which unfair discrimination affects an employer's decisions.

Legal scholars have identified three theories of discrimination: disparate treatment, disparate impact, and reasonable accommodation. In addition, there is protection for those participating in discrimination cases or opposing discriminatory actions. In the act, these theories are stated in very general terms. However, the court system has defined and delineated these theories through the cases brought before it. A comparison of the theories of discrimination is given in Table 3.3.

Disparate Treatment

Disparate treatment
A theory of discrimination based on different treatments given to individuals because of their race, color, religion, sex, national origin, age, or disability status.

Disparate treatment exists when individuals in similar situations are treated differently and the different treatment is based on the individual's race, color, religion, sex, national origin, age, or disability status. If two people with the same qualifications apply for a job and the employer decides whom to hire based on one individual's race, the individual not hired is a victim of disparate treatment. In the disparate treatment case the plaintiff must prove that there was a discriminatory motive—that is, that the employer *intended* to discriminate.

Whenever individuals are treated differently because of their race, sex, or the like, there is disparate treatment. For example, if a company fails to hire women with school-age children (claiming the women will be frequently absent) but hires men with school-age children, the applicants are being treated differently based on sex. Another example would be an employer who checks the references and investigates

TABLE 3.3

Comparison of Discrimination Theories

TYPES OF DISCRIMINATION	DISPARATE TREATMENT	DISPARATE IMPACT	REASONABLE ACCOMMODATION
Show intent?	Yes	No	Yes
Prima facie case	Individual is member of a protected group, was qualified for the job, and was turned down for the job, and the job remained open	Statistical disparity in the effects of a facially neutral employment practice	Individual has a belief or disability, provided the employer with notice (request to accommodate), and was adversely affected by a failure to be accommodated
Employer's defense	Produce a legitimate, nondiscriminatory reason for the employment decision or show bona fide occupational qualification (BFOQ)	Prove that the employment practice bears a manifest relationship with job performance	Job-relatedness and business necessity, undue hardship, or direct threat to health or safety
Plaintiff's rebuttal	Reason offered was merely a "pretext" for discrimination	Alternative procedures exist that meet the employer's goal without having disparate impact	
Monetary damages	Compensatory and punitive damages	Equitable relief (e.g., back pay)	Compensatory and punitive damages (if discrimination was intentional or employer failed to show good faith efforts to accommodate)

the conviction records of minority applicants but does not do so for white applicants. Why are managers advised not to ask about marital status? Because in most cases, a manager will either ask only the female applicants or, if the manager asks both males and females, he or she will make different assumptions about females (such as "She will have to move if her husband gets a job elsewhere") and males (such as "He's very stable"). In all these examples, notice that (1) people are being treated differently and (2) there is an actual intent to treat them differently.[16]

To understand how disparate treatment is applied in the law, let's look at how an actual court case, filed under disparate treatment, would proceed.

The Plaintiff's Burden

As in any legal case, the plaintiff has the burden of proving that the defendant has committed an illegal act. This is the idea of a "prima facie" case. In a disparate treatment case, the plaintiff meets the prima facie burden by showing four things:

1. The plaintiff belongs to a protected group.
2. The plaintiff applied for and was qualified for the job.
3. Despite possessing the qualifications, the plaintiff was rejected.
4. After the plaintiff was rejected, the position remained open and the employer continued to seek applicants with similar qualifications, or the position was filled by someone with similar qualifications.

Although these four things may seem easy to prove, it is important to note that what the court is trying to do is rule out the most obvious reasons for rejecting the plaintiff's claim (for example, the plaintiff did not apply or was not qualified, or the position was already filled or had been eliminated). If these alternative explanations are ruled out, the court assumes that the hiring decision was based on a discriminatory motive.

The Defendant's Rebuttal

Once the plaintiff has made the prima facie case for discrimination, the burden shifts to the defendant. The burden is different depending on whether the prima facie case presents only circumstantial evidence (there is no direct evidence of discrimination such as a formal policy to discriminate, but rather discriminatory intent must be inferred) or direct evidence (a formal policy of discrimination for some perceived legitimate reason). In cases of circumstantial evidence, the defendant simply must produce a legitimate, nondiscriminatory reason, such as that, although the plaintiff was qualified, the individual hired was more qualified.

However, in cases where direct evidence exists, such as a formal policy of hiring only women for waitress jobs because the business is aimed at catering to male customers, then the defendant is more likely to offer a different defense. This defense argues that for this job, a factor such as race, sex, or religion was a **bona fide occupational qualification (BFOQ).** For example, if one were hiring an individual to hand out towels in a women's locker room, being a woman might be a BFOQ. However, there are very few cases in which race or sex qualify as a BFOQ, and in these cases it must be a necessary, rather than simply a preferred, characteristic of the job.

UAW v. Johnson Controls, Inc., illustrates the difficulty in using a BFOQ as a defense.[17] Johnson Controls, a manufacturer of car batteries, had instituted a "fetal protection" policy that excluded women of childbearing age from a number of jobs in which they would be exposed to lead, which can cause birth defects in children. The company argued that sex was a BFOQ essential to maintaining a safe workplace. The Supreme Court did not uphold the company's policy, arguing that BFOQs are limited to policies that are directly related to a worker's ability to do the job.

The Plaintiff's Rebuttal

If the defendant provides a legitimate, nondiscriminatory reason for its employment decision, the burden shifts back to the plaintiff. The plaintiff must now show that the reason offered by the defendant was not in fact the reason for its decision but merely a "pretext" or excuse for its actual discriminatory decision. This could entail providing evidence that white applicants with very similar qualifications to the plaintiff have often been hired while black applicants with very similar qualifications were all rejected. To illustrate disparate treatment, let's look at the first major case dealing with disparate treatment, *McDonnell Douglas Corp. v. Green*.

McDonnell Douglas Corp. v. Green. This Supreme Court case was the first to delineate the four criteria for a prima facie case of discrimination. From 1956 to 1964, Green had been an employee at McDonnell Douglas, a manufacturing plant in St. Louis, Missouri, that employed about 30,000 people. In 1964 he was laid off during a general workforce reduction. While unemployed, he participated in some activities that the company undoubtedly frowned upon: a "lock-in," where he and others placed a chain and padlock on the front door of a building to prevent the employees from leaving; and a "stall-in," where a group of employees stalled their cars at the gates of

Bona fide occupational qualification (BFOQ)

A job qualification based on race, sex, religion, and so on that an employer asserts is a necessary qualification for the job.

the plant so that no one could enter or leave the parking lot. About three weeks after the lock-in, McDonnell Douglas advertised for qualified mechanics, Green's trade, and he reapplied. When the company rejected his application, he sued, arguing that the company didn't hire him because of his race and because of his persistent involvement in the civil rights movement.

In making his prima facie case, Green had no problem showing that he was a member of a protected group, that he had applied for and was qualified for the job (having already worked in the job), that he was rejected, and that the company continued to advertise the position. The company's defense was that the plaintiff was not hired because he participated in the lock-in and the stall-in. In other words, the company was merely refusing to hire a troublemaker.

The plaintiff responded that the company's stated reason for not hiring him was a pretext for discrimination. He pointed out that white employees who had participated in the same activities (the lock-in and stall-in) were rehired, whereas he was not. The court found in favor of the plaintiff.

This case illustrates how similarly situated individuals (white and black) can be treated differently (whites were hired back whereas blacks were not) with the differences in treatment based on race. As we discuss later, most plaintiffs bring cases of sexual harassment under this theory of discrimination, sexual harassment being a situation where individuals are treated differently because of their sex.

Mixed-Motive Cases

In a mixed-motive case, the defendant acknowledges that some discriminatory motive existed but argues that the same hiring decision would have been reached even without the discriminatory motive. In *Hopkins v. Price Waterhouse*, Elizabeth Hopkins was an accountant who had applied for partnership in her firm. Although she had brought in a large amount of business and had received high praise from her clients, she was turned down for a partnership on two separate occasions. In her performance reviews, she had been told to adopt more feminine dress and speech and received many other comments that suggested gender-based stereotypes. In court, the company admitted that a sex-based stereotype existed but argued that it would have come to the same decision (not promoted Hopkins) even if the stereotype had not existed.

One of the main questions that came out of this case was, Who has the burden of proof? Does the plaintiff have to prove that a different decision would have been made (that Hopkins would have been promoted) in the absence of the discriminatory motive? Or does the defendant have to prove that the same decision would have been made?

According to CRA 1991, if the plaintiff demonstrates that race, sex, color, religion, or national origin was a motivating factor for any employment practice, the prima facie burden has been met, and the burden of proof is on the employer to demonstrate that the same decision would have been made even if the discriminatory motive had not been present. If the employer can do this, the plaintiff cannot collect compensatory or punitive damages. However, the court may order the employer to quit using the discriminatory motive in its future employment decisions.

Disparate Impact

The second type of discrimination is called **disparate impact.** It occurs when a facially neutral employment practice disproportionately excludes a protected group from employment opportunities. A facially neutral employment practice is one that lacks

Disparate impact
A theory of discrimination based on facially neutral employment practices that disproportionately exclude a protected group from employment opportunities.

obvious discriminatory content yet affects one group to a greater extent than other groups, such as an employment test. Although the Supreme Court inferred disparate impact from Title VII in the *Griggs v. Duke Power* case, it has since been codified into the Civil Rights Act of 1991.

There is an important distinction between disparate impact and disparate treatment discrimination. For there to be discrimination under disparate treatment, there has to be intentional discrimination. Under disparate impact, intent is irrelevant. The important criterion is that the consequences of the employment practice are discriminatory.

For example, if, for some practical reason, you hired individuals based on their height, you may not have intended to discriminate against anyone, and yet using height would have a disproportionate impact on certain protected groups. Women tend to be shorter than men, so fewer women will be hired. Certain ethnic groups, such as those of Asian ancestry, also tend to be shorter than those of European ancestry. Thus, your facially neutral employment practice will have a disparate impact on certain protected groups.

This is not to imply that simply because a selection practice has disparate impact, it is necessarily illegal. Some characteristics (such as height) are not equally distributed across race and gender groups; however, the important question is whether the characteristic is related to successful performance on the job. To help you understand how disparate impact works, let's look at a court proceeding involving a disparate impact claim.

Four-fifths rule
A rule that states that an employment test has disparate impact if the hiring rate for a minority group is less than four-fifths, or 80 percent, of the hiring rate for the majority group.

The Plaintiff's Burden

In a disparate impact case, the plaintiff must make the prima facie case by showing that the employment practice in question disproportionately affects a protected group relative to the majority group. To illustrate this theory, let's assume that you are a manager who has 60 positions to fill. Your applicant pool has 80 white and 40 black applicants. You use a test that selects 48 of the white and 12 of the black applicants. Is this a disparate impact? Two alternative quantitative analyses are often used to determine whether a test has adverse impact.

The **four-fifths rule** states that a test has disparate impact if the hiring rate for the minority group is less than four-fifths (or 80 percent) of the hiring rate for the majority group. Applying this analysis to the preceding example, we would first calculate the hiring rates for each group:

$$\text{Whites} = 48/80 = 60\%$$

$$\text{Blacks} = 12/40 = 30\%$$

Standard deviation rule
A rule used to analyze employment tests to determine disparate impact; it uses the difference between the expected representation for minority groups and the actual representation to determine whether the difference between the two is greater than would occur by chance.

Then we would compare the hiring rate of the minority group (30%) with that of the majority group (60%). Using the four-fifths rule, we would determine that the test has adverse impact if the hiring rate of the minority group is less than 80% of the hiring rate of the majority group. Because it is less (that is, 30%/60% = 50%, which is less than 80%), we would conclude that the test has adverse impact. The four-fifths rule is used as a rule of thumb by the EEOC in determining adverse impact.

The **standard deviation rule** uses actual probability distributions to determine adverse impact. This analysis uses the difference between the expected representation (or hiring rates) for minority groups and the actual representation (or hiring rate) to determine whether the difference between these two values is greater than would occur by chance. Thus, in our example, 33% (40 of 120) of the applicants were blacks, so one would expect 33% (20 of 60) of those hired to be black. However, only 12 black applicants were hired. To determine if the difference between the expected representation and the actual representation is greater than we would expect by chance, we calculate the standard deviation (which, you might remember from your statistics class, is the standard deviation in a binomial distribution):

$$\sqrt{\text{Number hired} \times \frac{\text{Number of minority applicants}}{\text{Number of total applicants}} \times \frac{\text{Number of nonminority applicants}}{\text{Number of total applicants}}}$$

or in this case:

$$\sqrt{60 \times \frac{40}{120} \times \frac{80}{120}} = 3.6$$

If the difference between the actual representation and the expected representation ($20 - 12 = 8$ in this case) of blacks is greater than 2 standard deviations (2×3.6, $= 7.2$ in this case), we would conclude that the test had adverse impact against blacks, because we would expect this result less than 1 time in 20 if the test were equally difficult for both whites and blacks.

The *Wards Cove Packing Co. v. Atonio* case involved an interesting use of statistics. The plaintiffs showed that the jobs in the cannery (lower-paying jobs) were filled primarily with minority applicants (in this case, American Eskimos). However, only a small percentage of the noncannery jobs (those with higher pay) were filled by nonminorities. The plaintiffs argued that this statistical disparity in the racial makeup of the cannery and noncannery jobs was proof of discrimination. The federal district, appellate, and Supreme Courts all found for the defendant, stating that this disparity was not proof of discrimination.

Once the plaintiff has demonstrated adverse impact, he or she has met the burden of a prima facie case of discrimination.[18]

Defendant's Rebuttal

According to CRA 1991, once the plaintiff has made a prima facie case, the burden of proof shifts to the defendant, who must show that the employment practice is a "business necessity." This is accomplished by showing that the practice bears a relationship with some legitimate employer goal. With respect to job selection, this relationship is demonstrated by showing the job relatedness of the test, usually by reporting a validity study of some type, to be discussed in Chapter 6. For now, suffice it to say that the employer shows that the test scores are significantly correlated with measures of job performance.

Measures of job performance used in validation studies can include such things as objective measures of output, supervisor ratings of job performance, and success in training.[19] Normally, performance appraisal ratings are used, but these ratings must be valid for the court to accept the validation results. For example, in *Albermarle Paper v. Moody*, the employer demonstrated that the selection battery predicted performance (measured with supervisors' overall rankings of employees) in only some of the 13 occupational groups in which it was used. In this case, the court was especially critical of the supervisory ratings used as the measure of job performance. The court stated, "There is no way of knowing precisely what criteria of job performance the supervisors were considering."[20]

Plaintiff's Rebuttal

If the employer shows that the employment practice is the result of some business necessity, the plaintiff's last resort is to argue that other employment practices could sufficiently meet the employer's goal without adverse impact. Thus, if a plaintiff can demonstrate that selection tests other than the one used by the employer exist, do not have adverse impact, and correlate with job performance as highly as the employer's test, then the defendant can be found guilty of discrimination. Many cases deal with standardized tests of cognitive ability, so it is important to examine alternatives to these tests that have less adverse impact while still meeting the employer's goal. At least two separate studies reviewing alternative selection devices such as interviews, biographical data, assessment centers, and work sample tests have concluded that none of them met both criteria.[21] It seems that when the employment practice in question is a standardized test of cognitive ability, plaintiffs will have a difficult time rebutting the defendant's rebuttal.

Griggs v. Duke Power. To illustrate how this process works, let's look at the *Griggs v. Duke Power* case.[22] Following the passage of Title VII, Duke Power instituted a new system for making selection and promotion decisions. The system required either a high school diploma or a passing score on two professionally developed tests (the Wonderlic Personnel Test and the Bennett Mechanical Comprehension Test). A passing score was set so that it would be equal to the national median for high school graduates who had taken the tests.

The plaintiffs met their prima facie burden showing that both the high school diploma requirement and the test battery had adverse impacts on blacks. According to the 1960 census, 34 percent of white males had high school diplomas, compared with only 12 percent of black males. Similarly, 58 percent of white males passed the test battery, whereas only 6 percent of blacks passed.

Duke Power was unable to defend its use of these employment practices. A company vice president testified that the company had not studied the relationship between these employment practices and the employees' ability to perform the job. In addition, employees already on the job who did not have high school diplomas and had never taken the tests were performing satisfactorily. Thus Duke Power lost the case.

It is interesting to note that the court recognized that the company had not intended to discriminate, mentioning that the company was making special efforts to help undereducated employees through financing two-thirds of the cost of tuition for high school training. This illustrates the importance of the *consequences*, as opposed to the *motivation*, in determining discrimination under the disparate impact theory.

Reasonable Accommodation

Reasonable accommodation
Making facilities readily accessible to and usable by individuals with disabilities.

Reasonable accommodation presents a relatively new theory of discrimination. It began with regard to religious discrimination, but has recently been both expanded and popularized with the passage of the ADA. Reasonable accommodation differs from these two theories in that rather than simply requiring an employer to refrain from some action, reasonable accommodation places a special obligation on an employer to affirmatively *do* something to accommodate an individual's disability or religion. This theory is violated when an employer fails to make reasonable accommodation, where that is required, to a qualified person with a disability or to a person's religious observation and/or practices.

Religion and Accommodation

Often individuals with strong religious beliefs find that some observations and practices of their religion come into direct conflict with their work duties. For example, some religions forbid individuals from working on the sabbath day when the employer schedules them for work. Others might have beliefs that preclude them from shaving, which might conflict with a company's dress code. Although Title VII forbids discrimination on the basis of religion just like race or sex, religion also receives special treatment requiring employers to exercise an affirmative duty to accommodate individuals' religious beliefs and practices. As Figure 3.2 shows, the number of religious discrimination charges has consistently increased over the past few years, jumping significantly in 2002.

In cases of religious discrimination, an employee's burden is to demonstrate that he or she has a legitimate religious belief and provided the employer with notice of the need to accommodate the religious practice, and that adverse consequences occurred due to the employer's failure to accommodate. In such cases, the employer's major defense is to assert that to accommodate the employee would require an undue hardship.

Examples of reasonably accommodating a person's religious obligations might include redesigning work schedules (most often accommodating those who cannot work on their sabbath), providing alternative testing dates for applicants, not requiring union membership and/or allowing payment of "charitable contributions" in lieu of union dues, or altering certain dress or grooming requirements. Note that although an employer is required to make a reasonable accommodation, it need not be the one that is offered by the employee.[23]

In one recent case, Wal-Mart agreed to settle with a former employee who alleged that he was forced to quit in 1993 after refusing to work on Sunday. Wal-Mart has

FIGURE 3.2

Religious Discrimination Complaints, 1991–2003

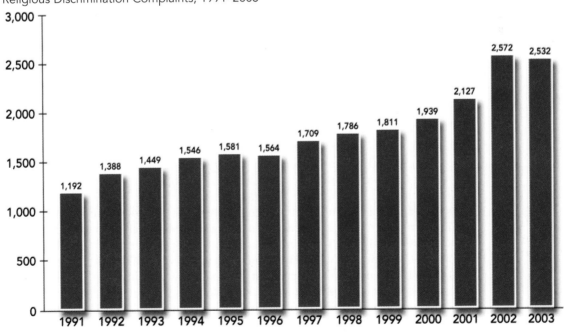

SOURCE: www.eeoc.gov/stats/religion.html.

agreed to pay the former employee unspecified damages, to instruct managers on employee's rights to have their religious beliefs accommodated, and to prepare a computer-based manual describing employees' rights and religious harassment.[24]

Following the attack of 9/11, a number of cases sprang up with regard to discrimination against Muslims, partly accounting for the significant increase in religious discrimination complaints in 2002. In one case, the EEOC and Electrolux Group settled a religious accommodation case brought by Muslim workers from Somalia. The Islamic faith requires Muslims to offer five prayers a day, with two of these prayers offered within restricted time periods (early morning and sunset). Muslim employees alleged that they were disciplined for using an unscheduled break traditionally offered to line employees on an as-needed basis to observe their sunset prayer. Electrolux worked with the EEOC to respect the needs of its Muslim workers without creating a business hardship by affording them with an opportunity to observe their sunset prayer.[25]

Disability and Accommodation

As previously discussed, the ADA made discrimination against individuals with disabilities illegal. However, the act itself states that the employer is obligated not just to refrain from discriminating, but to take affirmative steps to accommodate individuals who are protected under the act.

Under disability claims, the plaintiff must show that she or he is a qualified applicant with a disability and that adverse action was taken by a covered entity. The employer's defense then depends on whether the decision was made without regard to the disability or in light of the disability. For example, if the employer argues that the plaintiff is not qualified, then it has met the burden, and the question of reasonable accommodation becomes irrelevant.

If, however, the decision was made "in light of" the disability, then the question becomes one of whether the person could perform adequately with a reasonable accommodation. This leads to three potential defenses. First, the employer could allege job-relatedness or business necessity through demonstrating, for example, that it is using a test that assesses ability to perform essential job functions. However, then the question arises of whether the applicant could perform the essential job functions with a reasonable accommodation. Second, the employer could claim an undue hardship to accommodate the individual. In essence, this argues that the accommodation necessary is an action requiring significant difficulty or expense. Finally, the employer could argue that the individual with the disability might pose a direct threat to his own or others' health or safety in the workplace. This requires examining the duration of the risk, the nature and severity of potential harm, the probability of the harm occurring, and the imminence of the potential harm.

What are some examples of reasonable accommodation with regard to disabilities? First is providing readily accessible facilities such as ramps and/or elevators for disabled individuals to enter the workplace. Second, job restructuring might include eliminating marginal tasks, shifting these tasks to other employees, redesigning job procedures, or altering work schedules. Third, an employer might reassign a disabled employee to a job with essential job functions he or she could perform. Fourth, an employer might accommodate applicants for employment who must take tests through providing alternative testing formats, providing readers, or providing additional time for taking the test. Fifth, readers, interpreters, or technology to offer reading assistance might be given to a disabled employee. Sixth, an employer could allow employees to provide their own accommodation such as bringing a guide dog to work.[26] Note that most accommodations are inexpensive. A study by Sears Roebuck & Co. found

Nontraditional Solutions to a Traditional Employment Problem

Schukra Manufacturing of Toronto is an award-winning designer and manufacturer that has seen its production soar and workforce double over the past decade due to the popularity of its nontraditional seat installations. Its Schukra Lumbar Systems, which provide lower back support and encourage correct seating posture, have been adopted by a range of firms in the furniture manufacturing, health care, automotive, and aviation fields, including such household names as Air Canada, VIA Rail, Sears Manufacturing, Chrysler, and Ferrari.

In order to meet the demand for its products, Schukra has sought out employees with disabilities. For example, Schukra employs two hearing impaired press operators, while a mechanical engineer who has post-polio syndrome works for Sherwood Industries, its associated company. One of the hearing impaired employees was initially hired to work on a small press, but he now operates presses in the 400-ton to 600-ton range. Other than having an interpreter present for his annual review, no other ongoing accommodations have been required for this employee, he adds. The second hearing impaired employee was so comfortable with lip reading that an interpreter's services were never needed.

No major accommodations were made for the employee with post-polio syndrome, although the company did work with the person and the employment services co-ordinator to determine job duties that matched his current physical ability. For example, the majority of the work performed by the employee can be done sitting down and he is not assigned tasks that require heavy lifting. Also, once a week the person is allowed to leave work at 1 P.M. to attend physiotherapy appointments.

"Accommodations for these employees haven't been significant or costly," states Jim Carroll, the former head of human resources. "However, if their needs do change, we'll make accommodations to assist them to do their jobs or to improve the processes that affect their work, particularly where safety is concerned."

SOURCE: Canadian Ministry of Citizenship, "Qualified Workers with Disabilities, Found through TCG LINK-Up Employment Services, Allow Schukra Manufacturing to Save Money while Recruiting Staff," http://www.equalopportunity.on.ca (October 23, 2001).

that 69 percent of all accommodations cost nothing, 29 percent cost less than $1,000, and only 3 percent cost more than $1,000.[27] In addition, the "Competing through Technology" box illustrates how accommodating disabled individuals can actually provide competitive advantage.

Retaliation for Participation and Opposition

Suppose you overhear a supervisor in your workplace telling someone that he refuses to hire women because he knows they are just not cut out for the job. Believing this to be illegal discrimination, you face a dilemma. Should you come forward and report this statement? Or if someone else files a lawsuit for gender discrimination, should you testify on behalf of the plaintiff? What happens if your employer threatens to fire you if you do anything?

Title VII of the Civil Rights Act of 1964 protects you. It states that employers cannot retaliate against employees for either "opposing" a perceived illegal employment practice or "participating in a proceeding" related to an alleged illegal employment practice. *Opposition* refers to expressing to someone through proper channels that you believe that an illegal employment act has taken place or is taking place. *Participation* refers to actually testifying in an investigation, hearing, or court proceeding regarding an illegal employment act. Clearly, the purpose of this provision is to protect employees from employers' threats and other forms of intimidation aimed at discouraging the employees from bringing to light acts they believe to be illegal.

These cases can be extremely costly for companies because they are alleging acts of intentional discrimination, and therefore plaintiffs are entitled to punitive damages. For example, a 41-year-old former Allstate employee who claimed that a company official told her that the company wanted a "younger and cuter" image was awarded $2.8 million in damages by an Oregon jury. The jury concluded that the employee was forced out of the company for opposing age discrimination against other employees.[28]

This does not mean that employees have an unlimited right to talk about how racist or sexist their employers are. The courts tend to frown on employees whose activities result in a poor public image for the company unless those employees had attempted to use the organization's internal channels—approaching one's manager, raising the issue with the HRM department, and so on—before going public.

Current Issues Regarding Diversity and Equal Employment Opportunity

Because of recent changes in the labor market, most organizations' demographic compositions are becoming increasingly diverse. A study by the Hudson Institute projected that 85 percent of the new entrants into the U.S. labor force over the next decade will be females and minorities.[29] Integrating these groups into organizations made up predominantly of able-bodied white males will bring attention to important issues like sexual harassment, affirmative action, and the "reasonable accommodation" of employees with disabilities.

Sexual Harassment

Clarence Thomas's Supreme Court confirmation hearings in 1991 brought the issue of sexual harassment into increased prominence. Anita Hill, one of Thomas's former employees, alleged that he had sexually harassed her while she was working under his supervision at the Department of Education and the Equal Employment Opportunity Commission. Although the allegations were never substantiated, the hearing made many people more aware of how often employees are sexually harassed in the workplace and, combined with other events, resulted in a tremendous increase in the number of sexual harassment complaints being filed with the EEOC, as we see in Figure 3.3. In addition, after President Clinton took office and faced a sexual harassment lawsuit by Paula Corbin Jones for his alleged proposition to her in a Little Rock hotel room, the number of sexual harassment complaints took another jump from 1993 to 1994—again, potentially due to the tremendous amount of publicity regarding sexual harassment. However, the number of cases filed has actually decreased substantially since 2000.

FIGURE 3.3

Sexual Harassment Charges, 1991–2003

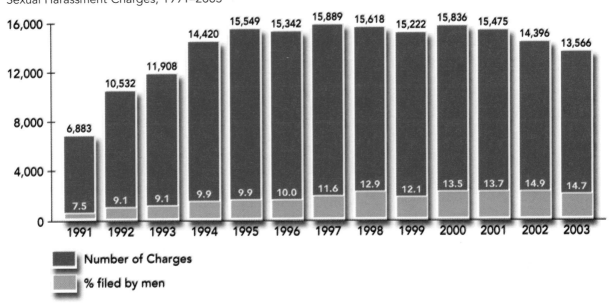

Number of Charges

% filed by men

SOURCE: www.eeoc.gov/stats/harass.html.

Sexual harassment refers to unwelcome sexual advances. (See Table 3.4.) It can take place in two basic ways. "Quid pro quo" harassment occurs when some kind of benefit (or punishment) is made contingent on the employee's submitting (or not submitting) to sexual advances. For example, a male manager tells his female secretary that if she has sex with him, he will help her get promoted, or he threatens to fire her if she fails to do so; these are clearly cases of quid pro quo sexual harassment.

The *Bundy v. Jackson* case illustrates quid pro quo sexual harassment.[30] Sandra Bundy was a personnel clerk with the District of Columbia Department of Corrections. She received repeated sexual propositions from Delbert Jackson, who was at the time a fellow employee (although he later became the director of the agency). She later began to receive propositions from two of her supervisors: Arthur Burton and James Gainey. When she raised the issue to their supervisor, Lawrence Swain, he dismissed her complaints, telling her that "any man in his right mind would want to rape you," and asked her to begin a sexual relationship with him. When Bundy became eligible for a promotion, she was passed over because of her "inadequate work performance,"

TABLE 3.4

EEOC Definition of Sexual Harassment

Unwelcome sexual advances, requests for sexual favors, and other verbal or physical contact of a sexual nature constitute sexual harassment when

1. Submission to such conduct is made either explicitly or implicitly a term of condition of an individual's employment,
2. Submission to or rejection of such conduct by an individual is used as the basis for employment decisions affecting such individual, or
3. Such conduct has the purpose or effect of unreasonably interfering with an individual's work performance or creating an intimidating, hostile, or offensive working environment.

SOURCE: EEOC guideline based on the Civil Rights Act of 1964, Title VII.

although she had never been told that her work performance was unsatisfactory. The U.S. Court of Appeals found that Bundy had been discriminated against because of her sex, thereby extending the idea of discrimination to sexual harassment.

A more subtle, and possibly more pervasive, form of sexual harassment is "hostile working environment." This occurs when someone's behavior in the workplace creates an environment that makes it difficult for someone of a particular sex to work. Many plaintiffs in sexual harassment lawsuits have alleged that men ran their fingers through the plaintiffs' hair, made suggestive remarks, and physically assaulted them by touching their intimate body parts. Other examples include having pictures of naked women posted in the workplace, using offensive sexually explicit language, or using sex-related jokes or innuendoes in conversations.[31]

Note that these types of behaviors are actionable under Title VII because they treat individuals differently based on their sex. In addition, although most harassment cases involve male-on-female harassment, any individual can be harassed. For example, male employees at Jenny Craig recently alleged that they were sexually harassed, and a federal jury recently found that a male employee had been sexually harassed by his male boss.[32]

In addition, Ron Clark Ford of Amarillo, Texas, recently agreed to pay $140,000 to six male plaintiffs who alleged that they and others were subjected to a sexually hostile work environment and different treatment because of their gender by male managers. Evidence gathered showed that the men were subjected to lewd, inappropriate comments of a sexual nature, and had their genitals and buttocks grabbed against their will by their male managers. The defendants argued that the conduct was "harmless horseplay."[33]

Finally, Babies 'R' Us agreed to pay $205,000 to resolve a same sex suit. The lawsuit alleged that Andres Vasquez was subjected to a sexually hostile working environment and was the target of unwelcome and derogatory comments as well as behavior that mocked him because he did not conform to societal stereotypes of how a male should appear or behave.

Sexual harassment charge filings with the EEOC by men have increased to 15 percent of all filings in 2002 from 10 percent of filings in 1994. While the Commission does not track same-sex, male-on-male charges, anecdotal evidence shows that most harassment allegations by men are against other men.[34]

There are three critical issues in these cases. First, the plaintiff cannot have "invited or incited" the advances. Often the plaintiff's sexual history, whether she or he wears provocative clothing, and whether she or he engages in sexually explicit conversations are used to prove or disprove that the advance was unwelcome. However, in the absence of substantial evidence that the plaintiff invited the behavior, courts usually lean toward assuming that sexual advances do not belong in the workplace and thus are unwelcome. In *Meritor Savings Bank v. Vinson*, Michelle Vinson claimed that during the four years she worked at a bank she was continually harassed by the bank's vice president, who repeatedly asked her to have sex with him (she eventually agreed) and sexually assaulted her.[35] The Supreme Court ruled that the victim's voluntary participation in sexual relations was not the major issue, saying that the focus of the case was on whether the vice president's advances were unwelcome.

A second critical issue is that the harassment must have been severe enough to alter the terms, conditions, and privileges of employment. Although it has not yet been consistently applied, many courts have used the "reasonable woman" standard in determining the severity or pervasiveness of the harassment. This consists of assessing whether a reasonable woman, faced with the same situation, would have reacted similarly. The reasonable woman standard recognizes that behavior that might be considered appropriate by a man (like off-color jokes) might not be considered appropriate by a woman.

The third issue is that the courts must determine whether the organization is liable for the actions of its employees. In doing so, the court usually examines two things. First, did the employer know about, or should he or she have known about, the harassment? Second, did the employer act to stop the behavior? If the employer knew about it and the behavior did not stop, the court usually decides that the employer did not act appropriately to stop it.

To ensure a workplace free from sexual harassment, organizations can follow some important steps. First, the organization can develop a policy statement that makes it very clear that sexual harassment will not be tolerated in the workplace. Second, all employees, new and old, can be trained to identify inappropriate workplace behavior. Third, the organization can develop a mechanism for reporting sexual harassment that encourages people to speak out. Fourth, management can prepare to take prompt disciplinary action against those who commit sexual harassment as well as appropriate action to protect the victims of sexual harassment.[36]

Affirmative Action and Reverse Discrimination

Few would disagree that having a diverse workforce in terms of race and gender is a desirable goal, if all individuals have the necessary qualifications. In fact, many organizations today are concerned with developing and managing diversity. To eliminate discrimination in the workplace, many organizations have affirmative action programs to increase minority representation. Affirmative action was originally conceived as a way of taking extra effort to attract and retain minority employees. This was normally done by extensively recruiting minorities on college campuses, advertising in minority-oriented publications, and providing educational and training opportunities to minorities.[37] However, over the years, many organizations have resorted to quotalike hiring to ensure that their workforce composition mirrors that of the labor market. Sometimes these organizations act voluntarily; in other cases, the quotas are imposed by the courts or by the EEOC. Whatever the impetus for these hiring practices, many white and/or male individuals have fought against them, alleging what is called *reverse discrimination*.

An example of an imposed quota program is found at the fire department in Birmingham, Alabama. Having admitted a history of discriminating against blacks, the department entered into a consent decree with the EEOC to hold 50 percent of positions at all levels in the fire department open for minorities even though minorities made up only 28 percent of the relevant labor market. The result was that some white applicants were denied employment or promotion in favor of black applicants who scored lower on a selection battery. The federal court found that the city's use of the inflexible hiring formula violated federal civil rights law and the constitutional guarantee of equal protection. The appellate court agreed, and the Supreme Court refused to hear the case, thus making the decision final.

The entire issue of affirmative action should evoke considerable attention and debate over the next few years. Although most individuals support the idea of diversity, few argue for the kinds of quotas that have to some extent resulted from the present legal climate. In fact, one recent survey revealed that only 16 percent of the respondents favored affirmative action with quotas, 46 percent favored it without quotas, and 28 percent opposed all affirmative action programs. One study found that people favor affirmative action when it is operationalized as recruitment, training, and attention to applicant qualifications but oppose it when it consists of discrimination, quotas, and preferential treatment.[38] Affirmative action and quotas constituted an important topic of debate for the 2000 presidential candidates, and there is reason to believe that some changes in the legal system will be observed over the next few years.

Outcomes of the Americans with Disabilities Act

The ADA was passed with the laudable goals of providing employment opportunities for the truly disabled who, in the absence of legislation, were unable to find employment. Certainly, some individuals with disabilities have found employment as a result of its passage. However, as often occurs with legislation, the impact is not necessarily what was intended. First, there has been increased litigation. The EEOC reports that over 91,000 complaints have been filed since passage of the act. Approximately 50 percent of the complaints filed have been found to be without reasonable cause. For example, in July 1992 GTE Data Services fired an employee for stealing from other employees and bringing a loaded gun to work. The fired employee sued for reinstatement under the ADA, claiming that he was the victim of a mental illness and thus should be considered disabled.[39]

A second problem is that the kinds of cases being filed are not what Congress intended to protect. Although the act was passed because of the belief that discrimination against individuals with disabilities occurred in the failure to hire them, 52.2 percent of the claims deal with firings, 28.9 percent with failure to make reasonable accommodation, and 12.5 percent with harassment. Only 9.4 percent of the complaints allege a failure to hire or rehire.[40] In addition, although the act was passed to protect people with major disabilities such as blindness, deafness, lost limbs, or paralysis, these disabilities combined account for a small minority of the disabilities claimed. As we see in Table 3.5, the biggest disability category is "other," meaning that the plaintiff claims a disability that is not one of the 35 types of impairment listed in the EEOC charge data system. The second largest category is "back impairment," accounting for 16.1 percent of all charges, followed by mental-illness-related claims at 12.2 percent.

Finally, it does not appear that the act has had its anticipated impact on the employment of Americans with disabilities. According to the National Organization on Disability, a private group, only 31 percent of working-age Americans with disabilities were employed as of December 1993, compared with 33 percent in 1986, before the law was passed.

For these reasons, Congress has explored the possibility of amending the act to more narrowly define the term *disability*.[41] The debate continues regarding the effectiveness of the ADA.

Employee Safety

Like equal employment opportunity, employee safety is regulated by both the federal and state governments. However, to fully maximize the safety and health of workers, employers need to go well beyond the letter of the law and embrace its spirit. With this in mind, we first spell out the specific protections guaranteed by federal legislation and then discuss various kinds of safety awareness programs that attempt to reinforce these standards.

TABLE 3.5
Types of Complaints Filed under the ADA

	1992	1993	1994	1995	1996	1997	1998	1999	2000	2001	2002	2003	TOTAL
Number of Complaints	1,048	15,274	18,859	19,798	18,046	18,108	17,806	17,007	15,864	16,470	15,964	15,337	189,621
% dealing with													**% Avg.**
Asthma	1.7%	1.8%	1.7%	1.7%	1.7%	1.5%	1.7%	1.8%	2.0%	1.6%	1.6%	1.6%	1.7%
Cancer	2.9	2.6	2.4	2.1	2.2	2.5	2.6	2.3	2.7	2.8	2.9	2.9	2.5
Diabetes	5.0	3.4	3.5	3.5	3.7	3.7	3.7	4.0	4.1	4.3	4.7	4.8	3.9
Hearing	4.6	3.2	3.0	2.7	2.6	2.8	2.9	2.9	3.1	2.9	3.2	3.1	2.9
Vision	4.6	3.2	2.7	2.3	2.3	2.4	2.4	2.5	2.3	2.3	2.6	2.6	2.5
Heart	4.4	5.1	4.3	3.7	3.5	3.7	3.8	3.8	3.3	3.6	4.0	3.7	3.9
Psychological disorders	8.7	9.7	3.8	2.8	2.9	3.1	2.8	2.7	2.6	2.6	2.6	2.6	3.5
Back	19.8	19.8	19.4	17.5	16.1	14.9	12.9	12.2	10.2	9.3	9.5	8.6	14.5
Neurological	3.3	4.0	3.2	2.7	3.0	2.7	2.8	2.8	2.9	2.7	2.8	3.3	3.0
Drug addiction	1.7	1.4	1.1	1.2	0.9	0.8	0.7	0.5	0.6	0.5	0.6	0.6	0.8

SOURCE: EEOC, http://www.eeoc.gov/stats/ada.receipts.html.

The Occupational Safety and Health Act (OSHA)

Occupational Safety and Health Act (OSHA)
The law that authorizes the federal government to establish and enforce occupational safety and health standards for all places of employment engaging in interstate commerce.

Although concern for worker safety would seem to be a universal societal goal, the **Occupational Safety and Health Act of 1970 (OSHA)**—the most comprehensive legislation regarding worker safety—did not emerge in this country until the early 1970s. At that time, there were roughly 15,000 work-related fatalities every year.

OSHA authorized the federal government to establish and enforce occupational safety and health standards for all places of employment engaging in interstate commerce. The responsibility for inspecting employers, applying the standards, and levying fines was assigned to the Department of Labor. The Department of Health was assigned responsibility for conducting research to determine the criteria for specific operations or occupations and for training employers to comply with the act. Much of this research is conducted by the National Institute for Occupational Safety and Health (NIOSH).

Employee Rights under OSHA

General duty clause
The provision of the Occupational Health and Safety Act that states that an employer has an overall obligation to furnish employees with a place of employment free from recognized hazards.

The main provision of OSHA states that each employer has a general duty to furnish each employee a place of employment free from recognized hazards that cause or are likely to cause death or serious physical harm. This is referred to as the **general duty clause.** Some specific rights granted to workers under this act are listed in Table 3.6. The Department of Labor recognizes many specific types of hazards, and employers are required to comply with all the occupational safety and health standards published by NIOSH.

A recent example is the development of OSHA standards for occupational exposure to blood-borne pathogens such as the AIDS virus. These standards identify 24 affected industrial sectors, encompassing 500,000 establishments and 5.6 million workers. Among other features, these standards require employers to develop an exposure control plan (ECP). An ECP must include a list of jobs whose incumbents might be exposed to blood, methods for implementing precautions in these jobs, post-exposure follow-up plans, and procedures for evaluating incidents in which workers are accidentally infected.

Although NIOSH publishes numerous standards, it is clearly not possible for regulators to anticipate all possible hazards that could occur in the workplace. Thus, the general duty clause requires employers to be constantly alert for potential sources of harm in the workplace (as defined by the standards of a reasonably prudent person) and to correct them. For example, managers at Amoco's Joliet, Illinois, plant realized that over the years some employees had created undocumented shortcuts and built them into their process for handling flammable materials. These changes appeared to be labor saving but created a problem: workers did not have uniform procedures for dealing with flammable products. This became an urgent issue because many of the

TABLE 3.6

Rights Granted to Workers under the Occupational Safety and Health Act

Employees have the right to
1. Request an inspection.
2. Have a representative present at an inspection.
3. Have dangerous substances identified.
4. Be promptly informed about exposure to hazards and be given access to accurate records regarding exposures.
5. Have employer violations posted at the work site.

experienced workers were reaching retirement age, and the plant was in danger of losing critical technical expertise. To solve this problem, the plant adopted a training program that met all the standards required by OSHA. That is, it conducted a needs analysis highlighting each task new employees had to learn and then documented these processes in written guidelines. New employees were given hands-on training with the new procedures and were then certified in writing by their supervisor. A computer tracking system was installed to monitor who was handling flammable materials, and this system immediately identified anyone who was not certified. The plant met requirements for both ISO 9000 standards and OSHA regulations and continues to use the same model for safety training in other areas of the plant.[42]

OSHA Inspections

OSHA inspections are conducted by specially trained agents of the Department of Labor called *compliance officers*. These inspections usually follow a tight "script." Typically, the compliance officer shows up unannounced. For obvious reasons, OSHA's regulations prohibit advance notice of inspections. The officer, after presenting credentials, tells the employer the reasons for the inspection and describes, in a general way, the procedures necessary to conduct the investigation.

There are four major components of an OSHA inspection. First, the compliance officer reviews the employer's records of deaths, injuries, and illnesses. OSHA requires this kind of record keeping from all firms with 11 or more full- or part-time employees. Second, the officer, typically accompanied by a representative of the employer (and perhaps by a representative of the employees), conducts a "walkaround" tour of the employer's premises. On this tour, the officer notes any conditions that may violate specific published standards or the less specific general duty clause. The third component of the inspection, employee interviews, may take place during the tour. At this time, any person who is aware of a violation can bring it to the attention of the officer. Finally, in a closing conference the compliance officer discusses the findings with the employer, noting any violations. The employer is given a reasonable time frame in which to correct these violations. If any violation represents imminent danger (that is, could cause serious injury or death before being eliminated through the normal enforcement procedures), the officer may, through the Department of Labor, seek a restraining order from a U.S. District Court. Such an order compels the employer to correct the problem immediately.

Citations and Penalties

If a compliance officer believes that a violation has occurred, he or she issues a citation to the employer that specifies the exact practice or situation that violates the act. The employer is required to post this citation in a prominent place near the location of the violation—even if the employer intends to contest it. Nonserious violations may be assessed up to $1,000 for each incident, but this may be adjusted downward if the employer has no prior history of violations or if the employer has made a good-faith effort to comply with the act. Serious violations of the act or willful, repeated violations may be fined up to $10,000 per incident. Fines for safety violations are never levied against the employees themselves. The assumption is that safety is primarily the responsibility of the employer, who needs to work with employees to ensure that they use safe working procedures.

In addition to these civil penalties, criminal penalties may also be assessed for willful violations that kill an employee. Fines can go as high as $20,000, and the employer or agents of the employer can be imprisoned. Criminal charges can also be brought against anyone who falsifies records that are subject to OSHA inspection or anyone who gives advance notice of an OSHA inspection without permission from the Department of Labor.

The Effect of OSHA

OSHA has been unquestionably successful in raising the level of awareness of occupational safety. Yet legislation alone cannot solve all the problems of work site safety. Indeed, the number of occupational illnesses increased fivefold between 1985 and 1990, according to a survey by the Bureau of Labor Statistics.[43] Many industrial accidents are a product of unsafe behaviors, not unsafe working conditions. Because the act does not directly regulate employee behavior, little behavior change can be expected unless employees are convinced of the standards' importance.[44] This has been recognized by labor leaders. For example, Lynn Williams, president of the United Steelworkers of America, has noted, "We can't count on government. We can't count on employers. We must rely on ourselves to bring about the safety and health of our workers."[45]

Because conforming to the statute alone does not necessarily guarantee safety, many employers go beyond the letter of the law. In the next section we examine various kinds of employer-initiated safety awareness programs that comply with OSHA requirements and, in some cases, exceed them.

Safety Awareness Programs

Safety awareness programs
Employer programs that attempt to instill symbolic and substantive changes in the organization's emphasis on safety.

Safety awareness programs go beyond compliance with OSHA and attempt to instill symbolic and substantive changes in the organization's emphasis on safety. These programs typically focus either on specific jobs and job elements or on specific types of injuries or disabilities. There are three primary components to a safety awareness program: identifying and communicating hazards, reinforcing safe practices, and promoting safety internationally.

Identifying and Communicating Job Hazards

Job hazard analysis technique
A breakdown of each job into basic elements, each of which is rated for its potential for harm or injury.

Employees, supervisors, and other knowledgeable sources need to sit down and discuss potential problems related to safety. The **job hazard analysis technique** is one means of accomplishing this.[46] With this technique, each job is broken down into basic elements, and each of these is rated for its potential for harm or injury. If there is consensus that some job element has high hazard potential, this element is isolated and potential technological or behavioral changes are considered.

Technic of operations review (TOR)
Method of determining safety problems via an analysis of past accidents.

Another means of isolating unsafe job elements is to study past accidents. The **technic of operations review (TOR)** is an analysis methodology that helps managers determine which specific element of a job led to a past accident.[47] The first step in a TOR analysis is to establish the facts surrounding the incident. To accomplish this, all members of the work group involved in the accident give their initial impressions of what happened. The group must then, through group discussion, reach a consensus on the single, systematic failure that most contributed to the incident as well as two or three major secondary factors that contributed to it.

An analysis of jobs at Burger King, for example, revealed that certain jobs required employees to walk across wet or slippery surfaces, which led to many falls. Specific corrective action was taken based on analysis of where people were falling and what conditions led to these falls. Now Burger King provides mats at critical locations and has generally upgraded its floor maintenance. The company also makes slip-resistant shoes available to employees in certain job categories.[48]

Communication of an employee's risk should take advantage of several media. Direct verbal supervisory contact is important for its saliency and immediacy. Written memos are important because they help establish a "paper trail" that can later document a history of concern regarding the job hazard. Posters, especially those placed near the hazard, serve as a constant reminder, reinforcing other messages.

In communicating risk, it is important to recognize two distinct audiences. Sometimes relatively young or inexperienced workers need special attention. Research by the National Safety Council indicates that 40 percent of all accidents happen to individuals in the 20-to-29 age group and that 48 percent of all accidents happen to workers during their first year on the job.[49] The employer's primary concern with respect to this group is to inform them. However, the employer must not overlook experienced workers. Here the key concern is to remind them. Research indicates that long-term exposure and familiarity with a specific threat lead to complacency.[50] Experienced employees need retraining to jar them from complacency about the real dangers associated with their work. This is especially the case if the hazard in question poses a greater threat to older employees. For example, falling off a ladder is a greater threat to older workers than to younger ones. Over 20 percent of such falls lead to a fatality for workers in the 55-to-65 age group, compared with just 10 percent for all other workers.[51]

Reinforcing Safe Practices

One common technique for reinforcing safe practices is implementing a safety incentive program to reward workers for their support and commitment to safety goals. Initially, programs are set up to focus on improving short-term monthly or quarterly goals or to encourage safety suggestions. These short-term goals are later expanded to include more wide-ranging, long-term goals. Prizes are typically distributed in highly public forums (like annual meetings or events). These prizes usually consist of merchandise rather than cash because merchandise represents a lasting symbol of achievement. A good deal of evidence suggests that such programs are effective in reducing injuries and their cost.[52]

Whereas the safety awareness programs just described focus primarily on the job, other programs focus on specific injuries or disabilities. Lower back disability (LBD), for example, is a major problem that afflicts many employees. LBD accounts for approximately 25 percent of all workdays lost, costing firms nearly $30 billion a year.[53] Human resource managers can take many steps to prevent LBD and rehabilitate those who are already afflicted. Eye injuries are another target of safety awareness programs. The National Society to Prevent Blindness estimates that 1,000 eye injuries occur every day in occupational settings.[54] A 10-step program to reduce eye injuries is outlined in Table 3.7. Similar guidelines can be found for everything from chemical burns to electrocution to injuries caused by boiler explosions.[55]

Promoting Safety Internationally

Given the increasing focus on international management, organizations also need to consider how to best ensure the safety of people regardless of the nation in which they operate. Cultural differences may make this more difficult than it seems. For example,

The Gap Hopes Honesty Pays Off

Retail firms have faced substantial criticism over the past 10 years for using outsourced "sweatshop" labor in low wage countries. The allegations usually suggest that the contractors who manufacture the clothing use child or slave labor, fail to provide safe working conditions, or verbally or physically abuse their workers.

The Gap, the largest U.S. specialty-apparel retailer with sales of $15.85 billion in 2003, has engaged in an unusual strategy for managing its reputation: Honesty. It commissioned and released a report that conceded that working conditions are far from perfect at many of the 3,000 factories that make its clothing. The report details code viola-

tions such as the fact that 25 percent of its Asian factories use psychological coercion or verbal abuse. In addition, the report states that more than 50 percent of its sub-Saharan factories run machinery without proper safety devices.

While this might not sound very positive, the report also notes that 90 percent of factories vying to win contracts fail the initial evaluation. In addition, The Gap cancelled contracts with 136 factories in 2003 because of persistent or severe violations, and in two cases it cut off factories upon discovering a problem with an underage worker.

To increase its credibility, The Gap invited input from some of the groups that have historically

criticized its labor record with positive results. The Rev. David M. Schilling, an official of the Interfaith Center on Corporate Responsibility, described The Gap's report as a "major step forward." In addition, Nikki Bas, executive director of Sweatshop Watch, which monitors labor conditions, states, "One of the challenges in this industry is that not only is production incredibly global, but there just isn't that much information shared with consumers. The more information companies like The Gap disclose, the better."

SOURCE: A. Merrick, "Gap Offers Unusual Look at Factory Conditions," http://online.wsj.com/article/ 0,,SB108432131254608813,00.html (May 12, 2004).

TABLE 3.7

A 10-Step Program for Reducing Eye-Related Injuries

1. Conduct an eye hazard job analysis.
2. Test all employees' vision to establish a baseline.
3. Select protective eyewear designed for specific operations.
4. Establish a 100 percent behavioral compliance program for eyewear.
5. Ensure that eyewear is properly fitted.
6. Train employees in emergency procedures.
7. Conduct ongoing education programs regarding eye care.
8. Continually review accident prevention strategies.
9. Provide management support.
10. Establish written policies detailing sanctions and rewards for specific results.

SOURCE: T. W. Turrif, "NSPB Suggests 10-Step Program to Prevent Eye Injury," *Occupational Health and Safety* 60 (1991), pp. 62–66.

a recent study examined the impact of one standardized corporationwide safety policy on employees in three different countries: the United States, France, and Argentina. The results of this study indicated that the same policy was interpreted differently because of cultural differences. The individualistic, control-oriented culture of the United States stressed the role of top management in ensuring safety in a top-down fashion. However, this policy failed to work in Argentina, where the collectivist culture made employees feel that safety was everyone's joint concern; therefore, programs needed to be defined from the bottom up.[56]

The "Competing through Sustainability" box illustrates how The Gap has strategically managed a measurement and reporting system with regard to its suppliers to ensure that it is being socially responsible. This reporting system reveals The Gap's concern with human rights and safety in the workplace.

A Look Back

At the beginning of the chapter we described the legal challenge Boeing faces with regard to potentially discriminating against women in their pay systems. They have already paid $4.5 million to the OFCCP in a fine, and face a potential liability of over $1 billion if they lose the class action lawsuit. However, the opening story did not present Boeing's side of the case.

Boeing spokesman Kenneth B. Mercer states that the company is committed to equal rights, and argues that the statistical studies were intended to help identify and eliminate pay disparities. In fact, Frank Marshall, the former senior compensation manager at Boeing, testified that he created a "stealth" compensation program to minimize the legal risks. The plan entailed embedding the fixes in the salary planning process so that even senior managers were not aware of them. Mercer says, "When the jury has the full story, they will find that the company did not practice discrimination of any kind."

SOURCE: S. Holmes, "A New Black Eye for Boeing?" *BusinessWeek* (April 26, 2004), pp. 90–91.

Questions

1. Based on what you read, do you think that Boeing will win or lose the class action pay discrimination case brought against them?
2. Assume that you have taken over the HR function at Boeing and want to make sure that your pay system is fair, so you commission a salary study that reveals pay differences between men and women. If you publicize the data and try to fix it, you open the company up to liability for past discrimination. What will you do?

Summary

Viewing employees as a source of competitive advantage results in dealing with them in ways that are ethical and legal as well as providing a safe workplace. An organization's legal environment—especially the laws regarding equal employment opportunity and safety—has a particularly strong effect on its HRM function. HRM is concerned with the management of people, and government is concerned with protecting individuals. One of HRM's major challenges, therefore, is to perform its function within the legal constraints imposed by the government.

Given the multimillion-dollar settlements resulting from violations of EEO laws (and the moral requirement to treat people fairly regardless of their gender or race), as well as the penalties for violating OSHA, HR and line managers need a good understanding of the legal requirements and prohibitions in order to manage their businesses in ways that are sound, both financially and ethically. Organizations that do so effectively will definitely have a competitive advantage.

Discussion Questions

1. Disparate impact theory was originally created by the court in the *Griggs* case before finally being codified by Congress 20 years later in the Civil Rights Act of 1991. Given the system of law in the United States, from what branch of government should theories of discrimination develop?

2. Disparate impact analysis (the four-fifths rule, standard deviation analysis) is used in employment discrimination cases. The National Assessment of Education Progress conducted by the U.S. Department of Education found that among 21- to 25-year-olds (a) 60 percent of whites, 40 percent of Hispanics, and 25 percent of blacks could locate information in a news article or almanac; (b) 25 percent of whites, 7 percent of Hispanics, and 3 percent of blacks could decipher a bus schedule; and (c) 44 percent of whites, 20 percent of Hispanics, and 8 percent of blacks could correctly determine the change they were due from the purchase of a two-item restaurant meal. Do these tasks (locating information in a news article, deciphering a bus schedule, and determining correct change) have adverse impact? What are the implications?

3. Many companies have dress codes that require men to wear suits and women to wear dresses. Is this discriminatory according to disparate treatment theory? Why?

4. Cognitive ability tests seem to be the most valid selection devices available for hiring employees, yet they also have adverse impact against blacks and Hispanics. Given the validity and adverse impact, and considering that race norming is illegal under CRA 1991, what would you say in response to a recommendation that such tests be used for hiring?

5. How might the ADA's reasonable accommodation requirement affect workers such as law enforcement officers and firefighters?

6. The reasonable woman standard recognizes that women have different ideas than men of what constitutes appropriate behavior. What are the implications of this distinction? Do you think it is a good or bad idea to make this distinction?

7. Employers' major complaint about the ADA is that the costs of making reasonable accommodations will make them less competitive relative to other businesses (especially foreign ones) that do not face these requirements. Is this a legitimate concern? How should employers and society weigh the costs and benefits of the ADA?

8. Many have suggested that OSHA penalties are too weak and misdirected (aimed at employers rather than employees) to have any significant impact on employee safety. Do you think that OSHA-related sanctions need to be strengthened, or are existing penalties sufficient? Defend your answer.

Self-Assessment Exercise

Take the following self-assessment quiz. For each statement, circle T if the statement is true or F is the statement is false.

What do you know about sexual harassment?

A man cannot be the victim of sexual harassment.   T F

The harasser can only be the victim's manager or a manager in another work area.   T F

Sexual harassment charges can be filed only by the person who directly experiences the harassment.   T F

The best way to discourage sexual harassment is to have a policy that discourages employees from dating each other.   T F

Sexual harassment is not a form of sex discrimination.   T F

After receiving a sexual harassment complaint, the employer should let the situation cool off before investigating the complaint.   T F

Sexual harassment is illegal only if it results in the victim being laid off or receiving less pay.   T F

Manager's Hot Seat Exercise: Office Romance: Groping for Answers

This case explores how intimate relationships conducted between coworkers can often result in problematic issues presenting themselves to the entire organization. The scenario portrayed in this video depicts such problems as decreased employee job performance, rampant organizational gossip, and employee misuse of work time. It also indicates that, quite possibly, the most devastating challenge that may manifest from such an occurrence is the potential for disastrous legal difficulties for the organization.

The video stresses how important it is for managers to utilize appropriate human resource management techniques when faced with challenging issues. The importance of maintaining a professional atmosphere during discussion of the problem, keeping the issue in focus, offering corrective actions, and seeking the immediate counsel of the organization's human resource department are identified as being paramount to achieving a suitable resolution to problematic issues.

Individual Activity:

Conduct library research, which focuses on a recent court case resulting from sexual harassment within the workplace. Prepare a short report on your individual findings. The context of this report should pay particular attention to exploring such information as the following:

- Identify the pertinent facts of the case.
- Define the type of sexual harassment involved.
- Describe how the court viewed the case.
- Identify how the organization defended itself.
- Identify any costs the organization faced as a result of the lawsuit (regardless of whether the organization won or lost the case).

Group Activity:

Have the class divided into groups of 4–5 students. From the individually prepared reports, compare and contrast the cases researched. During this discussion, group members must remember to explore such information as the following:

- The facts of the case.
- The type of sexual harassment involved.
- The current law that protects victims from the type of sexual harassment present.
- How victims should go about reporting this type of problem to supervisors.
- What responsibilities supervisors have when receiving such employee allegations.
- What duties organizations have to prevent such occurrences in the workplace.
- How this type of experience impacted the victim or victims, both at work and in their private life.
- The impact these cases had on the organization involved.
- Methodologies organizations can employ to prevent such problems in the future.

Identify one best case from each group to be presented to the class with details.

Exercising Strategy: Home Depot's Bumpy Road to Equality

Home Depot is the largest home products firm selling home repair products and equipment for the "do-it-yourselfer." Founded 20 years ago, it now boasts 100,000 employees and more than 500 warehouse stores nationwide. The company's strategy for growth has focused mostly on one task: build more stores. In fact, an unwritten goal of Home Depot executives was to position a store within 30 minutes of every customer in the United States. They've almost made it. In addition, Home Depot has tried hard to implement a strategy of providing superior service to its customers. The company has prided itself on hiring people who are knowledgeable about home repair and who can teach customers how to do home repairs on their own. This strategy, along with blanketing the country with stores, has led to the firm's substantial advantage over competitors, including the now-defunct Home Quarters (HQ) and still-standing Lowe's.

But Home Depot has run into some legal problems. During the company's growth, a statistical anomaly has emerged. About 70 percent of the merchandise employees (those directly involved in selling lumber, electrical supplies, hardware, and so forth) are men, whereas about 70 percent of operations employees (cashiers, accountants, back office staff, and so forth) are women. Because of this difference, several years ago a lawsuit was filed on behalf of 17,000 current and former employees as well as up to 200,000 rejected applicants. Home Depot explained the disparity by noting that most female job applicants have experience as cashiers, so they are placed in cashier positions; most male applicants express an interest or aptitude for home repair work such as carpentry or plumbing. However, attorneys argued that Home Depot was reinforcing gender stereotyping by hiring in this manner.

More recently, five former Home Depot employees sued the company, charging that it had discriminated against African American workers at two stores in southeast Florida. The five alleged that they were paid less than white workers, passed over for promotion, and given critical performance reviews based on race. "The company takes exception to the charges and believes they are without merit," said Home Depot spokesman Jerry Shields. The company has faced other racial discrimination suits as well, including one filed by the Michigan Department of Civil Rights.

To avoid such lawsuits in the future, Home Depot could resort to hiring and promoting by quota, ensuring an equal distribution of employees across all job categories—something that the company has wanted to avoid because it believes such action would undermine its competitive advantage. However, the company has taken steps to broaden and strengthen its own nondiscrimination policy by adding sexual orientation to the written policy. In addition, company president and CEO Bob Nardelli announced in the fall of 2001 that Home Depot would take special steps to protect benefits for its more than 500 employees who serve in the Army reserves and had been activated. "We will make up any difference between their Home Depot pay and their military pay if it's lower," said Nardelli. "When they come home [from duty], their jobs and their orange aprons are waiting for them."

In settling the gender discrimination suit the company agreed to pay $65 million to women who had been steered to cashier's jobs and had been denied promotions. In addition, the company promised that every applicant would get a "fair shot." Home Depot's solution to this has been to leverage technology to make better hiring decisions that ensure they are able to maximize their diversity.

Home Depot instituted its Job Preference Program, an automated hiring and promotion system, across its 900 stores at a cost of $10 million. It has set up kiosks where potential applicants can log on to a computer, complete an application, and undergo a set of prescreening tests. This process weeds out unqualified applicants. Then the system prints out test scores along with structured interview questions and examples of good and bad answers for the managers interviewing those who make it through the prescreening. In addition, the Home Depot system is used for promotions. Employees are asked to constantly update their skills and career aspirations so they can be considered for promotions at nearby stores.

The system has been an unarguable success. Managers love it because they are able to get high-quality applicants without having to sift through mounds of résumés. In addition, the system seems to have accomplished its main purpose. The number of female managers has increased 30 percent and the number of minority managers by 28 percent since the introduction of the system. In fact, David Borgen, the co-counsel for the plaintiffs in the original lawsuit, states, "No one can say it can't be done anymore, because Home Depot is doing it bigger and better than anyone I know."

SOURCE: "Home Depot Says Thanks to America's Military; Extends Associates/Reservists' Benefits, Announces Military Discount," company press release (October 9, 2001); S. Jaffe, "New Tricks in Home Depot's Toolbox?" *BusinessWeek Online* (June 5, 2001), www.businessweek.com; "HRC Lauds Home Depot for Adding Sexual Orientation to its Non-Discrimination Policy," *Human Rights Campaign* (May 14, 2001), www.hrc.org; "Former Home Depot Employees File Racial Discrimination Lawsuit," *Diversity at Work*, June 2000, www.diversityatwork.com; "Michigan Officials File Discrimination Suit against Home Depot," *Diversity at Work*, February 2000, www.diversityatwork.com; M. Boot, "For Plaintiffs' Lawyers, There's No Place Like Home Depot," *The Wall Street Journal*, interactive edition (February 12, 1997).

Questions

1. If Home Depot was correct in that it was not discriminating, but simply filling positions consistent with those who applied for them (and very few women were applying for customer service positions), given your reading of this chapter, was the firm guilty of discrimination? If so, under what theory?
2. How does this case illustrate the application of new technology to solving issues that have never been tied to technology? Can you think of other ways technology might be used to address diversity/EEO/affirmative action issues?

Managing People: From the Pages of *BusinessWeek*

BusinessWeek *Brown v. Board of Education:* A Bittersweet Birthday

Decades of Progress on Integration Have Been Followed by Disturbing Slippage May 17 marks the 50th anniversary of *Brown v. Board of Education*, the landmark Supreme Court ruling that declared racially segregated "separate but equal" schools unconstitutional. The case is widely regarded as one of the court's most important decisions of the 20th century, but the birthday celebration will be something of a bittersweet occasion. There's no question that African Americans have made major strides since—economically, socially, and educationally. But starting in the late 1980s, political backlash brought racial progress to a halt. Since then, schools have slowly been resegregating, and the achievement gap between white and minority schoolchildren has been widening again. Can the U.S. ever achieve the great promise of integration? Some key questions follow.

What Did the Court Strike Down in 1954? Throughout the South and in border states such as Delaware, black and white children were officially assigned to separate schools. In Topeka, Kan., the lead city in the famous case, there were 18 elementary schools for whites and just 4 for blacks, forcing many African American children to travel a long way to school. The idea that black schools were "equal" to those for whites was a cruel fiction, condemning most black kids to a grossly inferior education.

Surely We've Come a Long Way Since Then? Yes, though change took a long time. Over 99% of Southern black children were still in segregated schools in 1963. The 1960s civil rights movement eventually brought aggressive federal policies such as busing and court orders that forced extensive integration, especially in the South. So by 1988, 44% of Southern black children were attending schools where a majority of students were white, up from 2% in 1964. "We cut school desegregation almost in half between 1968 and 1990," says John Logan, director of the Lewis Mumford Center for Comparative Urban and Regional Research at State University of New York at Albany.

What's the Picture Today?

There have been some real gains. The share of blacks graduating from high school has nearly quadrupled since *Brown*, to 88% today, while the share of those ages 25 to 29 with a college degree has increased more than sixfold, to 18%.

Another important trend is in housing, which in turn helps determine the characteristics of school districts. Residential integration is improving, albeit at a glacial pace. There's still high housing segregation in major metropolitan areas, but it has fallen four percentage points, to 65%, on an index developed by the Mumford Center. Some of the gains are happening in fast-growing new suburbs where race lines aren't so fixed. A few big cities have improved, too. In Dallas, for example, black–white residential segregation fell from 78% in 1980 to 59% in 2000.

Why Haven't Schools Continued to Desegregate, Too?

The increased racial mixing in housing hasn't been nearly large enough to offset the sheer increase in the ranks of minority schoolchildren. While the number of white elementary school kids remained flat, at 15.3 million, between 1990 and 2000, the number of black children climbed by 800,000, to 4.6 million, while Hispanic kids jumped by 1.7 million, to 4.3 million. The result: Minorities now comprise 40% of public school kids, vs. 32% in 1990. And as the nonwhite population has expanded, so have minority neighborhoods—and schools.

So Minorities Have Lost Ground?

Yes, in some respects. By age 17, black students are still more than three years behind their white counterparts in reading and math. And whites are twice as likely to graduate from college. Taken as a whole, U.S. schools have been resegregating for 15 years or so, according to studies by the Harvard University Civil Rights Project. "We're celebrating [*Brown*] at a time when schools in all regions are becoming increasingly segregated," says project co-director Gary Orfield.

What Role Has the Political Backlash against Integration Played?

The courts and politicians have been pulling back from integration goals for quite a while. In 1974, the Supreme Court ruled that heavily black Detroit didn't have to integrate its schools with the surrounding white suburbs. Then, in the 1980s, the growing backlash against busing and race-based school assignment led politicians and the courts to all but give up on those remedies, too.

So What Are the Goals Now?

The approach has shifted dramatically. Instead of trying to force integration, the U.S. has moved toward equalizing education. In a growing number of states, the courts have been siding with lawsuits that seek equal or "adequate" funding for minority and low-income schools.

The No Child Left Behind Act goes even further. It says that all children will receive a "highly qualified" teacher by 2006 and will achieve proficiency in math and reading by 2014. It specifically requires schools to meet these goals for racial subgroups. Paradoxically, it sounds like separate but equal again. Both the equal-funding suits and No Child Left Behind aim to improve all schools, whatever their racial composition. Integration is no longer the explicit goal.

Can Schools Equalize without Integrating?

It's possible in some cases, but probably not for the U.S. as a whole. The Education Trust, a nonprofit group in Washington, D.C., has identified a number of nearly all-black, low-income schools that have achieved exceptional test results. But such success requires outstanding leadership, good teachers, and a fervent commitment to high standards.

These qualities are far more difficult to achieve in large urban schools with many poor kids—the kind most black and Hispanic students attend. The average minority student goes to a school in which two-thirds of the students are low-income. By contrast, whites attend schools that are just 30% low-income.

So Are Black–White Achievement Gaps as Much about Poverty as Race?

Yes, which is why closing them is difficult with or without racial integration. Studies show that middle-class students tend to have higher expectations, more engaged parents, and better teachers. Poor children, by contrast, often come to school with far more personal problems. Yet poor schools are more likely to get inferior teachers, such as those who didn't major in the subject they teach. Many poor schools also lose as many as 20% of their teachers each year, while most middle-class suburban schools have more stable teaching staffs. "Research suggests that when low-income students attend middle-class schools, they do substantially better," says Richard Kahlenberg, senior fellow at the Century Foundation, a public policy think tank in New York City.

Is It Possible to Achieve More Economic Integration?

There are a few shining examples, but they take enormous political commitment. One example that education-system reformers love to highlight is Wake County, N.C., whose 110,000-student school district includes Raleigh. In 2000, it adopted a plan to ensure that low-income students make up no more than 40% of any student body. It also capped those achieving under grade level at 25%. Moreover, it used magnet schools offering specialized programs, such as one for gifted children, to help attract middle-income children to low-income areas.

Already, 91% of the county's third- to eighth-graders work at grade level in math and reading, up from 84% in 1999. More impressive, 75% of low-income kids are reading at grade level, up from just 56% in 1999, as are 78% of black children, up from 61%. "The academic payoff has been pretty incredible," says Walter C. Sherlin, a 28-year Wake County schools veteran and interim director of the nonprofit Wake Education Partnership.

Could This Serve as a National Model?

For that to happen in many cities, school districts would have to merge with the surrounding suburbs. Wake County did this, but that was back in the 1970s and part of a long-term plan to bring about racial integration. In the metro Boston area, by contrast, students are balkanized into dozens of tiny districts, many of which are economically homogeneous. The result: Some 70% of white students attend schools that are over 90% white and overwhelmingly middle-class. Meanwhile, 97% of the schools that are over 90% minority are also high-poverty. Similar patterns exist in most major cities, but most affluent white suburbs aren't likely to swallow a move like Wake County's.

How Important Is Funding Equality within States?

It's critical, especially if segregation by income and race persists. Massachusetts, for instance, has nearly tripled state aid to schools since 1993, with over 90% of the money going to the poorest towns. That has helped make Massachusetts a national leader in raising academic achievement.

Nationally, though, there are still huge inequities in school spending, with the poorest districts receiving less money than the richest—even though low-income children are more expensive to educate. Fixing these imbalances would be costly. Even in Massachusetts, a lower

court judge ruled on Apr. 26 that the system still shortchanges students in the poorest towns. Nationally, it would cost more than $50 billion a year in extra funding to correct inequities enough to meet the goals of No Child, figures Anthony P. Carnevale, a vice president at Educational Testing Service.

If, Somehow, the U.S. Could Achieve More Economic Integration, Would Racial Integration Still Be Necessary?

Proficiency on tests isn't the only aim. As the Supreme Court said last year in a landmark decision on affirmative action in higher education: "Effective participation by members of all racial and ethnic groups in the civic life of our nation is essential if the dream of one nation, indivisible, is to be realized." It's hard to see how students attending largely segregated schools, no matter how proficient, could be adequately prepared for life in an increasingly diverse country. In this sense, integrating America's educational system remains an essential, though still elusive, goal.

SOURCE: W. Symonds, "A Bittersweet Birthday," *BusinessWeek* (May 17, 2004), pp. 66–62.

Questions

1. While segregation of public schools has been outlawed, the article notes that schools are not necessarily "desegregating" (i.e., there are still predominantly minority and predominantly nonminority schools). If students are to work in increasingly diverse workforces, is the current system failing them? Why or why not?

2. The black–white gap continues to exist with regard to reading, math, and graduation rates. What are the implications of this on organizations' selection systems (i.e., disparate impact)?

3. Given the lack of a "diverse" educational experience for a large percentage of black children, and the gap between them and their white counterparts, what must organizations do to leverage diversity as a source of competitive advantage?

Notes

1. J. Ledvinka, *Federal Regulation of Personnel and Human Resource Management* (Boston: Kent, 1982).
2. *Martin v. Wilks,* 49 FEP Cases 1641 (1989).
3. *Wards Cove Packing Co. v. Atonio,* FEPC 1519 (1989).
4. *Bakke v. Regents of the University of California,* 17 FEPC 1000 (1978).
5. *Patterson v. McLean Credit Union,* 49 FEPC 1814 (1987).
6. J. Friedman and G. Strickler, *The Law of Employment Discrimination: Cases and Materials,* 2nd ed. (Mineola, NY: The Foundation Press, 1987).
7. "Labor Letter," *The Wall Street Journal* (August 25, 1987), p. 1.
8. J. Woo, "Ex-Workers Hit Back with Age-Bias Suits," *The Wall Street Journal* (December 8, 1992), p. B1.
9. W. Carley, "Salesman's Treatment Raises Bias Questions at Schering-Plough," *The Wall Street Journal* (May 31, 1995), p. A1.
10. Special feature issue: "The New Civil Rights Act of 1991 and What It Means to Employers," *Employment Law Update* 6, December 1991, pp. 1–12.
11. "ADA: The Final Regulations (Title I): A Lawyer's Dream/An Employer's Nightmare," *Employment Law Update* 16, no. 9 (1991), p. 1.

12. "ADA Supervisor Training Program: A Must for Any Supervisor Conducting a Legal Job Interview," *Employment Law Update* 7, no. 6 (1992), pp. 1–6.

13. Equal Employment Opportunity Commission, *Uniform Guidelines on Employee Selection Procedures*, Federal Register 43 (1978), pp. 38290–315.

14. Ledvinka, *Federal Regulation*.

15. R. Pear, "The Cabinet Searches for Consensus on Affirmative Action," *The New York Times* (October 27, 1985), p. E5.

16. *McDonnell Douglas v. Green*, 411 U.S. 972 (1973).

17. *UAW v. Johnson Controls, Inc.* (1991).

18. Special feature issue: "The New Civil Rights Act of 1991," pp. 1–6.

19. *Washington v. Davis*, 12 FEP 1415 (1976).

20. *Albermarle Paper Company v. Moody*, 10 FEP 1181 (1975).

21. R. Reilly and G. Chao, "Validity and Fairness of Some Alternative Employee Selection Procedures," *Personnel Psychology* 35 (1982), pp. 1–63; J. Hunter and R. Hunter, "Validity and Utility of Alternative Predictors of Job Performance," *Psychological Bulletin* 96 (1984), pp. 72–98.

22. *Griggs v. Duke Power Company*, 401 U.S. 424 (1971).

23. B. Lindeman and P. Grossman, *Employment Discrimination Law* (Washington, DC: BNA Books, 1996).

24. M. Jacobs, "Workers' Religious Beliefs May Get New Attention," *The Wall Street Journal* (August 22, 1995), pp. B1, B8.

25. "EEOC and Electrolux Reach Voluntary Resolution in Class Religious Accommodation Case," www.eeoc.gov/press/9-24-03.

26. Lindeman and Grossman, *Employment Discrimination Law*.

27. J. Reno and D. Thornburgh, "ADA—Not a Disabling Mandate," *The Wall Street Journal* (July 26, 1995), p. A12.

28. Woo, "Ex-Workers Hit Back."

29. W. Johnston and A. Packer, *Workforce 2000* (Indianapolis, IN: Hudson Institute, 1987).

30. *Bundy v. Jackson*, 641 F.2d 934, 24 FEP 1155 (D.C. Cir., 1981).

31. L. A. Graf and M. Hemmasi, "Risqué Humor: How It Really Affects the Workplace," *HR Magazine*, November 1995, pp. 64–69.

32. B. Carton, "At Jenny Craig, Men Are Ones Who Claim Sex Discrimination," *The Wall Street Journal* (November 29, 1995), p. A1; "Male-on-Male Harassment Suit Won," *Houston Chronicle* (August 12, 1995), p. 21A.

33. EEOC, "Texas Car Dealership to Pay $140,000 to Settle Same-Sex Harassment Suit by EEOC," www.eeoc.gov/press/10-28-02 (October 28, 2002).

34. EEOC, "Babies 'R' Us to Pay $205,000, Implement Training Due to Same-Sex Harassment of Male Employee," www.eeoc.gov/press/1-15-03 (January 15, 2003).

35. *Meritor Savings Bank v. Vinson* (1986).

36. R. Paetzold and A. O'Leary-Kelly, "The Implications of U.S. Supreme Court and Circuit Court Decisions for Hostile Environment Sexual Harassment Cases," *in Sexual Harassment: Perspectives, Frontiers, and Strategies*, ed. M. Stockdale (Beverly Hills, CA: Sage); R. B. McAfee and D. L. Deadrick, "Teach Employees to Just Say 'No'!" *HR Magazine*, February 1996, pp. 586–89.

37. C. Murray, "The Legacy of the 60's," *Commentary*, July 1992, pp. 23–30.

38. D. Kravitz and J. Platania, "Attitudes and Beliefs about Affirmative Action: Effects of Target and of Respondent Sex and Ethnicity," *Journal of Applied Psychology* 78 (1993), pp. 928–38.

39. J. Mathews, "Rash of Unintended Lawsuits Follows Passage of Disabilities Act," *Houston Chronicle* (May 16, 1995), p. 15A.

40. C. Bell, "What the First ADA Cases Tell Us," *SHRM Legal Report* (Winter 1995), pp. 4–7.

41. K. Mills, "Disabilities Act: A Help, or a Needless Hassle," *B/CS Eagle* (August 23, 1995), p. A7.

42. V. F. Estrada, "Are Your Factory Workers Know-It-All?" *Personnel Journal*, September 1995, pp. 128–34.

43. R. L. Simison, "Safety Last," *The Wall Street Journal* (March 18, 1986), p. 1.

44. J. Roughton, "Managing a Safety Program through Job Hazard Analysis," *Professional Safety* 37 (1992), pp. 28–31.

45. M. A. Verespec, "OSHA Reform Fails Again," *Industry Week* (November 2, 1992), p. 36.

46. R. G. Hallock and D. A. Weaver, "Controlling Losses and Enhancing Management Systems with TOR Analysis," *Professional Safety* 35 (1990), pp. 24–26.

47. H. Herbstman, "Controlling Losses the Burger King Way," *Risk Management* 37 (1990), pp. 22–30.

48. L. Bryan, "An Ounce of Prevention for Workplace Accidents," *Training and Development Journal* 44 (1990), pp. 101–2.

49. J. F. Mangan, "Hazard Communications: Safety in Knowledge," *Best's Review* 92 (1991), pp. 84–88.

50. T. Markus, "How to Set Up a Safety Awareness Program," *Supervision* 51 (1990), pp. 14–16.

51. J. Agnew and A. J. Saruda, "Age and Fatal Work-Related Falls," *Human Factors* 35 (1994), pp. 731–36.

52. R. King, "Active Safety Programs, Education Can Help Prevent Back Injuries," *Occupational Health and Safety* 60 (1991), pp. 49–52.

53. J. R. Hollenbeck, D. R. Ilgen, and S. M. Crampton, "Lower Back Disability in Occupational Settings: A Review of the Literature from a Human Resource Management View," *Personnel Psychology* 45 (1992), pp. 247–78.

54. T. W. Turriff, "NSPB Suggests 10-Step Program to Prevent Eye Injury," *Occupational Health and Safety* 60 (1991), pp. 62–66.

55. D. Hanson, "Chemical Plant Safety: OSHA Rule Addresses Industry Concerns," *Chemical and Engineering News* 70 (1992), pp. 4–5; K. Broscheit and K. Sawyer, "Safety Exhibit Teaches Customers and Employees about Electricity," *Transmission and Distribution* 43 (1992), pp. 174–79; R. Schuch, "Good Training Is Key to Avoiding Boiler Explosions," *National Underwriter* 95 (1992), pp. 21–22.

56. M. Janssens, J. M. Brett, and F. J. Smith, "Confirmatory Cross-Cultural Research: Testing the Viability of a Corporation-wide Safety Policy," *Academy of Management Journal* 38 (1995), pp. 364–82.

4

Chapter

The Analysis and Design of Work

Objectives After reading this chapter, you should be able to:

1. Analyze an organization's structure and work-flow process, identifying the output, activities, and inputs in the production of a product or service.

2. Understand the importance of job analysis in strategic and human resource management.

3. Choose the right job analysis technique for a variety of human resource activities.

4. Identify the tasks performed and the skills required in a given job.

5. Understand the different approaches to job design.

6. Comprehend the trade-offs among the various approaches to designing jobs.

Bill's To-Do List

Gates keeps a tally of the top 50 tech initiatives he is responsible for pushing throughout the company. Here are six items on what is known at Microsoft as simply The List.

SEARCH Look out, Google. Microsoft plans to put search technology into the operating system. And it will let people search the Web and their PCs all at once.

SECURITY Spam and viruses and worms, oh my. Windows draws attacks like no other, and the company has drawn fire for not doing enough to plug security holes. Gates vows to do better.

TELEPHONY Forget old-fashioned phone calls. Gates wants to bring computer innovation to telecom. Think video voice mails. Or instant messaging with talk, not text.

VOICE RECOGNITION Who wants to type? Microsoft is developing voice recognition so you won't have to. It's also developing software to read you your e-mails or Word documents.

FILE SYSTEM Finding things on a PC is too cumbersome. New software will let you find not just digital photos but, for example, e-mails from the people in them.

DIGITAL-RIGHTS MANAGEMENT Photos, music, and video are going digital. Microsoft is developing software to let people use that content without violating intellectual-property rights.

Restructuring the nature of work within a company can increase its efficiency and effectiveness. How did this decentralization of Microsoft's structure allow groups to work more responsibly and competitively?

Enter the World of Business

Structural Realignment at Microsoft: Opening New Windows of Opportunity

Throughout the 1990s, revenue growth at Microsoft averaged over 30 percent per year, making it one of the most successful business organizations in the world. However, with success comes new challenges, and both external and internal pressures have created problems that have cut into Microsoft's dominance. In fact, over the last five years, growth has been in the single digits. In terms of external pressures, Linux stands as a free, open source code that directly challenges Microsoft's operating system. IBM is also challenging Microsoft with its emphasis on customer service and system integration that allows clients to bypass Microsoft's bundles of integrated products.

Internally, as the organization increased in size and scope, the decision-making process at Microsoft was slowing to a crawl, with some suggesting that the new operating system known as "Longhorn" should be renamed "Long Wait." Also, Microsoft experienced turnover among key personnel, many of whom became millionaires as the company grew, but whose intrinsic motivation was low because they did not feel that they had enough autonomy in their jobs. As

one manager noted, "In the past, the system was optimized for people to get stuff done. Now, everybody is always preparing for a meeting."

In order to turn this situation around, CEO Bill Ballmer took unprecedented steps in strategically restructuring the organization to respond to these new competitive pressures. The question guiding this reorganization was how best to divvy up the 55,000 Microsoft employees and define their jobs so that innovation and productivity could be maximized, while turnover and bureaucratic impediments could be minimized. Turning first to the organization's structure, it was clear that Microsoft was too centralized given its current size, and that too much decision-making authority rested with the CEO and its founder, Bill Gates.

Ballmer wanted to decentralize the organization and create a large number of semiautonomous business divisions (e.g., a Personal Computer Division, a Server Division, a Gaming Division) that had responsibility for their own profit and loss figures. Gates initially resisted this move, however, because he felt that all Microsoft products had to work seamlessly together, and independent divisions would not provide for effective coordination and collaboration across units. Ballmer realized, "We'd have to come up with a structure unlike anything out there, to simultaneously give divisions enough autonomy to manage themselves, yet make it easier for them to cooperate and integrate the technology."

The solution was a matrixlike organization structure that relied on seven autonomous divisions that were supported by a new concept in workflow design that formalized how product development would both proceed within divisions and then be transferred across divisions. The seven divisions divided the work up into separate units for operating systems (Windows Client), desktop applications (Information Worker), business services, (Business Solutions), server systems (Server and Tools), mobile devices (Mobile and Embedded Devices), Internet services (MSN), and X-Box and other gaming applications (Home Entertainment). Within each unit, a new product development process called the Software Engineering Strategy laid out a universally-applied procedure that dictated how a project moved from the "incubator phase" to the "definer phase," to the "owner phase," stipulating where the "participants," "reviewers" and "coaches" should provide input into the process. As Gates noted, "This is the first time we've really had a structure to formally deal with issues. So it's not just 'hey if you're confused, send an email to Bill.'"

On the one hand, one of the immediate results of the new structure was that it clearly revealed how much money was being lost in certain divisions such as MSN and the Home Entertainment Divisions relative to the tried-and-true Windows Client Division. Although disheartening in some cases, this at least provided a benchmark from which to measure improvement as the divisions moved forward. More critically, however, these structural changes at the organization level spilled down to individual jobs, both clarifying who was supposed to do what and motivating individuals to sink or swim in their new, more autonomous roles. This helped reduce the turnover rates among the key players by increasing their intrinsic motivation. As one of Microsoft's new division leaders noted, all the new divisional managers "sense a chance to do one last great thing in their working lives," and this is the type of attitude that may help propel Microsoft back to the lofty rates of growth that it once enjoyed.

SOURCE: J. Greene, "Microsoft's Midlife Crisis," *BusinessWeek* (April 19, 2004), pp. 88–98; J. Kerstetter, "Gates and Ballmer on Making the Transition," *BusinessWeek* (April 19, 2004), pp. 96–97; B. Schlender, "Ballmer Unbound: How Do You Impose Order on a Giant Runaway Mensa Meeting?" *Fortune* (January 26, 2004), pp. 117–24.

Introduction

In Chapter 2 we discussed the processes of strategy formulation and strategy implementation. Strategy formulation is the process by which a company decides how it will compete in the marketplace; this is often the energizing and guiding force for everything it does. Strategy implementation is the way the strategic plan gets carried out in activities of organizational members. We noted five important components in the strategy implementation process, three of which are directly related to the human resource management function and one of which we will discuss in this chapter: the task or job.[1]

Many central aspects of strategy formulation address how the work gets done, in terms of both individual job design as well as the design of organizational structures that link individual jobs to each other and the organization as a whole. The way a firm competes can have a profound impact on the ways jobs are designed and how they are linked via organizational structure. In turn, the fit between the company's structure and environment can have a major impact on the firm's competitive success.

For example, if a company wants to compete via a low-cost strategy, it needs to maximize efficiency and coordination. Efficiency is maximized by breaking jobs down into small, simple components that are executed repetitively by low-wage, low-skilled workers. Efficiency is also enhanced by eliminating any redundancy of support services, so that jobs are structured into functional clusters where everyone in the cluster is performing similar work. (Thus all marketing people work together in a single unit, all engineering personnel work together in a single unit, and so on.) People working together within these functional clusters learn a great deal about how the function can be used to leverage their skills into small amounts of increased efficiency via continuous, evolutionary improvements, and higher level managers focus exclusively on coordinating the different functional units.

On the other hand, if a company wants to compete via innovation, it needs to maximize flexibility. Flexibility is maximized by aggregating work into larger, holistic pieces that are executed by teams of higher-wage, higher-skilled workers. Flexibility is also enhanced by giving the units their own support systems and decision-making authority to take advantage of local opportunities in regional or specialized product markets. People working together in these cross-functional clusters generate a greater number of creative and novel ideas that can be leveraged into more discontinuous, revolutionary improvements.

Thus, it should be clear from the outset of this chapter that there is no "one best way" to design jobs and structure organizations. The organization needs to create a fit between its environment, competitive strategy, and philosophy on the one hand, with its jobs and organizational design on the other. Thus, in our opening story, Microsoft was changing its structure from a highly centralized and functional structure that focused on coordination between units (in order to maintain compatibility of software) into a more decentralized and divisional structure that placed the emphasis on innovation and autonomy of its separate divisions (in order to penetrate specific markets). This change in the overall structure then spills down into individual jobs, creating higher levels of responsibility (i.e., profit and loss responsibility) on the shoulders of managers lower in the hierarchy.

This chapter discusses the analysis and design of work and, in doing so, lays out some considerations that go into making informed decisions about how to create and link jobs. The chapter is divided into three sections, the first of which deals with "big-picture" issues related to work-flow analysis and organizational structure. The remaining two sections deal with more specific, lower-level issues related to job analysis and job design.

The fields of job analysis and job design have extensive overlap, yet in the past they have been treated differently.[2] Job analysis has focused on analyzing existing jobs to gather information for other human resource management practices such as selection, training, performance appraisal, and compensation.[3] Job design, on the other hand, has focused on redesigning existing jobs to make them more efficient or more motivating to jobholders.[4] Thus job design has had a more proactive orientation toward changing the job, whereas job analysis has had a passive, information-gathering orientation. However, as we will show in this chapter, these two approaches are interrelated.

Work-Flow Analysis and Organization Structure

In the past, HR professionals and line managers have tended to analyze or design a particular job in isolation from the larger organizational context. *Work-flow design* is the process of analyzing the tasks necessary for the production of a product or service, prior to allocating and assigning these tasks to a particular job category or person. Only after we thoroughly understand work-flow design can we make informed decisions regarding how to initially bundle various tasks into discrete jobs that can be executed by a single person.

Organization structure refers to the relatively stable and formal network of vertical and horizontal interconnections among jobs that constitute the organization. Only after we understand how one job relates to those above (supervisors), below (subordinates), and at the same level in different functional areas (marketing versus production) can we make informed decisions about how to redesign or improve jobs to benefit the entire organization.

Finally, work-flow design and organization structure have to be understood in the context of how an organization has decided to compete. Both work-flow design and organization structure can be leveraged to gain competitive advantage for the firm, but how one does this depends on the firm's strategy and its competitive environment.

Work-Flow Analysis

A theme common to nearly all organizations is the need to identify clearly the outputs of work, to specify the quality and quantity standards for those outputs, and to analyze the processes and inputs necessary for producing outputs that meet the quality standards.[5] This conception of the work-flow process is useful because it provides a means for the manager to understand all the tasks required to produce a number of high-quality products as well as the skills necessary to perform those tasks. This work-flow process is depicted in Figure 4.1. In this section we present an approach for analyzing the work process of a department as a means of examining jobs in the context of an organization.

FIGURE 4.1

Developing a Work-Unit Activity Analysis

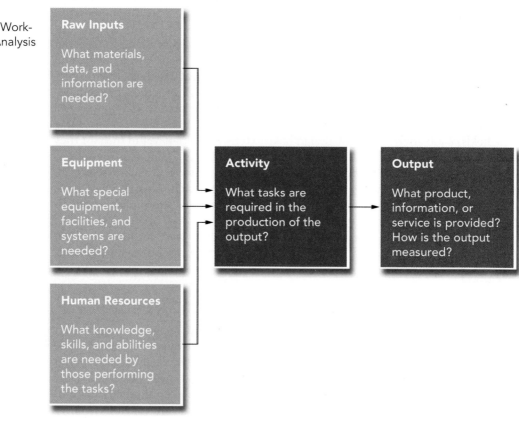

Raw Inputs

What materials, data, and information are needed?

Equipment

What special equipment, facilities, and systems are needed?

Human Resources

What knowledge, skills, and abilities are needed by those performing the tasks?

Activity

What tasks are required in the production of the output?

Output

What product, information, or service is provided? How is the output measured?

Analyzing Work Outputs

Every work unit—whether a department, team, or individual—seeks to produce some output that others can use. An output is the product of a work unit and is often an identifiable thing, such as a completed purchase order, an employment test, or a hot, juicy hamburger. However, an output can also be a service, such as the services provided by an airline that transports you to some destination, a housecleaning service that maintains your house, or a baby-sitter who watches over your children.

We often picture an organization only in terms of the product that it produces, and then we focus on that product as the output. So, for example, in our opening story, the products for Microsoft can be thought of in terms of its separate divisions, and therefore include things like Windows Software, X-boxes, MSN Internet Explorer, and so on. Indeed, although sometimes divisions are set up geographically (e.g., the Northeast Region versus the Southwest Region), more often one of the central features of a divisional structure is that it is organized around a specific product, and all the activities within that part of the organization are devoted to that one product. Merely identifying an output or set of outputs is not sufficient. Once these outputs have been identified, it is necessary to specify standards for the quantity or quality of these outputs. For example, a productivity improvement technique known as ProMES (productivity measurement and evaluation system) focuses attention on both identifying work-unit outputs and specifying the levels of required performance for different levels of effectiveness.[6] With ProMES, the members of a work unit identify each of the products (outputs) of the work unit for the various customers. They then evaluate the effectiveness of each level of products in the eyes of their customers.

The identification of work outputs has only recently gained attention among HRM departments. As discussed in Chapter 2, HR executives have begun to understand the role of the HRM department as they have attempted to analyze their customers inside the company and the products that those customers desire from the HRM function.[7] This has given HR managers a clearer understanding of the specific products that they supply to the company and allows them to focus on producing high-quality products. Without an understanding of the output of a work unit, any attempt at increasing work-unit effectiveness will be futile.

Analyzing Work Processes

Once the outputs of the work unit have been identified, it is possible to examine the work processes used to generate the output. The work processes are the activities that members of a work unit engage in to produce a given output. Every process consists of operating procedures that specify how things should be done at each stage of the development of the product. These procedures include all the tasks that must be performed in the production of the output. The tasks are usually broken down into those performed by each person in the work unit. Thus, one critical aspect of the reorganization at Microsoft was to spell out the roles defined by the new Software Engineering Strategy. This system described a formal procedure applied to all outputs that spelled out how a new product moved from "incubators" to the "definers" to the "owners" while also noting where the "participants," "reviewers" and "coaches" provide input into development.

Again, to design work systems that are maximally efficient, a manager needs to understand the processes required in the development of the products for that work unit. Often, as workloads increase within a work group, the group will grow by adding positions to meet these new requirements. However, when the workload lightens, members may take on tasks that do not relate to the work unit's product in an effort to appear busy. Without a clear understanding of the tasks necessary to the production of an output, it is difficult to determine whether the work unit has become overstaffed. Understanding the tasks required allows the manager to specify which tasks are to be carried out by which individuals and eliminate tasks that are not necessary for the desired end. This ensures that the work group maintains a high level of productivity.

For example, Microsoft, currently the most successful computer software company in the world, strategically manages the design of the total work-flow process for competitive advantage. To maintain the sense of being an underdog, Microsoft deliberately understaffs its product teams in "small bands of people with a mission." This ensures both a lean organization and high levels of motivation.[8]

Although this substitution was often focused formerly on production employees, more recently, the focus has been on eliminating midlevel managers. For example, at Unifi Inc., a textile producer, factory equipment is connected via high-speed data lines so that shop floor data can be relayed in real time to analysts at corporate headquarters, eliminating the need for local supervisors.[9] This kind of remote monitoring is becoming especially popular in multinational corporations as a means of standardizing work outputs. Although not all employees respond positively to technological changes in the nature of work, such changes are becoming increasingly critical in competing in the contemporary business environment.[10]

Analyzing Work Inputs

The final stage in work-flow analysis is to identify the inputs used in the development of the work unit's product. For example, assume that you were assigned a paper titled "The Importance of Human Resources to Organizational Performance." The output of your work process will be a paper that you will turn in to the professor. To produce this paper, you must perform a number of tasks, such as conducting research, reading articles, and writing the paper. What, however, are the inputs? As shown in Figure 4.1, these inputs can be broken down into the raw materials, equipment, and human skills needed to perform the tasks. *Raw materials* consist of the materials that will be converted into the work unit's product. Thus, for your assignment, the raw materials would be the information available in the library regarding the various effects of human resources on organizational performance.

Equipment refers to the technology and machinery necessary to transform the raw materials into the product. As you attempt to develop your paper, you may use the library computer search system to get a list of recent articles on the relationship between human resources and organizational performance. In addition, once you sit down to write, you will most likely have to use either a word processor or a personal computer to put your thoughts on paper.

The final inputs in the work-flow process are the *human skills* and efforts necessary to perform the tasks. Many skills are required of you in producing your paper. For example, you need to know how to use the library computer search facilities, you need some typing skill (or the phone number of a good typist), and you definitely need the ability to reason and write. Of course, in many situations where the work that needs to be done is highly complex, no single individual is likely to have all the required skills. In these situations, the work may be assigned to a team, and team-based job design is becoming increasingly popular in contemporary organizations.[11] In addition to providing a wider set of skills, team members can back each other up, share work when any member becomes overloaded, and catch each other's errors. Teams are not a panacea, however, and for teams to be effective, it is essential that the level of task interdependence (how much they have to cooperate) matches the level of outcome interdependence (how much they share the reward for task accomplishment).[12]

It is important to note that a flawed product can be caused by deficiencies at any phase in production. For example, if you fail to spell-check your paper before turning it in, you may receive a lower grade. Similarly, if you cannot obtain the best raw materials (if you cannot find the right articles), do not use the proper equipment (the computer is down), or do not possess the necessary skills (you do not write well), your paper will receive less than the maximum grade.

Organization Structure

Whereas work-flow design provides a longitudinal overview of the dynamic relationships by which inputs are converted into outputs, organization structure provides a cross-sectional overview of the static relationships between individuals and units that create the outputs. Organization structure is typically displayed via organizational charts that convey both vertical reporting relationships and horizontal functional responsibilities.

Dimensions of Structure

Two of the most critical dimensions of organization structure are centralization and departmentation. **Centralization** refers to the degree to which decision-making authority resides at the top of the organizational chart as opposed to being distributed throughout lower levels (in which case authority is *decentralized*). **Departmentalization** refers to the degree to which work units are grouped based on functional similarity or similarity of work flow.

For example, a school of business could be organized around functional similarity so that there would be a marketing department, a finance department, and an accounting department, and faculty within these specialized departments would each teach their area of expertise to all kinds of students. Alternatively, one could organize the same school around work-flow similarity, so that there would be an undergraduate unit, a graduate unit, and an executive development unit. Each of these units would have its own marketing, finance, and accounting professors who taught only their own respective students and not those of the other units.

Centralization
Degree to which decision-making authority resides at the top of the organizational chart.

Departmentalization
Degree to which work units are grouped based on functional similarity or similarity of work flow.

Structural Configurations

Although there are an infinite number of ways to combine centralization and departmentalization, two common configurations of organization structure tend to emerge in organizations. The first type, referred to as a *functional structure*, is shown in Figure 4.2. A functional structure, as the name implies, employs a functional departmentalization scheme with relatively high levels of centralization. High levels of centralization tend to go naturally with functional departmentalization because individual units in the structures are so specialized that members of the unit may have a weak conceptualization of the overall organization mission. Thus, they tend to identify with their department and cannot always be relied on to make decisions that are in the best interests of the organization as a whole.

FIGURE 4.2

The Functional Structure

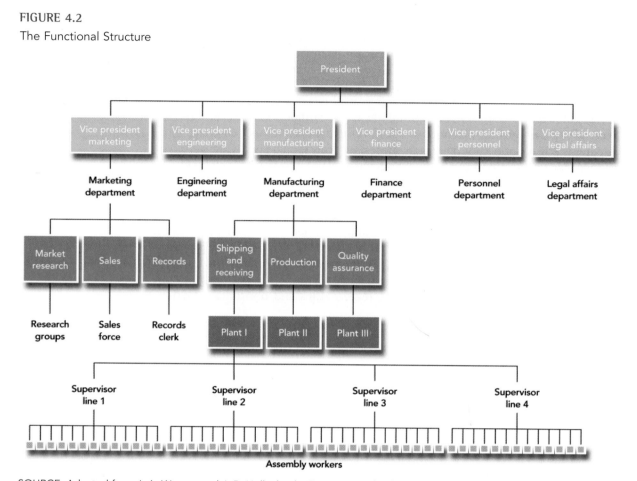

SOURCE: Adapted from J. A. Wagner and J. R. Hollenbeck, *Organizational Behavior: Securing Competitive Advantage*, 3rd ed. New York: Prentice Hall, 1998.

Alternatively, a second common configuration is a *divisional structure*, three examples of which are shown in Figures 4.3, 4.4, and 4.5. Divisional structures combine a divisional departmentalization scheme with relatively low levels of centralization. Units in these structures act almost like separate, self-sufficient, semi-autonomous organizations. The organization shown in Figure 4.3 is divisionally organized around different products; the organization shown in Figure 4.4 is divisionally organized around geographic regions; and the organization shown in Figure 4.5 is divisionally organized around different clients. This was the type of structure that Microsoft converted to in our opening story, where departments were organized around seven distinct products or services (i.e., Windows Client, Information Worker, Business Solutions, Server and Tools, Mobile Devices, MSN, and Home Entertainment).

Because of their work-flow focus, their semi-autonomous nature, and their proximity to a homogeneous consumer base, divisional structures tend to be more flexible and innovative. They can detect and exploit opportunities in their respective consumer base faster than the more centralized functionally-structured organizations. The perceived autonomy that goes along with this kind of structure also means that most employees prefer it and feel they are more fairly treated than when they are subject to centralized decision-making structures.[13] However, on the downside,

FIGURE 4.3
Divisional Structure: Product Structure

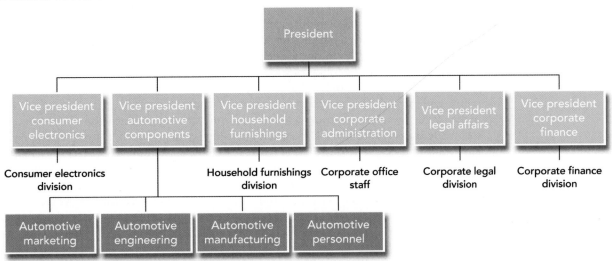

SOURCE: Adapted from J. A. Wagner and J. R. Hollenbeck, *Organizational Behavior: Securing Competitive Advantage*, 3rd ed. Prentice Hall, 1998.

FIGURE 4.4
Divisional Structure: Geographic Structure

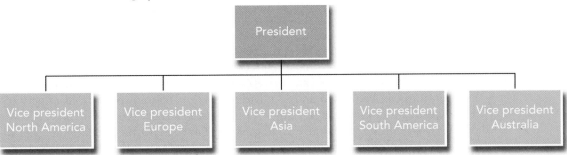

SOURCE: Adapted from J. A. Wagner and J. R. Hollenbeck, *Organizational Behavior: Securing Competitive Advantage*, 3rd ed. Prentice Hall, 1998.

FIGURE 4.5
Divisional Structure: Client Structure

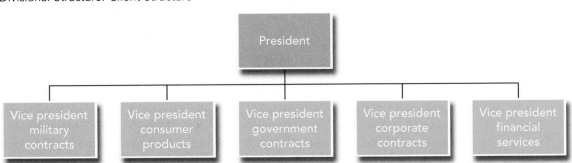

SOURCE: Adapted from J. A. Wagner and J. R. Hollenbeck, *Organizational Behavior: Securing Competitive Advantage*, 3rd ed. Prentice Hall, 1998.

divisional structures are not very efficient because of the redundancy associated with each group carrying its own functional specialists. Also, divisional structures can "self-cannibalize" if the gains achieved in one unit come at the expense of another unit (for example, if sales in one General Motors unit like Buick come at the expense of another GM unit like Chevrolet).

Alternatively, functional structures are very efficient, with little redundancy across units, and provide little opportunity for self-cannibalization. Also, although the higher level of oversight in centralized structures tends to reduce the number of errors made by lower level workers, when errors do occur in overly centralized systems, they tend to cascade through the system as a whole more quickly, and can therefore be more debilitating. For example, when there was a blackout throughout a large part of the East and Midwest in the summer of 2003, many felt that the overly centralized nature of the nation's power grid was a major source of this crisis.[14] However, these structures tend to be inflexible and insensitive to subtle differences across products, regions, or clients. Prior to the shift, Microsoft had two divisions split along technology lines—one for applications and one for operating systems. This promoted efficiency and coordination, and helped generate integrated products. At this stage of the organization's development, the strategic goal was to produce software that was so well-integrated that one did not need consulting services like those offered by IBM. Although this worked to some degree, the perception was that it did not allow for enough creativity, innovation, or specific focus on different markets, and thus when the strategic goal changed, the structure needed to change as well. The fear with the new structure, of course, would be that one of the new independent divisions might generate a product or service that was incompatible with other Microsoft products or services—or worse—steal business from one of the other Microsoft divisions. Thus, in general, no one structure is always the best.

Functional structures are most appropriate in stable, predictable environments, where demand for resources can be well anticipated and coordination requirements between jobs can be refined and standardized over consistent repetitions of activity. This type of structure also helps support organizations that compete on cost, because efficiency is central to make this strategy work. Divisional structures are most appropriate in unstable, unpredictable environments, where it is difficult to anticipate demands for resources, and coordination requirements between jobs are not consistent over time. This type of structure also helps support organizations that compete on differentiation or innovation, because flexible responsiveness is central to making this strategy work. Indeed, in the words of Microsoft founder Bill Gates, "we are now holding the leaders of our new business divisions accountable to think and act as if they are independent businesses so that will give us the flexibility to respond more quickly to changes in technology and the marketplace."[15]

Structure and the Nature of Jobs

Finally, moving from big-picture issues to lower-level specifics, the type of organization structure also has implications for the design of jobs. Jobs in functional structures need to be narrow and highly specialized, and people tend to work alone. Workers in these structures (even middle managers) tend to have little decision-making authority or responsibility for managing coordination between themselves and others. Jobs in divisional structures need to be more holistic, with people working in teams that tend to have greater decision-making authority. This, in turn, has implications for people who would assume the jobs created in functional versus divisional structures.

For example, managers of divisional structures often need to be more experienced or high in cognitive ability relative to managers of functional structures.[16] The relatively smaller scope and routine nature of jobs created in centralized and functional structures make them less sensitive to individual differences between workers. This is an important point because as the "Competing through Globalization" box shows, the degree to which work is routine versus nonroutine is an important determinant of whether or not it can be automated or shipped overseas. The nature of the structure also has implications for relationships, in the sense that in centralized and functional structures people tend to think of fairness in terms or rules and procedures, whereas in decentralized and divisional structures, they tend to think of fairness in terms of outcomes and how they are treated interpersonally.[17]

In our next section we cover specific approaches for analyzing and designing jobs. Although all of these approaches are viable, each focuses on a single, isolated job. These approaches do not necessarily consider how that single job fits into the overall work flow or structure of the organization. Thus, to use these techniques effectively, we have to understand the organization as a whole. Without this big-picture appreciation, we might redesign a job in a way that might be good for that one job but out of line with the work flow, structure, or strategy of the organization. In an effectively structured organization, people not only know how their job fits into the bigger picture, they know how everyone else fits as well. Thus, when one of Microsoft's managers says, "I'm not confused about who to go to in order to get something done—there's greater clarity now," this is a sign that the new structure may be meeting the internal needs of the organization's members.[18]

Job Analysis

Job analysis refers to the process of getting detailed information about jobs.[19] Job analysis has deep historical roots. For example, in his description of the "just" state, Socrates argued that society needed to recognize three things. First, there are individual differences in aptitudes for work, meaning that individuals differ in their abilities. Second, unique aptitude requirements exist for different occupations. Third, to achieve high-quality performance, society must attempt to place people in occupations that best suit their aptitudes. In other words, for society (or an organization) to succeed, it must have detailed information about the requirements of jobs (through job analysis) and it must ensure that a match exists between the job requirements and individuals' aptitudes (through selection).[20]

> **Job analysis**
> The process of getting detailed information about jobs.

Whereas Socrates was concerned with the larger society, it is even more important for organizations to understand and match job requirements and people to achieve high-quality performance. This is particularly true in today's competitive marketplace. Thus the information gained through job analysis is of utmost importance; it has great value to both human resource and line managers.

The Importance of Job Analysis to HR Managers

Job analysis is such an important activity to HR managers that it has been called the building block of everything that personnel does.[21] This statement refers to the fact that almost every human resource management program requires some type of information that is gleaned from job analysis: selection, performance appraisal, training and development, job evaluation, career planning, work redesign, and human resource planning.[22]

Wanted: Jobs That Do Not Travel Well

In 1999, then-President Bill Clinton visited Hazard, Kentucky, for the grand opening of one of the largest call centers ever built in the United States. Clinton said "I came here to show America who you are. I want people to know a lot of the good things are going on here." This was a shining moment for this small Appalachian town, but a mere four years later, the sprawling red brick call center that used to house 3,000 workers now stands empty. The jobs that once defined this facility have moved on—not just once but in some cases two or three times. The first stops for these jobs were the Philippines and Costa Rica, followed next by a stint in India and El Salvador. Many of those jobs then went on to China where they will probably stay until they are automated and then eliminated altogether.

Far from being an isolated case that happens only to U.S. workers, the call center phenomenon has been replicated with other industries in other countries. For example, work that used to be performed by Siemen's workers in Germany in 1999 has also moved twice in the ensuing years. As one German labor representative noted, "First it was Hungary, then Lithuania, and next will be Estonia. We are not going to be able to keep up with every low wage country."

After coming out of its last economic recession, the United States experienced its first "jobless recovery," that is, one marked by increased revenue growth and productivity, but stagnant or even reduced hiring. The lag of job growth in the United States has many concerned about the potential for high unemployment rates and a potentially large reduction in the standard of living. Understanding why this has oc-

Work Redesign. As previously discussed, job analysis and job design are interrelated. Often a firm will seek to redesign work to make it more efficient or effective. To redesign the work, detailed information about the existing job(s) must be available. In addition, redesigning a job will, in fact, be similar to analyzing a job that does not yet exist.

Human Resource Planning. In human resource planning, planners analyze an organization's human resource needs in a dynamic environment and develop activities that enable a firm to adapt to change. This planning process requires accurate information about the levels of skill required in various jobs to ensure that enough individuals are available in the organization to meet the human resource needs of the strategic plan.[23]

Selection. Human resource selection identifies the most qualified applicants for employment. To identify which applicants are most qualified, it is first necessary to determine the tasks that will be performed by the individual hired and the knowledge, skills, and abilities the individual must have to perform the job effectively. This information is gained through job analysis.[24]

Training. Almost every employee hired by an organization will require training. Some training programs may be more extensive than others, but all require the trainer

curred and what could be done to stop it has been an important goal for both politicians and workers alike. Indeed, any young person thinking about what career to choose might very well be interested in knowing what are the characteristics of jobs that make them more or less portable.

In general, the major factor determining whether a job travels well is the degree to which its activities are routine versus nonroutine. Routine jobs are highly predictable and their requirements can be easily summarized. As MIT economist Frank Levy notes, "If you can really write the whole job description down on paper, then someone else can do it." Nonroutine jobs are more variable, and their lack of stability can be traced to one of two primary sources. First, some jobs require complex pattern recognition skills that can only

be developed with many years of experience or training. These jobs are difficult both to teach and to learn because the patterns may rarely repeat themselves exactly the same way each time. Second, some jobs are nonroutine because they involve subtle communication and interpersonal skills that need to be executed in a face-to-face context. The need for physical proximity and sensitivity to the cultural milieu makes these jobs very difficult to offshore or automate.

In addition to work at call centers and production facilities that stamp out standardized products, this is bad news for jobs like sewing machine operator, word processor, telephone operator, travel agent, and computer programmer, but good news for jobs like manager, systems engineer, artist/designer, management consultant, and educator. Edu-

cation will surely be a critical factor in securing a stable job, with an ever-increasing premium on a college degree or an advanced college degree, but not all education ensures secure employment. Straightforward technical training like that experienced by computer programmers will be less helpful relative to skills in the "softer" areas of leadership and interpersonal skills. As Robert Best, chief information officer at UNUMProvidence Corporation concludes, "You used to be able to get away with being a technical nerd five years ago. Those days are over now."

SOURCE: D. Morse, "Kentucky Answered the Call of the Future—But Got Bad News," *The Wall Street Journal* (March 9, 2004), pp. 1–2; J. Ewing, "Is Siemens Still German?" *BusinessWeek* (May 17, 2004), pp. 50–51; P. Coy, "The Future of Work," *BusinessWeek* (March 22, 2004), pp. 50–52.

to have identified the tasks performed in the job to ensure that the training will prepare individuals to perform their jobs effectively.[25]

Performance Appraisal. Performance appraisal deals with getting information about how well each employee is performing in order to reward those who are effective, improve the performance of those who are ineffective, or provide a written justification for why the poor performer should be disciplined. Through job analysis, the organization can identify the behaviors and results that distinguish effective performance from ineffective performance.[26]

Career Planning. Career planning entails matching an individual's skills and aspirations with opportunities that are or may become available in the organization. This matching process requires that those in charge of career planning know the skill requirements of the various jobs. This allows them to guide individuals into jobs in which they will succeed and be satisfied.

Job Evaluation. The process of job evaluation involves assessing the relative dollar value of each job to the organization to set up internally equitable pay structures. If pay structures are not equitable, employees will be dissatisfied and quit, or they will not see the benefits of striving for promotions. To put dollar values on jobs, it is necessary to get information about different jobs to determine which jobs deserve higher pay than others.[27]

"There has never been a proven case against IBM that any of its employees have suffered any adverse effects from chemical exposure." That was the standard line that manager Beth Deisner-Gee was trained to recite to any employees who complained to her about the chemical odors that often pervaded their workplace. She had used this line many times, and thus recognized it immediately when the company doctor who was treating her husband for brain cancer mentioned to her that "By the way, there has never been a proven case that the IBM work environment causes cancer or any related illness." Her husband died two weeks after hearing this pronouncement.

Despite the standard denials, however, there has been growing concern about the safety associated with working in "clean rooms" at IBM and other semiconductor chip manufacturers. Although one tends to associate occupational dangers more with dirty environments like those encountered in the coal mining industry, the ironically named "clean rooms" associated with chip manufacturing are anything but pristine. A clean room is a highly controlled manufacturing environment that tightly limits the concentration of airborne particles. Compared to a typical office building, where a single cubic foot of air might contain 1,000,000 particles as large as 0.5 microns (for reference, the width of a human hair is roughly 100 microns), a clean room is designed to never allow more than 100 particles that size. This level of control is often needed for highly sensitive manufacturing work such as that associated with chip production.

Despite their name, however, clean rooms are actually filled with many potentially toxic substances, not the least of which is arsine gas that can kill on contact if inhaled. IBM is currently involved in over 250 lawsuits involving workers who

The Importance of Job Analysis to Line Managers

Job analysis is clearly important to the HR department's various activities, but it may not be as clear why it is important to line managers. There are many reasons. First, managers must have detailed information about all the jobs in their work group to understand the work-flow process. Earlier in this chapter we noted the importance of understanding the work-flow process—specifically, identifying the tasks performed and the knowledge, skills, and abilities required to perform them. In addition, an understanding of this work-flow process is essential if a manager chooses to redesign certain aspects to increase efficiency or effectiveness.

Second, managers need to understand the job requirements to make intelligent hiring decisions. Very seldom do employees get hired by the human resource department without a manager's input. Managers will often interview prospective applicants and recommend who should receive a job offer. However, if the manager does not clearly understand what tasks are performed on the job and the skills necessary to perform them, the hiring decision may result in employees whom the manager "likes" but who are not capable of performing the job successfully.

Third, a manager is responsible for ensuring that each individual is performing satisfactorily (or better). This requires the manager to evaluate how well each person is

feel they were chemically poisoned at work. In many ways, their experience reflects the broader problems of managing safety in an age when competitive pressures need to be balanced against the welfare of workers and the state of the current knowledge base regarding chemical exposure.

With respect to the current knowledge base, there are over 100,000 commercial chemicals used across various industries in the United States each year, and only 500 to 1,000 have ever been studied on their own, let alone in conjunction with other factors. If someone in business had to wait for 10–20 years to perform controlled systematic studies of the long-term effects of all of these chemicals, very little work would ever get done. Retrospective clinical studies that start with sick patients and then try to work backwards to trace their sickness to a single isolated chemical are also notoriously ambiguous because there are always hundreds of confounding factors other than the one single chemical that may explain the problem. Thus, the knowledge base is simply insufficient to justify many prescriptions.

Even where knowledge exists, it is often difficult to reliably apply this knowledge in real world manufacturing contexts that are not necessarily as tightly controlled as a standard scientific laboratory. Although many formalized procedures have been put into place to prevent workers from being exposed to toxic substances, many workers feel that under the pressure to get the job done, shortcuts are often taken that put the workers at risk. As one worker notes, "On paper, all the t's are crossed and the i's are dotted, but when you get to the reality of the situation, shortcuts are taken." In fact, the workers themselves often complain about the safety procedures as being too restrictive and time consuming, and are often their own worst enemy when it comes to promoting safe work practices.

The combination of lack of knowledge, the need for innovation and speed in manufacturing operations, and the inherent unreliability of human workers makes for a volatile fusion in many work contexts, and this is certainly the case in clean rooms. The evidence may never be able to definitively "prove" the case for one side versus another, and yet, decisions need to be made in a manner that allows for sustainable progress that meets production needs, while at the same time ensuring worker health and safety.

SOURCE: N. Varchaver, "What Really Happened in IBM's Clean Room?" *Fortune* (December 8, 2003), pp. 91–100; T. Poletti, "How Safe Are Clean Rooms?" *Mercury News* (January 18, 2004), pp. 8–9; L. Flynn, "Both Sides Like Chances in IBM Worker Safety Practices Trial," *The New York Times* (December 22, 2003), p. B1.

performing and to provide feedback to those whose performance needs improvement. Again, this requires that the manager clearly understand the tasks required in every job. It is also the manager's responsibility to ensure that the work is being done safely, knowing where potential hazards might manifest themselves and creating a climate where people feel free to interrupt the production process if dangerous conditions exist.[28] As the "Competing through Sustainability" box illustrates, balancing the needs for production and safety can be a difficult task, especially when one has less than complete knowledge regarding all the potential hazards in any given work environment.

Job Analysis Information

Nature of Information

Two types of information are most useful in job analysis: job descriptions and job specifications. A **job description** is a list of the tasks, duties, and responsibilities (TDRs) that a job entails. TDRs are observable actions. For example, a clerical job requires the jobholder to type. If you were to observe someone in that position for a day, you would certainly see some typing. When a manager attempts to evaluate job performance, it is most important to have detailed information about the work performed

Job description
A list of the tasks, duties, and responsibilities that a job entails.

149

TABLE 4.1

A Sample Job Description

Job Title: Maintenance Mechanic
General Description of Job: General maintenance and repair of all equipment used in the operations of a particular district. Includes the servicing of company vehicles, shop equipment, and machinery used on job sites.

1. *Essential Duty (40%):* *Maintenance of Equipment*
   Tasks: Keep a log of all maintenance performed on equipment. Replace parts and fluids according to maintenance schedule. Regularly check gauges and loads for deviances that may indicate problems with equipment. Perform nonroutine maintenance as required. May involve limited supervision and training of operators performing maintenance.

2. *Essential Duty (40%):* *Repair of Equipment*
   Tasks: Requires inspection of equipment and a recommendation that a piece be scrapped or repaired. If equipment is to be repaired, mechanic will take whatever steps are necessary to return the piece to working order. This may include a partial or total rebuilding of the piece using various hand tools and equipment. Will primarily involve the overhaul and troubleshooting of diesel engines and hydraulic equipment.

3. *Essential Duty (10%):* *Testing and Approval*
   Tasks: Ensure that all required maintenance and repair has been performed and that it was performed according to manufacturer specifications. Approve or reject equipment as being ready for use on a job.

4. *Essential Duty (10%):* *Maintain Stock*
   Tasks: Maintain inventory of parts needed for the maintenance and repair of equipment. Responsible for ordering satisfactory parts and supplies at the lowest possible cost.

Nonessential Functions
Other duties as assigned.

in the job (that is, the TDRs). This makes it possible to determine how well an individual is meeting each job requirement. Table 4.1 shows a sample job description.

A **job specification** is a list of the knowledge, skills, abilities, and other characteristics (KSAOs) that an individual must have to perform the job. *Knowledge* refers to factual or procedural information that is necessary for successfully performing a task. A *skill* is an individual's level of proficiency at performing a particular task. *Ability* refers to a more general enduring capability that an individual possesses. Finally, *other characteristics* might be personality traits such as one's achievement motivation or persistence. Thus KSAOs are characteristics about people that are not directly observable; they are observable only when individuals are carrying out the TDRs of the job. If someone applied for the clerical job discussed, you could not simply look at the individual to determine whether he or she possessed typing skills. However, if you were to observe that individual typing something, you could assess the level of typing skill. When a manager is attempting to fill a position, it is important to have accurate information about the characteristics a successful jobholder must have. This requires focusing on the KSAOs of each applicant.

Job specification
A list of the knowledge, skills, abilities, and other characteristics (KSAOs) that an individual must have to perform a job.

Sources of Job Analysis Information

In performing the job analysis, one question that often arises is, Who should make up the group of incumbents that are responsible for providing the job analysis information? Whatever job analysis method you choose, the process of job analysis entails obtaining information from people familiar with the job. We refer to these people as *subject-matter experts* because they are experts in their knowledge of the job.

In general, it will be useful to go to the job incumbent to get the most accurate information about what is actually done on the job. This is especially the case when it is difficult to monitor the person who does the job. However, particularly when the job analysis will be used for compensation purposes, incumbents might have an incentive to exaggerate their duties. Thus, you will also want to ask others familiar with the job, such as supervisors, to look over the information generated by the job incumbent. This serves as a check to determine whether what is being done is congruent with what is supposed to be done in the job. Although job incumbents and supervisors are the most obvious and frequently used sources of job analysis information, other sources can be helpful, particularly for service jobs.

It is important to understand the usefulness of different sources of job analysis information because this information is only as good as the source. Research has revealed some interesting findings regarding various sources of job analysis information, particularly regarding job incumbents and supervisors.

One question is whether supervisors and incumbents agree in their job analysis ratings. Some research has demonstrated significant differences in the job analysis ratings provided from these two different sources.[29] However, other research has found greater agreement between supervisors and subordinates when rating general job duties than when rating specific tasks.[30] One conclusion that can be drawn from this research is that incumbents may provide the most accurate estimates of the actual time spent performing job tasks. However, supervisors may be a more accurate source of information about the importance of job duties. Incumbents also seem more accurate in terms of assessing safety-related risk factors associated with various aspects of work, and in general the further one moves up the organizational hierarchy, the less accurate the risk assessments.[31]

Another question is whether a job incumbent's own performance level is related to the job analysis ratings. Although it is intuitively appealing to think that individuals who perform well in a job might give different ratings than individuals who do not perform well, research has not borne this out. One frequently cited study compared the job analysis ratings of effective and ineffective managers and found that they tended to give the same ratings despite their performance level.[32] However, more recent research has also examined the relationship between job analysis and employee performance. In this research no differences were observed between high and low performers regarding the tasks and KSAOs generated, the ratings made regarding the time spent, or importance of the tasks.[33] However, differences have been observed in the types of critical incidents generated[34] and the ratings of the level of effectiveness of various incidents.[35] Thus, research at present seems inconclusive regarding the relationship between the performance level of the job analyst and the job analysis information she or he provides.

Job Analysis Methods

There are various methods for analyzing jobs and no "one best way." In this section we discuss three methods for analyzing jobs: the position analysis questionnaire, the task analysis inventory, and the job analysis system. Although most managers may not have time to use each of these techniques in the exact manner suggested, the three provide some anchors for thinking about broad approaches, task-focused approaches, and person-oriented approaches to conducting job analysis.

Position Analysis Questionnaire (PAQ)

We lead this section off with the PAQ because this is one of the broadest and most well-researched instruments for analyzing jobs. Moreover, its emphasis on inputs, processes, relationships, and outputs is consistent with the work flow analysis approach that we used in leading off this chapter (Figure 4.1).

The PAQ is a standardized job analysis questionnaire containing 194 items.[36] These items represent work behaviors, work conditions, and job characteristics that can be generalized across a wide variety of jobs. They are organized into six sections:

1. *Information input*—Where and how a worker gets information needed to perform the job.
2. *Mental processes*—The reasoning, decision making, planning, and information processing activities that are involved in performing the job.
3. *Work output*—The physical activities, tools, and devices used by the worker to perform the job.
4. *Relationships with other persons*—The relationships with other people required in performing the job.
5. *Job context*—The physical and social contexts where the work is performed.
6. *Other characteristics*—The activities, conditions, and characteristics other than those previously described that are relevant to the job.

The job analyst is asked to determine whether each item applies to the job being analyzed. The analyst then rates the item on six scales: extent of use, amount of time, importance to the job, possibility of occurrence, applicability, and special code (special rating scales used with a particular item). These ratings are submitted to the PAQ headquarters, where a computer program generates a report regarding the job's scores on the job dimensions.

Research has indicated that the PAQ measures 32 dimensions and 13 overall dimensions of jobs (listed in Table 4.2) and that a given job's scores on these dimensions can be very useful. The significant database has linked scores on certain dimensions to scores on subtests of the General Aptitude Test Battery (GATB). Thus knowing the dimension scores provides some guidance regarding the types of abilities that are necessary to perform the job. Obviously, this technique provides information about the work performed in a format that allows for comparisons across jobs, whether those jobs are similar or dissimilar. Another advantage of the PAQ is that it covers the work context as well as inputs, outputs, and processes.

TABLE 4.2

Overall Dimensions of the Position Analysis Questionnaire

Decision/communication/general responsibilities
Clerical/related activities
Technical/related activities
Service/related activities
Regular day schedule versus other work schedules
Routine/repetitive work activities
Environmental awareness
General physical activities
Supervising/coordinating other personnel
Public/customer/related contact activities
Unpleasant/hazardous/demanding environment
Nontypical work schedules

In spite of its widespread use, the PAQ is not without problems. One problem is that to fill out the test, an employee needs the reading level of a college graduate; this disqualifies some job incumbents from the PAQ. In fact, it is recommended that only job analysts trained in how to use the PAQ should complete the questionnaire, rather than job incumbents or supervisors. Indeed, the ratings of job incumbents tend to be lower in reliability relative to ratings from supervisors or trained job analysts.[37] A second problem associated with the PAQ is that its general, standardized format leads to rather abstract characterizations of jobs. Thus it does not lend itself well to describing the specific, concrete task activities that comprise the actual job, and it is not ideal for developing job descriptions or redesigning jobs. Methods that do focus on this aspect of the work are needed if this is the goal.

Task Analysis Inventory

The **task analysis inventory** refers to several different methods, each with slight variations. However, common to these approaches is the focus on analyzing all the tasks performed in the focal job. (It is not uncommon to have over 100 tasks.)

Task analysis inventory
The process of identifying the tasks, knowledge, skills and behaviors that need to be emphasized in training.

For example, the task inventory–CODAP method[38] entails asking subject matter experts (SMEs) to generate a list of the tasks performed in a job. Once this list has been developed, the SMEs rate each task on dimensions such as the relative amount of time spent on the task, the frequency of task performance, the relative importance of the task, the relative difficulty of the task, and whether the task can be learned on the job relatively quickly. These ratings are then subjected to the CODAP computer program that organizes the tasks into dimensions of similar tasks.

Task inventories focus on providing detailed information about the work performed in a given job. The concrete and job-specific nature of the judgments made in a task inventory result in relatively higher levels of agreement between different sources like incumbents and supervisors.[39] Also the detail of the information can be helpful in developing both selection exam plans and performance appraisal criteria. Although a task inventory might indirectly suggest the types of KSAOs people might need to perform the job, these KSAOs do not come directly out of the process. Thus other approaches that do put the focus squarely on the people requirement associated with jobs have been developed.

Fleishman Job Analysis System[40]

Another job analysis technique that elicits information about the worker's characteristics is the Fleishman Job Analysis System (FJAS). This approach defines *abilities* as enduring attributes of individuals that account for differences in performance. The system is based on a taxonomy of abilities that adequately represent all the dimensions relevant to work. This taxonomy includes 52 cognitive, psychomotor, physical, and sensory abilities, listed in Table 4.3.[41]

The actual FJAS scales consist of descriptions of the ability, followed by behavioral benchmark examples of the different levels of the ability along a seven-point scale. An example of the written comprehension ability scale from the FJAS is presented in Figure 4.6.

In using the job analysis technique, SMEs are presented with each of the 52 scales. These experts indicate the point on the scale that best represents the level of that ability required in a particular job. These ratings provide an accurate picture of the ability requirements of the job. Substantial research has shown the value of this

TABLE 4.3

Abilities Included in the Fleishman Job Analysis System

1. Oral comprehension	27. Arm–hand steadiness
2. Written comprehension	28. Manual dexterity
3. Oral expression	29. Finger dexterity
4. Written expression	30. Wrist–finger speed
5. Fluency of ideas	31. Speed of limb movement
6. Originality	32. Static strength
7. Memorization	33. Explosive strength
8. Problem sensitivity	34. Dynamic strength
9. Mathematical reasoning	35. Trunk strength
10. Number facility	36. Extent flexibility
11. Deductive reasoning	37. Dynamic flexibility
12. Inductive reasoning	38. Gross body coordination
13. Information ordering	39. Gross body equilibrium
14. Category flexibility	40. Stamina
15. Speed of closure	41. Near vision
16. Flexibility of closure	42. Far vision
17. Spatial orientation	43. Visual color discrimination
18. Visualization	44. Night vision
19. Perceptual speed	45. Peripheral vision
20. Selective attention	46. Depth perception
21. Time sharing	47. Glare sensitivity
22. Control precision	48. Hearing sensitivity
23. Multilimb coordination	49. Auditory attention
24. Response orientation	50. Sound localization
25. Rate control	51. Speech recognition
26. Reaction time	52. Speech clarity

general approach for human resource activities such as career development, selection, and training.[42]

The Occupational Information Network (O*NET)

The *Dictionary of Occupational Titles* (DOT) was born during the 1930s and served as a vehicle for helping the new public employment system link the demand for skills and the supply of skills in the U.S. workforce. Given the high unemployment rate during that time (the "Great Depression"), federal intervention was perceived as being necessary to help create a match between workers and employers. The DOT provided descriptive information regarding over 12,000 jobs, as well as some of the requirements of successful job incumbents. The DOT was used by both public employment agencies and private employers to help efficiently staff jobs. It was also a valuable source for workers because it listed the skills and educational requirements they would need to have or develop to aspire to certain occupations.

Although this system served the country well for over 60 years, it became clear to officials at the U.S. Department of Labor that jobs in the new economy were so qualitatively different from jobs in the old economy, that the DOT no longer served its purpose. Technological changes in the nature of work, global competition, and a shift from stable, fixed manufacturing jobs to a more flexible, dynamic, service-based economy were quickly making the system obsolete.[43]

For all these reasons, the Department of Labor abandoned the DOT in 1998 and developed an entirely new system for classifying jobs referred to as the Occupational

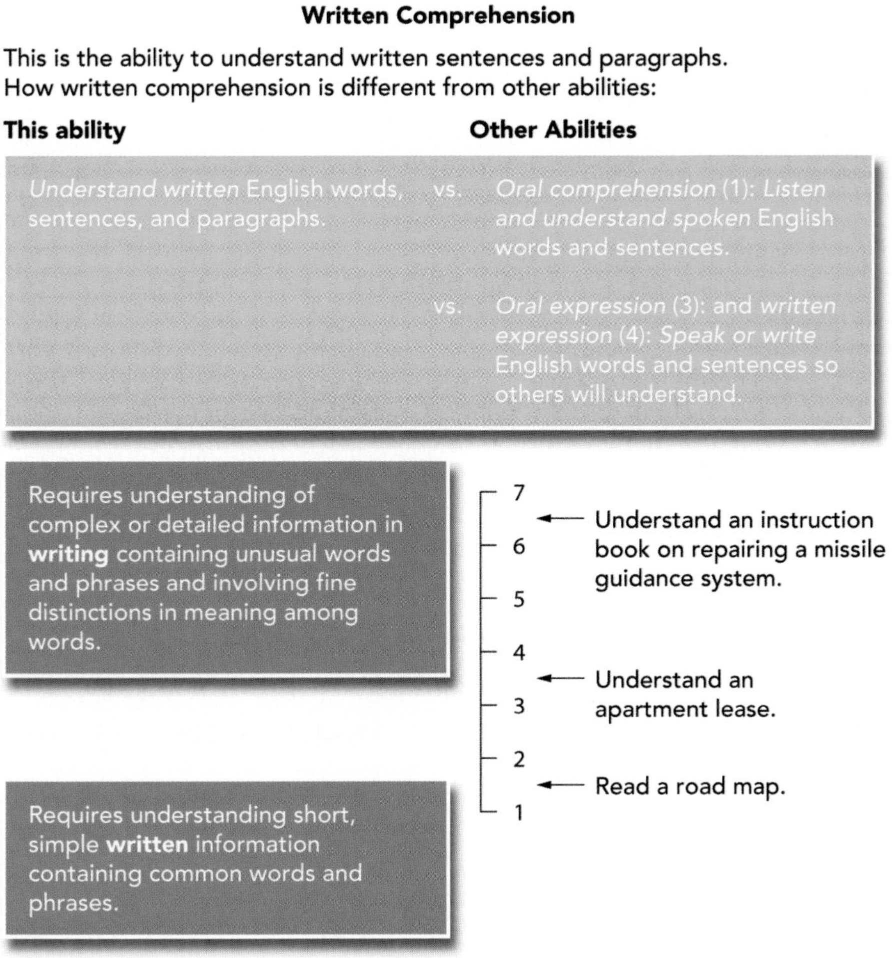

Written Comprehension

This is the ability to understand written sentences and paragraphs. How written comprehension is different from other abilities:

This ability		Other Abilities
Understand written English words, sentences, and paragraphs.	vs.	*Oral comprehension (1): Listen and understand spoken English words and sentences.*
	vs.	*Oral expression (3): and written expression (4): Speak or write English words and sentences so others will understand.*

FIGURE 4.6

Example of an Ability from the Fleishman Job Analysis System

Requires understanding of complex or detailed information in **writing** containing unusual words and phrases and involving fine distinctions in meaning among words.

7 —
6 — ← Understand an instruction book on repairing a missile guidance system.
5 —
4 —
3 — ← Understand an apartment lease.
2 —
1 — ← Read a road map.

Requires understanding short, simple **written** information containing common words and phrases.

SOURCE: E. A. Fleishman and M. D. Mumford, "Evaluating Classifications of Job Behavior: A Construct Validation of the Ability Requirements Scales," *Personnel Psychology* 44 (1991), pp. 523–76. The complete set of ability requirement scales, along with instructions for their use, may be found in E. A. Fleishman, *Fleishman Job Analysis Survey (F-JAS)* (Palo Alto, CA: Consulting Psychologists Press, 1992). Used with permission.

Information Network, or O*NET. Instead of relying on fixed job titles and narrow task descriptions, the O*NET uses a common language that generalizes across jobs to describe the abilities, work styles, work activities, and work context required for various occupations that are more broadly defined (e.g., instead of the 12,000 jobs in the DOT, the O*NET describes only 1,000 occupations).[44]

Although it is still being developed, the O*NET is already being used by many employers and employment agencies. For example, after closing its Seattle-based headquarters, Boeing used the O*NET system to help find new jobs for the workers who were laid off because of the impending move.[45] The State of Texas has used the O*NET to identify emerging occupations within the state whose requisite knowledge, skills, and abilities are underrepresented in the current occupational system. This information will be used to help train Texas residents to be prepared for the jobs of the future. Finally, educational organizations like the Boys and Girls Clubs of

"If You Want the Job Done Right . . ."

At a time when many organizations are increasingly trying to create competitive advantage by attracting, retaining, and developing human resources, it is also instructive to note areas where the goal is to totally eliminate human involvement from certain transactions. Indeed, in the last few years, technological developments have allowed an unprecedented shift of lower-level work from many organizations' workers to their customers. Where one used to encounter a "customer service representative," one now encounters a "self-service kiosk."

Kiosks are becoming increasingly ubiquitous in today's economy, and many different technological, cultural, and demographic developments are fueling the self-service movement. Technologically, many lower level jobs have been made so simple by technological advancements that it literally takes no skill or training whatsoever to perform certain transactions, thus eliminating the need for a worker to manage the transaction. For example, paying for items at the grocery store where every product is bar coded is so simple that any customer can easily perform the task without the aid of any kind of specialized staff member. Indeed, from 1999 to 2004, the percentage of grocery stores that offered self-service checkout went from 6 percent to 96 percent, representing one of the fastest and most comprehensive innovation transfers ever recorded.

Culturally, many customers are now very computer savvy and, unlike their parents or grandparents, trust the technology and have no qualms about interacting with automated equipment. As one technology expert has noted, "If you asked people even a few years ago which would be more likely to make a mistake, an ATM or a cashier, they would have said

America have used the O*NET to help design activities for children from disadvantaged backgrounds that would improve their standing on skills that are likely to be needed by future employers.[46]

Although these examples show its value for employers, the O*NET was also designed to help job seekers. To see if you think this new system meets the goal of promoting "the effective education, training, counseling, and employment needs of the American workforce," visit its website yourself at **http://online.onetcenter.org/** and see if the skills it lists for your current job or your "dream job" match what you know from your own experiences and expectations.

Dynamic Elements of Job Analysis

Although we tend to view jobs as static and stable, in fact, jobs tend to change and evolve over time. Those who occupy or manage the jobs often make minor, cumulative adjustments to the job that try to match either changing conditions in the environment or personal preferences for how to conduct the work.[47] Indeed, although there are numerous sources for error in the job analysis process,[48] most inaccuracy is likely to result from job descriptions simply being outdated. For this reason, in addian ATM. Now people would say a cashier." Indeed, Hilton Hotels offered self-check-in kiosk service back in 1999, but abandoned the service when customers showed little interest in it. Now, they are back at it, and intend to introduce kiosks back into 25 hotels in 2005.

Certainly, frequent fliers would fall under this category of technologically savvy customer, and hence, it should not be surprising to note that at the airport, there has been a 78 percent increase in the number of people who either obtain their boarding pass at a kiosk or simply print it out themselves at their home or office straight from the airlines' Web page. Northwest Airlines, one of the industry leaders in the self-service movement, has spent close to $10 million on self-service technology, and at its hub in Detroit one can even pay for the parking garage via a self-serve kiosk. Although this may seem like a large investment,

Northwest estimates that it saves $3.52 each time a customer takes advantage of some self-serve option.

In terms of demographics, because of the low scope and low pay for many of the positions that have been "kiosked," these jobs never attracted the best and brightest workers to begin with. Many incumbents of these jobs lacked social skills and the jobs themselves were dead-end propositions that often resulted in surly service. In addition, despite the fact that the jobs looked "idiot proof," the boring and low-scope nature of the work often resulted in errors caused by a lack of attention on the part of the worker. Clearly, the motivation to change one's initial seat assignment to a special seat (such as the aisle or exit row) is much higher when it's your seat and you do this only once a month, relative to when a person asks you to do this for them one thousand times a day.

Of course, there are still some glitches in these automated systems, and despite the cost efficiencies, some organizations think they can compete better by making the customer service encounter a "warm and friendly personal episode" that will create a positive and lasting impression in the consumer's mind. Time will tell whether improving the quality of service provided by human workers or eliminating the human element altogether is a more effective means of competing in various business markets. Increasingly, however, it looks like many customers feel that there is no service like self-service.

SOURCE: B. Horowitz, "It's a Do-It-Yourself" World," *USA Today* (April 27, 2004), pp. C1–C3; T. Newcombe, "Self-Service Takes Off," *Government Technology* (November 20, 2003), p. 33; B. De Lollis, "Hilton to Try Self-Service Kiosks in NYC, Chicago," *USA Today* (September 3, 2003), p. C1.

tion to statically defining the job, the job analysis process must also detect changes in the nature of jobs.

For example, in today's world of rapidly changing products and markets, some people have begun to question whether the concept of the job is simply a social artifact that has outlived its usefulness. Indeed, many researchers and practitioners are pointing to a trend referred to as "dejobbing" in organizations. This trend consists of viewing organizations as a field of work needing to be done rather than a set of discrete jobs held by specific individuals. For example, at Amazon.com, HR director Scott Pitasky notes, "Here, a person might be in the same 'job,' but three months later be doing completely different work."[49] This means Amazon.com puts more emphasis on broad worker specifications ("entrepreneurial and customer-focused") than on detailed job descriptions ("HTML programming") that may not be descriptive one year down the road.

Advances in technology have made it hard to keep up with some of the major changes in jobs, and automation has led to the elimination of certain jobs or the off-shoring of tasks or even the shifting of certain tasks from the worker to the customer. Indeed, as the "Competing through Technology" box shows, many low-scope features of some tasks have been taken on directly by consumers, as increasingly transactions become a "do-it-yourself" affair. This has created a win-win situation where workers shed boring, routine tasks, customers provide themselves better or faster service, and the organization saves money in terms of executing the transaction.

These changes in the nature of work and expanded use of "project-based" organizational structures require the type of broader understanding that comes from an analysis of work flows. Because the work can change so rapidly and it is impossible to rewrite job descriptions every week, more flexibility is needed in the writing of job descriptions and specifications. However, legal requirements (as discussed in Chapter 3) may discourage firms from writing flexible job descriptions. Thus firms seeking to use their employees as a source of competitive advantage must balance the need for flexibility with the need for legal documentation. This presents one of the major challenges faced by HRM departments in the next decade. Rather than a passive, job-analytic approach, these types of changes require an active approach to job design such as those discussed in our next section.

Job Design

So far we have approached the issue of managing work in a passive way, focusing only on understanding what gets done, how it gets done, and the skills required to get it done. Although this is necessary, it is a very static view of jobs, in that jobs must already exist and that they are already assumed to be structured in the one best way. However, a manager may often be faced with a situation in which the work unit does not yet exist, requiring jobs within the work unit to be designed from scratch. Sometimes work loads within an existing work unit are increased, or work group size is decreased while the same work load is required, a trend increasingly observed with the movement toward downsizing.[50] Finally, sometimes the work is not being performed in the most efficient manner. In these cases, a manager may decide to change the way that work is done in order for the work unit to perform more effectively and efficiently. This requires redesigning the existing jobs. For example, many organizations are currently developing "lean production systems." This is a systematic approach for identifying the total "value-added" of various activities along the production line, as well as the primary "sources of defects." Once identified, the entire production system is engineered to emphasize value-added activities, strip away nonproductive activities, and eliminate causes of defects.[51]

Job design is the process of defining how work will be performed and the tasks that will be required in a given job. **Job redesign** refers to changing the tasks or the way work is performed in an existing job. To effectively design jobs, one must thoroughly understand the job as it exists (through job analysis) and its place in the larger work unit's work-flow process (work-flow analysis). Having a detailed knowledge of the tasks performed in the work unit and in the job, a manager then has many alternative ways to design a job. This can be done most effectively through understanding the trade-offs between certain design approaches.

Research has identified four basic approaches that have been used among the various disciplines (such as psychology, management, engineering, and ergonomics) that have dealt with job design issues.[52] Although these four approaches comprehensively capture the historical approaches to this topic, one still needs to go below the category level to get a full appreciation of the exact nature of jobs and how they can be changed.[53] All jobs can be characterized in terms of how they fare according to each approach; thus a manager needs to understand the trade-offs of emphasizing one approach over another. In the next section we discuss each of these approaches and ex-

Job design
The process of defining the way work will be performed and the tasks that will be required in a given job.

Job redesign
The process of changing the tasks or the way work is performed in an existing job.

amine the implications of each for the design of jobs. Table 4.4 displays how jobs are characterized along each of these dimensions.

Strategic Use of HRM

The strategic importance of job redesign can be seen clearly in the recent experiences of Beth Israel Deaconess Medical Center. After a troubled merger with another hospital, dissatisfaction among the nursing staff had led to both high turnover and difficulty in recruiting new nurses to fill the positions of those who had left. In one year alone, over 200 nurses left the hospital, and since the cost of replacing a nurse is close to $35,000 each, this was a million-dollar problem. Dianne Anderson was hired as the new vice president of patient services and immediately went to work redesigning the jobs and then advertising the changes.

Working with teams of doctors and lawyers, Anderson rewrote the job descriptions for the nursing staff, giving them more autonomy and discretion to make their own decisions. Much of the administrative work that had traditionally fallen on the nursing staff was shifted over to newly hired clerical workers, allowing the nurses to focus on what got them into nursing in the first place—helping people. Opportunities to learn new skills were created via tuition reimbursement programs, and nurses that took those opportunities were shown new career paths that led to better jobs. All of these changes were then extolled in a radio and TV campaign that touted the hospital as a great place to work. In a period of just two years, turnover rates dropped from 16 percent to 6 percent, and vacancy rates (open positions) at the hospital went from 15 percent to under 5 percent.

SOURCE: G. Koprowski, "A Boston Hospital Finds a Cure for the Turnover Disease," *Workforce*, October 2003, pp. 77–78.

Mechanistic Approach

The mechanistic approach has roots in classical industrial engineering. The focus of the mechanistic approach is identifying the simplest way to structure work that maximizes efficiency. This most often entails reducing the complexity of the work to provide more human resource efficiency—that is, making the work so simple that anyone can be trained quickly and easily to perform it. This approach focuses on designing jobs around the concepts of task specialization, skill simplification, and repetition.

Scientific management was one of the earliest and best-known statements of the mechanistic approach.[54] According to this approach, productivity could be maximized by taking a scientific approach to the process of designing jobs. Scientific management first sought to identify the "one best way" to perform the job. This entailed performing time-and-motion studies to identify the most efficient movements for workers to make. Once the best way to perform the work is identified, workers should be selected based on their ability to do the job, they should be trained in the standard "one best way" to perform the job, and they should be offered monetary incentives to motivate them to work at their highest capacity.

The scientific management approach was built upon in later years, resulting in a mechanistic approach that calls for jobs to be designed so that they are very simple and lack any significant meaningfulness. By designing jobs in this way, the organization reduces its need for high-ability individuals and thus becomes less dependent on individual workers. Individuals are easily replaceable—that is, a new employee can be trained to perform the job quickly and inexpensively.

TABLE 4.4

Characterizing Jobs on Different Dimensions of Job Design

The motivational job design approach

1. *Autonomy:* Does the job allow freedom, independence, or discretion in work scheduling, sequence, methods, procedures, quality control, and other types of decisions?
2. *Intrinsic job feedback:* Do the work activities themselves provide direct, clear information about the effectiveness (in terms of quality and quantity) of job performance?
3. *Extrinsic job feedback:* Do other people in the organization (such as managers and coworkers) provide information about the effectiveness (in terms of quality and quantity) of job performance?
4. *Social interaction:* Does the job provide for positive social interaction (such as teamwork or coworker assistance)?
5. *Task/goal clarity:* Are the job duties, requirements, and goals clear and specific?
6. *Task variety:* Does the job have a variety of duties, tasks, and activities?
7. *Task identity:* Does the job require completion of a whole and identifiable piece of work? Does it give the incumbent a chance to do an entire piece of work from beginning to end?
8. *Ability/skill-level requirements:* Does the job require a high level of knowledge, skills, and abilities?
9. *Ability/skill variety:* Does the job require a variety of types of knowledge, skills, and abilities?
10. *Task significance:* Is the job significant and important compared with other jobs in the organization?
11. *Growth/learning:* Does the job allow opportunities for learning and growth in competence and proficiency?

The mechanistic job design approach

1. *Job specialization:* Is the job highly specialized in terms of purpose and/or activity?
2. *Specialization of tools and procedures:* Are the tools, procedures, materials, etc., used on this job highly specialized in terms of purpose?
3. *Task simplification:* Are the tasks simple and uncomplicated?
4. *Single activities:* Does the job require the incumbent to do only one task at a time? Does it not require the incumbent to do multiple activities at one time or in very close succession?
5. *Job simplification:* Does the job require relatively little skill and training time?
6. *Repetition:* Does the job require performing the same activity or activities repeatedly?
7. *Spare time:* Is there very little spare time between activities on this job?
8. *Automation:* Are many of the activities of this job automated or assisted by automation?

continued

SOURCE: Reprinted from *Organizational Dynamics*, Vol. 15, by M. A. Campion, et al., "Job Design: Approaches, Outcomes, and Trade-Offs." Copyright © 1987, with permission from Elsevier.

Motivational Approach

The motivational approach to job design has roots in organizational psychology and management literature and, in many ways, emerged as a reaction to mechanistic approaches to job design. It focuses on the job characteristics that affect psychological meaning and motivational potential, and it views attitudinal variables (such as satis-

The biological job design approach

1. *Strength:* Does the job require fairly little muscular strength?
2. *Lifting:* Does the job require fairly little lifting, and/or is the lifting of very light weights?
3. *Endurance:* Does the job require fairly little muscular endurance?
4. *Seating:* Are the seating arrangements on the job adequate (with ample opportunities to sit, comfortable chairs, good postural support, etc.)?
5. *Size difference:* Does the workplace allow for all size differences between people in terms of clearance, reach, eye height, leg room, etc.?
6. *Wrist movement:* Does the job allow the wrists to remain straight, without excessive movement?
7. *Noise:* Is the workplace free from excessive noise?
8. *Climate:* Is the climate at the workplace comfortable in terms of temperature and humidity, and is it free of excessive dust and fumes?
9. *Work breaks:* Is there adequate time for work breaks given the demands of the job?
10. *Shift work:* Does the job not require shift work or excessive overtime?

The perceptual–motor job design approach

1. *Lighting:* Is the lighting in the workplace adequate and free from glare?
2. *Displays:* Are the displays, gauges, meters, and computerized equipment used on this job easy to read and understand?
3. *Programs:* Are the programs in the computerized equipment for this job easy to learn and use?
4. *Other equipment:* Is the other equipment (all types) used on this job easy to learn and use?
5. *Printed job materials:* Are the printed materials used on this job easy to read and interpret?
6. *Workplace layout:* Is the workplace laid out so that the employee can see and hear well enough to perform the job?
7. *Information input requirements:* Is the amount of attention needed to perform this job fairly minimal?
8. *Information output requirements:* Is the amount of information that the employee must output on this job, in terms of both action and communication, fairly minimal?
9. *Information-processing requirements:* Is the amount of information that must be processed, in terms of thinking and problem solving, fairly minimal?
10. *Memory requirements:* Is the amount of information that must be remembered on this job fairly minimal?
11. *Stress:* Is there relatively little stress on this job?
12. *Boredom:* Are the chances of boredom on this job fairly small?

faction, intrinsic motivation, job involvement, and behavioral variables such as attendance and performance) as the most important outcomes of job design. The prescriptions of the motivational approach focus on increasing the complexity of jobs through such interventions as job enlargement, job enrichment, and the construction of jobs around sociotechnical systems.[55] Accordingly, a study of 213 different jobs found that the motivational attributes of jobs were positively related to the mental ability requirements of workers in those jobs.[56]

A model of how job design affects employee reactions is the "Job Characteristics Model."[57] According to this model, jobs can be described in terms of five characteristics. *Skill variety* is the extent to which the job requires a variety of skills to carry out the tasks. *Task identity* is the degree to which a job requires completing a "whole" piece of work from beginning to end. *Task significance* is the extent to which the job has an important impact on the lives of other people. *Autonomy* is the degree to which the job allows an individual to make decisions about the way the work will be carried out. *Feedback* is the extent to which a person receives clear information about performance effectiveness from the work itself.

These five job characteristics determine the motivating potential of a job by affecting the three critical psychological states of "experienced meaningfulness," "responsibility," and "knowledge of results." According to the model, when the core job characteristics (and thus the critical psychological states) are high, individuals will have a high level of internal work motivation. This is expected to result in higher quantity and quality of work as well as higher levels of job satisfaction.[58]

Job design interventions emphasizing the motivational approach tend to focus on increasing the motivating potential of jobs. Much of the work on job enlargement (broadening the types of tasks performed), job enrichment (empowering workers by adding more decision-making authority to jobs), and self-managing work teams has its roots in the motivational approach to job design. The critical psychological state one needs to create in the mind of the job incumbent is that the work is meaningful and that it contributes to accomplishing goals that are important to the individual.[59] Thus, although at some point it might be necessary to pay workers, it is even more important to show job incumbents why their jobs are important.

Finding and Keeping the Best Employees

A good example of how job design can be used to help retain the best employees can be seen in the experience of Atlanta law firm Alston & Bird. Whereas many paralegal workers complain about working long hours and unreasonable supervising attorneys, Alston & Bird have designed the paralegal job so that it entails a great deal of autonomy and clear communication channels between attorneys and paralegals. Paralegals work in teams, and together they generate their own collective schedules via job sharing and flexible work hours. The result: In an industry where turnover among paralegals averages 20 percent a year, turnover at Alston & Bird averages 7 percent a year. Moreover, when it comes time to fill the few vacancies that are created, the firm receives close to 15,000 applications for the 200 positions that are available, creating a highly desirable selection ratio. As one Alston & Bird employee notes, "I've got a tremendous amount of responsibility, and the lawyers respect me. I feel stimulated and challenged, and there are terrific opportunities to grow professionally. I can't imagine a more interesting job or a better place to work."

SOURCE: S. Greengard, "The Five-Alarm Job," *Workforce*, February 2004, pp. 43–48.

Biological Approach

The biological approach to job design comes primarily from the sciences of biomechanics (i.e., the study of body movements), work physiology, and occupational medicine, and it is usually referred to as *ergonomics*. **Ergonomics** is concerned with examining the interface between individuals' physiological characteristics and the physical work environment. The goal of this approach is to minimize physical strain on the worker by structuring the physical work environment around the way the human body works. It therefore focuses on outcomes such as physical fatigue, aches and pains, and health complaints.

The biological approach has been applied in redesigning equipment used in jobs that are physically demanding. Such redesign is often aimed at reducing the physical

Ergonomics
The interface between individuals' physiological characteristics and the physical work environment.

demands of certain jobs so that anyone can perform them. In addition, many biological interventions focus on redesigning machines and technology, such as adjusting the height of the computer keyboard to minimize occupational illnesses (like carpal tunnel syndrome). The design of chairs and desks to fit posture requirements is very important in many office jobs and is another example of the biological approach to job design. For example, one study found that having employees participate in an ergonomic redesign effort significantly reduced the number and severity of cumulative trauma disorders, lost production time, and restricted duty days.[60]

Often redesigning work to make it more worker-friendly also leads to increased efficiencies. For example, at International Truck and Engine Corporation, one of the most difficult aspects of truck production was pinning the axles to the truck frame. Traditionally, the frame was lowered onto the axle and a crew of six people, armed with oversized hammers and crowbars, forced the frame onto the axle. Because the workers could not see the bolts they had to tighten under the frame, the bolts were often not fastened properly, and many workers injured themselves in the process. After a brainstorming session, the workers and engineers figured that it would be better to flip the frame upside down and attach the axles from above instead of below. The result was a job that could be done twice as fast by half as many workers, who were much less likely to make mistakes or get injured.[61]

Because of the new Occupational Safety Health and Administration (OSHA) regulations that went into effect in 2001, one can expect that a number of employers will soon be looking to achieve the same kind of results from ergonomically focused changes in jobs. In particular, the regulations identify five specific high-risk work practices that employers need to avoid, including jobs that require a person to (a) use a keyboard for four hours straight without a break, (b) lift more than 75 pounds, (c) kneel or squat for more than two hours a day, (d) work with the back, neck, or wrists bent more than two hours a day, or (e) use large vibrating equipment such as chainsaws or jackhammers more than 30 minutes a day.[62] Although these new rules are controversial and may change over time, the fact that employers need to be vigilant about opportunities to improve the design of work for the benefit of both workers and shareholders is not likely to change.[63]

Perceptual–Motor Approach

The perceptual–motor approach to job design has roots in human-factors literature.[64] Whereas the biological approach focuses on physical capabilities and limitations, the perceptual–motor approach focuses on human mental capabilities and limitations. The goal is to design jobs in a way that ensures they do not exceed people's mental capabilities and limitations. This approach generally tries to improve reliability, safety, and user reactions by designing jobs to reduce their information-processing requirements. In designing jobs, one looks at the least capable worker and then constructs job requirements that an individual of that ability level could meet. Similar to the mechanistic approach, this approach generally decreases the job's cognitive demands.

Research on demanding jobs has made it clear than these can lead to fatigue, and depending upon the nature of the situation and the nature of the person, this can lead to dissatisfaction. In situations where the individual has little control over the pace of the demands and works in a context where there is low social support, high demands generally lead to low satisfaction. When the situation allows for control and provides social support, however, people often perceive the demands of the job as intrinsically motivating and enjoy the work, even though it creates fatigue.[65] In addition, some individuals that are high on "learning orientation" (i.e., motivated to learn new ideas and not afraid of making errors) also respond positively to demanding jobs, whereas those who have a "performance orientation" (i.e., motivated to avoid errors and caring little about learning) react negatively to highly demanding jobs.[66]

Recent changes in technological capacities hold the promise of helping to reduce job demands and errors, but in some cases, these developments have actually made the problem worse. The term "absence presence" has been coined to refer to the reduced attentive state that one might experience when simultaneously interacting with multiple media. For example, someone might be talking on a cell phone while driving a car, or surfing the net while attending a business meeting, or checking e-mail while preparing a presentation. In all these cases, the new technology serves as a source of distraction from the primary task, reducing performance and increasing the opportunities for errors.[67] Indeed, research shows that on complex tasks, even very short interruptions can break one's train of thought and derail performance. Thus, e-mail servers that have a feature that signals the arrival of each incoming message might best be turned off if the job incumbent cannot resist the temptation this creates to interrupt ongoing activity.[68]

Trade-Offs among Different Approaches to Job Design

A recent stream of research has aimed at understanding the trade-offs and implications of these different job design strategies.[69] Many authors have called for redesigning jobs according to the motivational approach so that the work becomes more psychologically meaningful. However, one study examined how the various approaches to job design are related to a variety of work outcomes. Table 4.5 summarizes the results. For example, in this study, job incumbents expressed higher satisfaction with jobs scoring high on the motivational approach. Also, jobs scoring high on the biological approach were ones for which incumbents expressed lower physical requirements. Finally, the motivational and mechanistic approaches were negatively related to each other, suggesting that designing jobs to maximize efficiency very likely results in a lower motivational component to those jobs.

Another recent study demonstrated that enlarging clerical jobs made workers more satisfied, less bored, more proficient at catching errors, and better at providing customer service. However, these enlarged jobs also had costs, such as higher training requirements, higher basic skill requirements, and higher compensation requirements based on job evaluation compensable factors.[70]

Although the motivational and mechanistic approaches to job design do work against one another somewhat, at the same time there is not a tight, one-on-one correspondence between the two. Thus, not all efficiency-producing changes result in dissatisfying work, and not all changes that promote satisfaction create inevitable inefficiencies. By carefully and simultaneously attending to both efficiency and satisfaction aspects of job redesign, managers can sometimes achieve the best of both worlds.[71] For example, at the new Indiana Heart Hospital in Indianapolis, much of the work was digitized in order to create a paperless organization. There are over 600 computer terminals placed throughout the facility, and the doctors and staff directly enter or access information from these terminals as needed. This has eliminated the need for nurses' stations, chart racks, medical records departments, file storage rooms, and copiers and has cut down paperwork, resulting in an increase in efficiency, but also increased job satisfaction by eliminating bureaucracy, allowing the staff more im-

JOB DESIGN APPROACH	POSITIVE OUTCOMES	NEGATIVE OUTCOMES
Motivational	Higher job satisfaction Higher motivation Greater job involvement Higher job performance Lower absenteeism	Increased training time Lower utilization levels Greater likelihood of error Greater chance of mental overload and stress
Mechanistic	Decreased training time Higher utilization levels Lower likelihood of error Less chance of mental overload and stress	Lower job satisfaction Lower motivation Higher absenteeism
Biological	Less physical effort Less physical fatigue Fewer health complaints Fewer medical incidents Lower absenteeism Higher job satisfaction	Higher financial costs because of changes in equipment or job environment
Perceptual–motor	Lower likelihood of error Lower likelihood of accidents Less chance of mental overload and stress Lower training time Higher utilization levels	Lower job satisfaction Lower motivation

TABLE 4.5

Summary of Outcomes from the Job Design Approaches

SOURCE: Reprinted from *Organizational Dynamics*, Vol. 15, by M. A. Campion, et al., "Job Design: Approaches, Outcomes, and Trade-Offs." Copyright © 1987, with permission from Elsevier.

mediate access to needed information. This has affected the bottom line by reducing the length of time a patient stays in the hospital from an average of five days at other hospitals to three days at Indiana Heart Hospital. This allows the hospital to process more patients per bed relative to the competition, giving them a direct source of competitive advantage.[72]

Finally, research has examined how job design approaches relate to compensation. Starting from the assumption that job evaluation (the process of determining the worth of jobs to organizations) links job design and market forces, researchers examined the relationship between job design approaches and both job evaluation results and pay. They found that jobs high on the motivational approach had higher job evaluation scores representing higher skill requirements and that these jobs had higher pay levels. Jobs high on the mechanistic and perceptual–motor dimensions had lower skill requirements and correspondingly lower wage rates. Finally, jobs high on the biological dimension had lower physical requirements and had a weak positive relationship to wage rates. Thus, it seems reasonable to conclude that jobs redesigned to increase the motivating potential result in higher costs in terms of ability requirements, training, and compensation.[73]

To summarize, in designing jobs it is important to understand the trade-offs inherent in focusing on one particular approach to job design. Managers who seek to design jobs in a way that maximizes all the outcomes for jobholders and the organization need to be aware of these different approaches, understand the costs and benefits associated with each, and balance them appropriately to give the organization a competitive advantage.

A Look Back

The chapter opening about Microsoft showed how drastically restructuring the nature of work could increase both the effectiveness and efficiency of operations. The specific changes in how work was designed created a better fit between the organization and its environment, as well as between the organization and its internal strategy.

Questions

1. Based on this chapter, how would you characterize the changes that were made in terms of the degree of centralization and departmentalization?
2. What would be some characteristics of the environments or internal strategy that might force a different firm to move in the opposite structural direction?
3. How would each of these changes in structure "trickle down" and affect the jobs of individual workers?

Summary

The analysis and design of work is one of the most important components to developing and maintaining a competitive advantage. Strategy implementation is virtually impossible without thorough attention devoted to work-flow analysis, job analysis, and job design. Managers need to understand the entire work-flow process in their work unit to ensure that the process maximizes efficiency and effectiveness. To understand this process, managers also must have clear, detailed information about the jobs that exist in the work unit, and the way to gain this information is through job analysis. Equipped with an understanding of the work-flow process and the existing job, managers can redesign jobs to ensure that the work unit is able to achieve its goals while individuals within the unit benefit on the various work outcome dimensions such as motivation, satisfaction, safety, health, and achievement. This is one key to competitive advantage.

Discussion Questions

1. Assume you are the manager of a fast food restaurant. What are the outputs of your work unit? What are the activities required to produce those outputs? What are the inputs?
2. Based on Question 1, consider the cashier's job. What are the outputs, activities, and inputs for that job?
3. Consider the "job" of college student. Perform a job analysis on this job. What are the tasks required in the job? What are the knowledge, skills, and abilities necessary to perform those tasks? What environmental trends or shocks (like computers) might change the job, and how would that change the skill requirements?
4. Discuss how the following trends are changing the skill requirements for managerial jobs in the United States: (a) increasing use of computers, (b) increasing

international competition, (c) increasing work–family conflicts.
5. Why is it important for a manager to be able to conduct a job analysis? What are the negative outcomes that would result from not understanding the jobs of those reporting to the manager?
6. What are the trade-offs between the different approaches to job design? Which approach do you think should be weighted most heavily when designing jobs?
7. For the cashier job in Question 2, which approach to job design was most influential in designing that job? In the context of the total work-flow process of the restaurant, how would you redesign the job to more heavily emphasize each of the other approaches?

Self-Assessment Exercise

The chapter described how the Department of Labor's Occupational Information Network (O*NET) can help employers. The system was also designed to help job seekers. To see if you think this new system meets the goal of promoting "the effective education, training, counseling, and employment needs of the American workforce," visit O*NET's website at http://online.onetcenter.org/.

Look up the listing for your current job or dream job. List the skills identified for that job. For each skill, evaluate how well your own experiences and abilities enable you to match the job requirements.

Manager's Hot Seat Exercise: Virtual Workplace: Out of Office Reply

This case takes a look into problems associated with one of the new workplace trends—performance of work duties from the employee's home. As the scene unfolds, a manager is talking with his employee. This employee has recently started conducting her job duties from her home. However lately, the employee has been late completing assignments and her work is no longer up to standard.

The discussion reveals that the employee has been feeling let down by the entire organization. She feels isolated and forgotten. The manager readily offers corrective suggestions to the employee. Unfortunately, the employee states she is determined to resign her position with the company.

This case clearly identifies the importance managerial skill can have on organizational operations. It depicts that managers must remain knowledgeable on problems generated by the changing dynamics of the workplace environment. It shows how effective utilization of acquired managerial skills can sometimes prevent organizations from losing the services of good employees.

Individual Activity:
Go to the library and find research on three new workplace trends. Prepare a two-page report discussing these trends. Identify how they can affect organizations. Identify how managers can foster these trends. Discuss how these trends may affect the manner in which organizations design and analyze work. Be prepared to share your findings with your class partners.

Group Activity:
Students should break into groups of 4. Share the individual reports each partner has created. Discuss the impact new workplace trends—for example, virtual workplaces—can produce on today's organizations. Discuss how the new trends will affect the ways in which organizations analyze their work processes. Discuss how the new trends may affect the overall design of work at organizations. Identify how these trends may necessitate change in the skills needed by employees and managers. Discuss new skills that may be required of managers when dealing with employees working in a different workplace environment. Discuss your personal opinions of the new trends.

Exercising Strategy: From Big Blue to Efficient Blue

IBM was long known as "Big Blue" because of its size, in terms of both the number of employees and the amount of revenue and costs associated with its operations. However, as the old saying goes, "the bigger they are, the harder they fall." In 1993 IBM racked up over $8 billion in losses when it was blindsided by the switch in consumer preferences from mainframe computers to smaller, networked personal computers.

The new incoming CEO, Lou Gerstner, needed to engineer one of the greatest turnarounds in modern business; he started with a new vision of what the company would become, as well as a strategy for getting where the company needed to be. The strategy had both an external aspect, focused on changing from an old-fashioned manufacturing company to a modern service provider, and an internal aspect of restructuring operations to reduce costs and promote efficiencies.

Nowhere was this internal strategy change felt more strongly than in the human resource division. In 1993, the HRM function at IBM was large, decentralized, and regionally based, with branch offices all over the world employing over 3,500 people. By the year 2000 there was only one single, centralized unit located in Raleigh, North Carolina, and this unit employed fewer than 1,000 people.

The key to the successful downsizing effort was its emphasis on matching size changes with changes in structure and the substitution of technology for labor. Instead of interacting face-to-face with the local human resources office, all communication would be technologically mediated and directed to the central Raleigh facility via telephone, e-mail, or fax. Moreover, user-friendly software was developed to help employees answer their questions without any other human involvement.

The sprawling, geographically dispersed units were replaced with an efficient three-tier system. The first tier was composed of broadly trained human resource generalists who received telephone calls from any of IBM's 700,000 HRM "customers" (employees) and tried to respond to any queries that could not be handled via the automated system. The second tier, a smaller number of highly trained specialists (such as in 401k plans, OSHA requirements, or selection standards), took any calls that exceeded the knowledge level of the generalists. Finally, the third tier consisted of even a smaller number of top executives charged with keeping the HRM practices in line with the overall corporate strategy being developed by Gerstner.

Amazingly, despite the radical downsizing of this unit, employee satisfaction with service actually increased to over 90 percent, and Gerstner singled out the reengineering of this department as a success story that should serve as a benchmark to the rest of the company's divisions. Moreover, the restructuring and redesign of these IBM jobs have formed a "blue"-print for many other HRM departments in other organizations.

SOURCE: S. N. Mehta, "What Lucent Can Learn from IBM," *Fortune* (June 25, 2001), p. 40; G. Flynn, "Out of the Red, Into the Blue," *Workforce*, March 2000, pp. 50–52; P. Gilster, "Making Online Self-Service Work," *Workforce*, January 2001, pp. 54–61; J. Hutchins, "The U.S. Postal Service Delivers an Innovative HR Strategy," *Workforce*, October 2000, pp. 116–18.

Questions

1. In terms of our discussion of organizational structure, in what ways did the structure at IBM change under Lou Gerstner and what impact did this have on individual jobs?

2. Compare and contrast the direction of structural change at IBM with the direction of change we saw in our opening story regarding the structural realignment at Microsoft.

3. Since both IBM and Microsoft achieved their goals by changing their structures and job design in opposite directions, what does this say about the relationship between organization structure and job design on the one hand and organizational performance and job satisfaction on the other?

Managing People: From the Pages of *BusinessWeek*

BusinessWeek Tech Jobs Are Sprouting Again

Companies Need More Warm Bodies to Meet New Demand for Gear and Services Back at the height of the boom, Mark Herleman spent many a heady day advising corporate clients on which technologies best suited their needs. But last February, Herleman's employer, FreeMarkets Inc., a Pittsburgh company that creates online corporate exchanges, gave him the pink slip. His job prospects got so bleak that Herleman took a gig digging ditches at a cemetery. It wasn't until April that the 25-year-old left his shovel behind. He landed a job at consulting giant Accenture Ltd.'s supply-chain practice, where he'll help companies buy more goods online. "I went from high tech to low tech to high tech again," Herleman says. "It was such a relief."

For the first time in three years, the tech job market is showing signs of life. After losing some 900,000 jobs since April 2001, the industry created 2,600 jobs in February and added 11,600 more in March, according to the Bureau of Labor Statistics. And with the tech recovery gaining steam, that appears to be just the beginning.

Broad-Based Trend Mark M. Zandi, chief economist at Economy.com Inc., expects tech to create 53,000 jobs this year and an additional 207,000 in 2005. While the pace of hiring pales in comparison with the late 1990s, tech employment remains a key component of U.S. job growth. Over the next five years, Zandi predicts, the industry will create 667,000, or 7.2%, of the projected 9.2 million new jobs.

Thanks to Corporate America's robust demand for tech gear and services, the hiring is relatively broad-based. Lehman Brothers Inc. economist Ethan S. Harris expects spending on business equipment and software to rise 14.5% this year, compared with 5.5% in 2003. The strong demand means tech providers can no longer rely solely on outsize productivity gains to keep their operations humming, as they've done for the past few years. Companies now need more warm bodies if they want to get products and services out the door.

As a result, everyone from Accenture and chipmaker Qualcomm to software maker Symantec is planning to take on more engineers, software jockeys, and project managers in '04. "We're hiring at twice the rate of last year," says Libby Sartain, a human resources executive at Yahoo! Inc., which has 305 openings.

Even better: Companies are filling positions that many feared would be sent to China or India. While software and chip companies will continue to shift their low-level support and maintenance tasks overseas, they are also beefing up their domestic engineering talent. In the first quarter, says the BLS, 3,200 engineers found jobs. These skilled folks will create such new products as Web applications and cutting-edge chips. Chipmaker Texas Instruments Inc. aims to hire 1,000 engineers this year to help design its wireless and broadband chips.

Handholders Needed Management consulting is another hot area, creating 10,500 new jobs in the first quarter, says the BLS. These positions are particularly resistant to moving offshore because consultants must spend a lot of face time with customers as they build or maintain technology systems. Accenture expects to add 8,000 people in the U.S. this year—its biggest hiring binge since 2001. The firm is taking over the computing, accounting, purchasing, and other systems of scores of corporations and needs lots of consultants and engineers to handle the load.

People adept at overseeing the development of software products also are in demand. Indeed, many with such skills are once again being snapped up. After losing her job at USF Corp. this January, Roshan Utamsingh, 35, pounded the pavement in search of another. It took just four weeks for her to land at Chicago software start-up Hubbard One. As a senior project manager, Utamsingh will create applications that help law firms use the Web to become more efficient. "I see lots of postings for project management," she says.

Of course, not every techie is finding it that easy. In sectors still plagued by overcapacity, such as telecommunications, layoffs will continue. In the first quarter, telcos shed 5,800 jobs, according to the BLS. Still, given the massive overcapacity that was built in the late '90s and the stop-and-start recovery since, this is the best jobs news techdom has seen for some time.

SOURCE: S. E. Ante, "Tech Jobs Are Sprouting Again," *BusinessWeek* (May 10, 2004), pp. 39–40.

Questions

1. What were some of the factors that led to widespread unemployment among technical workers prior to the recent upsurge in hiring?
2. In what ways are the technology jobs that are now emerging in the U.S. economy different from those that existed 10 years ago?
3. If you were a worker in the tech industry like Mark Herleman, what steps would you take to help buffer yourself from the ups and downs of this labor market?

Notes

1. J. Galbraith and R. Kazanjian, *Strategy Implementation: Structure, Systems, and Process* (St. Paul, MN: West, 1986).
2. D. Ilgen and J. Hollenbeck, "The Structure of Work: Job Design and Roles," in *Handbook of Industrial & Organizational Psychology*, 2nd ed., ed. M. Dunnette and L. Hough (Palo Alto, CA: Consulting Psychologists Press, 1991), pp. 165–208.
3. R. Harvey, "Job Analysis," in ibid., pp. 71–164.
4. R. Griffin, *Task Design: An Integrative Approach* (Glenview, IL: Scott Foresman, 1982).
5. B. Brocka and M. S. Brocka, *Quality Management: Implementing the Best Ideas of the Masters* (Homewood, IL: Business One Irwin, 1992).
6. R. Pritchard, D. Jones, P. Roth, K. Stuebing, and S. Ekeberg, "Effects of Group Feedback, Goal Setting, and Incentives on Organizational Productivity," *Journal of Applied Psychology* 73 (1988), pp. 337–60.
7. D. Bowen and E. Lawler, "Total Quality-Oriented Human Resources Management," *Organizational Dynamics* (1992), pp. 29–41.
8. M. Fefer, "Bill Gates' Next Challenge," *Fortune* (December 14, 1992), pp. 30–41.
9. D. Little, "Even the Supervisor Is Expendable: The Internet Allows Factories to Be Managed from Anywhere," *BusinessWeek* (July 23, 2001), p. 78.
10. M. G. Morris and V. Venkatesh, "Age Differences in Technology Adoption Decisions: Implications for a Changing Workforce," *Personnel Psychology* 53 (2000), pp. 375–403.
11. G. L. Stewart and M. R. Barrick, "Team Structure and Performance: Assessing the Mediating Role of Intrateam Process and the Moderating Role of Task Type," *Academy of Management Journal* 43 (2000), pp. 135–48.
12. G. S. Van der Vegt, B. J. M. Emans, and E. Van de Vliert, "Patterns of Interdependence in Work Teams: A Two-Level Investigation of the Relations with Job and Team Satisfaction," *Personnel Psychology* 54 (2001), pp. 51–70.
13. M. Schminke, M. L. Ambrose, and R. S. Cropanzano, "The Effect of Organizational Structure on Perceptions of Procedural Fairness," *Journal of Applied Psychology* 85 (2000), pp. 294–304.
14. B. Nussaum, "Technology, Just Make it Simpler," *BusinessWeek* (September 8, 2003), p. 38.
15. K. Rebello, "Visionary-in-Chief: A Talk with Bill Gates on the World beyond Windows," *BusinessWeek* (May 17, 1999), pp. 114–16.
16. J. R. Hollenbeck, H. Moon, A. Ellis, B. West, D. R. Ilgen, L. Sheppard, C. O. Porter, and J. A. Wagner, "Structural Contingency Theory and Individual Differences: Examination of External and Internal Person–Team Fit," *Journal of Applied Psychology* 87 (2002), pp. 599–606.
17. M. L. Ambrose and M. Schminke, "Organization Structure as a Moderator of the Relationship between Procedural Justice, Interactional Justice, Perceived Organizational Support, and Supervisory Trust," *Journal of Applied Psychology* 88 (2003), pp. 295–305.
18. B. Schlender, "Ballmer Unbound: How Do You Impose Order on a Giant Runaway Mensa Meeting?" *Fortune* (January 26, 2004), p. 123.

19. E. McCormick, "Job and Task Analysis," in *Handbook of Industrial & Organizational Psychology*, ed. M. Dunnette (Chicago: Rand McNalley, 1976), pp. 651–96.

20. E. Primoff and S. Fine, "A History of Job Analysis," in *The Job Analysis Handbook for Business, Industry, and Government*, ed. S. Gael (New York: Wiley, 1988), pp. 14–29.

21. W. Cascio, *Applied Psychology in Personnel Management*, 4th ed. (Englewood Cliffs, NJ: Prentice Hall, 1991).

22. P. Wright and K. Wexley, "How to Choose the Kind of Job Analysis You Really Need," *Personnel*, May 1985, pp. 51–55.

23. J. Walker, *Human Resource Strategy* (New York: McGraw-Hill, 1992).

24. R. Gatewood and H. Feild, *Human Resource Selection*, 2nd ed. (Hinsdale, IL: Dryden, 1990).

25. I. Goldstein, *Training in Organizations*, 3rd ed. (Pacific Grove, CA: Brooks/Cole, 1993).

26. K. Murphy and J. Cleveland, *Performance Appraisal: An Organizational Perspective* (Boston: Allyn & Bacon, 1991).

27. R. Harvey, L. Friedman, M. Hakel, and E. Cornelius, "Dimensionality of the Job Element Inventory (JEI): A Simplified Worker-Oriented Job-Analysis Questionnaire," *Journal of Applied Psychology* 73 (1988), pp. 639–46.

28. D. A. Hofmann, F. P. Morgeson, and S. J. Gerras, "Climate as a Moderator of the Relationship between Leader–Member Exchange and Content-Specific Citizenship: Safety Climate as an Exemplar," *Journal of Applied Psychology* 88 (2003), pp. 170–78.

29. A. O'Reilly, "Skill Requirements: Supervisor–Subordinate Conflict," *Personnel Psychology* 26 (1973), pp. 75–80.

30. J. Hazel, J. Madden, and R. Christal, "Agreement between Worker–Supervisor Descriptions of the Worker's Job," *Journal of Industrial Psychology* 2 (1964), pp. 71–79.

31. A. K. Weyman, "Investigating the Influence of Organizational Role on Perceptions of Risk in Deep Coal Mines," *Journal of Applied Psychology* 88 (2003), pp. 404–12.

32. K. Wexley and S. Silverman, "An Examination of Differences between Managerial Effectiveness and Response Patterns on a Structured Job-Analysis Questionnaire," *Journal of Applied Psychology* 63 (1978), pp. 646–49.

33. P. Conley and P. Sackett, "Effects of Using High- versus Low-Performing Job Incumbents as Sources of Job-Analysis Information," *Journal of Applied Psychology* 72 (1988), pp. 434–37.

34. W. Mullins and W. Kimbrough, "Group Composition as a Determinant of Job-Analysis Outcomes," *Journal of Applied Psychology* 73 (1988), pp. 657–64.

35. N. Hauenstein and R. Foti, "From Laboratory to Practice: Neglected Issues in Implementing Frame-of-Reference Rater Training," *Personnel Psychology* 42 (1989), pp. 359–78.

36. E. McCormick and R. Jeannerette, "The Position Analysis Questionnaire," in *The Job Analysis Handbook for Business, Industry, and Government*, pp. 880–901.

37. E. C. Dierdorff and M. A. Wilson, "A Meta-analysis of Job Analysis Reliability," *Journal of Applied Psychology* 88 (2003), pp. 635–46.

38. E. Primhoff, *How to Prepare and Conduct Job Element Examinations* (Washington, DC: U.S. Government Printing Office, 1975).

39. T. M. Manson, E. L. Levine, and M. T. Brannick, "The Construct Validity of Task Inventory Ratings: A Multitrait-Multimethod Analysis," *Human Performance* 13 (2000), pp. 1–22.

40. E. Fleishman and M. Reilly, *Handbook of Human Abilities* (Palo Alto, CA: Consulting Psychologists Press, 1992).

41. E. Fleishman and M. Mumford, "Ability Requirements Scales," in *The Job Analysis Handbook for Business, Industry, and Government*, pp. 917–35.

42. R. Christal, *The United States Air Force Occupational Research Project* (AFHRL-TR-73-75) (Lackland AFB, TX: Air Force Human Resources Laboratory, Occupational Research Division, 1974).

43. N. G. Peterson, M. D. Mumford, W. C. Borman, P. R. Jeanneret, and E. A. Fleishman, *An Occupational Information System for the 21st Century: The Development of O*NET* (Washington, DC: American Psychological Association, 1999).

44. N. G. Peterson, M. D. Mumford, W. C. Borman, P. R. Jeanneret, E. A. Fleishman, K. Y. Levin, M. A. Campion, M. S. Mayfield, F. P. Morgeson, K. Pearlman, M. K. Gowing, A. R. Lancaster, M. B. Silver, and D. M. Dye, "Understanding Work Using the Occupational Information Network (O*NET): Implications for Practice and Research," *Personnel Psychology* 54 (2001), pp. 451–92.

45. S. Holmes, "Lots of Green Left in the Emerald City," *BusinessWeek Online* (March 28, 2000).

46. D. Dyer, "O*NET in Action," O*NET website, http://online.onetcenter.org/.

47. M. K. Lindell, C. S. Clause, C. J. Brandt, and R. S. Landis, "Relationship between Organizational Context and Job Analysis Ratings," *Journal of Applied Psychology* 83 (1998), pp. 769–76.

48. F. P. Morgeson and M. A. Campion, "Social and Cognitive Sources of Potential Inaccuracy in Job Analysis," *Journal of Applied Psychology* 82 (1997), pp. 627–55.

49. S. Caudron, "Jobs Disappear When Work Becomes More Important," *Workforce*, January 2000, pp. 30–32.

50. K. Cameron, S. Freeman, and A. Mishra, "Best Practices in White Collar Downsizing: Managing Contradictions," *The Executive* 5 (1991), pp. 57–73.

51. S. K. Parker, "Longitudinal Effects of Lean Production on Employee Outcomes and the Mediating Role of Work Characteristics," *Journal of Applied Psychology* 88 (2003), pp. 620–34.

52. M. Campion and P. Thayer, "Development and Field Evaluation of an Interdisciplinary Measure of Job Design," *Journal of Applied Psychology* 70 (1985), pp. 29–34.

53. J. R. Edwards, J. A. Scully, and M. D. Brtek, "The Measurement of Work: Hierarchical Representation of the Multimethod Job Design Questionnaire," *Personnel Psychology* 52 (1999), pp. 305–24.

54. F. Taylor, *The Principles of Scientific Management* (New York: W. W. Norton, 1967) (originally published in 1911 by Harper & Brothers).

55. R. Griffin and G. McMahan, "Motivation through Job Design," in *OB: The State of the Science*, ed. J. Greenberg (Hillsdale, NJ: Lawrence Erlbaum Associates, 1993).

56. M. Campion, "Ability Requirement Implications of Job Design: An Interdisciplinary Perspective," *Personnel Psychology* 42 (1989), pp. 1–24.

57. R. Hackman and G. Oldham, *Work Redesign* (Boston: Addison-Wesley, 1980).

58. M. Schrage, "More Power to Whom?" *Fortune* (July 23, 2001), p. 270.

59. R. C. Liden, S. J. Wayne, R. T. Sparrowe, "An Examination of the Mediating Role of Psychological Empowerment on the Relations between the Job, Interpersonal Relationships, and Work Outcomes," *Journal of Applied Psychology* 85, pp. 407–16.

60. D. May and C. Schwoerer, "Employee Health by Design: Using Employee Involvement Teams in Ergonomic Job Redesign," *Personnel Psychology* 47 (1994), pp. 861–86.

61. S. F. Brown, "International's Better Way to Build Trucks," *Fortune* (February 19, 2001), pp. 210k–210v.

62. G. Flynn, "Now Is the Time to Prepare for OSHA's Sweeping New Ergonomics Standard," *Workforce*, March 2001, pp. 76–77.

63. J. Schlosser, "A Real Pain in the Workplace," *Fortune* (February 19, 2001), p. 246.

64. W. Howell, "Human Factors in the Workplace," in *Handbook of Industrial & Organizational Psychology*, 2nd ed., pp. 209–70.

65. N. W. Van Yperen and M. Hagedoorn, "Do High Job Demands Increase Intrinsic Motivation or Fatigue or Both? The Role of Job Support and Social Control," *Academy of Management Journal* 46 (2003), pp. 339–48.

66. N. W. Van Yperen and O. Janssen, "Fatigued and Dissatisfied or Fatigued but Satisfied? Goal Orientations and Responses to High Job Demands," *Academy of Management Journal* 45 (2002), pp. 1161–71.

67. D. K. Berman, "Technology Has Us So Plugged into Data, We Have Turned Off," *The Wall Street Journal* (November 10, 2003), pp. A1–A2.

68. J. Baker, "From Open Doors to Gated Communities," *Business-Week* (September 8, 2003), p. 36.

69. J. R. Edwards, J. A. Scully, and M. D. Brteck, "The Nature and Outcomes of Work: A Replication and Extension of Interdisciplinary Work-Design Research," *Journal of Applied Psychology* 85 (2000), pp. 860–68.

70. M. Campion and C. McClelland, "Interdisciplinary Examination of the Costs and Benefits of Enlarged Jobs: A Job-Design Quasi-experiment," *Journal of Applied Psychology* 76 (1991), pp. 186–98.

71. F. P. Morgeson and M. A. Campion, "Minimizing Trade-Offs When Redesigning Work: Evidence from a Longitudinal Quasi-Experiment," *Personnel Psychology* 55 (2002), pp. 589–612.

72. E. Florian, "IT Takes on the ER," *Fortune* (November 24, 2003), pp. 193–200.

73. M. Campion and C. Berger, "Conceptual Integration and Empirical Test of Job Design and Compensation Relationships," *Personnel Psychology* 43 (1990), pp. 525–53.

2
Part

Acquisition and Preparation of Human Resources

Chapter 5

Human Resource Planning and Recruitment

Chapter 6

Selection and Placement

Chapter 7

Training

5 Chapter

Human Resource Planning and Recruitment

Objectives After reading this chapter, you should be able to:

1. Discuss how to align a company's strategic direction with its human resource planning.

2. Determine the labor demand for workers in various job categories.

3. Discuss the advantages and disadvantages of various ways of eliminating a labor surplus and avoiding a labor shortage.

4. Describe the various recruitment policies that organizations adopt to make job vacancies more attractive.

5. List the various sources from which job applicants can be drawn, their relative advantages and disadvantages, and the methods for evaluating them.

6. Explain the recruiter's role in the recruitment process, the limits the recruiter faces, and the opportunities available.

Companies like IBM and Microsoft are outsourcing more mid-level professional jobs as well as factory jobs to countries like Ireland and India. Will this lead to more innovation and more jobs within the United States—is this an increasing risk for the U.S. economy?

Enter the World of Business

History Repeating Itself? The Impact of Offshoring

In the early 1800s, textile manufacturing was the domain of high-skilled workers who worked on hand looms. These workers were well paid. They also had a great deal of autonomy and power in determining product quality, quantity, and style. However, the introduction of steam-powered weaving machines threatened all this by allowing lower-skilled employees to do work of equal quantity and quality. Not only were these lower-skilled workers willing to work for much less money, they also worked much longer hours (14-hour days, six days a week) under much less desirable working conditions.

In order to stop this threatening new development, in 1811, gangs of skilled workers led by Ned Ludd raided the factories and destroyed hundreds of the new machines. The group became known as the "Luddites," and today they are a general symbol of the futility of trying to fight against progress of any kind. In the long run, the Luddites were powerless to stop the march of technological and social change. In fact, despite the best efforts of the Luddites, by 1830, the British textile industry, armed with the new machines was so efficient, it was destroying the textile industry in India. In reacting to the loss of good Indian textile jobs Governor William

Bentinck stated, "The misery hardly finds parallel in the history of commerce."

Well, maybe not. Jump ahead almost two hundred years. The advent and spread of fiber-optic lines throughout the world created the possibility of cheap and almost instantaneous global communication and sharing of data. All of a sudden, the work of a diverse set of occupations in the United States, including call center workers, software developers, mortgage processors, medical technicians, financial analysts, and tax accountants became open to competition from international labor markets. In these labor markets, many workers stood ready and able to do this work for longer hours for less pay and under less desirable working conditions. Governor Bentinck might take some solace knowing that, at the present time at least, Indian workers in cities such as Bangalore, Delhi, Madras, and Bombay are the prime beneficiaries of this latest development, much to the angst of U.S. workers, managers, and politicians.

India has been one of the primary beneficiaries of this new competition for several reasons. First, as one of the largest nations in the world, it has a huge surplus of labor and workers are willing to do the same jobs as American workers for 10 percent of the pay. Second, the Indian workforce is well educated, and one of the main features of their education is the development of strong English speaking skills that are, in many ways, superior to what one might encounter in large sections of the United States. Third, in terms of demographics, the Indian workforce is young and ambitious, and looking to break out of traditionally stratified social roles and gender roles. Thus, despite the repetitive and highly structured nature of some of the work, these workers still find it exciting and interesting. The work takes place in an exciting context, much of it at night, in an informal environment, where large groups of young people work and play together. In the process, this new generation of India's youth is exploring new and different ideas about family, marriage, romance, and material possessions.

Of course, back in the United States, the question becomes what to do about all these lost jobs, as well as the workers who are being displaced by this transfer of labor. On the one hand, the pain associated with job losses is clear and immediate, and so not surprisingly, the first reaction among politicians is to pass protectionist laws that would try to limit offshoring by U.S. companies. As this book is being written, there are no less than 20 different protectionist pieces of legislation being considered in federal and state legislatures. Many experts feel this is the legal equivalent of trying to smash the steam-powered weaving machines, and such politicians are often referred to as "Luddites."

Instead, others have argued that economic development is like a ladder, and that the highest returns result to those who extend the ladder ever upward, not to those who battle it out over the lower rungs. In that spirit, the need for U.S. workers and firms is to develop the next big industry, whether it be in biotech, nanotechnology, telecom or energy, and then dominate that until the time comes when this new technology becomes routine, and then repeat this process yet again. This strategy requires spending resources on education and research in order to ensure that the next major innovation of discovery occurs here rather than overseas. As one economist has noted, "The biggest danger to U.S. workers isn't overseas competition. It's that we worry too much about other countries trying to climb up the ladder and not enough about finding the next higher rung for ourselves."

Source: B. Davis, "Finding Lessons of Outsourcing in Four Historical Tales," *The Wall Street Journal* (March 28, 2004), pp. A1–A3; J. Fox, "Where Your Job Is Going," *Fortune* (November 24, 2003), pp. 84–94; J. Slater, "For India's Youth, New Money Fuels a Revolution," *The Wall Street Journal* (January 27, 2004), pp. A1–A3; B. Davis, "Migration of Skilled Jobs Abroad Unsettles Global-Economy Fans," *The Wall Street Journal* (January 26, 2004), pp. A1–A2; M. J. Mandel, "Outsourcing Jobs: Is It Bad?" *BusinessWeek* (August 25, 2003), pp. 36–38.

Introduction

As the opening story illustrates, firms and the workers they employ do not exist in a vacuum. Technological and social change can impact the competitive landscape, and firms and workers must either adapt or lose out in the global competition for revenue and resources. Few were able to foresee how the spread of fiber-optic cable, combined with social changes occurring in India, would combine to threaten the jobs of so many U.S. workers, but now that this change has became evident, the need to respond in some effective way becomes equally evident.

Organizations that ignored this trend and tried to compete against offshoring firms with higher priced U.S. labor often simply went of out business, leaving their workers unemployed in the end anyway.[1] Workers who lost their jobs to overseas competition and did not upgrade their own skills wound up in jobs that were much less secure and paid much less relative to their previous job.[2] Nations such as North Korea that operate in a protectionist mode and close themselves off from the rest of the world condemn their citizens to shorter life spans and ever lowering standards of living.[3]

As Carly Fiorina, CEO of Hewlett-Packard has noted, "We cannot protect the American people from reality"[4] and hence, individuals, firms and nations have to muster the will and strength to compete in ever more effective ways. The purpose of this chapter is to explore how this can be accomplished at the firm level via human resource planning and recruiting, so that firms can meet the challenges created by changes in the external environment.

Two of the major ways that societal trends and events affect employers are through (1) consumer markets, which affect the demand for goods and services, and (2) labor markets, which affect the supply of people to produce goods and services. In some cases, as we saw in the opening story, an event in the market might drastically alter the supply of labor, leading to a potential labor surplus. In other cases, increased demand for a product may result in an organization having a shortage of labor. For example, the increased demand for higher education to stay competitive means there is need for more college educators, and hence economists predict that jobs in this industry are likely to expand by 600,000 by 2012.[5] Reconciling the difference between the supply and demand for labor presents a challenge for organizations, and how they address this will affect their overall competitiveness.

There are three keys to effectively utilizing labor markets to one's competitive advantage. First, companies must have a clear idea of their current configuration of human resources. In particular, they need to know the strengths and weaknesses of their present stock of employees. Second, organizations must know where they are going in the future and be aware of how their present configuration of human resources relates to the configuration that will be needed. Third, where there are discrepancies between the present configuration and the configuration required for the future, organizations need programs that will address these discrepancies. Under conditions of a labor surplus, this may mean creating an effective downsizing intervention. Under conditions of a labor shortage, this may mean waging an effective recruitment campaign.

This chapter looks at tools and technologies that can help an organization develop and implement effective strategies for leveraging labor market "problems" into opportunities to gain competitive advantage. In the first half of the chapter, we lay out the actual steps that go into developing and implementing a human resource plan. Through each section, we focus especially on recent trends and practices (like downsizing, employing temporary workers, and outsourcing) that can have a major impact on the firm's bottom line and overall reputation. In the second half of the chapter, we familiarize you with the process by which individuals find and choose jobs and the role of personnel recruitment in reaching these individuals and shaping their choices.

The Human Resource Planning Process

An overview of human resource planning is depicted in Figure 5.1. The process consists of forecasting, goal setting and strategic planning, and program implementation and evaluation. We discuss each of these stages in the next sections of this chapter.

Forecasting

The first step in the planning process is **forecasting,** as shown in the top portion of Figure 5.1. In personnel forecasting, the HR manager attempts to ascertain the supply of and demand for various types of human resources. The primary goal is to predict areas within the organization where there will be future labor shortages or surpluses.

Forecasting
The attempts to determine the supply of and demand for various types of human resources to predict areas within the organization where there will be future labor shortages or surpluses.

FIGURE 5.1

Overview of the
Human Resource
Planning Process

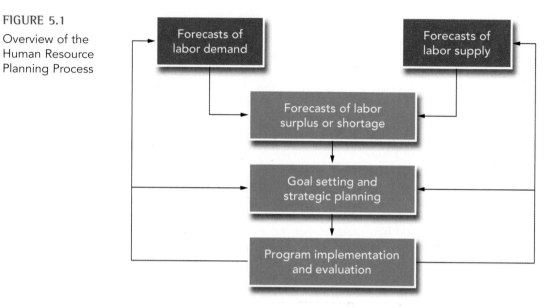

Forecasting, on both the supply and demand sides, can use either statistical methods or judgmental methods. Statistical methods are excellent for capturing historic trends in a company's demand for labor, and under the right conditions they give predictions that are much more precise than those that could be achieved through subjective judgments of a human forecaster. On the other hand, many important events that occur in the labor market, such as the introduction of global fiber optic cable, have no historical precedent; hence, statistical methods that work from historical trends are of little use in such cases. In these situations one must rely on the pooled subjective judgments of experts, and their "best guesses" might be the only source from which to make inferences about the future. Typically, because of the complementary strengths and weaknesses of the two methods, companies that engage in human resource planning use a balanced approach that includes both statistical and judgmental components.

Determining Labor Demand

Typically, demand forecasts are developed around specific job categories or skill areas relevant to the organization's current and future state. Once the job categories or skills are identified, the planner needs to seek information that will help predict whether the need for people with those skills or in that job category will increase or decrease in the future. Organizations differ in the sophistication with which such forecasts are derived.

At the most sophisticated level, an organization might have statistical models that predict labor demand for the next year given relatively objective statistics on leading indicators from the previous year. A **leading indicator** is an objective measure that accurately predicts future labor demand. For example, a manufacturer of automobile parts that sells its product primarily to the Big Three automakers would use several objective statistics on the Big Three automakers for one time period to predict how much demand there would be for the company's product at a later time period. As shown in Figure 5.2, inventory levels, sales levels, employment levels, and profits at the Big Three in one year might predict the demand for labor in the production assembler job category in the next year.

Leading indicator
An objective measure that accurately predicts future labor demand.

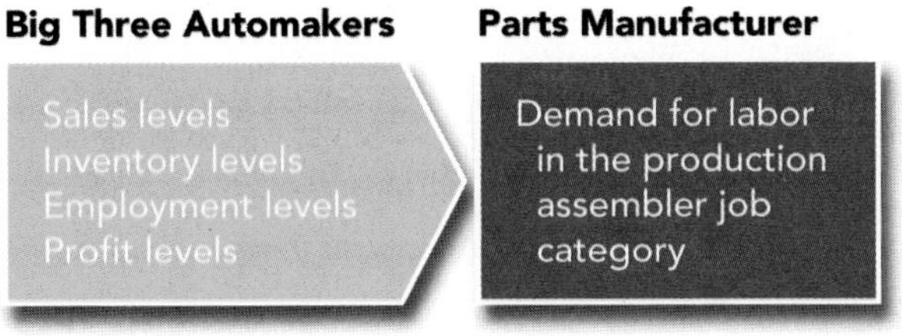

Big Three Automakers   **Parts Manufacturer**

Sales levels
Inventory levels
Employment levels
Profit levels

Demand for labor
in the production
assembler job
category

FIGURE 5.2

Leading Indicators
of the Demand for
Labor for a
Hypothetical Auto
Parts Manufacturer

For example, using historical records, one might use multiple regression techniques to assess the best predictive model for estimating demand for production assemblers from information on sales levels, inventory levels, employment levels, and profits at the Big Three. This is not a statistics book, so a detailed explanation of regression techniques is beyond our scope. Rather, we simply note here that this technique will convert information of four or more leading indicators into a single predicted value for demand for production assemblers that is optimal—at least according to the historical data.

Statistical planning models are useful when there is a long, stable history that can be used to reliably detect relationships among variables. However, these models almost always have to be complemented by subjective judgments of people who have expertise in the area. There are simply too many "once-in-a-lifetime" changes that have to be considered and that cannot be accurately captured in statistical models. For example, our small-parts manufacturer might learn that the leadership at one of the Big Three automakers changed and that the new leadership plans on closing 21 plants over the next 10 years. This event has no historical precedent, so the company might want to consult all its best managers to get their opinions on exactly how much this change would affect the demand for labor in different job categories.

Determining Labor Supply

Once a company has projected labor demand, it needs to get an indicator of the firm's labor supply. Determining the internal labor supply calls for a detailed analysis of how many people are currently in various job categories (or who have specific skills) within the company. This analysis is then modified to reflect changes in the near future caused by retirements, promotions, transfers, voluntary turnover, and terminations.

As in the case of labor demand, projections for labor supply can be derived either from historical statistical models or through judgmental techniques. One type of statistical procedure that can be employed for this purpose involves transitional matrices. **Transitional matrices** show the proportion (or number) of employees in different job categories at different times. Typically these matrices show how people move in one year from one state (outside the organization) or job category to another state or job category.[6]

Table 5.1 shows a hypothetical transitional matrix for our parts manufacturer, focusing on seven job categories. Although these matrices look imposing at first, you will see that they are easy to read and use in determining the internal labor supply. A matrix like the one in this table can be read in two ways. First, we can read the rows to answer the question "Where did people in this job category in 2001 go by 2004?" For example, 70 percent of those in the clerical job category (row 7) in 2001 were still in this job category in 2004, and the remaining 30 percent had left the organization. For the production assembler job category (row 6), 80 percent of those in this position in 2001 were still there in 2004. Of the remaining 20 percent, half (10 percent) were promoted to the production manager job category, and the other half (10 percent) left the

Transitional matrix
Matrix showing the proportion (or number) of employees in different job categories at different times.

TABLE 5.1

A Hypothetical Transitional Matrix for an Auto Parts Manufacturer

2001	2004							
	(1)	(2)	(3)	(4)	(5)	(6)	(7)	(8)
(1) Sales manager	.95							.05
(2) Sales representative	.05	.60						.35
(3) Sales apprentice		.20	.50					.30
(4) Assistant plant manager				.90	.05			.05
(5) Production manager				.10	.75			.15
(6) Production assembler					.10	.80		.10
(7) Clerical							.70	.30
(8) Not in organization	.00	.20	.50	.00	.10	.20	.30	

organization. Finally, 75 percent of those in the production manager job category in 2001 were still there in 2004, while 10 percent were promoted to assistant plant manager and 15 percent left the organization.

Reading these kinds of matrices across rows makes it clear that there is a career progression within this firm from production assembler to production manager to assistant plant manager. Although we have not discussed rows 1 through 3, it might also be noted that there is a similar career progression from sales apprentice to sales representative to sales manager. In this organization, the clerical category is not part of any career progression. That is, this job category does not feed any other job categories listed in Table 5.1.

A transitional matrix can also be read from top to bottom (in the columns) to answer the question "Where did the people in this job category in 2004 come from (Where were they in 2001)?" Again, starting with the clerical job (column 7), 70 percent of the 2004 clerical positions were filled by people who were also in this position in 2001, and the remaining 30 percent were external hires (they were not part of the organization in 2001). In the production assembler job category (column 6), 80 percent of those occupying this job in 2004 occupied the same job in 2001, and the other 20 percent were external hires. The most diversely staffed job category seems to be that of production manager (column 5): 75 percent of those in this position in 2004 held the same position in 2001; however, 10 percent were former production assemblers who were promoted, 5 percent were former assistant plant managers who were demoted, and 10 percent were external hires who were not with the company in 2001.

Matrices such as these are extremely useful for charting historical trends in the company's supply of labor. More important, if conditions remain somewhat constant, they can also be used to plan for the future. For example, if we believe that we are going to have a surplus of labor in the production assembler job category in the next three years, we note that by simply initiating a freeze on external hires, the ranks of this position will be depleted by 20 percent on their own. Similarly, if we believe that we will have a labor shortage in the area of sales representatives, the matrix informs us that we may want to (1) decrease the amount of voluntary turnover in this position, since 35 percent of those in this category leave every three years, (2) speed the training of those in the sales apprentice job category so that they can be promoted more quickly than in the past, and/or (3) expand external recruitment of individuals for this job category, since the usual 20 percent of job incumbents drawn from this source may not be sufficient to meet future needs. As with labor demand, historical precedents for labor supply may not always be reliable indicators of future trends. Thus statistical forecasts of labor supply also need to be complemented with judgmental methods.

Determining Labor Surplus or Shortage

Forecasting [handwritten]

Once forecasts for labor demand and supply are known, the planner can compare the figures to ascertain whether there will be a labor shortage or labor surplus for the respective job categories. When this is determined, the organization can determine what it is going to do about these potential problems.

Failure to address these issues can result in serious problems for the organization. For example, at NASA, some suspect that at least part of the blame for the Columbia disaster could be traced to poor human resource planning. Deep budget cuts led to a hiring freeze that lasted throughout the 1990s. This was followed up with a voluntary early retirement program where many of the most up-to-date and marketable scientists exited for new opportunities. This left the agency with an older workforce that some feel had outdated skills. The average age of NASA employees at the time of the shuttle disintegration was 45, and in the critical science and engineering divisions, workers 60 years and older outnumbered those who were 30 and under by a 3 to 1 margin. Moreover, due to the chronic levels of understaffing, those employees who were left faced unusually high workloads. As one critic noted, "They were pushing the people who remained too hard. They weren't bringing in new people, and the people who were left were stressed tremendously. At some point, a line is crossed when safety is compromised."[7]

A similar situation faces General Motors Corporation. It too has undergone several hiring freezes over the last few years, and by 2005, the average age of its workforce will be 48. In fact, a full 50 percent of GM workers will be able to retire within the next three years. However, based upon labor demand forecasts, GM also has estimated that it needs to reduce its workforce by close to 20 percent, and hence rather than lay workers off right now, it can afford to wait and let natural attrition and retirement processes perform the needed downsizing. While this is a fortuitous development in terms of solving the labor surplus problem, it does create another issue, because GM is responsible for the pension and health care costs of all these new retirees. Relative to its Japanese rivals, GM's pension and health care costs run $1,200 more per vehicle.[8] Having forecast this problem with pension and health care costs, the manufacturer has roughly three years to come up with a solution to this problem.

Goal Setting and Strategic Planning

Forecasting [handwritten]

The second step in human resource planning is goal setting and strategic planning, as shown in the middle of Figure 5.1. The purpose of setting specific quantitative goals is to focus attention on the problem and provide a benchmark for determining the relative success of any programs aimed at redressing a pending labor shortage or surplus. The goals should come directly from the analysis of labor supply and demand and should include a specific figure for what should happen with the job category or skill area and a specific timetable for when results should be achieved.

The auto parts manufacturer, for instance, might set a goal to reduce the number of individuals in the production assembler job category by 50 percent over the next three years. Similarly, the firm might set a goal to increase the number of individuals in the sales representative job category by 25 percent over the next three years.

Like many Mexican manufacturing operations, Jabil Circuit's Guadalajara plant succeeded by competing versus U.S. firms on costs. In 1998, labor costs in Mexico were roughly $1.50 per hour. This low wage rate, when combined with the passage of the North American Trade Act that gave Mexican firms privileged access to U.S. markets, helped the Guadalajara plant to grow to a size of 3,500 employees in 2001. However, by 2002, the demand for the products the company made had reduced to a trickle and the size of the workforce had been reduced to half of its former level.

Ironically, the same low cost strategy that helped to sustain the Jabil facility in the first place was now threatening to end its existence because Chinese firms could produce the same products with even lower labor costs. The impact of cheap Chinese labor has been felt by manufacturers all over the world, but nowhere is the impact larger than in Mexico, where so many firms have traditionally competed exclusively on labor costs. In the past three years, Mexico has lost an estimated 400,000 jobs to China, and now China—rather than Mexico—is the number 2 exporter to the U.S. market (after Canada). In response to this change in the competitive environment, many Mexican firms are attempting to compete in different ways, and the Jabil Guadalajara plant is illustrative of many of the potential strategies.

First, some firms shift from competing on the costs associated with simple products and instead try to compete on costs associated with more complex products. For example, at the Jabil Guadalajara plant, the

Once these goals are established, the firm needs to choose from the many different strategies available for redressing labor shortages and surpluses. Table 5.2 shows some of the options for a human resource planner seeking to reduce a labor surplus. Table 5.3 shows some options available to the same planner intent on avoiding a labor shortage.

This stage is critical because the many options available to the planner differ widely in their expense, speed, effectiveness, amount of human suffering, and revocability (how easily the change can be undone). For example, as we saw in the case of

TABLE 5.2

Options for Reducing an Expected Labor Surplus

OPTION	SPEED	HUMAN SUFFERING
1. Downsizing	Fast	High
2. Pay reductions	Fast	High
3. Demotions	Fast	High
4. Transfers	Fast	Moderate
5. Work sharing	Fast	Moderate
6. Hiring freeze	Slow	Low
7. Natural attrition	Slow	Low
8. Early retirement	Slow	Low
9. Retraining	Slow	Low

managers decided to stop producing simple electrical boards, and instead began trying to manufacture more complicated router systems. Currently, Chinese companies have little capacity for router production, which entails more than 3,000 parts, and this move put the Guadalajara plant back in competition with higher cost U.S. firms. Workers at the Mexican facility were used to long production runs of standardized products, and at first, struggled with router production. However, within seven months, the plant was producing routers that were equal to those produced in the United States, but cheaper.

In addition to producing more complex, nonroutine products, Mexican firms are also increasingly competing on speed. The Jabil plant manager in Guadalajara, Ernesto Sanchez notes, "The gate the Chinese cannot close is time and distance, and we have learned to exploit that." Indeed, U.S. retailers are increasingly interested in keeping fewer products on shelves and then replacing sold products back on the shelves as quickly as possible. While Chinese goods can take as long as two or three weeks to travel to the United States, many Mexican firms can get their products to retailers in two or three days. Thus, the Jabil plant also focused on producing products for retail outlets that were less willing to tolerate shipping delays associated with Chinese manufacturers.

Finally, Mexican firms are increasingly trying to compete on flexibility, and the key here is to both upgrade the skills of the workforce and eliminate turnover. For example, at the Jabil plant, Sanchez installed a new system for addressing worker complaints, a new financial bonus system that recognizes workers who get cross-trained on new tasks or develop new skills, and a fancy new cafeteria system for workers that offers top quality foods and produce. Turnover at the plant was reduced by 50 percent due to these steps, which is important now that the plant is growing again. Indeed, in 2004, the plant had not only gotten back to its original size prior to the Chinese entry into their market; it had actually exceeded its prior size.

SOURCE: C. Condon, "A Chillwind Blows from the East," *BusinessWeek* (September 1, 2003), pp. 44–45; F. Balfour, "China's Dream Team," *BusinessWeek* (September 1, 2003), pp. 50–51; D. Luhnow, "As Jobs Move East, Plants in Mexico Retool to Compete," *The Wall Street Journal* (March 5, 2004), pp. 1–2.

GM, if the organization can anticipate a labor surplus far enough in advance, it may be able to freeze hiring and then just let natural attrition adjust the size of the labor force. If successful, an organization may be able to avoid layoffs altogether, so that no one has to lose a job.

Unfortunately for many workers, in the past decade the typical organizational response to a surplus of labor has been downsizing, which is fast but high in human suffering. The widespread use of downsizing is a contributing factor in the largest number of personal bankruptcies ever recorded in the United States. Beyond this economic impact, the psychological impact spills over and affects families, increasing the rates of divorce, child abuse, and drug and alcohol addiction.[9] The typical organizational

OPTION	SPEED	REVOCABILITY
1. Overtime	Fast	High
2. Temporary employees	Fast	High
3. Outsourcing	Fast	High
4. Retrained transfers	Slow	High
5. Turnover reductions	Slow	Moderate
6. New external hires	Slow	Low
7. Technological innovation	Slow	Low

TABLE 5.3

Options for Avoiding an Expected Labor Shortage

Productivity Improvement: Who Wins and Who Loses?

The U.S. economy has traditionally followed business cycles marked by recessions and recoveries. However, the most recent turn of the recession and recovery cycle was unique in two important ways. First, productivity rates during the recession were actually rising, and these rates during the recovery were almost unprecedented. Between 2001 and 2004, output per hour had actually increased at a rate of over almost 5 percent per year, well ahead of the 1.5 percent rate associated with the recession and recovery cycle in the 1990s. Second, despite the unusually high spurt in the nation's gross national product in 2003 and 2004, close to 6 percent, the number of new jobs created

was minimal. If past business cycles were serving as guides to this most recent one, given this level of growth, the economy should have created 200,000 new jobs per month rather than one-tenth of this number.

As we saw in our opening story, many blame the lack of new jobs on offshoring and unfair foreign competition, but in reality, it is the increased level of productivity, rather than offshoring, that has led to such weak growth in jobs. Whereas most estimates suggest that offshoring has led to perhaps 300,000 lost jobs, the economy loses 1.3 million jobs for every 1 percent increase in the productivity rate. If one multiplies 1.3 million jobs times the pro-

ductivity growth rate of 5 percent, it becomes clear that in the overall scheme of things, offshoring is small change compared to productivity increases when it comes to explaining job losses.

The source of job growth in the current decade can be traced to technology investment that companies made in the 1990s in an effort to substitute technology for labor. These new technologies allow organizations to create more products with fewer people. For example, although some semiconductor manufacturing has moved overseas, Intel's newest plant opened up in New Mexico. Relative to Intel plants that started up five years ago, the workers in the New

response to a labor shortage has been either hiring temporary employees or outsourcing, responses that are fast and high in revocability. Given the pervasiveness of these choices, we will devote special subsections of this chapter to each of these options.

Downsizing

We define **downsizing** as the planned elimination of large numbers of personnel designed to enhance organizational competitiveness. Many organizations adopted this strategic option in the late 1980s and 1990s, especially in the United States. In fact, over 85 percent of the Fortune 1000 firms downsized between 1987 and 2001, resulting in more than 8 million permanent layoffs—an unprecedented figure in U.S. economic history. The jobs eliminated in these downsizing efforts should not be thought of as temporary losses due to business cycle downturns or a recession but as permanent losses due to the changing competitive pressures faced by businesses today. In fact, in over 80 percent of the cases where downsizing took place, the organizations initiating

Mexico facility can produce three times as many chips with the same number of workers. These types of gains are not limited to just high-tech industries. Although many might believe that U.S. steel production is dead, in fact, the industry generated 102 million tons of steel in 2002, up from 75 million tons in 1982. However, while it took close to 300,000 workers to produce the steel in 1982, it took less than 75,000 workers to produce the 2002 figure. Where once dozens of workers hand-guided huge ladles of melted ore from one location to another, now a single worker does the same task with a joystick operated from an air-conditioned cubicle.

Clearly, given the growth in the economy, someone must be making some money, and it is instructive to see who the winners and losers are in a world of increasing productivity. First, corporate profits were up $223 million in 2003, and managers and executives were the only category of workers whose real wages rose during the last recession. Second, corporate profits have resulted in stock gains, and thus, investors in the U.S. stock market achieved real gains of close to 25 to 30 percent over the last three years. Third, due in part to rising stock prices, foreign capital has flowed into the United States, resulting in low interest rates. This has translated into low mortgage rates, which in turn increase the values of home ownership. Finally, productivity gains have resulted in lower costs for many consumers, and low inflation rates help retirees and others on fixed incomes.

On the other hand, young, inexperienced workers and uneducated, older workers take a beating from these new productivity gains. Young workers suffer because the lack of new hiring makes it difficult for them to break into the labor market in the first place. Moreover, the jobs they are most suited for often lack complexity, and hence are the first ones to be automated or sent overseas. Older, uneducated workers also suffer because many of their jobs also lack complexity. However, unlike younger workers, it is more difficult for this group to retool their skills. It is questionable whether the gains for one group of people offset the losses experienced by others, and many have questioned the sustainability of an economy that fails to integrate young workers or utilize the skills of hardworking, but less educated workers over the long run. As one unemployed manufacturing worker has noted, "Over the last two centuries, America has developed a balanced society, with opportunities for a large cross section of people. We're gutting that."

SOURCE: B. Nussbaum, "Where Are the Jobs?" *BusinessWeek* (March 22, 2004), pp. 36–37; J. Cooper, "The Price of Efficiency," *BusinessWeek* (March 22, 2004), pp. 38–42; N. D. Schwartz, "Will 'Made in the USA' Fade Away?" *Fortune* (November 24, 2003), pp. 98–110; M. J. Mandel, "Productivity: Who Wins, Who Loses," *BusinessWeek* (March 22, 2004), pp. 44–46; C. Ansberry, "Laid-Off Factory Workers Find Jobs Are Drying Up for Good," *The Wall Street Journal* (July 21, 2003), pp. A1–A3.

the cutbacks were making a profit at the time.[10] For example, in 1998, General Electric Company set in motion a $2 billion restructuring program even though all of GE's divisions were generating double-digit returns on investments.[11]

Rather than trying to stem current losses, the major reasons for most downsizing efforts dealt with promoting future competitiveness. Surveys indicate four major reasons that organizations engaged in downsizing. First, many organizations were looking to reduce costs, and because labor costs represent a big part of a company's total costs, this is an attractive place to start. For example, when the Dow Jones industrial average dropped from over 11,000 points to below 9,000 in the year 2001, many Wall Street firms were faced with high overhead costs that could be eliminated only by reducing head counts. Merrill Lynch, Bank of America, Paine Webber, J. P. Morgan Chase, and Deutsche Bank all laid off roughly 10 percent of their workforce in an effort to stay profitable.[12]

Second, in some organizations, closing outdated plants or introducing technological changes to old plants reduced the need for labor. For example, Eastman Machine is a Buffalo, New York–based manufacturer of equipment that is used for cutting fabric. In order to stave off low-priced competition from Chinese rivals, Eastman expanded heavily into the market for highly automated, computer-driven cutting machines that are not currently available in Asia. This eliminated much of the manual work that was formerly performed at the plant, and now, the same amount of product and revenue that was once generated by a 120-person workforce can be produced with a staff of 80, requiring a downsizing of one-third of the workforce.[13] The experience of Eastman is not unique, and as the "Competing through Sustainability" box, on pages 184 and 185, shows, the impact of increased productivity on job creation has produced a number of winners and losers in terms of wealth and security.

A third reason for downsizing was that many mergers and acquisitions reduced the need for bureaucratic overhead, displacing many managers and some professional staff members. For example, the threat of health care reform in the mid-1990s prevented many pharmaceutical companies from raising prices. To maintain profitability in the face of price stagnation, many firms pursued merger strategies so that they would have more products but fewer people. For example, Rouche Holding Ltd. purchased Syntex Corporation for $5.3 billion, acquiring all its products, but then cut the Syntex payroll from 10,000 people to 5,000.[14]

A fourth reason for downsizing was that, for economic reasons, many firms changed the location of where they did business. Some of this shift was from one region of the United States to another—in particular, many organizations moved from the Northeast, the Midwest, and California to the South and the mountain regions of the West. For example, Universal Studios moved many of its operations out of Los Angeles to Orlando, Florida, where the costs of producing television shows are over 40 percent less than in Los Angeles.[15] Some of this shift was also due to jobs moving out of the United States altogether. For example, as we saw in our opening story on offshoring, close to 300,000 white-collar jobs were transferred from the United States to India in 2003 alone.[16]

Although the jury is still out on whether these downsizing efforts have enhanced organizational effectiveness, some early indications are that the results have not lived up to expectations. One study of 52 Fortune 100 firms shows that most firms that announce a downsizing campaign show worse, rather than better, financial performance in the following years.[17]

There seem to be a number of reasons for the failure of most downsizing efforts to live up to expectations in terms of enhancing firm performance. First, although the initial cost savings are a short-term plus, the long-term effects of an improperly managed downsizing effort can be negative. Downsizing not only leads to a loss of talent, but in many cases it disrupts the social networks needed to promote creativity and flexibility.[18] For example, in the Rouche Holding–Syntex merger discussed earlier, most employees who left did so voluntarily, taking advantage of a lucrative severance package. This "parachute" gave employees two to three years of full compensation, depending on their job level. Many felt that this strategy led to turnover among the best, most marketable scientists and managers. One former Syntex scientist asked, "What makes them think they can be successful scientifically and discover new drugs when they have lost most of their good discovery people?"[19]

Second, many downsizing campaigns let go of people who turn out to be irreplaceable assets. In fact, one survey indicated that in 80 percent of the cases, firms wind up replacing some of the very people who were let go. One senior manager of a Fortune 100 firm described a situation in which a bookkeeper making $9 an hour was let go; but then, when the company realized she knew many things about the company that no one else knew, she was hired back as a consultant for $42 an hour.[20] Indeed, the practice of hiring back formerly laid-off workers has become so routine that many organizations are increasingly using software formerly used for tracking job applicants to track their laid-off employees.[21]

A third reason downsizing efforts often fail is that employees who survive the purges often become narrow-minded, self-absorbed, and risk-averse. Motivation levels drop off because any hope of future promotions—or even a future—with the company dies out. Many employees also start looking for alternative employment opportunities. The negative publicity associated with a downsizing campaign can also hurt the company's image in the labor market, making it more difficult to recruit employees later. The key to avoiding this kind of reputation damage is to ensure that the need for the layoff is well explained and that procedures for implementing the layoff are fair.[22] Although this may seem to reflect common sense, organizations are often reluctant to provide this kind of information, especially if part of the reason for the layoff was top-level mismanagement.[23]

The key to a successful downsizing effort is to avoid indiscriminant across-the-board cuts, and instead perform surgical strategic cuts that not only reduce costs, but also improve the firm's competitive position. For example, Raven Industries, a Sioux Falls manufacturer of a wide variety of plastic products, had to cut its workforce, but went about the process in a manner that would help make the company "China proof." They went from having 10 different divisions to 4, eliminating manufacturing of certain low-margin products that could be produced cheaper in China (e.g., generic plastic covers for pickup trucks) and pouring more resources into more profitable custom-made covers for widely different agricultural machines. In the process, the organization decreased in size almost by half (from 1,500 workers to 750), but revenue was off by less than 20 percent. Two years after this strategic downsizing effort, the companies share price increased from $4.50 to over $30.[24]

Early Retirement Programs

Another popular means of reducing a labor surplus is to offer an early retirement program. As shown in Figure 5.3, the average age of the U.S. workforce is increasing. But although many baby boomers are approaching traditional retirement age, early

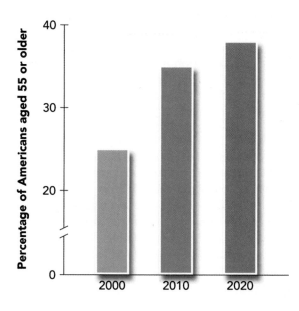

FIGURE 5.3

Aging of the U.S. Population, 2000–2020

indications are that this group has no intention of retiring any time soon.[25] Several forces fuel the drawing out of older workers' careers. First, the improved health of older people in general, in combination with the decreased physical labor in many jobs, has made working longer a viable option. Second, this option is attractive for many workers because they fear Social Security will be cut, and many have skimpy employer-sponsored pensions that may not be able to cover their expenses. Finally, age discrimination legislation and the outlawing of mandatory retirement ages have created constraints on organizations' ability to unilaterally deal with an aging workforce.

Although an older workforce has some clear advantages for employers in terms of experience and stability, it also poses problems. First, older workers are sometimes more costly than younger workers because of their higher seniority, higher medical costs, and higher pension contributions. When the value of the experience offsets these costs, then employers are fine; but if it does not, it becomes difficult to pass these costs to consumers. Second, because older workers typically occupy the best-paid jobs, they sometimes prevent the hiring or block the advancement of younger workers. This is frustrating for the younger workers and leaves the organization in a perilous position whenever the older workers decide to retire.

In the face of such demographic pressures, many employers try to induce voluntary attrition among their older workers through early retirement incentive programs. These programs come in an infinite variety. Depending on how lucrative they are, they meet with varied success. Although some research suggests that these programs do induce attrition among lower-performing older workers,[26] to a large extent, such programs' success is contingent upon accurate forecasting. For example, in 2003, Verizon needed to reduce its workforce and offered employees several incentives to retire early, including a 5 percent increase in pension benefits and a one-time severance payout of $30,000. Verizon's human resources department forecasted that 12,000 workers would opt for the program, but instead over 21,000 workers took the package. Verizon went from labor surplus to labor shortage almost overnight and had to hurriedly hire new and inexperienced people to take the place of the departed seasoned veterans. As one might expect, operational performance deteriorated, and as one industry analyst noted, "It's a mystery how they're even running that company today." Whereas the company hoped to save $1 billion dollars with the program, it instead lost $3 billion.[27]

For this and other reasons, many organizations are moving from early retirement programs to phased retirement programs. Phased retirement programs allow the organization to tap into the experience of older workers while reducing the number of hours they work (and hence reducing costs). This option is often helpful psychologically for the workers, who can ease into retirement rather than being thrust all at once into a markedly different way of life.[28]

Employing Temporary Workers

Whereas downsizing has been a popular method for reducing a labor surplus, hiring temporary workers and outsourcing has been the most widespread means of eliminating a labor shortage. Temporary employment affords firms the flexibility needed to operate efficiently in the face of swings in the demand for goods and services. In fact, a surge in temporary employment often precedes a jump in permanent hiring, and is often a leading indicator that the economy is expanding. For example, the number or temporary workers grew from 215 million to 230 million between 2003 and 2004, signaling to many the end of the recession.[29] In addition to flexibility, there are several other advantages of hiring temporary workers.

First, the use of temporary workers frees the firm from many administrative tasks and financial burdens associated with being the "employer of record." Second, small companies that cannot afford their own testing programs often get employees who have been tested by a temporary agency. Third, many temporary agencies train employees before to sending them to employers, which reduces training costs and eases the transition for both the temporary worker and the company. Finally, because the temporary worker has little experience in the host firm, she brings an objective perspective to the organization's problems and procedures that is sometimes valuable. Also, since the temporary worker may have a great deal of experience in other firms, she can sometimes identify solutions to the host organization's problems that were confronted at a different firm. For example, one temporary worker at Lord, Abbett and Company, an investment firm in New York, suggested an efficient software program for managing portfolios that she had been trained with at a different firm. Thus temporary employees can sometimes help employers to benchmark and improve their practices.

Certain disadvantages to employing temporary workers need to be overcome to effectively use this source of labor. For example, there is often tension between a firm's temporary employees and its full-time employees. Surveys indicate that 33 percent of full-time employees perceive the temporary help as a threat to their own job security. This can lead to low levels of cooperation and, in some cases, outright sabotage if not managed properly.

There are several keys to managing this problem. First, the organization needs to have bottomed out first in terms of any downsizing effort before it starts bringing in temporaries. A downsizing effort is almost like a death in the family for employees who survive, and a decent time interval needs to exist before new temporary workers are introduced into this context. Without this time delay, there will be a perceived association between the downsizing effort (which was a threat) and the new temporary employees (who may be perceived by some as outsiders who have been hired to replace old friends). Any upswing in demand for labor after a downsizing effort should probably first be met by an expansion of overtime granted to core full-time employees. If this demand persists over time, one can be more sure that the upswing is not temporary and that there will be no need for future layoffs. The extended stretches of overtime will eventually tax the full-time employees, who will then be more receptive to the prospect of hiring temporary employees to help lessen their load.

Second, if the organization is concerned about the reactions of full-time workers to the temporaries, it may want to go out of its way to hire "nonthreatening" temporaries. For example, although most temporary workers want their temporary assignments to turn into full-time work (75 percent of those surveyed expressed this hope), not all do. Some prefer the freedom of temporary arrangements. These workers are the ideal temporaries for a firm with fearful full-time workers.

Of course, in attempting to convince full-time employees that they are valued and not about to be replaced by temporary workers, the organization must not create the perception that temporary workers are second-class organizational citizens. For example, in 2000, in a case that went all the way to the Supreme Court, Microsoft's differential treatment of temporary versus full-time workers was deemed illegal, and the Court awarded close to $100 million to roughly 10,000 plaintiffs.[30] As with managing the full-time employee concerns, there are several keys to managing the concerns of temporary employees. First, as far as possible, the organization should treat temporary employees the same way it treats full-time workers. For example, unlike Microsoft, at Ford Motor Company in Detroit, temporary engineering employees were given the same memos, newsletters, and bulletins about the company as were regular employees, even though many of the projects they were working on had little to do with much of the organization's core business. Joe O'Hagan, principal engineer at Ford, notes, "We treated them as if they were an integral part of our team, and to be a part of our team, they had to know what everybody else knows. We worked to make sure they understood the big picture."[31]

HR staff can also prevent feelings of a two-tiered society by ensuring that the temporary agency provides benefits to the temporaries that are at least minimally comparable to those enjoyed by the full-time workers with whom they interact. For example, one temporary agency, MacTemps, gives its workers long-term health coverage, full disability insurance, and complete dental coverage. This not only reduces the benefit gap between the full-time and part-time workers but also helps attract the best part-time workers in the first place.

Outsourcing and Offshoring

Outsourcing

An organization's use of an outside organization for a broad set of services.

Whereas a temporary employee can be brought in to manage a single job, in other cases a firm may be interested in getting a much broader set of services performed by an outside organization; this is called **outsourcing.** For example, American Airlines established a contract with Johnson Controls Inc. to provide ticket agents for American's operations at 28 second-tier airports. In this case, cost control was the main reason—American paid its veteran agents at major airports $19 an hour plus benefits, the going market rate for this industry. Johnson Controls, on the other hand, pays the existing local market wage, only $8 an hour, for the 500 jobs that were handed over to it.

In other cases, outsourcing is driven by economies of scale that make it more efficient to hand over work to an outside agent. For example, several years ago Ford Motor Company had a unit that processed automobile financing applications. Now it hands this work over to Detroit-based MCN Corporation, which can do the same job with fewer people than Ford. MCN uses its dedicated computers and staff to process data for Ford (and over 25 other companies) with an efficiency that comes from a narrow focus on data entry and analysis, unfettered by the need to produce automobiles. APAC (a private telemarketing company in Cedar Rapids, Iowa) has a similar arrangement with Western Union, Compaq, Quill, Sears, and many other companies. APAC's specialty is answering the telephone, and its 4,000 operators take orders and provide information to customers of their clients. As Donald Gerryman, vice president of APAC, notes, "When you call our clients' 800 numbers, you get us."

Outsourcing is a logical choice when the firm simply does not have certain expertise and is not willing to invest the time and energy to develop it. For example, American Express Financial Advisors (AEFA) has a leadership development division that provides training services to clients based on a detailed needs analysis. Sometimes this needs analysis turns up training requirements in areas where AEFA has no established curriculum. Where once the firm might have developed such curriculum for the client, now, to keep a narrower focus, it searches for an outside supplier better able to meet this need. No new trainers are added to the AEFA payroll, and no costly curriculum development is initiated. As one manager notes, "There are just a lot of good programs out there, and we don't want to reinvent the wheel. . . . This allows us to keep ourselves very lean and focused."[32]

Offshoring

A special case of outsourcing where the jobs that move actually leave one country and go to another.

Offshoring is a special case of outsourcing where the jobs that move actually leave one country and go to another. As we saw in our opening story, this kind of job migration has always taken place; however, rapid technological changes have made the current trends in this area historically unprecedented. As we saw in our opening story, offshoring is controversial because close to 500,000 white-collar jobs have moved from the United States to India, Eastern Europe, Southeast Asia and China in the last five years. In addition to restricting job growth in the United States this has also affected wages, in the sense that while the average rate of salary growth during an economic recovery is usually around 6–8 percent, because of offshoring, salary growth in the most recent recovery was actually negative (–1 percent).

Although this may seem problematic for U.S. employers, in fact, if effectively managed, firms that offshore certain aspects of work gain an undeniable competitive advantage over their rivals. Ignoring this source of advantage is self-defeating, and akin to putting one's head in the sand. For example, Levi-Strauss tried for years to compete against other low-cost jeans manufacturers who offshored their labor. However, after years of one plant shutdown after another, in 2003 the firm finally gave up and closed down all of its U.S. manufacturing plants. The move, which many saw as inevitable, was long overdue and had it been made earlier, the company might have been able to avoid losing over $20 million. Indeed, as the earlier "Competing through Globalization" box on page 182 illustrated, even nations such as Mexico that are traditionally thought of as low-cost competitors have found that they too are not immune from even lower cost competitors.

When making the decision to offshore some product or service, organizations should consider several critical factors. Many who failed to look before they leaped onto the offshoring bandwagon have been disappointed by their results. Quality control problems, security violations, and poor customer service experiences have in many cases wiped out all the cost savings attributed to lower wages and more. There are several steps a company should take to ensure the success of this strategy. First, the best jobs to outsource are those that are repetitive, predictable and easily trained. For example, Dell computer sends almost all of its call center service work for home computers to India, but because of the more complex and unpredictable nature of problems confronted by business users, Dell employs a U.S. call center for its business-to-business work.[33] Second, when choosing an outsourcing vendor, it is usually the bigger and older the better. Small overseas upstarts often promise more than they can deliver and take risks that one is not likely to see in larger, more established contractors.[34] Third, do not offshore any work that is proprietary or requires tight security. One software developer that hired an Indian firm to debug its programs later found that the firm copied the software and sold it under its own brand name.[35] Finally, it is generally a good idea to start small and then monitor the work very closely, especially in the beginning. Typically, if problems are going to develop, they manifest themselves quickly to those who are paying close attention.[36]

Altering Pay and Hours

Companies facing a shortage of labor may be reluctant to hire new full-time or part-time employees. Under some conditions, these firms may have the option of trying to garner more hours out of the existing labor force. Many employers opted for this strategy during the 1990s. Indeed, 6 percent of the automobiles assembled in North America in 1997 resulted from overtime production. To put this in perspective, this is equivalent to the output of an additional four auto plants running on straight time.[37]

Despite having to pay workers time-and-a-half for overtime production, employers see this as preferable to hiring and training new employees—especially if they are afraid that current demand for products or services may not extend to the future. Also, for a short time at least, many workers enjoy the added compensation. However, over extended periods, employees experience stress and frustration from being overworked in this manner. Thus it is not surprising that during the 1998 General Motors strike, one employee demand was for the company to hire additional new workers.

In the face of a labor surplus, organizations can sometimes avoid layoffs if they can get their employees to take pay cuts. For example, when DiamondCluster Inc., a Chicago-based technology consulting firm, experienced a downturn in demand for its services, rather than reduce the workforce, it instead convinced the workers to take an across-the-board 20 percent pay cut. Although painful, the workers eventually accepted the need for this move and perceived that it was better than a series of layoffs.[38] Alternatively one can avoid layoffs and hold the pay rate constant but reduce the number of hours of all the workers. Hilton Hotels took this strategy when faced with a diminished occupancy rate that occurred in the wake of the 9/11 terrorist attacks. Some employees went from working five days per week to two, and although the reduction in income was significant, many could file for partial unemployment compensation and everyone kept benefits.[39] This is a particularly good strategy if the employer feels the downturn is just a short-term phenomenon, as was the case with the post-9/11 dearth in travel.

Strategic Use of HRM

Indeed, developing a flexible workforce is one the keys to avoiding layoffs on the one hand while still managing the ups and downs of business cycles on the other. For example, Lincoln Electric, an Ohio-based manufacturer of welding equipment, is committed to a no-layoff strategy, and yet does not experience a uniform demand for its products. During downtimes, it is not unusual for workers to move from one job to another, often experiencing a reduction in wages. Rick Willard, a 56-year-old veteran at Lincoln, is typical of Lincoln employees, having worked at 13 qualitatively different jobs over the course of the last five years. At one point, he was part of a division that produced electric motors, then he built circuit boards for electric welding machines, followed by a stint manufacturing the harnesses that hold wires together in welding machines, and so on. Each job paid a different rate, and Willard liked some, and hated others. However, through it all, he was able to retain his full health care and retirement benefits, and was never unemployed. Of course, it takes a certain type of person to weather these kinds of changes. As Willard notes, "Some people resent being moved. You accept it or you don't. It's good for the company. Sometimes it's good for the employees. You still have a place to go."

SOURCE: C. Ansberry, "Old Industries Adopt Flex Staffing to Adapt to Rapid Pace of Change," *The Wall Street Journal* (March 22, 2002), pp. A1–A2.

Program Implementation and Evaluation

The programs developed in the strategic-choice stage of the process are put into practice in the program-implementation stage, shown at the bottom of Figure 5.1. A critical aspect of program implementation is to make sure that some individual is held accountable for achieving the stated goals and has the necessary authority and resources to accomplish this goal. It is also important to have regular progress reports on the implementation to be sure that all programs are in place by specified times and that the early returns from these programs are in line with projections.

The final step in the planning process is to evaluate the results. Of course, the most obvious evaluation involves checking whether the company has successfully avoided any potential labor shortages or surpluses. Although this bottom-line evaluation is critical, it is also important to go beyond it to see which specific parts of the planning process contributed to success or failure.

A good example of the necessary diagnostic work can be seen in Bell Atlantic's recent failed downsizing effort. Convinced that the company would need fewer workers, but facing a union (the Communication Workers of America) that staunchly opposed layoffs, Bell Atlantic developed a high-priced buyout plan. Almost a third of its unionized workforce (14,000 people) stood ready to take the company up on its offer. However, forecasts for product demand were grossly underestimated. Whereas Bell Atlantic forecasted lower demand for copper wiring, instead orders surged as many industrial and residential consumers added second lines for faxes and modems. The smaller workforce could not keep up with demand, however. To avert disaster, the company had to offer a 25 percent hike in its already generous pension plan to any employee who would stay. The overall effect was to create an extravagant bonus system that rewarded employees for either staying or leaving.[40]

The Special Case of Affirmative Action Planning

We have argued that human resource planning is an important function that should be applied to an organization's entire labor force. It is also important to plan for various subgroups within the labor force. For example, affirmative action plans forecast and monitor the proportion of various protected group members, such as women and minorities, that are in various job categories and career tracks. The proportion of workers in these subgroups can then be compared with the proportion that each subgroup represents in the relevant labor market. This type of comparison is called a **workforce utilization review.** This process can be used to determine whether there is any subgroup whose proportion in the relevant labor market is substantially different from the proportion in the job category.

If such an analysis indicates that some group—for example, African Americans—makes up 35 percent of the relevant labor market for a job category but that this same group constitutes only 5 percent of the actual incumbents in that job category in that organization, then this is evidence of underutilization. Underutilization could come about because of problems in selection or from problems in internal movement, and this could be seen via the transitional matrices discussed earlier in this chapter.

This kind of review is critical for many different reasons. First, many firms adopt "voluntary affirmative action programs" to make sure underutilization does not occur and to promote diversity. Second, companies might also engage in utilization reviews because they are legally required to do so. For example, Executive Order 11246 requires that government contractors and subcontractors maintain affirmative action programs. Third, affirmative action programs can be mandated by the courts as part of the settlement of discrimination complaints.

Regardless of the motivation for adopting affirmative action planning, the steps required to execute such a plan are identical to the steps in the generic planning process discussed earlier in this chapter. That is, the company needs to assess current utilization patterns and then forecast how these are likely to change in the near future. If these analyses suggest current underutilization and if forecasts suggest that this problem is not likely to change, then the company may need to set goals and timetables for changing this situation. Certain strategic choices need to be made in the pursuit of these goals that might affect recruitment or selection practices, and then the success of these strategies has to be evaluated against the goals established earlier in the process.

Workforce utilization review
A comparison of the proportion of workers in protected subgroups with the proportion that each subgroup represents in the relevant labor market.

The Human Resource Recruitment Process

Human resource recruitment
The practice or activity carried on by the organization with the primary purpose of identifying and attracting potential employees.

As the first half of this chapter shows, it is difficult to always anticipate exactly how many (if any) new employees will have to be hired in a given year in a given job category. The role of human resource recruitment is to build a supply of potential new hires that the organization can draw on if the need arises. Thus **human resource recruitment** is defined as any practice or activity carried on by the organization with the primary purpose of identifying and attracting potential employees.[41] It thus creates a buffer between planning and actual selection of new employees, which is the topic of our next chapter.

Recruitment activities are designed to affect (1) the number of people who apply for vacancies, (2) the type of people who apply for them, and/or (3) the likelihood that those applying for vacancies will accept positions if offered.[42] The goal of an organizational recruitment program is to ensure that the organization has a number of reasonably qualified applicants (who would find the job acceptable) to choose from when a vacancy occurs.

The goal of the recruiting is not simply to generate large numbers of applicants. If the process generates a sea of unqualified applicants, the organization will incur great expense in personnel selection (as discussed more fully in the next chapter), but few vacancies will actually be filled.

The goal of personnel recruitment is not to finely discriminate among reasonably qualified applicants either. Recruiting new personnel and selecting new personnel are both complex processes. Each task is hard enough to accomplish successfully, even when one is well focused. Organizations explicitly trying to do both at the same time will probably not do either well. For example, research suggests that recruiters provide less information about the company when conducting dual-purpose interviews (interviews focused on both recruiting and selecting applicants).[43] Also, applicants apparently remember less information about the recruiting organization after dual-purpose interviews.[44]

Because of strategic differences among companies (see Chapter 2), the importance assigned to recruitment may differ.[45] In general, however, as shown in Figure 5.4, all companies have to make decisions in three areas of recruiting: (1) personnel policies, which affect the kinds of jobs the company has to offer; (2) recruitment sources used to solicit applicants, which affect the kinds of people who apply; and (3) the charac-

FIGURE 5.4

Overview of the Individual Job Choice—Organizational Recruitment Process

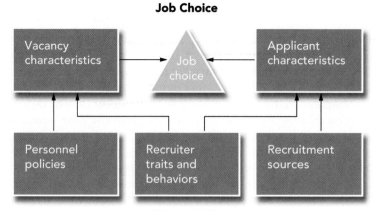

Job Choice

Recruitment Influences

teristics and behaviors of the recruiter. These in turn, influence both the nature of the vacancies and the nature of the people applying for jobs in a way that shapes job choice decisions.[46]

Personnel Policies

Personnel policies is a generic term we use to refer to organizational decisions that affect the nature of the vacancies for which people are recruited. If the research on recruitment makes one thing clear, it is that characteristics of the vacancy are more important than recruiters or recruiting sources when it comes to predicting job choice.[47]

Internal versus External Recruiting

One desirable feature of a vacancy is that it provides ample opportunity for advancement and promotion. One organizational policy that affects this is the degree to which the company "promotes from within"—that is, recruits for upper-level vacancies internally rather than externally. Indeed, a 2001 survey of MBA students found that this was their top consideration when evaluating a company.[48]

We discuss internal versus external recruiting both here and in the section "Recruitment Sources" later in this chapter because this policy affects the nature of both the job and the individuals who apply. For now, we focus on the effects that promote-from-within policies have on job characteristics, noting that such policies make it clear to applicants that there are opportunities for advancement within the company. These opportunities spring not just from the first vacancy but from the vacancy created when a person in the company fills that vacancy. Similarly, during downtimes, organizations with strong internal recruiting orientations typically have developed information systems that support reassigning potentially dislocated workers to different jobs in the company. For example, at Wachovia Corporation, stock market slumps in 2003 created a labor surplus of investment bankers and many employees in this job category were threatened with a layoff. Because all the company's openings and résumés were in a common database, Wachovia could search for matches in skills sets and job requirements and in the process place over 50 percent of the investment bankers that would have been laid off into other positions in the organization.[49] Thus, internal staffing systems provide both opportunities for advancement during growth and opportunities for stable employment during declining periods.

McDonald's restaurants provide a good example of the virtues of promoting from within. Phil Hagans, an African American who was once a cook at a McDonald's, now owns two franchises thanks to a program that encourages low-income managers, regardless of race, to buy franchises. Hagans's restaurants not only turn a profit, but also perform a valuable social function by providing needed employment and work experience for many inner-city youths in the Houston area.[50]

The retailing industry is an example of an entire sector of the economy that is increasingly being perceived as an area with good opportunities for internal advancement. This is especially the case for the superstores, such as Wal-Mart, Home Depot, and Target, where thousands of managers must be hired and promoted each year to run new outlets. Applicants who used to shun retailing jobs are now attracted to them because of the opportunities for advancement. A new college graduate who goes to Target can have responsibility for 20 employees and an $8 million department just 12 weeks out of school. These trainees, if successful, can become managers of small stores in as little as three years. Some employees who started with Target at 24 years of age are regional senior vice presidents by the time they are 30.[51]

Lead-the-Market Pay Strategies

Because pay is an important job characteristic for almost all applicants, companies that take a "lead-the-market" approach to pay—that is, a policy of paying higher-than-current-market wages—have a distinct advantage in recruiting. Pay can also make up for a job's less desirable features—for example, paying higher wages to employees who have to work midnight shifts. These kinds of specific shift differentials and other forms of more generic compensating differentials will be discussed in more detail in later chapters that focus on compensation strategies. We merely note here that "lead" policies make any given vacancy more attractive to applicants.

Increasingly, organizations that compete for applicants based on pay do so using pay forms other than wages and salary. In the 1990s many employers attempted to recruit employees with promises of stock option plans. However, the 2001 recession saw stock values drop sharply, thus reducing the attractiveness of this specific inducement. In addition, many people became aware of restrictions on stock option plans in the wake of the Enron bankruptcy in December 2001. Some low-level and midlevel Enron employees held stock options worth over $1 million. When Enron stock started to slide, the company prevented its employees from cashing out their options, leaving many to helplessly watch their stock become worthless. Other Enron employees whose 401(k) plans were entirely based on Enron stock (which they too could not sell) also suffered. It only made matters worse when the U.S. Securities and Exchange Commission suggested that Enron's top executives illegally made more than $1 billion off stock sales just prior to the bankruptcy announcement.

For many applicants restricted stock option plans are now perceived as having limited value, and in order to attract top talent, employers are returning to more traditional inducements such as salary and other benefits. Moreover, when the traditional benefit is a 401(k) plan, smart applicants are demanding diversified funds rather than funds that are heavily skewed toward the employer's own stock.[52]

Employment-at-Will Policies

Employment-at-will policies state that either party in the employment relationship can terminate that relationship at any time, regardless of cause. Companies that do not have employment-at-will provisions typically have extensive due process policies. **Due process policies** formally lay out the steps an employee can take to appeal a termination decision. Recent court decisions have increasingly eroded employers' rights to terminate employees with impunity.[53] To protect themselves from wrongful discharge suits, employers have been encouraged to state explicitly, in all formal recruiting documentation, that the employment is "at will."

Some authors have gone so far as to suggest that all mention of due process should be eliminated from company handbooks, personnel manuals, and recruiting brochures.[54] Although this may have some legal advantages, job security is an important feature to many job applicants. Organizational recruiting materials that emphasize due process, rights of appeal, and grievance mechanisms send a message that job security is high; employment-at-will policies suggest the opposite. Research indicates that job applicants find companies with due process policies more attractive than companies with employment-at-will policies.[55]

Image Advertising

Organizations often advertise specific vacancies (discussed below in the section "Recruitment Sources"). Sometimes, however, organizations advertise just to promote themselves as a good place to work in general.[56] Image advertising is particularly important for companies in highly competitive labor markets that perceive themselves as having a bad image.[57]

Even though it does not provide any information about any specific job, image advertising is often effective because job applicants develop ideas about the general reputation of the firm (i.e., its brand image) and then this spills over to influence their expectations about the nature of specific jobs or careers at the organization.[58] Although someone once said that there is no such thing as bad publicity, this is not always true when it comes to recruiting. Although familiarity is better than lack of familiarity in general, applicants seem to be especially sensitive to bad publicity, and thus advertising campaigns are often used to try to send a positive message about the organization.[59]

Research suggests that the language associated with the organization's brand image is often similar to personality trait descriptions that one might more commonly use to describe another person (such as innovative or competent or sincere).[60] These perceptions then influence the degree to which the person feels attracted to the organization, especially if there appears to be a good fit between the traits of the applicant and the traits that describe the organization.[61] Applicants seem particularly sensitive to issues of diversity and inclusion in these types of advertisements, and hence organizations that advertise their image need to go out of their way to ensure that the actors in their advertisements reflect the broad nature of the labor market constituencies that they are trying to appeal to in terms of race, gender, and culture.[62]

Whether the goal is to influence the perception of the public in general or specific segments of the labor market, research clearly shows that job seekers form beliefs about the nature of organizations well before they have any direct interviewing experience with those companies. Thus, it is critical for organizations to systematically assess their reputation in the labor market and redress any shortcomings they detect relative to their desired image.[63]

Recruitment Sources

The sources from which a company recruits potential employees are a critical aspect of its overall recruitment strategy. The total labor market is expansive; any single organization needs to draw from only a fraction of that total. The size and nature of the fraction that applies for an organization's vacancies will be affected by how (and to whom) the organization communicates its vacancies.[64] The type of person who is likely to respond to a job advertised on the Internet may be different from the type of person who responds to an ad in the classified section of a local newspaper. In this section we examine the different sources from which recruits can be drawn, highlighting the advantages and disadvantages of each.

Internal versus External Sources

We discussed internal versus external sources of recruits earlier in this chapter and focused on the positive effects that internal recruiting can have on recruits' perceptions of job characteristics. We will now discuss this issue again, but with a focus on how using internal sources affects the kinds of people who are recruited.

In general, relying on internal sources offers a company several advantages.[65] First, it generates a sample of applicants who are well known to the firm. Second, these applicants are relatively knowledgeable about the company's vacancies, which minimizes the possibility of inflated expectations about the job. Third, it is generally cheaper and faster to fill vacancies internally.

A good example of the value of an internal recruitment system can be seen in the experience of Sun Trust. In 2000, Sun Trust, a large and diversified banking institution with close to 30,000 employees, was organized into 28 separate regional centers, each with its own Human Resource Department. Each department operated independently, and thus they all had different technologies, different services, and different forms and procedures for all sorts of HR activities including recruiting. This precluded any form of coordinated activity across regions and also created huge redundancies and inefficiencies. In 2002, the organization restructured its Human Resource Department and went from being a decentralized and divisional structure to a more centralized and functional structure (see Chapter 4 for a discussion of these different dimensions of structure), Job descriptions and recruiting practices were standardized, and all existing employee's skill sets were entered into a central database to promote internal movement within the organization. One year later, the time it took to fill a vacancy went from 30 days to 20 days, and the cost per hire dropped from $1,100 to $900. Much of this was attributed to the more efficient utilization of internal applicants.[66]

Finding and Keeping the Best Employees

The value of a strong internal hiring system can also be seen in the experience of Whirlpool. In 2001, it was difficult for someone inside the company to know what jobs were or were not available within the huge manufacturing conglomerate. The job posting system was a paper and pencil process that was antiquated technologically and organized regionally, making it difficult and time consuming to obtain information about positions out of state. In order to rectify this situation, the company created a new Web-based system that allowed managers to enter open positions using a standardized format and employees to enter résumés in a standardized format, so that matches were identified instantly via an established search algorithm. In 2003, Whirlpool staffed over 50 percent of their new open positions with internal hires, saving the organization over $1 million in recruiting and training costs. The system also created a high degree of satisfaction among employees who could use it as a long-term career-planning tool. Indeed, relative to comparable manufacturers, where the average turnover rate is in the 10–15 percent range, the average turnover rate at Whirlpool in 2003 was less than 5 percent.

SOURCE: L. G. Klaff, "New Internal Hiring Systems Reduce Cost and Boost Morale," *Workforce*, March 2004, pp. 76–78.

With all these advantages, you might ask why any organization would ever employ external recruiting methods. There are several good reasons why organizations might decide to recruit externally.[67] First, for entry-level positions and perhaps even for some specialized upper-level positions, there may not be any internal recruits from which to draw. Second, bringing in outsiders may expose the organization to new ideas or new ways of doing business. Using only internal recruitment can result in a workforce whose members all think alike and who therefore may be poorly suited to innovation.[68]

Direct Applicants and Referrals

Direct applicants are people who apply for a vacancy without prompting from the organization. **Referrals** are people who are prompted to apply by someone within the organization. These two sources of recruits share some characteristics that make them excellent sources from which to draw.

First, many direct applicants are to some extent already "sold" on the organization. Most of them have done some homework and concluded that there is enough fit be-

Direct applicants
People who apply for a job vacancy without prompting from the organization.

Referrals
People who are prompted to apply for a job by someone within the organization.

tween themselves and the vacancy to warrant their submitting an application. This process is called *self-selection*. A form of aided self-selection occurs with referrals. Many job seekers look to friends, relatives, and acquaintances to help find employment, and evoking these social networks can greatly aid the job search process for both the job seeker and the organization.[69] Current employees (who are knowledgeable of both the vacancy and the person they are referring) do their homework and conclude that there is a fit between the person and the vacancy; they then sell the person on the job. Indeed, research shows that new hires that used at least one informal source reported having greater prehire knowledge of the organization than those who relied exclusively on formal recruitment sources. Those who report having multiple sources were even better, however, in terms of both prehire knowledge about the position and subsequent turnover. In fact, the turnover rate for applicants who came from multiple recruiting sources was half that of those recruited via campus interviews or newspaper advertisements.[70]

When one figures into these results the low costs of such sources, they clearly stand out as one of the best sources of new hires. Indeed, some employers even offer financial incentives to current employees for referring applicants who are accepted and perform acceptably on the job (stay 180 days, for example).[71] Other companies play off their good reputations in the labor market to generate direct applications. For example, minorities constitute 26 percent of the 6,500 managerial and professional employees at Avon Products, and this enhances the firm's ability to recruit other minorities. As Al Smith, director of managing diversity at Avon, notes, "I get a lot of résumés from people of all cultures and ethnicities because Avon has a good reputation," and this precludes the need for expensive and sometimes unreliable outreach programs.[72]

Of course, referrals do not necessarily have to come just from current employees. The importance of good community relations to recruitment can be seen in the experience of Papa John's Pizza, which was rated number one on *BusinessWeek*'s list of 100 Best Small Companies in America. Papa John's, one of the fastest-growing companies in the United States, once relied on classified ads to find drivers and store employees. This method was highly unreliable, however, because the company did not have the facilities to develop sophisticated tests of people's skills and attitudes. Store managers are now encouraged to make professional contacts within their communities, such as with the principal or guidance counselor at the local high school, leaders of church groups, and coaches in youth sports leagues. Store managers can then use these contacts to help generate referrals among promising young applicants. These community relationships help connect Papa John's to youths who have established good reputations in their community for reliability and trustworthiness. As one industry analyst notes, "I think the greatest advantage for Papa John's is recruitment. Once you get your feet wet recruiting that way, you can move on to bigger and better things."[73]

Advertisements in Newspapers and Periodicals

Advertisements to recruit personnel are ubiquitous, even though they typically generate less desirable recruits than direct applications or referrals—and do so at greater expense. However, because few employers can fill all their vacancies with direct applications and referrals, some form of advertising is usually needed. Moreover, an employer can take many steps to increase the effectiveness of this recruitment method.

The two most important questions to ask in designing a job advertisement are, What do we need to say? and To whom do we need to say it? With respect to the first question, many organizations fail to adequately communicate the specifics of the vacancy. Ideally, persons reading an ad should get enough information to evaluate the job and its requirements, allowing them to make a well-informed judgment regarding their qualifications. This could mean running long advertisements, which costs more. However, these additional costs should be evaluated against the costs of processing a huge number of applicants who are not reasonably qualified or who would not find the job acceptable once they learn more about it.

In terms of whom to reach with this message, the organization placing the advertisement has to decide which medium it will use. The classified section of local newspapers is the most common medium. It is a relatively inexpensive means of reaching many people within a specified geographic area who are currently looking for work (or at least interested enough to be reading the classifieds). On the downside, this medium does not allow an organization to target skill levels very well. Typically, classified ads are read by many people who are either over- or underqualified for the position. Moreover, people who are not looking for work rarely read the classifieds, and thus this is not the right medium for luring people away from their current employers. Specially targeted journals and periodicals may be better than general newspapers at reaching a specific part of the overall labor market. In addition, employers are increasingly using television—particularly cable television—as a reasonably priced way of reaching people.[74]

Electronic Recruiting

The growth of the information superhighway has opened up new vistas for organizations trying to recruit talent. There are many ways to employ the Internet, and increasingly organizations are refining their use of this medium. In fact, a recent 2001 survey of HR executives indicated that electronic job boards were the most effective source of recruits for 36 percent of the respondents, well ahead of local newspapers (21 percent), job fairs (4 percent), and walk-ins and referrals (1 percent).[75] Indeed, as the "Competing through Technology" box, on pages 202 and 203, reveals, the degree to which electronic recruiting media may someday totally replace newspapers has sparked a great deal of competition in this industry.

Obviously, one of the easiest ways to get into "e-cruiting" is to simply use the organization's own Web page to solicit applications. By using their own Web page, organizations can highly tune their recruitment message and focus in on specific people. For example, the interactive nature of this medium allows individuals to fill out surveys that describe what they are looking for and what they have to offer the organizations. These surveys can be "graded" immediately and recruits can be given direct feedback about how well they are matched for the organization. Research shows that this type of immediate feedback regarding their fit is both helpful to recruits and to the organization, by quickly and cheaply eliminating misfits for either side.[76]

Of course, smaller and less well-known organizations may not attract any attention to their own websites, and thus for them this is not a good option. A second way for organizations to use the Web is to interact with the large, well-known job sites such as Monster.com, HotJobs.com or CareerBuilder.com. These sites attract a vast array of applicants, who submit standardized résumés that can be electronically searched using key terms. Applicants can also search for companies in a similar fashion; the hope, of course, is that there may be a match between the employer and the applicant. The biggest downside to these large sites, however, is their sheer size and lack of differentiation. Because of this limitation of the large sites, smaller, more tailored websites called "niche boards" focus on certain industries, occupations, or geographic areas. For example, Telecommcareers.net is a site devoted to, as the name implies, the telecommunications industry. CIO.com, a companion site to *CIO Magazine,* is an occupational board that specializes in openings for chief information officers. The San Francisco Bay Area also features "craiglist.com"—a job board for applicants who live in that area and have no intentions of relocating. The best evidence regarding the growing popularity and effectiveness of these niche boards can be seen in the behaviors of the larger sites, which are scrambling to create more focused subsections of their own.[77] Clearly this dynamic area of human resource management is one where innovative, forward-thinking managers can gain competitive advantage.

Another technological innovation in recruiting that eliminates travel requirements but allows for a more personal meeting between employer and applicant is videoconferencing.[78] Used mostly on college campuses, videoconferencing allows applicants and employers to meet each other technologically "face-to-face."

Public and Private Employment Agencies

The Social Security Act of 1935 requires that everyone receiving unemployment compensation be registered with a local state employment office. These state employment offices work with the U.S. Employment Service (USES) to try to ensure that unemployed individuals eventually get off state aid and back on employer payrolls. To accomplish this, agencies collect information from the unemployed about their skills and experiences.

Employers can register their job vacancies with their local state employment office, and the agency will attempt to find someone suitable using its computerized inventory of local unemployed individuals. The agency makes referrals to the organization at no charge, and these individuals can be interviewed or tested by the employer for potential vacancies. Because of certain legislative mandates, state unemployment offices often have specialized "desks" for minorities, handicapped individuals, and Vietnam-era veterans. Thus, this is an excellent source for employers who feel they are currently underutilizing any of these subgroups.

Public employment agencies serve primarily the blue-collar labor market; private employment agencies perform much the same service for the white-collar labor market. Unlike public agencies, however, private employment agencies charge the organization for the referrals. Another difference between private and public employment agencies is that one doesn't have to be unemployed to use a private employment agency.

One special type of private employment agency is the so-called executive search firm (ESF). These agencies are often referred to as *headhunters* because, unlike the other sources we have examined, they operate almost exclusively with people who are currently employed. Dealing with executive search firms is sometimes a sensitive process because executives may not want to advertise their availability for fear of their current employer's reaction. Thus, ESFs serve as an important confidentiality buffer between the employer and the recruit.

Colleges and Universities

Most colleges and universities have placement services that seek to help their graduates obtain employment. Indeed, on-campus interviewing is the most important source of recruits for entry-level professional and managerial vacancies.[79] Organizations tend to focus especially on colleges that have strong reputations in areas for which they have critical needs (chemical engineering, public accounting, or the like).[80]

Taming the Monster

In one of the most popular advertisements run during the 2003 Superbowl, a driverless truck was depicted careening wildly down a major highway, narrowly avoiding one disaster after another. Meanwhile, at a truck stop that barely avoids being obliterated by the runaway semi, a depressed and dejected truck driver relates to another how difficult it is for him to find a driving job.

If only this truck and this driver could somehow get together! Which, of course, is just the matching service that is offered by the advertisement's sponsor, Monster.com. Unfortunately, like the truck in its advertisement, the fate of Monster.com is in no way assured, and the recent adventures of this company illustrate the difficulties of competing via technology in an ever-changing world.

Until very recently, Monster.com, along with eBay, Google, and Amazon.com, was considered one of the few dot-com success stories that survived the bust in the technology sector. The business model at Monster.com was not complicated. The basic idea was to use emerging Internet technology to pair up job seekers and employers in a way that was more comprehensive, cheaper, and efficient relative to what might be accomplished via a newspaper. Job seekers could post their résumés for free online, and employers could search these résumés and place their job listings online for 60 days for a fixed price. This business model was a huge success, and revenues at the company went from zero in 2000 to over $500 million dollars in 2001. At its peak, the stock price held at $87 and the founder and CEO, Andrew McKelvey, was worth over $2 billion. However, this monster is now under attack from many different angles, and in 2003 revenues were down so much that the company had to reduce its workforce by 250 people.

As we have noted elsewhere in this book, technology as a mean of securing competitive advantage is a two-edged sword, and one of the biggest problems with this source of advantage is that one's competitors can often use the same technology to fight back. Thus, after seeing newspaper revenues from classified job ads gutted by Monster, three of the major newspaper chains, Gannet, Knight-Ridder, and the Tribune, formed an alliance and created CareerBuilder as an Internet alternative to Monster.com. CareerBuilder encapsulated many of the same features of Monster.com's board. However, it created synergies with the print media by

For example, 3M has a five-part college recruiting strategy. First, the company concentrates its efforts on 25 to 30 selected universities, trying not to spread itself too thin. Second, it has a commitment to these selected universities and returns each year with new openings. Third, 3M uses a large number of line managers in its recruiting interviews, because they have better real-world knowledge about the jobs and working conditions relative to more narrowly informed human resource staff. Fourth, the HR staff is used to coordinate the line managers' activities with the university's staff, making sure that the same person works with the same university year in and year out to achieve "continuity of contact." Finally, 3M strives for continuous improvement by frequently asking students they have recruited to give them feedback on the process and, where possible, to compare and contrast 3M's process with the process used by other firms recruiting at the same university.[81]

offering a "free" 10-line advertisement in one of the sponsoring newspapers with each online job listed by the employer. Although the number of jobs listed on CareerBuilder is smaller than Monster.com at the moment, its traffic grew 37 percent in 2002 while traffic on Monster.com decreased by 20 percent. More ominously, CareerBuilder paid $50 million recently to replace Monster.com as the default job search engine for both AOL and MSN—a move that will shift 25 percent of Monster.com's traffic directly to CareerBuilder.

While these two giants battle it out, yet other competitive forces and changes in the labor market are conniving to bring down both of these giant sites. Indeed, one of the biggest complaints registered against the big boards like Monster.com, Career Builders, and Yahoo's Hotjobs, is that that they are too big, and that they generate too many low quality applicants. In a period of low demand for labor, the employer holding the job has the upper hand, and the emphasis shifts. As one expert has noted, "The war for talent has morphed into the war for the best talent, and employers don't necessarily want the largest database; they want the database with the most talent." This often works to the favor of niche boards, that is, smaller, more focused sites that are organized around professions such as Attorneys.jobs, Vets4hire, AMFMJobs, or any of a number of other sites. These niche sites use the same general technology as the big boards, but threaten them because of the quantity–quality trade-off.

Still, while the niche boards are busy attacking all the big boards, yet another source of competition is looking to destroy all boards that serve as "middlemen" between applicants and employers. That is, if we have learned one thing about Internet technology in the world of commerce, it is that it often works to eliminate the middleman by directly putting buyer and seller together (e.g., Amazon.com). Thus, both the big boards and the niche boards are threatened by new entrants such as DirectEmployers.com. This site is run by a consortium of employers and is really not a job posting service at all, but rather a search engine that sends job seekers directly to the employer's website, where they can get more information about the firm, and then apply online. As we have seen in this book, the research suggests that "walk-ins" or "direct applications" are one of the top sources for new recruits, and this new direct method of connecting employers with job seekers resembles this source, whereas the big boards and niche boards are more representative of newspapers as a source, which of course, was the original business that Monster.com was created to steal. Clearly, where this road is leading for Monster.com is hard to predict, and like the out-of-control truck that is used in its advertisements, the end of the story for this monster may not conclude with "they all lived happily ever after."

SOURCE: B. McLean, "A Scary Monster," *Fortune*, December 22, 2003, pp. 149–57; D. P. Shuit, "Board Games," *Workforce*, November 2003, pp. 37–44; D. P. Shuit, "Find a Niche, Fill a Job," *Workforce*, November 2003, p. 42; A. Harrington, "Can Anyone Build a Better Monster?" *Fortune* (May 13, 2002), pp. 189–190.

Many employers have found that to effectively compete for the best students, they need to do more than just sign prospective graduates up for interview slots. One of the best ways to establish a stronger presence on a campus is with a college internship program. For example, Dun & Bradstreet funds a summer intern program for minority MBA students and often hires these interns for full-time positions when they graduate.[82] These kinds of programs allow an organization to get early access to potential applicants and to assess their capacities directly.

Another way of increasing one's presence on campus is to participate in university job fairs. In general, a job fair is a place where many employers gather for a short time to meet large numbers of potential job applicants. Although job fairs can be held anywhere (such as at a hotel or convention center), campuses are ideal locations because of the many well-educated, yet unemployed, individuals who live there. Job fairs are a rather inexpensive means of generating an on-campus presence and can even provide one-on-one dialogue with potential recruits—dialogue that could not be achieved through less interactive media like newspaper ads.

Finally, as more organizations attempt to compete on a global level, the ability to recruit individuals who will be successful both at home and abroad is a growing concern. Many organizations feel that college campuses are one of the best places to search for this type of transportable talent. Molex Inc., for example, is a U.S. technology firm with 8,000 employees, only 2,000 of whom live in the United States. Molex derives 70 percent of its $950 million in annual sales from outside the United States, and thus the majority of workers are either expatriates, local nationals, or foreign service employees. Three critical aspects of Molex's recruitment strategy are critical to its success in attaining an internationally talented workforce.

First, Molex focuses on recruiting college students. As one manager at Molex states, "We have had more success molding younger people into this company and into overseas assignments than taking more experienced people who've worked for other companies." Second, Molex recruits many foreigners (especially MBA candidates) who are studying in the United States for assignments back in their native country. These individuals have the best of both worlds in terms of having a formal education in U.S. business practices and also understanding both the language and culture of their home country. Finally, when recruiting U.S. students, Molex requires that each person hired be fluent in both English and one other language. This commitment to multilingual competency can be seen at the national headquarters, where 15 different languages are spoken.[83]

Evaluating the Quality of a Source

Because there are few rules about the quality of a given source for a given vacancy, it is generally a good idea for employers to monitor the quality of all their recruitment sources. One means of accomplishing this is to develop and compare yield ratios for each source.[84] Yield ratios express the percentage of applicants who successfully move from one stage of the recruitment and selection process to the next. Comparing yield ratios for different sources helps determine which is best or most efficient for the type of vacancy being investigated. Data on cost per hire are also useful in establishing the efficiency of a given source.[85]

Table 5.4 shows hypothetical yield ratios and cost-per-hire data for five recruitment sources. For the job vacancies generated by this company, the best two sources of recruits are local universities and employee referral programs. Newspaper ads generate the largest number of recruits, but relatively few of these are qualified for the position. Recruiting at nationally renowned universities generates highly qualified applicants, but relatively few of them ultimately accept positions. Finally, executive search firms generate a small list of highly qualified, interested applicants, but this is an expensive source compared with other alternatives.

Recruiters

The last part of the model presented in Figure 5.4 that we will discuss is the recruiter. We consider the recruiter this late in the chapter to reinforce our earlier observation that the recruiter often gets involved late in the process. In many cases, by the time a recruiter meets some applicants, they have already made up their minds about what they desire in a job, what the current job has to offer, and their likelihood of receiving a job offer.[86]

TABLE 5.4

Hypothetical Yield Ratios for Five Recruitment Sources

	RECRUITING SOURCE				
	LOCAL UNIVERSITY	RENOWNED UNIVERSITY	EMPLOYEE REFERRALS	NEWSPAPER AD	EXECUTIVE SEARCH FIRMS
Résumés generated	200	400	50	500	20
Interview offers accepted	175	100	45	400	20
Yield ratio	87%	25%	90%	80%	100%
Applicants judged acceptable	100	95	40	50	19
Yield ratio	57%	95%	89%	12%	95%
Accept employment offers	90	10	35	25	15
Yield ratio	90%	11%	88%	50%	79%
Cumulative yield ratio	90/200 45%	10/400 3%	35/50 70%	25/500 5%	15/20 75%
Cost	$30,000	$50,000	$15,000	$20,000	$90,000
Cost per hire	$333	$5,000	$428	$800	$6,000

Moreover, many applicants approach the recruiter with some degree of skepticism. Knowing that it is the recruiter's job to sell them on a vacancy, some applicants may discount what the recruiter says relative to what they have heard from other sources (like friends, magazine articles, and professors). For these and other reasons, recruiters' characteristics and behaviors seem to have less impact on applicants' job choices than we might expect. Moreover, as shown in Figure 5.5, whatever impact a recruiter does have on an applicant lessens as we move from reaction criteria (how the applicant felt about the recruiter) toward job choice criteria (whether the applicant takes the job).[87]

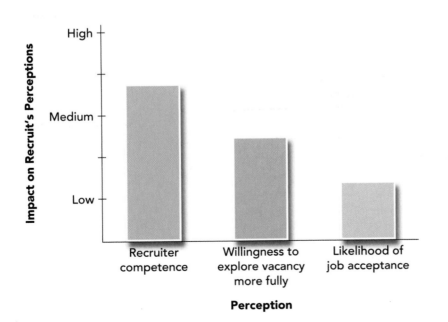

FIGURE 5.5

Relative Impact of the Recruiter on Various Recruitment Interview Outcomes

Recruiter's Functional Area. Most organizations must choose whether their recruiters are specialists in human resources or experts at particular jobs (supervisors or job incumbents). Some studies indicate that applicants find a job less attractive and the recruiter less credible when he is a personnel specialist.[88] This does not completely discount personnel specialists' role in recruiting, but it does indicate that such specialists need to take extra steps to ensure that applicants perceive them as knowledgeable and credible.

Recruiter's Traits. Two traits stand out when applicants' reactions to recruiters are examined. The first, which could be called "warmth," reflects the degree to which the recruiter seems to care about the applicant and is enthusiastic about her potential to contribute to the company. The second characteristic could be called "informativeness." In general, applicants respond more positively to recruiters who are perceived as warm and informative. These characteristics seem more important than such demographic characteristics as age, sex, or race, which have complex and inconsistent effects on applicant responses.[89]

Recruiter's Realism. Perhaps the most well-researched aspect of recruiting deals with the level of realism that the recruiter incorporates into his message. Since the recruiter's job is to attract candidates, there is some pressure to exaggerate the positive features of the vacancy while downplaying the negative features. Applicants are highly sensitive to negative information. Research suggests that the highest-quality applicants may be less willing to pursue jobs when this type of information comes out.[90] On the other hand, if the recruiter goes too far in a positive direction, the candidate can be misled and lured into taking the job under false pretenses.[91] This can lead to a serious case of unmet expectations and a high turnover rate.[92] In fact, unrealistic descriptions of a job may even lead new job incumbents to believe that the employer is deceitful.[93]

Many studies have looked at the capacity of "realistic job previews" to circumvent this problem and help minimize early job turnover. On the whole, the research suggests that the effect of realistic job previews on eventual turnover is weak and inconsistent.[94] Certainly, the idea that one can go overboard in selling a vacancy to a recruit has merit. However, the belief that informing people about the negative characteristics of the job will "inoculate" them to such characteristics seems unwarranted, based on the research conducted to date.[95] Thus we return to the conclusion that an organization's decisions about personnel policies that directly affect the job's attributes (pay, security, advancement opportunities, and so on) will probably be more important than recruiter traits and behaviors in affecting job choice. Indeed, research indicates that structured interventions that help applicants simply make good decisions about which jobs are best for them may work out best for both employers and applicants. That is, helping applicants better understand their own needs and qualifications and then linking this to the current openings may be best in the long run for all concerned, even if it does not result in an immediate hire.[96]

Enhancing Recruiter Impact. Although research suggests that recruiters do not have much influence on job choice, this does not mean recruiters cannot have an impact. Most recruiters receive little training.[97] One study has attempted to find conditions in which recruiters do make a difference. Based on this research, an organization can take several steps to increase the impact that recruiters have on those they recruit. First, recruiters can provide timely feedback. Applicants react very negatively to delays in feedback, often making unwarranted attributions for the delays (such as, the organization is uninterested in my application). Second, recruiters need to avoid

TABLE 5.5

Quotes from Recruits Who Were Repelled by Recruiters

One firm I didn't think of talking to initially, but they called me and asked me to talk with them. So I did, and then the recruiter was very, very rude. Yes, very rude, and I've run into that a couple of times. (engineering graduate)

I had a very bad campus interview experience . . . the person who came was a last-minute fill-in. . . . I think he had a couple of "issues" and was very discourteous during the interview. He was one step away from yawning in my face. . . . The other thing he did was that he kept making these (nothing illegal, mind you) but he kept making these references to the fact that I had been out of my undergraduate and first graduate programs for more than 10 years now. (MBA with 10 years of experience)

_____ has a management training program which the recruiter had gone through. She was talking about the great presentational skills that _____ teaches you, and the woman was barely literate. She was embarrassing. If that was the best they could do, I did not want any part of them. Also, _____ and _____'s recruiters appeared to have real attitude problems. I also thought they were chauvinistic. (arts undergraduate)

_____ had a set schedule for me which they deviated from regularly. Times overlapped, and one person kept me too long, which pushed the whole day back. They almost seemed to be saying that it was my fault that I was late for the next one! I guess a lot of what they did just wasn't very professional. Even at the point when I was done, where most companies would have a cab pick you up, I was in the middle of a snowstorm in Chicago and they said, "You can get a cab downstairs." There weren't any cabs. I literally had to walk 12 or 14 blocks with my luggage, trying to find some way to get to the airport. They didn't book me a hotel for the night of the snowstorm so I had to sit in the airport for eight hours trying to get another flight. . . . They wouldn't even reimburse me for the additional plane fare. (industrial relations graduate student)

The guy at the interview made a joke about how nice my nails were and how they were going to ruin them there due to all the tough work. (engineering undergraduate)

SOURCE: S. L. Rynes, R. D. Bretz, Jr., and B. Gerhart, "The Importance of Recruitment in Job Choice: A Different Way of Looking," *Personnel Psychology* 44 (1991), pp. 487–521. Used by permission.

behaviors that might convey the wrong organizational impression.[98] Table 5.5 lists quotes from applicants who felt that they had had extremely bad experiences with recruiters. Third, recruiting can be done in teams rather than by individuals. As we have seen, applicants tend to view line personnel (job incumbents and supervisors) as more credible than personnel specialists, so these kinds of recruiters should be part of any team. On the other hand, personnel specialists have knowledge that is not shared by line personnel (who may perceive recruiting as a small part of their "real" jobs), so they should be included as well.

A Look Back

The chapter opener showed how technological and social changes can often disrupt existing employment patterns, affecting the ability of nations, firm, and individuals to compete in contemporary labor markets. The speed and effectiveness of how nations, firms, and individuals respond to these changes is critical in determining their long-term success and well-being.

Questions

1. At the national level, what steps can politicians and labor leaders take to help their citizens and members compete in an ever-changing labor market?
2. At the firm level, what steps can organizational leaders and human resource professionals take to help their companies prosper in times of rapid change and turbulence?
3. At the individual level, what can you and other job seekers do to ensure that you will always have access to a high-paying, secure job that you find interesting and challenging?

Summary

Human resource planning uses labor supply and demand forecasts to anticipate labor shortages and surpluses. It also entails programs that can be utilized to reduce a labor surplus (such as downsizing and early retirement programs) and eliminate a labor shortage (like bringing in temporary workers or expanding overtime). When done well, human resource planning can enhance the success of the organization while minimizing the human suffering resulting from poorly anticipated labor surpluses or shortages. Human resource recruiting is a buffer activity that creates an applicant pool that the organization can draw from in the event of a labor shortage that is to be filled with new hires.

Organizational recruitment programs affect applications through personnel policies (such as promote-from-within policies or due process provisions) that affect the attributes of the vacancies themselves. They can also impact the nature of people who apply for positions by using different recruitment sources (like recruiting from universities versus advertising in newspapers). Finally, organizations can use recruiters to influence individuals' perceptions of jobs (eliminating misconceptions, clarifying uncertainties) or perceptions of themselves (changing their valences for various work outcomes).

Discussion Questions

1. Discuss the effects that an impending labor shortage might have on the following three subfunctions of human resource management: selection and placement, training and career development, and compensation and benefits. Which subfunction might be most heavily impacted? In what ways might these groups develop joint cooperative programs to avert a labor shortage?
2. Discuss the costs and benefits associated with statistical versus judgmental forecasts for labor demand and labor supply. Under what conditions might either of these techniques be infeasible? Under what conditions might both be feasible, but one more desirable than the other?
3. Some companies have detailed affirmative action plans, complete with goals and timetables, for women and minorities, and yet have no formal human resource plan for the organization as a whole. Why might this be

the case? If you were a human resource specialist interviewing with this company for an open position, what would this practice imply for the role of the human resource manager in that company?
4. Recruiting people for jobs that entail international assignments is increasingly important for many companies. Where might one go to look for individuals interested in these types of assignments? How might recruiting practices aimed at these people differ from those one might apply to the "average" recruit?
5. Discuss the relative merits of internal versus external recruitment. What types of business strategies might best be supported by recruiting externally, and what types might call for internal recruitment? What factors might lead a firm to decide to switch from internal to external recruitment or vice versa?

Self-Assessment Exercise

Most employers have to evaluate hundreds of résumés each week. If you want your résumé to have a good chance of being read by prospective employers, you must invest time and energy not only in its content, but also in its look. Review your résumé and answer yes or no to each of the following questions.

1. Does it avoid typos and grammatical errors?
2. Does it avoid using personal pronouns (such as I and me)?
3. Does it clearly identify what you have done and accomplished?
4. Does it highlight your accomplishments rather than your duties?
5. Does it exceed two pages in length?
6. Does it have correct contact information?
7. Does it have an employment objective that is specific and focuses on the employer's needs as well as your own?

8. Does it have at least one-inch margins?
9. Does it use a maximum of two typefaces or fonts?
10. Does it use bullet points to emphasize your skills and accomplishments?
11. Does it avoid use of underlining?
12. Is the presentation consistent? (Example: If you use all caps for the name of your most recent workplace, do you do that for previous workplaces as well?)

The more "yes" answers you gave, the more likely your résumé will attract an employer's attention and get you a job interview!

Manager's Hot Seat Exercise: Diversity: Mediating Morality

This Manager's Hot Seat case examines how employee diversity can affect the overall performance level of teams, departments, and organizations. In this scenario, an employee who has an alternate lifestyle claims this is why his coworker is complaining about him. The coworker staunchly disputes this claim. The human resource manager is attempting to assist the two workers in resolving their differences. Her ultimate goal is to redirect the attention of these employees back to achieving the established goals of the organization.

The case stresses the importance of understanding diversity in the workplace. Diversity surrounds each of us every day in the working environment. The differences in people must be acknowledged. Employees must be encouraged to gain appreciation for the many positive aspects diversity has to offer.

Individual Activity:
Prepare a one-page report, which thoroughly responds to the following questions:

- What does diversity mean to you?
- What exposure to diversity do you feel you have experienced?

- How did this diversity exposure affect you?
- What positives do you find in diversity?
- What negatives do you find in diversity?
- How can dealing with diversity in individuals be made easier?

Group Activity:
Divide the class in groups of 4-5 students per group. Each group is to discuss the individual reports members have prepared. As a group, identify problems diversity can create for organizational recruitment techniques. Discuss how organizations can defeat these types of problems. Discuss what organizations can do to assist recruiters to better understand the diversity in individuals. Identify both the positive and negative effects diversity can produce on organizations. Recommend methods organizations can utilize to diminish fear of diversity among its employees. Discuss how possessing a diverse workforce may affect human resource planning. Prepare a group response to be discussed as a class.

Exercising Strategy: Southwest Airlines: Focused on Take-Offs, Not Layoffs

In the summer of 2001, the airline industry was facing severe problems due to slumping business travel and vacationer demand. In fact, Northwest Airlines announced draconian cuts in both schedules and service; Midway Airlines declared bankruptcy in August of that year, citing "calamitous" decline in air traffic. However, as bad as things were, they soon got worse.

The September 11, 2001, terrorist attacks on New York and Washington, D.C., devastated the whole nation, but few segments of the economy felt the impact as dramati-

cally as the already struggling airline industry. Even after reducing scheduled flights by more than 20 percent, most planes were taking off with fewer than half their seats filled, and airline shares lost a third of their value on the stock exchange. Most airlines needed to cut costs drastically in order to make ends meet, and over 100,000 employees were eventually laid off from American Airlines, United Airlines, US Airways, Continental Airlines, and America West.

Southwest Airlines bucked this trend, however. Indeed, despite the regular ups and downs of the airline industry, in its 30 years of operation, Southwest has never laid off employees; remarkably, it was able to maintain this record even during the difficult Fall 2001 period. Southwest's no-layoff policy is one of the core values that underlie its human resource strategy, and insiders stress that it is one of the main reasons why the Southwest workforce is so fiercely loyal, productive, and flexible.

The high productivity of these workers helps keep labor costs low, and these savings are passed on to consumers in the form of lower prices that are sometimes half those offered by competitors. High levels of job security also promote a willingness on the part of Southwest employees to be innovative on the job without fearing that they will be punished for any mistakes. Southwest also finds that satisfied employees help create satisfied customers and can even help in recruiting new employees when economic conditions are conducive to growth.

In order to keep this perfect no-layoff record in 2001, Southwest executives assembled into an emergency command and control center in Dallas and brainstormed methods other than layoffs that could reduce costs. Decisions were made to delay the planned purchase of new planes, as well as to scrap ongoing plans to renovate the company's headquarters. The company, which had no debt and over a billion dollars in cash, also leaned heavily on this "rainy-day" fund to help get through tough times. It was a difficult and painful process, but as CEO Jim

Parker noted, "We are willing to suffer some damage, even to our stock price, to protect the jobs of our people."

SOURCE: M. Arndt, "Suddenly, Carriers Can't Get off the Ground," *BusinessWeek* (September 3, 2001), pp. 36–37; M. Arndt, "What Kind of Rescue?" *BusinessWeek* (October 1, 2001), pp. 36–37; W. Zeller, "Southwest: After Kelleher, More Blue Skies," *BusinessWeek* (April 2, 2001), p. 45; M. Conlin, "Where Layoffs Are a Last Resort," *BusinessWeek* (October 8, 2001), p. 42.

1. In this chapter, we explored several alternatives to layoffs as a mean of reducing a labor surplus. Compare and contrast the list we generated with what was done at Southwest in the wake of the 9/11 attacks. How did the response at Southwest differ from the other airlines'?
2. Southwest Airlines' "no layoff policy" is an important component of their overall culture and strategy. In what ways does this "no layoff policy," which clearly hurts the airline in the short term, give Southwest a competitive advantage over other airlines in the long term?
3. In the story that opened this chapter, we looked at the increased use of offshoring, where jobs are moved from the United States to other countries where labor rates are cheaper. In what ways is offshoring similar and different from a simple layoff? If there are some long-term benefits from avoiding layoffs, what might be the long-term advantages of trying to avoid offshoring?

Managing People: From the Pages of *BusinessWeek*

BusinessWeek Waking Up from the American Dream

Dead-End Jobs and the High Cost of College Could Be Choking Off Upward Mobility There has been much talk recently of the "Wal-Martization" of America, a reference to the giant retailer's fervent attempts to keep its costs—and therefore its prices—at rock-bottom levels. But for years, even during the 1990s boom, much of corporate America had already embraced Wal-Mart-like stratagems to control labor costs, such as hiring temps and part-timers, fighting unions, dismantling internal career ladders, and outsourcing to lower-paying contractors at home and abroad.

While these tactics have the admirable outcome of holding down consumer prices, they're costly in other ways. More than a quarter of the labor force, about 34 million workers, is trapped in low-wage, often dead-end jobs, according to a new book entitled *Low-Wage America: How Employers Are Reshaping Opportunity in the Workplace.* Many middle-income and high-skilled employees face fewer opportunities, too, as companies shift work to subcontractors and temp agencies and move white-collar jobs to China and India.

The result has been an erosion of one of America's most cherished values: giving its people the ability to move up the economic ladder over their lifetimes. Historically, most Americans, even low-skilled ones, were able to find poorly paid janitorial or factory jobs, then gradually climb into the middle class as they gained experience and moved up the wage curve. But the number of workers progressing upward began to slip in the 1970s, when the post–World War II productivity boom ran out of steam. Upward mobility diminished even more in the 1980s as globalization and technology slammed blue-collar wages.

Many experts expected the trend to reverse as productivity rebounded during the heated economy of the 1990s. Certainly, there were plenty of gains. The long decline in pay rates turned around as supertight labor markets raised the wages of almost everyone. College enrollment boomed, too, and home ownership shot up, extending the American dream to more families. Low interest rates and higher wages allowed even those on the bottom to benefit. There was even a slight decline in the ranks of the very poorest families, as measured by asset wealth—

those with a net worth of less than $5,000 —according to a study by New York University economics professor Edward N. Wolff.

But new research suggests that, surprisingly, the best economy in 30 years did little to get America's vaunted upward mobility back on track. The new studies, which follow individuals and families over many years, paint a paradoxical picture: Even as the U.S. economy was bursting with wealth in the 1990s, minting dot-com millionaires by the thousands, conventional companies were cutting the middle out of career ladders, leaving fewer people able to better their economic position over the decade.

During the 1990s, relative mobility—that is, the share of Americans changing income quintiles in any direction, up or down—slipped by two percentage points, to 62%, according to an analysis of decade-long income trends through 2001 by Jonathan D. Fisher and David S. Johnson, two economists at the Bureau of Labor Statistics. While two points may not sound like much, it's bad news given how much progress might have been made amid explosive growth. Essentially, says University of Chicago economics professor and Nobel laureate James J. Heckman, "the big finding in recent years is that the notion of America being a highly mobile society isn't as true as it used to be."

In fact, according to a study by two Federal Reserve Bank of Boston economists that analyzed families' incomes over three decades, the number of people who stayed stuck in the same income bracket—be it at the bottom or at the top—over the course of a decade actually increased in the 1990s. So, though the boom lifted pay rates for janitors and clerks by as much as 5% to 10% in the late 1990s, more of them remained janitors or clerks; fewer worked their way into better-paying positions. Imelda Roman, for one, makes about $30,000 a year as a counselor at a Milwaukee nonprofit—barely more than the $27,000 or so, after inflation adjustments, that the 33-year-old single mom earned as a school-bus driver more than 10 years ago. Says Roman, who hopes to return to college to improve her prospects: "It's hard to find a job with a career ladder these days, and a B.A. would be an edge."

What Roman faces is an economy that is slowly stratifying along class lines. Today, upward mobility is determined increasingly by a college degree that's attainable mostly by those whose parents already have money or education. "It's clear that unless you go to college, you can't achieve a high trajectory in life. Education is the key to success in America today," says Aramark Corp. CEO Joseph Neubauer. He gives scholarship money to hundreds of disadvantaged kids every year through the Horatio Alger Assn., a group of successful Americans who try to help others make it, too.

The gap in advancement shows up clearly in longitudinal studies such as Wolff's and the Boston Fed's, which track the same people over many years. These give a better picture of long-term economic mobility than the annual government surveys of wages and incomes, since even highly educated employees usually start at the bottom and work their way up the economic ladder.

For mobility to increase in relative terms, which is the standard way economists measure it, someone has to move down the pecking order to make room for another to move up. But the Boston Fed study found less movement in both directions. Some 40% of families didn't change income brackets over the decade, vs. 37% in the 1980s and 36% in the 1970s, according to the authors' analysis of annual longitudinal surveys by the University of Michigan.

The changing dynamic of the U.S. economy clearly has the most impact on those at the bottom. Some 49% of families who started the 1970s in poverty were still stuck there at the end of that decade, the Boston Fed study found. During the 1990s, the figure had jumped to 53%, even after accounting for two-earner families. A key reason lies with the creation of millions of jobs that pay less than a poverty-line wage of $8.70 an hour, according to *Low-Wage America,* a massive research project involving case studies by 38 academics. Most of the workers, such as nursing assistants or food preparers, "have no educational credentials beyond a high school diploma," the authors found.

Problem is, that all-important sheepskin is out of reach for most students from low-income families. Although college enrollment has soared for higher-income students, more children from poor families can only afford to go to community colleges, which typically don't offer bachelor's degrees. The number of poor students who get a degree— fewer than 5% in 2001—has barely budged in 30 years, according to an analysis of Census Bureau data by Thomas G. Mortenson, who publishes an education newsletter from Oskaloosa, Iowa.

In turn, the lack of mobility for those who don't or can't get a degree is putting a lid on the intergenerational progress that has long been a mainstay of the American experience. Last year, Wichita State University sociology professor David W. Wright and two colleagues updated a classic 1978 study that looked at how sons fared according to the social and economic class of their fathers. Defining class by a mix of education, income, and occupation, they found that sons from the bottom three-quarters of the socioeconomic scale were less likely to move up in the 1990s than in the 1960s. Just 10% of sons whose fathers were in the bottom quarter had made it to the top quarter by 1998, the authors found. By contrast, 23% of lower-class sons had done so by 1973, according to the earlier study. Similarly, only 51% of sons whose fathers belonged to the second-highest quarter equaled or surpassed the economic standing of their parents in the 1990s. In the 1960s, 63% did.

That's the pattern Michael A. McLimans and his family follows. Now 33, with two young children, the New Holland (Pa.) resident has spent the past decade working at pizza chains such as Domino's and Pizza Hut. He made it to assistant manager but found that he could earn more, $9 to $12 an hour with tips, as a delivery driver. He and his wife, a hotel receptionist, pull down about $40,000 a year—far from the $60,000 Michael's father, David I. McLimans, earns as a veteran steelworker. "I save every dime I can so my kids can go to college, which neither of us can afford to do," says Michael.

Increasingly, the story's the same for immigrants, who have been the most celebrated symbols of U.S. mobility. But compared with immigrants in the 1960s and '70s, a larger share of newcomers today are high school dropouts, including hundreds of thousands of poor villagers from Mexico. They encounter a plentiful job market that pays better than the one they left behind—but find fewer paths to a middle-class lifestyle, according to several recent studies. Over the long term, the spread between immigrant and native-born incomes is about three times greater today than it was a century ago, according to Harvard University sociology professor Christopher Jencks. Says Harvard economics professor George J. Borjas: "If you come here as an adult, it's very hard to get more education, which is the only way to get ahead today."

Restoring American mobility is less a question of knowing what to do than of making it happen. Experts have decried schools' inadequacy for years, but fixing them is a long, arduous struggle. Similarly, there have been plenty of warnings about declining college access, but finding funds was difficult even in eras of large surpluses. One radical approach: that college be treated the way high school is, as a public good paid for by taxpayers. Presidential candidate Senator John Edwards (D-N.C.) has proposed making the first year's tuition free at all community and public colleges for any student willing to work 10 hours a week. That may never happen, but clearly, if the U.S. couldn't shake off a creeping rigidity in the best of times, it will take a conscious change to reverse course now.

SOURCE: A. Bernstein, "Waking Up from the American Dream," *BusinessWeek* (December 1, 2003), pp. 54–58.

Questions

1. This article makes reference to the Horatio Alger Association, which offers scholarships to disadvantaged youths. Who was the real Horatio Alger and why was he symbolic of the U.S. labor market for the last 200 years?
2. In what ways is the current U.S. labor market different than it was over the last 200 years, and what is the objective evidence to indicate that there are fewer and fewer "Horatio Alger stories" out there today?
3. What are some of the factors that have limited upward mobility in the contemporary U.S. labor market?
4. What can be done at the national level by our government, the organizational level by U.S. firms, and the individual level by U.S. workers to help return to the days when upward mobility was the rule rather than the exception?

Please see the video case at the end of the book that correlates to this chapter: Jobless Recovery

Notes

1. W. Zellner, "Lessons from a Faded Levi-Strauss," *BusinessWeek* (December 25, 2003), p. 44.
2. M. Muray, "After Long Boom, Workers Confront Downward Mobility," *The Wall Street Journal* (August 13, 2003), pp. A1–A3.
3. T. Aeppel, "Offshore Face-Off," *The Wall Street Journal* (May 10, 2004), pp. B1–B2.
4. B. Davis, "Migration of Skilled Jobs Abroad Unsettles Global-Economy Fans," *The Wall Street Journal* (January 26, 2004), pp. A1–A2.
5. P. Coy, "The Future of Work," *BusinessWeek* (March 22, 2004), pp. 50–52.
6. D. W. Jarrell, *Human Resource Planning: A Business Planning Approach* (Englewood Cliffs, NJ: Prentice Hall, 1993).
7. D. P. Shuit, "Workforce Problems Imperil NASA" *Workforce*, March 2003, p. 15.
8. D. Welch, "A Contract the Big Three Can Take to the Bank," *BusinessWeek* (September 29, 2003), p. 46.
9. M. Conlin, "Savaged by the Slowdown," *BusinessWeek* (September 17, 2001), pp. 74–77.
10. W. F. Cascio, "Whither Industrial and Organizational Psychology in a Changing World of Work?" *American Psychologist* 50 (1995), pp. 928–39.
11. D. Greising, "It's the Best of Times—Or Is It?" *BusinessWeek* (January 12, 1998), pp. 35–38.
12. A. Serwer, "What's Hot on Wall Street in 2001? Cost Cutting and Layoffs," *Fortune* (February 19, 2001), pp. 34–36.
13. N. D. Schwartz, "Will 'Made in the USA' Fade Away?" *Fortune* (November 24, 2003), pp. 98–110.
14. R. T. King, "Is Job Cutting by Drug Makers Bad Medicine?" *The Wall Street Journal* (August 23, 1995), pp. B1–B3.
15. K. Labich, "The Geography of an Emerging America," *Fortune* (June 27, 1994), pp. 88–94.
16. J. E. Hilsenrath, "Behind the Outsourcing Debate: Surpisingly, Few Hard Numbers," *The Wall Street Journal* (April 22, 2004), pp. A1–A3.
17. K. P. DeMeuse, P. A. Vanderheiden, and T. J. Bergmann, "Announced Layoffs: Their Effect on Corporate Financial Performance," *Human Resource Management* 33 (1994), pp. 509–30.
18. P. P. Shaw, "Network Destruction: The Structural Implications

of Downsizing," *Academy of Management Journal* 43 (2000), pp. 101–12.

19. King, "Is Job Cutting by Drug Makers Bad Medicine?"

20. W. F. Cascio, "Downsizing: What Do We Know? What Have We Learned?" *Academy of Management Executive* 7 (1993), pp. 95–104.

21. J. Schu, "Internet Helps Keep Goodwill of Downsized Employees," *Workforce*, July 2001, p. 15.

22. D. Skarlicki, J. H. Ellard, and B. R. C. Kellin, "Third Party Perceptions of a Layoff: Procedural, Derogation, and Retributive Aspects of Justice," *Journal of Applied Psychology* 83 (1998), pp. 119–27.

23. R. Folger and D. P. Skarlicki, "When Tough Times Make Tough Bosses: Managerial Distancing as a Function of Layoff Blame," *Academy of Management Journal* 41 (1998), pp. 79–87.

24. J. E. Hilsenrath, "Adventures in Cost Cutting," *The Wall Street Journal* (May 10, 2004), pp. A1–A3.

25. R. Stodghill, "The Coming Job Bottleneck," *BusinessWeek* (March 24, 1997), pp. 184–85.

26. S. Kim and D. Feldman, "Healthy, Wealthy, or Wise: Predicting Actual Acceptances of Early Retirement Incentives at Three Points in Time," *Personnel Psychology* 51 (1998), pp. 623–42.

27. P. J. Kiger, "Early Retirement Plans Backfire, Driving Up Costs Instead of Cutting Them," *Workforce*, January 2004, pp. 66–68.

28. D. Fandray, "Gray Matters," *Workforce*, July 2000, pp. 27–32.

29. J. Weber, "Not Just a Temporary Lift," *BusinessWeek* (January 19, 2004).

30. M. Gimein, "The Bugs in Microsoft's Culture," *Fortune* (January 8, 2001), p. 128.

31. S. Caudron, "Are Your Temps Doing Their Best?" *Personnel Journal*, November 1995, pp. 32–38.

32. T. Cothran, "Outsourcing on the Inside Track," *Training*, May 1995, pp. 31–37.

33. L. D. Tyson, "Outsourcing: Who's Safe Anymore?" *BusinessWeek* (February 23, 2004), p. 26.

34. W. Zellner, "Lessons from a Faded Levi-Strauss," *BusinessWeek* (December 15, 2003), p. 44.

35. A. Meisler, "Think Globally, Act Rationally," *Workforce*, January 2004, pp. 40–45.

36. S. E. Ante, "Shifting Work Offshore? Outsourcer Beware," *BusinessWeek* (January 12, 2004, pp. 36–37.

37. G. Koretz, "Overtime versus New Factories," *BusinessWeek* (May 4, 1998), p. 34.

38. D. Foust, "A Smarter Squeeze?" *BusinessWeek* (December 31, 2001), pp. 42–44.

39. J. Eig, "Many Employers Cut Worker Hours to Avoid Layoffs," *The Wall Street Journal* (January 3, 2002), pp. A1–A2.

40. A. Bernstein, "Bell Atlantic North Faces a Monstrous Labor Crunch," *BusinessWeek* (June 8, 1998), p. 38.

41. A. E. Barber, *Recruiting Employees* (Thousand Oaks, CA: Sage, 1998).

42. J. A. Breaugh, *Recruitment: Science and Practice* (Boston: PWS-Kent, 1992).

43. C. K. Stevens, "Antecedents of Interview Interactions, Interviewers' Ratings, and Applicants' Reactions," *Personnel Psychology* 51 (1998), pp. 55–85.

44. A. E. Barber, J. R. Hollenbeck, S. L. Tower, and J. M. Phillips, "The Effects of Interview Focus on Recruitment Effectiveness: A Field Experiment," *Journal of Applied Psychology* 79 (1994), pp. 886–96.

45. J. D. Olian and S. L. Rynes, "Organizational Staffing: Integrating Practice with Strategy," *Industrial Relations* 23 (1984), pp. 170–83.

46. R. Kanfer, C. R. Wanberg, and T. M. Kantrowitz, "Job Search and Employment: A Personality–Motivational Analysis and Meta-Analytic Review," *Journal of Applied Psychology* 86 (2001), pp. 837–55.

47. G. T. Milkovich and J. M. Newman, *Compensation* (Homewood, IL: Richard D. Irwin, 1990).

48. S. J. Marks, "After School," *Human Resources Executive* (June 15, 2001), pp. 49–51.

49. P. J. Kiger, "The Center of Attention," *Workforce*, March 2004, pp. 51–52.

50. J. Kaufman, "A McDonald's Owner Becomes a Role Model for Black Teenagers," *The Wall Street Journal* (August 23, 1995), p. A1.

51. K. Helliker, "Sold on the Job: Retailing Chains Offer a Lot of Opportunity, Young Managers Find," *The Wall Street Journal* (August 25, 1995), p. A1.

52. W. Zellner, "The Fall of Enron," *BusinessWeek* (December 17, 2001), pp. 30–36.

53. M. Leonard, "Challenges to the Termination-at-Will Doctrine," *Personnel Administrator* 28 (1983), pp. 49–56.

54. C. Schowerer and B. Rosen, "Effects of Employment-at-Will Policies and Compensation Policies on Corporate Image and Job Pursuit Intentions," *Journal of Applied Psychology* 74 (1989), pp. 653–56.

55. M. Magnus, "Recruitment Ads at Work," *Personnel Journal* 64 (1985), pp. 42–63.

56. S. L. Rynes and A. E. Barber, "Applicant Attraction Strategies: An Organizational Perspective," *Academy of Management Review* 15 (1990), pp. 286–310.

57. Breaugh, *Recruitment*.

58. C. Collins and C. K. Stevens, "The Relationship between Early Recruitment-Related Activities and the Application Decisions of New Labor Market Entrants: A Brand Equity Approach to Recruitment," *Journal of Applied Psychology* 87 (2002), pp. 1121–33.

59. M. E. Brooks, S. Highhouse, S. S. Russell, and D. C. Mohr, "Familiarity, Ambivalence, and Firm Reputation: Is Corporate Fame a Double-Edged Sword?" *Journal of Applied Psychology* 88 (2003), pp. 904–14.

60. F. Lievens and S. Highhouse, "The Relation of Instrumental and Symbolic Attributes to a Company's Attractiveness as an Employer," *Personnel Psychology* 56 (2003), pp. 75–102.

61. J. E. Slaughter, M. J. Zickar, S. Highhouse, and D. C. Mohr, "Personality Trait Inferences about Organizations: Development of a Measure and Assessment of Construct Validity," *Journal of Applied Psychology* 89 (2004), pp. 85–103.

62. D. R. Avery, "Reactions to Diversity in Recruitment Advertising—Are Differences Black and White?" *Journal of Applied Psychology* 88 (2003), pp. 672–79.

63. D. M. Cable, L. Aiman-Smith, P. Mulvey, and J. R. Edwards, "The Sources and Accuracy of Job Applicants' Beliefs about Organizational Culture," *Academy of Management Journal* 43 (2000), pp. 1076–85.

64. M. A. Conrad and S. D. Ashworth, "Recruiting Source Effectiveness: A Meta-analysis and Re-examination of Two Rival Hypotheses," paper presented at the annual meeting of the Society of Industrial/Organizational Psychology, Chicago, 1986.

65. Breaugh, *Recruitment*.

66. M. Hammers, "One Out of Many," *Workforce*, November 2003, pp. 59–60.

67. Breaugh, *Recruitment*.

68. R. S. Schuler and S. E. Jackson, "Linking Competitive Strategies with Human Resource Management Practices," *Academy of Management Executive* 1 (1987), pp. 207–19.

69. C. R. Wanberg, R. Kanfer, and J.T. Banas, "Predictors and Outcomes of Networking Intensity among Job Seekers," *Journal of Applied Psychology* 85 (2000), pp. 491–503.

70. C. R. Williams, C. E. Labig, and T. H. Stone, "Recruitment Sources and Posthire Outcomes for Job Applicants and New Hires: A Test of Two Hypotheses," *Journal of Applied Psychology* 78 (1994), pp. 163–72.

71. A. Halcrow, "Employers Are Your Best Recruiters," *Personnel Journal* 67 (1988), pp. 42–49.

72. G. Flynn, "Do You Have the Right Approach to Diversity?" *Personnel Journal*, October 1995, pp. 68–75.

73. B. P. Sunoo, "Papa John's Rolls Out Hot HR Menu," *Personnel Journal*, September 1995, pp. 38–47.

74. Breaugh, *Recruitment*.

75. J. Smith, "Is Online Recruiting Getting Easier?" *Workforce* (September 2, 2001), p. 25.

76. B. R. Dineen, S. R. Ash, and R. A. Noe, "A Web of Applicant Attraction: Person–Organization Fit in the Context of Web-Based Recruitment," *Journal of Applied Psychology* 87(2002), pp. 723–34.

77. A. Salkever, "A Better Way to Float Your Résumé," *Business-Week Online* (October 9, 2000), pp. 1–2.

78. K. O. Magnusen and K. G. Kroeck, "Video Conferencing Maximizes Recruiting," *HRMagazine*, August 1995, pp. 70–72.

79. P. Smith, "Sources Used by Employers When Hiring College Grads," *Personnel Journal*, February 1995, p. 25.

80. J. W. Boudreau and S. L. Rynes, "Role of Recruitment in Staffing Utility Analysis," *Journal of Applied Psychology* 70 (1985), pp. 354–66.

81. D. Anfuso, "3M's Staffing Strategy Promotes Productivity and Pride," *Personnel Journal*, February 1995, pp. 28–34.

82. L. Winter, "Employers Go to School on Minority Recruiting," *The Wall Street Journal* (December 15, 1992), p. B1.

83. C. M. Solomon, "Navigating Your Search for Global Talent," *Personnel Journal*, May 1995, pp. 94–97.

84. R. Hawk, *The Recruitment Function* (New York: American Management Association, 1967).

85. K. D. Carlson, M. L. Connerly, and R. L. Mecham, "Recruitment Evaluation: The Case for Assessing the Quality of Applicants Attracted," *Personnel Psychology* 55 (2002), pp. 461–94.

86. C. K. Stevens, "Effects of Preinterview Beliefs on Applicants' Reactions to Campus Interviews," *Academy of Management Journal* 40 (1997), pp. 947–66.

87. C. D. Fisher, D. R. Ilgen, and W. D. Hoyer, "Source Credibility, Information Favorability, and Job Offer Acceptance," *Academy of Management Journal* 22 (1979), pp. 94–103; G. N. Powell, "Applicant Reactions to the Initial Employment Interview: Exploring Theoretical and Methodological Issues," *Personnel Psychology* 44 (1991), pp. 67–83; N. Schmitt and B. W. Coyle, "Applicant Decisions in the Employment Interview," *Journal of Applied Psychology* 61 (1976), pp. 184–92.

88. M. S. Taylor and T. J. Bergman, "Organizational Recruitment Activities and Applicants' Reactions at Different Stages of the Recruitment Process," *Personnel Psychology* 40 (1984), pp. 261–85; Fisher, Ilgen, and Hoyer, "Source Credibility."

89. L. M. Graves and G. N. Powell, "The Effect of Sex Similarity on Recruiters' Evaluations of Actual Applicants: A Test of the Similarity–Attraction Paradigm," *Personnel Psychology* 48 (1995), pp. 85–98.

90. R. D. Bretz and T. A. Judge, "Realistic Job Previews: A Test of the Adverse Self-Selection Hypothesis," *Journal of Applied Psychology* 83 (1998), pp. 330–37.

91. A. Meisler, "Little White Lies," *Workforce*, November 2003, pp. 88–89.

92. J. P. Wanous, *Organizational Entry: Recruitment, Selection and Socialization of Newcomers* (Reading, MA: Addison-Wesley, 1980).

93. P. Hom, R. W. Griffeth, L. E. Palich, and J. S. Bracker, "An Exploratory Investigation into Theoretical Mechanisms Underlying Realistic Job Previews," *Personnel Psychology* 51 (1998), pp. 421–51.

94. G. M. McEvoy and W. F. Cascio, "Strategies for Reducing Employee Turnover: A Meta-analysis," *Journal of Applied Psychology* 70 (1985), pp. 342–53; S. L. Premack and J. P. Wanous, "A Meta-analysis of Realistic Job Preview Experiments," *Journal of Applied Psychology* 70 (1985), pp. 706–19.

95. P. G. Irving and J. P. Meyer, "Reexamination of the Met-Expectations Hypothesis: A Longitudinal Analysis," *Journal of Applied Psychology* 79 (1995), pp. 937–49.

96. Y. Ganzach, A. Pazy, Y. Hohayun, "Social Exchange and Organizational Commitment: Decision-Making Training for Job Choice as an Alternative to the Realistic Job Preview," *Personnel Psychology* 55 (2002), pp. 613–37.

97. R. W. Walters, "It's Time We Become Pros," *Journal of College Placement* 12 (1985), pp. 30–33.

98. S. L. Rynes, R. D. Bretz, and B. Gerhart, "The Importance of Recruitment in Job Choice: A Different Way of Looking," *Personnel Psychology* 44 (1991), pp. 487–522.

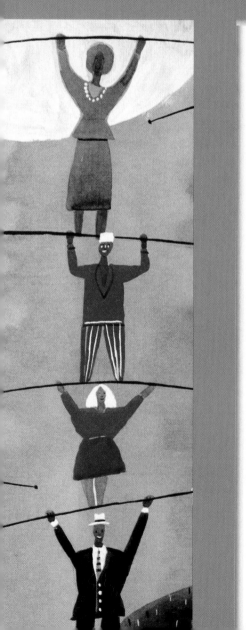

6 Chapter

Selection and Placement

Objectives After reading this chapter, you should be able to:

1. Establish the basic scientific properties of personnel selection methods, including reliability, validity, and generalizability.

2. Discuss how the particular characteristics of a job, organization, or applicant affect the utility of any test.

3. Describe the government's role in personnel selection decisions, particularly in the areas of constitutional law, federal laws, executive orders, and judicial precedent.

4. List the common methods used in selecting human resources.

5. Describe the degree to which each of the common methods used in selecting human resources meets the demands of reliability, validity, generalizability, utility, and legality.

Selection methods must be standardized so employees know what skills they need to move up within their organization.

Enter the World of Business

Standardizing Selection

The process for securing a management position at Wal-Mart was not a very standardized affair. Instead, as one observer has noted, "it was a tap-on-the-shoulder process, where Wal-Mart would reach down and anoint somebody and invite them into upper management." There are virtues to decentralized decision-making processes, and in many ways, Wal-Mart has exploited these when it comes to purchasing and merchandising. However, when applied to human resources, this aspect of Wal-Mart's decision-making process, when combined with the male-dominated Southern culture that pervaded the retailing giant, often worked against female employees. Many women workers who served the company for years, and who received glowing yearly evaluations, watched in frustration as they were passed over for management jobs that were given to seemingly less-qualified men.

Although the lack of standardization in the selection process made it hard to see what went into managerial selection decisions, the results of those decisions were easy to document. Specifically, although women made up over two-thirds of the hourly workers at Wal-Mart, women held fewer than one-third of the managerial positions. This led to a class action suit that

included 1.5 million current and former female employees—making it the largest such suit in history. To give an idea of the scope of this suit, in a similar case against Texaco in 1997, the oil company had to pay out, on average, roughly $125,000 to 1,400 African American workers who were bypassed for managerial positions. If Wal-Mart has to pay out a similar amount to the 1.5 million women, this would amount to over $150 billion. Indeed, given the number of claimants in the case, Wal-Mart has argued that there is no practical way that it could ever survive such a verdict.

There were two specific practices and one general philosophy that contributed to Wal-Mart's current predicament. First, in terms of specific practices, the company made it difficult for people to apply for managerial jobs because openings were not posted publicly. The local store manager, who was empowered by the company's decentralized philosophy, often filled positions without even notifying anyone that a position was open. Second, each store manager took his own idiosyncratic approach to selection decisions, and thus, the information that was used in deciding who was selected for managerial positions and who was rejected was never detailed or justified. Thus, when it became clear that the decision-making process was having an adverse impact on women in terms of both pay and advancement, the organization has had a hard time pointing to anything other than sex discrimination as the possible explanation for such a result.

On a more philosophical level, Wal-Mart also has had a history of taking a very minimalist approach to human resource management. The human resource staff was generally pulled from the ranks of former workers, rather than from professional programs or colleges that produced HR specialists. The human resource group was treated as an unfortunate cost of doing business, and consistent with the organization's culture, costs were to be minimized. In addition to making them liable to suits such as this one, this philosophy has also made them vulnerable to external competitors—particularly Costco —that directly compete with Wal-Mart by taking a more aggressive approach to human resource management issues.

Costco also tries to keep costs to customers low, but not at the expense of workers, who are well paid and who are given open opportunities for advancement regardless of gender. As Costco CEO James Sinegal notes, "We think when you take care of your customers and your employees, your shareholders are going to be rewarded in the long run. We're not going to do something for the sake of short-term share price that is going to destroy the fabric of our company and what we stand for." This philosophy has led to turnover rates at Costco stores that are half of that of Wal-Mart, which, along with its internal hiring practices that emphasize competence rather than gender, translates into more experienced and effective managerial ranks. Thus, although there are fewer of them, the average Costco store generates nearly double the revenue of a similarly sized Wal-Mart store. As one ex-Wal-Mart employee notes, "I don't think Wal-Mart realizes how important human resources is to them. They are learning, but they are learning the hard way."

Source: D. P. Shuit, "People Problems on Every Aisle," *Workforce*, February 2004, pp. 26–34; J. Useem, "Should We Admire Wal-Mart?" *Fortune* (March 8, 2004), pp. 118–120; W. Zellner, "A New Pay Scheme for Wal-Mart Workers," *BusinessWeek* (June 14, 2004), p. 39; J. Helyer, "The Only Company That Wal-Mart Fears," *Fortune* (November 24, 2003), pp. 158–166.

Introduction

Any organization that intends to compete through people must take the utmost care with how it chooses organizational members, especially those at managerial ranks. These decisions have a critical impact on the organization's ability to compete, as well as each and every job applicant's life. These decisions are too important to be left to the whim of untrained individuals, and as you can see from the opening story, legal actions can be taken against employers who fail to adequately discharge this responsibility. However, on top of the legal price that may be paid by organizations that fail to make the best selection decisions is the price they pay in term of economic competitiveness. By failing to consider female applicants for managerial positions, Wal-Mart is ignoring a large and potentially valuable source of managerial talent. Although the local store managers may have their own ideas about whether or not women make good leaders, their ideas may not be as sound as what can be gleaned from over 50 years of research on the topic.

Specifically, when it comes to managing workers, results from hundreds of studies support several conclusions. First, in terms of style, female leaders are more likely than male leaders to (a) appeal to workers' pride and need for respect, (b) rely on emotional appeals to inspire motivation, (c) provide more of an intellectual basis for their decisions, (d) give more individual consideration to employees (as opposed to relying on policies), and (e) apply performance-contingent rewards and bonuses. Studies

[handwritten: disadvantages to male managers]

show male leaders on the other hand are much less active leaders and are more likely to (a) lead by exception, that is, step in only when something goes wrong or (b) demonstrate laissez-faire tactics or a hands-off approach to management. In terms of results, the more active role of the female leaders results in employees who are (a) more likely to report putting forth extra effort, (b) more satisfied with their leader, and (c) more effective in terms of meeting work goals.[1]

The magnitude of the difference between the sexes, even on these dimensions, in the studies, was very, very small, and there were many men in these studies that outperformed women on the dimensions specified above. The key is not to decide which gender to hire, but rather to actually measure each individual's abilities, skills, experiences and temperaments in these critical areas, and then hire the best regardless of gender.

The purpose of this chapter is to familiarize you with ways to minimize errors in employee selection and placement and, in doing so, improve your company's competitive position. The chapter first focuses on five standards that should be met by any selection method. The chapter then evaluates several common selection methods according to those standards.

Selection Method Standards

Personnel selection is the process by which companies decide who will or will not be allowed into organizations. Several generic standards should be met in any selection process. We focus on five: (1) reliability, (2) validity, (3) generalizability, (4) utility, and (5) legality. The first four build off each other in the sense that the preceding standard is often necessary but not sufficient for the one that follows. This is less the case with legal standards. However, a thorough understanding of the first four standards helps us understand the rationale underlying many legal standards.

Reliability

Much of the work in personnel selection involves measuring characteristics of people to determine who will be accepted for job openings. For example, we might be interested in applicants' physical characteristics (like strength or endurance), their cognitive abilities (such as mathematical ability or verbal reasoning capacity), or aspects of their personality (like their initiative or integrity). Whatever the specific focus, in the end we need to quantify people on these dimensions (assign numbers to them) so we can order them from high to low on the characteristic of interest. Once people are ordered in this way, we can decide whom to hire and whom to reject.

One key standard for any measuring device is its reliability. We define **reliability** as the degree to which a measure is free from random error.[2] If a measure of some supposedly stable characteristic such as intelligence is reliable, then the score a person receives based on that measure will be consistent over time and in different contexts.

Reliability
The consistency of a performance measure; the degree to which a performance measure is free from random error.

True Scores and the Reliability of Measurement
Most measuring done in personnel selection deals with complex characteristics like intelligence, integrity, and leadership ability. However, to appreciate some of the complexities in measuring people, we will consider something concrete in discussing these concepts: the measurement of height. For example, if we were measuring an applicant's height, we might start by using a 12-inch ruler. Let's say the first person we

measure turns out to be 6 feet 1 and $^{4}/_{16}$ inches tall. It would not be surprising to find out that someone else measuring the same person a second time, perhaps an hour later, found this applicant's height to be 6 feet and $^{12}/_{16}$ inches. The same applicant, measured a third time, maybe the next day, might be measured at 6 feet 1 and $^{8}/_{16}$ inches tall.

As this example makes clear, even though the person's height is a stable characteristic, we get slightly different results each time he is assessed. This means that each time the person is assessed, we must be making slight errors. If a measurement device were perfectly reliable, there would be no errors of measurement. If we used a measure of height that was not as reliable as a ruler—for example, guessing someone's height after seeing her walk across the room—we might see an even greater amount of unreliability in the measure. Thus *reliability* refers to the measuring instrument (a ruler versus a visual guess) rather than to the characteristic itself.

Because one never really knows the true score for the person being measured, there is no direct way to capture the "true" reliability of the measure. We can estimate reliability in several different ways, however; and because most of these rely on computing a correlation coefficient, we will briefly describe and illustrate this statistic.

The *correlation coefficient* is a measure of the degree to which two sets of numbers are related. The correlation coefficient expresses the strength of the relationship in numerical form. A perfect positive relationship (as one set of numbers goes up, so does the other) equals +1.0; a perfect negative relationship (as one goes up, the other goes down) equals −1.0. When there is no relationship between the sets of numbers, the correlation equals .00. Although the actual calculation of this statistic goes beyond the scope of this book (see any introductory statistics book or spreadsheet program), it will be useful for us to conceptually examine the nature of the correlation coefficient and what this means in personnel selection contexts.

When assessing the reliability of a measure, for example, we might be interested in knowing how scores on the measure at one time relate to scores on the same measure at another time. Obviously, if the characteristic we are measuring is supposedly stable (like intelligence or integrity) and the time lapse is short, this relationship should be strong. If it were weak, then the measure would be inconsistent—hence unreliable. This is called assessing *test–retest reliability*.

Plotting the two sets of numbers on a two-dimensional graph often helps us to appreciate the meaning of various levels of the correlation coefficient. Figure 6.1, for example, examines the relationship between student scholastic aptitude in one's junior and senior years in high school, where aptitude for college is measured in three ways: (1) via the scores on the Scholastic Aptitude Test (SAT), (2) via ratings from a high school counselor on a 1-to-100 scale, and (3) via tossing dice. In this plot, each number on the graphs represents a person whose scholastic aptitude is assessed twice (in the junior and senior years), so in Figure 6.1a, 1_1 represents a person who scored 1580 on the SAT in the junior year and 1500 in the senior year; 20_{20} represents a person who scored 480 in the junior year and 620 in the senior year.

Figure 6.1a shows a very strong relationship between SAT scores across the two years. This relationship is not perfect in that the scores changed slightly from one year to the next, but not a great deal. Indeed, if there were a perfect 1.0 correlation, the plot would show a straight line at a 45-degree angle. The correlation coefficient for this set of data is in the .90 range. In this case, .90 is considered the test–retest estimate of reliability.

Turning to Figure 6.1b, we see that the relationship between the high school counselors' ratings across the two years, while still positive, is not as strong. That is, the

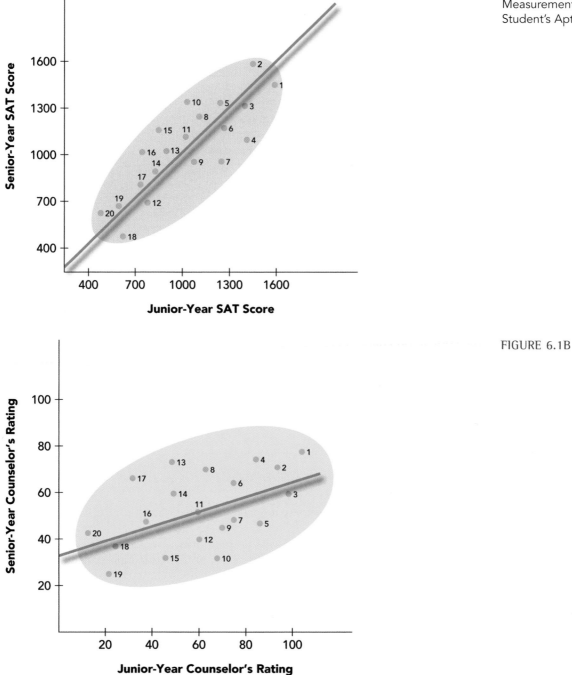

FIGURE 6.1A

Measurements of a
Student's Aptitude

FIGURE 6.1B

counselors' ratings of individual students' aptitudes for college are less consistent over
the two years than their test scores. The correlation, and hence test–retest reliability,
of this measure of aptitude is in the .50 range.

Finally, Figure 6.1c shows a worst-case scenario, where the students' aptitudes are
assessed by tossing two six-sided dice. As you would expect, the random nature of the

FIGURE 6.1C

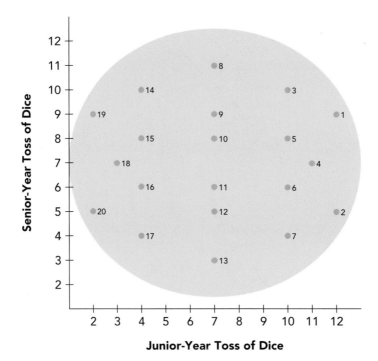

dice means that there is virtually no relationship between scores taken in one year and scores taken the next. Hence, in this instance, the correlation and test–retest estimate of reliability are .00. Although no one would seriously consider tossing dice to be a measure of aptitude, it is worth noting that research shows that the correlation of overall ratings of job applicants' suitability for jobs based on unstructured interviews is very close to .00. Thus, one cannot assume a measure is reliable without actually checking this directly. Novices in measurement are often surprised at exactly how unreliable many human judgments turn out to be.

Standards for Reliability

Regardless of what characteristic we are measuring, we want highly reliable measures. Thus, in the previous example, when it comes to measuring students' aptitudes for college, the SAT is more reliable than counselor ratings, which in turn are more reliable than tossing dice. But in an absolute sense, how high is high enough—.50, .70, .90? This is a difficult question to answer specifically because the required reliability depends in part on the nature of the decision being made about the people being measured.

For example, let's assume some college admissions officer was considering several students depicted in Figures 6.1a and 6.1b. Turning first to Figure 6.1b, assume the admissions officer was deciding between Student 1 (1_1) and Student 20 (20_{20}). For this decision, the .50 reliability of the ratings is high enough because the difference between the two students is so large that one would make the same decision for admission regardless of the year in which the rating was taken. That is, Student 1 (with scores of 100 and 80 in the junior and senior year, respectively) is always admitted and Student 20 (with scores of 12 and 42 for junior and senior years, respectively) is always rejected. Thus, although the ratings in this case are not all that reliable in an absolute sense, their reliability is high enough for this decision.

On the other hand, let's assume the same college admissions officer was deciding between Student 1 (1_1) and Student 2 (2_2). Looking at Figure 6.1a, it is clear that even with the highly reliable SAT scores, the difference between these students is so small that one would make a different admission decision depending on what year one obtained the score. Student 1 would be selected over Student 2 if the junior-year score was used, but Student 2 would be chosen over Student 1 if the senior-year score was used. Thus, even though the reliability of the SAT exam is high in an absolute sense, it is not high enough for this decision. Under these conditions, the admissions officer needs to find some other basis for making the decision regarding these two students (like high school GPA or rank in graduating class).

Although these two scenarios clearly show that no specific value of reliability is always acceptable, they also demonstrate why, all else being equal, the more reliable a measure is, the better. For example, turning again to Figures 6.1a and 6.1b, consider Student 9 (9_9) and Student 14 (14_{14}). One would not be able to make a decision between these two students based on scholastic aptitude scores if assessed via counselor ratings, because the unreliability in the ratings is so large that scores across the two years conflict. That is, Student 9 has a higher rating than Student 14 in the junior year, but Student 14 has a higher rating than Student 9 in the senior year.

On the other hand, one would be able to base the decision on scholastic aptitude scores if assessed via the SAT, because the unreliability of the SAT scores is so low that scores across the two years point to the same conclusion. That is, Student 9's scores are always higher than Student 14's scores. Clearly, all else being equal, the more reliable the measure, the more likely it is that we can base decisions on the score differences that it reveals.

There are many ways to increase the reliability of a test, including writing clear and unambiguous items and increasing the length of the test. In addition, as shown in the "Competing through Technology" box on pages 226–227, new technologies that allow for the development of computer adaptive testing can generate highly reliable tests by tailoring the item sequencing and selection process differently for each individual. Indeed, this and other technological changes associated with the Internet have required people to think differently about exactly what is meant by various terms that have long been taken for granted in this area.

Validity

We define **validity** as the extent to which performance on the measure is related to performance on the job. A measure must be reliable if it is to have any validity. On the other hand, we can reliably measure many characteristics (like height) that may have no relationship to whether someone can perform a job. For this reason, reliability is a necessary but insufficient condition for validity.

Criterion-Related Validation

One way of establishing the validity of a selection method is to show that there is an empirical association between scores on the selection measure and scores for job performance. If there is a substantial correlation between test scores and job-performance scores, **criterion-related validity** has been established. For example, Figure 6.2 shows the relationship between 2003 scores on the Scholastic Aptitude Test (SAT) and 2004 freshman grade point average (GPA). In this example, there is roughly a .50 correlation between the SAT and GPA. This .50 is referred to as a

Validity
The extent to which a performance measure assesses all the relevant—and only the relevant—aspects of job performance.

Criterion-related validity
A method of establishing the validity of a personnel selection method by showing a substantial correlation between test scores and job-performance scores.

FIGURE 6.2

Relationship
between 2003 SAT
Scores and 2004
Freshman GPA

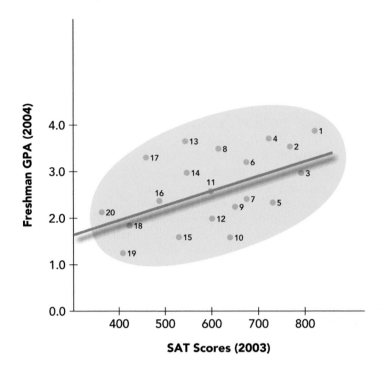

validity coefficient. Note that we have used the correlation coefficient to assess both reliability and validity, which may seem somewhat confusing. The key distinction is that the correlation reflects a reliability estimate when we are attempting to assess the same characteristic twice (such as SAT scores in the junior and senior years), but the correlation coefficient reflects a validity coefficient when we are attempting to relate one characteristic (SAT) to performance on some task (GPA).

Criterion-related validity studies come in two varieties. **Predictive validation** seeks to establish an empirical relationship between test scores taken prior to being hired and eventual performance on the job. Predictive validation requires one to administer tests to job applicants and then wait for some time after test administration to see how a subset of those applicants (those who were actually hired) performed.

Because of the time and effort required to conduct a predictive validation study, many employers are tempted to use a different design. **Concurrent validation** assesses the validity of a test by administering it to people already on the job and then correlating test scores with existing measures of each person's performance. The logic behind this strategy is that if the best performers currently on the job perform better on the test than those who are currently struggling on the job, the test has validity. (Figure 6.3 compares the two types of validation study.)

Despite the extra effort and time needed for predictive validation, it is superior to concurrent validation for a number of reasons, First, job applicants (because they are seeking work) are typically more motivated to perform well on the tests than are current employees (who already have jobs). Second, current employees have learned many things on the job that job applicants have not yet learned. Therefore, the correlation between test scores and job performance for current employees may not be the same as the correlation between test scores and job performance for less knowledgeable job applicants. Third, current employees tend to be homogeneous—that is, similar to each other on many characteristics.[3] Thus, on many of the characteristics

Predictive validation

A criterion-related validity study that seeks to establish an empirical relationship between applicants' test scores and their eventual performance on the job.

Concurrent validation

A criterion-related validity study in which a test is administered to all the people currently in a job and then incumbents' scores are correlated with existing measures of their performance on the job.

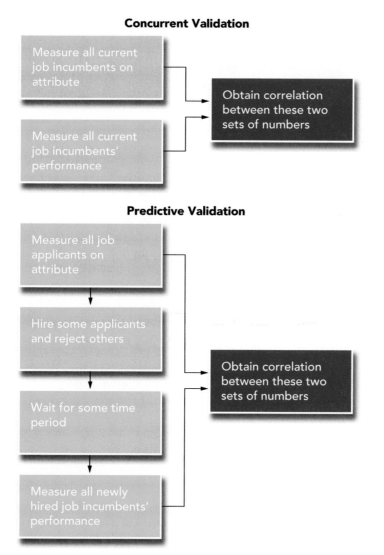

needed for success on the job, most current employees will show restriction in range. This restricted range makes it hard to detect a relationship between test scores and job-performance scores because few of the current employees will be very low on the characteristic you are trying to validate. For example, if emotional stability is required for a nursing career, it is quite likely that most nurses who have amassed five or six years' experience will score high on this characteristic. Yet to validate a test, you need both high test scorers (who should subsequently perform well on the job) and low test scorers (who should perform poorly on the job). Thus, although concurrent studies can sometimes help one anticipate the results of predictive studies, they do not serve as substitutes.[4]

Obviously, we would like our measures to be high in validity; but as with the reliability standard, we must also ask, how high is high enough? When trying to determine how much validity is enough, one typically has to turn to tests of statistical significance. A test of statistical significance answers the question, "How likely is it that a correlation of this size could have come about through luck or chance?"

New Technology Redefines the Language of Personnel Selection

Standardization of hiring practices serves a number of business goals, both legal and economic. Indeed, the major components of traditional testing paradigms have been relatively fixed for almost a century, in the sense that many intelligence tests in the 1990s looked highly similar to those first developed by Alfred Binet in 1912. However, new developments in technology have forced many human resource professionals to subtly reexamine what some standard terms, such as "applicant," "test," and "test taker," mean. As one former U.S. president noted, "it all depends on what the definition of 'is' is," and in the same fashion, many of the most basic terms, used by human resource management specialists have had to be reconsidered in light of changes in the technological landscape.

For example, the term "applicant" seems straightforward, and as we have seen in this chapter, one needs this figure to calculate many important human resource statistics, not the least of which is the selection ratio for members of various protected groups. In the old days, someone became an applicant when they filled out a formal application or a member of the hiring organization opened a résumé sent by an aspiring worker in the mail. However, today individuals can spam organizations with unsolicited résumés for jobs that are not even open, and the question becomes, does the employer have to open and then treat this with the same record-keeping rigor that is associated with formal applications that were solicited? The EEOC has looked into this matter and is developing new rules that would allow organizations to treat spammers differently from the "traditional applicants" in an effort to keep the documentation task more manageable.

Table 6.1 shows how big a correlation between a selection measure and a measure of job performance needs to be to achieve statistical significance at a level of .05 (that is, there is only a 5 out of 100 chance that one could get a correlation this big by chance alone). Although it is generally true that bigger correlations are better, the size of the sample on which the correlation is based plays a large role as well. Because many of the selection methods we examine in the second half of this chapter generate correlations in the .20s and .30s, we often need samples of 80 to 90 people.[5] A validation study with a small sample (such as 20 people) is almost doomed to failure from the start. Thus, many companies are too small to use a criterion-related validation strategy for most, if not all, of their jobs.

TABLE 6.1

Required Level of Correlation to Reach Statistical Significance as a Function of Sample Size

SAMPLE SIZE	REQUIRED CORRELATION
5	.75
10	.58
20	.42
40	.30
80	.21
100	.19

The term "test" also had a relatively clear traditional meaning, conjuring up paper and # 2 pencils, and a set of people who responded to all the same items in the same order, and then scored with the same answer sheet. If one applicant's score was two points higher than another's, everyone regardless of the testing sophistication understood how one outperformed the other. Today's technology allows for much more reliable and efficient testing, however, by tailoring the item-generating process to match the characteristics of the test taker.

For example, with computer adaptive testing, there is no standard set of questions that everyone takes, but instead, there is a massive pool of items, and the one that pops up on the test taker's screen depends partially on how that person did with past items. The program first sends some items of average difficulty, and if the respondent gets those correct, the computer sends a set of more difficult items. If these are answered correctly, then a different set of even more difficult items is sent. If these are missed, then the program ratchets downs and sends easier items. The program continues iteratively until the exact level of difficulty is achieved where the respondent can get the items right about half the time. Although incredibly efficient in terms of establishing the exact level of the person's ability, in the end, each test taker does not receive exactly the same test, and some may feel this is unfair.

Finally, who the "test taker" was could often be taken for granted because the testing typically took place in a face-to-face context where identity could be easily established. However, today, many organizations wish to test over the Internet, and in this context, it becomes a little more difficult to establish just who is on the other end of the line actually filling out the test. Although technologies are being developed to handle this problem, many organizations use Internet tests as just an initial screen to weed out masses of unqualified applicants. Once the masses are thinned, on-site "face-to-face" testing can be conducted to ferret out cheaters. These are just some of the challenges that rapidly changing technology is creating in the once stable world of testing.

SOURCE: D. P. Shuit, "Employers Beset by Résumé Span Might Get Break from the EEOC," *Workforce*, April 2004, pp. 54–55; D. Weichmann and A. M. Ryan, "Reactions to Computerized Testing in Selection Contexts," *International Journal of Selection and Assessment*, June–September 2003, pp. 215–29; K. Kersting, "How Do You Test on the Web? Responsibly," *Monitor on Psychology*, March 2004, pp. 26–27.

Content Validation

When sample sizes are small, an alternative test validation strategy, content validation, can be used. **Content validation** is performed by demonstrating that the items, questions, or problems posed by the test are a representative sample of the kinds of situations or problems that occur on the job.[6] A test that is content valid exposes the job applicant to situations that are likely to occur on the job, and then tests whether the applicant currently has sufficient knowledge, skill, or ability to handle such situations.

For example, one general contracting firm that constructed tract housing needed to hire one construction superintendent.[7] This job involved organizing, supervising, and inspecting the work of many subcontractors involved in the construction process. The tests developed for this position attempted to mirror the job. One test was a scrambled subcontractor test, where the applicant had to take a random list of subcontractors (roofing, plumbing, electrical, fencing, concrete, and so on) and put them in the correct order that each should appear on the site. A second test measured construction error recognition. In this test, the applicant went into a shed that was specially constructed to have 25 common and expensive errors (like faulty wiring and upside-down windows) and recorded whatever problems she could detect. Because the content of these tests so closely parallels the content of the job, one can safely make inferences from one to the other. Although criterion-related validity is established by empirical means, content validity is achieved primarily through a process of expert judgment.

Content validation
A test-validation strategy performed by demonstrating that the items, questions, or problems posed by a test are a representative sample of the kinds of situations or problems that occur on the job.

The ability to use content validation in small sample settings makes it generally more applicable than criterion-related validation. However, content validation has two limitations.[8] First, one assumption behind content validation is that the person who is to be hired must have the knowledge, skills, or abilities at the time she is hired. Thus it is not appropriate to use content validation in settings where the applicant is expected to learn the job in a formal training program conducted after selection.

Second, because subjective judgment plays such a large role in content validation, it is critical to minimize the amount of inference involved on the part of judges. Thus the judges' ratings need to be made with respect to relatively concrete and observable behaviors (for example, "applicant detects common construction errors" or "arranges optimal subcontractor schedules"). Content validation would be inappropriate for assessing more abstract characteristics such as intelligence, leadership capacity, and integrity.

Generalizability

Generalizability
The degree to which the validity of a selection method established in one context extends to other contexts.

Generalizability is defined as the degree to which the validity of a selection method established in one context extends to other contexts. There are three primary "contexts" over which we might like to generalize: different situations (jobs or organizations), different samples of people, and different time periods. Just as reliability is necessary but not sufficient for validity, validity is necessary but not sufficient for generalizability.

Strategic Use of HRM

A good example of how strategic differences translate into different hiring policies can be seen in the different approaches taken by two of the country's largest booksellers, Barnes and Noble versus Borders. Although selling books would seem to be a pretty set task, in fact, there are major differences between these two franchises in philosophy and strategy. In a very real sense, the differences between these two organizations are manifested most clearly in hiring practices, which in turn influence customer service. Barnes and Noble is the more traditional retailer and focuses on stocking the most popular books at the lowest prices. The goal for employees is to get the right book into the customer's hand, and then execute the financial transaction as quickly as possible. Mitchell Klipper, CEO, notes that "our booksellers are nice, educated people. They wear collared shirts and have a cleaner look, as opposed to tattoos and T-shirts."

In contrast, Julie Johnson, manager of the Borders Michigan Avenue store in Chicago, notes, "We want our people to be comfortable and to show their personality. We pride ourselves on diversity." As a consequence, Borders employees dress much less formally, and are almost famous for their tattoos, piercings, and wide-ranging fashion sense. This diversity is then reinforced by the kinds of books stocked, in the sense that unlike Barnes and Noble, where the stock is almost the same for all stores, roughly 50 percent of the stock at any one Borders store is unique to that store. Store holdings are idiosyncratic and based upon the input of employees, who are just as likely to shape the customers' preferences as respond to them. Although these are radically different recipes for the same dish, in their own way each is a viable business model, and to some extent, this limits the direct competition each faces in the labor market. In fact, as one Borders manager notes, "It's surprising how few people we hire from Barnes and Noble; their environment is very different from ours."

SOURCE: J. A. Trachtenberg, "Investors Brace for a Plot Twist from Barnes and Noble," *The Wall Street Journal* (May 27, 2004), p. A1; S. F. Gale, "The Bookstore Battle," *Workforce*, January 2003, pp. 51–53.

It was once believed, for example, that validity coefficients were situationally specific—that is, the level of correlation between test and performance varied as one went from one organization to another, even though the jobs studied seemed to be identical. Subsequent research has indicated that this is largely false. Rather, tests tend to show similar levels of correlation even across jobs that are only somewhat similar (at least for tests of intelligence and cognitive ability). Correlations with these kinds of tests change as one goes across widely different kinds of jobs, however. Specifically, the more complex the job, the higher the validity of many tests.[9]

It was also believed that tests showed differential subgroup validity, which meant that the validity coefficient for any test–job performance pair was different for people of different races or genders. This belief was also refuted by subsequent research, and, in general, one finds very similar levels of correlations across different groups of people.[10]

Because the evidence suggests that test validity often extends across situations and subgroups, *validity generalization* stands as an alternative for validating selection methods for companies that cannot employ criterion-related or content validation. Validity generalization is a three-step process. First, the company provides evidence from previous criterion-related validity studies conducted in other situations that shows that a specific test (such as a test of emotional stability) is a valid predictor for a specific job (like nurse at a large hospital). Second, the company provides evidence from job analysis to document that the job it is trying to fill (nurse at a small hospital) is similar in all major respects to the job validated elsewhere (nurse at a large hospital). Finally, if the company can show that it uses a test that is the same as or similar to that used in the validated setting, then one can "generalize" the validity from the first context (large hospital) to the new context (small hospital).[11]

Utility

Utility is the degree to which the information provided by selection methods enhances the bottom-line effectiveness of the organization.[12] Strategic approaches to human resource management place a great deal of importance in determining the financial worth of their human capital, and great strides have been made in assessing this value.[13] In general, the more reliable, valid, and generalizable the selection method is, the more utility it will have. On the other hand, many characteristics of particular selection contexts enhance or detract from the usefulness of given selection methods, even when reliability, validity, and generalizability are held constant.

Figures 6.4a and 6.4b, for example, show two different scenarios where the correlation between a measure of extroversion and the amount of sales revenue generated by a sample of sales representatives is the same for two different companies: Company A and Company B. Although the correlation between the measure of extroversion and sales is the same, Company B derives much more utility or practical benefit from the measure. That is, as indicated by the arrows proceeding out of the boxes (which indicate the people selected), the average sales revenue of the three people selected by Company B (Figure 6.4b) is $850,000 compared to $780,000 from the three people selected by Company A (Figure 6.4a).

The major difference between these two companies is that Company B generated twice as many applicants as Company A. This means that the selection ratio (the percentage of people selected relative to the total number of people tested) is quite low for Company B (3/20) relative to Company A (3/10). Thus the people selected by Company B have higher amounts of extroversion than those selected by Company A; therefore, Company B takes better advantage of the relationship between extroversion and sales. Although this might be somewhat offset by the cost of recruiting and

Utility
The degree to which the information provided by selection methods enhances the effectiveness of selecting personnel in real organizations.

FIGURE 6.4A

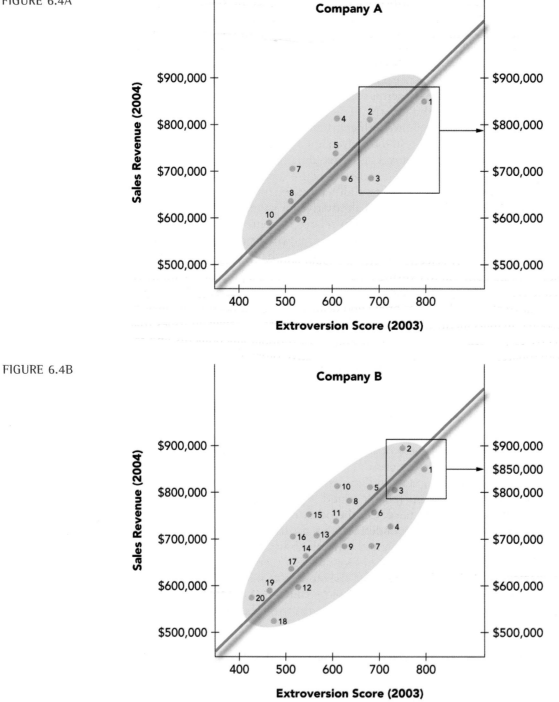

FIGURE 6.4B

measuring 20 more people, this added cost is probably trivial relative to the difference in revenue shown in this example ($70,000). Thus the utility of any test generally increases as the selection ratio gets lower, so long as the additional costs of recruiting and testing are not excessive.

Many other factors relate to the utility of a test. For example, the value of the product or service produced by the job incumbent plays a role: the more valuable the product or service, the more value there is in selecting the top performers. The cost of the test, of course, also plays a role. More expensive tests will on average have less utility unless they produce more valid predictions. A good recent example of this can be seen in the drug testing industry. Although few would dispute the reliability and validity of a properly conducted drug test, these can be relatively expensive, and employers are increasingly unwilling to pay the cost for these tests given the yield. Most drug tests yield few hard core drug abusers, and one study showed that given the hit rate of one test used in one department of the federal government, it cost the agency $77,000 per detected drug addict. Thus, although roughly 70 percent of companies were employing drug tests in 1996, that same figure is closer to 60 percent in 2003, due largely to cost/benefit questions such as this.[14]

Legality

The final standard that any selection method should adhere to is *legality*. All selection methods should conform to existing laws and existing legal precedents. Many issues related to selecting employees safely under U.S. law were discussed generically in Chapter 3. Our treatment there was broad and dealt with legal aspects in all areas of human resource management. In this chapter we focus more narrowly on issues that relate directly to personnel selection, bypassing constitutional amendments and focusing more squarely on federal legislation and executive orders.

Federal Legislation

Three primary federal laws form the basis for a majority of the suits filed by job applicants. First, the Civil Rights Act of 1991 (discussed in Chapter 3), an extension of the Civil Rights Act of 1964, protects individuals from discrimination based on race, color, sex, religion, and national origin with respect to hiring as well as compensation and working conditions. The 1991 act differs from the 1964 act in three important areas.

First, it establishes employers' explicit obligation to establish the business necessity of any neutral-appearing selection method that has had adverse impact on groups specified by the law. This is typically done by showing that the test has significant criterion-related or content validity. Thus, in our opening story, whatever the process was that was being used to select managers at Wal-Mart, it seemed to have an adverse impact on women, and thus, it is essential for the organization to show that the process was a business necessity, in the form of performance differences between men and women in managerial jobs. If they cannot show such a difference, which the research suggests will be difficult, then the process may be ruled illegal. It should also be noted that "customer preference" or "brand image" is not a legally defensible means of justifying a process that has adverse impact. For example, recently the retailer Abercrombie & Fitch was sued because it systematically screened out nonwhite applicants. Testimony in the trial suggested that one corporate representative visited a store, pointed to a blond-haired, blue-eyed model, and said, "This is the A&F look." She then told the manager that "she had better make the store look more like this."[15] This is not a legal defense, nor is the defense that "our customers prefer to buy from people of this or that race."

Second, the 1991 act allows the individual filing the complaint to have a jury decide whether he or she may recover punitive damages (in addition to lost wages and

Older but Wiser: Demographic Shifts Create Opportunities for the Over-50 Set

In late 2003 and early 2004, a U.S. congressional committee was engaged in an investigation of what caused some of the intelligence failures that led up to the 9/11 terrorist attacks. One of the conclusions that emerged from that committee was that a mandatory retirement program at the Federal Bureau of Investigation (FBI) that forced workers out of the agency when they reached the age of 57 led to a shortage of analytic skills that were needed to "connect the dots" in this case. Indeed, at the time of the attacks, over 40 percent of the agents at the FBI had less than five years of experience, and in a move that many saw as too little too late, the agency hurriedly rehired many of its retired agents to work as intelligence analysts and evidence examiners.

Although the stakes are much smaller than was the case at the FBI, the notion of rehiring older workers who were once retired is becoming an increasingly popular trend in many different areas of business and industry. In many instances, this is driven by a desire for the organization to appeal to a different segment of their customer base. For example, many of Home Depot customers are older individuals who, with more time on their hands relative to when they were younger and raising a family, prefer to manage their own home improvement projects. In order to appeal to this set of customers, Home Depot expanded its hiring of older workers. In other cases, the need to hire older workers is driven by demographic shifts in the population as a whole and the general unavailability of workers with certain skills in other age brackets. For example, St. Mary's Medical Center in Huntington, West Virginia, faced a critical nursing shortage and eliminated this problem by submitting applications from older alumni of a local nursing school as well as their own retired employees.

Employers who have taken this tack have found that the over-50 generation presents a unique set of opportunities and challenges that if properly managed can enhance the

benefits) for emotional injuries caused by the discrimination.[16] This can generate large financial settlements as well as poor public relations that can hinder the organization's ability to compete. Finally, the 1991 act explicitly prohibits the granting of preferential treatment to minority groups. For example, it specifically prohibits adjusting scores upward on tests just because someone is in a group with lower average scores (sometimes referred to as *race norming*). Adjusting scores in this way has been found to have a number of negative effects, not only on the attitudes of white males who claim it causes reverse discrimination,[17] but on the proposed beneficiaries of such preferential treatment. Research shows that when selection decisions are perceived as being based partially on group membership, it undermines the confidence and hurts the job performance of the women or minority group members the program was designed to help.[18]

The Age Discrimination in Employment Act of 1967 is also widely used in personnel selection. This act mirrors the Civil Rights Act of 1964 in its protections and, as amended in 1978, covers job applicants over the age of 40. The act does not protect younger workers (thus there is never a case for "reverse discrimination" here), and like the most recent civil rights act, it allows for jury trials and punitive damages. This

organization's competitive position. For example, older workers tend to have absenteeism rates that are lower than those associated with younger workers. Moreover, their skill set in certain critical areas exceeds that found with younger workers. CVS Drugstore's Director Steven Wing notes, "Many older people have a work ethic and sense of civility that the younger generation has not learned yet," and CVS has more than doubled the number of over-55 workers in the last 10 years. Finally, like Home Depot, CVS finds that many of its customers are also in the over-50 generation and appreciate dealing directly with people their own age.

A strategic decision to aggressively pursue older workers, however, also has to be accompanied by changes in other areas of human resources in order to fully realize the potential offered by this group. For example, training programs often have to expose former retirees to new technology. CVS likes to create mixed teams of older and younger workers in training programs so that the older workers can help the younger workers with leadership and customer service skills, while the younger workers help the older workers with computer and telecommunication skills. In other cases, jobs may need to be redesigned to accommodate older workers. For example, at Baptist Health South Florida, a nonprofit health care provider, spring lifts were installed on laundry containers so that older workers did not have to bend over and pick up heavy loads. Finally, in terms of compensation, human resource specialists need to work carefully to make sure that the financial package offered to older workers meets their needs. For older workers, health care benefits may be more important than salary, and pay and hours may need to be carefully managed so as not to disrupt pension benefits that workers may also be receiving.

Given demographic shifts with respect to the general aging of the U.S. population, many have questioned the degree to which sustainable growth and vitality of the U.S. economy can be achieved without somehow taking advantage of the unique contributions of older workers. Also, the better health associated with today's older workers places them in a position where many can benefit from the psychological value associated with work and productive activity. Organizations that can creatively tap this resource gain a source of competitive advantage that promotes their own goals and strategies, while at the same time promoting the psychological and economic health of an entire generation of workers.

SOURCE: J. Mullich, "They Don't Retire Them: They Hire Them," *Workforce*, December 2003, pp. 49–54; D. Jones, "Home Depot's Net Rises 39% Aided by Restructuring Efforts," *The Wall Street Journal* (February 24, 2004), p. A1; J. Mullich, "New Ideas Draw Older Workers," *Workforce*, March 2004, pp. 44–46.

act outlaws almost all "mandatory retirement" programs (company policies that dictate that everyone who reaches a set age must retire).

Litigation brought forward under this act surged by over 200 percent between 1991 and 2001. Two trends have combined to generate this increase: the general aging of the workforce and recent attempts by organizations to downsize. Together these trends have displaced many older workers, who have brought age discrimination suits against their former employers. The long list of companies sued under this act includes CBS Inc., McDonnell Douglas, Northwest Airlines, Disney, and Martin Marietta.[19] On the other hand, more recently, as the "Competing through Sustainability" box shows, many organizations have been reaching out to older workers as part of a strategic campaign to improve their performance and competitiveness.

Finally, the Americans with Disabilities Act (ADA) of 1991 protects individuals with physical and mental disabilities (or with a history of the same). It extends the Vocational Rehabilitation Act of 1973, requiring employers to make "reasonable accommodation" to disabled individuals whose handicaps may prevent them from performing essential functions of the job as currently designed. "Reasonable accommodation" could include restructuring jobs, modifying work schedules, making facilities accessible, providing readers, or modifying equipment. ADA does not require the organization to hire someone whose disability prevents them from performing either critical or routine aspects of the job nor does it require accommodations that would cause "undue hardship."[20] However, technological advancements in the area of accommodations, along with the general shift in jobs from those that are physically demanding to those that are more mentally challenging, is increasing the percentage of jobs that disabled workers can hold.[21] Largely due to this act, the percentage of disabled people participating full-time in the U.S. workforce has increased from under 45 percent in 1986 to over 55 percent in 2001.[22]

This act also restricts many preemployment inquiries.[23] For instance, it is legal to ask an applicant, "Can you meet the attendance requirements for this job?" but it is not legal to ask, "How many days did you miss work in your last job because you were sick?" because the latter question might reveal a disability. The ADA also prohibits tests that might reveal a psychological or physical disability. (These would fall under the heading of "illegal medical examinations.") If a manager is uncertain whether a test would be considered medical, she should review the test to determine whether it must be interpreted by a medical professional or whether the behavior or trait assessed by the test is so fundamental to the job that it can be interpreted by any line manager.

Executive Orders

As noted in Chapter 3, the executive branch of the government also regulates hiring decisions through the use of executive orders. Executive Order 11246 parallels the protections provided by the Civil Rights Act of 1964 but goes beyond the 1964 act in two important ways. First, not only do the executive orders prohibit discrimination, they actually mandate that employers take affirmative action to hire qualified minority applicants. The executive orders also allow the government to suspend all business with a contractor while an investigation is being conducted (rather than waiting for an actual finding), which puts a great deal of pressure on employers to comply with these orders. Executive orders are monitored by the Office of Federal Contract Compliance Procedures (OFCCP), which issues guidelines (like the Affirmative Action Program Guidelines published by the Bureau of National Affairs in 1983) to help companies comply.

Types of Selection Methods

The first half of this chapter laid out the five standards by which we can judge selection measures. In the second half of this chapter, we examine the common selection methods used in various organizations and discuss their advantages and disadvantages in terms of these standards.

Interviews

A selection interview has been defined as "a dialogue initiated by one or more persons to gather information and evaluate the qualifications of an applicant for employment."[24] The selection interview is the most widespread selection method employed in organizations, and there have been literally hundreds of studies examining their effectiveness.[25]

Unfortunately, the long history of research on the employment interview suggests that, without proper care, it can be unreliable, low in validity,[26] and biased against a number of different groups.[27] Moreover, interviews are relatively costly because they require at least one person to interview another person, and these persons have to be brought to the same geographic location. Finally, in terms of legality, the subjectivity embodied in the process often makes applicants upset, particularly if they fail to get a job after being asked apparently irrelevant questions. The Supreme Court ruled in *Watson v. Fort Worth Bank and Trust* that subjective selection methods like the interview must be validated by traditional criterion-related or content-validation procedures.[28]

Fortunately, more recent research has pointed to a number of concrete steps that one can employ to increase the utility of the personnel selection interview.[29] First, HR staff should keep the interview structured, standardized, and focused on accomplishing a small number of goals. That is, they should plan to come out of each interview with quantitative ratings on a small number of dimensions that are observable (like interpersonal style or ability to express oneself) and avoid ratings of abilities that may be better measured by tests (like intelligence). In addition to coming out of the interview with quantitative ratings, interviewers should also have a structured note-taking system that will aid recall when it comes to justifying the ratings.[30]

Second, ask questions dealing with specific situations that are likely to arise on the job, and use these to determine what the person is likely to do in that situation. These types of **situational interview** items have been shown to have quite high predictive validity.[31] Situational judgment items come in two varieties, as shown in Table 6.2. Some items are "experience-based" and require the applicant to reveal an actual experience he or she had in the past when confronting the situation. Other items are "future-oriented" and ask what the person is likely to do when confronting a certain hypothetical situation in the future. Research suggests that these types of items can

Situational interview
An interview procedure where applicants are confronted with specific issues, questions, or problems that are likely to arise on the job.

TABLE 6.2
Examples of Experience-Based and Future-Oriented Situational Interview Items

Experience-based	
Motivating employees:	"Think about an instance when you had to motivate an employee to perform a task that he or she disliked but that you needed to have done. How did you handle that situation?"
Resolving conflict:	"What was the biggest difference of opinion you ever had with a coworker? How did you resolve that situation?"
Overcoming resistance to change:	"What was the hardest change you ever had to bring about in a past job, and what did you do to get the people around you to change their thoughts or behaviors?"
Future-oriented	
Motivating employees:	"Suppose you were working with an employee who you knew greatly disliked performing a particular task. You needed to get this task completed, however, and this person was the only one available to do it. What would you do to motivate that person?"
Resolving conflict:	"Imagine that you and a coworker disagree about the best way to handle an absenteeism problem with another member of your team. How would you resolve that situation?"
Overcoming resistance to change:	"Suppose you had an idea for change in work procedures that would enhance quality, but some members of your work group were hesitant to make the change. What would you do in that situation?"

both show validity but that experience-based items often outperform future-oriented items.[32] Experience-based items also appear to reduce some forms of impression management such as ingratiation better than future-oriented items.[33] Regardless of the past or future frame, an additional benefit of situational interview items is that their standardization and the concrete behavioral nature of the information that is collected mean that they can be effectively employed, even by those who have little training in psychological assessment.[34]

Ameritech Cellular Services uses these types of situational questions in its interview procedures. Interviewees answer questions that directly relate to past experiences and future behaviors. As James Reicks, director of human resources, notes, "We're shifting toward competency-based systems which really zero in on the attributes of a candidate. We're looking for specific examples of how they succeeded in previous jobs rather than examining their entire work history."[35]

Finding and Keeping the Best Employees

A good example of the use of behavioral interview questions can be found in the experience of Women and Infants Hospital of Rhode Island. The hospital strives to create a culture of caring health care providers, and actively seeks to screen out doctors or nurses that are technically skilled but interpersonally challenged. Although the hospital looks for the same degrees and technical experiences that all hospitals seek, in order to get the person who has the right mix of compassion, energy, and diplomacy, it added a layer of behaviorally oriented interview questions on top of the standard screening devices. Applicants are asked questions such as "Have you ever had to work out a conflict with a coworker and how did you try to resolve it?" or "Could you describe a situation where you tried to solve a problem and it did not work the first time?" Answers are analyzed to determine if they fit the culture of the organization, and if there is a mismatch, the person is not hired regardless of their technical qualifications. Since adding the behavioral component to their assessment procedures, patient satisfaction rates jumped from the 70th percentile to the 90th percentile, and turnover dropped from 25 percent to 8 percent.

SOURCE: S. Greengard, "Gimme Attitude," *Workforce*, July 2003, pp. 56–60.

It is also important to use multiple interviewers who are trained to avoid many of the subjective errors that can result when one human being is asked to rate another. Many employers are now videotaping interviews and then sending the tapes (rather than the applicants) around from place to place. This is seen by some as a cost-effective means of allowing numerous raters to evaluate the candidate under standard conditions.[36]

Limiting the subjectivity of the process is central to much of this training, and research suggests that it is best to ask interviewers to be "witnesses" of facts that can later be integrated via objective formulas, as opposed to being "judges" allowed to idiosyncratically weigh how various facts should be combined to form the final recommendation.[37] In addition to being a witness, the interviewer sometimes has to be the prosecuting attorney, since in some cases the interviewees may be motivated to try to present an overly positive, if not outright false, picture of their qualifications. Interviewers need to be critical and look for inconsistencies or gaps in stories or experiences in those who are providing information. Increasingly, interviewers are seeking training that helps them detect nonverbal signs that someone is trying to be deceptive, such as hand tremors, darting eyes, mumbled speech, and failing to maintain eye contact that may be a cause for concern and increased scrutiny.[38] In fact, one such trained observer in the U.S. Customs Department was credited with thwarting a terrorist mission aimed at disrupting the nation's Millennium Celebrations in Los Angeles. The officer spotted several behavioral manifestations of deceptiveness, then pulled the driver over for a detailed search that uncovered a substantial amount of bombmaking materials.[39]

References and Biographical Data

Just as few employers would think of hiring someone without an interview, nearly all employers also use some method for getting background information on applicants before an interview. This information can be solicited from the people who know the candidate through reference checks.

The evidence on the reliability and validity of reference checks suggests that these are, at best, weak predictors of future success on the job.[40] The main reason for this low validity is that the evaluations supplied in most reference letters are so positive that it is hard to differentiate applicants. As Northwestern Bell's district manager of management employment notes, "They all say, 'This is the greatest individual the world has ever seen, the next president, at least.' . . . It isn't always accurate."[41]

This problem with reference letters has two causes. First, the applicant usually gets to choose who writes the letter and can thus choose only those writers who think the highest of her abilities. Second, because letter writers can never be sure who will read the letters, they may fear that supplying damaging information about someone could come back to haunt them. This fear is well placed. For example, in 2003, a jury awarded $283,000 to a truck driver whose past employer told a would-be employer that he "was late most of the time, regularly missed two days a week, had a problem with authority and a poor work ethic."[42] In fact, there are even companies that provide a reference checking service for people who feel that they may be getting a damaging reference from an employer. For roughly $90, BadReferences.com will call and document what information past employers are providing for individuals who have such concerns. Applicants who are armed with this kind of evidence are in a strong legal position, and Michael Rankin, chief services officer at BadReferences, notes that "we haven't lost a case in twenty years."[43] Thus, it is clearly not in the past employers' interest to reveal too much information beyond job title and years of service.

Intuit Corporation, the Menlo Park, California, software company that produces *Quicken*, tries to get around these problems by requesting references in bulk—sometimes asking for as many as 12 letters of reference. The first two or three people listed invariably have nothing but positive things to say about the candidate, but, according to Sharyn Vacunich, staffing manager for Intuit, once you get beyond those people, you hear more than just positive things.[44]

The evidence on the utility of biographical information collected directly from job applicants is much more positive, especially for certain occupational categories such as clerical and sales jobs[45] and for particular outcomes like turnover.[46] The low cost of obtaining such information significantly enhances its utility, especially when the information is used in conjunction with a well-designed, follow-up interview that complements, rather than duplicates, the biographical information bank.[47]

Again, as with the interview, the biggest concern with the use of biographical data is that applicants who supply the information may be motivated to misrepresent themselves. Background checks can help on this score, and many employers demand them.[48] However, this is often no guarantee, because of the increased sophistication of those in the dishonesty business. For example, there are now websites that will not only provide fake degrees, but also staffed telephone numbers that will provide further

Private Contractors Go to War: Impact of Work Context on Global Hiring Decisions

One of the more memorable images of the war in Iraq was the taped telecast of the kidnapping of Thomas Hamill. Hamill was a truck driver for Kellogg, Brown and Root (KBR), a subsidiary of Halliburton, and was part of a convoy that was providing fuel and food to U.S. soldiers. When Iraqi insurgents attacked the convoy, Hamill was captured and videotaped being placed into a car, and then whisked off to some unknown location. The tape was played over and over again on U.S. television, and the country tuned in every day to see how this story would turn out. Eventually, Hamill was able to escape from his captors, and made it to a U.S. checkpoint where he

was treated for injuries and then sent home.

Although this particular contract employee lived to tell of his harrowing experience in Iraq, the stories of other contract workers in Iraq did not share this happy ending. The images of the beheading of Nicholas Berg and the mutilation of four employees of Blackwater Incorporated at the main bridge in Fallujah also linger in the memories of those who watched the war closely. The fact that all of these individuals were not soldiers, but rather, contract workers working for private U.S. firms led many to question what role private contactors should play in war zones, and what type of people

are best and least suited for work that takes place in foreign and hostile contexts.

In terms of the role of private contractors, between 1991 and 2004, the U.S. armed forces were reduced by 29 percent, and private employers are now performing much of the work that was once done by soldiers. In fact, the military outsourced a full 30 percent of its services in the Iraq War, up from a mere 1 percent in the Gulf War of 1991. Although few question the practice of outsourcing tasks such as serving food and hauling away trash, increasingly, private firms are also engaged in security and interrogation tasks that encroach upon the core role of the military. For ex-

bogus information to callers. Some universities and state prison systems have even been hacked into by companies that try to insert or delete their clients names from databases.[49] Even the U.S. Transportation Safety Administration, the organization in charge of national security at airports struggles with this problem. In the ramp-up of hiring that followed the 9/11 attacks, the agency hired over 1,200 people for sensitive security jobs who later turned out to have criminal records.[50] Hiring individuals in the security industry is an especially sensitive task because of the threat they face, as well as the threat they pose to others, and as the "Competing through Globalization" box shows, this is especially the case when the employee is sent overseas into a war zone.

Although it is not a panacea, to some extent forcing applicants to elaborate on their responses to bio-data questions can sometimes be helpful.[51] A good elaboration forces applicants to support their answers with evidence that includes names of other people involved, dates, locations, and objective evidence that would support a thorough cross-checking. Thus, rather than just asking someone if they have ever led a sales team, an elaborated item would force the applicant to name all members of the team, where and when the team was together, and what sales they accomplished citing specific products, figures, and customers. The evidence suggests that forced elaboration reduces the traditional measures of faking behavior.[52]

ample, in his report on the abuses of prisoners, General Antonio Taguba concluded that two interrogators-for-hire, one from CACI and one from the Titan Corporation, "were either directly or indirectly responsible for the abuses at Abu Ghraib."

Indeed, from a military perspective one of the problems with outsourcing is that one loses control over the process of hiring and training people in critical positions, which in turn raises questions about how such people are selected and trained. "Thomas Hamill is exactly the kind of person you don't want," according to security specialist Philip Deming. Hamill was a former dairy farmer who had to sell the family farm when the bottom dropped out of milk prices. Unemployed and burdened with debt associated with medical bills from his wife's surgery, Hamill was desperate for money, and people with this profile are a poor fit for this kind of work according to Dem-

ing. "They're not in constant surveillance mode and take risks they cannot fully appreciate because they're desperate." According to Deming better candidates are people who are financially secure, but attracted to the work because of a sense of adventure or patriotism or high levels of commitment to their employer. People thrust into this situation need to have experience working in hostile environments; they need to be confident, flexible, innovative, and culturally sensitive to the region they are entering. Previous military service, although not a prerequisite, is a plus, and a security clearance stands as objective evidence that the person has been vetted to some degree.

Even with the most rigorous hiring standards, however, there are still those who object to handing over critical aspects of national defense to private contractors. After all, unlike soldiers, private employees can quit whenever they don't like a

job that they are assigned, and for that reason, many have argued for an increase in the size of the military. Better yet, in the case of Iraq, many have argued for speeding up the process whereby the Iraqis manage their own security. Early in the occupation, this was hampered by the fact that ex-Baathists (Saddam Hussein's political party) were not allowed to work in secure areas, but that policy has since been rescinded. Jean Abi-Nader, director of the Arab American Institute, advises private contractors to hire Iraqis because this reflects an investment in Iraq's future. "Ten years from now, they'll say, 'The Americans gave me skills and opportunities,' instead of feeling resentful about being exploited."

SOURCE: S. E. Ante, "The Other Military," *BusinessWeek* (May 31, 2004), pp. 76–78; J. Kahn and N. D. Schwartz, "Private Sector Soldiers," *Fortune* (May 3, 2004), pp. 33–36; S. A. Feeney, "Dangerous Business," *Workforce*, June 2004, pp. 32–40.

Physical Ability Tests

Although automation and other advances in technology have eliminated or modified many physically demanding occupational tasks, many jobs still require certain physical abilities or psychomotor abilities.[53] In these cases, tests of physical abilities may be relevant not only to predicting performance but to predicting occupational injuries and disabilities as well.[54] There are seven classes of tests in this area: ones that evaluate (1) muscular tension, (2) muscular power, (3) muscular endurance, (4) cardiovascular endurance, (5) flexibility, (6) balance, and (7) coordination.[55]

The criterion-related validities for these kinds of tests for certain jobs are quite strong.[56] Unfortunately, these tests, particularly the strength tests, are likely to have an adverse impact on some applicants with disabilities and many female applicants. For example, roughly two-thirds of all males score higher than the highest-scoring female on muscular tension tests.[57]

Because of this there are two key questions to ask in deciding whether to use these kinds of tests. First, is the physical ability essential to performing the job and is it mentioned prominently enough in the job description? Neither the Civil Rights Act nor the ADA requires employers to hire individuals who cannot perform essential job functions, and both accept a written job description as evidence of the essential functions of the job.[58] Second, is there a probability that failure to adequately perform the job would result in some risk to the safety or health of the applicant, coworkers, or clients? The "direct threat" clause of the ADA makes it clear that adverse impact against those with disabilities is warranted under such conditions.

Cognitive Ability Tests

Cognitive ability tests differentiate individuals: based on their mental rather than physical capacities. Cognitive ability has many different facets, although we will focus only on three dominant ones.[59] **Verbal comprehension** refers to a person's capacity to understand and use written and spoken language. **Quantitative ability** concerns the speed and accuracy with which one can solve arithmetic problems of all kinds. **Reasoning ability,** a broader concept, refers to a person's capacity to invent solutions to many diverse problems.

Some jobs require only one or two of these facets of cognitive ability. Under these conditions, maintaining the separation among the facets is appropriate. However, many jobs that are high in complexity require most, if not all, of the facets, and hence one general test is often as good as many tests of separate facets.[60] Highly reliable commercial tests measuring these kinds of abilities are widely available, and they are generally valid predictors of job performance in many different kinds of contexts, including widely different countries.[61] The validity of these kinds of tests is related to the complexity of the job, however, in that one sees higher criterion-related validation for complex jobs than for simple jobs.[62] The predictive validity for these tests is also higher in jobs that are dynamic and changing over time and thus require adaptability on the part of the job incumbent.[63] Given the changing nature of the economy, the adaptability of workers has become a critical concern of many employers. People who are high in adaptability have been found to be skilled at (a) handling emergencies, (b) managing stress, (c) solving problems, (d) learning new technologies, and (e) dealing with culturally diverse populations.[64]

One of the major drawbacks to these tests is that they typically have adverse impact on African Americans. Indeed, the size of the differences is so large that some have advocated abandoning these types of tests for making decisions regarding who will be accepted for certain schools or jobs.[65] In the past, the difference between the means for blacks and whites meant that an average black would score at the 16th percentile of the distribution of white scores.[66] The notion of race norming, alluded to earlier, was born of the desire to use these high-utility tests in a manner that avoided adverse impact. Although race norming was made illegal by the recent amendments to the Civil Rights Act, some have advocated the use of banding to both achieve the benefits of testing and minimize its adverse impact. The concept of *banding* suggests that similar groups of people whose scores differ by only a small amount all be treated as having the same score. Then, within any band, preferential treatment is given to minorities. Most observers feel preferential treatment of minorities is acceptable when scores are tied, and banding simply broadens the definition of what constitutes a tied score.[67]

For example, in many classes a score of 90–100 percent may constitute a 4.0 for the course. This means that even though someone scoring 99 outperformed someone with a score of 91, each gets the same grade (a 4.0). Banding uses the same logic for all kinds of tests. Thus, if one was going to use the grade in the class as a selection standard, this would mean that the person with the 91 is equal to the person with the 99 (that is, they both score a 4.0), and if their scores are tied, preference should be

Cognitive ability tests
Tests that include three dimensions: verbal comprehension, quantitative ability and reasoning ability.

Verbal comprehension
Refers to a person's capacity to understand and use written and spoken language.

Quantitative ability
Concerns the speed and accuracy with which one can solve arithmetic problems of all kinds.

Reasoning ability
Refers to a person's capacity to invent solutions to many diverse problems.

given to the minority. Like race norming, banding is very controversial, especially if the bands are set too wide.[68]

Personality Inventories

While ability tests attempt to categorize individuals relative to what they can do, personality measures tend to categorize individuals by what they are like. Two recent reviews of the personality literature independently arrived at five common aspects of personality.[69] We refer to these five major dimensions as "the Big Five," and they include (1) extroversion, (2) adjustment, (3) agreeableness, (4) conscientiousness, and (5) inquisitiveness. Table 6.3 lists each of these with a corresponding list of adjectives that fit each dimension.

Although it is possible to find reliable, commercially available measures of each of these traits, the evidence for their validity and generalizability is mixed at best.[70] Conscientiousness is one of the few factors that displays any validity across a number of different job categories, and many real-world managers rate this as one of the most important characteristics they look for in employees.[71] People high in conscientiousness show more stamina at work, which is helpful in many occupations. People who are high in conscientiousness strive to accomplish difficult goals and stand out relative to others, and hence are generally easier to motivate in work contexts.[72] For example, at the highest levels of management, many CEOs of the largest companies—such as Herb Kelleher of Southwest Airlines, Tony O'Reilly of H. J. Heinz, and Wolfgang Schmitt of Rubbermaid—report working 80 to 90 hours a week and get by on as little as 5 to 6 hours of sleep each night.[73] Conscientiousness seems to be a particularly good predictor when teamed with tests of mental ability because there is a stronger relationship between this trait and performance when ability is high.[74] When jobs have a large customer service component or when ratings of job performance are taken in the form of subjective supervisory evaluations, it also helps if people who are high on conscientiousness are also high in social skills. This helps ensure that the achievement striving behaviors they exhibit are noticed by critical stakeholders.[75]

Although conscientiousness is the only dimension of personality that seems to show predictive validity across all situations, there are contexts where other components of the Big Five relate to job performance. First, extroversion and agreeableness seem to be related to performance in jobs such as sales or management; it is easy to see why these types of attributes would be required for such jobs.[76] These two factors also seem to be predictive of performance in team contexts, although in many cases it is the score of the lowest team member that determines the whole group outcome. That is, one highly disagreeable, introverted, or unconscientious member can ruin an entire team.[77]

1.	Extroversion	Sociable, gregarious, assertive, talkative, expressive
2.	Adjustment	Emotionally stable, nondepressed, secure, content
3.	Agreeableness	Courteous, trusting, good-natured, tolerant, cooperative, forgiving
4.	Conscientiousness	Dependable, organized, persevering, thorough, achievement-oriented
5.	Inquisitiveness	Curious, imaginative, artistically sensitive, broad-minded, playful

TABLE 6.3

The Five Major Dimensions of Personality Inventories

Finally, the validity for almost all of the Big Five factors in terms of predicting job performance also seems to be higher when the scores are not obtained from the applicant but are instead taken from other people.[78] The lower validity associated with self-reports of personality can be traced to three factors. First, people sometimes lack insight into what their own personalities are actually like (or how they are perceived by others), so their scores are inaccurate or unreliable. Second, people's personalities sometime vary across different contexts. Thus, someone may be very conscientious when it comes to social activities such as planning a family wedding or a fraternity party, but less conscientious when it comes to doing a paid job. Someone else may work hard at the office, and then not lift a finger to do household chores. Indeed, the predictive validity of many personality measures can be enhanced by appending the frame "at work" to all of the items (e.g., "I tend to finish what I start *at work*" or "I am not afraid to put in long hours at a task *at work*").[79] Third, applicants can sometimes fake their responses to personality items.[80] The evidence suggests that faking may be particularly an issue with the traits of conscientiousness and emotional stability because of the transparent nature of how these items would be used in decision making.[81]

To some extent, the effect of faking in the area of personality traits is largely a problem at the top of the score distribution. That is, someone who demonstrates a high degree of conscientiousness may be getting a high score because they are actually high on the trait or they are faking. On the other hand, someone with a very low score on this trait is usually low because they are so low on the characteristic that they do not even know how to fake it. Thus, these kinds of tests are sometimes better for rejecting people with very low scores than they are for choosing people who have very high scores.[82]

Work Samples

Work-sample tests and job-performance tests attempt to simulate the job in miniaturized form. For example, many organizations use an "in-basket" test when assessing people who are applying for managerial jobs. In an in-basket test, job candidates are asked to respond to memos that typify the problems confronted by those who already hold the job. The key in this and other forms of work-sample tests is the behavioral consistency between the requirements of the job and the requirements of the test.[83]

Work-sample tests tend to be job specific—that is, tailored individually to each different job in each organization. On the positive side, this has resulted in tests that demonstrate a high degree of criterion-related validity. In addition, the obvious parallels between the test and the job make content validity high. In general, this reduces the likelihood that rejected applicants will challenge the procedure through litigation. Available evidence also suggests that these tests are low in adverse impact.[84]

With all these advantages come two drawbacks. First, by their very nature the tests are job-specific, so generalizability is low. Second, partly because a new test has to be developed for each job and partly because of their nonstandardized formats, these tests are relatively expensive to develop. It is much more cost-effective to purchase a commercially available cognitive ability test that can be used for a number of different job categories within the company than to develop a test for each job. For this reason, some have rated the utility of cognitive ability tests higher than work-sample tests, despite the latter's higher criterion-related validity.[85] On the other hand, technological developments in the area of communications have reduced the cost of many different kinds of work-sample tests. For example, many work-sample tests can now be delivered online from a remote location, creating some economies of scale.[86]

In the area of managerial selection, work-sample tests are typically the cornerstone in assessment centers. Generically, the term **assessment center** is used to describe a wide variety of specific selection programs that employ multiple selection methods to rate either applicants or job incumbents on their managerial potential. Someone attending an assessment center would typically experience work-sample tests such as an in-basket test and several tests of more general abilities and personality. Because assessment centers employ multiple selection methods, their criterion-related validity tends to be quite high. Assessment centers seem to tap a number of different characteristics, but "problem solving ability" stands out as probably the most important skill tapped via this method.[87] The idiosyncratic and unique nature of the different exercises, however, has led some to suggest that the exercises themselves should be scored for winners and losers without making any reference to higher order characteristics like skills, abilities, or traits.[88] Research indicates that one of the best combinations of selection methods includes work-sample tests with a highly structured interview and a measure of general cognitive ability. The validity coefficient expected from such a combined battery often exceeds .60.[89]

Assessment center
A process in which multiple raters evaluate employees' performance on a number of exercises.

Honesty Tests and Drug Tests

Many problems that confront society also exist within organizations, which has led to two new kinds of tests: honesty tests and drug-use tests. Many companies formerly employed polygraph tests, or lie detectors, to evaluate job applicants, but this changed with the passage of the Polygraph Act in 1988. This act banned the use of polygraphs in employment screening for most organizations. However, it did not eliminate the problem of theft by employees. As a result, the paper-and-pencil honesty testing industry was born.

Paper-and-pencil honesty tests come in a number of different forms. Some directly emphasize questions dealing with past theft admissions or associations with people who stole from employers. Other items are less direct and tap more basic traits such as social conformity, conscientiousness, or emotional stability.[90] Some sample items are shown in Table 6.4. A large-scale independent review of validity studies conducted by the publishers of many integrity tests suggests they can predict both theft and other disruptive behaviors.[91] One of the few predictive studies conducted by someone other than a publisher of honesty tests also suggests that these tests predict theft in convenience store settings.[92] Another positive feature of these tests is that one does not see large differences attributable to race or sex, so they are not likely to have adverse impact on these demographic groups.[93]

1. It's OK to take something from a company that is making too much profit.
2. Stealing is just a way of getting your fair share.
3. When a store overcharges its customers, it's OK to change price tags on merchandise.
4. If you could get into a movie without paying and not get caught, would you do it?
5. Is it OK to go around the law if you don't actually break it?

TABLE 6.4

Sample Items from a Typical Integrity Test

SOURCE: From *Inc.: The Magazine for Growing Companies.* Copyright © 1992 by Goldhirsh Group/Inc. Publishing. Reproduced with permission of Goldhirsh Group/Inc. Publishing via Copyright Clearance Center.

As is the case with measures of personality, some people are concerned that people confronting an honesty test can fake their way to a passing score. The evidence suggests that people instructed to fake their way to a high score (indicating honesty) can do so. However, it is not clear that this affects the validity of the predictions made using such tests. That is, it seems that despite this built-in bias, scores on the test still predict future theft. Thus, the effect of the faking bias is not large enough to detract from the test's validity.[94]

Although it is always a good rule to locally evaluate the reliability and validity of any selection method, because of the novelty of these kinds of measures this may be even more critical with honesty tests. For example, Nordstrom, the large department store chain, uses the Reid Survey to screen for violent tendencies, drug use, and dishonesty. Originally, the test was only one of many factors that went into the final hiring decision, so there were some people hired who were not recommended by the Reid test. Follow-up studies showed that the turnover rate for those recommended by the Reid test was only 22 percent, compared with 44 percent of those who did not pass the test but were hired anyway. Since the test costs only $5 to administer, this represents a major cost saving in the stores using the test.[95]

As with theft, there is a growing perception of the problems caused by drug use among employees. Indeed, 79 percent of *Fortune* 1,000 chief executives cited substance abuse as a significant problem in their organizations, and 50 percent of medium-size and large organizations test applicants for drug use.[96] Because the physical properties of drugs are invariant and subject to highly rigorous chemical testing, the reliability and validity of drug tests are very high.

The major controversies surrounding drug tests involve not their reliability and validity but whether they represent an invasion of privacy, an unreasonable search and seizure, or a violation of due process. Urinalysis and blood tests are invasive procedures, and accusing someone of drug use is a serious matter. Employers considering the use of drug tests would be well advised to make sure that their drug-testing programs conform to some general rules. First, these tests should be administered systematically to all applicants for the same job. Second, testing seems more defensible for jobs that involve safety hazards associated with failure to perform.[97] Test results should be reported back to the applicant, who should be allowed an avenue of appeal (and perhaps retesting). Tests should be conducted in an environment that is as unintrusive as possible, and results from those tests should be held in strict confidence. Finally, when testing current employees, the program should be part of a wider organizational program that provides rehabilitation counseling.[98]

A Look Back

In the story about Wal-Mart that opened this chapter, we saw how important hiring decisions are in terms of both legal and competitive issues. These are some of the most critical decisions that an organization will make, and thus, leaving these decisions to the idiosyncratic and nonstandardized subjective judgments of uninformed local managers may not be the best method of making such choices. Thankfully, there are numerous alternatives to this for making such decisions, many of which have been validated and supported by years of research, and these were highlighted in this chapter.

TABLE 6.5

A Summary of Personnel Selection Methods

METHOD	RELIABILITY	VALIDITY	GENERALIZABILITY	UTILITY	LEGALITY
Interviews	Low when unstructured and when assessing nonobservable traits	Low if unstructured and nonbehavioral	Low	Low, especially because of expense	Low because of subjectivity and potential interviewer bias; also, lack of validity makes job-relatedness low
Reference checks	Low, especially when obtained from letters	Low because of lack of range in evaluations	Low	Low, although not expensive to obtain	Those writing letters may be concerned with charges of libel
Biographical information	High test-retest, especially for verifiable information	High criterion-related validity; low in content validity	Usually job-specific, but have been successfully developed for many job types	High; inexpensive way to collect vast amounts of potentially relevant data	May have adverse impact; thus often develop separate scoring keys based on sex or race
Physical ability tests	High	Moderate criterion-related validity; high content validity for some jobs	Low; pertain only to physically demanding jobs	Moderate for some physical jobs; may prevent expensive injuries and disability	Often have adverse impact on women and people with disabilities; need to establish job-relatedness
Cognitive ability tests	High	Moderate criterion-related validity; content validation inappropriate	High; predictive for most jobs, although best for complex jobs	High; low cost and wide application across diverse jobs in companies	Often have adverse impact on race, especially for African Americans, though decreasing over time
Personality inventories	High	Low criterion-related validity for most traits; content validation inappropriate	Low; few traits predictive for many jobs	Low, although inexpensive for jobs where specific traits are relevant	Low because of cultural and sex differences on most traits, and low job-relatedness in general
Work-sample tests	High	High criterion and content validity	Usually job-specific, but have been successfully developed for many job types	High, despite the relatively high cost to develop	High because of low adverse impact and high job-relatedness
Honesty tests	Insufficient independent evidence	Insufficient independent evidence	Insufficient independent evidence	Insufficient independent evidence	Insufficient history of litigation, but will undergo scrutiny
Drug tests	High	High	High	Expensive, but may yield high payoffs for health-related costs	May be challenged on invasion-of-privacy grounds

Questions

1. Based on this chapter, what are the best methods of obtaining information about job applicants?
2. What are the best characteristics to look for in applicants, and how does this depend on the nature of the job?
3. If you could use only two of the methods described in this chapter and could assess only two of the characteristics discussed, which would you choose, and why?

Summary

In this chapter we examined the five critical standards with which all personnel selection methods should conform: reliability, validity, generalizability, utility, and legality. We also looked at nine different selection methods currently used in organizations and evaluated each with respect to these five standards. Table 6.5, on page 245, summarizes these selection methods and can be used as a guide in deciding which test to use for a specific purpose. Although we discussed each type of test individually, it is important to note in closing that there is no need to use only one type of test for any one job. Indeed, managerial assessment centers use many different forms of tests over a two- or three-day period to learn as much as possible about candidates for important executive positions. As a result, highly accurate predictions are often made, and the validity associated with the judicious use of multiple tests is higher than for tests used in isolation.

Discussion Questions

1. We examined nine different types of selection methods in this chapter. Assume that you were just rejected for a job based on one of these methods. Obviously, you might be disappointed and angry regardless of what method was used to make this decision, but can you think of two or three methods that might leave you most distressed? In general, why might the acceptability of the test to applicants be an important standard to add to the five we discussed in this chapter?
2. Videotaping applicants in interviews is becoming an increasingly popular means of getting multiple assessments of that individual from different perspectives. Can you think of some reasons why videotaping interviews might also be useful in evaluating the interviewer? What would you look for in an interviewer if you were evaluating one on videotape?

3. Distinguish between concurrent and predictive validation designs, discussing why the latter is preferred over the former. Examine each of the nine selection methods discussed in this chapter and determine which of these would have their validity most and least affected by the type of validation design employed.
4. Some have speculated that in addition to increasing the validity of decisions, employing rigorous selection methods has symbolic value for organizations. What message is sent to applicants about the organization through hiring practices, and how might this message be reinforced by recruitment programs that occur before selection and training programs that occur after selection?

Self-Assessment Exercise

Reviews of research about personality have identified five common aspects of personality, referred to as the Big Five personality traits. Find out which are your most prominent traits. Read each of the following statements, marking "Yes" if it describes you and "No" if it does not.

1. In conversations I tend to do most of the talking.
2. Often people look to me to make decisions.
3. I am a very active person.
4. I usually seem to be in a hurry.
5. I am dominant, forceful, and assertive.

6. I have a very active imagination.
7. I have an active fantasy life.
8. How I feel about things is important to me.
9. I find it easy to feel myself what others are feeling.
10. I think it's interesting to learn and develop new hobbies.
11. My first reaction is to trust people.
12. I believe that most persons are basically well intentioned.
13. I'm not crafty or shy.
14. I'd rather not talk about myself and my accomplishments.
15. I'd rather praise others than be praised myself.
16. I come into situations being fully prepared.
17. I pride myself on my sound judgment.
18. I have a lot of self-discipline.
19. I try to do jobs carefully so they don't have to be done again.
20. I like to keep everything in place so I know where it is.
21. I enjoy performing under pressure.
22. I am seldom sad or depressed.
23. I'm an even-tempered person.
24. I am levelheaded in emergencies.
25. I feel I am capable of coping with most of my problems.

The statements are grouped into categories. Statements 1–5 describe extroversion, 6–10 openness to experience, 11–15 agreeableness, 16–20 conscientiousness, and 21–25 emotional stability. The more times you wrote "Yes" for the statements in a category, the more likely you are to have the associated trait.

Manager's Hot Seat Exercise: Diversity in Hiring: Candidate Conundrum

This Manager's Hot Seat case takes a close look at problems that may hinder a company's ability to select the best available candidate. As the scene opens, two candidates are presented. There are also two interviewers on hand—one is the business owner and the other is a department manager. Both candidates have excellent qualifications, past experience, and possess the type of personality this company looks for in its employees.

As the case reveals, the interviewers are in disagreement over who should be selected for the position. The business owner feels the manager's opinion has been swayed by the candidate's personal appeal rather than the value of her qualifications. Ultimately, the owner makes the final decision in which candidate to hire.

This scenario depicts the importance of the interview process. It demonstrates the high organizational value of being able to select the best candidate based on the presence of qualifications that will prove beneficial. The case stresses how vital it is for personal preferences and biases to be removed from the selection process.

Group Activity:
Divide the class into groups of 4–5 individuals per group. Discuss the case. Identify what errors in the selection process you found. Discuss the importance of the selection process. Identify how this process impacts companies. Identify methods to prevent or alleviate candidate selection problems such as personal preference and bias from impeding the process. Discuss how the selection process, as depicted in the case, meets or fails to meet legal standards. Discuss other selection methods available for companies to engage. Express which one(s) you personally favor and why. Prepare the group notes to be discussed as a class.

Exercising Strategy: Never Having to Say "You Never Know"

Seymour Schlager had an impressive résumé. He had both MD and JD degrees, as well as a PhD in microbiology. He had experience as a director of established AIDS research at Abbott Laboratories, and as an entrepreneur in a small, upstart pharmaceutical company. He seemed like a perfect fit for the medical director job open at Becton Dickinson, a large medical device company, and was hired on the spot.

One fact about Schlager that did not come out of the application process was that he was convicted of attempted murder in 1991 and had spent several years in prison as a result of this crime. While any reader of this book could type Schlager's name into almost any Internet search engine and uncover at least one of the 24 articles written about his case—some of which were front-page material in the *Chicago Tribune*—apparently no one at Becton Dickinson felt this was necessary.

Although this is an extreme case, the practice of stretching, shading, spinning, and outright lying on one's résumé is hardly uncommon, and when one is in the business of hiring complete strangers, it pays to "be afraid—be very afraid." Although many firms fail to perform routine background checks on their hires, organizations that provide such checks can point to some startling statistics. For example, Kroll Associates, one of the leading investigative agencies for top-level executives, notes that of the 70 background checks it did in the year 2000, 39 percent turned up problems such as fraud, bankruptcy, and SEC violations that were serious enough to nix the employment offers being considered.

One reason for the lack of "due diligence" on the part of employers is that in a labor shortage, too many are in a rush to secure top talent. For example, when the firm Christian and Timbers narrowed the search for the new CEO of Pinpoint Networks Inc. down to six candidates, rather than let the firm finish its work, the young founders of this company were so infatuated with the résumé of one applicant that they immediately took over and closed the search. Unfortunately, when it became clear 13 weeks later that the new CEO, Anthony J. Blake, was not who he claimed to be, it was too late. Without a seasoned CEO, Pinpoint blew the opportunity to attract venture capital when it was still available. When the technology sector tanked later that year, Pinpoint was forced to lay off over a third of its workforce.

Experiences such as these are prompting other employers to slow down the hiring process so that they have a much better idea of exactly whom they are asking to join their organizational family. Some firms do not only background checks but also extensive psychological testing to ensure that a person is who he or she claims to be and also fits the culture of the organization. You never know what these kinds of investigations will uncover—unless, of course, you fail to perform them.

Questions

1. People applying for jobs are always motivated to display themselves in the best light, and as a result, this can sometimes lead to inaccurate portrayals of abilities, skills, experiences, and personality. Based upon what you have read in this chapter, how should you approach a job applicant's written application and résumé if your goal is to make sure that they accurately reflect the person's past experiences and accomplishments?

2. In the face-to-face interview process, what steps can be taken to ensure that the applicant is being frank and honest with you, and what steps should you take if you feel that he or she is portraying an inaccurate picture of himself or herself?

3. Beyond the traditional approaches of going over the application and conducting face-to-face interviews, what other steps can you as an employer take to ensure that the person who is being hired for the job has the right abilities, skills, past experiences and personality?

SOURCE: G. David, "You Just Hired Him: Should You Have Known Better," *Fortune* (October 29, 2001), pp. 205–6; D. Foust, "When the CEO Is Too Good to Be True," *BusinessWeek* (July 16, 2001), pp. 62–63; C. Daniels, "Does This Man Need a Shrink?" *Fortune* (February 5, 2001).

Managing People: From the Pages of *BusinessWeek*

BusinessWeek Coming Out in Corporate America

One chilly fall day last year, Gary Osifchin trooped into a mandatory training session at S.C. Johnson & Son Inc. The privately held company, located in Racine, Wis., which was voted 2003's "all-American city" by the National Civic League, manufactures Raid insecticide and Glade air fresheners. It's the kind of place where factory workers ride to the assembly line on Harley-Davidsons, dine on local bratwurst, and chase it down with Milwaukee beer.

About 20 plant managers were seated in a circle in a drab conference room. Osifchin, an S.C. Johnson marketing exec, walked into the center and started telling stories—about his boyfriend, his romantic life, and his experiences as a homosexual. He told co-workers, for instance, that one constant source of stress was having to come out anew every time he sat down with a new supervisor or switched units. "Somebody might see a picture of a guy on my desk, and that just sparks conversation," he said.

The frank talk was the kickoff of Gay 201, the upper-level course in gay sensitivity training offered at S.C. Johnson. It's available only to graduates of Gay 101, an introductory seminar that debunks stereotypes. The classes at Johnson are hardly anomalous. Eastman Kodak Co. offers similar sessions. Lucent Technologies, Microsoft, Southern California Edison, and dozens of others, meanwhile, send executives to weeklong training courses for gay managers at the University of California at Los Angeles' Anderson School of Management.

The programs are just one small piece of a growing gay, lesbian, bisexual, and transgender (GLBT) rights movement in Corporate America. Following in the footsteps of African Americans, women, and other traditionally marginalized groups, corporate gays are increasingly standing up for their rights. Defense contractors such as Raytheon Co. and Lockheed Martin Corp. now sponsor gay support groups. American Express Co. and Lehman Brothers Inc. promote their gay financial advisers in GLBT publications. Even culturally conservative Wal-Mart Stores Inc., which bans racy magazines and compact discs with offensive lyrics, this year adopted a nondiscrimination policy toward gays.

Galloping Change The new attitude of GLBT acceptance in the business world stems from the same cultural forces that, in recent months, have led to openly gay clergy, the television hit *Queer Eye for the Straight Guy*, the Supreme Court's landmark *Lawrence v. Texas* decision banning anti-sodomy laws, and the prospect of gay marriage in Massachusetts. Change is coming quite rapidly to corporations as well. Of the nation's top 500 companies, 95% now offer policies that preclude discrimination based on sexual orientation, and 70% offer domestic partner benefits for same-sex couples. In 2000, the numbers stood at 51% and 25%, respectively. "To be competitive, we need to be able to get the best from people when they're at work, and to do that they need to bring their whole self to the table," says Marge Connelly, director of operations at credit-card issuer Capital One Financial Corp. She should know—she's a lesbian. "Being out is imperative for me to be a good leader," Connelly says. "You've got to let people know you. People have to trust you."

Tougher at the Top Still, it comes as no surprise that, as is the case with society at large, gays still face plenty of discrimination in their jobs. In a study released on Oct. 1 by researcher Harris Interactive Inc. and marketer Witeck Combs Communications Inc., 41% of gay employees said they had been harassed, pressured to quit, or denied a promotion because of sexual orientation. Homosexuality is still legitimate legal grounds for firing an employee in 36 states. "For a lot of people, the fear is very real and justified that if you are openly gay in the workplace, it will jeopardize your earning potential," says Walter B. Schubert Jr., the first openly gay member of the New York Stock Exchange.

So while gays may have won more acceptance at work, that does not mean they have gained legal, financial, and occupational equality. Intolerance that has built up over centuries does not disappear because of the sudden emergence of harassment-training videos and rainbow flags in cubicles. Many members of the GLBT community believe that discrimination increases as they rise up the corporate hierarchy into the executive suites, boardrooms, and country clubs where true power is wielded.

Need proof? Just look at a list of openly gay corporate leaders. While there are some big names—including DreamWorks SKG co-founder David Geffen, former Quark CEO Tim Gill, and Ford Vice-Chairman Allan D. Gilmour—it is a pretty paltry roster for a highly educated minority that comprises, by some estimates, 6% of the population. In fact, many corporate CEOs who are widely believed to be gay are not comfortable discussing their sexuality on the record. The price of success, even in 2003, may be having to stay in the closet.

Ironically, many of the companies that are most progressive about GLBT rights are reluctant to stand up for them in public for fear of being identified too closely with the issue—an apprehension that is likely only to mount if gay marriage touches off a national culture battle in coming months.

Ordinary People The people driving the gay rights revolution in Corporate America by and large are not working in the executive suite. They're ordinary employees like Daniel Kline. The United Parcel Service Inc. supervisor last year applied for the company's Management Initiated Transfer, which allows employees to follow spouses to other cities and keep their jobs and seniority. An employee for more than two decades, Kline wanted to move with his longtime partner, who was reassigned by United Airlines Inc. from San Francisco to Chicago. After receiving approval at district and regional levels to take an open position in Chicago, Kline was rejected at the corporate level.

UPS backed down this August after the couple enlisted Lambda Legal Defense & Education Fund, a gay advocacy organization, to sue on their behalf, contending the company violated California antidiscrimination laws. A spokesman says UPS' policy on so-called trailing partners now includes same-sex couples. "I'm not looking to change the world. I simply want to live with the person with whom I've shared the last 27 years," says Kline.

Not all companies need to be pushed. Consider the story of Melissa Feinmel, who was asking for far greater accommodation than Kline. After boarding American Airlines Inc. planes for 10 years as pilot Mark Feinmel—and participating in the sports talk and sexual innuendo that suffuse the macho, military-influenced cockpit culture—she nevertheless decided to undergo a sex-change operation in 2000. Instead of opposing the move, American executives worked with Feinmel to clear the many federal regulatory hurdles that arose. For instance, the Federal Aviation Administration required Feinmel to undergo additional psychological and physical tests. The airline also had to figure out which bathroom to designate for her while she changed sexes. "There was a fear of losing my job, fear of losing my friends, fear of discrimination in the cockpit," says Feinmel. American "helped face all those issues." Now she happily flies 777s on transatlantic routes.

While the gay experience in Corporate America is far from monolithic, most gay managers interviewed by *BusinessWeek* say it has become easier in recent years to be themselves in the workplace. Displaying a picture of a same-sex lover on a desk or bringing a partner to a corporate gathering is no longer quite as intimidating as it used to be. Many now attend events such as the Out & Equal Workplace Summit, held this year in Minneapolis in October. "I used to keep my worklife and my private life separate, never talking about what I did on the weekend," says IBM Microelectronics Vice President Scottie Ginn. "Once you come out, you feel a much more whole person."

Broadly speaking, there is a generational divide among gay workers. Younger employees, typically those below 35, saw Roseanne Barr kiss another woman on TV and comedian Ellen DeGeneres declare publicly that she was a lesbian. They tend to come into the workplace as unashamedly gay and to demand equal rights more aggressively. Older workers, raised in times of greater stigma, tend to be quieter about their sexual identity to both co-workers and customers. Says James Law, a gay adviser at American Express Financial Advisors Inc: "With my older clients, I'm less prone to bring it up. With my younger clients, it's a nonissue."

Controversy Awaits The Massachusetts Supreme Court's recent decision supporting gay marriage is certain to shake up employee-benefits practices, but it is still too early to predict how widespread the victory will be. In the court's 50-page ruling, the justices held that gay couples working in the private sector should be entitled to the same health insurance, life insurance, and bereavement benefits that straight married couples receive. The court gave the state legislature until May to pass a law giving gays marriage-like rights, which will affect companies with offices in the state.

But not all issues are covered by the ruling. Veterans benefits, citizenship rights, and traditional retirement plans regulated by federal law, such as 401(k) plans and Social Security, are unaffected. Under the federal Defense of Marriage Act of 1996, which defines marriage as a legal union "between one man and one woman," gays are legally barred from claiming the same federal benefits as straight couples.

Now the action on this issue is likely to shift to Congress and state legislatures. Some gay advocacy groups want to challenge the Defense of Marriage Act. Their conservative counterparts want to broaden it. California and Minnesota have recently passed laws requiring employers to treat benefits for same-sex couples effectively the same as for married couples. But many other state legislatures are opposed to such a move.

The controversy will surely make life more complicated for CEOs trying to navigate this contentious issue.

While they may not want to alienate cultural conservatives, they will also be loath to drive away the gay community. After all, the GLBT universe in the U.S. includes some 15 million consumers. Many have high disposable incomes. Research from online company MarketResearch.com pegs GLBT buying power this year at $485 billion.

Of course, the path of gay rights in Corporate America is not a line angling boldly upward. When Exxon bought Mobil Oil in 1999, it rescinded the target company's policy of offering medical benefits to gay partners and disowned Mobil's written policy against discrimination based on sexual orientation (arguing that gay partners are not legal spouses and that gays are covered under its broader nondiscrimination policies). But despite such setbacks, far more companies are expanding gay rights than contracting them. There's no doubt that full legal equality for gays is many years away. But for the first time, it seems reasonable for gays in Corporate America to dream of a day when Gay 101 will no longer be necessary.

SOURCE: C. Edwards, "Coming Out in Corporate America," *BusinessWeek* (December 15, 2003), pp. 64–72.

Questions

1. The story that opened this chapter focused on sex discrimination at Wal-Mart, and our discussion of the Civil Rights Act focused on race discrimination. In what ways is discrimination on sexual orientation the same or different from these other types of discrimination?

2. In what ways has the experience of employers with previous dimensions of discrimination left them better able to manage discrimination on the basis of sexual orientation, and in what ways is the challenge associated with discrimination based on sexual orientation different from what employers have experienced in the past?

3. How does the age of the workforce affect implementation of programs aimed at reducing discrimination based upon sexual orientation, and what other factors associated with an organization's workforce or customer base may complicate program implementation?

Please see the video cases at the end of the book that correlate to this chapter:
1) Diversity in Hiring 2) Reality on Request—Digital Domain

Notes

1. A. Eagly, M. Johannesen-Schmidt, and M. von Engen, "Transformational, Transactional, and Laissez-Faire Leadership Styles: A Meta-Analysis Comparing Men and Women," *Psychological Bulletin*, July 2003, pp. 569–91.

2. J. C. Nunnally, *Psychometric Theory* (New York: McGraw-Hill, 1978).

3. B. Schneider, "An Interactionist Perspective on Organizational Effectiveness," in *Organizational Effectiveness: A Comparison of*

Multiple Models, ed. K. S. Cameron and D. A. Whetton (Orlando, FL: Academic Press, 1983), pp. 27–54.

4. N. Schmitt, R. Z. Gooding, R. A. Noe, and M. Kirsch, "Meta-Analysis of Validity Studies Published between 1964 and 1982 and the Investigation of Study Characteristics," *Personnel Psychology* 37 (1984), pp. 407–22.

5. J. Cohen, *Statistical Power Analysis for the Behavioral Sciences* (New York: Academic Press, 1977).

6. C. H. Lawshe, "Inferences from Personnel Tests and Their Validity," *Journal of Applied Psychology* 70 (1985), pp. 237–38.

7. D. D. Robinson, "Content-Oriented Personnel Selection in a Small Business Setting," *Personnel Psychology* 34 (1981), pp. 77–87.

8. P. R. Sackett, "Assessment Centers and Content Validity: Some Neglected Issues," *Personnel Psychology* 40 (1987), pp. 13–25.

9. F. L. Schmidt and J. E. Hunter, "The Future of Criterion-Related Validity," *Personnel Psychology* 33 (1980), pp. 41–60; F. L. Schmidt, J. E. Hunter, and K. Pearlman, "Task Differences as Moderators of Aptitude Test Validity: A Red Herring," *Journal of Applied Psychology* 66 (1982), pp. 166–85; R. L. Gutenberg, R. D. Arvey, H. G. Osburn, and R. P. Jeanneret, "Moderating Effects of Decision-Making/Information Processing Dimensions on Test Validities," *Journal of Applied Psychology* 68 (1983), pp. 600–8.

10. F. L. Schmidt, J. G. Berner, and J. E. Hunter, "Racial Differences in Validity of Employment Tests: Reality or Illusion," *Journal of Applied Psychology* 58 (1974), pp. 5–6.

11. Society for Industrial and Organizational Psychology, *Principles for the Validation and Use of Personnel Selection Procedures* (College Park, MD: University of Maryland Press, 1987).

12. J. W. Boudreau, "Utility Analysis for Decisions in Human Resource Management," in *Handbook of Industrial & Organizational Psychology,* ed. M. D. Dunnette and L. M. Hough (Palo Alto, CA: Consulting Psychologists Press, 1992).

13. E. Zimmerman, "What Are Employees Worth?" *Workforce,* February 2001, p. 36.

14. A. Meisler, "Negative Results," *Workforce,* October 2003, pp. 35–40.

15. A. Meisler, "When Bad Things Happen to Hot Brands," *Workforce,* July 2003, pp. 20–21.

16. K. F. Ebert, "New Civil Rights Act Invites Litigation," *Personnel Law* Update 6 (1991), p. 3.

17. G. Flynn, "The Reverse Discrimination Trap," *Workforce,* June 2003, pp. 106–7.

18. M. E. Heilman, W. S. Battle, C. E. Keller, and R. A. Lee, "Type of Affirmative Action Policy: A Determinant of Reactions to Sex-Based Preferential Selection," *Journal of Applied Psychology* 83 (1998), pp. 190–205.

19. R. Ableson, "Fighting Discrimination Takes Will and Cash," *Taipei Times* (July 2, 2001), pp. 21–22.

20. S. Sonnenberg, "Unreasonable Accommodations," *Workforce,* August 2003, pp. 16–17.

21. J. Mullich, "Hiring without Limits," *Workforce,* June 2002, pp. 53–58.

22. B. P. Sunoo, "Accommodating Workers with Disabilities," *Workforce,* February 2001, p. 93.

23. B. S. Murphy, "EEOC Gives Guidance on Legal and Illegal Inquiries under ADA," *Personnel Journal,* August 1994, p. 26.

24. R. L. Dipboye, *Selection Interviews: Process Perspectives* (Cincinnati, OH: South-Western, 1991).

25. R. A. Posthuma, F. R. Morgeson, and M. A. Campion, "Beyond Employment Interview Validity: A Comprehensive Narrative Review of Recent Research and Trends over Time," *Personnel Psychology* 55 (2002), pp. 1–81.

26. J. E. Hunter and R. H. Hunter, "Validity and Utility of Alternative Predictors of Job Performance," *Psychological Bulletin* 96 (1984), pp. 72–98.

27. R. Pingitore, B. L. Dugoni, R. S. Tindale, and B. Spring, "Bias against Overweight Job Applicants in a Simulated Interview," *Journal of Applied Psychology* 79 (1994), pp. 909–17.

28. *Watson v. Fort Worth Bank and Trust,* 108 Supreme Court 2791 (1988).

29. M. A. McDaniel, D. L. Whetzel, F. L. Schmidt, and S. D. Maurer, "The Validity of Employment Interviews: A Comprehensive Review and Meta-Analysis," *Journal of Applied Psychology* 79 (1994), pp. 599–616; A. I. Huffcutt and W. A. Arthur, "Hunter and Hunter (1984) Revisited: Interview Validity for Entry-Level Jobs," *Journal of Applied Psychology* 79 (1994), pp. 184–90.

30. C. H. Middendorf and T. H. Macan, "Note-Taking in the Interview: Effects on Recall and Judgments," *Journal of Applied Psychology* 87 (2002), pp. 293–303.

31. M. A. McDaniel, F. P. Morgeson, E. B. Finnegan, M. A. Campion, and E. P. Braverman, "Use of Situational Judgment Tests to Predict Job Performance: A Clarification of the Literature," *Journal of Applied Psychology* 86 (2001), pp. 730–40.

32. M. A. Campion, J. E. Campion, and J. P. Hudson, "Structured Interviewing: A Note of Incremental Validity and Alternative Question Types," *Journal of Applied Psychology* 79 (1994), pp. 998–1002; E. D. Pulakos and N. Schmitt, "Experience-Based and Situational Interview Questions: Studies of Validity," *Personnel Psychology* 48 (1995), pp. 289–308.

33. A. P. J. Ellis, B. J. West, A. M. Ryan, and R. P. DeShon, "The Use of Impression Management Tactics in Structured Interviews: A Function of Question Type?" *Journal of Applied Psychology* 87 (2002), pp. 1200–8.

34. S. Maurer, "A Practitioner-Based Analysis of Interviewer Job Expertise and Scale Format as Contextual Factors in Situational Interviews," *Personnel Psychology* 55 (2002), pp. 307–27.

35. S. Greengard, "Are You Well Armed to Screen Applicants?" *Personnel Journal,* December 1995, pp. 84–95.

36. T. Libby, "Surviving the Group Interview," *Forbes* (March 24, 1986), p. 190; Dipboye, *Selection Interviews,* p. 210.

37. Y. Ganzach, A. N. Kluger, and N. Klayman, "Making Decisions from an Interview: Expert Measurement and Mechanical Combination," *Personnel Psychology* 53 (2000), pp. 1–21.

38. S. F. Dingfelder, "To Tell the Truth," *Monitor on Psychology,* March 2004, pp. 22–23.

39. A. Davis, J. Pereira, and W. M. Bulkeley, "Security Concerns Bring Focus on Translating Body Language," *The Wall Street Journal* (August 15, 2002), pp. A1–A3.

40. Hunter and Hunter, "Validity and Utility."

41. L. McDonnell, "Interviews and Tests Counting More as Past Employers Clam Up," *Minneapolis Tribune* (May 3, 1981).

42. D. D. Hatch, "Bad Reference for Ex-Employee Judged Defamatory," *Workforce,* December 2003, p. 20.

43. E. Zimmerman, "A Subtle Reference Trap for Unwary Employers," *Workforce,* April 2003, p. 22.

44. Greengard, "Are You Well Armed to Screen Applicants?"

45. Hunter and Hunter, "Validity and Utility"; R. R. Reilly and G. T. Chao, "Validity and Fairness of Some Alternative Employee Selection Procedures," *Personnel Psychology* 35 (1982), pp. 1–62.

46. F. A. Mael and B. E. Ashforth, "Loyal from Day One: Biodata, Organizational Identification, and Turnover among Newcomers," *Personnel Psychology* 48 (1995), pp. 309–33.

47. T. W. Dougherty, D. B. Turban, and J. C. Callender, "Confirming First Impressions in the Employment Interview: A Field

Study of Interviewer Behavior," *Journal of Applied Psychology* 79 (1994), pp. 659–65.

48. C. Waxer, "Companies Demand that Staffing Agencies Check into Temps' Backgrounds," *Workforce,* June 2004, pp. 84–87.

49. S. Pustizzi, "Résumé Fraud Gets Slicker and Easier," CNN.com (March 11, 2004), p. 1.

50. K. Gordon, "Big, Fast and Easily Bungled, *Workforce,* August 2003, pp. 47–49.

51. N. Schmitt, F. L. Oswald, B. H. Kim, M. A. Gillespie, L. J. Ramsey, and T. Y. Yoo, "The Impact of Elaboration on Socially Desirable Responding and the Validity of Biodata Measures," *Journal of Applied Psychology* 88 (2003), pp. 979–88.

52. N. Schmitt and C. Kunce, "The Effects of Required Elaboration of Answers to Biodata Questions," *Personnel Psychology* 55 (2002), pp. 569–87.

53. L. C. Buffardi, E. A. Fleishman, R. A. Morath, and P. M. McCarthy, "Relationships between Ability Requirements and Human Errors in Job Tasks," *Journal of Applied Psychology* 85 (2000), pp. 551–64.

54. J. R. Hollenbeck, D. R. Ilgen, and S. M. Crampton, "Lower-Back Disability in Occupational Settings: A Human Resource Management View," *Personnel Psychology* 42 (1992), pp. 247–78.

55. J. Hogan, "Structure of Physical Performance in Occupational Tasks," *Journal of Applied Psychology* 76 (1991), pp. 495–507.

56. B. R. Blakely, M. A. Quinones, M. S. Crawford, and I. A. Jago, "The Validity of Isometric Strength Tests," *Personnel Psychology* 47 (1994), pp. 247–74.

57. J. Hogan, "Physical Abilities," in *Handbook of Industrial & Organizational Psychology,* 2nd ed., ed. M. D. Dunnette and L. M. Hough (Palo Alto, CA: Consulting Psychologists Press, 1991).

58. Americans with Disabilities Act of 1990, S. 933, Public Law 101-336 (1990).

59. Nunnally, *Psychometric Theory.*

60. M. J. Ree, J. A. Earles, and M. S. Teachout, "Predicting Job Performance: Not Much More Than g," *Journal of Applied Psychology* 79 (1994), pp. 518–24.

61. J. F. Salagado, N. Anderson, S. Moscoso, C. Bertua, and F. De Fruyt, "International Validity Generalization of GMA and Cognitive Abilities: A European Community Meta-Analysis," *Personnel Psychology* 56 (2003), pp. 573–605.

62. L. S. Gottfredson, "The g Factor in Employment," *Journal of Vocational Behavior* 29 (1986), pp. 293–96; Hunter and Hunter, "Validity and Utility"; Gutenberg et al., "Moderating Effects"; Schmidt, Berner, and Hunter, "Racial Differences in Validity."

63. J. A. LePine, J. A. Colquitt, and A. Erez, "Adaptability to Changing Task Contexts: Effects of General Cognitive Ability, Conscientiousness, and Openness to Experience," *Personnel Psychology* 53 (2000), pp. 563–93.

64. E. D. Pulakos, S. Arad, M. A. Donovan, K. E. Plamondon, "Adaptability in the Workplace: Development of a Taxonomy of Adaptive Performance," *Journal of Applied Psychology* 85 (2000), pp. 612–24.

65. R. J. Barro, "Why Colleges Shouldn't Dump the SAT," *Business-Week* (April 9, 2001), p. 20.

66. A. R. Jensen, "g: Artifact or Reality?" *Journal of Vocational Behavior* 29 (1986), pp. 301–31.

67. D. A. Kravitz and S. L. Klineberg, "Reactions to Versions of Affirmative Action among Whites, Blacks, and Hispanics," *Journal of Applied Psychology* (2000), pp. 597–611.

68. M. A. Campion, J. L. Outtz, S. Zedeck, F. S. Schmidt, J. E. Kehoe, K. R. Murphy, and R. M. Guion, "The Controversy over

Score Banding in Personnel Selection: Answers to 10 Key Questions," *Personnel Psychology* 54 (2001), pp. 149–85.

69. M. R. Barrick and M. K. Mount, "The Big Five Personality Dimensions and Job Performance: A Meta-Analysis," *Personnel Psychology* 44 (1991), pp. 1–26; L. M. Hough, N. K. Eaton, M. D. Dunnette, J. D. Camp, and R. A. McCloy, "Criterion-Related Validities of Personality Constructs and the Effect of Response Distortion on Test Validities," *Journal of Applied Psychology* 75 (1990), pp. 467–76.

70. G. M. Hurtz and J. J. Donovan, "Personality and Job Performance: The Big Five Revisited," *Journal of Applied Psychology* 85 (2000), pp. 869–79.

71. W. S. Dunn, M. K. Mount, M. R. Barrick, and D. S. Ones, "Relative Importance of Personality and General Mental Ability on Managers' Judgments of Applicant Qualifications," *Journal of Applied Psychology* 80 (1995), pp. 500–9.

72. M. R. Barrick, G. L. Stewart, and M. Piotrowski, "Personality and Job Performance: Test of the Mediating Effects of Motivation among Sales Representatives," *Journal of Applied Psychology* 87 (2002), pp. 43–51.

73. L. Smith, "Stamina: Who Has It, Why You Need It and How You Get It," *Fortune* (November 28, 1994).

74. P. M. Wright, K. M. Kacmar, G. C. McMahan, and K. Deleeuw, "P = f(M × A): Cognitive Ability as a Moderator of the Relationship between Personality and Job Performance," *Journal of Management* 21 (1995), pp. 1129–39.

75. L. A. Witt and G. R. Ferris, "Social Skill as Moderator of the Conscientiousness–Performance Relationship: Convergent Results across Four Studies," *Journal of Applied Psychology* 88 (2003), pp. 809–20.

76. M. Mount, M. R. Barrick, and J. P. Strauss, "Validity of Observer Ratings of the Big Five Personality Factors," *Journal of Applied Psychology* 79 (1994), pp. 272–80.

77. M. R. Barrick, G. L. Stewart, M. J. Neubert, and M. K. Mount, "Relating Member Ability and Personality to Work Team Processes and Team Effectiveness," *Journal of Applied Psychology* 83 (1998), pp. 377–91; J. L. LePine, J. R. Hollenbeck, D. R. Ilgen, and J. Hedlund, "Effects of Individual Differences on the Performance of Hierarchical Decision Making Teams: Much More Than g," *Journal of Applied Psychology* 82 (1997), pp. 803–11.

78. Mount, Barrick, and Strauss, "Validity of Observer Ratings."

79. J. M. Hunthausen, D. M. Truxillo, T. N. Bauer, and L. B. Hammer, "A Field Study of Frame of Reference Effects on Personality Test Validity," *Journal of Applied Psychology* 88 (2003), pp. 545–51.

80. J. G. Rosse, M. D. Stecher, J. L. Miller, and R. A. Levin, "The Impact of Response Distortion on Preemployment Personality Testing and Hiring Decisions," *Journal of Applied Psychology* 83 (1998), pp. 634–44.

81. L. A. McFarland and A. M. Ryan, "Variance in Faking across Noncognitive Measures," *Journal of Applied Psychology* 85 (2000), pp. 812–21.

82. R. Mueller-Hanson, E. D. Heggestad, and G. C. Thornton, "Faking and Selection: Considering the Use of Personality from Select-In and Select-Out Perspectives," *Journal of Applied Psychology* 88 (2003), pp. 348–55.

83. P. F. Wernimont and J. P. Campbell, "Signs, Samples and Criteria," *Journal of Applied Psychology* 46 (1968), pp. 417–19.

84. N. Schmitt and A. E. Mills, "Traditional Tests and Job Simulations: Minority and Majority Performance and Test Validities," *Journal of Applied Psychology* 86 (2001), pp. 451–58.

85. Hunter and Hunter, "Validity and Utility."

86. G. Nicholson, "Automated Assessments for Better Hire," *Workforce,* December 2000, pp. 102–09.

87. W. Arthur, E. A. Day, T. L. McNelly and P. S. Edens, "Meta-Analysis of the Criterion-Related Validity of Assessment Center Dimensions," *Personnel Psychology* 56 (2003), pp. 125–54.

88. C. E. Lance, T. A. Lambert, A. G. Gewin, F. Lievens, and J. M. Conway, "Revised Estimates of Dimension and Exercise Variance Components in Assessment Center Postexercise Dimension Ratings," *Journal of Applied Psychology* 89 (2004), pp. 377–85.

89. F. L. Schmidt and J. E. Hunter, "The Validity and Utility of Selection Methods in Personnel Psychology: Practical and Theoretical Implications of 85 Years of Research Findings," *Psychological Bulletin* 124 (1998), pp. 262–74.

90. J. E. Wanek, P. R. Sackett, and D. S. Ones, "Toward an Understanding of Integrity Test Similarities and Differences: An Item-Level Analysis of Seven Tests," *Personnel Psychology* 56 (2003), pp. 873–94.

91. D. S. One, C. Viswesvaran, and F. L. Schmidt, "Comprehensive Meta-Analysis of Integrity Test Validities: Findings and Implications for Personnel Selection and Theories of Job Performance," *Journal of Applied Psychology* 78 (1993), pp. 679–703.

92. H. J. Bernardin and D. K. Cooke, "Validity of an Honesty Test in Predicting Theft among Convenience Store Employees," *Academy of Management Journal* 36 (1993), pp. 1097–1106.

93. D. S. Ones and C. Viswesvaran, "Gender, Age, and Race Differences on Overt Integrity Tests: Results across Four Large-Scale Job Applicant Data Sets," *Journal of Applied Psychology* 83 (1998), pp. 35–42.

94. M. R. Cunningham, D. T. Wong, and A. P. Barbee, "Self-Presentation Dynamics on Overt Integrity Tests: Experimental Studies of the Reid Report," *Journal of Applied Psychology* 79 (1994), pp. 643–58.

95. Greengard, "Are You Well Armed to Screen Applicants?"

96. M. Freudenheim, "Workers Substance Abuse Increasing, Survey Says," *The New York Times* (December 13, 1988), p. 2; J. P. Guthrie and J. D. Olian, "Drug and Alcohol Testing Programs: The Influence of Organizational Context and Objectives" (paper presented at the Fourth Annual Conference of the Society for Industrial/Organizational Psychology, Boston, 1989).

97. M. E. Paronto, D. M. Truxillo, T. N. Bauer, and M. C. Leo, "Drug Testing, Drug Treatment, and Marijuana Use: A Fairness Perspective," *Journal of Applied Psychology* 87 (2002), pp. 1159–66.

98. K. R. Murphy, G. C. Thornton, and D. H. Reynolds, "College Students' Attitudes toward Drug Testing Programs, *Personnel Psychology* 43 (1990), pp. 615–31.

7
Chapter

Training

Nokia believes that an investment in training can help them gain a competitive advantage. Their programs offer employees the opportunity to develop and improve their ideas and professional growth opportunities. How might these programs help strengthen a company?

Enter the World of Business

Learning Is Business at Nokia

Nokia Corporation, the world leader in mobile communications, has over 50,000 employees and net sales of $30 billion. Nokia consists of two business groups: Nokia Networks and Nokia Mobile Phones. The company also includes the separate Nokia Ventures Organization and the corporate research unit, Nokia Research Center. Nokia's business strategy is to strengthen the company's position as the leading communications and systems provider. Nokia wants to create personalized communication technology that enables people to create their own mobile world. Nokia continues to target and enter segments of the communications market that the company believes will experience faster growth than the industry as a whole. As the demand for wireless access to services increases, Nokia plans to lead the development and commercialization of networks and systems required to make wireless content more accessible and rewarding for customers.

The management approach at Nokia, known as the "Nokia way," consists of the Nokia values, its organizational competencies, and its operations and processes used to maintain operational efficiency. The company has built its current and future strength on the Nokia way.

The Nokia way has resulted in a flat, networked company emphasizing speed and flexibility in decision making. Nokia's values include customer satisfaction, respect for the individual, achievement, and continuous learning. Continuous learning provides employees with the opportunity to develop themselves and to stay technologically current. Employees are encouraged to share experiences, take risks, and learn together. Continuous learning goes beyond formal training classes. At Nokia, continuous learning means that employees support each other's growth, developing and improving relationships through the exchange and development of ideas. E-learning is used to provide employees with the freedom to choose the best possible time and place for personal development.

Nokia's top management is committed to continuous learning. For example, the business group presidents are the "owners" of all global management and leadership programs for senior managers. They personally provide input into the development of these programs but they also appoint "godfathers" from their management teams. These godfathers participate actively throughout the program and are also designers of program content. Together with the training and development staff, the godfathers help the learning processes in the programs. Most of the programs involve strategic projects (action learning) that participants are responsible for completing. Top managers invest time in reviewing the projects and have the authority to take action based on the project team recommendations.

The value of continuous learning translates into personal and professional growth opportunities including a commitment to self-development, coaching, learning solutions and training, management training, a vibrant internal job market, and performance management. Employees are encouraged to create their own development plan and use available learning solutions and methods. Coaching with highly skilled colleagues helps employees develop and gives them the opportunity to share ideas and goals with each other. Nokia employees have access to a wide variety of training and development opportunities including learning centers and the Learning Market Place Internet, which has information on all the available learning solutions including e-learning and classroom training. Through the learning centers, Nokia has integrated the learning activities of all the business groups into one place. Nokia believes that by mixing participants from across business groups, knowledge is created because traditions and experiences can be shared between employees. In addition to formal programs offered in classrooms or on the Internet, Nokia emphasizes on-the-job learning through job rotation and through managers giving their employees challenging new job assignments. There is also a wide range of

opportunities for managers to improve their management and leadership skills. The emphasis on the internal labor market encourages employees to improve their skills by changing jobs. Nokia's performance management process, known as Investing in People (IIP), involves twice yearly discussions between employees and their managers. The IIP process consists of objective setting, coaching and achievement review, competence analysis, and personal development plan. The entire IIP process is supported electronically. Employees can choose their profile from the company intranet, conduct a self-evaluation, create a personal development plan, and investigate what learning solutions are available at the learning centers.

Nokia emphasizes that learning should result in improved operations and better business results. Therefore, the company uses a combination of measures to evaluate the value of training. Nokia always asks employees for their immediate reactions after they have completed a program. Other measures include attainment of competence and resource strategy in all parts of the company. Top management believes that the largest benefit of the learning is that employees have opportunities to network, creating more knowledge, reinforcing continuous learning, and creating committed employees.

Source: Based on the Nokia Corporation website, www.nokia.com, August 22, 2003; L. Masalin, "Nokia Leads Change through Continuous Learning," *Academy of Management Learning and Education* 2 (2003), pp. 68–72.

Introduction

As the chapter opening story shows, learning is an important part of Nokia's business strategy. Training helps employees at Nokia develop specific skills that enable them to succeed in their current job and develop for the future. Nokia also recognizes that learning involves not just formal training courses but also job experiences and interactions between employees. From Nokia's perspective, training and developing helps the company create a workforce that is able to cope with change, meet the increasing demands of the telecommunications industry, and prepare the future leadership of the company. Nokia recognizes that its industry is becoming complex—success will require smart, motivated employees who have the emotional strength to deal with change.

Why is the emphasis on strategic training important? Companies are in business to make money, and every business function is under pressure to show how it contributes to business success or face spending cuts and even outsourcing. To contribute to a company's success, training activities should help the company achieve its business strategy.

There is both a direct and indirect link between training and business strategy and goals. Training can help employees develop skills needed to perform their jobs, which directly affects the business. Giving employees opportunities to learn and develop creates a positive work environment, which supports the business strategy by attracting talented employees as well as motivating and retaining current employees.

Why do Nokia and many other companies believe that an investment in training can help them gain a competitive advantage? Training can

- Increase employees' knowledge of foreign competitors and cultures, which is critical for success in foreign markets.
- Help ensure that employees have the basic skills to work with new technology, such as robots and computer-assisted manufacturing processes.
- Help employees understand how to work effectively in teams to contribute to product and service quality.
- Ensure that the company's culture emphasizes innovation, creativity, and learning.
- Ensure employment security by providing new ways for employees to contribute to the company when their jobs change, their interests change, or their skills become obsolete.
- Prepare employees to accept and work more effectively with each other, particularly with minorities and women.[1]

In this chapter we emphasize the conditions through which training practices can help companies gain competitive advantage and how managers can contribute to a high-leverage training effort and create a learning organization. The chapter begins by discussing a systematic and effective approach to training design. Next we review training methods and training evaluation. The chapter concludes with a discussion of training issues including cross-cultural preparation, managing diversity, and socializing employees.

High-Leverage Training Strategy: A Systematic Approach

In general, **training** refers to a planned effort by a company to facilitate employees' learning of job-related competencies. These competencies include knowledge, skills, or behaviors that are critical for successful job performance. The goal of training is for employees to master the knowledge, skill, and behaviors emphasized in training programs and to apply them to their day-to-day activities. Recently it has been acknowledged that to offer a competitive advantage, training has to involve more than just basic skill development.[2] Training is moving from a primary focus on teaching employees specific skills to a broader focus of creating and sharing knowledge.[3] That is, to use training to gain a competitive advantage, a firm should view training broadly as a way to create intellectual capital. Intellectual capital includes basic skills (skills needed to perform one's job), advanced skills (such as how to use technology to share information with other employees), an understanding of the customer or manufacturing system, and self-motivated creativity.

Training
A planned effort to facilitate the learning of job-related knowledge, skills, and behavior by employees.

Traditionally most of the emphasis on training has been at the basic and advanced skill levels. But some estimate that 85 percent of the jobs in the United States and Europe require extensive use of knowledge. This requires employees to share knowledge and creatively use it to modify a product or serve the customer, as well as to understand the service or product development system.

Many companies have adopted this broader perspective, which is known as high-leverage training. **High-leverage training** is linked to strategic business goals and objectives, uses an instructional design process to ensure that training is effective, and compares or benchmarks the company's training programs against training programs in other companies.[4]

High-leverage training practices also help to create working conditions that encourage continuous learning. **Continuous learning** requires employees to understand the entire work system including the relationships among their jobs, their work units, and the company. (Continuous learning is similar to the idea of system understanding mentioned earlier.)[5] Employees are expected to acquire new skills and knowledge, apply them on the job, and share this information with other employees. Managers identify training needs and help to ensure that employees use training in their work. To facilitate the sharing of knowledge, managers may use informational maps that show where knowledge lies within the company (for example, directories that list what a person does as well as the specialized knowledge she possesses) and use technology such as groupware or the Internet that allows employees in various business units to work simultaneously on problems and share information.[6]

The emphasis on high-leverage training has been accompanied by a movement to link training to performance improvement or business strategy.[7] Companies have lost money on training because it is poorly designed, because it is not linked to a performance problem or business strategy, or because its outcomes are not properly evaluated.[8] That is, companies have been investing money into training simply because of beliefs that it is a good thing to do. The perspective that the training function exists to deliver programs to employees without a compelling business reason for doing so is being abandoned. Today, training is being evaluated not on the basis of the number of programs offered and training activity in the company but on how training addresses business needs related to learning, behavior change, and performance improvement. In fact, training is becoming more performance-focused. That is, training is used to improve employee performance, which leads to improved business results. Training is seen as one of several possible solutions to improve performance. Other solutions can include such actions as changing the job or increasing employee motivation through pay and incentives. Today there is a greater emphasis on[9]

- Providing educational opportunities for all employees. These educational opportunities may include training programs, but they also include support for taking courses offered outside the company, self-study, and learning through job rotation.
- An ongoing process of performance improvement that is directly measurable rather than organizing one-time training events.
- The need to demonstrate to executives, managers, and trainees the benefits of training.
- Learning as a lifelong event in which senior management, trainer managers, and employees have ownership.
- Training being used to help attain strategic business objectives, which help companies gain a competitive advantage.

FIGURE 7.1

The Strategic Training and Development Process

Business Strategy	Strategic Training and Development Initiatives	Training and Development Activities	Metrics That Show Value of Training
• Mission • Values • Goals	• Diversify the Learning Portfolio • Improve Customer Service • Accelerate the Pace of Employee Learning • Capture and Share Knowledge	• Use Web-Based Training • Make Development Planning Mandatory • Develop Websites for Knowledge Sharing • Increase Amount of Customer Participation	• Learning • Performance Improvement • Reduced Customer Complaints • Reduced Turnover • Employee Satisfaction

Figure 7.1 shows the strategic training and development process with examples of strategic initiatives, training activities, and metrics. The strategic training and development process involves identifying strategic training and development initiatives that will help achieve the business strategy. Employees participate in specific training and development activities that support these initiatives. The final step of the process involves collecting measures or metrics. The metrics are used to determine if training helped contribute to goals related to the business strategy.

Strategic Use of HRM

Medtronic is a good example of a company that uses high-leverage training. Medtronic is the world leader in medical technology, providing lifelong solutions for people with chronic heart and neurological diseases. Medtronic has 30,000 employees in more than 120 countries. Medtronic has set a goal of 15 percent annual growth, a goal of doubling the size of the company in five years.[10] To reach this goal, Medtronic believes that people development is important. Medtronic engages employees in learning and development, which links them to the company mission to restore many people to full and productive lives and to make sure that products are available to patients who need them.

Training and development occurs only after business strategies for achieving growth are identified by the company. For example, strong leadership is needed for a growing company. Strategies that the company uses to develop leadership skills include cross-functional, global job rotations as well as mentoring. To keep up with Medtronic's growth, training and development initiatives must be flexible. The training and development staff are continually scanning the company and the broader medical device industry to understand the issues and prepare training solutions to meet them. Because Medtronic is a global company, certain skills are needed by all managers wherever they are in the world. But the various offices have the ability to adapt programs to their locations. In the Medtronic Asia/Pacific location, for example, a developing managers' program placed more emphasis on cultural awareness because the managers were from many different locations and backgrounds. Training also supports new product launches to ensure that customers get a consistent message about the product. For example, Medtronic introduced a new heart therapy with a training event broadcast via satellite to salespeople located throughout the United States.

Measuring the return on investment in research and development, marketing, sales, and human resources is key for demonstrating the value to the business. Each of Medtronic's businesses uses a scorecard to measure success and return on investment. Medtronic is currently developing metrics to measure how training contributes to the company's success.

This discussion is not meant to underestimate the importance of "traditional training" (a focus on acquisition of knowledge, skills, and abilities), but it should alert you that for many companies training is evolving from a focus on skills to an emphasis on learning and creating and sharing knowledge.

Designing Effective Training Activities

Training design process
A systematic approach for developing training programs.

A key characteristic of training activities that contribute to competitiveness is that they are designed according to the instructional design process.[11] **Training design process** refers to a systematic approach for developing training programs. Instructional System Design (ISD) and the ADDIE model (analysis, design, development, implementation, evaluation) are two specific types of training design processes you may know. Table 7.1 presents the six steps of this process, which emphasizes that effective training practices involve more than just choosing the most popular or colorful training method.

Step 1 is to assess needs to determine if training is needed. Step 2 involves ensuring that employees have the motivation and basic skills to master training content. Step 3 addresses whether the training session (or the learning environment) has the

TABLE 7.1

The Training Process

1. Needs assessment
   - Organizational analysis
   - Person analysis
   - Task analysis
2. Ensuring employees' readiness for training
   - Attitudes and motivation
   - Basic skills
3. Creating a learning environment
   - Identification of learning objectives and training outcomes
   - Meaningful material
   - Practice
   - Feedback
   - Observation of others
   - Administering and coordinating program
4. Ensuring transfer of training
   - Self-management strategies
   - Peer and manager support
5. Selecting training methods
   - Presentational methods
   - Hands-on methods
   - Group methods
6. Evaluating training programs
   - Identification of training outcomes and evaluation design
   - Cost–benefit analysis

factors necessary for learning to occur. Step 4 is to ensure that trainees apply the content of training to their jobs. This requires support from managers and peers for the use of training content on the job as well as getting the employee to understand how to take personal responsibility for skill improvement. Step 5 involves choosing a training method. As we shall see in this chapter, a variety of training methods are available ranging from traditional on-the-job training to newer technologies such as the Internet. The key is to choose a training method that will provide the appropriate learning environment to achieve the training objectives. Step 6 is evaluation—that is, determining whether training achieved the desired learning outcomes and/or financial objectives.

The training design process should be systematic yet flexible enough to adapt to business needs. Different steps may be completed simultaneously. Keep in mind that designing training unsystematically will reduce the benefits that can be realized. For example, choosing a training method before determining training needs or ensuring employees' readiness for training increases the risk that the method chosen will not be the most effective one for meeting training needs. Also, training may not even be necessary and may result in a waste of time and money! Employees may have the knowledge, skills, or behavior they need but simply not be motivated to use them. Next we will discuss important aspects of the training design process.

Needs Assessment

The first step in the instructional design process, **needs assessment,** refers to the process used to determine if training is necessary. Figure 7.2 shows the causes and outcomes resulting from needs assessment. As we see, many different "pressure points" suggest that training is necessary. These pressure points include performance problems, new technology, internal or external customer requests for training, job redesign, new legislation, changes in customer preferences, new products, or employees' lack of basic skills as well as support for the company's business strategy (e.g., growth, global business expansion). Note that these pressure points do not guarantee that training is the correct solution. Consider, for example, a delivery truck driver whose job is to deliver anesthetic gases to medical facilities. The driver mistakenly hooks up the supply line of a mild anesthetic to the supply line of a hospital's oxygen system, contaminating the hospital's oxygen supply. Why did the driver make this mistake,

Needs assessment
The process used to determine if training is necessary.

FIGURE 7.2

The Needs Assessment Process

Reasons or "pressure points"   What is the context?

- Legislation
- Lack of basic skills
- Poor performance
- New technology
- Customer requests
- New products
- Higher performance standards
- New jobs
- Business growth or contraction
- Global business expansion

Organization analysis

Task analysis

Person analysis

In what do they need training?

Who needs training?

Outcomes

- What trainees need to learn
- Who receives training
- Type of training
- Frequency of training
- Buy-versus-build training decision
- Training versus other HR options such as selection or job redesign
- How training should be evaluated

Organizational analysis
A process for determining the business appropriateness of training.

Person analysis
A process for determining whether employees need training, who needs training, and whether employees are ready for training.

Task analysis
The process of identifying the tasks, knowledge, skills, and behaviors that need to be emphasized in training.

which is clearly a performance problem? The driver may have done this because of a lack of knowledge about the appropriate line hookup for the anesthetic, anger over a requested salary increase that his manager recently denied, or mislabeled valves for connecting the gas supply. Only the lack of knowledge can be addressed by training. The other pressure points require addressing issues related to the consequence of good performance (pay system) or the design of the work environment.

Needs assessment typically involves organizational analysis, person analysis, and task analysis.[12] Organizational analysis considers the context in which training will occur. That is, **organizational analysis** involves determining the business appropriateness of training, given the company's business strategy, its resources available for training, and support by managers and peers for training activities.

Person analysis helps identify who needs training. **Person analysis** involves (1) determining whether performance deficiencies result from a lack of knowledge, skill, or ability (a training issue) or from a motivational or work-design problem, (2) identifying who needs training, and (3) determining employees' readiness for training. **Task analysis** includes identifying the important tasks and knowledge, skill, and behaviors that need to be emphasized in training for employees to complete their tasks.

In practice, organizational analysis, person analysis, and task analysis are usually not conducted in any specific order. However, because organizational analysis is concerned with identifying whether training fits with the company's strategic objectives and whether the company wants to devote time and money to training, it is usually conducted first. Person analysis and task analysis are often conducted at the same time because it is often difficult to determine whether performance deficiencies are a training problem without understanding the tasks and the work environment.

What outcomes result from a needs assessment? As shown in Figure 7.2, needs assessment shows who needs training and what trainees need to learn, including the tasks in which they need to be trained plus knowledge, skill, behavior, or other job requirements. Needs assessment helps determine whether the company will purchase training from a vendor or consultant or develop training using internal resources.

Organizational Analysis

Managers need to consider three factors before choosing training as the solution to any pressure point: the company's strategic direction, the training resources available, and support of managers and peers for training activities.

Support of Managers and Peers
Various studies have found that peer and manager support for training is critical. The key factors to success are a positive attitude among peers and managers about participation in training activities; managers' and peers' willingness to tell trainees how they can more effectively use knowledge, skills, or behaviors learned in training on the job; and the availability of opportunities for the trainees to use training content in their jobs.[13] If peers' and managers' attitudes and behaviors are not supportive, employees are not likely to apply training content to their jobs.

Company Strategy
In Chapter 2 we discussed the importance of business strategy for a company to gain a competitive advantage. Several types of strategies were discussed including growth and disinvestment. As Figure 7.1 highlights training should help companies achieve the

TABLE 7.2

Strategic Training and Development Initiatives and Their Implications

STRATEGIC TRAINING AND DEVELOPMENT INITIATIVES	IMPLICATIONS
Diversify the Learning Portfolio	• Use new technology such as the Internet for training • Facilitate informal learning • Provide more personalized learning opportunities
Expand Who Is Trained	• Train customers, suppliers, and employees • Offer more learning opportunities to nonmanagerial employees
Accelerate the Pace of Employee Learning	• Quickly identify needs and provide a high-quality learning solution • Reduce the time to develop training programs • Facilitate access to learning resources on an as-needed basis
Improve Customer Service	• Ensure that employees have product and service knowledge • Ensure that employees have skills needed to interact with customers • Ensure that employees understand their roles and decision-making authority
Provide Development Opportunities and Communicate to Employees	• Ensure that employees have opportunities to develop • Ensure that employees understand career opportunities and personal growth opportunities • Ensure that training and development addresses employees' needs in current job as well as growth opportunities
Capture and Share Knowledge	• Capture insight and information from knowledgeable employees • Logically organize and store information • Provide methods to make information available (e.g., resource guides, websites)
Align Training and Development with the Company's Strategic Direction	• Identify needed knowledge, skills, abilities, or competencies • Ensure that current training and development programs support the company's strategic needs
Ensure That the Work Environment Supports Learning and Transfer of Training	• Remove constraints to learning, such as lack of time, resources, and equipment • Dedicate physical space to encourage teamwork, collaboration, creativity, and knowledge sharing • Ensure that employees understand the importance of learning • Ensure that managers and peers are supportive of training, development, and learning

SOURCE: Based on S. Tannenbaum, "A Strategic View of Organizational Training and Learning," in *Creating, Implementing and Managing Effective Training and Development*, ed. K. Kraiger (San Francisco: Jossey-Bass, 2002), pp. 10–52.

business strategy. Table 7.2 shows possible strategic training and development initiatives and their implications for training practices. **Strategic training and development initiatives** are learning related actions that a company should take to help achieve its business strategy.[14] The initiatives are based on the business environment, an understanding of the company's goals and resources, and insight into potential training and development options. They provide the company with a road map to guide specific training and development activities. They also show how training will help the company reach its goals and add value. The plan or goal the company chooses to achieve strategic objectives has a major impact on whether resources (money, trainers' time, program development) should be devoted to addressing a training pressure point.

It is important to identify the prevailing business strategy to ensure that the company allocates enough of its budget to training, that employees receive training on

Strategic training and development initiatives
Learning related actions that a company takes to achieve its business strategy.

relevant topics, and that employees get the right amount of training.[15] For example, Deluxe Corporation is a check printer based in Saint Paul, Minnesota. Factors such as electronic transactions, mergers and acquisitions among financial institutions, and a company reorganization resulted in downsizing and poor employee morale within the company.[16] Fewer than 140 of 400 account managers were still employed with the company. As a result of the downsizing, Deluxe lost many account managers with 5 to 10 years of experience. The account managers who remained had worked at Deluxe less than 3 years or more than 20 years. For these account managers, sales training involved only product training. Deluxe used training to capture and retain not only business but also the hearts and minds of employees.

Account managers developed fundamental sales skills through a combination of online and workshop courses. To build credibility for the training, three high-performing account managers assisted two trainers from Deluxe's training department. Simultaneously with the account managers' training, all employees providing field support for the sales team participated in a one-day training session that emphasized the change from selling product to building relationships with customers. Sales managers and directors participated in a field-coaching program so they could reinforce the account managers' learning. The sales managers now "shadow" the account managers once every business quarter to observe their sales skills and to provide coaching. Another training program focused on strategic time management skills. As a result of the training, customer retention rates have improved to 95 percent, up from 85 percent two years ago.

Companies with an internal growth strategy face the challenge of keeping employees up to date on new products and services. For example, Masimo Corporation, located in Orange County, California, develops, licenses, and markets advanced medical signal processing technologies for monitoring patient vital signs.[17] Because employees work with sophisticated technology and because new products are constantly being developed, Masimo is challenged to keep its sales force and distribution partners aware of the latest features, functions, and applications of its monitoring devices. Using an Internet-based corporate university, Masimo has been able to provide programs that enhance revenue by preparing the sales force more quickly to sell new products, and these programs have given the company the ability to bring products to the market faster. Also, the training benefits the clinical staff by increasing brand awareness and product competence among hospital staff and by building a community of users to drive future sales. The Internet-based corporate university is also important because it allows clinical staff who work long hours access to training and because it tracks and documents training as required by government regulations.

Training Resources

It is necessary to identify whether the company has the budget, time, and expertise for training. For example, if the company is installing computer-based manufacturing equipment in one of its plants, it has three possible strategies to have computer-literate employees. First, the company can use internal consultants to train all affected employees. Second, the company may decide that it is more cost-effective to identify computer-literate employees by using tests and work samples. Employees who fail the test or perform below standards on the work sample can be reassigned to other jobs. Choosing this strategy suggests that the company has decided to devote resources to selection and placement rather than training. Third, if it lacks time or expertise, the company may decide to purchase training from a consultant.

TABLE 7.3

Questions to Ask
Vendors and
Consultants

How much and what type of experience does your company have in designing and delivering training?

What are the qualifications and experiences of your staff?

Can you provide demonstrations or examples of training programs you have developed?

Would you provide references of clients for whom you worked?

What evidence do you have that your programs work?

Will the training program be customized to meet the company's needs?

How long will it take to develop the training program?

How much will your services cost?

SOURCE: Adapted from R. Zemke and J. Armstrong, "Evaluating Multimedia Developers." *Training Magazine*, November 1996.

Many companies identify vendors and consultants who can provide training services by using requests for proposals.[18] A **request for proposal (RFP)** is a document that outlines for potential vendors and consultants the type of service the company is seeking, the type and number of references needed, the number of employees who need to be trained, funding for the project, the follow-up process used to determine level of satisfaction and service, the expected completion date of the project, and the date when proposals must be received by the company. The request for proposal may be mailed to potential consultants and vendors or posted on the company's website. The request for proposal is valuable because it provides a standard set of criteria against which all consultants will be evaluated. The RFP also helps eliminate the need to evaluate outside vendors who cannot provide the needed services.

Usually the RFP helps identify several vendors who meet the criteria. The next step is to choose the preferred provider. Table 7.3 provides examples of questions to ask vendors.

Person Analysis

Person analysis helps the manager identify whether training is appropriate and which employees need training. In certain situations, such as the introduction of a new technology or service, all employees may need training. However, when managers, customers, or employees identify a problem (usually as a result of a performance deficiency), it is often unclear whether training is the solution.

A major pressure point for training is poor or substandard performance—that is, a gap between employees' current performance and their expected performance. Poor performance is indicated by customer complaints, low performance ratings, or on-the-job accidents or unsafe behavior. Another potential indicator of the need for training is if the job changes so current performance levels need improvement or employees must complete new tasks.

Figure 7.3 shows the factors that influence employees' performance and learning. These factors include person characteristics, input, output, consequences, and feedback.[19] **Person characteristics** refer to the employees' knowledge, skill, ability, and attitudes. **Input** relates to the instructions that tell employees what, how, and when to perform. Input also refers to the support given to employees to help them perform. This support includes resources such as equipment, time, or budget. Support also includes

Request for proposal (RFP)
A document that outlines for potential vendors and consultants the type of service the company is seeking, references needed, number of employees who should be trained, project funding, the follow-up process, expected completion date, and the date when proposals must be received by the company.

Person characteristics
An employee's knowledge, skills, abilities, and attitudes.

Input
Instructions that tell the employee what, how, and when to perform; also the support they are given to help them to perform.

FIGURE 7.3

Factors That Influence Employee Performance and Learning

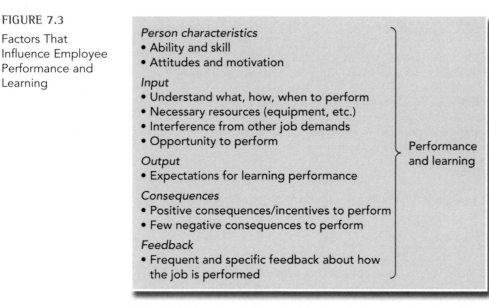

Person characteristics
• Ability and skill
• Attitudes and motivation

Input
• Understand what, how, when to perform
• Necessary resources (equipment, etc.)
• Interference from other job demands
• Opportunity to perform

Output
• Expectations for learning performance

Consequences
• Positive consequences/incentives to perform
• Few negative consequences to perform

Feedback
• Frequent and specific feedback about how the job is performed

Performance and learning

SOURCE: G. Rummler, "In Search of the Holy Performance Grail," *Training and Development,* April 1996, pp. 26–31. Reprinted with permission. All rights reserved.

Output
A job's performance standards.

Consequences
The incentives that employees receive for performing well.

Feedback
Information that employees receive while they are performing concerning how well they are meeting objectives.

feedback and reinforcement from managers and peers. **Output** refers to the job's performance standards. **Consequences** are the incentives employees receive for performing well. **Feedback** is the information employees receive while they are performing.

From a manager's perspective, to determine if training is needed, for any performance problem you need to analyze characteristics of the performer, input, output, consequences, and feedback. How might this be done? Based on the model in Figure 7.3, you should ask several questions to determine if training is the likely solution to a performance problem.[20] Assess whether

1. The performance problem is important and has the potential to cost the company a significant amount of money from lost productivity or customers.
2. Employees do not know how to perform effectively. Perhaps they received little or no previous training or the training was ineffective. (This problem is a characteristic of the person.)
3. Employees cannot demonstrate the correct knowledge or behavior. Perhaps they were trained but they infrequently or never used the training content (knowledge, skills, etc.) on the job. (This is an input problem.)
4. Performance expectations are clear (input) and there are no obstacles to performance such as faulty tools or equipment.
5. There are positive consequences for good performance, whereas poor performance is not rewarded. For example, if employees are dissatisfied with their compensation, their peers or a union may encourage them to slow down their pace of work. (This involves consequences.)
6. Employees receive timely, relevant, accurate, constructive, and specific feedback about their performance (a feedback issue).
7. Other solutions such as job redesign or transferring employees to other jobs are too expensive or unrealistic.

If employees lack the knowledge and skill to perform and the other factors are satisfactory, training is needed. If employees have the knowledge and skill to perform, but input, output, consequences, or feedback are inadequate, training may not be the best solution. For example, if poor performance results from faulty equipment, training cannot solve this problem, but repairing the equipment will! If poor performance results from lack of feedback, then employees may not need training, but their managers may need training on how to give performance feedback.

Task Analysis

A task analysis, defined on page 262, identifies the conditions in which tasks are performed. The conditions include identifying equipment and the environment the employee works in, time constraints (deadlines), safety considerations, or performance standards. Task analysis results in a description of work activities, including tasks performed by the employee and the knowledge, skills, and abilities required to successfully complete the tasks. A *job* is a specific position requiring the completion of specific tasks. A *task* is a statement of an employee's work activity in a specific job. There are four steps in task analysis:

1. Select the job(s) to be analyzed.
2. Develop a preliminary list of tasks performed on the job by interviewing and observing expert employees and their managers and talking with others who have performed a task analysis.
3. Validate or confirm the preliminary list of tasks. This involves having a group of subject matter experts (job incumbents, managers, and so on) answer in a meeting or on a written survey several questions regarding the tasks. The types of questions that may be asked include the following: How frequently is the task performed? How much time is spent performing each task? How important or critical is the task for successful performance of the job? How difficult is the task to learn? Is performance of the task expected of entry-level employees?[21]

   Table 7.4 presents a sample task analysis questionnaire. This information is used to determine which tasks will be focused on in the training program. The person or committee conducting the needs assessment must decide the level of ratings across dimensions that will determine that a task should be included in the training program. Tasks that are important, frequently performed, and of moderate-to-high levels of difficulty should be trained. Tasks that are not important and are infrequently performed will not be trained. It is difficult for managers and trainers to decide if tasks that are important, are performed infrequently, and require minimal difficulty should be included in training. Managers and trainers must determine whether important tasks—regardless of how frequently they are performed or their level of difficulty—will be included in training.
4. Identify the knowledge, skills, or abilities necessary to successfully perform each task. This information can be collected using interviews and questionnaires. Information concerning basic skill and cognitive ability requirements is critical for determining if certain levels of knowledge, skills, and abilities will be prerequisites for entrance to the training program (or job) or if supplementary training in underlying skills is needed. For training purposes, information concerning how difficult it is to learn the knowledge, skill, or ability is important—as is whether the knowledge, skill, or ability is expected to be acquired by the employee before taking the job.[22]

TABLE 7.4

Sample Task Statement Questionnaire

Name   Date
Position

Please rate each of the task statements according to three factors: the *importance* of the task for effective performance, how *frequently* the task is performed, and the degree of *difficulty* required to become effective in the task. Use the following scales in making your ratings.

Importance	*Frequency*
4 = Task is critical for effective performance.	4 = Task is performed once a day.
3 = Task is important but not critical for effective performance.	3 = Task is performed once a week.
2 = Task is of some importance for effective performance.	2 = Task is performed once every few months.
1 = Task is of no importance for effective performance.	1 = Task is performed once or twice a year.
0 = Task is not performed.	0 = Task is not performed.

Difficulty
4 = Effective performance of the task requires extensive prior experience and/or training (12–18 months or longer).
3 = Effective performance of the task requires minimal prior experience and training (6–12 months).
2 = Effective performance of the task requires a brief period of prior training and experience (1–6 months).
1 = Effective performance of the task does not require specific prior training and/or experience.
0 = This task is not performed.

Task	*Importance*	*Frequency*	*Difficulty*
1. Ensuring maintenance on equipment, tools, and safety controls			
2. Monitoring employee performance			
3. Scheduling employees			
4. Using statistical software on the computer			
5. Monitoring changes made in processes using statistical methods			

Example of a Task Analysis

Each of the four steps of a task analysis can be seen in this example from a utility company. Trainers were given the job of developing a training system in six months.[23] The purpose of the program was to identify tasks and knowledge, skills, abilities, and other considerations that would serve as the basis for training program objectives and lesson plans.

The first phase of the project involved identifying potential tasks for each job in the utility's electrical maintenance area. Procedures, equipment lists, and information provided by subject matter experts (SMEs) were used to generate the tasks. SMEs included managers, instructors, and senior technicians. The tasks were incorporated into a questionnaire administered to all technicians in the electrical maintenance department. The questionnaire included 550 tasks. Figure 7.4 shows sample items from the questionnaire for the electrical maintenance job. Technicians were asked to rate each task on importance, difficulty, and frequency of performance. The rating scale for frequency included zero. A zero rating indicated that the technician rating the task had never performed the task. Technicians who rated a task zero were asked not to evaluate the task's difficulty and importance.

Customized software was used to analyze the ratings collected via the questionnaire. The primary requirement used to determine whether a task required training was its importance rating. A task rated "very important" was identified as one requir-

FIGURE 7.4

Sample Items from Task Analysis Questionnaires for the Electrical Maintenance Job

Job: Electrical Maintenance Worker

Task Performance Ratings

Task #s	Task Description	Frequency of performance	Importance	Difficulty
199-264	Replace a light bulb	0 1 2 3 4 5	0 1 2 3 4 5	0 1 2 3 4 5
199-265	Replace an electrical outlet	0 1 2 3 4 5	0 1 2 3 4 5	0 1 2 3 4 5
199-266	Install a light fixture	0 1 2 3 4 5	0 1 2 3 4 5	0 1 2 3 4 5
199-267	Replace a light switch	0 1 2 3 4 5	0 1 2 3 4 5	0 1 2 3 4 5
199-268	Install a new circuit breaker	0 1 2 3 4 5	0 1 2 3 4 5	0 1 2 3 4 5

Frequency of performance	**Importance**	**Difficulty**
0=never 5=often	1=negligible 5=extremely high	1=easiest 5=most difficult

SOURCE: E. F. Holton III and C. Bailey, "Top-to-Bottom Curriculum Redesign," *Training and Development,* March 1995, pp. 40–44. Reprinted with permission of *Training & Development.*

ing training regardless of its frequency or difficulty. If a task was rated moderately important but difficult, it also was designated for training. Tasks rated unimportant, not difficult, and done infrequently were not designated for training.

The list of tasks designated for training was reviewed by the SMEs to determine if it accurately described job tasks. The result was a list of 487 tasks. For each of the 487 tasks, two SMEs identified the necessary knowledge, skills, abilities, and other factors required for performance. This included information on working conditions, cues that initiate the task's start and end, performance standards, safety considerations, and necessary tools and equipment. All data were reviewed by plant technicians and members of the training department. More than 14,000 knowledge, skill, ability, and other considerations were clustered into common areas. An identification code was assigned to each group that linked groups to task and knowledge, skill, ability, and other factors. These groups were then combined into clusters that represented qualification areas. That is, the task clusters related to linked tasks that the employees must be certified in to perform the job. The clusters were used to identify training lesson plans and course objectives; trainers also reviewed the clusters to identify prerequisite skills.

Ensuring Employees' Readiness for Training

The second step in the training design process is to evaluate whether employees are ready to learn. *Readiness for training* refers to whether (1) employees have the personal characteristics (ability, attitudes, beliefs, and motivation) necessary to learn program content and apply it on the job and (2) the work environment will facilitate learning and not interfere with performance.

Motivation to learn
The desire of the trainee to learn the content of a training program.

Although managers are not often trainers, they play an important role in influencing employees' readiness for training. **Motivation to learn** is the desire of the trainee to learn the content of the training program.[24] Various research studies have shown that motivation is related to knowledge gain, behavior change, or skill acquisition in training programs.[25] Managers need to ensure that employees' motivation to learn is as high as possible. They can do this by ensuring employees' self-efficacy; understanding the benefits of training; being aware of training needs, career interests, and goals; understanding work environment characteristics; and ensuring employees' basic skill levels. Managers should also consider input, output, consequences, and feedback because these factors influence motivation to learn.

Self-efficacy

Self-efficacy
The employees' belief that they can successfully learn the content of a training program.

Self-efficacy is the employees' belief that they can successfully learn the content of the training program. The training environment is potentially threatening to many employees who may not have extensive educational experience or who have little experience in the particular area emphasized by the training program. For example, training employees to use equipment for computer-based manufacturing represents a potential threat, especially if employees are intimidated by new technologies and do not have confidence in their ability to master the skills needed to use a computer. Research has demonstrated that self-efficacy is related to performance in training programs.[26] Managers can increase employees' self-efficacy level by

1. Letting employees know that the purpose of training is to try to improve performance rather than to identify areas in which employees are incompetent.
2. Providing as much information as possible about the training program and purpose of training prior to the actual training.
3. Showing employees the training success of their peers who are now in similar jobs.
4. Providing employees with feedback that learning is under their control and they have the ability and the responsibility to overcome any learning difficulties they experience in the program.

Understanding the Benefits or Consequences of Training

Employees' motivation to learn can be enhanced by communicating to them the potential job-related, personal, and career benefits they may receive as a result of attending the training program. These benefits may include learning a more efficient way to perform a process or procedure, establishing contacts with other employees in the firm (networking), or increasing opportunities to pursue different career paths. The communication from the manager about potential benefits should be realistic. Unmet expectations about training programs have been shown to adversely affect motivation to learn.[27]

Awareness of Training Needs, Career Interests, and Goals

To be motivated to learn in training programs, employees must be aware of their skill strengths and weaknesses and of the link between the training program and improvement of their weaknesses.[28] Managers should make sure that employees understand why they are asked to attend training programs, and they should communicate the link between training and improvement of skill weaknesses or knowledge deficiencies. This can be accomplished by sharing performance appraisal information with employees, holding career development discussions, or having employees complete self-evaluations of their skill strengths and weaknesses and career interests and goals.

If possible, employees need to choose programs to attend and must perceive how actual training assignments are made to maximize motivation to learn. Several recent studies have suggested that giving trainees a choice regarding which programs to attend and then honoring those choices maximizes motivation to learn. Giving employees choices but not necessarily honoring them can reduce motivation to learn.[29]

Work Environment Characteristics

Employees' perceptions of two characteristics of the work environment—situational constraints and social support—are critical determinants of motivation to learn. *Situational constraints* include lack of proper tools and equipment, materials and supplies, budgetary support, and time. *Social support* refers to managers' and peers' willingness to provide feedback and reinforcement.[30]

To ensure that the work environment enhances trainees' motivation to learn, managers need to

1. Provide materials, time, job-related information, and other work aids necessary for employees to use new skills or behavior before participating in training programs.
2. Speak positively about the company's training programs to employees.
3. Let employees know they are doing a good job when they use training content in their work.
4. Encourage work group members to involve each other in trying to use new skills on the job by soliciting feedback and sharing training experiences and situations in which training content was helpful.
5. Give employees time and opportunities to practice and apply new skills or behaviors to their work.

Basic Skills

Employees' motivation to learn in training activities can also be influenced by the degree to which they have **basic skills**—cognitive ability and reading and writing skills needed to understand the content of training programs. Recent forecasts of the skill levels of the U.S. workforce indicate that managers will likely have to work with employees who lack those skills.[31]

Managers need to conduct a literacy audit to determine employees' basic skill levels. Table 7.5 shows the activities involved in a literacy audit.

Cognitive Ability. **Cognitive ability** includes verbal comprehension (understand and use written and spoken language), quantitative ability (speed and accuracy in solving math problems), and reasoning ability (logic in solving problems).[32] Research shows that cognitive ability is related to successful performance in all jobs.[33] The importance of cognitive ability for job success increases as the job becomes more complex.

Cognitive ability influences job performance and ability to learn in training programs. If trainees lack the cognitive ability level necessary to perform job tasks, they will not perform well. Also, trainees' level of cognitive ability can influence whether they can learn in training programs.[34] Trainees with low levels of cognitive ability are more likely to fail to complete training or (at the end of training) receive low grades on tests to measure how much they have learned.

Basic skills
Reading, writing, and communication skills needed to understand the content of a training program.

Cognitive ability
Includes three dimensions: verbal comprehension, quantitative ability, and reasoning ability.

TABLE 7.5

Performing a
Literacy Audit

Step 1.	Observe employees to determine the basic skills they need to succeed in their jobs. Note the materials employees use on the job, the tasks performed, and the reading, writing, and computations completed by employees.
Step 2.	Collect all materials that are written and read on the job and identify computations that must be performed to determine the necessary level of basic skill proficiency. Materials include bills, memos, and forms such as inventory lists and requisition sheets.
Step 3.	Interview employees to determine the basic skills they believe are needed to do the job. Consider the basic-skill requirements of the job yourself.
Step 4.	Determine whether employees have the basic skills needed to successfully perform their jobs. Combine the information gathered by observing and interviewing employees and evaluating materials they use on their jobs. Write a description of each job in terms of reading, writing, and computation skills needed to perform successfully.
Step 5.	Develop or buy tests that ask questions relating specifically to the employees' jobs. Ask employees to complete the tests.
Step 6.	Compare test results with the description of the basic skills required for the job (from step 5). If the level of employees' reading, writing, and computation skills does not match the basic skills required by the job, then a basic skills problem exists.

SOURCE: U.S. Department of Education, U.S. Department of Labor. *The Bottom Line: Basic Skills in the Workplace* (Washington, DC: 1988), pp. 14–15.

As discussed in Chapter 6, to identify employees without the cognitive ability to succeed on the job or in training programs, companies use paper-and-pencil cognitive ability tests. Determining a job's cognitive ability requirement is part of the task analysis process discussed earlier in this chapter.

Reading Ability. Lack of the appropriate reading level can impede performance and learning in training programs. Material used in training should be evaluated to ensure that its reading level does not exceed that required by the job. **Readability** refers to the difficulty level of written materials.[35] A readability assessment usually involves analysis of sentence length and word difficulty.

Readability
The difficulty level of written materials.

If trainees' reading level does not match the level needed for the training materials, four options are available. First, determine whether it is feasible to use video or on-the-job training, which involves learning by watching and practicing rather than by reading. Second, employees without the necessary reading level could be identified through reading tests and reassigned to other positions more congruent with their skill levels. Third, again using reading tests, identify employees who lack the necessary reading skills and provide them with remedial training. Fourth, determine whether the job can be redesigned to accommodate employees' reading levels. The fourth option is certainly most costly and least practical. Therefore, alternative training methods need to be considered, or you can elect a nontraining option. Nontraining options include selecting employees for jobs and training opportunities on the basis of reading, computation, writing, and other basic skill requirements.

The "Competing through Sustainability" box shows how companies are partnering with nonprofit groups to develop worker skills and in return get a motivated and committed workforce.

Nonprofit groups or employment brokers serve as liaisons between employers and potential employees by developing training programs for low-income workers. The relationship is beneficial for both the employee and the companies. Employees receive wage-paying jobs, and companies throughout a region of the country and within a specific industry get the employees they need. Most of the companies are located in urban areas and help a wide range of people by raising living and working standards. For example, Jane Addams Resource Corporation (JARC) in Chicago was started as an industry-specific training organization in 1985 by local government and area businesses when the metalworking and stamping industry needed skilled workers. Chicago-based S&C Electric, a provider of equipment and services for the electric utility industry, partnered with JARC because it could no longer find skilled workers. S&C Electric and JARC worked together to help the company's 1,700 employees improve their machinery skills. Classes were also offered in math and English as a Second Language. Regence BlueShield, part of the Regence Group, which provides health plans in Idaho, Washington, Utah, and Oregon, teamed up with the Seattle Jobs Initiative (SJI) to create a curriculum that would train potential interns for customer service positions at Regence. SJI tailors its training to the company culture and requires that individuals show up for a 40-hour workweek and dress professionally. Trainees also are evaluated three times during training, similar to what they would encounter in a performance evaluation on the job.

Training partnerships to prepare economically disadvantaged workers benefit both the company and the employees. California-based Tucker Technology, which provides telecommunications installation and maintenance to large companies, was able to build 15 percent of its workforce from community-based organizations throughout the country. The company believes that it receives many benefits from hiring through community centers, including a trained work force without the training costs and a highly committed workforce with a low turnover rate. Participants of industry-specific training programs were surveyed before they entered the training program and after they completed the program, and the results suggest that the program also offers many benefits for the employees. Most employees improved their position in the labor market, and 66 percent remained employed two years after the survey was conducted. Seventy-eight percent had access to health insurance, paid vacation, sick leave, and a pension plan. Most employees felt that their job and their future employment opportunities were good.

SOURCE: Based on J. Gatewood, "Proactive Partnership," *Human Resource Executive,* May 16, 2003, pp. 36–38; C. Caggiano, "Insider Training," *Inc.,* May 1999, pp. 63–64.

Creating a Learning Environment

Learning permanently changes behavior. For employees to acquire knowledge and skills in the training program and apply this information in their jobs, the training program must include specific learning principles. Educational and industrial psychologists and instructional design specialists have identified several conditions under

TABLE 7.6

Conditions for Learning and Their Importance

CONDITIONS FOR LEARNING	IMPORTANCE
Employees need to know why they should learn	Learners need to understand the purpose or objectives of the training program.
Meaningful training content	Motivation to learn is enhanced when training is related to helping learner (such as related to current job tasks, problems, enhancing skills, or dealing with jobs or company changes).
Opportunities for practice	Practice is necessary to achieve proficiency in skill, behavior, task or acquire knowledge.
Feedback	Feedback helps learner modify behavior, skill, or use knowledge to meet objectives.
Observe experience, and interact with others	Adults learn best by doing. Gain new perspectives and insights by working with others. Can learn by observing the actions of models.
Good program coordination and administration	Eliminate distractions that could interfere with learning.
Commit training content to memory	Facilitate recall of training content after training.

SOURCE: Based on R. M. Gagne, "Learning Processes and Instruction," *Training Research Journal* 1 (1995/1996), pp. 17–28; M. Knowles, *The Adult Learner*, 4th ed. (Houston: Gulf, 1990); A. Bandura, *Social Foundations of Thought and Action* (Englewood Cliffs, NJ: Prentice Hall, 1986); E. A. Locke and G. D. Latham, *A Theory of Goal Setting and Task Performance* (Englewood Cliffs, NJ: Prentice Hall, 1990).

which employees learn best.[36] Table 7.6 shows the events that should take place for learning to occur in the training program and their implications for instruction.

Employees Need to Know Why They Should Learn. Employees learn best when they understand the objective of the training program. The **objective** refers to the purpose and expected outcome of training activities. There may be objectives for each training session as well as overall objectives for the program. Training objectives based on the training needs analysis help employees understand why they need training. Objectives are also useful for identifying the types of training outcomes that should be measured to evaluate a training program's effectiveness.

Objective

The purpose and expected outcome of training activities.

A training objective has three components:

1. A statement of what the employee is expected to do (performance or outcome).
2. A statement of the quality or level of performance that is acceptable (criterion).
3. A statement of the conditions under which the trainee is expected to perform the desired outcome (conditions).[37]

For example, a training objective for a retail customer service training program might be "After training, the employee will be able to express concern [performance] to all irate customers by a brief (fewer than 10 words) apology, only after the customer has stopped talking [criteria] and no matter how upset the customer is [conditions]."

Employees Need Meaningful Training Content. Employees are more likely to learn when the training is linked to their current job experiences and tasks—that is, when it is meaningful to them.[38] To enhance the meaningfulness of training content, the message should be presented using concepts, terms, and examples familiar to trainees.

Also, the training context should mirror the work environment. The *training context* refers to the physical, intellectual, and emotional environment in which the training occurs. For example, in a retail salesperson customer service program, the meaningfulness of the material will be increased by using scenarios of unhappy customers actually encountered by salespersons in stores. Recent research indicates that besides linking training to current job experiences, learning can be enhanced by letting trainees choose their practice strategy and other characteristics of the learning environment.[39]

Employees Need Opportunities to Practice. **Practice** involves having the employee demonstrate the learned capability (such as cognitive strategy or verbal information) emphasized in the training objectives under the conditions and performance standards specified by the objective. Effective practice actively involves the trainee, includes overlearning (repeated practice), takes the appropriate amount of time, and includes the appropriate unit of learning (amount of material). Practice also needs to be relevant to the training objectives.

Learning will not occur if employees practice only by talking about what they are expected to do. For example, using the objective for the customer service course previously discussed, practice would involve having trainees participate in role playing with unhappy customers (customers upset with poor service, poor merchandise, or exchange policies). Trainees need to continue to practice even if they have been able to perform the objective several times (**overlearning**). Overlearning helps the trainee become more comfortable using new knowledge and skills and increases the length of time the trainee will retain the knowledge, skill, or behavior.

For example, one objective of the retail customer service training is learning how to handle an unhappy customer. Salespersons are likely to have to learn three key behaviors: (1) greeting disgruntled customers, (2) understanding their complaints, and then (3) identifying and taking appropriate action. Practice sessions should be held for each of the three behaviors (part practice). Then another practice session should be held so that trainees can practice all three skills together (whole practice). If trainees were given the opportunity only to practice the behaviors individually, it is unlikely they would be able to deal with an unhappy customer.

Employees Need Feedback. *Feedback* is information about how well people are meeting the training objectives. To be effective, feedback should focus on specific behaviors and be provided as soon as possible after the trainees' behavior.[40] Also, positive trainee behavior should be verbally praised or reinforced. Videotape is a powerful tool for giving feedback because trainees can see the strengths and weaknesses of their behavior.

Employees Learn by Observing, Experience, and Interacting with Others. According to social learning theory, people learn by observing and imitating the actions of models. For the model to be effective, the desired behaviors or skills need to be clearly specified, and the model should have characteristics (such as age or position) similar to the target audience.[41] After observing the model, trainees should have the opportunity to reproduce the skills or behavior shown by the model in practice sessions.

Communities of practice are groups of employees who work together, learn from each other, and develop a common understanding of how to get work accomplished.[42] The idea of communities of practice suggests that learning occurs on the job as a result of social interaction. Communities of practice also take the form of discussion boards, list servers, or other forms of computer-mediated communication in which employees communicate electronically. In doing so, each employee's knowledge can be accessed relatively quickly. It is as if employees are having a conversation with a

Practice
Having the employee demonstrate what he or she has learned in training.

Overlearning
Trainees practice what they have learned several times.

Communities of practice
Groups of employees who work together, learn from each other, and develop a common understanding of how to get work accomplished.

group of experts. Every company has naturally occurring communities of practice that develop as a result of relationships employees develop to accomplish work and the design of the work environment. For example, at Siemens Power Transmission in Wendell, North Carolina, managers were wondering how to stop employees from gathering in the employee cafeteria for informal discussions.[43] But that was before the managers discovered that the informal discussions actually encouraged learning. In the discussions, employees were developing problem-solving strategies, sharing product and procedural information, and providing career counseling to each other. Now Siemens is placing pads of paper and overhead projectors in the lunchroom as aids for informal meetings. Managers who were previously focused on keeping workers on the job are now encouraging employees by providing essential tools and information and giving employees the freedom to meet.

Employees Need to Commit Training Content to Memory. Memory works by processing stimuli we perceive through our senses into short-term memory. If the information is determined to be "important," it moves to long-term memory where new interconnections are made between neurons or electrical connections in the brain. There are several things that trainers can do to help employees store knowledge, skills, behavior, and other training in long-term memory.[44] One is to create a concept map to show relationships among ideas. Another is to use multiple forms of review including writing, drawings, and role plays to access memory through multiple methods. Teaching key words, a procedure, or a sequence, or providing a visual image gives trainees another way to retrieve information. Reminding trainees of knowledge, behavior, and skills that they already know that are relevant to the current training content creates a link to long-term memory that provides a framework for recalling the new training content. External retrieval cues can also be useful. Consider a time when you misplaced your keys or wallet. In trying to remember, we often review all of the information we can recall that was close in time to the event or preceded the loss. We often go to the place where we were when we last saw the item because the environment can provide cues that aid in recall.

Research suggests that no more than four or five items can be attended to at one time. If a lengthy process or procedure is to be taught, instruction needs to be delivered in relatively small chunks or short sessions in order to not exceed memory limits.[45] Long-term memory is also enhanced by going beyond one-trial learning. That is, often once trainees correctly demonstrate a behavior or skill or correctly recall knowledge, it is assumed that they have learned it. However, that is often not the case. Making trainees review and practice over multiple days (overlearning) can help retain information in long-term memory. Overlearning also helps to automize a task.

Automatization refers to making performance of a task, recall of knowledge, or demonstration of a skill so automatic that it requires little thought or attention. Automatization also helps to reduce memory demands. The more automatization occurs, the more memory is freed up to concentrate on other learning and thinking. The more active a trainee is in rehearsal and practice, the greater the amount of information retained in long-term memory and the less memory decay occurs over time.

Training administration
Coordinating activities before, during, and after a training program.

Employees Need the Training Program to Be Properly Coordinated and Arranged.
Training coordination is one of several aspects of training administration. **Training administration** refers to coordinating activities before, during, and after the program.[46]

Good coordination ensures that trainees are not distracted by events (such as an uncomfortable room or poorly organized materials) that could interfere with learning.

Activities before the program include communicating to trainees the purpose of the program, the place it will be held, the name of a person to contact if they have questions, and any preprogram work they are supposed to complete. Books, speakers, handouts, and videotapes need to be prepared. Any necessary arrangements to secure rooms and equipment (such as VCRs) should be made. The physical arrangement of the training room should complement the training technique. For example, it would be difficult for a team-building session to be effective if the seats could not be moved for group activities. If visual aids will be used, all trainees should be able to see them. Make sure that the room is physically comfortable with adequate lighting and ventilation. Trainees should be informed of starting and finishing times, break times, and location of bathrooms. Minimize distractions such as phone messages. If trainees will be asked to evaluate the program or take tests to determine what they have learned, time for this activity at the end of the program.

Ensuring Transfer of Training

Transfer of training refers to on-the-job use of knowledge, skills, and behaviors learned in training. As Figure 7.5 shows, transfer of training is influenced by the climate for transfer, manager support, peer support, opportunity to use learned capabilities, technology support, and self-management skills. As we discussed earlier, learning is influenced by the learning environment (such as meaningfulness of the material and opportunities for practice and feedback) and employees' readiness for training (for example, their self-efficacy and basic skill level). If no learning occurs in the training program, transfer is unlikely.

Climate for Transfer

One way to think about the work environment's influence on transfer of training is to consider the overall climate for transfer. **Climate for transfer** refers to trainees' perceptions about a wide variety of characteristics of the work environment that facilitate or inhibit use of trained skills or behavior. These characteristics include manager and peer support, opportunity to use skills, and the consequences for using learned capabilities.[47] Research has shown that transfer of training climate is significantly related to positive changes in behaviors following training.

Transfer of training
The use of knowledge, skills, and behaviors learned in training on the job.

Climate for transfer
Trainees' perceptions of characteristics of the work environment (social support and situational constraints) that can either facilitate or inhibit use of trained skills or behavior.

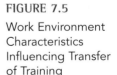

FIGURE 7.5

Work Environment Characteristics Influencing Transfer of Training

TABLE 7.7

What Managers Should Do to Support Training

Understand the content of the training.

Know how training relates to what you need employees to do.

In performance appraisals, evaluate employees on how they apply training to their jobs.

Support employees' use of training when they return to work.

Ensure that employees have the equipment and technology needed to use training.

Prior to training, discuss with employees how they plan to use training.

Recognize newly trained employees who use training content.

Give employees release time from their work to attend training.

Explain to employees why they have been asked to attend training.

Give employees feedback related to skills or behavior they are trying to develop.

SOURCE: Based on A. Rossett, "That Was a Great Class, but . . ." *Training and Development*, July 1997, p. 21.

Manager Support

Manager support refers to the degree to which trainees' managers (1) emphasize the importance of attending training programs and (2) stress the application of training content to the job. Table 7.7 shows what managers should do to support training. For example, at Men's Wearhouse, managers are expected to spend part of their budget on training. A series of meetings are held with managers to explain the purpose of training and the manager's role in helping employees learn and use skills in the stores. At Johnson and Johnson managers learn online how to support training and development. Using a Web-based resource, managers can assess employees' skills and develop learning plans.[48]

The greater the level of manager support, the more likely that transfer of training will occur.[49] The basic level of support that a manager should provide is acceptance, that is, allowing trainees to attend training. The highest level of support is to participate in training as an instructor (teaching in the program). Managers who serve as instructors are more likely to provide lower-level support functions such as reinforcing use of newly learned capabilities, discussing progress with trainees, and providing opportunities to practice. Managers can also facilitate transfer through use of action plans. An **action plan** is a written document that includes the steps that the trainee and manager will take to ensure that training transfers to the job. The action plan includes (1) a goal identifying what training content will be used and how it will be used (project, problem); (2) strategies for reaching the goal, including resources needed; (3) strategies for getting feedback (such as meetings with the manager); and (4) expected outcome (what will be different?). The action plan includes a schedule of specific dates and times when the manager and trainee agree to meet to discuss the progress being made in using learned capabilities on the job.

At a minimum, special sessions should be scheduled with managers to explain the purpose of the training and set expectations that they will encourage attendance at the training session, provide practice opportunities, reinforce use of training, and follow up with employees to determine the progress in using newly acquired capabilities.

Action plan
Document summarizing what the trainee and manager will do to ensure that training transfers to the job.

Finding and Keeping the Best Employees

Best Buy, the consumer electronics retailer based in Richfield, Minnesota, plans to grow the business through expansion.[50] Best Buy plans to open about 60 new stores each year. Training is important to make sure each new store provides the same quality of service and has efficient operations of inventory management and ordering. Best Buy uses Grand Opening University (GOU) to ensure consistency in all new stores. GOU involves several different phases of training prior to a new store opening. Supervisors work with a coach for two weeks in an existing store, learning leadership skills and how to open and operate a new store. Five weeks before the grand opening, one sales manager for each new store attends a five-day course held at Best Buy's corporate campus. The managers learn strategies for successfully training their new supervisors and employees. One day of the course is dedicated to managers' learning about the products they will be training their employees to sell. For example, supervisors who will be working in the digital imaging group are taken to a nature conservatory. The trainer for that group shows them how to take pictures using the functions on the digital cameras they will be selling and brings them back to the corporate campus to print out the pictures. This exercise helps the supervisors understand the strengths and limitations of the digital cameras so they can provide that knowledge to their own employees. What type of metrics does Best Buy use to evaluate whether training is contributing to the business? Best Buy uses turnover and survey data. Reducing turnover is important because if well-trained employees stay, Best Buy provides a consistent, high level of customer service. Otherwise, the company is faced with a constant churn of employees, which means spending more money on training for new employees. One estimate is that Best Buy employee turnover has dropped from between 110 percent and 120 percent to between 70 percent and 80 percent. GOU has also had a positive influence on employee satisfaction. Best Buy surveys employees about how much they like their jobs and the company. At new stores, the survey scores improved at the same time that GOU was started. Best Buy estimates that for every .01 increase in survey scores, the store can realize $100,000 in additional profits. Survey scores have increased .30, which translates into additional profit. Grand Opening University appears to be having a significant impact on Best Buy's bottom line!

Peer Support

Transfer of training can also be enhanced by creating a support network among the trainees.[51] A **support network** is a group of two or more trainees who agree to meet and discuss their progress in using learned capabilities on the job. This could involve face-to-face meetings or communications via e-mail. Trainees can share successful experiences in using training content on the job; they can also discuss how they obtained resources needed to use training content or how they coped with a work environment that interfered with use of training content.

Support network
Trainees who meet to discuss their progress in using learned capabilities on the job.

A newsletter might be written to show how trainees are dealing with transfer of training issues. Distributed to all trainees, the newsletter might feature interviews with trainees who were successful in using new skills. Managers may also provide trainees with a mentor—a more experienced employee who previously attended the same training program. The mentor, who may be a peer, can provide advice and support related to transfer of training issues (such as how to find opportunities to use the learned capabilities).

Opportunity to Use Learned Capabilities

Opportunity to use learned capabilities (**opportunity to perform**) refers to the extent to which the trainee is provided with or actively seeks experience with newly learned knowledge, skill, and behaviors from the training program.[52] Opportunity to perform is influenced by both the work environment and trainee motivation. One way trainees can use learned capabilities is through assigned work experiences (problems

Opportunity to perform
Trainee is provided with or actively seeks experience using newly learned knowledge, skills, or behavior.

or tasks) that require their use. The trainees' manager usually plays a key role in determining work assignments. Opportunity to perform is also influenced by the degree to which trainees take personal responsibility to actively seek out assignments that allow them to use newly acquired capabilities. Trainees given many opportunities to use training content on the job are more likely to maintain learned capabilities than trainees given few opportunities.[53]

Technological Support

Electronic performance support systems (EPSS) are computer applications that can provide, as requested, skills training, information access, and expert advice.[54] EPSSs may be used to enhance transfer of training by giving trainees an electronic information source that they can refer to as needed as they attempt to apply learned capabilities on the job.

For example, Atlanta-based poultry processor Cagle's Inc. uses an EPSS for employees who maintain the chicken-processing machines.[55] Because the machines that measure and cut chickens are constantly increasing in sophistication, it is impossible to continually train technicians so that they know the equipment's details. However, technicians are trained on the basic procedures they need to know to maintain these types of machines. When the machines encounter a problem, the technicians rely on what they have learned in training as well as on the EPSS, which provides more detailed instructions about the repairs. The EPSS also tells technicians the availability of parts and where in inventory to find replacement parts. The EPSS consists of a postage stamp–size computer monitor attached to a visor that magnifies the screen. The monitor is attached to a three-pound computer about half the size of a portable compact disc player. Attached to the visor is a microphone that the technician uses to give verbal commands to the computer. The EPSS helps employees diagnose and fix the machines very quickly. This is important given that the plant processes more than 100,000 chickens a day, and chicken is a perishable food product!

Self-Management Skills

Training programs should prepare employees to self-manage their use of new skills and behaviors on the job.[56] Specifically, within the training program, trainees should set goals for using skills or behaviors on the job, identify conditions under which they might fail to use them, identify the positive and negative consequences of using them, and monitor their use of them. Also, trainees need to understand that it is natural to encounter difficulty in trying to use skills on the job; relapses into old behavior and skill patterns do not indicate that trainees should give up. Finally, because peers and supervisors on the job may be unable to reward trainees using new behaviors or to provide feedback automatically, trainees need to create their own reward system and ask peers and managers for feedback.

Selecting Training Methods

A number of different methods can help employees acquire new knowledge, skills, and behaviors. Figure 7.6 shows the percentage of companies using different training methods. The figure shows that the instructor-led classroom is the most frequently used training method. Other common methods include the Internet, workbooks and manuals, and video. Figure 7.6 shows that traditional training methods, those that do

Electronic performance support systems (EPSS) Computer applications that can provide (as requested) skills training, information access, and expert advice.

FIGURE 7.6

Overview of Use of Instructional Methods

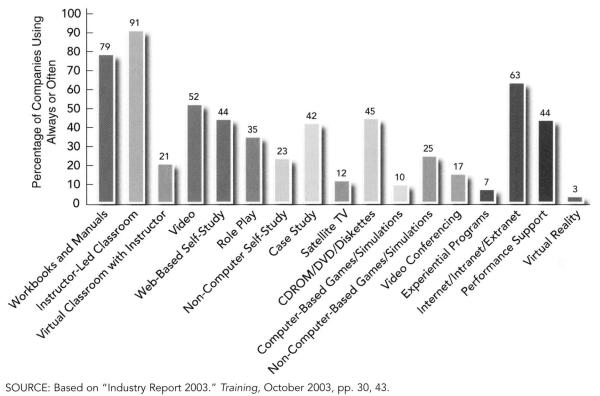

SOURCE: Based on "Industry Report 2003." *Training*, October 2003, pp. 30, 43.

not involve technology to deliver lessons, are more frequently used than is training that involves technology to deliver programs. For example, instructor-led classrooms, videos, workbooks and manuals, and role plays are used more frequently than virtual reality, computer-based games and simulations, and virtual classrooms with instructor. Note that there is one important exception: Technology-based programs involving CD-ROM/DVD/diskettes and Internet/intranet are frequently used by over 40 percent of the companies surveyed.

Regardless of whether the training method is traditional or technology based, for training to be effective it needs to be based on the training design model shown in Table 7.1. Needs assessment, a positive learning environment, and transfer of training are critical for training program effectiveness.

Presentation Methods

Presentation methods refer to methods in which trainees are passive recipients of information. Presentation methods include traditional classroom instruction, distance learning, and audiovisual techniques. These are ideal for presenting new facts, information, different philosophies, and alternative problem-solving solutions or processes.

Instructor-Led Classroom Instruction. Classroom instruction typically involves having the trainer lecture a group. In many cases the lecture is supplemented with question-and-answer periods, discussion, or case studies. Classroom instruction remains

Presentation methods
Training methods in which trainees are passive recipients of information.

a popular training method despite new technologies such as interactive video and computer-assisted instruction. Traditional classroom instruction is one of the least expensive, least time-consuming ways to present information on a specific topic to many trainees. The more active participation, job-related examples, and exercises that the instructor can build into traditional classroom instruction, the more likely trainees will learn and use the information presented on the job.

Distance learning is used by geographically dispersed companies to provide information about new products, policies, or procedures as well as skills training and expert lectures to field locations.[57] Distance learning features two-way communications between people. Distance learning currently involves two types of technology.[58] First, it includes teleconferencing. Teleconferencing refers to synchronous exchange of audio, video, and/or text between two or more individuals or groups at two or more locations. Trainees attend training programs in training facilities in which they can communicate with trainers (who are at another location) and other trainees using the telephone or personal computer. A second type of distance learning also includes individualized, personal-computer–based training.[59] Employees participate in training anywhere they have access to a personal computer. This type of distance learning may involve multimedia training methods such as Web-based training. Course material and assignments can be distributed using the company's intranet, video, or CD-ROM. Trainers and trainees interact using e-mail, bulletin boards, and conferencing systems.

Teleconferencing usually includes a telephone link so that trainees viewing the presentation can call in questions and comments to the trainer. Also, satellite networks allow companies to link up with industry-specific and educational courses for which employees receive college credit and job certification. IBM, Digital Equipment, and Eastman Kodak are among the many firms that subscribe to the National Technological University, which broadcasts courses throughout the United States that technical employees need to obtain advanced degrees in engineering.[60]

An advantage of distance learning is that the company can save on travel costs. It also allows employees in geographically dispersed sites to receive training from experts who would not otherwise be available to visit each location. FileNeT Corporation was concerned with how their sales force was going to keep up with new software and software updates.[61] FileNeT tried self-paced online learning but discovered that salespeople did not like to read a lot of material about new products on the Web. Enrollment in online courses dwindled, and salespeople flooded the company's training department with requests for one-on-one assistance. To solve the training problem, the company decided to use webcasting. Webcasting involves classroom instructions that are provided online through live broadcasts. Webcasting helped spread the sales force training throughout the year rather than cramming it into twice-a-year sales meetings. Webcasting also helped ensure that the salespeople all received the same information. The salespeople liked the webcasts because of the timely information that helped them have conversations with customers. The live sessions were also popular because participants could ask questions. Webcasting has not replaced face-to-face training at FileNeT; classroom training is still about 80 percent of training, but that percentage has decreased by 10 percent. Webcasting has also resulted in savings of $500,000 annually (one of the twice-yearly sales meetings was canceled).

The major disadvantage of distance learning is the potential for lack of interaction between the trainer and the audience. A high degree of interaction between trainees and the trainer is a positive learning feature that is missing from distance learning programs that merely use technology to broadcast a lecture to geographically dispersed employees. All that is done in this case is repurposing a traditional lecture (with its limitations for learning and transfer of training) for a new training technology! That's why establishing a communications link between employees and the trainer is important. Also, on-site instructors or facilitators should be available to answer questions and moderate question-and-answer sessions.

Audiovisual Techniques. *Audiovisual instruction* includes overheads, slides, and video. As Figure 7.6 shows, video is one of the most popular instructional methods.[62] It has been used for improving communications skills, interviewing skills, and customer-service skills and for illustrating how procedures (such as welding) should be followed. Video is, however, rarely used alone. It is usually used in conjunction with lectures to show trainees real-life experiences and examples. Video is also a major component of behavior modeling and, naturally, interactive video instruction. Morse Bros., located in Tangent, Oregon, is one of only a few ready-mix firms in the Northwest that provide regular training for their drivers. Drivers play a key role in determining the success of the business. Excessive idling at construction sites, avoiding rollovers at construction sites, and product training can reduce costs and raise customer satisfaction. Morse Bros. produces training videos, which are presented by mentor-drivers. The mentor-driver's job is to select the weekly video, schedule viewing sessions, keep attendance records, and guide a wrap-up discussion following each video. The mentor-drivers are trained to call attention to key learning points covered in the video and relate the topics to issues the drivers deal with on the job. Because training sessions are scheduled early in the morning at the beginning of the drivers' shift, time is limited. Videos seldom run more than 10 minutes. For example, one called *Another Pair of Eyes* trains drivers to observe test procedures used by testing agencies at job sites. Samples are tested several times a month. A sample that fails can leave the company liable for demolition and removal of the concrete structure. Morse Bros. provides training on test procedures because samples often fail a test due to contamination (such as dirt) that gets into the test cylinder. At each training session, drivers answer several questions related to the content of the program. At the end of a session, drivers and the mentor-driver discuss anything that might be interfering with the quality of the product or timeliness of delivery. Mentor-drivers then share this information with company managers.[63]

The use of video in training has a number of advantages. First, the trainer can review, slow down, or speed up the lesson, which permits flexibility in customizing the session depending on trainees' expertise. Second, trainees can be exposed to equipment, problems, and events that cannot be easily demonstrated, such as equipment malfunctions, angry customers, or emergencies. Third, trainees get consistent instruction; program content is not affected by the interests and goals of a particular trainer. Fourth, videotaping trainees allows them to see and hear their own performance without the interpretation of the trainer. As a result, trainees cannot attribute poor performance to the bias of external evaluators such as the trainer or peers.

Most problems in video result from the creative approach used.[64] These problems include too much content for the trainee to learn, poor dialogue between the actors (which hinders the credibility and clarity of the message), overuse of humor or music, and drama that makes it confusing for the trainee to understand the important learning points emphasized in the video.

Hands-on Methods

Hands-on methods are training methods that require the trainee to be actively involved in learning. Hands-on methods include on-the-job training, simulations, business games and case studies, behavior modeling, interactive video, and Web-based

Hands-on methods
Training methods that actively involve the trainee in learning.

training. These methods are ideal for developing specific skills, understanding how skills and behaviors can be transferred to the job, experiencing all aspects of completing a task, and dealing with interpersonal issues that arise on the job.

On-the-Job Training (OJT)

Companies spend between $90 billion and $180 billion annually on informal on-the-job training compared with $30 billion on formal off-the-job training.[65] On-the-job training (OJT) refers to new or inexperienced employees learning through observing peers or managers performing the job and trying to imitate their behavior. OJT can be useful for training newly hired employees, upgrading experienced employees' skills when new technology is introduced, cross-training employees within a department or work unit, and orienting transferred or promoted employees to their new jobs.

OJT takes various forms, including apprenticeships and self-directed learning programs. (Both are discussed later in this section.) OJT is an attractive training method because, compared to other methods, it needs less investment in time or money for materials, trainer's salary, or instructional design. Managers or peers who are job knowledge experts are used as instructors. As a result, it may be tempting to let them conduct the training as they believe it should be done.

There are several disadvantages to this unstructured approach to OJT.[66] Managers and peers may not use the same process to complete a task. They may pass on bad habits as well as useful skills. Also, they may not understand that demonstration, practice, and feedback are important conditions for effective on-the-job training. Unstructured OJT can result in poorly trained employees, employees who use ineffective or dangerous methods to produce a product or provide a service, and products or services that vary in quality.

OJT must be structured to be effective. Table 7.8 shows the principles of structured OJT. Because OJT involves learning by observing others, successful OJT is based on

TABLE 7.8

Principles of On-the-Job Training

PREPARING FOR INSTRUCTION	
1. Break down the job into important steps. 2. Prepare the necessary equipment, materials, and supplies.	3. Decide how much time you will devote to OJT and when you expect the employees to be competent in skill areas.
ACTUAL INSTRUCTION	
1. Tell the trainees the objective of the task and ask them to watch you demonstrate it. 2. Show the trainees how to do it without saying anything. 3. Explain the key points or behaviors. (Write out the key points for the trainees, if possible.) 4. Show the trainees how to do it again. 5. Have the trainees do one or more single parts of the task and praise them for correct reproduction (optional).	6. Have the trainees do the entire task and praise them for correct reproduction. 7. If mistakes are made, have the trainees practice until accurate reproduction is achieved. 8. Praise the trainees for their success in learning the task.

SOURCE: Based on W. J. Rothwell and H. C. Kazanas, "Planned OJT Is Productive OJT," *Training and Development Journal*, October 1990, pp. 53–55; P. J. Decker and B. R. Nathan, *Behavior Modeling Training* (New York: Praeger Scientific, 1985).

the principles emphasized by social learning theory. These include the use of a credible trainer, a manager or peer who models the behavior or skill, communication of specific key behaviors, practice, feedback, and reinforcement. For example, at Rochester Gas and Electric in Rochester, New York, radiation and chemistry instructors teach experienced employees how to conduct OJT.[67] While teaching these employees how to demonstrate software to new employees, the trainer may ask the employees to watch other OJT instructors as they train new recruits so they can learn new teaching techniques.

Self-directed learning involves having employees take responsibility for all aspects of learning—when it is conducted and who will be involved. For example, at Corning Glass, new engineering graduates participate in an OJT program called SMART (self-managed, awareness, responsibility, and technical competence).[68] Each employee seeks the answers to a set of questions (such as "Under what conditions would a statistician be involved in the design of engineering experiments?") by visiting plants and research facilities and meeting with technical engineering experts and managers. After employees complete the questions, they are evaluated by a committee of peers who have already completed the SMART program. Evaluations have shown that the program cuts employees' start-up time in their new jobs from six weeks to three weeks. It is effective for a number of reasons. It encourages active involvement of the new employees in learning and allows flexibility in finding time for training. It has a peer-review evaluation component that motivates employees to complete the questions correctly. And, as a result of participating in the program, employees make contacts throughout the company and better understand the technical and personal resources available within the company.

There are several advantages and disadvantages of self-directed learning.[69] It allows trainees to learn at their own pace and receive feedback about the learning performance. For the company, self-directed learning requires fewer trainers, reduces costs associated with travel and meeting rooms, and makes multiple-site training more realistic. Self-directed learning provides consistent training content that captures the knowledge of experts. Self-directed learning also makes it easier for shift employees to gain access to training materials. A major disadvantage of self-directed learning is that trainees must be willing and comfortable learning on their own; that is, trainees must be motivated to learn. From the company perspective, self-directed learning results in higher development costs, and development time is longer than with other types of training programs. Self-directed learning will likely be more common in the future as companies seek to train staff flexibly, to take advantage of technology, and to encourage employees to be proactive in their learning rather than driven by the employer.[70]

The Four Seasons Regent Hotel and Resorts is a luxury hotel operations and management group with 22,000 employees worldwide, including approximately 13,000 in international locations. The Four Seasons faced the challenge of opening a new hotel and resort at Jambaran Bay, Bali. To address training needs, the human resources staff created a self-directed learning center. The Self Access Learning Center emphasizes communication skills as well as English language skills. Its purpose is to teach skills and improve employees' confidence in their communications. The center includes video recorders, training modules, books, and magazines. Besides English, the center also teaches Japanese (the language of 20 percent of hotel visitors) and provides training for foreign managers in Bahasa Indonesian, the native language of Indonesia. The training process begins by administering an English test to potential employees to gauge the level of English training they need. As employees complete each level of the training, they receive a monetary incentive.

Self-directed learning
A program in which employees take responsibility for all aspects of learning.

How has the training paid dividends? Travel experts rated the Four Seasons Bali as one of the top hotels in the world. Business has increased steadily since the hotel opened, with guests from North America, Europe, Asia, Australia, and South America. As a result of the training, the Four Seasons is prepared for expansion. As the hotel industry expands in Asia, the Four Seasons now has a trained and talented staff that can be used to meet human resource needs as new resorts are developed. Four Seasons learned that the company must combine the training needs of the local culture with the standards of the company's culture to create a successful international business.[71]

Apprenticeship
A work-study training method with both on-the-job and classroom training.

Apprenticeship is a work-study training method with both on-the-job training and classroom training.[72] To qualify as a registered apprenticeship program under state or federal guidelines, at least 144 hours of classroom instruction and 2,000 hours, or one year, of on-the-job experience are required.[73] Apprenticeships can be sponsored by individual companies or by groups of companies cooperating with a union. The majority of apprenticeship programs are in the skilled trades, such as plumbing, carpentry, electrical work, and bricklaying.

The hours and weeks that must be devoted to completing specific skill units are clearly defined. OJT involves assisting a certified tradesperson (a journeyman) at the work site. The on-the-job training portion of the apprenticeship follows the guidelines for effective on-the-job training.[74] Modeling, practice, feedback, and evaluation are involved. First, the employer verifies that the trainee has the required knowledge of the operation or process. Next, the trainer (who is usually a more experienced, licensed employee) demonstrates each step of the process, emphasizing safety issues and key steps. The senior employee provides the apprentice with the opportunity to perform the process until all are satisfied that the apprentice can perform it properly and safely.

A major advantage of apprenticeship programs is that learners can earn pay while they learn. This is important because programs can last several years. Learners' wages usually increase automatically as their skills improve. Also, apprenticeships are usually effective learning experiences because they involve learning why and how a task is performed in classroom instruction provided by local trade schools, high schools, or community colleges. Apprenticeships also usually result in full-time employment for trainees when the program is completed. Will-Burt Corporation of Orrville, Ohio, started an apprenticeship program two years ago.[75] The program offers coursework for two career paths: machinist and brake press set-up operator. Each requires classroom study plus 160 hours of on-the-job training. Employees who want to become journeymen will take additional training off-site after completing their apprentice training. Classes are taught on-site through a partnership with Wayne College, University of Akron, and are free to employees. Many new employees work through the preapprenticeship program, while others take advantage of refreshing their skills in a single class or two. About 40 people signed up for geometric and tolerancing class as a refresher.

One disadvantage of many apprenticeship programs is limited access for minorities and women.[76] Another disadvantage is that there is no guarantee that jobs will be available when the program is completed. Finally, apprenticeship programs prepare trainees who are well trained in one craft or occupation. Due to the changing nature of jobs (thanks to new technology and use of cross-functional teams), many employers may be reluctant to employ workers from apprenticeship programs. Employers may believe that because apprentices are narrowly trained in one occupation or with one company, program graduates may have only company-specific skills and may be unable to acquire new skills or adapt their skills to changes in the workplace.

Simulations. A **simulation** is a training method that represents a real-life situation, with trainees' decisions resulting in outcomes that mirror what would happen if the trainee were on the job. Simulations, which allow trainees to see the impact of their decisions in an artificial, risk-free environment, are used to teach production and process skills as well as management and interpersonal skills.

Simulators need to have identical elements to those found in the work environment. The simulator needs to respond exactly as the equipment would under the conditions and response given by the trainee. For this reason simulators are expensive to develop and need constant updating as new information about the work environment is obtained.

Simulators replicate the physical equipment that employees use on the job. For example, Time Warner cable installers learn how to correctly install cable and high-speed Internet connections by crawling into two-story houses that have been built inside the company's training center.[77] Trainees drill through the walls and crawl around inside these houses, learning how to work with different types of homes. New call center employees at American Express learn in a simulated environment that replicates a real call center. Trainees go to a lab that contains cubicles identical to those in the call center. All materials (binders, reference materials, supplies) are exactly the same as they would be in the call center. The simulator uses a replica of the call center database and includes a role play that uses speech recognition software to simulate live calls. After the call center trainees learn transactions, they answer simulated calls that require them to practice the transactions. The simulator gives them feedback about errors they made during the calls and shows them the correct action. The simulator also tracks the trainees' performance and alerts the instructors if a trainee is falling behind. The simulator prepares call center employees in 32 days, an improvement over the previous 12-week program of classroom and on-the-job training. Turnover among call center employees is 50 percent lower since employees began training in the simulated environment. American Express believes that the reduction in turnover is because the training environment better prepares new employees to deal with the noise and pace of a real call center.

Simulations are also used to develop managerial skills. Looking Glass© is a simulation designed to develop both teamwork and individual management skills.[78] In this program, participants are assigned different roles in a glass company. On the basis of memos and correspondence, each participant interacts with other members of the management team over six hours. Participants' behavior and interactions in solving the problems described in correspondence are recorded and evaluated. At the conclusion of the simulation, participants are given feedback regarding their performance.

A recent development in simulations is the use of virtual reality technology. **Virtual reality** is a computer-based technology that provides trainees with a three-dimensional learning experience. Using specialized equipment or viewing the virtual model on the computer screen, trainees move through the simulated environment and interact with its components.[79] Technology is used to stimulate multiple senses of the trainee.[80] Devices relay information from the environment to the senses. For example, audio interfaces, gloves that provide a sense of touch, treadmills, or motion platforms are used to create a realistic, artificial environment. Devices also communicate information about the trainee's movements to a computer. These devices allow the trainee to experience the perception of actually being in a particular environment. For example, Motorola's advanced manufacturing courses for employees learning to run the Pager Robotic Assembly facility use virtual reality. Employees are fitted with a head-mount display that allows them to view the virtual world, which

Simulation
A training method that represents a real-life situation, allowing trainees to see the outcomes of their decisions in an artificial environment.

Virtual reality
Computer-based technology that provides trainees with a three-dimensional learning experience. Trainees operate in a simulated environment that responds to their behaviors and reactions.

includes the actual lab space, robots, tools, and the assembly operation. The trainees hear and see the actual sounds and sights as if they were using the real equipment. Also, the equipment responds to the employees' actions (such as turning on a switch or dial).

Business Games and Case Studies. Situations that trainees study and discuss (case studies) and business games in which trainees must gather information, analyze it, and make decisions are used primarily for management skill development. One organization that has effectively used case studies is the Central Intelligence Agency (CIA).[81] The cases are historically accurate and use actual data. For example, "The Libyan Attack" is used in management courses to teach leadership qualities. "The Stamp Case" is used to teach new employees about the agency's ethics structure. The CIA uses approximately 100 cases. One-third are focused on management; the rest focus on operations training, counterintelligence, and analysis. The cases are used in the training curriculum where the objectives include teaching students to analyze and resolve complex, ambiguous situations. The CIA found that for the cases used in training programs to be credible and meaningful to trainees, the material had to be as authentic as possible and stimulate students to make decisions similar to those they must make in their work environment. As a result, to ensure case accuracy, the CIA uses retired officers to research and write cases. The CIA has even developed a case writing workshop to prepare instructors to use the case method.

Games stimulate learning because participants are actively involved and they mimic the competitive nature of business. The types of decisions that participants make in games include all aspects of management practice, including labor relations (such as agreement in contract negotiations), marketing (the price to charge for a new product), and finance (financing the purchase of new technology). For example, Harley-Davidson, the motorcycle company, uses a business game to help prospective dealers understand how dealerships make money.[82] The game involves 15 to 35 people working in teams. The game consists of five simulated rounds, each round challenging a team to manage a Harley dealership in competition with other teams. Between rounds of the game, lectures and case studies reinforce key concepts. The facilitators change the business situation in each round of the game. The facilitators can increase or decrease interest rates, add new products, cause employee turnover, or even set up a bad event such as a fire at the business. The game helps dealers develop skills needed for business success. Participants must work well as a team, listen to each other, and think strategically.

Documentation on learning from games is anecdotal.[83] Games may give team members a quick start at developing a framework for information and help develop cohesive groups. For some groups (such as senior executives) games may be more meaningful training activities (because the game is realistic) than presentation techniques such as classroom instruction.

Cases may be especially appropriate for developing higher-order intellectual skills such as analysis, synthesis, and evaluation. These skills are often required by managers, physicians, and other professional employees. Cases also help trainees develop the willingness to take risks given uncertain outcomes, based on their analysis of the situation. To use cases effectively, the learning environment must let trainees prepare and discuss their case analyses. Also, face-to-face or electronic communication among trainees must be arranged. Because trainee involvement is critical for the effectiveness of the case method, learners must be willing and able to analyze the case and then communicate and defend their positions.

There are a number of available sources for preexisting cases (e.g., Harvard Business School). It is especially important to review preexisting cases to determine how meaningful they will be to the trainee.

Behavior Modeling. Research suggests that behavior modeling is one of the most effective techniques for teaching interpersonal skills.[84] Each training session, which typically lasts four hours, focuses on one interpersonal skill, such as coaching or communicating ideas. Each session presents the rationale behind key behaviors, a videotape of a model performing key behaviors, practice opportunities using role playing, evaluation of a model's performance in the videotape, and a planning session devoted to understanding how the key behaviors can be used on the job. In the practice sessions, trainees get feedback regarding how closely their behavior matches the key behaviors demonstrated by the model. The role playing and modeled performance are based on actual incidents in the employment setting in which the trainee needs to demonstrate success.

Interactive Video. Interactive video combines the advantages of video and computer-based instruction. Instruction is provided one-on-one to trainees via a personal computer. Trainees use the keyboard or touch the monitor to interact with the program. Interactive video is used to teach technical procedures and interpersonal skills. The training program may be stored on a compact disc (CD-ROM) or the company intranet. For example, the Shoney's and Captain D's restaurant chains have more than 350 restaurants in more than 20 states.[85] Over 8,000 employees each year must be trained on the basics of the operational parts of the business, including how to make french fries, hush puppies, and coleslaw. Also, each year 600 new managers must be trained in business issues and back-office operations of the restaurants. The biggest challenge that Shoney's faced was how to consistently train geographically dispersed employees. Shoney's solution was to implement OneTouch, a live integrated video and two-way voice and data application that combines synchronous video, voice, and data and live Web pages so that team members can interact with trainers. OneTouch can be delivered to desktop PCs as well as to warehouses and repair bays. Desktop systems can be positioned in any appropriate locations in the restaurant. Individuals or group of employees can gather around the PC for training. The training modules include such topics as orientation, kitchen, and dining room. Each module is interactive. Topics are introduced and are followed up by quizzes to ensure that learning occurs. For example, the coleslaw program shows trainees what the coleslaw ingredients are and where they can be found in the restaurant. The coleslaw program includes a video that trainees can watch and practice with. After they practice, they have to complete a quiz, and their manager has to verify that they completed the topic before they move on to the next program. The training is consistent and is easy to update so as to ensure it is current. The program also allows kitchen and counter staff to learn each other's skills, which gives Shoney's flexibility in its staffing (e.g., counter employees who know how to cook). The main disadvantage of interactive video is the high cost of developing the courseware. This may be a particular problem for courses in which frequent updates are necessary.[86]

E-Learning. **E-learning** or online learning refers to instruction and delivery of training by computers through the Internet or company intranets.[87] E-learning includes Web-based training, distance learning, virtual classrooms, and use of CD-ROMs. E-learning can include task support, simulation training, distance learning, and learning portals. There are three important characteristics of e-learning. First, e-learning

E-learning
Instruction and delivery of training by computers through the Internet or company intranet.

FIGURE 7.7

Characteristics of E-Learning

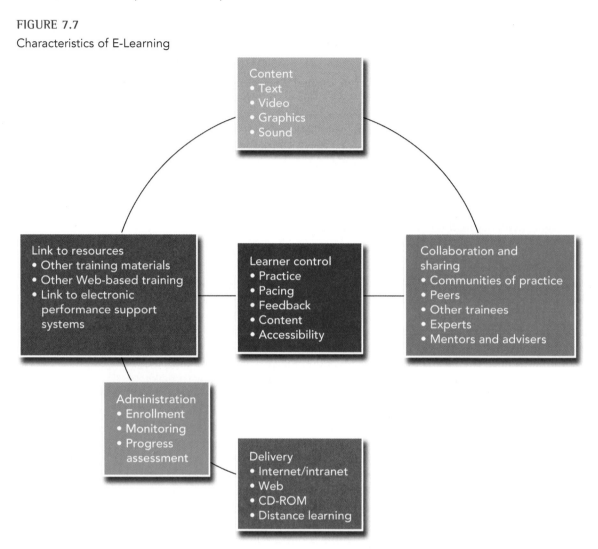

involves electronic networks that enable information and instruction to be delivered, shared, and updated instantly. Second, e-learning is delivered to the trainee via computers with Internet technology. Third, it focuses on learning solutions that go beyond traditional training to include information and tools that improve performance.

Figure 7.7 depicts the features of e-learning, which include collaboration and sharing, links to resources, learner control, delivery, and administration. As Figure 7.7 shows, e-learning not only provides training content but lets learners control what they learn, the speed at which they progress through the program, how much they practice, and even when they learn. E-learning also allows learners to collaborate or interact with other trainees and experts, and it provides links to other learning resources such as reference materials, company websites, and other training programs. Text, video, graphics, and sound can present course content. E-learning may also include various aspects of training administration such as course enrollment, testing and evaluating trainees, and monitoring learning progress. Various delivery methods can be incorporated into e-learning including distance learning, CD-ROM, and the Internet.

These features of e-learning give it advantages over other training methods. E-learning initiatives are designed to contribute to strategic business objectives.[88] E-learning supports company initiatives such as attracting customers, devising new ways to operate such as e-business, or quickly developing products or new services. E-learning may involve a larger audience than traditional training programs, which focused on employees; it may involve partners, suppliers, vendors, and potential customers.

For example, Lucent Technologies, which designs and delivers communications network technologies, has devoted significant resources to ensure that customers and business partners have access to e-learning.[89] Training affects customer satisfaction with Lucent's products and solutions. It also influences employees' ability to sell to and service customers. Product training courses that deal with installing, repairing, and operating Lucent equipment are available to customers on the company's website. Users can take the courses, register and pay for the classes, and track their progress. Lucent also provides training to its business partners, who are required to be certified in Lucent's products before they can receive special discounts. As Lucent increases its electronically delivered courses, the company is also trying to increase the percentage of learners who take courses online. Today, about half of the users attend classroom-based training.

Learning is enhanced through e-learning because trainees are more engaged through the use of video, graphics, sound, and text, which appeal to multiple senses of the learner. Also, e-learning requires that learners actively participate in practice, questions, and interaction with other learners and experts.

Besides enhancing the training experience, e-learning can reduce training costs and time. E-learning brings training to geographically dispersed employees at their locations, reducing travel costs. The "Competing through Technology" box on page 292 shows how e-learning benefits Cisco Systems account managers.

Effective e-learning is grounded on a thorough needs assessment and complete learning objectives. **Repurposing** refers to directly translating an instructor-led, face-to-face training program online. Online learning that merely repurposes an ineffective training program will remain ineffective. Unfortunately, in their haste to develop online learning, many companies are repurposing bad training! The best e-learning combines the advantages of the Internet with the principles of a good learning environment. Effective online learning takes advantage of the Web's dynamic nature and ability to use many positive learning features, including linking to other training sites and content through the use of hyperlinks, providing learner control, and allowing the trainee to collaborate with other learners. **Learner control** refers to the ability of trainees to actively learn through self-pacing, exercises, exploring links to other material, and conversations with other trainees and experts. That is, online learning allows activities typically led by the instructor (presentation, visuals, slides), trainees (discussion, questions), and group interaction (discussion of application of training content) to be incorporated into training without trainees or the instructor having to be physically present in a training room. Effective online learning gives trainees meaningful content, relevant examples, and the ability to apply content to work problems and issues. Also, trainees can practice and receive feedback through problems, exercises, assignments, and tests.

Blended Learning. Because of the limitations of online learning related to technology (e.g., insufficient bandwidth, lack of high-speed Web connections), because of trainee preference for face-to-face contact with instructors and other learners, and because of employees' inability to find unscheduled time during their workday to devote to learning from their desktops, many companies are moving to a hybrid, or blended,

Repurposing
Directly translating instructor-led training online.

Learner control
Ability of trainees to actively learn through self-pacing, exercises, links to other materials, and conversations with other trainees and experts.

Technology Makes Training an Easy Sale at Cisco Systems

Cisco Systems of San Jose, California, is a leading company that develops networking for the Internet. Cisco Systems grew from nothing in 1986 to a peak of 46,000 employees worldwide. However, Cisco fell on hard times during the 2001 economic downturn as the company's value fell by $430 billion and the company had to lay off more than 4,000 employees. Despite the downturn, Cisco did not cut back on its commitment to employee learning. CEO John Chambers believed that e-learning was an important force for helping Cisco recover from its economic woes, for creating strong ties with information

technology, and for demonstrating real business results. It doesn't hurt that the more e-learning that companies use, the more demand there will be for the video, voice, and data network products that Cisco provides! Cisco believes that the future of the Internet is the convergence of voice, video, and data (telephone, television, computer) networks into one common network.

Through a partnership with the company's Internet Learning Solutions Group, the Information Technology Unit, and Chambers, the Cisco Media Network was developed. This collaboration was neces-

sary to ensure a match between the company's tools and technology infrastructure, its business purpose, and effective learning principles. The Cisco Media Network is a large, private broadcasting network linked via satellite to a worldwide grid of servers. The network serves about 1,000 users. The content comes from business units, technology groups, and product marketing groups. The network broadcasts include the company's annual meeting, video briefings by executives, and learning portals for employees and customers. The Media Network allows Cisco to broadcast high-quality

learning approach. *Blended learning* combines online learning, face-to-face instruction, and other methods for distributing learning content and instruction. CAN, a Chicago-based company with employees across the United States and Canada, developed a blended learning approach.[90] Live seminars kick off a class and conclude it. But in between are online case studies, question-and-answer sessions, and simulations. Trainees work in teams of 10 people. They communicate with each other through chat rooms, threaded discussions, and virtual meetings. For example, employees might be assigned to come up with 10 questions. The instructor answers the questions, and the trainees discuss them. Trainees may be asked to put ideas into practice, using message rooms to provide updates and ask questions. Coaches or mentors may guide the trainees to additional reference materials. To be certified that they have completed training, trainees must complete an accountability plan. The plan summarizes actions that the trainees will take to prove to their managers that they have achieved proficiency.

Learning Portals. *Learning portals* are websites or online learning centers that provide, via e-commerce transactions, access to training courses, services, and online learning communities from many sources.[91] Learning portals provide not only one-stop shopping for a variety of training programs from different vendors but also access to online classes. Learning portals may also offer services to track employees' enroll-

material over the intranet. Sound and images are production quality.

The Media Network has been useful for developing e-learning for Cisco's account managers, who are the company's frontline sales force. To determine the account managers' needs, Cisco carried out a needs assessment that included interviews with them. The needs assessment helped identify what they needed to learn and the time they had available for learning. A common concern raised by the account managers was that learning content was not delivered to them in a way that fit their work patterns or learning styles. Because account managers spend a lot of time traveling, they wanted to get on the Internet, find what they needed, and get out again. They preferred not to sit in front of a personal computer for a long e-learning course.

As a result, the Account Manager Learning Environment (AMLE) was created. The AMLE is a development tool and performance support system based on four business objectives: increase sales, increase time-to-revenue, increase speed that account managers become competent in a topic, and reduce travel and costs. The goal in developing AMLE was to create a learning environment that would motivate the account managers to use it. The AMLE consists of a suite of learning tools, each with its own characteristics. The learning tools include small chunks of information to meet the managers' "get in and get out" needs, short skill-building sessions to help develop account managers' competencies, and a scenario-based, sales call simulator that provides real-world practice. The virtual sales calls are designed to make the account managers field difficult questions. The questions are provided by a realistic audio feed, and once a response is selected, feedback is immediate and specific about what the account manager could have done better.

Account managers can choose remote access or can download lessons to their hard drive. They are offered two ways to access lessons while traveling. First, a talk show can be accessed remotely, saved to a laptop, or downloaded to an MP3 player. The talk show discusses key issues of account management and the sales process. Second, a magazine is available to give account managers fast facts and advice.

SOURCE: Based on M. Delahoussaye and R. Zemke, "Ten Things We Know For Sure about On-Line Learning," *Training,* September 2001, pp. 48–59; P. Galagan, "Delta Force," *T&D,* July 2002, pp. 21–28.

ment and progress in training programs. They were initially set up with the idea that an individual purchaser (an employee or other "customer") could purchase training using a credit card. The characteristics of learning portals vary.[92] Some allow users to pay, register, and attend courses online; others offer access only to classroom training programs at colleges or universities. In addition to instruction, some sites provide mentors who can tutor students as well as discussion groups where students can communicate with each other. W. R. Grace, a specialty chemicals company, uses its online learning center to support employee development, to link learning to performance and talent management, and to improve communications.[93] The learning center is organized around a set of core competencies that define the knowledge, skills, and abilities all employees are expected to achieve. A search option is provided so that employees can explore and access resources relevant to a specific topic. The learning center includes training sessions, recommended readings, a rental library (providing videotapes and CD-ROMs for self-paced learning), and a strategy guide (providing quick ideas and learning assignments to develop a competency). Every six weeks the learning center sends an electronic newsletter to every employee's personal computer. The newsletter keeps employees up to date on the latest learning center offerings, reports on how employees are effectively using the learning center, and encourages employees to use the center.

Group-building methods
Training techniques that help trainees share ideas and experiences, build group identity, understand the dynamics of interpersonal relationships, and get to know their own strengths and weaknesses and those of their coworkers.

Group Building Methods. **Group building methods** are training methods designed to improve team or group effectiveness. Training is directed at improving the trainees' skills as well as team effectiveness. In group building methods, trainees share ideas and experiences, build group identity, understand the dynamics of interpersonal relationships, and get to know their own strengths and weaknesses and those of their coworkers. Group techniques focus on helping teams increase their skills for effective teamwork. A number of training techniques are available to improve work group or team performance, to establish a new team, or to improve interactions among different teams. All involve examination of feelings, perceptions, and beliefs about the functioning of the team; discussion; and development of plans to apply what was learned in training to the team's performance in the work setting. Group building methods include adventure learning, team training, and action learning.

Group building methods often involve experiential learning. *Experiential learning* training programs involve gaining conceptual knowledge and theory; taking part in a behavioral simulation; analyzing the activity; and connecting the theory and activity with on-the-job or real-life situations.[94]

For experiential training programs to be successful, several guidelines should be followed. The program needs to tie in to a specific business problem. The trainees need to be moved outside their personal comfort zones but within limits so as not to reduce trainee motivation or ability to understand the purpose of the program. Multiple learning modes should be used, including audio, visual, and kinesthetic. When preparing activities for an experiential training program, trainers should ask trainees for input on the program goals. Clear expectations about the purpose, expected outcomes, and trainees' role in the program are important. Finally, training programs that include experiential learning should be linked to changes in employee attitudes, behaviors, and other business results.

California-based Quantum Corporation developed a project to overhaul the company's online infrastructure across global operations.[95] The project included a diverse group of team members from the information technology, engineering, marketing, and graphic design departments. The team consisted of very talented employees who were not used to working with each other. Many of the team members were geographically dispersed, which increased the difficulties in working together. Quantum hired an actors' group to lead the team through a series of improvisational activities designed to get the team members to share personal stories. Using music, props, lighting, and costumes, the actors interpreted the stories told by team members. The actors portrayed team members who, for example, expressed isolation and frustration. Other times, team members would play the parts. The sessions allowed each team member to ask questions of the actors or each other. The team came away from the activity with more empathy and understanding for each other. Development of the personal relationships created positive interpersonal bonds that helped the team meet deadlines and complete projects.

Adventure learning
Learning focused on the development of teamwork and leadership skills by using structured outdoor activities.

Adventure Learning. **Adventure learning** develops teamwork and leadership skills using structured outdoor activities.[96] Adventure learning appears to be best suited for developing skills related to group effectiveness, such as self-awareness, problem solving, conflict management, and risk taking. Adventure learning may involve strenuous, challenging physical activities such as dogsledding or mountain climbing. It can also use structured individual and group outdoor activities such as climbing walls, going through rope courses, making trust falls (in which each trainee stands on a table and falls backward into the arms of fellow group members), climbing ladders, and traveling from one tower to another using a device attached to a wire that connects the two towers.

For example, a Chili's restaurant manager in adventure learning was required to scale a three-story-high wall.[97] About two-thirds away from the top of the wall the manager became very tired. She successfully reached the top of the wall using the advice and encouragement shouted from team members on the ground below. When asked to consider what she learned from the experience, she reported that the exercise made her realize that reaching personal success depends on other people. At her restaurant, everyone has to work together to make the customers happy.

For adventure learning programs to succeed, the exercises should be related to the types of skills that participants are expected to develop. Also, after the exercises, a skilled facilitator should lead a discussion about what happened in the exercise, what was learned, how the exercise relates to the job situation, and how to set goals and apply what was learned on the job.[98]

Does adventure learning work? Rigorous evaluations of the impact of adventure learning on productivity and performance have not been conducted. However, participants often report that they gained a greater understanding of themselves and the ways they interact with their coworkers. One key to the success of an adventure learning program may be the insistence that whole work groups participate together so that group dynamics that inhibit effectiveness can emerge and be discussed.

The physically demanding nature of adventure learning and the requirement that trainees often have to touch each other in the exercises may increase the company's risk for negligence claims due to personal injury, intentional infliction of emotional distress, and invasion of privacy. Also, the Americans with Disabilities Act (discussed in Chapter 3) raises questions about requiring employees with disabilities to participate in physically demanding training experiences.[99]

Team Training. Team training coordinates the performance of individuals who work together to achieve a common goal. Such training is an important issue when information must be shared and individuals affect the overall performance of the group. For example, in the military as well as the private sector (think of nuclear power plants or commercial airlines), much work is performed by crews, groups, or teams. Success depends on coordination of individual activities to make decisions, team performance, and readiness to deal with potentially dangerous situations (like an overheating nuclear reactor).

Team training strategies include cross-training and coordination training.[100] In **cross-training** team members understand and practice each other's skills so that members are prepared to step in and take another member's place. **Coordination training** trains the team in how to share information and decisions to maximize team performance. Coordination training is especially important for commercial aviation and surgical teams, who monitor different aspects of equipment and the environment but must share information to make the most effective decisions regarding patient care or aircraft safety and performance. **Team leader training** refers to training the team manager or facilitator. This may involve training the manager how to resolve conflict within the team or help the team coordinate activities or other team skills.

Team training usually involves multiple methods. For example, a lecture or video may disseminate knowledge regarding communication skills to trainees. Role plays or simulations may let trainees practice the communication skills emphasized in the lecture. Boeing utilized team training to improve the effectiveness of teams used to design the Boeing 777.[101] At Boeing, 250 teams with 8 to 15 members each worked

Cross-training
Team members understand and practice each other's skills.

Coordination training
Trains the team in how to share information and decisions.

Team leader training
Training the team manager or facilitator.

on the design of the aircraft. Team members included engineers with different specialties (such as design engineers and production engineers), reliability specialists, quality experts, and marketing professionals. This type of team is known as a *concurrent engineering team* because employees from all the business functions who are needed to design the aircraft work together at the same time. Concurrent engineering team members must understand how the process or product they are working on fits with the finished product. Because each 777 aircraft contains millions of parts, it is important that they fly together!

Boeing's team training approach began with an extensive orientation emphasizing how team members were supposed to work together. Following orientation, the teams were given their work assignments. Trainers helped the teams work through issues and problems as needed; that is, trainers were available to help the teams if they requested help in communication skills, conflict resolution, and leadership.

Research suggests that effective teams develop procedures to identify and resolve errors, coordinate information gathering, and reinforce each other.[102]

Action learning
Teams work on an actual business problem, commit to an action plan, and are accountable for carrying out the plan.

Action Learning. In **action learning** teams or work groups get an actual business problem, work on solving it and commit to an action plan, and are accountable for carrying out the plan.[103] Typically, action learning involves between 6 and 30 employees; it may also include customers and vendors. There are several variations on the composition of the group. In one variation the group includes a single customer for the problem being dealt with. Sometimes the groups include cross-functional team members (members from different company departments) who all have a stake in the problem. Or the group may involve employees from multiple functions who all focus on their own functional problems, each contributing to helping solve the problems identified. For example, ATC, a public transportation services management company in Illinois, used action learning to help boost profitability by reducing operating costs.[104] Employees were divided into Action Workout Teams to identify ways of reducing costs and to brainstorm effective solutions. The process assumed that employees closest to where the work gets done have the best ideas about how to solve problems. Teams of five to seven employees met once a week for a couple of hours for 45 to 60 days. For example, a team working on parts inventory might have had a parts clerk, a couple of people from maintenance, a supervisor, and an operations employee. These teams studied problems and issues such as overtime, preventive maintenance, absenteeism, parts inventory, and inefficient safety inspection procedures. The teams brainstormed ideas, prioritized them according to their highest potential, developed action plans, installed them, tested them, and measured the outcomes. The solutions that the teams generated resulted in more than $1.8 million in savings for the company.

Six Sigma Training
An action training program that provides employees with defect-reducing tools to cut costs; and certifies employees as green belts, champions, or black belts.

Six Sigma and black belt training programs involve principles of action learning. **Six Sigma Training** provides employees with measurement and statistical tools to help reduce defects and to cut costs.[105] Six Sigma is a quality standard with a goal of only 3.4 defects per million processes. Six Sigma was born at Motorola. It has saved the company an estimated $15 billion since the early 1990s. There are several levels of Six Sigma training, resulting in employees becoming certified as green belts, champions, or black belts.[106] To become black belts, trainees must participate in workshops and written assignments coached by expert instructors. The training involves four 4-day sessions over about 16 weeks. Between training sessions, candidates apply what they learn to assigned projects and then use them in the next training session. Trainees are also required to complete not only oral and written exams but also two or more projects that have a significant impact on the company's bottom line. After completing black belt training, employees are able to develop, coach, and lead Six Sigma teams; mentor and advise management on determining Six Sigma projects; and provide Six Sigma tools and statistical methods to team members. After black belts lead several project teams, they can take additional training and be certified as master black belts. Master black belts can teach other black belts and help senior managers integrate Six Sigma into the company's business goals.

McKesson Corporation trained 15 to 20 black belts and reassigned them to their original business units as their team's Six Sigma representatives.[107] When the two-year commitment ends, the black belts return to the business at higher positions, helping to spread the approach throughout the organization and ensuring that key leaders are committed to the Six Sigma philosophy. In most divisions of the company, Six Sigma training is mandated for senior vice presidents, who attend training that introduces Six Sigma and details how to identify a potential Six Sigma project. Across the company, every manager and director is expected to attend basic training. The Six Sigma effort has shown benefits every year since the program started in 1999.

Advice for Choosing a Training Method

As a manager, you will likely be asked to choose a training method. Given the large number of training methods available to you, this task may seem difficult. One way to choose a training method is to compare methods. The first step in choosing a method is to identify the type of learning outcome that you want training to influence. These outcomes include verbal information, intellectual skills, cognitive strategies, attitudes, and motor skills. Training methods may influence one or several learning outcomes. Once you have identified a learning method, the next step is to consider the extent to which the method facilitates learning and transfer of training, the costs related to development and use of the method, and its effectiveness.

For learning to occur, trainees must understand the objectives of the training program, training content should be meaningful, and trainees should have the opportunity to practice and receive feedback. Also, a powerful way to learn is through observing and interacting with others. Transfer of training refers to the extent to which training will be used on the job. In general, the closer the training content and environment prepare trainees for use of learning outcomes on the job, the greater the likelihood that transfer will occur. Two types of costs are important: development costs and administrative costs. Development costs relate to design of the training program, including costs to buy or create the program. Administrative costs are incurred each time the training method is used. These include costs related to consultants, instructors, materials, and trainers.

Several trends are worth noting. First, there is considerable overlap between learning outcomes across the training methods. Group building methods are unique because they focus on individual as well as team learning (e.g., improving group processes). If you are interested in improving the effectiveness of groups or teams, you should choose one of the group building methods (e.g., action learning, team training, action learning). Second, comparing the presentation methods to the hands-on methods illustrates that most hands-on methods provide a better learning environment and transfer of training than do the presentation methods. The presentation methods are also less effective than the hands-on methods. E-learning or blended learning can be an effective training method for geographically dispersed trainees if it includes meaningful content, links to other resources, collaboration and sharing, and learner

TABLE 7.9

Outcomes Used in Evaluating Training Programs

OUTCOME	WHAT IS MEASURED	HOW MEASURED	EXAMPLE
Cognitive Outcomes	• Acquisition of knowledge	• Pencil-and-paper tests • Work sample	• Safety rules • Electrical principles • Steps in appraisal interview
Skill-Based Outcomes	• Behavior • Skills	• Observation • Work sample • Ratings	• Jigsaw use • Listening skills • Coaching skills • Airplane landings
Affective Outcomes	• Motivation • Reaction to program • Attitudes	• Interviews • Focus groups • Attitude surveys	• Satisfaction with training • Beliefs regarding other cultures
Results	• Company payoff	• Observation • Data from information system or performance records	• Absenteeism • Accidents • Patents
Return on Investment	• Economic value of training	• Identification and comparison of costs and benefits of the program	• Dollars

control. E-learning and other technology-driven training methods have higher development costs, but travel and housing cost savings will likely offset development costs over time. The training budget for developing training methods can influence the method chosen. If you have a limited budget for developing new training methods, use structured on-the-job training—a relatively inexpensive yet effective hands-on method. If you have a larger budget, you might want to consider hands-on methods that facilitate transfer of training, such as simulators.

Evaluating Training Programs

Training outcomes
A way to evaluate the effectiveness of a training program based on cognitive, skill-based, affective, and results outcomes.

Examining the outcomes of a program helps in evaluating its effectiveness. These outcomes should be related to the program objectives, which help trainees understand the purpose of the program. **Training outcomes** can be categorized as cognitive outcomes, skill-based outcomes, affective outcomes, results, and return on investment.[108] Table 7.9 shows the types of outcomes used in evaluating training programs and what is measured and how it is measured.

Which training outcomes measure is best? The answer depends on the training objectives. For example, if the instructional objectives identified business-related outcomes such as increased customer service or product quality, then results outcomes should be included in the evaluation. Both reaction and cognitive outcomes are usually collected before the trainees leave the training site. As a result, these measures do not help determine the extent to which trainees actually use the training content in their jobs (transfer of training). Skill-based, affective, and results outcomes measured following training can be used to determine transfer of training—that is, the extent to which training has changed behavior, skills, or attitudes or directly influenced objective measures related to company effectiveness (such as sales).

Reasons for Evaluating Training

Many companies are beginning to invest millions of dollars in training programs to gain a competitive advantage. Firms with high-leverage training practices not only invest large sums of money in developing and administering training programs but also evaluate training programs. Why should training programs be evaluated?

1. To identify the program's strengths and weaknesses. This includes determining whether the program is meeting the learning objectives, the quality of the learning environment, and whether transfer of training to the job is occurring.
2. To assess whether the content, organization, and administration of the program (including the schedule, accommodations, trainers, and materials) contribute to learning and the use of training content on the job.
3. To identify which trainees benefited most or least from the program.
4. To gather marketing data by asking participants whether they would recommend the program to others, why they attended the program, and their level of satisfaction with the program.
5. To determine the financial benefits and costs of the program.
6. To compare the costs and benefits of training to nontraining investments (such as work redesign or better employee selection).
7. To compare the costs and benefits of different training programs to choose the best program.

Walgreens is a good example of a company that has reconsidered the role of training based on evaluation data. A Walgreens training course for new technicians was developed to replace on-the-job training they received from the pharmacists who hired them. This course involved 20 hours of classroom training and 20 hours of supervision on the job. Because the company has several thousand stores, large amounts of money and time were invested in the training, so the company decided to evaluate the program.

The evaluation consisted of comparing technicians who had completed the program with some who had not. Surveys about new employees' performance were sent to the pharmacists who supervised the technicians. Some questions related to speed of entering patient and drug data into the store computer and how often the technician offered customers generic drug substitutes. The results showed that formally trained technicians were more efficient and wasted less of the pharmacist's time than those who received traditional on-the-job training. Sales in pharmacies with formally trained technicians exceeded sales in pharmacies with on-the-job–trained technicians by an average of $9,500 each year.[109]

Evaluation Designs

A number of different evaluation designs can be applied to training programs.

Pretest/Posttest with Comparison Group. This method compares a group of employees who receive training and a group who do not. Outcome measures are collected from both groups before and after training. If improvement is greater for the training group than the comparison group, this provides evidence that training is responsible for the change.

Pretest/Posttest. This method is similar to the pretest/posttest comparison group design but has one major difference: no comparison group is used. The lack of a comparison group makes it difficult to rule out the effects of business conditions or other factors as explanations for changes. This design is often used by companies that want to evaluate a training program but are uncomfortable with excluding certain employees or that intend to train only a small group of employees.

Posttest Only. In this method only training outcomes are collected. This design can be strengthened by adding a comparison group (which helps to rule out alternative explanations for changes). The posttest-only design is appropriate when trainees (and the comparison group, if one is used) can be expected to have similar levels of knowledge, behavior, or results outcomes (same number of sales, equal awareness of how to close a sale) prior to training.

Time Series. In the time-series method, training outcomes are collected at periodic intervals before and after training. (In the other evaluation designs we have discussed, training outcomes are collected only once before and after training.) A comparison group can also be used with a time-series design. One advantage of the time-series design is that it allows analysis of the stability of training outcomes over time. This type of design is frequently used to evaluate training programs that focus on improving readily observable outcomes (such as accident rates, productivity, and absenteeism) that vary over time. For example, a time-series design was used to evaluate the extent to which a training program helped improve the number of safe work behaviors in a food manufacturing plant.[110] Observations of safe work behaviors were made for 25 weeks. Training directed at increasing the number of safe behaviors was introduced after approximately five weeks. The number of safe acts observed varied across the observation period. However, the number of safe behaviors increased after training and remained stable across the observation period.

There is no one appropriate evaluation design. Several factors need to be considered in choosing one:[111]

- Size of the training program.
- Purpose of training.
- Implications if a training program does not work.
- Company norms regarding evaluation.
- Costs of designing and conducting an evaluation.
- Need for speed in obtaining program effectiveness information.

For example, if a manager is interested in determining how much employees' communications skills have changed as a result of a behavior-modeling training program, a pretest/posttest comparison group design is necessary. Trainees should be randomly assigned to training and no-training conditions. These evaluation design features give the manager a high degree of confidence that any communication skill change is the result of participating in the training program.[112] This type of evaluation design is also necessary if the manager wants to compare the effectiveness of two training programs.

Evaluation designs without pretesting or comparison groups are most appropriate if the manager is interested in identifying whether a specific level of performance has been achieved (for example, can employees who participated in behavior-modeling training adequately communicate their ideas?). In this situation the manager is not interested in determining how much change has occurred.

Determining Return on Investment

Cost–benefit analysis
The process of determining the economic benefits of a training program using accounting methods.

Cost–benefit analysis is the process of determining the economic benefits of a training program using accounting methods, which involves determining training costs and benefits. Training cost information is important for several reasons:

1. To understand total expenditures for training, including direct and indirect costs.
2. To compare the costs of alternative training programs.
3. To evaluate the proportion of money spent on training development, administration, and evaluation, as well as to compare monies spent on training for different groups of employees (such as exempt versus nonexempt).
4. To control costs.[113]

Determining Costs. As we discussed earlier, training costs include direct and indirect costs.[114] One method for comparing costs of alternative training programs is the resource requirements model.[115] This model compares equipment, facilities, personnel, and materials costs across different stages of the training process (training design, implementation, needs assessment, development, and evaluation). The resource requirements model can help determine overall differences in costs between training programs. Also, costs incurred at different stages of the training process can be compared across programs.

Determining Benefits. To identify the potential benefits of training, the company must review the original reasons for the training. For example, training may have been conducted to reduce production costs or overtime costs or to increase repeat business. A number of methods may help identify the benefits of training:

1. Technical, academic, and practitioner literature summarizes the benefits that have been shown to relate to a specific training program.
2. Pilot training programs assess the benefits for a small group of trainees before a company commits more resources.
3. Observing successful job performers can help a company determine what they do differently than unsuccessful job performers.[116]
4. Trainees and their managers can provide estimates of training benefits.

Making the Analysis. A cost–benefit analysis is best explained by an example. A training and development consultant at Apple Computer was concerned with the quality and consistency of the training program used in assembly operations.[117] She wanted to show that training was not only effective but also resulted in financial benefits. To do this, the consultant chose an evaluation design that involved two separately trained groups—each consisting of 27 employees—and two untrained groups (comparison groups). The consultant collected a pretraining history of what was happening on the production line in each outcome she was measuring (productivity, quality, and labor efficiency). She determined the effectiveness of training by comparing performance between the comparison and training groups for two months after training. The consultant was able to show that the untrained comparison group had 2,000 more minutes of downtime than the trained group did. This finding meant that the trained employees built and shipped more products to customers—showing definitively that training was contributing to Apple's business objectives.

To conduct a cost–benefit analysis, the consultant had each employee in the training group estimate the effect of behavior change on a specific business measure (e.g., breaking down tasks will improve productivity or efficiency). The trainees assigned a confidence percentage to the estimates. To get a cost–benefit estimate for each group of trainees, the consultant multiplied the monthly cost–benefit by the confidence level and divided by the number of trainees. For example, one group of 20 trainees estimated a total overall monthly cost benefit of $336,000 related to business improvements and showed an average 70 percent confidence level with that estimate. Seventy percent multiplied by $336,000 gave a cost benefit of $235,200. This number was divided by

20 ($235,200/20 trainees) to give an average estimated cost benefit for the 20 trainees ($11,760). To calculate return on investment, follow these steps:

1. Identify outcomes (e.g., quality, accidents).
2. Place a value on the outcomes.
3. Determine the change in performance after eliminating other potential influences on training results.
4. Obtain an annual amount of benefits (operational results) from training by comparing results after training to results before training (in dollars).
5. Determine the training costs (direct costs + indirect costs + development costs + overhead costs + compensation for trainees).
6. Calculate the total savings by subtracting the training costs from benefits (operational results).
7. Calculate the ROI by dividing benefits (operational results) by costs. The ROI gives an estimate of the dollar return expected from each dollar invested in training.

Special Training Issues

To meet the competitive challenges of sustainability, globalization, and technology discussed in Chapter 1, companies must successfully deal with several special training issues. The special training issues include preparing employees to work in different cultures abroad, managing workforce diversity, and socializing and orienting new employees.

Cross-Cultural Preparation

Expatriate
Employee sent by his or her company to manage operations in a different country.

As we mentioned in Chapter 1, companies today are challenged to expand globally. Because of the increase in global operations, employees often work outside their country of origin or work with employees from other countries. An **expatriate** works in a country other than his or her country of origin. For example, Microsoft is headquartered in the United States but has facilities around the world. To be effective, expatriates in the Microsoft Mexico operations in Mexico City must understand the region's business and social culture. Because of a growing pool of talented labor around the world, greater use of host-country nationals is occurring.[118] *Host country nationals* are employees with citizenship in the country where a company is located. A key reason is that a host-country national can more easily understand the values and customs of the workforce than an expatriate can. Also, training and transporting U.S. employees and their families to a foreign assignment and housing them there tend to be more expensive than hiring a host-country national. We discuss international human resource management in detail in Chapter 15. Here the focus is on understanding how to prepare employees for expatriate assignments.

Cross-cultural preparation
The process of educating employees (and their families) who are given an assignment in a foreign country.

Cross-cultural preparation educates employees (expatriates) and their families who are to be sent to a foreign country. To successfully conduct business in the global marketplace, employees must understand the business practices and the cultural norms of different countries.

Steps in Cross-Cultural Preparation

To prepare employees for cross-cultural assignments, companies need to provide cross-cultural training. Most U.S. companies send employees overseas without any preparation. As a result, the number of employees who return home before completing their assignments is higher for U.S. companies than for European and Japanese companies.[119] U.S. companies lose more than $2 billion a year as a result of failed overseas assignments.

To succeed overseas, expatriates (employees on foreign assignments) need to be

1. Competent in their areas of expertise.
2. Able to communicate verbally and nonverbally in the host country.
3. Flexible, tolerant of ambiguity, and sensitive to cultural differences.
4. Motivated to succeed, able to enjoy the challenge of working in other countries, and willing to learn about the host country's culture, language, and customs.
5. Supported by their families.[120]

One reason for U.S. expatriates' high failure rate is that companies place more emphasis on developing employees' technical skills than on preparing them to work in other cultures. Research suggests that the comfort of an expatriate's spouse and family is the most important determinant of whether the employee will complete the assignment.[121] Studies have also found that personality characteristics are related to expatriates' desire to terminate the assignment and performance in the assignment.[122] Expatriates who were extroverted (outgoing), agreeable (cooperative and tolerant), and conscientious (dependable, achievement oriented) were more likely to want to stay on the assignment and perform well. This suggests that cross-cultural training may be effective only when expatriates' personalities predispose them to be successful in assignments in other cultures.

The key to a successful foreign assignment is a combination of training and career management for the employee and family. The "Competing through Globalization" box shows the importance of language and cultural training. Foreign assignments involve three phases: predeparture, on-site, and repatriation (preparing to return home). Training is necessary in all three phases.

Predeparture Phase

Before departure, employees need to receive language training and an orientation to the new country's culture and customs. It is critical that the family be included in orientation programs.[123] Expatriates and their families need information about housing, schools, recreation, shopping, and health care facilities in the areas where they will live. Expatriates also must discuss with their managers how the foreign assignment fits into their career plans and what types of positions they can expect upon return.

Cross-cultural training methods range from presentational techniques, such as lectures that expatriates and their families attend on the customs and culture of the host country, to actual experiences in the home country in culturally diverse communities.[124] Experiential exercises, such as miniculture experiences, allow expatriates to spend time with a family in the United States from the ethnic group of the host country.

Research suggests that the degree of difference between the United States and the host country (cultural novelty), the amount of interaction with host country citizens and host nationals (interaction), and the familiarity with new job tasks and work environment (job novelty) all influence the "rigor" of the cross-cultural training method used.[125] Hands-on and group building methods are most effective (and most needed) in assignments with a high level of cultural and job novelty that require a good deal of interpersonal interaction with host nationals.

On-Site Phase

On-site training involves continued orientation to the host country and its customs and cultures through formal programs or through a mentoring relationship. Expatriates

English is the common language at many multinational companies. But failing to speak the native language can cause employees to risk being misinterpreted or fail to understand informal conversations. Speaking and understanding the local language can help employees avoid misunderstandings and gain greater respect from business partners, subordinates, and customers.

At Intel, employees with a business need can take classes in Mandarin, Japanese, and Spanish at various offices throughout the United States, free of charge. The courses are not designed for expatriates destined for assignments abroad, but instead target employees who, through technology, are in direct contact with foreign clients or who work on cross-cultural teams within the company. With 78,000 employees in 294 offices in 48 countries, Intel has teams that are regularly made up of employees from different cultures working in different locations. The optional 12-week courses, taught at three levels by contracting companies, are designed to help minimize the culture gaps within these teams. The classes meet for two hours a week and cost the company approximately $300 per person. Employees are allowed to repeat courses.

Marcos Garciaacosta, a business alliance manager at Intel who is based in Arizona, has been taking Japanese classes since he joined the company seven years ago. He says that the "ease and flexibility of on-site classes" keep him motivated to continue to learn. And while he says he is far from fluent, he is now at a proficiency level that enables him to

and their families may be paired with an employee from the host country who helps them understand the new, unfamiliar work environment and community.[126]

A major reason that employees refuse expatriate assignments is that they can't afford to lose their spouse's income or are concerned that their spouse's career could be derailed by being out of the workforce for a few years.[127] Some "trailing" spouses decide to use the time to pursue educational activities that could contribute to their long-term career goals. But it is difficult to find these opportunities in an unfamiliar place. Pfizer, the pharmaceutical firm, is taking action to help trailing spouses. It provides a $10,000 allowance that the spouse can use in many different ways. A person at the expatriate location is assigned to help the spouse with professional development and locating educational or other resources. In countries where spouses are allowed to work, Pfizer tries to find them jobs within the company. Pfizer also provides cross-cultural counseling and language assistance. The company tries to connect the family with the expatriate community.

Repatriation Phase

Repatriation prepares expatriates for return to the parent company and country from the foreign assignment. Expatriates and their families are likely to experience high levels of stress and anxiety when they return because of the changes that have occurred since their departure. Employees should be encouraged to self-manage the repatriation process.[128] Before they go on the assignment they need to consider what skills they want to develop and the types of jobs that might be available in the com-

Repatriation
The preparation of expatriates for return to the parent company and country from a foreign assignment.

better communicate with business contacts and customers in Japan.

The in-house strategy is not new. Company spokeswoman Tracy Koon says that Intel offered its first language programs in Japanese in the 1980s. But despite its 20-year history, the program is still relatively small. Since January 2002, Intel has spent only $54,000 to train 180 employees in these three languages, a tiny fraction of its workforce, and one that does not include expatriates, who are compensated for language training outside these company classes. Without making a huge investment in the concept, Intel is receiving some positive results. Kathy Powell, the foundational development manager for Intel University, the division of the company that manages training, says the demand for foreign-language courses is increasing. Intel plans to expand the language-training program to overseas offices and to train 300 more employees by the end of this year.

The language classes are part of a larger in-house cultural-training curriculum for Intel employees. The company also offers optional one-day classes with titles such as "Working with Russia" and "Doing Business with the Japanese," which are designed to give employees basic information that they need to build relationships and do business cross-culturally. Class size is about 15 students, and subjects include culture, history and an overview of various countries and their business practices. Classes about other cultures are also becoming more popular. During the past 27 months, Intel has spent more than $762,000 on the program and has trained 2,495 employees. It plans to offer the classes to 2,300 more employees by the end of this year, at a cost of about $450,000.

"Our business is very global, and there are a large number of people here working across cultures," Koon says. "By having these language and cultural tools at your disposal when you work with employees from different countries, you can understand the do's and don'ts of the cultures. You're not going to be an effective team if you are constantly offending the other members without knowing it."

SOURCE: Based on G. Weber, "Intel's Internal Approach," *Workforce Management* 83 (2004), p. 49; K. Kranhold, D. Bileklan, M. Karnitschnig, and G. Parker, "Lost in Translation," *The Wall Street Journal* (May 18, 2004), pp. B1 and B6.

pany for an employee with those skills. Because the company changes and colleagues, peers, and managers may leave while the expatriate is on assignment, they need to maintain contact with key company and industry contacts. Otherwise, on return the employees' reentry shock will be heightened due to having to deal with new colleagues, a new job, and a company culture that may have changed. This includes providing expatriates with company newsletters and community newspapers and by ensuring that they receive personal and work-related mail from the United States while they are on foreign assignment. It is also not uncommon for employees and their families to have to readjust to a lower standard of living in the United States than they had in the foreign country, where they may have enjoyed maid service, a limousine, private schools, and clubs. Salary and other compensation arrangements should be worked out well before employees return from overseas assignments.

Aside from reentry shock, many expatriates decide to leave the company because the assignments they are given upon returning to the United States have less responsibility, challenge, and status than their foreign assignments.[129] As noted earlier, career planning discussions need to be held before the employees leave the United States to ensure that they understand the positions they will be eligible for upon repatriation.

Royal Dutch Shell, a joint Dutch and United Kingdom oil and gas company, has one of the world's largest expatriate work forces. To avoid expatriates who feel undervalued and leave the company, Royal Dutch gets involved with expatriates and their career. Resource planners track workers abroad, helping to identify their next assignment. Most expatriates know their next assignment three to six months before the move, and all begin the next assignment with a clear job description. Expatriates who have the potential to reach top-level management positions are placed in the home office every third assignment to increase their visibility to company executives. Expatriates are also assigned technical mentors who evaluate their skills and help them improve their skills through training at Royal Dutch's training center.

Because of family issues, poor economic times, and security issues, many companies are using virtual expatriates, relying more on short-time assignments, frequent business travel, and international commutes in which an employee lives in one country and works in another.[130] *Virtual expatriates* have an assignment to manage an operation abroad without being located permanently in that country. The employees periodically travel to the overseas location, return, and later use videoconferencing and communications technology to manage the operation.[131] Virtual expatriates eliminate exposing the family to the culture shock of an overseas move. This setup also allows the employee to manage globally while keeping in close touch with the home office. Virtual expatriates are less expensive than traditional expatriates, who can cost companies over three times as much as a host national employee. One major disadvantage of virtual expatriates is that visiting a foreign operation on a sporadic basis may lengthen the time needed to build a local management team, so it will take longer to solve problems because of the lack of a strong personal relationship with local employees. One of the potential difficulties of short-term international assignments is that employees may be perceived as foreigners rather than colleagues because they haven't had the time to build relationships and develop trust among coworkers in their short-term location. Another is that traveling can take a physical and emotional toll on employees as they try to juggle business responsibilities with maintaining contact with family and friends. Procter & Gamble helps employees on short-term assignments by providing a trip fund that is based on the length of time an employee is on an extended business trip. For example, a U.S.-based employee working in western Europe for six months would get a fund containing the cost of five business-class round-trips. The employee can use money from the fund to take trips home or to cover family visits to the employee's location.

Managing Workforce Diversity

The goals of diversity training are (1) to eliminate values, stereotypes, and managerial practices that inhibit employees' personal development and therefore (2) to allow employees to contribute to organizational goals regardless of their race, sexual orientation, gender, family status, religious orientation, or cultural background.[132] Because of Equal Opportunity Employment laws, companies have been forced to ensure that women and minorities are adequately represented in their labor force. That is, companies have focused on ensuring equal access to jobs. As was discussed in Chapter 1, the impact of culture on the workplace, and specifically on training and development, has received heightened attention. Cultural factors that companies need to consider include the terrorist attacks of 9/11; employees' fear of discussing cultural differences; more work being conducted in teams whose members have many different characteristics; the realization that people from diverse cultures represent an important customer market; and, especially for professional and technical jobs, the availability of highly trained employees that has many companies seeking workers from overseas. These new immigrants need diversity training to help them understand such facets of American culture as obsession with time, individualistic attitudes, and capitalistic ideas.[133]

Managing diversity involves creating an environment that allows all employees to contribute to organizational goals and experience personal growth. This environment

Managing diversity
The process of creating an environment that allows all employees to contribute to organizational goals and experience personal growth.

includes access to jobs as well as fair and positive treatment of all employees. The company must develop employees who are comfortable working with people from a wide variety of ethnic, racial, and religious backgrounds. Managing diversity may require changing the company culture. It includes the company's standards and norms about how employees are treated, competitiveness, results orientation, innovation, and risk taking. The value placed on diversity is grounded in the company culture.

Managing Diversity through Adherence to Legislation

One approach to managing diversity is through affirmative action policies and by making sure that human resource management practices meet standards of equal employment opportunity laws.[134] This approach rarely changes employees' values, stereotypes, and behaviors that inhibit productivity and personal development. Figure 7.8 shows the cycle of disillusionment resulting from managing diversity by relying solely on adherence to employment laws. The cycle begins when the company realizes that it must

FIGURE 7.8

Cycle of Disillusionment Resulting from Managing Diversity through Adherence to Legislation

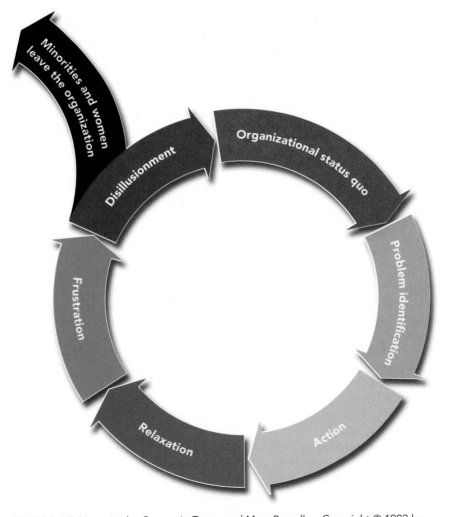

SOURCE: *HR Magazine* by Cresencio Torres and Mary Bruxelles. Copyright © 1992 by Society for Human Resource Management. Reproduced with permission of Society for Human Resource Management via Copyright Clearance Center.

change policies regarding women and minorities because of legal pressure or a discrepancy between the number or percentage of women and minorities in the company's workforce and the number available in the broader labor market. To address these concerns, a greater number of women and minorities are hired by the company. Managers see little need for additional action because women and minority employment rates reflect their availability in the labor market. However, as women and minorities gain experience in the company, they may become frustrated. Managers and coworkers may avoid providing coaching or performance feedback to women and minorities because they are uncomfortable interacting with individuals from different gender, ethnic, or racial backgrounds. Coworkers may express beliefs that women and minorities are employed only because they received special treatment (hiring standards were lowered).[135] As a result of their frustration, women and minorities may form support groups to voice their concerns to management. Because of the work atmosphere, women and minorities may fail to fully utilize their skills and leave the company.

Managing Diversity through Diversity Training Programs

The preceding discussion is not to suggest that companies should be reluctant to engage in affirmative action or pursue equal opportunity employment practices. However, affirmative action without additional supporting strategies does not deal with issues of assimilating women and minorities into the workforce. To successfully manage a diverse workforce, companies need to ensure that

- Employees understand how their values and stereotypes influence their behavior toward others of different gender, ethnic, racial, or religious backgrounds.
- Employees gain an appreciation of cultural differences among themselves.
- Behaviors that isolate or intimidate minority group members improve.

Diversity training
Training designed to change employee attitudes about diversity and/or develop skills needed to work with a diverse workforce.

This can be accomplished through diversity training programs. **Diversity training** refers to training designed to change employee attitudes about diversity and/or develop skills needed to work with a diverse workforce. Diversity training programs differ according to whether attitude or behavior change is emphasized.[136]

Attitude Awareness and Change Programs

Attitude awareness and change program
Program focusing on increasing employees' awareness of differences in cultural and ethnic backgrounds, physical characteristics, and personal characteristics that influence behavior toward others.

Attitude awareness and change programs focus on increasing employees' awareness of differences in cultural and ethnic backgrounds, physical characteristics (such as disabilities), and personal characteristics that influence behavior toward others. The assumption underlying these programs is that, by increasing their awareness of stereotypes and beliefs, employees will be able to avoid negative stereotypes when interacting with employees of different backgrounds. The programs help employees consider the similarities and differences between cultural groups, examine their attitudes toward affirmative action, or analyze their beliefs about why minority employees are successful or unsuccessful in their jobs. Many of these programs use videotapes and experiential exercises to increase employees' awareness of the negative emotional and performance effects of stereotypes, values, and behaviors on minority group members. For example, 3M conducts workshops in which managers are asked to assess their attitudes toward stereotypical statements about race, age, and gender.[137] The participants select two stereotypes they hold and consider how these stereotypes affect their ability to manage. One of the most popular video training packages, Copeland Griggs Productions' "Valuing Diversity Training Program," involves three days of training that focus on managing differences, diversity in the workplace, and cross-cultural communications.

The attitude awareness and change approach has been criticized for several reasons.[138] First, by focusing on group differences, the program may communicate that certain stereotypes and attitudes are valid. For example, in diversity training a male manager may learn that women employees prefer to work by building consensus rather than by arguing until others agree with their point. He might conclude that the training has validated his stereotype. As a result, he will continue to fail to give women important job responsibilities that involve heated negotiations with customers or clients. Second, encouraging employees to share their attitudes, feelings, and stereotypes toward certain groups may cause employees to feel guilty, angry, and less likely to see the similarities among racial, ethnic, or gender groups and the advantages of working together.

Behavior-Based Programs

Behavior-based programs focus on changing the organizational policies and individual behaviors that inhibit employees' personal growth and productivity. These programs can take three approaches.

One approach of these programs is to identify incidents that discourage employees from working up to their potential. Groups of employees are asked to identify specific promotion opportunities, sponsorship, training opportunities, or performance management practices that they believe were handled unfairly. Their views regarding how well the work environment and management practices value employee differences and provide equal opportunity may also be collected. Specific training programs may be developed to address the issues presented in the focus groups.

Another approach is to teach managers and employees basic rules of behavior in the workplace.[139] For example, managers and employees should learn that it is inappropriate to use statements and engage in behaviors that have negative racial, sexual, or cultural content. Companies that have focused on teaching rules and behavior have found that employees react less negatively to this type of training than to other diversity training approaches.

A third approach is **cultural immersion:** sending employees directly into communities where they have to interact with persons from different cultures, races, and nationalities. The degree of interaction varies but may involve talking with community members, working in community organizations, or learning about religious, cultural, or historically significant events. For example, the United Parcel Service (UPS) Community Internship Program is designed to help UPS senior managers understand the needs of diverse customers and a diverse workforce through exposure to poverty and inequality.[140] UPS is the world's largest package delivery company and a leading global provider of transportation and logistic services. Since 1968, over 1,200 senior managers have completed the program, an internship that typically lasts four weeks. The internships take the managers to cities throughout the United States, where they work on the problems facing local populations. UPS managers may find themselves serving meals to the homeless, working in AIDS centers, helping migrant farm workers, building temporary housing and schools, and managing children in a Head Start program. These experiences take the managers outside their comfort zones, and the problems that they encounter—from transportation to housing to education to health care—help them better understand the issues that many UPS employees face daily. This enlightenment is a business necessity for UPS because three out of four managers are white whereas 35 percent of the employees are minorities. UPS has not formally evaluated the program, but the company continues to invest $10,000 per intern. The company has invested a total of more than $13.5 billion in the program since its start

Behavior-based program
A program focusing on changing the organizational policies and individual behaviors that inhibit employees' personal growth and productivity.

Cultural immersion
A behavior-based diversity program that sends employees into communities where they interact with persons from different cultures, races, and nationalities.

in 1968. Despite the lack of hard evaluation data, UPS managers report that the program helps them look for unconventional solutions to problems. One manager who spent a month working at a halfway house in New York was impressed by the creative ideas of uneducated addicts for keeping teens away from drugs. The manager realized that she had failed to capitalize on the creativity of the employees she supervised. As a result, when she returned to her job and faced problems, she started brainstorming with her entire staff, not just senior managers. Other managers report that the experience helped them empathize with employees facing crises at home.

Characteristics of Successful Diversity Efforts

Is a behavior-based or an attitude awareness and change program most effective? Increasing evidence shows that attitude awareness programs are ineffective and that one-time diversity training programs are unlikely to succeed. For example, R. R. Donnelley & Sons suspended its diversity awareness training program even though the company has spent more than $3 million on it as a result of a racial discrimination lawsuit.[141]

At various training sessions participants were encouraged to voice their concerns. Many said that they were experiencing difficulty in working effectively due to abuse and harassment. The managers attending the training disputed the concerns. Also, after training, an employee who applied for an open position was rejected, because, she was told, she had been too honest in expressing her concerns during the diversity training session. Although R. R. Donnelley held many diversity training sessions, little progress was made in increasing the employment and promotion rates of women and minorities. Because of the low ratio of black employees to white employees, many black employees were asked to attend multiple training sessions to ensure diverse groups, which they resented. The company declined to release data requested by shareholders that it provided to the Equal Employment Opportunity Commission regarding female and minority representation in jobs throughout the company. The firm also failed to act on recommendations made by company-approved employee "diversity councils."

More generally, a survey of diversity training efforts found that[142]

- The most common area addressed through diversity efforts is the pervasiveness of stereotypes, assumptions, and biases.
- Fewer than one-third of companies do any kind of long-term evaluation or follow-up. The most common indicators of success were reduced grievances and lawsuits, increased diversity in promotions and hiring, increased self-awareness of biases, and increased consultation of HRM specialists on diversity-related issues.
- Most programs lasted only one day or less.
- Three-fourths of the survey respondents indicated that they believed the typical employee leaves diversity training with positive attitudes toward diversity. However, over 50 percent reported that the programs have no effect over the long term.

Little research addresses the impact of diversity or diversity-management practices on financial success. Diversity may enhance performance when organizations have an environment that promotes learning from diversity. There is no evidence to support the direct relationship between diversity and business.[143] Rather, a company will see the success of its diversity efforts only if it makes a long-term commitment to managing diversity. Successful diversity requires that it be viewed as an opportunity for employees to (1) learn from each other how to better accomplish their work, (2) be provided with a supportive and cooperative organizational culture, and (3) be taught

- Top management provides resources, personally intervenes, and publicly advocates diversity.
- The program is structured.
- Capitalizing on a diverse workforce is defined as a business objective.
- Capitalizing on a diverse workforce is seen as necessary to generate revenue and profits.
- The program is evaluated.
- Manager involvement is mandatory.
- The program is seen as a culture change, not a one-shot program.
- Managers and demographic groups are not blamed for problems.
- Behaviors and skills needed to successfully interact with others are taught.
- Managers are rewarded on progress toward meeting diversity goals.
- Management collects employee feedback and responds to it.

TABLE 7.10

Characteristics Associated with Diversity Programs' Long-Term Success

SOURCE: S. Rynes and B. Rosen, "What Makes Diversity Programs Work?" *HR Magazine*, October 1994, pp. 67–73; S. Rynes and B. Rosen, "A Field Survey of Factors Affecting the Adoption and Perceived Success of Diversity Training," *Personnel Psychology* 48 (1995), pp. 247–70; J. Gordon, "Different from What? Diversity as a Performance Issue," *Training*, May 1995, pp. 25–33; Corporate Leadership Council, *The Evolution of Corporate Diversity* (Washington, DC: Corporate Executive Board, 2002).

leadership and process skills that can facilitate effective team functioning. Diversity is a reality in labor and customer markets and is a social expectation and value. Managers should focus on building an organizational environment, on human resource practices, and on managerial and team skills that all capitalize on diversity. As you will see in the discussion that follows, managing diversity requires difficult cultural change, not just slogans on the wall!

Table 7.10 shows the characteristics associated with the long-term success of diversity programs. It is critical that a diversity program be tied to business objectives. For example, cultural differences affect the type of skin cream consumers believe they need or the fragrance they may be attracted to. Understanding cultural differences is part of understanding the consumer (which is critical to the success of companies such as Avon). Top management support can be demonstrated by creating a structure to support the initiative.

Bank of America in San Francisco has a diversity department to handle day-to-day issues. The CEO of the bank created a corporate diversity task force involving 28 executives from different geographical locations and business functions whose goals were to gather employee feedback, review current programs, and suggest new ways to promote diversity. Diversity business councils were created to formulate strategies to ensure that the diversity effort was related to business needs. Diversity networks are available to assist white males, women, Hispanics, and African Americans in their personal and professional development.[144]

Consider Texaco's diversity effort, shown in Table 7.11. Prior to becoming a subsidiary of Chevron Texaco, Texaco developed a state-of-the-art diversity program after the company had to pay more than $175 million to settle a racial discrimination lawsuit.[145] The lawsuit made public accusations that company executives were using racial slurs. As Table 7.11 shows, managing diversity at Texaco went far beyond workshop attendance. Managing diversity became part of a culture change. Texaco's diversity effort included programs designed to stop discrimination in hiring, retention, and promotion. Managers were held accountable for diversity goals in their performance evaluations.

TABLE 7.11

Texaco's Diversity
Effort

Recruitment and Hiring
- Ask search firms to identify wider arrays of candidates.
- Enhance the interviewing, selection, and hiring skills of managers.
- Expand college recruitment at historically minority colleges.

Identifying and Developing Talent
- Form a partnership with INROADS, a nationwide internship program that targets minority students for management careers.
- Establish a mentoring process.
- Refine the company's global succession planning system to improve identification of talent.
- Improve the selection and development of managers and leaders to help ensure that they are capable of maximizing team performance.

Ensuring Fair Treatment
- Conduct extensive diversity training.
- Implement an alternative dispute resolution process.
- Include women and minorities on all human resources committees throughout the company.

Holding Managers Accountable
- Link managers' compensation to their success in creating "openness and inclusion in the workplace."
- Implement 360-degree feedback for all managers and supervisors.
- Redesign the company's employee attitude survey and begin using it annually to monitor employee attitudes.

Improving Relationships with External Stakeholders
- Broaden the company's base of vendors and suppliers to incorporate more minority- and women-owned businesses.
- Increase banking, investment, and insurance business with minority- and women-owned firms.
- Add more independent, minority retailers and increase the number of minority managers in company-owned gas stations and Xpress Lube outlets.

SOURCE: D. Hellriegel, S. E. Jackson, and J. W. Slocum, Jr., *Management*, 8th ed. (Cincinnati, OH: South-Western College Publishing, 1999). Originally adapted from V. C. Smith, "Texaco Outlines Comprehensive Initiatives," *Human Resource Executive*, February 1997, p. 13; A. Bryant, "How Much Has Texaco Changed? A Mixed Report Card on Anti-bias Efforts," *The New York Times* (November 2, 1997), pp. 3-1, 3-16, 3-17; and "Texaco's Worldforce Diversity Plan," as reprinted in *Workforce*, March 1997, supp. from D. Daft and R. Noe, *Organizational Behavior* (Fort Worth, TX: Dryden Press, 2001), p. 58.

The company also realized that to capitalize on diversity from a business perspective, it needed to give more opportunities to minority vendors, suppliers, and customers.

There is considerable evidence that the program has transformed the culture. From 1996 to October 2001, Chevron and Texaco contracted $2.7 billion in products and services from women-owned or minority-owned suppliers.[146] Chevron Texaco also supports diversity networks, which are open to all employees. These formally structured organizations must show how they support the company's diversity objectives, vision, values, and strategy. Currently, there are nine groups with 3,360 members (approximately 5 percent of all employees). These groups include a Native American network, a lesbian and gay network, a women's network, a black employees network, and a Filipino-American network. These networks are more than social clubs. Their goals are to increase members' cultural awareness and leadership skills, to sponsor learning activities that help develop a more cross-culturally sensitive workforce, and to communicate new ideas.

Successful diversity programs involve more than just an effective training program. They require an ongoing process of culture change that includes top management support as well as diversity policies and practices in the areas of recruitment and hiring, training and development, and administrative structures, such as conducting diversity surveys and evaluating managers' progress on diversity goals.[147]

Socialization and Orientation

Organizational socialization is the process by which new employees are transformed into effective members of the company. As Table 7.12 shows, effective socialization involves being prepared to perform the job effectively, learning about the organization, and establishing work relationships. Socialization involves three phases: anticipatory socialization, encounter, and settling in.[148]

Anticipatory Socialization

Anticipatory socialization occurs before the individual joins the company. Through **anticipatory socialization,** expectations about the company, job, working conditions, and interpersonal relationships are developed through interactions with representatives of the company (recruiters, prospective peers, and managers) during recruitment and selection. The expectations are also based on prior work experiences in similar jobs.

Potential employees need realistic job information. A **realistic job preview** provides accurate information about the attractive and unattractive aspects of the job, working conditions, company, and location to ensure that employees develop appropriate expectations. This information should come early in recruiting and selection. It is usually given in brochures, in videos, or by the company recruiter during an interview. Although research specifically investigating the influence of realistic job previews on employee turnover is weak and inconsistent, we do know that unmet expectations resulting from recruitment and selection relate to dissatisfaction and turnover.[149] As we will see, employees' expectations about a job and a company may be formed by interactions with managers, peers, and recruiters rather than from specific messages about the job.

Organizational socialization
The process used to transform new employees into effective company members.

Anticipatory socialization
Process that helps individuals develop expectations about the company, job, working conditions, and interpersonal relationships.

Realistic job preview
Provides accurate information about the unattractive and attractive aspects of the job, working conditions, company, and location.

History	The company's traditions, customs, and myths; background of members
Company goals	Rules, values, or principles directing the company
Language	Slang and jargon unique to the company; professional technical language
Politics	How to gain information regarding the formal and informal work relationships and power structures in the company
People	Successful and satisfying work relationships with other employees
Performance proficiency	What needs to be learned; effectiveness in using and acquiring the knowledge, skills, and abilities needed for the job.

TABLE 7.12

What Employees Should Learn and Develop through the Socialization Process

SOURCE: Based on G. T. Chao, A. M. O'Leary-Kelly, S. Wolf, H. Klein, and P. D. Gardner, "Organizational Socialization: Its Content and Consequences," *Journal of Applied Psychology* 79 (1994), pp. 730–43.

Encounter

Encounter phase
Phase of
socialization that
occurs when an
employee begins a
new job.

The **encounter phase** occurs when the employee begins a new job. No matter how realistic the information provided during interviews and site visits, individuals beginning new jobs will experience shock and surprise.[150] Employees need to become familiar with job tasks, receive appropriate training, and understand company practices and procedures.

Challenging work plus cooperative and helpful managers and peers have been shown to enhance employees' learning a new job.[151] New employees view managers as an important source of information about their jobs and the company. Research suggests that the nature and quality of the new employee's relationship with the manager has a significant impact on socialization.[152] In fact, the negative effects of unmet expectations can be reduced by the new employee having a good relationship with her or his manager! Managers can help create high-quality work relationships by helping new employees understand their roles, providing information about the company, and understanding the stresses and issues that new employees experience.

Settling In

Settling-in phase
Phase of
socialization that
occurs when
employees are
comfortable with job
demands and social
relationships.

In the **settling-in phase,** employees begin to feel comfortable with their job demands and social relationships. They begin to resolve work conflicts (like too much work or conflicting job demands) and conflicts between work and nonwork activities. Employees are interested in the company's evaluation of their performance and in learning about potential career opportunities within the company.

Employees need to complete all three socialization phases to fully contribute to the company. For example, employees who do not feel that they have established good working relationships with coworkers will likely spend time and energy worrying about those relationships rather than being concerned with product development or customer service. Employees who experience successful socialization are more motivated, more committed to the company, and more satisfied with their jobs.[153]

Socialization and Orientation Programs

Socialization and orientation programs play an important role in socializing employees. Orientation involves familiarizing new employees with company rules, policies, and procedures. Typically, a program includes information about the company, department in which the employees will be working, and the community they will live in.

Although the content of orientation programs is important, the process of orientation cannot be ignored. Too often, orientation programs consist of completing payroll forms and reviewing personnel policies with managers or human resource representatives. The new employee, a passive recipient of information, has little opportunity to ask questions or interact with peers and managers.

Effective orientation programs actively involve the new employee. Table 7.13 shows the characteristics of effective orientation. An important characteristic of effective orientation is that peers, managers, and senior coworkers are actively involved in helping new employees adjust to the work group.[154]

Several companies offer programs that include the characteristics shown in Table 7.13.[155] For example, Mission Bell Winery exposes new hires to every department for up to five days. New hires see how each department works and meet that department's employees. An online scavenger hunt as well as a Lunch and Learn program in which

Employees are encouraged to ask questions.
Program includes information on both technical and social aspects of the job.
Orientation is the responsibility of the new employee's manager.
Debasing or embarrassing new employees is avoided.
Formal and informal interactions with managers and peers occur.
Programs involve relocation assistance (such as house hunting or information sessions on the community for employees and their spouses).
Employees are told about the company's products, services, and customers.

TABLE 7.13

Characteristics of Effective Orientation Programs

new hires visit with the leaders of the company are part of StorageTek's orientation program. The Mayo Clinic rewards employees with movie tickets and coupons for free food in the cafeteria for answering questions correctly during a game show exercise that reviews orientation materials. The Verizon Wireless orientation program includes three "tours": an online virtual tour that includes information such as the code of conduct and benefits; a team tour that helps new employees become comfortable with peers and bosses; and a classroom visit that highlights the company history, mission, and values.

An example of how orientation and socialization can reduce turnover and contribute to business is National City Corporation's Early Success program. National City Corporation, a bank and financial services company based in Cleveland, Ohio, was challenged by the high level of turnover that occurred among new employees within 90 days of being hired.[156] Turnover was 51 percent. Because it is difficult to provide excellent service and retain customers if customers are always dealing with a new employee, National City developed the National City Institute. Within the institute, the Early Success program provides a comfortable environment, a support network, and a series of classes where new hires learn product knowledge and customer service skills. For example, one course called Plus provides an overview of National City's corporate objectives, employee benefits, and information about the brand.

Another course, called People, Policies, and Practices, complements the employee handbook. Top-Notch Customer Care focuses on how to provide service and work in teams. New employees are matched with a peer (known as a buddy). The buddies are a support network for new hires that provides someone to answer their questions. The peer mentor is trained in coaching skills. The hiring managers also attend training designed to help them select buddy mentors, create a supportive work environment, communicate clearly, understand how to allow the new hire to gradually take on more responsibility, and help new hires achieve career goals. With the new program, new employees are 50 percent less likely to quit in the first three months on the job, resulting in a savings of approximately $1.35 million per year.

Onboarding refers to the orientation process for newly hired managers. Onboarding gives new managers an introduction to the work they will be supervising and an understanding of the culture and operations of the entire company. For example, at Pella Corporation, an Iowa-based manufacturer of windows and doors, new managers are sent on a tour of production plants, meeting and observing employees and department heads. These tours ensure that the managers will get a better sense of the market and how the company's products are designed, built, and distributed.[157] At The Limited, the Columbus, Ohio, retail clothing company, new vice presidents and regional directors spend their days talking to customers, reading company history, working the floor of retail stores, investigating the competition, and studying the company's current and past operations. They spend a month with no responsibilities for the tasks related to their new positions. Limited's philosophy is that managers are better able to perform their job by first taking time to understand the people, customers, company, and operations they will be working with.

A Look Back

As the chapter opener highlighted, Nokia uses training to support the company's business strategy. Nokia provides extensive training, encourages continuous learning, and evaluates the value of training.

Questions

1. Suppose a manager asked you to determine whether training was supporting a company's business strategy. How would you conduct this type of analysis? What kind of information would you look for?
2. Is there a difference between a company supporting learning and a company supporting training? Explain.

Summary

Technological innovations, new product markets, and a diverse workforce have increased the need for companies to reexamine how their training practices contribute to learning. In this chapter we discussed a systematic approach to training, including needs assessment, design of the learning environment, consideration of employee readiness for training, and transfer-of-training issues. We reviewed numerous training methods and stressed that the key to successful training was to choose a method that would best accomplish the objectives of training. We also emphasized how training can contribute to effectiveness through establishing a link with the company's strategic direction and demonstrating through cost–benefit analysis how training contributes to profitability. Managing diversity and cross-cultural preparation are two training issues that are relevant given company needs to capitalize on a diverse workforce and global markets.

Discussion Questions

1. Noetron, a retail electronics store, recently invested a large amount of money to train sales staff to improve customer service. The skills emphasized in the program include how to greet customers, determine their needs, and demonstrate product convenience. The company wants to know whether the program is effective. What outcomes should it collect? What type of evaluation design should it use?
2. "Melinda," bellowed Toran, "I've got a problem and you've got to solve it. I can't get people in this plant to work together as a team. As if I don't have enough trouble with the competition and delinquent accounts, now I have to put up with running a zoo. It's your responsibility to see that the staff gets along with each other. I want a human relations training proposal on my desk by Monday." How would you determine the need for human relations training? How would you determine whether you actually had a training problem? What else could be responsible?
3. Assume you are general manager of a small seafood company. Most training is unstructured and occurs on the job. Currently, senior fish cleaners are responsible for teaching new employees how to perform the job. Your company has been profitable, but recently wholesale fish dealers that buy your product have been complaining about the poor quality of your fresh fish. For example, some fillets have not had all the scales removed and abdomen parts remain attached to the fillets. You have decided to change the on-the-job training received by the fish cleaners. How will you modify the training to improve the quality of the product delivered to the wholesalers?

4. A training needs analysis indicates that managers' productivity is inhibited because they are reluctant to delegate tasks to their subordinates. Suppose you had to decide between using adventure learning and interactive video for your training program. What are the strengths and weaknesses of each technique? Which would you choose? Why? What factors would influence your decision?

5. To improve product quality, a company is introducing a computer-assisted manufacturing process into one of its assembly plants. The new technology is likely to substantially modify jobs. Employees will also be required to learn statistical process control techniques. The new technology and push for quality will require employees to attend numerous training sessions. Over 50 percent of the employees who will be affected by the new technology completed their formal education over 10 years ago. Only about 5 percent of the company's employees have used the tuition reimbursement benefit. How should management maximize employees' readiness for training?

6. A training course was offered for maintenance employees in which trainees were supposed to learn how to repair and operate a new, complex electronics system. On the job, maintenance employees were typically told about a symptom experienced by the machine operator and were asked to locate the trouble. During training, the trainer would pose various problems for the maintenance employees to solve. He would point out a component on an electrical diagram and ask, "What would happen if this component was faulty?" Trainees would then trace the circuitry on a blueprint to uncover the symptoms that would appear as a result of the problem. You are receiving complaints about poor troubleshooting from maintenance supervisors of employees who have completed the program. The trainees are highly motivated and have the necessary prerequisites. What is the problem with the training course? What recommendations do you have for fixing this course?

7. What factors contribute to the effectiveness of Web training programs?

Self-Assessment Exercise

In the chapter we discussed the need for learners to be motivated so that training will be effective. What is your motivation to learn? Find out by answering the following questions. Read each statement and indicate how much you agree with it, using the following scale:

5 = Strongly Agree
4 = Somewhat Agree
3 = Neutral
2 = Somewhat Disagree
1 = Strongly Disagree

1. I try to learn as much as I can from the courses I take.	5	4	3	2	1
2. I believe I tend to learn more from my courses than other students do.	5	4	3	2	1
3. When I'm involved in courses and can't understand something, I get so frustrated I stop trying to learn.	5	4	3	2	1

Manager's Hot Seat Exercise: Working in Teams

This Manager's Hot Seat case explores problems associated with teams and teamwork in the workplace. As the video begins, a team leader is trying to conduct a productive meeting to initiate a new project for the company. However, his efforts are thwarted by the blasé attitudes of the team members who are present at the meeting. These members allow personal issues, other commitments, and time pressures to divert their attention from the task at hand. The meeting is concluded without the necessary answers or decisions being derived. Because of their attitudes and lack of organizational commitment, the leader feels extremely disappointed by the team.

This case depicts the importance of employee commitment and focus to the organization. It clearly shows how the inability to commit to organizational needs can manifest in overall workplace negativity. This negativity can, in turn, result in decreased accomplishment of established business goals.

Group Activity:

Divide the class in groups of 4–5 students. The groups are to discuss the situation portrayed in the case. Each student should pay particular attention to details such as: (1) identifying what you felt went well in the meeting, and (2) discussing what you would have handled differently during the meeting.

Next, the group should discuss the role employee training plays within organizations. Did you perceive the case study actors as being well trained—for the positions they fictitiously held in the company? Explain why or why not.

Discuss what organizations can do to ensure effective training is rendered to employees. Identify organizational advantages and disadvantages of employee training. Discuss how effectively trained employees create a competitive advantage for organizations. Prepare the group notes for class discussion.

Exercising Strategy:　"Learning Is Key for Smooth Flying"

Rockwell Collins manufactures cockpit instruments, in-flight entertainment systems, and ground communications tools. Rockwell Collins is trying to reduce operating costs in all areas through developing employees skills so they can work more efficiently and improve product quality. The company's new learning strategy involves expanding training courses 40 percent. In a recent survey, over half of their employees reported that work demands had forced them to cancel their attendance at a training session or to leave a session without completing it. Currently, most training is instructor-led classroom training.

Questions

1. What training method(s) should Rockwell Collins use to reach their goal of reducing operating costs as well as improving employees' ability to attend training? Why?
2. How would you suggest that the company evaluate training to determine if it is helping the company reach its business goals?

Managing People:　From the Pages of *BusinessWeek*

BusinessWeek　Look Who's Building Online Classrooms

Since investment moguls such as Michael Milken began granting huge sums of money to online education ventures in the late 1990s, debates about e-learning have focused on its impact on traditional universities or K–12 schools. Would traditional universities be forced out of business? Would kindergarten students watch a teacher on a screen all day, instead of sitting in a circle with one at story time?

Given such questions, primary schools and universities have been cautious about getting into the e-learning game. But corporations have been far more adventurous. In fact, e-learning is becoming commonplace in offices and work-places across the country, spawning a multimillion-dollar industry. The trend isn't limited to just tech courses. Online programs now teach so-called "soft" skills, such as leadership, coaching, and global teamwork.

The new learning models have the potential to make education a high priority on the job. After all, analysts write volumes on the value of having an educated, skilled, and speedy workforce. When a lesson can be transmitted quickly to managers and sales teams worldwide through an e-learning program, it begins to show on the bottom line. Says James Moore, Sun Microsystems' director of work-force: "If you look at product development at Sun, by the time I got everyone trained [the traditional way, the product] would be obsolete."

Is e-learning here to stay? *BusinessWeek Online* explores this question in a series that looks at the companies investing heavily in adult learning on the job. Later parts of this series will examine how private e-learning companies are trying to cash in on the potential boom and will look at how companies are affected by the change.

While no reliable estimates on the current U.S. market for corporate education exist, by 2003 the Net-based corporate education market should be worth a hefty $11.4 billion, according to International Data Corp. The stack of dough could be that tall thanks to a conversion by training directors to use the Net to teach employees. It saves money and time, and managers can pack more information into a lesson, missionaries say.

Publicly traded e-learning companies—long victims of a skeptical market—are beginning to report improved earnings, too. Chris J. Nguyen, CEO of Baltimore's Caliber Learning Network (CLBR), says when his company reports quarterly earnings on July 26, investors can expect sequential growth over the first quarter of 2000. Smart-Force (SMTF), a Redwood (California) e-learning company that focuses on adults, saw revenues increase to $36.4 million in the second quarter of 2000. And in San Francisco, DigitalThink (DTHK), an e-learning company offering programs for corporations, also reported stronger earnings in its fiscal first quarter of 2001, ending June 30. The $6.3 million in earnings is a 433 percent increase since last year. That's right, 433 percent.

"Our customers want learning strategies to integrate all the learning that goes on in their organization with the corporate strategy," says John W. Humphrey, chairman of Forum Corp., a 30-year-old private-sector provider of leadership training. FT Knowledge, an e-learning company spun off from British publishing giant Pearson, announced earlier in July that it will acquire Forum for $90 million. The move points to a race among old economy training groups to use the Web to meet company needs. The idea is to mix e-learning with some classroom sessions, using content from varied sources—executives, university professors, or private training companies.

Other online learning companies are struggling to stay on top of demand. General Manager Robert Brodo of 15-year-old SMG Net, the online business unit of SMG Strategic Management Group in Philadelphia, says each of the company's 40 top clients—Boeing is its largest—has had a conversation about bringing courses online. Eighty percent are implementing courses such as SMG's "simulated company." In the two-day simulation, execs can play out five to six years of business experience. "We can't keep up with the demand, and it's scary when you have to tell a customer that you can't start a project for them until October and November." Privately held SMG says it will generate revenues of $31 million in 2000—$5 million from online programs. Next year, Brodo estimates $48 million to $50 million in revenues. "The growth is from online corporate universities," he says.

Cushing Anderson, program manager for learning-services research at International Data Corp., is in the process of researching how companies are using e-learning for everyone from managers to sales teams and programmers. In 1999, 6 percent of all corporate training was done online, he says. Anderson's preliminary findings show that doubling to 12 percent this year. In 2001, that figure should double again. "Large companies tend to be more adventurous and have larger budgets" to put courses online, he says, though most buy programs from outside vendors.

That isn't the case at IBM. Nancy J. Lewis, IBM's director of management development worldwide, says Big Blue will move its training programs online for 5,000 new managers, saving the company $16 million in 2000, half of which has already been realized. She adds that producing five times the content at a third of the cost has helped convince all of IBM's training units to adopt the model. Her unit alone has reduced its staff from about 500 trainers worldwide to 70 this year.

IBM is so confident about its training that the company has packaged its programs to sell to customers—a side business that is already bringing in "small amounts of revenue" says Lewis's second in command, Robert MacGregor. If IBM's models for e-corporate universities works, it could become a profitable new business.

Heads of training and development have grander plans than simply offering a course online. They expect to change adults' learning habits. Pippa Wicks, CEO of FT Knowledge, says in January 2001 the company will launch a new learning program called Insight Forum. "You do your job through the training program," she says. For in-

stance, a customer service manager would use the program to perform her daily tasks and then receive feedback about her decisions. Employees could take the training individually, or entire departments can share information in open sessions. FT Knowledge says it is already billing an unnamed company $3,500 an hour to link a handful of its execs with one of FT's management gurus for advice via videoconferencing.

Los Altos (California)-based Pensare, a four-year-old e-learning company, has a different vision. The company uses a model that lets employees, not trainers, decide what they need to learn, and when. "Tell [employees] what they need to do to help [execute] company strategy, then say, 'what do you think you need to know to help us?'" says Pensare cofounder Dean Hovey.

Online learning, delivered quickly and in a setting where the information can be commonly shared, will make the training process more engaging and less of a chore, experts say. And it'll give companies an advantage over competitors. 3Com, for one, places a high value on e-learning. "I've got senior people saying that they want more [online training]," says Geoff Roberts, 3Com's director of education. 3Com's agility with technology makes it imperative to train not only internal employees but also its customers. "We're selling into a market where 80 percent of the people don't understand the industry," he says, adding that 3Com's investment in e-learning is fed from the company's marketing budget, not training.

As companies convert lessons to be delivered over intranets, one massive obstacle remains: unless it's mandatory, most employees drop out of training. "Getting 2 percent to 3 percent [of a workforce to sign on] can't happen," says Forum's Humphrey. "There have to be more breakthroughs to make learning less intrusive to the worker." His suggestion to clients: make lessons relevant.

The good news is that generation-Y workers—recent college grads—are more comfortable using the Web. In 2003, analysts expect 95 percent of college students to use the Internet; only 41.7 percent did in 1996. This means college grads entering the workforce in 2003, and beyond, may be more receptive to e-learning. In fact, they may expect it. In 1998, 700,000 students were enrolled in distance learning programs. By 2002, 2.2 million will be, according to Credit Suisse First Boston analysts.

The plans sound grand. More and more companies will log their workers on to lessons on the Net. But getting the 45-year-old manager or executive to adopt e-learning models as easily as they've grown to employ e-mail is a challenge. No matter how fancy the program, if no one logs on, it'll be a hard to convince any CFO that investing in e-learning is worth it.

SOURCE: Reprinted from July 25, 2000 issue of *BusinessWeek* by special permission. Copyright © 2000 by The McGraw-Hill Companies, Inc.

Questions

1. What features are necessary for online learning to be effective? Explain.
2. Online learning blurs the distinction between training and work. Trainees are expected to be motivated to complete online learning during breaks in their workday or on their personal time. As a manager, is this realistic? How would you "schedule" online learning for your employees?

Please see the video case at the end of the book that corresponds to this chapter: Abbott Laboratories

Notes

1. I. I. Goldstein and P. Gilliam, "Training Systems Issues in the Year 2000," *American Psychologist* 45 (1990), pp. 134–43.
2. J. B. Quinn, P. Anderson, and S. Finkelstein, "Leveraging Intellect," *Academy of Management Executive* 10 (1996), pp. 7–27.
3. T. T. Baldwin, C. Danielson, and W. Wiggenhorn, "The Evolution of Learning Strategies in Organizations: From Employee Development to Business Redefinition," *Academy of Management Executive* 11 (1997), pp. 47–58; J. J. Martocchio and T. T. Baldwin, "The Evolution of Strategic Organizational Training," in *Research in Personnel and Human Resource Management* 15, ed. G. R. Ferris (Greenwich, CT: JAI Press, 1997), pp. 1–46.
4. A. P. Carnevale, "America and the New Economy," *Training and Development Journal*, November 1990, pp. 31–52.
5. J. M. Rosow and R. Zager, *Training: The Competitive Edge* (San Francisco: Jossey-Bass, 1988).
6. L. Thornburg, "Accounting for Knowledge," *HR Magazine*, October 1994, pp. 51–56; T. A. Stewart, "Mapping Corporate Brainpower," *Fortune* (October 30, 1995), p. 209.
7. D. Miller, "A Preliminary Typology of Organizational Learning: Synthesizing the Literature," *Strategic Management Journal* 22 (1996), pp. 484–505; ed., S. Jackson, M. Hitt, and A. DeNisi, *Managing Knowledge for Sustained Competitive Advantage* (San Francisco: Jossey-Bass, 2003).
8. D. Delong and L. Fahey, "Diagnosing Cultural Barriers to Knowledge Management," *Academy of Management Executive* 14 (2000), pp. 113–27; A. Rossett, "Knowledge Management Meets Analysis," *Training and Development*, May 1999, pp. 71–78.
9. I. Nonaka and H. Takeuchi, *The Knowledge Creating Company* (New York: Oxford University Press, 1995).
10. D. Tobin, *The Knowledge-Enabled Organization* (New York: AMACOM, 1998).
11. R. Noe, *Employee Training and Development*, 3rd ed. (Burr Ridge, IL: Irwin/McGraw-Hill, 2005).
12. I. L. Goldstein, E. P. Braverman, and H. Goldstein, "Needs Assessment," in *Developing Human Resources*, ed. K. N. Wexley (Washington, DC: Bureau of National Affairs, 1991), pp. 5-35 to 5-75.
13. J. Z. Rouillier and I. L. Goldstein, "Determinants of the Climate for Transfer of Training" (presented at Society of Industrial/Organizational Psychology meetings, St. Louis, MO, 1991); J. S. Russell, J. R. Terborg, and M. L. Powers, "Organizational Performance and Organizational Level Training and Support," *Personnel Psychology* 38 (1985), pp. 849–63; H. Baumgartel, G. J. Sullivan, and L. E. Dunn, "How Organizational Climate and Personality Affect the Payoff from Advanced Management Training Sessions," *Kansas Business Review* 5 (1978), pp. 1–10.
14. S. Tannenbaum, "A Strategic View of Organizational Training and Learning," in *Creating, Implementing, and Managing Effective Training and Development*, ed. K. Kraiger (San Francisco: Jossey-Bass, 2002), pp. 10–52.
15. A. P. Carnevale, L. J. Gainer, and J. Villet, *Training in America* (San Francisco: Jossey-Bass, 1990).
16. K. Ellis, "Smarter, Faster, Better," *Training*, April 2003, pp. 27–31.
17. B. Manville, "Organizing Enterprise-Wide E-Learning and Human Capital Management," *Chief Learning Officer*, May 2003, pp. 50–55.
18. B. Gerber, "How to Buy Training Programs," *Training*, June 1989, pp. 59–68.
19. G. Rummler, "In Search of the Holy Performance Grail," *Training and Development*, April 1996, pp. 26–31; D. G. Langdon, "Selecting Interventions," *Performance Improvement* 36 (1997), pp. 11–15.
20. R. F. Mager and P. Pipe, *Analyzing Performance Problems: Or You Really Oughta Wanna*, 2nd ed. (Belmont, CA: Pittman Learning, 1984); A. P. Carnevale, L. J. Gainer, and A. S. Meltzer, *Workplace Basics Training Manual*, 1990 (San Francisco: Jossey-Bass, 1990); G. Rummler, "In Search of the Holy Performance Grail."
21. C. E. Schneier, J. P. Guthrie, and J. D. Olian, "A Practical Approach to Conducting and Using Training Needs Assessment," *Public Personnel Management*, Summer 1988, pp. 191–205.
22. I. Goldstein, "Training in Organizations," in *Handbook of Industrial/Organizational Psychology*, 2nd ed., ed. M. D. Dunnette and L. M. Hough (Palo Alto, CA: Consulting Psychologists Press, 1991), vol. 2, pp. 507–619.
23. E. F. Holton III and C. Bailey, "Top-to-Bottom Curriculum Redesign," *Training and Development*, March 1995, pp. 40–44.
24. R. A. Noe, "Trainees' Attributes and Attitudes: Neglected Influences on Training Effectiveness," *Academy of Management Review* 11 (1986), pp. 736–49.
25. T. T. Baldwin, R. T. Magjuka, and B. T. Loher, "The Perils of Participation: Effects of Choice on Trainee Motivation and Learning," *Personnel Psychology* 44 (1991), pp. 51–66; S. I. Tan-

nenbaum, J. E. Mathieu, E. Salas, and J. A. Cannon-Bowers, "Meeting Trainees' Expectations: The Influence of Training Fulfillment on the Development of Commitment, Self-Efficacy, and Motivation," *Journal of Applied Psychology* 76 (1991), pp. 759–69.

26. M. E. Gist, C. Schwoerer and B. Rosen, "Effects of Alternative Training Methods on Self-Efficacy and Performance in Computer Software Training," *Journal of Applied Psychology* 74 (1989), pp. 884–91; J. Martocchio and J. Dulebohn, "Performance Feedback Effects in Training: The Role of Perceived Controllability," *Personnel Psychology* 47 (1994), pp. 357–73; J. Martocchio, "Ability Conceptions and Learning," *Journal of Applied Psychology* 79 (1994), pp. 819–25.

27. W. D. Hicks and R. J. Klimoski, "Entry into Training Programs and Its Effects on Training Outcomes: A Field Experiment," *Academy of Management Journal* 30 (1987), pp. 542–52.

28. R. A. Noe and N. Schmitt, "The Influence of Trainee Attitudes on Training Effectiveness: Test of a Model," *Personnel Psychology* 39 (1986), pp. 497–523.

29. M. A. Quinones, "Pretraining Context Effects: Training Assignments as Feedback," *Journal of Applied Psychology* 80 (1995), pp. 226–38; Baldwin, Magjuka, and Loher, "The Perils of Participation."

30. L. H. Peters, E. J. O'Connor, and J. R. Eulberg, "Situational Constraints: Sources, Consequences, and Future Considerations," in *Research in Personnel and Human Resource Management*, ed. K. M. Rowland and G. R. Ferris (Greenwich, CT: JAI Press, 1985), vol. 3, pp. 79–114; E. J. O'Connor, L. H. Peters, A. Pooyan, J. Weekley, B. Frank, and B. Erenkranz, "Situational Constraints Effects on Performance, Affective Reactions, and Turnover: A Field Replication and Extension," *Journal of Applied Psychology* 69 (1984), pp. 663–72; D. J. Cohen, "What Motivates Trainees?" *Training and Development Journal*, November 1990, pp. 91–93; Russell, Terborg, and Powers, "Organizational Performance."

31. A. P. Carnevale, "America and the New Economy."

32. J. Nunally, *Psychometric Theory* (New York: McGraw-Hill, 1978).

33. L. Gottsfredson, "The g Factor in Employment," *Journal of Vocational Behavior* 19 (1986), pp. 293–96.

34. M. J. Ree and J. A. Earles, "Predicting Training Success: Not Much More Than g," *Personnel Psychology* 44 (1991), pp. 321–32.

35. D. R. Torrence and J. A. Torrence, "Training in the Face of Illiteracy," *Training and Development Journal*, August 1987, pp. 44–49.

36. C. E. Schneier, "Training and Development Programs: What Learning Theory and Research Have to Offer," *Personnel Journal*, April 1974, pp. 288–93; M. Knowles, "Adult Learning," in *Training and Development Handbook*, 3rd ed., ed. R. L. Craig (New York: McGraw-Hill, 1987), pp. 168–79; R. Zemke and S. Zemke, "30 Things We Know for Sure about Adult Learning," *Training*, June 1981, pp. 45–52; B. J. Smith and B. L. Delahaye, *How to Be an Effective Trainer*, 2nd ed. (New York: John Wiley and Sons, 1987).

37. B. Mager, *Preparing Instructional Objectives*, 2nd ed. (Belmont, CA: Lake, 1984); B. J. Smith and B. L. Delahaye, *How to Be an Effective Trainer*, 2nd ed. (New York: John Wiley and Sons, 1987).

38. K. A. Smith-Jentsch, F. G. Jentsch, S. C. Payne, and E. Salas, "Can Pretraining Experiences Explain Individual Differences in Learning?" *Journal of Applied Psychology* 81 (1996), pp. 110–16.

39. J. K. Ford, D. A. Weissbein, S. M. Guly, and E. Salas, "Relationship of Goal Orientation, Metacognitive Activity and Practice Strategies with Learning Outcomes and Transfer," *Journal of Applied Psychology* 83 (1998), pp. 218–33.

40. R. M. Gagne and K. L. Medsker, *The Condition of Learning* (Fort Worth, TX: Harcourt-Brace, 1996).

41. P. J. Decker and B. R. Nathan, *Behavior Modeling Training: Principles and Applications* (New York: Praeger, 1985).

42. D. Stamps, "Communities of Practice," *Training*, February 1997, pp. 35–42.

43. D. Goldwasser, "Me, a Trainer," *Training*, April 2001, pp. 61–66.

44. R. Weiss, "Memory and Learning," *Training and Development*, October 2000, pp. 46–50; R. Zemke, "Toward a Science of Training," *Training*, July 1999, pp. 32–36.

45. J. C. Naylor and G. D. Briggs, "The Effects of Tasks Complexity and Task Organization on the Relative Efficiency of Part and Whole Training Methods," *Journal of Experimental Psychology* 65 (1963), pp. 217–24.

46. Smith and Delahaye, *How to Be an Effective Trainer*; M. Van Wart, N. J. Cayer, and S. Cook, *Handbook of Training and Development for the Public Sector* (San Francisco: Jossey-Bass, 1993).

47. J. B. Tracey, S. I. Tannenbaum, and M. J. Kavanaugh, "Applying Trained Skills on the Job: The Importance of the Work Environment," *Journal of Applied Psychology* 80 (1995), pp. 239–52; P. E. Tesluk, J. L. Farr, J. E. Mathieu, and R. J. Vance, "Generalization of Employee Involvement Training to the Job Setting: Individual and Situational Effects," *Personnel Psychology* 48 (1995), pp. 607–32; J. K. Ford, M. A. Quinones, D. J. Sego, and J. S. Sorra, "Factors Affecting the Opportunity to Perform Trained Tasks on the Job," *Personnel Psychology* 45 (1992), pp. 511–27.

48. D. Goldwasser, "Me, a Trainer."

49. J. M. Cusimano, "Managers as Facilitators," *Training and Development* 50 (1996), pp. 31–33.

50. "Grand Opening University," *Training*, July/August 2003, p. 16.

51. C. M. Petrini, ed., "Bringing It Back to Work," *Training and Development Journal*, December 1990, pp. 15–21.

52. Ford, Quinones, Sego, and Sorra, "Factors Affecting the Opportunity to Perform Trained Tasks on the Job."

53. Ibid.; M. A. Quinones, J. K. Ford, D. J. Sego, and E. M. Smith, "The Effects of Individual and Transfer Environment Characteristics on the Opportunity to Perform Trained Tasks," *Training Research Journal* 1 (1995/96), pp. 29–48.

54. G. Stevens and E. Stevens, "The Truth about EPSS," *Training and Development* 50 (1996), pp. 59–61.

55. "In Your Face EPSSs," *Training*, April 1996, pp. 101–2.

56. R. D. Marx, "Relapse Prevention for Managerial Training: A Model for Maintenance of Behavior Change," *Academy of Management Review* 7 (1982), pp. 433–41; G. P. Latham and C. A. Frayne, "Self-Management Training for Increasing Job Attendance: A Follow-up and Replication," *Journal of Applied Psychology* 74 (1989), pp. 411–16.

57. "Putting the Distance into Distance Learning," *Training*, October 1995, pp. 111–18.

58. D. Picard, "The Future Is Distance Training," *Training*, November 1996, pp. s3–s10.

59. A. F. Maydas, "On-line Networks Build the Savings into Employee Education," *HR Magazine*, October 1997, pp. 31–35.

60. J. M. Rosow and R. Zager, *Training: The Competitive Edge* (San Francisco: Jossey-Bass, 1988).

61. S. Alexander, "Reducing the Learning Burden," *Training*, September 2002, pp. 32–34.

62. C. Lee, "Who Gets Trained in What?"; A. P. Carnevale, L. J. Gainer, and A. S. Meltzer, *Workplace Basics Training Manual* (San Francisco: Jossey-Bass, 1990).

63. T. Skylar, "When Training Collides with a 35-Ton Truck," *Training*, March 1996, pp. 32–38.

64. R. B. Cohn, "How to Choose a Video Producer," *Training*, July 1996, pp. 58–61.

65. A. P. Carnevale, "The Learning Enterprise," *Training and Development Journal*, February 1989, pp. 26–37.

66. B. Filipczak, "Who Owns Your OJT?" *Training*, December 1996, pp. 44–49.

67. Ibid.

68. D. B. Youst and L. Lipsett, "New Job Immersion without Drowning," *Training and Development Journal*, February 1989, pp. 73–75; G. M. Piskurich, *Self-Directed Learning* (San Francisco: Jossey-Bass, 1993).

69. G. M. Piskurich, "Self-Directed Learning," in *The ASTD Training and Development Handbook*, 4th ed., pp. 453–72; G. M. Piskurich, "Developing Self-Directed Learning," *Training and Development*, March 1994, pp. 31–36.

70. P. Warr and D. Bunce, "Trainee Characteristics and the Outcomes of Open Learning," *Personnel Psychology* 48 (1995), pp. 347–75.

71. C. M. Solomon, "When Training Doesn't Translate," *Workforce* 76, no. 3 (1997), pp. 40–44.

72. R. W. Glover, *Apprenticeship Lessons from Abroad* (Columbus, OH: National Center for Research in Vocational Education, 1986).

73. Commerce Clearing House, Inc., *Orientation–Training* (Chicago, IL: Personnel Practices Communications, Commerce Clearing House, 1981), pp. 501–905.

74. A. H. Howard III, "Apprenticeships," in *The ASTD Training and Development Handbook*, pp. 803–13.

75. K. Ellis, "More Than an Assembly Line," *Training*, January 2002, p. 33.

76. *Eldredge v. Carpenters JATC* (1981), 27 Fair Employment Practices (Bureau of National Affairs), p. 479.

77. M. Pramik, "Installers Learn on Practice Dwellings," *Columbus Dispatch* (February 7, 2003), p. F1.

78. M. W. McCall Jr. and M. M. Lombardo, "Using Simulation for Leadership and Management Research," *Management Science* 28 (1982), pp. 533–49.

79. N. Adams, "Lessons from the Virtual World," *Training*, June 1995, pp. 45–48.

80. Ibid.

81. T. W. Shreeve, "On the Case at the CIA," *Training and Development*, March 1997, pp. 53–54.

82. "Business War Games," *Training*, December 2002, p. 18.

83. M. Hequet, "Games That Teach," *Training*, July 1995, pp. 53–58.

84. G. P. Latham and L. M. Saari, "Application of Social Learning Theory to Training Supervisors through Behavior Modeling," *Journal of Applied Psychology* 64 (1979), pp. 239–46.

85. E. Hollis, "Shoney's: Workforce Development on the Side," *Chief Learning Officer*, March 2003, pp. 32–34.

86. Hannum, *Application of Emerging Training Technology*.

87. M. Rosenberg, *E-Learning: Strategies for Delivering Knowledge in the Digital Age* (New York: McGraw-Hill, 2001).

88. P. Galagan, "The E-Learning Revolution," *Training and Development*, December 2000, pp. 24–30; D. Khirallah, "A New Way to Learn," *Information Week Online* (May 22, 2000).

89. M. Gold, "E-Learning, the Lucent Way," *TD*, July 2003, pp. 46–50.

90. G. Yohe, "The E-Collaborators," *Human Resource Executive*, August 2002, pp. 41–44.

91. J. Armstrong, "The Biggest, Baddest Learning Portals," *Training*, June 2000, pp. 61–63.

92. Ibid.; B. Hall, "One-Stop Shopping: Learning Portals Proliferate," from www.internetconnect.net/bhall/portals/portals.html, 1999–2000.

93. K. Boxer and B. Johnson, "How to Build an Online Learning Center," *TD*, August 2002, pp. 36–42.

94. D. Brown and D. Harvey, *An Experiential Approach to Organizational Development* (Englewood Cliffs, NJ: Prentice Hall, 2000); J. Schettler, "Learning by Doing," *Training*, April 2002, pp. 38–43.

95. J. Schettler, "Learning by Doing."

96. R. J. Wagner, T. T. Baldwin, and C. C. Rowland, "Outdoor Training: Revolution or Fad?" *Training and Development Journal*, March 1991, pp. 51–57; C. J. Cantoni, "Learning the Ropes of Teamwork," *The Wall Street Journal* (October 2, 1995), p. A14.

97. C. Steinfeld, "Challenge Courses Can Build Strong Teams," *Training and Development*, April 1997, pp. 12–13.

98. P. F. Buller, J. R. Cragun, and G. M. McEvoy, "Getting the Most out of Outdoor Training," *Training and Development Journal*, March 1991, pp. 58–61.

99. C. Clements, R. J. Wagner, C. C. Roland, "The Ins and Outs of Experiential Training," *Training and Development*, February 1995, pp. 52–56.

100. Ibid.

101. P. Froiland, "Action Learning," *Training*, January 1994, pp. 27–34.

102. R. L. Oser, A. McCallum, E. Salas, and B. B. Morgan, Jr., "Toward a Definition of Teamwork: An Analysis of Critical Team Behaviors," Technical Report 89-004 (Orlando, FL.: Naval Training Research Center, 1989).

103. Froiland, "Action Learning."

104. "A Team Effort," *Training*, September 2002, p. 18.

105. H. Lancaster, "This Kind of Black Belt Can Help You Score Some Points at Work," *The Wall Street Journal* (September 14, 1999), p. B1; S. Gale, "Building Frameworks for Six Sigma Success," *Workforce*, May 2003, pp. 64–66.

106. J. DeFeo, "An ROI Story," *Training and Development*, July 2000, pp. 25–27.

107. S. Gale, "Six Sigma Is a Way of Life," May 2003, pp. 67–68.

108. K. Kraiger, J. K. Ford, and E. Salas, "Application of Cognitive, Skill-Based, and Affective Theories of Learning Outcomes to New Methods of Training Evaluation," *Journal of Applied Psychology* 78 (1993), pp. 311–28; J. J. Phillips, "ROI: The Search for Best Practices," *Training and Development*, February 1996, pp. 42–47; D. L. Kirkpatrick, "Evaluation of Training," in *Training and Development Handbook*, 2nd ed., ed. R. L. Craig (New York: McGraw-Hill, 1976), pp. 18-1 to 18-27.

109. B. Gerber, "Does Your Training Make a Difference? Prove It!" *Training*, March 1995, pp. 27–34.

110. J. Komaki, K. D. Bardwick, and L. R. Scott, "A Behavioral Approach to Occupational Safety: Pinpointing and Reinforcing Safe Performance in a Food Manufacturing Plant," *Journal of Applied Psychology* 63 (1978), pp. 434–45.

111. A. P. Carnevale and E. R. Schulz, "Return on Investment: Accounting for Training," *Training and Development Journal*, July 1990, pp. S1–S32; P. R. Sackett and E. J. Mullen, "Beyond Formal Experimental Design: Toward an Expanded View of the Training Evaluation Process," *Personnel Psychology* 46 (1993),

pp. 613–27; S. I. Tannenbaum and S. B. Woods, "Determining a Strategy for Evaluating Training: Operating within Organizational Constraints," *Human Resource Planning* 15 (1992), pp. 63–81; R. D. Arvey, S. E. Maxwell, and E. Salas, "The Relative Power of Training Evaluation Designs under Different Cost Configurations," *Journal of Applied Psychology* 77 (1992), pp. 155–60.

112. D. A. Grove and C. O. Ostroff, "Program Evaluation," in *Developing Human Resources,* ed. K. N. Wexley (Washington, DC: BNA Books, 1991), pp. 185–219.

113. Carnevale and Schulz, "Return on Investment."

114. Ibid.; G. Kearsley, *Costs, Benefits, and Productivity in Training Systems* (Boston: Addison-Wesley, 1982).

115. Ibid.

116. D. G. Robinson and J. Robinson, "Training for Impact," *Training and Development Journal,* August 1989, pp. 30–42.

117. A. Purcell, "20/20 ROI," *Training and Development,* July 2000, pp. 28–33.

118. B. Ettorre, "Let's Hear It for Local Talent," *Management Review,* October 1994, p. 9; S. Franklin, "A New World Order for Business Strategy," *Chicago Tribune* (May 15, 1994), sec. 19, pp. 7–8.

119. R. L. Tung, "Selection and Training of Personnel for Overseas Assignments," *Columbia Journal of World Business* 16 (1981), pp. 18–78.

120. W. A. Arthur, Jr., and W. Bennett, Jr., "The International Assignee: The Relative Importance of Factors Perceived to Contribute to Success," *Personnel Psychology* 48 (1995), pp. 99–114; G. M. Spreitzer, M. W. McCall, Jr., and Joan D. Mahoney, "Early Identification of International Executive Potential," *Journal of Applied Psychology* 82 (1997), pp. 6–29.

121. J. S. Black and J. K. Stephens, "The Influence of the Spouse on American Expatriate Adjustment and Intent to Stay in Pacific Rim Overseas Assignments," *Journal of Management* 15 (1989), pp. 529–44.

122. P. Caligiuri, "The Big Five Personality Characteristics as Predictors of Expatriate's Desire to Terminate the Assignment and Supervisor-Rated Performance," *Personnel Psychology* 53 (2000), pp. 67–88.

123. E. Dunbar and A. Katcher, "Preparing Managers for Foreign Assignments," *Training and Development Journal,* September 1990, pp. 45–47.

124. J. S. Black and M. Mendenhall, "A Practical but Theory-Based Framework for Selecting Cross-Cultural Training Methods," in *Readings and Cases in International Human Resource Management,* ed. M. Mendenhall and G. Oddou (Boston: PWS-Kent, 1991), pp. 177–204.

125. S. Ronen, "Training the International Assignee," in *Training and Development in Organizations,* ed. I. L. Goldstein (San Francisco: Jossey-Bass, 1989), pp. 417–53.

126. P. R. Harris and R. T. Moran, *Managing Cultural Differences* (Houston: Gulf, 1991).

127. C. Solomon, "Unhappy Trails," *Workforce,* August 2000, pp. 36–41.

128. H. Lancaster, "Before Going Overseas, Smart Managers Plan Their Homecoming," *The Wall Street Journal* (September 28, 1999), p. B1; A. Halcrow, "Expats: The Squandered Resource," *Workforce,* April 1999, pp. 42–48.

129. Harris and Moran, *Managing Cultural Differences.*

130. J. Cook, "Rethinking Relocation," *Human Resources Executive,* June 2, 2003, pp. 23–26.

131. J. Flynn, "E-Mail, Cellphones, and Frequent-Flier Miles Let 'Virtual' Expats Work Abroad but Live at Home," *The Wall Street Journal* (October 25, 1999), p. A26; J. Flynn, "Multinationals Help Career Couples Deal with Strains Affecting Expatriates," *The Wall Street Journal* (August 8, 2000), p. A19; C. Solomon, "The World Stops Shrinking," *Workforce,* January 2000, pp. 48–51.

132. S. E. Jackson and Associates, *Diversity in the Workplace: Human Resource Initiatives* (New York: Guilford Press, 1992).

133. M. Lee, "Post-9/11 Training," *TD,* September 2002, pp. 33–35.

134. R. R. Thomas, "Managing Diversity: A Conceptual Framework," in *Diversity in the Workplace* (New York: Guilford Press), pp. 306–18.

135. M. E. Heilman, C. J. Block, and J. A. Lucas, "Presumed Incompetent? Stigmatization and Affirmative Action Efforts," *Journal of Applied Psychology* 77 (1992), pp. 536–44.

136. B. Gerber, "Managing Diversity," *Training,* July 1990, pp. 23–30; T. Diamante, C. L. Reid, and L. Ciylo, "Making the Right Training Moves," *HR Magazine,* March 1995, pp. 60–65.

137. C. M. Solomon, "The Corporate Response to Workforce Diversity," *Personnel Journal,* August 1989, pp. 43–53; A. Morrison, *The New Leaders: Guidelines on Leadership Diversity in America* (San Francisco: Jossey-Bass, 1992).

138. S. M. Paskoff, "Ending the Workplace Diversity Wars," *Training,* August 1996, pp. 43–47; H. B. Karp and N. Sutton, "Where Diversity Training Goes Wrong," *Training,* July 1993, pp. 30–34.

139. Paskoff, "Ending the Workplace Diversity Wars."

140. L. Lavelle, "For UPS Managers, a School of Hard Knocks," *BusinessWeek* (July 22, 2002), pp. 58–59; M. Berkley, "UPS Community Internship Program (CIP) Fact Sheet" (Atlanta, GA: United Parcel Service, 2003).

141. A. Markels, "Diversity Program Can Prove Divisive," *The Wall Street Journal* (January 30, 1997), pp. B1–B2; "R. R. Donnelley Curtails Diversity Training Moves," *The Wall Street Journal* (February 13, 1997), p. B3.

142. S. Rynes and B. Rosen, "A Field Study of Factors Affecting the Adoption and Perceived Success of Diversity Training," *Personnel Psychology* 48 (1995), pp. 247–70.

143. T. Kochan, K. Bezrukova, R. Ely, S. Jackson, A. Joshi, K. Jehn, J. Leonard, D. Levine, and D. Thomas, "The Effects of Diversity on Business Performance: Report of the Diversity Research Network," *Human Resource Management* 42 (2003), pp. 8–21; F. Hansen, "Diversity's Business Case Just Doesn't Add Up," *Workforce,* June 2003, pp. 29–32.

144. G. Flynn, "Do You Have the Right Approach to Diversity?" *Personnel Journal,* October 1995, pp. 68–72; M. Galen and A. T. Palmer, "Diversity: Beyond the Numbers Game, *BusinessWeek* (August 14, 1995), pp. 60–61.

145. H. Rosin, "Cultural Revolution at Texaco," *The New Republic* (February 2, 1998), pp. 15–18; K. Labich, "No More Crude at Texaco," *Fortune* (September 6, 1999), pp. 205–12.

146. See Social Responsibility section of www.chevrontexaco.com, website for Chevron Texaco.

147. C. T. Schreiber, K. F. Price, and A. Morrison, "Workforce Diversity and the Glass Ceiling: Practices, Barriers, Possibilities," *Human Resource Planning* 16 (1994), pp. 51–69.

148. D. C. Feldman, "A Contingency Theory of Socialization," *Administrative Science Quarterly* 21 (1976), pp. 433–52; D. C. Feldman, "A Socialization Process That Helps New Recruits Succeed," *Personnel* 57 (1980), pp. 11–23; J. P. Wanous, A. E. Reichers, and S. D. Malik, "Organizational Socialization and Group Development: Toward an Integrative Perspective," *Academy of Management Review* 9 (1984), pp. 670–83; C. L. Adkins, "Previous Work Experience and Organizational Socialization:

A Longitudinal Examination," *Academy of Management Journal* 38 (1995), pp. 839–62; E. W. Morrison, "Longitudinal Study of the Effects of Information Seeking on Newcomer Socialization," *Journal of Applied Psychology* 78 (1993), pp. 173–83.

149. G. M. McEnvoy and W. F. Cascio, "Strategies for Reducing Employee Turnover: A Meta-Analysis," *Journal of Applied Psychology* 70 (1985), pp. 342–53.

150. M. R. Louis, "Surprise and Sense Making: What Newcomers Experience in Entering Unfamiliar Organizational Settings," *Administrative Science Quarterly* 25 (1980), pp. 226–51.

151. R. F. Morrison and T. M. Brantner, "What Enhances or Inhibits Learning a New Job? A Basic Career Issue," *Journal of Applied Psychology* 77 (1992), pp. 926–40.

152. D. A. Major, S. W. J. Kozlowski, G. T. Chao, and P. D. Gardner, " A Longitudinal Investigation of Newcomer Expectations, Early Socialization Outcomes, and the Moderating Effect of Role Development Factors," *Journal of Applied Psychology* 80 (1995), pp. 418–31.

153. D. C. Feldman, *Managing Careers in Organizations* (Glenview, IL: Scott Foresman, 1988).

154. Ibid.; D. Reed-Mendenhall and C. W. Millard, "Orientation: A Training and Development Tool," *Personnel Administrator* 25, no. 8 (1980), pp. 42–44; M. R. Louis, B. Z. Posner, and G. H. Powell, "The Availability and Helpfulness of Socialization Practices," *Personnel Psychology* 36 (1983), pp. 857–66; C. Ostroff and S. W. J. Kozlowski, Jr., "Organizational Socialization as a Learning Process: The Role of Information Acquisition," *Personnel Psychology* 45 (1992), pp. 849–74; D. R. France and R. L. Jarvis, "Quick Starts for New Employees," *Training and Development,* October 1996, pp. 47–50.

155. J. Schettler, "Welcome to ACME Inc." *Training,* August 2002, pp. 36–43.

156. M. Hammers, "Quashing Quick Quits," *Workforce,* May 2003, p. 50.

157. K. Rhodes, "Breaking in the Top Dogs," *Training,* February 2000, pp. 67–71.

3
Part

Assessment and Development of HRM

8

Chapter

Performance Management

Objectives After reading this chapter, you should be able to:

1. Identify the major determinants of individual performance.

2. Discuss the three general purposes of performance management.

3. Identify the five criteria for effective performance management systems.

4. Discuss the four approaches to performance management, the specific techniques used in each approach, and the way these approaches compare with the criteria for effective performance management systems.

5. Choose the most effective approach to performance measurement for a given situation.

6. Discuss the advantages and disadvantages of the different sources of performance information.

7. Choose the most effective source(s) for performance information for any situation.

8. Distinguish types of rating errors and explain how to minimize each in a performance evaluation.

9. Identify the characteristics of a performance measurement system that follows legal guidelines.

10. Conduct an effective performance feedback session.

When Jack Welch was CEO of GE, he instituted a forced distribution system as a way to evaluate company and employee performance. What are the advantages and disadvantages to this type of performance system?

Enter the World of Business

Performance Management ABCs: Is This the Way to Manage Human Resources?

In many U.S. companies, including Ford Motors, General Electric, Microsoft, and Hewlett-Packard, performance evaluation systems, known as *forced ranking systems,* in which employees are ranked against each other, or *forced distribution systems* in which a certain percentage of employees have to be designated as top, average, and subpar performers, have generated lawsuits and negative publicity and have caused poor employee morale. Forced distribution was advocated by former General Electric CEO Jack Welch, who insisted that GE annually identify and remove the bottom 10 percent of the workforce. Such performance ranking takes several forms. Most commonly, employees are grouped into three, four, or five categories usually of unequal size indicating the best workers, the worst workers, and one or more categories in between. For example, at General Electric managers were to place employees into top (20 percent), middle (70 percent), and bottom (10 percent) categories. The bottom 10 percent usually receive no bonuses and can be terminated.

Why are forced distribution systems popular? Top level managers at many companies have observed that despite corporate performance and return to shareholders being flat or decreasing, compensation costs have continued to spiral upward and performance ratings continue to be high. They question how there can be such a disconnect between corporate performance and employees' evaluations and compensation. Forced distribution systems provide a mechanism to help align company performance and employee performance and compensation. Managers are asked to differentiate between good, average, and poor performers, a distinction that many managers find difficult to make. Because pay increases are related to performance appraisals, a forced distribution system helps better link pay to performance. That is, poor performers receive no salary increase, and average performers do not receive as large an increase as top performers. Also, a forced distribution system helps managers tailor development activities to employees based on their performance. For example, poor performers are given specific feedback about what they need to improve in their job and a timetable is set for their improvement. If they do not improve their performance, they are dismissed. Top performers are encouraged to participate in development activities such as job experiences, mentoring, and completion of leadership programs which will help prepare them for top management positions. The use of a forced distribution system is seen as a way for companies to increase performance, motivate employees, and open the door for new talent to join the company to replace poor performers.

Despite its potential merits, forced distribution systems have been difficult to implement. In 2002, Ford Motors settled two class action lawsuits for $10.5 million. Ford said it needed the forced ranking system because its culture discouraged candor in performance evaluations. Ford Motors Performance Management System involved grading 1,800 middle managers as A, B, or C. Managers who received a C for one year received no bonus; two years at the C level meant possible demotion and termination. Ten percent of the managers were to be graded as C. But some employees claimed the system had a negative impact on older, white workers because they received a larger proportion of C grades. Eventually, Ford eliminated the forced ranking system.

Dow Chemical Global had a forced ranking system until the mid-1990s. The system caused a lot of problems. A study showed that the system took too much time and energy to use and that managers were focused on the appraisal instead of improving employee performance. The same employees consistently were evaluated in the top 15 percent, which caused other employees to wonder how they could ever achieve a higher ranking. The company also found that the system was used to deny employees raises and did not fit with Dow's philosophy of recruiting the best employees when it then designated a certain percentage of them as poor performers. Dow's new performance management system involves

managers' defining performance expectations to employees. The company values are clearly explained to workers, as is the employee's role in maintaining those values. The department mission and goals, as well as the employee's performance expectations, are explained and employees are compared against those standards.

Goodyear Tire and Rubber used a system in which 10 percent of its staff would be rated as A performers who would be singled out for promotion. Another 10 percent of the tire company's workforce would be rated as C performers and targeted for improvement or dismissal. After getting a second C rating in two years, a chemist at Goodyear was fired. He was fired a few days before he received a patent for a new kind of aircraft tire. The chemist and seven other Goodyear employees sued the company, claiming the new forced ranking system targeted older employees and not poor performers. Goodyear is fighting the lawsuit, but the company has abandoned the labeling of employees as A, B, or C and rates them as "exceeds expectations," "meets expectations," or "unsatisfactory." Nonetheless, after eliminating the categories (and with them the implication that employees in the bottom category have to leave), employees who are "unsatisfactory" still have to improve or they face reassignment or even firing.

Source: S. Bates, "Forced Ranking," *HR Magazine*, June 2003, pp. 63–68; A. Meisler, "Deadman's Curve," *Workforce Management*, July 2003, pp. 44–49; M. Lowery, "Forcing the Issue," *Human Resource Executive* (October 16, 2003), pp. 26–29; M. Boyle, "Performance Reviews: Perilous Curves Ahead," *Fortune* (May 28, 2001), pp. 187–88.

Introduction

Companies that seek competitive advantage through employees must be able to manage the behavior and results of all employees. The opening story illustrates that one of the most difficult challenges is how to get managers to distinguish between good, average, and poor performers. Ford Motors had decided to rely on a performance appraisal system that forced managers to evaluate some employees as poor performers. The system was met with great resistance because to correctly use it the system compelled managers to make artificial distinctions between employees. Also, such a system makes sense only if those being ranked perform exactly the same job. In this chapter we will discuss characteristics that performance appraisal systems need for administrative purposes such as this. For example, Ford must ensure that the system is job-related; the rationale for performance evaluations is well-documented, and managers have to discuss improvements with employees in the "Improvement Required" category.

Traditionally, the formal performance appraisal system was viewed as the primary means for managing employee performance. Performance appraisal was an administrative duty performed by managers and was primarily the responsibility of the human resource function. Managers now view performance appraisal as an annual ritual—they quickly complete the form and use it to catalog all the negative information they have collected on an employee over the previous year. Because they may dislike confrontation and not feel that they know how to give effective evaluations, some managers spend as little time as possible giving employees feedback. Not surprisingly, most managers and employees dislike performance appraisals! The major reasons for this dislike include the lack of ongoing review, lack of employee involvement, and lack of recognition for good performance.[1]

Some have argued that all performance appraisal systems are flawed to the point that they are manipulative, abusive, autocratic, and counterproductive. Table 8.1 shows some of the criticism of performance appraisals and how the problems can be fixed. It is important to realize that the deficiencies shown in Table 8.1 are not the result of evaluating employee performance. Rather, they result from how the appraisal system is developed and used. As we will see in this chapter, if done correctly, performance appraisal can provide several valuable benefits to both employees and the company. An important part of appraising performance is to establish employee goals, which should be tied to the company's strategic goals. The performance appraisal process tells top performers that they are valued by the company. It requires managers to at least annually communicate to employees their performance strengths and deficiencies. A good appraisal process ensures that all employees doing similar jobs are

TABLE 8.1

Problems and Possible Solutions in Performance Management

PROBLEM	SOLUTION
Discourages teamwork	Make collaboration a criterion on which employees will be evaluated.
Evaluators are inconsistent or use different criteria and standards	Provide training for managers; have the HR department look for patterns on appraisals that suggest bias or over- or underevaluation.
Only valuable for very good or very poor employees	Evaluate specific behaviors or results to show specifically what employees need to improve.
Encourages employees to achieve short-term goals	Include both long-term and short-term goals in the appraisal process.
Manager has complete power over the employee	Managers should be appraised for how they appraise their employees.
Too subjective	Evaluate specific behavior or results.
Produces emotional anguish	Focus on behavior; do not criticize employees; conduct appraisal on time.

SOURCE: Based on J. A. Siegel, "86 Your Appraisal Process?" *HR Magazine*, October 2000, pp. 199–202.

evaluated according to the same standards. A properly conducted appraisal can help the company identify the strongest and weakest employees. It can help legally justify many HRM decisions such as promotions, salary increases, discipline, and layoffs. Annually, *Fortune* magazine ranks the most globally admired companies. The Hay Group, which produces the Global Most Admired report for *Fortune,* says the companies on the list have chief executive officers who understand that performance measurement is about learning how to motivate people and link performance to rewards.[2] Many of the executives report that performance measurement encourages collaboration and cooperation. They believe performance measures help companies focus on operational excellence, customer loyalty, and development of people.

We believe that performance appraisal is only one part of the broader process of performance management. We define **performance management** as the process through which managers ensure that employees' activities and outputs are congruent with the organization's goals. Performance management is central to gaining competitive advantage.

Our performance management system has three parts: defining performance, measuring performance, and feeding back performance information. First, a performance management system specifies which aspects of performance are relevant to the organization, primarily through *job analysis* (discussed in Chapter 4). Second, it measures those aspects of performance through **performance appraisal,** which is only one method for managing employee performance. Third, it provides feedback to employees through **performance feedback** sessions so they can adjust their performance to the organization's goals. Performance feedback is also fulfilled through tying rewards to performance via the compensation system (such as through merit increases or bonuses), a topic to be covered in Chapters 11 and 12.

In this chapter we examine a variety of approaches to performance management. We begin with a model of the performance management process that helps us examine the system's purposes. Then we discuss specific approaches to performance management and the strengths and weaknesses of each. We also look at various sources of performance information. The errors resulting from subjective assessments of performance are presented, as well as the means for reducing those errors. Then we discuss some effective components to performance feedback. Finally, we address components of a legally defensible performance management system.

An Organizational Model of Performance Management

For many years, researchers in the field of HRM and industrial–organizational psychology focused on performance appraisal as a measurement technique.[3] The goal of these performance appraisal systems was to measure individual employee performance reliably and validly. This perspective, however, tended to ignore some important influences on the performance management process. Thus we begin this section by presenting the major purposes of performance management from an organizational rather than a measurement perspective. To do this, we need to understand the process of performance. Figure 8.1 depicts our process model of performance.

As the figure shows, individuals' attributes—their skills, abilities, and so on—are the raw materials of performance. For example, in a sales job, an organization wants someone who has good interpersonal skills and knowledge of the products. These raw

---

Performance management
The means through which managers ensure that employees' activities and outputs are congruent with the organization's goals.

Performance appraisal
The process through which an organization gets information on how well an employee is doing his or her job.

Performance feedback
The process of providing employees information regarding their performance effectiveness.

FIGURE 8.1

Model of
Performance
Management in
Organizations

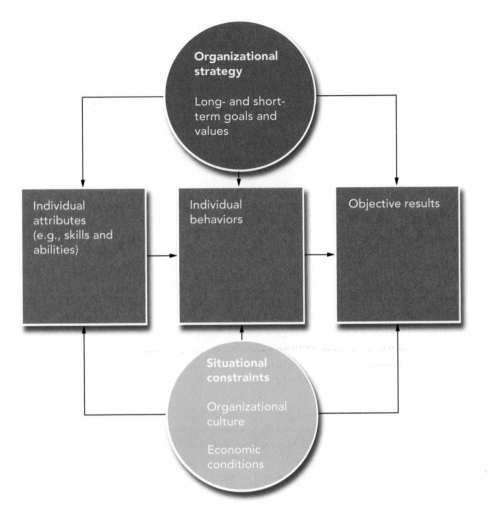

materials are transformed into objective results through the employee's behavior. Employees can exhibit behaviors only if they have the necessary knowledge, skills, abilities, and other characteristics. Thus, employees with good product knowledge and interpersonal skills can talk about the advantages of various brands and can be friendly and helpful (not that they necessarily display those behaviors, only that they *can* display them). On the other hand, employees with little product knowledge or indifferent interpersonal skills cannot effectively display those behaviors. The objective results are the measurable, tangible outputs of the work, and they are a consequence of the employee's or the work group's behavior. In our example, a salesperson who displays the correct behaviors will likely make a number of sales.

Another important component in our organizational model of the performance management system is the organization's strategy. The link between performance management and the organization's strategies and goals is often neglected. Chapter 2 pointed out that most companies pursue some type of strategy to attain their revenue, profit, and market share goals. Divisions, departments, work groups, and individuals within the company must align their activities with these strategies and goals. If they are not aligned, then the likelihood of achieving the goals becomes small. How is this link made in organizations? Primarily by specifying what needs to be accomplished

Performance planning and evaluation (PPE) system
Any system that seeks to tie the formal performance appraisal process to the company's strategies by specifying at the beginning of the evaluation period the types and level of performance that must be accomplished in order to achieve the strategy.

and what behaviors must be exhibited for the company's strategy to be implemented. This link is being recognized as necessary more and more often, through the increasing popularity of **performance planning and evaluation (PPE) systems.** PPE systems seek to tie the formal performance appraisal process to the company's strategies by specifying at the beginning of the evaluation period the types and level of performance that must be accomplished to achieve the strategy. Then at the end of the evaluation period, individuals and groups are evaluated based on how closely their actual performance met the performance plan. In an ideal world, performance management systems would ensure that all activities support the organization's strategic goals.

Finally, our model notes that situational constraints are always at work within the performance management system. As discussed previously, an employee may have the necessary skills and yet not exhibit the necessary behaviors. Sometimes the organizational culture discourages the employee from doing effective things. Work group norms often dictate what the group's members do and the results they produce. On the other hand, some people are simply not motivated to exhibit the right behaviors. This often occurs if the employees do not believe their behaviors will be rewarded with pay raises, promotions, and so forth. Finally, people may be performing effective behaviors, and yet the right results do not follow. For example, an outstanding salesperson may not have a large dollar volume because the economy is bad and people are not buying.

Thus, as you can see in Figure 8.1, employees must have certain attributes to perform a set of behaviors and achieve some results. To gain competitive advantage, the attributes, behaviors, and results must be tied to the company's strategy. Regardless of the job or company, effective performance management systems measure performance criteria (such as behaviors or sales) as precisely as possible. Effective performance management systems also serve a strategic function by linking performance criteria to internal and external customer requirements. Effective performance management systems include a process for changing the system based on situational constraints. Besides serving a strategic purpose, performance management systems also have administrative and developmental purposes. We will next examine the various purposes of performance management systems.

Purposes of Performance Management

The purposes of performance management systems are of three kinds: strategic, administrative, and developmental.

Strategic Purpose

First and foremost, a performance management system should link employee activities with the organization's goals. One of the primary ways strategies are implemented is through defining the results, behaviors, and, to some extent, employee characteristics that are necessary for carrying out those strategies, and then developing measurement and feedback systems that will maximize the extent to which employees exhibit the characteristics, engage in the behaviors, and produce the results. To achieve this strategic purpose, the system must be flexible, because when goals and strategies change, the results, behaviors, and employee characteristics usually need to change correspondingly. Performance management systems do not commonly achieve any strategic purpose, however. A survey indicates that only 13 percent of the companies questioned were using their performance appraisal system to communicate company objectives.[4] In addition, surveys of HRM practitioners regarding the purposes of performance appraisal suggest that most systems focus on administrative and developmental purposes.[5]

Performance management systems can even help develop global business (see the "Competing through Globalization" box on page 334).

Administrative Purpose

Organizations use performance management information (performance appraisals, in particular) in many administrative decisions: salary administration (pay raises), promotions, retention–termination, layoffs, and recognition of individual performance.[6] Despite the importance of these decisions, however, many managers, who are the source of the information, see the performance appraisal process only as a necessary evil they must go through to fulfill their job requirements. They feel uncomfortable evaluating others and feeding those evaluations back to the employees. Thus, they tend to rate everyone high or at least rate them the same, making the performance appraisal information relatively useless. For example, one manager stated, "There is really no getting around the fact that whenever I evaluate one of my people, I stop and think about the impact—the ramifications of my decisions on my relationship with the guy and his future here. . . . Call it being politically minded, or using managerial discretion, or fine-tuning the guy's ratings, but in the end, I've got to live with him, and I'm not going to rate a guy without thinking about the fallout."[7]

Developmental Purpose

A third purpose of performance management is to develop employees who are effective at their jobs. When employees are not performing as well as they should, performance management seeks to improve their performance. The feedback given during a performance evaluation process often pinpoints the employee's weaknesses. Ideally, however, the performance management system identifies not only any deficient aspects of the employee's performance but also the causes of these deficiencies—for example, a skill deficiency, a motivational problem, or some obstacle holding the employee back.

Managers are often uncomfortable confronting employees with their performance weaknesses. Such confrontations, although necessary to the effectiveness of the work group, often strain everyday working relationships. Giving high ratings to all employees enables a manager to minimize such conflicts, but then the developmental purpose of the performance management system is not fully achieved.[8]

As you will see from this chapter there are many aspects to consider and a variety of choices for managers to make regarding performance management systems (e.g., source of performance information, approaches to measuring performance, and others). There is no one correct system that fits all companies. However, to make a performance management system that can best meet strategic, administrative, and developmental goals there are several things that should occur.[9] Table 8.2 provides recommendations for developing an effective performance management system that can meet strategic, administrative and developmental purposes. First, the system should ensure that values and beliefs are integrated into the system. For example, if employee involvement is an important value then self and/or peer appraisals should be part of the performance measurement process. Second, visible CEO and senior management support for the system is necessary. Studies show that senior management plays an important role in the design and implementation of the performance management system in most companies. The stronger the role of senior management the more likely lower level managers will

The Transition from Expatriates to Local Talent

Expatriates are employees assigned to work in another country. Although in developing countries there is a tendency for employees to want an American expatriate manager in charge because they believe that they will have better communications with headquarters and get greater experience in Western business techniques, the goal of many foreign operations is to turn over control to local managers. Locally run businesses are less expensive and they provide advantages from a cultural and business perspective. The transition to local talent may add time and complexity to a project though. ORINCON Corporation International, a San Diego–based technology company, wanted to open an office in Manchester, England, from which to expand overseas. The vice president of human resources was sent over with the job of leasing the office, creating a benefits package, and working out the legal details of the new operations with United Kingdom attorneys. He believed he could accomplish enough in two weeks that he could turn over the project to the British and assist them from the San Diego headquarters. He was not able to completely open the office during his stay in Manchester, however, but finished the job from San Diego (which took more time).

Performance management plays an important role in keeping expatriate performance expectations realistic and providing goals against which their performance can be evaluated. For example, Andrew Corporation, a global communications and equipment provider in Orland Park, Illinois, assigns expatriates to a one-year assignment and reviews their performance after six or eight months before lengthening the assignment. Valerie McGuire, group HR manager explains, "It helps me set the parameters of what is going to be accomplished, especially since the scope of projects always gets bigger. We always find in two or three areas that the individual's not going to accomplish all of what was hoped in a year." As a result, the company extends the assignment until the goals are reached.

Steven Miranda, vice president of human resources at Lucent Technologies, recommends overmonitoring expatriates' performance in the first five or six months to make sure their accomplishments suggest they should be given more authority to run their own operation. This involves not only accelerated and more frequent performance appraisals but meeting periodically face-to-face and communicating via phone and e-mail. While on a three-year assignment in Hong Kong, Miranda and other Lucent managers would meet around the world to report their progress to senior managers and to share information. Careful monitoring is especially useful in identifying expatriates who are not working out.

Performance management is also important for determining whether the expatriate has successfully developed and prepared local staff members to take over the operations. In a successful transition, local managers will have had enough training and will have the leadership ability to take over the operations, and the expatriate will have met the company's goals—as well as personal goals such as gaining more knowledge about global management and international markets that could lead the expatriate to a different position.

SOURCE: F. Jossi, "Successful Handoff," *HR Magazine*, October 2002, pp. 49–52.

TABLE 8.2

Recommendations for Developing an Effective Performance Management System

- Mirror the corporate culture and values.
- Have visible CEO and senior management support.
- Focus on the right company performance measures.
  Vital or "critical few"—relate to strategy, mission, and goals.
  Cascade company goals down the organization.
  Goals are linked to business drivers.
- Link job descriptions to the performance management system.
  Employees need to see the direct relationship between their job competencies, job description, and goals and objectives targeted in the performance plan.
  Establish accountabilities.
- Differentiate performance fairly and effectively.
- Train managers in performance management.
- Link compensation to the performance management system.
  Merit increases.
  Annual incentives.
  Long-term incentives.
  Discretionary incentives.
- Communicate the total rewards system.
- Require managers to actively search out, offer, and acquire performance feedback on a regular basis.
  Be involved in completing the performance cycle: planning, forecasting, progress review, end-of-year evaluation.
- Set clear expectations for employee development.
- Track effectiveness of the performance management system.
  Is it able to identify trends in performance differentiation, pay differentiation, performance gaps/developmental needs?
  Can data be shared with other applications (pay, development, workforce analysis, succession planning)?
- Adjust the system as required.

SOURCE: Based on L. Weatherly, *Performance Management: Getting It Right from the Start* (Alexandria, VA: Society for Human Resource Management, 2004); H. J. Bernardin, C. M. Hagan, J. S. Kane, and P. Villanova, "Effective Performance Management: A Focus on Precision Customers, and Situational Constraints," in *Performance Appraisal: State of the Art in Practice*, ed. J. S. Smither (San Francisco: Jossey-Bass, 1998), pp. 3–48.

take responsibility for ensuring that appraisals are completed and the system is used consistently across the company.[10] Third, the critical company performance measures should be identified. These should provide the best barometer of how the company is doing in relation to achieving its strategy and business goals. Fourth, job descriptions should be linked to the performance management system. Employees need to be able to see the link between their job requirements, their job descriptions, and the goals and objectives included in their performance plans. Fifth, be sure that the performance management system assesses employees fairly and objectively based on clearly understood standards of performance or in terms of their contribution relative to other employees. The system needs to identify poor, good, and excellent performance. Sixth, managers need to be trained in how to use the performance measurement system and how to give performance feedback on a daily basis as well as during the formal performance appraisal interview. Seventh, effective performance management systems link appraisals to financial rewards. Also, to effectively motivate employee performance with rewards, the program must be communicated and understood by employees. Eighth, employee training and development should be linked to the results of performance appraisals. Some companies establish a minimum number of training and development hours per year for each employee to set expectations. Finally, the effectiveness of the performance management system should be evaluated to make sure employee performance is linked to business goals and objectives and financial indicators such as Return on Investment. Based on the evaluation, the performance management system should be adjusted.

Strategic Use of HRM

General Semiconductor has a workforce that is spread from North America to Asia and includes employees who speak five languages. Although General Semiconductor is headquartered on Long Island, New York, only 200 of its 5,600 employees are located in the United States. General Semiconductor makes power magnet components for the high-tech industry. These components power everything from automobiles to cell phones to dishwashers. It manufactures over 17 million parts each day from facilities in Europe, Taiwan, Ireland, and China.

The company's interest in growth created the need to identify a core set of company values and make sure these values were adhered to at all of the worldwide facilities. The company has eight values that are referred to as "culture points." They include integrity; a passion for customer satisfaction; respect for, responsiveness to, and empowerment of employees; technology and innovation; continual improvement; teamwork; job satisfaction; and a winning, competitive spirit. A leadership and problem-solving program developed by the company's HRM staff was used to spread these values throughout the company. The company also developed a program called People Plus that involves a 360-degree review of each employee, including an employee self-assessment matched with feedback from managers, peers, and subordinates chosen by the employee. Once the evaluations are completed, each employee meets with a psychologist to discuss the evaluations and make recommendations on how to improve the weaknesses identified.

Employees believe that the program brings the company together despite its global locations. The program focuses on identifying the unique talents and contributions of every employee. It also helps employees understand how others on the work team view them. The positive results of the program are measurable. Two years after the program was implemented, a survey of the senior management group showed that of 39 development areas, 36 showed improvement. The program has also contributed to a very stable workforce with a low turnover rate across all locations. This has helped General Semiconductor take pride in having the most knowledgeable and well-trained employees in its industry.[11]

As the example of General Semiconductor highlights, an important step in performance management is to develop the measures by which performance will be evaluated. We next discuss the issues involved in developing and using different measures of performance.

Performance Measures Criteria

In Chapter 4 we discussed how, through job analysis, one can analyze a job to determine exactly what constitutes effective performance. Once the company has determined, through job analysis and design, what kind of performance it expects from its employees, it needs to develop ways to measure that performance. This section presents the criteria underlying job performance measures. Later sections discuss approaches to performance measurement, sources of information, and errors.

Although people differ about criteria to use to evaluate performance management systems, we believe that five stand out: strategic congruence, validity, reliability, acceptability, and specificity.

Strategic Congruence

Strategic congruence is the extent to which a performance management system elicits job performance that is congruent with the organization's strategy, goals, and culture. If a company emphasizes customer service, then its performance management system should assess how well its employees are serving the company's customers. Strategic congruence emphasizes the need for the performance management system to guide employees in contributing to the organization's success. This requires systems flexible enough to adapt to changes in the company's strategic posture.

Many companies such as Hewlett-Packard, Federal Express, and Coca-Cola have introduced measures of critical success factors (CSFs) into their performance management systems.[12] CSFs are factors in a company's business strategy that give it a competitive edge. Companies measure employee behavior that relates to attainment of CSFs, which increases the importance of these behaviors for employees. Employees can be held accountable and rewarded for behaviors that directly relate to the company attaining the CSFs.

Take, for example, a drug company whose business strategy is to penetrate the North American market for dermatology compounds.[13] The company needs to shorten the drug development cycle, attract and retain research and development talent, and maximize the effectiveness of research teams. These are core competencies of the business; performance measures are linked directly to the core competencies. These include number of dermatology compound submissions to the Food and Drug Administration (FDA), number of compound approvals by the FDA, turnover of senior engineers, and team leadership and collaboration. The sources for information regarding these performance measures include FDA decisions, team member feedback on surveys, and turnover rates. Team and individual accountabilities are directly linked to the performance measures. For example, research teams' performance goals include FDA submission and approval of three compounds.

One challenge that companies face is how to measure customer loyalty, employee satisfaction, and other nonfinancial performance areas that affect profitability. To effectively use nonfinancial performance measures managers need to:[14]

- Develop a model of how nonfinancial performance measures link to the company's strategic goals. Identify the performance areas that are critical to success.
- Using already existing databases identify data that exists on key performance measures (e.g. customer satisfaction, employee satisfaction surveys). If data is not available, identify a performance area that affects the company's strategy and performance. Develop measures for those performance areas.
- Use statistical and qualitative methods for testing the relationship between the performance measures and financial outcomes. Regression and correlation analysis as well as focus groups and interviews can be used. For example, studies show that employees' involvement, satisfaction and enthusiasm for work are significantly related to business performance including customer satisfaction, productivity, and profitability.[15]
- Revisit the model to ensure that the nonfinancial performance measures are appropriate and determine whether new measures should be added. This is important to understand the drivers of financial performance and to ensure that the model is appropriate as the business strategy and economic conditions change.

Strategic congruence
The extent to which the performance management system elicits job performance that is consistent with the organization's strategy, goals, and culture.

- Act on conclusions that the model demonstrates. For example, Sears found that employee attitudes about the supervision they received and the work environment had a significant impact on customer satisfaction and shareholder results. As a result, Sears invested in managerial training to help managers do a better job of holding employees accountable for their jobs while giving them autonomy to perform their roles.[16]
- Audit whether the actions taken and the investments made produced the desired result.

Most companies' appraisal systems remain constant over a long time and through a variety of strategic emphases. However, when a company's strategy changes, its employees' behavior needs to change too.[17] The fact that appraisal systems often do not change may account for why many managers see performance appraisal systems as having little impact on a firm's effectiveness.

Validity

Validity

The extent to which a performance measure assesses all the relevant—and only the relevant—aspects of job performance.

Validity is the extent to which a performance measure assesses all the relevant—and only the relevant—aspects of performance. This is often referred to as "content validity." For a performance measure to be valid, it must not be deficient or contaminated. As you can see in Figure 8.2, one of the circles represents "true" job performance—all the aspects of performance relevant to success in the job. On the other hand, companies must use some measure of performance, such as a supervisory rating of performance on a set of dimensions or measures of the objective results on the job. Validity is concerned with maximizing the overlap between actual job performance and the measure of job performance (the green portion in the figure).

A performance measure is deficient if it does not measure all aspects of performance (the cranberry portion in the figure). An example is a system at a large university that assesses faculty members based more on research than teaching, thereby relatively ignoring a relevant aspect of performance.

A contaminated measure evaluates irrelevant aspects of performance or aspects that are not job related (the gold portion in the figure). The performance measure should seek to minimize contamination, but its complete elimination is seldom possible. An example of a contaminated measure is the use of actual sales figures for evaluating salespersons across very different regional territories. Often sales are highly dependent upon the territory (number of potential customers, number of competitors, economic conditions) rather than the actual performance of the salesperson. A sales-

FIGURE 8.2

Contamination and Deficiency of a Job Performance Measure

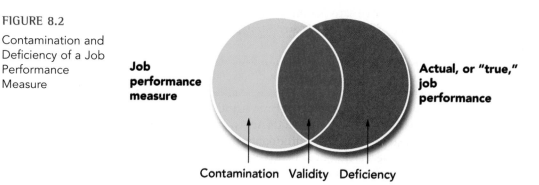

Job performance measure

Actual, or "true," job performance

Contamination   Validity   Deficiency

person who works harder and better than others might not have the highest sales totals because the territory simply does not have as much sales potential as others. Thus, these figures alone would be a measure that is strongly affected by things beyond the control of the individual employee.

Reliability

Reliability refers to the consistency of a performance measure. One important type of reliability is *interrater reliability*: the consistency among the individuals who evaluate the employee's performance. A performance measure has interrater reliability if two individuals give the same (or close to the same) evaluations of a person's job performance. Evidence seems to indicate that most subjective supervisory measures of job performance exhibit low reliability.[18] With some measures, the extent to which all the items rated are internally consistent is important (*internal consistency reliability*).

In addition, the measure should be reliable over time (*test–retest reliability*). A measure that results in drastically different ratings depending on when the measures are taken lacks test–retest reliability. For example, if salespeople are evaluated based on their actual sales volume during a given month, it would be important to consider their consistency of monthly sales across time. What if an evaluator in a department store examined sales only during May? Employees in the lawn and garden department would have high sales volumes, but those in the men's clothing department would have somewhat low sales volumes. Clothing sales in May are traditionally lower than other months. One needs to measure performance consistently across time.

Reliability
The consistency of a performance measure; the degree to which a performance measure is free from random error.

Acceptability

Acceptability refers to whether the people who use a performance measure accept it. Many elaborate performance measures are extremely valid and reliable, but they consume so much of managers' time that they refuse to use it. Alternatively, those being evaluated by a measure may not accept it.

Acceptability is affected by the extent to which employees believe the performance management system is fair. As Table 8.3 shows, there are three categories of perceived fairness: procedural, interpersonal, and outcome fairness. The table also shows specifically how the performance management system's development, use, and outcomes affect perceptions of fairness. In developing and using a performance management system, managers should take the steps shown in the column labeled "Implications" in Table 8.3 to ensure that the system is perceived as fair. Research suggests that performance management systems that are perceived as unfair are likely to be legally challenged, be used incorrectly, and decrease employee motivation to improve.[19]

Acceptability
The extent to which a performance measure is deemed to be satisfactory or adequate by those who use it.

Specificity

Specificity is the extent to which a performance measure tells employees what is expected of them and how they can meet these expectations. Specificity is relevant to both the strategic and developmental purposes of performance management. If a measure does not specify what an employee must do to help the company achieve its strategic goals, it does not achieve its strategic purpose. Additionally, if the measure fails to point out employees' performance problems, it is almost impossible for the employees to correct their performance.

Specificity
The extent to which a performance measure gives detailed guidance to employees about what is expected of them and how they can meet these expectations.

TABLE 8.3

Categories of Perceived Fairness and Implications for Performance Management Systems

FAIRNESS CATEGORY	IMPORTANCE FOR PERFORMANCE MANAGEMENT SYSTEM	IMPLICATIONS
Procedural fairness	Development	• Give managers and employees opportunity to participate in development of system. • Ensure consistent standards when evaluating different employees. • Minimize rating errors and biases.
Interpersonal fairness	Use	• Give timely and complete feedback. • Allow employees to challenge the evaluation. • Provide feedback in an atmosphere of respect and courtesy.
Outcome fairness	Outcomes	• Communicate expectations regarding performance evaluations and standards. • Communicate expectations regarding rewards.

SOURCE: Adapted from S. W. Gilliland and J. C. Langdon, "Creating Performance Management Systems That Promote Perceptions of Fairness," in *Performance Appraisal: State of the Art in Practice*, ed. J. W. Smither. Copyright © 1998 by Jossey-Bass, Inc. This material is used by permission of John Wiley & Sons, Inc.

The "Competing through Sustainability" box shows how Children's Hospital's team-based appraisal system demonstrated strategic congruence, validity, acceptability, and specificity of a performance management system.

Approaches to Measuring Performance

The model of performance management presented in Figure 8.1 shows that we can manage performance by focusing on employee attributes, behaviors, or results. In addition, we can measure performance in a relative way, making overall comparisons among individuals' performance. Finally, we can develop a performance measurement system that incorporates some variety of the preceding measures, as evidenced by the quality approach to measuring performance. Various techniques combine these approaches. In this section we explore these approaches to measuring and managing performance, discussing the techniques that are associated with each approach and evaluating these approaches against the criteria of strategic congruence, validity, reliability, acceptability, and specificity.

The Comparative Approach

The comparative approach to performance measurement requires the rater to compare an individual's performance with that of others. This approach usually uses some overall assessment of an individual's performance or worth and seeks to develop some

Team Performance Helps Get the Bills Paid

Children's Hospital in Boston was determined to improve cash flow and shorten the billing cycle. The hospital's accounts receivable department was taking more than 100 days to receive payment after bills were being sent out. The hospital wanted to design an incentive plan that would show employees the relationship between quarterly cash flow and the number of days a bill spent in the hospital. The hospital decided to use a team-based incentive plan. Managers had to determine who would be rewarded and on what basis, and they had to communicate the plan and its payoffs to employees. Team members were given three possible goals—threshold, target, and optimal—defined in terms of how long a bill remained in accounts receivable. A dollar value was linked to the attainment of each

goal: a quarterly payment of $500, $1,000, or $1,500. Each team member would receive a prorated portion of the payment based on the number of scheduled hours they worked. To earn the incentive team members had to work together, bill by bill, to process the paperwork more quickly. The incentive payment would be added to their checks within 30 days of the close of the quarter and celebrated. To make sure that employees understood the plan, a series of meetings were held in which the dollar value of each day a bill spends in accounts receivable and how the lack of cash flow affects the hospital were explained.

After employees understood how their work affected cash flow at the hospital as well as how their extra efforts could increase their personal cash flow, they began working as a team.

Employees started to take personal initiative and to follow up with patients, insurers, and medical records. If any team members were not carrying their weight there was peer pressure that forced them to pick up the pace and complete their jobs. Employees received weekly progress reports so they could monitor their performance.

The teamwork netted very positive results. At the end of the first year of the plan, employees reduced the average number of days a bill spent in accounts receivable from 100 to 75.8. The plan also helped recruit new employees and keep employees from going to competitors.

SOURCE: Based on D. Cadrain, "Put Success in Sight," *HR Magazine*, May 2003, pp. 85–92.

ranking of the individuals within a work group. At least three techniques fall under the comparative approach: ranking, forced distribution, and paired comparison.

Ranking

Simple ranking requires managers to rank employees within their departments from highest performer to poorest performer (or best to worst). *Alternation ranking,* on the other hand, consists of a manager looking at a list of employees, deciding who is the best employee, and crossing that person's name off the list. From the remaining names, the manager decides who the worst employee is and crosses that name off the list—and so forth.

Ranking is one method of performance appraisal that has received specific attention in the courts. In the *Albermarle v. Moody* case, the validation of the selection system was conducted using employee rankings as the measure of performance. The court actually stated, "There is no way of knowing precisely what criteria of job performance that supervisors were considering, whether each supervisor was considering the same criteria—or whether, indeed, any of the supervisors actually applied a focused and stable body of criteria of any kind."[20]

Forced Distribution

The *forced distribution* method also uses a ranking format, but employees are ranked in groups. This technique requires the manager to put certain percentages of employees into predetermined categories as depicted in Table 8.4. The example in the table shows how Merck combines the performance of the division with individual performance to recommend the distributions of employees that should fall into each category. For example, among poorly performing divisions (Not Acceptable), only 1 percent of employees should receive the highest rating (TF = Top 5 percent), whereas among top-performing divisions (Exceptional), 8 percent of employees should receive the highest rating. In some situations, the forced distribution method forces managers to categorize employees based on distribution rules, not on their performance. For example, even if a manager's employees are all above average performers, the manager is forced to rate some employees as "Not Acceptable."

Forced distribution and ranking systems were discussed in the chapter opener "Enter the World of Business." Advocates of these systems say that they are the best way to identify high potential employees who should be given training, promotions, and financial rewards and to identify the poorest performers who should be helped or asked to leave. Employees in the bottom 10 percent cause performance standards to be lowered, influence good employees to leave, and keep good employees from joining the company. Advocates say these systems force managers to make hard decisions about employee performance based on job-related criteria, rather than to be lenient

TABLE 8.4

Proposed Guidelines for Targeted Distribution of Performance Ratings
Targeted Employee Rating Distribution, by Divisional Performance

PERFORMANCE RATING FOR EMPLOYEES	RATING TYPE	PERFORMANCE RATING FOR DIVISIONS				
		EX EXCEPTIONAL	WD WITH DISTINCTION	HS HIGH STANDARD	RI ROOM FOR IMPROVEMENT	NA NOT ACCEPTABLE
TF Top 5%	Relative	8%	6%	5%	2%	1%
TQ Top quintile	Relative	20%	17%	15%	12%	10%
OU Outstanding	Absolute					
VG Very good	Absolute	71%	75%	75%	78%	79%
GD Good	Absolute					
LF Lower 5%	Relative					
NA Not acceptable	Absolute	1%	2%	5%	8%	10%
PR Progressing		Not Applicable				

SOURCE: Reprinted with permission of The Conference Board, New York City. Data supplied by Merck & Co.; chart by Kevin J. Murphy, University of Rochester.

in evaluating employees. Critics, on the other hand, say the systems in practice are arbitrary, may be illegal, and cause poor morale. For example, one workgroup might have 20 percent poor performers while another might have only high performers, but the process mandates that 10 percent of employees be eliminated from both groups. Also, in many forced distribution systems an unintended consequence is the bottom category tends to consist of minorities, women, and people over 40 years of age, causing discrimination lawsuits. Finally, it is difficult to rank employees into distinctive categories when criteria are subjective or when it is difficult to differentiate employees on the criteria (such as teamwork or communications skills).

Despite the potential problems with these systems, companies that have clear goals and management criteria, train evaluators, use the rankings along with other HR metrics, and reward good performers may find them useful. Forced ranking is ethical as long as the system is clearly communicated, the system is part of a positive dimension of the organization culture (innovation, continuous improvement), and the employees have the chance to appeal decisions.

Paired Comparison

The *paired comparison* method requires managers to compare every employee with every other employee in the work group, giving an employee a score of 1 every time he or she is considered the higher performer. Once all the pairs have been compared, the manager computes the number of times each employee received the favorable decision (that is, counts up the points), and this becomes the employee's performance score.

The paired comparison method tends to be time-consuming for managers and will become more so as organizations become flatter with an increased span of control. For example, a manager with 10 employees must make 45 (10 × ½) comparisons. However, if the group increases to 15 employees, 105 comparisons must be made.

Evaluating the Comparative Approach

The comparative approach to performance measurement is an effective tool in differentiating employee performance; it virtually eliminates problems of leniency, central tendency, and strictness. This is especially valuable if the results of the measures are to be used in making administrative decisions such as pay raises and promotions. In addition, such systems are relatively easy to develop and in most cases easy to use; thus, they are often accepted by users.

One problem with these techniques, however, is their common failure to be linked to the strategic goals of the organization. Although raters can evaluate the extent to which individuals' performances support the strategy, this link is seldom made explicit. In addition, because of the subjective nature of the ratings, their actual validity and reliability depend on the raters themselves. Some firms use multiple evaluators to reduce the biases of any individual, but most do not. At best, we could conclude that their reliability and validity are modest.

These techniques lack specificity for feedback purposes. Based only on their relative rankings, individuals are completely unaware of what they must do differently to improve their ranking. This puts a heavy burden on the manager to provide specific feedback beyond that of the rating instrument itself. Finally, many employees and managers are less likely to accept evaluations based on comparative approaches. Evaluations depend on how employees' performance relates to other employees in a group, team, or department (normative standard) rather than on absolute standards of excellent, good, fair, and poor performance.

The Attribute Approach

The attribute approach to performance management focuses on the extent to which individuals have certain attributes (characteristics or traits) believed desirable for the company's success. The techniques that use this approach define a set of traits—such as initiative, leadership, and competitiveness—and evaluate individuals on them.

Graphic Rating Scales

The most common form that the attribute approach to performance management takes is the *graphic rating scale*. Table 8.5 shows a graphic rating scale used in a manufacturing company. As you can see, a list of traits is evaluated by a five-point (or some other number of points) rating scale. The manager considers one employee at a time, circling the number that signifies how much of that trait the individual has. Graphic rating scales can provide a number of different points (a discrete scale) or a continuum along which the rater simply places a check mark (a continuous scale).

The legal defensibility of graphic rating scales was questioned in the *Brito v. Zia* (1973) case. In this case Spanish-speaking employees had been terminated as a result of their performance appraisals. These appraisals consisted of supervisors' rating subordinates on a number of undefined dimensions such as volume of work, quantity of work, job knowledge, dependability, and cooperation. The court criticized the subjective appraisals and stated that the company should have presented empirical data demonstrating that the appraisal was significantly related to actual work behavior.

Mixed-Standard Scales

Mixed-standard scales were developed to get around some of the problems with graphic rating scales. To create a mixed-standard scale, we define the relevant performance dimensions and then develop statements representing good, average, and poor performance along each dimension. These statements are then mixed with the statements from other dimensions on the actual rating instrument. An example of a mixed-standard scale is presented in Table 8.6.

TABLE 8.5

Example of a Graphic Rating Scale

The following areas of performance are significant to most positions. Indicate your assessment of performance on each dimension by circling the appropriate rating.

PERFORMANCE DIMENSION	RATING				
	DISTINGUISHED	EXCELLENT	COMMENDABLE	ADEQUATE	POOR
Knowledge	5	4	3	2	1
Communication	5	4	3	2	1
Judgment	5	4	3	2	1
Managerial skill	5	4	3	2	1
Quality performance	5	4	3	2	1
Teamwork	5	4	3	2	1
Interpersonal skills	5	4	3	2	1
Initiative	5	4	3	2	1
Creativity	5	4	3	2	1
Problem solving	5	4	3	2	1

TABLE 8.6

An Example of a
Mixed-Standard
Scale

Three traits being assessed:
    Initiative (INTV)
    Intelligence (INTG)
    Relations with others (RWO)

Levels of performance in statements:
    High (H)
    Medium (M)
    Low (L)

Instructions: Please indicate next to each statement whether the employee's performance is above (+), equal to (0), or below (–) the statement.

INTV	H	1.	This employee is a real self-starter. The employee always takes the initiative and his/her superior never has to prod this individual.	+
INTG	M	2.	While perhaps this employee is not a genius, s/he is a lot more intelligent than many people I know.	+
RWO	L	3.	This employee has a tendency to get into unnecessary conflicts with other people.	0
INTV	M	4.	While generally this employee shows initiative, occasionally his/her superior must prod him/her to complete work.	+
INTG	L	5.	Although this employee is slower than some in understanding things, and may take a bit longer in learning new things, s/he is of average intelligence.	+
RWO	H	6.	This employee is on good terms with everyone. S/he can get along with people even when s/he does not agree with them.	–
INTV	L	7.	This employee has a bit of a tendency to sit around and wait for directions.	+
INTG	H	8.	This employee is extremely intelligent, and s/he learns very rapidly.	–
RWO	M	9.	This employee gets along with most people. Only very occasionally does s/he have conflicts with others on the job, and these are likely to be minor.	–

Scoring Key:

STATEMENTS			SCORE
HIGH	MEDIUM	LOW	
+	+	+	7
0	+	+	6
–	+	+	5
–	0	+	4
–	–	+	3
–	–	0	2
–	–	–	1

Example score from preceding ratings:

	STATEMENTS			SCORE
	HIGH	MEDIUM	LOW	
Initiative	+	+	+	7
Intelligence	0	+	+	6
Relations with others	–	–	0	2

As we see in the table, the rater is asked to complete the rating instrument by indicating whether the employee's performance is above (+), at (0), or below (−) the statement. A special scoring key is then used to score the employee's performance for each dimension. Thus, for example, an employee performing above all three statements receives a 7. If the employee is below the good statement, at the average statement, and above the poor statement, a score of 4 is assessed. An employee below all three statements is given a rating of 1. This scoring is applied to all the dimensions to determine an overall performance score.

Note that mixed-standard scales were originally developed as trait-oriented scales. However, this same technique has been applied to instruments using behavioral rather than trait-oriented statements as a means of reducing rating errors in performance appraisal.[21]

Evaluating the Attribute Approach

Attribute-based performance methods are the most popular methods in organizations. They are quite easy to develop and are generalizable across a variety of jobs, strategies, and organizations. In addition, if much attention is devoted to identifying those attributes relevant to job performance and carefully defining them on the rating instrument, they can be as reliable and valid as more elaborate measurement techniques.

However, these techniques fall short on several of the criteria for effective performance management. There is usually little congruence between the techniques and the company's strategy. These methods are used because of the ease in developing them and because the same method (list of traits, comparisons) is generalizable across any organization and any strategy. In addition, these methods usually have very vague performance standards that are open to different interpretations by different raters. Because of this, different raters often provide extremely different ratings and rankings. The result is that both the validity and reliability of these methods are usually low.

Virtually none of these techniques provides any specific guidance on how an employee can support the company's goals or correct performance deficiencies. In addition, when raters give feedback, these techniques tend to elicit defensiveness from employees. For example, how would you feel if you were told that on a five-point scale, you were rated a "2" in maturity? Certainly you might feel somewhat defensive and unwilling to accept that judgment, as well as any additional feedback. Also, being told you were rated a "2" in maturity doesn't tell you how to improve your rating.

The Behavioral Approach

The behavioral approach to performance management attempts to define the behaviors an employee must exhibit to be effective in the job. The various techniques define those behaviors and then require managers to assess the extent to which employees exhibit them. We discuss five techniques that rely on the behavioral approach.

Critical Incidents

The *critical incidents* approach requires managers to keep a record of specific examples of effective and ineffective performance on the part of each employee. Here's an example of an incident described in the performance evaluation of an appliance repair person:

A customer called in about a refrigerator that was not cooling and was making a clicking noise every few minutes. The technician prediagnosed the cause of the problem and checked his truck for the necessary parts. When he found he did not have them, he checked the parts out from inventory so that the customer's refrigerator would be repaired on his first visit and the customer would be satisfied promptly.

These incidents give specific feedback to employees about what they do well and what they do poorly, and they can be tied to the company's strategy by focusing on incidents that best support that strategy. However, many managers resist having to keep a daily or weekly log of their employees' behavior. It is also often difficult to compare employees because each incident is specific to that individual.

Behaviorally Anchored Rating Scales

A *behaviorally anchored rating scale (BARS)* builds on the critical incidents approach. It is designed to specifically define performance dimensions by developing behavioral anchors associated with different levels of performance.[22] An example of a BARS is presented in Figure 8.3. As you can see, the performance dimension has a number of examples of behaviors that indicate specific levels of performance along the dimension.

To develop a BARS, we first gather a large number of critical incidents that represent effective and ineffective performance on the job. These incidents are classified into performance dimensions, and the ones that experts agree clearly represent a particular level of performance are used as behavioral examples (or anchors) to guide the rater. The manager's task is to consider an employee's performance along each dimension and determine where on the dimension the employee's performance fits using the behavioral anchors as guides. This rating becomes the employee's score for that dimension.

Behavioral anchors have advantages and disadvantages. They can increase interrater reliability by providing a precise and complete definition of the performance dimension. A disadvantage is that they can bias information recall—that is, behavior that closely approximates the anchor is more easily recalled than other behavior.[23] Research has also demonstrated that managers and their subordinates do not make much of a distinction between BARS and trait scales.[24]

Behavioral Observation Scales

A *behavioral observation scale (BOS)* is a variation of a BARS. Like a BARS, a BOS is developed from critical incidents.[25] However, a BOS differs from a BARS in two basic ways. First, rather than discarding a large number of the behaviors that exemplify effective or ineffective performance, a BOS uses many of them to more specifically define all the behaviors that are necessary for effective performance (or that would be considered ineffective performance). Instead of using, say, 4 behaviors to define 4 levels of performance on a particular dimension, a BOS may use 15 behaviors. An example of a BOS is presented in Table 8.7.

A second difference is that rather than assessing which behavior best reflects an individual's performance, a BOS requires managers to rate the frequency with which the employee has exhibited each behavior during the rating period. These ratings are then averaged to compute an overall performance rating.

The major drawback of a BOS is that it may require more information than most managers can process or remember. A BOS can have 80 or more behaviors, and the

FIGURE 8.3

Task-BARS Rating
Dimension: Patrol
Officer

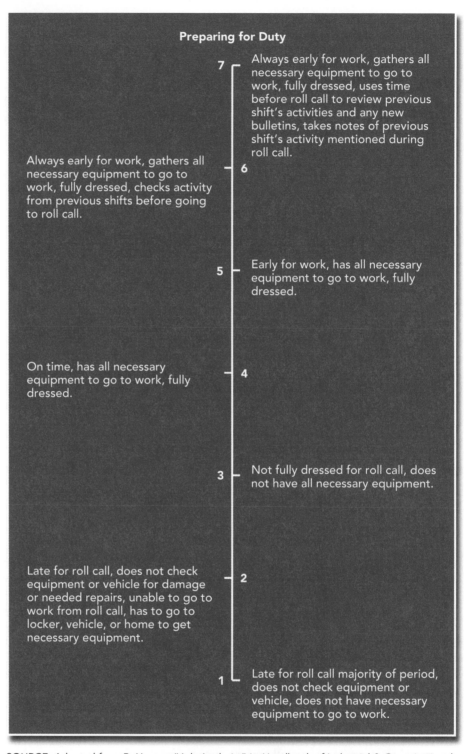

Preparing for Duty

7 — Always early for work, gathers all necessary equipment to go to work, fully dressed, uses time before roll call to review previous shift's activities and any new bulletins, takes notes of previous shift's activity mentioned during roll call.

6 — Always early for work, gathers all necessary equipment to go to work, fully dressed, checks activity from previous shifts before going to roll call.

5 — Early for work, has all necessary equipment to go to work, fully dressed.

4 — On time, has all necessary equipment to go to work, fully dressed.

3 — Not fully dressed for roll call, does not have all necessary equipment.

2 — Late for roll call, does not check equipment or vehicle for damage or needed repairs, unable to go to work from roll call, has to go to locker, vehicle, or home to get necessary equipment.

1 — Late for roll call majority of period, does not check equipment or vehicle, does not have necessary equipment to go to work.

SOURCE: Adapted from R. Harvey, "Job Analysis," in *Handbook of Industrial & Organizational Psychology*, 2nd ed., ed. M. Dunnette and L. Hough (Palo Alto, CA.: Consulting Psychologists Press, 1991), p. 138.

Overcoming Resistance to Change						
(1) Describes the details of the change to subordinates.						
Almost Never	1	2	3	4	5	Almost Always
(2) Explains why the change is necessary.						
Almost Never	1	2	3	4	5	Almost Always
(3) Discusses how the change will affect the employee.						
Almost Never	1	2	3	4	5	Almost Always
(4) Listens to the employee's concerns.						
Almost Never	1	2	3	4	5	Almost Always
(5) Asks the employee for help in making the change work.						
Almost Never	1	2	3	4	5	Almost Always
(6) If necessary, specifies the date for a follow-up meeting to respond to the employee's concerns.						
Almost Never	1	2	3	4	5	Almost Always

Total = _____

Below Adequate	Adequate	Full	Excellent	Superior
6–10	11–15	16–20	21–25	26–30

TABLE 8.7

An Example of a Behavioral Observation Scale (BOS) for Evaluating Job Performance

Scores are set by management.
SOURCE: G. Latham and K. Wexley, *Increasing Productivity through Performance Appraisal*, p. 56. © 1964. Reprinted by permission of Pearson Education, Inc., Upper Saddle River, New Jersey.

manager must remember how frequently an employee exhibited each of these behaviors over a 6- or 12-month rating period. This is taxing enough for one employee, but managers often must rate 10 or more employees.

A direct comparison of BOS, BARS, and graphic rating scales found that both managers and employees prefer BOS for differentiating good from poor performers, maintaining objectivity, providing feedback, suggesting training needs, and being easy to use among managers and subordinates.[26]

Organizational Behavior Modification

Organizational behavior modification (OBM) entails managing the behavior of employees through a formal system of behavioral feedback and reinforcement. This system builds on the behaviorist view of motivation, which holds that individuals' future behavior is determined by past behaviors that have been positively reinforced. The techniques vary, but most have four components. First, they define a set of key behaviors necessary for job performance. Second, they use a measurement system to assess whether these behaviors are exhibited. Third, the manager or consultant informs employees of those behaviors, perhaps even setting goals for how often the employees should exhibit those behaviors. Finally, feedback and reinforcement are provided to employees.[27]

OBM techniques have been used in a variety of settings. For example, OBM was used to increase the rates and timeliness of critical job behaviors by showing the connection between job behaviors and the accomplishments of a community mental health agency.[28] Job behaviors were identified that related to administration, record keeping, and service provided to clients. Feedback and reinforcement improved staff performance. Figure 8.4 shows increases in staff performance in record keeping following the feedback and reinforcement intervention. "Baseline" refers to measures of

FIGURE 8.4

Increases in Record Keeping as a Result of OBM

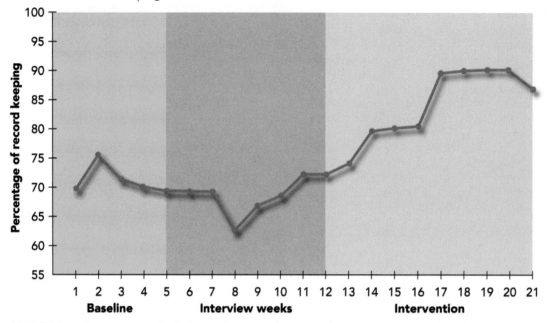

SOURCE: Based on K. L. Langeland, C. M. Johnson, and T. C. Mawhinney, "Improving Staff Performance in a Community Mental Health Setting: Job Analysis, Training, Goal Setting, Feedback, and Year of Data," *Journal of Organizational Behavior Management* 18 (1998), pp. 211–43.

record keeping prior to the intervention. "Interview" refers to record keeping when interviews were being conducted with staff to better explain their jobs. Similar results have been observed with the frequency of safety behaviors in a processing plant.[29]

Assessment Centers

Although assessment centers are usually used for selection and promotion decisions, they have also been used as a way of measuring managerial performance.[30] At an **assessment center,** individuals usually perform a number of simulated tasks, such as leaderless group discussions, in-basket management, and role playing. Assessors observe the individuals' behavior and evaluate their skill or potential as managers. We discuss assessment centers more in Chapter 9.

Assessment centers
A process in which multiple raters evaluate employees' performance on a number of exercises.

The advantage of assessment centers is that they provide a somewhat objective measure of an individual's performance at managerial tasks. In addition, they allow specific performance feedback, and individualized developmental plans can be designed. For example, ARCO Oil & Gas Corporation sends its managers through assessment centers to identify their individual strengths and weaknesses and to create developmental action plans for each manager.

An interesting public sector application of assessment centers is in the state government of North Carolina. Managers there can be assessed to become "certified middle managers." This process includes an assessment center at the beginning of the certification program, from which an individualized developmental action plan is created. The developmental plan, implemented over approximately two years, consists of training and on-the-job developmental experiences. At the end of the two years, the manager attends the certification assessment center. Those who successfully meet the criteria set forth then become certified.

Evaluation of the Behavioral Approach

The behavioral approach can be very effective. It can link the company's strategy to the specific behavior necessary for implementing that strategy. It provides specific guidance and feedback for employees about the performance expected of them. Most of the techniques rely on in-depth job analysis, so the behaviors that are identified and measured are valid. Because those who will use the system develop the measures, the acceptability is also often high. Finally, with a substantial investment in training raters, the techniques are reasonably reliable.

The major weaknesses have to do with the organizational context of the system. Although the behavioral approach can be closely tied to a company's strategy, the behaviors and measures must be constantly monitored and revised to ensure that they are still linked to the strategic focus. This approach also assumes that there is "one best way" to do the job and that the behaviors that constitute this best way can be identified. One study found that managers seek to control behaviors when they perceive a clear relationship between behaviors and results. When this link is not clear, they tend to rely on managing results.[31] The behavioral approach might be best suited to less complex jobs (where the best way to achieve results is somewhat clear) and least suited to complex jobs (where there are multiple ways, or behaviors, to achieve success).

The Results Approach

The results approach focuses on managing the objective, measurable results of a job or work group. This approach assumes that subjectivity can be eliminated from the measurement process and that results are the closest indicator of one's contribution to organizational effectiveness.[32] We will examine two performance management systems that use results: management by objectives and the productivity measurement and evaluation system.

Management by Objectives

Management by objectives (MBO) is popular in both private and public organizations.[33] The original concept came from the accounting firm of Booz, Allen, and Hamilton and was called a "manager's letter." The process consisted of having all the subordinate managers write a letter to their superiors, detailing what their performance goals were for the coming year and how they planned to achieve them. Harold Smiddy applied and expanded this idea at General Electric in the 1950s, and Douglas McGregor has since developed it into a philosophy of management.[34]

In an MBO system, the top management team first defines the company's strategic goals for the coming year. These goals are passed on to the next layer of management, and these managers define the goals they must achieve for the company to reach its goals. This goal-setting process cascades down the organization so that all managers set goals that help the company achieve its goals.[35] These goals are used as the standards by which an individual's performance is evaluated.[36]

MBO systems have three common components.[37] They require specific, difficult, objective goals. (An example of MBO-based goals used in a financial service firm is

KEY RESULT AREA	OBJECTIVE	% COMPLETE	ACTUAL PERFORMANCE
Loan portfolio management	Increase portfolio value by 10% over the next 12 months	90	Increased portfolio value by 9% over the past 12 months
Sales	Generate fee income of $30,000 over the next 12 months	150	Generated fee income of $45,000 over the past 12 months

presented in Table 8.8.) The goals are not usually set unilaterally by management but with the managers' and subordinates' participation. And the manager gives objective feedback throughout the rating period to monitor progress toward the goals.

Research on MBO has revealed two important findings regarding its effectiveness.[38] Of 70 studies examined, 68 showed productivity gains, while only 2 showed productivity losses, suggesting that MBO usually increases productivity. Also, productivity gains tend to be highest when there is substantial commitment to the MBO program from top management: an average increase of 56 percent when commitment was high, 33 percent when commitment was moderate, and 6 percent when commitment was low.

Clearly, MBO can have a very positive effect on an organization's performance. Considering the process through which goals are set (involvement of staff in setting objectives), it is also likely that MBO systems effectively link individual employee performance with the firm's strategic goals. For example, Pier 1 Imports was able to give store managers and salespeople access to real-time sales totals and analyses, telling them exactly how they were doing compared with, say, the previous day or month. Instead of creating a sweatshop atmosphere, as some critics worried, employees took the figures as a challenge. "The more information you give the associates, the more ownership they feel in the store's performance," says Dave Self, a regional manager for 33 Pier 1 stores.

Pier 1 employees agree. "It adds to the excitement," claims Alicia Winchell, an assistant manager. During the day, clerks at the store rotate their use of a backroom computer that gives them up-to-the-minute sales data. They learn not only how many items were sold and at what price but also how many people entered the store and the percentage of those who bought something. They know how many items are new and how many were imported from overseas. These figures help managers and sales staff create better value for customers, paying close attention to everyone who walks in the door. Paula Hankins, a store manager, spent a half hour one day helping an interior designer select some small decorations. The designer hadn't planned to spend $250 that day but said that Hankins "did a great job pointing out what I wanted."

Pier 1 management makes an important distinction about the data: they are an informational tool, not an instrument of discipline. If a store fails to meet a certain short-term goal, "It's not like they're blaming us for it," says employee Kim Smith. Results provide valuable insight into the whole performance management picture.[39]

Productivity Measurement and Evaluation System (ProMES)

The main goal of ProMES is to motivate employees to higher levels of productivity.[40] It is a means of measuring and feeding back productivity information to personnel.

ProMES consists of four steps. First, people in an organization identify the products, or the set of activities or objectives, the organization expects to accomplish. The organization's productivity depends on how well it produces these products. At a repair shop, for example, a product might be something like "quality of repair." Second, the staff defines indicators of the products. Indicators are measures of how well the products are being generated by the organization. Quality of repair could be indicated by (1) return rate (percentage of items returned that did not function immediately after repair) and (2) percentage of quality-control inspections passed. Third, the staff establishes the contingencies between the amount of the indicators and the level of evaluation associated with that amount. Fourth, a feedback system is developed that provides employees and work groups with information about their specific level of performance on each of the indicators. An overall productivity score can be computed by summing the effectiveness scores across the various indicators.

Because this technique is somewhat new, it has been applied in only a few situations. However, research thus far strongly suggests it is effective in increasing productivity. (Figure 8.5 illustrates the productivity gains in the repair shop described previously.) The research also suggests the system is an effective feedback mechanism.

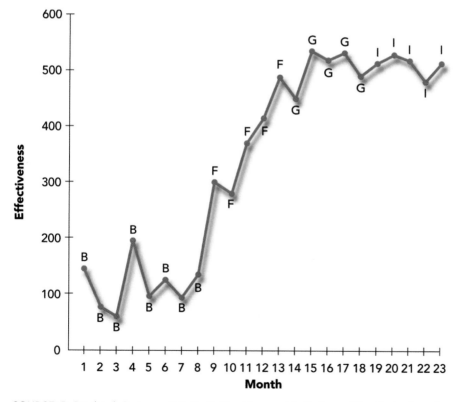

FIGURE 8.5

Increases in Productivity for a Repair Shop Using ProMES Measures

SOURCE: R. Pritchard, S. Jones, P. Roth, K. Stuebing, and S. Ekeberg, "The Evaluation of an Integrated Approach to Measuring Organizational Productivity," *Personnel Psychology* 42 (1989), pp. 69–115. Used by permission.

However, users found it time-consuming to develop the initial system. Future research on ProMES needs to be conducted before we draw any firm conclusions, but the existing research indicates that this may be a useful performance management tool.

Evaluation of the Results Approach

The results approach minimizes subjectivity, relying on objective, quantifiable indicators of performance. Thus, it is usually highly acceptable to both managers and employees. Another advantage is that it links an individual's results with the organization's strategies and goals.

However, objective measurements can be both contaminated and deficient—contaminated because they are affected by things that are not under the employee's control, such as economic recessions, and deficient because not all the important aspects of job performance are amenable to objective measurement. Another disadvantage is that individuals may focus only on aspects of their performance that are measured, neglecting those that are not. For example, if the large majority of employees' goals relate to productivity, it is unlikely they will be concerned with customer service. One study found that objective performance goals led to higher performance but that they also led to helping coworkers less.[41] A final disadvantage is that, though results measures provide objective feedback, the feedback may not help employees learn how they need to change their behavior to increase their performance. If baseball players are in a hitting slump, simply telling them that their batting average is .190 may not motivate them to raise it. Feedback focusing on the exact behavior that needs to be changed (like taking one's eye off the ball or dropping one's shoulder) would be more helpful.[42]

The Quality Approach

Thus far we have examined the traditional approaches to measuring and evaluating employee performance. Two fundamental characteristics of the quality approach are a customer orientation and a prevention approach to errors. Improving customer satisfaction is the primary goal of the quality approach. Customers can be internal or external to the organization. A performance management system designed with a strong quality orientation can be expected to

- Emphasize an assessment of both person and system factors in the measurement system.
- Emphasize that managers and employees work together to solve performance problems.
- Involve both internal and external customers in setting standards and measuring performance.
- Use multiple sources to evaluate person and system factors.[43]

Based on this chapter's earlier discussion of the characteristics of an effective performance management system, it should be apparent to you that these characteristics are not just unique to the quality approach but are characteristics of an effective appraisal system!

Advocates of the quality approach believe that most U.S. companies' performance management systems are incompatible with the quality philosophy for a number of reasons:

1. Most existing systems measure performance in terms of quantity, not quality.
2. Employees are held accountable for good or bad results to which they contribute but do not completely control.
3. Companies do not share the financial rewards of successes with employees according to how much they have contributed to them.
4. Rewards are not connected to business results.[44]

Sales, profit margins, and behavioral ratings are often collected by managers to evaluate employees' performance. These are person-based outcomes. An assumption of using these types of outcomes is that the employee completely controls them. However, according to the quality approach, these types of outcomes should not be used to evaluate employees' performance because they do not have complete control over them (that is, they are contaminated). For example, for salespersons, performance evaluations (and salary increases) are often based on attainment of a sales quota. It is assumed that salespersons' abilities and motivation are directly responsible for their performance. However, quality approach advocates argue that better determinants of whether a salesperson reaches the quota are "systems factors" (such as competitors' product price changes) and economic conditions (which are not under the salesperson's control).[45] Holding employees accountable for outcomes affected by systems factors is believed to result in dysfunctional behavior, such as falsifying sales reports, budgets, expense accounts, and other performance measures, as well as lowering employees' motivation for continuous improvement.

Quality advocates suggest that the major focus of performance evaluations should be to provide employees with feedback about areas in which they can improve. Two types of feedback are necessary: (1) subjective feedback from managers, peers, and customers about the personal qualities of the employee and (2) objective feedback based on the work process itself using statistical quality control methods.

Performance feedback from managers, peers, and customers should be based on such dimensions as cooperation, attitude, initiative, and communication skills. Performance evaluation should include a discussion of the employee's career plans. The quality approach also strongly emphasizes that performance appraisal systems should avoid providing overall evaluations of employees (like ratings such as excellent, good, poor). Categorizing employees is believed to encourage them to behave in ways that are expected based on their ratings. For example, "average" performers may not be motivated to improve their performance but rather may continue to perform at the expected level. Also, because employees do not have control over the quality of the system in which they work, employee performance evaluations should not be linked to compensation. Compensation rates should be based on prevailing market rates of pay, seniority, and business results, which are distributed equitably to all employees.

Statistical process control techniques are very important in the quality approach. These techniques provide employees with an objective tool to identify causes of problems and potential solutions. These techniques include process-flow analysis, cause-and-effect diagrams, Pareto charts, control charts, histograms, and scattergrams.

Process-flow analysis identifies each action and decision necessary to complete work, such as waiting on a customer or assembling a television set. Process-flow analysis is useful for identifying redundancy in processes that increase manufacturing or service time. For example, one business unit at Owens-Corning was able to confirm that customer orders were error-free only about 25 percent of the time (an unacceptable level of service). To improve the service level, the unit mapped out the process to identify bottlenecks and problem areas. As a result of this mapping, one simple change (installing an 800 number for the fax machine) increased overall accuracy of orders as well as transaction speed.[46]

In *cause-and-effect diagrams,* events or causes that result in undesirable outcomes are identified. Employees try to identify all possible causes of a problem. The feasibility of the causes is not evaluated, and as a result, cause-and-effect diagrams produce a large list of possible causes.

A *Pareto chart* highlights the most important cause of a problem. In a Pareto chart, causes are listed in decreasing order of importance, where *importance* is usually defined as the frequency with which that cause resulted in a problem. The assumption of Pareto analysis is that the majority of problems are the result of a small number of causes. Figure 8.6 shows a Pareto chart listing the reasons managers give for not selecting current employees for a job vacancy.

Control charts involve collecting data at multiple points in time. By collecting data at different times, employees can identify what factors contribute to an outcome and when they tend to occur. Figure 8.7 shows the percentage of employees hired internally for a company for each quarter between 1993 and 1995. Internal hiring increased dramatically during the third quarter of 1994. The use of control charts helps employees understand the number of internal candidates who can be expected to be hired each year. Also, the control chart shows that the amount of internal hiring conducted during the third quarter of 1994 was much larger than normal.

Histograms display distributions of large sets of data. Data are grouped into a smaller number of categories or classes. Histograms are useful for understanding the amount of variance between an outcome and the expected value or average outcome. Figure 8.8 is a histogram showing the number of days it took a company to fill nonexempt job vacancies. The histogram shows that most nonexempt jobs took from 18 to 21 days to fill, and the amount of time to fill nonexempt jobs ranged from 1 to 33 days.

FIGURE 8.6
Pareto Chart

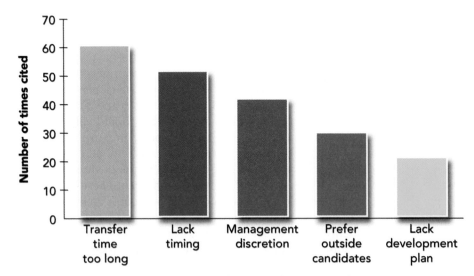

SOURCE: From *HR Magazine* by Clara Carter. Copyright 1992, by Society for Human Resource Management. Reprinted with permission of Society for Human Resource Management via Copyright Clearance Center.

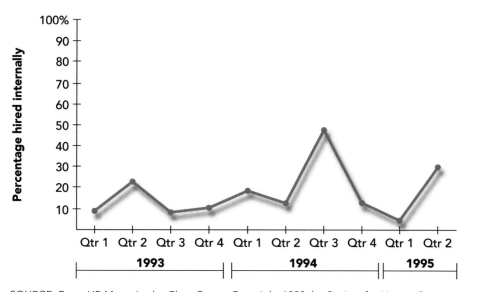

FIGURE 8.7

Control Chart

SOURCE: From *HR Magazine* by Clara Carter. Copyright 1992, by Society for Human Resource Management. Reprinted with permission of Society for Human Resource Management via Copyright Clearance Center.

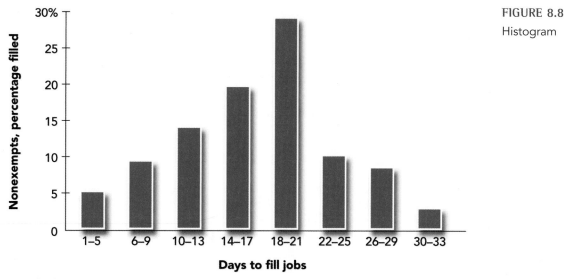

FIGURE 8.8

Histogram

SOURCE: From *HR Magazine* by Clara Carter. Copyright 1992, by Society for Human Resource Management. Reprinted with permission of Society for Human Resource Management via Copyright Clearance Center.

If an HR manager relied simply on data from personnel files on the number of days it took to fill nonexempt positions, it would be extremely difficult to understand the variation and average tendency in the amount of time to fill the positions.

Scattergrams show the relationship between two variables, events, or different pieces of data. Scattergrams help employees determine whether the relationship between two variables or events is positive, negative, or zero.

Evaluation of the Quality Approach

The quality approach relies primarily on a combination of the attribute and results approaches to performance measurement. However, traditional performance appraisal systems focus more on individual employee performance, while the quality approach adopts a systems-oriented focus.[47] Many companies may be unwilling to completely abandon their traditional performance management system because it serves as the basis for personnel selection validation, identification of training needs, or compensation decisions. Also, the quality approach advocates evaluation of personal traits (such as cooperation), which are difficult to relate to job performance unless the company has been structured into work teams.

In summary, organizations can take five approaches to measuring performance: comparative, attribute, behavioral, results, and quality. Table 8.9 summarizes the various approaches to measuring performance based on the criteria we set forth earlier and illustrates that each approach has strengths and weaknesses. As the quality approach illustrates, the most effective way of measuring performance is to rely on a combination of two or more alternatives. For example, performance management systems in

TABLE 8.9

Evaluation of Approaches to Performance Measurement

| | CRITERIA | | | | |
APPROACH	STRATEGIC CONGRUENCE	VALIDITY	RELIABILITY	ACCEPTABILITY	SPECIFICITY
Comparative	Poor, unless manager takes time to make link	Can be high if ratings are done carefully	Depends on rater, but usually no measure of agreement used	Moderate; easy to develop and use but resistant to normative standard	Very low
Attribute	Usually low; requires manager to make link	Usually low; can be fine if developed carefully	Usually low; can be improved by specific definitions of attributes	High; easy to develop and use	Very low
Behavioral	Can be quite high	Usually high; minimizes contamination and deficiency	Usually high	Moderate; difficult to develop, but accepted well for use	Very high
Results	Very high	Usually high; can be both contaminated and deficient	High; main problem can be test–retest— depends on timing of measure	High; usually developed with input from those to be evaluated	High regarding results, but low regarding behaviors necessary to achieve them
Quality	Very high	High, but can be both contaminated and deficient	High	High; usually developed with input from those to be evaluated	High regarding results, but low regarding behaviors necessary to achieve them

many companies evaluate the extent to which managers reach specific performance goals or results as well as evaluate their behavior. Figure 8.9 shows an example of a performance management system that evaluates behavior and results. The results (project development) are linked to the goals of the business. The performance standards include behaviors that the employee can demonstrate to reach the results. The system provides for feedback to the employee and holds both the employee and manager accountable for changing behavior.

Choosing a Source for Performance Information

Whatever approach to performance management is used, it is necessary to decide whom to use as the source of the performance measures. Each source has specific strengths and weaknesses. We discuss five primary sources: managers, peers, subordinates, self, and customers.

Managers

Managers are the most frequently used source of performance information. It is usually safe to assume that supervisors have extensive knowledge of the job requirements and that they have had adequate opportunity to observe their employees—in other words, that they have the ability to rate their employees. In addition, because supervisors have something to gain from the employees' high performance and something to lose from low performance, they are motivated to make accurate ratings.[48] Finally, feedback from supervisors is strongly related to performance and to employee perceptions of the accuracy of the appraisal if managers attempt to observe employee behavior or discuss performance issues in the feedback session.[49]

Burlington Northern Santa Fe Corporation of Fort Worth, Texas, improved its performance management process by holding leaders accountable in setting annual goals, creating individual development plans, providing feedback and coaching to employees, and self-evaluation.[50] An online performance management system supports the process. The company's executive team creates the overall company objectives, which cascade down to each department and individual employees who can now see how they contribute to the company's success. The online system allows managers and employees to see how they and the department are progressing on the objectives. Required to be engaged in the performance management process, managers are more focused on the necessary communications, coaching, and giving feedback, and they are more inclined to seek out training to be sure that they have the necessary communications, feedback, and coaching skills. Managers' effectiveness is monitored by periodic employee surveys that ask questions about whether the manager discusses performance, whether the dialogue with the manager is two-way, and whether the employee receives ongoing feedback.

Problems with using supervisors as the source of performance information can occur in particular situations. In some jobs, for example, the supervisor does not have an adequate opportunity to observe the employee performing his job duties. For example, in outside sales jobs, the supervisor does not have the opportunity to see the salesperson at work most of the time. This usually requires that the manager occasionally spend a day accompanying the salesperson on sales calls. However, on those occasions the employee will be on best behavior, so there is no assurance that performance that day accurately reflects performance when the manager is not around.

FIGURE 8.9

Example of a Performance Management System That Includes Behavior and Results

Accountabilities and Key Results	Performance Standards	Interim Feedback	Actual Results	Performance Rating	Areas for Development	Action
Key result areas that the employee will accomplish during the review period. Should align with company values, business goals, and job description.	How the key result area will be measured (quality, cost, quantity). Focus on work methods and accomplishments.	Employee and manager discuss performance on an ongoing basis.	Review actual performance for each key result.	Evaluate performance on each key result. 1 = Outstanding 2 = Highly effective 3 = Acceptable 4 = Unsatisfactory	Specific knowledge, skills, and behaviors to be developed that will help employee achieve key results.	What employee and manager will do to address development needs.
Project Development Manage the development of project scope, cost estimate studies, and schedules for approval.	Develop preliminary project material for approval within four weeks after receiving project scope. Eighty percent of new projects receive approval. Initial cost estimates are within 5% of final estimates.	Preliminary project materials are developed on time.	By end of year, approvals were at 75%, 5% less than standard.	3	Increase knowledge of project management software.	Read articles, research, and meet with software vendors.

Also, some supervisors may be so biased against a particular employee that to use the supervisor as the sole source of information would result in less-than-accurate measures for that individual. Favoritism is a fact of organizational life, but it is one that must be minimized as much as possible in performance management.[51] Thus, the performance evaluation system should seek to minimize the opportunities for favoritism to affect ratings. One way to do this is not to rely on only a supervisor's evaluation of an employee's performance.

While managers are the most frequently used source of performance information, it is ironic that upper level managers or chief executive officers, whose decisions affect all of the company's shareholders, rarely receive performance evaluation. This situation is beginning to change. For example, Thomas Loarie (chairman and CEO of KeraVision Inc., a vision correction company in California) is evaluated by the company's six directors.[52] The six nonmanagement directors evaluate Loarie each August during a retreat that lasts two or three days. The process is separate from that used to set his annual compensation. Directors use a 17-item questionnaire that focuses on four key areas: company performance, leadership, team building and management succession, and leadership of external stakeholders such as customers. The board rated him lower than he expected on involving its members. As a result of the appraisal, he has taken steps to get the board involved in setting the company's objectives. He has encouraged more interactions between senior managers and board members.

Although CEOs view appraisals such as Loarie's with anxiety, these appraisals are helpful in building an understanding with the board of directors. Such feedback is also useful for changing the CEO's strategy and policies, likely improving the bottom line. This translates into benefits for employees and shareholders alike!

Peers

Another source of performance information is the employee's coworkers. Peers are an excellent source of information in a job such as law enforcement, where the supervisor does not always observe the employee. Peers have expert knowledge of job requirements, and they often have the most opportunity to observe the employee in day-to-day activities. Peers also bring a different perspective to the evaluation process, which can be valuable in gaining an overall picture of the individual's performance. In fact, peers have been found to provide extremely valid assessments of performance in several different settings.[53]

One disadvantage of using peer ratings is the potential for friendship to bias ratings.[54] Little empirical evidence suggests that this is often a problem, however. Another disadvantage is that when the evaluations are made for administrative decisions, peers often find the situation of being both rater and ratee uncomfortable. When these ratings are used only for developmental purposes, however, peers react favorably.[55]

Subordinates

Subordinates are an especially valuable source of performance information when managers are evaluated. Subordinates often have the best opportunity to evaluate how well a manager treats employees. One recent study found that managers viewed receiving upward feedback more positively when receiving feedback from subordinates who were identified, but subordinates preferred to provide anonymous feedback. When subordinates were identified, they inflated their ratings of the manager.[56]

One problem with subordinate evaluations is that they give subordinates power over their managers, thus putting the manager in a difficult situation.[57] This can lead to managers' emphasizing employee satisfaction over productivity. However, this happens only when administrative decisions are made from these evaluations. As with peer evaluations, it is a good idea to use subordinate evaluations only for developmental purposes. To assure subordinates that they need not fear retribution from their managers, it is necessary to use anonymous evaluations and at least three subordinates for each manager.

Self

Although self-ratings are not often used as the sole source of performance information, they can still be valuable.[58] Obviously, individuals have extensive opportunities to observe their own behavior, and they usually have access to information regarding their results on the job. For example, hoping to quicken the pace of decision making and create a sense of urgency in its global workforce, General Motors has given salaried employees the chance to contribute to innovation and use of new technology.[59] Employees are given individual responsibility to contribute to corporate business results through a program known as the Performance Management Process (PMP). The PMP program established individual business objectives for salaried employees that must be linked to the employee's unit and to overall company goals. A recent survey indicates that 80 percent of GM's managers believe they are being held personally accountable for business results, compared to only 50 percent a few years ago.

One problem with self-ratings, however, is a tendency toward inflated assessments. This stems from two sources. If the ratings are going to be used for administrative decisions (like pay raises), it is in the employees' interests to inflate their ratings. And there is ample evidence in the social psychology literature that individuals attribute their poor performance to external causes, such as a coworker who they think has not provided them with timely information. Although self-ratings are less inflated when supervisors provide frequent performance feedback, it is not advisable to use them for administrative purposes.[60] The best use of self-ratings is as a prelude to the performance feedback session to get employees thinking about their performance and to focus discussion on areas of disagreement.

Customers

Service industries are expected to account for a major portion of job growth between 2002 and 2012.[61] As a result, we would expect many companies to move toward involving customers in their evaluation systems. One writer has defined *services* this way: "Services is something which can be bought and sold but which you cannot drop on your foot."[62] Because of the unique nature of services—the product is often produced and consumed on the spot—supervisors, peers, and subordinates often do not have the opportunity to observe employee behavior. Instead, the customer is often the only person present to observe the employee's performance and thus is the best source of performance information.

Many companies in service industries have moved toward customer evaluations of employee performance. Marriott Corporation provides a customer satisfaction card in every room and mails surveys to a random sample of customers after their stay in a Marriott hotel. Whirlpool's Consumer Services Division conducts both mail and telephone surveys of customers after factory service technicians have serviced their ap-

	SOURCE				
	SUPERVISOR	PEERS	SUBORDINATES	SELF	CUSTOMERS
Task					
Behaviors	Occasional	Frequent	Rare	Always	Frequent
Results	Frequent	Frequent	Occasional	Frequent	Frequent
Interpersonal					
Behaviors	Occasional	Frequent	Frequent	Always	Frequent
Results	Occasional	Frequent	Frequent	Frequent	Frequent

TABLE 8.10

Frequency of Observation for Various Sources of Performance Information

SOURCE: Adapted from K. Murphy and J. Cleveland, *Performance Appraisal: An Organizational Perspective* (Boston: Allyn & Bacon, 1991).

pliances. These surveys allow the company to evaluate an individual technician's customer-service behaviors while in the customer's home.

Using customer evaluations of employee performance is appropriate in two situations.[63] The first is when an employee's job requires direct service to the customer or linking the customer to other services within the company. Second, customer evaluations are appropriate when the company is interested in gathering information to determine what products and services the customer wants. That is, customer evaluations serve a strategic goal by integrating marketing strategies with human resource activities and policies. Customer evaluations collected for this purpose are useful for both evaluating the employee and helping to determine whether changes in other HRM activities (such as training or the compensation system) are needed to improve customer service.

The weakness of customer surveys is their expense. Printing, postage, telephone, and labor can add up to hundreds of dollars for the evaluation of one individual. Thus many companies conduct such evaluations only once a year for a short time.

In conclusion, the best source of performance information often depends on the particular job. One should choose the source or sources that provide the best opportunity to observe employee behavior and results. Table 8.10 summarizes this information for most jobs. Often, eliciting performance information from a variety of sources results in a performance management process that is accurate and effective. In fact, one recent popular trend in organizations is called **360-degree appraisals.**[64] This technique consists of having multiple raters (boss, peers, subordinates, customers) provide input into a manager's evaluation. The major advantage of the technique is that it provides a means for minimizing bias in an otherwise subjective evaluation technique. It has been used primarily for strategic and developmental purposes and is discussed in greater detail in Chapter 9.[65]

The "Competing through Technology" box shows how Seagate Technologies and Baxter Healthcare Corporation use technology to ensure that company, supervisor, and employee performance goals are aligned and understood.

360-degree appraisal
A performance appraisal process for managers that includes evaluations from a wide range of persons who interact with the manager. The process includes self-evaluations as well as evaluations from the manager's boss, subordinates, peers, and customers.

Rater Errors in Performance Measurement

Research consistently reveals that humans have tremendous limitations in processing information. Because we are so limited, we often use "heuristics," or simplifying mechanisms, to make judgments, whether about investments or about people.[66] These

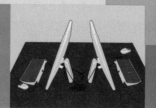

Online Goals Provide Clear Line of Site

Interest in the high-tech approach to performance management is growing. Surveys indicate that employee performance management is one of the top application initiatives among human resource executives with a greater priority than e-learning and employee self-service applications. Seagate Technologies and Baxter Healthcare Corporation are both using technology to ensure that employees understand the companies' priorities and that their efforts are aligned with the companies' business objectives. The biggest drawbacks of these systems are employees who procrastinate on setting goals, lack of involvement of managers, and lack of guidance on how to set goals. The systems in use at Seagate Technologies and Baxter Healthcare Corporation were designed to overcome these potential flaws.

Employees at Seagate Technologies receive annual performance reviews that are based on how close employees come to achieving their personal goals. The disk-drive company asked its professional workforce to consider the CEO's top five goals for the company in developing their own. The resulting 56,000 goals from 15,000 employees can now be viewed online by every employee in the company. The process started when the CEO added his goals to the Web application. In the following weeks, senior managers, executives, and professional workers signed onto the system, reviewed the goals set by their managers, and developed their own. Performance goal setting is an ongoing process. Each quarter managers work with employees on updating goals and a section of the website provides coaching on how to develop and align personal goals with the company goals. An employee can see all of the goals that have been set by managers above her or him all the way to the CEO. Online reminders alert employees of due dates for meeting goals and allow managers to transfer goals from one worker to others who might benefit from the same goals. When performance appraisals are conducted, software assigns a score to each employee based on his or her success at meeting goals through desired behaviors. Performance appraisals are based 70 percent on how well employees achieved their goals and 30 percent on the behaviors used to reach the goals. Scores are sent to a compensation system that helps determine raises. The system is also linked to the company's human resource database.

Baxter Healthcare Corporation has an automated goal-alignment system that about half of its 55,000 employees participate in. At Baxter the process starts with the company's top strategic goals known as the four B's (Best Team, Best Partner, Best Investments, Best Citizen). The executive team creates goals under each category. The top 150 executives then develop their goals, which are distributed to employees. The goals are collected in a performance management system. A website provides guidance on how to write goals, and achievement results are shared with the company's performance review and compensation systems. A manager of e-procurement of suppliers at Baxter who reports to the VP of purchasing says, "The biggest value is the digitization and consistent fashion of performance information. Historically we'd put this information into filing cabinets and pull it out once or twice a year. What this process is, really, is a tool that provides me with an opportunity to better understand Baxter's expectations of me and my team."

heuristics, which appear often in subjective measures of performance, can lead to rater errors. Performance evaluations may also be purposefully distorted. We discuss rater errors and appraisal politics next.

Similar to Me

"Similar to me" is the error we make when we judge those who are similar to us more highly than those who are not. Research has demonstrated that this effect is strong, and when similarity is based on demographic characteristics such as race or sex, it can result in discriminatory decisions.[67] Most of us tend to think of ourselves as effective, and so if others are like us—in race, gender, background, attitudes, or beliefs—we assume that they too are effective.

Contrast

Contrast error occurs when we compare individuals with one another instead of against an objective standard. Consider a completely competent performer who works with a number of peers who are outstanding. If the competent employee receives lower-than-deserved ratings because of the outstanding colleagues, that is contrast error.

Distributional Errors

Distributional errors are the result of a rater's tendency to use only one part of the rating scale. *Leniency* occurs when a rater assigns high (lenient) ratings to all employees. *Strictness* occurs when a manager gives low ratings to all employees—that is, holds all employees to unreasonably high standards. *Central tendency* reflects that a manager rates all employees in the middle of the scale. These errors pose two problems. First, they make it difficult to distinguish among employees rated by the same person. Second, they create problems in comparing the performance of individuals rated by different raters. If one rater is lenient and the other is strict, employees of the strict rater will receive significantly fewer rewards than those rated by the lenient rater.

Halo and Horns

These errors refer to a failure to distinguish among different aspects of performance. *Halo error* occurs when one positive performance aspect causes the rater to rate all other aspects of performance positively—for example, professors who are rated as outstanding researchers because they are known to be outstanding teachers. *Horns error* works in the opposite direction: one negative aspect results in the rater assigning low ratings to all the other aspects.

Halo and horns errors preclude making the necessary distinctions between strong and weak performance. Halo error leads to employees believing that no aspects of their performance need improvement. Horns error makes employees frustrated and defensive.

Reducing Rater Errors

Two approaches to reducing rating errors have been offered.[68] *Rater error training* attempts to make managers aware of rating errors and helps them develop strategies for minimizing those errors.[69] These programs consist of having the participants view

videotaped vignettes designed to elicit rating errors such as "contrast." They then make their ratings and discuss how the error influenced the rating. Finally, they get tips to avoid committing those errors. This approach has been shown to be effective for reducing errors, but there is evidence that reducing rating errors can also reduce accuracy.[70]

Rater accuracy training, also called *frame-of-reference training,* attempts to emphasize the multidimensional nature of performance and thoroughly familiarize raters with the actual content of various performance dimensions. This involves providing examples of performance for each dimension and then discussing the actual or "correct" level of performance that the example represents.[71] Accuracy training seems to increase accuracy, provided that in addition the raters are held accountable for ratings, job-related rating scales are used, and raters keep records of the behavior they observe.[72]

Appraisal Politics

Appraisal politics
A situation in which evaluators purposefully distort ratings to achieve personal or company goals.

Appraisal politics refer to evaluators purposefully distorting a rating to achieve personal or company goals. Research suggests that several factors promote appraisal politics. These factors are inherent in the appraisal system and the company culture. Appraisal politics are most likely to occur when raters are accountable to the employee being rated, there are competing rating goals, and a direct link exists between performance appraisal and highly desirable rewards. Also, appraisal politics are likely to occur if top executives tolerate distortion or are complacent toward it, and if distortion strategies are part of "company folklore" and are passed down from senior employees to new employees.

It is unlikely that appraisal politics can be completely eliminated. Unfortunately, there is little research on the best methods to eliminate appraisal politics. To minimize appraisal politics, managers should keep in mind the characteristics of a fair appraisal system shown in Table 8.3. In addition, managers should

- Train raters on the appropriate use of the process as discussed previously.
- Build top management support for the appraisal system and actively discourage distortion.
- Give raters some latitude to customize performance objectives and criteria for their ratees.
- Recognize employee accomplishments that are not self-promoted.
- Make sure constraints such as budget do not drive the process.
- Make sure appraisal processes are consistent across the company.
- Foster a climate of openness to encourage employees to be honest about weaknesses.[73]

Performance Feedback

Once the expected performance has been defined and employees' performances have been measured, it is necessary to feed that performance information back to the employees so they can correct any deficiencies. The performance feedback process is complex and provokes anxiety for both the manager and the employee. Table 8.11 provides examples of feedback that managers have given employees. You be the judge as to these statements' effectiveness in improving employees' performance!

Few of us feel comfortable sitting in judgment of others. The thought of confronting others with what we perceive to be their deficiencies causes most of us to

Since my last report; this employee has reached rock bottom and has started to dig.
His men would follow him anywhere, but only out of morbid curiosity.
I would not allow this employee to breed.
This associate is really not so much of a "has-been," but more of a "definitely won't-be."
Works well when under constant supervision and cornered like a rat in a trap.
When she opens her mouth, it seems that this is only to change whichever foot was previously in there.
He would be out of his depth in a parking-lot puddle.
This young lady has delusions of adequacy.
He sets low personal standards, then consistently fails to achieve them.
This employee should go far—and the sooner he starts, the better.
This employee is depriving a village somewhere of an idiot.

TABLE 8.11

Examples of Performance Feedback

SOURCE: Y. Harari, *The Daily Dose* (www.harari.org/index.html), July 22, 1997. Reprinted with permission.

shake in our shoes. If giving negative feedback is painful, receiving it can be excruciating—thus the importance of the performance feedback process.

Finding and Keeping the Best Employees

Synergy, Inc., headquartered in a Philadelphia suburb, provides incentive compensation plan management software for large companies. An important part of Synergy's culture is open communications and continuous feedback—not just between employee and manager but also between client and employee and between employees.

When the company consisted of only seven employees, Synergy had a very informal appraisal process. The seven employees would sit around a table and discuss performance issues. The informal appraisal process is no longer realistic because Synergy has grown to 260 employees. To maintain positive teamwork, Synergy has developed a unique employee evaluation program. One of the most important features is that Synergy employees are evaluated every quarter instead of the typical once-a-year evaluation. Management believes that to change behavior more frequent feedback is necessary. For their evaluations, employees are given a numerical score from 1 to 5 in addition to written comments. To motivate employees to improve their numbers, the evaluations are linked to compensation. The evaluation determines up to 40 percent of the quarterly bonus, which can be from 5 to 100 percent of an employee's base pay. Another important feature of the evaluation system is that employees can receive feedback from their managers, colleagues, and employees and managers in other departments. All feedback is anonymous except that provided by an employee's manager. Staff members are even encouraged to give feedback to managers and executives. Customers also contribute feedback to Synergy teams they work with. The feedback from multiple sources shows employees that others besides their managers see their performance similarly. The feedback also builds managers' confidence in their own evaluations when it matches the evaluations of others. If other evaluators disagree or identify possible barriers that inhibited performance, a manager may reconsider an evaluation.

One challenge of the evaluation program is that it requires a major commitment from both employees and managers to make it work. Employees can write comments for as many as 20 other employees in addition to their own self-evaluations and setting personal performance goals. For managers the process may take an entire week each quarter. But despite this large effort, the system has had some positive payoffs. Because the system gives managers plenty of opportunities to help employees improve, Synergy has terminated only 10 employees in the past eight years. Employees also appreciate the program because it helps them focus on what is important for themselves and for Synergy's success.[74]

The Manager's Role in an Effective Performance Feedback Process

If employees are not made aware of how their performance is not meeting expectations, their performance will almost certainly not improve. In fact, it may get worse. Effective managers provide specific performance feedback to employees in a way that elicits positive behavioral responses. To provide effective performance feedback managers should consider the following recommendations.

Feedback Should Be Given Frequently, Not Once a Year. There are two reasons for this. First, managers have a responsibility to correct performance deficiencies immediately on becoming aware of them. If performance is subpar in January, waiting until December to appraise the performance could mean an 11-month productivity loss. Second, a major determinant of the effectiveness of a feedback session is the degree to which the subordinate is not surprised by the evaluation. An easy rule to follow is that employees should receive such frequent performance feedback that they already know almost exactly what their formal evaluation will be.

Create the Right Context for the Discussion. Managers should choose a neutral location for the feedback session. The manager's office may not be the best place for a constructive feedback session because the employee may associate the office with unpleasant conversations. Managers should describe the meeting as an opportunity to discuss the role of the employee, the role of the manager, and the relationship between them. Managers should also acknowledge that they would like the meeting to be an open dialogue.

Ask the Employee to Rate His or Her Performance before the Session. Having employees complete a self-assessment before the feedback session can be very productive. It requires employees to think about their performance over the past rating period, and it encourages them to think about their weaknesses. Although self-ratings used for administrative decisions are often inflated, there is evidence that they may actually be lower than supervisors' ratings when done for developmental purposes. Another reason a self-assessment can be productive is that it can make the session go more smoothly by focusing discussion on areas where disagreement exists, resulting in a more efficient session. Finally, employees who have thought about past performance are more able to participate fully in the feedback session.

Encourage the Subordinate to Participate in the Session. Managers can take one of three approaches in performance feedback sessions. In the "tell-and-sell" approach, managers tell the employees how they have rated them and then justify these ratings. In the "tell-and-listen" approach, managers tell employees how they have rated them and then let the employees explain their side of the story. In the "problem-solving" approach, managers and employees work together to solve performance problems in an atmosphere of respect and encouragement. In spite of the research demonstrating the superiority of the problem-solving approach, most managers still rely on the tell-and-sell approach.[75]

When employees participate in the feedback session, they are consistently satisfied with the process. (Recall our discussion of fairness earlier in this chapter.) Participation includes allowing employees to voice their opinions of the evaluation, as well as discuss performance goals.[76] One study found that, other than satisfaction with one's supervisor, participation was the single most important predictor of satisfaction with the feedback session.[77]

Recognize Effective Performance through Praise. One usually thinks of performance feedback sessions as focusing on the employee's performance problems. This should never be the case. The purpose of the session is to give accurate performance feedback, which entails recognizing effective performance as well as poor performance. Praising effective performance provides reinforcement for that behavior. It also adds credibility to the feedback by making it clear that the manager is not just identifying performance problems.

Focus on Solving Problems. A common mistake that managers make in providing performance feedback is to try to use the session as a chance to punish poorly performing employees by telling them how utterly lousy their performance is. This only reduces the employees' self-esteem and increases defensiveness, neither of which will improve performance.

To improve poor performance, a manager must attempt to solve the problems causing it. This entails working with the employee to determine the actual cause and then agreeing on how to solve it. For example, a salesperson's failure to meet a sales goal may be the result of lack of a proper sales pitch, lack of product knowledge, or stolen sales by another salesperson. Each of these causes requires a different solution. Without a problem-solving approach, however, the correct solution might never be identified.

Focus Feedback on Behavior or Results, Not on the Person. One of the most important things to do when giving negative feedback is to avoid questioning the employee's worth as a person. This is best accomplished by focusing the discussion on the employee's behaviors or results, not on the employee. Saying "You're screwing up! You're just not motivated!" will bring about more defensiveness and ill feelings than stating "You did not meet the deadline that you agreed to because you spent too much time on another project."

Minimize Criticism. Obviously, if an individual's performance is below standard, some criticism must take place. However, an effective manager should resist the temptation to reel off a litany of offenses. Having been confronted with the performance problem, an employee often agrees that a change is in order. However, if the manager continues to come up with more and more examples of low performance, the employee may get defensive.

Agree to Specific Goals and Set a Date to Review Progress. The importance of goal setting cannot be overemphasized. It is one of the most effective motivators of performance.[78] Research has demonstrated that it results in increased satisfaction, motivation to improve, and performance improvement.[79] Besides setting goals, the manager must also set a specific follow-up date to review the employee's performance toward the goal. This provides an added incentive for the employee to take the goal seriously and work toward achieving it.

What Managers Can Do to Manage the Performance of Marginal Employees

As we emphasized in the previous discussion, employees need performance feedback to improve their current job performance. As we will discuss in Chapter 9, "Employee Development," performance feedback is also needed for employees to develop their knowledge and skills for the future. In addition to understanding how to effectively give employees performance feedback, managers need to be aware of what types of actions are likely to improve and maintain that performance. For example, giving performance feedback to marginal employees may not be sufficient for improving their performance. **Marginal employees** are those employees who are performing at a bare minimum level because of a lack of ability and/or motivation to perform well.[80]

marginal employee
An employee performing at a barely acceptable level because of lack of ability and/or motivation to perform well, not poor work conditions.

Table 8.12 shows actions for the manager to take with four different types of employees. As the table highlights, managers need to take into account whether employees lack ability, motivation, or both in considering ways to improve performance. To determine an employee's level of ability, a manager should consider if he or she has the knowledge, skills, and abilities needed to perform effectively. Lack of ability may be an issue if an employee is new or the job has recently changed. To determine employees' level of motivation, managers need to consider if employees are doing a job they want to do and if they feel they are being appropriately paid or rewarded. A sudden negative change in an employee's performance may indicate personal problems.

Employees with high ability and motivation are likely good performers (*solid performers*). Table 8.12 emphasizes that managers should not ignore employees with high

TABLE 8.12

Ways to Manage Employees' Performance

		ABILITY	
		HIGH	**LOW**
MOTIVATION	**High**	Solid performers • Reward good performance • Identify development opportunities • Provide honest, direct feedback	Misdirected effort • Coaching • Frequent performance feedback • Goal setting • Training or temporary assignment for skill development • Restructured job assignment
	Low	Underutilizers • Give honest, direct feedback • Provide counseling • Use team building and conflict resolution • Link rewards to performance outcomes • Offer training for needed knowledge or skills • Manage stress levels	Deadwood • Withholding pay increases • Demotion • Outplacement • Firing • Specific, direct feedback on performance problems

SOURCE: Based on M. London, *Job Feedback* (Mahwah, NJ: Lawrence Erlbaum Associates, 1997), pp. 96–97. Used by permission.

ability and high motivation. Managers should provide development opportunities to keep them satisfied and effective. Poor performance resulting from lack of ability but not motivation (*misdirected effort*) may be improved by skill development activities such as training or temporary assignments. Managers with employees who have the ability but lack motivation (*underutilizers*) need to consider actions that focus on interpersonal problems or incentives. These actions include making sure that incentives or rewards that the employee values are linked to performance and making counseling available to help employees deal with personal problems or career or job dissatisfaction. Chronic poor performance by employees with low ability and motivation (*deadwood*) indicates that outplacement or firing may be the best solution.

Developing and Implementing a System That Follows Legal Guidelines

We now discuss the legal issues and constraints affecting performance management. Because performance measures play a central role in such administrative decisions as promotions, pay raises, and discipline, employees who sue an organization over these decisions ultimately attack the measurement systems on which the decisions were made. Two types of cases have dominated: discrimination and unjust dismissal.

In discrimination suits, the plaintiff often alleges that the performance measurement system unjustly discriminated against the plaintiff because of race or gender. Many performance measures are subjective, and we have seen that individual biases can affect them, especially when those doing the measuring harbor racial or gender stereotypes.

In *Brito v. Zia*, the Supreme Court essentially equated performance measures with selection tests.[81] It ruled that the *Uniform Guidelines on Employee Selection Procedures* apply to evaluating the adequacy of a performance appraisal instrument. This ruling presents a challenge to those involved in developing performance measures, because a substantial body of research on race discrimination in performance rating has demonstrated that both white and black raters give higher ratings to members of their own racial group, even after rater training.[82] There is also evidence that the discriminatory biases in performance rating are worse when one group makes up a small percentage of the work group. When the vast majority of the group is male, females receive lower ratings; when the minority is male, males receive lower ratings.[83]

In the second type of suit, an unjust dismissal suit, the plaintiff claims that the dismissal was for reasons other than those the employer claims. For example, an employee who works for a defense contractor might blow the whistle on the company for defrauding the government. If the company fires the employee, claiming poor performance, the employee may argue that the firing was, in fact, because of blowing the whistle on the employer—in other words, that the dismissal was unjust. The court case will likely focus on the performance measurement system used as the basis for claiming the employee's performance was poor.

Because of the potential costs of discrimination and unjust dismissal suits, an organization needs to determine exactly what the courts consider a legally defensible performance management system. Based on reviews of such court decisions, we offer the following characteristics of a system that will withstand legal scrutiny.[84]

1. The system should be developed by conducting a valid job analysis that ascertains the important aspects of job performance. The requirements for job success should be clearly communicated to employees.

2. The system should be based on either behaviors or results; evaluations of ambiguous traits should be avoided.

3. Raters should be trained in how to use the system rather than simply given the materials and left to interpret how to conduct the appraisal.

4. There should be some form of review by upper-level managers of all the performance ratings, and there should be a system for employees to appeal what they consider to be an unfair evaluation.

5. The organization should provide some form of performance counseling or corrective guidance to help poor performers improve their performance before being dismissed. Both short- and long-term performance goals should be included.

6. Multiple raters should be used, particularly if an employee's performance is unlikely to be seen by only one rating source such as manager or customer. At a minimum, employees should be asked to comment on their appraisals. There should be a dialogue between the manager and the employee.

Use of Technology for Performance Management: Electronic Monitoring

An increasing trend in companies is using sophisticated electronic tracking systems to ensure that employees are working when they should be. The systems are used on both blue-collar and white-collar employees.[85] For example, at a New York law firm Akin & Smith LLC, paralegals, receptionists, and clerks clock in by placing their finger on a sensor kept at a secretary's desk. The managing partners believe the system improves productivity and keeps everyone honest, holding them to their lunch times. At Mitsubishi Motors North American plant in Normal, Illinois, accounting managers can check from their desktop computers how many of the plant's 500 white-collar employees have shown up for work. The employees clock in using a Web-based system on their desk computers. The 2,600 assembly line workers are also tracked. They "clock in" for work with an identification badge instead of a paper time card.

Economic Advantages Corporation, a mortgage service company with offices in Vermont and New York, installed an attendance tracking system. The new system implies that the company's salaried workers, client services representatives, get paid by the hour. The company's president believes that most employees put in an honest day's work, but those employees who decide to take time off won't get paid for it. Illiana Financial Credit Union in Calumet City, Illinois, uses a fingerprint recognition system to track its tellers and loan officers. This has saved the company payroll costs by preventing employees from exaggerating their hours worked by staying late or starting early.

Some argue that electronic tracking systems are needlessly surveilling and tracking employees when there is no reason to believe that anything is wrong. Good managers know what their employees are doing, and electronic systems should not be a substitute for good management. Critics also argue that such systems result in less productivity and motivation, demoralize employees, and create unnecessary stress. A mentality is created that employees have to always be at their desks to be productive. Advocates, on the other hand, counter that these systems ensure that time is not abused, they improve scheduling, and they help managers identify lazy workers. To avoid the potential negative effects of electronic monitoring, managers must communicate why employees are being monitored. Monitoring can also be used as a way for more experienced employees to coach less experienced employees.

In addition to monitoring, other types of electronic systems are being used to track attendance. TriB Nursery Inc., an Oklahoma plant wholesaler, is testing a hand-recognition system to replace a punch time-clock to track employees who work across 300 acres during the company's busiest season. The hand readers make it easier for managers to figure out how many workers are on the job at any given time. The system allows the nursery to identify employees and to shift them to areas where they are most needed, increasing efficiency. The system also prevents friends' clocking in for each other.

Using Performance Management Applications for Decision Making

Performance management applications are available to help managers monitor performance problems.[86] Software is available to help the manager customize performance rating forms for each job. The manager determines the performance standard for each job and rates each employee according to the appropriate standards. The manager receives a report summarizing the employees' strengths and weaknesses. The report also shows how different the employee's performance was from the established standard.

Performance diagnosis applications ask the manager for information about performance problems (e.g., Has the employee been trained in the skills that caused the performance problem?) and the work environment (e.g., Does the employee work under time pressure?). The software analyzes the information and provides solutions to consider in dealing with the performance problem.

A Look Back

The chapter opener on forced distribution highlighted the problems that companies are having with forced ranking appraisal systems that are used to differentiate above-average, average, and below-average employees. Companies remain challenged to find a performance management system that is acceptable to employees and managers alike yet allows managers to make important administrative decisions (like promotions, salary increases, and terminations).

Questions

1. Based on what was covered in the chapter, what type of performance system would you recommend that Goodyear, Ford, or Dow Chemical adopt to improve managers' performance and ability to deal with future business challenges?
2. What advantages will your system have over their current systems?

Summary

Measuring and managing performance is a challenging enterprise and one of the keys to gaining competitive advantage. Performance management systems serve strategic, administrative, and developmental purposes—their importance cannot be overestimated. A performance measurement system should be evaluated against the criteria of strategic congruence, validity, reliability, acceptability, and specificity. Measured against these criteria, the comparative, attribute, behavioral, results, and quality approaches have different strengths and weaknesses. Thus, deciding which approach and which source of performance information are best depends on the job in question. Effective managers need to be aware of the issues involved in determining the best method or combination of methods for their particular situations. In addition, once performance has been measured, a major component of a manager's job is to feed that performance information back to employees in a way that results in improved performance rather than defensiveness and decreased motivation. Managers should take action based on the causes for poor performance: ability, motivation, or both. Managers must be sure that their performance management system can meet legal scrutiny, especially if it is used to discipline or fire poor performers.

Discussion Questions

1. What are examples of administrative decisions that might be made in managing the performance of professors? Developmental decisions?
2. What would you consider the strategy of your university (e.g., research, undergraduate teaching, graduate teaching, a combination)? How might the performance management system for faculty members fulfill its strategic purpose of eliciting the types of behaviors and results required by this strategy?
3. If you were developing a performance measurement system for faculty members, what types of attributes would you seek to measure? Behaviors? Results?
4. What sources of performance information would you use to evaluate faculty members' performance?
5. The performance of students is usually evaluated with an overall results measure of grade point average. How is this measure contaminated? How is it deficient? What other measures might you use to more adequately evaluate student performance?
6. Think of the last time you had a conflict with another person, either at work or at school. Using the guidelines for performance feedback, how would you provide effective performance feedback to that person?
7. Explain what fairness has to do with performance management.
8. Why might a manager intentionally distort appraisal results? What would you recommend to minimize this problem?
9. Can computer monitoring of performance ever be acceptable to employees? Explain.

Self-Assessment Exercise

How do you like getting feedback? To test your attitudes toward feedback, take the following quiz. Read each statement, and write A next to each statement you agree with. If you disagree with the statement, write D.

_____ 1. I like being told how well I am doing on a project.

_____ 2. Even though I may think I have done a good job, I feel a lot more confident when someone else tells me so.

_____ 3. Even when I think I could have done something better, I feel good when other people think well of me for what I have done.

_____ 4. It is important for me to know what people think of my work.

_____ 5. I think my instructor would think worse of me if I asked him or her for feedback.

_____ 6. I would be nervous about asking my instructor how she or he evaluates my behavior in class.

_____ 7. It is not a good idea to ask my fellow students for feedback; they might think I am incompetent.

_____ 8. It is embarrassing to ask other students for their impression of how I am doing in class.

_____ 9. It would bother me to ask the instructor for feedback.

_____ 10. It is not a good idea to ask the instructor for feedback because he or she might think I am incompetent.

_____ 11. It is embarrassing to ask the instructor for feedback.

_____ 12. It is better to try to figure out how I am doing on my own, rather than to ask other students for feedback.

For statements 1–4, add the total number of As: _____

For statements 5–12, add the total number of As: _____

For statements 1–4, the greater the number of As, the greater your preference for and trust in feedback from others. For statements 5–12, the greater the number of As, the greater the risk you believe there is in asking for feedback.

How might this information be useful in understanding how you react to feedback in school or on the job?

SOURCE: Based on D. B. Fedor, R. B. Rensvold, and S. M. Adams, "An Investigation of Factors Expected to Affect Feedback Seeking: A Longitudinal Field Study," *Personnel Psychology* 45 (1992), pp. 779–805; S. J. Asford, "Feedback Seeking in Individual Adaptation: A Resource Perspective," *Academy of Management Journal* 29 (1986), pp. 465–87.

Manager's Hot Seat Exercise: Project Management: Steering the Committee

This Manager's Hot Seat case explores the dynamics often associated with conducting business meetings. As the scenario depicts, varying personalities, different levels of member participation, and differing agendas are vital components that strongly impact the success of business meetings. These components can strongly affect whether the meeting accomplishes its goals or not.

Group Activity:
All members of the class should form into a circle. Here is the scenario: Three production supervisors have just concluded a nonproductive meeting. The meeting was all about finger pointing, blaming other departments, and what was for lunch. The original purpose of this meeting was to identify department problems and determine how to get production levels back on track for the company.

In discussion, each class member is to identify how he or she feels the nonproductive meeting between these three manufacturing supervisors would impact the work performance of the department's workers. Discuss why focus during business meetings is vital to accomplishing established business goals. Identify ways meetings can be handled more successfully. Discuss how gaining knowledge on how to successfully conduct a business meeting may impact employee and organizational performance. Discuss how secure you would feel knowing your next performance evaluation would be handled by a supervisor that is known to goof off in important business meetings. Be descriptive and thorough in your responses.

Exercising Strategy: Are All Employees above Average?

Despite the problems with forced ranking systems, First Consulting Group, an IT health care consulting firm based in Long Beach, California, uses a forced ranking system. The company's system has five numerical grades that do not mandate the exact proportion of employees to be placed in different categories or what will happen to those employees. Rankings are combined with the results of traditional employee evaluations and project reviews to provide a comprehensive picture of each employee's strengths and weaknesses. Managers and coaches discuss each employee's performance for about 10 minutes and then each evaluator gives employees a numerical score. The scores for each employee are averaged. In a recent session rating 11 employees on a scale of 1 to 5 almost every employee was placed in the 2s and 3s. After discussion, the employ-

ees were spread out along the full scale. By the end of the discussion there was one top performer and one bottom performer with the other employees spread out between.

SOURCE: S. Bates, "Forced Ranking," *HR Magazine*, June 2003, pp. 63–68.

Questions
1. How does this type of performance management system potentially affect training and development and compensation?
2. Why might this type of ranking system work in comparison to those systems discussed in the chapter opener?
3. What recommendations would you give to First Consulting Group to make this system even more effective?

Managing People: From the Pages of *BusinessWeek*

BusinessWeek Focusing on the Softer Side of Managing

In the construction business, interpersonal skills are valued about as highly as rain on wet cement. It's a culture of muscle, not mouth.

Granite Construction, a $1.3 billion company in Watsonville, California, was no exception. For most of its 80 years, a call from the boss's office meant bad news. "Employees were only contacted when something went wrong," says division manager Bruce McGowan, a 20-year

veteran who oversees a staff of 700. Because it was corrective, feedback "tended to be negative."

No longer. Spurred by a tight labor market, Granite is starting to deliver feedback of the positive kind. And to make sure the idea takes, starting next year 20 percent of every manager's bonus—which sometimes exceeds 500 percent of base salary—will depend on the person's "people skills." Explains Mike Thomas, director of human resources, "In a market where everyone is struggling to keep people, we want to foster a culture that employees choose to be part of." `

Tying compensation to nonfinancial objectives isn't new—General Electric and Hewlett-Packard have done it for years. But more companies are embracing the idea. In a recent survey of 721 North American companies by management consultants Towers Perrin, 66 percent of respondents said they focused exclusively on financial results when assessing employee performance back in 1998. Today only 43 percent do. And that group will shrink to 16 percent by 2004, projects Towers Perrin, as greater attention is paid to softer skills, such as listening to subordinates and giving them opportunities to grow.

Granite, which already uses an anonymous rating system to let its 400 managers see how their coworkers, peers, and superiors perceive them, plans to use 20 touchy-feely metrics—chosen by employees themselves—when calculating bonuses next year. Two weeks ago, the company's 4,300 employees received an e-mail survey asking which skills best serve the company. According to Thomas, 81 percent mentioned integrity and ethics. An additional 79 percent cited teamwork, and 76 percent said knowledge-sharing abilities. The company is still deciding which criteria it will use next year.

Granite is modeling its approach on companies that have gone before. Wells Fargo has made worker satisfaction a top goal since its 1998 acquisition by Norwest, which took the Wells Fargo name. Accomplishing "people goals" at Wells Fargo is linked to 16–25 percent of every manager's annual bonus, which ranges from 10–30 percent of base salary.

Wells Fargo requires its 117,000 employees to take an automated phone survey every 18 months to answer such questions as "Do you get enough communication from management?" and "How was your training?" Now subordinates and managers talk more. Says Patricia Callahan, the company's human resources director, "Everyone is much clearer about what constitutes success." Julie Shriver, a recruitment director who has spent nine years at Wells Fargo, says, "It's nice that if you have people skills, you can be rewarded."

Still, it's unclear how much business sense it makes for companies to monkey with manager evaluations. According to Roland Van der Meer, a partner at ComVentures, a venture capital firm in Palo Alto, "An executive is a leader. He's driving a company and a team. Some of the best leaders aren't necessarily people we'd want to have a beer with."

In fact, in a Watson Wyatt Worldwide study last year

of 400 U.S. and Canadian companies, employee participation in a manager's review seemed to hurt shareholder return. Explains Brian Anderson, a senior consultant at the firm, "It's largely about implementation. If the appraisal isn't communicated properly, it can create disruption or tension that really takes you in the wrong direction."

That isn't the case at Wells Fargo, insists Callahan, a 25-year veteran. During her review last year, she heard from her nine direct reports that new employees weren't being trained well enough. "I'm not saying I didn't walk away feeling disappointed, or wishing I'd done something differently," she says. But, she adds, "Feedback is still a precious thing, even if it's not what you expect. Otherwise, you just don't know."

That explains why a manager's people skills may be key to a company's future performance. "Financial outcomes are results. They don't really get you ready for the future, or help you manage the process," says Jeffrey Pfeffer, a professor of organizational behavior at Stanford University's business school. Relying on them exclusively, he adds, is a little like "purchasing the present at the price of the future. If you get results in a way that's destructive of your people and culture, that performance won't last."

Granite's McGowan agrees. "Employees today are much more concerned about life satisfaction than they used to be, and that isn't something you ignore," he says. "Besides," he adds, "if you can't figure out how to help your people improve, and accelerate the rate at which they do, you're probably not going to meet the goals you've set for your overall business."

SOURCE: Reprinted from April 10, 2001 issue of *BusinessWeek* by special permission. Copyright © 2001 by The McGraw-Hill Companies, Inc.

Questions

1. Having direct reports, peers, and customers evaluate managers' people skills is a new idea for some companies. What steps would you recommend a company take if they were going to introduce an evaluation system to help ensure that managers accept this type of evaluation system?

2. Advocates of the quality approach argue that systems factors (factors not under the control of the person being evaluated) need to be taken into account in performance management systems. What systems factors might affect how managers' direct reports evaluate their people skills? If you were asked to design an evaluation system that focused on managers' "people skills," what features would you include to either eliminate the influence of or take account of systems factors?

Notes

1. C. Lee, "Performance Appraisal: Can We Manage Away the Curse?" *Training,* May 1996, pp. 44–49.
2. "Measuring People Power," *Fortune* (October 2, 2000).
3. K. Murphy and J. Cleveland, *Performance Appraisal: An Organizational Perspective* (Boston: Allyn & Bacon, 1991).
4. Commerce Clearing House, *Performance Appraisal: What Three*

Companies Are Doing (Chicago, IL: Commerce Clearing House, 1985).

5. J. Cleveland, K. Murphy, and R. Williams, "Multiple Uses of Performance Appraisal: Prevalence and Correlates," *Journal of Applied Psychology* 74 (1989), pp. 130–35.

6. Ibid.

7. C. Longenecker, "Behind the Mask: The Politics of Employee Appraisal," *Academy of Management Executive* 1 (1987), p. 183.

8. M. Beer, "Note on Performance Appraisal," in *Readings in Human Resource Management*, ed. M. Beer and B. Spector (New York: Free Press, 1985).

9. L. Weatherly, *Performance Management: Getting It Right from the Start* (Alexandria, VA: Society for Human Resource Management, 2004).

10. E. Lawler and M. McDermott, "Current Performance Management Practices," *World at Work Journal* 12, no. 2, (2003), pp. 49–60.

11. C. Cole, "Eight Values Bring Unity to a Worldwide Force," *Workforce*, March 2001, pp. 44–45; General Semiconductor website, www.generalsemiconductor.com, September 2, 2001.

12. C. G. Banks and K. E. May, "Performance Management: The Real Glue in Organizations," in *Evolving Practices in Human Resource Management*, ed. A. Kraut and A. Korman (San Francisco: Jossey-Bass, 1999), pp. 118–45.

13. C. E. Schneier, D. G. Shaw, and R. W. Beatty, "Performance Measurement and Management: A Tool for Strategic Execution," *Human Resource Management* 30 (1991), pp. 279–301.

14. C. D. Ittner and D. F. Larcker, "Coming Up Short on Nonfinancial Performance Measurement," *Harvard Business Review*, December 2003, pp. 88–95.

15. J. K. Harter, F. Schmidt, and T. L. Hayes, "Business-Unit Level Relationships between Employee Satisfaction, Employee Engagement, and Business Outcomes: A Meta-Analysis," *Journal of Applied Psychology* 87 (2002), pp. 268–79.

16. A. J. Rucci, S. P. Kirn, and R. T. Quinn, "The Employee-Customer-Profit Chain at Sears," *Harvard Business Review*, January–February 1998, pp. 82–97.

17. R. Schuler and S. Jackson, "Linking Competitive Strategies with Human Resource Practices," *Academy of Management Executive* 1 (1987), pp. 207–19.

18. L. King, J. Hunter, and F. Schmidt, "Halo in a Multidimensional Forced-Choice Performance Evaluation Scale," *Journal of Applied Psychology* 65 (1980), pp. 507–16.

19. B. R. Nathan, A. M. Mohrman, and J. Millman, "Interpersonal Relations as a Context for the Effects of Appraisal Interviews on Performance and Satisfaction: A Longitudinal Study," *Academy of Management Journal* 34 (1991), pp. 352–69; M. S. Taylor, K. B. Tracy, M. K. Renard, J. K. Harrison, and S. J. Carroll, "Due Process in Performance Appraisal: A Quasi-experiment in Procedural Justice," *Administrative Science Quarterly* 40 (1995), pp. 495–523; J. M. Werner and M. C. Bolino, "Explaining U.S. Courts of Appeals Decisions Involving Performance Appraisal: Accuracy, Fairness, and Validation," *Personnel Psychology* 50 (1997), pp. 1–24.

20. *Albermarle Paper Company v. Moody*, 10 FEP 1181 (1975).

21. F. Blanz and E. Ghiselli, "The Mixed Standard Scale: A New Rating System," *Personnel Psychology* 25 (1973), pp. 185–99; K. Murphy and J. Constans, "Behavioral Anchors as a Source of Bias in Rating," *Journal of Applied Psychology* 72 (1987), pp. 573–77.

22. P. Smith and L. Kendall, "Retranslation of Expectations: An Approach to the Construction of Unambiguous Anchors for Rating Scales," *Journal of Applied Psychology* 47 (1963), pp. 149–55.

23. Murphy and Constans, "Behavioral Anchors"; M. Piotrowski, J. Barnes-Farrel, and F. Esrig, "Behaviorally Anchored Bias: A Replication and Extension of Murphy and Constans," *Journal of Applied Psychology* 74 (1989), pp. 823–26.

24. U. Wiersma and G. Latham, "The Practicality of Behavioral Observation Scales, Behavioral Expectation Scales, and Trait Scales," *Personnel Psychology* 39 (1986), pp. 619–28.

25. G. Latham and K. Wexley, *Increasing Productivity through Performance Appraisal* (Boston: Addison-Wesley, 1981).

26. Wiersma and Latham, "The Practicality of Behavioral Observation Scales, Behavioral Expectation Scales, and Trait Scales."

27. D. C. Anderson, C. Crowell, J. Sucec, K. Gilligan, and M. Wikoff, "Behavior Management of Client Contacts in a Real Estate Brokerage: Getting Agents to Sell More," *Journal of Organizational Behavior Management* 4 (1983), pp. 67–96; A. D. Stajkovic and F. Luthans, "Differential Effects of Incentive Motivation on Work Performance," *Academy of Management Journal* 4 (2001), pp. 580–90; F. Luthans and R. Kreitner, *Organizational Behavior Modification and Beyond* (Glenview, IL: Scott Foresman, 1975).

28. K. L. Langeland, C. M. Jones, and T. C. Mawhinney, "Improving Staff Performance in a Community Mental Health Setting: Job Analysis, Training, Goal Setting, Feedback, and Years of Data," *Journal of Organizational Behavior Management* 18 (1998), pp. 21–43.

29. J. Komaki, R. Collins, and P. Penn, "The Role of Performance Antecedents and Consequences in Work Motivation," *Journal of Applied Psychology* 67 (1982), pp. 334–40.

30. Latham and Wexley, *Increasing Productivity through Performance Appraisal*.

31. S. Snell, "Control Theory in Strategic Human Resource Management: The Mediating Effect of Administrative Information," *Academy of Management Journal* 35 (1992), pp. 292–327.

32. T. Patten, Jr., *A Manager's Guide to Performance Appraisal* (New York: Free Press, 1982).

33. M. O'Donnell and R. O'Donnell, "MBO—Is It Passe?" *Hospital and Health Services Administration* 28, no. 5 (1983), pp. 46–58; T. Poister and G. Streib, "Management Tools in Government: Trends over the Past Decade," *Public Administration Review* 49 (1989), pp. 240–48.

34. D. McGregor, "An Uneasy Look at Performance Appraisal," *Harvard Business Review* 35, no. 3 (1957), pp. 89–94.

35. E. Locke and G. Latham, *A Theory of Goal Setting and Task Performance* (Englewood Cliffs, NJ: Prentice Hall, 1990).

36. S. Carroll and H. Tosi, *Management by Objectives* (New York: Macmillan, 1973).

37. G. Odiorne, *MBO II: A System of Managerial Leadership for the 80's* (Belmont, CA: Pitman, 1986).

38. R. Rodgers and J. Hunter, "Impact of Management by Objectives on Organizational Productivity," *Journal of Applied Psychology* 76 (1991), pp. 322–26.

39. Kevin Helliker, "Pressure at Pier 1: Beating Sales Numbers of Year Earlier Is a Storewide Obsession," *The Wall Street Journal* (December 7, 1995), pp. B1, B2.

40. R. Pritchard, S. Jones, P. Roth, K. Stuebing, and S. Ekeberg, "The Evaluation of an Integrated Approach to Measuring Organizational Productivity," *Personnel Psychology* 42 (1989), pp. 69–115.

41. P. Wright, J. George, S. Farnsworth, and G. McMahan, "Productivity and Extra-Role Behavior: The Effects of Goals and Incentives on Spontaneous Helping," *Journal of Applied Psychology* 78, no. 3 (1993), pp. 374–81.

42. Latham and Wexley, *Increasing Productivity through Performance Appraisal*.

43. R. L. Cardy, "Performance Appraisal in a Quality Context: A New Look at an Old Problem," in *Performance Appraisal: State of the Art in Practice,* ed. J. W. Smither (San Francisco: Jossey-Bass, 1998), pp. 132–62.

44. E. C. Huge, *Total Quality: An Executive's Guide for the 1990s* (Homewood, IL: Richard D. Irwin, 1990): see Chapter 5, "Measuring and Rewarding Performance," pp. 70–88; W. E. Deming, *Out of Crisis* (Cambridge, MA: MIT Center for Advanced Engineering Study, 1986).

45. M. Caroselli, *Total Quality Transformations* (Amherst, MA: Human Resource Development Press, 1991); Huge, *Total Quality.*

46. J. D. Cryer and R. B. Miller, *Statistics for Business: Data Analysis and Modeling* (Boston: PWS-Kent, 1991); C. Carter, "Seven Basic Quality Tools," *HR Magazine,* January 1992, pp. 81–83; D. K. Denton, "Process Mapping Trims Cycle Time," *HR Magazine,* February 1995, pp. 56–61.

47. D. E. Bowen and E. E. Lawler III, "Total Quality-Oriented Human Resource Management," *Organizational Dynamics* 21 (1992), pp. 29–41.

48. R. Heneman, K. Wexley, and M. Moore, "Performance Rating Accuracy: A Critical Review," *Journal of Business Research* 15 (1987), pp. 431–48.

49. T. Becker and R. Klimoski, "A Field Study of the Relationship between the Organizational Feedback Environment and Performance," *Personnel Psychology* 42 (1989), pp. 343–58; H. M. Findley, W. F. Giles, K. W. Mossholder, "Performance Appraisal and Systems Facets: Relationships with Contextual Performance," *Journal of Applied Psychology* 85 (2000) pp. 634–40.

50. K. Ellis, "Developing for Dollars," *Training,* May 2003, pp. 34–39.

51. L. Axline, "Performance Biased Evaluations," *Supervisory Management,* November 1991, p. 3.

52. T. Schellhardt, "Behind the Scenes at One CEO's Performance Review," *The Wall Street Journal* (April 27, 1998), pp. B1–B2. Reprinted by permission.

53. K. Wexley and R. Klimoski, "Performance Appraisal: An Update," in *Research in Personnel and Human Resource Management* (vol. 2), ed. K. Rowland and G. Ferris (Greenwich, CT: JAI Press, 1984).

54. F. Landy and J. Farr, *The Measurement of Work Performance: Methods, Theory, and Applications* (New York: Academic Press, 1983).

55. G. McEvoy and P. Buller, "User Acceptance of Peer Appraisals in an Industrial Setting," *Personnel Psychology* 40 (1987), pp. 785–97.

56. D. Antonioni, "The Effects of Feedback Accountability on Upward Appraisal Ratings," *Personnel Psychology* 47 (1994), pp. 349–56.

57. Murphy and Cleveland, *Performance Appraisal: An Organizational Perspective.*

58. J. Bernardin and L. Klatt, "Managerial Appraisal Systems: Has Practice Caught Up with the State of the Art?" *Public Personnel Administrator,* November 1985, pp. 79–86.

59. D. Shuit, "GM Goes Fast," *Workforce Management,* March 2004, pp. 36–38.

60. R. Steel and N. Ovalle, "Self-Appraisal Based on Supervisor Feedback," *Personnel Psychology* 37 (1984), pp. 667–85; L. E. Atwater, "The Advantages and Pitfalls of Self-Assessment in Organizations," in *Performance Appraisal: State of the Art in Practice,* pp. 331–65.

61. M. W. Horrigan, "Employment Projections to 2012: Concepts and Context," *Monthly Labor Review* 127 (2004), pp. 3–11.

62. E. Gummerson, "Lip Services—A Neglected Area of Service Marketing," *Journal of Services Marketing* 1 (1987), pp. 1–29.

63. J. Bernardin, B. Hagan, J. Kane, and P. Villanova, "Effective Performance Management: A Focus on Precision, Customers, and Situational Constraints," in *Performance Appraisal: State of the Art in Practice,* ed. J. W. Smither (San Francisco: Jossey-Bass, 1998), pp. 3–48.

64. R. Hoffman, "Ten Reasons You Should Be Using 360-Degree Feedback," *HR Magazine,* April 1995, pp. 82–84.

65. S. Sherman, "How Tomorrow's Best Leaders Are Learning Their Stuff," *Fortune* (November 27, 1995), pp. 90–104; W. W. Tornow, M. London, and Associates, *Maximizing the Value of 360-Degree Feedback* (San Francisco: Jossey-Bass, 1998); D. A. Waldman, L. E. Atwater, and D. Antonioni, "Has 360-Degree Feedback Gone Amok?" *Academy of Management Executive* 12 (1988), pp. 86–94.

66. A. Tversky and D. Kahneman, "Availability: A Heuristic for Judging Frequency and Probability," *Cognitive Psychology* 5 (1973), pp. 207–32.

67. K. Wexley and W. Nemeroff, "Effects of Racial Prejudice, Race of Applicant, and Biographical Similarity on Interviewer Evaluations of Job Applicants," *Journal of Social and Behavioral Sciences* 20 (1974), pp. 66–78.

68. D. Smith, "Training Programs for Performance Appraisal: A Review," *Academy of Management Review* 11 (1986), pp. 22–40.

69. G. Latham, K. Wexley, and E. Pursell, "Training Managers to Minimize Rating Errors in the Observation of Behavior," *Journal of Applied Psychology* 60 (1975), pp. 550–55.

70. J. Bernardin and E. Pence, "Effects of Rater Training: Creating New Response Sets and Decreasing Accuracy," *Journal of Applied Psychology* 65 (1980), pp. 60–66.

71. E. Pulakos, "A Comparison of Rater Training Programs: Error Training and Accuracy Training," *Journal of Applied Psychology* 69 (1984), pp. 581–88.

72. H. J. Bernardin, M. R. Buckley, C. L. Tyler, and D. S. Wiese, "A Reconsideration of Strategies in Rater Training," in *Research in Personnel and Human Resource Management,* vol. 18, ed. G. R. Ferris (Greenwich, CT: JAI Press, 2000), pp. 221–74.

73. S. W. J. Kozlowski, G. T. Chao, and R. F. Morrison, "Games Raters Play: Politics, Strategies, and Impression Management in Performance Appraisal," in *Performance Appraisal: State of the Art in Practice,* pp. 163–205.

74. P. Kiger, "Frequent Employee Feedback Is Worth the Cost and Time," *Workforce,* March 2001, pp. 62–65.

75. K. Wexley, V. Singh, and G. Yukl, "Subordinate Participation in Three Types of Appraisal Interviews," *Journal of Applied Psychology* 58 (1973), pp. 54–57; K. Wexley, "Appraisal Interview," in *Performance Assessment,* ed. R. A. Berk (Baltimore: Johns Hopkins University Press, 1986), pp. 167–85.

76. D. Cederblom, "The Performance Appraisal Interview: A Review, Implications, and Suggestions," *Academy of Management Review* 7 (1982), pp. 219–27; B. D. Cawley, L. M. Keeping, and P. E. Levy, "Participation in the Performance Appraisal Process and Employee Reactions: A Meta-analytic Review of Field Investigations," *Journal of Applied Psychology* 83, no. 3 (1998), pp. 615–63.

77. W. Giles and K. Mossholder, "Employee Reactions to Contextual and Session Components of Performance Appraisal," *Journal of Applied Psychology* 75 (1990), pp. 371–77.

78. E. Locke and G. Latham, *A Theory of Goal Setting and Task Performance* (Englewood Cliffs, NJ: Prentice Hall, 1990).

79. H. Klein, S. Snell, and K. Wexley, "A Systems Model of the Performance Appraisal Interview Process," *Industrial Relations* 26 (1987), pp. 267–80.

80. M. London and E. M. Mone, "Managing Marginal Performance

in Organizations Striving for Excellence," in *Human Resource Dilemmas in Work Organizations: Strategies for Resolution*, ed. A. K. Korman (New York: Guilford, 1993), pp. 95–124.

81. *Brito v. Zia Co.*, 478 F.2d 1200 (10th. Cir. 1973).

82. K. Kraiger and J. Ford, "A Meta-Analysis of Ratee Race Effects in Performance Rating," *Journal of Applied Psychology* 70 (1985), pp. 56–65.

83. P. Sackett, C. DuBois, and A. Noe, "Tokenism in Performance Evaluation: The Effects of Work Groups Representation on Male–Female and White–Black Differences in Performance Ratings," *Journal of Applied Psychology* 76 (1991), pp. 263–67.

84. G. Barrett and M. Kernan, "Performance Appraisal and Terminations: A Review of Court Decisions since *Brito v. Zia* with Implications for Personnel Practices," *Personnel Psychology* 40 (1987), pp. 489–503; H. Field and W. Holley, "The Relationship of Performance Appraisal System Characteristics to Verdicts in Selected Employment Discrimination Cases," *Academy of Management Journal* 25 (1982), pp. 392–406; J. M. Werner and M. C. Bolino, "Explaining U.S. Courts of Appeals Decisions Involving Performance Appraisal: Accuracy, Fairness, and Validation," *Personnel Psychology* 50 (1997), pp. 1–24; J. A. Segal, "86 Your Appraisal Process," *HR Magazine*, October 2000, pp. 199–202.

85. K. Maher, "Big Employer Is Watching," *The Wall Street Journal* (November 4, 2003), pp. B1 and B6.

86. G. Bylinsky, "How Companies Spy on Employees," *Fortune* (November 4, 1991), pp. 131–40; T. L. Griffith, "Teaching Big Brother to Be a Team Player: Computer Monitoring and Quality," *Academy of Management Executive* (1993), pp. 73–80.

9 Chapter

Employee Development

Objectives After reading this chapter, you should be able to:

1. Discuss current trends in using formal education for development.

2. Relate how assessment of personality type, work behaviors, and job performance can be used for employee development.

3. Develop successful mentoring programs.

4. Explain how job experiences can be used for skill development.

5. Tell how to train managers to coach employees.

6. Discuss the steps in the development planning process.

7. Explain the employees' and company's responsibilities in planning development.

8. Discuss what companies are doing for management development issues including succession planning, melting the glass ceiling, and helping dysfunctional managers.

9. Explain how employee development contributes to strategies related to employee retention, developing intellectual capital, and business growth.

Booz | Allen | Hamilton
90 years **delivering results that endure**   about us   services   industries   careers   publications

strategy and technology consulting   search

delivering results that endure

SITE MAP | FEEDBACK | CONTACT   TEXT ONLY   LANGUAGE PREFERENCE

Booz Allen Quicklinks

alumni
careers
clients
community relations
global presence
gov't contract vehicles
media inquiries
multimedia library
news & ideas
press highlights
strategy+business
Booz Allen Classic

about us : : news & ideas

Study Says RFID is Still in its Infancy
Booz Allen believes that, for many companies, investment in
RFID technology still presents risks.

No-Frills CRM
By leveraging the customer data it already possesses, a
company can improve customer profitability and uncover
new opportunities.

**Channel Strategy and Trade Management in Book
Publishing**
VPs say today's approach to the trade does not meet the
needs of publishers or retailers.

**Europe's Service Sector May Be the Next to Adopt a Low-
Cost Business Model**

global presence

> Asia, Australia, &
  South Pacific
> Europe, Middle East,
  & Africa
> Latin America
> North America

spotlight on

**Measuring and
Analyzing
Corporate Values
During Major
Transformations**

Not so long ago,
corporate values were

*The Booz Allen Hamilton development framework
allows employees to strengthen their performance
and manage their careers—at any level within the
company. What employee development tools might
be important to you in your career?*

Enter the World of Business

Developing Employees Increases Intellectual Capital at Booz Allen Hamilton

Booz Allen Hamilton, a strategy and technology
consulting company headquartered in McLean,
Virginia, uses a program they call the
Development Framework to help managers and
employees choose the right combination of
development activities to strengthen
competencies and manage their careers.
Employee development is especially important at
a firm like Booz Allen Hamilton whose business
success is based on the ability of its workforce to
sell and deliver consulting and technology
solutions. These solutions are only as good as
the intellectual capital (knowledge, skills,
competencies, abilities) of the employees
creating them. The Development Framework
consists of four sections:

1. *Development roles:* Managers, mentors,
   development staff, and other roles in the
   development process.
2. *Performance expectations:* A description of
   competencies, performance results, and major
   job experiences required to succeed at each
   level of the company.

3. *Development needs:* Needs that frequently
   occur at each career level, those that vary by
   individual, and the derailers that can stall
   career progress and negatively affect
   performance. Ways to prevent or deal with
   derailers are provided.
4. *Development road map:* Descriptions of
   development activities that should occur at
   each career level and that support
   development needs and prevent derailers.
   These activities include job experiences,
   training and education, coaching and
   mentoring, and self-directed experiences.

Employees can access the Development
Framework online via the company's virtual
campus and website. Managers can use the tool
to discuss development needs in their
departments. The framework includes the
competencies for each staff level and for each
employee, which allows employees to view their
personal development needs online. By
identifying the competencies that employees
want to strengthen, the framework provides a list
of activities employees can use to develop those
competencies. Employees can use the
Development Framework to take charge of their
own careers. The framework helps employees
answer questions such as "I'm at this level and
this person is above me; how can I get there?"

The framework was provided by Booz Allen Hamilton to help employees better understand how to develop themselves. Booz Allen Hamilton views development as a shared responsibility between employees and the company. The framework helps employees realize that development can occur through activities other than training classes. The framework makes a strong business case for employee development by aligning development to the business strategy and to different levels of the company; the program provides a process for simultaneously building the company's intellectual capital and helping employees build successful careers. The framework also provides a map for preparing potential leaders, which is important because the company is growing 20 percent per year.

Source: Based on G. Johnson, "The Development Framework," *Training,* February 2003, pp. 32–36.

Introduction

As the Booz Allen Hamilton example illustrates, employee development is a key contributor to a business strategy based on developing intellectual capital, helps develop managerial talent, and allows employees to take responsibility for their careers. Employee development is a necessary component of a company's efforts to compete in the new economy, to meet the challenges of global competition and social change, and to incorporate technological advances and changes in work design. Employee development is key to ensuring that employees have the competencies necessary to serve customers and create new products and customer solutions. Employee development is also important to ensure that companies have the managerial talent needed to successfully execute a growth strategy. Regardless of the business strategy, development is important for retaining talented employees. Also because companies (and their employees) must constantly learn and change to meet customer needs and compete in new markets, the emphasis placed on both training and development has increased. As we noted in Chapter 1, employee commitment and retention are directly related to how employees are treated by their managers.

Finding and Keeping the Best Employees

To "win the war for talent," managers need to be able to identify high-potential employees, make sure their talents are used, and reassure them of their value before they become dissatisfied and leave the company. Managers also need to be able to listen. Although new employees need strong direction and bosses who can make quick decisions, they expect to be able to challenge managers' thinking and be treated with respect and dignity. Because of their skills, many employees are in high demand and can easily leave for a competitor.

Development activities can help companies reduce turnover in two ways: (1) by showing employees that the company is investing in the employees' skill development, and (2) by developing managers who can create a positive work environment that makes employees want to come to work and contribute to the company goals. One of the major reasons that good employees leave companies is poor relationships with their managers. Companies need to retain their talented employees or risk losing their competitive advantage. Development activities can help companies with employee retention by developing managers' skills. Sprint PCS used 360-degree feedback as a way to help develop people skills in its managers of customer contact centers.[1] That is, the company wanted its managers to develop skills in communication, creating trust, coaching, and other interpersonal actions that would help the company retain good employees. Managers who scored high on the 360-degree assessment were also ranked by their employees as high in providing career development help and support (key reasons employees stayed with Sprint). The 360-degree assessment was linked to a development plan, and each interpersonal skill could be developed through online training. Sprint set a goal to reduce turnover to 48 percent. Every Sprint location that completed the 360-degree assessment met the goal!

This chapter begins by discussing the relationship between development, training, and careers. Second, we look at development approaches, including formal education, assessment, job experiences, and interpersonal relationships. The chapter emphasizes the types of skills, knowledge, and behaviors that are strengthened by each development method. Choosing an approach is one part of development planning. Before one or multiple developmental approaches are used, the employee and the company must have an idea of the employee's development needs and the purpose of development. Identifying the needs and purpose of development is part of its planning. The third section of the chapter describes the steps of the development planning process. Employee and company responsibilities at each step of the process are emphasized. The chapter concludes with a discussion of special issues in employee development, including succession planning, dealing with dysfunctional managers, and using development to help women and minorities move into upper-level management positions (referred to as "melting the glass ceiling").

The Relationship between Development, Training, and Careers

Development and Training

Development refers to formal education, job experiences, relationships, and assessment of personality and abilities that help employees prepare for the future. Because it is future-oriented, it involves learning that is not necessarily related to the employee's current job.[2] Table 9.1 shows the differences between training and development. Traditionally, training focuses on helping employees' performance in their current jobs. Development prepares them for other positions in the company and increases their ability to move into jobs that may not yet exist.[3] Development also helps employees prepare for changes in their current jobs that may result from new technology, work designs, new customers, or new product markets. Chapter 7 emphasized the strategic role of training. As training continues to become more strategic (that is, related to business goals), the distinction between training and development will blur.

Development
The acquisition of knowledge, skills, and behaviors that improve an employee's ability to meet changes in job requirements and in client and customer demands.

	TRAINING	DEVELOPMENT
Focus	Current	Future
Use of work experiences	Low	High
Goal	Preparation for current job	Preparation for changes
Participation	Required	Voluntary

TABLE 9.1

Comparison between Training and Development

Development and Careers

Traditionally, careers have been described in various ways.[4] Careers have been described as a sequence of positions held within an occupation. For example, a university faculty member can hold assistant, associate, and full professor positions. A career has also been described in the context of mobility within an organization. For example, an engineer may begin her career as a staff engineer. As her expertise, experience, and performance increase, she may move through advisory engineering, senior engineering, and senior technical positions. Finally, a career has been described as a characteristic of the employee. Each employee's career consists of different jobs, positions, and experiences.

Protean career
A career that is frequently changing due to both changes in the person's interests, abilities, and values and changes in the work environment.

The new concept of the career is often referred to as a "protean career."[5] A **protean career** is a career that frequently changes based on changes in the person's interests, abilities, and values and also in the work environment. Compared to the traditional career view, employees here take major responsibility for managing their careers. For example, an engineer may decide to take a sabbatical from her position to work in management at the United Way Agency for a year. The purpose of this assignment could be to develop her managerial skills as well as help her personally evaluate if she likes managerial work more than engineering.

Psychological contract
The expectations that employers and employees have about each other.

Changes in the psychological contract between employees and their companies have influenced the development of the protean career.[6] A **psychological contract** is the expectations that employers and employees have about each other. Traditionally, the psychological contract emphasized that the company would provide continued employment (job security) and advancement opportunities if the employee remained with the company and performed well. Pay increases and status were linked directly to vertical movement in the company (promotions).

Instead of offering job security, companies can offer employees opportunities to attend training programs and participate in work experiences that can increase their employability with their current and future employers. For example, the term *blue-collar work* has always meant manufacturing work, but technology has transformed the meaning dramatically.[7] Traditional assembly-line jobs that required little skill and less education have been sent overseas. Today's blue-collar workers are more involved in customized manufacturing. At U.S. Steel employees make more than 700 different kinds of steel, requiring greater familiarity with additives and more understanding of customers and markets. Jobs once considered as lifetime employment are now more temporary, forcing employees to adapt by moving from one factory to another or by changing work shifts. Employees are taking classes to keep up with the latest developments in steelmaking, such as lathes and resins. Despite the lack of guaranteed lifetime employment, many blue-collar jobs are safer and better paying than they were 10 years ago.

Psychological success
The feeling of pride and accomplishment that comes from achieving life goals.

The protean career has several implications for employee development. The goal of the new career is **psychological success:** the feeling of pride and accomplishment that comes from achieving life goals that are not limited to achievements at work (such as raising a family and having good physical health). Psychological success is more under the employee's control than the traditional career goals, which were not only influenced by employee effort but were controlled by the availability of positions in the company. Psychological success is self-determined rather than solely determined through signals the employee receives from the company (like salary increase and promotion). Psychological success appears to be especially important to the new generation of persons entering the workforce. "Generation X" is often unimpressed with status symbols, wants flexibility in doing job tasks, and desires meaning from work.[8]

Employees need to develop new skills rather than rely on a static knowledge base. This has resulted from companies' need to be more responsive to customers' service and product demands. The types of knowledge an employee needs have changed.[9] In the traditional career, "knowing how" (having the appropriate skills and knowledge to provide a service or produce a product) was critical. Although knowing how remains important, employees also need to "know why" and "know whom." Knowing why refers to understanding the company's business and culture so the employee can develop and apply knowledge and skills that can contribute to the business. Knowing whom refers to relationships the employee may develop to contribute to company success. These relationships may include networking with vendors, suppliers, community members, customers, or industry experts. Learning to know whom and know why requires more than formal courses and training programs. Learning and development in the protean career are increasingly likely to involve relationships and job experiences rather than formal courses.

The emphasis on continuous learning and learning beyond knowing how as well as changes in the psychological contract are altering the direction and frequency of movement within careers (career pattern).[10]

Traditional career patterns consisted of a series of steps arranged in a linear hierarchy, with higher steps related to increased authority, responsibility, and compensation. Expert career patterns involve a lifelong commitment to a field or specialization (such as law, medicine, or management). These types of career patterns will not disappear. Rather, career patterns involving movement across specializations or disciplines (a spiral career pattern) will become more prevalent. These new career patterns mean that developing employees (as well as employees taking control of their own careers) will require providing them with the opportunity to (a) determine their interests, skill strengths, and weaknesses and (b) based on this information, seek appropriate development experiences that will likely involve job experiences and relationships as well as formal courses.

The most appropriate view of a career is that it is "boundaryless."[11] It may include movement across several employers or even different occupations. Statistics indicate that the average employment tenure for all American workers is only five years.[12] For example, Craig Matison, 33 years old, took a job with Cincinnati Bell Information System, a unit of Cincinnati Bell Corporation that manages billing for phone and cable companies.[13] Although he had been on the job only six months, he was already looking to make his next career move. Not wanting to stay on the technical career path, he regularly explored company databases for job postings, looking for sales and marketing opportunities within the company. A career may also involve identifying more with a job or profession than with the present employer. A career can also be considered boundaryless in the sense that career plans or goals are influenced by personal or family demands and values. Finally, *boundaryless* may refer to the fact that career success may be tied not to promotions but to achieving goals that are personally meaningful to the employee rather than those set by parents, peers, or the company.

As this discussion shows, to retain and motivate employees companies need to provide a system to identify and meet employees' development needs. This is especially important to retain good performers and employees who have potential for managerial positions. This system is often known as a **career management** or **development planning system.** We will discuss these systems in detail later in the chapter.

Approaches to Employee Development

Four approaches are used to develop employees: formal education, assessment, job experiences, and interpersonal relationships.[14] Many companies use a combination of these approaches. Cardinal Health, the largest provider of health care products and

Career management system
A system to retain and motivate employees by identifying and meeting their development needs (also called *development planning systems*).

services in the world, is headquartered in Dublin, Ohio.[15] The company has 50,000 employees in 22 countries. Cardinal Health has 10 leadership core competencies: customer orientation, personal leadership, business acumen, team player, innovation/risk taker, results orientation, integrity, strategic thinker, interpersonal skills, and maturity. Development activities are designed to assess the strengths and weaknesses of managers (or potential managers) in these core competencies. Training programs, job experiences, and mentoring programs are designed to improve individuals' competencies and the leadership capabilities of the company.

Keep in mind that although much development activity is targeted at managers, all levels of employees may be involved in development. For example, grocery store clerks usually receive performance appraisal feedback (a development activity related to assessment). As part of the appraisal process they are asked to complete individual development plans outlining (1) how they plan to change their weaknesses and (2) their future plans (including positions or locations desired and education or experience needed). Next we explore each type of development approach.

Formal Education

Formal education programs
Employee development programs, including short courses offered by consultants or universities, executive MBA programs, and university programs.

Formal education programs include off-site and on-site programs designed specifically for the company's employees, short courses offered by consultants or universities, executive MBA programs, and university programs in which participants actually live at the university while taking classes. These programs may involve lectures by business experts, business games and simulations, adventure learning, and meetings with customers. Many companies (such as Motorola, IBM, GE, Metropolitan Financial, and Dow) have training and development centers that offer development programs including classroom and online training as well as job experiences. Table 9.2 shows examples of the types of development programs used at GE and their target audiences. For example, the Communication Leadership Program is a 21-month, entry-level training program that consists of three six-month rotational assignments and a project in one of GE's businesses.[16] The program provides experiences in areas such as public relations, financial communication, electronic media and Internet development. Formal training is given in leadership and presentational skills. Participants are mentored by experienced communication leaders. They receive formal evaluation on their progress and feedback.

TABLE 9.2

Examples of Development Programs at General Electric

PROGRAM	DESCRIPTION	TARGET AUDIENCE	EXAMPLE
Corporate master's program	Classroom and online training Job rotation	Employees with work experience	Risk management leadership program Commercial leadership program Human Resources leadership program
Entry-level leadership	Formal classroom studies and job assignments	New employees	Communication leadership program Financial management program Operations management leadership program

SOURCE: Adapted from http://www.gecareers.com.

TABLE 9.3

Example of Institutions for Executive Education

PROVIDER (LOCATION)	2000–01 REVENUE (MILLIONS)	NO. OF EXECUTIVE NONDEGREE PROGRAMS	NO. OF EXECUTIVES ATTENDING PROGRAMS	RANGE OF COSTS FOR PROGRAMS	TOP CORPORATE CLIENTS
Harvard (Boston)	$91.0	47	4,051	$2,450–$47,000	NA
University of Pennsylvania Wharton School (Philadelphia)	43.0	43	3,946	4,750– 49,000	Merrill Lynch Verizon Merck
University of Michigan (Ann Arbor)	28.6	50	4,175	2,400– 25,000	AT&T Ford Motor Company Pfizer
Center for Creative Leadership (Greensboro, North Carolina)	49.0	13	8,679	2,900– 8,900	General Motors SAP America Maytag Corporation
INSEAD (Fontainbleau, France)	47.7	41	2,932	4,410– 22,660	IBM Credit Suisse Dow Chemical

SOURCE: Based on "Exec-Ed Rankings and Profiles," *BusinessWeek Online,* October 15, 2001, www.businessweek.com; M. Schneider and B. Hindo, "A Mid-Career Boost," *BusinessWeek Online,* October 15, 2001, www.businessweek.com.

Table 9.3 shows examples of institutions for executive education. There are several important trends in executive education. Leadership, entrepreneurship, and e-business are the most important topics in executive education programs. Programs directed at developing executives' understanding of global business issues and management of change are other important parts of executive development.[17] More and more companies and universities are using distance learning (which we discussed in Chapter 7) to reach executive audiences.[18] For example, Duke University's Fuqua School of Business offers an electronic executive MBA program in both Frankfurt, Germany, and Durham, North Carolina. Using their personal computers, students "attend" CD-ROM video lectures as well as traditional face-to-face lectures. They can download study aids and additional video and audio programs. Students discuss lectures and work on team projects using computer bulletin boards, e-mail, and live chat rooms. They use the Internet to research specific companies and class topics. Besides their work in the electronic learning environment students spend time in traditional face-to-face instructions for several weeks at home. They also attend courses held either in Germany or on the U.S. campus. The "Competing through Technology" box shows how IBM is using the Web for its management development program.

Another trend in executive education is for companies and the education provider (business school or other educational institution) to create short custom courses with content designed specifically for the audience. For example, in the Global Leadership Program run by Columbia University's business school, executives work on real problems they face in their jobs. A manager for window maker Pella Corporation left the program with a plan for international sales.[19]

The final important trend in executive education is to supplement formal courses from consultants or university faculty with other types of development activities. Avon Products' "Passport Program" is targeted at employees the company thinks can become general managers.[20] To learn Avon's global strategy, they meet for each

E-Learning Helps Build Management Talent

To succeed, companies need to identify employees with managerial talent and help managers develop skills needed to be more effective. To attract and retain talented employees who are in short supply, companies must offer training and development opportunities on the Web to meet the needs of a geographically dispersed workforce dealing with many work demands. IBM's "Basic Blue for Managers" program uses e-learning and face-to-face classroom experiences. The program helps managers understand their responsibilities in managing performance, employee relations, diversity, and multicultural issues. It moves the learning of all basic management skills to the Web, using classroom experiences for more complex management issues. It also gives managers and their bosses greater responsibility for development, while the company provides support in the form of unlimited access to development activities and support networks. The learning model includes four levels:

- Management quick views: These provide practical information on over 40 common management topics related to how to conduct business, leadership and management competencies, productivity, and HRM issues.
- Interactive learning modules and simulations: These interactive simulations emphasize people and task management. Employees learn by viewing videos, interacting with models and problem employees, deciding how to deal with a problem, issue, or request, and getting feedback on their decisions. Case studies are also available for review.
- Collaborative learning: The learner can connect on the company intranet with tutors, team members, customers, or other learners to discuss problems, issues, and approaches to share learning.
- Learning labs: Five-day class workshops build on the learning acquired during the previous phases of e-learning. The workshops emphasize peer learning and the development of a learning community. Through challenging activities and assignments managers gain increased awareness of themselves, their work teams, and IBM.

The program recognizes the roles of the boss as coach, supporter, and role model. The boss is involved in the program through providing coaching and feedback, on-the-job learning experiences, assessment of the manager's development needs and progress, and assistance to complete individual development plans.

IBM believes that by utilizing e-learning and the classroom environment, managers participate in self-directed learning, try out skills in a "safe" environment, and gain access to communities of learning and just-in-time learning. The advantages of e-learning are complemented by the strengths of an interactive classroom experience and support from the manager's boss to create the best development program possible.

Evaluations of the program have been positive. Participants report they are satisfied with the program content and delivery. Most of the participants have mastered the 15 subject areas included in the program. It is estimated that the business value related to leadership skill improvement averages $450,000 per employee.

SOURCE: N. Lewis and P. Orton, "The Five Attributes of Innovative E-Learning," *Training and Development*, June 2000, pp. 47–51; K. Mantyla, Blending E-learning (Alexandria, VA: ASTD, 2001).

session in a different country. The program brings a team of employees together for six-week periods spread over 18 months. Participants are provided with general background of a functional area by university faculty and consultants. The team then works with senior executives on a country project, such as how to penetrate a new market. The team projects are presented to Avon's top managers.

Managers who attend the Center for Creative Leadership development program take psychological tests; receive feedback from managers, peers, and direct reports; participate in group-building activities (like adventure learning, discussed in Chapter 7); receive counseling; and set improvement goals and write development plans.[21]

Most companies consider the primary purpose of education programs to be providing the employee with job-specific skills.[22] Unfortunately, there has been little research on the effectiveness of formal education programs. In a study of Harvard University's Advanced Management Program, participants reported that they had acquired valuable knowledge from the program (like how globalization affects a company's structure). They said the program broadened their perspectives on issues facing their companies, increased their self-confidence, and helped them learn new ways of thinking and looking at problems.[23]

Assessment

Assessment involves collecting information and providing feedback to employees about their behavior, communication style, or skills.[24] The employees, their peers, managers, and customers may provide information. Assessment is most frequently used to identify employees with managerial potential and to measure current managers' strengths and weaknesses. Assessment is also used to identify managers with the potential to move into higher-level executive positions, and it can be used with work teams to identify the strengths and weaknesses of individual team members and the decision processes or communication styles that inhibit the team's productivity.

Companies vary in the methods and the sources of information they use in developmental assessment. Many companies appraise employee performance. Companies with sophisticated development systems use psychological tests to measure employees' skills, personality types, and communication styles. Self, peer, and managers' ratings of employees' interpersonal styles and behaviors may also be collected. Popular assessment tools include the Myers-Briggs Type Indicator®, assessment centers, benchmarks, performance appraisal, and 360-degree feedback.

Assessment
Collecting information and providing feedback to employees about their behavior, communication style, or skills.

Myers-Briggs Type Indicator®

Myers-Briggs Type Indicator (MBTI)® is the most popular psychological assessment tool for employee development. As many as 2 million people take the MBTI® in the United States each year. The test consists of more than 100 questions about how the person feels or prefers to behave in different situations (such as "Are you usually a good 'mixer' or rather quiet and reserved?"). The MBTI® is based on the work of Carl Jung, a psychologist who believed that differences in individuals' behavior resulted from preferences in decision making, interpersonal communication, and information gathering. The MBTI® identifies individuals' preference for energy (introversion versus extroversion), information gathering (sensing versus intuition), decision making (thinking versus feeling), and lifestyle (judging versus perceiving).[25] The energy dimension determines where individuals gain interpersonal strength and vitality. Extroverts (E) gain energy through interpersonal relationships. Introverts (I) gain energy

Myers-Briggs Type Indicator (MBTI)®
A psychological test used for team building and leadership development that identifies employees' preferences for energy, information gathering, decision making, and lifestyle.

by focusing on personal thoughts and feelings. The information-gathering preference relates to the actions individuals take when making decisions. Individuals with a Sensing (S) preference tend to gather facts and details. Intuitives (I) tend to focus less on facts and more on possibilities and relationships between ideas. Decision-making preferences differ based on the amount of consideration the person gives to others' feelings in making a decision. Individuals with a Thinking (T) preference tend to be objective in making decisions. Individuals with a Feeling (F) preference tend to evaluate the impact of potential decisions on others and be more subjective in making a decision. The lifestyle preference reflects an individual's tendency to be flexible and adaptable. Individuals with a Judging (J) preference focus on goals, establish deadlines, and prefer to be conclusive. Individuals with a Perceiving (P) preference tend to enjoy surprises, like to change decisions, and dislike deadlines.

Sixteen unique personality types result from the combination of the four MBTI® preferences. (See Table 9.4.) Each person has developed strengths and weaknesses as a result of using these preferences. For example, individuals who are Introverted, Sensing, Thinking, and Judging (known as ISTJs) tend to be serious, quiet, practical, orderly, and logical. These persons can organize tasks, be decisive, and follow through on plans and goals. ISTJs have several weaknesses because they have not used the opposite preferences: Extroversion, Intuition, Feeling, and Perceiving. Potential weaknesses for ISTJs include problems dealing with unexpected opportunities, appearing too task-oriented or impersonal to colleagues, and making overly quick decisions. Visit the website www.keirsey.com for more information on the personality types.

The MBTI® is used for understanding such things as communication, motivation, teamwork, work styles, and leadership. For example, it can be used by salespeople or executives who want to become more effective at interpersonal communication by learning about their own personality styles and the way they are perceived by others. The MBTI® can help develop teams by matching team members with assignments that allow them to capitalize on their preferences and helping employees understand how the different preferences of team members can lead to useful problem solving.[26] For example, employees with an Intuitive preference can be assigned brainstorming tasks. Employees with a Sensing preference can evaluate ideas.

Research on the validity, reliability, and effectiveness of the MBTI® is inconclusive.[27] People who take the MBTI® find it a positive experience and say it helps them change their behavior. MBTI® scores appear to be related to one's occupation. Analysis of managers' MBTI® scores in the United States, England, Latin America, and Japan suggests that a large majority of all managers have certain personality types (ISTJ, INTJ, ESTJ, or ENTJ). However, MBTI® scores are not necessarily stable over time. Studies in which the MBTI® was administered at two different times found that as few as 24 percent of those who took the test were classified as the same type the second time.

The MBTI® is a valuable tool for understanding communication styles and the ways people prefer to interact with others. Because it does not measure how well employees perform their preferred functions, it should not be used to appraise performance or evaluate employees' promotion potential. Furthermore, MBTI® types should not be viewed as unchangeable personality patterns.

Assessment Center

Assessment center
A process in which multiple raters evaluate employees' performance on a number of exercises.

At an **assessment center** multiple raters or evaluators (assessors) evaluate employees' performance on a number of exercises.[28] An assessment center is usually an off-site location such as a conference center. From 6 to 12 employees usually participate at one

TABLE 9.4

The 16 Personality Types Used in the Myers-Briggs Type Indicator Assessment

	SENSING TYPES (S)		INTUITIVE TYPES (N)	
	THINKING (T)	FEELING (F)	FEELING (F)	THINKING (T)
Introverts (I) Judging (J)	**ISTJ** Quiet, serious, earn success by thoroughness and dependability. Practical, matter-of-fact, realistic, and responsible. Decide logically what should be done and work toward it steadily, regardless of distractions. Take pleasure in making everything orderly and organized—their work, their home, their life. Value traditions and loyalty.	**ISFJ** Quiet, friendly, responsible, and conscientious. Committed and steady in meeting their obligations. Thorough, painstaking, and accurate. Loyal, considerate, notice and remember specifics about people who are important to them, concerned with how others feel. Strive to create an orderly and harmonious environment at work and at home.	**INFJ** Seek meaning and connection in ideas, relationships, and material possessions. Want to understand what motivates people and are insightful about others. Conscientious and committed to their firm values. Develop a clear vision about how best to serve the common good. Organized and decisive in implementing their vision.	**INTJ** Have original minds and great drive for implementing their ideas and achieving their goals. Quickly see patterns in external events and develop long-range explanatory perspectives. When committed, organize a job and carry it through. Skeptical and independent, have high standards of competence and performance—for themselves and others.
Perceiving (P)	**ISTP** Tolerant and flexible, quiet observers until a problem appears, then act quickly to find workable solutions. Analyze what makes things work and readily get through large amounts of data to isolate the core of practical problems. Interested in cause and effect, organize facts using logical principles, value efficiency.	**ISFP** Quiet, friendly, sensitive, and kind. Enjoy the present moment, what's going on around them. Like to have their own space and to work within their own time frame. Loyal and committed to their values and to people who are important to them. Dislike disagreements and conflicts, do not force their opinions or values on others.	**INFP** Idealistic, loyal to their values and to people who are important to them. Want an external life that is congruent with their values. Curious, quick to see possibilities, can be catalysts for implementing ideas. Seek to understand people and to help them fulfill their potential. Adaptable, flexible, and accepting unless a value is threatened.	**INTP** Seek to develop logical explanations for everything that interests them. Theoretical and abstract, interested more in ideas than in social interaction. Quiet, contained, flexible, and adaptable. Have unusual ability to focus in depth to solve problems in their area of interest. Skeptical, sometimes critical, always analytical.
Extroverts (E) Perceiving (P)	**ESTP** Flexible and tolerant, they take a pragmatic approach focused on immediate results. Theories and conceptual explanations bore them—they want to act energetically to solve the problem. Focus on the here-and-now, spontaneous, enjoy each moment that they can be active with others. Enjoy material comforts and style. Learn best through doing.	**ESFP** Outgoing, friendly, and accepting. Exuberant lovers of life, people, and material comforts. Enjoy working with others to make things happen. Bring common sense and a realistic approach to their work, and make work fun. Flexible and spontaneous, adapt readily to new people and environments. Learn best by trying a new skill with other people.	**ENFP** Warmly enthusiastic and imaginative. See life as full of possibilities. Make connections between events and information very quickly, and confidently proceed based on the patterns they see. Want a lot of affirmation from others, and readily give appreciation and support. Spontaneous and flexible, often rely on their ability to improvise and their verbal fluency.	**ENTP** Quick, ingenious, stimulating, alert, and outspoken. Resourceful in solving new and challenging problems. Adept at generating conceptual possibilities and then analyzing them strategically. Good at reading other people. Bored by routine, will seldom do the same thing the same way, apt to turn to one new interest after another.
Judging (J)	**ESTJ** Practical, realistic, matter-of-fact. Decisive, quickly move to implement decisions. Organize projects and people to get things done, focus on getting results in the most efficient way possible. Take care of routine details. Have a clear set of logical standards, systematically follow them and want others to also. Forceful in implementing their plans.	**ESFJ** Warmhearted, conscientious, and cooperative. Want harmony in their environment, work with determination to establish it. Like to work with others to complete tasks accurately and on time. Loyal, follow through even in small matters. Notice what others need in their day-by-day lives and try to provide it. Want to be appreciated for who they are and for what they contribute.	**ENFJ** Warm, empathetic, responsive, and responsible. Highly attuned to the emotions, needs, and motivations of others. Find potential in everyone, want to help others fulfill their potential. May act as catalysts for individual and group growth. Loyal, responsive to praise and criticism. Sociable, facilitate others in a group, and provide inspiring leadership.	**ENTJ** Frank, decisive, assume leadership readily. Quickly see illogical and inefficient procedures and policies, develop and implement comprehensive systems to solve organizational problems. Enjoy long-term planning and goal setting. Usually well informed, well read, enjoy expanding their knowledge and passing it on to others. Forceful in presenting their ideas.

Leaderless group discussion
Process in which a team of five to seven employees solve an assigned problem together within a certain time period.

Interview
Employees are questioned about their work and personal experiences, skills, and career plans.

In-basket
A simulation of the administrative tasks of a manager's job.

Role plays
A participant taking the part or role of a manager or other employee.

time. Assessment centers are primarily used to identify if employees have the personality characteristics, administrative skills, and interpersonal skills needed for managerial jobs. They are also increasingly being used to determine if employees have the necessary skills to work in teams.

The types of exercises used in assessment centers include leaderless group discussions, interviews, in-baskets, and role plays.[29] In a **leaderless group discussion,** a team of five to seven employees is assigned a problem and must work together to solve it within a certain time period. The problem may involve buying and selling supplies, nominating a subordinate for an award, or assembling a product. In the **interview,** employees answer questions about their work and personal experiences, skill strengths and weaknesses, and career plans. An **in-basket** is a simulation of the administrative tasks of the manager's job. The exercise includes a variety of documents that may appear in the in-basket on a manager's desk. The participants read the materials and decide how to respond to them. Responses might include delegating tasks, scheduling meetings, writing replies, or completely ignoring the memo! **Role plays** refer to the participant taking the part or role of a manager or other employee. For example, an assessment center participant may be asked to take the role of a manager who has to give a negative performance review to a subordinate. The participant is told about the subordinate's performance and is asked to prepare for and actually hold a 45-minute meeting with the subordinate to discuss the performance problems. The role of the subordinate is played by a manager or other member of the assessment center design team or company. The assessment center might also include interest and aptitude tests to evaluate an employee's vocabulary, general mental ability, and reasoning skills. Personality tests may be used to determine if employees can get along with others, their tolerance for ambiguity, and other traits related to success as a manager.

Assessment center exercises are designed to measure employees' administrative and interpersonal skills. Skills typically measured include leadership, oral and written communication, judgment, organizational ability, and stress tolerance. Table 9.5 shows

TABLE 9.5

Examples of Skills Measured by Assessment Center Exercises

| | EXERCISES | | | | |
	IN-BASKET	SCHEDULING EXERCISE	LEADERLESS GROUP DISCUSSION	PERSONALITY TEST	ROLE PLAY
SKILLS					
Leadership (Dominance, coaching, influence, resourcefulness)	X		X	X	X
Problem solving (Judgment)	X	X	X		X
Interpersonal (Sensitivity, conflict resolution, cooperation, oral communication)			X	X	X
Administrative (Organizing, planning, written communications)	X	X	X		
Personal (Stress tolerance, confidence)			X	X	X

X indicates skill measured by exercise.

an example of the skills measured by the assessment center. As we see, each exercise gives participating employees the opportunity to demonstrate several different skills. For example, the exercise requiring scheduling to meet production demands evaluates employees' administrative and problem-solving ability. The leaderless group discussion measures interpersonal skills such as sensitivity toward others, stress tolerance, and oral communication skills.

Managers are usually used as assessors. The managers are trained to look for employee behaviors that are related to the skills that will be assessed. Typically, each assessor observes and records one or two employees' behaviors in each exercise. The assessors review their notes and rate each employee's level of skills (for example, 5 = high level of leadership skills, 1 = low level of leadership skills). After all employees have completed the exercises, the assessors discuss their observations of each employee. They compare their ratings and try to agree on each employee's rating for each of the skills.

As we mentioned in Chapter 6, research suggests that assessment center ratings are related to performance, salary level, and career advancement.[30] Assessment centers may also be useful for development because employees who participate in the process receive feedback regarding their attitudes, skill strengths, and weaknesses.[31] For example, Steelcase, the office furniture manufacturer based in Grand Rapids, Michigan, uses assessment centers for first-level managers.[32] The assessment center exercises include in-basket, interview simulation, and a timed scheduling exercise requiring participants to fill positions created by absences. Managers are also required to confront an employee on a performance issue, getting the employee to commit to improve. Because the exercises relate closely to what managers are required to do at work, feedback given to managers based on their performance in the assessment center can target specific skills or competencies that they need to be successful managers.

Benchmarks

Benchmarks© is an instrument designed to measure the factors that are important to being a successful manager. The items measured by Benchmarks are based on research that examines the lessons executives learn at critical events in their careers.[33] This includes items that measure managers' skills in dealing with subordinates, acquiring resources, and creating a productive work climate. Table 9.6 shows the 16 skills and perspectives believed to be important for becoming a successful manager. These skills and perspectives have been shown to be related to performance evaluations, bosses' ratings of promotability, and actual promotions received.[34] To get a complete picture of managers' skills, the managers' supervisors, their peers, and the managers themselves all complete the instrument. A summary report presenting the self-ratings and ratings by others is provided to the manager, along with information about how the ratings compare with those of other managers. A development guide with examples of experiences that enhance each skill and how successful managers use the skills is also available.

Performance Appraisals and 360-Degree Feedback Systems

As we mentioned in Chapter 8, **performance appraisal** is the process of measuring employees' performance. Performance appraisal information can be useful for employee development under certain conditions.[35] The appraisal system must tell employees specifically about their performance problems and how they can improve their performance. This includes providing a clear understanding of the differences between current performance and expected performance, identifying causes of the performance discrepancy, and developing action plans to improve performance. Managers must be trained in frequent performance feedback. Managers also need to monitor employees' progress in carrying out action plans.

Benchmarks©
An instrument designed to measure the factors that are important to managerial success.

Performance appraisal
The process through which an organization gets information on how well an employee is doing his or her job.

TABLE 9.6

Skills Related to Managerial Success

Resourcefulness	Can think strategically, engage in flexible problem solving, and work effectively with higher management.
Doing whatever it takes	Has perseverance and focus in the face of obstacles.
Being a quick study	Quickly masters new technical and business knowledge.
Building and mending relationships	Knows how to build and maintain working relationships with coworkers and external parties.
Leading subordinates	Delegates to subordinates effectively, broadens their opportunities, and acts with fairness toward them.
Compassion and sensitivity	Shows genuine interest in others and sensitivity to subordinates' needs.
Straightforwardness and composure	Is honorable and steadfast.
Setting a developmental climate	Provides a challenging climate to encourage subordinates' development.
Confronting problem subordinates	Acts decisively and fairly when dealing with problem subordinates.
Team orientation	Accomplishes tasks through managing others.
Balance between personal life and work	Balances work priorities with personal life so that neither is neglected.
Decisiveness	Prefers quick and approximate actions to slow and precise ones in many management situations.
Self-awareness	Has an accurate picture of strengths and weaknesses and is willing to improve.
Hiring talented staff	Hires talented people for the team.
Putting people at ease	Displays warmth and a good sense of humor.
Acting with flexibility	Can behave in ways that are often seen as opposites.

SOURCE: Adapted with permission from C. D. McCauley, M. M. Lombardo, and C. J. Usher, "Diagnosing Management Development Needs: An Instrument Based on How Managers Develop," *Journal of Management* 15 (1989), pp. 389–403.

Upward feedback
A performance appraisal process for managers that includes subordinates' evaluations.

A recent trend in performance appraisals for management development is the use of upward feedback and 360-degree feedback. **Upward feedback** refers to appraisal that involves collecting subordinates' evaluations of managers' behaviors or skills. The 360-degree feedback process is a special case of upward feedback. In **360-degree feedback systems,** employees' behaviors or skills are evaluated not only by subordinates but by peers, customers, their bosses, and themselves. The raters complete a questionnaire asking them to rate the person on a number of different dimensions. Table 9.7 provides an example of the types of competencies that are rated in a 360-degree feedback questionnaire. This example evaluates the management competency

TABLE 9.7

Sample Competency and Items from a 360-Degree Feedback Instrument

Decision Making
Identifies the key decisions that have the greatest impact on business goals.
Understands and integrates conflicting or contradictory information.
Balances business sense with data and logic to make effective decisions.
Takes accountability for results of individual and team decisions.
Makes appropriate trade-offs between complete analysis and speed when making decisions.

1. **Understand strengths and weaknesses.**
   Review ratings for strengths and weaknesses.
   Identify skills or behaviors where self and others' (manager, peer, customer) ratings agree and disagree.
2. **Identify a development goal.**
   Choose a skill or behavior to develop.
   Set a clear, specific goal with a specified outcome.
3. **Identify a process for recognizing goal accomplishment.**
4. **Identify strategies for reaching the development goal.**
   Establish strategies such as reading, job experiences, courses, and relationships.
   Establish strategies for receiving feedback on progress.
   Establish strategies for reinforcing the new skill or behavior.

TABLE 9.8

Activities in Development Planning

360-degree feedback systems
A performance appraisal system for managers that includes evaluations from a wide range of persons who interact with the manager. The process includes self-evaluations as well as evaluations from the manager's boss, subordinates, peers, and customers.

of decision making. Each of the five items relates to a specific aspect of decision making (e.g., takes accountability for results of individual and team decisions). Typically, raters are asked to assess the manager's strength in a particular item or whether development is needed. Raters may also be asked to identify how frequently they observe a competency or skill (e.g., always, sometimes, seldom, never).

The results of a 360-degree feedback system show how the manager was rated on each item. The results also show how self-evaluations differ from evaluations from the other raters. Typically managers review their results, seek clarification from the raters, and set specific development goals based on the strengths and weaknesses identified.[36] Table 9.8 shows the type of activities involved in development planning using 360-degree feedback.[37] Consider how U.S. West used development planning with 360-degree feedback.[38] The 360-degree feedback results showed that one manager tended to avoid confrontation. Knowing this helped her focus her training and development activity on role plays and discussions that would help her become more comfortable with confrontation. She left the program with an individualized list of training and development activities linked directly to the skill she needed to improve.

The benefits of 360-degree feedback include collecting multiple perspectives of managers' performance, allowing employees to compare their own personal evaluations with the views of others, and formalizing communications about behaviors and skills ratings between employees and their internal and external customers. Several studies have shown that performance improves and behavior changes as a result of participating in upward feedback and 360-degree feedback systems.[39] The most change occurs in individuals who receive lower ratings from others than they gave themselves (overraters).

Potential limitations of 360-degree feedback include the time demands placed on the raters to complete the evaluations, managers seeking to identify and punish raters who provided negative information, the need to have a facilitator help interpret results, and companies' failure to provide ways that managers can act on the feedback they receive (development planning, meeting with raters, taking courses).

In effective 360-degree feedback systems, reliable or consistent ratings are provided, raters' confidentiality is maintained, the behaviors or skills assessed are job-related (valid), the system is easy to use, and managers receive and act on the feedback.[40]

Technology allows 360-degree questionnaires to be delivered to the raters via their personal computers. This increases the number of completed questionnaires returned, makes it easier to process the information, and speeds feedback reports to managers.

Regardless of the assessment method used, the information must be shared with the employee for development to occur. Along with assessment information, the employee needs suggestions for correcting skill weaknesses and using skills already learned. These suggestions might be to participate in training courses or develop skills through new job experiences. Based on the assessment information and available development opportunities, employees should develop action plans to guide their self-improvement efforts.

Capital One has developed effective 360-degree feedback systems.[41] Capitol One, a consumer credit company, has included a number of features in its 360-degree feedback system to minimize the chance that the ratings will be used as ways to get back at an employee or turned into popularity contests. The 360-degree assessments are based on the company's competency model, so raters are asked for specific feedback on a competency area. Rather than a lengthy form that places a large burden on raters to assess many different competencies, Capital One's assessment asks the raters to concentrate on three or four strengths or development opportunities. It also seeks comments rather than limiting raters to merely circling numbers corresponding to how much of each competency the employee has demonstrated. These comments often provide specific information about what aspect of a competency needs to be developed or identifies work situations in which a competency needs to be improved. This comment system helps tailor development activities to fit competency development. To increase the chances that the assessment will result in change, the feedback from the 360-degree assessment is linked to development plans, and the company offers coaching and training to help employees strengthen their competencies. Employees are encouraged to share feedback with their coworkers. This creates a work environment based on honest and open feedback that helps employees personally grow.

Job Experiences

Job experiences
The relationships, problems, demands, tasks, and other features that employees face in their jobs.

Most employee development occurs through **job experiences:**[42] relationships, problems, demands, tasks, or other features that employees face in their jobs. A major assumption of using job experiences for employee development is that development is most likely to occur when there is a mismatch between the employee's skills and past experiences and the skills required for the job. To succeed in their jobs, employees must stretch their skills—that is, they are forced to learn new skills, apply their skills and knowledge in a new way, and master new experiences.[43] For example, to prepare employees to grow overseas business markets, companies are using international job experiences.

Most of what we know about development through job experiences comes from a series of studies conducted by the Center for Creative Leadership.[44] Executives were asked to identify key career events that made a difference in their managerial styles and the lessons they learned from these experiences. The key events included those involving the job assignment (such as fixing a failing operation), those involving interpersonal relationships (getting along with supervisors), and the specific type of transition required (situations in which the executive did not have the necessary background). The job demands and what employees can learn from them are shown in Table 9.9.

One concern in the use of demanding job experiences for employee development is whether they are viewed as positive or negative stressors. Job experiences that are seen as positive stressors challenge employees to stimulate learning. Job challenges viewed as negative stressors create high levels of harmful stress for employees exposed to them. Recent research findings suggest that all of the job demands, with the excep-

TABLE 9.9

Job Demands and the Lessons Employees Learn from Them

Making transitions	*Unfamiliar responsibilities:* The manager must handle responsibilities that are new, very different, or much broader than previous ones.
	Proving yourself: The manager has added pressure to show others she can handle the job.
Creating change	*Developing new directions:* The manager is responsible for starting something new in the organization, making strategic changes in the business, carrying out a reorganization, or responding to rapid changes in the business environment.
	Inherited problems: The manager has to fix problems created by a former incumbent or take over problem employees.
	Reduction decisions: Decisions about shutting down operations or staff reductions have to be made.
	Problems with employees: Employees lack adequate experience, are incompetent, or are resistant.
Having high level of responsibility	*High stakes:* Clear deadlines, pressure from senior managers, high visibility, and responsibility for key decisions make success or failure in this job clearly evident.
	Managing business diversity: The scope of the job is large with responsibilities for multiple functions, groups, products, customers, or markets.
	Job overload: The sheer size of the job requires a large investment of time and energy.
	Handling external pressure: External factors that affect the business (e.g., negotiating with unions or government agencies; working in a foreign culture; coping with serious community problems) must be dealt with.
Being involved in nonauthority relationships	*Influencing without authority:* Getting the job done requires influencing peers, higher management, external parties, or other key people over whom the manager has no direct authority.
Facing obstacles	*Adverse business conditions:* The business unit or product line faces financial problems or difficult economic conditions.
	Lack of top management support: Senior management is reluctant to provide direction, support, or resources for current work or new projects.
	Lack of personal support: The manager is excluded from key networks and gets little support and encouragement from others.
	Difficult boss: The manager's opinions or management style differs from those of the boss, or the boss has major shortcomings.

SOURCE: C. D. McCauley, L. J. Eastman, and J. Ohlott, "Linking Management Selection and Development through Stretch Assignments," *Human Resource Management* 84 (1995), pp. 93–115. Copyright © 1995 Wiley Periodicals, Inc., a Wiley Company.

tion of obstacles, are related to learning.[45] Managers reported that obstacles and job demands related to creating change were more likely to lead to negative stress than the other job demands. This suggests that companies should carefully weigh the potential negative consequences before placing employees in development assignments involving obstacles or creating change.

Although the research on development through job experiences has focused on executives and managers, line employees can also learn from job experiences. As we noted earlier, for a work team to be successful, its members now need the kinds of skills that only managers were once thought to need (such as dealing directly with customers, analyzing data to determine product quality, and resolving conflict among team members). Besides the development that occurs when a team is formed, employees can further develop their skills by switching work roles within the team.

FIGURE 9.1

How Job
Experiences Are
Used for Employee
Development

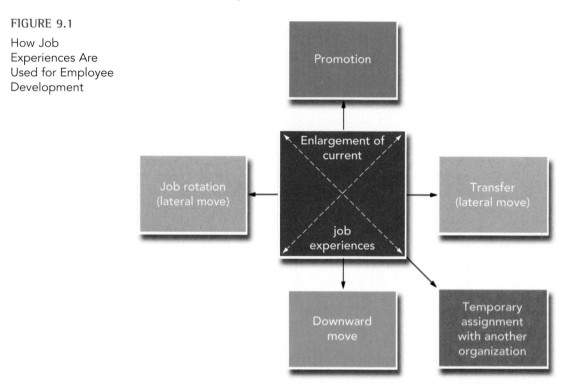

Figure 9.1 shows the various ways that job experiences can be used for employee development. These include enlarging the current job, job rotation, transfers, promotions, downward moves, and temporary assignments with other companies. For companies with global operations (multinationals) it is not uncommon for employee development to involve international assignments that require frequent travel or relocation.

Job enlargement
Adding challenges
or new
responsibilities
to an employee's
current job.

Enlarging the Current Job

Job enlargement refers to adding challenges or new responsibilities to employees' current jobs. This could include special project assignments, switching roles within a work team, or researching new ways to serve clients and customers. For example, an engineering employee may join a task force developing new career paths for technical employees. Through this project work, the engineer may lead certain aspects of career path development (such as reviewing the company's career development process). As a result, the engineer not only learns about the company's career development system, but uses leadership and organizational skills to help the task force reach its goals.

Job rotation
The process of
systematically
moving a single
individual from one
job to another over
the course of time.
The job assignments
may be in various
functional areas of
the company or
movement may be
between jobs in a
single functional
area or department.

Job Rotation

Job rotation gives employees a series of job assignments in various functional areas of the company or movement among jobs in a single functional area or department. Arrow Electronics allows employees to take a 10-week sabbatical after seven years with the company.[46] While an employee is taking the sabbatical, the company uses the job vacancy as a job rotation for a different employee. Assignments to open positions are based on an employee's development needs. Employees who rotate to new positions are required to document their experiences and learning, especially emphasizing how the position helped them better understand the business. W. W. Grainger, a distributor of business maintenance products in Lake Forest, Illinois, regularly moves employees across functions—for example, from marketing to information technology, from field-office work to corporate-office work, from regional sales offices to distribution centers—to help employees think strategically about different parts of the business.[47] Each employee has a customized development plan, and employees are assigned new positions based on the skills they need. The length of time in each position varies, depending on the skills and experience the employees need. Some employees return to their original jobs, while others may move to another department.

Job rotation helps employees gain an overall appreciation of the company's goals, increases their understanding of different company functions, develops a network of contacts, and improves problem-solving and decision-making skills.[48] Job rotation has also been shown to be related to skill acquisition, salary growth, and promotion rates. But there are several potential problems with job rotation for both the employee and the work unit. The rotation may create a short-term perspective on problems and solutions in rotating employees and their peers. Employees' satisfaction and motivation may be adversely affected because they find it difficult to develop functional specialties and they don't spend enough time in one position to receive a challenging assignment. Productivity losses and work load increases may be experienced by both the department gaining a rotating employee and the department losing the employee due to training demands and loss of a resource.

The characteristics of effective job rotation systems are shown in Table 9.10. As we see, effective job rotation systems are linked to the company's training, development, and career management systems. Also, job rotation should be used for all types of employees, not just those with managerial potential.

Transfers, Promotions, and Downward Moves

Upward, lateral, and downward mobility is available for development purposes in most companies.[49] In a **transfer,** an employee is assigned a job in a different area of the company. Transfers do not necessarily increase job responsibilities or compensation. They are likely lateral moves (a move to a job with similar responsibilities). **Promotions** are advancements into positions with greater challenges, more responsibility, and more authority than in the previous job. Promotions usually include pay increases.

Transfers may involve relocation within the United States or to another country. This can be stressful not only because the employee's work role changes, but if the

Transfer
The movement of an employee to a different job assignment in a different area of the company.

Promotions
Advances into positions with greater challenge, more responsibility, and more authority than the employee's previous job.

TABLE 9.10

Characteristics of Effective Job Rotation Systems

1. Job rotation is used to develop skills as well as give employees experience needed for managerial positions.
2. Employees understand specific skills that will be developed by rotation.
3. Job rotation is used for all levels and types of employees.
4. Job rotation is linked with the career management process so employees know the development needs addressed by each job assignment.
5. Benefits of rotation are maximized and costs are minimized through managing timing of rotations to reduce work load costs and helping employees understand job rotation's role in their development plans.
6. All employees have equal opportunities for job rotation assignments regardless of their demographic group.

SOURCE: Based on L. Cheraskin and M. Campion, "Study Clarifies Job Rotation Benefits," *Personnel Journal,* November 1996, pp. 31–38.

employee is in a two-career family, the spouse must find new employment. Also, the family has to join a new community. Transfers disrupt employees' daily lives, interpersonal relationships, and work habits.[50] People have to find new housing, shopping, health care, and leisure facilities, and they may be many miles from the emotional support of friends and family. They also have to learn a new set of work norms and procedures; they must develop interpersonal relationships with their new managers and peers; and they are expected to be as productive in their new jobs as they were in their old jobs even though they may know little about the products, services, processes, or employees for whom they are responsible.

Because transfers can provoke anxiety, many companies have difficulty getting employees to accept them. Research has identified the employee characteristics associated with a willingness to accept transfers:[51] high career ambitions, a belief that one's future with the company is promising, and a belief that accepting a transfer is necessary for success in the company. Employees who are not married and not active in the community are generally most willing to accept transfers. Among married employees, the spouse's willingness to move is the most important influence on whether an employee will accept a transfer.

Downward move
A job change involving a reduction in an employee's level of responsibility and authority.

A **downward move** occurs when an employee is given less responsibility and authority.[52] This may involve a move to another position at the same level (lateral demotion), a temporary cross-functional move, or a demotion because of poor performance. Temporary cross-functional moves to lower-level positions, which give employees experience working in different functional areas, are most frequently used for employee development. For example, engineers who want to move into management often take lower-level positions (like shift supervisor) to develop their management skills.

Because of the psychological and tangible rewards of promotions (such as increased feelings of self-worth, salary, and status in the company), employees are more willing to accept promotions than lateral or downward moves. Promotions are more readily available when a company is profitable and growing. When a company is restructuring or experiencing stable or declining profits—especially if numerous employees are interested in promotions and the company tends to rely on the external labor market to staff higher-level positions—promotion opportunities may be limited.[53]

Unfortunately, many employees have difficulty associating transfers and downward moves with development. They see them as punishments rather than as opportunities to develop skills that will help them achieve long-term success with the company. Many employees decide to leave a company rather than accept a transfer. Companies need to successfully manage transfers not only because of the costs of replacing employees but because of the costs directly associated with them. For example, GTE spends approximately $60 million a year on home purchases and other relocation costs such as temporary housing and relocation allowances.[54] One challenge companies face is learning how to use transfers and downward moves as development opportunities—convincing employees that accepting these opportunities will result in long-term benefits for them.

To ensure that employees accept transfers, promotions, and downward moves as development opportunities, companies can provide

- Information about the content, challenges, and potential benefits of the new job and location.
- Involvement in the transfer decision by sending the employees to preview the new location and giving them information about the community.
- Clear performance objectives and early feedback about their job performance.

- A host at the new location to help them adjust to the new community and workplace.
- Information about how the job opportunity will affect their income, taxes, mortgage payments, and other expenses.
- Reimbursement and assistance in selling and purchasing or renting a place to live.
- An orientation program for the new location and job.
- Information on how the new job experiences will support the employee's career plans.
- Assistance for dependent family members, including identifying schools and child care and elder care options.
- Help for the spouse in identifying and marketing skills and finding employment.[55]

Temporary Assignments with Other Organizations

Externship refers to a company allowing employees to take a full-time operational role at another company. Mercer Management, a consulting firm, uses externship to develop employees interested in gaining experience in a specific industry.[56] Mercer Management promises to employ the externs after their assignments end. For example, one employee who has been a Mercer consultant for five years is now vice president of Internet services for Binney & Smith, the maker of Crayola crayons. A year ago he was consulting on an Internet project for Binney & Smith. But he wanted to actually implement his recommendations rather than just give them to the client and move on to another project—so he started working at Binney & Smith. He remains on Mercer Management's payroll, though his salary comes from Binney & Smith. Mercer believes that employees who participate in the externship program will remain committed to the company because they have had the opportunity to learn and grow professionally and have not had to disrupt their personal and professional lives with a job search. Although externships give employees other employment options and some employees will leave, Mercer believes that it not only is a good development strategy but also helps in recruitment. The externship program signals to potential employees that Mercer is creative and flexible with its employees.

First Chicago National Bank and Kodak participated in an employee exchange program so that the two companies could better understand each other's business and how to improve the services provided.[57] For example, a First Chicago employee helped Kodak's business imaging division identify applications for compact disc technology. A Kodak employee helped First Chicago understand areas within the bank that could benefit from imaging technology.

Temporary assignments can include a **sabbatical** (a leave of absence from the company to renew or develop skills). Employees on sabbatical often receive full pay and benefits. Sabbaticals let employees get away from the day-to-day stresses of their jobs and acquire new skills and perspectives. Sabbaticals also allow employees more time for personal pursuits such as writing a book or spending more time with young children. Sabbaticals are common in a variety of industries ranging from consulting firms to the fast food industry.[58] Fallon Worldwide, an advertising agency, offers a program called Dreamcatchers to staff members who want to work on a project or travel.[59] Dreamcatchers was developed to help the agency avoid having employees burn out and lose their creative edge. Employees have taken time off to write novels, kayak, and motorcycle through the Alps. Fallon Worldwide matches employee contributions of up to $1,000 annually for two years and offers up to two extra weeks of paid vacation. The agency partners believe that the program has helped in the retention of key employees and the recruiting of new ones. The partners also believe that the program

Externship
When a company allows an employee to take a full-time operational role at another company.

Sabbatical
A leave of absence from the company to renew or develop skills.

helps recharge employees' creativity, which is key for employees to do their best work for customers.

Interpersonal Relationships

Employees can also develop skills and increase their knowledge about the company and its customers by interacting with a more experienced organization member. Mentoring and coaching are two types of interpersonal relationships that are used to develop employees.

Mentoring

Mentor

An experienced, productive senior employee who helps develop a less experienced employee.

A **mentor** is an experienced, productive senior employee who helps develop a less experienced employee (the protégé). Most mentoring relationships develop informally as a result of interests or values shared by the mentor and protégé. Research suggests that employees with certain personality characteristics (like emotional stability, the ability to adapt their behavior based on the situation, and high needs for power and achievement) are most likely to seek a mentor and be an attractive protégé for a mentor.[60] Mentoring relationships can also develop as part of a planned company effort to bring together successful senior employees with less experienced employees.

Developing Successful Mentoring Programs. Although many mentoring relationships develop informally, one major advantage of formalized mentoring programs is that they ensure access to mentors for all employees, regardless of gender or race. An additional advantage is that participants in the mentoring relationship know what is expected of them.[61] One limitation of formal mentoring programs is that mentors may not be able to provide counseling and coaching in a relationship that has been artificially created.[62]

Table 9.11 presents the characteristics of a successful formal mentoring program. Mentors should be chosen based on interpersonal and technical skills. They also need

TABLE 9.11

Characteristics of Successful Formal Mentoring Programs

1. Mentor and protégé participation is voluntary. Relationship can be ended at any time without fear of punishment.
2. The mentor–protégé matching process does not limit the ability of informal relationships to develop. For example, a mentor pool can be established to allow protégés to choose from a variety of qualified mentors.
3. Mentors are chosen on the basis of their past record in developing employees, willingness to serve as a mentor, and evidence of positive coaching, communication, and listening skills.
4. The purpose of the program is clearly understood. Projects and activities that the mentor and protégé are expected to complete are specified.
5. The length of the program is specified. Mentor and protégé are encouraged to pursue the relationship beyond the formal period.
6. A minimum level of contact between the mentor and protégé is specified.
7. Protégés are encouraged to contact one another to discuss problems and share successes.
8. The mentor program is evaluated. Interviews with mentors and protégés give immediate feedback regarding specific areas of dissatisfaction. Surveys gather more detailed information regarding benefits received from participating in the program.
9. Employee development is rewarded, which signals managers that mentoring and other development activities are worth their time and effort.

to be trained. For example, New York Hospital–Cornell Medical Center developed a mentoring program for housekeeping employees. Each mentor has between 5 and 10 protégés to meet with on a quarterly basis. To qualify as mentors, employees have to receive outstanding performance evaluations, demonstrate strong interpersonal skills, and be able to perform basic cleaning tasks and essential duties of all housekeeping positions including safety procedures (such as handling infectious waste).

Mentors undergo a two-day training program that emphasizes communication skills. They are also taught how to convey information about the job and give directions effectively without criticizing employees.[63]

A key to successful mentoring programs is that the mentor and protégé actually interact with each other. Face-to-face contact may be difficult, but with e-mail, Web cameras, and videoconferencing, virtual mentoring is possible.

Benefits of Mentoring Relationships. Both mentors and protégés can benefit from a mentoring relationship. Research suggests that mentors provide career and psychosocial support to their protégés. **Career support** includes coaching, protection, sponsorship, and providing challenging assignments, exposure, and visibility. **Psychosocial support** includes serving as a friend and a role model, providing positive regard and acceptance, and creating an outlet for the protégé to talk about anxieties and fears. Additional benefits for the protégé include higher rates of promotion, higher salaries, and greater organizational influence.[64]

Mentoring relationships provide opportunities for mentors to develop their interpersonal skills and increase their feelings of self-esteem and worth to the organization. For individuals in technical fields such as engineering or health services, the protégé may help them gain knowledge about important new scientific developments in their field (and therefore prevent them from becoming technically obsolete). For example, General Electric recently launched an initiative in e-business. However, many veteran managers faced the challenge of trying to understand how to effectively use the Internet. Jack Welch, former CEO of General Electric, created a mentoring program for his top 600 managers.[65] The program involves having younger employees who have more experience with the Internet serving as mentors for the top managers. Welch generated interest in the program by getting his own mentor, who is approximately half his age and has much less business experience than he does—but is a Web expert who runs the company's website. The purpose of the program is to help managers become familiar with competitors' websites, experience the difficulty of ordering products online, and understand what the best websites are doing right. Welch started the program because he believes that e-business knowledge is generally inversely related to age and position in the company hierarchy. GE managers meet with their mentors for Web lessons, where they critique websites, discuss articles and books about e-commerce they have have been given to read, and ask the mentors questions. The sessions benefit both the mentors and the protégés. The protégés learn about the Web, and the mentoring sessions make the younger employees more comfortable talking to their bosses. The mentors also learn about the skills that a manager needs to run a large business operation (such as the ability to communicate with different people).

Purposes of Mentoring Programs. Mentor programs socialize new employees, increase the likelihood of skill transfer from training to the work setting, and provide opportunities for women and minorities to gain the exposure and skills needed to evolve into managerial positions. Consider the New York Hospital–Cornell Medical Center mentoring program. The program is designed to help new employees more quickly learn housekeeping duties and understand the culture of the hospital. One

Career support
Coaching, protection, sponsorship, and providing challenging assignments, exposure, and visibility.

Psychosocial support
Serving as a friend and role model, providing positive regard and acceptance, and creating an outlet for a protégé to talk about anxieties and fears.

benefit of the program is that new employees' performance deficiencies are more quickly corrected. Although the formal mentoring of new employees lasts only two weeks, mentors are available to provide support many months later.

At E. I. Du Pont de Nemours and Company's corporate headquarters, Steve Croft and Janet Graham have met at least once a month for the past seven years to share problems, information, and advice as part of Du Pont's mentoring program.[66] He is a planning manager in Du Pont's research division. She is an administrative assistant in the toxicology lab where Steve used to work. From a list of volunteers, protégés choose mentors (managers and executives) whose skills and experience they want to learn about. Croft, the mentor, has answered Graham's questions about corporate programs and given her the opportunity to meet scientists and managers in the company. Graham has also learned more about the role of other departments in the company and budgetary priorities. Croft too has benefited from the relationship. He has learned about how management decisions affect employees. For example, when the toxicology lab was forced to begin to charge departments for its services (rather than being supported from the company's general fund), Croft learned about employees' reactions and anxieties from Graham.

Because of the lack of potential mentors or a formal reward system supporting mentoring, and the belief that the quality of mentorships developed in a formal program is poorer than informal mentoring relationships, some companies have initiated group mentoring programs. In **group mentoring programs,** a successful senior employee is paired with a group of four to six less experienced protégés. One potential advantage of the mentoring group is that protégés can learn from each other as well as from a more experienced senior employee. The leader helps protégés understand the organization, guides them in analyzing their experiences, and helps them clarify career directions. Each member of the group may complete specific assignments, or the group may work together on a problem or issue.[67]

The "Competing through Sustainability" box shows how mentoring programs can lead to value for different company stakeholders.

Coaching

A **coach** is a peer or manager who works with an employee to motivate him, help him develop skills, and provide reinforcement and feedback. There are three roles that a coach can play.[68] Part of coaching may be one-on-one with an employee (such as giving feedback). Another role is to help employees learn for themselves. This involves helping them find experts who can assist them with their concerns and teaching them how to obtain feedback from others. Third, coaching may involve providing resources such as mentors, courses, or job experiences that the employee may not be able to gain access to without the coach's help. For example, a middle manager at PG&E, an energy company, was hurting her relationships with her associates, and her management career, by her brash personality.[69] PG&E hired a coach to work with her. The coach videotaped her as she role-played an actual clash that she had had with another manager over a new information system. During the confrontation (and the role play), she was aloof, abrasive, cold, and condescending. The coach helped her see the limitations of her approach. She apologized to the colleague and listened to the colleague's ideas. Coaching helped this manager learn how to maintain her composure and focus on what was being said rather than on the person.

To develop coaching skills, training programs need to focus on four issues related to managers' reluctance to provide coaching.[70] First, managers may be reluctant to discuss performance issues even with a competent employee because they want to avoid con-

---

Group mentoring program
A program pairing a successful senior employee with a group of four to six less experienced protégés.

Coach
A peer or manager who works with an employee to motivate her, help her develop skills, and provide reinforcement and feedback.

Mentoring Programs
Have Potential to Pay
Individual, Corporate, and
Societal Dividends

A company's sustainability is determined by the extent to which it satisfies the needs of shareholders, customers, employees, community, and society. KLA-Tencor, Fannie Mae, and Cardinal Health are using mentoring programs to help employees learn new skills, encourage women and minorities to move into management positions, and develop management talent that can help sustain a business strategy.

KLA-Tencor, a supplier of process control solutions for the semiconductor industry, uses mentoring to improve senior managers' skills. The senior managers receive mentoring from company board members as well as retired company executives. The senior managers are expected to increase their functional expertise, identify specific performance goals and developmental activities to address job-related weaknesses, and increase their understanding of the company's culture, vision, and political structure. KLA-Tencor also has an online mentoring program for managers identified as having high potential for upper-level posi-

tions. The program includes an automated relationship pairing function and a 360-degree assessment that is used in the mentoring relationship to improve skill weaknesses.

Fannie Mae provides financial products and services that make it possible for families to purchase homes. At Fannie Mae, the company's mentoring program is designed to encourage the advancement of high-potential employees, especially women and minorities. To ensure that the mentor and protégé are compatible, a pairing committee conducts detailed screening and matching based on the mentor's and protégé's interests and expectations (e.g., What skills, experiences, and knowledge would you like your mentor to possess?). Fannie Mae provides guidelines to both mentors and protégés that identify what is expected of the relationship. Orientation sessions help the mentor and protégé become acquainted with each other. Both mentor and protégé sign a confidentiality agreement to build trust between the parties. To help ensure the success of the mentoring program, Fannie

Mae uses surveys to conduct formal and informal evaluations that help the company understand the strengths and weaknesses of the program.

Cardinal Health's mentoring program is designed to expose mentors and protégés to the company's different business units (e.g., pharmaceutical formulation, manufacturing, packaging, and distribution) for the purpose of developing managers who have a broad understanding of the Cardinal Health businesses. This cross-unit perspective is especially important because Cardinal Health has grown to be a global business through acquisitions. To ensure that mentors and protégés interact, Cardinal Health's program includes four formal sessions in which mentors and protégés meet at a business location. Both mentors and protégés are expected to make a specific time commitment to the program each month.

SOURCE: Based on T. Galvin, "Best Practices: Mentoring, KLA-Tencor Corp.," *Training*, March 2003, p. 58; A. Poe, "Establishing Positive Mentoring Relationships," *HR Magazine*, February 2002, pp. 62–69.

frontation. This is especially an issue when the manager is less of an expert than the employee. Second, managers may be better able to identify performance problems than to help employees solve them. Third, managers may also feel that the employee interprets coaching as criticism. Fourth, as companies downsize and operate with fewer employees, managers may feel that there is not enough time for coaching.

Career Management and Development Planning Systems

Companies' career management systems vary in the level of sophistication and the emphasis they place on different components of the process. Steps and responsibilities in the career management system are shown in Figure 9.2.

Self-Assessment

Self-assessment refers to the use of information by employees to determine their career interests, values, aptitudes, and behavioral tendencies. It often involves psychological tests such as the Myers-Briggs Type Indicator (described earlier in the chapter), the Strong-Campbell Interest Inventory, and the Self-Directed Search. The Strong-Campbell helps employees identify their occupational and job interests; the Self-Directed Search identifies employees' preferences for working in different types of environments (like sales, counseling, landscaping, and so on). Tests may also help employees identify the relative values they place on work and leisure activities. Self-assessment can involve exercises such as the one in Table 9.12. This type of exercise helps an employee consider where she is now in her career, identify future plans, and gauge how her career fits with her current situation and available resources. In some companies, counselors assist employees in the self-assessment process and interpret the results of psychological tests.

Through the assessment, a development need can be identified. This need can result from gaps between current skills and/or interests and the type of work or position the employee wants. For example, a branch manager at Wells Fargo Bank for 14 years enjoyed both working with computers and researching program development issues.[71] He was having difficulty in choosing whether to pursue further work experiences with computers or enter a new career in developing software applications. Psychological

FIGURE 9.2

Steps and Responsibilities in the Career Management Process

	Self-assessment	Reality check	Goal setting	Action planning
Employee responsibility	Identify opportunities and needs to improve.	Identify what needs are realistic to develop.	Identify goal and method to determine goal progress.	Identify steps and timetable to reach goal.
Company responsibility	Provide assessment information to identify strengths, weaknesses, interests, and values.	Communicate performance evaluation, where employee fits in long-range plans of the company, changes in industry, profession, and workplace.	Ensure that goal is specific, challenging, and attainable; commit to help employee reach the goal.	Identify resources employee needs to reach goal, including courses, work experiences, relationships.

TABLE 9.12

Example of a Self-Assessment Exercise

ACTIVITY   (PURPOSE)
Step 1:   *Where am I?* (Examine current position of life and career.) Think about your life from past and present to the future. Draw a time line to represent important events.
Step 2:   *Who am I?* (Examine different roles.) Using 3 × 5 cards, write down one answer per card to the question "Who am I?"
Step 3:   *Where would I like to be and what would I like to happen?*   (This helps in future goal setting.) Consider your life from present to future. Write an autobiography answering three questions: What do you want to have accomplished? What milestones do you want to achieve? What do you want to be remembered for?
Step 4:   *An ideal year in the future* (Identify resources needed.) Consider a one-year period in the future. If you had unlimited resources, what would you do? What would the ideal environment look like? Does the ideal environment match step 3?
Step 5:   *An ideal job* (Create current goal.) In the present, think about an ideal job for you with your available resources. Consider your role, resources, and type of training or education needed.
Step 6:   *Career by objective inventory* (Summarize current situation.) • What gets you excited each day? • What do you do well? What are you known for? • What do you need to achieve your goals? • What could interfere with reaching your goals? • What should you do now to move toward reaching your goals? • What is your long-term career objective?

SOURCE: Based on J. E. McMahon and S. K. Merman, "Career Development," in *The ASTD Training and Development Handbook*, 4th ed., ed. R. L. Craig. Copyright © 1996 The McGraw–Hill Companies. Reprinted with permission.

tests he completed as part of the company's career assessment program confirmed his strong interests in research and development. As a result, he began his own software design company.

Reality Check

Reality check refers to the information employees receive about how the company evaluates their skills and knowledge and where they fit into the company's plans (potential promotion opportunities, lateral moves). Usually this information is provided by the employee's manager as part of performance appraisal. It is not uncommon in well-developed career management systems for the manager to hold separate performance appraisals and career development discussions. For example, in Coca-Cola USA's system, employees and managers have a separate meeting after the annual performance review to discuss the employee's career interests, strengths, and possible development activities.[72]

Goal Setting

Goal setting refers to the process of employees developing short- and long-term career objectives. These goals usually relate to desired positions (such as becoming sales manager within three years), level of skill application (use one's budgeting skills to improve the unit's cash flow problems), work setting (move to corporate marketing within two years), or skill acquisition (learn how to use the company's human resource information system). These goals are usually discussed with the manager and written into a development plan. A development plan for a product manager is shown in Figure 9.3. Development plans usually include descriptions of strengths and weaknesses, career goals, and development activities for reaching the career goal.

FIGURE 9.3

Career Development Plan

Name: **Title:** Project Manager   **Immediate Manager:**

Competencies
Please identify your three greatest strengths and areas for improvement.
Strengths
- Strategic thinking and execution (confidence, command skills, action orientation)
- Results orientation (competence, motivating others, perseverance)
- Spirit for winning (building team spirit, customer focus, respect colleagues)

Areas for Improvement
- Patience (tolerance of people or processes and sensitivity to pacing)
- Written communications (ability to write clearly and succinctly)
- Overly ambitious (too much focus on successful completion of projects rather than developing relationships with individuals involved in the projects)

Career Goals
Please describe your overall career goals.
- **Long-term:** Accept positions of increased responsibility to a level of general manager (or beyond). The areas of specific interest include but are not limited to product and brand management, technology and development, strategic planning, and marketing.
- **Short-term:** Continue to improve my skills in marketing and brand management while utilizing my skills in product management, strategic planning, and global relations.

Next Assignments
Identify potential next assignments (including timing) that would help you develop toward your career goals.
- Manager or director level in planning, development, product, or brand management. Timing estimated to be Spring 2006.

Training and Development Needs
List both training and development activities that will either help you develop in your current assignment or provide overall career development.
- Master's degree classes will allow me to practice and improve my written communications skills. The dynamics of my current position, teamwork, and reliance on other individuals allow me to practice patience and to focus on individual team members' needs along with the success of the projects.

Employee _____   **Date** _____
Immediate Manager _____   **Date** _____
Mentor _____   **Date** _____

Action Planning

During this phase, employees determine how they will achieve their short- and long-term career goals. Action plans may involve any one or combination of development approaches discussed in the chapter (such as enrolling in courses and seminars, getting additional assessment, obtaining new job experiences, or finding a mentor or coach).[73] The development approach used depends on the needs and developmental goal.

Strategic Use of HRM

Banking conglomerate First USA created its Opportunity Knocks program in response to employee dissatisfaction with professional growth opportunities following the company's merger with Bank One. Development is a key component of a strategy to retain employees and ensure employees are ready to assume new jobs, duties, and responsibilities as new financial programs and services are offered to customers. The goals of the Opportunity Knocks program are to improve job satisfaction, reduce turnover, and increase the number of employees promoted. First USA also wants its employees to take charge of their own careers and to realize that promotions are not the only desirable career path. For example, lateral moves within the company help employees develop a greater range of experience and perspective by working at a different job at the same level. First USA has adopted "five Ps" as the core philosophy of the program—person, perspective, place, possibility, and plan. The "five Ps" relate to the steps and responsibilities in the career management process shown in Figure 9.2. The person, or individual employee, needs to understand his or her skills, values, and interests and communicate them so that career development is possible. Employees conduct self-assessments and seek feedback on them by talking to peers and managers (perspective). Employees need to understand not only First USA and their jobs but also developments in the industry, profession, and workplace requiring changes in employees' skills (place). Employees need to consider different possibilities within First USA: moving laterally or vertically or enriching the current job. And, employees need plans for developing new skills and competencies that will help them reach their career goals. The program includes career management skills workshops, and at each worksite career resource centers were set up with business publications, career management literature, and computers for preparing résumés. First USA also hired employment development advisers to counsel employees about their careers.

The program has had many positive benefits. Internal promotions at First USA have increased by 50 percent. When First USA repeated the employee attitude survey, it found that employee satisfaction with career development issues had increased more than 25 percent. The turnover rate among employees who participated in the Opportunity Knocks program was approximately 65 percent lower than that of employees who did not participate, saving the company an estimated $2.2 million in employee replacement costs.[74]

The "Competing through Globalization" box highlights the role of career management and development planning in successful global work assignments. Several important design factors should be considered in the process of developing a career management system (see Table 9.13).

Example of an Employee's Use of a Career Management System

Robert Brown, a program manager in an information systems department, needs to increase his knowledge of available project management software. His performance appraisal indicates that only 60 percent of the projects he is working on are being

Many companies are entering international markets by exporting their products overseas, building manufacturing facilities in other countries, entering into alliances with foreign companies, and engaging in e-commerce. This requires sending managers to work in international locations. As discussed in Chapter 8, these managers are known as expatriates. Expatriates work in a country other than their country of origin. For multinational companies, expatriate assignments are important for the business as well as developing managers who have the skills necessary for global business operations. Although many expatriate assignments can last several years, development planning is an important issue in successful repatriation (return to parent company and country).

Aside from the reentry stress and anxiety expatriates feel, many expatriates decide to leave the company because the assignment they are given upon returning to the parent country has less responsibility, challenge, and status than the foreign assignment. Career planning discussions need to be held before the employees leave to ensure that they understand the positions they will be eligible for upon repatriation.

Employees should be encouraged to self-manage the repatriation process. Before they go on the assignment, they need to consider what skills they want to develop and the types of jobs that might be available in the company for an employee with those skills. Because the company changes and because colleagues, peers, and managers may leave while the expatriate is on assignment, he or she needs to maintain contact with key company and industry people. Otherwise, the employee's reentry shock will be heightened from having to deal with new colleagues, a somewhat changed job, and a company culture that may have shifted.

Royal Dutch Shell, a joint Dutch and United Kingdom oil and gas company, has one of the world's largest expatriate workforces. To avoid expatriates who feel undervalued and leave the company, Royal Dutch gets involved with expatriates and their careers. Resource planners track workers abroad, helping to identify their next assignment. Most expatriates know their next assignment three to six months before the move, and all begin the next assignment with a clear job description. Expatriates who have the potential to reach top-level management positions are placed in the home office every third assignment to increase their visibility to company executives. Expatriates are also assigned technical mentors who evaluate their skills and help them improve their skills through training at Royal Dutch's training center.

SOURCE: Based on C. Solomon, "Unhappy Trails," *Workforce*, August 2000, pp. 36–41; H. Lancaster, "Before Going Overseas, Smart Managers Plan Their Homecoming," *The Wall Street Journal* (September 28, 1999), p. B1; A. Halcrow, "Expats: The Squandered Resource," *Workforce*, April 1999, pp. 42–48; J. Barbian, "Return to Sender," *Training*, January 2002, pp. 40–43.

approved due to incomplete information. (Assessment identified his development need.) As a result, Robert and his manager agree that his development goal is to increase his knowledge of available project management software, which can boost his effectiveness in project management. To raise his knowledge of project management software, Robert will read articles (formal education), meet software vendors, and contact vendors' customers for evaluations of the project management software they have used (job experiences). His manager will provide the names of customers to contact. Robert and his manager set six months as the target date for completion of these activities.

1. System is positioned as a response to a business need.
2. Employees and managers participate in development of the system.
3. Employees are encouraged to take an active role in career management.
4. Evaluation is ongoing and used to improve the system.
5. Business units can customize the system for their own purposes (with some constraints).
6. Employees need access to career information sources (including advisers and positions available).
7. Senior management supports the career system.
8. Career management is linked to other human resource practices such as performance management, training, and recruiting systems.

TABLE 9.13

Design Factors of Effective Career Management Systems

SOURCE: Based on B. Baumann, J. Duncan, S. E. Former, and Z. Leibowitz, "Amoco Primes the Talent Pump," *Personnel Journal*, February 1996, pp. 79–84.

Special Issues in Employee Development

Melting the Glass Ceiling

A major development issue facing companies today is how to get women and minorities into upper-level management positions—how to break the **glass ceiling.** The glass ceiling is a barrier to advancement to the higher levels of the organization. This barrier may be due to stereotypes or company systems that adversely affect the development of women or minorities.[75] The glass ceiling is likely caused by lack of access to training programs, appropriate developmental job experiences, and developmental relationships (such as mentoring).[76] Research has found no gender differences in access to job experiences involving transitions or creating change.[77] However, male managers receive significantly more assignments involving high levels of responsibility (high stakes, managing business diversity, handling external pressure) than female managers of similar ability and managerial level. Also, female managers report experiencing more challenge due to lack of personal support (a type of job demand considered to be an obstacle that has been found to relate to harmful stress) than male managers. Managers making developmental assignments need to carefully consider whether gender biases or stereotypes are influencing the types of assignments given to women versus men.

Women and minorities often have trouble finding mentors because of their lack of access to the "old boy network," managers' preference to interact with other managers of similar status rather than with line employees, and intentional exclusion by managers who have negative stereotypes about women's and minorities' abilities, motivation, and job preferences.[78] Potential mentors may view minorities and women as a threat to their job security because they believe affirmative action plans give those groups preferential treatment.

Wal-Mart's strong corporate culture—emphasizing leadership, trust, willingness to relocate on short notice, and promotion from within—may have unintentionally created a glass ceiling.[79] Eighty-six percent of store manager positions are held by men. More than two-thirds of Wal-Mart managers started as hourly employees. Hourly job openings are posted at each store, but Wal-Mart never posted openings for management training positions that allowed hourly employees to move up into salaried, management positions. Part of the reason for this practice was that Wal-Mart values efficiency and never saw the need for job postings to fill open management

Glass ceiling
A barrier to advancement to higher-level jobs in the company that adversely affects women and minorities. The barrier may be due to lack of access to training programs, development experiences, or relationships (e.g., mentoring).

positions. The other reason is that Wal-Mart trusts its managers to promote individuals who deserve promotion. However, women at Wal-Mart claim that it is difficult to find out about manager jobs. Traditionally, managers at Wal-Mart had to be willing to move with short notice. At Wal-Mart, this relocation requirement results in more opportunities for management jobs for men than for women. Male employees had more access to information about management job openings because they spent more time socializing and talking with management employees (who are primarily male). Wal-Mart is taking steps to ensure that the company remains a good place to work. For example, to give women more opportunities for management positions, Wal-Mart is developing a posting system for all management jobs. The company also plans on providing employees with a database that will notify them of job openings at stores across the country.

Consider Deloitte & Touche's efforts to melt the glass ceiling. Deloitte & Touche is an accounting, tax, and consulting firm with offices throughout the United States. The company had been experiencing high turnover of talented women and set out to understand why this was occurring and what the company could do to stop it.[80] Table 9.14 shows Deloitte & Touche's recommendations for melting the glass ceiling. Deloitte's Initiative for the Retention and Advancement of Women grew from a task force chaired by the company's chief executive officer. Deloitte & Touche made a business case for change by showing the senior partners of the company that half of the new hires were women, and half of them left the company before becoming candidates for upper management positions (partners). Data on the problem were gathered by having every management professional in the company attend a workshop designed to explore how gender attitudes affected the work environment (and led to the loss of talented women). The workshops included discussions, videos, and case studies. For example, a case scenario involved having partners evaluate two promising employees, one male and one female, with identical skills. One issue that was raised through the case analysis was that men get evaluated based on their potential, women based on their performance. Discussion suggested that the male could be expected to grow into the position through mentoring and other types of development. The female was evaluated based on performance in her current position. Her potential was not considered; rather, her past performance indicated that she was good in her current job but didn't have the necessary skills to move into executive management. The workshop also focused on how work assignments were allocated. High-profile, high-revenue assignments were important for advancement in the company. Workshop discussion showed that women were passed over for these desirable assignments because of false assumptions that male partners made about what women wanted, such as no travel. Also, women tended to get assigned to projects that were in the non-

TABLE 9.14

Deloitte & Touche's Recommendations for Melting the Glass Ceiling

Make sure senior management supports and is involved in the program.
Make a business case for change.
Make the change public.
Gather data on problems causing the glass ceiling using task forces, focus groups, and questionnaires.
Create awareness of how gender attitudes affect the work environment.
Force accountability through reviews of promotion rates and assignment decisions.
Promote development for all employees.

SOURCE: Based on D. McCracken, "Winning the Talent War for Women," *Harvard Business Review,* November–December 2000, pp. 159–67.

profit, health care, and retail sectors—important segments but not as visible as areas like manufacturing, financial services, or mergers and acquisitions.

As a result of the workshops, Deloitte & Touche began discussing assignment decisions to make sure women had opportunities for highly visible assignments. Also, the company started formal career planning for both women and men. The company also sponsored networking events for women, where they had the opportunity to hear from successful women partners and meet other women at their level and higher in the company.

To measure the effectiveness of the program, Deloitte & Touche offices were given a menu of goals that they could choose from as evaluation criteria, including recruiting more women and reducing turnover. The compensation and promotability of office managers depended in part on their meeting these objectives. The company communicated to top management results on turnover and promotion rates for each office. Low-performing offices were visited by top managers to facilitate more progress.

Melting the glass ceiling takes time. Currently 14 percent of Deloitte & Touche's partners and directors are women, and women's and men's turnover rates are comparable. Reducing the turnover rate for women has saved the company an estimated $250 million in hiring and training costs. Deloitte is still striving to make sure that more women are partners and directors. In a global business world, one challenge is to extend the values of the initiative while respecting local cultural norms that might view women as less desirable employees or business partners.

Many companies, as part of their approach to managing a diverse workforce, are using mentoring programs to ensure that women and minorities gain the skills and visibility needed to move into managerial positions. Procter and Gamble (P&G) has a unique program called "Mentoring Up," which asks mid- and junior-level female managers to mentor senior-level managers to raise their awareness of work-related issues affecting women.[81] The goals of the program are to reduce turnover of promising female managers, to give women managers greater exposure to P&G's top decision makers, and to improve cross-gender communications. Mentoring Up was developed because of turnover of high-potential female employees who in exit interviews cited not feeling valued (rather than money, promotions, or better assignments) as the reason why they were leaving the company. Although the program was designed to help upper-level managers better understand how to manage women, the program also includes five upper-level female managers who are participating as mentees.

How does the program work? It incorporates many characteristics of effective mentoring programs. All eligible female junior-level managers and male senior-level managers are expected to participate. The female managers must have at least one year of tenure and be good performers. Junior mentors are matched with senior mentors based on their responses to a questionnaire. Both mentors and protégés attend an orientation session that includes a panel discussion by past participants in the program and a series of exercises probing women's workplace issues and reasons for success at P&G. The mentor-mentee pairs are required to meet at least once every two months. Mentors and mentees receive discussion guides designed to help facilitate dialogue. For example, one guide asked the mentor-mentee pairs to explore the keys to success and failure for women and men in company leadership positions. The discussion guides also include questions designed to elicit feelings about when women feel valued. The mentor and mentee explore differences and similarities in responses to these questions to identify how people like to be recognized. Two issues have frequently been raised in the mentor-mentee relationships: first, the barriers that women face in achieving a balance between work and life and, second, differences in managerial and decision-making styles between men and women.

Succession Planning

Many companies are losing sizable numbers of upper-level managers due to retirement and company restructurings that reduced the number of potential upper-level managers. They are finding that their middle managers are not ready to move into upper management positions due to skill weaknesses or lack of needed experience. This creates the need for succession planning. Succession planning refers to the process of identifying and tracking high-potential employees. **Succession planning** helps organizations in several different ways.[82] It requires senior management to systematically review leadership talent in the company. It assures that top-level managerial talent is available. It provides a set of development experiences that managers must complete to be considered for top management positions; this avoids premature promotion of managers who are not ready for upper management ranks. Succession planning systems also help attract and retain managerial employees by providing them with development opportunities that they can complete if upper management is a career goal for them. **High-potential employees** are those the company believes are capable of being successful in higher-level managerial positions such as general manager of a strategic business unit, functional director (such as director of marketing), or chief executive officer (CEO).[83] High-potential employees typically complete an individual development program that involves education, executive mentoring and coaching, and rotation through job assignments. Job assignments are based on the successful career paths of the managers whom the high-potential employees are being prepared to replace. High-potential employees may also receive special assignments, such as making presentations and serving on committees and task forces.

Research suggests that the development of high-potential employees involves three stages.[84] A large pool of employees may initially be identified as high-potential employees, but the numbers are reduced over time because of turnover, poor performance, or a personal choice not to strive for a higher position. In stage 1, high-potential employees are selected. Those who have completed elite academic programs (like an MBA at Stanford) or who have been outstanding performers are identified. Psychological tests such as assessment centers may also be used.

In stage 2, high-potential employees receive development experiences. Those who succeed are the ones who continue to demonstrate good performance. A willingness to make sacrifices for the company is also necessary (such as accepting new assignments or relocating to a different region). Good oral and written communication skills, an ease in interpersonal relationships, and a talent for leadership are critical. In what is known as a "tournament model" of job transitions, high-potential employees who meet their senior managers' expectations in this stage advance into the next stage of the process.[85] Employees who do not meet the expectations are ineligible for higher-level managerial positions in the company.

To reach stage 3, high-potential employees usually have to be seen by top management as fitting into the company's culture and having the personality characteristics needed to successfully represent the company. These employees have the potential to occupy the company's top positions. In stage 3, the CEO becomes actively involved in developing the employees, who are exposed to the company's key personnel and are given a greater understanding of the company's culture. It is important to note that the development of high-potential employees is a slow process. Reaching stage 3 may take 15 to 20 years.

Table 9.15 shows the process used to develop a succession plan. The first step is to identify what positions are included in the succession plan, such as all management positions or only certain levels of management. The second step is to identify which

---

Succession planning
The identification and tracking of high-potential employees capable of filling higher-level managerial positions.

High-potential employees
Employees the company believes are capable of being successful in high-level management positions.

1. Identify what positions are included in the plan.
2. Identify the employees who are included in the plan.
3. Develop standards to evaluate positions (e.g., competencies, desired experiences, desired knowledge, developmental value).
4. Determine how employee potential will be measured (e.g., current performance and potential performance).
5. Develop the succession planning review.
6. Link the succession planning system with other human resource systems, including training and development, compensation, and staffing systems.
7. Determine what feedback is provided to employees.

TABLE 9.15

The Process of Developing a Succession Plan

SOURCE: Based on B. Dowell, "Succession Planning," in *Implementing Organizational Interventions,* ed. J. Hedge and E. Pulaskos (San Francisco: Jossey-Bass, 2002), pp. 78–109.

employees are part of the succession planning system. For example, in some companies only high-potential employees are included in the succession plan. Third, the company needs to identify how positions will be evaluated. For example, will the emphasis be on competencies needed for each position or on the experiences an individual needs to have before moving into the position? Fourth, the company should identify how employee potential will be measured. That is, will employees' performance in their current jobs as well as ratings of potential be used? Will employees' position interests and career goals be considered? Fifth, the succession planning review process needs to be developed. Typically, succession planning reviews first involve employees' managers and human resources. A talent review could also include an overall assessment of leadership talent in the company, an identification of high-potential employees, and a discussion of plans to keep key managers from leaving the company. Sixth, succession planning is dependent on other human resource systems, including compensation, training and development, and staffing. Incentives and bonuses may be linked to completion of development opportunities. Activities such as training courses, job experiences, mentors, and 360-degree feedback can be used to meet development needs. Companies need to make decisions such as will they fill an open management position internally with a less-experienced employee who will improve in the role over time, or will they hire a manager from outside the company who can immediately deliver results. Finally, employees need to be provided with feedback on future moves, expected career paths, and development goals and experiences.

A good example of succession planning is the system at WellPoint, a health care company headquartered in Thousand Oaks, California.[86] WellPoint has a Web-based corporate database that identifies employees for management jobs throughout the company and tracks the development of employee talent. WellPoint has operations across the United States, including locations in California and Georgia. The succession planning system includes 600 managers and executives across five levels of the company. The Human Resource Planning System (HRPS) has detailed information on possible candidates, including performance evaluations, summaries of the candidates' accomplishments at the company, self-evaluations, information about career goals, and personal data such as the candidates' willingness to relocate to another part of the company. Part of the development of HRPS involved identifying the company's strength and weaknesses at each position. Senior management team members developed standards, or benchmarks, to use to identify the best candidates for promotion. The HRPS system allows managers and the human resource team to identify and evaluate candidates for every management position in the company. It helps identify and track the development of promising internal candidates and also identifies areas where internal candidates are weak, so that (1) external candidates can be recruited, (2) a special development program can be initiated to develop employee talent, and (3) the company can place more emphasis on developing the missing skills and competencies in internal candidates. For example, because WellPoint lacked candidates for two levels of management, the company created a special training program that used business case simulations for 24 managers and executives who had been identified as high-potential candidates for upper-level management positions.

WellPoint's process of succession planning includes several steps. First, each employee who is eligible for succession planning completes a self-evaluation that is sent to his or her manager. The manager adds a performance appraisal, a rating on the employee's core competencies, and a promotion assessment, that is, an assessment of the employee's potential for promotion. The promotion assessment includes the manager's opinion regarding what positions the employee might be ready for and when the employee should be moved. It also includes the manager's view on who could fill the open position if the employee is promoted. The information from the employee and the manager is used to create an online résumé for each eligible employee. The system has benefited the company's bottom line. WellPoint realized an 86 percent internal promotion rate, which exceeded its goal of filling 75 percent of management positions from within. By improving employees' opportunities for promotion, WellPoint has reduced its turnover rate by 6 percent since 1997 and has saved $21 million on recruitment and training expenses. The time to fill open management positions has been reduced from 60 days to 35 days.

Helping Managers with Dysfunctional Behaviors

A number of studies have identified managerial behavior that can cause an otherwise competent manager to be a "toxic" or ineffective manager. Such behavior includes insensitivity to others, inability to be a team player, arrogance, poor conflict management skills, inability to meet business objectives, and inability to change or adapt during a transition.[87] For example, a skilled manager who is interpersonally abrasive, aggressive, and an autocratic leader may find it difficult to motivate subordinates, may alienate internal and external customers, and may have trouble getting ideas accepted by superiors. These managers are in jeopardy of losing their jobs and have little chance of future advancement because of the dysfunctional behavior. Typically, a combination of assessment, training, and counseling is used to help managers change the dysfunctional behavior.

One example of a program designed specifically to help managers with dysfunctional behavior is the Individual Coaching for Effectiveness (ICE) program.[88] Although such programs' effectiveness needs to be further investigated, research suggests that managers' participation in them improves skill and reduces likelihood of termination.[89] The ICE program includes diagnosis, coaching, and support activities, tailored to the manager's needs. Clinical, counseling, or industrial-organizational psychologists are involved in all phases of the ICE program. They conduct the diagnosis, coach and counsel the manager, and develop action plans for implementing new skills on the job.

The first step in the ICE program, diagnosis, involves collecting information about the manager's personality, skills, and interests. Interviews with the manager, his or her supervisor, and colleagues as well as psychological tests collect this information to determine whether the manager can actually change the dysfunctional behavior. For example, personality traits such as extreme defensiveness may make behavior change difficult. If it is determined that the manager can benefit from the program, then specific developmental objectives are set. The manager and supervisor are typically involved in this process.

The coaching phase of the program first involves presenting the manager with information about the targeted skills or behavior. This may include information about principles of effective communication or teamwork, tolerance of individual differences in the workplace, or conducting effective meetings. The second step is for the manager to participate in behavior modeling training (discussed in Chapter 7). The manager also receives psychological counseling to overcome beliefs that may inhibit learning the desired behavior.

The support phase of the program creates conditions to ensure that the manager can use the new behaviors and skills acquired in the ICE program on the job. The supervisor provides feedback to the manager and the psychologist about progress made in using the new skills and behavior. The psychologist and manager identify situations in which the manager may tend to rely on dysfunctional behavior. The coach and manager also develop action plans that outline how the manager should try to use new behavior in daily work activities.

A Look Back

The chapter opener described Booz Allen Hamilton's development program designed to help employees develop and take charge of their careers.

Questions
1. How might job experiences be useful for helping employees develop?
2. To be effective, what should a development plan include that an employee at Booz Allen Hamilton might complete as part of the Development Framework?

Summary

This chapter emphasized the various development methods that companies use: formal education, assessment, job experiences, and interpersonal relationships. Most companies use one or more of these approaches to develop employees. Formal education involves enrolling employees in courses or seminars offered by the company or educational institutions. Assessment involves measuring the employee's performance, behavior, skills, or personality characteristics. Job experiences include job enlargement, rotating to a new job, promotions, or transfers. A more experienced, senior employee (a mentor) can help employees better understand the company and gain exposure and visibility to key persons in the organization. Part of a manager's job responsibility may be to coach employees. Regardless of the development approaches used, employees should have a development plan to identify (1) the type of development needed, (2) development goals, (3) the best approach for development, and (4) whether development goals have been reached. For development plans to be effective, both the employee and the company have responsibilities that need to be completed.

Discussion Questions

1. How could assessment be used to create a productive work team?
2. List and explain the characteristics of effective 360-degree feedback systems.
3. Why do companies develop formal mentoring programs? What are the potential benefits for the mentor? For the protégé?
4. Your boss is interested in hiring a consultant to help identify potential managers among current employees of a fast food restaurant. The manager's job is to help

wait on customers and prepare food during busy times, oversee all aspects of restaurant operations (including scheduling, maintenance, on-the-job training, and food purchase), and help motivate employees to provide high-quality service. The manager is also responsible for resolving disputes that might occur between employees. The position involves working under stress and coordinating several activities at one time. She asks you to outline the type of assessment program you believe would do the best job of identifying employees who will be successful managers. What will you tell her?

5. Many employees are unwilling to relocate because they like their current community, and spouses and children prefer not to move. Yet employees need to develop new skills, strengthen skill weaknesses, and be exposed to new aspects of the business to prepare for management positions. How could an employee's current job be changed to develop management skills?

6. What is coaching? Is there one type of coaching? Explain.

7. Why are many managers reluctant to coach their employees?

8. Why should companies be interested in helping employees plan their careers? What benefits can companies gain? What are the risks?

9. What are the manager's roles in a career management system? Which role do you think is most difficult for the typical manager? Which is the easiest role? List the reasons why managers might resist involvement in career management.

10. What are the characteristics of the most effective company development strategies? Which characteristic do you believe is most important? Why?

11. Nationwide Financial, a 5,000-employee life insurance company based in Columbus, Ohio, found that their management development program contained four types of managers. One type, unknown leaders, have the right skills but their talents are unknown to top managers in the company. Another group, arrogant leaders, believe they have all the skills they need. What types of development program would you recommend for these managers?

Self-Assessment Exercise

Career Key is an online tool that can be used for career management and employee development. Use it to try some planning of your own career. Visit the site at www.careerkey.org. Click first on "You," then on "Take the Career Key." After you have completed the assessment, review your scores on the six dimensions.

1. What do the six dimensions represent? (Hint: Go back to the Career Key home page.)

2. On what three personality types do you receive the highest score?

3. Review the jobs listed under your three highest dimensions. Of these jobs, which are you most interested in?

4. Do any of these jobs match your college major, current job, or career interests?

5. How might the Career Key help you develop or manage your career? How might a company benefit from using the Career Key for employee development or career management?

Manager's Hot Seat Exercise: Personal Disclosure: Confession Coincidence?

This Manager's Hot Seat case examines the role managers can take in assisting the development of employees. In this case, a manager counsels one of her employees. The employee's job performance has become significantly compromised. She has been missing deadlines and reporting in late for work on a regular basis.

The discussion, which ensues between these two individuals, reveals the employee has been battling a problem—alcoholism. The manager offers suggestions to the employee and the employee is able to improve on her performance. However, an organizational layoff creates ten-

sion and the employee feels she is being let go because she revealed her problem. The manager disputes this claim.

This case identifies how important it is for managers to be involved in helping their employees develop into the type of worker who is best suited for the organization.

Group Activity:

The class should divide into groups of 4–5 students. The members of each group are to discuss how they would have handled the scenario that was presented in the case. Each member should identify what they would have done the same? What they would have done differently? Have the group response prepared for class discussion.

Next, the group members are to discuss the overall issue of employee development. Suggestions for topics to discuss should include the following:

- What is employee development?
- Why is employee development important?

- What can organizations do to further the development of their employees?
- Why should organizations concern themselves with this matter?
- How can managers effectively assist with the employee development process?
- What organizational gains can be had through effective employee development?

Exercising Strategy: Employees in Motion at PPG Industries

PPG Industries, based in Pittsburgh, Pennsylvania, manufactures coatings for transportation and other industries. PPG is a decentralized company with 16 different businesses. Although the businesses differ in many aspects, they share a need: to develop employees to fill the role of general manager, an important position within PPG. General management positions help employees build competencies needed for top leadership positions with PPG. Recently, senior executives of PPG have taken an aggressive approach to developing the company's future leaders by moving employees to new positions. For example, a sales position is now occupied by a human resource manager. A new plant manager was previously an experienced salesperson. What's the reason for putting employees in mo-

tion, that is, moving them to new positions? PPG anticipates a significant need for leaders because of retirements and turnover. Replacements for these leaders are not available from the positions that are traditionally used to staff leadership positions.

Questions
1. PPG is relying on moving employees to new positions as a development strategy. What things should PPG do to ensure this is a successful strategy? Are other development activities necessary? Why?
2. What data on outcomes should be collected to monitor the effectiveness of PPG Industries' development program?

Managing People: From the Pages of *BusinessWeek*

BusinessWeek How to Groom the Next Boss

Of all the challenges confronting managers and directors, few are as difficult or as critical as finding and training a chief executive-in-waiting. At Coca-Cola, Xerox, and Procter & Gamble, CEO successions have been marked by long searches, poor choices, or fumbled transitions. But a company with a well-prepared No. 2 can quell uncertainty, even in the worst emergencies. When McDonald's Corp. CEO James Cantalupo died of a heart attack on April 19, the board named Chief Operating Officer Charles H. Bell to his post within hours.

Kenneth W. Freeman, CEO of Quest Diagnostics Inc., was determined not to leave his company in the lurch. He started grooming his handpicked successor five years ago. When he transfers management of the $4.7 billion medical-testing company to Surya N. Mohapatra at the May 4 annual meeting, it will be the culmination of a meticulous succession process that experts say is a case study in how to choose a future CEO and prepare him for the job. Marc S. Effron, global practice leader for consultants Hewitt Associates Inc., says the careful succession planning at the Teterboro (N.J.)–based company will pay

off with a new CEO who can hit the ground running. "It's incredibly unusual," says Effron of Freeman's efforts. "They're going to see the benefits."

Freeman's search for a successor started in 1999. He was on the brink of an acquisition spree that would triple Quest's revenues in five years. But he knew the buying binge couldn't last and that Quest's next CEO would need a science background to exploit advances in medicine and technology to generate internal growth. To identify candidates, he put 200 executives from Quest and a recently acquired rival through an *Apprentice*-like challenge: day-long case assignments that allowed him to see their leadership skills in action. "This was his legacy," says Audrey B. Smith, a consultant with Development Dimensions International who worked with Freeman. "He felt huge pressure to make the right decision."

Of all the executives, one stood out: his new chief operating officer. Mohapatra came to Quest in February, 1999, from Picker International, a maker of medical imaging systems. He had extensive experience in cardiovascular disease and information technology—areas that would be crucial to Quest's future. What's more, he was CEO material. Says Freeman: "Here was a guy who was incredibly smart, who could balance a whole bunch of priorities at the same time, who could be incredibly focused, and who did not know the meaning of failure."

Four months after Mohapatra's arrival, Freeman named him president, giving him a clear—but by no means guaranteed—shot at the top job. The two men could not be more different. Mohapatra, a scientist with several patents to his name, grew up in India. Freeman, a New Yorker, had a long finance career at Corning Inc. When Corning Clinical Laboratories was spun off as Quest in 1996, Freeman became CEO, a position he says he had no intention of occupying for more than 10 years.

Front-runner or not, it quickly became clear that if Mohapatra was to be CEO he would need basic leadership skills. During his first week, one of the most glaring deficiencies, poor public speaking skills, became apparent. At a "town meeting" with employees in Baltimore, Mohapatra told the crowd of 800 that he was glad to be there—then clammed up. Freeman decided the best way to coax Mohapatra out of his shell was trial by fire. In the months that followed, he had Mohapatra make unscripted comments to employees, meet with shareholders, and field questions from analysts on conference calls. He is now a more polished, confident speaker.

As a scientist, Mohapatra had come to Quest with habits that Freeman felt could undermine him as a CEO. A deep thinker, he took weeks to make decisions that should only take days. And he was far more "hands-on" than he needed to be, sometimes reopening interviews for jobs that his subordinates were ready to fill. Freeman challenged Mohapatra to make faster decisions and give his executive team more authority. Every Sunday afternoon for five years, the two engaged in lengthy telephone conversations during which Freeman would analyze Mohapatra's evolving management style and suggest further improvements. It was, Freeman now concedes, "pure browbeating."

Perhaps, but it worked. "Am I more ready now than I was four years ago? Absolutely," says Mohapatra.

Fine-tuning Mohapatra's management skills was only part of the challenge. Making him an active board participant was equally important. When he arrived, Mohapatra deferred to Freeman in board debates, contributing little. Freeman forced him to be more assertive—at first surreptitiously, by leaving the room during discussions, and later by asking him to conduct formal board presentations. Even after joining the board in 2002, Mohapatra continued to strike some directors as aloof. By changing the seating chart, Freeman was able to increase Mohapatra's face time with other directors. "You want someone to be able to speak their mind and participate," says Gail R. Wilensky, an independent director. "It helped."

When his long incubation ends, Mohapatra's success will be far from assured. Maintaining double-digit growth won't be easy as takeover targets become scarce. That's the way it is in business; the future is never assured. But Freeman has done about as much to increase the odds as a CEO can.

SOURCE: Reprinted from May 10, 2004, issue of *BusinessWeek* by special permission. L. Lavelle, "How to Groom the Next Boss," *BusinessWeek* (May 10, 2004), pp. 93–94.

Questions

1. What development activities did Kenneth Freeman use to strengthen the skills of Surya Mohapatra (his successor)? List the activities and the skills they were designed to improve. What other development activities could he have used? Identify the development activities and the skills they would be targeted to improve.
2. Could a coach help Mohapatra develop the skills needed to be an effective CEO? Explain.
3. What recommendations do you have for identifying and preparing managers for CEO positions? Indicate the succession planning process as well as the development activities you would recommend.

Please see the video cases at the end of the book that correspond to this chapter: 1) Patagonia, 2) Women are Working in Jobs Once Almost Exclusively Filled by Men.

Notes

1. C. Taylor, "Focus on Talent," *TD*, December 2002, pp. 26–31.
2. M. London, *Managing the Training Enterprise* (San Francisco: Jossey-Bass, 1989).
3. R. W. Pace, P. C. Smith, and G. E. Mills, *Human Resource Development* (Englewood Cliffs, NJ: Prentice Hall, 1991); W. Fitzgerald, "Training versus Development," *Training and Development Journal*, May 1992, pp. 81–84; R. A. Noe, S. L. Wilk,

E. J. Mullen, and J. E. Wanek, "Employee Development: Issues in Construct Definition and Investigation of Antecedents," in *Improving Training Effectiveness in Work Organizations*, ed. J. K. Ford (Mahwah, NJ: Lawrence Erlbaum, 1997), pp. 153–89.
4. J. H. Greenhaus and G. A. Callanan, *Career Management*, 2nd ed. (Fort Worth, TX: Dryden Press, 1994); D. C. Feldman, *Managing Careers in Organizations* (Glenview, IL: Scott Foresman,

1988); D. Hall, *Careers In and Out of Organizations* (Thousand Oaks, CA: Sage, 2002).

5. D. T. Hall, "Protean Careers of the 21st Century," *Academy of Management Executive* 11 (1996), pp. 8–16.

6. D. M. Rousseau, "Changing the Deal while Keeping the People," *Academy of Management Executive* 11 (1996), pp. 50–61; D. M. Rousseau and J. M. Parks, "The Contracts of Individuals and Organizations," in *Research in Organizational Behavior* 15, ed. L. L. Cummings and B. M. Staw (Greenwich, CT: JAI Press, 1992), pp. 1–47.

7. C. Ansberry, "A New Blue-Collar World," *The Wall Street Journal* (June 30, 2003), p. B1.

8. P. Sellers, "Don't Call Me a Slacker," *Fortune* (December 12, 1994), pp. 181–96.

9. M. B. Arthur, P. H. Claman, and R. J. DeFillippi, "Intelligent Enterprise, Intelligent Careers," *Academy of Management Executive* 9 (1995), pp. 7–20.

10. K. R. Brousseau, M. J. Driver, K. Eneroth, and R. Larsson, "Career Pandemonium: Realigning Organizations and Individuals," *Academy of Management Executive* 11 (1996), pp. 52–66.

11. M. B. Arthur, "The Boundaryless Career: A New Perspective of Organizational Inquiry," *Journal of Organization Behavior* 15 (1994), pp. 295–309; P. H. Mirvis and D. T. Hall, "Psychological Success and the Boundaryless Career," *Journal of Organization Behavior* 15 (1994), pp. 365–80.

12. B. P. Grossman and R. S. Blitzer, "Choreographing Careers," *Training and Development*, January 1992, pp. 67–69.

13. J. S. Lubin and J. B. White, "Throwing Off Angst, Workers Are Feeling in Control of Their Careers," *The Wall Street Journal* (September 11, 1997), pp. A1, A6.

14. R. J. Campbell, "HR Development Strategies," in *Developing Human Resources*, ed. K. N. Wexley (Washington, DC: BNA Books, 1991), pp. 5-1–5-34; M. A. Sheppeck and C. A. Rhodes, "Management Development: Revised Thinking in Light of New Events of Strategic Importance," *Human Resource Planning* 11 (1988) pp. 159–72; B. Keys and J. Wolf, "Management Education: Current Issues and Emerging Trends," *Journal of Management* 14 (1988), pp. 205–29; L. M. Saari, T. R. Johnson, S. D. McLaughlin, and D. Zimmerle, "A Survey of Management Training and Education Practices in U.S. Companies," *Personnel Psychology* 41 (1988), pp. 731–44.

15. *Cardinal Health: A Tradition of Performance* (Dublin, OH: Cardinal Health, 2003), brochure.

16. www.gecareers.com/GECAREERS/jsp/campus/cldp_program_guide.jsp.

17. J. Bolt, *Executive Development* (New York: Harper Business, 1989); M. A. Hitt, B. B. Tyler, C. Hardee, and D. Park, "Understanding Strategic Intent in the Global Marketplace," *Academy of Management Executive* 9 (1995), pp. 12–19.

18. J. A. Byrne, "Virtual Business Schools," *BusinessWeek* (October 23, 1995), pp. 64–68; T. Bartlett, "The Hottest Campus on the Internet," *BusinessWeek* (October 20, 1997), pp. 77–80.

19. J. Reingold, "Corporate America Goes to School," *BusinessWeek* (October 20, 1997), pp. 66–72.

20. Ibid.

21. L. Bongiorno, "How'm I Doing," *BusinessWeek* (October 23, 1995), pp. 72, 74.

22. T. A. Stewart, "GE Keeps Those Ideas Coming," *Fortune* (August 12, 1991), pp. 41–49.

23. G. P. Hollenbeck, "What Did You Learn in School? Studies of a University Executive Program," *Human Resource Planning* 14 (1991), pp. 247–60.

24. A. Howard and D. W. Bray, *Managerial Lives in Transition: Advancing Age and Changing Times* (New York: Guilford, 1988);

Bolt, *Executive Development*; J. R. Hinrichs and G. P. Hollenbeck, "Leadership Development," in *Developing Human Resources*, ed. K. N. Wexley (Washington, DC: BNA Books, 1991), pp. 5-221 to 5-237.

25. S. K. Hirsch, *MBTI Team Member's Guide* (Palo Alto, CA: Consulting Psychologists Press, 1992); A. L. Hammer, *Introduction to Type and Careers* (Palo Alto, CA: Consulting Psychologists Press, 1993).

26. A. Thorne and H. Gough, *Portraits of Type* (Palo Alto, CA: Consulting Psychologists Press, 1991).

27. D. Druckman and R. A. Bjork, eds., *In the Mind's Eye: Enhancing Human Performance* (Washington, DC: National Academy Press, 1991); M. H. McCaulley, "The Myers-Briggs Type Indicator and Leadership," in *Measures of Leadership*, ed. K. E. Clark and M. B. Clark (West Orange, NJ: Leadership Library of America, 1990), pp. 381–418.

28. G. C. Thornton III and W. C. Byham, *Assessment Centers and Managerial Performance* (New York: Academic Press, 1982); L. F. Schoenfeldt and J. A. Steger, "Identification and Development of Management Talent," in *Research in Personnel and Human Resource Management*, ed. K. N. Rowland and G. Ferris (Greenwich, CT: JAI Press, 1989), vol. 7, pp. 151–81.

29. Thornton and Byham, *Assessment Centers and Managerial Performance*.

30. B. B. Gaugler, D. B. Rosenthal, G. C. Thornton III, and C. Bentson, "Metaanalysis of Assessment Center Validity," *Journal of Applied Psychology* 72 (1987), pp. 493–511; D. W. Bray, R. J. Campbell, and D. L. Grant, *Formative Years in Business: A Long-Term AT&T Study of Managerial Lives* (New York: Wiley, 1974).

31. R. G. Jones and M. D. Whitmore, "Evaluating Developmental Assessment Centers as Interventions," *Personnel Psychology* 48 (1995), pp. 377–88.

32. J. Schettler, "Building Bench Strength," *Training*, June 2002, pp. 55–58.

33. C. D. McCauley and M. M. Lombardo, "Benchmarks: An Instrument for Diagnosing Managerial Strengths and Weaknesses," in *Measures of Leadership*, pp. 535–45.

34. C. D. McCauley, M. M. Lombardo, and C. J. Usher, "Diagnosing Management Development Needs: An Instrument Based on How Managers Develop," *Journal of Management* 15 (1989), pp. 389–403.

35. S. B. Silverman, "Individual Development through Performance Appraisal," in *Developing Human Resources*, pp. 5-120 to 5-151.

36. J. S. Lublin, "Turning the Tables: Underlings Evaluate Bosses," *The Wall Street Journal* (October 4, 1994), pp. B1, B14; B. O'Reilly, "360-Degree Feedback Can Change Your Life," *Fortune* (October 17, 1994), pp. 93–100; J. F. Milliman, R. A. Zawacki, C. Norman, L. Powell, and J. Kirksey, "Companies Evaluate Employees from All Perspectives," *Personnel Journal*, November 1994, pp. 99–103.

37. Center for Creative Leadership, *Skillscope for Managers: Development Planning Guide* (Greensboro, NC: Center for Creative Leadership, 1992); G. Yukl and R. Lepsinger, "360-Degree Feedback," *Training*, December 1995, pp. 45–50.

38. S. Caudron, "Building Better Bosses," *Workforce*, May 2000, pp. 33–39.

39. L. Atwater, P. Roush, and A. Fischthal, "The Influence of Upward Feedback on Self- and Follower Ratings of Leadership," *Personnel Psychology* 48 (1995), pp. 35–59; J. F. Hazucha, S. A. Hezlett, and R. J. Schneider, "The Impact of 360-Degree Feedback on Management Skill Development," *Human Resource Management* 32 (1993), pp. 325–51; J. W. Smither, M. London, N. Vasilopoulos, R. R. Reilly, R. E. Millsap, and N. Salvemini,

"An Examination of the Effects of an Upward Feedback Program over Time," *Personnel Psychology* 48 (1995), pp. 1–34.

40. D. Bracken, "Straight Talk about Multirater Feedback," *Training and Development*, September 1994, pp. 44–51; K. Nowack, J. Hartley, and W. Bradley, "How to Evaluate Your 360-Feedback Efforts," *Training and Development*, April 1999, pp. 48–52.

41. A. Freedman, "The Evolution of 360s," *Human Resource Executive*, December 2002, pp. 47–51.

42. M. W. McCall, Jr., M. M. Lombardo, and A. M. Morrison, *Lessons of Experience* (Lexington, MA: Lexington Books, 1988).

43. R. S. Snell, "Congenial Ways of Learning: So Near yet So Far," *Journal of Management Development* 9 (1990), pp. 17–23.

44. McCall, Lombardo, and Morrison, *Lessons of Experience*; M. W. McCall, "Developing Executives through Work Experiences," *Human Resource Planning* 11 (1988), pp. 1–11; M. N. Ruderman, P. J. Ohlott, and C. D. McCauley, "Assessing Opportunities for Leadership Development," in *Measures of Leadership*, pp. 547–62; C. D. McCauley, L. J. Estman, and P. J. Ohlott, "Linking Management Selection and Development through Stretch Assignments," *Human Resource Management* 34 (1995), pp. 93–115.

45. C. D. McCauley, M. N. Ruderman, P. J. Ohlott, and J. E. Morrow, "Assessing the Developmental Components of Managerial Jobs," *Journal of Applied Psychology* 79 (1994), pp. 544–60.

46. T. Galvin, "Best Practice: Job Rotation, Arrow Electronics," *Training*, March 2003, p. 59.

47. M. Solomon, "Trading Places," *ComputerWorld* (November 5, 2002), www.computerworld.com/careertopics/careers/labor/story/0,10801,75527,00.html.

48. M. London, *Developing Managers* (San Francisco: Jossey-Bass, 1985); M. A. Campion, L. Cheraskin, and M. J. Stevens, "Career-Related Antecedents and Outcomes of Job Rotation," *Academy of Management Journal* 37 (1994), pp. 1518–42; M. London, *Managing the Training Enterprise* (San Francisco: Jossey-Bass, 1989).

49. D. C. Feldman, *Managing Careers in Organizations* (Glenview, IL: Scott Foresman, 1988).

50. J. M. Brett, L. K. Stroh, and A. H. Reilly, "Job Transfer," in *International Review of Industrial and Organizational Psychology: 1992*, ed. C. L. Cooper and I. T. Robinson (Chichester, England: John Wiley and Sons, 1992); D. C. Feldman and J. M. Brett, "Coping with New Jobs: A Comparative Study of New Hires and Job Changers," *Academy of Management Journal* 26 (1983), pp. 258–72.

51. R. A. Noe, B. D. Steffy, and A. E. Barber, "An Investigation of the Factors Influencing Employees' Willingness to Accept Mobility Opportunities," *Personnel Psychology* 41 (1988), pp. 559–80; S. Gould and L. E. Penley, "A Study of the Correlates of Willingness to Relocate," *Academy of Management Journal* 28 (1984), pp. 472–78; J. Landau and T. H. Hammer, "Clerical Employees' Perceptions of Intraorganizational Career Opportunities," *Academy of Management Journal* 29 (1986), pp. 385–405; R. P. Duncan and C. C. Perruci, "Dual Occupation Families and Migration," *American Sociological Review* 41 (1976), pp. 252–61; J. M. Brett and A. H. Reilly, "On the Road Again: Predicting the Job Transfer Decision," *Journal of Applied Psychology* 73 (1988), pp. 614–620.

52. D. T. Hall and L. A. Isabella, "Downward Moves and Career Development," *Organizational Dynamics* 14 (1985), pp. 5–23.

53. H. D. Dewirst, "Career Patterns: Mobility, Specialization, and Related Career Issues," in *Contemporary Career Development Issues*, ed. R. F. Morrison and J. Adams (Hillsdale, NJ: Lawrence Erlbaum, 1991), pp. 73–108.

54. N. C. Tompkins, "GTE Managers on the Move," *Personnel Journal*, August 1992, pp. 86–91.

55. J. M. Brett, "Job Transfer and Well-Being," *Journal of Applied Psychology* 67 (1992), pp. 450–63; F. J. Minor, L. A. Slade, and R. A. Myers, "Career Transitions in Changing Times," in *Contemporary Career Development Issues*, pp. 109–20; C. C. Pinder and K. G. Schroeder, "Time to Proficiency Following Job Transfers," *Academy of Management Journal* 30 (1987), pp. 336–53; G. Flynn, "Heck No—We Won't Go!" *Personnel Journal*, March 1996, pp. 37–43.

56. R. E. Silverman, "Mercer Tries to Keep Employees Through Its 'Externship' Program," *The Wall Street Journal* (November 7, 2000), p. B18.

57. D. Gunsch, "Customer Service Focus Prompts Employee Exchange," *Personnel Journal*, October 1992, pp. 32–38.

58. C. J. Bachler, "Workers Take Leave of Job Stress," *Personnel Journal*, January 1995, pp. 38–48.

59. F. Jossi, "Taking Time Off from Advertising," *Workforce*, April 2002, p. 15.

60. D. B. Turban and T. W. Dougherty, "Role of Protégé Personality in Receipt of Mentoring and Career Success," *Academy of Management Journal* 37 (1994), pp. 688–702; E. A. Fagenson, "Mentoring: Who Needs It? A Comparison of Protégés' and Nonprotégés' Needs for Power, Achievement, Affiliation, and Autonomy," *Journal of Vocational Behavior* 41 (1992), pp. 48–60.

61. A. H. Geiger, "Measures for Mentors," *Training and Development Journal*, February 1992, pp. 65–67.

62. K. E. Kram, *Mentoring at Work: Developmental Relationships in Organizational Life* (Glenview, IL: Scott Foresman, 1985); K. Kram, "Phases of the Mentoring Relationship," *Academy of Management Journal* 26 (1983), pp. 608–25; G. T. Chao, P. M. Walz, and P. D. Gardner, "Formal and Informal Mentorships: A Comparison of Mentoring Functions and Contrasts with Nonmentored Counterparts," *Personnel Psychology* 45 (1992), pp. 619–36; C. Wanberg, E. Welsh, and S. Hezlett, "Mentoring Research: A Review and Dynamic Process Model," in *Research in Personnel and Human Resources Management*, ed. J. Martocchio and G. Ferris (New York: Elsevier Science, 2003), pp. 39–124.

63. C. M. Solomon, "Hotel Breathes Life Into Hospital's Customer Service," *Personnel Journal*, October 1995, p. 120.

64. G. F. Dreher and R. A. Ash, "A Comparative Study of Mentoring among Men and Women in Managerial, Professional, and Technical Positions," *Journal of Applied Psychology* 75 (1990), pp. 539–46; T. D. Allen, L. T. Eby, M. L. Poteet, E. Lentz, and L. Lima, "Career Benefits Associated with Mentoring for Protégés: A Meta-Analysis," *Journal of Applied Psychology* 89 (2004), pp. 127–36; R. A. Noe, D. B. Greenberger, and S. Wang, "Mentoring: What We Know and Where We Might Go," in *Research in Personnel and Human Resources Management*, ed. G. Ferris and J. Martucchio (New York: Elsevier Science, 2002), pp. 129–74; R. A. Noe, "An Investigation of the Determinants of Successful Assigned Mentoring Relationships," *Personnel Psychology* 41 (1988), pp. 457–79; B. J. Tepper, "Upward Maintenance Tactics in Supervisory Mentoring and Nonmentoring Relationships," *Academy of Management Journal* 38 (1995), pp. 1191–205; B. R. Ragins and T. A. Scandura, "Gender Differences in Expected Outcomes of Mentoring Relationships," *Academy of Management Journal* 37 (1994), pp. 957–71.

65. M. Murray, "GE Mentoring Program Turns Underlings Into Teachers of the Web," *The Wall Street Journal* (February 15, 2000), pp. B1, B16.

66. F. Jossi, "Mentoring in Changing Times," *Training*, August 1997, pp. 50–54.

67. B. Kaye and B. Jackson, "Mentoring: A Group Guide," *Training and Development* (April 1995), pp. 23–27.

68. D. B. Peterson and M. D. Hicks, *Leader as Coach* (Minneapolis, MN: Personnel Decisions, 1996).

69. J. Lublin, "Did I Just Say That?! How You Can Recover from Foot-in-Mouth," *The Wall Street Journal* (June 18, 2002), p. B1.

70. R. Zemke, " The Corporate Coach," *Training* (December 1996), pp. 24–28.

71. Consulting Psychologists Press, "Wells Fargo Helps Employees Change Careers," *Strong Forum* 8, no. 1 (1991), p. 1.

72. L. Slavenski, "Career Development: A Systems Approach," *Training and Development Journal*, February 1987, pp. 56–60.

73. D. T. Jaffe and C. D. Scott, "Career Development for Empowerment in a Changing Work World," in *New Directions in Career Planning and the Workplace*, ed. J. M. Kummerow (Palo Alto, CA: Consulting Psychologists Press, 1991), pp. 33–60; L. Summers, "A Logical Approach to Development Planning," *Training and Development* 48 (1994), pp. 22–31; D. B. Peterson and M. D. Hicks, *Development First* (Minneapolis, MN: Personnel Decisions, 1995).

74. P. Kiger, "At First USA Bank, Promotions and Job Satisfaction Are Up," *Workforce*, March 2001, pp. 54–56.

75. U.S. Dept. of Labor, *A Report on the Glass Ceiling Initiative* (Washington, DC: U.S. Dept. of Labor, 1991).

76. P. J. Ohlott, M. N. Ruderman, and C. D. McCauley, "Gender Differences in Managers' Developmental Job Experiences," *Academy of Management Journal* 37 (1994), pp. 46–67.

77. L. A. Mainiero, "Getting Anointed for Advancement: The Case of Executive Women," *Academy of Management Executive* 8 (1994), pp. 53–67; J. S. Lublin, "Women at Top Still Are Distant from CEO Jobs," *The Wall Street Journal* (February 28, 1995), pp. B1, B5; P. Tharenov, S. Latimer, and D. Conroy, "How Do You Make It to the Top? An Examination of Influences on Women's and Men's Managerial Advancement," *Academy of Management Journal* 37 (1994), pp. 899–931.

78. U.S. Dept. of Labor, *A Report on the Glass Ceiling Initiative*; R. A. Noe, "Women and Mentoring: A Review and Research Agenda," *Academy of Management Review* 13 (1988), pp. 65–78; B. R. Ragins and J. L. Cotton, "Easier Said Than Done: Gender Differences in Perceived Barriers to Gaining a Mentor," *Academy of Management Journal* 34 (1991), pp. 939–51.

79. C. Daniels, "Women vs. Wal-Mart," *Fortune* (July 21, 2003), pp. 78–82.

80. D. McCracken, "Winning the Talent War for Women," *Harvard Business Review*, November–December 2000, pp. 159–67.

81. D. Zielinski, "Mentoring Up," *Training*, October 2000, pp. 136–40.

82. W. J. Rothwell, *Effective Succession Planning*, 2nd ed. (New York: AMACOM, 2001).

83. C. B. Derr, C. Jones, and E. L. Toomey, "Managing High-Potential Employees: Current Practices in Thirty-Three U.S. Corporations," *Human Resource Management* 27 (1988), pp. 273–90.

84. Ibid.; K. M. Nowack, "The Secrets of Succession," *Training and Development* 48 (1994), pp. 49–54; J. S. Lublin, "An Overseas Stint Can Be a Ticket to the Top," *The Wall Street Journal* (January 29, 1996), pp. B1, B2.

85. Nowack, "The Secrets of Succession," Lublin, "An Overseas Stint Can Be a Ticket to the Top."

86. P. Kiger, "Succession Planning Keeps WellPoint Competitive," *Workforce*, April 2002, pp. 50–54.

87. M. W. McCall, Jr., and M. M. Lombardo, "Off the Track: Why and How Successful Executives Get Derailed," *Technical Report* no. 21 (Greensboro, NC: Center for Creative Leadership, 1983); E. V. Veslor and J. B. Leslie, "Why Executives Derail: Perspectives across Time and Cultures," *Academy of Management Executive* 9 (1995), pp. 62–72.

88. L. W. Hellervik, J. F. Hazucha, and R. J. Schneider, "Behavior Change: Models, Methods, and a Review of Evidence," in *Handbook of Industrial and Organizational Psychology*, vol. 3, 2nd ed., ed. M. D. Dunnette and L. M. Hough (Palo Alto, CA: Consulting Psychologists Press, 1992), pp. 823–99.

89. D. B. Peterson, "Measuring and Evaluating Change in Executive and Managerial Development," paper presented at the annual conference of the Society for Industrial and Organizational Psychology, Miami, 1990.

10 Chapter

Employee Separation and Retention

Objectives After reading this chapter, you should be able to:

1. Distinguish between involuntary and voluntary turnover, and discuss how each of these forms of turnover can be leveraged for competitive advantage.

2. List the major elements that contribute to perceptions of justice and how to apply these in organizational contexts involving discipline and dismissal.

3. Specify the relationship between job satisfaction and various forms of job withdrawal, and identify the major sources of job satisfaction in work contexts.

4. Design a survey feedback intervention program and use this to promote retention of key organizational personnel.

Enter the World of Business

When Family-Friendly Policies Attack

Raising children has never been easy, and in an age when both parents work or where families are being run by single parents, this task is not getting any easier. Thus, the idea that employers might use family-friendly policies to help recruit and retain valued workers is one that has been used for years by many employers. Over time the sophistication of these programs has evolved and currently this support can take any of a number of forms. This would include referral services, corporate sponsored community child care centers, corporate-owned on-site child-care centers, on-site backup emergency care centers for parents whose primary care provider is unavailable, after-school care for older children, and even employer matching of tax deferred spending accounts earmarked for child care. The effectiveness of these programs can be well documented, in the sense that over 40 percent of the workers at companies that provided on-site care cited this as one of the primary reasons they chose their current employer, and over 20 percent said they spurned outside offers from competing employers because they wanted to keep their kids at their current company center.

These centers also reduce absenteeism among employees, which directly affects the

employer's bottom line. Even beyond this, however, these programs can be instrumental in keeping many people who are living on the margins of society in the workforce. Particularly among the working poor, failure to find affordable and reliable child care is the single biggest contributing factor to chronic tardiness and absenteeism. This, in turn, often leads to employee dismissals and spotty work histories, which in turn leads to high unemployment rates and an increased need for government aid to such individuals. Thus, employee-sponsored child-care provisions help support both the goals of specific employers, employees, and the overall society as well, right?

Well, maybe yes and maybe no. Increasingly, family-friendly work practices such as child-care provision, benefits to the spouses of employees, and even company-sponsored "family picnics" are being criticized by "family-free" workers who see this as a form of unfair compensation that is not paid to single workers. That is, even though two workers may be performing exactly the same work for the same pay, because one is enjoying benefits that accrue to his or her spouse and children, the worker with the family is in effect receiving much more compensation than the worker who lives alone. As Tom Coleman, director of the advocacy group Unmarried America notes, "Employees without children have lives outside of work and consider their needs and responsibilities just as important as those of workers with kids."

Indeed, demographic shifts are resulting in a large increase in the number of individuals who are classified as "singletons," that is, people living alone. This can be attributed to the fact that people are marrying much later in life or not at all, people are postponing having children or not having them at all, people are divorcing more and retiring later, meaning that they live alone after their children have grown and left home. Taken together, it has been estimated that by the year 2010, 30 percent of U.S. households will be inhabited by someone who lives alone.

Responding to the needs of this increasingly diverse workforce will be a challenge for employers. On the one hand, trying to cover every possible contingency in a highly centralized, formal HR policy is impossible, because the opportunities for one group to be slighted relative to another on some dimension of compensation are endless. On the other hand,

creating decentralized systems that leave too much discretion in the hands of individual supervisors can also lead to problems. If supervisors strike idiosyncratic deals for how they are going to support workers with families versus those without families, perceptions of favoritism are likely to be created. Clearly, keeping everyone happy is going to be a difficult challenge for both human resource professionals and the managers they support, and those who successfully respond to this challenge can gain a competitive advantage in recruitment, retention, and productivity.

Source: P. J. Kiger, "A Case for Child-Care," *Workforce*, April 2004, pp. 34–40; M. Conlin and A. Bernstein, "Working and Poor," *Business-Week* (October 20, 2003), pp. 58–68; M. Conlin, "Unmarried America," *BusinessWeek* (October 20, 2003), pp. 106–16; M. Hammers, "Family-Friendly Benefits Prompt Non-Parent Backlash," *Workforce*, August 2003, pp. 77–79; A. Fisher, "The Rebalancing Act," *Fortune* (October 6, 2003), pp. 110–13.

Introduction

Every executive recognizes the need for satisfied, loyal customers. If the firm is publicly held, it is also safe to assume that every executive appreciates the need to have satisfied, loyal investors. Customers and investors provide the financial resources that allow the organization to survive. Not every executive understands the need to generate satisfaction and loyalty among employees, however. Yet, retention rates among employees are related to retention rates among both customers[1] and investors.[2] In fact, research has established a direct link between employee retention rates and sales growth[3] and companies that are cited as one of the "100 Best Companies to Work For" routinely outperform their competition on many other financial indicators of performance.[4] Job satisfaction and retention are related to organizational performance. Firms that fail to secure a loyal base of workers constantly place an inexperienced group of noncohesive units on the front lines of their organization, much to their own detriment.[5] This is especially the case in service industries, where confused and disgruntled workers often create large numbers of dissatisfied customers.[6] As we can see in our opening story, however, satisfying a diverse set of employees can often be a difficult challenge, and the opportunity to please one group while creating displeasure within another group always exists. Thus, this provides yet another area where one organization can gain competitive advantage over another.

In addition to holding onto key personnel, another hallmark of successful firms is their ability and willingness to dismiss employees who are engaging in counterproductive behavior. Indeed, it is somewhat ironic that one of the keys to retaining productive employees is ensuring that these people are not being made miserable by supervisors or coworkers who are engaging in unproductive, disruptive, or dangerous behavior. For example, as we noted in Chapter 8, more companies are turning to "rank and yank" systems, where all employees are listed on performance from top to bottom, and then the bottom 5–10 percent are dismissed.[7] Former Chairman of General Electric Jack Welch has noted that "while the top and middle performers sometimes trade places, the bottom 10 percent, in our experience, tend to stay there, and delaying the inevitable in their case is a form of cruelty."[8] Welch believes strongly that culling the bottom of the organization like this makes room for new members and helps maintain the company's vitality. However, as we saw in the opening story, some workers, particularly low wage single parents, struggle on the job not because of the job requirements, but because of difficulty managing their off-work responsibilities. Employee-sponsored programs that support these individuals often take what were once marginal employees and turn them into top performers.

Thus, to compete effectively, organizations must take steps to ensure that good performers are motivated to stay with the organization, whereas chronically low performers are allowed, encouraged, or, if necessary, forced to leave. Retaining top performers is not always easy, however. Recent developments have made this more difficult than ever. For example, the rash of layoffs and downsizings of the early and mid-1990s has reduced company loyalty. Couple this general attitude of mistrust with the tight labor markets characterizing the 2001–2004 period, and we have a workforce that is both willing and able to leave on a moment's notice. For example, one recent survey found that 83 percent of managerial employees stated that they were "likely or extremely likely" to search for new jobs when the economy turns around.[9] Similarly, the increased willingness of people to sue their employer, combined with an unprecedented level of violence in the workplace, has made discharging employees legally complicated and personally dangerous.[10]

The purpose of this chapter (the last in Part III of this book) is to focus on employee separation and retention. The material presented in Part III's previous two chapters ("Performance Management" and "Employee Development") can be used to help establish who are the current effective performers as well as who is likely to respond well to future developmental opportunities. This chapter completes Part III by discussing what can be done to retain high-performing employees who warrant further development as well as managing the separation process for low-performing employees who have not responded well to developmental opportunities.

Since much of what needs to be done to retain employees involves compensation and benefits, this chapter also serves as a bridge to Part IV, which addresses these issues in more detail. The chapter is divided in two sections. The first examines **involuntary turnover,** that is, turnover initiated by the organization (often among people who would prefer to stay). The second deals with **voluntary turnover,** that is, turnover initiated by employees (often whom the company would prefer to keep). Although both types of turnover reflect employee separation, they are clearly different phenomena that need to be examined separately.[11]

Involuntary turnover
Turnover initiated by the organization (often among people who would prefer to stay).

Voluntary turnover
Turnover initiated by employees (often whom the company would prefer to keep).

Managing Involuntary Turnover

Despite a company's best efforts in the area of personnel selection, training, and design of compensation systems, some employees will occasionally fail to meet performance requirements or will violate company policies while on the job. When this happens, organizations need to invoke a discipline program that could ultimately lead to the individual's discharge. For a number of reasons, discharging employees can be a very difficult task that needs to be handled with the utmost care and attention to detail.

First, there are legal aspects to this decision that can have important repercussions for the organization. Historically, in the absence of a specified contract, either the employer or the employee could sever the employment relationship at any time. The severing of this relationship could be for "good cause," "no cause," or even "bad cause." Over time, this policy has been referred to as the **employment-at-will doctrine.** This employment-at-will doctrine has eroded significantly over time, however. Today employees who are fired sometimes sue their employers for wrongful discharge. Some judges have been willing to consider employees who meet certain criteria regarding longevity, promotions, raises, and favorable past performance reviews as having an implied contract to dismissal only for good cause—even in the face of direct language in the company handbook that states an employment-at-will relationship.[12]

> **Employment-at-will doctrine**
> The doctrine that, in the absence of a specific contract, either an employer or employee could sever the employment relationship at any time.

A wrongful discharge suit typically attempts to establish that the discharge either (1) violated an implied contract or covenant (that is, the employer acted unfairly) or (2) violated public policy (that is, the employee was terminated because he or she refused to do something illegal, unethical, or unsafe). Courts have been quite willing to listen to such cases, and employees win settlements over 70 percent of the time. The average award is more than $500,000, and the cost for mounting a defense can be anywhere from $50,000 to $250,000.[13] Thus there is great financial risk associated with any termination decision.

In addition to the financial risks associated with a dismissal, there are issues related to personal safety. Although the fact that some former employees use the court system to get back at their former employers may be distressing, even more problematic are employees who respond to a termination decision with violence directed at the employer. Violence in the workplace has become a major organizational problem. Workplace homicide is the fastest-growing form of murder in the United States—especially for women, for whom homicide is the leading cause of death in the workplace.[14] Although any number of organizational actions or decisions may incite violence among employees, the "nothing else to lose" aspect of employee dismissal cases makes for a dangerous situation, especially in the presence of other risk factors associated with the nature of the work.[15]

Given the critical financial and personal risks associated with employee dismissal, it is easy to see why the development of a standardized, systematic approach to discipline and discharge is critical to all organizations. These decisions should not be left solely to the discretion of individual managers or supervisors. In the next section we explore aspects of an effective discipline and discharge policy.

Principles of Justice

In Chapter 8 ("Performance Management") we touched on the notion of justice, particularly as this relates to the notions of outcome justice, procedural justice, and interactional justice. There we noted that employees are more likely to respond positively to negative feedback regarding their performance if they perceive the appraisal process as being fair on these three dimensions. Obviously, if fairness is important with respect to ongoing feedback, this is even more critical in the context of a final termination decision. Therefore, we will explore the three types of fairness perceptions in greater detail here, with an emphasis on how these need to be operationalized in effective discipline and discharge policies.[16] Indeed, a thorough understanding of these justice principles will make it clear why many organizations have enacted various policies regarding progressive discipline, Employee Assistance Programs (EAPs), alternative dispute resolution, and outplacement.

(1) **Consistency.** The procedures are applied consistently across time and other persons.

(2) **Bias suppression.** The procedures are applied by a person who has no vested interest in the outcome and no prior prejudices regarding the individual.

(3) **Information accuracy.** The procedure is based on information that is perceived to be true.

(4) **Correctabilty.** The procedure has built-in safeguards that allow one to appeal mistakes or bad decisions.

(5) **Representativeness.** The procedure is informed by the concerns of all groups or stakeholders (coworkers, customers, owners) affected by the decision, including the individual being dismissed.

(6) **Ethicality.** The procedure is consistent with prevailing moral standards as they pertain to issues like invasion of privacy or deception.

(1) **Explanation.** Emphasize aspects of procedural fairness that justify the decision.
(2) **Social Sensitivity.** Treat the person with dignity and respect.
(3) **Consideration.** Listen to the person's concerns.
(4) **Empathy.** Identify with the person's feelings.

As we noted earlier in Chapter 8, **outcome fairness** refers to the judgment that people make with respect to the *outcomes received* relative to the outcomes received by other people with whom they identify (referent others). Clearly, a situation where one person is losing his or her job while others are not is conducive to perceptions of outcome unfairness on the part of the discharged employee. The degree to which this potentially unfair act translates into the type of anger and resentment that might spawn retaliation in the form of violence or litigation, however, depends on perceptions of procedural and interactional justice.[17]

Whereas outcome justice focuses on the ends, procedural and interactional justice focus on means. If methods and procedures used to arrive at and implement decisions that impact the employee negatively are seen as fair, the reaction is likely to be much more positive than if this is not the case. **Procedural justice** focuses specifically on the *methods used to determine the outcomes received.* Table 10.1 details six key principles that determine whether people perceive procedures as being fair. Even given all the negative ramifications of being dismissed from one's job, the person being dismissed may accept the decision with minimum anger if the procedures used to arrive at the decision are consistent, unbiased, accurate, correctable, representative, and ethical.

Whereas procedural justice deals with how a decision was made, **interactional justice** refers to the *interpersonal nature of how the outcomes were implemented.* Table 10.2 lists the four key determinants of interactional justice. When the decision is explained well and implemented in a fashion that is socially sensitive, considerate, and empathetic, this helps defuse some of the resentment that might come about from a decision to discharge an employee. As the "Competing through Sustainability" box shows, even some of the world's most experienced executives can sometimes struggle with this aspect of the managerial process. Indeed, beyond the context of employee termination, the use of systems that promote procedural and interactive justice across the organization results in both more satisfied employees[18] and more a productive workforce.[19]

Outcome fairness

The judgment that people make with respect to the outcomes received relative to the outcomes received by other people with whom they identify.

Procedural justice

A concept of justice focusing on the methods used to determine the outcomes received.

Interactional justice

A concept of justice referring to the interpersonal nature of how the outcomes were implemented.

COMPETING THROUGH SUSTAINABILITY

You're Fired! What You Should (and Shouldn't) Learn from "The Donald"

Employee terminations came into American living rooms with a great deal of frequency in 2003, thanks to the television show, "The Apprentice." In this reality show, which was basically a business version of the old "Survivor" series, a number of people competed at various tasks in groups. Each week, real estate magnate Donald Trump, acting as the group's supervisor, terminated one employee— using his signature declaration —"You're fired!" The show lasted until there was one person left standing and this person was awarded a six-figure job working with The Donald.

This show was highly popular, and it was also controversial in many circles as people argued about whether it was a "reality show" or a "total lack of reality show" when it comes to understanding how the business world operates. Many felt that the show accurately reflected the scheming and backstabbing that often takes place at high levels of corporate politics, but also noted that the overtly sexual nature of much of the action made it look more like a TV show than a regular day at the office for most folks.

Leaving this aside, if one takes a more focused look at specifically how Trump executed the terminations, one can spot both positive and negative aspects to his approach. Clearly, on the negative side,

his use of sarcasm, humor, and humiliation at the point of execution is certainly something that makes for good television, but horrible management. In the real world, as we noted in this text, it is critical to provide interactional justice to the person who is being fired, and if anything, steps need to be taken to restore and build up the person's self-worth—not tear it down. Someone who is humiliated is much more likely to come back with a lawyer (or with a gun), and juries that are shown evidence of cruel intent during the termination process are much more likely to find for the plaintiff in a wrongful discharge suit. In such cases, juries award larger settlements in order to rectify the pain and anguish inflicted upon the plaintiff in terms of outcome justice.

On the positive side, whereas many real managers often try to avoid conflict by sugarcoating the message, Trump gets high marks for candor and frankness—which are also critical in terms of establishing procedural justice. Trump lays out the reasons behind the decision-making process, focusing on specific behavioral incidents that support the decision, making it clear what aspects of the person's performance were not up to the standards he had set. In all too many real world firings, conflict avoidant managers hem and haw, and in the spirit of not trying to humiliate the

person, fail to convincingly present the case for why the person is being fired, which could also invite legal action.

Indeed, perhaps the worst move a manager can make is to pretend that the termination decision was not performance based, when in fact it was. For example, in many court cases, the employer's true intent is to fire the person because of performance deficiencies but instead of stating this directly, says the person is being laid off or the job is being eliminated as part of a restructuring. If the terminated employee then learns that someone was actually hired as his or her replacement, he or she now has the organization trapped in a lie. In particular, if the plaintiff is part of any protected group, it is going to be very difficult for the manager—already admitting to having lied once—to convince the jury that he or she is not lying that the decision was not based upon age, race, sex or other protected characteristic. Clearly, it is very unlikely that "The Donald" would ever wind up in front of "Judge Judy" for this reason.

SOURCE: J. Merritt, "What Trump Saw in Bill: The Donald," *BusinessWeek* (April 16, 2004), pp. 31–32; J. Merritt, "A Gut Course in Post-Grad Scheming," *BusinessWeek* (February 2, 2004), p. 41; A. L. Rupe, "Horrors from the Bad-Firing Files," *Workforce*, November 2003, pp. 16–18; A. L. Rupe, "Plain and Simple: Liars Lose," *Workforce*, March 2004, pp. 14–16.

OFFENSE FREQUENCY	ORGANIZATIONAL RESPONSE	DOCUMENTATION
First offense	Unofficial verbal warning	Witness present
Second offense	Official written warning	Document filed
Third offense	Second official warning, with threat of temporary suspension	Document filed
Fourth offense	Temporary suspension and "last chance notification"	Document filed
Fifth offense	Termination (with right to go to arbitration)	Document filed

TABLE 10.3

An Example of a Progressive Discipline Program

Progressive Discipline

Except in the most extreme cases, employees should generally not be terminated for a first offense. Rather, termination should come about at the end of a systematic discipline program. Effective discipline programs have two central components: documentation (which includes specific publication of work rules and job descriptions that should be in place prior to administering discipline) and progressive punitive measures. Thus, as shown in Table 10.3, punitive measures should be taken in steps of increasing magnitude, and only after having been clearly documented. This may start with an unofficial warning for the first offense, followed by a written reprimand for additional offenses. At some point, later offenses may lead to a temporary suspension. Before a company suspends an employee, it may even want to issue a "last chance notification," indicating that the next offense will result in termination. Such procedures may seem exasperatingly slow, and they may fail to meet one's emotional need for quick and satisfying retribution. In the end, however, when problem employees are discharged, the chance that they can prove they were discharged for poor cause has been minimized.

Alternative Dispute Resolution

At various points in the discipline process, the individual or the organization might want to bring in outside parties to help resolve discrepancies or conflicts. As a last resort, the individual might invoke the legal system to resolve these types of conflicts, but in order to avoid this, more and more companies are turning to **alternative dispute resolution (ADR)** techniques that show promise in resolving disputes in a timely, constructive, cost-effective manner.

Alternative dispute resolution can take on many different forms, but in general, ADR proceeds through the four stages shown in Table 10.4. Each stage reflects a somewhat broader involvement of different people, and the hope is that the conflict will be resolved at earlier steps. However, the last step may include binding arbitration, where an agreed upon neutral party resolves the conflict unilaterally if necessary.

Experience shows that ADR can be highly effective in terms of cost and time savings. For example, over a four-year period, one large company, Houston-based Kellogg, Brown and Root, found that legal fees dropped 90 percent after instituting ADR. Indeed, of the 2,000 disputes initiated by employees at that time, only 30 ever reached the binding arbitration stage.[20]

Alternative dispute resolution (ADR)
A method of resolving disputes that does not rely on the legal system. Often proceeds through the four stages of open door policy, peer review, mediation, and arbitration.

TABLE 10.4

Stages in Alternative Dispute Resolution

Stage 1: Open door policy The two people in conflict (e.g., supervisor and subordinate) attempt to arrive at a settlement together. If none can be reached, they proceed to
Stage 2: Peer review A panel composed of representatives from the organization that are at the same level of those people in the dispute hears the case and attempts to help the parties arrive at a settlement. If none can be reached, they proceed to
Stage 3: Mediation A neutral third party from outside the organization hears the case and, via a nonbinding process, tries to help the disputants arrive at a settlement. If none can be reached, the parties proceed to
Stage 4: Arbitration A professional arbitrator from outside the organization hears the case and resolves it unilaterally by rendering a specific decision or award. Most arbitrators are experienced employment attorneys or retired judges.

Whereas ADR is effective in dealing with problems related to performance and interpersonal differences in the workplace, many of the problems that lead an organization to want to terminate an individual's employment relate to drug or alcohol abuse. In these cases, the organization's discipline and dismissal program should also incorporate an employee assistance program. Due to the increased prevalence of EAPs in organizations, we describe them in detail here.

Employee Assistance Programs

Drug and alcohol abuse have been estimated to cost U.S. companies nearly $100 billion a year in lost productivity.[21] Although health care costs in general have risen sharply, treatment costs for mental and chemical dependency disorders appear to be rising even faster.[22] To lower these costs and to help get unproductive employees back on track, many employers are turning to EAPs.

An **EAP** is a referral service that supervisors or employees can use to seek professional treatment for various problems. EAPs began in the 1950s with a focus on treating alcoholism, but in the 1980s they expanded into drug treatment as well. EAPs continue to evolve, and many are now fully integrated into companies' overall health benefits plans, serving as gatekeepers for health care utilization—especially for mental health.[23] For example, when the Campbell Soup Company incorporated mental health treatment into its EAP, claims costs associated with psychiatrists decreased 28 percent in a single year.[24] This kind of program is frequently referred to as a *carve-out plan*. In carve-out plans, mental health and chemical dependency benefits are provided by a single vendor that has responsibility for all of the company's health benefits.

EAPs vary widely, but most share some basic elements. First, the programs are usually identified in official documents published by the employer (such as employee handbooks). Supervisors (and union representatives, where relevant) are trained to use the referral service for employees whom they suspect of having health-related problems. Employees are also trained to use the system to make self-referrals when necessary. Finally, costs and benefits of the programs (as measured in positive employee outcomes such as return-to-work rates) are evaluated, typically annually.

Given EAPs' wide range of options and evolving nature, we need to constantly analyze their effectiveness. For example, there is a current debate about the desirability

Employee assistance programs (EAPs)
Employer programs that attempt to ameliorate problems encountered by workers who are drug dependent, alcoholic, or psychologically troubled.

of costly, intensive, inpatient alcoholism and substance abuse services over less costly outpatient care. Some fear that the lower initial costs of outpatient treatment might be offset by higher long-term costs because of relapse or other forms of failure. To settle this question, General Electric performed an experiment at its plant in Lynn, Massachusetts. To evaluate the relative effectiveness of three possible treatment courses, GE researchers assessed the experiences of 227 workers who were randomly assigned to one of the three treatments: (1) compulsory hospitalization followed by participation in Alcoholics Anonymous (AA), (2) compulsory AA without hospitalization, or (3) the employee's choice of treatments (1) or (2).

The results of this study indicated that after two years, workers who received hospital care fared the best despite the fact that this option was chosen less often by the employees themselves.[25] A study of drug dependency has shown comparable results.[26] The message from these studies is clear: although both employers (for cost reasons) and employees (for convenience reasons) may be attracted to short-term, low-cost treatments, everyone might be better served by focusing on long-term costs and well-being. This difference in short-term versus long-term costs is now being waged in the area of treating depression. In the past, hospitalization, plus psychiatric care was the main way to treat employees who were clinically depressed. However, the advent of managed care and the widespread effectiveness of Prozac and other pharmaceutical interventions for depression have made it possible for regular physicians to treat depression with medication.[27] By eliminating hospitalization and psychiatric care, employers can save a great deal of money in treating this problem, but some have questioned its long-term effectiveness relative to more traditional treatments.[28]

Outplacement Counseling

The terminal nature of an employee discharge not only leaves the person angry, it also leads to confusion as to how to react and in a quandary regarding what happens next. If the person feels there is nothing to lose and nowhere else to turn, the potential for violence or litigation is higher than most organizations are willing to tolerate. Therefore, many organizations provide **outplacement counseling,** which tries to help dismissed employees manage the transition from one job to another.

Some organizations have their own in-house staff for conducting this counseling. In other companies, outside consultants are kept on a retainer basis to help with individual cases. Regardless, goals of outplacement programs are to help the former employee deal with the psychological issues associated with losing one's job (grief, depression, fear) while at the same time helping him or her find new employment.

Outplacement counseling is aimed at helping people realize that losing a job is not the end of the world and that other opportunities exist. Indeed, for many people, losing a job can be a critical learning experience that plants the seed for future success. For example, when John Morgridge was fired from his job as branch manager at Honeywell 20 years ago, it made him realize that his own assertiveness and need for independence were never going to cut it in a large, bureaucratic institution like Honeywell. Morgridge took his skills and went on to build computer network maker Cisco Systems, which is now worth over $1 billion.[29]

This is a success story for Morgridge, but the fact that a major corporation like Honeywell let his talent go certainly reflects a lost opportunity for the company. Retaining people who can make such contributions is a key to gaining and maintaining competitive advantage. The second half of this chapter is devoted to issues related to retention.

Outplacement counseling
Counseling to help displaced employees manage the transition from one job to another.

Managing Voluntary Turnover

In the story that opened this chapter, we showed how the availability of family-friendly policies helps to both recruit and retain employees. This in turn helps fuel organizational performance. In fact, one recent study showed that firms who were in the top quartile in terms of employee job satisfaction had profit rates that were 4 percent higher than firms in the bottom quartile. The impact of human resource policies on job satisfaction has also been documented,[30] as has the link between employee retention and customer satisfaction.[31] Indeed, the whole employee satisfaction–firm performance relationship can become part of a virtuous cycle, where firms with more highly satisfied employees perform better and increase their profits, which in turn they use to shore up employee pay and benefits—further adding to their competitive advantage.[32]

In this section of the chapter, we examine the job withdrawal process that characterizes voluntary employee turnover, and we illustrate the central role that job satisfaction plays in this process. We also discuss what aspects of job satisfaction seem most critical to retention and how to measure these facets. Finally, we show how survey–feedback interventions, designed around these measures, can be used to strategically manage the voluntary turnover process so that high performers are retained while marginal performers are allowed to leave.

Process of Job Withdrawal

Job withdrawal is a set of behaviors that dissatisfied individuals enact to avoid the work situation. The right side of Figure 10.1 shows a model grouping the overall set of behaviors into three categories: behavior change, physical job withdrawal, and psychological job withdrawal.

We present the various forms of withdrawal in a progression, as if individuals try the next category only if the preceding is either unsuccessful or impossible to implement. This theory of **progression of withdrawal** has a long history and many adherents.[33] Others have suggested that there is no tight progression in that any one of the categories can compensate for another, and people choose the category that is most likely to redress the specific source of dissatisfaction.[34] Either way, the withdrawal behaviors are clearly related to one another, and they are all at least partially caused by job dissatisfaction.[35]

Progression of withdrawal
Theory that dissatisfied individuals enact a set of behaviors in succession to avoid their work situation.

FIGURE 10.1

An Overall Model of the Job Dissatisfaction–Job Withdrawal Process

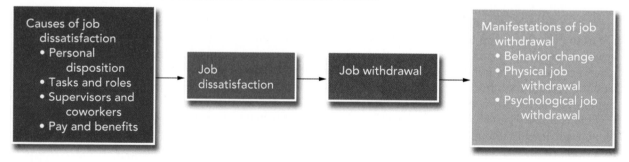

Behavior Change

One might expect that an employee's first response to dissatisfaction would be to try to change the conditions that generate the dissatisfaction. This can lead to supervisor–subordinate confrontation, perhaps even conflict, as dissatisfied workers try to bring about changes in policy or upper-level personnel. Where employees are unionized, it can lead to an increased number of grievances being filed.[36] Although at first this type of conflict can feel threatening to the manager, on closer inspection, this is really an opportunity for the manager to learn about and perhaps solve an important problem. For example, Don McAdams, a manager at Johnsonville Foods, recalls an incident where one particular employee had been very critical of the company's incentive system. McAdams listened to the person's concerns and then asked him to head a committee charged with developing a better incentive system. At first the employee was taken aback, but he eventually accepted the challenge and became so enthusiastic about the project that he was the one who presented the new system to the general membership. Because this person was known to be highly critical of the old system, he had a high level of credibility with the other workers, who felt, "If this guy likes it, it must be pretty good." In the end, this critic-turned-champion was immensely successful in solving a specific organizational problem.[37]

Less constructively, employees can initiate change through **whistle-blowing** (making grievances public by going to the media).[38] The damage that a single well-placed whistle-blower can do to an organization was revealed at Archer Daniels Midland (ADM). Top executive Mark Whitacre, working in cooperation with the FBI, taped many conversations that were later used to charge ADM with price fixing in one of the biggest antitrust cases in the 1990s.[39]

Employees can also sue their employers when the disputed policies relate to race, sex, safe working conditions, or any other aspect of employment regulated by state or federal laws. As we have seen, such suits are costly, both financially and in terms of the firm's image, regardless of whether the firm wins or loses. Most employers would prefer to avoid litigation altogether. Keeping a majority of their employees happy is one means of achieving this.

Whistle-blowing
Making grievances public by going to the media or government.

Physical Job Withdrawal

If the job conditions cannot be changed, a dissatisfied worker may be able to solve the problem by leaving the job. This could take the form of an internal transfer if the dissatisfaction is job-specific (the result of an unfair supervisor or unpleasant working conditions). On the other hand, if the source of the dissatisfaction relates to organizationwide policies (lack of job security or below-market pay levels), organizational turnover is likely.

In addition to the overall turnover rate, we need to be concerned with the nature of the turnover in terms of who is staying and who is leaving. For example, turnover rates among minorities at the managerial level are often two to three times that of white males, and this is often attributable to a perceived lack of opportunities for promotions. Lawrence Perlman, CEO of Ceridian Corporation of Minneapolis, states, "The combination of women and people of color dropping out is really discouraging . . . it just isn't good business." To prevent this exodus, Ceridian set diversity goals for promotions and career-enhancing experiences. Similar steps are being taken at Polaroid, Ameritech, Texaco, and Dow Chemical.[40]

Many employees who would like to quit their jobs have to stay on if they have no other employment opportunities. For example, the weak job market that characterized the U.S. economy in the 2000–2003 time period meant that many dissatisfied employees could not quit even though job dissatisfaction levels were at historic highs.[41] Another way of physically removing oneself from the dissatisfying work short of quitting altogether is to be absent.[42] One recent survey indicated that, on average, companies spend 15 percent of their payroll costs to make up for absent workers.[43] Short of missing the whole day, a dissatisfied employee may be late for work. Although not as disruptive as absenteeism, tardiness can be costly and is related to job satisfaction.[44] Tardiness can be especially costly when companies are organized around teams because the tardy individual often creates difficulties that spill over and affect the other team members.

Psychological Withdrawal

When dissatisfied employees are unable to change their situation or remove themselves physically from their jobs, they may psychologically disengage themselves from their jobs. Although they are physically on the job, their minds may be somewhere else.

This psychological disengagement can take several forms. First, if the primary dissatisfaction has to do with the job itself, the employee may display a very low level of job involvement. **Job involvement** is the degree to which people identify themselves with their jobs. People who are uninvolved with their jobs consider their work an unimportant aspect of their lives. A second form of psychological disengagement, which can occur when the dissatisfaction is with the employer as a whole, is a low level of organizational commitment. **Organizational commitment** is the degree to which an employee identifies with the organization and is willing to put forth effort on its behalf.[45] Individuals who have low organizational commitment are often just waiting for the first good opportunity to quit their jobs. Like job involvement, organizational commitment is strongly related to job satisfaction.

Job Satisfaction and Job Withdrawal

As we see in Figure 10.1, the key driving force behind all the different forms of job withdrawal is **job satisfaction,** which we will define as a pleasurable feeling that results from the perception that one's job fulfills or allows for the fulfillment of one's important job values.[46] This definition reflects three important aspects of job satisfaction. First, job satisfaction is a function of *values,* defined as "what a person consciously or unconsciously desires to obtain." Second, this definition emphasizes that different employees have different views of which values are important, and this is critical in determining the nature and degree of their job satisfaction. One person may value high pay above all else; another may value the opportunity to travel; another may value staying within a specific geographic region. The third important aspect of job satisfaction is perception. An individual's perceptions may not be a completely accurate reflection of reality, and different people may view the same situation differently.

In particular, people's perceptions are often strongly influenced by their frame of reference. A **frame of reference** is a standard point that serves as a comparison for other points and thus provides meaning. For example, an upper-level executive who offers a 6 percent salary increase to a lower-level manager might expect this to make the manager happy because inflation (the executive's frame of reference) is only 3 percent. The manager, on the other hand, might find the raise quite unsatisfactory because it is less

---

Job involvement
The degree to which people identify themselves with their jobs.

Organizational commitment
The degree to which an employee identifies with the organization and is willing to put forth effort on its behalf.

Job satisfaction
A pleasurable feeling that results from the perception that one's job fulfills or allows for the fulfillment of one's important job values.

Frame of reference
A standard point that serves as a comparison for other points and thus provides meaning.

than the 9 percent raise received by a colleague who does similar work (the manager's frame of reference). So, for example, in our opening story, childless workers who were dissatisfied with their company's family-friendly policies were using workers with spouses and children as their frame of reference. Thus values, perceptions, and importance are the three components of job satisfaction. People will be satisfied with their jobs as long as they perceive that their jobs meet their important values.

Sources of Job Dissatisfaction

Many aspects of people and organizations can cause dissatisfaction among employees. Managers and HR professionals need to be aware of these because they are the levers which can raise job satisfaction and reduce employee withdrawal. This is an issue that is particularly salient in the current economy where pressures to raise productivity have pushed many workers to the limit, and the opportunity for changing jobs is enhanced by a market where the demand for labor is heating up.[47]

Personal Dispositions

Because dissatisfaction is an emotion that ultimately resides within the person, it is not surprising that many who have studied these outcomes have focused on individual differences. **Negative affectivity** is a term used to describe a dispositional dimension that reflects pervasive individual differences in satisfaction with any and all aspects of life. Individuals who are high in negative affectivity report higher levels of aversive mood states, including anger, contempt, disgust, guilt, fear, and nervousness across all contexts (work and nonwork).[48]

People who are high in negative affectivity tend to focus extensively on the negative aspects of themselves and others.[49] Indeed, people who are low in emotional stability (see Chapter 6) tend be less satisfied with work regardless of the nature of the job.[50] In addition, workers who are depressed (one facet of emotional stability) experience off-work problems that result in higher rates of absenteeism even if one holds the level of job satisfaction constant.[51] Research has even shown that negative affectivity in early adolescence is predictive of overall job dissatisfaction in adulthood. There were also significant relationships between work attitudes measured over 5-year[52] and 10-year[53] periods, even for workers who changed employers and/or occupations. All of this implies that some individuals tend to bring low satisfaction with them to work. Thus these people may be relatively dissatisfied regardless of what steps the organization or the manager takes.

Although the causes of negative affectivity are not completely known, research that examined identical twins who were raised apart suggests that there may be a genetic component.[54] Thirty-four pairs of twins were measured for their general job satisfaction and their satisfaction with intrinsic and extrinsic aspects of the job. The researchers found a significant relationship between the ratings for each member of a pair, despite the fact that the twins were raised apart and worked at different jobs. Other research on genetic twins reared apart has shown similar effects on perceptions of the degree to which one's organization provides a supportive climate.[55]

Another construct useful in understanding dispositional aspects of job satisfaction is the notion of core self-evaluations. *Core self-evaluations* have been defined as a basic positive or negative bottom-line opinion that individuals hold about themselves. A positive core evaluation reflects the person's self-image on a number of more specific traits, including high self-esteem, high self-efficacy, internal locus of control, and

Negative affectivity
A dispositional dimension that reflects pervasive individual differences in satisfaction with any and all aspects of life.

emotional stability. These factors, both alone and together, have been found to be quite predictive of job satisfaction.[56]

Part of the reason why individuals with positive core self-evaluations have higher job satisfaction is that they tend to seek out and obtain jobs with more desirable characteristics, such as allowing discretion or dealing with complex tasks.[57] They also tend to take more socially approved proactive steps when it comes to trying to personally change a situation that is not to their liking. People with negative core self-evaluations tend to attribute dissatisfying features of their lives or work to the acts of other people, whom they blame for all their problems. They are less likely to work toward change, instead either doing nothing or acting aggressively toward those they blame for their misfortunes.[58]

The evidence on the linkage between these kinds of traits and job satisfaction suggests the importance of personnel selection as a way of raising overall levels of employee satisfaction. Interviews should assess the degree to which any job applicant has a history of chronic dissatisfaction with employment. If an applicant states that he was dissatisfied with his past six jobs, what makes the employer think he won't be dissatisfied with this one?

Tasks and Roles

As a predictor of job dissatisfaction, nothing surpasses the nature of the task itself.[59] Many aspects of a task have been linked to dissatisfaction. Several elaborate theories relating task characteristics to worker reactions have been formulated and extensively tested. We discussed several of these in Chapter 4. In this section we focus on three primary aspects of tasks that affect job satisfaction: the complexity of the task, the degree of physical strain and exertion on the job, and the value the employee puts on the task.[60]

With a few exceptions, there is a strong positive relationship between task complexity and job satisfaction. That is, the boredom generated by simple, repetitive jobs that do not mentally challenge the worker leads to frustration and dissatisfaction.[61] One intervention that employees themselves often introduce to low-complexity situations is to bring personal stereo headsets to work. Many supervisors disapprove of this practice, which can be understood in situations where employees need to interact with customers. However, in simple jobs with minimal customer contact (like processing paperwork or data entry) the research actually suggests that personal stereo headsets can improve performance. For example, one study examined stereo headset use among workers in 32 jobs within a large retailing organization. The results indicated the stereo group outperformed a no-stereo control group on simple jobs (like invoice processor) but performed worse than controls on jobs high in complexity (such as accountant).[62]

The second primary aspect of a task that affects job satisfaction is the degree to which the job involves physical strain and exertion.[63] This aspect is sometimes overlooked at a time when automation has removed much of the physical strain associated with jobs. Indeed, the fact that technology has aimed to lessen work-related physical exertion indicates that such exertion is almost universally considered undesirable. Nevertheless, many jobs can still be characterized as physically demanding.

The third primary aspect is whether the object of the work promotes something valued by the worker. Over 1 million volunteer workers in the United States perform their jobs almost exclusively because of the meaning they attach to the work. Some of these jobs are even low in complexity and high in physical exertion. These volunteers view themselves as performing a worthwhile service, however, and this overrides the other two factors and increases satisfaction with the job. Similarly, several low-paying occupations (such as social services and religious orders) explicitly try to make up for pay deficiencies by appealing to the prospective employee's nonfinancial values. The Peace Corps, for example, attempts to recruit applicants by describing its work as "the toughest job you will ever love."

One of the major interventions aimed at reducing job dissatisfaction is job enrichment, which explicitly focuses on the task as a source of dissatisfaction. **Job enrichment** refers to specific ways to add complexity and meaningfulness to a person's work. As the term suggests, this intervention is directed at jobs that are "impoverished" or boring because of their repetitive nature or low scope. Many job enrichment programs are based on the job characteristics theory discussed earlier in Chapter 4.

For example, at Xerox, work was once structured along four large functional units: manufacturing, research, marketing, and finance. Segmenting the work this way reduces the meaningfulness of many jobs. It also isolates workers from each other and distances them from customers. Thus CEO Paul Allaire restructured the organization into separate product divisions that each did its own manufacturing, research, marketing, and finance. Dan Cholish, a Xerox veteran, had been a "one-dimensional" engineer, but under the new system he has learned a little about manufacturing, finance, and marketing as he concentrates on customer needs. According to Cholish, "I've probably visited more customers in the last six months than I had in my last six years on my old assignment.[64] Including people who have minimal customer contact in meetings with the end users of the product or service has been found to reliably increase the perceived meaningfulness of work, which in turn raises job satisfaction.[65]

As another example, at Motorola "total customer satisfaction" teams are given authority to change production or any other work procedures, and are then given bonuses tied to improved defect rates or cycle times. One team used basic industrial engineering techniques to analyze inventory and ultimately reduced average levels of supply from seven weeks to four weeks, saving the company $2.4 million. Such results often breed functional internal competition because, as one team member noted, "Other workers were all jealous of our team." Internal competition can drive other teams to raise their standards of excellence and greatly contributes to the organization's overall competitive advantage.[66]

Another task-based intervention is **job rotation.** This is a process of systematically moving a single individual from one job to another over the course of time. Although employees may not feel capable of putting up with the dissatisfying aspects of a particular job indefinitely, they often feel they can do so temporarily. Job rotation can do more than simply spread out the dissatisfying aspects of a particular job. It can increase work complexity for employees and provide valuable cross-training in jobs so that employees eventually understand many different jobs. This makes for a more flexible workforce and increases workers' appreciation of the other tasks that have to be accomplished for the organization to complete its mission.[67]

In addition to the specific task performed by an individual, in the broader scheme of work, each person also has a role in the organization.[68] The person's **role** in the organization can be defined as the set of expected behaviors that both the person and other people who make up the social environment have for the person in that job. These expected behaviors include all the formal aspects of the job and usually much more as well. That is, coworkers, supervisors, and clients or customers have expectations for the person that go beyond what is formally described as the person's job. Expectations have a large impact on how the person responds to the work.

Three aspects of organizational roles stand out as significant influences on job satisfaction: role ambiguity, role conflict, and role overload. **Role ambiguity** refers to the

Job enrichment
Ways to add complexity and meaningfulness to a person's work.

Job rotation
The process of systematically moving a single individual from one job to another over the course of time. The job assignments may be in various functional areas of the company or movement may be between jobs in a single functional area or department.

Role
What an organization expects from an employee in terms of what to do and how to do it.

Role ambiguity
Uncertainty about what an organization expects from an employee in terms of what to do and how to do it.

level of uncertainty about what the organization expects from the employee in terms of what to do or how to do it. Ambiguity associated with work methods and scheduling are two of the most problematic forms of ambiguity, but by far the most critical dimension in terms of predicting job satisfaction is ambiguity around performance criteria. Employees have strong needs to know precisely how they are going to be evaluated on the job—and when this is unclear, job satisfaction suffers.[69]

Role conflict
Recognition of incompatible or contradictory demands by the person occupying the role.

A second source of dissatisfaction is **role conflict:** recognition of incompatible or contradictory demands by the person who occupies the role. Role conflict occurs in many different forms. For example, a member of a cross-functional project team might have a project manager as well as a manager in her functional area who hold mutually exclusive expectations for the employee. Another form of role conflict occurs when the employee may be occupying more than one role at a time and the roles have incompatible expectations. Conflict between work roles and family roles, for example, is common in organizations.

As we saw in the discussion that opened this chapter, in order to help employees manage role conflict, companies have turned to a number of family-friendly policies in order to both recruit new talent and hold onto the talent they already have. These policies may include provisions for child care, elder care, flexible work schedules, job sharing, telecommuting, and extended maternal and paternal leaves.[70] Although these programs create some headaches for managers in terms of scheduling work and reporting requirements, they have a number of demonstrable benefits. First, the provision of these sorts of benefits is a recruitment aid that helps employers attract potential job applicants.[71] Second, once hired, flexible work arrangements result in reduced absenteeism.[72] This is particularly true for firms that employ large numbers of women with children. In fact, one nonprofit company that could not compete on wages, was able to reduce its turnover rate from 30 percent to 7 percent just by initiating a program that let mothers bring their babies to work.[73] Third, over the long term, these program result in higher levels of employee commitment to the organization.[74] They have also been linked to increased organizational citizenship behaviors on the part of individual employees,[75] as well as enhanced organizational performance, especially in organizations that employ a large percentage of female employees.[76] Indeed, the benefits of these kinds of programs are so well documented that the mere announcement that an organizations is initiating some sort of flexible work policy has a positive impact on the share price of the company's stock.[77]

Role overload
A state in which too many expectations or demands are placed on a person.

Dissatisfaction can also arise from **role overload,** a state in which too many expectations or demands are placed on the person. Role overload is often a precursor to role conflict because high role load on the job creates more opportunities for conflict with family roles.[78] As we have noted, role overload seems to be an increasingly prevalent problem in today's organizations because of their emphasis on downsizing and cost cutting.[79] A 2001 survey, for example, indicated that 46 percent of American workers felt they were working too many hours. Roughly a quarter of those surveyed worked six days and over 50 hours a week.[80] The picture is even worse for members of managerial ranks, where a 2003 study found that many middle- and upper-level managers were working over 60 hours a week.[81] This upward trend in work hours does not necessarily reflect a global trend, however, and as our "Competing through Globalization" box shows, the number of hours worked in some European countries has actually decreased over the same period.

One by-product of this situation is that there has been an increase in the number of lawsuits filed by people who are suing for overtime pay. Although managers and professionals are supposedly "exempt" from the Fair Standards Act that dictates a 40-

hour week, increasingly members of this group have been claiming they are misclassified and should be treated as nonexempt workers. Companies such as U-Haul, Taco Bell, PepsiCo, Auto Zone, Borders Books, Pacific Bell, Bridgestone, and Wal-Mart have been slapped with such suits. Plaintiffs argue that while their job titles may make it sound like they are managers, in reality their day-to-day activities have a lot more to do with production and much less with supervision. When the work starts taking longer than 40 hours a week, this becomes important. As one legal expert has noted, "Companies that are not addressing these issues are sitting ducks waiting to get shot at."[82]

Because role problems rank just behind job problems in creating job dissatisfaction, interventions that aim directly at role elements have been created. One such intervention, the role analysis technique shown in Figure 10.2, is designed to increase the communication and understanding of the various sets of role expectations that exist for a

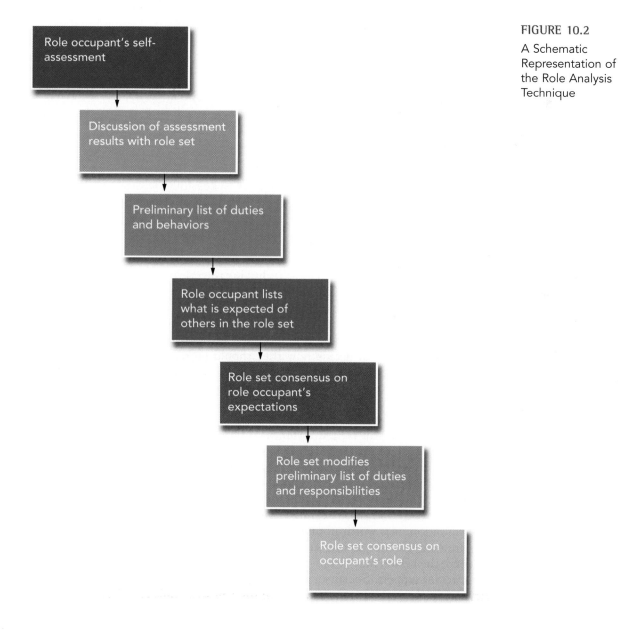

FIGURE 10.2

A Schematic Representation of the Role Analysis Technique

"Work itself is the enemy, and the less you do the better." That—declares Jean-Paul Pollin, a leading French economist—is exactly the message that is being sent by a four-year-old law in France that reduced the national workweek from 40 to 35 hours. At a time when many Americans are experiencing a crushing expansion of role overload that translates into more hours worked, the French have enjoyed historically low levels of role overload. In fact, the French now rank last in the developed world when it comes to hours worked, fully 25 per-cent less than workers in the United States, Japan, or Britain. This may seem like a dream come true to many overworked American workers who have to practically sue their employer to receive any overtime pay. However, increasingly French business leaders and workers alike are coming to realize that the costs of working fewer hours may surpass its joys.

First, one of the assumptions upon which the law was based was that the overall amount of work available in France was a fixed pie, and thus lowering the length of the workweek could reduce the national unemploy-ment rate. That is, employers would have to hire more workers to cover the same amount of work. This assumption not only denies the hope that the French economy might expand, it actually is instrumental in turning that pessimistic attitude into reality. Rather than hiring more French workers, employ-ers have responded by reducing their level of output or offshoring work to other coun-tries. These moves do little to help the average French citizen and have certainly been unsuc-cessful in improving unemployment rates as had been hoped.

Role analysis technique
A method that enables a role occupant and other members of the role occupant's role set to specify and examine their expectations for the role occupant.

specific employee.[83] In the **role analysis technique** the role occupant and each member of the role occupant's *role set* (supervisors, coworkers, subordinates) are asked to write down their expectations for the role occupant. Then everybody is gathered together, and each person goes through his or her list. All the expectations are written out so that ambiguities can be removed and conflicts identified. Where there are conflicts, the group as a whole tries to decide how they should be resolved. When this is done throughout an organization, instances of overload and underload may be discovered, and role requirements may be traded off so that more balanced roles are developed.

Supervisors and Coworkers

The two primary sets of people in an organization who affect job satisfaction are coworkers and supervisors. A person may be satisfied with her supervisor and cowork-ers for one of three reasons. First, she may have many of the same values, attitudes, and philosophies that the coworkers and supervisors have. Most individuals find this very important. Indeed, many organizations try to foster a culture of shared values among employees. Even if one cannot generate a unifying culture throughout an en-tire organization, it is worth noting that increases in job satisfaction can be derived simply from congruence among supervisors and subordinates at one level.[84]

Second, the person may be satisfied with his supervisor and coworkers because they provide social support. Social support means the degree to which the person is sur-rounded by other people who are sympathetic and caring. Considerable research

Second, even French citizens who may see some potential advantage in working less themselves are now beginning to realize that they are also consumers of goods or services, and the reduced workweek harms them from this perspective. In the public sector, the reduced workweek has led to a decrease in public services, as well as longer delays in receiving needed government services. This is particularly salient in a country where medical care is nationalized, and the reduced workweek thus creates shortages of doctors, nurses, and other medical professionals. Indeed, in the heat wave that enveloped Europe in the summer of 2003, 14,000 French citizens perished, and many attributed this to a lack of responsiveness of public medical services and public utilities to that crisis.

Other European countries share France's liberal labor policies; however, public unrest has led to some pressures to change national policy. For example, in Germany, the youth wing of the Christian-Democratic party and the new Young Socialists party have criticized labor policies that attempt to maintain the security of entrenched workers and retirees, at the expense of job creation, growth and opportunities for young people. Bjorn Boerning, head of the Young Socialists, notes, "Germany's laws, above all, protect those who are already in a completely insured eight-hour-a-day jobs, and we have long given up any expectation of receiving even a dime from the government when we're 60."

However, even in Germany, the entrenched culture works against such changes. When German Chancellor Gerhard Schroder announced modest reforms in state pension plans and work hour rules, over 100,000 demonstrators marched in the streets of Berlin to oppose the moves. French officials took notice of this and have made no attempt to revise their work rules, even though they cost the country $17 billion a year in lost productivity. Apparently, these economic costs are outweighed by the political costs, and unlike Germany, there seems to be no political pressure from young French workers on the French government.

SOURCE: J. Rossant, "Give This Policy the Guillotine," *BusinessWeek* (October 27, 2003), p. 58; A. Weintraub, "Revenge of the Overworked Nerds," *BusinessWeek* (December 8, 2003), p. 41; J. Ewing, "Revolt of the Young," *BusinessWeek* (September 22, 2003), p. 48; G. S. Becker, "A Little German Reform Would Go a Long Way," *BusinessWeek* (December 1, 2003), p. 22.

indicates that social support is a strong predictor of job satisfaction, whether the support comes from supervisors or coworkers.[85] Support from other organizational members is also related to lower employee turnover.[86]

Third, one's supervisor or coworkers may help the person attain some valued outcome.[87] For example, a new employee may be uncertain about what goals to pursue or what paths to take to achieve those goals. This person will likely be satisfied with a supervisor or with coworkers who can help clarify those goals and paths.[88]

Because a supportive environment reduces dissatisfaction, many organizations foster team building both on and off the job (such as via softball or bowling leagues). The idea is that group cohesiveness and support for individual group members will be increased through exposure and joint efforts. Although management certainly cannot ensure that each stressed employee develops friends, it can make it easier for employees to interact—a necessary condition for developing friendship and rapport.

For example, American Airlines teamed up with the environmental group The Nature Conservancy to sponsor a "Teamwork for Nature" day in several U.S. cities. Employee teams reported for cleanup duty and helped by gathering litter, pulling weeds, and constructing fences. Some teams even worked on more elaborate projects such as installing irrigation systems or controlling erosion problems. Flight attendant Jacqueline Grant noted, "The nice thing about it is every employee group, regardless of their job description, can participate in their own way. I think it has brought a lot of departments closer together."[89]

Pay and Benefits

We should not discount the influence of the job incumbent, the job itself, and the surrounding people in terms of influencing job satisfaction, but for most people, work is their primary source of income and financial security. Pay is also seen as an indicator of status within the organization as well as in society at large. Thus, for some people, pay is a reflection of self-worth, so pay satisfaction takes on critical significance when it comes to retention. Indeed, the role of pay and benefits is so large that we devote the entire next part of this book to these topics. Within this chapter we focus primarily on satisfaction with two aspects of pay (pay levels and benefits) and how these are assessed within the organization. Methods for addressing these issues are discussed in Part IV of this book.

One of the main dimensions of satisfaction with pay deals with pay levels—that is, the absolute amount of income associated with the job. Indeed, when it comes to retention, employees being recruited away from one organization by another are often lured with promises of higher pay levels. Satisfaction with benefits is another important dimension of overall pay satisfaction. Because many individuals have a difficult time ascertaining the true dollar value of their benefits package, however, this dimension may not always be as salient to people as pay itself. In order to derive competitive advantage from benefits' expenditures, it is critical not only to make them highly salient to employees, however, but also link them to the organization's strategic direction.

Strategic Use of HRM

A good example of matching the organization's benefit package to its culture can be seen at Google, the Internet search engine software developer. The company began work in 1998 with two employees, founders Larry Page and Sergey Brin, working out of a garage in Menlo Park, California. In five short years, the company rose to the top of their industry by creatively finding answers to tough technical questions that lie at the heart of structuring the inherently unstructured World Wide Web. Google places an intense focus on human resource management issues, and its two founders often get highly involved in what many would consider low level hiring decisions and the nitty-gritty details of HR benefits. At Google, employees become eligible for health benefits and 401(k) savings plans on Day 1, and get up to three weeks' vacation their first year. Sick days are not monitored, but few of the firm's young workers report in sick because they would miss the free breakfast, lunch, and dinner offered on site. The firm also added an on-site medical facility, preschool, and day care center.

With respect to the work itself, many talented young people flock to Google because the work is challenging, complex, and compelling in terms of social recognition for what the firm has accomplished in such a short time. Information is freely shared in weekly meetings where the founders discuss upcoming product launches or new advertising revenues. All of these benefits are aimed at keeping employees' minds on their tasks and not having them worried about other problems. As Google's HR director notes, the benefits package mirrors the company's values. "It's about creativity, and enabling people to be creative about their jobs. It's not a culture of standardization."

SOURCE: T. Raphael, "At Google, the Proof Is in the People," *Workforce*, March 2003, pp. 50–51.

In order to make costs better reflect revenues, organizations are increasingly adopting variable pay schemes that reward employees for specific accomplishments related to either individual or organizational performance.[90] Although "paying for performance" is an easy idea to express in general terms, it is often difficult to put into practice without creating certain negative side effects. For example, reward schemes that target the performance of individuals (merit raises or incentives for being the top salesperson) often detract from teamwork because the motivation to win the award makes it against the person's own self-interest to help colleagues succeed. For example, in one company, an individual who learned of a new idea that reduced costs kept it a secret, even though this information, if shared companywide, could have saved the organization millions of dollars. On the other hand, incentives that are targeted at performance at the unit or organizational level often fail to recognize the difference between "star performers" and "social loafers," each of which gets the same reward. For example, in another company, an individual whose idea saved the company millions of dollars received a $2,000 bonus after this was figured into the organization-wide cost saving program—the same amount received by those who came up with no ideas of their own.[91] Thus, although simple in theory, organizations that opt for variable reward schemes need to think out these kinds of issues carefully to avoid negative side effects.

Measuring and Monitoring Job Satisfaction

Most attempts to measure job satisfaction rely on workers' self-reports. There is a vast amount of data on the reliability and validity of many existing scales as well as a wealth of data from companies that have used these scales, allowing for comparisons across firms. Established scales are excellent places to begin if employers wish to assess the satisfaction levels of their employees. An employer would be foolish to "reinvent the wheel" by generating its own versions of measures of these broad constructs. Of course, in some cases, organizations want to measure their employees' satisfaction with aspects of their work that are specific to that organization (such as satisfaction with one particular health plan versus another). In these situations the organization may need to create its own scales, but this will be the exception rather than the rule.

One standardized, widely used measure of job satisfaction is the Job Descriptive Index (JDI). The JDI emphasizes various facets of satisfaction: pay, the work itself, supervision, coworkers, and promotions. Table 10.5 presents several items from the JDI scale. Other scales exist for those who want to get even more specific about different facets of satisfaction. For example, although the JDI we just examined assesses satisfaction with pay, it does not break pay up into different dimensions.[92] The Pay

TABLE 10.5

Sample Items from a Standardized Job Satisfaction Scale (the JDI)

Instructions: Think of your present work. What is it like most of the time? In the blank beside each word given below, write

_Y_	for "Yes" if it describes your work
_N_	for "No" if it does NOT describe your work
_?_	if you cannot decide

Work Itself	**Pay**	**Promotion Opportunities**
___ Routine	___ Less than I deserve	___ Dead-end job
___ Satisfying	___ Highly paid	___ Unfair policies
___ Good	___ Insecure	___ Based on ability

Supervision	**Coworkers**
___ Impolite	___ Intelligent
___ Praises good work	___ Responsible
___ Doesn't supervise enough	___ Boring

SOURCE: W. K. Balzar, D. C. Smith, D. E. Kravitz, S. E. Lovell, K. B. Paul, B. A. Reilly, and C. E. Reilly, *User's Manual for the Job Descriptive Index (JDI)* (Bowling Green, OH: Bowling Green State University, 1990).

Satisfaction Questionnaire (PSQ) focuses on these more specific dimensions (pay levels, benefits, pay structure, and pay raises); thus this measure gives a more detailed view of exactly what aspects of pay are most or least satisfying.[93] Taking this even further, we can find scales that take just one of these dimensions—benefits—and then break this down even further into multiple facets of satisfaction with benefits.

Clearly there is no end to the number of satisfaction facets that we might want to measure, but the key in operational contexts, where the main concern is retention, is making sure that scores on whatever measures taken truly relate to voluntary turnover among valued people. For example, satisfaction with coworkers might be low, but if this aspect of satisfaction is not too central to employees, it may not translate into voluntary turnover. Similarly, in an organization that bases raises on performance, low performers might report being dissatisfied with raises, but this may not reflect any operational problem. Indeed, the whole strategic purpose of many pay-for-performance plans is to create this type of dissatisfaction among low performers to motivate them to higher levels of performance.

Survey-Feedback Interventions

Regardless of what measures are used or how many facets of satisfaction are assessed, a systematic, ongoing program of *employee survey research* should be a prominent part of any human resource strategy for a number of reasons. First, it allows the company to monitor trends over time and thus prevent problems in the area of voluntary turnover before they happen. For example, Figure 10.3 shows the average profile for different facets of satisfaction for a hypothetical company in 2000, 2002, and 2004. As the figure makes clear, the level of satisfaction with promotion opportunities in

FIGURE 10.3

Average Profile for Different Facets of Satisfaction over Time

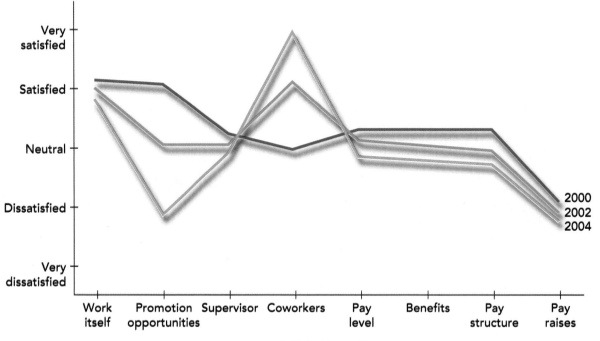

this company has eroded over time, whereas the satisfaction with coworkers has improved. If there was a strong relationship between satisfaction with promotion opportunities and voluntary turnover among high performers, this would constitute a threat that the organization might need to address via some of the techniques discussed in our previous chapter, "Employee Development." For example, First USA Bank saw exactly this kind of profile in its job satisfaction survey of all its managers. As Jeff Brown, vice president of organizational effectiveness, noted, "We already had a sense that career development was an issue, but the survey data really threw it in our faces and made us realize we had to do something about it." This led to First USA's "Opportunity Knocks" program, an employee-led career development effort that clarified the opportunities available within the firm as well as what skills and experiences were needed to take advantage of those opportunities. As a result of this program, two years later when the survey was conducted again, satisfaction with promotion opportunities increased by 40 percent.[94]

A second reason for engaging in an ongoing program of employee satisfaction surveys is that it provides a means of empirically assessing the impact of changes in policy (such as introduction of a new performance appraisal system) or personnel (introduction of a new CEO, for example) on worker attitudes. Figure 10.4 shows the average profile for different satisfaction facets for a hypothetical organization one year before and one year after a merger. An examination of the profile makes it clear that since the merger, satisfaction with supervision and pay structure have gone down dramatically, and this has not been offset by any increase in satisfaction along other dimensions. Again, this might point to the need for training programs for supervisors (like those discussed in Chapter 7) or changes in the job evaluation system (like those discussed in Chapter 11).

FIGURE 10.4

Average Profile for Different Facets of Satisfaction before and after a Major Event

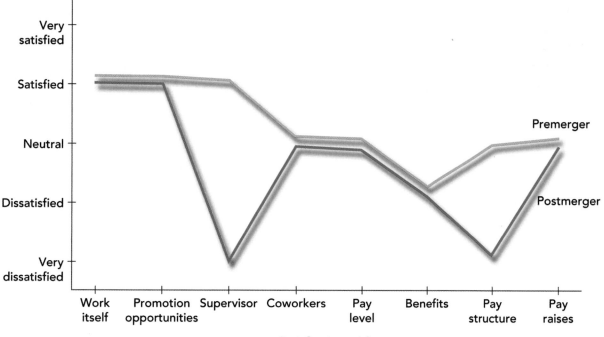

Finding and Keeping the Best Employees

A good example of linking survey results to a major organizational change can be seen in the experience of Cendant Mobility, a Connecticut-based global relocation service. After a rocky series of mergers with two other companies, managers at Cendant faced a workforce where morale was low and turnover was high. It was clear to all involved that reducing turnover would produce cost savings associated with recruiting, hiring, and training new replacements, who were often less productive than the people who had left those jobs. An employee attitude survey revealed that most of the workers were women in the 30–40 age bracket who were struggling with work/life balance issues. Indeed, most felt that the lack of flexibility in work schedules was the one of the top problems they faced at Cendant. Acting on these findings, Cendant offered a flexible start and end schedule with a small range of core time (10 AM–2 PM), as well as a four-day compressed workweek option. Turnover dropped from over 30 percent to less than 10 percent in less than two years, and Cendant wound up saving $8.6 million from a program that cost very little to implement.

SOURCE: E. Zimmerman, "The Joy of Flex," *Workforce*, March 2004, pp. 38–40.

Third, when these surveys incorporate standardized scales like the JDI, they often allow the company to compare itself with others in the same industry along these dimensions. For example, Figure 10.5 shows the average profile for different satisfaction facets for a hypothetical organization and compares this to the industry average. Again, if we detect major differences between one organization and the industry as a whole (on overall pay levels, for example), this might allow the company to react and change its policies before there is a mass exodus of people moving to the competition.

FIGURE 10.5

Average Profile for Different Facets of Satisfaction versus the Industry Average

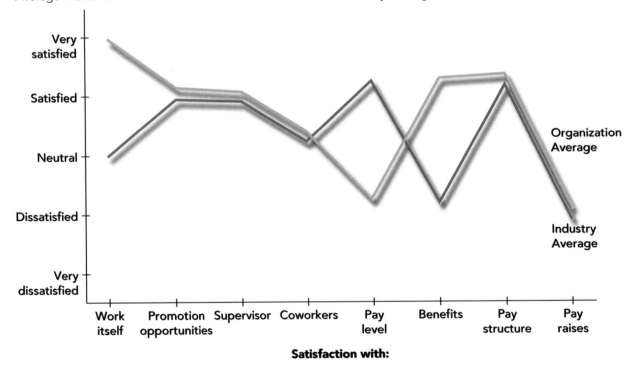

FIGURE 10.6

Average Profile for Different Facets of Satisfaction for Different Regional Divisions

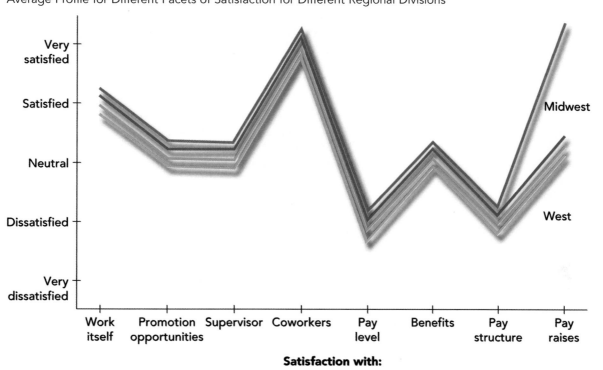

According to Figure 10.5, the satisfaction with pay levels is low relative to the industry, but this is offset by higher-than-industry-average satisfaction with benefits and the work itself. As we showed in Chapter 6 ("Selection and Placement"), the organization might want to use this information to systematically screen people. That is, the fit between the person and the organization would be best if the company selected applicants who reported being most interested in the nature of the work itself and benefits, and rejected those applicants whose sole concern was with pay levels.

Within the organization, a systematic survey program also allows the company to check for differences between units and hence benchmark "best practices" that might be generalized across units. For example, Figure 10.6 shows the average profile for five different regional divisions of a hypothetical company. The figure shows that satisfaction with pay raises is much higher in one of the regions relative to the others. If the overall amount of money allocated to raises was equal through the entire company, this implies that the manner in which raises are allocated or communicated in the Midwest region might be something that the other regions should look into.

Finally, yearly surveys give employees a constructive outlet for voicing their concerns and frustrations. Employees' ability to handle dissatisfying work experiences is enhanced when they feel they have an opportunity to air their problems. Formalized opportunities to state complaints about one's work situation have been referred to as **voicing.**[95] Research has shown that voicing gives employees an active, constructive outlet for their work frustrations.[96] For example, a study of nurses indicated that providing such voicing mechanisms as an employee attitude survey and question-and-answer sessions between employees and management enhanced worker attitudes and

Voicing
A formal
opportunity to
complain about
one's work situation.

Taking the Pulse of Your Organization: Don't Wait for Your Annual Checkup

Assessing employee attitudes is a critical process; however, most organizations treat it more like an "annual checkup" rather than a day-to-day activity. In the past, the very nature of paper-and-pencil interviews dictated this approach. Paper-and-pencil annual surveys at large companies were typically large, complex undertakings that generated tons of paperwork, and often dictated large travel budgets, high mailing costs, and the need for a large staff to enter, analyze, interpret and report back on the data. In fact, when one thinks of all the logistics associated with paper-and-pencil surveys at large companies, it seems like a miracle that they could even be executed once a year.

New technologies, however, have changed all of this, and increasingly organizations are conducting surveys on the Web, using automated software to help perform the analysis and reporting process. One of the primary virtues of using technology-based surveys is their reduced cost. However, if all the organization does is shift their annual survey from paper to the Web, they are missing three other features embodied in this technology that make them even more valuable— speed, frequency, and richness.

In terms of speed, the problem with many annual surveys is that by the time problems are identified, it is often too late to act upon them in any meaningful fashion. SAP, a software company that has been carrying out computer-administered surveys for over eight years, can now deliver online results to organizations in a mere four days. The timely nature of the data collected makes it highly suitable for taking action, and all organizations that conduct surveys need to realize that the key to their continued effectiveness is showing demonstrable actions that were taken based upon the survey. Without ac-

cut turnover.[97] The value of voicing opportunities has been expressed well by Norman Plummer, president of Monitrex (a San Francisco–based health care provider): "If you don't provide an environment for open communication, you'll suffer through revolutions rather than evolutions."[98]

Obviously a great deal can be learned from employee satisfaction surveys. It is surprising that many companies conducting regular consumer satisfaction surveys fail to show the same concern for employee satisfaction. Retention is an issue involving both customers and employees, however, and—as we've noted throughout this chapter—the two types of retention are substantially related. For example, sales agents at State Farm Insurance stay with the company for an average of 18 to 20 years—two to three times the average tenure in this industry. This kind of tenure allows the average State Farm agent to learn the job and develop long-term customer relations that cannot be matched by competitors who may lose half of their sales staff each year. State Farm also benefits from this experienced staff by systematically surveying its agents to get their views about where customer satisfaction is high, where it is low, and what can be done to improve service.[99] The result in terms of the bottom line is that State Farm achieves 40 percent higher sales per agent compared to the competition. In addition, as an indicator of quality of service, the retention rate among State Farm customers exceeds 95 percent.[100]

tion, the survey process is soon viewed as a waste of time, and the quality of data collected quickly falls off.

In terms of frequency, the problem with annual surveys is that their once-a-year nature makes it difficult to detect changes in attitudes and sentiments. In terms of importance, the next most critical aspect of the survey process beyond taking actions is documenting results, and this can be achieved much more convincingly when the survey is repeated over shorter time intervals. For example, eePulse Inc., an Ann Arbor–based survey firm, provides its clients with weekly survey results that provide highly detailed data on changes from week to week. The timely nature of this data makes it much easier to link specific changes or actions on the part of the employer to specific changes in attitudes and sentiments on the part of the employees because the two can be isolated in time. In contexts where the employer is making many changes or taking many actions over the course of a year, it is hard to attribute yearly changes in attitudes to any single change or action, thus reducing the ability to learn from the process.

Finally, in terms of richness, a common critique associated with annual surveys is that the data is "a mile wide and an inch thick." Overall averages on items that capture moods and sentiments across a wide number of domains (quality, leadership, coworkers, pay, benefits, and so on) often identify generic problems, but provide little guidance on the source or solutions to the problems identified. Much of the information on sources of problems and solutions could sometimes be found in the "write in comments" of traditional paper-and-pencil surveys, but sifting through this nonstandardized data was a subjective and time-consuming process. Automated search software can now handle this valuable write-in material much more efficiently, searching for key terms and themes, efficiently sorting and categorizing content, and then concisely reporting this content in a clear fashion. Clearly the cheaper, faster, more frequent and richer data that is generated via electronic surveys is just what the doctor ordered for many companies.

SOURCE: N. Eason, "Tech Lends an Ear to the Workplace," *CNN.com* (September 8, 2003), p. 1; K. Thomas, "Ticking the Right Boxes," *Financial Times* (April 28, 2004), pp. 2–4; S. Raphael, "Employers Start to Listen as eePulse Delivers," *Business Direct Weekly* (July 24, 2003), pp. 1–2; S. Jones, "Ever Sharp Eyes Are Watching You," *BusinessWeek* (July 22, 2003), pp. 22–23.

Although findings such as these are leading more companies to do such surveys, conducting an organizational opinion survey is not something that should be taken lightly. Especially in the beginning, surveys such as this often raise expectations. If people fail to see any timely actions taken on matters identified as problems in the survey, satisfaction is likely to be even lower than it would be in the absence of a survey. Fortunately, as the "Competing through Technology" box shows, current advancements in electronic survey technology are speeding the process of moving from problem identification to problem solving.

Finally, although the focus in this section has been on surveys of current employees, any strategic retention policy also has to consider surveying people who are about to become ex-employees. Exit interviews with departing workers can be a valuable tool for uncovering systematic concerns that are driving retention problems. If properly conducted, an exit interview can reveal the reasons why people are leaving, and perhaps even set the stage for their later return.[101] Indeed, in the new economy, it is now so common for people who once left their firm to return that they are given a special name—"boomerangs."[102] A good exit interview sets the stage for this phenomenon because if a recruiter is armed with information about what caused a specific person to leave (such as an abusive supervisor or a lack of family-friendly policies), when the situation changes, the person may be willing to come back.[103] Indeed, in the war for talent, the best way to manage retention is to engage in a battle for every valued employee, even in situations when it looks like the battle may have been lost.

A Look Back

In the discussion that opened this chapter, we examined how family-friendly policies were perceived by various groups of workers, and how this in turn affected work attitudes and retention.

Questions

1. Based upon our discussion of outcome fairness, procedural fairness, and interactional fairness, do you think that family-friendly policies are unfair to single employees? If so, what could be done to reduce this unfairness without significantly increasing costs?
2. What specific facets of job satisfaction or role problems are being targeted by these kinds of policies, and what facets or problems do they ignore? What facets of job satisfaction or role problems might be more of a concern for single people, and what steps can organizations take to address such issues?
3. Given the increased diversity of workers and their personal situations, how can a systematic employee survey process be used to quickly identify problems and solutions for different subgroups?

Summary

This chapter examined issues related to employee separation and retention. Involuntary turnover reflects a separation initiated by the organization, often when the individual would prefer to stay a member of the organization. Voluntary turnover reflects a separation initiated by the individual, often when the organization would prefer that the person stay a member. Organizations can gain competitive advantage by strategically managing the separation process so that involuntary turnover is implemented in a fashion that does not invite retaliation, and voluntary turnover among high performers is kept to a minimum. Retaliatory reactions to organizational discipline and dismissal decisions can be minimized by implementing these decisions in a manner that promotes feelings of procedural and interactive justice. Voluntary turnover can be minimized by measuring and monitoring employee levels of satisfaction with critical facets of job and organization, and then addressing any problems identified by such surveys.

Discussion Questions

1. The discipline and discharge procedures described in this chapter are systematic but rather slow. In your opinion, should some offenses lead to immediate dismissal? If so, how would you justify this to a court if you were sued for wrongful discharge?
2. Organizational turnover is generally considered a negative outcome, and many organizations spend a great deal of time and money trying to reduce it. What situations would indicate that an increase in turnover might be just what an organization needs? Given the difficulty of terminating employees, what organizational policies

might promote the retention of high-performing workers but voluntary turnover among low performers?
3. Three popular interventions for enhancing worker satisfaction are job enrichment, job rotation, and role analysis. What are the critical differences between these interventions, and under what conditions might one be preferable to the others?
4. If off-the-job stress and dissatisfaction begin to create on-the-job problems, what are the rights and responsibilities of the human resource manager in helping the employee to overcome these problems? Are intrusions

into such areas an invasion of privacy, a benevolent and altruistic employer practice, or simply a prudent financial step taken to protect the firm's investment?
5. Discuss the advantages of using published, standardized measures in employee attitude surveys. Do employers ever need to develop their own measures for such surveys? Where would one turn to learn how to do this?

Self-Assessment Exercise

The characteristics of your job influence your overall satisfaction with the job. One way to be satisfied at work is to find a job with the characteristics that you find desirable. The following assessment is a look at what kind of job is likely to satisfy you.

The following phrases describe different job characteristics. Read each phrase, then circle a number to indicate how much of the job characteristic you would like. Use the following scale: 1 = very little; 2 = little; 3 = a moderate amount; 4 = much; 5 = very much.

1. The opportunity to perform a number of different activities each day   1 2 3 4 5
2. Contributing something significant to the company   1 2 3 4 5
3. The freedom to determine how to do my job   1 2 3 4 5
4. The ability to see projects or jobs through to completion, rather than performing only one piece of the job   1 2 3 4 5
5. Seeing the results of my work, so I can get an idea of how well I am doing the job   1 2 3 4 5
6. A feeling that the quality of my work is important to others in the company   1 2 3 4 5
7. The need to use a variety of complex skills   1 2 3 4 5
8. Responsibility to act and make decisions independently of managers or supervisors   1 2 3 4 5
9. Time and resources to do an entire piece of work from beginning to end   1 2 3 4 5
10. Getting feedback about my performance from the work itself   1 2 3 4 5

Add the scores for the pairs of items that measure each job characteristic. A higher score for a characteristic means that characteristic is more important to you.

Skill Variety: The degree to which a job requires you to use a variety of skills.

Item 1: ____ + Item 7: ____ = ____

Task Identity: The degree to which a job requires completion of a whole and identifiable piece of work.

Item 4: ____ + Item 9: ____ = ____

Task Significance: The degree to which a job has an impact on the lives or work of others.

Item 2: ____ + Item 6: ____ = ____

Autonomy: The degree to which a job provides freedom, empowerment, and discretion in scheduling the work and determining processes and procedures for completing the work.

Item 3: ____ + Item 8: ____ = ____

Feedback: The degree to which carrying out job-related tasks and activities provides you with direct and clear information about your effectiveness.

Item 5 ____ + Item 10: ____ = ____

SOURCE: Adapted from R. Daft and R. Noe, *Organizational Behavior* (New York: Harcourt, 2001).

Manager's Hot Seat Exercise: Whistleblowing: Code Red or Red Ink?

This Manager's Hot Seat case looks at the issue of employees who "blow the whistle" on perceived illegal or unethical business practices. Two varying viewpoints are presented in this case study. One perspective displays the determination of an employee to bring to light the company's alleged life-threatening activities. The other demonstrates the determination of management to protect the pursuit of obtaining business objectives. The case explores this difficult issue in detail and points out how sensitive such situations can quickly become.

The video stresses how important it is for managers and organizations to conduct business in an ethical manner.

Acting in any other manner can create significant problems for the company. These problems most often include substantial legal difficulties, resulting in large financial losses to the company.

Individual Activity:

Identify a hypothetical business situation in which you would willingly "blow the whistle" on the offense and offender to organizational management and/or the press. Identify what you would expect the company to do to correct the problem. Identify what repercussions, if any, you would expect to experience for bringing the subject to light. Be clear and descriptive in your response, as you will be sharing this information with your team partner. Be prepared to justify your rationale for whistleblowing.

Group Activity:
Divide the class into groups of 3–4 students. Exchange the hypothetical business situations you individually constructed with your group members. Carefully read over the new situations you now have in front of you. Discuss with your team members how you would handle the situation he or she created. Defend your rationale with your group. Have your team members explain and defend his or her ra-

tionale to you. Do not avoid disagreement; just remember to remain professional! If you do not feel the situation your team member created would cause you to whistleblow, be honest about it. Simply be able to validate and defend your reasoning.

After concluding both hypothetical situation discussions, each group should discuss the best and the worst possible outcomes from engaging in whistleblowing. Discuss how inaction on the part of the company would impact your decision to remain with the organization. Describe how the action of whistleblowing could impact on your level of job satisfaction.

Exercising Strategy: Feeling Insecure about Airline Security

Becoming an expert in any field takes some degree of training and on-the-job experience. When working as part of a team, it also takes some time to learn about the strengths and weaknesses of one's team members so that a unit can operate like a well-oiled machine. For this reason, turnover in just one position can drastically reduce the effectiveness of work units. However, imagine the case where the entire work unit changes *every four months!*

Although it may seem hard to believe, this was the turnover rate at the security checkpoints at Logan International Airport in September 2001, when two planes were hijacked and used as guided missiles in the attacks on the World Trade Center. And Logan was not even the worst airport in this regard. The turnover rates at both St. Louis and Atlanta were over 400 percent—meaning that the entire crew turned over every three months. Given the lack of experience that workers in these positions had on the job, as well as their lack of experience working together, it is not at all surprising that performance of these work units was abysmal. In fact, as Max Cleland, chairman of the Senate Armed Services Subcommittee on Personnel, noted, "This was our front line, and what we found is we didn't have security, we had a sieve."

A number of factors explain the incredibly high turnover rates in these jobs. First, the job is low in pay. Most airport security personnel make less than $6 an hour, well below the rate of even those who work in the airport's fast food restaurants. Second, these are dead-end jobs. There is no career progression that would lead the incumbent to think that if he or she worked hard and stuck with it, he or she could climb into some managerial position. Third, the work itself is boring and monotonous. In addition, it is performed in a context of resentment, where hurried passengers look down on the security personnel who are perceived as being beneath those they are trying to serve. Finally, there is very little job security. A person can be fired for a single mistake, and the notion that a quality job is demanded is undermined by airline pressure to keep people moving during peak departure periods.

The airlines, which are currently responsible for security, blame this situation on the economics of the industry, where costs need to be kept low in order to maintain profitability. However, most airlines need to fill 65 percent of cabin capacity to clear a profit, and even two months after the terrorist attacks, fear of flying kept the capacity levels below 35 percent, putting even greater financial pressure on the carriers. As Cleland notes, as far as the industry is concerned, "Security is No. 1 in a series of confidence-building measures that will bring people back to fly."

Many of the security measures that are being considered will be imported from Europe and Israel, which have far better records than the United States in this area. There, airline security screening is treated as a police function, and the pay, training, and benefits are all much higher than what is seen in the United States. Moreover, a close emotional attachment between the security personnel and the airlines, many of which are nationalized, makes this work seem like a patriotic duty. This type of emotional attachment never develops in the revolving door that serves as the context for airline security work in the United States.

SOURCE: M. Fish, "Airport Security: A System Driven by the Minimum Wage," *CNN.com* (October 31, 2001), pp. 1–5; M. Fish, "Many Warnings over Security Preceded Terrorist Attacks," *CNN.com* (November 1, 2001), pp. 1–3; S. Candiotti, "FBI Arrests Man Who Tried to Board Flight Armed with Knives," *CNN.com* (November 5, 2001), pp. 1–2; M. Fish, "Outside the U.S., a Different Approach to Air Security," *CNN.com* (November 1, 2001), pp. 1–2.

Questions
1. Many now look back at the way airport security was selected and managed prior to the 9/11 attacks with disbelief. What was the relationship between the airlines, the airports, the government, and the security agents prior to the attacks? How did the nature of these relationships explain why airport security agents were managed so poorly?
2. How has the relationship between the airlines, airports, government, and security agents changed since

9/11, and it what ways has the new Transportation Safety Administration changed the nature of airport security work?

3. Much of the task in keeping air travel safe requires teamwork between the airlines, the airports, the gov-

ernment, and the security agents. In what way does high interdependence between people working together heighten the negative impact of employee turnover and performance?

Managing People: From the Pages of *BusinessWeek*

BusinessWeek The Costco Way

Higher Wages Mean Higher Profits, but Try Telling Wall Street Costco Wholesale Corp. handily beat Wall Street expectations on March 3, posting a 25% profit gain in its most recent quarter on top of a 14% sales hike. The warehouse club even nudged up its profit forecast for the rest of 2004. So how did the market respond? By driving the Issaquah (Wash.) company's stock down by 4%. One problem for Wall Street is that Costco pays its workers much better than archrival Wal-Mart Stores Inc. does and analysts worry that Costco's operating expenses could get out of hand. "At Costco, it's better to be an employee or a customer than a shareholder," says Deutsche Bank analyst Bill Dreher.

The market's view of Costco speaks volumes about the so-called Wal-Martization of the U.S. economy. True, the Bentonville (Ark.) retailer has taken a public-relations pounding recently for paying poverty-level wages and shouldering health insurance for fewer than half of its 1.2 million U.S. workers. Still, it remains the darling of the Street, which, like Wal-Mart and many other companies, believes that shareholders are best served if employers do all they can to hold down costs, including the cost of labor.

Surprisingly, however, Costco's high-wage approach actually beats Wal-Mart at its own game on many measures. *BusinessWeek* ran through the numbers from each company to compare Costco and Sam's Club, the Wal-Mart warehouse unit that competes directly with Costco. We found that by compensating employees generously to motivate and retain good workers, one-fifth of whom are unionized, Costco gets lower turnover and higher productivity. Combined with a smart business strategy that sells a mix of higher-margin products to more affluent customers, Costco actually keeps its labor costs lower than Wal-Mart's as a percentage of sales, and its 68,000 hourly workers in the U.S. sell more per square foot. Put another way, the 102,000 Sam's employees in the U.S. generated some $35 billion in sales last year, while Costco did $34 billion with one-third fewer employees.

Bottom line: Costco pulled in $13,647 in U.S. operating profit per hourly employee last year, vs. $11,039 at Sam's. Over the past five years, Costco's operating income grew at an average of 10.1% annually, slightly besting Sam's 9.8%. Most of Wall Street doesn't see the broader picture, though, and only focuses on the up-front savings

Costco would gain if it paid workers less. But a few analysts concede that Costco suffers from the Street's bias toward the low-wage model. "Costco deserves a little more credit than it has been getting lately, [since] it's one of the most productive companies in the industry," says Citigroup/Smith Barney retail analyst Deborah Weinswig. Wal-Mart spokeswoman Mona Williams says that Sam's pays competitively with Costco when all factors are considered, such as promotion opportunities.

Passing the Buck The larger question here is which model of competition will predominate in the U.S. Costco isn't alone; some companies, even ones like New Balance Athletic Shoe Inc. that face cheap imports from China, have been able to compete by finding ways to lift productivity instead of cutting pay. But most executives find it easier to go the Wal-Mart route, even if shareholders fare just as well either way over the long run.

Yet the cheap-labor model turns out to be costly in many ways. It can fuel poverty and related social ills and dump costs on other companies and taxpayers, who indirectly pick up the health-care tab for all the workers not insured by their parsimonious employers. What's more, the low-wage approach cuts into consumer spending and, potentially, economic growth. "You can't have every company adopt a Wal-Mart strategy. It isn't sustainable," says Rutgers University management professor Eileen Appelbaum, who in 2003 edited a vast study by 38 academics that found employers taking the high road in dozens of industries.

Given Costco's performance, the question for Wall Street shouldn't be why Costco isn't more like Wal-Mart. Rather, why can't Wal-Mart deliver high shareholder returns and high living standards for its workforce? Says Costco CEO James D. Sinegal: "Paying your employees well is not only the right thing to do but it makes for good business."

Look at how Costco pulls it off. Although Sam's $11.52 hourly average wage for full-timers tops the $9.64 earned by a typical Wal-Mart worker, it's still nearly 40% less than Costco's $15.97. Costco also shells out thousands more a year for workers' health and retirement and includes more of them in its health care, 401(k), and profit-sharing plans. "They take a very pro-employee attitude," says Rome Aloise, chief Costco negotiator for the Teamsters, which represents 14,000 Costco workers.

In return for all this generosity, Costco gets one of the most productive and loyal workforces in all of retailing. Only 6% of employees leave after the first year, compared with 21% at Sam's. That saves tons, since Wal-Mart says it costs $2,500 per worker just to test, interview, and train a new hire. Costco's motivated employees also sell more: $795 of sales per square foot, vs. only $516 at Sam's and $411 at BJ's Wholesale Club Inc., its other primary club rival. "Employees are willing to do whatever it takes to get the job done," says Julie Molina, a 17-year Costco worker in South San Francisco, Calif., who makes $17.82 an hour, plus bonuses.

Management Savvy Costco's productive workforce more than offsets the higher expense. Its labor and overhead tab, also called its selling, general, and administrative costs (SG&A), total just 9.8% of revenue. While Wal-Mart declines to break out Sam's SG&A, it's likely higher than Costco's but lower than Wal-Mart's 17%. At Target, it's 24%. "Paying higher wages translates into more efficiency," says Costco Chief Financial Officer Richard Galanti.

Of course, it's by no means as simple as that sounds, and management has to hustle to make the high-wage strategy work. It's constantly looking for ways to repackage goods into bulk items, which reduces labor, speeds up Costco's just-in-time inventory and distribution system, and boosts sales per square foot. Costco is also savvier than Sam's and BJ's about catering to small shop owners and more affluent customers, who are more likely to buy in bulk and purchase higher-margin goods. Neither rival has been able to match Costco's innovative packaging or merchandising mix, either. Costco was the first wholesale club to offer fresh meat, pharmacies, and photo labs.

Wal-Mart defenders often focus on the undeniable benefits its low prices bring consumers, while ignoring the damage it does to U.S. wages. Costco shows that with enough smarts, companies can help consumers and workers alike.

SOURCE: S. Holmes and W. Zellner, "The Costco Way," *BusinessWeek* (April 12, 2004), pp. 76–77.

Questions

1. Many organizations that skimp on pay, benefits, and working conditions attribute this to the intense competition they face. Does Costco face competitive pressures, and if so, how does their "pro-employee attitude" help them overcome these pressures?
2. In what ways are there hidden costs associated with the "cheap-labor model" epitomized by Costco's major competitor, Wal-Mart?
3. In the article, one investment analyst states "At Costco, it is better to be an employee or a customer than a shareholder." From a strategic perspective, when are the goals of these three different groups of stakeholders (customers, employees, shareholders) the same or different? If you are a manager, how do you balance the needs of these three constituencies?

Notes

1. M. L. Schmit and S. P. Allscheid, "Employee Attitudes and Customer Satisfaction: Making Theoretical and Empirical Connections," *Personnel Psychology* 48 (1995), pp. 521–36.
2. F. Reichheld, *The Loyalty Effect* (Cambridge, MA: Harvard Business School Press).
3. R. Batt, "Managing Customer Services: Human Resource Practices, Quit Rates, and Sales Growth," *Academy of Management Journal* 45 (2002), pp. 587–97.
4. I. S. Fulmer, B. Gerhart, & K. S. Scott, "Are the 100 Best Better? An Empirical Investigation of the Relationship between Being a 'Great Place to Work' and Firm Performance," *Personnel Psychology* 56 (2003), pp. 965–93.
5. J. P. Guthrie, "High-Involvement Work Practices, Turnover, and Productivity: Evidence from New Zealand," *Academy of Management Journal* 44 (2001), pp. 180–90.
6. S. S. Masterson, "A Trickle-Down Model of Organizational Justice: Relating Employees' and Customers' Perceptions of and Reactions to Fairness," *Journal of Applied Psychology* 86 (2001), pp. 594–604.
7. J. Greenwald, "Rank and Fire," *Time* (June 18, 2001), pp. 38–40.
8. D. Jones, "More Firms Cut Workers Ranked at Bottom," USA Today.com (May 5, 2001), pp. 1–2.
9. E. Tahmincioglu, "Close to the Breaking Point," *Workforce*, March 2004, p. 44.
10. S. A. Feeney, "The High Cost of Employee Violence," *Workforce*, August 2003, pp. 23–24.
11. J. D. Shaw, J. E. Delery, C. D. Jenkins, and N. Gupta, "An Organizational-Level Analysis of Voluntary Turnover," *Academy of Management Journal* 41 (1998), pp. 511–25.
12. M. Heller, "A Return to At-Will Employment," *Workforce*, May 2001, pp. 42–46.
13. J. B. Copeland, W. Turque, L. Wright, and D. Shapiro, "The Revenge of the Fired," *Newsweek* (February 16, 1987), pp. 46–47.
14. A. Q. Nomani, "Women Likelier to Face Violence in the Workplace," *The Wall Street Journal* (October 31, 1995), p. A16.
15. M. M. Le Blanc and K. Kelloway, "Predictors and Outcomes of Workplace Violence and Aggression," *Journal of Applied Psychology* 87 (2002), pp. 444–53.
16. N. D. Cole and G. P. Latham, "Effects of Training in Procedural Justice on Perceptions of Disciplinary Fairness by Unionized Employees and Disciplinary Subject Matter Experts," *Journal of Applied Psychology* 82 (1997), pp. 699–705.
17. D. P. Skarlicki and R. Folger, "Retaliation in the Workplace: The Roles of Distributive, Procedural, and Interactional Justice," *Journal of Applied Psychology* 82 (1997), pp. 434–43.

18. B. J. Tepper, "Relationship among Supervisors' and Subordinates' Procedural Justice Perceptions and Organizational Citizenship Behaviors," *Academy of Management Journal* 46 (2003), pp. 97–105.

19. T. Simons and Q. Roberson, "Why Managers Should Care About Fairness: The Affects of Aggregate Justice Perceptions on Organizational Outcomes," *Journal of Applied Psychology* 88 (2003), pp. 432–43.

20. S. Caudron, "Blowing the Whistle on Employee Disputes," *Workforce,* May 1997, pp. 50–57.

21. M. McGarvey, "The Challenge of Containing Health-Care Costs," *Financial Executive* 8 (1992), pp. 34–40.

22. B. B. Pflaum, "Seeking Sane Solutions: Managing Mental Health and Chemical Dependency Costs," *Employee Benefits Journal* 16 (1992), pp. 31–35.

23. J. Smith, "EAPs Evolve to Health Plan Gatekeeper," *Employee Benefit Plan Review* 46 (1992), pp. 18–19.

24. E. Stetzer, "Bringing Sanity to Mental Health," *Business Health* 10 (1992), p. 72.

25. S. Johnson, "Results, Relapse Rates Add to Cost of Non-Hospital Treatment," *Employee Benefit Plan Review* 46 (1992), pp. 15–16.

26. C. Mulcany, "Experts Eye Perils of Mental Health Cuts," *National Underwriter* 96 (1992), pp. 17–18.

27. A. Meisler, "Mind Field," *Workforce* (2003), pp. 57–60.

28. S. Sonnenberg and C. McEnerney, "Medical Leave: A Prescription," *Workforce,* April 2004, pp. 16–17.

29. J. Jones, "How to Bounce Back if You're Bounced Out," *BusinessWeek* (January 27, 1998), pp. 22–23.

30. J. Z. Carr, A. M. Schmidt, K. Ford, and R. P. DeShon, "Climate Perceptions Matter: A Meta-Analytic Path Analysis Relating Molar Climate, Cognitive and Affective States and Individual Level Outcomes," *Journal of Applied Psychology* 88 (2003), pp. 605–19.

31. G. A. Gelade and M. Ivery, "The Impact of Human Resource Management and Work Climate on Organizational Performance," *Personnel Psychology* 56 (2003), pp. 383–404.

32. B. Schneider, P. J. Hanges, D. B. Smith, and A. N. Salvaggio, "Which Come First, Employee Attitudes or Organizational Financial and Market Performance?" *Journal of Applied Psychology* 88 (2003), pp. 838–51.

33. D. W. Baruch, "Why They Terminate," *Journal of Consulting Psychology* 8 (1944), pp. 35–46; J. G. Rosse, "Relations among Lateness, Absence and Turnover: Is There a Progression of Withdrawal?" *Human Relations* 41 (1988), pp. 517–31.

34. C. Hulin, "Adaptation, Persistence and Commitment in Organizations," in *Handbook of Industrial & Organizational Psychology* 2nd ed., ed. M. D. Dunnette and L. M. Hough (Palo Alto, CA: *Consulting Psychologists Press,* 1991), pp. 443–50.

35. C. Hulin, M. Roznowski, and D. Hachiya, "Alternative Opportunities and Withdrawal Decisions," *Psychological Bulletin* 97 (1985), pp. 233–50.

36. C. E. Labig and I. B. Helburn, "Union and Management Policy Influences on Grievance Initiation," *Journal of Labor Research* 7 (1986), pp. 269–84.

37. J. Cook, "Positively Negative," *Human Resource Executive* (June 15, 2001), pp. 101–4.

38. M. P. Miceli and J. P. Near, "Characteristics of Organizational Climate and Perceived Wrongdoing Associated with Whistle-Blowing Decisions," *Personnel Psychology* 38 (1985), pp. 525–44.

39. M. Whitacre, "My Life as a Corporate Mole for the FBI," *Fortune* (September 4, 1995).

40. M. Galen, "Diversity: Beyond the Numbers Game," *BusinessWeek* (August 14, 1995), pp. 60–61.

41. L. Lavelle, "After the Jobless Recovery, a War for Talent," *BusinessWeek* (September 29, 2003), p. 92.

42. R. D. Hackett and R. M. Guion, "A Re-evaluation of the Job Satisfaction–Absenteeism Relation," *Organizational Behavior and Human Decision Processes* 35 (1985), pp. 340–81.

43. S. F. Gale, "Sickened by Costs of Absenteeism, Companies Look for Solutions," *Workforce,* September 2003, pp. 72–75.

44. J. G. Rosse and H. E. Miller, "Relationship between Absenteeism and Other Employee Behaviors," in *New Approaches to Understanding, Measuring, and Managing Employee Absence,* ed. P. S. Goodman and R. S. Atkin (San Francisco: Jossey-Bass, 1984).

45. R. T. Mowday, R. M. Steers, and L. W. Porter, "The Measurement of Organizational Commitment," *Journal of Vocational Behavior* 14 (1979), pp. 224–47.

46. E. A. Locke, "The Nature and Causes of Job Dissatisfaction," in *The Handbook of Industrial & Organizational Psychology,* ed. M. D. Dunnette (Chicago: Rand McNally, 1976), pp. 901–69.

47. E. Tahmincioglu, "More, More, More," *Workforce,* May 2004, pp. 41–44.

48. D. Watson, L. A. Clark, and A. Tellegen, "Development and Validation of Brief Measures of Positive and Negative Affect: The PANAS Scales," *Journal of Personality and Social Psychology* 54 (1988), pp. 1063–70.

49. T. A. Judge, E. A. Locke, C. C. Durham, and A. N. Kluger, "Dispositional Effects on Job and Life Satisfaction: The Role of Core Evaluations," *Journal of Applied Psychology* 83 (1998), pp. 17–34.

50. T. A. Judge, D. Heller, and M. K. Mount, "Five-factor Model of Personality and Job Satisfaction: A Meta-Analysis," *Journal of Applied Psychology* 87 (2002), pp. 530–41.

51. G. E. Hardy, D. Woods, and T. D. Wall, "The Impact of Psychological Distress on Absence from Work," *Journal of Applied Psychology* 88 (2003), pp. 306–14.

52. B. M. Staw, N. E. Bell, and J. A. Clausen, "The Dispositional Approach to Job Attitudes: A Lifetime Longitudinal Test," *Administrative Science Quarterly* 31 (1986), pp. 56–78; B. M. Staw and J. Ross, "Stability in the Midst of Change: A Dispositional Approach to Job Attitudes," *Journal of Applied Psychology* 70 (1985), pp. 469–80.

53. R. P. Steel and J. R. Rentsch, "The Dispositional Model of Job Attitudes Revisited: Findings of a 10-Year Study," *Journal of Applied Psychology* 82 (1997), pp. 873–79.

54. R. D. Arvey, T. J. Bouchard, N. L. Segal, and L. M. Abraham, "Job Satisfaction: Genetic and Environmental Components," *Journal of Applied Psychology* 74 (1989), pp. 187–93.

55. S. L. Hershberger, P. Lichenstein, and S. S. Knox, "Genetic and Environmental Influences on Perceptions of Organizational Climate," *Journal of Applied Psychology* 79 (1994), pp. 24–33.

56. T. A. Judge and J. E. Bono, "Relationship of Core Self-Evaluations Traits—Self-Esteem, Generalized Self-Efficacy, Locus of Control, and Emotional Stability—With Job Satisfaction and Job Performance: A Meta-Analysis," *Journal of Applied Psychology* 86 (2001), pp. 80–92.

57. T. A. Judge, J. E. Bono, and E. A. Locke, "Personality and Job Satisfaction: The Mediating Role of Job Characteristics," *Journal of Applied Psychology* 85 (2000), pp. 237–49.

58. S. C. Douglas and M. J. Martinko, "Exploring the Role of Individual Differences in the Prediction of Workplace Aggression," *Journal of Applied Psychology* 86 (2001), pp. 547–59.

59. B. A. Gerhart, "How Important Are Dispositional Factors as Determinants of Job Satisfaction? Implications for Job Design and Other Personnel Programs," *Journal of Applied Psychology* 72 (1987), pp. 493–502.

60. E. F. Stone and H. G. Gueutal, "An Empirical Derivation of the Dimensions along Which Characteristics of Jobs Are Perceived," *Academy of Management Journal* 28 (1985), pp. 376–96.

61. L. W. Porter and R. M. Steers, "Organizational, Work and Personal Factors in Employee Absenteeism and Turnover," *Psychological Bulletin* 80 (1973), pp. 151–76.

62. G. R. Oldham, A. Cummings, L. J. Mischel, J. M. Schmidtke, and J. Zhou, "Listen While You Work? Quasi-experimental Relations between Personal-Stereo Headset Use and Employee Work Responses," *Journal of Applied Psychology* 80 (1995), pp. 547–64.

63. Locke, "The Nature and Causes of Job Dissatisfaction."

64. L. Jones, "Xerox Is Rewriting the Book on Organization 'Architecture'," *Chicago Tribune* (December 29, 1992), pp. 3-1, 3-2.

65. S. Wellner, "What Makes Employees Want to Stick Around?" *BusinessWeek Online* (March 20, 2000), pp. 1–2.

66. G. C. Hill and K. Yamada, "Motorola Illustrates How an Aged Giant Can Remain Vibrant," *The Wall Street Journal* (December 9, 1992), p. A1.

67. J. R. Hackman and G. R. Oldham, "Motivation through the Design of Work," *Organizational Behavior and Human Performance* 16 (1976), pp. 250–79.

68. D. R. Ilgen and J. R. Hollenbeck, "The Structure of Work: Job Design and Roles," in *Handbook of Industrial & Organizational Psychology*, 2nd ed.

69. J. A. Breaugh and J. P. Colihan, "Measuring Facets of Job Ambiguity: Construct Validity Evidence," *Journal of Applied Psychology* 79 (1994), pp. 191–201.

70. B. Kaye, "Wake Up and Smell the Coffee: People Flock to Family Friendly," *BusinessWeek Online* (January 28, 2001), pp. 1–2.

71. B. L. Rau and M. M. Hyland, "Role Conflict and Flexible Work Arrangements: The Effects on Applicant Attraction," *Personnel Psychology* 55 (2002), pp. 111–36.

72. G. Weber, "Flexible Jobs Mean Fewer Absences," *Workforce*, November 2003, pp. 26–28.

73. M. Hammers, "Babies Deliver a Loyal Workforce," *Workforce*, April 2003, p. 52.

74. G. Flynn, "The Legalities of Flextime," *Workforce*, October 2001, pp. 62–66.

75. S. L. Lambert, "Added Benefits: The Link between Work–Life Benefits and Organizational Citizenship Behaviors," *Academy of Management Journal* 43 (2000), pp. 801–15.

76. J. E. Perry-Smith, "Work Family Human Resource Bundles and Perceived Organizational Performance," *Academy of Management Journal* 43 (2000), pp. 1107–17.

77. M. M. Arthur, "Share Price Reactions to Work-Family Initiatives: An Institutional Perspective," *Academy of Management Journal* 46 (2003), pp. 497–505.

78. V. S. Major, K. J. Klein, and M. G. Ehrhart, "Work Time, Work Interference with Family, and Psychological Distress," *Journal of Applied Psychology* 87 (2002), pp. 427–36.

79. T. J. Newton and R. S. Keenan, "Role Stress Reexamined: An Investigation of Role Stress Predictors," *Organizational Behavior and Human Decision Processes* 40 (1987), pp. 346–68.

80. B. Sorrell, "Many U.S. Employees Feel Overworked, Stressed, Study Says," *CNN.com* (May 16, 2001), pp. 1–2.

81. J. M. Brett and L. K. Stroh, "Working 61 Plus Hours a Week: Why Do Managers Do It?" *Journal of Applied Psychology* 88 (2003), pp. 67–78.

82. M. Conlin, "Revenge of the Managers," *BusinessWeek* (March 12, 2001), pp. 60–61.

83. I. Dayal and J. M. Thomas, "Operation KPE: Developing a New Organization," *Journal of Applied Behavioral Sciences* 4 (1968), pp. 473–506.

84. B. M. Meglino, E. C. Ravlin, and C. L. Adkins, "A Work Values Approach to Corporate Culture: A Field Test of the Value Congruence Process and Its Relationship to Individual Outcomes," *Journal of Applied Psychology* 74 (1989), pp. 424–33.

85. G. C. Ganster, M. R. Fusilier, and B. T. Mayes, "Role of Social Support in the Experience of Stress at Work," *Journal of Applied Psychology* 71 (1986), pp. 102–11.

86. R. Eisenberger, F. Stinghamber, C. Vandenberghe, I. L. Sucharski, and L. Rhoades, "Perceived Supervisor Support: Contributions to Perceived Organizational Support and Employee Retention," *Journal of Applied Psychology* 87 (2002), pp. 565–73.

87. M. A. Donovan, F. Drasgow, and L. J. Munson, "The Perceptions of Fair Interpersonal Treatment Scale: Development and Validation of a Measure of Interpersonal Treatment in the Workplace," *Journal of Applied Psychology* 83 (1998), pp. 683–92.

88. R. T. Keller, "A Test of the Path–Goal Theory of Leadership with Need for Clarity as a Moderator in Research and Development Organizations," *Journal of Applied Psychology* 74 (1989), pp. 208–12.

89. J. Lawrence, "American Airlines: A Profile in Employee Involvement," *Personnel Journal*, August 1992, p. 63.

90. J. S. Lubin, "Bottom Up," *The Wall Street Journal* (April 14, 2003), pp. 1–3.

91. E. Tahmincioglu, "Gifts That Gall," *Workforce*, April 2004, pp. 43–46.

92. H. G. Heneman and D. S. Schwab, "Pay Satisfaction: Its Multidimensional Nature and Measurement," *International Journal of Applied Psychology* 20 (1985), pp. 129–41.

93. T. Judge and T. Welbourne, "A Confirmatory Investigation of the Dimensionality of the Pay Satisfaction Questionnaire," *Journal of Applied Psychology* 79 (1994), pp. 461–66.

94. P. K. Kiger, "At First USA Bank, Promotions and Job Satisfaction Are Up," *Workforce*, March 2001, pp. 54–56.

95. A. O. Hirshman, *Exit Voice and Loyalty* (Cambridge, MA: Harvard University Press, 1970).

96. D. Farrell, "Exit, Voice, Loyalty and Neglect as Responses to Job Dissatisfaction: A Multidimensional Scaling Study," *Academy of Management Journal* 26 (1983), pp. 596–607.

97. D. G. Spencer, "Employee Voice and Employee Retention," *Academy of Management Journal* 29 (1986), pp. 488–502.

98. B. Lambert, "Give Your Company a Check-up," *Personnel Journal*, September 1995, pp. 143–46.

99. B. Schneider, S. D. Ashworth, A. C. Higgs, and L. Carr, "Design, Validity and Use of Strategically Focused Employee Attitude Surveys," *Personnel Psychology* 49 (1996), pp. 695–705.

100. M. Loeb, "Wouldn't It Be Good to Work for the Good Guys?" *Fortune* (October 14, 1996), pp. 223–24.

101. J. Applegaste, "Plan an Exit Interview," *CNNMoney.com* (November 13, 2000), pp. 1–2.

102. M. Conlin, "Job Security, No. Tall Latte, Yes," *BusinessWeek* (April 2, 2001), pp. 62–63.

103. J. Lynn, "Many Happy Returns," *CNNMoney.com* (March 2, 2001), pp. 1–2.

Compensation of Human Resources

Part 4

11 Chapter

Pay Structure Decisions

Objectives After reading this chapter, you should be able to:

1. List the main decision areas and concepts in employee compensation management.

2. Describe the major administrative tools used to manage employee compensation.

3. Explain the importance of competitive labor market and product market forces in compensation decisions.

4. Discuss the significance of process issues such as communication in compensation management.

5. Describe new developments in the design of pay structures.

6. Explain where the United States stands from an international perspective on pay issues.

7. Explain the reasons for the controversy over executive pay.

8. Describe the regulatory framework for employee compensation.

Enter the World of Business

AMR Unions Express Fury over Management Benefits

The disclosure of special payments for top executives at AMR Corp.'s American Airlines touched off a firestorm among employees and threatened to send the world's largest airline into federal bankruptcy court after all.

Retention bonuses and creation of a trust to protect executive pensions were disclosed in a filing AMR made just as three unions were wrapping up voting on whether to accept deep cuts in pay and benefits.

Workers now say they were betrayed. The Transport Workers Union, for one, threatened to refuse to sign a new contract that the company says it needs to avoid filing for bankruptcy-court protection. "I believe if our members had known this, it might have changed the outcome," said Jim Little, head of the union's air transport division. As it was, only 53 percent of TWU members voted for contract concessions.

On the ramp at O'Hare International Airport in Chicago, crew chief Joseph Szubryt, who recently made buttons saying, "For Your Future, Vote Yes," was dismayed. "This feels like a stab in the back," he said Thursday. "On the day we voted for all this stuff, giving up $10,000 a year when we only make $45,000 or $50,000, they disclose this? How the heck could these guys do that?"

Amid cost cutting and enormous losses, AMR's board last year agreed to spend an undisclosed cash sum to create a trust to protect supplemental pension benefits for 45 senior American executives. In addition, the board last year offered "retention bonuses"—equal to twice base salary—to American's top six executives if they stay with the troubled airline through January 2005.

Meanwhile, the company asked workers to swallow pay cuts of between 15.6 percent and 23 percent starting May 1, and to accept cuts in their own benefits and looser work rules. Most troubling, workers said, was that AMR didn't disclose the executive benefits until it filed its annual report on Tuesday with the Securities and Exchange Commission. The filing had been delayed while workers considered pay cuts, then was made within hours of the close of voting. "Knowledge of this outrage would probably have doomed any agreement, and rightly so," said John Ward, president of the Association of Professional Flight Attendants.

Union leaders demanded that executives give up the bonuses and the pension trust. But that may not be easily done. Under terms of the trust, it appears that each of the 45 executives may individually have to relinquish rights to the funds before AMR could get the money back.

Managers and top executives are giving up $100 million of the $1.8 billion in worker savings.

But the disclosure of extra benefits undermined those givebacks.

A senior executive at American said the airline last year faced losing a significant number of retirement-eligible operations executives key to day-to-day operations. The executives were concerned that their pension benefits weren't protected and realized they could leave at that time and take their pensions in a lump sum, before the danger of imminent bankruptcy. As a result, the board decided to fund the pension

trust. "We needed these guys to try to save the company," the senior official said.

American's three unions have yet to sign the concessionary contracts and said they are consulting lawyers and studying their options. "The credibility of the company is at stake. This was supposed to be shared sacrifice," said the transport workers union's Mr. Little.

Source: From *The Wall Street Journal, Online,* by Scott McCartney. Copyright 2003 by Dow Jones & Co., Inc. Reproduced with permission of Dow Jones & Co., Inc. via Copyright Clearance Center.

Introduction

From the employer's point of view, pay is a powerful tool for furthering the organization's strategic goals. First, pay has a large impact on employee attitudes and behaviors. It influences the kind of employees who are attracted to (and remain with) the organization, and it can be a powerful tool for aligning current employees' interests with those of the broader organization. Second, employee compensation is typically a significant organizational cost and thus requires close scrutiny. As Table 11.1 shows, total compensation (cash and benefits) averages 23 percent of revenues and varies both within and across industries, with the ratio of companies at the 75th percentile being approximately four times that of companies at the 25th percentile across all industries. In the chapter opener, American Airlines sought labor cost savings to avoid bankruptcy.

From the employees' point of view, policies having to do with wages, salaries, and other earnings affect their overall income and thus their standard of living. Both the level of pay and its seeming fairness compared with others' pay are important. Pay is also often considered a sign of status and success. Employees attach great importance to pay decisions when they evaluate their relationship with the organization. Therefore, pay decisions must be carefully managed and communicated.

Pay decisions can be broken into two areas: pay structure and individual pay. In this chapter we focus on **pay structure,** which in turn entails a consideration of pay level and job structure. **Pay level** is defined here as the average pay (including wages, salaries, and bonuses) of jobs in an organization. (Benefits could also be included, but these are discussed separately in Chapter 13.) **Job structure** refers to the relative pay of jobs in an organization. Consider the same two jobs in two different organizations. In Organization 1, jobs A and B are paid an annual average compensation of $40,000

Pay structure
The relative pay of different jobs (job structure) and how much they are paid (pay level).

Pay level
The average pay, including wages, salaries, and bonuses, of jobs in an organization.

Job structure
The relative pay of jobs in an organization.

TABLE 11.1

Total Compensation as a Percentage of Revenues

INDUSTRY	PERCENTILE		
	10TH	50TH	75TH
Hospitals/health care	43%	46%	49%
Manufacturing	22	27	34
Insurance/health care	6	8	11
All industries	12	23	43

SOURCE: Data from Saratoga Institute, *Human Capital Benchmarking Report 2000.*

and $60,000, respectively. In Organization 2, the pay rates are $45,000 and $55,000, respectively. Organizations 1 and 2 have the same pay level ($50,000), but the job structures (relative rates of pay) differ.

Both pay level and job structure are characteristics of organizations and reflect decisions about jobs rather than about individual employees. This chapter's focus is on why and how organizations attach pay policies to jobs. In the next chapter we look within jobs to discuss the different approaches that can determine the pay of individual employees as well as the advantages and disadvantages of these different approaches.

Why is the focus on jobs in developing a pay structure? As the number of employees in an organization increases, so too does the number of human resource management decisions. In determining compensation, for example, each employee must be assigned a rate of pay that is acceptable in terms of external, internal, and individual equity (defined later) and in terms of the employer's cost. Although each employee is unique and thus requires some degree of individualized treatment, standardizing the treatment of similar employees (those with similar jobs) can help greatly to make compensation administration and decision making more manageable and more equitable. Thus pay policies are often attached to particular jobs rather than tailored entirely to individual employees.

Equity Theory and Fairness

In discussing the consequences of pay decisions, it is useful to keep in mind that employees often evaluate their pay relative to that of other employees, as we saw in the chapter opening describing pay decisions at American Airlines. Chairman and CEO Don Carty eventually resigned over the fallout caused by employees' perceptions of inequity. Equity theory suggests that people evaluate the fairness of their situations by comparing them with those of other people.[1] According to the theory, a person (P) compares her own ratio of perceived outcomes O (pay, benefits, working conditions) to perceived inputs I (effort, ability, experience) to the ratio of a comparison other (o).

$$O_P/I_P <, >, \text{ or } = O_o/I_o?$$

If P's ratio (O_P/I_P) is smaller than the comparison other's ratio (O_o/I_o), underreward inequity results. If P's ratio is larger, overreward inequity results, although evidence suggests that this type of inequity is less likely to occur and less likely to be sustained because P may rationalize the situation by reevaluating her outcomes less favorably or inputs (self-worth) more favorably.[2]

The consequences of P's comparisons depend on whether equity is perceived. If equity is perceived, no change is expected in P's attitudes or behavior. In contrast, perceived inequity may cause P to restore equity. Some ways of restoring equity are counterproductive, including (1) reducing one's own inputs (not working as hard), (2) increasing one's outcomes (such as by theft), (3) leaving the situation that generates perceived inequity (leaving the organization or refusing to work or cooperate with employees who are perceived as overrewarded).

Equity theory's main implication for managing employee compensation is that to an important extent, employees evaluate their pay by comparing it with what others get paid, and their work attitudes and behaviors are influenced by such comparisons. Consider the contract that shortstop Alex Rodriquez (now a New York Yankee) signed in 2000 with the Texas Rangers baseball team. Rodriguez will earn a minimum of $21 million to $27 million per year (plus incentives) during the 10-year span of the

TABLE 11.2

Pay Structure Concepts and Consequences

PAY STRUCTURE DECISION AREA	ADMINISTRATIVE TOOL	FOCUS OF EMPLOYEE PAY COMPARISONS	CONSEQUENCES OF EQUITY PERCEPTIONS
Pay level	Market pay surveys	External equity	External employee movement (attraction and retention of quality employees); labor costs; employee attitudes
Job structure	Job evaluation	Internal equity	Internal employee movement (promotion, transfer, job rotation); cooperation among employees; employee attitudes

contract. However, two key provisions could result in him earning substantially more money. One provision states that during the 2001 to 2004 seasons, his base compensation must be at least $2 million higher than any other shortstop's in major league baseball. A second provision permits Rodriquez to void seasons after 2008 unless his 2009 and 2010 base compensation is at least $1 million higher than any position player's in major league baseball. Otherwise, Rodriguez is free to leave his current team. These provisions that peg Rodriguez's pay to other players' pay is a compelling example of the importance of being paid well in *relative* terms.

Another implication is that employee perceptions are what determine their evaluation. The fact that management believes its employees are paid well compared with those of other companies does not necessarily translate into employees' beliefs. Employees may have different information or make different comparisons than management.

Two types of employee social comparisons of pay are especially relevant in making pay level and job structure decisions. (See Table 11.2.) First, *external equity* pay comparisons focus on what employees in other organizations are paid for doing the same general job. Such comparisons are likely to influence the decisions of applicants to accept job offers as well as the attitudes and decisions of employees about whether to stay with an organization or take a job elsewhere. (See Chapters 5 and 10.) The organization's choice of pay level influences its employees' external pay comparisons and their consequences. A market pay survey is the primary administrative tool organizations use in choosing a pay level.

Second, *internal equity* pay comparisons focus on what employees within the same organization, but in different jobs, are paid. Employees make comparisons with lower-level jobs, jobs at the same level (but perhaps in different skill areas or product divisions), and jobs at higher levels. These comparisons may influence general attitudes of employees; their willingness to transfer to other jobs within the organization; their willingness to accept promotions; their inclination to cooperate across jobs, functional areas, or product groups; and their commitment to the organization. The organization's choice of job structure influences its employees' internal comparisons and their consequences. Job evaluation is the administrative tool organizations use to design job structures.

In addition, employees make internal equity pay comparisons with others performing the same job. Such comparisons are most relevant to the following chapter, which focuses on using pay to recognize individual contributions and differences.

We now turn to ways to choose and develop pay levels and pay structures, the consequences of such choices, and the ways two administrative tools—market pay surveys and job evaluation—help in making pay decisions.

Developing Pay Levels

Market Pressures

Any organization faces two important competitive market challenges in deciding what to pay its employees: product market competition and labor market competition.

Product Market Competition

First, organizations must compete effectively in the product market. In other words, they must be able to sell their goods and services at a quantity and price that will bring a sufficient return on their investment. Organizations compete on multiple dimensions (quality, service, and so on), and price is one of the most important dimensions. An important influence on price is the cost of production.

An organization that has higher labor costs than its product market competitors will have to charge higher average prices for products of similar quality. Thus, for example, if labor costs are 30 percent of revenues at Company A and Company B, but Company A has labor costs that are 20 percent higher than those of Company B, we would expect Company A to have product prices that are higher by $(.30 \times .20) = 6$ percent. At some point, the higher price charged by Company A will contribute to a loss of its business to competing companies with lower prices (like Company B). One study, for example, found that in the early 1990s the wage and benefit cost to produce a small car was approximately $1,700 for Ford, $1,800 for Chrysler, and $2,400 for General Motors.[3] Thus, if all other costs were equal, General Motors would have to sell the same quality car for $600 to $700 more than Ford or Chrysler.

Therefore, *product market competition* places an *upper bound* on labor costs and compensation. This upper bound is more constrictive when labor costs are a larger share of total costs and when demand for the product is affected by changes in price (that is, when demand is *elastic*). Although costs are only one part of the competitive equation (productivity is just as important), higher costs may result in a loss of business. In the absence of clear evidence on productivity differences, costs need to be closely monitored.

What components make up labor costs? A major component is the average cost per employee. This is made up of both direct payments (such as wages, salaries, and bonuses) and indirect payments (such as health insurance, Social Security, and unemployment compensation). A second component of labor cost is the staffing level (number of employees). Not surprisingly, financially troubled organizations often seek to cut costs by focusing on one or both components. Staff reductions, hiring freezes, wage and salary freezes, and sharing benefits costs with employees are several ways of enhancing the organization's competitive position in the product market.

Labor Market Competition

A second important competitive market challenge is *labor market competition*. Essentially, labor market competition is the amount an organization must pay to compete against other companies that hire similar employees. These labor market competitors typically include not only companies that have similar products but also those in different product markets that hire similar types of employees. If an organization is not competitive in the labor market, it will fail to attract and retain employees of sufficient numbers and quality. For example, even if a computer manufacturer offers newly graduated electrical engineers the same pay as other computer manufacturers, if automobile manufacturers and other labor market competitors offer salaries $5,000 higher, the computer company may not be able to hire enough qualified electrical engineers. Labor market competition places a *lower bound* on pay levels.

Employees as a Resource

Because organizations have to compete in the labor market, they should consider their employees not just as a cost but as a resource in which the organization has invested and from which it expects valuable returns. Although controlling costs directly affects an organization's ability to compete in the product market, the organization's competitive position can be compromised if costs are kept low at the expense of employee productivity and quality. Having higher labor costs than your competitors is not necessarily bad if you also have the best and most effective workforce, one that produces more products of better quality.

Pay policies and programs are one of the most important human resource tools for encouraging desired employee behaviors and discouraging undesired behaviors. Therefore, they must be evaluated not just in terms of costs but in terms of the returns they generate—how they attract, retain, and motivate a high-quality workforce. For example, if the average revenue per employee in Company A is 20 percent higher than in Company B, it may not be important that the average pay in Company A is 10 percent higher than in Company B.

Deciding What to Pay

Although organizations face important external labor and product market pressures in setting their pay levels, a range of discretion remains.[4] How large the range is depends on the particular competitive environment the organization faces. Where the range is broad, an important strategic decision is whether to pay above, at, or below the market average. The advantage of paying above the market average is the ability to attract and retain the top talent available, which can translate into a highly effective and productive workforce. The disadvantage, however, is the added cost.

Under what circumstances do the benefits of higher pay outweigh the higher costs? According to **efficiency wage theory**, one circumstance is when organizations have technologies or structures that depend on highly skilled employees. For example, organizations that emphasize decentralized decision making may need higher-caliber employees. Another circumstance where higher pay may be warranted is when an organization has difficulties observing and monitoring its employees' performance. It may therefore wish to provide an above-market pay rate to ensure the incentive to put forth maximum effort. The theory is that employees who are paid more than they would be paid elsewhere will be reluctant to shirk because they wish to retain their good jobs.[5]

Efficiency wage theory
A theory stating that wages influence worker productivity.

Benchmarking
Comparing an organization's practices against those of the competition.

Market Pay Surveys

To compete for talent, organizations use **benchmarking,** a procedure in which it compares its own practices against those of the competition. In compensation management, benchmarking against product market and labor market competitors is typically accomplished through the use of one or more pay surveys, which provide information on going rates of pay among competing organizations.

The use of pay surveys requires answers to several important questions:[6]

1. Which employers should be included in the survey? Ideally, they would be the key labor market and product market competitors.
2. Which jobs are included in the survey? Because only a sample of jobs is ordinarily used, care must be taken that the jobs are representative in terms of level, functional area, and product market. Also, the job content must be sufficiently similar.
3. If multiple surveys are used, how are all the rates of pay weighted and combined? Organizations often have to weight and combine pay rates because different surveys are often tailored toward particular employee groups (labor markets) or product markets. The organization must decide how much relative weight to give to its labor market and product market competitors in setting pay.

Several factors affect decisions on how to combine surveys.[7] Product market comparisons that focus on labor costs are likely to deserve greater weight when (1) labor costs represent a large share of total costs, (2) product demand is elastic (it changes in response to product price changes), (3) the supply of labor is inelastic, and (4) employee skills are specific to the product market (and will remain so). In contrast, labor market comparisons may be more important when (1) attracting and retaining qualified employees is difficult and (2) the costs (administrative, disruption, and so on) of recruiting replacements are high.

As this discussion suggests, knowing what other organizations are paying is only one part of the story. It is also necessary to know what those organizations are getting in return for their investment in employees. To find that out, some organizations examine ratios such as revenues/employees and revenues/labor cost. The first ratio includes the staffing component of employee cost but not the average cost per employee. The second ratio, however, includes both. Note that comparing these ratios across organizations requires caution. For example, different industries rely on different labor and capital resources. So comparing the ratio of revenues to labor costs of a petroleum company (capital intensive, high ratio) to a bank (labor intensive, low ratio) would be like comparing apples and oranges. But within industries, such comparisons can be useful. Besides revenues, other return-on-investment data might include product quality, customer satisfaction, and potential workforce quality (such as average education levels).

Strategic Use of HRM

At Procter & Gamble compensation for executives is based on the principles that compensation must (a) be competitive with other quality companies in order to help attract, motivate, and retain the talent needed to lead and grow Procter & Gamble's business; (b) provide a strong incentive for key managers to achieve the company's goals; and (c) make prudent use of the company's resources. Procter & Gamble has an enviable record of recruiting, retaining, and developing its executive talent from within—an achievement few other corporations have matched.

Executive compensation is based on performance against a combination of financial and nonfinancial measures, including business results and developing organizational capacity. In addition, executives are expected to uphold the fundamental principles embodied in the company's Statement of Purpose, Values, and Principles plus the Sustainability Report and the Environmental Quality Policy. These include a commitment to integrity, doing the right thing, maximizing the development of each individual, developing a diverse organization, and continually improving the environmental quality of products and operations. In upholding these objectives, executives not only contribute to their own success, but also help ensure that the company's business, employees, shareholders, and communities will prosper.

SOURCE: Excerpt from Procter & Gamble proxy statement.

Rate Ranges

As the preceding discussion suggests, obtaining a single "going rate" of market pay is a complex task that involves a number of subjective decisions; it is both an art and a science. Once a market rate has been chosen, how is it incorporated into the pay structure? Typically—especially for white-collar jobs—it is used for setting the midpoint of pay ranges for either jobs or pay grades (discussed next). Market survey data are also often collected on minimum and maximum rates of pay as well. The use of **rate ranges** permits a company to recognize differences in employee performance, seniority, training, and so forth in setting individual pay (discussed in the next chapter). For some blue-collar jobs, however, particularly those covered by collective bargaining contracts, there may be a single rate of pay for all employees within the job.

Key Jobs and Nonkey Jobs

In using pay surveys, it is necessary to make a distinction between two general types of jobs: key jobs (or benchmark jobs) and nonkey jobs. **Key jobs** have relatively stable content and—perhaps most important—are common to many organizations. Therefore, it is possible to obtain market pay survey data on them. Note, however, that to avoid too much of an administrative burden, organizations may not gather market pay data on all such jobs. In contrast to key jobs, **nonkey jobs** are, to an important extent, unique to organizations; thus, by definition, they cannot be directly valued or compared through the use of market surveys. Therefore, they are treated differently in the pay-setting process.

Developing a Job Structure

Although external comparisons of the sort we have been discussing are important, employees also evaluate their pay using internal comparisons. So, for example, a vice president of marketing may expect to be paid roughly the same amount as a vice president of information systems because they are at the same organizational level, with similar levels of responsibility and similar impacts on the organization's performance. A job structure can be defined as the relative worth of various jobs in the organization, based on these types of internal comparisons. We now discuss how such decisions are made.

Job Evaluation

One typical way of measuring internal job worth is to use an administrative procedure called **job evaluation.** A job evaluation system is composed of compensable factors and a weighting scheme based on the importance of each **compensable factor** to the organization. Simply stated, compensable factors are the characteristics of jobs that an organization values and chooses to pay for. These characteristics may include job complexity, working conditions, required education, required experience, and responsibility. Most job evaluation systems use several compensable factors. Job analysis

---

Rate ranges
Different employees in the same job may have different pay rates.

Key jobs
Benchmark jobs, used in pay surveys, that have relatively stable content and are common to many organizations.

Nonkey jobs
Jobs that are unique to organizations and that cannot be directly valued or compared through the use of market surveys.

Job evaluation
An administrative procedure used to measure internal job worth.

Compensable factors
The characteristics of jobs that an organization values and chooses to pay for.

(discussed in Chapter 4) provides basic descriptive information on job attributes, and the job evaluation process assigns values to these compensable factors.

Scores can be generated in a variety of ways, but they typically include input from a number of people. A job evaluation committee commonly generates ratings. Although there are numerous ways to evaluate jobs, the most widely used is the point-factor system, which yields job evaluation points for each compensable factor.[8]

The Point-Factor System

After generating scores for each compensable factor on each job, job evaluators often apply a weighting scheme to account for the differing importance of the compensable factors to the organization. Weights can be generated in two ways. First, *a priori* weights can be assigned, which means factors are weighted using expert judgments about the importance of each compensable factor. Second, weights can be derived empirically based on how important each factor seems in determining pay in the labor market. (Statistical methods such as multiple regression can be used for this purpose.) For the sake of simplicity, we assume in the following example that equal a priori weights are chosen, which means that the scores on the compensable factors can be simply summed.

Table 11.3 shows an example of a three-factor job evaluation system applied to three jobs. Note that the jobs differ in the levels of experience, education, and complexity required. Summing the scores on the three compensable factors provides an internally oriented assessment of relative job worth in the organization. In a sense, the computer programmer job is worth 41 percent (155/110 − 1) more than the computer operator job, and the systems analyst job is worth 91 percent (210/110 − 1) more than the computer operator job. Whatever pay level is chosen (based on benchmarking and competitive strategy), we would expect the pay differentials to be somewhat similar to these percentages. The internal job evaluation and external survey-based measures of worth can, however, diverge.

Developing a Pay Structure

In the example provided in Table 11.4, there are 15 jobs, 10 of which are key jobs. For these key jobs, both pay survey and job evaluation data are available. For the five nonkey jobs, by definition, no survey data are available, only job evaluation information. Note that, for simplicity's sake, we work with data from only two pay surveys and we use a weighted average that gives twice as much weight to survey 1. Also, our example works with a single structure. Many organizations have multiple structures that correspond to different job families (like clerical, technical, and professional) or product divisions.

How are the data in Table 11.4 combined to develop a pay structure? First, it is important to note that both internal and external comparisons must be considered in

| JOB TITLE | COMPENSABLE FACTORS | | | |
	EXPERIENCE	EDUCATION	COMPLEXITY	TOTAL
Computer operator	40	30	40	110
Computer programmer	40	50	65	155
Systems analyst	65	60	85	210

TABLE 11.3

Example of a Three-Factor Job Evaluation System

TABLE 11.4

Job Evaluation and Pay Survey Data

JOB	KEY JOB?	JOB TITLE	JOB EVALUATION	SURVEY 1 (S1)	SURVEY 2 (S2)	SURVEY COMPOSITE (2/3*S1 + 1/3*S2)
A	y	Computer operator	110	$2,012	$1,731	$1,919
B	y	Engineering tech I	115	2,206	1,908	2,106
C	y	Computer programmer	155	2,916	2,589	2,807
D	n	Engineering tech II	165	—	—	—
E	n	Compensation analyst	170	—	—	—
F	y	Accountant	190	3,613	3,099	3,442
G	y	Systems analyst	210	4,275	3,854	4,134
H	n	Computer programmer—senior	225	—	—	—
I	y	Director of personnel	245	4,982	4,506	4,823
J	y	Accountant—senior	255	5,205	4,270	4,893
K	y	Systems analyst—senior	270	5,868	5,652	5,796
L	y	Industrial engineer	275	5,496	4,794	5,262
M	n	Chief accountant	315	—	—	—
N	y	Senior engineer	320	7,026	6,572	6,875
O	n	Senior scientist	330	—	—	—

SOURCE: Adapted from S. Rynes, B. Gerhart, G. T. Milkovich, and J. Boudreau, *Current Compensation Professional Institute* (Scottsdale, AZ: American Compensation Association, 1988). Reprinted with permission.

making compensation decisions. However, because the pay structures suggested by internal and external comparisons do not necessarily converge, employers must carefully balance them. Studies suggest that employers may differ significantly in the degree to which they place priority on internal- or external-comparison data in developing pay structures.[9]

At least three pay-setting approaches, which differ according to their relative emphasis on external or internal comparisons, can be identified.[10]

Market Survey Data

The approach with the greatest emphasis on external comparisons (market survey data) is achieved by directly basing pay on market surveys that cover as many key jobs as possible. For example, the rate of pay for job A in Table 11.5 would be $1,919; for job B, $2,106; and for job C, $2,807. For nonkey jobs (jobs D, E, H, M, and O), however, pay survey information is not available, and we must proceed differently. Basically, we develop a market **pay policy line** based on the key jobs (for which there are both job evaluation and market pay survey data available). As Figure 11.1 shows, the data can be plotted with a line of best fit estimated. This line can be generated using a statistical procedure (regression analysis). Doing so yields the equation –$661 + $22.69 × job evaluation points. In other words, the predicted monthly salary (based on fitting a line to the key job data) is obtained by plugging the number of job evaluation points into this equation. Thus, for example, job D, a nonkey job, would have a predicted monthly salary of –$661 + $22.69 × 165 = $3,083.

As Figure 11.1 also indicates, it is not necessary to fit a straight line to the job evaluation and pay survey data. In some cases, a pay structure that provides increasing monetary rewards to higher-level jobs may be more consistent with the organization's

Pay policy line
A mathematical expression that describes the relationship between a job's pay and its job evaluation points.

TABLE 11.5

Pay Midpoints under Different Approaches

JOB	KEY JOB?	JOB TITLE	JOB EVALUATION	(1) SURVEY + POLICY	(2) PAY MIDPOINTS POLICY	(3) GRADES
A	y	Computer operator	110	$1,919	$1,835	$2,175
B	y	Engineering tech I	115	2,106	1,948	2,175
C	y	Computer programmer	155	2,807	2,856	3,310
D	n	Engineering tech II	165	3,083	3,083	3,310
E	n	Compensation analyst	170	3,196	3,196	3,310
F	y	Accountant	190	3,442	3,650	3,310
G	y	Systems analyst	210	4,134	4,104	4,444
H	n	Computer programmer—senior	225	4,444	4,444	4,444
I	y	Director of personnel	245	4,823	4,898	4,444
J	y	Accountant—senior	255	4,893	5,125	5,579
K	y	Systems analyst—senior	270	5,796	5,465	5,579
L	y	Industrial engineer	275	5,262	5,579	5,579
M	n	Chief accountant	315	6,486	6,486	6,713
N	y	Senior engineer	320	6,875	6,600	6,713
O	n	Senior scientist	330	6,826	6,826	6,713

SOURCE: Adapted from S. Rynes, B. Gerhart, G.T. Milkovich, and J. Boudreau, *Current Compensation Professional Institute* (Scottsdale, AZ: American Compensation Association, 1988). Reprinted with permission.

goals or with the external market. For example, nonlinearity may be more appropriate if higher-level jobs are especially valuable to organizations and the talent to perform such jobs is rare. The curvilinear function in Figure 11.1 is described by the equation:

$$\text{Natural logarithm of pay} = \$6.98 + .006 \times \text{job evaluation points}$$

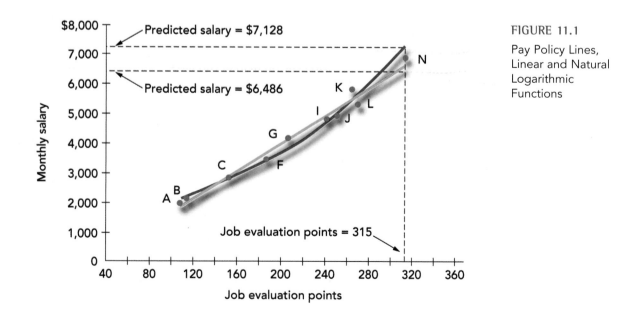

FIGURE 11.1

Pay Policy Lines, Linear and Natural Logarithmic Functions

TABLE 11.6

Sample Pay Grade Structure

PAY GRADE	JOB EVALUATION POINTS RANGE		MONTHLY PAY RATE RANGE		
	MINIMUM	MAXIMUM	MINIMUM	MIDPOINT	MAXIMUM
1	100	150	$1,740	$2,175	$2,610
2	150	200	2,648	3,310	3,971
3	200	250	3,555	4,444	5,333
4	250	300	4,463	5,579	6,694
5	300	350	5,370	6,713	8,056

Pay Policy Line

A second pay-setting approach that combines information from external and internal comparisons is to use the pay policy line to derive pay rates for both key and nonkey jobs. This approach differs from the first approach in that actual market rates are no longer used for key jobs. This introduces a greater degree of internal consistency into the structure because the pay of all the jobs is directly linked to the number of job evaluation points.

Pay Grades

Pay grades
Jobs of similar worth or content grouped together for pay administration purposes.

A third approach is to group jobs into a smaller number of pay classes or **pay grades.** Table 11.6 (see also Table 11.5, last column), for example, demonstrates one possibility: a five-grade structure. Each job within a grade would have the same rate range (that is, would be assigned the same midpoint, minimum, and maximum). The advantage of this approach is that the administrative burden of setting separate rates of pay for hundreds (even thousands) of different jobs is reduced. It also permits greater flexibility in moving employees from job to job without raising concerns about, for example, going from a job having 230 job evaluation points to a job with 215 job evaluation points. What might look like a demotion in a completely job-based system is often a nonissue in a grade-based system. Note that the **range spread** (the distance between the minimum and maximum) is larger at higher levels, in recognition of the fact that performance differences are likely to have more impact on the organization at higher job levels. (See Figure 11.2.)

Range spread
The distance between the minimum and maximum amounts in a pay grade.

The disadvantage of using grades is that some jobs will be underpaid and others overpaid. For example, job C and job F both fall within the same grade. The midpoint for job C under a grade system is $3,310 per month, or about $400 or so more than under the two alternative pay-setting approaches. Obviously, this will contribute to higher labor costs and potential difficulties in competing in the product market. Unless there is an expected return to this increased cost, the approach is questionable. Job F, on the other hand, is paid between $130 and $340 less per month under the grades system than it would be otherwise. Therefore, the company may find it more difficult to compete in the labor market.

Conflicts between Market Pay Surveys and Job Evaluation

An examination of Table 11.5 suggests that the relative worth of jobs is quite similar overall, whether based on job evaluation or pay survey data. However, some inconsistencies typically arise, and these are usually indicated by jobs whose average survey

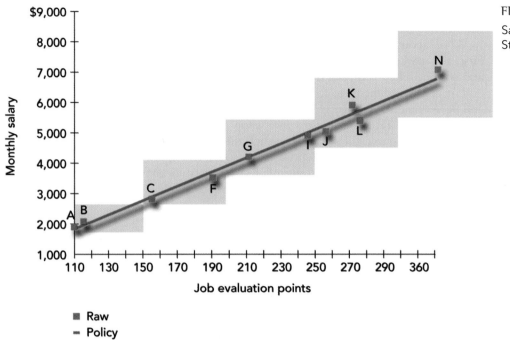

FIGURE 11.2

Sample Pay Grade Structure

pay is significantly below or above the pay policy line. The closest case in Table 11.5 is job L, for which the average pay falls significantly below the policy line. One possible explanation is that a relatively plentiful supply of people in the labor market are capable of performing this job, so the pay needed to attract and retain them is lower than would be expected given the job evaluation points. Another kind of inconsistency occurs when market surveys show that a job is paid higher than the policy line (like job K). Again, this may reflect relative supply and demand, in this case driving pay higher.

How are conflicts between external and internal equity resolved, and what are the consequences? The example of the vice presidents of marketing and information processing may help illustrate the type of choice faced. The marketing VP job may receive the same number of job evaluation points, but market survey data may indicate that it typically pays less than the information-processing VP job, perhaps because of tighter supply for the latter. Does the organization pay based on the market survey (external comparison) or on the job evaluation points (internal comparison)?

Emphasizing the internal comparison would suggest paying the two VPs the same. In doing so, however, either the VP of marketing would be "overpaid" or the VP of information processing would be "underpaid." The former drives up labor costs (product market problems); the latter may make it difficult to attract and retain a quality VP of information processing (labor market problems).

Another consideration has to do with the strategy of the organization. In some organizations (like Pepsi and Nike) the marketing function is critical to success. Thus, even though the market for marketing VPs is lower than that for information technology VPs, an organization may choose to be a pay leader for the marketing position (pay at the 90th percentile, for example) but only meet the market for the information systems position (perhaps pay at the 50th percentile). In other words, designing a pay structure requires careful consideration of which positions are most central to dealing with critical environmental challenges and opportunities in reaching the organization's goals.[11]

What about emphasizing external comparisons? Two potential problems arise. First, the marketing VP may be dissatisfied because she expects a job of similar rank and responsibility to that of the information technology VP to be paid similarly. Second, it becomes difficult to rotate people through different VP positions (for training and development) because going to the marketing VP position might appear as a demotion to the VP of information processing.

There is no one right solution to such dilemmas. Each organization must decide which objectives are most essential and choose the appropriate strategy. However, there seems to be a growing sentiment that external comparisons deserve greater weight because organizations are finding it increasingly difficult to ignore market competitive pressures.

Monitoring Compensation Costs

Pay structure influences compensation costs in a number of ways. Most obviously, the pay level at which the structure is pegged influences these costs. However, this is only part of the story. The pay structure represents the organization's intended policy, but actual practice may not coincide with it. Take, for example, the pay grade structure presented earlier. The midpoint for grade 1 is $2,175, and the midpoint for grade 2 is $3,310. Now, consider the data on a group of individual employees in Table 11.7. One frequently used index of the correspondence between actual and intended pay is the **compa-ratio,** computed as follows:

Compa-ratio
An index of the correspondence between actual and intended pay.

$$\text{Grade compa-ratio} = \text{Actual average pay for grade/Pay midpoint for grade}$$

The compa-ratio directly assesses the degree to which actual pay is consistent with the pay policy. A compa-ratio less than 1.00 suggests that actual pay is lagging behind the policy, whereas a compa-ratio greater than 1.00 indicates that pay (and costs) exceeds that of the policy. Although there may be good reasons for compa-ratios to differ from 1.00, managers should also consider whether the pay structure is allowing costs to get out of control.

TABLE 11.7

Compa-Ratios for Two Grades

EMPLOYEE	JOB	PAY	MIDPOINT	EMPLOYEE COMPA-RATIOS
	Grade 1			
1	Engineering tech I	$2,306	$2,175	1.06
2	Computer programmer	2,066	2,175	.95
3	Engineering tech I	2,523	2,175	1.16
4	Engineering tech I	2,414	2,175	1.11
				1.07
	Grade 2			
5	Computer programmer	3,906	3,310	1.18
6	Accountant	3,773	3,310	1.14
7	Accountant	3,674	3,310	1.11
				1.15

Globalization, Geographic Region, and Pay Structures

As Figure 11.3 shows, market pay structures can differ substantially across countries both in terms of their level and in terms of the relative worth of jobs. Compared with the labor market in Frankfurt, markets in Budapest and Bombay provide much lower levels of pay overall and much lower payoffs to skill, education, and advancement. These differences create a dilemma for global companies. For example, should a German engineer posted to Bombay be paid according to the standard in Frankfurt or Bombay? If Frankfurt, a sense of inequity is likely to exist among peers in Bombay. If the Bombay market standard is used, it may be all but impossible to find a German engineer willing to accept an assignment in Bombay. Typically, expatriate pay and benefits (like housing allowance and tax equalization) continue to be linked more closely to the home country. However, this link appears to be slowly weakening and now depends more on the nature and length of the assignment.[12]

Within the United States, Runzheimer International reports that 56 percent of companies have either a formal (30 percent) or informal (26 percent) policy that provides for pay differentials based on geographic location.[13] These differentials are intended to prevent inequitable treatment of employees who work in more expensive parts of the country. For example, according to Runzheimer, the cost of living index for New York City is 24 percent higher than in the average metropolitan area, whereas it is about average in Milwaukee. Therefore, an employee receiving annual pay of $50,000 in Milwaukee would require annual pay of more than $60,000 in New York City to retain the same purchasing power. The most common approach (74 percent of companies) is to move an employee higher in the pay structure to compensate

FIGURE 11.3

Earnings in Selected Occupations in Seven Cities

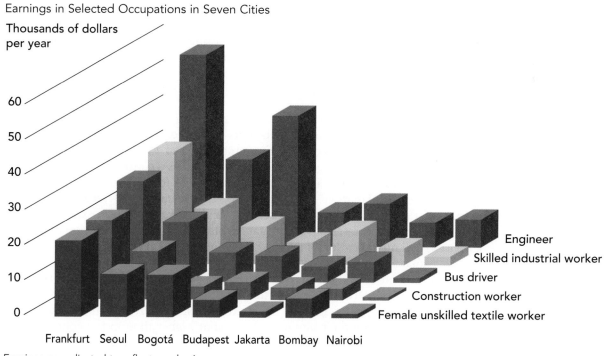

Earnings are adjusted to reflect purchasing power.
SOURCE: Data from World Bank, *World Development Report 1995*, p. 11.

for higher living costs. However, the drawback of this approach is that it may be difficult to adjust the salary downward if costs in that location fall or the employee moves to a lower-cost area. Thus 22 percent of the companies choose to pay an ongoing supplement that changes or disappears in the event of such changes.

The Importance of Process: Participation and Communication

Compensation management has been criticized for following the simplistic belief that "if the right technology can be developed, the right answers will be found."[14] In reality, however, any given pay decision is rarely obvious to the diverse groups that make up organizations, regardless of the decision's technical merit or basis in theory. Of course, it is important when changing pay practices to decide which program or combination of programs makes most sense, but it also matters how such decisions are made and how they are communicated.[15]

Participation

Employee participation in compensation decision making can take many forms. For example, employees may serve on task forces charged with recommending and designing a pay program. They may also be asked to help communicate and explain its rationale. This is particularly true in the case of job evaluation as well as many of the programs discussed in the next chapter. To date, for what are perhaps obvious reasons, employee participation in pay level decisions remains fairly rare.

It is important to distinguish between participation by those affected by policies and those who must actually implement the policies. Managers are in the latter group (and often in the former group at the same time). As in other areas of human resource management, line managers are typically responsible for making policies work. Their intimate involvement in any change to existing pay practices is, of course, necessary.

Communication

A dramatic example of the importance of communication was found in a study of how an organization communicated pay cuts to its employees and the effects on theft rates and perceived equity.[16] Two organization units received 15 percent across-the-board pay cuts. A third unit received no pay cut and served as a control group. The reasons for the pay cuts were communicated in different ways to the two pay-cut groups. In the "adequate explanation" pay-cut group, management provided a significant amount of information to explain its reasons for the pay cut and also expressed significant remorse. In contrast, the "inadequate explanation" group received much less information and no indication of remorse. The control group received no pay cut (and thus no explanation).

The control group and the two pay-cut groups began with the same theft rates and equity perceptions. After the pay cut, the theft rate was 54 percent higher in the "adequate explanation" group than in the control group. But in the "inadequate explanation" condition, the theft rate was 141 percent higher than in the control group. In this case communication had a large, independent effect on employees' attitudes and behaviors.

Communication is likely to have other important effects. We know, for example, that not only actual pay but the comparison standard influences employee attitudes.[17]

Under two-tier wage plans, employees doing the same jobs are paid two different rates, depending on when they were hired. Moreover, the lower-paid employees do not ordinarily move into the higher-paying tier. Common sense might suggest that the lower-paid employees would be less satisfied, but this is not necessarily true. In fact, a study by Peter Cappelli and Peter Sherer found that the lower-paid employees were more satisfied on average.[18] Apparently, those in the lower tier used different (lower) comparison standards than those in the higher tier. The lower-tier employees compared their jobs with unemployment or lower-paying jobs they had managed to avoid. As a result, they were more satisfied, despite being paid less money for the same work. This finding does not mean that two-tier wage plans are necessarily a good idea; indeed, they seem to be diminishing in number. Rather, consistent with equity theory, it shows that the way employees compare their pay with other jobs matters, and managers need to take this into consideration. Employees increasingly have access to salary survey information, which is likely to result in more comparisons and thus a greater need for effective communication.

Managers play the most crucial communication role because of their day-to-day interactions with their employees. Therefore, they must be prepared to explain why the pay structure is designed as it is and to judge whether employee concerns about the structure need to be addressed with changes to the structure. One common issue is deciding when a job needs to be reclassified because of substantial changes in its content. If an employee takes on more responsibility, she will often ask the manager for assistance in making the case for increased pay for the job.

Finding and Keeping the Best Employees

Military action relies on the call-up of reservists and National Guard members. This poses challenges for employers, who must cover the work ordinarily done by employees away on military duty, and for employees, who can suffer financial hardship because their military pay often falls short of what they would be paid in their civilian jobs. In response, some employers have chosen to support their employees by paying them the difference between their military and civilian earnings. One employer making this decision is the City of Los Angeles. Other companies adopting such a policy include Walt Disney Company, which will extend its policy from the normal 30 days of coverage to 180 days. Northrop Grumman will make up any difference in pay for one full year. Although such policies are expensive, these employers have decided that their relationship with employees is sufficiently important that they want to support them in what is already a very difficult time for them and their families.

SOURCE: *Daily News*, Los Angeles, California (October 3, 2001).

Current Challenges

Problems with Job–Based Pay Structures

The approach taken in this chapter, that of defining pay structures in terms of jobs and their associated responsibilities, remains the most widely used in practice. However, job-based pay structures have a number of potential limitations.[19] First, they may encourage bureaucracy. The job description sets out specific tasks and activities for which the incumbent is responsible and, by implication, those for which the incumbent is not responsible. Although this facilitates performance evaluation and control by the manager, it can also encourage a lack of flexibility and a lack of initiative on the part of employees: "Why should I do that? It's not in my job description." Second, the structure's hierarchical nature reinforces a top-down decision making

A Chill East Wind

Eastern Europe's Dynamos Are Losing Jobs to Asia

Dutch electronics maker Royal Philips Electronics and Singapore contract manufacturer Flextronics International Ltd. have moved 1,500 Hungarian jobs to China in the past 18 months. Flextronics also has closed a 1,000-worker plant in the Czech Republic. IBM closed its computer disk-drive factory in Szekesfehervar, Hungary, which was built just eight years ago, moving the work to China where wages are 75 percent cheaper. The closings are sending shudders across eight formerly communist countries just as they are gearing up to celebrate their entry into the European Union on May 1.

The most successful of that group—Hungary, Poland, and the Czech Republic—have been put on warning even before the party starts that EU membership is no economic panacea. The labor markets of Asia, especially China, are beginning to pull away industrial investments that helped this region rebuild after communism's collapse. "Their whole goal has been to join the EU," says Humphrey W. Porter, president of Flextronics Europe. "The risk is that they don't realize this is a rat race. And it's just the beginning, not the end."

"If they try to keep attracting [investment based on] cheap labor, they'll have problems. Their real future test will be how well they emphasize knowledge-based jobs," says Philips regional CEO Wim Wielens.

The competition will be harsh. India, the Philippines, and Russia are rising powers in information technology and customer support. But Eastern Europe has some advantages. EU law prohibits storage of banking data outside the union. So joining the EU will help the region grab back-office financial jobs. EU membership also will increase the feeling of security for foreign investors.

But Eastern Europe's cost advantage is shrinking by the day. Take Hungary. In the past two years, real wages have risen by 20 percent, according to Vienna-based Erste Bank. That explains why Hungary has seen the worst job losses as foreign manufacturers head for the exits. Czech wages have jumped by 11.5 percent in two years. Even in Poland, where unemployment is estimated at 20 percent, wages have risen by 3 percent.

Despite the recent runup, wages in Eastern Europe's most dynamic economies are still 25 percent lower than those in Western Europe. But the gap is widening with China, where wages have stayed roughly the

and information flow as well as status differentials, which do not lend themselves to taking advantage of the skills and knowledge of those closest to production. Third, the bureaucracy required to generate and update job descriptions and job evaluations can become a barrier to change because wholesale changes to job descriptions can involve a tremendous amount of time and cost. Fourth, the job-based pay structure may not reward desired behaviors, particularly in a rapidly changing environment where the knowledge, skills, and abilities needed yesterday may not be very helpful today and tomorrow. Fifth, the emphasis on job levels and status differentials encourages promotion-seeking behavior but may discourage lateral employee movement because employees are reluctant to accept jobs that are not promotions or that appear to be steps down.

same, at about $100 per month for unskilled factory workers. Factor in the greater access to China's vast domestic market as the country dismantles trade and investment barriers, and the case for moving production is more compelling. Even Eastern European companies are shifting work to Asia. Bela Karsai, president of Karsai Plastics Holding in Szekesfehervar, boosted annual revenues from $2.7 million to $37 million since 1995. Now he's keen to be an international player. But rather than expand at home in Hungary, Karsai is opening a plastics plant outside Shanghai. "If you want to be a global supplier, there is no way you cannot be in China," he says.

Wages don't dictate every investment decision. Proximity to Western Europe, not to mention Eastern Europe's blossoming consumer markets, can be an advantage. For large appliances or autos, shipping costs are high. PSA Peugeot-Citroën and Toyota Motor Corp. will open a joint plant in the Czech Republic in 2005 employing 3,000. PSA will open a 3,500-worker factory in 2006 in Slovakia. And since moving production of Microsoft Corp.'s Xbox game consoles to China, Flextronics has hired more Hungarians to make goods such as TVs for France's Schneider Electric.

Thanks to such investment, the number of overall manufacturing jobs in Hungary and the Czech Republic has remained steady for the last two years, while the two economies are growing at 2.7 percent and 2.2 percent, respectively. But that's following years of heady manufacturing growth. And Poland has lost 250,000 manufacturing jobs in two years.

Some of the manufacturing work is being replaced by higher-skilled jobs. Just about three miles from IBM's mothballed factory in Szekesfehervar, Alcoa has just hired 210 service workers. Tucked away in quiet offices, two-thirds of these staffers handle finance and administration tasks. The rest, mostly young techies dressed in T-shirts and shorts, run and help design applications for a computer system that serves 10,000 Alcoa Inc. workstations in 14 countries across the continent.

Alcoa isn't alone in pooling information technology and back-office support tasks in the region. Lufthansa and Philips have each recently announced they will centralize accounting operations for Europe in Poland. In the Czech Republic, IBM, Axa, and Honeywell have gotten into the act. ING Group, General Electric, and British distiller Diageo are adding back-office jobs in Hungary. Plano (Tex.)-based Electronic Data Systems Corp. has offices in all three countries, including a call center in Budapest where 140 employees handle remote information technology support for companies like General Motors, Coca-Cola, and Sweden's Ericsson. "There's going to be a huge wave in the next three to five years in the transition to commoditized back-office services," says Laszlo Szakal, EDS's client sales executive for Hungary. Consultancy A. T. Kearney Inc. forecasts that German, Austrian, and Swiss banks alone could move up to 100,000 back-office jobs from their home countries to cheaper locales by 2008.

To keep pace in the global economic race, the new EU members will have to use their heads more than their hands.

SOURCE: From "A Chill East Wind," by Christopher Condon and Rick Butler, *BusinessWeek* September 1, 2003. Reprinted with permission.

Responses to Problems with Job-Based Pay Structures

Delayering and Banding

In response to the problems caused by job-based pay structures, some organizations are **delayering,** or reducing the number of job levels to achieve more flexibility in job assignments and in assigning merit increases. Pratt and Whitney, for example, changed from 11 pay grades and 3,000 job descriptions for entry-level through middle-management positions to 6 pay grades and several hundred job descriptions.[20] These broader groupings of jobs are also known as *broad bands*. Table 11.8 shows how banding might work for a small sample of jobs. IBM's change to broad bands was accompanied by a change away from a point-factor job evaluation system to a more streamlined approach to evaluating jobs, as Figure 11.4 shows.

Delayering
Reducing the number of job levels within an organization.

TABLE 11.8

Example of Pay
Bands

TRADITIONAL STRUCTURE		BANDED STRUCTURE	
GRADE	TITLE	BAND	TITLE
14	Senior accountant	6	Senior accountant
12	Accountant III		
10	Accountant II	5	Accountant
8	Accountant I		

SOURCE: P. LeBlanc, *Perspectives in Total Compensation* 3, no. 3 (March 1992), pp. 1–6. Used with permission of the National Practice Director, Sibson & Company, Inc.

FIGURE 11.4

IBM's New Job Evaluation Approach

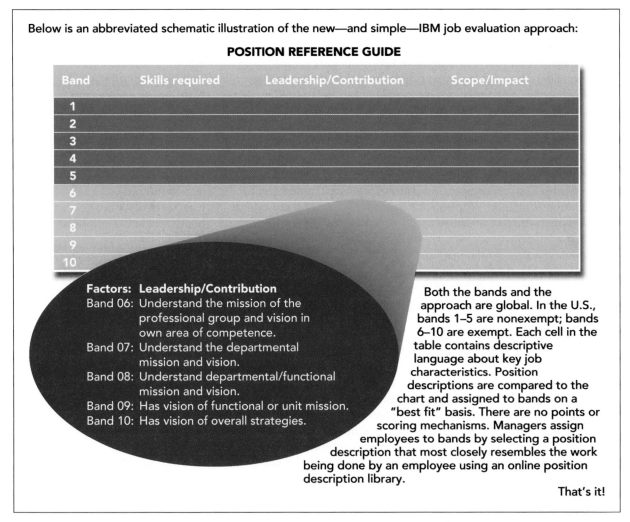

Below is an abbreviated schematic illustration of the new—and simple—IBM job evaluation approach:

POSITION REFERENCE GUIDE

Band	Skills required	Leadership/Contribution	Scope/Impact
1			
2			
3			
4			
5			
6			
7			
8			
9			
10			

Factors: Leadership/Contribution
Band 06: Understand the mission of the professional group and vision in own area of competence.
Band 07: Understand the departmental mission and vision.
Band 08: Understand departmental/functional mission and vision.
Band 09: Has vision of functional or unit mission.
Band 10: Has vision of overall strategies.

Both the bands and the approach are global. In the U.S., bands 1–5 are nonexempt; bands 6–10 are exempt. Each cell in the table contains descriptive language about key job characteristics. Position descriptions are compared to the chart and assigned to bands on a "best fit" basis. There are no points or scoring mechanisms. Managers assign employees to bands by selecting a position description that most closely resembles the work being done by an employee using an online position description library.

That's it!

SOURCE: A. S. Richter, "Paying the People in Black at Big Blue," *Compensation and Benefits Review*, May–June 1998, pp. 51–59. Copyright © 1998 by Sage Publications, Inc. Reprinted with permission of Sage Publications, Inc.

At the same time, IBM greatly reduced the bureaucratic nature of the system, going from 5,000 job titles and 24 salary grades to a simpler 1,200 jobs and 10 bands. Within their broad bands, managers were given more discretion to reward high performers and to choose pay levels that were competitive in the market for talent.

One possible disadvantage of delayering and banding is a reduced opportunity for promotion. Therefore, organizations need to consider what they will offer employees instead. In addition, to the extent that there are separate ranges within bands, the new structure may not represent as dramatic a change as it might appear. These distinctions can easily become just as entrenched as they were under the old system. Broad bands, with their greater spread between pay minimums and maximums, can also lead to weaker budgetary control and rising labor costs. Alternatively, the greater spread can permit managers to better recognize high performers with high pay. It can also permit the organization to reward employees for learning.

Paying the Person: Pay for Skill, Knowledge, and Competency

A second, related response to job-based pay structure problems has been to move away from linking pay to jobs and toward building structures based on individual characteristics such as skill or knowledge.[21] Competency-based pay is similar but usually refers to a plan that covers exempt employees (such as managers). The basic idea is that if you want employees to learn more skills and become more flexible in the jobs they perform, you should pay them to do it. (See Chapter 7 for a discussion of the implications of skill-based pay systems on training.) According to Gerald Ledford, however, it is "a fundamental departure" because employees are now "paid for the skills they are capable of using, not for the job they are performing at a particular point in time."[22]

Skill-based pay systems seem to fit well with the increased breadth and depth of skill that changing technology continues to bring.[23] For example, in a production environment, workers might be expected not only to operate machines but also to take responsibility for maintenance and troubleshooting, quality control, even modifying computer programs.[24] Toyota concluded years ago that "none of the specialists [e.g., quality inspectors, many managers, and foremen] beyond the assembly worker was actually adding any value to the car. What's more . . . assembly workers could probably do most of the functions of specialists much better because of their direct acquaintance with conditions on the line."[25]

In other words, an important potential advantage of skill-based pay is its contribution to increased worker flexibility, which in turn facilitates the decentralization of decision making to those who are most knowledgeable. It also provides the opportunity for leaner staffing levels because employee turnover or absenteeism can now be covered by current employees who are multiskilled.[26] In addition, multiskilled employees are important in cases where different products require different manufacturing processes or where supply shortages or other problems call for adaptive or flexible responses—characteristics typical, for example, of many newer so-called advanced manufacturing environments (like flexible manufacturing and just-in-time systems).[27] More generally, it has been suggested that skill-based plans also contribute to a climate of learning and adaptability and give employees a broader view of how the organization functions. Both changes should contribute to better use of employees' know-how and ideas. Consistent with the advantages just noted, a field study found that a change to a skill-based plan led to better quality and lower labor costs in a manufacturing plant.[28]

Of course, skill-based and competency-based approaches also have potential disadvantages.[29] First, although the plan will likely enhance skill acquisition, the organization may find it a challenge to use the new skills effectively. Without careful planning,

Skill-based pay
Pay based on the skills employees acquire and are capable of using.

Can the German Labor Force Compete?

DaimlerChrysler AG reached a cost-cutting deal with its German workers Friday in return for job security guarantees after contentious talks marked by a week of protests and brief work stoppages.

The deal involves €500 million ($612 million) in annual labor-cost savings in return for securing the jobs of more than 6,000 German workers through 2012, DaimlerChrysler Chief Executive Juergen Schrempp and chief worker representative Erich Klemm told reporters. "After tough and constructive negotiations, we have reached a good solution for DaimlerChrysler and for Germany," Mr. Schrempp said.

As part of the deal, DaimlerChrysler's management board, the top executives running the company day to day, agreed to accept a 10 percent cut in compensation, and other senior managers will also make unspecified pay concessions, the company said.

The deal, reached in talks that dragged into early Friday morning, removed DaimlerChrysler's threat to move production of its Mercedes C-Class cars away from its main factory in Sindelfingen, near Stuttgart, to cheaper plants unless workers agreed to labor-cost cuts.

Savings from the agreement are due to take effect by 2007, when the next C-Class generation is due to go into production, the company said. The deal will also have some white-collar workers work longer hours and includes a 20 percent wage cut for new staff in service jobs, such as security and cafeteria workers.

it may find itself with large new labor costs but little payoff. In other words, if skills change, work design must change as quickly to take full advantage. Second, if pay growth is based entirely on skills, problems may arise if employees "top out" by acquiring all the skills too quickly, leaving no room for further pay growth. (Of course, this problem can also afflict job-based systems.) Third, and somewhat ironically, skill-based plans may generate a large bureaucracy—usually a criticism of job-based systems. Training programs need to be developed. Skills must be described, measured, and assigned monetary values. Certification tests must be developed to determine whether an employee has acquired a certain skill. Finally, as if the challenges in obtaining market rates under a job-based system were not enough, there is almost no body of knowledge regarding how to price combinations of skills (versus jobs) in the marketplace. Obtaining comparison data from other organizations will be difficult until skill-based plans become more widely used.

Can the U.S. Labor Force Compete?

We often hear that U.S. labor costs are simply too high to allow U.S. companies to compete effectively with companies in other countries. The average hourly labor costs (cash and benefits) for manufacturing production workers in the United States and in other advanced industrialized and newly industrialized countries are given in the following table in U.S. dollars:[30]

With further labor strife averted at one of Germany's industrial flagships, German Chancellor Gerhard Schroeder welcomed the deal as "a victory of common sense." The accord will help Germany's fragile economic recovery and proves that the country's tradition of cooperation between labor and management is "superior and successful," Mr. Schroeder said in a statement.

After the announcement, DaimlerChrysler shares were trading 0.4 percent higher in midday trading at €36.37 apiece on the Frankfurt exchange.

A main sticking point had been employee demands that the company guarantee jobs for longer than four or five years.

The company says the Sindelfingen workers have perks such as five minutes of paid break time accumulated per hour and higher premiums for late shifts than workers at German plants elsewhere. It threatened to move the C-Class work to plants in Bremen, Germany, and East London, South Africa, where costs are lower—a move that would wipe out 6,000 jobs at Sindelfingen.

The paid breaks remain for now under Friday's deal.

Tens of thousands of DaimlerChrysler workers across the country have staged protests, which they had said would escalate if no agreement could be reached.

DaimlerChrysler has been pressing for cost cuts at its luxury Mercedes division, an earnings mainstay for the past several years, as it comes under increasing sales pressure from a slew of new models from German competitor BMW.

"The result, in sum, is pleasing," DaimlerChrysler board member Juergen Hubbert said. "I am grateful for the willingness to reach a compromise."

Other big German industrial firms have been pressing for similar concessions. Engineering giant Siemens AG achieved what is widely viewed as a groundbreaking deal by getting workers at phone-repair facilities in northern Germany to work 40 hours rather than 35 for no added pay. The 35-hour week was won through a 1984 strike by the industrial union IG Metall, and union leaders have been highly critical of proposals to give it up.

SOURCE: "DaimlerChrysler," Workers Reach Cost-Saving Deal, Union Says," *The Wall Street Journal Online* (July 23, 2004).

	1985	1990	1995	2000	2002
Industrialized					
United States	$13.01	$14.77	$17.19	$19.76	$21.33
Canada	10.95	15.95	16.10	16.04	16.02
Czech Republic					3.50[c]
Germany[a]	9.57	21.53	30.26	23.38	25.08
France	7.52	15.49	20.01	15.70	17.42
Japan	6.43	12.64	23.82	22.27	18.83
Newly industrialized					
Mexico	1.60	1.80	1.51	2.08	2.38
Hong Kong[b]	1.73	3.20	4.82	5.63	5.83
Korea	1.25	3.82	7.29	8.19	9.16

[a] West Germany for 1985 and 1990 data.
[b] Special Administrative Region of China.
[c] Estimate using World Bank and OECD data.

Based solely on a cost approach, it would perhaps make sense to try to shift many types of production from Germany and Japan to the United States and from the United States to other countries, particularly the newly industrialized countries. Would this be a good idea? Not necessarily. There are several factors to consider.

IBM Documents Give Rare Look at Sensitive Plans on "Offshoring"

In a rare look at the numbers and verbal nuances a big U.S. company chews over when moving jobs abroad, internal documents from International Business Machines Corp. show that it expects to save $168 million annually starting in 2006 by shifting several thousand high-paying programming jobs overseas.

Among other things, the documents indicate that for internal IBM accounting purposes, a programmer in China with three to five years experience would cost about $12.50 an hour, including salary and benefits. A person familiar with IBM's internal billing rates says that's less than one-fourth of the $56-an-hour cost of a comparable U.S. employee, which also includes salary and benefits.

According to the documents, which also provide managers with detailed advice on how to talk about the moves and their effect, IBM plans to shift the jobs from various U.S. locations to China, India and Brazil, where wages for skilled programmers are substantially lower.

At IBM headquarters in Armonk, N.Y., a spokesman said that the company expects to shift 3,000 U.S. jobs overseas this year. He declined to comment on plans for next year. He said IBM expects to add 15,000 jobs world-wide this year, with a net total of 5,000 of them in the U.S. That would increase IBM's world-wide employment to 330,000, the highest level since 1991.

IBM hasn't announced the plan to shift workers overseas—elements of which were reported in *The Wall Street Journal* last month—either internally or externally. It isn't clear if the documents are final versions; most carry dates of late November and December 2003. The spokesman declined to comment on the documents seen by the *Journal*.

Like other high-tech companies, IBM is moving knowledge work to cheap-labor sites outside the U.S. This "offshoring" process has raised fears that even high-skill jobs that were supposed to represent the U.S.'s future are being lost to countries that have already taken over low-skill factory work.

IBM's human resources department has prepared a draft "suggested script" for managers to use in telling employees that their jobs are being moved. The managers will tell the employees that "this is not a resource action"—IBM language for layoff—and that they will help the employees try to find a job elsewhere in IBM, although they can't promise to pay for any needed relocation.

The documents describe work done by IBM's Application Management Services division, part of Big Blue's giant global-services operation, which comprises more than half of the company's 315,000 employees. The affected workers don't deal directly with customers; they write code and perform other programming tasks for applications software used inside IBM.

Instability of Country Differences in Labor Costs

First, note that relative labor costs are very unstable over time. For example, in 1985, U.S. labor costs were (13.01/9.57) or 36 percent greater than those of (West) Germany. But by 1990, the situation was reversed, with (West) German labor costs exceeding those of the United States by (21.53/14.77), or 46 percent, and remaining higher. Did German employers suddenly become more generous while U.S. employers clamped down on pay growth? Not exactly. Because all our figures are expressed in U.S. dollars, currency exchange rates influence such comparisons, and these ex-

Some of the foreign programmers will come to the U.S. for several weeks of on-the-job training by the people whose jobs they will take over. That's an aspect of offshoring that many high-tech workers regard as particularly humiliating.

With revenue growing slowly throughout the information-technology business, IBM and other vendors are under great pressure to reduce costs to boost earnings. Last week, when reporting fourth-quarter earnings, IBM's chief financial officer, John Joyce, said the company reduced costs $7 billion during 2003 and expects similar savings this year. Mr. Joyce said competitive price pressures in computer services are holding down profitability.

IBM's competitors are making similar moves. Accenture Ltd., one of IBM's main rivals in the computer-services field, said recently it expects to double its work force in India this year to nearly 10,000. Google Inc., the online search leader, said last month that it plans to open an engineering center in India this year as part of an expansion.

For all these companies, lower-cost labor is the biggest lure.

A chart of internal billing rates developed by IBM's Chinese group in Shanghai shows how dramatic the labor savings can be. The chart doesn't show actual wages, but instead reflects IBM's internal system by which one unit bills another for the work it does.

Besides the low-level programmers billing at $12.50 an hour, the chart shows that a Chinese senior analyst or application-development manager with more than five years experience would be billed at $18 an hour. The person familiar with IBM's operations said that person would be equivalent to a U.S. "Band 7" employee billed at about $66 an hour. And a Chinese project manager with seven years experience would be billed at $24 an hour, equivalent to a U.S. "Band 8" billed at about $81 hourly.

Dean Davidson, an analyst who follows outsourcing for Meta Group, in Stamford, Conn., says that companies usually find their actual cost savings from moving offshore are less than they would expect based on straight wage comparisons. "The reality is a general savings of 15 percent to 20 percent during the first year," Mr. Davidson says. That's far less than the 50 percent to 80 percent savings based on hourly labor rates, he says.

The person familiar with IBM's plans says that implementation could be slowed if the company isn't able to hire enough qualified programmers to do the work in its overseas software centers. He said that those facilities are already very busy doing work for IBM's big U.S. customers.

According to the IBM documents, the company expects severance costs for laying off U.S. employees in conjunction with the plan to be $30.6 million in 2004 and $47.4 million in 2005. Including other transition costs, the documents say, the offshoring plan will result in a loss of $19 million this year. Savings will amount to $40 million in 2005 and $168 million annually thereafter.

In the draft script prepared for managers, IBM suggests the workers be told: "This action is a statement about the rate and pace of change in this demanding industry. . . . It is in no way a comment on the excellent work you have done over the years." The script also suggests saying: "For the people whose jobs are affected by this consolidation, I understand this is difficult news."

SOURCE: From *The Wall Street Journal, Online,* by William M. Bulkeley. Copyright 2004 by Dow Jones & Co., Inc. Reproduced with permission of Dow Jones & Co., Inc. via Copyright Clearance Center.

change rates often fluctuate significantly from year to year. For example, in 1985, when German labor costs were 74 percent of those in the United States, the U.S. dollar was worth 2.94 German marks. But in 1990 the U.S. dollar was worth 1.62 German marks. If the exchange rate in 1990 were still 1 to 2.94, the average German hourly wage in U.S. dollars would have been $11.80, or about 80 percent of the U.S. average. In any event, relative to countries like Germany, U.S. labor costs are now a bargain; this explains, in part, decisions by BMW and Mercedes-Benz to locate production facilities in South Carolina and Alabama, respectively, where labor costs are lower than Germany's by 30 percent or more.

Skill Levels

Second, the quality and productivity of national labor forces can vary dramatically. This is an especially important consideration in comparisons between labor costs in industrialized countries like the United States and developing countries like Mexico. For example, the high school graduation rate in the United States is 88 percent versus 25 percent in Mexico.[31] Thus, lower labor costs may reflect the lower average skill level of the workforce; certain types of skilled labor may be less available in low–labor-cost countries. On the other hand, any given company needs only enough skilled employees for its own operations. Some companies have found that low labor costs do not necessarily preclude high quality.

Productivity

Third, and most directly relevant, are data on comparative productivity and unit labor costs, essentially meaning labor cost per hour divided by productivity per hour worked. One indicator of productivity is gross domestic product (or total output of the economy) per person, adjusted for differences in purchasing power. On this measure, the United States fares well. In 2002 these figures (in U.S. dollars) were[32]

United States	$36,100
Japan	$26,900
Korea	$17,000
Germany	$25,900
France	$27,200
Czech Republic	$15,100
Mexico	$ 9,200
Canada	$30,300

The combination of lower labor costs and higher productivity translates into lower unit labor costs in the United States than in Japan and Western Europe.[33]

Nonlabor Considerations

Fourth, any consideration of where to locate production cannot be based on labor considerations alone. For example, although the average hourly labor cost in Country A may be $15 versus $10 in Country B, if labor costs are 30 percent of total operating costs and nonlabor operating costs are roughly the same, then the total operating costs might be $65 (50 + 15) in Country A and $60 (50 + 10) in Country B. Although labor costs in Country B are 33 percent less, total operating costs are only 7.7 percent less. This may not be enough to compensate for differences in skills and productivity, transportation costs, taxes, and so on. Further, the direct labor component of many products, particularly high-tech products (such as electronic components), may often be 5 percent or less. Thus the effect on product price competitiveness may be insignificant.[34]

In fact, an increasing number of organizations have decided that it is more important to focus on nonlabor factors in deciding where to locate production. Product development speed may be greater when manufacturing is physically close to the design group. Quick response to customers (like making a custom replacement product) is difficult when production facilities are on the other side of the world. Inventory levels can be dramatically reduced through the use of manufacturing methods like just-in-time production, but suppliers need to be in close physical proximity.

Executive Pay

The issue of executive pay has been given widespread attention in the press. The topic has received more coverage than it deserves because there are very few top executives and their compensation accounts for only a small share of an organization's total labor costs. On the other hand, top executives have a disproportionate ability to influence organization performance, so decisions about their compensation are critical. Top executives also help set the tone or culture of the organization. If, for example, the top executive's pay seems unrelated to the organization's performance, staying high even when business is poor, employees may not understand why some of their pay should be at risk and depend on how the organization is performing.

How much do executives make? Table 11.9 provides some data. Long-term compensation, typically in the form of stock plans, is the major component of CEO pay, which means that CEO pay varies with the performance of the stock market (see the "change in S&P 500" column). Table 11.10 shows that some CEOs are paid well above the averages shown in Table 11.9.

TABLE 11.9

CEO Compensation: *BusinessWeek* Survey ("365 of the Country's Largest Companies")

YEAR	SALARY PLUS BONUS	LONG-TERM COMPENSATION	TOTAL COMPENSATION	CHANGE IN PAY	CHANGE IN S&P 500*	CEO/WORKER**
2003	—	—	$ 8.1 million	9%	29%	276[a]
2002	—	—	7.4 million	−33	−22	259
2001	—	—	11.0 million	−16	−12	397
2000	$2.7 million[a]	$10.4 million[a]	13.1 million	6	−9	484
1999	2.3 million	10.1 million	12.4 million	17	21	475
1998	2.1 million	8.5 million	10.6 million	36	27	419
1997	2.2 million	5.6 million	7.8 million	35	31	326
1996	2.3 million	3.2 million	5.8 million	54	23	209

*Change in market value of the Standard & Poor's 500 group of companies.

**Ratio of CEO pay to hourly employee pay.

[a]Estimated.

SOURCE: Data from April 19, 2004 issue of *BusinessWeek*.

TABLE 11.10

Highest-Paid CEOs

	SALARY PLUS BONUS	LONG-TERM COMPENSATION	TOTAL COMPENSATION
Reuben Mark, Colgate-Palmolive	$5 million	$136 million	$141 million
Steven P. Jobs, Apple Computer	0 million	75 million	75 million
George David, United Technologies	4 million	66 million	70 million

SOURCE: Data from April 19, 2004, issue of *BusinessWeek*.

TABLE 11.11

Total Remuneration of CEOs in Selected Countries (U.S. dollars)

COUNTRY	CEO TOTAL REMUNERATION	CEO/MANUFACTURING EMPLOYEE TOTAL REMUNERATION MULTIPLE
United States	$1,404,000	31
Brazil	597,000	60
France	540,000	15
Argentina	861,000	48
Germany	422,000	11
Japan	546,000	11
Mexico	649,000	46

Notes: Data based on a company with $500 million in sales; total remuneration includes salary, bonus, company contributions, perquisites, and long-term incentives. Table 11.11 values are based on much smaller companies than those in Table 11.9, thus explaining the table differences.
SOURCE: Towers Perrin, "2000 Worldwide Total Remuneration," New York, 2000.

As Table 11.11 shows, U.S. top executives are also the highest paid in the world. (These figures are lower than those from *BusinessWeek* because the latter pertain to larger companies.) The fact that the differential between top-executive pay and that of an average manufacturing worker is so much higher in the United States has been described as creating a "trust gap"—that is, in employees' minds, a "frame of mind that mistrusts senior management's intentions, doubts its competence, and resents its self-congratulatory pay." The issue becomes even more salient at a time when so many of the same companies with high executive pay are simultaneously engaging in layoffs or other forms of employment reduction. Employees might ask, "If the company needs to cut costs, why not cut executive pay rather than our jobs?"[35] The issue is one of perceived fairness in difficult economic times. One study, in fact, reported that business units with higher pay differentials between executives and rank-and-file employees had lower customer satisfaction, which was speculated to result from employees' perceptions of inequity coming through in customer relations.[36] Perhaps more important than how much top executives are paid is how they are paid. This is an issue we return to in the next chapter.

Government Regulation of Employee Compensation
Equal Employment Opportunity

Equal Employment Opportunity (EEO) regulation (such as Title VII and the Civil Rights Act) prohibits sex- and race-based differences in employment outcomes such as pay, unless justified by business necessity (like pay differences stemming from differences in job performance). In addition to regulatory pressures, organizations must deal with changing labor market and demographic realities. At least two trends are directly relevant in discussing EEO. First, women have gone from 33 percent of all employees in 1960 to 47 percent in 2001. Second, between 1960 and 2001, whites have gone from 90 percent to 84 percent of all employees. The percentage of white males in organizations will probably continue to decline, making attention to EEO issues in compensation even more important.

Is there equality of treatment in pay determination? Typically, the popular press focuses on raw earnings ratios. For example, in 2000, among full-time workers, the ratio of female-to-male median earnings was .76, and the ratio of black-to-white earnings was .79.[37] These percentages have generally risen over the last two to three decades, but significant race and sex differences in pay clearly remain.[38]

The usefulness of raw percentages is limited, however, because some portion of earnings differences arises from differences in legitimate factors: education, labor market experience, and occupation. Adjusting for such factors reduces earnings differences based on race and sex, but significant differences remain. With few exceptions, such adjustments rarely account for more than half of the earnings differential.[39]

What aspects of pay determination are responsible for such differences? In the case of women, it is suggested that their work is undervalued. Another explanation rests on the "crowding" hypothesis, which argues that women were historically restricted to entering a small number of occupations. As a result, the supply of workers far exceeded demand, resulting in lower pay for such occupations. If so, market surveys would only perpetuate the situation.

Comparable worth (or pay equity) is a public policy that advocates remedies for any undervaluation of women's jobs. The idea is to obtain equal pay, not just for jobs of equal content (already mandated by the Equal Pay Act of 1963) but for jobs of equal value or worth. Typically, job evaluation is used to measure worth. Table 11.12, which is based on State of Washington data from one of the first comparable worth cases, suggests that measures of worth based on internal comparisons (job evaluation) and external comparisons (market surveys) can be compared. In this case many disagreements between the two measures appear. Internal comparisons suggest that women's jobs are underpaid, whereas external comparisons are less supportive of this argument. For example, although the licensed practical nurse job receives 173 job evaluation points and the truck driver position receives 97 points, the market rate (and thus the State of Washington employer rate) for the truck driver position is $1,493 per month versus only $1,030 per month for the nurse. The truck driver is paid nearly 127 percent more than the pay policy line would predict, whereas the nurse is paid only 75 percent of the pay policy line prediction.

One potential problem with using job evaluation to establish worth independent of the market is that job evaluation procedures were never designed for this purpose.[40] Rather, as demonstrated earlier, their major use is in helping to capture the market pay policy and then applying that to nonkey jobs for which market data are not available. In other words, job evaluation has typically been used to help apply the market pay policy, quite the opposite of replacing the market in pay setting.

As with any regulation, there are also concerns that EEO regulation obstructs market forces, which, according to economic theory, provide the most efficient means of pricing and allocating people to jobs. In theory, moving away from a reliance on market forces would result in some jobs being paid too much and others too little, leading to an oversupply of workers for the former and an undersupply for the latter. In addition, some empirical evidence suggests that a comparable worth policy would not have much impact on the relative earnings of women in the private sector.[41] One limitation of such a policy is that it targets single employers, ignoring that men and women tend to work for different employers.[42] To the extent that segregation by employer contributes to pay differences between men and women, comparable worth would not be effective. In other words, to the extent that sex-based pay differences are the result of men and women working in different organizations with different pay levels, such policies will have little impact.

TABLE 11.12

Job Evaluation Points, Monthly Prevailing Market Pay Rates, and Proportion of Incumbents in Job Who Are Female

BENCHMARK TITLE	MONTHLY EVALUATION POINTS	PREVAILING RATES[a]	PREVAILING RATE AS PERCENTAGE OF PREDICTED[b]	PERCENTAGE OF FEMALE INCUMBENTS
Warehouse worker	97	$1,286	109.1%	15.4%
Truck driver	97	1,493	126.6	13.6
Laundry worker	105	884	73.2	80.3
Telephone operator	118	887	71.6	95.7
Retail sales clerk	121	921	74.3	100.0
Data entry operator	125	1,017	82.1	96.5
Intermediate clerk typist	129	968	76.3	96.7
Highway engineering tech	133	1,401	110.4	11.1
Word processing equipment operator	138	1,082	83.2	98.3
Correctional officer	173	1,436	105.0	9.3
Licensed practical nurse	173	1,030	75.3	89.5
Automotive mechanic	175	1,646	120.4	0.0
Maintenance carpenter	197	1,707	118.9	2.3
Secretary	197	1,122	78.1	98.5
Administrative assistant	226	1,334	90.6	95.1
Chemist	277	1,885	116.0	20.0
Civil engineer	287	1,885	116.0	0.0
Highway engineer 3	345	1,980	110.4	3.0
Registered nurse	348	1,368	76.3	92.2
Librarian 3	353	1,625	90.6	84.6
Senior architect	362	2,240	121.8	16.7
Senior computer systems analyst	384	2,080	113.1	17.8
Personnel representative	410	1,956	101.2	45.6
Physician	861	3,857	128.0	13.6

[a]Prevailing market rate as of July 1, 1980. Midpoint of job range set equal to this amount.

[b]Predicted salary is based on regression of prevailing market rate on job evaluation points $2.43 × job evaluation points + 936.19, r = .77.

SOURCE: Reprinted with permission of *Public Personnel Management*, published by the International Personnel Management Association.

Perhaps most important, despite potential problems with market rates, the courts have consistently ruled that using the going market rates of pay is an acceptable defense in comparable worth litigation suits.[43] The rationale is that organizations face competitive labor and product markets. Paying less or more than the market rate will put the organization at a competitive disadvantage. Thus there is no comparable worth legal mandate in the U.S. private sector. On the other hand, by the early 1990s, almost one-half of the states had begun or completed comparable worth adjustments to public-sector employees' pay. In addition, in 1988 the Canadian province of Ontario mandated comparable worth in both the private and public sectors.

Another line of inquiry has focused on pinpointing where women's pay falls behind that of men. Some evidence indicates that women lose ground at the time they are hired and actually do better once they are employed for some time.[44] One interpretation is that when actual job performance (rather than the limited general qualification information available on applicants) is used in decisions, women may be less likely to encounter unequal treatment. If so, more attention needs to be devoted to ensuring fair treatment of applicants and new employees.[45] On the other hand, a "glass ceiling" is believed to exist in some organizations that allows women (and minorities) to come within sight of the top echelons of management, but not advance to them.

It is likely, however, that organizations will differ in terms of where women's earnings disadvantages arise. For example, advancement opportunities for women and other protected groups may be hindered by unequal access to the "old boy" or informal network. This, in turn, may be reflected in lower rates of pay. Mentoring programs have been suggested as one means of improving access. Indeed, one study found that mentoring was successful, having a significant positive effect on the pay of both men and women, with women receiving a greater payoff in percentage terms than men.[46]

Minimum Wage, Overtime, and Prevailing Wage Laws

The 1938 **Fair Labor Standards Act (FLSA)** establishes a **minimum wage** for jobs that now stands at $5.15 per hour. State laws may specify higher minimum wages. The FLSA also permits a subminimum training wage that is approximately 85 percent of the minimum wage, which employers are permitted to pay most employees under the age of 20 for a period of up to 90 days.

The FLSA also requires that employees be paid at a rate of one and a half times their hourly rate for each hour of overtime worked beyond 40 hours in a week. The hourly rate includes not only the base wage but also other components such as bonuses and piece-rate payments. The FLSA requires overtime pay for any hours beyond 40 in a week that an employer "suffers or permits" the employee to perform, regardless of whether the work is done at the workplace or whether the employer explicitly asked or expected the employee to do it. If the employer knows the employee is working overtime but neither moves to stop it nor pays time and a half, a violation of the FLSA may have occurred. A department store was the target of a lawsuit that claimed employees were "encouraged" to, among other things, write thank-you notes to customers outside of scheduled work hours but were not compensated for this work. Although the company denied encouraging this off-the-clock work, it reached an out-of-court settlement to pay between $15 million and $30 million in back pay (plus legal fees of $7.5 million) to approximately 85,000 sales representatives it employed between 1987 and 1990.[47]

Executive, professional, administrative, outside sales and certain "computer employees" occupations are **exempt** from FLSA coverage. *Nonexempt* occupations are covered and include most hourly jobs. One estimate is that just over 20 percent of employees fall into the exempt category.[48] Exempt status depends on job responsibilities and salary. All exemptions (except for outside sales) require that an employee be paid no less than $455 per week. The job responsibility criteria vary. For example, the executive exemption is based on whether two or more people are supervised, whether there is authority to hire and fire (or whether particular weight is given to the employee's recommendations), and whether the employee's primary duty is managing the enterprise, recognized department, or subdivision of the enterprise. The Wage and Hour Division, Employment Standards Administration (www.dol.gov/esa), U.S. Department of Labor, and its local offices can provide further information on these definitions. (The exemptions do *not* apply to police, firefighters, paramedics, and first responders.)

Two pieces of legislation—the 1931 Davis-Bacon Act and the 1936 Walsh-Healy Public Contracts Act—require federal contractors to pay employees no less than the

Fair Labor Standards Act (FLSA)
The 1938 law that established the minimum wage and overtime pay.

Minimum wage
The lowest amount that employers are legally allowed to pay; the 1990 amendment of the Fair Labor Standards Act permits a subminimum wage to workers under the age of 20 for a period of up to 90 days.

Exempt
Employees who are not covered by the Fair Labor Standards Act. Exempt employees are not eligible for overtime pay.

Give to ZoK

prevailing wages in the area. Davis-Bacon covers construction contractors receiving federal money of more than $2,000. Typically, prevailing wages have been based on relevant union contracts, partly because only 30 percent of the local labor force is required to be used in establishing the prevailing rate. Walsh-Healy covers all government contractors receiving $10,000 or more in federal funds.

Finally, employers must take care in deciding whether a person working on their premises is classified as an employee or independent contractor. We address this issue in Chapter 13.

A Look Back

We began this chapter by showing how one company encountered serious employee relations problems because of the inequity perceptions created by its pay structure decisions, as well as its apparent attempt to keep these decisions from being known by employees. On a more positive note, we have seen how Procter & Gamble pays its executives in a way that supports its strategy, and we have seen how IBM realigned its pay structure to support changes to its strategy for competing in evolving markets. We have seen in this chapter that pay structure decisions influence the success of strategy execution by influencing costs, employee perceptions of equity, and the way that different structures provide flexibility and incentives for employees to learn and be productive.

Questions

1. What types of changes have the companies discussed in this chapter made to their pay structures to support execution of their business strategies?
2. Would other companies seeking to better align their pay structures with their business strategies benefit from imitating the changes made at these companies?

Summary

In this chapter we have discussed the nature of the pay structure and its component parts, the pay level, and the job structure. Equity theory suggests that social comparisons are an important influence on how employees evaluate their pay. Employees make external comparisons between their pay and the pay they believe is received by employees in other organizations. Such comparisons may have consequences for employee attitudes and retention. Employees also make internal comparisons between what they receive and what they perceive others within the organization are paid. These types of comparisons may have consequences for internal movement, cooperation, and attitudes (like organization commitment). Such comparisons play an important role in the controversy over executive pay, as illustrated by the focus of critics on the ratio of executive pay to that of lower-paid workers.

Pay benchmarking surveys and job evaluation are two administrative tools widely used in managing the pay level and job structure components of the pay structure, which influence employee social comparisons. Pay surveys also permit organizations to benchmark their labor costs against other organizations'. Globalization is increasing the need for organizations to be competitive in both their labor costs and productivity.

The nature of pay structures is undergoing a fundamental change in many organizations. One change is the move to fewer pay levels to reduce labor costs and bureaucracy. Second, some employers are shifting from paying employees for narrow jobs to giving them broader responsibilities and paying them to learn the necessary skills.

Finally, a theme that runs through this chapter and the next is the importance of process in managing employee compensation. How a new program is designed, decided on, implemented, and communicated is perhaps just as important as its core characteristics.

Discussion Questions

1. You have been asked to evaluate whether your organization's current pay structure makes sense in view of what competing organizations are paying. How would you determine what organizations to compare your organization with? Why might your organization's pay structure differ from those in competing organizations? What are the potential consequences of having a pay structure that is out of line relative to those of your competitors?
2. Top management has decided that the organization is too bureaucratic and has too many layers of jobs to compete effectively. You have been asked to suggest innovative alternatives to the traditional "job-based" approach to employee compensation and to list the advantages and disadvantages of these new approaches.

3. If major changes of the type mentioned in question 2 are to be made, what types of so-called process issues need to be considered? Of what relevance is equity theory in helping to understand how employees might react to changes in the pay structure?
4. Are executive pay levels unreasonable? Why or why not?
5. Your company plans to build a new manufacturing plant but is undecided where to locate it. What factors would you consider in choosing in which country (or state) to build the plant?
6. You have been asked to evaluate whether a company's pay structure is fair to women and minorities. How would you go about answering this question?

Self-Assessment Exercise

Consider your current job or a job you had in the past. For each of the following pay characteristics, indicate your level of satisfaction by using the following scale: 1 = very dissatisfied; 2 = somewhat dissatisfied; 3 = neither satisfied nor dissatisfied; 4 = somewhat satisfied; 5 = very satisfied.

____ 1. My take-home pay
____ 2. My current pay
____ 3. My overall level of pay
____ 4. Size of my current salary
____ 5. My benefit package
____ 6. Amount the company pays toward my benefits
____ 7. The value of my benefits
____ 8. The number of benefits I receive
____ 9. My most recent raise
____ 10. Influence my manager has over my pay
____ 11. The raises I have typically received in the past
____ 12. The company's pay structure
____ 13. Information the company gives about pay issues of concern to me
____ 14. Pay of other jobs in the company
____ 15. Consistency of the company's pay policies

____ 16. How my raises are determined
____ 17. Differences in pay among jobs in the company
____ 18. The way the company administers pay

These 18 items measure four dimensions of pay satisfaction. Find your total score for each set of item numbers to measure your satisfaction with each dimension.
Pay Level
Total of items 1, 2, 3, 4, 9, 11: _____
Benefits
Total of items 5, 6, 7, 8: _____
Pay Structure and Administration
Total of items 12, 13, 14, 15, 17, 18: _____
Pay Raises
Total of items 10, 11, 16: _____
Considering the principles discussed in this chapter, how could your company improve (or how could it have improved) your satisfaction on each dimension?

SOURCE: Based on H. G. Heneman III and D. P. Schwab, "Pay Satisfaction: Its Multidimensional Nature and Measurement," *International Journal of Psychology*, 20 (1985), pp. 129–41.

Manager's Hot Seat Exercise: Negotiation: Thawing the Salary Freeze

This Manager's Hot Seat case explores the issue of labor–management negotiations. The scenario presented introduces a newly hired, disgruntled labor representative. This labor representative wishes to challenge management's decision to freeze employees' salaries while continuing to award large bonuses to its executives. Management's representative is introduced as a well-informed, decisive and experienced individual who defends the organization's salary-freeze decision. This representative takes a firm stance in justifying the company's seemingly unbalanced rationales for its decisions on allocation of funds.

Negotiation serves the purpose of assisting the parties involved with reaching a give-and-take resolution that is acceptable to all. The video depicts some of the varying negotiation techniques that either side may employ during this very important and highly stressful time. It clearly indicates the importance of both parties possessing strong skills in this area.

Group Activity:

The class is to divide into two groups, with one group acting the part of management personnel and the other as labor. Here is the scenario the groups are to negotiate: It is time for contract benefit negotiation. Top managerial leaders are being awarded new, extensive perks such as free personal transportation, valet parking at work, newly renovated office suites, and an extensive time-off-with-pay package. Labor, on the other hand, is to be provided only a five-cent per hour increment, are expected to pay for all of their health insurances now, and have to sacrifice one paid holiday per year.

The two groups should prepare to defend their respective positions. Each group should engage various negotiation strategies. It is up to the capabilities of each group to enhance and justify their individual positions. Negotiate this situation until a suitable resolution is obtained. The instructor will act as the consultant, final judge, and the arbitrator if needed.

Exercising Strategy: Changing Compensation to Support Changes in Corporate Strategy

By realigning its strategy and compensation and benefits programs, Corning Inc., once a traditional economy company, hopes to compete successfully in the new economy. First, the company divested itself of several business units, including Corning Consumer Products. These divestitures reduced its annual revenues from $5 billion to $3 billion. Next Corning pursued a "high-octane" growth strategy in optical communications (optical fiber, cable systems, photo technologies, optical networking devices), environmental technologies, display technologies, and specialty materials. To support this shift in corporate strategy, Corning sought to support growth by creating an environment that bolstered innovation, risk taking, teaming, and speed. One major change was in its compensation system. The salary structure was streamlined from 11 grades to 5 broad bands for exempt employees and from 7 grades to 3 broad bands for nonexempt employees. In a new economy company, products have a short life cycle and change in markets is a way of life. This means that the nature of work also changes rapidly, so the detailed job descriptions and traditional promotion paths of the past may not fit this fluid environment. By changing its salary structure, Corning hopes to increase its ability to move quickly in responding to and anticipating customer needs in rapidly changing markets by encouraging flexibility, teamwork, and learning among its employees. Decentralizing more pay decisions to managers contributes to this flexibility, and giving employees an increasing stake in the success of the company by making more employees eligible for stock options contributes to the increased focus on teamwork. Finally, employee compensation is increasingly tied to individual employee learning and performance as the broad bands allow managers more flexibility to recognize outstanding achievements.

SOURCE: B. Parus, "How an Old Economy Company Became a New Economy Enterprise," *Workspan* 44:6 (June 2001), pp. 34–41.

Questions

1. What are the pros and cons of Corning's new pay structure?
2. How did shifting product market conditions affect Corning's restructuring and its success?

Managing People: From the Pages of *BusinessWeek*

BusinessWeek Revenge of the Overworked Nerds

They're Suing for Overtime Pay—And the Outcome Could Change the Tech Industry When Gary R. Oberholtz signed on as a salaried network engineer for Computer Sciences Corp. in 2000, he thought he'd found the ideal job. Especially appealing: He says he was promised a 40-hour workweek. But soon Oberholtz was routinely working 48-hour weeks and many weekends, he says. When he asked about overtime, his bosses at the El Segundo (Calif.)–based provider of tech services told him he wasn't eligible under state and federal employment laws.

Now, four months after being laid off, Oberholtz is suing. He joined a class action filed on Nov. 12, alleging that CSC dodged paying overtime to some of its employees by improperly classifying them as exempt. "I want to send a message," Oberholtz says. "If you're going to make us work all these hours, you have to compensate us."

CSC, which cited the pending litigation in declining to comment, isn't the only target of overworked techies. Last April, two trainers for Oracle Corp. launched a class action seeking unpaid overtime pay. A spokesman for the software giant says it believes it pays employees in accord with all prevailing laws. Yet lawyers for both cases say they've been fielding calls from employees of other tech companies. If successful, the suits could touch off a wave of new charges. Says Jill Springer, a human resources consultant who has worked for several large Silicon Valley companies: "These lawsuits are red flags."

Lawyers for the plaintiffs insist they are on solid footing. They point to the hundreds of millions of dollars in back pay doled out over the past two years for workers from companies ranging from RadioShack Corp. to Starbucks Corp. In 2001, a jury found Farmers Insurance Group guilty of denying overtime pay to 2,400 claims adjusters and ordered it to pay $90 million. The case is under appeal. "This whole area has the plaintiff's bar drooling," says Joyce L. Oliner, a partner with Shaw Pittman, a Washington, D.C., law firm that defends employers in labor suits.

"Not Creative" One reason lawyers find such cases enticing is that labor laws on overtime are vague. The Labor Dept. is working on clarifying federal law and hopes to have a list of proposed changes finalized by early 2004. (Update: These rules changes were issued. These changes are incorporated in our discussion of overtime rules in the text.) In the meantime, lawyers have been having a field day alleging that companies withhold overtime pay from workers by misclassifying them as "administrators" or "professionals."

The tech industry, though, is a special case. A 1992 amendment to the federal Fair Labor Standards Act stipulates that any computer professional who is an analyst, programmer, or software engineer shouldn't be paid overtime. But James M. Finberg, who represents the plaintiffs in the CSC case, says thousands of workers who've been denied overtime are responsible for maintaining their clients' networks, not designing them. "Their jobs are not creative," says Finberg, a partner with Lieff Cabraser Heimann & Bernstein LLP in San Francisco. "These people perform mechanical functions. The law says they're entitled to overtime."

The industry is making changes. In September, Oracle quietly reclassified its California-based trainers as eligible for overtime pay under state laws. To cushion the potential financial blow, the company says it cut base compensation 10% and told workers they can't work extra hours without asking permission.

For employees who continue to work long hours, overtime compensation will remain fertile ground for lawsuits. "There's a lot of abuse of employees going on," claims Daniel Gabel, one of the lead plaintiffs in the Oracle case. And many more of his cohorts could decide to raise a stink.

Questions

1. Do you think the "cachet" of being a manager makes up for longer hours at the same pay?
2. Even though the law permits it, are there any potential drawbacks for an organization that works its managers long hours without paying them more? Are there consequences for perceived equity or motivation?
3. Do you think the government should allocate more or fewer resources to enforcing the Fair Labor Standards Act? Why?

SOURCE: Arlene Weintraub and Jim Kerstetter, "Revenge of the Overworked Nerds," *BusinessWeek Online* (December 8, 2003). Reprinted from the December 8, 2003 issue of *BusinessWeek* by special permission. Copyright 2003 by the McGraw-Hill Company.

Notes

1. J. S. Adams, "Inequity in Social Exchange," in *Advances in Experimental Social Psychology*, ed. L. Berkowitz (New York: Academic Press, 1965); P. S. Goodman, "An Examination of Referents Used in the Evaluation of Pay," *Organizational Behavior and Human Performance* 12 (1974), pp. 170–95.
2. J. B. Miner, *Theories of Organizational Behavior* (Hinsdale, IL: Dryden Press, 1980); B. Gerhart and S. L. Rynes, *Compensation: Theory, Evidence, and Strategic Implications* (Thousand Oaks, CA: Sage, 2003).
3. Steve Lohr, "Ford and Chrysler Outpace Japanese in Reducing Costs," *The New York Times* (June 18, 1992), p. D1.
4. B. Gerhart and G. T. Milkovich, "Organizational Differences in Managerial Compensation and Financial Performance," *Academy of Management Journal* 33 (1990), pp. 663–91; E. L. Groshen, "Why Do Wages Vary among Employers?" *Economic Review* 24 (1988), pp. 19–38; Gerhart and Rynes, *Compensation*.
5. G. A. Akerlof, "Gift Exchange and Efficiency-Wage Theory: Four Views," *American Economic Review* 74 (1984), pp. 79–83; J. L. Yellen, "Efficiency Wage Models of Unemployment," *American Economic Review* 74 (1984), pp. 200–5.
6. S. L. Rynes and G. T. Milkovich, "Wage Surveys: Dispelling Some Myths about the 'Market Wage,'" *Personnel Psychology* 39 (1986), pp. 71–90.
7. B. Gerhart and G. T. Milkovich, "Employee Compensation: Research and Practice," in *Handbook of Industrial and Organizational Psychology*, 2nd ed., ed. M. D. Dunnette and L. M. Hough (Palo Alto, CA: Consulting Psychologists Press, 1992).
8. G. T. Milkovich and J. M. Newman, *Compensation*, 7th ed. (New York: Irwin/McGraw-Hill, 2002).
9. B. Gerhart, G. T. Milkovich, and B. Murray, "Pay, Performance, and Participation," in *Research Frontiers in Industrial Relations and Human Resources*, ed. D. Lewin, O. S. Mitchell, and P. D. Sherer (Madison, WI: IRRA, 1992).
10. C. H. Fay, "External Pay Relationships," in *Compensation and Benefits*, ed. L. R. Gomez-Mejia (Washington, DC: Bureau of National Affairs, 1989).
11. J. P. Pfeffer and A. Davis-Blake, "Understanding Organizational Wage Structures: A Resource Dependence Approach," *Academy of Management Journal* 30 (1987), pp. 437–55; M. A. Carpenter and J. B. Wade, "Micro-Level Opportunity Structures as Determinants of Non-CEO Executive Pay," *Academy of Management Journal* 45 (2002), pp. 1085–1103.
12. C. M. Solomon, "Global Compensation: Learn the ABCs," *Personnel Journal*, July 1995, p. 70; R. A. Swaak, "Expatriate Management: The Search for Best Practices," *Compensation and Benefits Review*, March–April 1995, p. 21.

13. *1997–1998 Survey of Geographic Pay Differential Policies and Practices* (Rochester, WI: Runzeimer International). Actually, data from the American Chamber of Commerce Research Association (ACCRA) estimate the cost of living in New York City (in 2001) to be 239.2, compared to 100 for the average metropolitan area.

14. E. E. Lawler III, *Pay and Organizational Development* (Reading, MA: Addison-Wesley, 1981).

15. R. Folger and M. A. Konovsky, "Effects of Procedural and Distributive Justice on Reactions to Pay Raise Decisions," *Academy of Management Journal* 32 (1989), pp. 115–30; H. G. Heneman III and T. A. Judge, "Compensation Attitudes," in S. L. Rynes and B. Gerhart, eds., *Compensation in Organizations* (San Francisco: Jossey-Bass (2002), pp. 61–103; J. Greenberg, "Determinants of Perceived Fairness of Performance Evaluations," *Journal of Applied Psychology* 71 (1986), pp. 340–42; H. G. Heneman III, "Pay Satisfaction," *Research in Personnel and Human Resource Management* 3 (1985), pp. 115–39.

16. J. Greenberg, "Employee Theft as a Reaction to Underpayment of Inequity: The Hidden Cost of Pay Cuts," *Journal of Applied Psychology* 75 (1990), pp. 561–68.

17. Adams, "Inequity in Social Exchange"; C. J. Berger, C. A. Olson, and J. W. Boudreau, "The Effect of Unionism on Job Satisfaction: The Role of Work-Related Values and Perceived Rewards," *Organizational Behavior and Human Performance* 32 (1983), pp. 284–324; P. Cappelli and P. D. Sherer, "Assessing Worker Attitudes under a Two-Tier Wage Plan," *Industrial and Labor Relations Review* 43 (1990), pp. 225–44; R. W. Rice, S. M. Phillips, and D. B. McFarlin, "Multiple Discrepancies and Pay Satisfaction," *Journal of Applied Psychology* 75 (1990), pp. 386–93.

18. Cappelli and Sherer, "Assessing Worker Attitudes."

19. R. M. Kanter, *When Giants Learn to Dance* (New York: Simon & Schuster, 1989); E. E. Lawler III, *Strategic Pay* (San Francisco: Jossey-Bass, 1990); "Farewell, Fast Track," *BusinessWeek* (December 10, 1990), pp. 192–200; R. L. Heneman, G. E. Ledford, Jr., and M. T. Gresham, "The Changing Nature of Work and Its Effects on Compensation Design and Delivery," in S. L. Rynes and B. Gerhart, eds., *Compensation in Organizations*.

20. P. R. Eyers, "Realignment Ties Pay to Performance," *Personnel Journal*, January 1993, p. 74.

21. Lawler, *Strategic Pay*; G. Ledford, "3 Cases on Skill-Based Pay: An Overview," *Compensation and Benefits Review*, March–April 1991, pp. 11–23; G. E. Ledford, "Paying for the Skills, Knowledge, Competencies of Knowledge Workers," *Compensation and Benefits Review*, July–August 1995, p. 55; Heneman et al., "The Changing Nature of Work."

22. Ledford, "3 Cases."

23. Heneman et al., "The Changing Nature of Work."

24. T. D. Wall, J. M. Corbett, R. Martin, C. W. Clegg, and P. R. Jackson, "Advanced Manufacturing Technology, Work Design, and Performance: A Change Study," *Journal of Applied Psychology* 75 (1990), pp. 691–97.

25. Womack et al., *The Machine That Changed the World*, p. 56.

26. Lawler, *Strategic Pay*.

27. Ibid.; Gerhart and Milkovich, "Employee Compensation."

28. B. C. Murray and B. Gerhart, "An Empirical Analysis of a Skill-Based Pay Program and Plant Performance Outcomes," *Academy of Management Journal* 41, no. 1 (1998), pp. 68–78.

29. Ibid.; N. Gupta, D. Jenkins, and W. Curington, "Paying for Knowledge: Myths and Realities," *National Productivity Review*, Spring 1986, pp. 107–23.

30. Data from U.S. Bureau of Labor Statistics website, www.bls.gov.

31. *Education at a Glance—OECD Indicators 2001* (Paris: OECD, 2001).

32. Annual National Accounts, www.oecd.org.

33. C. Sparks and M. Greiner, "U.S. and Foreign Productivity and Labor Costs," *Monthly Labor Review*, February 1997, pp. 26–35.

34. E. Faltermayer, "U.S. Companies Come Back Home," *Fortune* (December 30, 1991), pp. 106ff; M. Hayes, "Precious Connection: Companies Thinking about Using Offshore Outsourcing Need to Consider More than Just Cost Savings," *Information Week Online*, www.informationweek.com (October 20, 2003).

35. A. Farnham, "The Trust Gap," Fortune (December 4, 1989), pp. 56ff; Scott McCartney, "AMR Unions Express Fury," *The Wall Street Journal*, April 17, 2003.

36. D. M. Cowherd and D. I. Levine, "Product Quality and Pay Equity between Lower-Level Employees and Top Management: An Investigation of Distributive Justice Theory," *Administrative Science Quarterly* 37 (1992), pp. 302–20.

37. Bureau of Labor Statistics, *Current Population Surveys* (website).

38. Bureau of Labor Statistics, U.S. Department of Labor, "Highlights of Women's Earnings in 2002," Report 972 (2003).

39. B. Gerhart, "Gender Differences in Current and Starting Salaries: The Role of Performance, College Major, and Job Title," *Industrial and Labor Relations Review* 43 (1990), pp. 418–33; G. G. Cain, "The Economic Analysis of Labor-Market Discrimination: A Survey," in *Handbook of Labor Economics*, ed. O. Ashenfelter and R. Layard (New York: North-Holland, 1986), pp. 694–785.

40. D. P. Schwab, "Job Evaluation and Pay-Setting: Concepts and Practices," in *Comparable Worth: Issues and Alternatives*, ed. E. R. Livernash (Washington, DC: Equal Employment Advisory Council, 1980).

41. B. Gerhart and N. El Cheikh, "Earnings and Percentage Female: A Longitudinal Study," *Industrial Relations* 30 (1991), pp. 62–78; R. S. Smith, "Comparable Worth: Limited Coverage and the Exacerbation of Inequality," *Industrial and Labor Relations Review* 61 (1988), pp. 227–39.

42. W. T. Bielby and J. N. Baron, "Men and Women at Work: Sex Segregation and Statistical Discrimination," *American Journal of Sociology* 91 (1986), pp. 759–99.

43. Rynes and Milkovich, "Wage Surveys"; G. T. Milkovich and J. Newman, Compensation (Homewood, IL: BPI/Irwin, 1993).

44. Gerhart, "Gender Differences in Current and Starting Salaries"; B. Gerhart and G. T. Milkovich, "Salaries, Salary Growth, and Promotions of Men and Women in a Large, Private Firm," in *Pay Equity: Empirical Inquiries*, ed. R. Michael, H. Hartmann, and B. O'Farrell (Washington, DC: National Academy Press, 1989).

45. Gerhart, "Gender Differences in Current and Starting Salaries"; B. Gerhart and S. Rynes, "Determinants and Consequences of Salary Negotiations by Graduating Male and Female MBAs," *Journal of Applied Psychology* 76 (1991), pp. 256–62.

46. G. F. Dreher and R. A. Ash, "A Comparative Study of Mentoring among Men and Women in Managerial, Professional, and Technical Positions," *Journal of Applied Psychology* 75 (1990), pp. 539–46.

47. G. A. Patterson, "Nordstrom Inc. Sets Back-Pay Accord on Suit Alleging 'Off-the-Clock' Work," *The Wall Street Journal* (January 12, 1993), p. A2; for additional information on overtime legal issues, see A. Weintraub and J. Kerstetter, "Revenge of the Overworked Nerds," *BusinessWeek Online*, www.businessweek.com (December 8, 2003).

48. R. I. Henderson, *Compensation Management in a Knowledge-Based World* (Upper-Saddle River, NJ: Prentice Hall, 2003).

12

Chapter

Recognizing Employee Contributions with Pay

Objectives After reading this chapter, you should be able to:

1. Describe the fundamental pay programs for recognizing employees' contributions to the organization's success.

2. List the advantages and disadvantages of the pay programs.

3. List the major factors to consider in matching the pay strategy to the organization's strategy.

4. Explain the importance of process issues such as communication in compensation management.

5. Describe how U.S. pay practices compare with those of other countries.

Changes in the external environment and in company strategy may require a revised compensation strategy. What are the advantages and disadvantages to the changes Microsoft has made in terms of stock options?

Enter the World of Business

Microsoft Ushers Out Golden Era of Options

The golden age of stock options is over.

Microsoft Corp., the quintessential high-tech success story whose stock options turned thousands of employees into millionaires, sounded the knell [July 2003] when it announced it would stop issuing options and instead begin giving its 50,000 employees restricted stock. Those shares typically can be sold only in future years and only if the employee is still at the company.

Microsoft also offered employees the opportunity to sell the nearly worthless options they already hold, in an unusual arrangement with J.P. Morgan Chase & Co. But in most cases they'll make far less than what they had once hoped to reap by exercising them.

The company's decision comes amid mounting pressures on stock options, long a pay perk for senior executives. More recently companies began doling them out to rank-and-file employees, making them an iconic trapping of wealth during the boom of the 1990s. Because options carry the right to buy stock at a fixed price during a specified period, they have the potential to create enormous windfalls if the stock goes up.

Today they face a multifront assault. Employees are unhappy because after three years of stock-market declines many of their options are close to worthless. A growing chorus of critics argue that they tend to warp managers' views by emphasizing short-term performance and giving them an incentive to play accounting games to inflate the stock price.

Federal Reserve Chairman Alan Greenspan last year blamed "poorly structured" options as a major contributor to the "infectious greed" that gripped business in the 1990s. "The incentives they created overcame the good judgment of too many corporate managers," he testified before the Senate Banking Committee. Investors howled when leaders of companies including Enron Corp. and Qwest Communications International Inc. reaped huge gains from exercising options and selling shares just before bad corporate news broke.

Some investors and regulators are pushing to change the favorable accounting treatment for options, under which companies aren't required to show option-based compensation as an expense on their income statements.

For Microsoft, the move to abolish options signals that the once-fast-growing tech business is becoming a mature industry. Microsoft Chief Executive Steve Ballmer said in an interview that grants of restricted stock will prove more valuable to employees than options at a time when Microsoft shares are unlikely to rise as rapidly as they did in the 1990s.

After its initial public offering in 1986, Microsoft stock price soared as the company turned its control of the standard for personal-computer software into one of the most lucrative franchises in business history. Its co-founder Bill Gates became the world's richest man. But following the slowdown in the PC market, Microsoft's share price dropped from its high of $59.56, adjusted for stock splits. Microsoft says that most of the options held by its employees are now "underwater," meaning that exercising them wouldn't yield any money.

"It is very important to me that we absolutely have an environment where we are attracting [talented employees] and our compensation has to be part of our attraction," said Mr. Ballmer. He said Microsoft employees have been expressing "angst" about compensation that he thinks "reflects nothing more than the drop in stock price."

Increasingly Microsoft has come to grips with the possibility that its soaring share price, and the rich rewards of options, are a thing of the past. "If you think what happened in the nineties is going to happen again—it's not," said Microsoft Chief Financial Officer John Connors. In a recent interview he described the PC market boom as a "phenomenon" that "nobody will ever likely repeat."

Compensation experts said Microsoft's move is the latest, and most significant, in a migration away from stock options. About 216 companies—including a handful of tech firms—have announced plans in the last year to count options as an expense. Dozens of others are switching to restricted stock.

"It is a watershed moment because of [Microsoft's] size and the size of their options program," said Brian Foley, managing director of Brian Foley & Co., a pay-consulting firm in White Plains, N.Y. "When a player of this size takes an action like this, it forces other people to rethink what they should be doing." Mr. Foley thinks that other companies "will do the same thing because they want a more predictable accounting expense."

To be sure, options will remain a valuable tool for many companies, particularly fast growing start-ups that don't have a lot of money to pay employees.

The move could significantly change Microsoft's financial statements. The company said that in the future it will record an expense for the restricted stock. It did not immediately offer an estimate of the financial effect. But in an SEC filing in May, Microsoft said that counting stock options as an expense would have reduced its net income in the nine months ended March 31 [2003] by a fourth to $6.05 billion from $8.07 billion.

Microsoft's shift away from stock options reflects an astonishingly quick reversal in public sentiment. Just a few years ago, consultants, professors, investors and politicians championed options as the ideal incentive for executives and rank-and-file employees. The idea was that they aligned staffers' fortunes with those of shareholders. Government tax and accounting policies helped, by giving companies tax breaks when employees exercised options and allowing them not to count options as expenses.

But options have fallen out of favor amid a wave of corporate scandals and the end of the 90s bull market. The Financial Accounting Standards Board has been moving toward requiring that options be treated as expenses in financial statements.

There are still many holdouts, most notably chip giant Intel Corp. and networking titan Cisco Systems Inc. An Intel spokesman said Microsoft's plan "in no way affects our resolve, or affects our argument" that treating stock options as an expense is a bad idea. In the past, Intel Chairman Andy Grove has defended options as a way to link employees and shareholders.

Mr. Grove and Cisco Chief Executive John Chambers have argued that it doesn't make sense to treat options as an expense, because companies don't expend any cash. They argue that financial statements already recognize that options reduce the ownership stake of existing shareholders and per-share earnings. Moreover, these executives say, there's no way to accurately estimate the value of options, so counting them as expenses will make financial statements less reliable.

The Microsoft move "is not going to have any impact on our coalition because they remain committed to broad-based stock option plans,"

said Jeff Peck, a lobbyist for the International Employee Stock Options Coalition. Members include more than two dozen companies, such as Intel, Cisco and AOL/Time Warner Inc.

Source: From *The Wall Street Journal* (Eastern edition), by Robert A. Guth and Joann S. Lublin. Copyright 2003 by Dow Jones & Co., Inc. Reproduced with permission of Dow Jones & Co., Inc. via Copyright Clearance Center.

Introduction

The opening story illustrates how changes in the external environment and in company strategy may require a rethinking of compensation strategy.

The preceding chapter discussed setting pay for jobs. In this chapter we focus on using pay to recognize and reward employees' contributions to the organization's success. Employees' pay does not depend solely on the jobs they hold. Instead, differences in performance (individual, group, or organization), seniority, skills, and so forth are used as a basis for differentiating pay among employees.[1]

Several key questions arise in evaluating different pay programs for recognizing contributions. First, what are the costs of the program? Second, what is the expected return (in terms of influences on attitudes and behaviors) from such investments? Third, does the program fit with the organization's human resource strategy and its overall business strategy?

Organizations have a relatively large degree of discretion in deciding how to pay, especially compared with the pay level decisions discussed in the previous chapter. The same organizational pay level (or "compensation pie") can be distributed ("sliced") among employees in many ways. Whether each employee's share is based on individual performance, profits, seniority, or other factors, the size of the pie (and thus the cost to the organization) can remain the same.

Regardless of cost differences, different pay programs can have very different consequences for productivity and return on investment. Indeed, a study of how much 150 organizations paid found not only that the largest differences between organizations had to do with how they paid but that these differences resulted in different levels of profitability.[2]

How Does Pay Influence Individual Employees?

Pay plans are typically used to energize, direct, or control employee behavior. Equity theory, described in the previous chapter, is relevant here as well. Most employees compare their own pay with that of others, especially those in the same job. Perceptions of inequity may cause employees to take actions to restore equity. Unfortunately, some of these actions (like quitting or lack of cooperation) may not help the organization.

Three additional theories also help explain compensation's effects: reinforcement, expectancy, and agency theories.

Reinforcement Theory

E. L. Thorndike's Law of Effect states that a response followed by a reward is more likely to recur in the future. The implication for compensation management is that high employee performance followed by a monetary reward will make future high performance more likely. By the same token, high performance not followed by a reward will make it less likely in the future. The theory emphasizes the importance of a person's actual experience of a reward.

Expectancy Theory

Expectancy theory
The theory that says motivation is a function of valence, instrumentality, and expectancy.

Although **expectancy theory** also focuses on the link between rewards and behaviors, it emphasizes expected (rather than experienced) rewards. In other words, it focuses on the effects of incentives. Behaviors (job performance) can be described as a function of ability and motivation. In turn, motivation is hypothesized to be a function of expectancy, instrumentality, and valence perceptions. Compensation systems differ according to their impact on these motivational components. Generally speaking, the main factor is instrumentality: the perceived link between behaviors and pay. Valence of pay outcomes should remain the same under different pay systems. Expectancy perceptions (the perceived link between effort and performance) often have more to do with job design and training than pay systems. A possible exception would be skill-based pay, which directly influences employee training and thus expectancy perceptions.

Although expectancy theory implies that linking an increased amount of rewards to performance will increase motivation and performance, some authors have questioned this assumption, arguing that monetary rewards may increase extrinsic motivation but decrease intrinsic motivation. Extrinsic motivation depends on rewards (such as pay and benefits) controlled by an external source, whereas intrinsic motivation depends on rewards that flow naturally from work itself (like performing interesting work).[3] In other words, paying a child to read books may diminish the child's natural interest in reading, and the child may in the future be less likely to read books unless there are monetary incentives. Although monetary incentives may reduce intrinsic motivation in some settings (such as education), the evidence suggests that such effects are small and isolated in work settings.[4] Therefore, while it is important to keep in mind that money is not the only effective way to motivate behavior and that monetary rewards will not always be the answer to motivation problems, it does not appear that monetary rewards run much risk of compromising intrinsic motivation in most work settings.

Agency Theory

Principal
In agency theory, a person (e.g., an owner) who seeks to direct another person's behavior.

Agent
In agency theory, a person (e.g., a manager) who is expected to act on behalf of a principal (e.g., an owner).

This theory focuses on the divergent interests and goals of the organization's stakeholders and the ways that employee compensation can be used to align these interests and goals. We cover agency theory in some depth because it provides especially relevant implications for compensation design.

An important characteristic of the modern corporation is the separation of ownership from management (or control). Unlike the early stages of capitalism, where owner and manager were often the same, today, with some exceptions (mostly smaller companies), most stockholders are far removed from the day-to-day operation of companies. Although this separation has important advantages (like mobility of financial capital and diversification of investment risk), it also creates agency costs—the interests of the **principals** (owners) and their **agents** (managers) may no longer converge. What is best for the agent, or manager, may not be best for the owner.

Three types of agency costs arise in managerial compensation.[5] First, although shareholders seek to maximize their wealth, management may spend money on things such as perquisites (corporate jets, for example) or "empire building" (making acquisitions that do not add value to the company but may enhance the manager's prestige or pay). Second, managers and shareholders may differ in their attitudes toward risk. Shareholders can diversify their investments (and thus their risks) more easily than managers (whose only major source of income may be their jobs), so managers are typically more averse to risk. They may be less likely to pursue projects or acquisitions with high potential payoff. It also suggests a preference on the part of managers for relatively little risk in their pay (high emphasis on base salary, low emphasis on uncertain bonuses or incentives). Indeed, research shows that managerial compensation in manager-controlled firms is more often designed in this manner.[6] Third, decision making horizons may differ. For example, if managers change companies more than owners change ownership, managers may be more likely to maximize short-run performance (and pay), perhaps at the expense of long-term success.

Agency theory is also of value in the analysis and design of nonmanagers' compensation. In this case, interests may diverge between managers (now in the role of principals) and their employees (who take on the role of agents).

In designing either managerial or nonmanagerial compensation, the key question is, How can such agency costs be minimized? Agency theory says that the principal must choose a contracting scheme that helps align the interests of the agent with the principal's own interests (that is, it reduces agency costs). These contracts can be classified as either behavior-oriented (such as merit pay) or outcome-oriented (stock options, profit sharing, commissions, and so on).[7]

At first blush, outcome-oriented contracts seem to be the obvious solution. If profits are high, compensation goes up. If profits drop, compensation goes down. The interests of "the company" and employees are aligned. An important drawback, however, is that such contracts increase the agent's risk. And because agents are averse to risk, they may require higher pay (a compensating wage differential) to make up for it.[8]

Behavior-based contracts, on the other hand, do not transfer risk to the agent and thus do not require a compensating wage differential. However, the principal must be able to monitor with little cost what the agent has done. Otherwise, the principal must either invest in monitoring and information or structure the contract so that pay is linked at least partly to outcomes.[9]

Which type of contract should an organization use? It depends partly on the following factors:[10]

- *Risk aversion.* Risk aversion among agents makes outcome-oriented contracts less likely.
- *Outcome uncertainty.* Profit is an example of an outcome. Agents are less willing to have their pay linked to profits to the extent that there is a risk of low profits. They would therefore prefer a behavior-oriented contract.
- *Job programmability.* As jobs become less programmable (less routine), outcome-oriented contracts become more likely because monitoring becomes more difficult.[11]
- *Measurable job outcomes.* When outcomes are more measurable, outcome-oriented contracts are more likely.
- *Ability to pay.* Outcome-oriented contracts contribute to higher compensation costs because of the risk premium.
- *Tradition.* A tradition or custom of using (or not using) outcome-oriented contracts will make such contracts more (or less) likely.

In summary, the reinforcement, expectancy, and agency theories all focus on the fact that behavior–reward contingencies can shape behaviors. However, agency theory is of particular value in compensation management because of its emphasis on the risk–reward trade-off, an issue that needs close attention when companies consider variable pay plans, which can carry significant risk.

How Does Pay Influence Labor Force Composition?

Traditionally, using pay to recognize employee contributions has been thought of as a way to influence the behaviors and attitudes of current employees, whereas pay level and benefits have been seen as a way to influence so-called membership behaviors: decisions about whether to join or remain with the organization. However, there is increasing recognition that individual pay programs may also affect the nature and composition of an organization's workforce.[12] For example, it is possible that an organization that links pay to performance may attract more high performers than an organization that does not link the two. There may be a similar effect with respect to job retention.[13]

Continuing the analysis, different pay systems appear to attract people with different personality traits and values.[14] Organizations that link pay to individual performance may be more likely to attract individualistic employees, whereas organizations relying more heavily on team rewards are more likely to attract team-oriented employees. The implication is that the design of compensation programs needs to be carefully coordinated with the business and human resource strategy. Increasingly, both in the United States and abroad, employers are seeking to establish stronger links between pay and performance.

Programs

In compensating employees, an organization does not have to choose one program over another. Instead, a combination of programs is often the best solution. For example, one program may foster teamwork and cooperation but not enough individual initiative. Another may do the opposite. Used in conjunction, a balance may be attained.[15]

Table 12.1 provides an overview of the programs for recognizing employee contributions. Each program shares a focus on paying for performance. The programs differ according to three design features: (1) payment method, (2) frequency of payout, and (3) ways of measuring performance. In a perhaps more speculative vein, the table also suggests the potential consequences of such programs for (1) performance motivation of employees, (2) attraction of employees, (3) organization culture, and (4) costs. Finally, there are two contingencies that may influence whether each pay program fits the situation: (1) management style and (2) type of work. We now discuss the different programs and some of their potential consequences in more depth.

Merit Pay

In merit pay programs, annual pay increases are usually linked to performance appraisal ratings. (See Chapter 8.) Some type of merit pay program exists in almost all organizations (although evidence on merit pay effectiveness is surprisingly scarce).[16]

TABLE 12.1

Programs for Recognizing Employee Contributions

	MERIT PAY	INCENTIVE PAY	PROFIT SHARING	OWNERSHIP	GAIN SHARING	SKILL-BASED
Design features						
Payment method	Changes in base pay	Bonus	Bonus	Equity changes	Bonus	Change in base pay
Frequency of payout	Annually	Weekly	Semiannually or annually	When stock sold	Monthly or quarterly	When skill or competency acquired
Performance measures	Supervisor's appraisal of individual performance	Individual output, productivity, sales	Company profit	Company stock returns	Production or controllable costs of stand-alone work unit	Skill or competency acquisition of individuals
Consequences						
Performance motivation	Relationship between pay and performance varies	Clear performance–reward connection	Stronger in smaller firms	Stronger in smaller firms	Stronger in smaller units	Encourages learning
Attraction	Over time pays better performers more	Pays higher performers more	Helps with all employees if plan pays out	Can help lock in employees	Helps with all employees if plan pays out	Attracts learning-oriented employees
Culture	Individual competition	Individual competition	Knowledge of business and cooperation	Sense of ownership and cooperation	Supports cooperation, problem solving	Learning and flexible organization
Costs	Requires well-developed performance appraisal system	Setting and maintaining acceptable standards	Relates costs to ability to pay	Relates costs to ability to pay	Setting and maintaining acceptable standards	Training and certification
Contingencies						
Management style	Some participation desirable	Control	Fits participation	Fits participation	Fits participation	Fits participation
Type of work	Individual unless group appraisals done	Stable, individual, easily measurable	All types	All types	All types	Significant skill depth or breadth

SOURCE: Adapted and modified from E. E. Lawler III, "Pay for Performance: A Strategic Analysis," in *Compensation and Benefits,* ed. L. R. Gomez-Mejia (Washington, DC: Bureau of National Affairs, 1989).

One reason for the widespread use of merit pay is its ability to define and reward a broad range of performance dimensions. (See Figure 12.1 for an example.) Indeed, given the pervasiveness of merit pay programs, we devote a good deal of attention to them here.

FIGURE 12.1

Performance Dimensions for Lower to Midlevel Managers, Arrow Electronics

1. Exercises good business judgment
2. Inspires enthusiasm, energy, understanding, loyalty for company goals
3. Attracts, grows, and retains outstanding talent
4. Shows initiative
5. Has position-specific knowledge
6. Delivers results
7. Builds internal good will

SOURCE: From "Compensation and Performance Evaluation at Arrow Electronics," Harvard Business School Case 9-800-290. Copyright © 2000 by the President and Fellows of Harvard College. Reprinted with permission.

Basic Features

Merit increase grid
A grid that combines an employee's performance rating with the employee's position in a pay range to determine the size and frequency of his or her pay increases.

Many merit pay programs work off of a **merit increase grid.** As Table 12.2 indicates, the size and frequency of pay increases are determined by two factors. The first factor is the individual's performance rating (because better performers should receive higher pay). The second factor is position in range (that is, an individual's compa-ratio). So, for example, an employee with a performance rating of EX and a compa-ratio of 120 would receive a pay increase of 9 to 11 percent. By comparison, an employee with a performance rating of EX and a compa-ratio of 85 would receive an increase of 13 to 15 percent. (Note that the general magnitude of increases in such a table is influenced by inflation rates. Thus the percentage increases in such a grid would have been considerably lower in recent years.) One reason for factoring in the compa-ratio is to control compensation costs and maintain the integrity of the pay structure. If a person with a compa-ratio of 120 received a merit increase of 13 to 15 percent, she would soon exceed the pay range maximum. Not factoring in the compa-ratio would also result in uncontrolled growth of compensation costs for employees who continue to perform the same job year after year. Instead, some organizations think in terms of assessing where the employee's pay is now and where it should be, given a particular performance level. Consider Table 12.3. An employee who consistently performs at the EX level should be paid at 115 to 125 percent of the market (that is, a compa-ratio of 115 to 125). To the extent that the employee is far from that

TABLE 12.2

Example of Merit Increase Grid from Merck & Co., Inc.

PERFORMANCE RATING		SUGGESTED MERIT INCREASE PERCENTAGE			
		COMPA-RATIO 80.00–95.00	COMPA-RATIO 95.01–110.00	COMPA-RATIO 110.01–120.00	COMPA-RATIO 120.01–125.00
EX	(Exceptional within Merck)	13–15%	12–14%	9–11%	To maximum of range
WD	(Merck Standard with Distinction)	9–11	8–10	7–9	—
HS	(High Merck Standard)	7–9	6–8	—	—
RI	(Merck Standard Room for Improvement)	5–7	—	—	—
NA	(Not Adequate for Merck)	—	—	—	—

SOURCE: K. J. Murphy, "Merck & Co., Inc., (B)" (Boston: Harvard Business School), Case 491-006. Copyright © 1990 by the President and Fellows of Harvard College. Reprinted with permission.

PERFORMANCE RATING	COMPA-RATIO TARGET
EX (Exceptional within Merck)	115–125
WD (Merck Standard with Distinction)	100–120
HS (High Merck Standard)	90–110
RI (Merck Standard Room for Improvement)	80–95
NA (Not Adequate for Merck)	None

TABLE 12.3

Performance Ratings and Compa-ratio Targets

SOURCE: K. J. Murphy, "Merck & Co., Inc., (B)" (Boston: Harvard Business School), Case 491-006. Copyright © 1990 by the President and Fellows of Harvard College. Reprinted with permission.

pay level, larger and more frequent pay increases are necessary to move the employee to the correct position. On the other hand, if the employee is already at that pay level, smaller pay increases will be needed. The main objective in the latter case would be to provide pay increases that are sufficient to maintain the employee at the targeted compa-ratio.

In controlling compensation costs, another factor that requires close attention is the distribution of performance ratings. (See Chapter 8.) In many organizations, 60 to 70 percent of employees fall into the top two (out of four to five) performance rating categories.[17] This means tremendous growth in compensation costs because most employees will eventually be above the midpoint of the pay range, resulting in compa-ratios well over 100. To avoid this, some organizations provide guidelines regarding the percentage of employees who should fall into each performance category, usually limiting the percentage that can be placed in the top two categories. These guidelines are enforced differently, ranging from true guidelines to strict forced-distribution requirements.

In general, merit pay programs have the following characteristics. First, they identify individual differences in performance, which are assumed to reflect differences in ability or motivation. By implication, system constraints on performance are not seen as significant. Second, the majority of information on individual performance is collected from the immediate supervisor. Peer and subordinate ratings are rare, and where they exist, they tend to receive less weight than supervisory ratings.[18] Third, there is a policy of linking pay increases to performance appraisal results.[19] Fourth, the feedback under such systems tends to occur infrequently, often once per year at the formal performance review session. Fifth, the flow of feedback tends to be largely unidirectional, from supervisor to subordinate.

Criticisms of Traditional Merit Pay Programs

Criticisms of this process have been raised. For example, W. Edwards Deming, a leader of the total quality management movement, argued that it is unfair to rate individual performance because "apparent differences between people arise almost entirely from the system that they work in, not from the people themselves."[20] Examples of system factors include coworkers, the job, materials, equipment, customers, management, supervision, and environmental conditions. These are believed to be largely outside the worker's control, instead falling under management's responsibility. Deming argued that the performance rating is essentially "the result of a lottery."[21]

Deming also argued that the individual focus of merit pay discourages teamwork: "Everyone propels himself forward, or tries to, for his own good, on his own life preserver. The organization is the loser."[22] As an example, if people in the purchasing department are evaluated based on the number of contracts negotiated, they may have little interest in materials quality, even though manufacturing is having quality problems.

Deming's solution was to eliminate the link between individual performance and pay. This approach reflects a desire to move away from recognizing individual contributions. What are the consequences of such a move? It is possible that fewer employees with individual-achievement orientations would be attracted to and remain with the organization. One study of job retention found that the relationship between pay growth and individual performance over time was weaker at higher performance levels. As a consequence, the organization lost a disproportionate share of its top performers.[23] In other words, too little emphasis on individual performance may leave the organization with average and poor performers.[24]

Thus, although Deming's concerns about too much emphasis on individual performance are well taken, one must be careful not to replace one set of problems with another. Instead, there needs to be an appropriate balance between individual and group objectives. At the very least, ranking and forced-distribution performance-rating systems need to be considered with caution, lest they contribute to behavior that is too individualistic and competitive.

Another criticism of merit pay programs is the way they measure performance. If the performance measure is not perceived as being fair and accurate, the entire merit pay program can break down. One potential impediment to accuracy is the almost exclusive reliance on the supervisor for providing performance ratings, even though peers, subordinates, and customers (internal and external) often have information on a person's performance that is as good as or better than that of the supervisor. A 360-degree performance feedback approach (discussed in Chapter 9) gathers feedback from each of these sources. To date, however, organizations have been reluctant to use these multisource data for making pay decisions.[25]

In general, process issues appear to be important in administering merit pay. In any situation where rewards are distributed, employees appear to assess fairness along two dimensions: distributive (based on how much they receive) and procedural (what process was used to decide how much).[26] Some of the most important aspects of procedural fairness, or justice, appear in Table 12.4. These items suggest that employees desire clear and consistent performance standards, as well as opportunities to provide input, discuss their performance, and appeal any decision they believe to be incorrect.

Perhaps the most basic criticism is that merit pay does not really exist. High performers are not paid significantly more than mediocre or even poor performers in most cases.[27] For example, in the late 1980s and early 1990s, merit increase budgets often did not exceed 4 to 5 percent. Thus high performers might receive 6 percent raises, versus 3.5 to 4 percent raises for average performers. On a salary of $40,000 per year, the difference in take-home pay would not be more than about $300 per year, or about $6 per week. Critics of merit pay point out that this difference is probably not significant enough to influence employee behaviors or attitudes. Indeed, as Figure 12.2 indicates, many employees do not believe there is any payoff to higher levels of performance.

Of course, small differences in pay can accumulate into large differences over time. The present value of the salary advantage would be $29,489 (based on a discount rate of 5 percent). For example, over a 30-year career, an initial annual salary difference of $740 with equal merit increases thereafter of 7 percent would accumulate into a career salary advantage of $75,738.[28] Whether employees think in these terms is open to question. But even if they do not, nothing prevents an organization from explaining to employees that what may appear to be small differences in pay can add up to large differences over time. It should also be kept in mind that merit ratings are often

Indicate the extent to which your supervisor did each of the following:
1. Was honest and ethical in dealing with you.
2. Gave you an opportunity to express your side.
3. Used consistent standards in evaluating your performance.
4. Considered your views regarding your performance.
5. Gave you feedback that helped you learn how well you were doing.
6. Was completely candid and frank with you.
7. Showed a real interest in trying to be fair.
8. Became thoroughly familiar with your performance.
9. Took into account factors beyond your control.
10. Got input from you before a recommendation.
11. Made clear what was expected of you.

Indicate how much of an opportunity existed, after the last raise decision, for you to do each of the following things:
12. Make an appeal about the size of a raise.
13. Express your feelings to your supervisor about the salary decision.
14. Discuss, with your supervisor, how your performance was evaluated.
15. Develop, with your supervisor, an action plan for future performance.

TABLE 12.4

Aspects of Procedural Justice in Pay Raise Decisions

SOURCE: From *Academy of Management Journal* by R. Folger and M. A. Konovsky. Reprinted with permission of *Academy of Management* via Copyright Clearance Center.

closely linked to promotions, which in turn are closely linked to salary. Thus, even in merit pay settings where performance differences are not recognized in the short run, high performers are likely to have significantly higher career earnings.

Finally, the accumulation effect just described can also be seen as a drawback if it contributes to an entitlement mentality. Here the concern is that a big merit increase given early in an employee's career remains part of base salary "forever." It does not have to be re-earned each year, and the cost to the organization grows over time, perhaps more than either the employee's performance or the organization's profitability

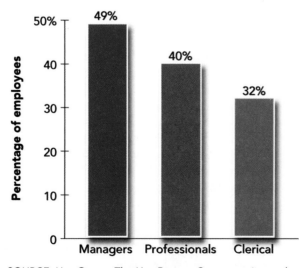

FIGURE 12.2

Percentage of Employees Who Agreed That Better Performers Get Better Increases

SOURCE: Hay Group, *The Hay Report: Compensation and Benefit Strategies for 1995 and Beyond*, Philadelphia: Hay Group, 1994. Reprinted with permission.

would always warrant. Merit bonuses (payouts that do not become part of base salary), in lieu of traditional merit increases, are thus used by some organizations instead.

Individual Incentives

Like merit pay, individual incentives reward individual performance, but with two important differences. First, payments are not rolled into base pay. They must be continuously earned and re-earned. Second, performance is usually measured as physical output (such as number of water faucets produced) rather than by subjective ratings. Individual incentives have the potential to significantly increase performance. Locke and his colleagues found that monetary incentives increased production output by a median of 30 percent—more than any other motivational device studied.[29]

Nevertheless, individual incentives are relatively rare for a variety of reasons.[30] Most jobs (like those of managers and professionals) have no physical output measure. Instead, they involve what might be described as "knowledge work." Also, many potential administrative problems (such as setting and maintaining acceptable standards) often prove intractable. Third, individual incentives may do such a good job of motivating employees that they do whatever they get paid for and nothing else. (See the Dilbert cartoon in Figure 12.3.) Fourth, as the name implies, individual incentives typically do not fit well with a team approach. Fifth, they may be inconsistent with the goals of acquiring multiple skills and proactive problem solving. Learning new skills often requires employees to slow or stop production. If the employees are paid based on production volume, they may not want to slow down or stop. Sixth, some incentive plans reward output volume at the expense of quality or customer service.

Therefore, although individual incentives carry potential advantages, they are not likely to contribute to a flexible, proactive, problem-solving workforce. In addition, such programs may not be particularly helpful in the pursuit of total quality management objectives.

Profit sharing
A compensation plan in which payments are based on a measure of organization performance (profits) and do not become part of the employees' base salary.

Profit Sharing and Ownership

Profit Sharing
At the other end of the individual–group continuum are profit sharing and stock ownership plans. Under **profit sharing,** payments are based on a measure of organization performance (profits), and the payments do not become part of the base salary.

FIGURE 12.3

How Incentives Sometimes "Work"

SOURCE: DILBERT reprinted by permission of United Feature Syndicate, Inc.

BMW's Labor Practices Are Cutting-Edge, Too

Germany is renowned for its rigid labor laws. But consider this curious contradiction: Munich-based Baverische Motoren Werke (BMW) operates some of the most flexible and productive factories in the global auto industry right in its own backyard. Booming demand? No problem. BMW ramps up assembly lines to 110 hours per week, with negligible overtime costs. When sales slide, production managers can dial back weekly operating hours to 78, but they don't fire employees. A new plant in Leipzig will be even more flexible, swinging from 60 hours a week to 140 when demand booms. "That's the secret of BMW Group's success," says CFO Stefan Krause. "Our [machines] sweat more than other people's because they work longer hours."

BMW pioneered innovative labor practices in Germany, introducing Saturday shifts back in 1985. The goal is to boost productivity by matching output with demand. That means making sure capital-intensive press and paint shops run practically around the clock. In addition, highly skilled assembly workers have to be available to work longer workweeks without costing a fortune. "They are ahead of the pack," says Christoph Stürmer, senior analyst at Global Insight Automotive in Frankfurt.

How does it work? When workers exceed the union-agreed 35-hour work week, they bank the extra hours in an account. When demand drops, they can withdraw from the account and take days off. As long as the work-time model respects compensation levels dictated in union pay contracts, BMW and its worker representatives are free to forge innovative schedules. The basic model: A four-day week at 9 hours a day with three days off. That gives most workers long weekends in exchange for working some Saturdays. At first, workers balked. But now they love the system. "Bavarians aren't dumb. *They realized they would win more free time if they collaborated to boost productivity*," says Rudolf Braun, a *Meister* in vehicle assembly at BMW's Dingolfing plant. Thanks to the flexible shifts, BMW's plants operate near full capacity, avoiding loss-making periods when capacity use plunges.

BMW also can juggle model lines from plant to plant. All of its factories can produce at least two different models. When demand on the 3 Series surged last year, BMW bumped up production at the Dingolfing plant, which was built chiefly to make the 5 Series and the 7 Series, but also can make the highly profitable 3 Series. By stretching production at the Munich and Regensburg plants, as well as adding capacity at Dingolfing for 70,000 vehicles, BMW cranked out an extra 160,000 autos. "That's an entire car plant," says Norbert Reithofer, BMW board member in charge of production. And if one factory in Bavaria is slack while another is straining, the company reroutes its workers to the factory under stress. Every day, more than 300 buses shuttle 15,500 employees to and from Dingolfing.

But the ultimate manufacturing acrobatic act at BMW is build-to-order. Some 80 percent of European BMW buyers custom-design their own cars, choosing everything from special engine configurations to headlights with sensors that track the bend in the road. And BMW offers customers the chance to change every detail on the car until five days before production. For each vehicle, the total number of possible variations is 10 to the power of 17—yes, that's 10 with 17 zeros after it. Most of those finicky last-minute changes are costly upgrades to bigger engines or more luxurious interiors, says Reithofer. Even with these demands, BMW's software can handle up to 120,000 customers a month who change their mind about what they want. You can be sure the Dingolfing dream team is already thinking about how to double that number.

SOURCE: Gail Edmondson, "BMW's Labor Practices Are Cutting-Edge Too," *BusinessWeek* (June 9, 2003). Reprinted with permission.

Profit sharing has two potential advantages. First, it may encourage employees to think more like owners, taking a broad view of what needs to be done to make the organization more effective. Thus, the sort of narrow self-interest encouraged by individual incentive plans (and perhaps also by merit pay) is presumably less of an issue. Instead, increased cooperation and citizenship are expected. Second, because payments do not become part of base pay, labor costs are automatically reduced during difficult economic times, and wealth is shared during good times. Consequently, organizations may not need to rely on layoffs as much to reduce costs during tough times.[31]

Does profit sharing contribute to better organization performance? The evidence is not clear. Although there is consistent support for a correlation between profit sharing payments and profits, questions have been raised about the direction of causality.[32] For example, Ford, Chrysler, and GM all have profit sharing plans in their contracts with the United Auto Workers (UAW). (See Figure 12.4 for provisions of the GM–UAW plan.) The average profit sharing payment at Ford one year was $4,000 per worker versus an average of $550 per worker at GM and $8,000 at Chrysler. Given that the profit sharing plans are similar, it seems unlikely they caused Ford and Chrysler to be more profitable. Rather, it would appear that profits were higher at Ford for other reasons, resulting in higher profit sharing payments.

This example also helps illustrate the fundamental drawback of profit sharing. Why should automobile workers at GM receive profit sharing payments that are only 1/15th the size received by those doing the same type of work at Chrysler? Is it because Chrysler UAW members performed 15 times better than their counterparts at GM that year? Probably not. Rather, workers are likely to view top management decisions regarding products, engineering, pricing, and marketing as more important. As

FIGURE 12.4

Profit Sharing in the General Motors–UAW Contract

2.14 **"Profits"** . . . means income earned by U.S. operations before income taxes and "extraordinary" items. . . . Profits are before any profit sharing charges are deducted. Profits also are before incentive program charges for U.S. operations.

2.18 **"Total Profit Share"** . . . means an obligation of the corporation for any plan year in an amount equal to the sum of:

(a) 6 percent of the portion of profits . . . which exceeds 0.0 percent of sales and revenues . . . but does not exceed 1.8 percent . . .;

(b) 8 percent of the portion of profits . . . which exceeds 1.8 percent of sales and revenues . . . but does not exceed 2.3 percent . . .;

(c) 10 percent of the portion of profits . . . which exceeds 2.3 percent of sales and revenues . . . but does not exceed 4.6 percent . . .;

(d) 14 percent of the portion of profits . . . which exceeds 4.6 percent of sales and revenues . . . but does not exceed 6.9 percent . . .;

(e) 17 percent of the portion of profits . . . which exceeds 6.9 percent of sales and revenues.

4.02 **Allocation of Profit Sharing Amount to Participants**

The portion of the total profit share for the plan year allocated to this plan . . . will be allocated to each participant entitled to a distribution . . . in the proportion that (a) the participant's compensation hours for the plan year bears to (b) the total compensated hours for all participants in the plan entitled to a distribution for the plan year.

SOURCE: From J. A. Fossum, *Labor Relations: Development, Structure and Process,* 2002. Copyright © 2002 The McGraw-Hill Companies, Inc. Reprinted with permission.

a result, with the exception of top (and perhaps some middle) managers, most employees are unlikely to see a strong connection between what they do and what they earn under profit sharing. This means that performance motivation is likely to change very little under profit sharing. Consistent with expectancy theory, motivation depends on a strong link between behaviors and valued consequences such as pay (instrumentality perceptions).

Another factor that reduces the motivational impact of profit sharing plans is that most plans are of the deferred type. Roughly 16 percent of full-time employees in medium-size and large private establishments participate in profit sharing plans, but only 1 percent of employees overall (about 6 percent of those in profit sharing plans) are in cash plans where profits are paid to employees during the current time period.[33]

Not only may profit sharing fail to increase performance motivation, but employees may also react very negatively when they learn that such plans do not pay out during business downturns.[34] First, they may not feel they are to blame because they have been performing their jobs well. Other factors are beyond their control, so why should they be penalized? Second, what seems like a small amount of risked pay for a manager earning $80,000 per year can be very painful to someone earning $15,000 or $20,000.

Consider the case of the Du Pont Fibers Division, which had a plan that linked a portion of employees' pay to division profits.[35] After the plan's implementation, employees' base salary was about 4 percent lower than similar employees' in other divisions unless 100 percent of the profit goal (a 4 percent increase over the previous year's profits) was reached. Thus, there was what might be called downside risk. However, there was also considerable upside opportunity: if 100 percent of the profit goal was exceeded, employees would earn more than similar employees in other divisions. For example, if the division reached 150 percent of the profit goal (6 percent growth in profits), employees would receive 12 percent more than comparable employees in other divisions.

Initially, the plan worked fine. The profit goal was exceeded, and employees earned slightly more than employees in other divisions. In the following year, however, profits were down 26 percent, and the profit goal was not met. Employees received no profit sharing bonus; instead, they earned 4 percent less than comparable employees in other divisions. Profit sharing was no longer seen as a very good idea. Du Pont management responded to employee concerns by eliminating the plan and returning to a system of fixed base salaries with no variable (or risk) component. This outcome is perhaps not surprising from an agency theory perspective, which suggests that employees must somehow be compensated before they will be willing to assume increased risk.

One solution some organizations choose is to design plans that have upside but not downside risk. In such cases, when a profit sharing plan is introduced, base pay is not reduced. Thus, when profits are high, employees share in the gain, but when profits are low, they are not penalized. Such plans largely eliminate what is purported to be a major advantage of profit sharing: reducing labor costs during business downturns. During business upturns, labor costs will increase. Given that the performance benefits of such plans are not assured, an organization runs the risk under such plans of increasing its labor costs with little return on its investment.

In summary, although profit sharing may be useful as one component of a compensation system (to enhance identification with broad organizational goals), it may need to be complemented with other pay programs that more closely link pay to outcomes that individuals or teams can control (or "own"), particularly in larger companies. In addition, profit sharing runs the risk of contributing to employee dissatisfaction or higher labor costs, depending on how it is designed.

Ownership

Employee ownership is similar to profit sharing in some key respects, such as encouraging employees to focus on the success of the organization as a whole. In fact, with ownership, this focus may be even stronger. Like profit sharing, ownership may be less motivational the larger the organization. And because employees may not realize any financial gain until they actually sell their stock (typically upon leaving the organization), the link between pay and performance may be even less obvious than under profit sharing. Thus, from a reinforcement theory standpoint (with its emphasis on actually experiencing rewards), performance motivation may be especially low.

Stock options
An employee ownership plan that gives employees the opportunity to buy the company's stock at a previously fixed price.

One way of achieving employee ownership is through **stock options,** which give employees the opportunity to buy stock at a fixed price. Say the employees receive options to purchase stock at $10 per share in 1995, and the stock price reaches $30 per share in 2000. They have the option of purchasing stock ("exercising" their stock options) at $10 per share in 2000, thus making a tidy return on investment if the shares are then sold. If the stock price goes down to $8 per share in the year 2000, however, there will be no financial gain. Therefore, employees are encouraged to act in ways that will benefit the organization.

For many years, stock options had typically been reserved for executives in larger, established companies. More recently, there was a trend toward pushing eligibility farther down in the organization.[36] In fact, many companies, including PepsiCo, Merck, McDonald's, Wal-Mart, and Procter & Gamble, now grant stock options to employees at all levels. Among start-up companies like these in the technology sector, these broad-based stock option programs have long been popular and companies like Microsoft and Cisco Systems attribute much of their growth and success to these option plans. Some studies suggest that organization performance is higher when a large percentage of top and midlevel managers are eligible for long-term incentives such as stock options, which is consistent with agency theory's focus on the problem of encouraging managers to think like owners.[37] However, it is not clear whether these findings would hold up for lower-level employees, particularly in larger companies, who may see much less opportunity to influence overall organization performance.

The Golden Age of stock options may be coming to an end. Investors have long questioned the historically favorable tax treatment of stock options. In 2004, the Financial Accounting Standards Board (FASB) proposed a landmark change that would require companies to expense options on their financial statements, which reduces reported net income, dramatically in some cases. As we saw in the chapter opener, Microsoft has decided to eliminate stock options in favor of actual stock grants. This is partly in response to the new accounting standards and partly in recognition of the fact that Microsoft's stock price is not likely to grow as rapidly as it once did, making options less effective in recruiting, retaining, and motivating its employees.

Employee stock ownership plan (ESOP)
An employee ownership plan that gives employers certain tax and financial advantages when stock is granted to employees.

Employee stock ownership plans (ESOPs), under which employers give employees stock in the company, are the most common form of employee ownership, with the number of employees in such plans increasing from 4 million in 1980 to over 10 million in 1999 in the United States.[38] In Japan, 91 percent of companies listed on Japanese stock markets have an ESOP, and these companies appear to have higher average productivity than non-ESOP companies.[39] ESOPs raise a number of unique issues. On the negative side, they can carry significant risk for employees. An ESOP must, by law, invest at least 51 percent of assets in its company's stock, resulting in less diversification of investment risk (in some cases, no diversification). Consequently, when employees buy out companies in poor financial condition to save their jobs, or when the ESOP is used to fund pensions, employees risk serious financial difficulties if the company does poorly.[40] This is not just a concern for employees, because, as agency theory suggests, employees may require higher pay to offset increased risks of this sort.

ESOPs can be attractive to organizations because they have tax and financing advantages and can serve as a takeover defense (under the assumption that employee owners will be "friendly" to management). ESOPs give employees the right to vote their securities (if registered on a national exchange).[41] As such, some degree of participation in a select number of decisions is mandatory, but overall participation in decision making appears to vary significantly across organizations with ESOPs. Some studies suggest that the positive effects of ownership are larger in cases where employees have greater participation,[42] perhaps because the "employee–owner comes to psychologically experience his/her ownership in the organization."[43]

Finding and Keeping the Best Employees
Will fewer risk takers apply?

As Microsoft Corp. and other companies retreat from stock options, they may find it harder to attract entrepreneurial staffers vitally needed to spur innovation, recruiters and pay consultants believe.

Microsoft management initially worried that its shift from stock options to restricted stock (see "Enter the World of Business" at the beginning of this chapter) might hurt employee retention and recruitment. Based on focus groups with employees, Microsoft tweaked the new restricted-stock program to make sure it "appeals to the kind of talent we want, entrepreneurial and otherwise," says Ken DiPietro, Microsoft's vice president of human resources. For example, he notes, a midlevel technical developer mulling an offer elsewhere accepted a position with Microsoft after hearing about its new pay plan Tuesday. The developer was among four prospects to whom Microsoft initially had offered stock options. "They had not accepted and were vacillating," says Mark Murray, a Microsoft spokesman. "We went back to them with the new [restricted] stock plan and they accepted on the spot." Microsoft hasn't had difficulty attracting applicants. Indeed, it often gets 1,000 resumes a day. Moreover, in this depressed downturn, it is a buyer's market for technology staff.

Other businesses that have trimmed or eliminated their option usage are hiring new staffers. None say they fear the shift will damage the caliber of their applicants.

Dell Computer, for example, intends to grant about half as many stock options this fiscal year as in the previous year. "Our compensation package reflects what's necessary to hire and retain people in the marketplace," says Dell spokesman Mike Maher. "It's a different time than it was three years ago" when the talent market was red-hot and the stock market was booming. Equally important, he notes, options alone don't attract innovative, entrepreneurial individuals to a good company. Dell doesn't have any plans to offer restricted stock to employees.

It's a similar story at Amazon. The Seattle Internet retailer switched to restricted stock from options last year, saying it would help retain workers whose options were close to worthless. Amazon gives employees fewer restricted shares than it used to offer options. "We find we can still get great people and our attrition rate is below the industry average," says Bill Curry, an Amazon spokesman. "We hire people on a lot of different metrics. Entrepreneurship is [just] one."

SOURCE: From *The Wall Street Journal* (Eastern edition) by Joann S. Lublin. Copyright 2003 by Dow Jones & Co., Inc. Reproduced with permission of Dow Jones & Co., Inc. via Copyright Clearance Center.

Gainsharing, Group Incentives, and Team Awards

Gainsharing

Gainsharing
A form of compensation based on group or plant performance (rather than organization-wide profits) that does not become part of the employee's base salary.

Gainsharing programs offer a means of sharing productivity gains with employees. Although sometimes confused with profit sharing plans, gainsharing differs in two key respects. First, instead of using an organization-level performance measure (profits), the programs measure group or plant performance, which are likely to be seen as more controllable by employees. Second, payouts are distributed more frequently and not deferred. In a sense, gainsharing programs represent an effort to pull out the best features of organization-oriented plans like profit sharing and individual-oriented plans like merit pay and individual incentives. Like profit sharing, gainsharing encourages pursuit of broader goals than individual-oriented plans do. But, unlike profit sharing, gainsharing can motivate employees much as individual plans do because of the more controllable nature of the performance measure and the frequency of payouts. Indeed, studies indicate that gainsharing improves performance.[44]

Table 12.5 shows the workings of one type of gainsharing, the Scanlon plan (developed in the 1930s by Joseph N. Scanlon, president of a local union at Empire Steel and Tin Plant in Mansfield, Ohio). The Scanlon plan provides a monetary bonus to employees (and the organization) if the ratio of labor costs to the sales value of production is kept below a certain standard, $240,000 (20 percent of $1.2 million) in this example. Because actual labor costs were $210,000, there is a savings of $30,000. The organization receives 50 percent of the savings, and the employees receive the other 50 percent, although part of the employees' share is set aside in the event that actual labor costs exceed the standard in upcoming months.

Gainsharing plans like the Scanlon plan and pay-for-performance plans in general often encompass more than just a monetary component. As Table 12.6 indicates, there is often a strong emphasis on taking advantage of employee know-how to improve the production process through teams and suggestion systems. A number of recommendations have been made about the organization conditions that should be in place for gainsharing to succeed. Commonly mentioned factors include (1) management commitment, (2) a need to change or a strong commitment to continuous improvement, (3) management's acceptance and encouragement of employee input, (4) high levels of cooperation and interaction, (5) employment security, (6) informa-

TABLE 12.5

Example of Gainsharing (Scanlon Plan) Monthly Report

1.	Sales	$1,100,000
2.	Less sales returns, allowances, discounts	25,000
3.	Net sales	1,075,000
4.	Add: increase in inventory (at cost or selling price)	125,000
5.	Value of production	1,200,000
6.	Allowed payroll costs (20% of value of production)	240,000
7.	Actual payroll costs	210,000
8.	Bonus pool	30,000
9.	Company share (50%)	15,000
	Subtotal	15,000
10.	Reserve for deficit months (25%)	3,750
11.	Employee share—immediate distribution	11,250

SOURCE: Reprinted with permission, p. 57 from *Gainsharing: Plans for Improving Performance*, by Brian Graham-Moore and Timothy L. Ross. Copyright © 1990 by the Bureau of National Affairs, Inc., Washington, DC 20037.

TYPE OF EMPLOYEE INVOLVEMENT PROGRAM	PERCENTAGE USING PROGRAM	MEDIAN PERCENTAGE OF EMPLOYEES PARTICIPATING	MEDIAN NUMBER OF HOURS SPENT PER PARTICIPATING EMPLOYEE PER YEAR
Individual suggestion plans	42%	20%	5
Ad hoc problem solving groups	44	20	22
Team group suggestion plans	28	25	10
Employee–management teams	19	15	40
Quality circles	26	16	50
Percentage of all plans using any type of employee involvement program	66		

TABLE 12.6

Employee Involvement Plans for Nonmanagement Employees

SOURCE: J. L. McAdams, "Design, Implementation, and Results: Employee Involvement and Performance Reward Plans," *Compensation and Benefits Review,* March–April 1995, pp. 45–55. Copyright © 1995 by Sage Publications, Inc. Reprinted with permission of Sage Publications, Inc.

tion sharing on productivity and costs, (7) goal setting, (8) commitment of all involved parties to the process of change and improvement, and (9) agreement on a performance standard and calculation that is understandable, seen as fair, and closely related to managerial objectives.[45]

Group Incentives and Team Awards

Whereas gainsharing plans are often plantwide, group incentives and team awards typically pertain to a smaller work group.[46] Group incentives (like individual incentives) tend to measure performance in terms of physical output, whereas team award plans may use a broader range of performance measures (like cost savings, successful completion of product design, or meeting deadlines). As with individual incentive plans, these plans have a number of potential drawbacks. Competition between individuals may be reduced, but it may be replaced by competition between groups or teams. Also, as with any incentive plan, a standard-setting process must be developed that is seen as fair by employees, and these standards must not exclude important dimensions such as quality.

Balanced Scorecard

As the preceding discussion indicates, every pay program has advantages and disadvantages. Therefore, rather than choosing one program, some companies find it useful to design a mix of pay programs, one that has just the right chemistry for the situation at hand. Relying exclusively on merit pay or individual incentives may result in high levels of work motivation but unacceptable levels of individualistic and competitive behavior and too little concern for broader plant or organization goals. Relying too heavily on profit sharing and gainsharing plans may increase cooperation and concern for the welfare of the entire plant or organization, but it may reduce individual work motivation to unacceptable levels. However, a particular mix of merit pay, gainsharing, and profit sharing could contribute to acceptable performance on all these performance dimensions.

One approach that seeks to balance multiple objectives is the balanced scorecard (see Chapter 1), which Kaplan and Norton describe as a way for companies to "track

TABLE 12.7

Illustration of Balanced Scorecard Incentive Concept

PERFORMANCE MEASURE	INCENTIVE SCHEDULE				
	TARGET INCENTIVE	PERFORMANCE	% TARGET	ACTUAL PERFORMANCE	INCENTIVE EARNED
Financial	$100	20%+	150%	18%	$100
• Return on capital employed		16–20%	100%		
		12–16%	50%		
		Below 12%	0%		
Customer	$ 40	1 in:		1 in 876	$ 20
• Product returns		1,000 +	150%		
		900–999	100%		
		800–899	50%		
		Below 800	0%		
Internal	$ 30	9%+	150%	11%	$ 45
• Cycle time reduction (%)		6–9%	100%		
		3–6%	50%		
		0–3%	0%		
Learning and growth	$ 30	Below 5%	150%	7%	$ 30
• Voluntary employee turnover		5–8%	100%		
		8–12%	50%		
Total	$200				$195

SOURCE: F. C. McKenzie and M. P. Shilling, "Avoiding Performance Traps: Ensuring Effective Incentive Design and Implementation," *Compensation and Benefits Review*, July–August 1998, pp. 57–65. Copyright © 1998 by Sage Publications, Inc. Reprinted with permission of Sage Publications, Inc.

financial results while simultaneously monitoring progress in building the capabilities and acquiring the intangible assets they would need for future growth."[47]

Table 12.7 shows how a mix of measures might be used by a manufacturing firm to motivate improvements in a balanced set of key business drivers.

Strategic Use of HRM

When Florence Phillips was told by her doctor two years ago that she had congestive heart failure, she didn't have to worry about how she would manage the disease.

A health educator from her doctor's practice, the Hill Physicians Medical Group in San Ramon, California, called her immediately to talk about her condition and sent along a packet of material about it. Over the next several weeks, Ms. Phillips, 86, received more information and follow-up calls. She learned how to deal with her illness daily by watching her weight, restricting her salt intake and keeping up with her medications. She learned to look for signs of problems that would require her doctor's immediate attention, and to schedule regular checkups to monitor her condition.

In recent years, disease management programs have sprung up nationwide as employers and insurers grapple with rising medical costs. Nearly two-thirds of those costs go toward treating chronic illnesses like congestive heart failure.

But Ms. Phillips's experience is uncommon in one very notable way: the disease management services are being sponsored by her doctor and her doctor's medical group, not by a health insurer or an employer. And her doctor stands to make more money from the Hill Physicians Medical Group, in the form of an annual bonus of roughly 10 percent of his compensation, if he can keep her and his other patients out of the emergency room, keep their cholesterol under control and make sure they're taking their medications, among other things.

This is not the way doctors normally practice medicine, but maybe it should be. "The American medical system has been designed around heroic efforts, not around creeping diseases," said Steve McDermott, chief executive of Hill Physicians, an independent-practice association with 2,000 doctors and 350,000 patients in Northern California.

For example, he said, heart surgeons are among the highest-paid doctors and often perform heroically during emergencies.

"You want your reactive systems to work very well," Mr. McDermott said, "but that's a talent and a skill and a mind-set that's very different than the teamwork that's required in disease management."

Doctors are only beginning to embrace this approach. A study published last month in the Journal of the American Medical Association found that the average physician group with 20 or more doctors used just 5 out of 16 "care management processes" prescribed by the authors, like case management and patient education, to treat patients with four chronic diseases—diabetes, asthma, congestive heart failure and depression.

Because smaller practices lack the people and resources to put these systems in place, they "are almost certainly doing even less of this," said Dr. Lawrence Casalino, an assistant professor of health studies at the University of Chicago and a principal author of the study.

Disease management programs sponsored by health plans or employers may do an excellent job, but they're often perceived—sometimes accurately—as limiting care rather than encouraging it. Catherine Marschilok, manager of the Northeast Health Diabetes Centers at Albany Memorial Hospital and Samaritan Hospital in Troy, N.Y., described the not-uncommon experience of a patient whose doctor referred him to Northeast Health for a five-session diabetes self-management course after the diagnosis. The man's insurance company refused to pay unless he had been hospitalized or admitted to the emergency room twice, citing the contract with his employer. "I was shocked," Ms. Marschilok said. "What they paid in disease management they could actually save in hospital costs."

From a patient's perspective, it makes sense that a doctor would be the point person in managing care: the doctor, after all, does the examining and sees the patient regularly. Traditionally, however, doctors haven't been paid to monitor and manage patients' care. Instead, their compensation has often been based on diagnosis and treatment. In other words, they've been paid to make you healthy, but not to keep you that way.

Offering financial incentives to doctors, as Hill Physicians has done through its bonus program, is an effort to shift the focus toward better patient care management.

Will performance incentives for doctors work on a broad scale? It's too early to tell. "We currently have a payment system that's very wrong-headed," said Margaret O'Kane, president of the National Committee for Quality Assurance, which accredits managed-care plans and last year began accrediting disease management programs. "The question is how do you get people motivated," she said. "They're running out of tools to drive better quality, and this is a new approach."

SOURCE: Michelle Andrews, "A Doctor's Bonus Could Also Help the Patients," *The New York Times Online* (February 16, 2003).

Managerial and Executive Pay

Because of their significant ability to influence organization performance, top managers and executives are a strategically important group whose compensation warrants special attention. In the previous chapter we discussed how much this group is paid. Here we focus on the issue of how their pay is determined.

Each year *BusinessWeek* publishes a list of top executives who did the most for their pay and those who did the least. The latter group has been the impetus for much of the attention to executive pay. The problem seems to be that in some companies, top executive pay is high every year, regardless of profitability or stock market performance. One study, for example, found that CEO pay changes by $3.25 for every $1,000 change in shareholder wealth. This relationship was interpreted to mean that "the compensation of top executives is virtually independent of corporate performance."[48]

How can executive pay be linked to organization performance? From an agency theory perspective, the goal of owners (shareholders) is to encourage the agents (managers and executives) to act in the best interests of the owners. This may mean less emphasis on noncontingent pay, such as base salary, and more emphasis on outcome-oriented "contracts" that make some portion of executive pay contingent on the organization's profitability or stock performance.[49] Among midlevel and top managers, it is common to use both short-term bonus and long-term incentive plans to encourage the pursuit of both short- and long-term organization performance objectives. Indeed, in the *BusinessWeek* surveys discussed in Chapter 11, the bulk of executive compensation comes from stock options and other forms of long-term compensation.

To what extent do organizations use such pay-for-performance plans, and what are their consequences? Research suggests that organizations vary substantially in the extent to which they use both long-term and short-term incentive programs. Further, greater use of such plans among top and midlevel managers was associated with higher subsequent levels of profitability. As Table 12.8 indicates, greater reliance on short-term bonuses and long-term incentives (relative to base pay) resulted in substantial improvements in return on assets.[50]

Earlier, we saw how the balanced scorecard approach could be applied to paying manufacturing employees. It is also useful in designing executive pay. Table 12.9 shows how the choice of performance measures can be guided by a desire to balance shareholder, customer, and employee objectives. Former Sears CEO Arthur Martinez has described financial results as a lagging indicator that tells the company how it has done in the past, whereas customer and employee metrics like those in Table 12.9 are leading indicators that tell the company how its financial results will be in the future.

TABLE 12.8

The Relationship between Managerial Pay and Organization Return on Assets

		PREDICTED RETURN ON ASSETS	
BONUS/BASE RATIO	LONG-TERM INCENTIVE ELIGIBILITY	%	$[a]
10%	28%	5.2%	$250 million
20	28	5.6	269 million
10	48	5.9	283 million
20	48	7.1	341 million

[a]Based on the assets of the average *Fortune* 500 company in 1990.

SOURCE: B. Gerhart and G. T. Milkovich, "Organizational Differences in Managerial Compensation and Financial Performance," *Academy of Management Journal* 33 (1990), pp. 663–91.

STAKEHOLDER	MEASURES
Shareholder value	Economic value added Earnings per share Cash flow Total cost productivity
Customer value	Quality Market share Customer satisfaction
Employee value	High-performance culture index High-performance culture deployment Training and development diversity

TABLE 12.9

Whirlpool's Three-Stakeholder Scorecard

SOURCE: From E. L. Gubman, *The Talent Solution*, 1998. Copyright © 1998 The McGraw-Hill Companies, Inc. Reproduced with permission of The McGraw-Hill Companies.

Thus, Sears ties its executive compensation to achievement of objectives to "(1) drive profitable growth, (2) become customer-centric, (3) foster the development of a diverse, high-performance culture, and (4) focus on productivity and returns."[51]

Finally, there has been pressure from regulators and shareholders to better link pay and performance since 1992. The Securities and Exchange Commission (SEC) has required companies to more clearly report executive compensation levels and the company's performance relative to that of competitors over a five-year period. The Omnibus Budget Reconciliation Act of 1993 eliminated the deductibility of executive pay that exceeds $1 million. However, most companies have been able to avoid the cap by taking advantage of an exemption for plans that link executive pay to company performance (such as by using stock options).

Large retirement fund investors such as TIAA-CREF and CalPERS have proposed guidelines to better ensure that boards of directors act in shareholders' best interests when making executive pay decisions, rather than being beholden to management. Some of the governance practices believed to be related to director independence from management are shown in Table 12.10. In addition, when a firm's future is at risk, the board may well need to demonstrate its independence from management by taking dramatic action, which may include removing the chief executive.

Process and Context Issues

In Chapter 11 we discussed the importance of process issues such as communication and employee participation. Significant differences in how such issues are handled can be found both across and within organizations, suggesting that organizations have considerable discretion in this aspect of compensation management.[52] As such, it represents another strategic opportunity to distinguish one's organization from the competition.

Employee Participation in Decision Making

Consider employee participation in decision making and its potential consequences. Involvement in the design and implementation of pay policies has been linked to higher pay satisfaction and job satisfaction, presumably because employees have a better understanding of and greater commitment to the policy when they are involved.[53]

TABLE 12.10

Guidelines for Board of Directors Structure and Effective Governance

Interlocking boards	Top executives should not serve on each other's boards. Otherwise, there may be an incentive for executives to heed the Golden Rule too closely.
Outside versus inside directors	Inside directors are part of the management team and thus report to the top executive. Therefore, the number of inside directors should be kept to a minimum. Some committees, such as the nominating committee and the compensation committee, should be composed entirely of outside directors.
Outside directors meet without top executive	Such meetings permit directors to speak freely and consider actions that might be in the best interests of shareholders but unattractive to the top executive.
Director pensions	Directors with pensions may be reluctant to have conflicts with the top executive for fear of losing their directorships and thus their pensions.
Director pay	Directors should be required to own a minimum amount of stock to align their interests with those of shareholders.

SOURCE: Adapted from J. A. Byrne, "The CEO and the Board," *BusinessWeek* (September 15, 1997), p. 12.

What about the effects on productivity? Agency theory provides some insight. The delegation of decision making by a principal to an agent creates agency costs because employees may not act in the best interests of top management. In addition, the more agents there are, the higher the monitoring costs.[54] Together, these suggest that delegation of decision making can be very costly.

On the other hand, agency theory suggests that monitoring would be less costly and more effective if performed by employees because they have knowledge about the workplace and behavior of fellow employees that managers do not have. As such, the right compensation system might encourage self-monitoring and peer monitoring.[55]

Researchers have suggested that two general factors are critical to encouraging such monitoring: monetary incentives (outcome-oriented contracts in agency theory) and an environment that fosters trust and cooperation. This environment, in turn, is a function of employment security, group cohesiveness, and individual rights for employees—in other words, respect for and commitment to employees.[56]

Communication

Another important process issue is communication. Earlier, we spoke of its importance in the administration of merit pay, both from the perspective of procedural fairness and as a means of obtaining the maximum impact from a merit pay program. More generally, a change in any part of the compensation system is likely to give rise to employee concerns. Rumors and assumptions based on poor or incomplete information are always an issue in administering compensation, partly because of its importance to employee economic security and well-being. Therefore, in making any changes, it is crucial to determine how best to communicate reasons for the changes to employees. Some organizations now rely heavily on videotaped messages from the chief executive officer to communicate the rationale for major changes. Brochures that include scenarios for typical employees are also used, as are focus group sessions where small groups of employees are interviewed to obtain feedback about concerns that can be addressed in later communication programs.

Pay and Process: Intertwined Effects

The preceding discussion treats process issues such as participation as factors that may facilitate the success of pay programs. At least one commentator, however, has described an even more important role for process factors in determining employee performance:

> Worker participation apparently helps make alternative compensation plans . . . work better—and also has beneficial effects of its own. . . . It appears that changing the way workers are treated may boost productivity more than changing the way they are paid.[57]

This suggestion raises a broader question: How important are pay decisions, per se, relative to other human resource practices? Although it may not be terribly useful to attempt to disentangle closely intertwined programs, it is important to reinforce the notion that human resource programs, even those as powerful as compensation systems, do not work alone.

Consider gainsharing programs. As described earlier, pay is often only one component of such programs. (See Table 12.6.) How important are the nonpay components?[58] There is ample evidence that gainsharing programs that rely almost exclusively on the monetary component can have substantial effects on productivity.[59] On the other hand, a study of an automotive parts plant found that adding a participation component (monthly meetings with management to discuss the gainsharing plan and ways to increase productivity) to a gainsharing pay incentive plan raised productivity. In a related study, employees were asked about the factors that motivated them to engage in active participation (such as suggestion systems). Employees reported that the desire to earn a monetary bonus was much less important than a number of nonpay factors, particularly the desire for influence and control in how their work was done.[60] A third study reported that productivity and profitability were both enhanced by the addition of employee participation in decisions, beyond the improvement derived from monetary incentives such as gainsharing.[61]

Organization Strategy and Compensation Strategy: A Question of Fit

Although much of our focus has been on the general, or average, effects of different pay programs, it is also useful to think in terms of matching pay strategies to organization strategies. To take an example from medicine, using the same medical treatment regardless of the symptoms and diagnosis would be foolish. In choosing a pay strategy, one must consider how effectively it will further the organization's overall business strategy. Consider again the findings reported in Table 12.8. The average effect of moving from a pay strategy with below-average variability in pay to one with above-average variability is an increase in return on assets of almost two percentage points (from 5.2 percent to 7.1 percent). But in some organizations, the increase could be smaller. In fact, greater variability in pay could contribute to a lower return on assets in some organizations. In other organizations, greater variability in pay could

Technology Alters How Performance Is Gauged— and Rewarded

During the boom, workers often shrugged off annual reviews as exercises in utter meaninglessness. Companies were so desperate to keep people that grade and bonus inflation ran rampant, creating a kind of corporate Lake Wobegon, in which all performances were strong and all cube dwellers above average.

Now, in the New Economy's first recession, the glow is gone as harsh reviews pummel grades, batter bonuses, and often turn the closed-door sessions into tense, stony-faced affairs. True, economists note lots of encouraging data sup-porting an upturn. But by then, many reviews will likely be altered for good. That's because what was once a smushy, subjective effort by finger-in-the-wind managers is hitting new levels of scientific precision—with the help of the latest technology. More and more, companies are turning to Web-enabled employee performance software that allows them to analyze with cold, hard data just how effective their ranks are. Back in the 1980s and 90s, the focus was on business units, with compensation tied to the group's overall performance. Today, tracking software can zoom in on the finest-grained measure of an individual's output, so that everyone from customer service reps to marketing execs can be paid in the modern equivalent of a piece-rate system.

Think of it as a kind of Six Sigma program for human capital. By identifying which workers are best at which skills, companies can quickly assemble the most stellar teams. The technology's performance data help managers identify whom to lay off, thus helping to cut costs and lift productivity—even in the midst of a downturn. Moreover, it's another tool in

contribute to increases in return on assets of greater than two percentage points. Obviously, being able to tell where variable pay works and where it does not could have substantial consequences.

In Chapter 2 we discussed directional business strategies, two of which were growth (internal or external) and concentration ("sticking to the knitting"). How should compensation strategies differ according to whether an organization follows a growth strategy or a concentration strategy? Table 12.11 provides some suggested matches. Basically, a growth strategy's emphasis on innovation, risk taking, and new markets is linked to a pay strategy that shares risk with employees but also gives them the opportunity for high future earnings by having them share in whatever success the organization has. This means relatively low levels of fixed compensation in the short run but the use of bonuses and stock options, for example, that can pay off handsomely in the long run. Stock options have been described as the pay program "that built Silicon Valley," having been used by companies such as Apple, Microsoft, and others.[62] When such companies become successful, everyone from top managers to secretaries can become millionaires if they own stock. Growth organizations are also thought to benefit from a less bureaucratic orientation, in the sense of having more decentralization and flexibility in pay decisions and in recognizing individual skills, rather than being constrained by job or grade classification systems. On the other hand, concentration-oriented organizations are thought to require a very different set

the emerging corporate star system, in which top players are lavished with rewards, while the middling make do with less. It was all part of the larger development in corporate America of transforming labor from a fixed to a more flexible cost.

The methods are attracting a growing group of adherents, including Hewlett-Packard, General Electric, DuPont, and Sun Microsystems. British Airways PLC uses the new software to ensure that customer service reps' time in the break room or on personal calls doesn't count on the clock. Customer-complaint resolutions and ticket sales also are calculated. The technology can keep track so that extra incentive dollars are eventually kicked directly into the paychecks of those whose digital records merit the boost. "We knew how many hours our planes were on the ground or in the air—the productivity of our capital," says Steven Pruneau, British Airways' manager in charge of the project. "But we didn't have a fraction of that kind of information about the productivity of our other assets—our human capital."

While the technology is most commonly deployed in customer service departments, it is reaching into other layers of companies, too. At Hewlett-Packard, a new incentive calculator allows sales and marketing executives to see just how much they'll earn if they double their goals. At Bayer, executives were able to instantly rejigger incentive metrics after the September 11–related run on Cipro. Bayer wanted sales staffers to reap windfalls only if they were putting in extra physician and hospital calls, not just riding on the unprecedented demand.

Critics say these developments can take on an Orwellian cast. Some software experts predict companies will soon be able to blend in the monitoring information they already have—how much time their employees spend pleasure-surfing the Net, what time they arrive at work via their key cards, and what they do when they get there through concealed security cameras—with the new goal data. If that happens, there will likely be a huge dustup over employee privacy. But in the near term, the new technology is bound to make it easier for companies to single out the coasters—as well as identify who the above average really are.

SOURCE: Michelle Conlin, "The Software Says You're Just Average," *BusinessWeek*. Reprinted with permission.

of pay practices by virtue of their lower rate of growth, more stable workforce, and greater need for consistency and standardization in pay decisions. As we saw earlier, Microsoft recently eliminated stock options in favor of stock grants to its employees, in part because it is not the growth company it once was.

PAY STRATEGY DIMENSIONS	ORGANIZATION STRATEGY	
	CONCENTRATION	GROWTH
Risk sharing (variable pay)	Low	High
Time orientation	Short-term	Long-term
Pay level (short run)	Above market	Below market
Pay level (long-run potential)	Below market	Above market
Benefits level	Above market	Below market
Centralization of pay decisions	Centralized	Decentralized
Pay unit of analysis	Job	Skills

TABLE 12.11

Matching Pay Strategy and Organization Strategy

SOURCE: Adapted from L. R. Gomez-Mejia and D. B. Balkin, *Compensation, Organizational Strategy, and Firm Performance* (Cincinnati: South-Western, 1992), Appendix 4b.

A Look Back

In this chapter, we have discussed the potential advantages and disadvantages of different types of incentive or pay for performance plans. We have also seen that these pay plans can have both intended and unintended consequences. Designing a pay for performance strategy typically seeks to balance the pros and cons of different plans and reduce the chance of unintended consequences. To an important degree, pay strategy will depend on the particular goals and strategy of the organization and its units. For example, as we saw at the beginning of the chapter, Microsoft determined that its pay strategy needed to be revised (less emphasis on stock options, more on stock grants) to support a change in its business strategy and to recognize the slower-paced growth of its stock price.

Questions

1. Does money motivate? Use the theories and examples discussed in this chapter to address this question.
2. Think of a job that you have held. Design an incentive plan. What would be the potential advantages and disadvantages of your plan? If your money was invested in the company, would you adopt the plan?

Summary

Our focus in this chapter has been on the design and administration of programs that recognize employee contributions to the organization's success. These programs vary as to whether they link pay to individual, group, or organization performance. Often, it is not so much a choice of one program or the other as it is a choice between different combinations of programs that seek to balance individual, group, and organization objectives.

Wages, bonuses, and other types of pay have an important influence on an employee's standard of living. This carries at least two important implications. First, pay can be a powerful motivator. An effective pay strategy can substantially promote an organization's success; conversely, a poorly conceived pay strategy can have detri-

mental effects. Second, the importance of pay means that employees care a great deal about the fairness of the pay process. A recurring theme is that pay programs must be explained and administered in such a way that employees understand their underlying rationale and believe it is fair.

The fact that organizations differ in their business and human resource strategies suggests that the most effective compensation strategy may differ from one organization to another. Although benchmarking programs against the competition is informative, what succeeds in some organizations may not be a good idea for others. The balanced scorecard suggests the need for organizations to decide what their key objectives are and use pay to support them.

Discussion Questions

1. To compete more effectively, your organization is considering a profit sharing plan to increase employee effort and to encourage employees to think like owners. What are the potential advantages and disadvantages of such a plan? Would the profit sharing plan have the same impact on all types of employees? Is the size of your organization an important consideration? Why? What alternative pay programs should be considered?
2. Gainsharing plans have often been used in manufacturing settings but can also be applied in service or-

ganizations. How could performance standards be developed for gainsharing plans in hospitals, banks, insurance companies, and so forth?
3. Your organization has two business units. One unit is a long-established manufacturer of a product that competes on price and has not been subject to many technological innovations. The other business unit is just being started. It has no products yet, but it is working on developing a new technology for testing the effects of drugs on people via simulation instead of through

lengthy clinical trials. Would you recommend that the two business units have the same pay programs for recognizing individual contributions? Why?

4. The opening vignette describes a change in pay strategy at Microsoft and the Finding and Keeping Employees section also discusses this change as well as similar changes at Dell and Amazon. Do you believe the changes at these companies make sense? What are the potential payoffs and pitfalls of their new pay strategies?

Self-Assessment Exercise

Pay is only one type of incentive that can motivate you to perform well and contribute to your satisfaction at work. This survey will help you understand what motivates you at work. Consider each aspect of work and rate its importance to you, using the following scale: 5 = very important, 4 = somewhat important, 3 = neutral, 2 = somewhat unimportant, 1 = very unimportant.

Salary or wages	1	2	3	4	5
Cash bonuses	1	2	3	4	5
Boss's management style	1	2	3	4	5
Location of workplace	1	2	3	4	5
Commute	1	2	3	4	5
Job security	1	2	3	4	5
Opportunity for advancement	1	2	3	4	5
Work environment	1	2	3	4	5
Level of independence in job	1	2	3	4	5
Level of teamwork required for job	1	2	3	4	5

Other (enter your own):

_____	1	2	3	4	5
_____	1	2	3	4	5
_____	1	2	3	4	5

Which aspects of work received a score of 5? A score of 4? These are the ones you believe motivate you to perform well and make you happy in your job. Which aspects of work received a score of 1 or 2? These are least likely to motivate you. Is pay the only way to motivate you?

SOURCE: Based on the "Job Assessor" found at www.salarymonster.com, accessed August 2002.

Exercising Strategy: Paying for Good Employee Relations

Organizations understand that reaching financial objectives, or satisfying shareholders, depends to a considerable degree on how well they manage relationships with other important stakeholders such as customers and employees. One suggestion has been to link compensation, in part, to customer satisfaction and employee satisfaction. Is this a good idea in the case of employee satisfaction? There is some disagreement on this issue. Eastman Kodak has, since 1995, used employee opinion survey results as one factor in deciding executive bonuses. Likewise, United Airlines, which is employee-owned, is moving to a system where executive bonuses will depend to some degree on employee-satisfaction surveys. Although the idea of rewarding managers for good employee relations has some intuitive appeal, there may be unintended consequences. Indeed, Gordon Bethune, CEO of Continental Airlines, described such an idea as "absolutely stupid." Bethune argues, "Being an effective leader and having a company where people enjoy coming to work is not a popularity contest. When you run popularity contests, you tend to do things that may get you more points. That may not be good for shareholders and may not be good for the company." This is not to say that Bethune and Continental do not see employee relations as an important part of their competitive advantage. Continental was named the 2001 airline of the year by *Air Transport World* and number 18 on Fortune's 2001 list of best companies to work for in America. And many companies use employee opinion survey results to adjust their employee relations policies as needed. Rather, the issue is whether an incentive plan that explicitly rewards employee satisfaction will produce only intended positive consequences or might also produce unintended, less desirable consequences. Eastman Kodak and United are two examples of companies that have decided some direct incentive makes sense, even if it is small relative to other factors (like financial performance) that determine executive pay. Other companies, even those that use strong employee relations as an important source of competitive advantage, have been too concerned about unintended consequences to use explicit incentives.

SOURCE: "Bottom-up Pay: Companies Regularly Survey How Employees Feel about Their Bosses, But They Rarely Use Ratings to Set Compensation," *The Wall Street Journal* (April 6, 2000), pp. R5+.

Questions

1. Should companies worry about employee attitudes? Why or why not?
2. If positive employee attitudes are an objective, should organizations directly link pay incentives to attitudes?

BusinessWeek The CEOs' Gravy Train May Be Drying Up

Finally, Boards Are Reining in Executive Pay and Tying It More to Performance Two years ago, Boise Cascade Corp.'s CEO, George J. Harad, received a large grant of stock options with no strings attached. A rising market, regardless of his performance, would make them worth a tidy sum. But last April, Boise investors staged a small revolt, with 12% backing a resolution to do away with traditional stock options. A few months later, they got the next best thing. Instead of options, the board decided that the bulk of Harad's $9 million 2003 pay package would be paid in restricted stock that vests in 2006. But if he misses his cash-flow targets, he could lose it all. Says Harad: "I have the opportunity to make a lot of money, but only if the company meets the goals."

Across corporate America, boards are getting the message. While big pay packages will continue as long as executives exercise options awarded years ago, they will almost certainly fall in coming years. A mix of forces—from accounting changes to enraged investors—has prompted many compensation committees to make changes likely to keep future increases well below the double-digit gains of the 1990s. Among the reforms: a closer link between pay and performance. "This isn't a transition," says Pearl Meyer, a New York pay adviser. "This is a transformation."

In 2003, CEOs got a taste of the future. Initial results indicate that the overall rise in executive compensation—the first such jump in three years—was modest. Among 252 of the largest U.S. companies in the Standard & Poor's ExecuComp database that have filed proxies so far, average CEO pay was up 5.2% in 2003, to $7.8 million. That tally includes salary, bonus, and stock as well as gains from the exercise of options awarded in earlier years. The key reasons for the increase: Boards awarded bigger bonuses amid a surge in profits and rising stocks allowed many CEOs to cash in once-worthless options. Moreover, more boards are paying CEOs with stock grants, which *BusinessWeek* counts toward compensation, rather than in stock options, which it does not.

Of course, there will always be gravity-defying pay packages. The highest-paid exec so far for 2003 was not even a CEO. Nigel W. Morris, vice chairman of Capital One Financial Corp., cashed in options for a haul of $147.3 million. Among CEOs at companies that have filed their proxies so far, Steven P. Jobs of Apple Computer Inc. comes out on top. Although he can't collect until 2006, Jobs swapped 2.7 million underwater options for a restricted stock grant worth $74.8 million.

In the future, though, such sky-high pay may become the exception. CEOs are no longer being handed huge fistfuls of options, and their current stockpiles are dwindling. At companies such as Alcoa, Verizon Communications, and Sun Microsystems, CEOs saw option grants reduced or replaced by stock. Mandatory option expensing, expected to start in 2005, will keep pressure on boards to reduce grants. "We're going to see more reductions in CEO pay," says PepsiCo Inc. CEO Steven S. Reinemund, who's girding for his own cut in 2004. "Expensing options has caused everyone to focus on it."

The governance reforms of the past three years have also provided a big push. At General Electric Co. and at IBM, which both added independent directors in recent years, boards have performed radical surgery to better tie pay to performance. GE's Jeffrey R. Immelt could lose all 250,000 shares of stock GE awarded him last year unless he meets performance goals. And IBM's Samuel J. Palmisano will get options, but they'll be worthless until the stock rises by 10%. "Shareholders have been uncomfortable with [traditional] options," says J. Randall MacDonald, IBM's senior vice president for human resources. "We listened."

But it's not just boards with fresh blood that are making changes. At Procter & Gamble Co., CEO Alan G. Lafley must now own six times his base salary in P&G stock and hold shares he acquires through option exercises for a year. At Alcoa Inc., the board is reducing option terms from 10 years to 6 and phasing out a "reload" feature that replaces exercised options—potentially reducing CEO Alain J. P. Belda's future pay.

Some Holdouts One reason directors might be getting tougher: They're afraid of losing their jobs. A Securities & Exchange Commission plan would allow big investors to nominate directors in 2005 if this year 35% of shareholders withhold support for a nominee. Proxy advisers Institutional Shareholder Services and Glass Lewis & Co., Big Labor, and mutual funds are all gunning for such directors.

Of course, while most boards are revamping pay, some seem impervious to reform. At SBC Communications Inc., 2003 operating income was down 25% and the stock lagged its peers. Yet CEO Edward E. Whitacre Jr. earned $19.6 million, including a $5.7 million bonus and a $7.2 million stock grant—a 93% increase over 2002. The company notes that net profit jumped 50%, but that was due largely to accounting changes. A spokesman also adds that the increase was justified because Whitacre met all the board's goals, including targets for free cash flow and customer satisfaction.

At Apple, Jobs's $74.8 million options-for-stock swap last March came after a three-year stretch in which the stock plummeted 80%, and then barely moved. What's more, Jobs will receive them in 2006, regardless of performance. But Apple notes he earns just $1 a year in salary and argues that only a third of the three-year grant should be counted in any given year. Moreover, compensation committee chairman William V. Campbell says the stock was intended to keep Jobs, who saved Apple in the late 90s and devised its digital music business, at the helm. Says Campbell: "We did what we thought was a good and fair practice."

There will always be exceptions, but most boards are making changes that will result in fewer riches for CEOs.

Is $7.8 million exorbitant? Probably, but investors can take comfort in the fact that it's unlikely to get much worse.

SOURCE: Louis Lavelle and Diane Brady, "The CEOs' Gravy Train May Be Drying Up," *BusinessWeek Online* (April 5, 2004).

Questions
1. Have CEOs been overpaid? Why or why not?
2. How can boards of directors and their governance procedures be structured so as to better serve shareholders? Should they serve other stakeholders as well?
3. What are your predictions for the future regarding the level and appropriateness of CEO pay?

Please see the video case at the end of the book that corresponds to this chapter: Container Store: Working for the Best.

Notes

1. We draw freely in this chapter on several literature reviews: B. Gerhart and G. T. Milkovich, "Employee Compensation: Research and Practice," in *Handbook of Industrial and Organizational Psychology*, vol. 3, 2nd ed., ed. M. D. Dunnette and L. M. Hough (Palo Alto, CA: Consulting Psychologists Press, 1992); B. Gerhart and S. L. Rynes, *Compensation: Theory, Evidence, and Strategic Implications* (Thousand Oaks, CA: Sage, 2003).

2. B. Gerhart and G. T. Milkovich, "Organizational Differences in Managerial Compensation and Financial Performance," *Academy of Management Journal* 33 (1990), pp. 663–91; B. Gerhart, "Compensation Strategy and Organization Performance," in S. L. Rynes and B. Gerhart, eds., *Compensation in Organizations: Current Research and Practice* (San Francisco: Jossey-Bass, 2000), pp. 151–94.

3. E. Deci and R. Ryan, *Intrinsic Motivation and Self-Determination in Human Behavior* (New York: Plenum, 1985); A. Kohn, "Why Incentive Plans Cannot Work," *Harvard Business Review*, September–October 1993.

4. R. Eisenberger and J. Cameron "Detrimental Effects of Reward: Reality or Myth?" *American Psychologist* 51, no. 11 (1996), pp. 1153–66; S. L. Rynes, B. Gerhart, and L. Parks, "Personnel Psychology: Performance Evaluation and Compensation," *Annual Review of Psychology* (2005).

5. R. A. Lambert and D. F. Larcker, "Executive Compensation, Corporate Decision Making, and Shareholder Wealth," in *Executive Compensation*, ed. F. Foulkes (Boston: Harvard Business School Press, 1989), pp. 287–309.

6. L. R. Gomez-Mejia, H. Tosi, and T. Hinkin, "Managerial Control, Performance, and Executive Compensation," *Academy of Management Journal* 30 (1987), pp. 51–70; H. L. Tosi Jr. and L. R. Gomez-Mejia, "The Decoupling of CEO Pay and Performance: An Agency Theory Perspective," *Administrative Science Quarterly* 34 (1989), pp. 169–89.

7. K. M. Eisenhardt, "Agency Theory: An Assessment and Review," *Academy of Management Review* 14 (1989), pp. 57–74.

8. R. E. Hoskisson, M. A. Hitt, and C.W. L. Hill, "Managerial Incentives and Investment in R&D in Large Multiproduct Firms," *Organizational Science* 4 (1993), pp. 325–41; M. Bloom and G. T. Milkovich, "Relationships among Risk, Incentive Pay, and Organizational Performance," *Academy of Management Journal* 41 (1998), pp. 283–97.

9. Eisenhardt, "Agency Theory."

10. Ibid.; E. J. Conlon and J. M. Parks, "Effects of Monitoring and Tradition on Compensation Arrangements: An Experiment with Principal–Agent Dyads," *Academy of Management Journal* 33 (1990), pp. 603–22; K. M. Eisenhardt, "Agency- and Institutional-Theory Explanations: The Case of Retail Sales Compensation," *Academy of Management Journal* 31 (1988), pp. 488–511; Gerhart and Milkovich, "Employee Compensation."

11. G. T. Milkovich, J. Hannon, and B. Gerhart, "The Effects of Research and Development Intensity on Managerial Compensation in Large Organizations," *Journal of High Technology Management Research* 2 (1991), pp. 133–50.

12. G. T. Milkovich and A. K. Wigdor, *Pay for Performance* (Washington, DC: National Academy Press, 1991); Gerhart and Milkovich, "Employee Compensation"; Gerhart and Rynes, *Compensation: Theory, Evidence, and Strategic Implications*.

13. C. Trevor, B. Gerhart, and J. W. Boudreau, "Voluntary Turnover and Job Performance: Curvilinearity and the Moderating Influences of Salary Growth and Promotions," *Journal of Applied Psychology* 82 (1997), pp. 44–61.

14. R. D. Bretz, R. A. Ash, and G. F. Dreher, "Do People Make the Place? An Examination of the Attraction–Selection–Attrition Hypothesis," *Personnel Psychology* 42 (1989), pp. 561–81; T. A. Judge and R. D. Bretz, "Effect of Values on Job Choice Decisions," *Journal of Applied Psychology* 77 (1992), pp. 261–71; D. M. Cable and T. A. Judge, "Pay Performances and Job Search Decisions: A Person–Organization Fit Perspective," *Personnel Psychology* 47 (1994), pp. 317–48.

15. E. E. Lawler III, *Strategic Pay* (San Francisco: Jossey-Bass, 1990);

Gerhart and Milkovich, "Employee Compensation"; Gerhart and Rynes, *Compensation: Theory, Evidence, and Strategic Implications.*

16. R. D. Bretz, G. T. Milkovich, and W. Read, "The Current State of Performance Appraisal Research and Practice," *Journal of Management* 18 (1992), pp. 321–52; R. L. Heneman, "Merit Pay Research," *Research in Personnel and Human Resource Management* 8 (1990), pp. 203–63; Milkovich and Wigdor, *Pay for Performance;* Rynes, Gerhart, and Parks, "Personnel Psychology: Performance Evaluation and Compensation."

17. Bretz et al., "Current State of Performance Appraisal."

18. Ibid.

19. Ibid.

20. W. E. Deming, *Out of the Crisis* (Cambridge, MA: Center for Advanced Engineering Study, Massachusetts Institute of Technology, 1986), p. 110.

21. Ibid.

22. Ibid.

23. Trevor et al., "Voluntary Turnover."

24. Rynes and Gerhart, *Compensation: Theory, Evidence, and Strategic Implications.*

25. Rynes, Gerhart, and Parks, "Personnel Psychology: Performance Evaluation and Compensation."

26. R. Folger and M. A. Konovsky, "Effects of Procedural and Distributive Justice on Reactions to Pay Raise Decisions," *Academy of Management Journal* 32 (1989), pp. 115–30; J. Greenberg, "Determinants of Perceived Fairness of Performance Evaluations," *Journal of Applied Psychology* 71 (1986), pp. 340–42.

27. Rynes, Gerhart, and Parks, "Personnel Psychology: Performance Evaluation and Compensation."

28. B. Gerhart and S. Rynes, "Determinants and Consequences of Salary Negotiations by Graduating Male and Female MBAs," *Journal of Applied Psychology* (1991), pp. 256–62; Gerhart and Rynes, *Compensation: Theory, Evidence, and Strategic Implications.*

29. E. A. Locke, D. B. Feren, V. M. McCaleb, K. N. Shaw, and A. T. Denny, "The Relative Effectiveness of Four Methods of Motivating Employee Performance," in *Changes in Working Life,* ed. K. D. Duncan, M. M. Gruenberg, and D. Wallis (New York: Wiley, 1980), pp. 363–88; for a summary of additional evidence, see also Gerhart and Rynes, *Compensation: Theory, Evidence, and Strategic Implications.*

30. Gerhart and Milkovich, "Employee Compensation."

31. This idea has been referred to as the "share economy." See M. L. Weitzman, "The Simple Macroeconomics of Profit Sharing," *American Economic Review* 75 (1985), pp. 937–53. For supportive empirical evidence, see the following studies: J. Chelius and R. S. Smith, "Profit Sharing and Employment Stability," *Industrial and Labor Relations Review* 43 (1990), pp. 256S–73S; B. Gerhart and L. O. Trevor, "Employment Stability under Different Managerial Compensation Systems," working paper 1995 (Cornell University: Center for Advanced Human Resource Studies); D. L. Kruse, "Profit Sharing and Employment Variability: Microeconomic Evidence on the Weitzman Theory," *Industrial and Labor Relations Review* 44 (1991), pp. 437–53.

32. Gerhart and Milkovich, "Employee Compensation"; M. L. Weitzman and D. L. Kruse, "Profit Sharing and Productivity," in *Paying for Productivity,* ed. A. S. Blinder (Washington, DC: Brookings Institution, 1990); D. L. Kruse, *Profit Sharing: Does It Make a Difference?* (Kalamazoo, MI: Upjohn Institute, 1993).

33. "GM/UAW: The Battle Goes On," *Ward's Auto World* (May 1995), p. 40; E. M. Coates III, "Profit Sharing Today: Plans and Provisions," *Monthly Labor Review* (April 1991), pp. 19–25.

34. Gerhart and Rynes, *Compensation: Theory, Evidence, and Strategic Implications.*

35. American Management Association, *CompFlash,* April 1991, p. 3.

36. "Executive Compensation: Taking Stock," *Personnel* 67 (December 1990), pp. 7–8; "Another Day, Another Dollar Needs Another Look," *Personnel* 68 (January 1991), pp. 9–13.

37. Gerhart and Milkovich, "Organizational Differences in Managerial Compensation."

38. *EBRI Databook on Employee Benefits* (Washington, DC: Employee Benefit Research Institute, 1995). www.nceo.org (National Center for Employee Ownership website).

39. D. Jones and T. Kato, "The Productivity Effects of Employee Stock Ownership Plans and Bonuses: Evidence from Japanese Panel Data," *American Economic Review* 185, no. 3 (June 1995), pp. 391–414.

40. "Employees Left Holding the Bag," *Fortune* (May 20, 1991), pp. 83–93; M. A. Conte and J. Svejnar, "The Performance Effects of Employee Ownership Plans," in *Paying for Productivity,* pp. 245–94.

41. Conte and Svejnar, "Performance Effects of Employee Ownership Plans."

42. Ibid.; T. H. Hammer, "New Developments in Profit Sharing, Gainsharing, and Employee Ownership," in *Productivity in Organizations,* ed. J. P. Campbell, R. J. Campbell and Associates (San Francisco: Jossey-Bass, 1988); K. J. Klein, "Employee Stock Ownership and Employee Attitudes: A Test of Three Models," *Journal of Applied Psychology* 72 (1987), pp. 319–32.

43. J. L. Pierce, S. Rubenfeld, and S. Morgan, "Employee Ownership: A Conceptual Model of Process and Effects," *Academy of Management Review* 16 (1991), pp. 121–44.

44. R. T. Kaufman, "The Effects of Improshare on Productivity," *Industrial and Labor Relations Review* 45 (1992), pp. 311–22; M. H. Schuster, "The Scanlon Plan: A Longitudinal Analysis," *Journal of Applied Behavioral Science* 20 (1984), pp. 23–28; M. M. Petty, B. Singleton, and D. W. Connell, "An Experimental Evaluation of an Organizational Incentive Plan in the Electric Utility Industry," *Journal of Applied Psychology* 77 (1992), pp. 427–36; W. N. Cooke, "Employee Participation Programs, Group-Based Incentives, and Company Performance: A Union–Nonunion Comparison," *Industrial and Labor Relations Review* 47 (1994), pp. 594–609; J. B. Arthur and L. Aiman-Smith, "Gainsharing and Organizational Learning: An Analysis of Employee Suggestions over Time," *Academy of Management Journal* 44 (2001), pp. 737–54; J. B. Arthur and G. S. Jelf, "The Effects of Gainsharing on Grievance Rates and Absenteeism over Time," *Journal of Labor Research* 20 (1999), pp. 133–45.

45. T. L. Ross and R. A. Ross, "Gainsharing: Sharing Improved Performance," in *The Compensation Handbook,* 3rd ed., ed. M. L. Rock and L. A. Berger (New York: McGraw-Hill, 1991).

46. T. M. Welbourne and L. R. Gomez-Mejia, "Team Incentives in the Workplace," in *The Compensation Handbook,* 3rd ed.

47. R. S. Kaplan and D. P. Norton "Using the Balanced Scorecard as a Strategic Management System," *Harvard Business Review,* January–February 1996, pp. 75–85.

48. M. C. Jensen and K. J. Murphy, "Performance Pay and Top-Management Incentives," *Journal of Political Economy* 98 (1990), pp. 225–64; A stronger relationship between CEO pay and performance was found by R. K. Aggarwal and A. A. Samwick, "The Other Side of the Trade-off: The Impact of Risk on Executive Compensation," *Journal of Political Economy* 107 (1999), pp. 65–105. Also, these observed relationships actually translate into significant changes in CEO pay in response to

modest changes in financial performance of a company, as made clear by Gerhart and Rynes, *Compensation: Theory, Evidence, and Strategic Implications*.

49. M. C. Jensen and K. J. Murphy, "CEO Incentives—It's Not How Much You Pay, but How," *Harvard Business Review* 68 (May–June 1990), pp. 138–53. The definitive resource on executive pay is B. R. Ellis, *The Complete Guide to Executive Compensation* (New York: McGraw-Hill, 2002).

50. Gerhart and Milkovich, "Organizational Differences in Managerial Compensation."

51. Sears and Roebuck proxy statement to shareholders, March 22, 2004. Available at www.sec.gov.

52. J. Cutcher-Gershenfeld, "The Impact on Economic Performance of a Transformation in Workplace Relations," *Industrial and Labor Relations Review* 44 (1991), pp. 241–60; Irene Goll, "Environment, Corporate Ideology, and Involvement Programs," *Industrial Relations* 30 (1991), pp. 138–49.

53. L. R. Gomez-Mejia and D. B. Balkin, *Compensation, Organizational Strategy, and Firm Performance* (Cincinnati: South-Western, 1992); G. D. Jenkins and E. E. Lawler III, "Impact of Employee Participation in Pay Plan Development," *Organizational Behavior and Human Performance* 28 (1981), pp. 111–28.

54. D. I. Levine and L. D. Tyson, "Participation, Productivity, and the Firm's Environment," in *Paying for Productivity*.

55. T. Welbourne, D. Balkin, and L. Gomez-Mejia, "Gainsharing and Mutual Monitoring: A Combined Agency–Organizational Justice Interpretation," *Academy of Management Journal* 38 (1995), pp. 881–99.

56. Ibid.

57. Blinder, *Paying for Productivity*.

58. Hammer, "New Developments in Profit Sharing"; Milkovich and Wigdor, *Pay for Performance*; D. J. B. Mitchell, D. Lewin, and E. E. Lawler III, "Alternative Pay Systems, Firm Performance and Productivity," in *Paying for Productivity*.

59. Kaufman, "The Effects of Improshare on Productivity"; M. H. Schuster, "The Scanlon Plan: A Longitudinal Analysis," *Journal of Applied Behavioral Science* 20 (1984), pp. 23–28; J. A. Wagner III, P. Rubin, and T. J. Callahan, "Incentive Payment and Non-managerial Productivity: An Interrupted Time Series Analysis of Magnitude and Trend," *Organizational Behavior and Human Decision Processes* 42 (1988), pp. 47–74.

60. C. R. Gowen III and S. A. Jennings, "The Effects of Changes in Participation and Group Size on Gainsharing Success: A Case Study," *Journal of Organizational Behavior Management* 11 (1991), pp. 147–69.

61. L. Hatcher, T. L. Ross, and D. Collins, "Attributions for Participation and Nonparticipation in Gainsharing-Plan Involvement Systems," *Group and Organization Studies* 16 (1991), pp. 25–43; Mitchell et al., "Alternative Pay Systems."

62. A. J. Baker, "Stock Options—a Perk That Built Silicon Valley," *The Wall Street Journal* (June 23, 1993), p. A20.

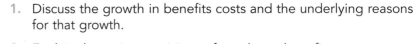

13

Chapter

Employee Benefits

Objectives After reading this chapter, you should be able to:

1. Discuss the growth in benefits costs and the underlying reasons for that growth.

2. Explain the major provisions of employee benefits programs.

3. Describe the effects of benefits management on cost and workforce quality.

4. Discuss how employee benefits in the United States compare with those in other countries.

5. Explain the importance of effectively communicating the nature and value of benefits to employees.

6. Describe the regulatory constraints that affect the way employee benefits are designed and administered.

Rising health care costs are a big concern to employees. What can employers do to try to reduce the costs that are passed on to their workers?

Enter the World of Business

Shifting Burden Helps Employers Cut Health Costs

Employers slowed their runaway health-care costs more sharply than expected this year, but they did it mostly by shifting an unprecedented share of the expense to employees.

The average cost of employer health plans rose 10 percent per employee in 2003, less than the 14 percent that was predicted heading into 2003, a new survey of 3,000 employers found. Earlier surveys this year indicated that soaring costs were finally slowing after several years of ever-larger increases. But the new study, conducted by Mercer Human Resource Consulting, offers a more comprehensive picture of 2003 health care costs and suggests employers have been even more successful at reining in health care expenses than anticipated.

Still, health care costs continued to climb at a double-digit pace. And without raising employees' premium contributions and deductibles and trimming coverage, employers wouldn't have seen costs slow much at all. "The last three or four years, employers really didn't pass on much of the cost increases," says Blaine Bos, a Mercer health benefits consultant. But this year, "they took out their scalpels."

Another wave of cost shifting is likely next year. A quarter of the companies surveyed said they expected to increase employee contributions, and 23 percent said they would pass on more costs by making changes to the health plans they offer workers. Nonetheless, companies in the survey said they anticipate that their health care costs in 2004 will surge again, this time by 13 percent. Mr. Bos notes that chief financial officers at many companies believe that unless they are able to cut annual health benefit cost increases to 8 percent sometime soon, those costs soon will become unsustainable. "But that's very difficult to do without creating a huge disruption with your work force," he says.

Some employers, particularly larger ones, are trying to find additional solutions to the rising costs, rather than just passing them on to employees. The number of companies that adopted disease-management programs for employees' chronic conditions and other wellness initiatives to make workforces healthier jumped this year. "To the extent these bear fruit, we may see a lessening of more draconian measures over time," Mr. Bos says.

In the meantime, though, the struggle over shifting costs has made health benefits a hot-button issue at companies around the country. In California, 70,000 workers at several grocery chains, including Albertsons Inc., Kroger Co. and Safeway Inc., have been involved in a protracted strike over proposed cuts to their health care. The three grocers say that competition from Wal-Mart Inc. requires them to cut costs.

At Lucent Technologies Inc., hundreds of retired workers reacted angrily earlier this fall to plans to raise premiums and make other benefit cuts. The Murray Hill, N.J., company says that after watching its health benefit expenses soar 50 percent in the past five years, it had no choice. Health benefits for Lucent's retirees and their dependents alone cost the company $850 million a year, about 10 percent of the company's annual revenue.

"We are still committed to a subsidy for our retirees' health benefits, but we have had to make some changes," says Bill Price, a Lucent spokesman. "We have to make sure we're going to be around as a competitive company to offer those benefits in the first place."

Many companies have been paring, and even phasing out, retiree benefits for years. According to the survey, only 21 percent of large employers still offered medical coverage to Medicare-eligible retirees, down from 40 percent a decade ago. Just 28 percent offered coverage to early retirees, compared with 46 percent 10 years ago.

Cost shifting by employers is prompting some employees to cut back on their use of prescription drugs and other medical care rather than absorb the extra costs. In a study of two employer plans published last week in the *New England Journal of Medicine,* in some cases as many as half of the employees changed from an expensive drug to a cheaper generic one after

their employers switched to plans that charged more for brand-name medications. But many other employees quit filling prescriptions for chronic conditions, with as many as 21 percent at one employer, for example, giving up taking cholesterol-lowering statins.

The researchers, from Harvard Medical School and pharmacy-benefit manager Medco Health Solutions Inc., said it was unclear how the switch has affected people's health.

One company taking a longer-term approach to the problem of rising health benefit costs is Worthington Industries Inc., a Columbus, Ohio, metal-processing company. Worthington hadn't charged employees a monthly premium for their health benefits, but after health care costs rose 30 percent last year and another 14 percent this year, the company decided "we really needed to start sharing the costs," says John McConnell, Worthington's chairman and chief executive.

This fall, the company said it would begin charging $25 a month for individual employees and $50 for family coverage. Employees don't have to pay, though, if they join the company's new health-management program administered by Gordian Health Solutions Inc. In the program workers set health-related goals, such as losing weight, reducing cholesterol levels, or quitting smoking.

So far, 65 percent of Worthington's 3,500 U.S. employees have signed up. "We're not just going to shift costs," Mr. McConnell says. "We're taking a longer-term view."

Source: Vanessa Fuhrmans, "Shifting Burden Helps Employers Cut Health Costs," *The Wall Street Journal Online* (December 8, 2003).

Introduction

If we think of benefits as a part of total employee compensation, many of the concepts discussed in the two previous chapters on employee compensation apply here as well. This means, for example, that both cost and behavioral objectives are important. The cost of benefits adds an average of 37 percent to every dollar of payroll, thus account-ing for about 27 percent of the total employee compensation package. Controlling labor costs is not possible without controlling benefits costs. When General Motors pays $1300 in health care costs per car produced, more than it spends on steel, its ability to sell automobiles at a competitive price is challenged, when health care costs per vehicle are $180 at Toyota (U.S. plants), and $107 at Honda (U.S. plants).[1] On the behavioral side, benefits seem to influence whether potential employees come to work for a company, whether they stay, when they retire—perhaps even how they perform (although the empirical evidence, especially on the latter point, is surprisingly limited). Different employees look for different types of benefits. Employers need to regularly reexamine their benefits to see whether they fit the needs of today rather than yesterday. The chapter opening story indicates that some employers are shifting growing benefits costs to employees. Other companies have managed to avoid this. All must deal with the issue.

Although it makes sense to think of benefits as part of total compensation, benefits have unique aspects. First, there is the question of legal compliance. Although direct compensation is subject to government regulation, the scope and impact of regulation on benefits is far greater. Some benefits, such as Social Security, are mandated by law. Others, although not mandated, are subject to significant regulation or must meet certain criteria to achieve the most favorable tax treatment; these include pensions and savings plans. The heavy involvement of government in benefits decisions reflects the central role benefits play in maintaining economic security.

A second unique aspect of benefits is that organizations so typically offer them that they have come to be institutionalized. Providing medical and retirement benefits of some sort has become almost obligatory for many employers. A large employer that did not offer such benefits to its full-time employees would be highly unusual, and the employer might well have trouble attracting and retaining a quality workforce. However, the chapter opening story provides an example of how the relationship between employers and employees is changing and how it may influence the types of benefits offered. The story also shows how serious the consequences can be if employers and employees do not recognize the risks that particular benefits decisions may create.

A third unique aspect of benefits, compared with other forms of compensation, is their complexity. It is relatively easy to understand the value of a dollar as part of a salary, but not as part of a benefits package. The advantages and disadvantages of different types of medical coverage, pension provisions, disability insurance, and so forth are often difficult to grasp, and their value (beyond a general sense that they are good to have) is rarely as clear as the value of one's salary. Most fundamentally, employees may not even be aware of the benefits available to them; and if they are aware, they may not understand how to use them. When employers spend large sums of money on benefits but employees do not understand the benefits or attach much value to them, the return on employers' benefits investment will be fairly dismal.[2] Thus, another reason for giving more responsibility to employees for retirement planning and other benefits is to increase their understanding of the value of such benefits.

Reasons for Benefits Growth

In thinking about benefits as part of total compensation, a basic question arises: Why do employers choose to channel a significant portion of the compensation dollar away from cash (wages and salaries) into benefits? Economic theory tells us that people prefer a dollar in cash over a dollar's worth of any specific commodity because the cash can be used to purchase the commodity or something else.[3] Thus cash is less restrictive. Several factors, however, have contributed to less emphasis on cash and more on

FIGURE 13.1

Growth of Employee Benefits, Percentage of Wages and Salaries, 1929–99

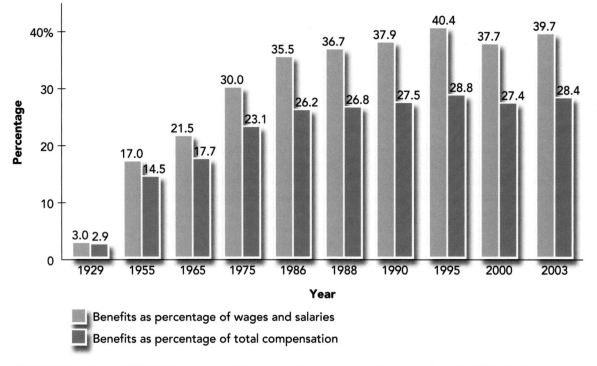

SOURCE: Data through 1990, U.S. Chamber of Commerce Research Center, *Employee Benefits 1990, Employee Benefits 1997, Employee Benefits 2000* (Washington, DC: U.S. Chamber of Commerce, 1991, 1997, and 2000). Data from 1995 onward, "Employer Cost for Employer Compensation," www.bls.gov.

benefits in compensation. To understand these factors, it is useful to examine the growth in benefits over time and the underlying reasons for that growth.

Figure 13.1 gives an indication of the overall growth in benefits. Note that in 1929, on the eve of the Great Depression, benefits added an average of only 3 percent to every dollar of payroll. By 1955 this figure had grown to 17 percent, and it has continued to grow, now accounting for about 40 cents on top of every payroll dollar.

Many factors contributed to this tremendous growth.[4] First, during the 1930s several laws were passed as part of Franklin Roosevelt's New Deal, a legislative program aimed at buffering people from the devastating effects of the Great Depression. The Social Security Act and other legislation established legally required benefits (such as the Social Security retirement system) and modified the tax structure in such a way as to effectively make other benefits—such as workers' compensation (for work-related injuries) and unemployment insurance—mandatory. Second, wage and price controls instituted during World War II, combined with labor market shortages, forced employers to think of new ways to attract and retain employees. Because benefits were not covered by wage controls, employers channeled more resources in this direction. Once institutionalized, such benefits tended to remain even after wage and price controls were lifted.

Third, the tax treatment of benefits programs is often more favorable for employees than the tax treatment of wages and salaries, meaning that a dollar spent on benefits has the potential to generate more value for the employees than the same dollar

	NOMINAL TAX RATE	EFFECTIVE TAX RATE
Federal	25.0%	25.0%
State (New York)	6.8	5.1
City (New York)	3.7	2.8
Social Security	6.2	6.2
Medicare	1.45	1.45
Total tax rate		40.55

TABLE 13.1

Example of Marginal Tax Rates for an Employee Salary of $50,000

Note: State and city taxes are deductible on the federal tax return, reducing their effective tax rate.

spent on wages and salaries. The **marginal tax rate** is the percentage of additional earnings that goes to taxes. Consider the hypothetical employee in Table 13.1 and the effect on take-home pay of a $1,000 increase in salary. The total effective marginal tax rate is higher for higher-paid employees and also varies according to state and city. (New York State and New York City are among the highest.) A $1,000 annual raise for the employee earning $50,000 per year would increase net pay $594.50 ($1,000 × [1 − .4055]). In contrast, an extra $1,000 put into benefits would lead to an increase of $1,000 in "take-home benefits."

Employers, too, realize tax advantages from certain types of benefits. Although both cash compensation and most benefits are deductible as operating expenses, employers (like employees) pay Social Security tax on salaries below a certain amount ($87,900 in 2004) and Medicare tax on the entire salary, as well as other taxes like workers' compensation and unemployment compensation. However, no such taxes are paid on most employee benefits. The bottom line is that the employer may be able to provide more value to employees by spending the extra $1,000 on benefits instead of salary.

The tax advantage of benefits also takes another form. Deferring compensation until retirement allows the employee to receive cash, but at a time (retirement) when the employee's tax rate is sometimes lower because of a lower income level. More important, perhaps, is that investment returns on the deferred money typically accumulate tax free, resulting in much faster growth of the investment.

A fourth factor that has influenced benefits growth is the cost advantage that groups typically realize over individuals. Organizations that represent large groups of employees can purchase insurance (or self-insure) at a lower rate because of economies of scale, which spread fixed costs over more employees to reduce the cost per person. Insurance risks can be more easily pooled in large groups, and large groups can also achieve greater bargaining power in dealing with insurance carriers or medical providers.

A fifth factor influencing the growth of benefits was the growth of organized labor from the 1930s through the 1950s. This growth was partly a result of another piece of New Deal legislation, the National Labor Relations Act, which greatly enhanced trade unions' ability to organize workers and negotiate contracts with employers. Benefits were often a key negotiation objective. (Indeed, they still are. It is estimated that more than half of workers who struck in the early 1990s did so over health care coverage issues.)[5] Unions were able to successfully pursue their members' interests in benefits, particularly when tax advantages provided an incentive for employers to shift money from cash to benefits. For unions, a new benefit such as medical coverage was

Marginal tax rate
The percentage of an additional dollar of earnings that goes to taxes.

TABLE 13.2

Differentiating via Benefits

CMP Media	$30,000 for infertility treatments or adoption
Fannie Mae	10 paid hours per month for volunteer work
Microstrategy	One-week Caribbean cruise each January
Eli Lilly	Free Lilly drugs (including Prozac)
Pfizer	Free Pfizer drugs (including Viagra)
Intel	Eight-week sabbatical after seven years

SOURCE: From "100 Best Companies to Work For," *Fortune.* Copyright © 2001 Time, Inc. All rights reserved.

a tangible success that could have more impact on prospective union members than a wage increase of equivalent value, which might have amounted to only a cent or two per hour. Also, many nonunion employers responded to the threat of unionization by implementing the same benefits for their own employees, thus contributing to benefits growth.

Finally, employers may also provide unique benefits as a means of differentiating themselves in the eyes of current or prospective employees. In this way, employers communicate key aspects of their culture that set them apart from the rest of the pack. Table 13.2 shows some examples.

Benefits Programs

Most benefits fall into one of the following categories: social insurance, private group insurance, retirement, pay for time not worked, and family-friendly policies.[6] Table 13.3, based on Bureau of Labor Statistics (BLS) data, provides an overview of the prevalence of specific benefits programs. As Table 13.3 shows, the percentage of employees covered by these benefits programs increases with employer size. Among the largest employers, these percentages would be higher still.

TABLE 13.3

Percentage of Full-Time Workers in U.S. Private Sector Who Participated in Selected Benefits Programs, 2003

	ESTABLISHMENTS HAVING 100 WORKERS OR MORE	ESTABLISHMENTS HAVING LESS THAN 100 WORKERS
Medical care	55%	36%
Dental care	44	21
Short-term disability insurance	50	26
Long-term disability insurance	40	18
All retirement	65	35
Defined benefit pension	33	8
Defined contribution plan	51	31
Life insurance	64	33
Paid leave		
Holidays	86	74
Vacation	87	73

SOURCE: http://stats.bls.gov/ebshome.htm.

Social Insurance (Legally Required)

Social Security

Among the most important provisions of the Social Security Act of 1935 was the establishment of old-age insurance and unemployment insurance. The act was later amended to add survivor's insurance (1939), disability insurance (1956), hospital insurance (Medicare Part A, 1965), and supplementary medical insurance (Medicare Part B, 1965) for the elderly. Together these provisions constitute the federal Old Age, Survivors, Disability, and Health Insurance (OASDHI) program. Over 90 percent of U.S. employees are covered by the program, the main exceptions being railroad and federal, state, and local government employees, who often have their own plans. Note, however, that an individual employee must meet certain eligibility requirements to receive benefits. To be fully insured typically requires 40 quarters of covered employment and minimum earnings of $900 per quarter in 2004. However, the eligibility rules for survivors' and disability benefits are somewhat different.

Social Security retirement (old-age insurance) benefits for fully insured workers begin at age 65 and 6 months (full benefits) or age 62 (at a permanent reduction in benefits) for those born in 1940. The full retirement age now rises with birth year, reaching age 67 for those born in 1960 or later. Although the amount of the benefit depends on one's earnings history, benefits go up very little after a certain level (the maximum monthly benefit in 2004 was $1,825); thus high earners help subsidize benefit payments to low earners. Cost-of-living increases are provided each year that the consumer price index increases.

An important attribute of the Social Security retirement benefit is that it is free from state tax in about half of the states and entirely free from federal tax. However, the federal tax code has an earnings test for those who are still earning wages (and not yet at full retirement age). In 2004, beneficiaries ages 62–64 were allowed to make $11,640; in the year an individual reaches full retirement age, the earnings test is $31,080. If these amounts are exceeded, the Social Security benefit is reduced $1 for every $2 in excess earnings for those ages 62 to 64 and $1 for every $3 in the year a worker turns 65. These provisions are important because of their effects on the work decisions of those between 62 and full retirement age. The earnings test increases a person's incentive to retire (otherwise full Social Security benefits are not received), and if she continues to work, the incentive to work part-time rather than full-time increases.

A major change made in January 2000 is that there is no earnings test once full retirement age is reached. Therefore, these workers no longer incur any earnings penalty (and thus have no tax-related work disincentive).

How are retirement and other benefits financed? Both employers and employees are assessed a payroll tax. In 2004, each paid a tax of 7.65 percent (a total of 15.3 percent) on the first $87,900 of the employee's earnings. Of the 7.65 percent, 6.2 percent funds OASDHI, and 1.45 percent funds Medicare (Part A). In addition, the 1.45 percent Medicare tax is assessed on all earnings.

What are the behavioral consequences of Social Security benefits? Because they are legally mandated, employers do not have discretion in designing this aspect of their benefits programs. However, Social Security does affect employees' retirement decisions. The eligibility age for benefits and any tax penalty for earnings influence retirement decisions. The elimination of the tax penalty on earnings for those at full retirement age should mean a larger pool of older workers in the labor force for employers to tap into.

Unemployment Insurance

Established by the 1935 Social Security Act, this program has four major objectives: (1) to offset lost income during involuntary unemployment, (2) to help unemployed workers find new jobs, (3) to provide an incentive for employers to stabilize employment, and (4) to preserve investments in worker skills by providing income during short-term layoffs (which allows workers to return to their employer rather than start over with another employer).

The unemployment insurance program is financed largely through federal and state taxes on employers. Although, strictly speaking, the decision to establish the program is left to each state, the Social Security Act created a tax incentive structure that quickly led every state to establish a program. The federal tax rate is currently 0.8 percent on the first $7,000 of wages. The state tax rate varies, the minimum being 5.4 percent on the first $7,000 of wages. Many states have a higher rate or impose the tax on a greater share of earnings.[7]

A very important feature of the unemployment insurance program is that no state imposes the same tax on every employer. Instead, the size of the tax depends on the employer's experience rating. Employers that have a history of laying off a large share of their workforces pay higher taxes than those who do not. In some states, an employer that has had very few layoffs may pay no state tax. In contrast, an employer with a poor experience rating could pay a tax as high as 5 to 10 percent, depending on the state.[8]

Unemployed workers are eligible for benefits if they (1) have a prior attachment to the workforce (often 52 weeks or four quarters of work at a minimum level of pay), (2) are available for work, (3) are actively seeking work (including registering at the local unemployment office), and (4) were not discharged for cause (such as willful misconduct), did not quit voluntarily, and are not out of work because of a labor dispute.

Benefits also vary by state, but they are typically about 50 percent of a person's earnings and last for 26 weeks. Extended benefits for up to 13 weeks are also available in states with a sustained unemployment rate above 6.5 percent. Emergency extended benefits are also sometimes funded by Congress. All states have minimum and maximum weekly benefit levels. In contrast to Social Security retirement benefits, unemployment benefits are taxed as ordinary income.

Because unemployment insurance is, in effect, legally required, management's discretion is limited here, too. Management's main task is to keep its experience rating low by avoiding unnecessary workforce reductions (by relying, for example, on the sorts of actions described in Chapter 5).

Workers' Compensation

Workers' compensation laws cover job-related injuries and death.[9] Prior to enactment of these laws, workers suffering work-related injuries or diseases could receive compensation only by suing for damages. Moreover, the common-law defenses available to employers meant that such lawsuits were not usually successful. In contrast, these laws operate under a principle of no-fault liability, meaning that an employee does not need to establish gross negligence by the employer. In return, employers receive immunity from lawsuits. (One exception is the employer who intentionally contributes to a dangerous workplace.) Employees are not covered when injuries are self-inflicted or stem from intoxication or "willful disregard of safety rules."[10] Approximately 90 percent of all U.S. workers are covered by state workers' compensation laws, although again there are differences among states, with coverage ranging from 70 percent to over 95 percent.

Workers' compensation benefits fall into four major categories: (1) disability income, (2) medical care, (3) death benefits, and (4) rehabilitative services.

Disability income is typically two-thirds of predisability earnings, although each state has its own minimum and maximum. In contrast to unemployment insurance benefits, disability benefits are tax free. The system is financed differently by different states, some having a single state fund, most allowing employers to purchase coverage from private insurance companies. Self-funding by employers is also permitted in most states. The cost to the employer is based on three factors. The first factor is the nature of the occupations and the risk attached to each. Premiums for low-risk occupations may be less than 1 percent of payroll; the cost for some of the most hazardous occupations may be as high as 100 percent of payroll. The second factor is the state where work is located. For example, the loss of a leg may be worth $264,040 in Pennsylvania versus $67,860 in Colorado.[11] The third factor is the employer's experience rating.

The cost of the workers' compensation system to U.S. employers grew dramatically through 1992, leading to an increased focus on ways of controlling workers' compensation costs.[12] The experience rating system again provides an incentive for employers to make their workplaces safer. Dramatic injuries (like losing a finger or hand) are less prevalent than minor ones, such as sprains and strains. Back strain is the most expensive benign health condition in developed countries. Each year in the United States, 3–4 percent of the population is temporarily disabled and 1 percent is permanently and totally disabled.[13] Many actions can be taken to reduce workplace injuries, such as work redesign and training; and to speed the return to health, and thus to work (e.g., exercise).[14] Some changes can be fairly simple (such as permitting workers to sit instead of having them bend over). It is also important to hold managers accountable (in their performance evaluations) for making workplaces safer and getting employees back to work promptly following an injury. With the recent passage of the Americans with Disabilities Act, employers are under even greater pressure to deal effectively and fairly with workplace injuries. See the discussion in Chapter 3 on safety awareness programs for some of the ways employers and employees are striving to make the workplace safer.

Private Group Insurance

As we noted earlier, group insurance rates are typically lower than individual rates because of economies of scale, the ability to pool risks, and the greater bargaining power of a group. This cost advantage, together with tax considerations and a concern for employee security, helps explain the prevalence of employer-sponsored insurance plans. We discuss two major types: medical insurance and disability insurance. Note that these programs are not legally required; rather, they are offered at the discretion of employers.

Medical Insurance
Not surprisingly, public opinion surveys indicate that medical benefits are by far the most important benefit to the average person.[15] As Table 13.3 indicates, most full-time employees, particularly in medium-size and large companies, get such benefits.

Doctor "Scorecards" Are Proposed in a Health Care Quality Drive

In one of the most ambitious efforts yet to provide health care quality ratings for consumers, 28 large employers, including Sprint Corp., Lowe's Cos., BellSouth Corp., J.C. Penney Co. and Morgan Stanley are teaming up to develop "scorecards" to help employees choose doctors based on how well they care for patients—and how cost-efficient they are.

The companies, which cover two million employees and their dependents, say they plan to use claims data provided by insurance carriers to measure how individual physicians stack up against well-established and generally accepted quality standards based on medical evidence.

Although the scorecard format is still in the development phase, employers in the program hope to provide within a year or so something as simple as a Consumer Report or Zagat type of guide, ranking doctors as well as hospitals with easy-to-understand points and stars, says David Rahill, of Mercer Human Resource Consulting, who is acting as project leader. But unlike with a restaurant review or appliance-buying guide, "we are trying to have ratings that are quantitative and unassailable, not in the eye of a reviewer on a particular Thursday night," he says.

Care Focused Purchasing, as the scorecard effort is called, marks the latest entry by big employers in the growing pay-for-quality movement in health care, which includes rewarding doctors and hospitals for providing higher-quality care at a reasonable price, and offering patients financial incentives to use more cost-efficient providers. And it comes as consumers are asked to dig deeper into their own pockets for health care and take on more decision-making about doctors and treatments.

The plan is sure to be controversial among doctors. Measures of quality, some doctors point out, might not take into account factors such as whether physicians are generally treating sicker patients with multiple chronic conditions whose outcomes may not look good even if they are providing excellent care. Similarly, they say, claims data won't take into account how well a doctor communicates or relates to patients. And then there are intangible issues, such as trust.

Yank D. Coble Jr., immediate past president of the American Medical Association and chair of its Quality Task Force, says quality measures must be "science-based, objective, meaningful, and not misleading to patients." For example, rating a doctor on how closely he or she monitors a diabetic patient's blood-sugar counts "is focusing on just one thing, but there are so many other components and other things that need to be checked," Dr. Coble says.

But companies involved say the scorecards can help employees not only choose care based on quality and cost, but also deal with troubling issues about inconsistent quality, varied outcomes and unacceptable error rates in their care.

"We have an obligation to give our employees more information. We can't just say, 'You are responsible for your health care, now go at it,'" says Sharon Leight, manager of benefits at J.C. Penney. "When you go buy a car you look at Consumer Reports to find out about both price and value," she says, "but we don't do that in health care because we don't have the same information."

E. J. Holland Jr., vice president of compensation, benefits, labor and employee relations at Sprint, says companies want to change health care so that employers don't have to pay all over again when a doctor's lapses have to be corrected with additional care or repeated procedures. "If we go out and install a phone system and it doesn't work, we have to come back and fix it for free—the customer doesn't have to pay us all over again," he says. "What other industry besides health care makes the customer pay for re-work?"

Under the scorecard system, insurance and pharmacy claims data would be used to measure whether accepted, standard practices are being followed. For instance, a doctor who regularly treats patients with congestive heart failure using ACE inhibitors—medicines used to treat high-blood pressure—would get more points than a doctor who wasn't providing a medically proven treatment. Likewise, doctors who ensure that patients with diabetes got all the recommended checkups for blood sugar and cholesterol would be higher-ranked than those who didn't follow the standard regimen. Recognized standards are set by independent nonprofit groups such as the National Committee on Quality Assurance, which accredits managed-care plans, the Joint Commission on Accreditation of Healthcare Organizations, which accredits hospitals, and the National Quality Forum.

While it would seem that all or at least most doctors follow accepted procedures, a Rand Corp. study last year said Americans get the right treatment only half the time and other research shows the U.S. could reduce health care spending by 30 percent merely by eliminating unnecessary care, operating more efficiently and improving quality.

Employers would put the doctor rankings up on their employee-benefits Web sites, perhaps rating doctors with dollar signs for price and hearts for care. A user, for instance, could check the site to see ratings on

a dozen doctors who treat diabetes in their area, then choose those with the best ratings for relative efficiency and quality.

Employers are expected to offer incentive programs such as lower co-pays and deductibles for choosing the best providers on both quality and cost.

One of the biggest challenges for the scorecard consortium will be to persuade a wide swath of insurers to provide data, to ensure statistically solid samplings and useful, accurate ratings. The program wouldn't be viable with only one or two insurers participating.

So far, the group has commitments from Humana Inc., based in Louisville, Ky., Cigna Corp. of Philadelphia, and Empire Blue Cross Blue Shield of New York to contribute their data. It is also discussing the plan with Aetna Inc., Hartford, Conn., which has its own pilot "Aexcel" network in three cities rating doctors in six medical specialties, using established quality and cost measures.

The participating insurers say it fits with their goals as well. "We support efforts to develop standardized provider performance measures," says Michael A. Stocker, president and CEO of Empire Blue Cross Blue Shield.

While health care quality experts laud such efforts as a good start, the plan, with its reliance on insurance claims data, is likely to add to the fractious and often emotional debate in health care about what constitutes doctor quality—and how to reliably measure it. There are numerous hospital "report card" programs out there because standard data about hospital performance is widely

available from accreditation groups and government agencies, such as mortality rates, readmission rates and the number of surgeries or other procedures performed at a given institution. But when it comes to the country's 600,000-plus individual physicians, many of whom are in small groups or solo practices, there is little public reporting required. Thus, few quality data are available.

Arnold Milstein, a physician and Mercer Human Resources consultant who has helped design pay-for-performance programs for large employer coalitions, says there are only a handful of voluntary doctor quality-assessment programs, and claims data remains the only reliable source to verify the treatments doctors use and the drugs they prescribe. "It's imperfect, but it's better than being totally blind," he says.

Medical specialty groups so far haven't had much luck reaching consensus on how to rate doctor quality, though they have been working on it for years. One effort, the Physician Consortium for Performance Improvement, a group of experts led by the American Medical Association, offers online worksheets for doctors to gather data from their own practices and measure their own level of performance in certain diseases. But it doesn't offer such information on all diseases and conditions, and offers no data for consumers to judge quality.

In general, doctors have resisted efforts to come up with a standard way to assess clinical performance, according to

(concluded on next page)

Three basic types of medical expenses are typically covered: hospital expenses, surgical expenses, and physicians' visits. Other benefits that employers may offer include dental care, vision care, birthing centers, and prescription drug programs. Perhaps the most important issue in benefits management is the challenge of providing quality medical benefits while controlling costs, a subject we return to in a later section.

Consolidated Omnibus Budget Reconciliation Act (COBRA)
The 1985 act that requires employers to permit employees to extend their health insurance coverage at group rates for up to 36 months following a qualifying event, such as a layoff.

The **Consolidated Omnibus Budget Reconciliation Act (COBRA)** of 1985 requires employers to permit employees to extend their health insurance coverage at group rates for up to 36 months following a "qualifying event" such as termination (except for gross misconduct), a reduction in hours that leads to the loss of health insurance, death, and other events. The beneficiary (whether the employee, spouse, or dependent) must have access to the same services as employees who have not lost their health insurance. Note that the beneficiaries do not get free coverage. Rather, they receive the advantage of purchasing coverage at the group rather than the individual rate.

Disability Insurance

Two basic types of disability coverage exist.[16] As Table 13.3 indicates, 26 to 50 percent of employees are covered by short-term disability plans and 18 to 40 percent are covered by long-term disability plans. Short-term plans typically provide benefits for six months or less, at which point long-term plans take over, potentially covering the person for life. The salary replacement rate is typically between 50 and 70 percent, although short-term plans are sometimes higher. There are often caps on the amount that can be paid each month. Federal income taxation of disability benefits depends on the funding method. Where employee contributions completely fund the plan, there is no federal tax. Benefits based on employer contributions are taxed. Finally, disability benefits, especially long-term ones, need to be coordinated with other programs, such as Social Security disability benefits.

Retirement

Earlier we discussed the old-age insurance part of Social Security, a legally required source of retirement income. Although this remains the largest single component of the elderly's overall retirement income (39 percent), the combination of private pensions (18 percent) and earnings from assets (savings and other investments like stock) account for an even larger share (16 percent). The remainder of the elderly's income comes from earnings (24 percent) and other sources (3 percent).[17]

Employers have no legal obligation to offer private retirement plans, but many do. As we note later, if a private retirement plan is provided, it must meet certain standards set forth by the Employee Retirement Income Security Act.

COMPETING THROUGH SUSTAINABILITY

Employers Consider Insurance Pools

Millions of Americans work for companies that provide health insurance but don't qualify for it because they are part-time or contract workers.

On Monday, 45 of the nation's largest employers, including IBM, Sears Roebuck, Ford Motor, Gap, Home Depot, and Textron, will unveil a possible solution—pooling all of their uninsured workers, then seeking an insurer willing to offer them a variety of health policies at prices lower than the workers could get individually.

They're betting that such a pool would be attractive business to a large insurer, as it would include a wide mix of about 4 million people, including part-timers, contractors and early retirees.

"We're tired of waiting for people to figure out what to do about the uninsured," says Randy MacDonald, senior vice president of human resources at IBM.

"We could not get that reform through the halls of Congress," he says, "so we are reforming the marketplace."

The idea comes as health insurance becomes increasingly unaffordable for many workers, but critics question whether uninsured employees will be able to afford insurance even at the group price, as the companies are not going to help pay for the coverage.

The number of uninsured is growing rapidly and is now estimated at more than 43 million.

Even employers who offer most of their workers health benefits say they are affected because the cost of paying for uninsured patients' medical costs is reflected in insurance premiums.

Details of the program have not been finalized. The idea, formed by the HR Policy Association, a group of senior company executives, may result in a new insurance pool by early next year.

The group, working with benefit consultant Hewitt Associates, expects to offer a range of insurance options, from low-cost cards offering discounts on medical services to comprehensive benefit packages.

"The more affordable we can make it, the fewer uninsured we will have," says Greg Lee, senior vice president of human resources at Sears, which provides health benefits to many of its workers, but has about 100,000 uninsured employees.

The companies say they cannot afford to offer insurance to all workers, so they are attempting to make affordable options available for noncovered employees.

It is not known how many employees might sign up. Purchasing pools can fail if not enough workers of average health join.

"The question is, who would actually participate, absent some sort of compulsion or subsidy?" says Gary Claxton, vice president at the Kaiser Family Foundation, a nonprofit research group.

Aetna President Ron Williams says the insurer is talking with the employers about the pool. "We see the uninsured as the alignment of two important interests: the opportunity to do good for society and an important business opportunity to attract new customers," he says.

SOURCE: Julie Appleby, "Employers Consider Insurance Pools," *USA Today* (May 9, 2004).

Defined Benefit

A *defined benefit plan* guarantees ("defines") a specified retirement benefit level to employees based typically on a combination of years of service and age as well as on the employee's earnings level (usually the five highest earnings years). For instance, an organization might guarantee a monthly pension payment of $1,500 to an employee retiring at age 65 with 30 years of service and an average salary over the final 5 years of $40,000. As Table 13.3 indicates, full-time employees in 33 percent of larger companies and 8 percent in smaller companies are covered by such plans. (As recently as the mid-1990s 50 percent of larger companies and 15 percent of smaller companies had such plans.) The replacement ratio (pension payment/final salary) ranges from about 21 percent for a worker aged 55 with 30 years of service who earned $35,000 in her last year to about 36 percent for a 65-year-old worker with 40 years of service who earned the same amount. With Social Security added in, the ratio for the 65-year-old worker increases to about 77 percent.[18]

Defined benefit plans insulate employees from investment risk, which is borne by the company. In the event of severe financial difficulties that force the company to terminate or reduce employee pension benefits, the **Pension Benefit Guaranty Corporation (PBGC)** provides some protection of benefits. Established by the **Employee Retirement Income Security Act (ERISA)** of 1974, the PBGC guarantees a basic benefit, not necessarily complete pension benefit replacement, for employees who were eligible for pensions at the time of termination. It insures the retirement benefits of 44 million workers in about 31,000 plans. The maximum monthly benefit is limited to the lesser of 1/12 of an employee's annual gross income during a PBGC-defined period or $3,699 in 2004. The PBGC is funded by an annual contribution of $19 per plan participant, plus an additional variable rate premium for underfunded plans that can reach $72 per participant.[19] Note that the PBGC does not guarantee health care benefits.

Defined Contribution

Unlike defined benefit plans, *defined contribution plans* do not promise a specific benefit level for employees upon retirement. Rather, an individual account is set up for each employee with a guaranteed size of contribution. The advantage of such plans for employers is that they shift investment risk to employees and present fewer administrative challenges because there is no need to calculate payments based on age and service and no need to make payments to the PBGC. As Table 13.3 indicates, defined contribution plans are especially preferred in smaller companies, perhaps because of small employers' desire to avoid long-term obligations or perhaps because small companies tend to be younger, often being founded since the trend toward defined contribution plans. Some companies have both defined benefit and defined contribution plans.

There is a wide variety of defined contribution plans, a few of which are briefly described here. One of the simplest is a money purchase plan, under which an employer specifies a level of annual contribution (such as 10 percent of salary). At retirement age, the employee is entitled to the contributions plus the investment returns. The term "money purchase" stems from the fact that employees often use the money to purchase an annuity rather than taking it as a lump sum. Profit sharing plans and employee stock ownership plans are also often used as retirement vehicles. Both permit contributions (cash and stock, respectively) to vary from year to year, thus allowing employers to avoid fixed obligations that may be burdensome in difficult financial times. Section 401(k) plans (named after the tax code section) permit employees to defer compensation on a pretax basis. Annual contributions in 2004 are limited to $13,000, increasing to $14,000 in 2005, to $15,000 in 2006, and by up to $500 annually thereafter through 2010, depending on inflation.[20]

Defined contribution plans continue to grow in importance, while as we saw above, defined benefit plans have become less common. An important implication is that defined contribution plans put the responsibility for wise investing squarely on

Pension Benefit Guaranty Corporation (PBGC)
The agency that guarantees to pay employees a basic retirement benefit in the event that financial difficulties force a company to terminate or reduce employee pension benefits.

Employee Retirement Income Security Act (ERISA)
The 1974 act that increased the fiduciary responsibilities of pension plan trustees, established vesting rights and portability provisions, and established the Pension Benefit Guaranty Corporation (PBGC).

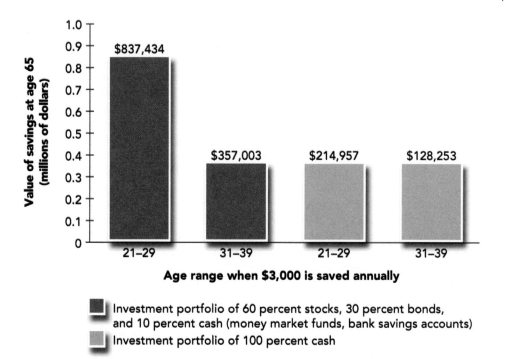

FIGURE 13.2

The Relationship of Retirement Savings to Age When Savings Begins and Type of Investment Portfolio

the shoulders of the employee. These investment decisions will become more critical because 401(k) plans continue to grow rapidly, covering 64 million people in 2003, up from 16 million in 1978.[21] Several factors affect the amount of income that will be available to an employee upon retirement. First, the earlier the age at which investments are made, the longer returns can accumulate. As Figure 13.2 shows, an annual investment of $3,000 made between ages 21 and 29 will be worth much more at age 65 than a similar investment made between ages 31 and 39. Second, different investments have different historical rates of return. Between 1946 and 1990, the average annual return was 11.4 percent for stocks, 5.1 percent for bonds, and 5.3 percent for cash (bank savings accounts).[22] As Figure 13.2 shows, if historical rates of return were to continue, an investment in a mix of 60 percent stock, 30 percent bonds, and 10 percent cash between the ages of 21 and 29 would be worth almost four times as much at age 65 as would the same amount invested in a bank savings account. A third consideration is the need to counteract investment risk by diversification because stock and bond prices can be volatile in the short run. Although stocks have the greatest historical rate of return, that is no guarantee of future performance, particularly over shorter time periods. Thus some investment advisers recommend a mix of stock, bonds, and cash, as shown in Figure 13.2, to reduce investment risk. Younger investors may wish to have more stock, while those closer to retirement age typically have less stock in their portfolios. It's also important not to invest too heavily in any single stock. Some Enron employees had 100% of their 401k assets in Enron stock. When the price dropped from $90 to less than $1 in 2001, their retirement money was gone. Risk is further compounded by risk of job loss when one's employer struggles financially.

Cash Balance Plans

An increasingly popular way to combine the advantages of defined benefit plans and defined contribution plans is to use a **cash balance plan.** This type of retirement plan consists of individual accounts, as in a 401(k) plan. But in contrast to a 401(k), all

cash balance plan
Retirement plan in which the employer sets up an individual account for each employee and contributes a percentage of the employee's salary; the account earns interest at a predefined rate.

the contributions come from the employer. Usually, the employer contributes a percentage of the employee's salary, say, 4 or 5 percent. The money in the cash balance plan earns interest according to a predetermined rate, such as the rate paid on U.S. Treasury bills. Employers guarantee this rate as in a defined benefit plan. This arrangement helps employers plan their contributions and helps employees predict their retirement benefits. If employees change jobs, they generally can roll over the balance into an individual retirement account.

Many organizations have switched from traditional defined benefit plans to cash balance plans. The change, like any major change, requires employers to consider the effects on employees as well as on the organization's bottom line. Defined benefit plans are most generous to older employees with many years of service, and cash balance plans are most generous to young employees who will have many years ahead in which to earn interest. For an organization with many experienced employees, switching from a defined benefit plan can produce great savings in pension benefits. In that case, the older workers are the greatest losers, unless the organization adjusts the program to retain their benefits.

For the time being, however, few if any companies are converting their defined benefit plans to cash balance plans because of legal uncertainties. In a closely watched case, IBM was successfully sued for age discrimination after converting its plan in 1999, and IBM has said it could cost as much as $5.7 billion to comply if its appeal is unsuccessful. The U.S. Treasury Department recently proposed rules on cash balance plans (www.treas.gov), but it is unclear when or if Congress will act on these.

Funding, Communication, and Vesting Requirements

ERISA does not require organizations to have pension plans, but those that are set up must meet certain requirements. In addition to the termination provisions discussed earlier, plans must meet certain guidelines on management and funding. For example, employers are required to make yearly contributions that are sufficient to cover future obligations. (As noted previously, underfunded plans require higher premiums.) ERISA also specifies a number of reporting and disclosure requirements involving the IRS, the Department of Labor, and employees.[23] Employees, for example, must receive within 90 days after entering a plan a **summary plan description (SPD)** that describes the plan's funding, eligibility requirements, risks, and so forth. Upon request, an employer must also make available to an employee an individual benefit statement, which describes the employee's vested and unvested benefits. Obviously, employers may wish to provide such information on a regular basis anyway as a means of increasing the understanding and value employees attach to their benefits.

ERISA guarantees employees that when they become participants in a pension plan and work a specified minimum number of years, they earn a right to a pension upon retirement. These are referred to as *vesting rights*.[24] Vested employees have the right to their pension at retirement age, regardless of whether they remain with the employer until that time. Employee contributions to their own plans are always completely vested. The vesting of employer-funded pension benefits must take place under one of two schedules. Employers may choose to vest employees after five years; until that time, employers can provide zero vesting if they choose. Alternatively, employers may vest employees over a three- to seven-year period, with at least 20 percent vesting in the third year and each year thereafter. These two schedules represent minimum requirements; employers are free to vest employees more quickly. These are the two choices relevant to the majority of employers. However, so-called "top-heavy" plans, where pension benefits for "key" employees (like highly paid top man-

Summary plan description (SPD)
A reporting requirement of the Employee Retirement Income Security Act (ERISA) that obligates employers to describe the plan's funding, eligibility requirements, risks, and so forth within 90 days after an employee has entered the plan.

agers) exceed a certain share of total pension benefits, require faster vesting for non-key employees. On the other hand, multiemployer pension plans need not provide vesting until after 10 years of employment.

These requirements were put in place to prevent companies from terminating employees before they reach retirement age or before they reach their length-of-service requirements in order to avoid paying pension benefits. It should also be noted that transferring employees or laying them off as a means of avoiding pension obligations is not legal either, even if such actions are motivated partly by business necessity.[25] On the other hand, employers are free to choose whichever of the two vesting schedules is most advantageous. For example, an employer that experiences high quit rates during the fourth and fifth years of employment may choose five-year vesting to minimize pension costs.

The traditional defined benefit pension plan discourages employee turnover or delays it until the employer can recoup the training investment in employees.[26] Even if an employee's pension benefit is vested, it is usually smaller if the employee changes employers, mainly because the size of the benefit depends on earnings in the final years with an employer. Consider an employee who earns $30,000 after 20 years and $60,000 after 40 years.[27] The employer pays an annual retirement benefit equal to 1.5 percent of final earnings times the number of years of service. If the employee stays with the employer for 40 years, the annual benefit level upon retirement would be $36,000 (.015 × $60,000 × 40). If, instead, the employee changes employers after 20 years (and has the same earnings progression), the retirement benefit from the first employer would be $9,000 (.015 × $30,000 × 20). The annual benefit from the second employer would be $18,000 (.015 × $60,000 × 20). Therefore, staying with one employer for 40 years would yield an annual retirement benefit of $36,000, versus a combined annual retirement benefit of $27,000 ($9,000 + $18,000) if the employee changes employers once. It has also been suggested that pensions are designed to encourage long-service employees, whose earnings growth may eventually exceed their productivity growth, to retire. This is consistent with the fact that retirement benefits reach their maximum at retirement age.[28]

The fact that in recent years many employers have sought to reduce their workforces through early retirement programs is also consistent with the notion that pensions are used to retain certain employees while encouraging others to leave. One early retirement program approach is to adjust years-of-service credit upward for employees willing to retire, resulting in a higher retirement benefit for them (and less monetary incentive to work). These workforce reductions may also be one indication of a broader trend toward employees becoming less likely to spend their entire careers with a single employer.[29] On one hand, if more mobility across employers becomes necessary or desirable, the current pension system's incentives against (or penalties for) mobility may require modification. On the other hand, perhaps increased employee mobility will reinforce the continued trend toward defined contribution plans [like 401(k)s], which have greater portability (ease of transfer of funds) across employers.[30]

International Comparisons

About 45 percent of the U.S. private-sector labor force is covered by pension plans, compared with 100 percent in France, 92 percent in Switzerland, 42 percent in Germany, and 39 percent in Japan. Among those covered by pensions, U.S. workers are significantly less likely to be covered by defined benefit plans (see Table 13.3, page 538) than Japanese workers (100 percent) or German workers (90 percent).

Finding and Keeping the Best Employees

There's something comforting and classy about Starbucks. It's not just the enticing aromas and blues tunes wafting through the air, the handsome surroundings or the likelihood of running into a friend or neighbor. It's more the way the baristas (never called "counter help") greet people, perhaps offering a blueberry scone sample, or remembering a customer's preference for nonfat soy latte with extra foam.

Starbucks attracts a near-cult following, serving 25 million drinks a week at nearly 7,000 locations worldwide. In a four-week period ending in August, the company—which is growing by three to four stores a day—reported net revenues of $335 million, an increase of 26 percent over the same period last year. The Seattle-based coffee empire was among the top 10 on *Fortune*'s most recent "America's Most Admired Companies" list. The magazine also rated it the most admired food-services company in 2001 and 2002. *BusinessWeek* named founder Howard Schultz one of the country's top 25 managers in 2001.

Since Starbucks began with a single store in 1971, its overriding philosophy has been this: "Leave no one behind." With that in mind, new employees get 24 hours of in-store training, steeping themselves in information about coffee and how to meet, greet and serve customers. Full health care benefits (medical, dental, vision and alternative services) are offered to all employees, including part-timers who work at least 240 hours per calendar quarter. The EAP is available to all employees. Employees share in the company's growth via "Bean Stock" (stock options) of up to 14 percent of their gross pay, and a stock-investment plan allows them to buy shares of Starbucks common stock at a discount (85 percent of fair market value) through payroll deductions. The company also matches employees' contributions to their "Future Roast" 401(k) plans, adding from 25 to 150 percent of the first 4 percent of pay, depending on length of service.

As a result of such measures, Starbucks employees have an 82 percent job-satisfaction rate, according to a Hewitt Associates Starbucks Partner View Survey. This compares to a 50 percent satisfaction rate for all employers and 74 percent for Hewitt's "Best Place to Work" employers. Though the company won't release specific numbers, it also claims that its turnover is lower than that of most fast-food establishments. But it's not just the benefits that attract employees. Another company survey found that the top two reasons why people work for Starbucks are "the opportunity to work with an enthusiastic team" and "to work in a place where I feel I have value."

Omollo Gaya, who grew up on a coffee farm in Kenya and emigrated to San Diego to attend college, was drawn inside a Starbucks store seven years ago by the heady aroma. He bought a pound of coffee, struck up a conversation with the employee behind the counter, and was impressed by the barista's knowledge. As he sipped his brew, "something clicked," Gaya says. After researching Starbucks, he applied for a job and spent the next four years in a San Diego store before being promoted to his current position as one of eight coffee tasters at company headquarters. After six years, Gaya exercised his Bean Stock options, which netted about $25,000 after payment of the exercise price, to build a new four-bedroom house for his widowed mother on 15 acres in her home village.

"The health benefits, the 401(k) and the stock options really surprised me, and confirmed what this company is all about," Gaya says. "From my first day on the job, I got a lot of satisfaction when I offered a cup of coffee to customers and saw the smile on their faces, when I answered their questions about coffee, and when I saw their enthusiasm when they returned with a friend or colleague. My love for coffee started when I was 5 years old, but I never thought it would come to mean so much to me. Buying a home for my mother is the highlight of my being with Starbucks."

Maintaining that kind of feel-good atmosphere in a small mom-and-pop company is one thing. The question is how Starbucks manages to keep the spirit flowing with 11,000 full-time and 60,000 part-time employees in North America, and an additional 7,400 workers globally. "Staying 'small' while we grow is one of our biggest challenges," says Dave Pace, executive vice president of partner resources (the company's term for human resources). "It sounds clichéd, but we do it by taking our mission statement seriously. Almost all companies have a mission, but at Starbucks, we use it as our guiding principle and hold it up as a filter for decision making.

Providing a great work environment and treating employees with respect is number one on Starbucks' six-point mission statement. The list also includes a commitment to diversity; excellence in purchasing, roasting and delivering coffee; keeping customers satisfied; contributing to communities and the environment; and, of course, achieving profitability.

Starbucks encourages its employees, who are called partners, to keep in mind its mission statement, monitor management decisions, and submit comments and questions if they encounter anything that runs counter to any of the six points. Employees submit about 200 such Mission Review queries a month, and a two-person team considers and responds to each one. As a result of one such review request, Starbucks extended its military-reserve policy to protect the jobs, salaries, and health care benefits of employees who were called into action after September 11 and again during the Iraq war.

The company also encourages community involvement by donating $10 for each hour that an employee volunteers to a nonprofit or charitable organization. Profits from sales of the company's logo-emblazoned "coffee gear" are channeled into clubs and services for employees, which include everything from running groups and bowling leagues to quilting and book clubs. Employees can donate an amount of their choice to a voluntary "CUP (Caring Unites Partners) fund," which is used to provide grants to fellow employees who fall on hard times. And every year, as part of its Earthwatch program, the company selects a few employees to travel to coffee-producing parts of the world, where they learn firsthand about environmental and conservation issues from the growers. Last year two were selected; this year five are going.

"People come to Starbucks to socialize and interact, so our partners do much more than just make coffee," Pace says. "They are the ones who create that environment in our stores and make this a place that people feel good about. So they feel empowered and know they are making a contribution. This is a company where we look out for each other and look out for the community. And when people see us responding to them, they feel like this company really 'gets it.'"

SOURCE: From *Workforce Management* by Maryann Hammers. Copyrigh t © 2003 by *Workforce Management*. Reproduced with permission of *Workforce Management* via Copyright Clearance Center.

Pay for Time Not Worked

At first blush, paid vacation, holidays, sick leave, and so forth may not seem to make economic sense. The employer pays the employee for time not spent working, receiving no tangible production value in return. Therefore, some employers may see little direct advantage. Perhaps for this reason, a minimum number of vacation days (20) is mandated by law in the European Community. As many as 30 days of vacation is not uncommon for relatively new employees in Europe. By contrast, there is no legal minimum in the United States, but 10 days is typical for large companies. U.S. workers must typically be with an employer for 20 to 25 years before they receive as much paid vacation as their Western European counterparts.[31]

Sick leave programs often provide full salary replacement for a limited period of time, usually not exceeding 26 weeks. The amount of sick leave is often based on length of service, accumulating with service (one day per month, for example). Sick leave policies need to be carefully structured to avoid providing employees with the wrong incentives. For example, if sick leave days disappear at the end of the year (rather than accumulate), a "use it or lose it" mentality may develop among employees, contributing to greater absenteeism. Organizations have developed a number of measures to counter this.[32] Some allow sick days to accumulate, then pay employees for the number of sick days when they retire or resign. Employers may also attempt to communicate to their employees that accumulated sick leave is better saved to use as a bridge to long-term disability, because the replacement rate (the ratio of sick leave or disability payments to normal salary) for the former is typically higher. Sick leave payments may equal 100 percent of usual salary, whereas the replacement ratio for long-term disability might be 50 percent, so the more sick leave accumulated, the longer an employee can avoid dropping to 50 percent of usual pay when unable to work.

Although vacation and other paid leave programs help attract and retain employees, there is a cost to providing time off with pay, especially in a global economy. The fact that vacation and other paid leave practices differ across countries contributes to the differences in labor costs described in Chapter 11. Consider that, on average, in manufacturing, German workers work 375 fewer hours per year than their U.S. counterparts, who work 1,815 hours per year, and over 500 fewer hours than workers in the central European country, the Czech Republic. (See Figure 13.3.) In other words, German workers are at work approximately 9 fewer weeks per year than their U.S. counterparts and 12 to 13 fewer weeks than workers in the Czech Republic next door (and as of 2004, a member of the European community). It is perhaps not surprising then that German manufacturers have looked outside Germany in many cases for alternative production sites.

FIGURE 13.3

Normal Annual Hours Worked in Manufacturing Relative to United States

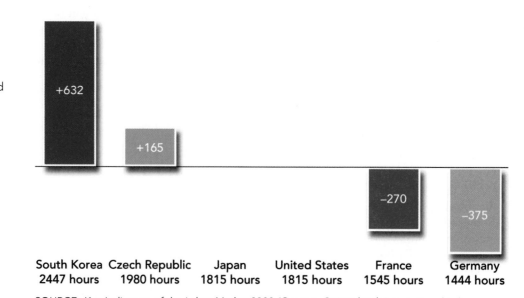

SOURCE: *Key Indicators of the Labor Market* 2003 (Geneva, Switzerland: International Labour Office, 2003).

Family-Friendly Policies

To ease employees' conflicts between work and nonwork, organizations may use *family-friendly policies* such as family leave policies and child care. Although the programs discussed here would seem to be targeted to a particular group of employees, these programs often have "spillover effects" on other employees, who see them as symbolizing a general corporate concern for human resources, thus promoting loyalty even among employee groups that do not use the programs possibly resulting in improved organizational performance.[33]

Since 1993 the **Family and Medical Leave Act** requires organizations with 50 or more employees within a 75-mile radius to provide as much as 12 weeks of unpaid leave after childbirth or adoption; to care for a seriously ill child, spouse, or parent; or for an employee's own serious illness. Employees are guaranteed the same or a comparable job on their return to work. Employees with less than one year of service or who work under 25 hours per week or who are among the 10 percent highest paid are not covered.

Many employers had already taken steps to deal with this issue, partly to help attract and retain key employees. Less than 10 percent of American families fit the image of a husband working outside the home and a wife who stays home to take care of the children.[34]

The United States still offers significantly less unpaid leave than most Western European countries and Japan. Moreover, paid family leave remains rare in the United States (fewer than 5 percent are eligible for paid leave, despite some state laws), in even sharper contrast to Western Europe and Japan, where it is typically mandated by law.[35] Until the passage of the Americans with Disabilities Act, the only applicable law was the Pregnancy Discrimination Act of 1978, which requires employers that offer disability plans to treat pregnancy as they would any other disability.

Experience with the Family and Medical Leave Act suggests that a majority of those opting for this benefit fail to take the full allotment of time. This is especially the case among female executives. Many of these executives find they do not enjoy maternity leave as much as they expected they would and miss the challenges associated with their careers. Others fear that their careers would be damaged in the long run by missing out on opportunities that might arise while they are out on leave.[36]

Family and Medical Leave Act
The 1993 act that requires employers with 50 or more employees to provide up to 12 weeks of unpaid leave after childbirth or adoption; to care for a seriously ill child, spouse, or parent; or for an employee's own serious illness.

Child Care

U.S. companies increasingly provide some form of child care support to their employees. This support comes in several forms that vary in their degree of organizational involvement.[37] The lowest level of involvement, offered by 36 percent of companies, is when an organization supplies and helps employees collect information about the cost and quality of available child care. At the next level, organizations provide vouchers or discounts for employees to use at existing child care facilities (5 percent of companies). At the highest level, firms provide child care at or near their worksites (9 percent of companies). Toyota's Child Development Program provides 24-hours-a-day care for children of workers at its Georgetown, Kentucky, plant. This facility is designed to meet the needs of employees working evening and night shifts who want their children to be on the same schedule. In this facility, the children are kept awake all night. At the end of the night shift, the parents pick up their children and the whole family goes home to bed.[38]

An organization's decision to staff its own child care facility should not be taken lightly. It is typically a costly venture with important liability concerns. Moreover, the results, in terms of reducing absenteeism and enhancing productivity, are often mixed.[39] One reason for this is that many organizations are "jumping on the day care bandwagon" without giving much thought to the best form of assistance for their specific employees.

As an alternative example, Memphis-based First Tennessee Bank, which was losing 1,500 days of productivity a year because of child care problems, considered creating its own on-site day care center. Before acting, however, the company surveyed its employees. This survey indicated that the only real problem with day care occurred when the parents' regular day care provisions fell through because of sickness on the part of the child or provider. Based on these findings, the bank opted to establish a sick-child care center, which was less costly and smaller in scope than a full-time center and yet still solved the employees' major problem. As a result, absenteeism dropped so dramatically that the program paid for itself in the first nine months of operation.[40]

Managing Benefits: Employer Objectives and Strategies

Although the regulatory environment places some important constraints on benefits decisions, employers retain significant discretion and need to evaluate the payoff of such decisions.[41] As discussed earlier, however, this evaluation needs to recognize that employees have come to expect certain things from employers. Employers who do not meet these expectations run the risk of violating what has been called an "implicit contract" between the employer and its workers. If employees believe their employers feel little commitment to their welfare, they can hardly be expected to commit themselves to the company's success.

Clearly, there is much room for progress in the evaluation of benefits decisions. Despite some of the obvious reasons for benefits—group discounts, regulation, and minimizing compensation-related taxes—organizations do not do as well as they could in spelling out what they want their benefits package to achieve and evaluating how well they are succeeding. Research suggests that most organizations do not have written benefits objectives.[42] Obviously, without clear objectives to measure progress, evaluation is difficult (and less likely to occur). Table 13.4 provides an example of one organization's written benefits objectives.

Surveys and Benchmarking

As with cash compensation, an important element of benefits management is knowing what the competition is doing. Survey information on benefits packages is available from private consultants, the U.S. Chamber of Commerce, and the Bureau of Labor Statistics (BLS).[43] BLS data of the sort in Table 13.3 and the more detailed information on programs and provisions available from consultants are useful in designing competitive benefits packages. To compete effectively in the product market, cost information is also necessary. A good source is again the BLS, which provides information on benefits costs for specific categories as well as breakdowns by industry, occupation, union status, and organization size. Table 13.5 shows some of these data for 2003.

- To establish and maintain an employee benefit program that is based primarily on the employees' needs for leisure time and on protection against the risks of old age, loss of health, and loss of life.
- To establish and maintain an employee benefit program that complements the efforts of employees on their own behalf.
- To evaluate the employee benefit plan annually for its effect on employee morale and productivity, giving consideration to turnover, unfilled positions, attendance, employees' complaints, and employees' opinions.
- To compare the employee benefit plan annually with that of other leading companies in the same field and to maintain a benefit plan with an overall level of benefits based on cost per employee that falls within the second quintile of these companies.
- To maintain a level of benefits for nonunion employees that represents the same level of expenditures per employee as for union employees.
- To determine annually the costs of new, changed, and existing programs as percentages of salaries and wages and to maintain these percentages as much as possible.
- To self-fund benefits to the extent that a long-run cost savings can be expected for the firm and catastrophic losses can be avoided.
- To coordinate all benefits with social insurance programs to which the company makes payments.
- To provide benefits on a noncontributory basis except for dependent coverage, for which employees should pay a portion of the cost.
- To maintain continual communications with all employees concerning benefit programs.

TABLE 13.4

One Company's Written Benefits Objectives

SOURCE: *Employee Benefits*, 3rd ed., Burton T. Beam, Jr., and John J. McFadden. © 1992 by Dearborn Financial Publishing, Inc. Published by Dearborn Financial Publishing, Inc., Chicago. All rights reserved.

	PERCENTAGE OF PAYROLL
Legally required	11.2%
Retirement and savings plans	5.0
Medical and other insurance	10.5
Payments for time not worked	9.4
Miscellaneous[a]	3.6
Total Benefits	39.7

TABLE 13.5

Employee Benefits by Category, Cost and Total Compensation, 2003

[a] Includes employee services and extra cash payment categories.
SOURCE: "Employer Cost for Employee Compensation," www.bls.gov.

Cost Control

In thinking about cost control strategies, it is useful to consider several factors. First, the larger the cost of a benefit category, the greater the opportunity for savings. Second, the growth trajectory of the benefit category is also important: even if costs are currently acceptable, the rate of growth may result in serious costs in the future.

Third, cost containment efforts can only work to the extent that the employer has significant discretion in choosing how much to spend in a benefit category. Much of the cost of legally required benefits (like Social Security) is relatively fixed, which constrains cost reduction efforts. Even with legally required benefits, however, employers can take actions to limit costs because of "experience ratings," which impose higher taxes on employers with high rates of unemployment or workers' compensation claims.

One benefit—medical and other insurance—stands out as a target for cost control for two reasons. Its costs are substantial; they have, except for the 1994 to 1999 period, grown at a significant pace, and this growth is expected to continue. Second, employers have many options for attacking costs and improving quality.

Health Care: Controlling Costs and Improving Quality

As Table 13.6 indicates, the United States spends more on health care than any other country in the world. U.S. health care expenditures have gone from 5.3 percent of the gross national product ($27 billion) in 1960 to 14 percent (approximately $1.45 trillion) recently. Yet the percentage of full-time workers receiving job-related health benefits has declined, with over 43 million Americans uninsured as of 2002.[44] The United States also trails Japan and Western Europe on measures of life expectancy and infant mortality.

Unlike workers in most Western European countries, who have nationalized health systems, the majority of Americans receiving health insurance get it through their (or a family member's) employers.[45] Consequently, health insurance, like pensions, discourages employee turnover because not all employers provide health insurance benefits.[46] Not surprisingly, the fact that many Americans receive coverage through their employers has meant that many efforts at controlling costs and increasing quality and coverage have been undertaken by employers. These efforts, broadly referred to as managed care, fall into six major categories: (1) plan design, (2) use of alternative providers, (3) use of alternative funding methods, (4) claims review, (5) education and prevention, and (6) external cost control systems.[47] Examples appear in Table 13.7.

One trend in plan design has been to shift costs to employees through the use of deductibles, coinsurance, exclusions and limitations, and maximum benefits.[48] These

TABLE 13.6

Health Care Costs and Outcomes in Various Countries

	LIFE EXPECTANCY	INFANT MORTALITY RATE	HEALTH EXPENDITURES AS A PERCENTAGE OF GDP
Japan	82	3.1	8%
Korea	74	6.2	6
Canada	79	5.3	10
United Kingdom	78	5.5	8
France	79	4.6	10
Germany	78	4.5	11
Mexico	75	21.4	7
United States	77	6.9	14

SOURCE: Organization for Economic Cooperation and Development, *OECD in Figures, 2003 edition* (Paris: 2003).

TABLE 13.7

Ways Employers Use Managed Care to Control Health Care Costs

Plan design
Cost shifting to employees
    Deductibles
    Coinsurance
    Exclusions and limitations
    Maximum benefits
Cost reduction
    Preadmission testing
    Second surgical opinions
    Coordination of benefits
    Alternatives to hospital stays (such as home health care)
Alternative providers
Health maintenance organizations (HMOs)
Preferred provider organizations (PPOs)
Alternative funding methods
Self-funding
Claims review
Health education and preventive care
Wellness programs
Employee assistance programs (EAPs)
Encouragement of external control systems
National Council on Health Planning and Development
Employer coalitions

SOURCE: Adapted from B. T. Beam Jr. and J. J. McFadden, *Employee Benefits*, 3rd ed. (Chicago: Dearborn Financial Publishing, 1992).

costs can be structured such that employees act on incentives to shift to less expensive plans.[49] Another trend has been to focus on reducing, rather than shifting, costs through such activities as preadmission testing and second surgical opinions. The use of alternative providers like **health maintenance organizations (HMOs)** and **preferred provider organizations (PPOs)** has also increased. HMOs differ from more traditional providers by focusing on preventive care and outpatient treatment, requiring employees to use only HMO services, and providing benefits on a prepaid basis. Many HMOs pay physicians and other health care workers a flat salary instead of using the traditional fee-for-service system, under which a physician's pay may depend on the number of patients seen. Paying on a salary basis is intended to reduce incentives for physicians to schedule more patient visits or medical procedures than might be necessary. (Of course, there is the risk that incentives will be reduced too much, resulting in inadequate access to medical procedures and specialists.) PPOs are essentially groups of health care providers that contract with employers, insurance companies, and so forth to provide health care at a reduced fee. They differ from HMOs in that they do not provide benefits on a prepaid basis and employees often are not required to use the preferred providers. Instead, employers may provide incentives for employees to choose, for example, a physician who participates in the plan. In general, PPOs seem to be less expensive than traditional delivery systems but more expensive than HMOs.[50] Another trend in employers' attempts to control costs has been to vary required employee contributions based on the employee's health and risk factors rather than charging each employee the same premium.

Health maintenance organization (HMO)
A health care plan that provides benefits on a prepaid basis for employees who are required to use only HMO medical service providers.

Preferred provider organization (PPO)
A group of health care providers who contract with employers, insurance companies, and so forth to provide health care at a reduced fee.

Employee Wellness Programs. Employee wellness programs (EWPs) focus on changing behaviors both on and off work time that could eventually lead to future health problems. EWPs are preventive in nature; they attempt to manage health care costs by decreasing employees' needs for services. Typically, these programs aim at specific health risks such as high blood pressure, high cholesterol levels, smoking, and obesity. They also try to promote positive health influences such as physical exercise and good nutrition.[51]

EWPs are either passive or active. Passive programs use little or no outreach to individuals, nor do they provide ongoing support to motivate them to use the resources. Active wellness centers assume that behavior change requires not only awareness and opportunity but support and reinforcement.

One example of a passive wellness program is a health education program. Health education programs have two central goals: raising awareness levels of health-related issues and informing people on health-related topics. In these kinds of programs, a health educator usually conducts classes or lunchtime lectures (or coordinates outside speakers). The program may also have various promotions (like an annual mile run or a "smoke-out") and include a newsletter that reports on current health issues.

Another kind of passive employee wellness program is a fitness facility. In this kind of program, the company sets up a center for physical fitness equipped with aerobic and muscle-building exercise machines and staffed with certified athletic trainers. The facility is publicized within the organization, and employees are free to use it on their own time. Aetna, for example, has created five state-of-the-art health clubs that serve over 7,500 workers.[52] Northwestern Mutual Life's fitness facilities are open 24 hours a day to its 3,300 employees.[53] Health education classes related to smoking cessation and weight loss may be offered in addition to the facilities.

Although fitness facility programs are usually more expensive than health education programs, both are classified as passive because they rely on individual employees to identify their problems and take corrective action. In contrast, active wellness centers assume that behavior change also requires encouragement and assistance. One kind of active wellness center is the outreach and follow-up model. This type of wellness center contains all the features of a passive model, but it also has counselors who handle one-on-one outreach and provide tailored, individualized programs for employees. Typically, tailored programs obtain baseline measures on various indicators (weight, blood pressure, lung capacity, and so on) and measure individuals' progress relative to these indicators over time. The programs set goals and provide small, symbolic rewards to individuals who meet their goals.

This encouragement needs to be particularly targeted to employees in high-risk categories (like those who smoke, are overweight, or have high blood pressure) for two reasons. First, a small percentage of employees create a disproportionate amount of health care costs; therefore, targeted interventions are more efficient. Second, research shows that those in high-risk categories are the most likely to perceive barriers (like family problems or work overload)[54] to participating in company-sponsored fitness programs. Thus untargeted interventions are likely to miss the people that most need to be included.

Research on these different types of wellness centers leads to several conclusions.[55] First, the costs of health education programs are significantly less than those associated with either fitness facility programs or the follow-up model. Second, as indicated in Figure 13.4, all three models are effective in reducing the risk factors associated with cardiovascular disease (obesity, high blood pressure, smoking, and lack of exercise). However, the follow-up model is significantly better than the other two in reducing the risk factors.

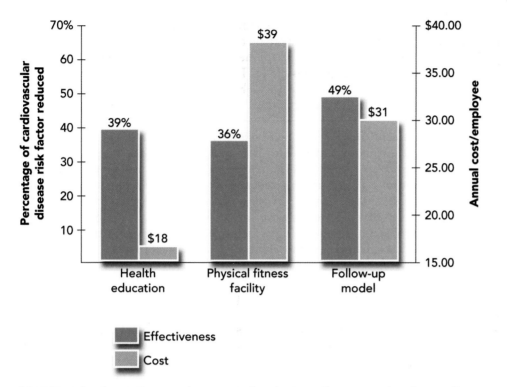

FIGURE 13.4

The Cost and Effectiveness of Three Different Types of Employee Wellness Designs

SOURCE: J. C. Erfurt, A. Foote, and M. A. Heirich, "The Cost Effectiveness of Worksite Wellness Programs for Hypertension Control, Weight Loss, Smoking Cessation and Exercise," *Personnel Psychology* 45 (1992), pp. 5–27. Used with permission.

Whether the added cost of follow-up programs compared with health education programs is warranted is a judgment that only employers, employees, and unions can make. However, employers like Sony and Quaker Oats believe that incentives are worth the extra cost, and their employees can receive up to several hundred dollars for reducing their risk factors. There appears to be no such ambiguity associated with the fitness facility model, however. This type of wellness center costs as much or more than the follow-up model but is only as effective as the health education model. Providing a fitness facility that does not include systematic outreach and routine long-term follow-up to assist people with risk factors is not cost-effective in reducing health risks. "Attendants may sit in the fitness center like the 'Maytag repairman' waiting for people to come."[56]

Health Care Costs and Quality: Progress and Prospects. Efforts to control health care cost growth have borne fruit. Whereas from 1980 through 1993 there was double-digit annual growth in health care costs, as noted earlier, between 1994 and 1999 employer expenditures on health care actually fell (by 17 percent). However, these reductions proved to be temporary, as costs increased 22 percent from 1999 to 2003.[57] A report by the Health Care Financing Administration projects that health care spending in the United States will continue to grow. Why? Because 85 percent of working Americans with health care are already covered by managed care, so few additional savings can be obtained by further switches. Moreover, many managed care companies have existed on small profit margins, but this cannot continue indefinitely.

Two important phenomena are often encountered in cost control efforts. First, piecemeal programs may not work well because steps to control one aspect (such as medical cost shifting) may lead employees to "migrate" to other programs that provide medical treatment at no cost to them (like workers' compensation). Second, there is often a so-called Pareto group, which refers to a small percentage (perhaps 20 percent) of employees being responsible for generating the majority (often 60 to 80 percent) of health care costs. Obviously, cost control efforts will be more successful to the extent that the costs generated by the Pareto group can be identified and managed effectively.[58]

Although cost control will continue to require a good deal of attention, there is a growing emphasis on monitoring health care quality, which has been described as "the next battlefield." A major focus is on identifying best medical practices by measuring and monitoring the relative success of alternative treatment strategies using large-scale databases and research.[59] In addition, employers increasingly cooperate with one another to develop "report cards" on health care provider organizations to facilitate better choices by their employers and to receive improved health care. General Motors, Ford, and Chrysler, for example, have developed this type of system and made it Web-accessible.[60]

Staffing Responses to Control Benefits Cost Growth

Employers may change staffing practices to control benefits costs. First, because benefits costs are fixed (in that they do not usually go up with hours worked), the benefits cost per hour can be reduced by having employees work more hours. However, there are drawbacks to having employees work more hours. The Fair Labor Standards Act (FLSA), introduced in Chapter 11, requires that nonexempt employees be paid time-and-a-half for hours in excess of 40 per week. Yet the decline in U.S. work hours tapered off in the late 1940s; work hours have actually gone up since then. It is estimated that Americans were working the equivalent of one month longer in 1987 than they were in 1969, and these higher levels have continued.[61] Increased benefits were identified as one of the major reasons for this.

A second possible effect of FLSA regulations (though this is more speculative) is that organizations will try to have their employees classified as exempt whenever possible (though such attempts may run afoul of FLSA law). The growth in the number of salaried workers (many of whom are exempt) may also reflect an effort by organizations to limit the benefits cost per hour without having to pay overtime. A third potential effect is the growth in part-time employment and the use of temporary workers, which may be a response to rising benefits costs. Part-time workers are less likely to receive benefits than full-time workers although labor market shortages in recent years have reduced this difference.[62] Benefits for temporary workers are also usually quite limited.

Third, employers may be more likely to classify workers as independent contractors rather than employees, which eliminates the employer's obligation to provide legally required employee benefits. However, the Internal Revenue Service (IRS) scrutinizes such decisions carefully, as Microsoft and other companies have discovered. Microsoft was compelled to reclassify a group of workers as employees (rather than as independent contractors) and to grant them retroactive benefits. The IRS looks at several factors, including the permanency of the relationship between employer and worker, how much control the employer exercises in directing the worker, and whether the worker offers services to only that employer. Permanency, control, and dealing with a single employer are viewed by the IRS as suggestive of an employment relationship.

Nature of the Workforce

Although general considerations such as cost control and "protection against the risks of old age and loss of health and life" (see Table 13.4) are important, employers must also consider the specific demographic composition and preferences of their current workforces in designing their benefits packages.

At a broad level, basic demographic factors such as age and sex can have important consequences for the types of benefits employees want. For example, an older workforce is more likely to be concerned about (and use) medical coverage, life insurance, and pensions. A workforce with a high percentage of women of childbearing age may care more about disability leave. Young, unmarried men and women often have less interest in benefits generally, preferring higher wages and salaries.

Although some general conclusions about employee preferences can be drawn based on demographics, more finely tuned assessments of employee benefit preferences need to be done. One approach is to use marketing research methods to assess employees' preferences the same way consumers' demands for products and services are assessed.[63] Methods include personal interviews, focus groups, and questionnaires. Relevant questions might include

- What benefits are most important to you?
- If you could choose one new benefit, what would it be?
- If you were given x dollars for benefits, how would you spend it?

As with surveys generally, care must be taken not to raise employee expectations regarding future changes. If the employer is not prepared to act on the employees' input, surveying may do more harm than good.

The preceding discussion may imply that the current makeup of the workforce is a given, but such is not the case. As discussed earlier, the benefits package may influence the composition of the workforce. For example, a benefits package that has strong medical benefits and pensions may be particularly attractive to older people or those with families. An attractive pension plan may be a way to attract workers who wish to make a long-term commitment to an organization. Where turnover costs are high, this type of strategy may have some appeal. On the other hand, a company that has very lucrative health care benefits may attract and retain people with high health care costs. Sick leave provisions may also affect the composition of the workforce. Organizations need to think about the signals their benefits packages send and the implications of these signals for workforce composition. In this vein, the benefits shown in Table 13.8 are designed to attract a particular type of employee—those in the Silicon Valley information technology and biotechnology labor markets.

Communicating with Employees

Effective communication of benefits information to employees is critical if employers are to realize sufficient returns on their benefits investments. Research makes it clear that current employees and job applicants often have a very poor idea of what benefits provisions are already in place and the cost or market value of those benefits. One study asked employees to estimate both the amount contributed by the employer to their medical insurance and what it would cost the employees to provide their own health insurance. Table 13.9 shows that employees significantly underestimated both the cost and market value of their medical benefits. In the case of family coverage, employees estimated that the employer contributed $24, only 38 percent of the

TABLE 13.8

A Field Guide to
High-Tech Perks

Gentech	This biotech pioneer, known for its "casual intensity," offers big-company perks like a hair salon, dry-cleaning services, and sushi in the cafeteria while keeping bureaucracy to a minimum.
Yahoo! Inc.	Office attire for cofounder David Filo is typically "T-shirts, shorts, and bare feet," says Diane Hunt, director of corporate communications.
Qualcomm Inc.	Employees "go off on one-month junkets," says John Major, executive vice president, who adds, "I've never seen long pants on my chief engineer." Flexible holiday policy allows employees to change any of the ten company-approved days to better suit their needs.
Adobe Systems Inc.	Employees get a three-week paid sabbatical every five years. And "a really neat benefit is everybody in the building has an office with a door," says Linda White, spokeswoman. A new high-rise at the San Jose campus will include a basketball court.

SOURCE: From *The Wall Street Journal* (Eastern edition), by Q. Hardy. Copyright 1998 by Dow Jones & Co., Inc. Reproduced with permission of Dow Jones & Co., Inc. via Copyright Clearance Center.

TABLE 13.9

Employee
Perceptions versus
Actual Cost and
Market Value of
Employer
Contributions to
Employee Medical
Insurance

	EMPLOYER CONTRIBUTION			MARKET VALUE[a]		
COVERAGE	ACTUAL	EMPLOYEE PERCEPTION	RATIO	ACTUAL	EMPLOYEE PERCEPTION	RATIO
Individual	$34	$23	68%	$ 61	$37	61%
Family	64	24	38	138	43	31

Note: Dollar values in table represent means across three different insurance carriers for individual coverage and three different carriers for family coverage.

[a]Defined as the amount a nonemployee would have to pay to obtain the same level of coverage.

SOURCE: Adapted from M. Wilson, G. B. Northcraft, and M. A. Neale, "The Perceived Value of Fringe Benefits," *Personnel Psychology* 38 (1985), pp. 309–20. Used with permission.

employer's actual contribution. This employer was receiving a very poor return on its benefits investment: $0.38 for every $1.00 spent.[64]

The situation with job applicants is no better. One study of MBAs found that 46 percent believed that benefits added 15 percent or less on top of direct payroll. Not surprisingly, perhaps, benefits were dead last on the applicants' priority lists in making job choices.[65] A study of undergraduate business majors found similar results, with benefits ranked 15th (out of 18) in importance in evaluating jobs. These results must be interpreted with caution, however. Some research suggests that job attributes can be ranked low in importance, not because they are unimportant per se, but because all employers are perceived to be about the same on that attribute. If some employers offered noticeably poorer benefits, the importance of benefits could become much greater.

Organizations can help remedy the problem of applicants' and employees' lack of knowledge about benefits. One study found that employees' awareness of benefits information was significantly increased through several media, including memoranda, question-and-answer meetings, and detailed brochures. The increased awareness, in turn, contributed to significant increases in benefits satisfaction. Another study suggests, however, that increased employee knowledge of benefits can have a positive or negative effect, depending on the nature of the benefits package. For example, there was a negative, or inverse, correlation between cost to the employee and benefits satisfaction overall, but the correlation was more strongly negative among employees with greater knowledge of their benefits.[66] The implication is that employees will be least satisfied with their benefits if their cost is high and they are well informed.

One thing an employer should consider with respect to written benefits communication is that over 27 million employees in the United States may be functionally illiterate. Of course, there are many alternative ways to communicate benefits information. (See Table 13.10.) Nevertheless, most organizations spend less than $10 per year per employee to communicate information about benefits, and almost all of this is spent on written communication rather than on more personalized or "innovative" approaches such as benefits fairs, videos, and Web-based efforts. Considering that organizations spend an average of nearly $15,000 per worker per year on benefits, together with the complex nature of many benefits and the poor understanding of most employees, the typical communication effort seems woefully inadequate.[67] Organizations are spending less than $1 to communicate every $1,000 in benefits.

Rather than a single standard benefits package for all employees, flexible benefit plans (flex-plans or cafeteria-style plans) permit employees to choose the types and amounts of benefits they want for themselves. The plans vary according to such things as whether minimum levels of certain benefits (such as health care coverage) are prescribed and whether employees can receive money for having chosen a "light" benefits package (or have to pay extra for more benefits). One example is vacation, where some plans permit employees to give up vacation days for more salary or, alternatively, purchase extra vacation days through a salary reduction.

What are the potential advantages of such plans?[68] In the best case, almost all of the objectives discussed previously can be positively influenced. First, employees can gain a greater awareness and appreciation of what the employer provides them, particularly with plans that give employees a lump sum to allocate to benefits. Second, by permitting employee choice, there should be a better match between the benefits package and the employees' preferences. This, in turn, should improve employee

TABLE 13.10

Benefits Communication Techniques

Word of mouth	Booklets
Employee meetings	Web-based statements
Manuals	Letters to employees
Paycheck inserts	Posters
Annual reports	Check stubs
Personal counseling	Benefits fairs
Web-based tools	Annual benefits review
Television and videotapes	Slide presentations
Benefits quizzes	Telephone hot lines

SOURCE: "An Evaluation of Benefit Communication Strategy" by Michael C. Giallourakis and G. Stephen Taylor, which appeared in the 4th Quarter 1991 issue, was reprinted with permission from the *Employee Benefits Journal*, published by the International Foundation of Employee Benefit Plans, Brookfield, WI. All rights reserved. No further transmission or electronic distribution of this material is permitted.

attitudes and retention.[69] Third, employers may achieve overall cost reductions in their benefits programs. Cafeteria plans can be thought of as similar to defined contribution plans, whereas traditional plans are more like defined benefit plans. The employer can control the size of the contribution under the former, but not under the latter, because the cost and utilization of benefits is beyond the employer's control. Costs can also be controlled by designing the choices so that employees have an incentive to choose more efficient options. For example, in the case of a medical flex-plan, employees who do not wish to take advantage of the (presumably more cost-effective) HMO have to pay significant deductibles and other costs under the alternative plans.

One drawback of cafeteria-style plans is their administrative cost, especially in the initial design and start-up stages. However, software packages and standardized flex-plans developed by consultants offer some help in this regard. Another possible drawback to these plans is adverse selection. Employees are most likely to choose benefits that they expect to need the most. Someone in need of dental work would choose as much dental coverage as possible. As a result, employer costs can increase significantly as each employee chooses benefits based on their personal value. Another result of adverse selection is the difficulty in estimating benefits costs under such a plan, especially in small companies. Adverse selection can be controlled, however, by limiting coverage amounts, pricing benefits that are subject to adverse selection higher, or using a limited set of packaged options, which prevents employees from choosing too many benefits options that would be susceptible to adverse selection.

Flexible Spending Accounts

A flexible spending account permits pretax contributions to an employee account that can be drawn on to pay for uncovered health care expenses (like deductibles or copayments). A separate account of up to $5,000 per year is permitted for pretax contributions to cover dependent care expenses. The federal tax code requires that funds in the health care and dependent care accounts be earmarked in advance and spent during the plan year. Remaining funds revert to the employer. Therefore, the accounts work best to the extent that employees have predictable expenses. The major advantage of such plans is the increase in take-home pay that results from pretax payment of health and dependent care expenses. Consider again the hypothetical employee with annual earnings of $50,000 and an effective total marginal tax rate of 41 percent from Table 13.1. The take-home pay from an additional $10,000 in salary with and without a flexible dependent care account is as follows:

	NO FLEXIBLE SPENDING CARE ACCOUNT	FLEXIBLE SPENDING CARE ACCOUNT
Salary portion	$10,000	$10,000
Pretax dependent care contribution	–$ 0	–$ 5,000
Taxable salary	$10,000	$ 5,000
Tax (41 percent)	–$ 4,100	–$ 2,050
Aftertax cost of dependent care	–$ 5,000	–$ 0
Take-home pay	$ 900	$ 2,950

Therefore, the use of a flexible spending account saves the employee $2,050 ($2,950 – $900) per year.

General Regulatory Issues

Although we have already discussed a number of regulatory issues, some additional ones require attention.

Nondiscrimination Rules and Qualified Plans

As a general rule, all benefits packages must meet certain rules to be classified as qualified plans. What are the advantages of a qualified plan? Basically, it receives more favorable tax treatment than a nonqualified plan. In the case of a qualified retirement plan, for example, these tax advantages include (1) an immediate tax deduction for employers for their contributions to retirement funds, (2) no tax liability for the employee at the time of the employer deduction, and (3) tax-free investment returns (from stocks, bonds, money markets, or the like) on the retirement funds.[70]

What rules must be satisfied for a plan to obtain qualified status? Each benefit area has different rules. It would be impossible to describe the various rules here, but some general observations are possible. Taking pensions as an example again, vesting requirements must be met. More generally, qualified plans must meet so-called nondiscrimination rules. Basically, this means that a benefit cannot discriminate in favor of "highly compensated employees." One rationale behind such rules is that the tax benefits of qualified benefits plans (and the corresponding loss of tax revenues for the U.S. government) should not go disproportionately to the wealthy.[71] Rather, the favorable tax treatment is designed to encourage employers to provide important benefits to a broad spectrum of employees. The nondiscrimination rules discourage owners or top managers from adopting plans that benefit them exclusively.

Sex, Age, and Disability

Beyond the Pregnancy Discrimination Act's requirements that were discussed earlier in the chapter, a second area of concern for employers in ensuring legal treatment of men and women in the benefits area has to do with pension benefits. Women tend to live longer than men, meaning that pension benefits for women are more costly, all else being equal. However, in its 1978 *Manhart* ruling, the Supreme Court declared it illegal for employers to require women to contribute more to a defined benefit plan than men: Title VII protects individuals, and not all women outlive all men.[72]

Two major age-related issues have received attention under the Age Discrimination in Employment Act (ADEA) and later amendments such as the Older Workers Benefit Protection Act (OWBPA). First, employers must take care not to discriminate against workers over age 40 in the provision of pay or benefits. As one example, employers cannot generally cease accrual (stop the growth) of retirement benefits at some age (like 65) as a way of pressuring older employees to retire.[73] Second, early retirement incentive programs need to meet the following standards to avoid legal liability: (1) the employee is not coerced to accept the incentive and retire, (2) accurate information is provided regarding options, and (3) the employee is given adequate time (is not pressured) to make a decision.

Employers also have to comply with the Americans with Disabilities Act (ADA), which went into effect in 1992. The ADA specifies that employees with disabilities must have "equal access to whatever health insurance coverage the employer provides other employees." However, the act also notes that the terms and conditions of health insurance can be based on risk factors as long as this is not a subterfuge for denying the benefit to those with disabilities. Employers with risk-based programs in place would be in a stronger position, however, than employers who make changes after hiring employees with disabilities.[74]

Monitoring Future Benefits Obligations

Financial Accounting Statement (FAS) 106

The rule issued by the Financial Accounting Standards Board in 1993 requiring companies to fund benefits provided after retirement on an accrual rather than a pay-as-you-go basis and to enter these future cost obligations on their financial statements.

Financial Accounting Statement (FAS) 106, issued by the Financial Accounting Standards Board, became effective in 1993. This rule requires that any benefits (excluding pensions) provided after retirement (the major one being health care) can no longer be funded on a pay-as-you-go basis. Rather, they must be paid on an accrual basis, and companies must enter these future cost obligations on their financial statements. The effect on financial statements can be substantial. For AT&T, a company with a large retiree population, the initial effect of adopting FAS 106 was a reduction in net income of between $5.5 billion and $7.5 billion. General Motors (GM) took a $20.8 billion reduction in net income, resulting in a total loss of $23.5 billion in 1992, the largest loss in corporate history.[75] In 2002, GM's retiree health care cost was over 15 percent of its operating cash flow and it currently has an unfunded obligation here of more than $50 billion.[76]

Increasing retiree health care costs (and the change in accounting standards) have led companies like GM to require its white-collar employees and retirees to pay insurance premiums for the first time in its history and to increase copayments and deductibles. Survey data indicate that some companies are ending retiree health care benefits altogether, while most have reduced benefits or increased retiree contributions. Obviously, such changes hit the elderly hard, especially those with relatively fixed incomes. Not surprisingly, legal challenges have arisen. The need to balance the interests of shareholders, current employees, and retirees in this area will be one of the most difficult challenges facing managers in the future.

A Look Back

We have seen that many organizations have become less paternalistic in their employee benefits strategies. Employees now have more responsibility, and sometimes more risk, regarding their benefits choices. One change has been in the area of retirement income plans, where employers have moved toward greater reliance on defined contribution plans. Such plans require employees to understand investing; otherwise, their retirement years may not be so happy. The risk to employees is especially great when defined contribution plans invest a substantial portion of their assets in company stock. One reason companies do this is because they wish to move away from an entitlement mentality and instead link benefits to company performance. However, if the company has financial problems, employees risk losing not only their jobs, but also their retirement money. As we saw in the beginning of the chapter, another change has been in the area of health care benefits for retirees, where companies have reduced or sometimes eliminated such benefits. Again, the responsibility for anticipating this possibility increasingly falls with employees. In the health care area, employees are being asked to increase the proportion of costs that they pay and also to use data on health care quality to make better choices about health care. Finally, although these trends characterize many employers, some employers follow different benefit strategies. SAS, the subject of the end of chapter *BusinessWeek* case, provides an example.

Questions

1. Why do employers offer benefits? Is it because the law requires it, because it makes good business sense, or because it is the right thing to do? How much responsibility should employers have for the health and well-being of their employees? Take the perspective of both a shareholder and an employee in answering this question.
2. If you were advising a new company on how to design its health care plan, what would you recommend?

Summary

Effective management of employee benefits is an important means by which organizations successfully compete. Benefits costs are substantial and continue to grow rapidly in some areas, most notably health care. Control of such costs is necessary to compete in the product market. At the same time, employers must offer a benefits package that permits them to compete in the labor market. Beyond investing more money in benefits, this attraction and retention of quality employees can be helped by better communication of the value of the benefits package and by allowing employees to tailor benefits to their own needs through flexible benefits plans.

Employers continue to be a major source of economic security for employees, often providing health insurance, retirement benefits, and so forth. Changes to benefits can have a tremendous impact on employees and retirees. Therefore, employers carry a significant social responsibility in making benefits decisions. At the same time, employees need to be aware that they will increasingly become responsible for their own economic security. Health care benefit design is changing to encourage employees to be more informed consumers, and retirement benefits will depend more and more on the financial investment decisions employees make on their own behalf.

Discussion Questions

1. The chapter opening story described how relationships between employers and employees are changing. What are the likely consequences of this change? Where does the social responsibility of employers end, and where does the need to operate more efficiently begin?
2. Your company, like many others, is experiencing double-digit percentage increases in health care costs. What suggestions can you offer that may reduce the rate of cost increases?
3. Why is communication so important in the employee benefits area? What sorts of programs can a company use to communicate more effectively? What are the potential positive consequences of more effective benefits communication?
4. What are the potential advantages of flexible benefits and flexible spending accounts? Are there any potential drawbacks?
5. Although benefits account for a large share of employee compensation, many feel there is little evidence on whether an employer receives an adequate return on the benefits investment. One suggestion has been to link benefits to individual, group, or organization performance. Explain why you would or would not recommend this strategy to an organization.

Self-Assessment Exercise

One way companies determine which types of benefits to provide is to use a survey asking employees which types of benefits are important to them. Read the following list of employee benefits. For each benefit, mark an X in the column that indicates whether it is important to you or not.

Benefit	Important to Have	Not Important to Have	% Employers Offering
Dependent-care flexible spending account			70%
Flextime			64
Ability to bring child to work in case of emergency			30
Elder-care referral services			21
Adoption assistance			21
On-site child care center			6
Gym subsidy			28
Vaccinations on site (e.g., flu shots)			61
On-site fitness center			26
Casual dress days (every day)			53
Organization-sponsored sports teams			39
Food services/subsidized cafeteria			29
Travel-planning services			27
Dry-cleaning services			15
Massage therapy services at work			12
Self-defense training			6
Concierge services			4

Compare your importance ratings for each benefit to the corresponding number in the right-hand column that indicates the percentage of employers that offer the benefit. Are you likely to find jobs that provide the benefits you want? Explain.

SOURCE: Based on Figure 2, "Percent of Employers Offering Work/Life Benefits (by Year)," in *Workplace Visions* 4 (2002), p. 3, published by the Society for Human Resource Management.

Manager's Hot Seat Exercise: Listening Skills: Yeah, Whatever

This Manager's Hot Seat case explores how important it is for individuals to possess skill in communicating with others. As the video displays, possession of communication skills is especially vital within the organizational setting. The presented case study also clearly shows the significance of effective listening skills. Without adequate listening skills, misunderstanding of information is very likely to occur. Should this occur, the end result can prove to be quite costly for organizations.

Group Activity

All members of the class will participate in this activity. The purpose of this exercise is to see how vital communication skills, especially listening skills, truly are. Here is the scenario: Everyone works for the same company. This company has decided to change insurance plans and coverage for its employees. It will now have a $200 annual deductible for single employees, $450 for families, $20,000 life insurance coverage after providing four years of service with the company, no eyeglass coverage at all, and a dental plan that pays 35% of all services for teeth except enamel fillings, which will have 75 percent coverage paid.

The first person in row one will review this information. He or she has three minutes to read over and study it. He or she should make notes—to be used later in the exercise—of what the information says. Prepare a 2- to 3- sentence assessment of this insurance information. Now, this first row person must relay the insurance information and the assessment of it to the individual sitting behind him or her. The second row person onward should not take notes but rely on listening. **Remember, no notes are to be used yet!** Keep this going until all students have been informed of the new information. The last person to receive the information is to write down what he or she is told and read it aloud to the class. The first person is to read aloud the original notes.

In open class discussion, identify any differences that were found in the two lists. Discuss how this exercise demonstrates the importance of effective communication and listening skills. Discuss the effects ineffective communication can have on organizations. Discuss how ineffective communication can affect an organization's employee benefits plan and the level of employee understanding of such plans. Discuss methods to improve communication and listening skills.

Exercising Strategy: Companies Learn that It Pays to Keep Employees Fit

Physical fitness—or at least wellness—does matter, as more and more companies and their insurers are learning. A healthy workforce means better productivity and fewer workdays lost, not to mention reduced medical costs by keeping injuries and illnesses to a minimum. A study published by the Presidents' Council on Physical Fitness and Sports found that fitness programs provided by companies saved from $1.15 to $5.52 for every dollar spent.

At 3Com, the network communications company, employees spend their lunch hours at the WellCom Center, a 13,500-square-foot fitness facility right on site. There they can cycle, walk a treadmill, lift weights, take a fitness class, or relax in the sauna. Or they can play a game of basketball or beach volleyball outside. Afterward, they can cool off at the juice bar with a fruit smoothie. The center is open 24 hours a day, seven days a week, to meet the needs of employees who work at all hours. More than 40 percent of the 4,200 workers at 3Com are WellCom members, and 70 percent take advantage of the center's seminars on wellness, smoking cessation, or weight loss. "A healthy workforce is good for employees and good for 3Com," says Peter Sandman, a manager of strategic planning at the company. "It helps recruiting and it helps retention, especially in a competitive environment like Silicon Valley [California]."

Applied Materials Inc. of Santa Clara, California, conducted its own study that showed that for fitness center participants, medical payments were reduced by 20 percent, hospital admissions were 70 percent lower, costs for accident-related disability claims were 30 percent less, and workers' compensation claims were 79 percent less than those of employees who didn't use the company's fitness center. Even a five-minute stretch break has been shown to reduce strains and sprains by as much as 65 percent. "Just moving and getting away from their PC makes them feel better," says Judy Webster, director of corporate wellness for the company.

Boeing's health care package also includes access to its fitness centers as part of its overall recreation program. "When you're happy and healthy, you're able to perform at your best," explains the aircraft manufacturer's website. The recreation program includes indoor and outdoor facilities as well as discount packages for sports and cultural events. These companies have embraced the wisdom of the old adage, "an ounce of prevention is worth a pound of cure," and it has literally paid off.

SOURCE: Boeing website, www.boeing.com, accessed October 30, 2001; D. Beck, "Your Company Needs Its Own Best Practices," *Career Journal* from *The Wall Street Journal* (July 30–August 5, 2001), www.careerjournal.com; M. Chase, "Healthy Assets," *The Wall Street Journal* (May 1. 2000), http://interactive.wsj.

Questions

1. Why don't more companies emphasize employee wellness? Does it work better for some companies than for others?
2. The companies here have on-site facilities. Is that the right model for all companies?

Managing People: From the Pages of *BusinessWeek*

BusinessWeek Dr. Goodnight's Company Town

The war for talent has businesses transforming their corporate campuses into country clubs—offering everything from five-star lunches to concierges willing to arrange employees' lawn mowing and haircuts. But long before the words "labor crunch" put employee perks in vogue, SAS Institute Inc. founder James Goodnight was lavishing money on programmers instead of headhunters. It worked: SAS turnover is 4 percent in an industry for which 20 percent is typical. The Cary (North Carolina)-based company may compete against PeopleSoft Inc. and Oracle Corp., but SAS employees aren't asked to mimic their Silicon Valley brethren's sleep-starved lifestyle. Goodnight, a shy billionaire who until recently drove a Buick Roadmaster wagon, believes in leaving the office at 5 p.m. sharp. Dinner, he says, should be spent with your family, not at your desk.

The Perk Factory Goodnight remembers working as a programmer for NASA—a place so cheap it wouldn't even spring for workers' sodas. Insulted, he vowed to do things differently. Today he's become a Willy Wonka to his workers, creating a corporate perk factory where even the plain and peanut-filled M&M's, replenished like clockwork every Wednesday, are free. Goodnight believes that if you treat people as if they make a difference, they will. The turnover savings he reaps from his largesse are huge: an estimated $75 million a year. This means Goodnight can afford all those banana trees and cracker-and-cheese–stocked snack rooms. It may be too Stepford-like for cynics, but the T-shirt- and Teva-sporting SAS employees say they wouldn't have it any other way.

On-site benefits at the Institute include day care, Montessori school, the Atrium, and lunchtime entertainment.

For $25 a month, the center will take babies after SAS's six-week paid maternity leave. Sixty percent of the employees use the on-site day care; parents can visit or pick up their kids for lunch. Employees also get private offices and open spaces for impromptu meetings and breaks.

The perks aren't limited to the on-site stuff. Goodnight offers discounts on everything from land in his ritzy subdivision to memberships at his country club. Employees make only industry-average salaries, but they get a generous year-end bonus, profit sharing, and an extra week of paid vacation at Christmas. Employees can also enjoy Shiatsu, Swedish, and deep tissue massages—all available between meetings—right down the hall. A free clinic is also available so employees can get care at work—even when a child is ill.

What They Want   This is just the beginning. SAS also has a 55,000-square-foot athletic facility worthy of Olympic games—plus tennis courts, walking trails, picnic shelters, and a lake, canoes provided. In summer the place looks more like a raucous college campus than a headquarter for wireheads. After your workout, the company takes your gym clothes and returns them to you freshly laundered the next day. Hungry? Head over to the subsidized cafeteria, where it's hard to spend more than $3 for a feast.

What They Like   When Goodnight decided he didn't like Cary's local high school, he built a new private college prep called Cary Academy right next to SAS. (His own son didn't want to switch schools to attend.) Employees receive a 10 percent discount off the $9,000-per-year tuition. If that's too steep, they can still enjoy a smorgasbord of free services like the car wash and detailing, farmer's market, and advice on financial planning for college and retirement. But the all-time favorite SAS perk is the seven-hour workday, which leaves time for family or personal obligations. While the Silicon Valley set grinds away, SAS's gates close shut. For Goodnight, seven hours of work a day are plenty.

Why They Stay   Goodnight believes that workers' environments can inspire or depress them. To that end, he has hired a full-time ergonomics specialist and built an on-site greenhouse that provides fresh flowers. His 7,000 employees also enjoyed the $16 million in bonuses and $30 million in profit sharing shelled out last year, when the company's revenues hit $1.02 billion. The payoff: similar software companies lose and replace 1,000 people a year, while SAS loses 130. Says one SAS employee, "We're spoiled rotten."

SOURCE: Reprinted from June 19, 2000 issue of *BusinessWeek* by special permission. Copyright © 2000 by The McGraw-Hill Companies, Inc.

Questions

1. Would you like to work at SAS? Why or why not? Would you prefer to work at SAS or at Microsoft?
2. What are the advantages and disadvantages of SAS's benefits strategy?
3. SAS is sometimes criticized for being too paternalistic. What is your opinion?

Please see the video case at the end of the book that corresponds to this chapter: Finding and Keeping the Best Employees: SAS.

Notes

1. D. Zoia, "DCC Attacks High Health Care Costs," *Ward's Auto World*, September 1999, p. 75; P. Welch, "A Small Reprieve for Detroit, But . . . ," *BusinessWeek* (September 22, 2003), p. 38.
2. H. W. Hennessey, "Using Employee Benefits to Gain a Competitive Advantage," *Benefits Quarterly* 5, no. 1 (1989), pp. 51–57; B. Gerhart and G.T. Milkovich, "Employee Compensation: Research and Practice," in *Handbook of Industrial and Organizational Psychology*, vol. 3, 2nd ed., ed. M. D. Dunnette and L. M. Hough (Palo Alto, CA: *Consulting Psychologists Press*, 1992); J. Swist, "Benefits Communications: Measuring Impact and Value," *Employee Benefit Plan Review*, September 2002, pp. 24–26.
3. R. Ehrenberg and R. S. Smith. *Modern Labor Economics: Theory and Public Policy*, 7th ed. (Upper Saddle River, NJ: Addison Wesley Longman, 2000).
4. B. T. Beam Jr. and J. J. McFadden, *Employee Benefits*, 6th ed. (Chicago: Dearborn Financial Publishing, 2000).
5. Bureau of National Affairs, "Most Workers Who Struck in 1990 Did So over Health Coverage, AFL–CIO Says," *Daily Labor Report* (August 20, 1991), p. A12; M. Herper, "GE Strike Sounds Health Care Alarm," *Forbes* (January 14, 2003), www.forbes.com.
6. The organization and description in this section draws heavily on Beam and McFadden, *Employee Benefits*.
7. See www.doleta.gov for further information.
8. J. A. Penczak, "Unemployment Benefit Plans," in *Employee Benefits Handbook*, 3rd ed., ed. J. D. Mamorsky (Boston: Warren, Gorham & Lamont, 1992).
9. J. V. Nackley, *Primer on Workers' Compensation* (Washington, DC: Bureau of National Affairs, 1989).
10. Beam and McFadden, *Employee Benefits*, 6th ed., p. 81.
11. www.dol.gov/esa.
12. M. D. Fefer, "What to Do about Workers' Comp," *Fortune* (June 29, 1992), pp. 80ff; National Academy of Social Insurance, "Re-

cession Affects Workers' Compensation Trends" (July 15, 2003), www.nasi.org.

13. A. H. Wheeler, "Pathophysiology of Chronic Back Pain," www.emedicine.com (2002).

14. J. R. Hollenbeck, D. R. Ilgen, and S. M. Crampton, "Lower Back Disability in Occupational Settings: A Review of the Literature from a Human Resource Management View," *Personnel Psychology* 45 (1992), pp. 247–78; J. J. Martocchio, D. A. Harrison, and H. Berkson, "Connections between Lower Back Pain, Interventions, and Absence from Work: A Time-Based Meta-Analysis," *Personnel Psychology* (2000), p. 595.

15. Employee Benefit Research Institute, "Value of Employee Benefits Constant in a Changing World," www.ebri.org (March 28, 2002).

16. Beam and McFadden, *Employee Benefits*, 6th ed.

17. Social Security Administration, "Fast Facts and Figures about Social Security." Data for 2001, published 2003, www.ssa.gov.

18. L. M. Dailey and J. A. Turner, "Private Pension Coverage in Nine Countries," *Monthly Labor Review*, May 1992, pp. 40–43; Hewitt Associates, *Salaried Employee Benefits Provided by Major Employers in 1990* (Lincolnshire, IL: Hewitt Associates, 1990); W. J. Wiatrowski, "New Survey Data on Pension Benefits," *Monthly Labor Review*, August 1991, pp. 8–21; K. A. Bender, "Pension Integration and Retirement Benefits," *Monthly Labor Review*, February 2001, pp. 49–58, http://stats.bls.gov/opub/mlr.

19. www.pbgc.gov.

20. www.irs.gov. Those age 50 and over have higher contribution limits.

21. R. A. Ippolito, "Toward Explaining the Growth of Defined Contribution Plans," *Industrial Relations* 34 (1995), pp. 1–20; Employee Benefit Research Institute, "Historical Statistics," EBRI May 2004 Policy Forum, www.ebri.org.

22. J. Fierman, "How Secure Is Your Nest Egg?" *Fortune* (August 12, 1991), pp. 50–54.

23. Beam and McFadden, *Employee Benefits*, 6th ed.

24. B. J. Coleman, *Primer on Employee Retirement Income Security Act*, 3rd ed. (Washington, DC: Bureau of National Affairs, 1989).

25. *Continental Can Company v. Gavalik*, summary in *Daily Labor Report* (December 8, 1987): "Supreme Court Lets Stand Third Circuit Ruling That Pension Avoidance Scheme Is ERISA Violation," No. 234, p. A-14.

26. A. L. Gustman, O. S. Mitchell, and T. L. Steinmeier, "The Role of Pensions in the Labor Market: A Survey of the Literature," *Industrial and Labor Relations* 47 (1994), pp. 417–38.

27. D. A. DeCenzo and S. J. Holoviak, *Employee Benefits* (Englewood Cliffs, NJ: Prentice-Hall, 1990).

28. E. P. Lazear, "Why Is There Early Retirement?" *Journal of Political Economy* 87 (1979), pp. 1261–84; Gustman et al., "The Role of Pensions."

29. P. Cappelli, *The New Deal at Work: Managing the Market-Driven Workforce* (Boston: Harvard Business School Press, 1999).

30. S. Dorsey, "Pension Portability and Labor Market Efficiency," *Industrial and Labor Relations* 48, no. 5 (1995), pp. 276–92.

31. Commission of the European Communities, European Community Directive 93/104/EC, issued November 23, 1993 and amended June 22, 2000, by Directive 2000/34/EC, http://europa/eu.int/comm/index_en.htm.

32. DeCenzo and Holoviak, *Employee Benefits*, 6th ed.

33. S. L. Grover and K. J. Crooker, "Who Appreciates Family Responsive Human Resource Policies: The Impact of Family-Friendly Policies on the Organizational Attachment of Parents and Non-parents," *Personnel Psychology* 48 (1995), pp. 271–88;

T. J. Rothausen, J. A. Gonzalez, N. E. Clarke, and L. L. O'Dell, "Family-Friendly Backlash: Fact or Fiction? The Case of Organizations' On-Site Child Care Centers," *Personnel Psychology* 51 (1998), p. 685; M. A. Arthur, "Share Price Reactions to Work-Family Initiatives: An Institutional Perspective," *Academy of Management Journal* 46 (2003), p. 497; J. E. Perry-Smith and T. Blum, "Work-Family Human Resource Bundles and Perceived Organizational Performance," *Academy of Management Journal* 43 (2000), pp. 1107–17.

34. "The Employer's Role in Helping Working Families." For examples of child care arrangements in some well-known companies (e.g., AT&T, Apple, Exxon, IBM, Merck), see "A Look at Child-Care Benefits," *USA Today* (March 14, 1989), p. 4B; U.S. Census Bureau, "America's Families and Living Arrangements," June 2001, www.census.gov.

35. J. Waldfogel, "International Policies toward Parental Leave and Child Care," *Future of Children* 11(1) (2001), pp. 99–111.

36. P. Hardin, "Women Execs Should Feel at Ease about Taking Full Maternity Leave," *Personnel Journal*, September 1995, p. 19.

37. "The Families and Work Institute's 1998 Business Work–Life Study," www.familiesandwork.org. Results based on a nationally representative survey of employers having 100 or more employees.

38. J. Fierman, "It's 2 A.M.: Let's Go to Work," *Fortune* (August 21, 1995), pp. 82–88.

39. E. E. Kossek, "Diversity in Child Care Assistance Needs: Employee Problems, Preferences, and Work-Related Outcomes," *Personnel Psychology* 43 (1990), pp. 769–91.

40. "A Bank Profits from Its Work/Life Program," *Workforce*, February 1997, p. 49.

41. R. Broderick and B. Gerhart, "Nonwage Compensation," in *The Human Resource Management Handbook*, ed. D. Lewin, D. J. B. Mitchell, and M. A. Zadi (San Francisco: JAI Press, 1996).

42. Hennessey, "Using Employee Benefits to Gain a Competitive Advantage."

43. U.S. Bureau of Labor Statistics, "Employer Cost for Employee Compensation," www.bls.gov; U.S. Chamber of Commerce Research Center, Employee Benefits Study, annual (Washington, D.C.: U.S. Chamber of Commerce).

44. www.census.gov.

45. Employee Benefit Research Institute, "Health Care Reform."

46. A. C. Monheit and P. F. Cooper, "Health Insurance and Job Mobility: The Effects of Public Policy on Job-Lock," *Industrial and Labor Relations Review* 48 (1994), pp. 86–102.

47. Beam and McFadden, *Employee Benefits*, 6th ed.

48. R. Lieber, "New Way to Curb Medical Costs: Make Employees Feel the Sting," *The Wall Street Journal* (June 23, 2004), p. A1.

49. M. Barringer and O. S. Mitchell, "Workers' Preferences among Company-Provided Health Insurance Plans," *Industrial and Labor Relations Review* 48 (1994), pp. 141–52.

50. Beam and McFadden, *Employee Benefits*, 6th ed.

51. Wellness Councils of America, "101 Ways to Wellness," www.welcoa.org, 2001; Wellness Councils of America, "A Guide to Developing Your Worksite Wellness Program," www.welcoa.org, 1997.

52. S. Tully, "America's Healthiest Companies," *Fortune* (June 12, 1995), pp. 98–106.

53. G. Flynn, "Companies Make Wellness Work," *Personnel Journal*, February 1995, pp. 63–66.

54. D. A. Harrison and L. Z. Liska, "Promoting Regular Exercise in Organizational Fitness Programs: Health-Related Differences in Motivational Building Blocks," *Personnel Psychology* 47 (1994), pp. 47–71.

55. J. C. Erfurt, A. Foote, and M. A. Heirich, "The Cost-Effective-

ness of Worksite Wellness Programs for Hypertension Control, Weight Loss, Smoking Cessation and Exercise," *Personnel Psychology* 45 (1992), pp. 5–27.

56. Ibid.

57. U.S. Bureau of Labor Statistics, www.bls.gov.

58. H. Gardner, unpublished manuscript (Cheyenne, WY: Options & Choices, Inc., 1995).

59. H. B. Noble, "Quality Is Focus for Health Plans," *The New York Times* (July 3, 1995), p. A1; J. D. Klinke, "Medicine's Industrial Revolution," *The Wall Street Journal* (August 21, 1995), p. A8.

60. J. B. White, "Business Plan," *The Wall Street Journal* (October 19, 1998), p. R18.

61. J. Schor, *The Overworked American: The Unexpected Decline of Leisure* (New York: Basic Books, 1991); U.S. Bureau of Labor Statistics, "Workers Are on the Job More Hours over the Course of a Year," *Issues in Labor Statistics*, February 1997.

62. Hewitt Associates. http://www.hewitt.com.

63. Beam and McFadden, *Employee Benefits*, 6th ed.

64. M. Wilson, G. B. Northcraft, and M. A. Neale, "The Perceived Value of Fringe Benefits," *Personnel Psychology* 38 (1985), pp. 309–20. Similar results were found in other studies reviewed by H. W. Hennessey, P. L. Perrewe, and W. A. Hochwarter, "Impact of Benefit Awareness on Employee and Organizational Outcomes: A Longitudinal Field Experiment," *Benefits Quarterly* 8, no. 2 (1992), pp. 90–96.

65. R. Huseman, J. Hatfield, and R. Robinson, "The MBA and Fringe Benefits," *Personnel Administrator* 23, no. 7 (1978), pp. 57–60. See summary in H. W. Hennessey Jr., "Using Employee Benefits to Gain a Competitive Advantage," *Benefits Quarterly* 5, no. 1 (1989), pp. 51–57.

66. Hennessey et al., "Impact of Benefit Awareness"; the same study found no impact of the increased awareness and benefits satisfaction on overall job satisfaction. G. F. Dreher, R. A. Ash, and R. D. Bretz, "Benefit Coverage and Employee Cost: Critical Factors in Explaining Compensation Satisfaction," *Personnel Psychology* 41 (1988), pp. 237–54.

67. M. C. Giallourakis and G. S. Taylor, "An Evaluation of Benefit Communication Strategy," *Employee Benefits Journal* 15, no. 4 (1991), pp. 14–18.

68. Beam and McFadden, *Employee Benefits*, 6th ed.

69. For supportive evidence, see A. E. Barber, R. B. Dunham, and R. A. Formisano, "The Impact of Flexible Benefits on Employee Satisfaction: A Field Study," *Personnel Psychology* 45 (1992), pp. 55–75; E. E. Lawler, *Pay and Organizational Development* (Reading, MA: Addison-Wesley, 1981).

70. Beam and McFadden, *Employee Benefits*.

71. Ibid.

72. *Los Angeles Dept. of Water & Power v. Manhart*, 435 US SCt 702 (1978), 16 EPD, 8250.

73. S. K. Hoffman, "Discrimination Litigation Relating to Employee Benefits," *Labor Law Journal*, June 1992, pp. 362–81.

74. Ibid., p. 375.

75. W. A. Reimert, "Accounting for Retiree Health Benefits," *Compensation and Benefits Review* 23, no. 5 (September–October, 1991), pp. 49–55; D. P. Levin, "20.8 Billion G. M. Charge for Benefits," *The New York Times* (February 2, 1993), p. D4.

76. A. Tergesen, "The Hidden Bite of Retiree Health," *BusinessWeek* (January 19, 2004); D. Welch, "Has GM Outrun Its Pension Problems?" *BusinessWeek* (January 19, 2004).

5
Part

Special Topics in Human Resource Management

14 Chapter

Collective Bargaining and Labor Relations

Objectives After reading this chapter, you should be able to:

1. Describe what is meant by collective bargaining and labor relations.

2. Identify the labor relations goals of management, labor unions, and society.

3. Explain the legal environment's impact on labor relations.

4. Describe the major labor–management interactions: organizing, contract negotiations, and contract administration.

5. Describe new, less adversarial approaches to labor–management relations.

6. Explain how changes in competitive challenges (e.g., product market competition and globalization) are influencing labor–management interactions.

7. Explain how labor relations in the public sector differ from labor relations in the private sector.

No terms & concepts for final

Enter the World of Business

The American Dream

Not long ago, the top managers and 80,000 employees at the world's largest airline were barely on speaking terms. The only time they really talked was over the bargaining table. But in a classroom dotted with inspirational posters (JUST BECAUSE THE SITUATION IS TENSE . . . YOU DON'T HAVE TO BE!), managers from American Airlines sat down recently to do something unheard of—exchange ideas with employees. From the back, a consultant acting as a "marriage counselor" observed silently as flight attendants and pilots, airport workers and reservationists, and even skycaps made suggestions about how to improve service for American's premium passengers. The rancor of early meetings was gone, replaced by—what's this?—a raucous cheer that went up when flight attendants learned they had won a round in a yearlong battle for . . . half-and-half. Yes, the real thing is again part of coffee service in first class on American. "They've been through a lot, but they're still passionate," says counselor Marc Bridgham, beaming.

Thanks in part to such sessions, American Airlines is coming back from the brink. In the aftermath of 9/11, when two of its planes went down, American suffered from a collapse in air travel, two wars, a rotten economy, the outbreak of SARS and the rise of low-cost carriers—all of which conspired to put the airline on the verge

of bankruptcy in April 2003. What's more, employees were in open revolt after they discovered that CEO Don Carty had secretly handed out retention bonuses and pension guarantees to executives, even as he was negotiating $1.8 billion in salary cuts and eliminating 14,000 jobs. Sliding into the pilot seat, new CEO Gerard Arpey brought in corporate counselors to change the company's culture and slashed the airline's operating costs, making American the most efficient big-network carrier. But the airline's troubles aren't over. Despite increasing revenue and posting a modest $30 million profit in March, the airline is still losing money because of rising fuel prices. Huge pension costs, soft business travel and competition from low-cost carriers like Southwest and JetBlue could still wipe out the airline's mini-recovery.

When he took over a year ago, Arpey had little choice but to introduce radical therapy. The CEO, whose first job as a college student was stowing luggage for Delta, remembers sitting alone in a conference room a year ago, exhausted from negotiating with flight attendants and facing American's grim future. The company had lost $1 billion in the first quarter of 2003. "We had no cash, no flight attendants' deal, no access to the [financial] markets, no real understanding by our employees or Wall Street of where we needed to take the company," says Arpey, 45. Forget about the short-term cash-flow problem of a $20 billion company with just $1 billion in the bank and debt payments coming due, he says. "We had a long-term 'Where is the company going?' crisis."

Arpey launched a plan to cut annual costs by $4 billion, or 25 percent of American's pre-9/11 operating costs. But with pay cuts of up to 23 percent and morale at an all-time low, he also brought in corporate therapist Overland Resource Group, which has helped giants like Ford Motor Co. and its unions rethink old habits. Overland told the unions and management that they should see each other not as warring parties but as businesses that need each other to survive. Overland set up a structure, called Joint Leadership Teams, to make sure the old "silos" (management in one silo, unions in another, never talking) came tumbling down. The meetings haven't exactly been love-ins. One blew up over employee travel passes, but the company called the unions the next day to work on a solution. "Gerard really gets it," says John Darrah, head of the Allied Pilots Association.

To carve out savings, Arpey says he shamelessly borrowed ideas from competitors. He reversed his predecessor's policy of expanding legroom, adding seats in one-fourth of the fleet so American could cut fares even further. Emulating low-cost carrier Southwest, American is simplifying its fleet, from 14 types of planes to six by September. Picking up on an idea from TWA, which American bought in 2001, pilots suggested taxiing on one engine instead of two to save fuel. Not all the changes were bloodless. The company's 10,500 pilots agreed to the biggest layoff in airline history: 2,400 jobs, 1 in 5 pilots, saving $660 million a year.

Gradually, employees started embracing the idea of rethinking the old ways of doing things. Arpey likes to hold up a set of plastic cutlery to show how far the two sides have come in helping management cut some $2.2 billion in costs annually. Plastic forks and spoons used to cost $2 million a year, but employees at headquarters came up with the idea of reverse auctioning on the Internet and saved $600,000 by buying them in Asia. Of all the changes in operating

methods, some of the most productive have come in aircraft maintenance. Workers on MD-80 heavy overhauls realized they could reuse perfectly good windows, lightbulbs and fasteners on the plane's outer skin without compromising safety. They saved $30,000 on each overhaul—trimming at least $5 million a year. Shop-floor workers in Tulsa, Oklahoma, taking lean-manufacturing tips from a Toyota sensei, or master, trimmed time and inventory, freeing up room to in-source aircraft repair work from American Eagle.

Even longtime veterans got into the act. In a corner of the huge maintenance complex in Tulsa, Ralph Dwain Garrison and Jack (Robin) Hood schemed to save drill bits costing as much as $200 each that were routinely being tossed after a few uses. Garrison took the motor from his son's science project and slapped on a vacuum-cleaner belt to create "Thumpin' Ralph"—a machine to sharpen old drill bits for reuse. Savings? Over $300,000. "The old mind-set—unions versus management—it's still there for about 10 percent of the people," says machinist Jim Messick. "But if we want to survive as unions and as a company, we have to work together."

Not everyone is happy, of course. Morale is lowest among the 19,500 beleaguered flight attendants, who took 15 percent pay cuts and frequently work on quick turnarounds with little sleep. They plan to hold a press conference in Washington this week to raise concerns that exhaustion could compromise safety. "Company relations with employees, in particular flight attendants, are as strained as ever—if not worse," says John Ward, president of the Association of Professional Flight Attendants, pointing to an "insulting" management memo leaked on the Internet last month. The letter quoted corporate travel agents complaining that American attendants were "not enthusiastic" and aired the airline's "dirty laundry" on flights. "You can hire all the suits you want to give advice," says Ward. "But we're the ones being taken to task when customers are unhappy that service is not what is once was."

Keeping business travelers happy is crucial to American's future. Once the darling of such premium-paying customers, who liked the airline's service along with being able to rack up frequent-flyer miles on transcontinental flights, American has lost some even to the likes of JetBlue, a low-cost alternative with amenities like seat-back TVs. "The business traveler used to be American's bread and butter, but the butter is a little thinner these days," admits executive vice president Dan Garton. But American's elite clientele will see improvements this summer—a low-carb, high-protein breakfast as well as more power ports—and more frequent service on the main bicoastal routes, like New York to Los Angeles.

The company's pension burden weighs on profitability, though Congress recently allowed American to defer some payments to under-funded pensions for two years. This year management has put $319 million away for pensions and will spend an additional $300 million on retirees' medical benefits—an expense its younger competitors don't have. These low-cost carriers "pay people a lot less, and they don't provide good benefits," says Arpey. "I do believe people in big public companies should retire with benefits, but we've got to find a way to pay for it."

While American's turnaround has surprised skeptics, the long-term survival of such old-line carriers is still an open question. No-frills carriers, once just 8 percent of the U.S. market, now grab about 25 percent and compete with American on 8 out of every 10 routes the airline flies. Last week vintage carrier U.S. Airways said it may have to consider its second bankruptcy filing in two years, while United Airlines is still waiting to hear if the government will guarantee a $1.6 billion loan. Delta and its pilots' union are headed for a dustup that could roil the company's future. At American, losses for the first three months this year were lower: $166 million versus $1 billion last year. But jet fuel prices are up more than 40 percent in the past year, and every penny of increase costs American $30 million annually. Arpey is acutely aware that his airline still faces a bumpy ride. Sitting on his desk is a purple papier-mache dinosaur his 6-year-old daughter gave him for his first "show and tell" with executives after the near miss with bankruptcy. "She says it has special flying powers," says Arpey, "and boy, do we need that right now."

Source: Cathy Booth Thomas, "The American Dream," *Time Online* (May 10, 2004). Copyright © 2004 *Time Inc.* Reprinted by permission.

Introduction

In Chapter 11, we saw that the chief executive of American resigned in response to an employee relations firestorm over the fairness of executive pay. New CEO Gerard Arpey is trying to bring American "back from the brink" by building a better relationship with employees, while at the same time, asking for shared sacrifice to do so.

The events at American illustrate both the important role of labor relations in running a business and the influence of competitive challenges on the nature of labor relations. Deregulation in the airlines industry and low-fare competitors have forced a re-thinking of core strategies. To be more competitive, American must reduce cost, but also improve the customer experience. Employees don't want pay cuts, but their employment depends on the company's remaining financially viable. This common goal is what binds management and labor together in a search for improved competitiveness.

The Labor Relations Framework

John Dunlop, former secretary of labor and a leading industrial relations scholar, suggested in the book *Industrial Relations Systems* (1958) that such a system consists of four elements: (1) an environmental context (technology, market pressures, and the legal framework, especially as it affects bargaining power); (2) participants, including employees and their unions, management, and the government; (3) a "web of rules" (rules of the game) that describe the process by which labor and management interact and resolve disagreements (such as the steps followed in settling contract grievances); and (4) ideology.[1] For the industrial relations system to operate properly, the three participants must, to some degree, have a common ideology (like acceptance of the capitalist system) and must accept the roles of the other participants. Acceptance does not translate into convergence of interests, however. To the contrary, some degree of worker–management conflict is inevitable because, although the interests of the two parties overlap, they also diverge in key respects (such as how to divide the economic profits).[2]

Therefore, according to Dunlop and other U.S. scholars of like mind, an effective industrial relations system does not eliminate conflict. Rather, it provides institutions (and a "web of rules") that resolve conflict in a way that minimizes its costs to management, employees, and society. The collective bargaining system is one such institution, as are related mechanisms such as mediation, arbitration, and participation in decision making. These ideas formed the basis for the development in the 1940s of schools and departments of industrial and labor relations to train labor relations professionals who, working in both union and management positions, would have the skills to minimize costly forms of conflict such as strikes (which were reaching record levels at the time) and maximize integrative (win–win) solutions to such disagreements.

A more recent industrial relations model, developed by Harry Katz and Thomas Kochan, is particularly helpful in laying out the types of decisions management and unions make in their interactions and the consequences of such decisions for attainment of goals in areas such as wages and benefits, job security, and the rights and responsibilities of unions and managements.[3] According to Katz and Kochan, these choices occur at three levels.

First, at the strategic level, management makes basic choices such as whether to work with its union(s) or to devote its efforts to developing nonunion operations. Environmental factors (or competitive challenges) offer both constraints and opportunities in implementing strategies. For example, if public opinion toward labor unions becomes negative during a particular time period, some employers may see that as an opportunity to rid themselves of unions, whereas other employers may seek a better working relationship with their unions. Similarly, increased competition may dictate the need to increase productivity or reduce labor costs, but whether this is accomplished by shifting work to nonunion facilities or by working with unions to become more competitive is a strategic choice that management faces.

Although management has often been the initiator of change in recent years, unions face a similar choice between fighting changes to the status quo and being open to new labor–management relationships (like less adversarial forms of participation in decision making, such as labor–management teams).

Katz and Kochan suggest that labor and management choices at the strategic level in turn affect the labor–management interaction at a second level, the functional level, where contract negotiations and union organizing occur, and at the final workplace level, the arena in which the contract is administered. In the opening story, American's strategic-level choice was to work toward its labor unions being not part of the problem, but part of the solution. By doing so, they hope to have labor peace (functional level) and an effective day-to-day working relationship (workplace level). Although the relationships between labor and management at each of the three levels are somewhat interdependent, the relationship at the three levels may also differ. For example, while management may have a strategy of building an effective relationship with its unions at the strategic level, there may be significant day-to-day conflicts over work rules, grievances, and so forth at any given facility or bargaining unit (workplace level).

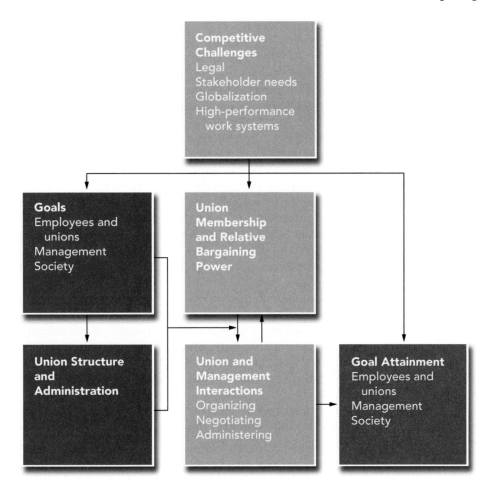

FIGURE 14.1

A Labor Relations
Framework

The labor relations framework depicted in Figure 14.1 incorporates many of the ideas discussed so far, including the important role of the environment (the competitive challenges); union, management, and societal goals; and a separation of union–management interactions into categories (union organizing, contract negotiation, contract administration) that can have important influences on one another but may also be analyzed somewhat independently. The model also highlights the important role that relative bargaining power plays in influencing goals, union–management interactions, and the degree to which each party achieves its goals. Relative bargaining power, in turn, is significantly influenced by the competitive environment (legal, social, quality, high-performance work systems, and globalization competitive challenges) and the size and depth of union membership.[4]

We now describe the components of this model in greater depth. The remainder of the chapter is organized into the following sections: the goals and strategies of society, management, and unions; union structure (including union administration and membership); the legal framework, perhaps the key aspect of the competitive environment for labor relations; union and management interactions (organizing, contract negotiation, contract administration); and goal attainment. Environmental factors (other than legal) and bargaining power are discussed in the context of these sections. In addition, two special topics, international comparisons and public sector labor relations, are discussed.

Goals and Strategies

Society

In one sense, labor unions, with their emphasis on group action, do not fit well with the individualistic orientation of U.S. capitalism. However, industrial relations scholars such as Beatrice and Sidney Webb and John R. Commons argued in the late 1800s and early 1900s that individual workers' bargaining power was far smaller than that of employers, who were likely to have more financial resources and the ability to easily replace workers.[5] Effective institutions for worker representation (like labor unions) were therefore seen as a way to make bargaining power more equal.

Labor unions' major benefit to society is the institutionalization of industrial conflict, which is therefore resolved in the least costly way. Thus, although disagreements between management and labor continue, it is better to resolve disputes through discussion (collective bargaining) than by battling in the streets. As an influential group of industrial relations scholars put it in describing the future of advanced industrial relations around the world, "Class warfare will be forgotten. The battles will be in the corridors instead of the streets, and memos will flow instead of blood."[6] In this sense, collective bargaining not only has the potential to reduce economic losses caused by strikes but may also contribute to societal stability. For this reason, industrial relations scholars have often viewed labor unions as an essential component of a democratic society.[7] These were some of the beliefs that contributed to the enactment of the National Labor Relations Act (NLRA) in 1935, which sought to provide an environment conducive to collective bargaining and has since regulated labor and management activities and interactions.

Even Senator Orrin Hatch, described by *BusinessWeek* as "labor's archrival on Capitol Hill," has spoken of the need for unions:

> There are always going to be people who take advantage of workers. Unions even that out, to their credit. We need them to level the field between labor and management. If you didn't have unions, it would be very difficult for even enlightened employers not to take advantage of workers on wages and working conditions, because of [competition from] rivals. I'm among the first to say I believe in unions.[8]

Although an industrial relations system based on collective bargaining has drawbacks, so too do the alternatives. Unilateral control by management sacrifices workers' rights. Extensive involvement of government and the courts can result in conflict resolution that is expensive, slow, and imposed by someone (a judge) with much less firsthand knowledge of the circumstances than either labor or management.

Management

One of management's most basic decisions is whether to encourage or discourage the unionization of its employees. It may discourage unions because it fears higher wage and benefit costs, the disruptions caused by strikes, and an adversarial relationship with its employees or, more generally, greater constraints placed on its decision-making flexibility and discretion. Historically, management has used two basic strategies to avoid unionization.[9] It may seek to provide employment terms and conditions that employees will perceive as sufficiently attractive and equitable so that they see little gain from union representation. Or it may aggressively oppose union representation, even where there is significant employee interest. Use of the latter strategy has increased significantly during the last 20 to 30 years.

If management voluntarily recognizes a union or if employees are already represented by a union, the focus is shifted from dealing with employees as individuals to employees as a group. Still, certain basic management objectives remain: controlling labor costs and increasing productivity (by keeping wages and benefits in check) and maintaining management prerogatives in important areas such as staffing levels and work rules. Of course, management always has the option of trying to decertify a union (that is, encouraging employees to vote out the union in a decertification election) if it believes that the majority of employees no longer wish to be represented by the union.

Labor Unions

Labor unions seek, through collective action, to give workers a formal and independent voice in setting the terms and conditions of their work. Table 14.1 shows typical provisions negotiated by unions in collective bargaining contracts. Labor unions attempt to represent their members' interests in these decisions.

A major goal of labor unions is bargaining effectiveness, because with it comes the power and influence to make the employees' voices heard and to effect changes in the workplace.[10] The right to strike is one important component of bargaining power. In turn, the success of a strike (actual or threatened) depends on the relative magnitude of the costs imposed on management versus those imposed on the union. A critical factor is the size of union membership. More members translate into a greater ability to halt or disrupt production and also into greater financial resources for continuing a strike in the face of lost wages.

Union Structure, Administration, and Membership

A necessary step in discussing labor–management interactions is a basic knowledge of how labor and management are organized and how they function. Management has been described throughout this book. We now focus on labor unions.

National and International Unions

Most union members belong to a national or international union. In turn, most national unions are composed of multiple local units, and most are affiliated with the American Federation of Labor and Congress of Industrial Organizations (AFL-CIO).

The largest national unions are listed in Table 14.2. (The National Education Association, with 2.5 million members, is not affiliated with the AFL-CIO.) An important characteristic of a union is whether it is a craft or industrial union. The electrical workers' and carpenters' unions are craft unions, meaning that the members all have a particular skill or occupation. Craft unions often are responsible for training their members (through apprenticeships) and for supplying craft workers to employers. Requests for carpenters, for example, would come to the union hiring hall, which would decide which carpenters to send out. Thus craft workers may work for many employers over time, their constant link being to the union. A craft union's bargaining power depends greatly on the control it can exercise over the supply of its workers.

In contrast, industrial unions are made up of members who are linked by their work in a particular industry (such as steelworkers and autoworkers). Typically they represent many different occupations. Membership in the union is a result of working for a particular employer in the industry. Changing employers is less common than it is among craft workers, and employees who change employers remain members of the same union only if they happen to move to other employers covered by that union. Whereas a craft union may restrict the number of, say, carpenters to maintain higher wages, industrial unions try to organize as many employees in as wide a range of skills as possible.

TABLE 14.1

Typical Provisions in Collective Bargaining Contracts

Establishment and administration of the agreement	**Wage determination and administration**	**Plant operations**
Bargaining unit and plant supplements	General provisions	Work and shop rules
Contract duration and reopening and renegotiation provisions	Rate structure and wage differentials	Rest periods and other in-plant time allowances
Union security and the checkoff	Allowances	Safety and health
Special bargaining committees	Incentive systems and production bonus plans	Plant committees
Grievance procedures	Production standards and time studies	Hours of work and premium pay practices
Arbitration and mediation	Job classification and job evaluation	Shift operations
Strikes and lockouts	Individual wage adjustments	Hazardous work
Contract enforcement	General wage adjustments during the contract period	Discipline and discharge
Functions, rights, and responsibilities	**Job or income security**	**Paid and unpaid leave**
Management rights clauses	Hiring and transfer arrangements	Vacations and holidays
Plant removal	Employment and income guarantees	Sick leave
Subcontracting	Reporting and call-in pay	Funeral and personal leave
Union activities on company time and premises	Supplemental unemployment benefit plans	Military leave and jury duty
Union–management cooperation	Regulation of overtime, shift work, etc.	**Employee benefit plans**
Regulation of technological change	Reduction of hours to forestall layoffs	Health and insurance plans
Advance notice and consultation	Layoff procedures; seniority; recall	Pension plans
	Worksharing in lieu of layoff	Profit-sharing, stock purchase, and thrift plans
	Attrition arrangements	Bonus plans
	Promotion practices	**Special groups**
	Training and retraining	Apprentices and learners
	Relocation allowances	Workers with disabilities and older workers
	Severance pay and layoff benefit plans	Women
	Special funds and study committees	Veterans
		Union representatives
		Nondiscrimination clauses

SOURCE: From H. C. Katz and T. A. Kochan, *Collective Bargaining and Industrial Relations*, 1980. Copyright © 1980 The McGraw-Hill Companies, Inc. Reprinted with permission.

Local Unions

Even when a national union plays the most critical role in negotiating terms of a collective bargaining contract, negotiation occurs at the local level as well as over work rules and other issues that are locally determined. In addition, administration of the contract is largely carried out at the local union level. Consequently, the bulk of day-to-day interaction between labor and management takes place at the local union level.

The local of an industrial-based union may correspond to a single large facility or to a number of small facilities. In a craft-oriented union, the local may cover a city or a region. The local union typically elects officers (like president, vice president, trea-

TABLE 14.2

Largest Labor Unions in the United States

ORGANIZATION	NUMBER OF MEMBERS
National Education Association	2,495,826
International Brotherhood of Teamsters	1,400,700
United Food and Commercial Workers International Union	1,391,399
Service Employees International Union	1,321,790
American Federation of State, County and Municipal Employees	1,300,000
Laborers' International Union of North America	774,696
International Union, United Automobile, Aerospace and Agricultural Implement Workers of America	762,439
International Association of Machinists and Aerospace Workers	737,510
International Brotherhood of Electrical Workers	718,742
American Federation of Teachers	686,518
United Steelworkers of America	636,297
United Brotherhood of Carpenters and Joiners of America	515,986
Communications Workers of America	490,621
National Postal Mail Handlers Union	419,987
International Union of Operating Engineers	372,527
American Postal Workers Union	315,582
National Association of Letter Carriers	307,761
United Association of Journeymen and Apprentices of the Plumbing and Pipe Fitting Industry of the United States and Canada	299,136
Paper, Allied-Industrial, Chemical Employees International Union	292,160
Hotel Employees and Restaurant Employees International Union	245,327
International Association of Fire Fighters	235,527
Union of Needletrades, Industrial and Textile Employees	216,261
American Federation of Government Employees	191,171
American Association of Classified School Employees	166,512
Amalgamated Transit Union	165,678
Sheet Metal Workers International Association	142,500
Graphic Communications International Union	141,874
International Association of Bridge, Structural and Ornamental Iron Workers	126,004
United Mine Workers of America	124,803
Bakery, Confectionery, Tobacco Workers and Grain Millers International Union	121,379
Office and Professional Employees International Union	117,997
International Brotherhood of Painters and Allied Trades	113,445
International Union of Electronic, Electrical, Salaried, Machine and Furniture Workers	112,331
Transportation Communications International Union	110,652
American Federation of Musicians of the United States and Canada	110,000
Transport Workers Union of America	109,000

SOURCE: Reprinted with permission from Directory of U.S. Labor Organizations, 2000 edition by Courtney D. Gifford. Copyright © 2000 by the Bureau of National Affairs Washington, DC 20037. For copies of BNA Books publications call toll free 1-800-960-1220.

surer). Responsibility for contract negotiation may rest with the officers, or a bargaining committee may be formed for this purpose. Typically the national union provides assistance, ranging from background data about other settlements and technical advice to sending a representative to lead the negotiations.

Checkoff provision
A union contract provision that requires an employer to deduct union dues from employees' paychecks.

Closed shop
A union security provision requiring a person to be a union member before being hired. Illegal under NLRA.

Union shop
A union security provision that requires a person to join the union within a certain amount of time after being hired.

Agency shop
A union security provision that requires an employee to pay union membership dues but not to join the union.

Maintenance of membership
Union rules requiring members to remain members for a certain period of time (such as the length of the union contract).

Right-to-work laws
State laws that make union shops, maintenance of membership, and agency shops illegal.

Individual members' participation in local union meetings includes the election of union officials and strike votes. However, most union contact is with the shop steward, who is responsible for ensuring that the terms of the collective bargaining contract are enforced. The shop steward represents employees in contract grievances. Another union position, the business representative, performs some of the same functions, especially where the union deals with multiple employers, as is often the case with craft unions.

American Federation of Labor and Congress of Industrial Organizations (AFL–CIO)

The AFL–CIO is not a labor union but rather an association that seeks to advance the shared interests of its member unions at the national level, much as the Chamber of Commerce and the National Association of Manufacturers do for their member employers. As Figure 14.2 indicates, there are approximately 72 affiliated national and international unions and 60,000 locals. An important responsibility of the AFL–CIO is to represent labor's interests in public policy issues such as civil rights, economic policy, safety, and occupational health. It also provides information and analysis that member unions can use in their activities: organizing new members, negotiating new contracts, and administering contracts.

Union Security

The survival and security of a union depends on its ability to ensure a regular flow of new members and member dues to support the services it provides. Therefore, unions typically place high priority on negotiating two contract provisions with an employer that are critical to a union's security or viability: checkoff provisions and union membership or contribution. First, under a **checkoff provision,** the employer, on behalf of the union, automatically deducts union dues from employees' paychecks.

A second union security provision focuses on the flow of new members (and their dues). The strongest union security arrangement is a **closed shop,** under which a person must be a union member (and thus pay dues) before being hired. A closed shop is, however, illegal under the NLRA. A **union shop** requires a person to join the union within a certain amount of time (30 days) after beginning employment. An **agency shop** is similar to a union shop but does not require union membership, only that dues be paid. **Maintenance of membership** rules do not require union membership but do require that employees who choose to join must remain members for a certain period of time (such as the length of the contract).

Under the 1947 Taft–Hartley Act (an amendment to the NLRA), states may pass so-called **right-to-work laws,** which make union shops, maintenance of membership, and agency shops illegal. The idea behind such laws is that compulsory union membership (or making employees pay union dues) infringes on the employee's right to freedom of association. From the union perspective, a big concern is "free riders," employees who benefit from union activities without belonging to a union. By law, all members of a bargaining unit, whether union members or not, must be represented by the union. If the union is required to offer service to all bargaining unit members, even those who are not union members, it may lose its financial viability.

FIGURE 14.2

Structure of the American Federation of Labor and Congress of Industrial Organizations (AFL-CIO)

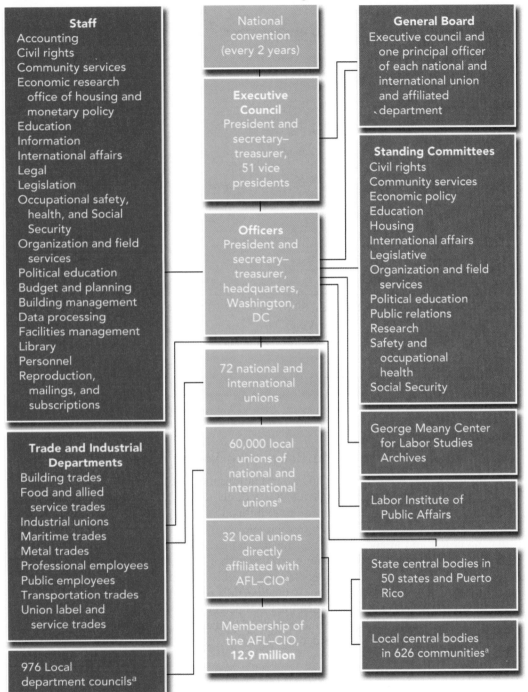

Staff
Accounting
Civil rights
Community services
Economic research
 office of housing and
 monetary policy
Education
Information
International affairs
Legal
Legislation
Occupational safety,
 health, and Social
 Security
Organization and field
 services
Political education
Budget and planning
Building management
Data processing
Facilities management
Library
Personnel
Reproduction,
 mailings, and
 subscriptions

**Trade and Industrial
Departments**
Building trades
Food and allied
 service trades
Industrial unions
Maritime trades
Metal trades
Professional employees
Public employees
Transportation trades
Union label and
 service trades

976 Local
department councils[a]

National
convention
(every 2 years)

**Executive
Council**
President and
secretary–
treasurer,
51 vice
presidents

Officers
President and
secretary–
treasurer,
headquarters,
Washington,
DC

72 national and
international
unions

60,000 local
unions of
national and
international
unions[a]

32 local unions
directly
affiliated with
AFL–CIO[a]

Membership of
the AFL–CIO,
12.9 million

General Board
Executive council and
 one principal officer
 of each national and
 international union
 and affiliated
 department

Standing Committees
Civil rights
Community services
Economic policy
Education
Housing
International affairs
Legislative
Organization and field
 services
Political education
Public relations
Research
Safety and
 occupational
 health
Social Security

George Meany Center
 for Labor Studies
 Archives

Labor Institute of
 Public Affairs

State central bodies in
 50 states and Puerto
 Rico

Local central bodies
 in 626 communities[a]

[a] 1989 data.

SOURCES: J. A. Fossum, *Labor Relations*, 5th ed. (Homewood, IL: Richard D. Irwin, 1992), p. 118. Updated with data from C. D. Gifford, *Directory of U.S. Labor Organizations*, 1998 (Washington, DC: Bureau of National Affairs, 1998).

FIGURE 14.3

Union Membership Density among U.S. Wage and Salary Workers, 1973–2003

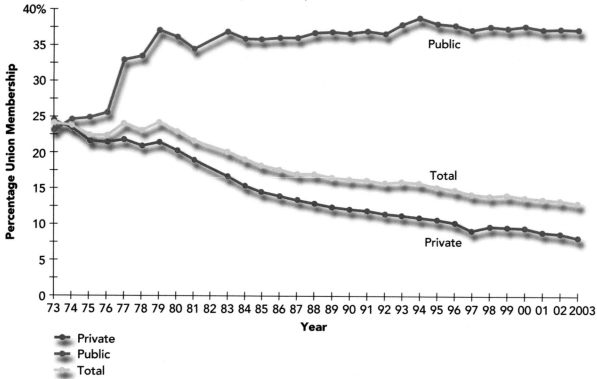

SOURCE: From B. T. Hirsch and D. A. MacPherson, *Union Membership and Earnings Data Book 2001* (Washington, DC: The Bureau of National Affairs, Inc., 2001). Reprinted with permission. Data for 2001 to 2003 obtained from U.S. Bureau of Labor Statistics, www.bls.gov.

Union Membership and Bargaining Power

At the strategic level, management and unions meet head-on over the issue of union organizing. Increasingly, employers are actively resisting unionization in an attempt to control costs and maintain their flexibility. Unions, on the other hand, must organize new members and hold on to their current members to have the kind of bargaining power and financial resources needed to achieve their goals in future organizing and to negotiate and administer contracts with management. For this reason we now discuss trends in union membership and possible explanations for those trends.

Since the 1950s, when union membership rose to 35 percent of employment, membership has consistently declined as a percentage of employment. It now stands at 12.9 percent of all employment and 8.2 percent of private-sector employment.[11] As Figure 14.3 indicates, this decline shows no indication of reversing (or even slowing down).[12]

What factors explain the decline in union membership? Several have been identified.[13]

Structural Changes in the Economy

At the risk of oversimplifying, we might say that unions have traditionally been strongest in urban workplaces (especially those outside the South) that employ middle-aged men in blue-collar jobs. However, much recent job growth has occurred among women and youth in the service sector of the economy. Although unionizing such groups is possible, unions have so far not had much success organizing these groups in the private sector. Despite the importance of structural changes in the economy, studies show that they account for no more than one-quarter of the overall union membership decline.[14] Also, Canada, which has been undergoing similar structural changes, has experienced growth in union membership since the early 1960s. Union membership in Canada now stands at over 30 percent of employment, compared with roughly 13 percent in the United States.

Increased Employer Resistance

Almost one-half of large employers in a survey reported that their most important labor goal was to be union-free. This contrasts sharply with 50 years ago, when Jack Barbash wrote that "many tough bargainers [among employers] prefer the union to a situation where there is no union. Most of the employers in rubber, basic steel and the automobile industry fall in this category." The idea then was that an effective union could help assess and communicate the interests of employees to management, thus helping management make better decisions. But product-market pressures, such as foreign competition and deregulation (e.g., trucking, airlines, telecommunications), have contributed to increasing employer resistance to unions.[15] These changes in the competitive environment have contributed to a change in management's perspective and goals.[16]

In the absence of significant competition from foreign producers, unions were often able to organize entire industries. For example, the UAW organized all four major producers in the automobile industry (GM, Ford, Chrysler, and American Motors). The UAW usually sought and achieved the same union–management contract at each company. As a consequence, a negotiated wage increase in the industry could be passed on to the consumer in the form of higher prices. No company was undercut by its competitors because the labor cost of all major producers in the industry was determined by the same union–management contract, and the U.S. public had little option but to buy U.S.-made cars. However, the onset of foreign competition in the automobile market changed the competitive situation as well as the UAW's ability to organize the industry.[17] U.S. automakers were slow to recognize and respond to the competitive threat from foreign producers, resulting in a loss of market share and employment.

Competitive threats have contributed to increased employer resistance to union organizing and, in some cases, to an increased emphasis on ridding themselves of existing unions. Unionized workers receive, on average, 10 to 15 percent higher wages than their nonunion counterparts and this advantage is still larger if benefits are also included. Many employers have decided that they can no longer compete with these higher labor costs, and union membership has suffered as a result.[18] One measure of increased employer resistance is the dramatic increase in the late 1960s in the number of unfair employer labor practices (violations of sections of the NLRA such as section 8(a)(3), which prohibits firing employees for union organizing, as we discuss later) even though the number of elections held did not change much. (See Figure 14.4.) The use of remedies such as back pay for workers also grew, but the costs to employers of such penalties does not appear to have been sufficient to prevent the growth in employer unfair labor practices. Not surprisingly, the union victory rate in representation elections has decreased from almost 59 percent in 1960 to below 50 percent by 1975. Although the union victory rate in recent years has been over 50 percent, the number of elections has declined by more than 50 percent since the

FIGURE 14.4

Employer Resistance to Union Organizing, 1950–2003

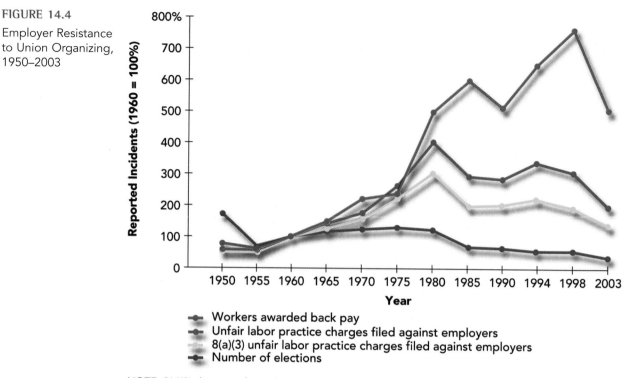

- ● Workers awarded back pay
- ● Unfair labor practice charges filed against employers
- ● 8(a)(3) unfair labor practice charges filed against employers
- ● Number of elections

NOTE: 8(a)(3) charges refer to the section of the NLRA that makes it an unfair employer labor practice to discriminate against (e.g., fire) employees who engage in union activities such as union organizing.

SOURCE: Adapted and updated from R. B. Freeman and J. L. Medoff, *What Do Unions Do?* (New York: BasicBooks, 1984). Data for 1985, 1989, 1990, 1994, 1998, and 2003 from National Labor Relations Board annual reports.

1960s and 1970s. Moreover, decertification elections have gone from about 4 percent of elections in 1960 to about 14 percent of elections in 2003.[19]

At a personal level, some managers may face serious consequences if a union successfully organizes a new set of workers or mounts a serious organizing drive. One study indicated that 8 percent of the plant managers in companies with organizing drives were fired, and 10 percent of those in companies where the union was successful were fired (compared with 2 percent in a control group).[20] Furthermore, only 3 percent of the plant managers facing an organizing drive were promoted, and none of those ending up with a union contract were promoted (compared with 21 percent of the managers in the control group). Therefore, managers are often under intense pressure to oppose unionization attempts.

Substitution with HRM

A major study of the human resource management strategies and practices among large, nonunion employers found that union avoidance was often an important employee relations objective.[21] Top management's values in such companies drive specific policies such as promotion from within, an influential personnel–human resource department, and above-average pay and benefits. These policies, in turn, contribute to a number of desirable outcomes such as flexibility, positive employee attitudes, and responsive and committed employees, which ultimately lead to higher productivity and better employee relations. In other words, employers attempt to remain nonunion by offering most of the things a union can offer, and then some, while still maintaining a productivity advantage over their competitors. Of course, one aspect of union representation that employers cannot duplicate is the independent employee voice that a union provides.

Substitution by Government Regulation

Since the 1960s, regulation of many employment areas has increased, including equal employment opportunity, pensions, and worker displacement. Combined with existing regulations, this increase may result in fewer areas in which unions can provide worker rights or protection beyond those specified by law. Yet Western European countries generally have more regulations and higher levels of union membership than the United States.[22]

Worker Views

Industrial relations scholars have long argued that the absence in the United States of a history of feudalism and of strong class distinctions found in Western Europe have contributed to a more pragmatic, business-oriented (versus class-conscious) unionism. Although this may help explain the somewhat lower level of union membership in the United States, its relevance in explaining the downward trend is not clear.

Strategic Use of HRM

On December 16, 2003, Boeing's new CEO, Harry C. Stonecipher, stood up in a Seattle convention center and announced that the company would go ahead with its 7e7 jetliner and build it in nearby Everett, Washington. "The 7e7 is a real game-changer," he declared as commercial-plane division chief Allan Mulally looked on approvingly. "Now let's go sell it."

What Stonecipher didn't tell the assembled 3,000 Boeing Co. employees was that 10 days earlier, he had quietly approached the chief of the company's biggest and feistiest union, the International Association of Machinists, to offer an olive branch. At that meeting, Stonecipher not only told Machinists President R. Thomas Buffenbarger that Boeing would build the plane in Everett, he went much further—offering to work hand in hand with the unions to end decades of bitter labor relations that have sunk employee morale to an all-time low.

Why would Stonecipher, long considered a foe of organized labor, have such a radical change of heart? Company insiders say it's because he realizes that Boeing's future rests in part on its ability to deliver the 7e7 cheaper and faster than it has any previous jetliner. An angry Machinists union could disrupt those plans. Besides, Stonecipher has already wrested significant concessions from labor—including 17,400 union layoffs since 2001 and an agreement to allow Boeing to outsource a large chunk of the 7e7 assembly work to Asia and Europe.

By winning labor peace, Stonecipher can focus on shoring up Boeing's defense business. He also must reassure the Pentagon and Congress that the company's ethical scandals are over.

Buying labor peace is crucial. Boeing will face the IAM at the end of May, when the contract expires for 6,000 workers at the military-aircraft division in St. Louis. A potential strike is the last thing Stonecipher needs as he tries to restore Boeing's credibility in Washington.

Company insiders also say Stonecipher is betting that a closer relationship with the unions will help Boeing build planes faster and cheaper. The union is pushing an initiative called High Performance Work Organization, which gives workers more responsibility for making continuous productivity improvements. Execs at Harley Davidson Inc. and International Specialty Products, a maker of chemicals and pharmaceuticals, credit the initiative for helping to revitalize inefficient factories. Using a similar program at Boeing would free up capital and resources that could be devoted to engineering and product improvement.

So what did the Machinists give up? First, they've accepted that outsourcing is a reality—even though they still officially oppose it. Second, union leaders acknowledge that as Boeing plants become more efficient, there will be fewer jobs.

With Boeing falling behind Airbus in orders and deliveries, the stakes are just too high to continue the bitter divisiveness. If Stonecipher succeeds in making some kind of peace with Boeing's combative unions, it could be one of his most ironic but enduring legacies.

SOURCE: From "Boeing: Putting Out the Labor Fires," by Stanley Holmes, *BusinessWeek*, December 29, 2003. Reprinted with permission.

Union Actions

In some ways, unions have hurt their own cause. First, corruption in unions such as the Teamsters may have had a detrimental effect. Second, questions have been raised about how well unions have adapted to recent changes in the economic structure. Employee groups and economic sectors with the fastest growth rates tend to have the lowest rates of unionization.[23] Women are less likely to be in unions than men (11 percent versus 14 percent), and nonmanufacturing industries such as finance, insurance, and real estate have a lower union representation (2 percent) than does manufacturing (14 percent). The South is also less heavily organized than the rest of the country, with, for example, South Carolina having a unionization rate of 4 percent, compared with 25 percent in New York State.[24]

Legal Framework

Although competitive challenges have a major impact on labor relations, the legal framework of collective bargaining is an especially critical determinant of union membership and relative bargaining power and, therefore, of the degree to which employers, employees, and society are successful in achieving their goals. The legal framework also constrains union structure and administration and the manner in which unions and employers interact. Perhaps the most dramatic example of labor laws' influence is the 1935 passage of the Wagner Act (also known as the National Labor Relations Act or NLRA), which actively supported collective bargaining rather than impeding it. As a result, union membership nearly tripled, from 3 million in 1933 (7.7 percent of all employment) to 8.8 million (19.2 percent of employment) by 1939.[25] With increased membership came greater union bargaining power and, consequently, more success in achieving union goals.

Before the 1930s, the legal system was generally hostile to unions. The courts generally viewed unions as coercive organizations that hindered free trade. Unions' focus on collective voice and collective action (strikes, boycotts) did not fit well with the U.S. emphasis on capitalism, individualism, freedom of contract, and property rights.[26]

TABLE 14.3

Are You Excluded from the NLRA's Coverage?

The NLRA specifically excludes from its coverage individuals who are
- Employed as a supervisor.
- Employed by a parent or spouse.
- Employed as an independent contractor.
- Employed in the domestic service of any person or family in a home.
- Employed as agricultural laborers.
- Employed by an employer subject to the Railway Labor Act.
- Employed by a federal, state, or local government.
- Employed by any other person who is not an employer as defined in the NLRA.

SOURCE: http://www.nlrb.gov/publications/engulp.html.

The Great Depression of the 1930s, however, shifted public attitudes toward business and the free-enterprise system. Unemployment rates as high as 25 percent and a 30 percent drop in the gross national product between 1929 and 1933 focused attention on employee rights and on the shortcomings of the system as it existed then. The nation was in a crisis, and President Franklin Roosevelt responded with dramatic action, the New Deal. On the labor front, the 1935 NLRA ushered in a new era of public policy for labor unions, enshrining collective bargaining as the preferred mechanism for settling labor–management disputes.

The introduction to the NLRA states:

> It is in the national interest of the United States to maintain full production in its economy. Industrial strife among employees, employers, and labor organizations interferes with full production and is contrary to our national interest. Experience has shown that labor disputes can be lessened if the parties involved recognize the legitimate rights of each in their relations with one another. To establish these rights under the law, Congress enacted the National Labor Relations Act. Its purpose is to define and protect the rights of employees and employers, to encourage collective bargaining, and to eliminate certain practices on the part of labor and management that are harmful to the general welfare.[27]

The rights of employees are set out in Section 7 of the act, including the "right to self-organization, to form, join, or assist labor organizations, to bargain collectively through representatives of their own choosing, and to engage in other concerted activities for the purpose of collective bargaining. The act also gives employees the right to refrain from any or all of such activities except [in cases] requiring membership in a labor organization as a condition of employment."[28] Examples of protected activities include

- Union organizing.
- Joining a union, whether it is recognized by the employer or not.
- Going out on strike to secure better working conditions.
- Refraining from activity on behalf of the union.[29]

Although the NLRA has broad coverage in the private sector, Table 14.3 shows that there are some notable exclusions.

Unfair Labor Practices—Employers

The NLRA prohibits certain activities by both employers and labor unions. Unfair labor practices by employers are listed in Section 8(a) of the NLRA. Section 8(a)(1) prohibits employers from interfering with, restraining, or coercing employees in

TABLE 14.4

Examples of Employer Unfair Labor Practices

- Threatening employees with loss of their jobs or benefits if they join or vote for a union.
- Threatening to close down a plant if organized by a union.
- Questioning employees about their union membership or activities in a manner that restrains or coerces them.
- Spying or pretending to spy on union meetings.
- Granting wage increases that are timed to discourage employees from forming or joining a union.
- Taking an active part in organizing a union or committee to represent employees.
- Providing preferential treatment or aid to one of several unions trying to organize employees.
- Discharging employees for urging other employees to join a union or refusing to hire applicants because they are union members.
- Refusing to reinstate workers when job openings occur because the workers participated in a lawful strike.
- Ending operation at one plant and opening the same operation at another plant with new employees because employees at the first plant joined a union.
- Demoting or firing employees for filing an unfair labor practice or for testifying at an NLRB hearing.
- Refusing to meet with employees' representatives because the employees are on strike.
- Refusing to supply the employees' representative with cost and other data concerning a group insurance plan covering employees.
- Announcing a wage increase without consulting the employees' representative.
- Failing to bargain about the effects of a decision to close one of employer's plants.

SOURCE: National Labor Relations Board, *A Guide to Basic Law and Procedures under the National Labor Relations Act* (Washington, DC: U.S. Government Printing Office, 1991). See also www.nlrb.gov.

exercising their rights to join or assist a labor organization or to refrain from such activities. Section 8(a)(2) prohibits employer domination of or interference with the formation or activities of a labor union. Section 8(a)(3) prohibits discrimination in any aspect of employment that attempts to encourage or discourage union-related activity. Section 8(a)(4) prohibits discrimination against employees for providing testimony relevant to enforcement of the NLRA. Section 8(a)(5) prohibits employers from refusing to bargain collectively with a labor organization that has standing under the act. Examples of employer unfair labor practices are listed in Table 14.4.

Unfair Labor Practices—Labor Unions

Taft-Hartley Act, 1947
The 1947 act that outlawed unfair union labor practices.

Originally the NLRA did not list any union unfair labor practices. These were added through the 1947 **Taft-Hartley Act.** The 1959 *Landrum-Griffin* Act further regulated unions' actions and their internal affairs (like financial disclosure and conduct of elections). Section 8(b)(1)(a) of the NLRA states that a labor organization is not to "restrain or coerce employees in the exercise of the rights guaranteed in section 7" (described earlier). Table 14.5 provides examples of union unfair labor practices.

Enforcement

Enforcement of the NLRA rests with the National Labor Relations Board (NLRB), which is composed of a five-member board, the general counsel, and 33 regional offices. The basis for the NLRA is the commerce clause of the U.S. Constitution. Therefore, the NLRB's jurisdiction is limited to employers whose operations affect commerce generally and interstate commerce in particular. In practice, only purely local firms are

TABLE 14.5

Examples of Union Unfair Labor Practices

- Mass picketing in such numbers that nonstriking employees are physically barred from entering the plant.
- Acts of force or violence on the picket line or in connection with a strike.
- Threats to employees of bodily injury or that they will lose their jobs unless they support the union's activities.
- Fining or expelling members for crossing a picket line that is unlawful.
- Fining or expelling members for filing unfair labor practice charges or testifying before the NLRB.
- Insisting during contract negotiations that the employer agree to accept working conditions that will be determined by a group to which it does not belong.
- Fining or expelling union members for the way they apply the bargaining contract while carrying out their supervisory responsibilities.
- Causing an employer to discharge employees because they spoke out against a contract proposed by the union.
- Making a contract that requires an employer to hire only members of the union or employees "satisfactory" to the union.
- Insisting on the inclusion of illegal provisions in a contract.
- Terminating an existing contract and striking for a new one without notifying the employer, the Federal Mediation and Conciliation Service, and the state mediation service (where one exists).
- Attempting to compel a beer distributor to recognize a union (the union prevents the distributor from obtaining beer at a brewery by inducing the brewery's employees to refuse to fill the distributor's orders).
- Picketing an employer to force it to stop doing business with another employer who has refused to recognize the union (a "secondary boycott").

SOURCE: National Labor Relations Board, *A Guide to Basic Law and Procedures under the National Labor Relations Act* (Washington, DC: U.S. Government Printing Office, 1991). See also www.nlrb.gov.

likely to fall outside the NLRB's jurisdiction. Specific jurisdictional standards (nearly 20) that vary by industry are applied. Two examples of businesses that are covered (and the standards) are retail businesses that had more than $500,000 in annual business and newspapers that had more than $200,000 in annual business.

The NLRB's two major functions are to conduct and certify representation elections and prevent unfair labor practices. In both realms, it does not initiate action. Rather, it responds to requests for action. The NLRB's role in representation elections is discussed in the next section. Here we discuss unfair labor practices.

Unfair labor practice cases begin with the filing of a charge, which is investigated by a regional office. A charge must be filed within six months of the alleged unfair practice, and copies must be served on all parties. (Registered mail is recommended.) If the NLRB finds the charge to have merit and issues a complaint, there are two possible actions. It may defer to a grievance procedure agreed on by the employer and union. Otherwise, a hearing is held before an administrative law judge. The judge makes a recommendation, which can be appealed by either party. The NLRB has the authority to issue cease-and-desist orders to halt unfair labor practices. It can also order reinstatement of employees, with or without back pay. In 2003, for example, $91.4 million in back pay was awarded and 1,838 workers were offered reinstatement (of whom 77 percent accepted). Note, however, that the NLRA is not a criminal statute, and punitive damages are not available. If an employer or union refuses to comply with an NLRB order, the board has the authority to petition the U.S. Court of Appeals. The court can choose to enforce the order, remand it to the NLRB for modification, change it, or set it aside altogether.

How Briggs Is Revving the Engines

Briggs & Stratton Corp. was at a crossroads. Since 1955, the company had been cranking out small gasoline-powered engines by the millions at a titanic 2-million-square-foot factory outside Milwaukee. The setup paid off for the longest time, enabling Briggs to claim two-thirds of the U.S. lawn-mower market and helping it post a profit every year except 1988, when drought scorched sales.

In 1993, though, Briggs executives concluded that the plant had become a millstone. Organized labor had pushed up costs just as retailers, trawling the global market for cheaper goods, were demanding lower

prices. The facility itself had grown so unwieldy that no one could even tell which products were making money. "We had become a battleship," says John S. Shiely, chairman and CEO.

Check out Briggs today. The company is on track to build 10.4 million engines—more than any other manufacturer in the world. Despite a lackluster economy, Briggs has made money every year since 1988. In fact, net income is forecast to surge 32 percent to $75 million in the fiscal year ending June 30 on record revenue of $1.6 billion, with exports accounting for 25 percent of sales. Briggs

is also getting into new products, including outboard boat motors and portable power generators, at prices that undercut those of Japanese competitors by nearly half.

The secret? Instead of scurrying to China and other low-wage countries as many other U.S. manufacturers have done, the Wauwatosa, Wisconsin–based company relocated its assembly work to a clutch of factories in America's rural South. The facilities are all nonunion, which means much lower labor expenses. The new plants are also smaller and focus on only one or two product lines, making them more man-

Union and Management Interactions: Organizing

To this point we have discussed macro trends in union membership. Here we shift our focus to the more micro questions of why individual employees join unions and how the organizing process works at the workplace level.

Why Do Employees Join Unions?

Virtually every model of the decision to join a union focuses on two questions.[30] First, is there a gap between the pay, benefits, and other conditions of employment that employees actually receive versus what they believe they should receive? Second, if such a gap exists and is sufficiently large to motivate employees to try to remedy the situation, is union membership seen as the most effective or instrumental means of change? The outcome of an election campaign hinges on how the majority of employees answer these two questions.

The Process and Legal Framework of Organizing

The NLRB is responsible for ensuring that the organizing process follows certain steps. At the most general level, the NLRB holds a union representation election if at least 30 percent of employees in the bargaining unit sign authorization cards (see

ageable. And they're highly automated, allowing Briggs to cut jobs and bring the union at its headquarters plant to heel. "Briggs wouldn't be in business today with the old system," says L. Michael Braig, an equity analyst with A. G. Edwards & Sons Inc. in St. Louis.

Management decided to go all out with its Southern strategy in 1993, after the company's union—now Local 7-232 of the Paper, Allied-Industrial, Chemical & Energy Workers International Union (PACE)—refused to go along with pay and benefit concessions. Briggs now operates a total of six "focus factories." They may not match China's rock-bottom wages, but the plants keep Briggs in the game.

Take its Murray, Kentucky, factory, which each year produces about 3.4 million basic 3- and 4.5-horsepower engines for walk-behind mowers. The plant employs about 950 people, in-cluding 80 to 90 students from Murray State University, who are let go every summer when demand ebbs. Pay starts at $9.64 an hour, plus productivity bonuses that add $1.72 an hour to the base wage. Because of that incentive, "our workers go to extremes to take even a half a cent of cost out of each engine," notes Paul M. Neylon, senior vice president for engine products. Engines that took one hour to build at the old plant now require just 30 minutes.

The company's new ways have also hurt many people. To compete with the nonunion shops, PACE now allows Briggs to pay new hires at Wauwatosa $11 an hour—instead of the going union rate of $16 an hour or more—and to exclude them from retiree health care benefits. Still, Briggs continues to shrink the facility's payroll. By next year, total head count will fall to roughly 1,000, down from 6,000 hourly workers in 1984.

"It just seems like corporate greed," charges Local 7-232 President Gregory Gorecki. He warns the company's nonunion workers that Briggs will abandon them, too, if their pay and benefits rise too high.

CEO Shiely acknowledges that Briggs may, in fact, transfer assembly work to Asia one day. Already, the company outsources components from low-wage foreign manufacturers and has a joint venture in China that builds engines, primarily for Asian markets. But for now, he says, Briggs intends to rely on its new plants. Granted, the company's payroll is smaller, but its factory jobs are still largely in America. That's something fewer and fewer U.S. manufacturers can claim.

SOURCE: From "How Briggs Is Revving Its Engines," *BusinessWeek*, May 5, 2003. Reprinted with permission.

Figure 14.5). If over 50 percent of the employees sign authorization cards, the union may request that the employer voluntarily recognize it. If 50 percent or fewer of the employees sign, or if the employer refuses to recognize the union voluntarily, the NLRB conducts a secret-ballot election. The union is certified by the NLRB as the exclusive representative of employees if over 50 percent of employees vote for the union. If more than one union appears on the ballot and neither gains a simple majority, a runoff election is held. Once a union has been certified as the exclusive representative of a group of employees, no additional elections are permitted for one year. After the negotiation of a contract, an election cannot be held for the contract's duration or for three years, whichever comes first. The parties to the contract may agree not to hold an election for longer than three years, but an outside party cannot be barred for more than three years.

As mentioned previously, union members' right to be represented by leaders of their own choosing was expanded under the Taft–Hartley Act to include the right to vote an existing union out—that is, to decertify it. The process follows the same steps as a representation election. A decertification election is not permitted when a contract is in effect. Research indicates that when decertification elections are held, unions typically do not fare well, losing about 70 percent of the time during the mid 1990s. Moreover, the number of such elections has increased from roughly 5 percent of all elections in the 1950s and 1960s to about 14 percent in the mid-1990s.[31]

FIGURE 14.5
Authorization Card

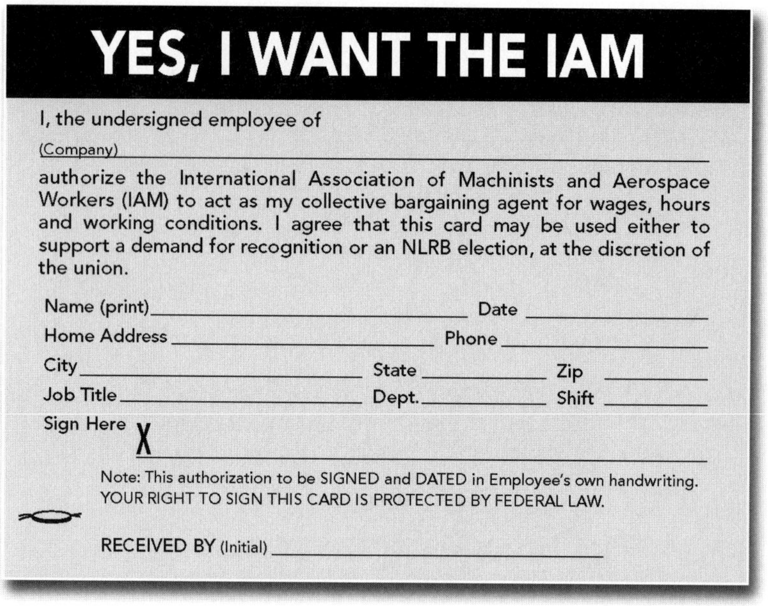

YES, I WANT THE IAM

I, the undersigned employee of

(Company) _____

authorize the International Association of Machinists and Aerospace Workers (IAM) to act as my collective bargaining agent for wages, hours and working conditions. I agree that this card may be used either to support a demand for recognition or an NLRB election, at the discretion of the union.

Name (print)_____ Date _____

Home Address _____ Phone _____

City_____ State _____ Zip _____

Job Title_____ Dept._____ Shift _____

Sign Here X
_____

Note: This authorization to be SIGNED and DATED in Employee's own handwriting.
YOUR RIGHT TO SIGN THIS CARD IS PROTECTED BY FEDERAL LAW.

RECEIVED BY (Initial) _____

SOURCE: From J. A. Fossum, *Labor Relations: Development, Structure and Process*, 2002. Copyright © 2002 The McGraw-Hill Companies, Inc. Reprinted with permission.

The NLRB also is responsible for determining the appropriate bargaining unit and the employees who are eligible to participate in organizing activities. A unit may cover employees in one facility or multiple facilities within a single employer, or the unit may cover multiple employers. In general, employees on the payroll just prior to the ordering of an election are eligible to vote, although this rule is modified in some cases where, for example, employment in the industry is irregular. Most employees who are on strike and who have been replaced by other employees are eligible to vote in an election (such as a decertification election) that occurs within 12 months of the onset of the strike.

As shown in Table 14.3, the following types of employees cannot be included in bargaining units: agricultural laborers, independent contractors, supervisors, and managers. Beyond this, the NLRB attempts to group together employees who have a community of interest in their wages, hours, and working conditions. In many cases this grouping will be sharply contested, with management and the union jockeying to include or exclude certain employee subgroups in the hope of influencing the outcome of the election.

Organizing Campaigns: Management and Union Strategies and Tactics

Tables 14.6 and 14.7 list common issues that arise during most campaigns. Unions attempt to persuade employees that their wages, benefits, treatment by employers, and opportunity to influence workplace decisions are not sufficient and that the union will be effective in obtaining improvements. Management emphasizes that it has provided a good package of wages, benefits, and so on. It also argues that, whereas a union is unlikely to provide improvements in such areas, it will likely lead to certain costs for employees, such as union dues and the income loss resulting from strikes.

As Table 14.8 indicates, employers use a variety of methods to oppose unions in organizing campaigns, some of which may go beyond what the law permits, especially

UNION ISSUES	PERCENTAGE OF CAMPAIGNS
Union will prevent unfairness and will set up a grievance procedure and seniority system.	82%
Union will improve unsatisfactory wages.	79
Union strength will give employees voice in wages, working conditions.	79
Union, not outsider, bargains for what employees want.	73
Union has obtained gains elsewhere.	70
Union will improve unsatisfactory sick leave and insurance.	64
Dues and initiation fees are reasonable.	64
Union will improve unsatisfactory vacations and holidays.	61
Union will improve unsatisfactory pensions.	61
Employer promises and good treatment may not be continued without union.	61
Employees choose union leaders.	55
Employer will seek to persuade or frighten employees to vote against union.	55
No strike without vote.	55
Union will improve unsatisfactory working conditions.	52
Employees have legal right to engage in union activity.	52

TABLE 14.6

Prevalence of Certain Union Issues in Campaigns

SOURCE: From J. A. Fossum, *Labor Relations: Development, Structure and Process*, 1992. Copyright © 1992 The McGraw-Hill Companies, Inc. Reprinted with permission.

MANAGEMENT ISSUES	PERCENTAGE OF CAMPAIGNS
Improvements not dependent on unionization.	85%
Wages good, equal to, or better than under union contract.	82
Financial costs of union dues outweigh gains.	79
Union is outsider.	79
Get facts before deciding; employer will provide facts and accept employee decision.	76
If union wins, strike may follow.	70
Loss of benefits may follow union win.	67
Strikers will lose wages; lose more than gain.	67
Unions not concerned with employee welfare.	67
Strike may lead to loss of jobs.	64
Employer has treated employees fairly and/or well.	60
Employees should be certain to vote.	54

TABLE 14.7

Prevalence of Certain Management Issues in Campaigns

SOURCE: From J. A. Fossum, *Labor Relations: Development, Structure and Process*, 1992. Copyright © 1992 The McGraw-Hill Companies, Inc. Reprinted with permission.

in the eyes of union organizers. This perception is supported by our earlier discussion, which noted a significant increase in employer unfair labor practices since the late 1960s. (See Figure 14.4.)

Why would employers increasingly break the law? Fossum suggests that the consequences (like back pay and reinstatement of workers) of doing so are "slight."[32] His review of various studies suggests that discrimination against employees involved in

TABLE 14.8

Percentage of Firms Using Various Methods to Oppose Union Organizing Campaigns

Survey of employers	
Consultants used	41%
Unfair labor practice charges filed against employer	24
Survey of union organizers	
Consultants and/or lawyers used	70
Unfair labor practices by employer	
Charges filed	36
Discharges or discriminatory layoffs	42[a]
Company leaflets	80
Company letters	91
Captive audience speech	91[b]
Supervisor meetings with small groups of employees	92
Supervisor intensity in opposing union	
Low	14
Moderate	34
High	51

[a] This percentage is larger than the figure for charges filed because it includes cases in which no unfair labor practice charge was actually filed against the employer.

[b] Refers to management's requiring employees to attend a session on company time at which the disadvantages of union membership are emphasized.

SOURCE: R. B. Freeman and M. M. Kleiner, "Employer Behavior in the Face of Union Organizing Drives," *Industrial and Labor Relations Review* 43, no. 4 (April 1990), pp. 351–65. © Cornell University.

union organizing decreases union organizing success significantly and that the cost of back pay to union activists reinstated in their jobs is far smaller than the costs that would be incurred if the union managed to organize and gain better wages, benefits, and so forth.

Still, the NLRB attempts to maintain a noncoercive atmosphere under which employees feel they can exercise free choice. It will set aside an election if it believes that either the union or the employer has created "an atmosphere of confusion or fear of reprisals."[33] Examples of conduct that may lead to an election result being set aside include

- Threats of loss of jobs or benefits by an employer or union to influence votes or organizing activities.
- A grant of benefits or a promise of benefits as a means of influencing votes or organizing activities.
- An employer or union making campaign speeches to assembled groups of employees on company time less than 24 hours before an election.
- The actual use or threat of physical force or violence to influence votes or organizing activities.[34]

Supervisors have the most direct contact with employees. Thus, as Table 14.9 indicates, it is critical that they be proactive in establishing good relationships with employees if the company wishes to avoid union organizing attempts. It is also important for supervisors to know what not to do should a drive take place.

In response to organizing difficulties, the union movement has tried alternative approaches. **Associate union membership** is not linked to an employee's workplace and does not provide representation in collective bargaining. Instead the union provides other services, such as discounts on health and life insurance or credit cards.[35] In return, the union receives membership dues and a broader base of support for its activ-

Associate union membership
A form of union membership by which the union receives dues in exchange for services (e.g., health insurance, credit cards) but does not provide representation in collective bargaining.

TABLE 14.9

What Supervisors Should and Should Not Do to Stay Union-Free

WHAT TO DO:

Report any direct or indirect signs of union activity to a core management group.
Deal with employees by carefully stating the company's response to pro-union arguments. These responses should be coordinated by the company to maintain consistency and to avoid threats or promises.
Take away union issues by following effective management practice all the time:
    Deliver recognition and appreciation.
    Solve employee problems.
    Protect employees from harassment or humiliation.
    Provide business-related information.
    Be consistent in treatment of different employees.
    Accommodate special circumstances where appropriate.
    Ensure due process in performance management.
    Treat all employees with dignity and respect.

WHAT TO AVOID:

Threatening employees with harsher terms and conditions of employment or employment loss if they engage in union activity.
Interrogating employees about pro-union or anti-union sentiments that they or others may have or reviewing union authorization cards or pro-union petitions.
Promising employees that they will receive favorable terms or conditions of employment if they forgo union activity.
Spying on employees known to be, or suspected of being, engaged in pro-union activities.

SOURCE: *HR Magazine* by J. A. Segal. Copyright © 1998 by Society for Human Resource Management. Reproduced with permission of Society for Human Resource Management via Copyright Clearance Center.

ities. Associate membership may be attractive to employees who wish to join a union but cannot because their workplace is not organized by a union.

Corporate campaigns seek to bring public, financial, or political pressure on employers during the organizing (and negotiating) process.[36] For example, the Building and Construction Trades Department of the AFL-CIO successfully lobbied Congress to eliminate $100 million in tax breaks for a Toyota truck plant in Kentucky until Toyota agreed to use union construction workers and pay union wages.[37] The Amalgamated Clothing and Textile Workers Union (ACTWU) corporate campaign against J. P. Stevens during the late 1970s was one of the first and best known. The ACTWU organized a boycott of J. P. Stevens products and threatened to withdraw its pension funds from financial institutions where J. P. Stevens officers acted as directors. J. P. Stevens subsequently agreed to a contract with the ACTWU.[38]

Unions also hope to use their financial assets to influence companies. Prior to the rebound of the stock market in 2003, unions directly controlled roughly $250 billion in pension funds and shared control with employers over another $1.04 trillion.[39] In addition, public sector pension funds controlled another $2.0 trillion. The AFL-CIO and the United Steelworkers have also set up a separate fund, the Heartland Labor Capital Network, which invests in worker-friendly companies.[40]

In some recent success stories unions have eschewed elections in favor of strikes and negative publicity to pressure corporations to accept a union. The Hotel Employees and Restaurant Employees (HERE) organized 9,000 workers in 2001, with 80 percent

Corporate campaigns
Union activities designed to exert public, financial, or political pressure on employers during the union-organizing process.

of these memberships resulting from pressure on employers rather than a vote. The Union of Needletrade, Industrial and Textile Employees (UNITE), which organized 15,000 workers in 2001, has also succeeded with this approach. After losing an election by just two votes among employees of Up-to-Date Laundry, which cleans linens for Baltimore hotels and hospitals, UNITE decided to try other tactics, including a corporate campaign. It called a strike to demand that Up-to-Date recognize the union. It also persuaded several major customers of the laundry to threaten to stop using the laundry's services, shared claims of racial and sexual harassment with state agencies and the NAACP, and convinced the Baltimore city council to require testimony from Up-to-Date. Eventually, the company gave in, recognized the union, and negotiated a contract that raised the workers' $6-an-hour wages and gave them better benefits.

Another winning union organizing strategy is to negotiate employer neutrality and card-check provisions into a contract. Under a *neutrality provision,* the employer pledges not to oppose organizing attempts elsewhere in the company. A *card-check provision* is an agreement that if a certain percentage—by law, at least a majority—of employees sign an authorization card, the employer will recognize their union representation. An impartial outside agency, such as the American Arbitration Association, counts the cards. The Communication Workers of America negotiated these provisions in its dispute with Verizon. Evidence suggests that this strategy can be very effective for unions.

Union and Management Interactions: Contract Negotiation

The majority of contract negotiations take place between unions and employers that have been through the process before. In most cases, management has come to accept the union as an organization that it must work with. But when the union has just been certified and is negotiating its first contract, the situation can be very different. In fact, unions are unable to negotiate a first contract in 27 to 37 percent of the cases.[41]

Labor–management contracts differ in their bargaining structures—that is, the range of employees and employers that are covered. As Table 14.10 indicates, the contracts differ, first, according to whether narrow (craft) or broad (industrial) employee interests are covered. Second, they differ according to whether they cover multiple employers or multiple plants within a single employer. (A single employer may have multiple plants, some union and some nonunion.) Different structures have different implications for bargaining power and the number of interests that must be incorporated in reaching an agreement.

The Negotiation Process

Richard Walton and Robert McKersie suggested that labor–management negotiations could be broken into four subprocesses: distributive bargaining, integrative bargaining, attitudinal structuring, and intraorganizational bargaining.[42] **Distributive bargaining** focuses on dividing a fixed economic "pie" between the two sides. A wage increase, for example, means that the union gets a larger share of the pie, management a smaller share. It is a win–lose situation. **Integrative bargaining** has a win–win focus; it seeks solutions beneficial to both sides. So if management needs to reduce labor costs, it could reach an agreement with the union to avoid layoffs in return for the union agreeing to changes in work rules that might enhance productivity.

Distributive bargaining
The part of the labor–management negotiation process that focuses on dividing a fixed economic "pie."

Integrative bargaining
The part of the labor–management negotiation process that seeks solutions beneficial to both sides.

TABLE 14.10

Types and Examples of Bargaining Structures

EMPLOYEE INTERESTS COVERED	EMPLOYER INTERESTS COVERED		
	MULTIEMPLOYER (CENTRALIZED)	SINGLE-EMPLOYER— MULTIPLANT	SINGLE-EMPLOYER— SINGLE PLANT (DECENTRALIZED)
Craft (Narrow)	Construction trades Interstate trucking Longshoring Hospital association	Airline Teacher Police Firefighters Railroad	Craft union in small manufacturing plant Hospital
Industrial or Multiskill (Broad)	Coal mining (underground) Basic steel (pre-1986) Hotel association	Automobiles Steel (post-1986) Farm equipment State government Textile	Industrial union in small manufacturing plant

SOURCE: Adapted from H. C. Katz and T. A. Kochan, *An Introduction to Collective Bargaining and Industrial Relations* (New York: McGraw-Hill, 2004). © 2004 The McGraw-Hill Companies, Inc. Used with permission.

Attitudinal structuring refers to the relationship and trust between labor and management negotiators. Where the relationship is poor, it may be difficult for the two sides to engage in integrative bargaining because there is little trust that the other side will carry out its part of the deal. For example, the union may be reluctant to agree to productivity-enhancing work-rule changes to enhance job security if, in the past, it has made similar concessions but believes that management did not stick to its assurance of greater job security. Thus the long-term relationship between the two parties can have a very important impact on negotiations and their outcomes.

Intraorganizational bargaining reminds us that labor–management negotiations involve more than just two parties. Within management, and to an even greater extent within the union, different factions can have conflicting objectives. High-seniority workers, who are least likely to be laid off, may be more willing to accept a contract that has layoffs (especially if there is also a significant pay increase for those whose jobs are not at risk). Less senior workers would likely feel very differently. Thus negotiators and union leaders must simultaneously satisfy both the management side and their own internal constituencies. If they do not, they risk the union membership's rejecting the contract, or they risk being voted out of office in the next election. Management, too, is unlikely to be of one mind about how to approach negotiations. Some will focus more on long-term employee relations, others will focus on cost control, and still others will focus on what effect the contract will have on stockholders.

Attitudinal structuring
The aspect of the labor–management negotiation process that refers to the relationship and level of trust between the negotiators.

Intraorganizational bargaining
The part of the labor–management negotiation process that focuses on the conflicting objectives of factions within labor and management.

Management's Preparation for Negotiations

Clearly, the outcome of contract negotiations can have important consequences for labor costs and labor productivity and, therefore, for the company's ability to compete in the product market. Adapting Fossum's discussion, we can divide management preparation into the following seven areas, most of which have counterparts on the union side.[43]

1. *Establishing interdepartmental contract objectives:* The employer's industrial relations department needs to meet with the accounting, finance, production, marketing, and other departments and set contract goals that will permit each department to meet its responsibilities. As an example, finance may suggest a cost figure above which a contract settlement would seriously damage the company's financial health. The bargaining team needs to be constructed to take these various interests into account.

2. *Reviewing the old contract:* This step focuses on identifying provisions of the contract that might cause difficulties by hindering the company's productivity or flexibility or by leading to significant disagreements between management and the union.

3. *Preparing and analyzing data:* Information on labor costs and the productivity of competitors, as well as data the union may emphasize, needs to be prepared and analyzed. The union data might include cost-of-living changes and agreements reached by other unions that could serve as a target. Data on employee demographics and seniority are relevant for establishing the costs of such benefits as pensions, health insurance, and paid vacations. Finally, management needs to know how much it would be hurt by a strike. How long will its inventory allow it to keep meeting customer orders? To what extent are other companies positioned to step in and offer replacement products? How difficult would it be to find replacement workers if the company decided to continue operations during a strike?

4. *Anticipating union demands:* Recalling grievances over the previous contract, having ongoing discussions with union leaders, and becoming aware of settlements at other companies are ways of anticipating likely union demands and developing potential counterproposals.

5. *Establishing the cost of possible contract provisions:* Wages have not only a direct influence on labor costs but often an indirect effect on benefit costs (such as Social Security and paid vacation). Recall that benefits add 35 to 40 cents to every dollar's worth of wages. Also, wage or benefit increases that seem manageable in the first year of a contract can accumulate to less manageable levels over time.

6. *Preparing for a strike:* If management intends to operate during a strike, it may need to line up replacement workers, increase its security, and figure out how to deal with incidents on the picket line and elsewhere. If management does not intend to operate during a strike (or if the company will not be operating at normal levels), it needs to alert suppliers and customers and consider possible ways to avoid the loss of their business. This could even entail purchasing a competitor's product in order to have something to sell to customers.

7. *Determining strategy and logistics:* Decisions must be made about the amount of authority the negotiating team will have. What concessions can it make on its own, and which ones require it to check with top management? On which issues can it compromise, and on which can it not? Decisions regarding meeting places and times must also be made.

Negotiation Stages and Tactics

Negotiations go through various stages.[44] In the early stages, many more people are often present than in later stages. On the union side, this may give all the various internal interest groups a chance to participate and voice their goals. This, in turn, helps send a message to management about what the union feels it must do to satisfy its members, and it may also help the union achieve greater solidarity. Union negotiators often present an extensive list of proposals at this stage, partly to satisfy their constituents and partly to provide themselves with issues on which they can show flexibility later in the process. Management may or may not present proposals of its own; sometimes it prefers to react to the union's proposals.

During the middle stages, each side must make a series of decisions, even though the outcome is uncertain. How important is each issue to the other side? How likely is it that disagreement on particular issues will result in a strike? When and to what extent should one side signal its willingness to compromise on its position?

In the final stage, pressure for an agreement increases as the deadline for a strike approaches. Public negotiations may be only part of the process. Negotiators from each side may have one-on-one meetings or small-group meetings where public-relations pressures are reduced. In addition, a neutral third party may become involved, someone who can act as a go-between or facilitator. In some cases, the only way for the parties to convince each other of their resolve (or to convince their own constituents of the other party's resolve) is to allow an impasse to occur.

Various books suggest how to avoid impasses by using mutual gains or integrative bargaining tactics. For example, *Getting to Yes* (New York: Penguin Books, 1991), by Roger Fisher and William Ury, describes four basic principles:

1. Separate the people from the problem.
2. Focus on interests, not positions.
3. Generate a variety of possibilities before deciding what to do.
4. Insist that the results be based on some objective standard.

Bargaining Power, Impasses, and Impasse Resolution

Employers' and unions' conflicting goals are resolved through the negotiation process just described. An important determinant of the outcome of this process is the relative bargaining power of each party, which can be defined as the "ability of one party to achieve its goals when faced with opposition from some other party to the bargaining process."[45] In collective bargaining, an important element of power is the relative ability of each party to withstand a strike. Although strikes are rare, the threat of a strike often looms large in labor–management negotiations. The relative ability to take a strike, whether one occurs or not, is an important determinant of bargaining power and, therefore, of bargaining outcomes.

Management's Willingness to Take a Strike

Management's willingness to take a strike comes down to two questions:

1. *Can the company remain profitable over the long run if it agrees to the union's demands?* The answer is more likely to be yes to the extent that higher labor costs can be passed on to consumers without losing business. This, in turn, is most likely when (1) the price increase is small because labor costs are a small fraction of total costs or (2) there is little price competition in the industry. Low price competition can result from regulated prices, from competition based on quality (rather than price), or from the union's organizing all or most of the employers in the industry, which eliminates labor costs as a price factor.

    Unions share part of management's concern with long-term competitiveness because a decline in competitiveness can translate into a decline in employment levels. On the other hand, the majority of union members may prefer to have higher wages, despite employment declines, particularly if a minority of the members (those with low seniority) suffer more employment loss and the majority keep their employment with higher wages.

2. *Can the company continue to operate in the short run despite a strike?* Although "hanging tough" on its bargaining goals may pay off for management in the long run, the short-run concern is the loss of revenues and profits from production being disrupted. The cost to strikers is a loss of wages and possibly a permanent loss of jobs.

Under what conditions is management most able to take a strike? The following factors are important:[46]

1. *Product demand:* Management is less able to afford a strike when the demand for its product is strong because that is when more revenue and profits are lost.

2. *Product perishability:* A strike by certain kinds of employees (farm workers at harvest time, truckers transporting perishable food, airline employees at peak travel periods) will result in permanent losses of revenue, thus increasing the cost of the strike to management.

3. *Technology:* An organization that is capital intensive (versus labor intensive) is less dependent on its employees and more likely to be able to use supervisors or others as replacements. Telephone companies are typically able to operate through strikes, even though installing new equipment or services and repair work may take significantly longer than usual.

4. *Availability of replacement workers:* When jobs are scarce, replacement workers are more available and perhaps more willing to cross picket lines. Using replacement workers to operate during a strike raises the stakes considerably for strikers who may be permanently replaced. Most strikers are not entitled to reinstatement until there are job openings for which they qualify. If replacements were hired, such openings may not occur for some time (if at all).

5. *Multiple production sites and staggered contracts:* Multiple sites and staggered contracts permit employers to shift production from the struck facility to facilities that, even if unionized, have contracts that expire at different times (so they are not able to strike at the same time).

6. *Integrated facilities:* When one facility produces something that other facilities need for their products, the employer is less able to take a strike because the disruption to production goes beyond that single facility. The just-in-time production system, which provides very little stockpiling of parts, further weakens management's ability to take a strike.

7. *Lack of substitutes for the product:* A strike is more costly to the employer if customers have a readily available alternative source from which to purchase the goods or services the company provides.

Bargaining outcomes also depend on the nature of the bargaining process and relationship, which includes the types of tactics used and the history of labor relations. The vast majority of labor–management negotiations do not result in a strike because a strike is typically not in the best interests of either party. Furthermore, both the union and management usually realize that if they wish to interact effectively in the future, the experience of a strike can be difficult to overcome. When strikes do occur, the conduct of each party during the strike can also have a lasting effect on labor–management relations. Violence by either side or threats of job loss by hiring replacements can make future relations difficult.

Impasse Resolution Procedures: Alternatives to Strikes

Given the substantial costs of strikes to both parties, procedures that resolve conflicts without strikes have arisen in both the private and public sectors. Because many public sector employees do not have the right to strike, alternatives are particularly important in that arena.

Three often-used impasse resolution procedures are mediation, fact finding, and arbitration. All of them rely on the intervention of a neutral third party, most typically provided by the Federal Mediation and Conciliation Service (FMCS), which must be notified 30 days prior to a planned change in contract terms (including a strike). **Mediation** is the least formal but most widely used of the procedures (in both the public and private sectors). One survey found it was used by nearly 40 percent of all large private sector bargaining units.[47] A mediator has no formal authority but, rather, acts as a facilitator and go-between in negotiations.

A **fact finder,** most commonly used in the public sector, typically reports on the reasons for the dispute, the views and arguments of both sides, and (in some cases) a recommended settlement, which the parties are free to decline. That these recommendations are made public may give rise to public pressure for a settlement. Even if a fact finder's settlement is not accepted, the hope is that he or she will identify or frame issues in such a way as to facilitate an agreement. Sometimes, for the simple reason that fact finding takes time, the parties reach a settlement during the interim.

The most formal type of outside intervention is **arbitration,** under which a solution is actually chosen by an arbitrator (or arbitration board). In some instances the arbitrator can fashion a solution (conventional arbitration). In other cases the arbitrator must choose either the management's or union's final offer (final offer arbitration) on either the contract as a whole or on an issue-by-issue basis. Traditionally, arbitrating the enforcement or interpretation of contract terms (rights arbitration) has been widely accepted, whereas arbitrating the actual writing or setting of contract terms (interest arbitration, our focus here) has been reserved for special circumstances. These include some public sector negotiations, where strikes may be especially costly (such as those by police or firefighters) and a very few private sector situations, where strikes have been especially debilitating to both sides (the steel industry in the 1970s).[48] One reason for avoiding greater use of interest arbitration is a strong belief that the parties closest to the situation (unions and management, not an arbitrator) are in the best position to effectively resolve their conflicts.

Mediation
A procedure for resolving collective bargaining impasses by which a mediator with no formal authority acts as a facilitator and go-between in the negotiations.

Fact finder
A person who reports on the reasons for the labor–management dispute, the views and arguments of both sides, and a nonbinding recommendation for settling the dispute.

Arbitration
A procedure for resolving collective bargaining impasses by which an arbitrator chooses a solution to the dispute.

Union and Management Interactions: Contract Administration

Grievance Procedure

Although the negotiation process (and the occasional resulting strike) receive the most publicity, the negotiation process typically occurs only about every three years, whereas contract administration goes on day after day, year after year. The two processes—negotiation and administration—are linked, of course. Vague or incomplete contract language developed in the negotiation process can make administration of the contract difficult. Such difficulties can, in turn, create conflict that can spill over into the next negotiation process.[49] Furthermore, events during the negotiation process—strikes, the use of replacement workers, or violence by either side—can lead to management and labor difficulties in working successfully under a contract.

As Jobs Head East in Europe, Power Shifts Away from Unions

Since the late 1990s, when the European Union began laying plans to admit new members from Central and Eastern Europe, manufacturers have been building plants and moving production east to take advantage of lower wages, more accommodating unions—and the prospect of relaxed trade barriers. With them have gone tens of thousands of union jobs. Unions fear more will follow as nine Eastern European nations plus Malta join the EU in May, cementing ties between the low-cost East and expensive West—and creating the world's largest economic entity.

In response, some unions are beginning to give ground in hopes of preserving jobs. For the past few months, Stuttgart auto giant DaimlerChrysler AG has been ramping up production at a new engine plant in Kölleda, in Germany. The factory probably would have been built in Central Europe, if the traditionally hard-line IG Metall union hadn't agreed to new flexible rules, including the use of temporary workers who could be let go after a few years, something the union has long opposed.

"We were very clear in the talks," Chief Executive Jürgen Schrempp explains in an interview. "We said, 'We have Poland. We have Hungary. We have the Czech Republic.'"

Western Europe still has some of the most generous labor laws in the world. France legally limits all workers to a 35-hour work week. In Sweden, married couples are entitled to a total of 480 paid days off when children are born. German unions still negotiate nationwide contracts that set one-size-fits-all wages on companies across whole sectors.

Changed Landscape

But unions have to realize the landscape has changed, says Klaus Volkert, the top labor representative on VW's supervisory board, the equivalent of a U.S. board of directors. By sticking to the old, hard-line approach, he says, "you only hurt yourself."

Volkswagen provides a vivid example. Most labor leaders at the car maker come from a wing of the IG Metall union that recognizes the threat Central Europe poses to workers in the West. This faction has increasingly turned away from the union leadership's hard line and is now pushing brethren across Western Europe to be more flexible before more jobs move away.

In 1999, Bratislava started assembling the VW Polo, a subcompact that previously had been built only in Pamplona. Output in Bratislava soared to 180,000 cars in 2000 from 40,000 in 1997. For VW, the advantage was obvious: Slovak workers earn about $7.40 an hour—a fifth of the cost of workers in Germany.

The arrival of Polo production in Bratislava seemed to pose little threat to VW workers in the West. With a starting price of

A key influence on successful contract administration is the grievance procedure for resolving labor–management disputes over the interpretation and execution of the contract. During World War II, the War Labor Board helped institutionalize the use of arbitration as an alternative to strikes to settle disputes that arose during the term of the contract. The soon-to-follow Taft–Hartley Act further reinforced this preference. Today the great majority of grievance procedures have binding arbitration as a final step, and only a minority of strikes occur during the term of a contract. (Most occur during the negotiation stage.) Strikes during the term of a contract can be es-

about $17,200, the Polo must be built under tight cost controls. For more profitable and luxurious cars, German plants were still preferred, despite their higher costs.

Then in 2000, workers in Germany were taken aback when VW announced that a much-anticipated upscale sport-utility vehicle would be built in Bratislava. Later named the Touareg, the car was launched last year with a starting price of about $41,000.

The decision marked the start of a strategy to foster competition between VW's plants, says Peter Hartz, VW's veteran personnel chief. "For every car VW makes, the plants have to apply to get the assignment. If Wolfsburg wants to get a new model, it must make an offer, in terms of its costs," against other VW plants in Spain, Mexico, Slovakia and elsewhere.

For VW's German workers, Bratislava's victory was a shock. "Suddenly globalization was in the minds of the workers, not just something happening in China or Vietnam," says Mr. Volkert, the highest-ranking labor representative on VW's supervisory board. "There's now low-cost labor that can build high-value products—and it's right next to Germany."

Bratislava, he noted, is closer to Wolfsburg than Munich.

Shaken, the workers in Wolfsburg and their IG Metall representatives realized they had to do something to make German labor more competitive, or VW would continue shifting production east. The next big chance arrived when VW was deciding where to build another new vehicle, a compact minivan called the Touran.

To win the assignment for VW's massive plant in Wolfsburg, Mr. Volkert and other union representatives at VW started talks aimed at creating a new class of employees who would work longer than allowed under VW's standard contract with IG Metall. After a year of negotiations, they had a deal. VW would hire about 5,000 unemployed workers to build the Touran, and they would earn 5,000 marks ($2,303 at exchange rates then) a month, about the same starting rate as in the standard contract.

But these new workers would put in 35 hours a week and work Saturdays and some night shifts at the regular hourly pay. Moreover, if cars came off the assembly line with defects, these workers would have to put in unpaid hours to fix the problems.

The deal sparked a rift within IG Metall. VW's workers and some in the union hierarchy hailed the deal because it created jobs in Germany and persuaded VW not to move more

production to Central Europe. But union hard-liners were concerned. For years, IG Metall had fought to force healthy companies to stick to union contracts. The hard-liners feared BMW, DaimlerChrysler and other companies would try to push through similar deals to extend work hours or hire workers to lower pay levels.

Spreading the Word

At VW, Messrs. Widuckel and Volkert set out to spread the gospel of accommodation. In 2001 they began holding seminars at VW plants in Brussels, Portugal, Britain, Brazil, Mexico and Spain. The idea was to explain the approach they had taken in Germany and encourage local labor leaders to take note of the threat from Eastern Europe.

"A cow that gives milk must also be fed," he says, recalling the core of his message. "And you can't only milk the company, either." At the beginning of 2003, after weeks of meetings and talks, the Spanish workers gave in and agreed to the 5 percent pay cut.

pecially disruptive because they are more unpredictable than strikes during the negotiation phase, which occur only at regular intervals.

Beyond its ability to reduce strikes, a grievance procedure can be judged using three criteria.[50] First, how well are day-to-day contract questions resolved? Time delays and heavy use of the procedure may indicate problems. Second, how well does the grievance procedure adapt to changing circumstances? For example, if the company's business turns downward and the company needs to cut costs, how clear are the provisions relating to subcontracting of work, layoffs, and so forth? Third, in multiunit contracts, how well does the grievance procedure permit local contract issues (like work rules) to be included and resolved?

From the employees' perspective, the grievance procedure is the key to fair treatment in the workplace, and its effectiveness rests both on the degree to which employees feel they can use it without fear of recrimination and whether they believe their case will be carried forward strongly enough by their union representative. The **duty of fair representation** is mandated by the NLRA and requires that all bargaining unit members, whether union members or not, have equal access to and representation by the union in the grievance procedure. Too many grievances may indicate a problem, but so may too few. A very low grievance rate may suggest a fear of filing a grievance, a belief that the system is not effective, or a belief that representation is not adequate.

As Table 14.11 suggests, most grievance procedures have several steps prior to arbitration. Moreover, the majority of grievances are settled during the earlier steps of the process, which is desirable both to reduce time delays and to avoid the costs of arbitration. If the grievance does reach arbitration, the arbitrator makes the final ruling in the matter. A series of Supreme Court decisions in 1960, commonly known as the Steelworkers' Trilogy, established that the courts should essentially refrain from reviewing the merits of arbitrators' decisions and, instead, limit judicial review to the question of whether the issue was subject to arbitration under the contract.[51] Furthermore, unless the contract explicitly states that an issue is not subject to arbitration, it will be assumed

Duty of fair representation
The National Labor Relations Act requirement that all bargaining unit members have equal access to and representation by the union.

TABLE 14.11

Steps in a Typical Grievance Procedure

Employee-initiated grievance
Step 1
a. Employee discusses grievance or problem orally with supervisor.
b. Union steward and employee may discuss problem orally with supervisor.
c. Union steward and employee decide (1) whether problem has been resolved or (2) if not resolved, whether a contract violation has occurred.

Step 2
a. Grievance is put in writing and submitted to production superintendent or other designated line manager.
b. Steward and management representative meet and discuss grievance. Management's response is put in writing. A member of the industrial relations staff may be consulted at this stage.

Step 3
a. Grievance is appealed to top line management and industrial relations staff representatives. Additional local or international union officers may become involved in discussions. Decision is put in writing.

Step 4
a. Union decides on whether to appeal unresolved grievance to arbitration according to procedures specified in its constitution and/or bylaws.
b. Grievance is appealed to arbitration for binding decision.

Discharge grievance
a. Procedure may begin at step 2 or step 3.
b. Time limits between steps may be shorter to expedite the process.

Union or group grievance
a. Union representative initiates grievance at step 1 or step 2 on behalf of affected class of workers or union representatives.

SOURCE: H. C. Katz and T. A. Kochan, *Collective Bargaining and Industrial Relations*, 1980. Copyright © 1980 The McGraw-Hill Companies, Inc. Reprinted with permission.

that arbitration is an appropriate means of deciding the issue. Giving further strength to the role of arbitration is the NLRB's general policy of deferring to arbitration.

What types of issues most commonly reach arbitration? Data from the FMCS on a total of 3,460 grievances in 1997 show that discharge and disciplinary issues topped the list with 1,941 cases.[52] Other frequent issues include the use of seniority in promotion, layoffs, transfers, work assignments, and scheduling (684 cases); distribution of overtime or use of compulsory overtime (105 cases); and subcontracting (79 cases).

What criteria do arbitrators use to reach a decision? In the most common case—discharge or discipline—the following due process questions are important:[53]

1. *Did the employee know what the rule or expectation was and what the consequences of not adhering to it were?*
2. *Was the rule applied in a consistent and predictable way?* In other words, are all employees treated the same?
3. *Are facts collected in a fair and systematic manner?* An important element of this principle is detailed record keeping. Both employee actions (such as tardiness) and management's response (verbal or written warnings) should be carefully documented.
4. *Does the employee have the right to question the facts and present a defense?* An example in a union setting is a hearing with a shop steward present.
5. *Does the employee have the right to appeal a decision?* An example is recourse to an impartial third party, such as an arbitrator.
6. *Is there progressive discipline?* Except perhaps for severe cases, an arbitrator will typically look for evidence that an employee was alerted as early as possible that behavior was inappropriate and the employee was given a chance to change prior to some form of severe discipline, such as discharge.
7. *Are there unique mitigating circumstances?* Although discipline must be consistent, individuals differ in terms of their prior service, performance, and discipline record. All of these factors may need to be considered.

New Labor–Management Strategies

Jack Barbash has described the nature of the traditional relationship between labor and management (during both the negotiation and administration phases) as follows:

> Bargaining is a love–hate, cooperation–conflict relationship. The parties have a common interest in maximizing the total revenue which finances their respective returns. But they take on adversarial postures in debating how the revenue shall be divided as between wages and profits. It is the adversarial posture which has historically set the tone of the relationship.[54]

Although there have always been exceptions to the adversarial approach, there are signs of a more general transformation to less adversarial workplace relations (at least where the union's role is accepted by management).[55] This transformation has two basic objectives: (1) to increase the involvement of individuals and work groups in overcoming adversarial relations and increasing employee commitment, motivation, and problem solving and (2) to reorganize work so that work rules are minimized and flexibility in managing people is maximized. These objectives are especially important for companies (like steel minimills) that need to be able to shift production quickly in response to changes in markets and customer demands. The specific programs aimed at achieving these objectives include employee involvement in decision making, self-managing employee teams, labor–management problem-solving teams, broadly defined jobs, and sharing of financial gains and business information with employees.[56]

Union resistance to such programs has often been substantial, precisely because the programs seek to change workplace relations and the role that unions play. Without the union's support, these programs are less likely to survive and less likely to be effective if they do survive.[57] Union leaders have often feared that such programs will weaken unions' role as an independent representative of employee interests. Indeed, according to the NLRA, to "dominate or interfere with the formation or administration of any labor organization or contribute financial or other support to it" is an unfair labor practice. An example of a prohibited practice is "taking an active part in organizing a union or committee to represent employees."[58]

One case that has received much attention is that of Electromation, a small electrical parts manufacturer. In 1992 the NLRB ruled that the company had violated Section 8(a)(2) of the NLRA by setting up worker–management committees (typically about six workers and one or two managers) to solve problems having to do with absenteeism and pay scales.[59] The original complaint was filed by the Teamsters union, which was trying to organize the (nonunion) company and felt that the committees were, in effect, illegally competing with them to be workers' representatives. Similarly, Polaroid dissolved an employee committee that had been in existence for over 40 years in response to the U.S. Department of Labor's claim that it violated the NLRA. The primary functions of the employee committee had been to represent employees in grievances and to advise senior management on issues such as pay and company rules and regulations. In a third case, the NLRB ruled in 1993 that seven worker–management safety committees at DuPont Co. were illegal under the NLRB because they were dominated by management. The committee members were chosen by management and their decisions were subject to the approval of the management members of the committees. Finally, the committees made decisions about issues that were mandatory subjects of bargaining with the employees' elected representative—the chemical workers' union.[60] The impact of such cases will be felt both in nonunion companies, as union organizers move to fill the worker representation vacuum, and in unionized companies, as managers find they must deal more directly and effectively with their unions.

In 1994 the Commission on the Future of Worker–Management Relations (also referred to as the Dunlop Commission, after its chair, former Secretary of Labor John Dunlop) recommended that Congress clarify Section 8(a)(2) and give employers more freedom to use employee involvement programs without risking legal challenges. In 1996 the U.S. Congress passed the Teamwork for Employees and Managers Act, which supporters said would remove legal roadblocks to greater employee involvement. Critics claimed the act went too far and would bring back employer-dominated labor organizations, which existed prior to the passage of the NLRA in 1935. The Clinton administration vetoed the bill, meaning that employers will continue to face some uncertainty about legal issues. Table 14.12 provides some guidance on when the use of teams might be illegal.

Employers must take care that employee involvement meets the legal test, but the NLRB has clearly supported the legality of involvement in important cases. For example, in a 2001 ruling, the NLRB found that the use of seven employee participation committees at a Crown Cork & Seal aluminum can manufacturing plant did not violate federal labor law. The committees in question make and implement decisions regarding a wide range of issues, including production, quality, training, safety, and certain types of worker discipline. The NLRB determined that these committees were not employer-dominated labor organizations, which would have violated federal labor law. Instead of "dealing with" management in a bilateral manner where proposals are made

Primary factors to look for that could mean a team violates national labor law:	
Representation	Does the team address issues affecting nonteam employees? (Does it represent other workers?)
Subject matter	Do these issues involve matters such as wages, grievances, hours of work, and working conditions?
Management involvement	Does the team deal with any supervisors, managers, or executives on any issue?
Employer domination	Did the company create the team or decide what it would do and how it would function?

TABLE 14.12

When Teams May Be Illegal

SOURCE: From *BusinessWeek* January 25, 1993. Reprinted with permission.

that are either rejected or accepted by management, the teams and committees exercise authority, delegated by management, to operate the plant within certain parameters. Indeed, the NLRB noted that rather than "dealing with management," the evidence indicated that within delegated areas of authority, the teams and committees "are management." This authority was found to be similar to that delegated to a first-line supervisor. Thus the charge that the teams and committees did not have final decision-making authority (and so were not acting in a management capacity) did not weigh heavily with the NLRB, which noted, "Few, if any, supervisors in a conventional plant have authority that is final and absolute." Instead, it was noted that managers typically make recommendations that move up through "the chain of command."[61]

Although there are legal concerns to address, some evidence suggests that these new approaches to labor relations—incorporating greater employee participation in decisions, using employee teams, multiskilling, rotating jobs, and sharing financial gains—can contribute significantly to an organization's effectiveness.[62] One study, for example, compared the features of traditional and transformational approaches to labor relations at Xerox.[63] As Table 14.13 indicates, the transformational approach was characterized by better conflict resolution, more shop-floor cooperation, and greater worker autonomy and feedback in decision making. Furthermore, compared with the traditional approach, transformational labor relations were found to be associated with lower costs, better product quality, and higher productivity. The Commission on the Future of Worker–Management Relations concluded that the evidence is "overwhelming that employee participation and labor–management partnerships are good for workers, firms, and the national economy." National survey data also indicate that most employees want more influence in workplace decisions and believe that such influence leads to more effective organizations.[64]

Labor Relations Outcomes

The effectiveness of labor relations can be evaluated from management, labor, and societal perspectives. Management seeks to control costs and enhance productivity and quality. Labor unions seek to raise wages and benefits and exercise control over how employees spend their time at work (such as through work rules). Each of the three parties typically seeks to avoid forms of conflict (like strikes) that impose significant costs on everyone. In this section we examine several outcomes.

TABLE 14.13

Patterns in
Labor–Management
Relations Using
Traditional and
Transformational
Approaches

DIMENSION	PATTERN	
	TRADITIONAL	TRANSFORMATIONAL
Conflict resolution		
Frequency of conflicts	High	Low
Speed of conflict resolution	Slow	Fast
Informal resolution of grievances	Low	High
Third- and fourth-step grievances	High	Low
Shop-floor cooperation		
Formal problem-solving groups (such as quality, reducing scrap, employment security)	Low	High
Informal problem-solving activity	Low	High
Worker autonomy and feedback		
Formal autonomous work groups	Low	High
Informal worker autonomous activity	Low	High
Worker-initiated changes in work design	Low	High
Feedback on cost, quality, and schedule	Low	High

SOURCE: Adapted from J. Cutcher-Gershenfeld, "The Impact of Economic Performance of a Transformation in Workplace Relations," *Industrial and Labor Relations Review* 44 (1991), pp. 241–60. Reprinted with permission.

Strikes

Table 14.14 presents data on strikes in the United States that involved 1,000 or more employees. Because strikes are more likely in large units, the lack of data on smaller units is probably not a major concern, although such data would, of course, raise the figure on the estimated time lost to strikes. For example, for the 1960s, this estimate is .12 percent using data on strikes involving 1,000 or more employees versus .17 percent for all strikes. Although strikes impose significant costs on union members, employers, and society, it is clear from Table 14.14 that strikes are the exception rather than the rule. Very little working time is lost to strikes in the United States (with annual work hours of 1800, about 11 minutes per union member in 2003), and their frequency in recent years is generally low by historical standards. Does this mean that the industrial relations system is working well? Not necessarily. Some would view the low number of strikes as another sign of labor's weakness.

Wages and Benefits

In 2000, private-sector unionized workers received, on average, wages 19 percent higher than their nonunion counterparts.[65] Total compensation was 36 percent higher for union-covered employees because of an even larger effect of unions on benefits.[66] However, these are raw differences. To assess the net effect of unions on wages more accurately, adjustments must be made. We now briefly highlight a few of these.

The union wage effect is likely to be overestimated to the extent that unions can more easily organize workers who are already highly paid or who are more productive.

YEAR	STOPPAGES	NUMBER OF WORKERS (THOUSANDS)	PERCENTAGE OF TOTAL WORKING TIME
1950	424	1,698	0.26%
1955	363	2,055	0.16
1960	222	896	0.09
1965	268	999	0.10
1970	381	2,468	0.29
1975	235	965	0.09
1980	187	795	0.09
1985	54	324	0.03
1990	44	185	0.02
1995	31	192	0.02
1999	17	73	0.01
2000	39	394	0.06
2001	29	99	<.005
2002	19	46	<.005
2003	14	129	.01

TABLE 14.14

Work Stoppages Involving 1,000 or More Workers

SOURCE: http://stats.bls.gov.

The gap is likely to be underestimated to the extent that nonunion employers raise wages and benefits in response to the perceived "union threat" in the hope that their employees will then have less interest in union representation. When these and other factors are taken into account, the net union advantage in wages, though still substantial, is reduced to 10 to 15 percent. The union benefits advantage is also reduced, but it remains larger than the union wage effect, and the union effect on total compensation is therefore larger than the wage effect alone.[67]

Beyond differences in pay and benefits, unions typically influence the way pay and promotions are determined. Whereas management often seeks to deal with employees as individuals, emphasizing performance differences in pay and promotion decisions, unions seek to build group solidarity and avoid the possibly arbitrary treatment of employees. To do so, unions focus on equal pay for equal work. Any differences among employees in pay or promotions, they say, should be based on seniority (an objective measure) rather than on performance (a subjective measure susceptible to favoritism). It is very common in union settings for there to be a single rate of pay for all employees in a particular job classification.

Productivity

There has been much debate regarding the effects of unions on productivity.[68] Unions are believed to decrease productivity in at least three ways: (1) the union pay advantage causes employers to use less labor and more capital per worker than they would otherwise, which reduces efficiency across society; (2) union contract provisions may limit permissible workloads, restrict the tasks that particular workers are allowed to perform, and require employers to use more employees for certain jobs than they otherwise would; and (3) strikes, slowdowns, and working-to-rule (slowing down production by following every workplace rule to an extreme) result in lost production.[69]

What Goodyear Got from Its Union

When leaders of the United Steelworkers union sat down last April to negotiate a new labor pact with Goodyear Tire & Rubber Co., they knew they were headed for trouble. After all, the nation's largest tire maker had lost $1.1 billion in the previous year as rivals selling cheap tires made in low-wage countries sliced its market share by three points, to 19.5 percent. Just as bad, a revolving door of top executives had racked up a crushing $5 billion in debt by investing in acquisitions and new tire products that didn't pan out. The union's options? Allow Goodyear to replace some of its 14 U.S. plants with ones in Asia, or fight the company with a strike that could force it into bankruptcy.

"We'll Make You Profitable"

Instead, USW President Leo Gerard came up with a third choice. Tapping the expertise of former Lazard Frères investment banker Ron Bloom, who joined the USW as a strategy advisor in 1996, the union hired a boutique Wall Street firm to devise a long-term strategic plan for the company. The goal: to make Goodyear globally competitive in a way that would preserve as many of the union's 19,000 jobs as possible.

In the end, that's just what happened in a new contract ratified in mid-September. The USW offered to slash labor costs by $1.15 billion over three years and to cut 3,000 jobs. In exchange, Goodyear promised to keep—and invest in—all but two of its U.S. factories and to limit imports from its factories in Brazil and Asia. The company also promised to go along with the more aggressive debt restructuring timetable the USW's Wall Street advisers recommended as a way to rein in management. In fact, to hold the company's feet to the fire, the USW got Goodyear to agree to pay $1,000 to each union worker and $500 apiece to all 22,000 retirees if the debt goals aren't met by 2007. "We

On the other hand, unions can have positive effects on productivity.[70] Employees, whether members of a union or not, communicate to management regarding how good a job it is doing by either the "exit" or "voice" mechanisms. "Exit" refers to simply leaving the company to work for a better employer. "Voice" refers to communicating one's concerns to management without necessarily leaving the employer. Unions are believed to increase the operation and effectiveness of the voice mechanism.[71] This, in turn, is likely to reduce employee turnover and its associated costs. More broadly, voice can be seen as including the union's contribution to the success of labor–management cooperation programs that make use of employee suggestions and increased involvement in decisions. A second way that unions can increase productivity is (perhaps ironically) through their emphasis on the use of seniority in pay, promotion, and layoff decisions. Although management typically prefers to rely more heavily on performance in such decisions, using seniority has a potentially important advantage—namely, it reduces competition among workers. As a result, workers may be less reluctant to share their knowledge with less senior workers because they do not have to worry about less senior workers taking their jobs. Finally, the introduction of a union may have a "shock effect" on management, pressuring it into tightening standards and accountability and paying greater heed to employee input in the design and management of production.[72]

told Goodyear, 'We'll make you profitable, but you're going to adopt this strategy,'" says Bloom. Says Jonathan D. Rich, president of Goodyear's North American tire business: "We got what we needed" to become competitive again.

The innovative Goodyear pact is a reprise of the strategy Gerard used to help restructure the ailing U.S. steel industry in the past year. Foreign competition has savaged steel even worse than tires, driving several steelmakers into bankruptcy or liquidation. To stop the hemorrhaging, the USW agreed to massive job and benefit cuts, which have helped stabilize leading steelmakers. Now Gerard hopes to use the Goodyear deal as a model to pull off the same feat with other tire makers. Instead of making tires in overseas factories, he wants Bridgestone/Firestone Inc. and Continental Tire North America Inc. to invest in their U.S. plants and compete via higher productivity. "We're trying to bargain public policy," says Gerard.

Breathing Room

It's an ambitious goal, given the huge wage differentials with other tire-producing countries. In Brazil, Goodyear pays workers just a fraction of the $22 an hour it pays USW members. That's why the union took some painful medicine to try to put Goodyear's U.S. factories back on a competitive footing. In addition to the job cuts, USW members won't get a raise for three years. Plus, union workers and retirees will pay more for health care coverage, saving $50 million a year. Management also agreed to limit executive salaries, including options, and to cut the salaried workforce by 15 percent more than the hourly staff.

Will even all this be enough? UBS Warburg analyst Saul Rubin says Goodyear needs to close several plants, not just the one the union agreed to shutter, with a possible second closure if productivity targets aren't met. Plus, the $1.15 billion in cuts slice only $450 million off existing expenses, with the remaining $700 million coming in future wage and benefit hikes the company now won't have to pay.

Still, Goodyear clearly has won some breathing room. The other U.S. tire makers, whose USW pacts also expired last April, are suffering too and may be willing to go along with a similar approach. If Goodyear and the USW can figure out how to keep up as globalization drives down costs, there may be some hope that this old-line manufacturing industry can be competitive—and remain in the United States.

SOURCE: From "What Goodyear Got from Its Union," *BusinessWeek*, October 20, 2003. Reprinted with permission.

Although there is evidence that unions have both positive and negative effects on productivity, most studies have found that union workers are more productive than nonunion workers. Nevertheless, it is generally recognized that most of the findings on this issue are open to a number of alternative explanations, making any clear conclusions difficult. For example, if unions raise productivity, why has union representation of employees declined over time, even within industries?[73] A related concern is that unionized establishments are more likely to survive where there is some inherent productivity advantage unrelated to unionism that actually offsets a negative impact of unionism. If so, these establishments would be overrepresented, whereas establishments that did not survive the negative impact of unions would be underrepresented. Consequently, any negative impact of unions on productivity would be underestimated.

Profits and Stock Performance

Even if unions do raise productivity, a company's profits and stock performance may still suffer if unions raise costs (such as wages) or decrease investment by a greater amount. Evidence shows that unions have a large negative effect on profits and that union coverage tends to decline more quickly in firms experiencing lower shareholder returns, suggesting that some firms become more competitive partly by reducing union strength.[74] Similarly, one study finds that each dollar of unexpected increase in collectively bargained labor costs results in a dollar reduction in shareholder wealth. Other research suggests that investment in research and development is lower in unionized firms.[75] Strikes, although infrequent, lower shareholder returns in both the struck companies and firms (like suppliers) linked to those companies.[76] These research findings describe the average effects of unions. The consequences of more innovative union–management relationships for profits and stock performance are less clear.

The International Context

Except for China, Russia, and the Ukraine, the United States has more union members than any other country. Yet, as Table 14.15 indicates, aside from France and Korea, the United States has the lowest unionization rate (union density) of any country in the table. Even more striking are differences in union coverage, the percentage of employees whose terms and conditions of employment are governed by a union contract. (See Table 14.15.) In Western Europe, it is common to have coverage rates of 80 to 90 percent, meaning that the influence of labor unions far outstrips what would be implied by their membership levels.[77] Why are the unionization rate and coverage comparatively low? One explanation is that the United States does not have as strong a history of deep class-based divisions in society as other countries do. For example, labor and social democratic political parties are commonplace in Western Europe, and they are major players in the political process. Furthermore, the labor movement in Western Europe is broader than that in the United States. It extends not just to the workplace but—through its own or closely related political parties—directly into the national political process.

TABLE 14.15

Union Membership and Union Coverage, Selected Countries

	MEMBERSHIP		COVERAGE
COUNTRY	NUMBER (THOUSANDS)	PERCENTAGE OF EMPLOYMENT (DENSITY)	PERCENTAGE OF EMPLOYMENT
United States	16,360	14	12
Canada	4,128[a]	37	37[b]
Japan	12,410[b]	24	25
Korea	1,615	13	—
Germany	9,300	29	90[b]
France	1,758	9	90
United Kingdom	7,280	33	37
Sweden	3,180[c]	91	85
Mexico	7,000[d]	43	—
Argentina	3,200	39	73
Brazil	15,205	44[d]	—

[a] 1993.

[b] 1996.

[c] 1994.

[d] 1991.

SOURCE: International Labour Office, *World Labour Report, 1997–98* (Geneva, Switzerland, 2001).

What is the trend in union membership rates and coverage? In the United States, we have seen earlier that the trend is clearly downward, at least in the private sector. Although there have also been declines in membership rates in many other countries, coverage rates have stayed high in many of these countries. In the United States, deregulation and competition from foreign-owned companies have forced companies to become more efficient. Combined with the fact that the union wage premium in the United States is substantially larger than in other advanced industrialized countries, it is not surprising that management opposition would be higher in the United States than elsewhere.[78] This, in turn, may help explain why the decline in union influence has been especially steep in the United States.

It seems likely that—with the growing globalization of markets—labor costs and productivity will continue to be key challenges. The European Union (EU) added 10 new member countries in 2004, bringing its total to 25 countries and 455 million people, or about 50 percent larger than the United States. The new EU countries (e.g., the Czech Republic, Slovakia, Poland) have much lower wages than the existing EU countries. Closer to home, we have the North American Free Trade Agreement among the United States, Canada, and Mexico. These common market agreements mean that goods, services, and production will continue to move more freely across international borders. Where substantial differences in wages, benefits, and other costs of doing business (such as regulation) exist, there will be a tendency to move to areas that are less costly, unless skills are unavailable or productivity is significantly lower there. Unless labor unions can increase their productivity sufficiently or organize new production facilities, union influence is likely to decline.

In addition to membership and coverage, the United States differs from Western Europe in the degree of formal worker participation in decision making. Works' councils (joint labor–management decision-making institutions at the enterprise level) and worker representation on supervisory boards of directors (codetermination) are mandated by law in countries such as Germany. The Scandinavian countries, Austria, and Luxembourg have similar legislation. German works' councils make decisions about changes in work or the work environment, discipline, pay systems, safety, and other human resource issues. The degree of codetermination on supervisory boards depends on the size and industry of the company. For example, in German organizations having more than 2,000 employees, half of the board members must be worker representatives. (However, the chairman of the board, a management representative, can cast a tie-breaking vote.) In contrast, worker representation on boards of directors in the United States is still rare.[79]

The works' councils exist in part because collective bargaining agreements in countries such as Germany tend to be oriented toward industrywide or regional issues, with less emphasis on local issues. However, competitive forces have led employers to increasingly opt out of centralized bargaining, even in the countries best known for centralized bargaining, like Sweden and Germany.[80]

The Public Sector

Unlike the private sector, union membership in the public sector grew in the 1960s and 1970s and remained fairly stable through the 1980s. As of 2003, 37 percent of government employees were union members, and 42 percent of all government employees were covered by a collective bargaining contract.[81] Like the NLRA in the private sector, changes in the legal framework contributed significantly to union growth in the public sector. One early step was the enactment in Wisconsin of collective bargaining legislation in 1959 for its state employees.[82] Executive Order 10988 provided collective bargaining rights for federal employees in 1962. By the end of the 1960s, most states had passed similar laws. The Civil Service Reform Act of 1978, Title VII, later established the Federal Labor Relations Authority (modeled after the NLRB). Many states have similar administrative agencies to administer their own laws.

An interesting aspect of public sector union growth is that much of it has occurred in the service industry and among white-collar employees—groups that have traditionally been viewed as difficult to organize. The American Federation of State, County, and Municipal Employees (AFSCME) with 1.3 million members, has about 325,000 members in health care, 325,000 in clerical jobs, and over 400,000 in all white-collar occupations.[83]

In contrast to the private sector, strikes are illegal at the federal level of the public sector and in most states. At the local level, all states prohibit strikes by police (Hawaii being a partial exception) and firefighters (Idaho being the exception). Teachers and state employees are somewhat more likely to have the right to strike, depending on the state. Legal or not, strikes nonetheless do occur in the public sector. In 2000, of the 39 strikes involving 1,000 or more workers, 8 were in state and local government.

A Look Back

The membership rate, and thus influence, of labor unions in the United States and in many other countries has been on the decline in the private sector. In the meantime, however, as we saw in the opening to this chapter, there are many companies where labor unions represent a large share of employees and thus play a major role in the operation and success of those companies. In such companies, whatever the national trend, effective labor relations are crucial for both companies and workers.

Questions

1. Many people picture labor union members as being men in blue-collar jobs in manufacturing plants. Is that accurate? Are there certain types of jobs where an employer can be fairly certain that employees will not join a union? Give examples.
2. Why do people join labor unions? Would you be interested in joining a labor union if given the opportunity? Why or why not? As a manager, would you prefer to work with a union or would you prefer that employees be unrepresented by a union? Explain.
3. What led to a change in labor relations at American Airlines? What was the nature of the change and do you think it is an important and sustainable change?

Summary

Labor unions seek to represent the interests of their members in the workplace. Although this may further the cause of industrial democracy, management often finds that unions increase labor costs while setting limits on the company's flexibility and discretion in decision making. As a result, the company may witness a diminished ability to compete effectively in a global economy. Not surprisingly, management in nonunion companies often feels compelled to actively resist the unionization of its employees. This, together with a host of economic, legal, and other factors, has contributed to union losses in membership and bargaining power in the private sector. There are some indications, however, that managements and unions are seeking new, more effective ways of working together to enhance competitiveness while giving employees a voice in how workplace decisions are made.

Discussion Questions

1. Why do employees join unions?
2. What has been the trend in union membership in the United States, and what are the underlying reasons for the trend?
3. What are the consequences for management and owners of having a union represent employees?
4. What are the general provisions of the National Labor Relations Act, and how does it affect labor–management interactions?

5. What are the features of traditional and nontraditional labor relations? What are the potential advantages of the "new" nontraditional approaches to labor relations?
6. How does the U.S. industrial and labor relations system compare with systems in other countries, such as those in Western Europe?

Self-Assessment Exercise

Would you join a union? Each of the following phrases expresses an opinion about the effects of a union on employees' jobs. For each phrase, circle a number on the scale to indicate whether you agree that a union would affect your job as described by the phrase.

Having a union would result in . . .	Strongly Disagree				Strongly Agree
1. Increased wages	1	2	3	4	5
2. Improved benefits	1	2	3	4	5
3. Protection from being fired	1	2	3	4	5
4. More promotions	1	2	3	4	5
5. Better work hours	1	2	3	4	5
6. Improved productivity	1	2	3	4	5
7. Better working conditions	1	2	3	4	5
8. Fewer accidents at work	1	2	3	4	5

9. More interesting work	1	2	3	4	5
10. Easier handling of employee problems	1	2	3	4	5
11. Increased work disruptions	5	4	3	2	1
12. More disagreements between employees and management	5	4	3	2	1
13. Work stoppages	5	4	3	2	1

Add up your total score. The highest score possible is 65, the lowest 13. The higher your score, the more you see value in unions, and the more likely you would be to join a union.

SOURCE: Based on S. A. Youngblood, A. S. DeNisi, J. L. Molleston, and W. H. Mobley, "The Impact of Work Environment, Instrumentality Beliefs, Perceived Union Image, and Subjective Norms on Union Voting Intentions," *Academy of Management Journal* 27 (1984), pp. 576–90.

Manager's Hot Seat Exercise: Partnerships: The Unbalancing Act

This Manager's Hot Seat case looks at problematic issues that can surround partnerships—especially when those partnerships are formed between friends. As the case study reveals, one partner has become seriously lax in handling his business responsibilities due to the advent of personal life challenges. The other partner has become somewhat resentful of the careless way her partner is handling his obligations to the business.

A discussion between the two brings forth the fact that the male partner wishes to sell his part of the business, but only to the buyer of his choice. He stresses that after all it is investment return, which will be affected by the buyer's purchase price. The female partner disagrees with him and contends that she is the one who ultimately will have to

deal with the new partner in the business. She reminds him of the initial contractual agreement set up between the two of them when the company was first formed. This agreement set forth the guidelines for the conditions of sale in the event either party wanted to leave the partnership. After serious consultation, the two partners finally agree to meet with their attorney to discuss the best method for proceeding with the sale.

The video stresses the importance of contractual relationships and indicates how imperative outlining contingency plans can be. It clearly depicts that the responsibilities associated with partnerships are to be shared between the partners involved. This case also identifies the significance of keeping communication lines open and well used.

Group Activity

Students should divide into two groups. One group will act as management while the other will represent labor. Here is the issue facing the two groups: The labor group has declared that it is being exposed to unsafe working conditions. Three life-threatening accidents have occurred to workers within the last year. The management group contends that it is providing a safe workplace for each of its employees. It claims the accidents resulted from employee horseplay while on the job.

The groups are to devise a satisfactory resolution to this situation. Keep in mind, this resolution is to result in an amendment being incorporated into the current contract. As this hypothetical situation is discussed, each group is to pay particular attention to such details as the following (this list is presented only as a guide and should not be looked upon as all-inclusive of the necessary information):

- What are the primary concerns of labor in this situation?
- What are the primary concerns of management in this situation?
- How would utilization of a mediator or arbitrator affect this situation?
- Would enlisting a fact finder assist this situation?
- What rights do both sides have in such a case?
- How important are contractual agreements in this situation?
- What alternatives do labor and management each have in such a situation?

Have a prepared statement from each group for the negotiation with the other party and have your concessions prepared and discussed. The instructor will act as the consultant, judge, and the arbitrator if needed.

 Please see the video case at the end of the book that corresponds to this chapter: Luv in the Workplace: Southwest Airlines.

Exercising Strategy: How Nissan Laps Detroit

Jonathan Gates slaps a wide slab of tan-colored, hard foam rubber on his workbench. He fastens a numbered tag in one corner and some black foam insulation at the edges. As soon as he puts a number on the piece of foam, which will become the top of a dashboard for a Nissan Quest minivan, the vehicle has an identity. All of the parts for a big chunk of the minivan's interior, decked out with the customer's choice of colors, fabrics, and options, will come together in the next 42 minutes.

Gates and his co-workers fill a crucial role at Nissan Motor Co.'s new Canton, Mississippi, assembly plant: Almost everything a driver touches inside a new Quest, Titan pickup, or Armada sport-utility vehicle is put together in a single module, starting at Gates's workbench. "This is the most important job," he says. And yet, amazingly, Gates doesn't even work for Nissan. He works for Lextron/Visteon Automotive Systems, a parts supplier that also builds the center console between the front seats and a subassembly of the car's front end. The finished modules pass over a wall to be bolted into a car or truck body rolling down the assembly line. Lextron/Visteon does the work faster than Nissan could and pays $3 an hour less than the carmaker pays assembly workers. Nissan is using a similar strategy for its vehicle frames, seats, electrical systems, and completed doors.

It's a level of efficiency that Detroit auto makers are only beginning to attempt. Along with other features in Nissan's eight-month-old, $1.4 billion factory, the whole-

sale integration of outside suppliers is another reason why General Motors, Ford, and Chrysler are still playing catch-up with Japanese car manufacturers. The Big Three have made great strides in productivity in recent years: General Motors Corp.'s best plants now actually beat Toyota's factories. But overall, every time Detroit gets close, the competition seems to get a little better.

Nissan's secret? Sure, its plants use cheaper, nonunion labor. Besides lower wages, its Smyrna, Tennessee, workers get about $3 an hour less in benefits than Big Three assemblers represented by the United Auto Workers. But there's more to it. Outsourcing offers huge savings, whereas the Big Three must negotiate the outsourcing of subassembly work with the union. And Nissan's plants are far more flexible in adjusting to market twists and turns. Nissan's Canton plant can send a minivan, pickup truck, and sport-utility vehicle down the same assembly line, one after the other, without interruption. At first glance, a Nissan factory does not look much different than one you would see in Detroit or St. Louis. But talk to the workers, and it soon becomes clear how relentlessly the company squeezes mere seconds out of the assembly process.

The United Auto Workers is slowly allowing more outsourcing. But the UAW wants to outsource work only to union-friendly suppliers. And even then it has to be negotiated. Nissan, meanwhile, has free rein to outsource jobs. Two of Smyrna's vehicles—the Maxima and Altima sedans—were engineered to be built using modules built by suppliers. Every vehicle built in Canton was designed that way. All together, buying modules saves 15 percent to 30 percent on the total cost of that section of the car, according to the Center for Automotive Research (CAR) in Ann Arbor, Michigan. And the Big Three? GM is the most "modular" of the domestic manufacturers, but only a few of its plants have been designed to build cars using many big modules.

Detroit is slowly making headway. Prudential says half of GM's 35 North American assembly lines can make multiple vehicles. GM's two-year-old Cadillac plant in Lansing, Michigan, will make three luxury vehicles: the CTS and STS sedans and SRX SUV. It has also been designed to get some large, preassembled modules from suppliers. GM is using the Cadillac plant as a model for upgrading other plants. "We're getting much more flexible," says Gary L. Cowger, president of GM North America.

But it's much easier to design a new factory to be flexible from the ground up than to refurbish those built 30 or more years ago. And with so much excess capacity, the Big Three have no room to build new plants. Even if they could match the Japanese in productivity, they would have to account for the costs of laid-off workers, whose contracts entitle them to 75 percent of their pay.

By contrast, Nissan runs a tight ship and works its employees harder. During the UAW's failed attempt to organize Smyrna in 2001, workers told the union that line speeds were too fast and people were getting injured, says Bob King, the UAW's vice president of organizing. The union says that in 2001, Nissan reported 31 injuries per 1,000 workers—twice the average at Big Three plants—according to logs reported to the Occupational Safety and Health Administration.

Nissan does not dispute the OSHA figures, but it denies its assembly lines are any less safe than Detroit's. Although the company won't release current numbers, executives do say that they have taken steps to reduce injuries. For instance, the company has workers do four different jobs during a typical eight-hour shift, to try to cut down on repetitive-motion injuries. Nissan claims that injury rates have fallen 60 percent in the past two years.

SOURCE: From "How Nissan Laps Detroit," *BusinessWeek*, December 22, 2003. Reprinted with permission.

Questions

1. Can unionized plants compete with Nissan's nonunion plants?
2. Why isn't there a union at Nissan? Would a union be a good thing or a bad thing for Nissan workers? Nissan shareholders?

Managing People: From the Pages of *BusinessWeek*

BusinessWeek Sweatshops: Finally, Airing the Dirty Linen

For more than a decade, consumer-product and retail companies have been fending off sweatshop critics by hiring auditors to inspect their overseas factories for labor violations. The companies use the reports to reassure consumers that they're grappling with the sweatshop conditions prevalent in low-wage countries. But the entire effort has been of limited public-relations value. For one thing, companies such as Nike, Wal-Mart Stores, and Walt Disney have largely refused to release the audits to the public. Essentially, they have asked critics to trust that they're taking care of the problem—which of course few are willing to do.

Now, a handful of companies—among them Nike, Reebok, and Phillips-Van Heusen—have for the first time gone public. Their factory labor audits were posted in early June on the Web site of the Fair Labor Assn., a sweatshop-monitoring group started in 1997 with help from the Clinton Administration. (Nike Inc. released only limited information, citing its pending U.S. Supreme Court case.)

This is a major and long-overdue step in the whole sweatshop debate. The FLA, which includes a dozen brand-name firms as well as 175 colleges, has promised for years to publicize audits of factories, most of which are owned by subcontractors. Now that it has, human rights groups will be able to see for themselves whether the process is valid. The move also puts pressure on Wal-Mart, Disney, Gap, and every other company that does labor monitoring, to release their audits, too. "When you put these reports in the public domain, it creates a huge incentive for companies to remedy the problems," says Michael Posner, an FLA founder and head of the Lawyers Committee for Human Rights, a New York advocacy group. "It's like the old Reagan line: 'Trust, but verify.'"

Commendable as it is, the FLA companies' gutsy move still leaves plenty of fundamental problems unsolved. For example, the FLA doesn't even try to make sure that factories pay a living wage by the standards of the countries in which they operate—a frequent activist demand. Nor do FLA inspectors report on whether factories respect the right to form independent unions in countries like China that repress them. The FLA, under pressure from its member companies, also declined to require that the actual factories inspected be named, making it more difficult for watchdog groups to check up on the reports.

In addition, some critics say the FLA has watered down its overall inspection regime as it has struggled to get up and running. Currently, the group requires companies to inspect just 5% of their factories—too few to be credible, says Heather White, the head of Verite, the only major nonprofit doing global factory inspections. Indeed, White recently stopped doing FLA audits partly for this reason, though she applauds their public release as a milestone.

Another complaint: Most of the FLA monitoring is handled by for-profit auditing firms that don't usually talk to workers off-site. Although this is considered the best way to uncover systematic labor abuses, it's also more expensive, and many companies don't want to spend the money.

Still, the first batch of audits is remarkably candid. In fact, one depressing result of seeing them for the first time is the realization of just how little has changed after all these years. In more than 40 factories inspected, the audits found all the ills that have plagued low-wage producers for years, from arbitrary firings to forced overtime. "There's not much sense of progress being made on these long-standing issues," says Prakash Sethi, a Baruch College management professor who heads the independent monitoring effort at Mattel Inc., the only other company to publicly release its audits.

On the plus side, though, the FLA audits list what the factories are doing to fix the problems, such as training managers and giving workers pay stubs. It's too early to tell how far the factories are willing to go with the reforms, but this should become clear as follow-up reports come out next year. "Over time, you'll be able to judge the progress being made," says Doug Cahn, Reebok International Ltd.'s vice-president of human rights programs. "Our goal is to be sure that the factories have systems to find problems and fix them, so we don't keep finding the same things day in and day out."

So why do other companies refuse to let the public see their audits? Wal-Mart Stores Inc. and Walt Disney Co., like many other consumer-product companies, have been dogged by sweatshop allegations for years. Says Disney spokesman Gary Foster, whose company does audits on a regular basis: "We're an easy target because we have one of the most highly recognized names out there, but this is an issue we take very seriously." Problem is, outsiders have no way to know whether Disney does in fact do thorough auditing. Foster concedes this is a problem and says he is looking into whether releasing audits is a good idea. Wal-Mart declined to comment.

Airing dirty linen is always painful. If critics respond solely by focusing on all the problems the companies have voluntarily exposed, the Disneys and Wal-Marts of the world are sure to keep their own labor conditions under wraps. The better approach: to praise the FLA's openness while insisting that more be done—and holding other companies to the same standard.

SOURCE: Aaron Bernstein, "Sweatshops: Finally, Airing the Dirty Linen," *BusinessWeek* (June 23, 2003). Reprinted from *BusinessWeek* by special permission. Copyright © 2003 by The McGraw-Hill Companies, Inc.

Questions

1. Why should American companies care about work conditions overseas?
2. Are these kinds of working conditions necessary for poorer countries to attract jobs?
3. Why do people work under such conditions?
4. What is the best way to improve conditions? How did working conditions improve over time in the United States?

Notes

1. J. T. Dunlop, *Industrial Relations Systems* (New York: Holt, 1958).
2. C. Kerr, "Industrial Conflict and Its Mediation," *American Journal of Sociology* 60 (1954), pp. 230–45.
3. T. A. Kochan, *Collective Bargaining and Industrial Relations* (Homewood, IL: Richard D. Irwin, 1980), p. 25; H. C. Katz and T. A. Kochan, *An Introduction to Collective Bargaining and Industrial Relations*, 3rd ed. (New York: McGraw-Hill, 2004).
4. Katz and Kochan, *An Introduction to Collective Bargaining*, 3rd ed.
5. S. Webb and B. Webb, *Industrial Democracy* (London: Longmans, Green, 1897); J. R. Commons, *Institutional Economics* (New York: Macmillan, 1934).
6. C. Kerr, J. T. Dunlop, F. Harbison, and C. Myers, "Industrialism and World Society," *Harvard Business Review*, February 1961, pp. 113–26.
7. T. A. Kochan and K. R. Wever, "American Unions and the Future of Worker Representation," in *The State of the Unions*, ed. G. Strauss et al. (Madison, WI: Industrial Relations Research Association, 1991).
8. "Why America Needs Unions, but Not the Kind It Has Now," *BusinessWeek* (May 23, 1994), p. 70.
9. Katz and Kochan, *An Introduction to Collective Bargaining*, 3rd ed.
10. J. Barbash, *The Elements of Industrial Relations* (Madison, WI: University of Wisconsin Press, 1984).
11. U.S. Bureau of Labor Statistics, www.bls.gov.
12. J. T. Bennett and B. E. Kaufman, *The Future of Private Sector Unionism in the United States* (Armonk, NY: M. E. Sharpe, 2002).
13. Katz and Kochan, *An Introduction to Collective Bargaining*, 3rd ed. Katz and Kochan in turn build on work by J. Fiorito and C. L. Maranto, "The Contemporary Decline of Union Strength," *Contemporary Policy Issues* 3 (1987), pp. 12–27.
14. G. N. Chaison and J. Rose, "The Macrodeterminants of Union Growth and Decline," in *The State of the Unions*, George Strauss et al. (eds.) (Madison, WI: Industrial Relations Research Association, 1991).
15. D. L. Belman and K. A. Monaco, "The Effects of Deregulation, Deunionization, Technology, and Human Capital on the Work and Work Lives of Truck Drivers, *Industrial and Labor Relations Review* 54 (2001), pp. 502–24.

16. T. A. Kochan, R. B. McKersie, and J. Chalykoff, "The Effects of Corporate Strategy and Workplace Innovations in Union Representation," *Industrial and Labor Relations Review* 39 (1986), pp. 487–501; Chaison and Rose, "The Macrodeterminants of Union Growth"; J. Barbash, *Practice of Unionism* (New York: Harper, 1956), p. 210; W. N. Cooke and D. G. Meyer, "Structural and Market Predictors of Corporate Labor Relations Strategies," *Industrial and Labor Relations Review* 43 (1990), pp. 280–93; T. A. Kochan and P. Cappelli, "The Transformation of the Industrial Relations and Personnel Function," in *Internal Labor Markets*, ed. P. Osterman (Cambridge, MA: MIT Press, 1984).

17. Kochan and Cappelli, "The Transformation of the Industrial Relations and Personnel Function."

18. S. B. Jarrell and T. D. Stanley, "A Meta-Analysis of the Union–Nonunion Wage Gap," *Industrial and Labor Relations Review* 44 (1990), pp. 54–67; P. D. Lineneman, M. L. Wachter, and W. H. Carter, "Evaluating the Evidence on Union Employment and Wages," *Industrial and Labor Relations Review* 44 (1990), pp. 34–53; L. Mischel and M. Walters, "How Unions Help All Workers," Economic Policy Institute Briefing Paper (2003).

19. National Labor Relations Board annual reports.

20. R. B. Freeman and M. M. Kleiner, "Employer Behavior in the Face of Union Organizing Drives," *Industrial and Labor Relations Review* 43 (1990), pp. 351–65.

21. F. K. Foulkes, "Large Nonunionized Employers," in *U.S. Industrial Relations 1950–1980: A Critical Assessment*, eds. J. Steiber et al. (Madison, WI: Industrial Relations Research Association, 1981).

22. Katz and Kochan, *An Introduction to Collective Bargaining*, 3rd ed.

23. E. E. Herman, J. L. Schwarz, and A. Kuhn, *Collective Bargaining and Labor Relations* (Englewood Cliffs, NJ: Prentice–Hall, 1992), p. 32.

24. BLS website; AFL-CIO website.

25. Herman et al., *Collective Bargaining*, p. 33.

26. Kochan, *Collective Bargaining and Industrial Relations*, p. 61.

27. National Labor Relations Board, *A Guide to Basic Law and Procedures under the National Labor Relations Act* (Washington, DC: U.S. Government Printing Office, 1991).

28. Ibid.

29. Ibid.

30. H. N. Wheeler and J. A. McClendon, "The Individual Decision to Unionize," in *The State of the Unions*.

31. National Labor Relations Board annual reports.

32. J. A. Fossum, *Labor Relations*, 8th ed. (New York: McGraw-Hill, 2002), p. 149.

33. National Labor Relations Board, *A Guide to Basic Law*, p. 17.

34. Ibid.

35. Herman et al., *Collective Bargaining*; P. Jarley and J. Fiorito, "Associate Membership: Unionism or Consumerism?" *Industrial and Labor Relations Review* 43 (1990), pp. 209–24.

36. Katz and Kochan, *An Introduction to Collective Bargaining*; 3rd ed., R. L. Rose, "Unions Hit Corporate Campaign Trail," *The Wall Street Journal* (March 8, 1993), p. B1.

37. P. Jarley and C. L. Maranto, "Union Corporate Campaigns: An Assessment," *Industrial and Labor Relations Review* 44 (1990), pp. 505–24.

38. Katz and Kochan, *An Introduction to Collective Bargaining*, 3rd ed.

39. A. Fung, T. Hebb, and J. Rogers (eds.), *Working Capital: The Power of Labor's Pensions* (Ithaca, NY: Cornell University Press, 2001).

40. A. Bernstein, "Working Capital: Labor's New Weapon?" *BusinessWeek* (September 27, 1997); A. Michaud, "Investments with the Union Label, *BusinessWeek* (August 22, 2001).

41. Chaison and Rose, "The Macrodeterminants of Union Growth."

42. R. E. Walton and R. B. McKersie, *A Behavioral Theory of Negotiations* (New York: McGraw-Hill, 1965).

43. Fossum, *Labor Relations*. See also C. S. Loughran, *Negotiating a Labor Contract: A Management Handbook*, 2nd ed. (Washington, DC: Bureau of National Affairs, 1990).

44. C. M. Steven, *Strategy and Collective Bargaining Negotiations* (New York: McGraw-Hill, 1963); Katz and Kochan, *An Introduction to Collective Bargaining*.

45. Kochan, *Collective Bargaining and Industrial Relations*.

46. Fossum, *Labor Relations*.

47. Kochan, *Collective Bargaining and Industrial Relations*, p. 272.

48. Herman et al., *Collective Bargaining*.

49. Katz and Kochan, *An Introduction to Collective Bargaining*, 3rd ed.

50. Kochan, *Collective Bargaining and Industrial Relations*, p. 386.

51. *United Steelworkers v. American Manufacturing Co.*, 363 U.S. 564 (1960); *United Steelworkers v. Warrior Gulf and Navigation Co.*, 363 U.S. 574 (1960); *United Steelworkers v. Enterprise Wheel and Car Corp.*, 363 U.S. 593 (1960).

52. Original data from U.S. Federal Mediation and Conciliation Service, *Fiftieth Annual Report, Fiscal Year 1997* (Washington, DC: U.S. Government Printing Office, 1997); www.fmcs.gov.

53. J. R. Redecker, *Employee Discipline: Policies and Practices* (Washington, DC: Bureau of National Affairs, 1989).

54. Barbash, *The Elements of Industrial Relations*, p. 6.

55. T. A. Kochan, H. C. Katz, and R. B. McKersie, *The Transformation of American Industrial Relations* (New York: BasicBooks, 1986), chap. 6.

56. J. B. Arthur, "The Link between Business Strategy and Industrial Relations Systems in American Steel Minimills," *Industrial and Labor Relations Review* 45 (1992), pp. 488–506; M. Schuster, "Union Management Cooperation," in *Employee and Labor Relations*, ed. J. A. Fossum (Washington, DC: Bureau of National Affairs, 1990); E. Cohen-Rosenthal and C. Burton, *Mutual Gains: A Guide to Union–Management Cooperation*, 2nd ed. (Ithaca, NY: ILR Press, 1993); T. A. Kochan and P. Osterman, *The Mutual Gains Enterprise* (Boston: Harvard Business School Press, 1994); E. Applebaum and R. Batt, *The New American Workplace* (Ithaca, NY: ILR Press, 1994).

57. A. E. Eaton, "Factors Contributing to the Survival of Employee Participation Programs in Unionized Settings," *Industrial and Labor Relations Review* 47, no. 3 (1994), pp. 371–89.

58. National Labor Relations Board, *A Guide to Basic Law*.

59. A. Bernstein, "Putting a Damper on That Old Team Spirit," *BusinessWeek* (May 4, 1992), p. 60.

60. Bureau of National Affairs, "Polaroid Dissolves Employee Committee in Response to Labor Department Ruling," *Daily Labor Report* (June 23, 1992), p. A-3; K. G. Salwen, "DuPont Is Told It Must Disband Nonunion Panels," *The Wall Street Journal* (June 7, 1993), p. A-2.

61. "NLRB 4-0 Approves Crown Cork & Seal's Use of Seven Employee Participation Committees." *HR News* (September 3, 2001).

62. Kochan and Osterman, *Mutual Gains*; J. P. MacDuffie, "Human Resource Bundles and Manufacturing Performance: Organizational Logic and Flexible Production Systems in the World Auto Industry," *Industrial and Labor Relations Review* 48, no. 2 (1995), pp. 197–221; W. N. Cooke, "Employee Participation Programs, Group-Based Incentives, and Company Performance: A Union–Nonunion Comparison," *Industrial and Labor Relations Review* 47, no. 4 (1994), pp. 594–609; C. Doucouliagos, "Worker Participation and Productivity in Labor-Managed and Participatory Capitalist Firms: A Meta-Analysis," *Industrial and Labor Relations Review* 49, no. 1 (1995), pp. 58–77.

63. J. Cutcher-Gershenfeld, "The Impact of Economic Performance of a Transformation in Workplace Relations," *Industrial and Labor Relations Review* 44 (1991), pp. 241–60.

64. R. B. Freeman and J. Rogers, *Proceedings of the Industrial Relations Research Association*, 1995. A survey of workers represented by the United Autoworkers at six Chrysler manufacturing plants found generally positive worker reactions to the implementation of work teams, streamlined job classifications, and skill-based pay. See L. W. Hunter, J. P. Macduffie, and L. Doucet, "What Makes Teams Take? Employee Reactions to Work Reforms," *Industrial and Labor Relations Review* 55 (2002), p. 448. A study of the airline industry, moreover, concludes that relational factors, such as conflict and workplace culture, also play an important role in firm performance. See J. H. Gittell, A. vonNordenflycht, and T. A. Kochan, "Mutual Gains or Zero Sum? Labor Relations and Firm Performance in the Airline Industry," *Industrial and Labor Relations Review* 57 (2004), p. 163.

65. http://stats.bls.gov.

66. Ibid.

67. Jarrell and Stanley, "A Meta-Analysis"; R. B. Freeman and J. Medoff, *What Do Unions Do?* (New York: BasicBooks, 1984); L. Mishel and M. Walters, "How Unions Help All Workers," *Economic Policy Institute Briefing Paper*, August 2003, www.epinet.org.

68. J. T. Addison and B. T. Hirsch, "Union Effects on Productivity, Profits, and Growth: Has the Long Run Arrived?" *Journal of Labor Economics* 7 (1989), pp. 72–105.

69. R. B. Freeman and J. L. Medoff, "The Two Faces of Unionism," *Public Interest* 57 (Fall 1979), pp. 69–93.

70. Ibid., L. Mishel and P. Voos, *Unions and Economic Competitiveness* (Armonk, NY: M. E. Sharpe, 1991); Ibid., M. Ash and J. A. Seago, "The Effect of Registered Nurses' Unions on Heart-Attack Mortality," *Industrial and Labor Relations Review* 57 (2004), p. 422; C. Doucouliagos and P. Laroche, What Do Unions Do to Productivity? A Meta-Analysis, *Industrial Relations* 42 (2003), pp. 650–91.

71. Freeman and Medoff, "Two Faces."

72. S. Slichter, J. Healy, and E. R. Livernash, *The Impact of Collective Bargaining on Management* (Washington, DC: Brookings Institution, 1960); Freeman and Medoff, "Two Faces."

73. Freeman and Medoff, *What Do Unions Do?*; Herman et al., *Collective Bargaining*; Addison and Hirsch, "Union Effects on Productivity"; Katz and Kochan, *An Introduction to Collective Bargaining*; Lineneman et al., "Evaluating the Evidence."

74. B. E. Becker and C. A. Olson, "Unions and Firm Profits," *Industrial Relations* 31, no. 3 (1992), pp. 395–415; B. T. Hirsch and B. A. Morgan, "Shareholder Risks and Returns in Union and Nonunion Firms," *Industrial and Labor Relations Review* 47, no. 2 (1994), pp. 302–18.

75. Addison and Hirsch, "Union Effects on Productivity." See also B. T. Hirsch, *Labor Unions and the Economic Performance of Firms* (Kalamazoo, MI: W. E. Upjohn Institute, 1991); J. M. Abowd, "The Effect of Wage Bargains on the Stock Market Value of the Firm," *American Economic Review* 79 (1989), pp. 774–800; Hirsch, *Labor Unions*.

76. B. E. Becker, and C. A. Olson, "The Impact of Strikes on Shareholder Equity," *Industrial and Labor Relations Review* 39, no. 3 (1986), pp. 425–38; O. Persons, "The Effects of Automobile Strikes on the Stock Value of Steel Suppliers," *Industrial and Labor Relations Review* 49, no. 1 (1995), pp. 78–87.

77. C. Brewster, "Levels of Analysis in Strategic HRM: Questions Raised by Comparative Research," Conference on Research and Theory in HRM, Cornell University, October 1997.

78. C. Chang and C. Sorrentino, "Union Membership in 12 Countries," *Monthly Labor Review* 114, no. 12 (1991), pp. 46–53; D. G. Blanchflower and R. B. Freeman, "Going Different Ways: Unionism in the U.S. and Other Advanced O.E.C.D. Countries" (Symposium on the Future Role of Unions, Industry, and Government in Industrial Relations. University of Minnesota), cited in Chaison and Rose, "The Macrodeterminants of Union Growth," p. 23.

79. J. P. Begin and E. F. Beal, *The Practice of Collective Bargaining* (Homewood, IL: Richard D. Irwin, 1989); T. H. Hammer, S. C. Currall, and R. N. Stern, "Worker Representation on Boards of Directors: A Study of Competing Roles," *Industrial and Labor Relations Review* 44 (1991), pp. 661–80; Katz and Kochan, *An Introduction to Collective Bargaining*; H. Gunter and G. Leminsky, "The Federal Republic of Germany," in *Labor in the Twentieth Century*, ed. J. T. Dunlop and W. Galenson (New York: Academic Press, 1978), pp. 149–96.

80. "Adapt or Die," *The Economist* (July 1, 1995), p. 54; G. Steinmetz, "German Firms Sour on Stem That Keeps Peace with Workers: Centralized Bargaining, a Key to Postwar Gains, Inflates Costs, Companies Fear," *The Wall Street Journal* (October 17, 1995), p. A1.

81. Herman et al., *Collective Bargaining*, p. 348; B. T. Hirsch and D. A. MacPherson, *Union Membership and Earnings Data Book 1994* (Washington, DC: Bureau of National Affairs, 1995).

82. J. F. Burton and T. Thomason, "The Extent of Collective Bargaining in the Public Sector," in *Public Sector Bargaining*, ed. B. Aaron, J. M. Najita, and J. L. Stern (Washington, DC: Bureau of National Affairs, 1988).

83. www.afscme.org.

15 Chapter

Managing Human Resources Globally

Objectives After reading this chapter, you should be able to:

1. Identify the recent changes that have caused companies to expand into international markets.

2. Discuss the four factors that most strongly influence HRM in international markets.

3. List the different categories of international employees.

4. Identify the four levels of global participation and the HRM issues faced within each level.

5. Discuss the ways companies attempt to select, train, compensate, and reintegrate expatriate managers.

Businesses are competing in a rapidly globalizing environment. How does the practice of offshoring that companies like IBM are practicing affect existing domestic workforces?

Enter the World of Business

Global Sourcing of Talent: IBM's Dilemma

As the global economy becomes more and more interdependent, companies are forced to make tough decisions regarding the sourcing of their work. It used to be that when a company based in the United States needed to manufacture goods closer to their global customers, the rationale seemed obvious and few people balked. Then, as companies found that locating manufacturing overseas could capitalize on lower labor costs, enabling them to then ship those goods to the United States (consequently, not needing U.S. manufacturing plants as much), public sentiment began occasionally to turn negative. However, most recently, enabled by global telecommunications technology, companies have discovered that they can locate call center jobs and information technology jobs (such as software coding or computer chip design) in countries such as India or China and realize as much as a 75 percent labor cost savings. For instance, Stephanie Moore, vice president of outsourcing at Forrester Research states "You can get crackerjack Java programmers in India right out of college for $5,000 a year versus $60,000 here. The technology is such, why be in New York City

when you can be 9,000 miles away with far less expense?" Such savings cannot be ignored by companies whose customers want low costs and shareholders want high profits.

For instance, General Electric has thousands of call center, research and development, and information technology workers in India. Peter Stack, a G.E. spokesman, stated "The outsourcing presence in India definitely gives us a competitive advantage in the businesses that use it. Those businesses are some of our growth businesses, and I would say that they're businesses where our overall employment is increasing."

In addition to cost savings, the global sourcing of talent provides capability that is difficult to build within one country or one time zone. For instance, Oracle's spokesman David Samson argues "Our aim here is not cost driven. It's to build a 24/7 follow-the-sun model for development and support. When a software engineer goes to bed at night in the U.S., his or her colleague in India picks up development when they get into work. They're able to continually develop products."

However, in spite of the cost and capability advantages, offshoring of jobs can result in considerable negative publicity. For instance, IBM's efforts to develop offshore call center and information technology capability has elicited significant backlash in the United States. Internal IBM employees have recorded calls and released internal memos that provide negative grist for opponents to focus on. For instance, a recorded phone call of IBM's director of global employee relations, Tom Lynch, was released, in which he and other executives were suggesting they should move some jobs now done in the United States to India or other countries. "Our competitors are doing it, and we have to do it," he stated. He also suggested, "Governments are going to find out that they're fairly limited as to what they can do, so unionizing becomes an attractive option."

Ultimately the dilemma is what to do about those whose jobs are being replaced. In the call Mr. Lynch stated, "One of our challenges that we deal with every day is trying to balance what the business needs to do versus impact on people. This is one of these areas where this challenge hits us squarely between the eyes."

Source: From "IBM Explores Shift of White-Collar Jobs Overseas," by S. Greenhouse, *New York Times,* July 22, 2003. Copyright © 2003 by The New York Times Co. Reprinted with permission. W. Bulkeley (July 29, 2004) IBM now plans fewer layoffs from offshoring. http://online.wsj.com/article_print/0,,SB109105951415677179,00.html.

Introduction

The environment in which business competes is rapidly becoming globalized. More and more companies are entering international markets by exporting their products overseas, building plants in other countries, and entering into alliances with foreign companies. Back in the middle of the 1980s, 61 of the top 100 organizations had their headquarters in the United States. By 2004, that number has dropped to 35, and, as you can see in Table 15.1, of the world's largest 25 organizations, only 11 are headquartered in the United States, with 10 in Europe and 4 in Asia. Within the banking industry, only 5 U.S. companies make the top 25 list.

A survey of 12,000 managers from 25 different countries indicates how common international expansion has become, both in the United States and in other countries.[1] Of the U.S. managers surveyed, 26 percent indicated that their companies had recently expanded internationally. Among the larger companies (10,000 or more employees), 45 percent had expanded internationally during the previous two years. Currently, exports account for 11 percent of the gross domestic product in the United States, and they have been growing at a rate of 12 percent a year since 1987.[2]

Indeed, most organizations now function in the global economy. Thus U.S. businesses are entering international markets at the same time foreign companies are entering the U.S. market.

What is behind the trend toward expansion into global markets? Companies are attempting to gain a competitive advantage, which can be provided by international expansion in a number of ways. First, these countries are new markets with large numbers of potential customers. For companies that are producing below their capacity, they provide a means of increasing sales and profits. Second, many companies are building production facilities in other countries as a means of capitalizing on those countries' lower labor costs for relatively unskilled jobs. For example, many of the *maquiladora* plants (foreign-owned plants located in Mexico that employ Mexican laborers) provide low-skilled labor at considerably lower cost than in the United States. In 1999, the average manufacturing hourly wage in Mexico was $2.12.[3] Third, the rapid increasing in telecommunications and information technology enables work to be done more rapidly, efficiently, and effectively around the globe. With the best col-

TABLE 15.1

Fortune Global
500—25 Largest
Organizations
Ranked by Revenues

RANK	COMPANY	REVENUES ($ MILLIONS)	PROFITS ($ MILLIONS)
1	Wal-Mart Stores	263,009.0	9,054.0
2	BP	232,571.0	10,267.0
3	Exxon Mobil	222,883.0	21,510.0
4	Royal Dutch/Shell Group	201,728.0	12,496.0
5	General Motors	195,324.0	3,822.0
6	Ford Motor	164,505.0	495.0
7	DaimlerChrylser	156,602.2	507.0
8	Toyota Motor	153,111.0	10,288.1
9	General Electric	134,187.0	15,002.0
10	Total	118,441.4	7,950.6
11	Allianz	114,949.9	1,828.9
12	ChevronTexaco	112,937.0	7,230.0
13	AXA	111,912.2	1,137.4
14	ConocoPhillips	99,468.0	4,735.0
15	Volkswagen	98,636.6	1,239.3
16	Nippon Telegraph & Telephone	98,229.1	5,700.1
17	ING Group	95,893.3	4,575.7
18	Citigroup	94,713.0	17,853.0
19	International Business Machines	89,131.0	7,583.0
20	American International Group	81,303.0	9,274.0
21	Siemens	80,501.0	2,651.4
22	Carrefour	79,773.8	1,843.8
23	Hitachi	76,423.3	140.6
24	Hewlett-Packard	73,061.0	2,539.0
25	Honda Motor	72,263.7	4,110.8

From Fortune Global 500: The 25 Largest Companies, Fortune, July 26, 2004. Copyright © 2004 Time Inc. All rights reserved.

lege graduates available for $2.00 an hour in India versus $12–18 an hour in the United States, companies can hire the best talent (resulting in better work) at a lower cost. And because their day is our night, work done in the United Srates can be handed off to those in India for a 24/7 work process.[4]

According to a survey of almost 3,000 line executives and HR executives from 12 countries, international competition is the number one factor affecting HRM. The globalization of business structures and globalization of the economy ranked fourth and fifth, respectively.[5] Deciding whether to enter foreign markets and whether to develop plants or other facilities in other countries, however, is no simple matter, and many human resource issues surface.

This chapter discusses the human resource issues that must be addressed to gain competitive advantage in a world of global competition. This is not a chapter on international human resource management (the specific HRM policies and programs companies use to manage human resources across international boundaries).[6] The chapter focuses instead on the key factors that must be addressed to strategically manage human resources in an international context. We discuss some of the important events that have increased the global nature of business over the past few years. We then identify some of the factors that are most important to HRM in global environments. Finally, we examine particular issues related to managing expatriate managers. These issues present unique opportunities for firms to gain competitive advantage.

Current Global Changes

Several recent social and political changes have accelerated the movement toward international competition. The effects of these changes have been profound and far-reaching. Many are still evolving. In this section we discuss the major developments that have accentuated the need for organizations to gain a competitive advantage through effectively managing human resources in a global economy.

European Economic Community

European countries have managed their economies individually for years. Because of the countries' close geographic proximity, their economies have become intertwined. This created a number of problems for international businesses; for example, the regulations of one country, such as France, might be completely different from those of another country, such as Germany. In response, most of the European countries agreed to participate in the European Economic Community, which began in 1992. The EEC is a confederation of most of the European nations that agree to engage in free trade with one another, with commerce regulated by an overseeing body called the European Commission (EC). Under the EEC, legal regulation in the participating countries has become more, although not completely, uniform. Assuming the EEC's trend toward free trade among members continues, Europe has become one of the largest free markets in the world. In addition, as of 1999, all of the members of the European Economic Community share a common currency, the euro. This ties the members' economic fates even more closely with one another. In addition to the previous 15 EU states, as of May 1, 2004, 10 EU accession states—Cyprus, the Czech Republic, Estonia, Hungary, Latvia, Lithuania, Malta, Poland, Slovakia, and Slovenia—were added to the EU, expanding the economic zone covered by the European Union.

North American Free Trade Agreement (NAFTA)

NAFTA is an agreement among Canada, the United States, and Mexico that has created a free market even larger than the European Economic Community. The United States and Canada already had a free trade agreement since 1989, but NAFTA brought Mexico into the consortium. The agreement has been prompted by Mexico's increasing willingness to open its markets and facilities in an effort to promote economic growth.[7] As previously discussed, the *maquiladora* plants exemplify this trend. In addition, some efforts have been made to expand the membership of NAFTA to other Latin American countries, such as Chile.

NAFTA has increased U.S. investment in Mexico because of Mexico's substantially lower labor costs for low-skilled employees. This has had two effects on employment in the United States. First, many low-skilled jobs went south, decreasing employment opportunities for U.S. citizens who lack higher-level skills. Second, it has increased employment opportunities for Americans with higher-level skills beyond those already being observed.[8]

The Growth of Asia

An additional global market that is of economic consequence to many firms lies in Asia. Whereas Japan has been a dominant economic force for over 20 years, recently countries such as Singapore, Hong Kong, and Malaysia have become significant economic forces. In addition, China, with its population of over 1 billion and trend toward opening its markets to foreign investors, presents a tremendous potential market for goods. In fact, a consortium of Singaporean companies and governmental agencies has jointly developed with China a huge industrial township in eastern China's Suzhou City that will consist of ready-made factories for sale to foreign companies.[9] Although Asia has recently been the victim of a large-scale economic recession termed the "Asian flu," it is fully expected to regain its stature as an attractive market for products and investment over the next few years.

General Agreement on Tariffs and Trade (GATT)

GATT is an international framework of rules and principles for reducing trade barriers across countries around the world. It currently consists of over 100 member nations. The most recent round of GATT negotiations resulted in an agreement to cut tariffs (taxes on imports) by 40 percent, reduce government subsidies to businesses, expand protection of intellectual property such as copyrights and patents, and establish rules for investing and trading in services. It also established the World Trade Organization (WTO) to resolve disputes among GATT members.

These changes—the European Economic Community, NAFTA, the growth of Asia, and GATT—all exemplify events that are pushing companies to compete in a global economy. These developments are opening new markets and new sources of technology and labor in a way that has never been seen in history. However, this era of increasing international competition accentuates the need to manage human resources effectively to gain competitive advantage in a global marketplace. This requires understanding some of the factors that can determine the effectiveness of various HRM practices and approaches.

Factors Affecting HRM in Global Markets

Companies that enter global markets must recognize that these markets are not simply mirror images of their home country. Countries differ along a number of dimensions that influence the attractiveness of direct foreign investment in each country. These differences determine the economic viability of building an operation in a foreign location, and they have a particularly strong impact on HRM in that operation. Researchers in international management have identified a number of factors that can affect HRM in global markets, and we focus on four factors, as depicted in Figure 15.1: culture, education–human capital, the political–legal system, and the economic system.[10]

Culture

By far the most important factor influencing international HRM is the culture of the country in which a facility is located. Culture is defined as "the set of important assumptions (often unstated) that members of a community share."[11] These assumptions consist of beliefs about the world and how it works and the ideals that are worth striving for.[12]

Culture is important to HRM for two reasons. First, it often determines the other three factors affecting HRM in global markets. Culture can greatly affect a country's laws, in that laws are often the codification of right and wrong as defined by the culture. Culture also affects human capital, because if education is greatly valued by the culture, then members of the community try to increase their human capital. Finally, as we will discuss later, cultures and economic systems are closely intertwined.[13]

FIGURE 15.1

Factors Affecting Human Resource Management in International Markets

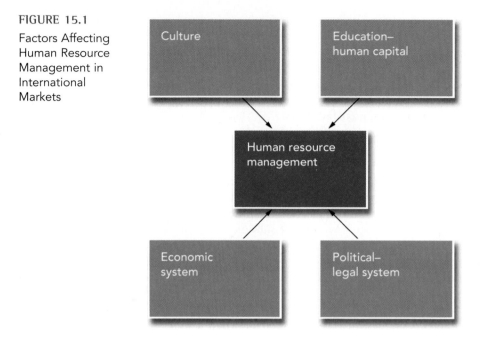

However, the most important reason that culture is important to HRM is that it often determines the effectiveness of various HRM practices. Practices found to be effective in the United States may not be effective in a culture that has different beliefs and values.[14] For example, U.S. companies rely heavily on individual performance appraisal, and rewards are tied to individual performance. In Japan, however, individuals are expected to subordinate their wishes and desires to those of the larger group. Thus, individual-based evaluation and incentives are not nearly as effective there and, in fact, are seldom observed among Japanese organizations.[15]

In this section we examine a model that attempts to characterize different cultures. This model illustrates why culture can have a profound influence on HRM.

Hofstede's Cultural Dimensions

In a classic study of culture, Geert Hofstede identified four dimensions on which various cultures could be classified.[16] In a later study he added a fifth dimension that aids in characterizing cultures.[17] The relative scores for 10 major countries are provided in Table 15.2. **Individualism–collectivism** describes the strength of the relation between an individual and other individuals in the society—that is, the degree to which people act as individuals rather than as members of a group. In individualist cultures, such as the United States, Great Britain, and the Netherlands, people are expected to look after their own interests and the interests of their immediate families. The individual is expected to stand on her own two feet rather than be protected by the group. In collectivist cultures, such as Colombia, Pakistan, and Taiwan, people are expected to look after the interest of the larger community, which is expected to protect people when they are in trouble.

The second dimension, **power distance**, concerns how a culture deals with hierarchical power relationships—particularly the unequal distribution of power. It describes the degree of inequality among people that is considered to be normal. Cultures with

Individualism–collectivism
One of Hofstede's cultural dimensions; describes the strength of the relation between an individual and other individuals in a society.

Power distance
One of Hofstede's cultural dimensions; describes how a culture deals with hierarchical power relationships.

	PDᵃ	ID	MA	UA	LT
United States	40 Lᵇ	91 H	62 H	46 L	29 L
Germany	35 L	67 H	66 H	65 M	31 M
Japan	54 M	45 M	95 H	92 H	80 H
France	68 H	71 H	43 M	86 H	30ᶜ L
Netherlands	38 L	80 H	14 L	53 M	44 M
Hong Kong	68 H	25 L	57 H	29 L	96 H
Indonesia	78 H	14 L	46 M	48 L	25ᶜ L
West Africa	77 H	20 L	46 M	54 M	16 L
Russia	95ᶜ H	50ᶜ M	40ᶜ L	90ᶜ H	10ᶜ L
China	80ᶜ H	20ᶜ L	50ᶜ M	60ᶜ M	118 H

TABLE 15.2

Cultural Dimension Scores for 10 Countries

ᵃPD = power distance; ID = individualism; MA = masculinity; UA = uncertainty avoidance; LT = long-term orientation.

ᵇH = top third; M = medium third; L = bottom third (among 53 countries and regions for the first four dimensions; among 23 countries for the fifth).

ᶜEstimated.

SOURCE: From *Academy of Management Executive* by G. Hofstede. Copyright © 1993 by Academy of Management. Reproduced with permission of Academy of Management via Copyright Clearance Center.

small power distance, such as those of Denmark and Israel, seek to eliminate inequalities in power and wealth as much as possible, whereas countries with large power distances, such as India and the Philippines, seek to maintain those differences.

Differences in power distance often result in miscommunication and conflicts between people from different cultures. For example, in Mexico and Japan individuals are always addressed by their titles (Señor Smith or Smith-san, respectively). Individuals from the United States, however, often believe in minimizing power distances by using first names. Although this is perfectly normal, and possibly even advisable in the United States, it can be offensive and a sign of disrespect in other cultures.

The third dimension, **uncertainty avoidance,** describes how cultures seek to deal with the fact that the future is not perfectly predictable. It is defined as the degree to which people in a culture prefer structured over unstructured situations. Some cultures, such as those of Singapore and Jamaica, have weak uncertainty avoidance. They socialize individuals to accept this uncertainty and take each day as it comes. People from these cultures tend to be rather easygoing and flexible regarding different views. Other cultures, such as those of Greece and Portugal, socialize their people to seek security through technology, law, and religion. Thus these cultures provide clear rules as to how one should behave.

The **masculinity–femininit**y dimension describes the division of roles between the sexes within a society. In "masculine" cultures, such as those of Germany and Japan, what are considered traditionally masculine values—showing off, achieving something visible, and making money—permeate the society. These societies stress assertiveness, performance, success, and competition. "Feminine" cultures, such as those of Sweden and Norway, promote values that have been traditionally regarded as feminine, such as putting relationships before money, helping others, and preserving the environment. These cultures stress service, care for the weak, and solidarity.

Finally, the fifth dimension comes from the philosophy of the Far East and is referred to as the **long-term–short-term orientation.** Cultures high on the long-term

Uncertainty avoidance
One of Hofstede's cultural dimensions; describes how cultures seek to deal with an unpredictable future.

Masculinity–femininity dimension
One of Hofstede's cultural dimensions; describes the division of roles between the sexes within a society.

Long-term–short-term orientation
One of Hofstede's cultural dimensions; describes how a culture balances immediate benefits with future rewards.

orientation focus on the future and hold values in the present that will not necessarily provide an immediate benefit, such as thrift (saving) and persistence. Hofstede found that many Far Eastern countries such as Japan and China have a long-term orientation. Short-term orientations, on the other hand, are found in the United States, Russia, and West Africa. These cultures are oriented toward the past and present and promote respect for tradition and for fulfilling social obligations.

The current Japanese criticism of management practices in the United States illustrates the differences in long-term–short-term orientation. Japanese managers, traditionally exhibiting a long-term orientation, engage in 5- to 10-year planning. This leads them to criticize U.S. managers, who are traditionally much more short-term in orientation because their planning often consists of quarterly to yearly time horizons.

These five dimensions help us understand the potential problems of managing employees from different cultures. Later in this chapter we will explore how these cultural dimensions affect the acceptability and utility of various HRM practices. However, it is important to note that these differences can have a profound influence on whether a company chooses to enter a given country. One interesting finding of Hofstede's research was the impact of culture on a country's economic health. He found that countries with individualist cultures were more wealthy. Collectivist cultures with high power distance were all poor.[18] Cultures seem to affect a country's economy through their promotion of individual work ethics and incentives for individuals to increase their human capital. Figure 15.2 maps the countries Hofstede studied on the two characteristics of individualism–collectivism and economic success.

Implications of Culture for HRM

Cultures have an important impact on approaches to managing people. As we discuss later, the culture can strongly affect the education–human capital of a country, the political–legal system, and the economic system. As Hofstede found, culture also has a profound impact on a country's economic health by promoting certain values that either aid or inhibit economic growth.

More important to this discussion, however, is that cultural characteristics influence the ways managers behave in relation to subordinates, as well as the perceptions of the appropriateness of various HRM practices. First, cultures differ strongly on such things as how subordinates expect leaders to lead, how decisions are handled within the hierarchy, and (most important) what motivates individuals. For example, in Germany, managers achieve their status by demonstrating technical skills, so employees look to them to assign their tasks and resolve technical problems. In the Netherlands, on the other hand, managers focus on seeking consensus among all parties and must engage in an open-ended exchange of views and balancing of interests.[19] Clearly, these methods have different implications for selecting and training managers in the different countries.

Second, cultures strongly influence the appropriateness of HRM practices. For example, as previously discussed, the extent to which a culture promotes an individualistic versus a collectivist orientation will impact the effectiveness of individually oriented human resource management systems. In the United States, companies often focus selection systems on assessing an individual's technical skill and, to a lesser extent, social skills. In collectivist cultures, on the other hand, companies focus more on assessing how well an individual will perform as a member of the work group.

Similarly, cultures can influence compensation systems. Individualistic cultures such as those found in the United States often exhibit great differences between the

FIGURE 15.2

The Position of the Studied Countries on Their Individualism Index (IDV) versus Their 1970 National Wealth

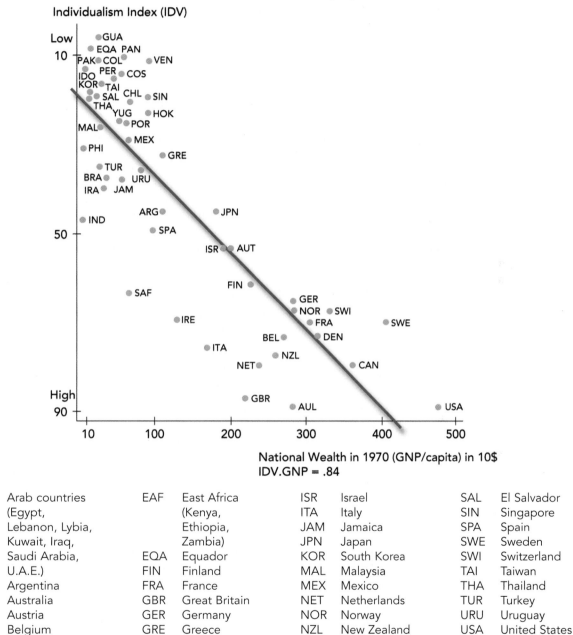

ARA	Arab countries (Egypt, Lebanon, Lybia, Kuwait, Iraq, Saudi Arabia, U.A.E.)	EAF	East Africa (Kenya, Ethiopia, Zambia)	ISR Israel
ARG	Argentina			ITA Italy
AUL	Australia	EQA	Equador	JAM Jamaica
AUT	Austria	FIN	Finland	JPN Japan
BEL	Belgium	FRA	France	KOR South Korea
BRA	Brazil	GBR	Great Britain	MAL Malaysia
CAN	Canada	GER	Germany	MEX Mexico
CHL	Chile	GRE	Greece	NET Netherlands
COL	Colombia	GUA	Guatemala	NOR Norway
COS	Costa Rica	HOK	Hong Kong	NZL New Zealand
DEN	Denmark	IDO	Indonesia	PAK Pakistan
		IND	India	PAN Panama
		IRA	Iran	PER Peru
		IRE	Ireland	PHI Philippines
				POR Portugal
				SAF South Africa

ISR Israel · ITA Italy · JAM Jamaica · JPN Japan · KOR South Korea · MAL Malaysia · MEX Mexico · NET Netherlands · NOR Norway · NZL New Zealand · PAK Pakistan · PAN Panama · PER Peru · PHI Philippines · POR Portugal · SAF South Africa

SAL El Salvador · SIN Singapore · SPA Spain · SWE Sweden · SWI Switzerland · TAI Taiwan · THA Thailand · TUR Turkey · URU Uruguay · USA United States · VEN Venezuela · WAF West Africa (Nigeria, Ghana, Sierra Leone) · YUG Yugoslavia

SOURCE: G. Hofstede, "The Cultural Relativity of Organizational Practices and Theories," *Journal of International Business Studies* 14, no. 2 (Fall 1983), p. 89. Reprinted with permission of Palgrave Macmillan.

highest- and lowest-paid individuals in an organization, with the highest-paid individual often receiving 200 times the salary of the lowest. Collectivist cultures, on the other hand, tend to have much flatter salary structures, with the top-paid individual receiving only about 20 times the overall pay of the lowest-paid one.

Cultural differences can affect the communication and coordination processes in organizations. Collectivist cultures, as well as those with less of an authoritarian orientation, value group decision making and participative management practices more highly than do individualistic cultures. When a person raised in an individualistic culture must work closely with those from a collectivist culture, communication problems and conflicts often appear. Much of the emphasis on "cultural diversity" programs in organizations focuses on understanding the cultures of others in order to better communicate with them.

While national culture is important, recent research also suggests that its importance may be overstated. Researchers reexamining Hofstede's original work found that while differences existed across nations, significant cultural differences also existed within nations. They also found that the differences in cultures across organizations within countries was larger than the differences across countries. Their results imply that while one cannot ignore national culture, one must not think that certain HR practices may not be effective simply based on a regard for national culture.[20] People of varying cultural backgrounds within a nation will be drawn to organizations whose cultures better match their individual, as opposed to national, value systems. The "Competing through Technology" box illustrates how technological and economic forces are impacting the culture of India.

Education–Human Capital

A company's potential to find and maintain a qualified workforce is an important consideration in any decision to expand into a foreign market. Thus a country's human capital resources can be an important HRM issue. *Human capital* refers to the productive capabilities of individuals—that is, the knowledge, skills, and experience that have economic value.[21]

Countries differ in their levels of human capital. For example, as discussed in Chapter 1, the United States suffers from a human capital shortage because the jobs being created require skills beyond those of most new entrants into the workforce.[22] In former East Germany, there is an excess of human capital in terms of technical knowledge and skill because of that country's large investment in education. However, East Germany's business schools did not teach management development, so there is a human capital shortage for managerial jobs.[23] Similarly, companies in what used to be West Germany have shifted toward types of production and service that require high-skilled workers; this is creating a human capital shortage for high-skill jobs, yet the unemployment rate remains high because of a large number of low-skilled workers.[24] However, the high skills and low wages of workers in many countries make their labor forces quite attractive.

A country's human capital is determined by a number of variables. A major variable is the educational opportunities available to the labor force. In the Netherlands, for instance, government funding of school systems allows students to go all the way through graduate school without paying.[25] Similarly, the free education provided to citizens in the former Soviet bloc resulted in high levels of human capital, in spite of the poor infrastructure and economy that resulted from the socialist economic sys-

Technology's Impact on Culture

By now you are well aware of the issue of offshoring and its impact on the U.S. workforce. However, great value can be gained by understanding how technological advances leading to offshoring are impacting the beneficiaries: the Indian workforce.

The telecommunications and information technology advances that made possible the ability to locate call centers halfway around the globe are having a tremendous impact in those locations. The outsourced jobs bring much more than just money to India. They are creating a young, affluent class that embraces Western values and attitudes, quite contrary to the time-honored social mores. In India the thought of women working at night was unimaginable, and young people are expected to marry someone their parents choose.

Nowhere is the cultural transformation more apparent than in the call centers, filled with workers in their 20s. These jobs bring money, independence, and an informal environment where people can wear and say what they like. They are trained in American accents and geography, and absorb new ideas about family, material possessions, and romance. For instance, Nikesh Soares used to be a "little gentleman" adhering to traditional Indian mores. However, his outlook changed when he joined e-Funds, a Bombay call center. He answered calls from Americans responding to infomercials, and his $220 a month salary—twice what he had been paid in his previous job—was empowering. He and his friends would frequent all-night bars after work, stumbling home for a few hours sleep before heading back to work. He married Sophia D'Souza, who sat in the next cubicle. Her independence and preference for jeans stand in dark contrast to old-fashioned values. They both seem to embrace American values now. In the United States, "there is this idea that at 18 years old, you go out, work, and parents don't interfere," Mr. Soares says. "I think that is very excellent."

However, others are not so enamored by the rapid importation of American values. Arundhati Roy, a novelist and activist in India, argues that call centers strip young Indian workers of their cultural identities. She wrote that call centers show "how easily an ancient civilization can be made to abase itself completely."

SOURCE: From *The Wall Street Journal, Online*, by J. Slater. Copyright by Dow Jones & Co., Inc. Reproduced with permission of Dow Jones & Co., Inc. via Copyright Clearance Center.

tems. In contrast, some Third World countries, such as Nicaragua and Haiti, have relatively low levels of human capital because of a lack of investment in education.

A country's human capital may profoundly affect a foreign company's desire to locate there or enter that country's market. Countries with low human capital attract facilities that require low skills and low wage levels. This explains why U.S. companies desire to move their currently unionized low-skill–high-wage manufacturing and assembly jobs to Mexico, where they can obtain low-skilled workers for substantially lower wages. Similarly, Japan ships its messy, low-skill work to neighboring countries while maintaining its high-skill work at home.[26] Countries like Mexico, with relatively low levels of human capital, might not be as attractive for operations that consist of more high-skill jobs.

Countries with high human capital are attractive sites for direct foreign investment that creates high-skill jobs. In Ireland, for example, over 25 percent of 18-year-olds attend college, a rate much higher than other European countries. In addition, Ireland's economy supports only 1.1 million jobs for a population of 3.5 million. The combination of high education levels, a strong work ethic, and high unemployment makes the country attractive for foreign firms because of the resulting high productivity and low turnover. The Met Life insurance company set up a facility for Irish workers to analyze medical insurance claims. It has found the high levels of human capital and the high work ethic provide such a competitive advantage that the company is currently looking for other work performed in the United States to be shipped to Ireland. Similarly, as already discussed, the skills of newly graduated technology workers in India are as high or higher than those found among their counterparts in the United States. In addition, because jobs are not as plentiful in India, the worker attitudes are better in many of these locations.[27]

The "Competing through Sustainability" box describes how the HIV/AIDS epidemic is impacting the human capital in Africa.

Political–Legal System

The regulations imposed by a country's legal system can strongly affect HRM. The political–legal system often dictates the requirements for certain HRM practices, such as training, compensation, hiring, firing, and layoffs. In large part, the legal system is an outgrowth of the culture in which it exists. Thus the laws of a particular country often reflect societal norms about what constitutes legitimate behavior.[28]

For example, the United States has led the world in eliminating discrimination in the workplace. Because of the importance this has in our culture, we also have legal safeguards such as equal employment opportunity laws (discussed in Chapter 3) that strongly affect the hiring and firing practices of firms. As a society, we also have strong beliefs regarding the equity of pay systems; thus the Fair Labor Standards Act (discussed in Chapter 11), among other laws and regulations, sets the minimum wage for a variety of jobs. We have regulations that dictate much of the process for negotiation between unions and management. These regulations profoundly affect the ways human resources are managed in the United States.

Similarly, the legal regulations regarding HRM in other countries reflect their societal norms. For example, in Germany employees have a legal right to "codetermination" at the company, plant, and individual levels. At the company level, a firm's employees have direct influence on the important decisions that affect them, such as large investments or new strategies. This is brought about through having employee representatives on the supervisory council (*Aufsichtsrat*). At the plant level, codetermination exists through works councils. These councils have no rights in the economic management of the company, but they can influence HRM policies on such issues as working hours, payment methods, hirings, and transfers. Finally, at the individual level, employees have contractual rights, such as the right to read their personnel files and the right to be informed about how their pay is calculated.[29]

The EEC provides another example of the effects of the political–legal system on HRM. The EEC's Community Charter of December 9, 1989, provides for the fundamental social rights of workers. These rights include freedom of movement, freedom to choose one's occupation and be fairly compensated, guarantee of social protection via Social Security benefits, freedom of association and collective bargaining, equal treatment for men and women, and a safe and healthful work environment, among others.

Sustainable development calls upon business to address social issues. Quite possibly the most pressing global social issue of our time is the HIV/AIDS pandemic ravaging Africa and spreading rapidly across other areas of the world. Depriving communities and nations of their people, HIV/AIDS drains the human and institutional capacities that fuel sustainable development.

According to a December 2003 AIDS epidemic update by the Joint United Nations Programme on HIV/AIDS (UNAIDS) and the World Health Organization (WHO), an estimated three million people died from HIV/AIDS complications and an additional five million acquired the disease in 2003, bringing the total number of people living with the virus to 40 million. Thirty percent of these individuals are concentrated in Southern Africa, while Asia and Eastern Europe are experiencing rapid spread of the disease.

While causing disastrous social consequences, the HIV/AIDS pandemic has serious implications for organizations as well. They may be subjected to lower productivity stemming from absenteeism, turnover, skill shortages, and lower morale. In fact, a recent study conducted by several South African countries estimated that productivity would fall by 5 percent and profits by 6–8 percent as a result of absenteeism, health and insurance payments, and training costs.

The International Labor Office (ILO) developed a code of practice in 2001 which is widely used as a set of guidelines for designing an AIDS response. The ILO has developed four focus areas which are: prevention of HIV/AIDS, management and mitigation of the impact of HIV/AIDS on the world of work, care and support of workers infected and affected by HIV/AIDS, and elimination of stigma and discrimination on the basis of real or perceived HIV status.

As a conduit between the workforce and management, the HR function directly influences business response to HIV/AIDS and will be a key player in formulating future responses to the epidemic. It is reasonable to conclude that business at the very least will need a greater understanding of the epidemic for planning purposes. The direct costs associated with HIV/AIDS will drive business response. The sustainability of business operations in parts of the world greatly depends on business partnering with government and communities to implement prevention and care strategies.

SOURCE: D. Bloom, L. Bloom, D. Steven, and M. Weston, "Business and HIV/AIDS: Who Me? A Global Review of the Business Response to HIV/AIDS," *World Economic Forum and the Joint United Nations Program on HIV/AIDS*, World Economic Forum (2003), http://www.weforum.org, February 16, 2004; International Labor Organization, *An ILO Code of Practice on HIV/AIDS and the World of Work*, http://www.ilo.org/public/english/protection/trav/aids/code/codemain.htm 2001; Joint United Nations Programme on HIV/AIDS and World Health Organization, "AIDS Epidemic Update," UNAIDS (December 2003), http://www.unaids.org, February 27, 2004.

Economic System

A country's economic system influences HRM in a number of ways. As previously discussed, a country's culture is integrally tied to its economic system, and these systems provide many of the incentives for developing human capital. In socialist economic systems there are ample opportunities for developing human capital because the education system is free. However, under these systems, there is little economic incentive to develop human capital because there are no monetary rewards for increasing human capital. In addition, in former Soviet bloc countries, an individual's investment in human capital did not always result in a promotion. Rather, it was investment in the Communist Party that led to career advancements.

In capitalist systems the opposite situation exists. There is less opportunity to develop human capital without higher costs. (You have probably observed tuition increases at U.S. universities.) However, those who do invest in their individual human capital, particularly through education, are more able to reap monetary rewards, thus providing more incentive for such investment. In the United States, individuals' salaries usually reflect differences in human capital (high-skill workers receive higher compensation than low-skill workers). In fact, research estimates that an individual's wages increase by between 10 and 16 percent for each additional year of schooling.[30]

In addition to the effects of an economic system on HRM, the health of the system can have an important impact. For example, we referred earlier to lower labor costs in India. In developed countries with a high level of wealth, labor costs tend to be quite high relative to those in developing countries. While labor costs are related to the human capital of a country, they are not perfectly related, as shown by Table 15.3. This table provides a good example of the different hourly labor costs for manufacturing jobs in various countries.

An economic system also affects HRM directly through its taxes on compensation packages. Thus the differential labor costs shown in Table 15.3 do not always reflect the actual take-home pay of employees. Socialist systems are characterized by tax systems that redistribute wealth by taking a higher percentage of a person's income as she moves up the economic ladder. Capitalist systems attempt to reward individuals for their efforts by allowing them to keep more of their earnings. Companies that do business in other countries have to present compensation packages to expatriate managers that are competitive in take-home, rather than gross, pay. HRM

TABLE 15.3

Average Gross Hourly Compensation in Several Countries

Germany	$26.18
Switzerland	24.11
Sweden	20.18
Austria	21.07
Netherlands	21.74
Japan	18.83
United States	21.33
France	17.42
Italy	14.93
Britain	17.47
Australia	15.55
Singapore	7.27
Mexico	2.38
Sri Lanka	.42[a]
Canada	16.02
Taiwan	5.41

[a]2001 data.

SOURCE: U.S. Department of Labor, *International Comparisons of Hourly Compensation Costs for Production Workers in Manufacturing, 2002;* Bureau of Labor Statistics, www.bls.gov/fls/hccompreport.htm, 2001.

responses to these issues affecting expatriate managers will be discussed in more detail later in this chapter.

These differences in economies can have a profound impact on pay systems, particularly among global companies seeking to develop an international compensation and reward system that maintains cost controls while enabling local operations to compete in the war for talent. One recent study examining how compensation managers design these systems indicates that they look at a number of factors including the global firm strategy, the local regulatory/political context, institutions and stakeholders, local markets, and national culture. While they try to learn from the best practices that exist globally, they balance these approaches with the constraints imposed by the local environment.[31]

In conclusion, every country varies in terms of its culture, human capital, legal system, and economic systems. These variations directly influence the types of HRM systems that must be developed to accommodate the particular situation. The extent to which these differences affect a company depends on how involved the company is in global markets. In the next sections we discuss important concepts of global business and various levels of global participation, particularly noting how these factors come into play.

Managing Employees in a Global Context
Types of International Employees

Before discussing the levels of global participation, we need to distinguish between parent countries, host countries, and third countries. A **parent country** is the country in which the company's corporate headquarters are located. For example, the United States is the parent country of General Motors. A **host country** is the country in which the parent country organization seeks to locate (or has already located) a facility. Thus Great Britain is a host country for General Motors because GM has operations there. A **third country** is a country other than the host country or parent country, and a company may or may not have a facility there.

There are also different categories of employees. **Expatriate** is the term generally used for employees sent by a company in one country to manage operations in a different country. With the increasing globalization of business, it is now important to distinguish among different types of expatriates. **Parent-country nationals (PCNs)** are employees who were born and live in the parent country. **Host-country nationals (HCNs)** are those employees who were born and raised in the host, as opposed to the parent, country. Finally, **third-country nationals (TCNs)** are employees born in a country other than the parent country and host country but who work in the host country. Thus a manager born and raised in Brazil employed by an organization located in the United States and assigned to manage an operation in Thailand would be considered a TCN.

Research shows that countries differ in their use of various types of international employees. One study revealed that Japanese multinational firms have more ethnocentric HRM policies and practices (they tend to use Japanese expatriate managers more than local host-country nationals) than either European or U.S. firms. This study also found that the use of ethnocentric HRM practices is associated with more HRM problems.[32]

Parent country
The country in which a company's corporate headquarters is located.

Host country
The country in which the parent country organization seeks to locate or has already located a facility.

Third country
A country other than a host or parent country.

Expatriate
An employee sent by his or her company in one country to manage operations in a different country.

Parent-country nationals (PCNs)
Employees who were born and live in a parent country.

Host-country nationals (HCNs)
Employees who were born and raised in the host, not the parent, country.

Third-country nationals (TCNs)
Employees born in a country other than the parent or host country.

FIGURE 15.3

Levels of Global Participation

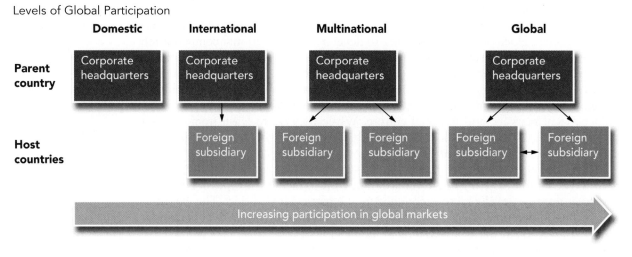

Levels of Global Participation

We often hear companies referred to as "multinational" or "international." However, it is important to understand the different levels of participation in international markets. This is especially important because as a company becomes more involved in international trade, different types of HRM problems arise. In this section we examine Nancy Adler's categorization of the various levels of international participation from which a company may choose.[33] Figure 15.3 depicts these levels of involvement.

Domestic

Most companies begin by operating within a domestic marketplace. For example, an entrepreneur may have an idea for a product that meets a need in the U.S. marketplace. This individual then obtains capital to build a facility that produces the product or service in a quantity that meets the needs of a small market niche. This requires recruiting, hiring, training, and compensating a number of individuals who will be involved in the production process, and these individuals are usually drawn from the local labor market. The focus of the selection and training programs is often on the employees' technical competence to perform job-related duties and to some extent on interpersonal skills. In addition, because the company is usually involved in only one labor market, determining the market rate of pay for various jobs is relatively easy.

As the product grows in popularity, the owner might choose to build additional facilities in different parts of the country to reduce the costs of transporting the product over large distances. In deciding where to locate these facilities, the owner must consider the attractiveness of the local labor markets. Various parts of the country may have different cultures that make those areas more or less attractive according to the work ethics of the potential employees. Similarly, the human capital in the different areas may vary greatly because of differences in educational systems. Finally, local pay rates may differ. It is for these reasons that the U.S. economy in the past 10 years has experienced a movement of jobs from northern states, which are characterized by strong unions and high labor costs, to the Sunbelt states, which have lower labor costs and are less unionized.

Incidentally, even domestic companies face problems with cultural diversity. In the United States, for example, the representation of women and minorities is increasing within the workforce. These groups come to the workplace with worldviews that differ from those of the traditional white male. Thus we are seeing more and more emphasis on developing systems for managing cultural diversity within single-country organizations, even though the diversity might be on a somewhat smaller scale than the diversity of cultures across national boundaries.[34]

It is important to note that companies functioning at the domestic level face an environment with very similar cultural, human capital, political–legal, and economic situations, although some variation might be observed across states and geographic areas.

International

As more competitors enter the domestic market, companies face the possibility of losing market share; thus they often seek other markets for their products. This usually requires entering international markets, initially by exporting products but ultimately by building production facilities in other countries. The decision to participate in international competition raises a host of human resource issues. All the problems regarding locating facilities are magnified. One must consider whether a particular location provides an environment where human resources can be successfully acquired and managed.

Now the company faces an entirely different situation with regard to culture, human capital, the political–legal system, and the economic system. For example, the availability of human capital is of utmost importance, and there is a substantially greater variability in human capital between the United States and other countries than there is among the various states in the United States.

A country's legal system may also present HRM problems. For example, France has a relatively high minimum wage, which drives labor costs up. In Germany companies are legally required to offer employees influence in the management of the firm. Companies that develop facilities in other countries have to adapt their HRM practices to conform to the host country's laws. This requires the company to gain expertise in the country's HRM legal requirements and knowledge about how to deal with the country's legal system, and it often requires the company to hire one or more HCNs. In fact, some countries legally require companies to hire a certain percentage of HCNs for any foreign-owned subsidiary.

Finally, cultures have to be considered. To the extent that the country's culture is vastly different from that of the parent organization, conflicts, communication problems, and morale problems may occur. Expatriate managers must be trained to identify these cultural differences, and they must be flexible enough to adapt their styles to those of their host country. This requires an extensive selection effort to identify individuals who are capable of adapting to new environments and an extensive training program to ensure that the culture shock is not devastating. The "Competing through Globalization" box illustrates how even small start-up companies are being pressured to become international.

Multinational

Whereas international companies build one or a few facilities in another country, they become multinational when they build facilities in a number of different countries, attempting to capitalize on lower production and distribution costs in different

locations. The lower production costs are gained by shifting production from higher-cost locations to lower-cost locations. For example, some of the major U.S. automakers have plants all over the world. They continue to shift their production from the United States, where labor unions have gained high wages for their members, to *maquiladora* facilities in Mexico, where the wages are substantially lower. Similarly, these companies minimize distribution costs by locating facilities in Europe for manufacturing and assembling automobiles to sell in the European market. They are also now expanding into some of the former Soviet bloc countries to produce automobiles for the European market.

The HRM problems multinational companies face are similar to those international companies face, only magnified. Instead of having to consider only one or two countries' cultural, human capital, legal, and economic systems, the multinational company must address these differences for a large number of countries. This accentuates the need to select managers capable of functioning in a variety of settings, give them necessary training, and provide flexible compensation systems that take into account the different market pay rates, tax systems, and costs of living.

Multinational companies now employ many "inpatriates"—managers from different countries who become part of the corporate headquarters staff. This creates a need to integrate managers from different cultures into the culture of the parent company. In addition, multinational companies now take more expatriates from countries other than the parent country and place them in facilities of other countries. For example, a manager from Scotland, working for a U.S. company, might be assigned to run an operation in South Africa. This practice accentuates the need for cross-cultural training to provide managerial skills for interaction with individuals from different cultures.

Global

Many researchers now propose a fourth level of integration: global organizations. Global organizations compete on state-of-the-art, top-quality products and services and do so with the lowest costs possible. Whereas multinational companies attempt to develop identical products distributed worldwide, global companies increasingly emphasize flexibility and mass customization of products to meet the needs of particular clients. Multinational companies are usually driven to locate facilities in a country as a means of reaching that country's market or lowering production costs, and the company must deal with the differences across the countries. Global firms, on the other hand, choose to locate a facility based on the ability to effectively, efficiently, and flexibly produce a product or service and attempt to create synergy through the cultural differences.

This creates the need for HRM systems that encourage flexible production (thus presenting a host of HRM issues). These companies proactively consider the cultures, human capital, political–legal systems, and economic systems to determine where production facilities can be located to provide a competitive advantage. Global companies have multiple headquarters spread across the globe, resulting in less hierarchically structured organizations that emphasize decentralized decision making. This results in the need for human resource systems that recruit, develop, retain, and use managers and executives who are competent transnationally.

A transnational HRM system is characterized by three attributes.[35] **Transnational scope** refers to the fact that HRM decisions must be made from a global rather than a national or regional perspective. This creates the need to make decisions that balance the need for uniformity (to ensure fair treatment of all employees) with the need for flexibility (to meet the needs of employees in different countries). **Transnational representation** reflects the multinational composition of a company's managers. Global participation does not necessarily ensure that each country is providing managers to the company's ranks. This is a prerequisite if the company is to achieve the next attribute. **Transnational process** refers to the extent to which the company's planning and decision-making processes include representatives and ideas from a variety of cultures. This attribute allows for diverse viewpoints and knowledge associated with different cultures, increasing the quality of decision making.

These three characteristics are necessary for global companies to achieve cultural synergy. Rather than simply integrating foreigners into the domestic organization, a successful transnational company needs managers who will treat managers from other cultures as equals. This synergy can be accomplished only by combining selection, training, appraisal, and compensation systems in such a way that managers have a transnational rather than a parochial orientation. However, a survey of 50 companies in the United States and Canada found that global companies' HRM systems are far less transnational in scope, representation, and process than the companies' strategic planning systems and organizational structures.[36]

In conclusion, entry into international markets creates a host of HRM issues that must be addressed if a company is to gain competitive advantage. Once the choice has been made to compete in a global arena, companies must seek to manage employees who are sent to foreign countries (expatriates and third-country nationals). This

Transnational scope
A company's ability to make HRM decisions from an international perspective.

Transnational representation
Reflects the multinational composition of a company's managers.

Transnational process
The extent to which a company's planning and decision-making processes include representatives and ideas from a variety of cultures.

causes the need to shift from focusing only on the culture, human capital, political–legal, and economic influences of the host country to examining ways to manage the expatriate managers who must be located there. Selection systems must be developed that allow the company to identify managers capable of functioning in a new culture. These managers must be trained to identify the important aspects of the new culture in which they will live as well as the relevant legal–political and economic systems. Finally, these managers must be compensated to offset the costs of uprooting themselves and their families to move to a new situation vastly different from their previous lives. In the next section we address issues regarding management of expatriates.

Managing Expatriates in Global Markets

We have outlined the major macro-level factors that influence HRM in global markets. These factors can affect a company's decision whether to build facilities in a given country. In addition, if a company does develop such facilities, these factors strongly affect the HRM practices used. However, one important issue that has been recognized over the past few years is the set of problems inherent in selecting, training, compensating, and reintegrating expatriate managers.

According to a recent study by the National Foreign Trade Council (NFTC), there were 250,000 Americans on assignments overseas and that number was expected to increase. In addition, the NFTC estimates that the average one-time cost for relocating an expatriate is $60,000.[37] The importance to the company's profitability of making the right expatriate assignments should not be underestimated. Expatriate managers' average compensation package is approximately $250,000,[38] and the cost of an unsuccessful expatriate assignment (that is, a manager returning early) is approximately $100,000.[39] It used to be believed that the failure rate for expatriate assignments among U.S. firms was between 15 and 40 percent. However, more recent research suggests that the current figure is much lower. Some recent studies of European multinationals put the rate at 5 percent for most firms. While it is generally recognized that the failure rate is higher among U.S. multinationals, it is doubtful that the number reaches the 15–40 percent range.[40]

In this final section of the chapter, we discuss the major issues relevant to the management of expatriate managers. These issues cover the selection, training, compensation, and reacculturation of expatriates.

Selection of Expatriate Managers

One of the major problems in managing expatriate managers is determining which individuals in the organization are most capable of handling an assignment in a different culture. Expatriate managers must have technical competence in the area of operations; otherwise they will be unable to earn the respect of subordinates. However, technical competence has been almost the sole variable used in deciding whom to send on overseas assignments, despite the fact that multiple skills are necessary for successful performance in these assignments.[41]

A successful expatriate manager must be sensitive to the country's cultural norms, flexible enough to adapt to those norms, and strong enough to make it through the inevitable culture shock. In addition, the manager's family must be similarly capable of adapting to the new culture. These adaptive skills have been categorized into three dimensions:[42] (1) the self dimension (the skills that enable a manager to maintain a positive self-image and psychological well-being); (2) the relationship dimension (the skills required to foster relationships with the host-country nationals); and (3) the perception dimension (those skills that enable a manager to accurately perceive and evaluate the host environment). One study of international assignees found that they considered the following five factors to be important in descending order of importance: family situation, flexibility and adaptability, job knowledge and motivation, relational skills, and extracultural openness.[43] Table 15.4 presents a series of considerations and questions to ask potential expatriate managers to assess their ability to adapt to a new cultural environment.

TABLE 15.4

Interview Worksheet for International Candidates

Motivation
- Investigate reasons and degree of interest in wanting to be considered.
- Determine desire to work abroad, verified by previous concerns such as personal travel, language training, reading, and association with foreign employees or students.
- Determine whether the candidate has a realistic understanding of what working and living abroad requires.
- Determine the basic attitudes of the spouse toward an overseas assignment.

Health
- Determine whether any medical problems of the candidate or his or her family might be critical to the success of the assignment.
- Determine whether he or she is in good physical and mental health, without any foreseeable change.

Language ability
- Determine potential for learning a new language.
- Determine any previous language(s) studied or oral ability (judge against language needed on the overseas assignment).
- Determine the ability of the spouse to meet the language requirements.

Family considerations
- How many moves has the family made in the past among different cities or parts of the United States?
- What problems were encountered?
- How recent was the last move?
- What is the spouse's goal in this move?
- What are the number of children and the ages of each?
- Has divorce or its potential, or death of a family member, weakened family solidarity?
- Will all the children move? Why or why not?
- What are the location, health, and living arrangements of grandparents and the number of trips normally made to their home each year?
- Are there any special adjustment problems that you would expect?
- How is each member of the family reacting to this possible move?
- Do special educational problems exist within the family?

Resourcefulness and initiative
- Is the candidate independent; can he make and stand by his decisions and judgments?
- Does she have the intellectual capacity to deal with several dimensions simultaneously?
- Is he able to reach objectives and produce results with whatever personnel and facilities are available, regardless of the limitations and barriers that might arise?
- Can the candidate operate without a clear definition of responsibility and authority on a foreign assignment?
- Will the candidate be able to explain the aims and company philosophy to the local managers and workers?
- Does she possess sufficient self-discipline and self-confidence to overcome difficulties or handle complex problems?

(continues)

TABLE 15.4

Interview Worksheet for International Candidates *concluded*

Resourcefulness and initiative *continued*
- Can the candidate work without supervision?
- Can the candidate operate effectively in a foreign environment without normal communications and supporting services?

Adaptability
- Is the candidate sensitive to others, open to the opinions of others, cooperative, and able to compromise?
- What are his reactions to new situations, and efforts to understand and appreciate differences?
- Is she culturally sensitive, aware, and able to relate across the culture?
- Does the candidate understand his own culturally derived values?
- How does the candidate react to criticism?
- What is her understanding of the U.S. government system?
- Will he be able to make and develop contacts with peers in the foreign country?
- Does she have patience when dealing with problems?
- Is he resilient; can he bounce back after setbacks?

Career planning
- Does the candidate consider the assignment anything other than a temporary overseas trip?
- Is the move consistent with her progression and that planned by the company?
- Is his career planning realistic?
- What is the candidate's basic attitude toward the company?
- Is there any history or indication of interpersonal problems with this employee?

Financial
- Are there any current financial and/or legal considerations that might affect the assignment, such as house purchase, children and college expenses, car purchases?
- Are financial considerations negative factors? Will undue pressures be brought to bear on the employee or her family as a result of the assignment?

SOURCE: Reprinted with permission from *Multinational People Management*, pp. 55–57, by D. M. Noer. Copyright © 1989 by the Bureau of National Affairs, Inc., Washington, DC 20037.

Little evidence suggests that U.S. companies have invested much effort in attempting to make correct expatriate selections. One researcher found that only 5 percent of the firms surveyed administered any tests to determine the degree to which expatriate candidates possessed cross-cultural skills.[44] More recent research reveals that only 35 percent of firms choose expatriates from multiple candidates and that those firms emphasize only technical job-related experience and skills in making these decisions.[45] These findings glaringly demonstrate that U.S. organizations need to improve their success rate in overseas assignments. As discussed in Chapter 6, the technology for assessing individuals' knowledge, skills, and abilities has advanced. The potential for selection testing to decrease the failure rate and productivity problems of U.S. expatriate managers seems promising. For instance, recent research has examined the "Big Five" personality dimensions as predictors of expatriate success (remember these from Chapter 6). For instance, one study distinguished between expatriate success as measured by not terminating the assignment and success as measured by supervisory evaluations of the expatriate. The researcher found that agreeableness, emotional stability, and extraversion were negatively related to the desire to terminate the assignment (i.e., they wanted to stay on the assignment longer), and conscientiousness was positively related to supervisory evaluations of the expatriate.[46]

A final issue with regard to expatriate selection is the use of women in expatriate assignments. For a long time U.S. firms believed that women would not be successful managers in countries where women have not traditionally been promoted to management positions (such as in Japan and other Asian countries). However, recent evidence indicates that this is not true. Robin Abrams, an expatriate manager for Apple Computer's Hong Kong office, states that nobody cares whether "you are wearing trousers or a skirt if you have demonstrated core competencies." In fact, some women believe that the novelty of their presence among a group of men increases their credibility with locals. In fact, some research suggests that male and female expatriates can perform equally well in international assignments, regardless of the country's cultural predispositions toward women in management. However, female expatriates self-rate their adjustment lower in countries that have few women in the workforce.[47] Also research has shown that female expatriates were perceived as being effective regardless of the cultural toughness of the host country.[48] And the fact is that female expatriates feel more strongly than their supervisors that prejudice does not limit women's ability to be successful.[49]

Training and Development of Expatriates

Once an expatriate manager has been selected, it is necessary to prepare that manager for the upcoming assignment. Because these individuals already have job-related skills, some firms have focused development efforts on cross-cultural training. A review of the cross-cultural training literature found support for the belief that cross-cultural training has an impact on effectiveness.[50] However, in spite of this, cross-cultural training is hardly universal. According to one 1995 survey, nearly 40 percent of the respondents offered no cross-cultural preparation to expatriates.[51]

What exactly is emphasized in cross-cultural training programs? The details regarding these programs were discussed in Chapter 7. However, for now, it is important to know that most attempt to create an appreciation of the host country's culture so that expatriates can behave appropriately.[52] This entails emphasizing a few aspects of cultural sensitivity. First, expatriates must be clear about their own cultural background, particularly as it is perceived by the host nationals. With an accurate cultural self-awareness, managers can modify their behavior to accentuate the effective characteristics while minimizing those that are dysfunctional.[53]

Second, expatriates must understand the particular aspects of culture in the new work environment. Although culture is an elusive, almost invisible phenomenon, astute expatriate managers must perceive the culture and adapt their behavior to it. This entails identifying the types of behaviors and interpersonal styles that are considered acceptable in both business meetings and social gatherings. For example, Germans value promptness for meetings to a much greater extent than do Latin Americans. Table 15.5 displays some ways body language conveys different messages in different countries.

Finally, expatriates must learn to communicate accurately in the new culture. Some firms attempt to use expatriates who speak the language of the host country, and a few provide language training. However, most companies simply assume that the host-country nationals all speak the parent-country's language. Although this assumption might be true, seldom do these nationals speak the parent-country language fluently. Thus expatriate managers must be trained to communicate with others when language barriers exist. Table 15.6 offers some tips for communicating across language barriers.

TABLE 15.5

International Body Language

COUNTRY	NONVERBAL MESSAGES
Argentina	If the waiter approaches pointing to the side of his head and making a spinning gesture with their finger, don't think they've lost it—they're trying to say you have a phone call.
Bangladesh	Bursting to go the toilet? Hold it. It is considered very rude to excuse yourself from the table to use the bathroom.
Bolivia	Don't make "the sign of the fig" (thumb protruding between index and middle finger), historically a sign that you couldn't care less—it is very insulting.
Bulgaria	Bulgarians nod the head up and down to mean no, not yes. To say yes, a Bulgarian nods the head back and forth.
China	In Eastern culture, silence really can be golden. So don't panic if long periods of silence form part of your meeting with Chinese clients. It simply means they are considering your proposal carefully.
Egypt	As across the Arab world the left hand is unclean, use your right to accept business cards and to greet someone. Use only your right hand for eating.
Fiji	To show respect to your Fijian hosts when addressing them, stand with your arms folded behind your back.
France	The French don't like strong handshakes, preferring a short, light grip or air kissing. If your French colleague is seen to be playing an imaginary flute, however, it means he thinks you are not being truthful.
Germany	When Germans meet across a large conference table and it is awkward to reach over and shake hands, they will instead rap their knuckles lightly on the table by way of a greeting.
Greece	Beware of making the okay sign to Greek colleagues as it signifies bodily orifices. A safer bet is the thumbs-up sign. The thumbs-down, however, is the kind of gesture reserved for when a Greek motorist cuts you off on the highway.
Hong Kong	When trying to attract someone's attention, don't use your index finger with palm extended upward. This is how the Cantonese call their dogs.
India	Beware of whistling in public—it is the height of rudeness here.
Japan	Japan is a real minefield for Western businesspeople, but one that always gets to them is the way the Japanese heartily slurp their noodles at lunch. Far from being rude, it actually shows appreciation of the food in Japanese culture.
Jordan	No matter how hungry you are, it is customary to refuse seconds from your host twice before finally accepting a third time.
Lebanon	Itchy eyebrow? Don't scratch it. Licking your little finger and brushing it across your eyebrow is provocative.
Malaysia	If you find a Malaysian standing with hands on hips before you, you've clearly said something wrong. It means he's livid.
Mexico	Mexicans are very tactile and often perform a bizarre handshake whereby, after pressing together the palms, they will slide their hands upward to grasp each other's thumbs.
Netherlands	The Dutch may seem open-minded, but if Dutch people tap the underside of their elbow, it means they think you're unreliable.
Pakistan	The overt display of a closed fist is an incitement to war.
Philippines	The "Roger Moore" is a common greeting here—a quick flash of the eyebrows supersedes the need for handshakes.
Russia	The Russians are highly tactile meet and greeters, with bear hugs and kisses direct on the lips commonplace. Don't take this habit to nearby Uzbekistan, however. They'd probably shoot you.
Saudi Arabia	If a Saudi man takes another's hand on the street, it's a sign of mutual respect.
Samoa	When your new Samoan host offers you a cup of the traditional drink, kava, make sure to deliberately spill a few drops on the ground before taking your first sip.
Turkey	Be careful not to lean back on your chair and point the sole of your foot at anyone in a meeting in Istanbul. Pointing with the underside of the foot is highly insulting.

SOURCE: http://www.businesstravelerusa.com/articles.php?articleID=490 Business Traveler Center, R. Axtell, *Gestures: The Dos and Taboos of Body Language Around the World,* John Wiley and Sons, N.Y., 1991 P. Harris and R. Moran (1991). Managing cultural differences (3rd ed.). Houston, TX: Gulf Publishing Company; R. Linowes (1993). The Japanese manager's traumatic entry into the United States: Understanding the American-Japanese cultural divide, *Academy of Management Executive,* 7 (4): 26. D. Doke, "Perfect strangers," HR Magazine, December 2004:62–68.

TABLE 15.6

Communicating across Language Barriers

Verbal behavior
- *Clear, slow speech.* Enunciate each word. Do not use colloquial expressions.
- *Repetition.* Repeat each important idea using different words to explain the same concept.
- *Simple sentences.* Avoid compound, long sentences.
- *Active verbs.* Avoid passive verbs.

Nonverbal behavior
- *Visual restatements.* Use as many visual restatements as possible, such as pictures, graphs, tables, and slides.
- *Gestures.* Use more facial and hand gestures to emphasize the meaning of words.
- *Demonstration.* Act out as many themes as possible.
- *Pauses.* Pause more frequently.
- *Summaries.* Hand out written summaries of your verbal presentation.

Attribution
- *Silence.* When there is a silence, wait. Do not jump in to fill the silence. The other person is probably just thinking more slowly in the nonnative language or translating.
- *Intelligence.* Do not equate poor grammar and mispronunciation with lack of intelligence; it is usually a sign of second-language use.
- *Differences.* If unsure, assume difference, not similarity.

Comprehension
- *Understanding.* Do not just assume that they understand; assume that they do not understand.
- *Checking comprehension.* Have colleagues repeat their understanding of the material back to you. Do not simply ask whether they understand or not. Let them explain what they understand to you.

Design
- *Breaks.* Take more frequent breaks. Second-language comprehension is exhausting.
- *Small modules.* Divide the material into smaller modules.
- *Longer time frame.* Allocate more time for each module than usual in a monolingual program.

Motivation
- *Encouragement.* Verbally and nonverbally encourage and reinforce speaking by nonnative language participants.
- *Drawing out.* Explicitly draw out marginal and passive participants.
- *Reinforcement.* Do not embarrass novice speakers.

SOURCE: From *International Dimensions of Organizational Behavior*, 2nd ed. by Nancy Adler, pp. 84–85. Copyright © 1991. Reprinted with permission of South-Western, a division of Thomson Learning: www.thomsonrights.com. Fax 800-730-2215.

Effective cross-cultural training helps ease an expatriate's transition to the new work environment. It can also help avoid costly mistakes, such as the expatriate who attempted to bring two bottles of brandy into the Muslim country of Qatar. The brandy was discovered by customs; not only was the expatriate deported, the company was also "disinvited" from the country.[54]

Compensation of Expatriates

One of the more troublesome aspects of managing expatriates is determining the compensation package. As previously discussed, these packages average $250,000, but it is necessary to examine the exact breakdown of these packages. Most use a balance

FIGURE 15.4

The Balance Sheet for Determining Expatriate Compensation

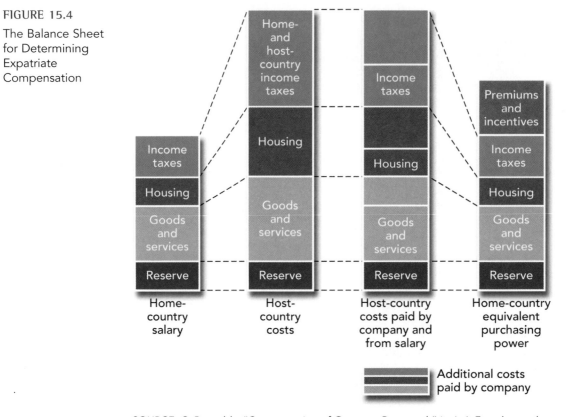

SOURCE: C. Reynolds, "Compensation of Overseas Personnel," in J. J. Famularo, ed., *Handbook of Human Resource Administration*, 2nd ed., 1986. Copyright © 1986 The McGraw-Hill Companies, Inc. Reprinted with permission.

sheet approach to determine the total package level. This approach entails developing a total compensation package that equalizes the purchasing power of the expatriate manager with that of employees in similar positions in the home country and provides incentives to offset the inconveniences incurred in the location. Purchasing power includes all of the expenses associated with the expatriate assignment. Expenses include goods and services (food, personal care, clothing, recreation, and transportation), housing (for a principal residence), income taxes (paid to federal and local governments), reserve (savings, payments for benefits, pension contributions), and shipment and storage (costs associated with moving and/or storing personal belongings). A typical balance sheet is shown in Figure 15.4.

As you can see from this figure, the employee starts with a set of costs for taxes, housing, goods and services, and reserve. However, in the host country, these costs are significantly higher. Thus the company must make up the difference between costs in the home and those in the host country, and then provide a premium and/or incentive for the employee to go through the trouble of living in a different environment. Table 15.7 provides an idea of just how much these add-ons can cost for an expatriate. As we see, these combined benefits amount to a 114 percent increase in compensation cost above the base pay.

Total pay packages have four components. First, there is the base salary. Determining the base salary is not a simple matter, however. Fluctuating exchange rates be-

Housing (purchase)	38%
Goods and services (cost of living)	24
Education	22
Position	17
Hardship	13

TABLE 15.7

Average Amount of Allowance as a Percentage of Base Pay

SOURCE: From *HR Magazine* by B. Fitzgerald-Turner. Copyright © 1997 by Society for Human Resource Management. Reproduced with permission of Society for Human Resource Management via Copyright Clearance Center.

tween countries may make an offered salary a raise some of the time, a pay cut at other times. In addition, the base salary may be based on comparable pay in the parent country, or it may be based on the prevailing market rates for the job in the host country. Expatriates are often offered a salary premium beyond that of their present salary as an inducement to accept the expatriate assignment.

Tax equalization allowances are a second component. They are necessary because of countries' different taxation systems in high-tax countries. For example, a senior executive earning $100,000 in Belgium (with a maximum marginal tax rate of 70.8 percent) could cost a company almost $1 million in taxes over five to seven years.[55] Under most tax equalization plans, the company withholds the amount of tax to be paid in the home country, then pays all of the taxes accrued in the host country.

A third component, benefits, presents additional compensation problems. Most of the problems have to do with the transportability of the benefits. For example, if an expatriate contributing to a pension plan in the United States is moved to a different country, does the individual have a new pension in the host country, or should the individual be allowed to contribute to the existing pension in her home country? What about health care systems located in the United States? How does the company ensure that expatriate employees have equal health care coverage? For example, in one company, the different health care plans available resulted in situations where it might cost significantly less to have the employee fly to the United States to have a procedure performed rather than to have it done in the host country. However, the health plans did not allow this alternative.

Finally, allowances are often offered to make the expatriate assignment less unattractive. Cost-of-living allowances are payments that offset the differences in expenditures on day-to-day necessities between the host country and the parent country. Housing allowances ensure that the expatriate can maintain the same home-country living standard. Education allowances reimburse expatriates for the expense of placing their children in private English-speaking schools. Relocation allowances cover all the expenses of making the actual move to a new country, including transportation to and from the new location, temporary living expenses, and shipping and/or storage of personal possessions. Figure 15.5 illustrates a typical summary sheet for an expatriate manager's compensation package.

Reacculturation of Expatriates

A final issue of importance to managing expatriates is dealing with the reacculturation process when the managers reenter their home country. Reentry is no simple feat. Culture shock takes place in reverse. The individual has changed, the company has changed, and the culture has changed while the expatriate was overseas. According

FIGURE 15.5

International
Assignment
Allowance Form

John H. Doe
Name

1 October 2004
Effective date

Singapore
Location of assignment

Manager, SLS./Serv. AP/ME
Title

Houston, Texas	1234	202	202
Home base	**Emp. no.**	**LCA code**	**Tax code**

Reason for Change: International Assignment

	Old	New
Monthly base salary		$5,000.00
Living cost allowance		$1,291.00
Foreign service premium		$ 750.00
Area allowance		-0-
Gross monthly salary		$7,041.00
Housing deduction		$ 500.00
Hypothetical tax		$ 570.00
Other		
Net monthly salary		$5,971.00

Prepared by   **Date**

Vice President, Human Resources   **Date**

to one source, 60 to 70 percent of expatriates did not know what their position would be upon their return, and 46 percent ended up with jobs that gave them reduced autonomy and authority.[56] Twenty percent of workers want to leave the company when they return from an overseas assignment, and this presents potentially serious morale and productivity problems.[57] In fact, the most recent estimates are that 25 percent of expatriate managers leave the company within one year of returning from their expatriate assignments.[58] If these repatriates leave, the company has virtually no way to recoup its substantial investment in human capital.[59]

Finding and Keeping the Best Employees

Companies are increasingly making efforts to help expatriates through reacculturation. Two characteristics help in this transition process: communication and validation.[60] *Communication* refers to the extent to which the expatriate receives information and recognizes changes while abroad. The closer the contact with the home organization while abroad, the more proactive, effective, and satisfied the expatriate will be upon reentry. *Validation* refers to the amount of recognition received by the expatriate upon return home. Expatriates who receive recognition from their peers and their bosses for their foreign work and their future potential contribution to the company have fewer troubles with reentry compared with those who are treated as if they were "out of the loop." Given the tremendous investment that firms make in expatriate employees, usually aimed at providing global experience that will help the company, firms certainly do not want to lose expatriates after their assignments have concluded.

Finally, one research study noted the role of an expatriate manager's expectations about the expatriate assignment in determining repatriation adjustment and job performance. This study found that managers whose job expectations (constraints and demands in terms of volume and performance standards) and nonwork expectations (living and housing conditions) were met exhibited a greater degree of repatriation adjustment and higher levels of job performance.[61] Monsanto has an extensive repatriation program that begins long before the expatriate returns. The program entails

Staffing and Selection
• Communicate the value of international assignments for the company's global mission.
• Ensure that those with the highest potential move internationally.
• Provide short-term assignments to increase the pool of employees with international experience.
• Recruit employees who have lived or who were educated abroad.
Training and Career Development
• Make international assignment planning a part of the career development process.
• Encourage early international experience.
• Create learning opportunities during the assignment.
• Use international assignments as a leadership development tool.
Performance Appraisal and Compensation
• Differentiate performance management based on expatriate roles.
• Align incentives with expatriation objectives.
• Tailor benefits to the expatriate's needs.
• Focus on equality of opportunities, not cash.
• Emphasize rewarding careers rather than short-term outcomes.
Expatriation and Repatriation Activities
• Involve the family in the orientation program at the beginning and the end of the assignment.
• Establish mentor relationships between expatriates and executives from the home location.
• Provide support for dual careers.
• Secure opportunities for the returning manager to use knowledge and skills learned while on the international assignment.

TABLE 15.8

Human Resource Practices That Support Effective Expatriation

SOURCE: P. Evans, V. Pucik, and J. Barsoux, *The Global Challenge: Framework for International Human Resource Management*, 2002. Copyright © 2002 The McGraw-Hill Companies, Inc. Reprinted with permission.

providing extensive information regarding the potential culture shock of repatriation and information on how family members, friends, and the office environment might have changed. Then, a few months after returning, expatriate managers hold "debriefing" sessions with several colleagues to help work through difficulties. Monsanto believes that this program provides them with a source of competitive advantage in international assignments.[62]

In sum, there are a variety of HR practices that can support effective expatriation. In general, the selection system must rigorously assess potential expatriates' skills and personalities and even focus on the candidate's spouse. Training should be conducted prior to and during the expatriate assignment, and the assignment itself should be viewed as a career development experience. Effective reward systems must go beyond salary and benefits, and while keeping the employee "whole" and even offering a monetary premium, should also provide access to career development and learning opportunities. Finally, serious efforts should be made to manage the repatriation process.[63] A summary of the key points is provided in Table 15.8 on page 655.

A Look Back

At the beginning of this chapter we examined the challenge that companies, in particular IBM, face as they seek to build global capability at low cost. Such efforts have potentially negative effects on their existing domestic workforce. How do they deal with these challenges?

IBM is increasing employment for the first time in three years, expecting to boost worldwide headcount by 15,000 to 330,000. Over 2,000 of that net increase will occur in the United States. In addition, IBM recently adopted a new internal-transfer policy which would enable employees who would otherwise be laid off to fill more open positions within IBM. IBM Vice President of Learning Ted Hoff states that this policy will result in fewer offshored jobs, and a person familiar with IBM suggests that IBM may lay off only 2,000 U.S. workers in 2004, down from the previous estimate of 3,000.

Some transfers may mean working for lower pay. The policy allows employees to transfer to "comparable jobs" but "comparable" is defined within IBM as up to a 10 percent pay cut and a shift or schedule change. IBM also says it will pay for retraining, allocating $25 million over the next two years, and give employees threatened by offshoring more time (60 days warning, as opposed to the previous 30 days) to find an in-house job.

Such a move will not only help alleviate insecurity among existing workers, but actually will help the bottom line. Stephanie Moore, an analyst at Forrester Research, suggests that IBM is not alone in this effort as companies increasingly discover some of the problems with offshoring. "Some people say they don't believe it, but the fact is it's less expensive to repurpose the people than it is to fire them and hire different ones."

Questions
1. How does the issue of offshoring impact existing workforces? What can firms do to alleviate concerns or address potentially negative consequences?
2. Is offshoring the same thing as "global sourcing of talent"? While the strategy hurts U.S. workers, can and should a global company be patriotic in making its talent sourcing decisions?

3. What are some of the ethical concerns with regard to offshoring? Consider this question both from the standpoint of the parent country (e.g., the United States) and from that of the host country (e.g., India).

Summary

Today's organizations are more involved in international commerce than ever before, and the trend will continue. Recent historic events such as the development of the EEC, NAFTA, the growth of Asia, and GATT have accelerated the movement toward a global market. Companies competing in the global marketplace require top-quality people to compete successfully. This requires that managers be aware of the many factors that significantly affect HRM in a global environment, such as culture, human capital, and the political–legal and economic systems, and that they understand how these factors come into play in the various levels of global participation. Finally, it requires that they be adept at developing HRM systems that maximize the effectiveness of all human resources, particularly with regard to expatriate managers. Managers cannot overestimate the importance of effectively managing human resources to gain competitive advantage in today's global marketplace.

Discussion Questions

1. What current trends and/or events (besides those mentioned at the outset of the chapter) are responsible for the increased internationalization of the marketplace?
2. According to Hofstede (in Table 15.2), the United States is low on power distance, high on individuality, high on masculinity, low on uncertainty avoidance, and low on long-term orientation. Russia, on the other hand, is high on power distance, moderate on individuality, low on masculinity, high on uncertainty avoidance, and low on long-term orientation. Many U.S. managers are transplanting their own HRM practices into Russia while companies seek to develop operations there. How acceptable and effective do you think the following practices will be and why? (a) Extensive assessments of individual abilities for selection? (b) Individually based appraisal systems? (c) Suggestion systems? (d) Self-managing work teams?
3. The chapter notes that political–legal and economic systems can reflect a country's culture. The former Eastern bloc countries seem to be changing their political–legal and economic systems. Is this change brought on by their cultures, or will culture have an impact on the ability to change these systems? Why?
4. Think of the different levels of global participation. What companies that you are familiar with exhibit the different levels of participation?
5. Think of a time when you had to function in another culture (on a vacation or job). What were the major obstacles you faced, and how did you deal with them? Was this a stressful experience? Why? How can companies help expatriate employees deal with stress?
6. What types of skills do you need to be able to manage in today's global marketplace? Where do you expect to get those skills? What classes and/or experiences will you need?

Self-Assessment Exercise

The following list includes a number of qualities that have been identified as being associated with success in an expatriate assignment. Rate the degree to which you possess each quality, using the following scale:

1 = very low
2 = low
3 = moderate
4 = high
5 = very high

____ Resourcefulness/resilience
____ Adaptability/flexibility
____ Emotional stability
____ Ability to deal with ambiguity/uncertainty/differences
____ Desire to work with people who are different
____ Cultural empathy/sensitivity
____ Tolerance of others' views, especially when they differ from your own
____ Sensitivity to feelings and attitudes of others
____ Good health and wellness

Add up your total score for the items. The higher your score, the greater your likelihood of success. Qualities that you rated low would be considered weaknesses for an expatriate assignment. Keep in mind that you will also need to be technically competent for the assignment, and your spouse and family (if applicable) must be adaptable and willing to live abroad.

SOURCE: Based on "Rating Scale on Successful Expatriate Qualities," from P. R. Harris and R. T. Moran, *Managing Cultural Differences*, 3rd ed. (Houston: Gulf, 1991), p. 569.

Manager's Hot Seat Exercise: Cultural Differences: Let's Break a Deal

This Manager's Hot Seat case explores the impact that varying cultures can have on whether successful completion of business between differing countries is achieved or not. As the video begins, a new American representative has been appointed by the company to close a large deal with a Japanese buyer. The Japanese buyer would like to proceed slowly with the contract process while the American wants a fast closure. Ultimately, the deal is lost due to the lack of understanding of how foreign cultures prefer to conduct business.

The case stresses how important it is for managers to understand and adapt to foreign customers' preferences. In this instance, the American way of quick decisions and fast closure proved unacceptable to the Japanese customer. Japanese culture prefers a much slower progression through the stages of closing a deal. Gaining knowledge and understanding of different cultures is essential for achieving business success when conducting operations in today's global marketplace.

Individual Activity

Conduct library research focusing on how foreign cultures prefer to conduct business deals. Be specific about the selected entity's mannerisms and accepted behaviors. Suggested countries to explore are: Japan, China, India, and Saudi Arabia—feel free to select another nation of your choice. Prepare a two-page report on your findings. Bear in mind that this information will be discussed with your class partner.

Group Activity

Divide into groups of three. Discuss the findings from the research each group member has performed. Discuss how these cultural differences vary from the United States. Discuss how these variations may impact upon a business deal between the foreign country and the United States. Identify methods companies can engage in to prevent cultural mistakes during business dealings with foreign cultures. Discuss how cultural differences can affect future globalization. Discuss why cultural awareness is essential to the successful future of business operations.

Exercising Strategy: Terrorism and Global Human Resource Management

Globalization has continued to increase as companies expand their operations in a number of countries, employing an increasingly global workforce. Although this process has resulted in a number of positive outcomes, it has also occasionally presented new types of problems for firms to face.

On September 11, 2001, terrorists with Middle Eastern roots (alleged to be part of Osama bin Laden's al-Qaida network) hijacked four U.S. planes, crashing two of them into the World Trade Center's twin towers and one into the Pentagon (a fourth was crashed in Pennsylvania in a scuffle with passengers). President Bush and U.K. Prime Minister Tony Blair, after their demands that the Taliban government in Afghanistan turn over bin Laden and his leaders were ignored, began military action against that country on October 7, 2001. At the writing of this chapter, we do not know what the ultimate result of this action will be, but we do know that both the terrorist acts and

the subsequent war on terrorism have created a host of issues for multinational companies.

First, companies doing business overseas, particularly in Muslim-dominated countries such as the Arab states and Indonesia, must manage their expatriate workforce (particularly U.S. and British citizens) in what has the potential to become hostile territory. These employees fear for their security, and some have asked to return to their home countries.

Second, companies with global workforces must manage across what have become increasingly nationalistic boundaries. Those of us in the United States may view the terrorist attacks as an act of war and our response as being entirely justified. However, those in the Arab world, while not justifying the terrorist attacks, may similarly feel that the military response toward Afghanistan (and later Iraq) is hostile aggression. One executive at a global oil company noted the difficulty in managing a workforce that is approximately 25 percent Arab. He stated that many of the Arab executives have said, "While we know that you are concerned about the events of September 11, you should know that we are equally concerned about the events of October 7 and since."

Questions

1. How can a global company manage the inevitable conflicts that will arise among individuals from different religious, racial, ethnic, and national groups who must work together within firms? How can these conflicts be overcome to create a productive work environment?

2. What will firms have to do differently in managing expatriates, particularly U.S. or British citizens who are asked to take assignments in predominantly Muslim countries?

Managing People: From the Pages of *BusinessWeek*

BusinessWeek   Poland and the EU

Early on the morning of May 1, Polish Prime Minister Leszek Miller will hoist the European Union's blue flag with gold stars above the arched doorway leading to his vast 19th century office building. Fifteen years after casting off communism and embarking on a process of wrenching economic change, Poland is finally joining the EU—the ultimate confirmation that it is now a mature, liberal democracy with a dynamic free-market economy. "This is a turning point in our history," says Miller, a former communist. "At last we are rejoining the West."

Poland is by far the largest of the 10 primarily Central and Eastern European countries that will become members of the common market on May 1. With a population of 38.6 million and a gross domestic product of $230 billion, it accounts for over half of the newcomers' population and 41% of their total GDP. To many Western politicians and executives, bringing Poland into the fold is what EU expansion is all about. "Enlargement without the Poles would be unthinkable," says German Chancellor Gerhard Schröder.

What happens in Poland will determine whether history will judge enlargement a success or a failure. By dint of its size and the forcefulness with which it has so far defended its interests in Brussels, Poland has something of a leadership role in Central and Eastern Europe. If the country learns to play a constructive part in decision making and continues growing fast economically, it could help reenergize the EU, which has lost much of its vitality in recent years. Poland's GDP growth, almost 6% this year, is decidedly brisker than anything the old EU has to offer. Reflecting that success, the Warsaw stock index has soared more than 70% in the past year.

But there are two Polands vying with each other today, and which one prevails will determine the success of Poland's EU experiment. One is the Poland of scrappy entrepreneurs, hardworking, well-educated factory hands, and eager foreign investors who have poured around $70 billion into the country in the past 14 years. This is the Poland that could give Europe a shot in the arm and shake up things in Brussels—by forcing the EU to meet sharper competition from the new members. The other Poland is a quasi-

dysfunctional political system grafted onto a communist-era welfare state and form-happy bureaucracy. This is the Poland that makes applicants wait up to 230 days to set up a business. The Poland with the biggest budget deficit, as a share of GDP, in Europe (it could hit 7.5% this year). The Poland that cannot even build a decent road from Warsaw to Gdansk. "It's hard to imagine anything worse than the Polish bureaucracy," says Piotr Bielski, an economist at Bank Zachodni WBK in Warsaw. The idea of this overbearing system merging with the faceless bureaucracy in Brussels makes many informed Poles worry whether they can keep up their record of growth and transformation. "The EU offers a chance for us, but it gives no guarantees," says former Finance Minister Leszek Balcerowicz, who now heads the National Bank of Poland.

There are precedents for a happy entry into the EU from which Poland is trying to learn. Spain boomed after joining in 1986 because successive governments spent the funds they received from the EU shrewdly, restructured state finances successfully, and continued to liberalize and deregulate the economy. The results were rapid growth, rising living standards, and, after a period of painful restructuring, lower unemployment. Spain's per capita GDP is now about $22,500, almost 90% of the EU average. Polish GDP per capita, in contrast, is less than $6,000. "If we could do what the Spanish did, I'd be very happy," says Janusz Onyszkiewicz, senior fellow at the Center for International Relations in Warsaw and a former Defense Minister. But Poland could just as easily go the way of Greece, which wasted billions in EU subsidies on propping up state-owned companies.

The Poles know the economic challenges. But they see EU membership as a way to reclaim their historic place at the heart of Europe. Although Poland ceased to exist as a country for more than 120 years after being divided up among Russia, Prussia, and Austria in 1795, it has traditionally been a powerful, creative force in the Old World. Poles still proudly recite their countrymen's historic and scientific achievements. Europeans thought the earth was the center of the universe before the great 16th century astronomer, Nicolaus Copernicus, a Pole from

Torun, proved otherwise. When Western civilization was threatened by Turkish and Tatar invaders in the late 1600s, Polish King Jan III Sobieski came to its rescue with an army that destroyed the Ottoman forces at the Battle of Vienna in 1683. The first woman to win a Nobel prize was Poland's Maria Sklodowska Curie, who discovered radium in 1898. "Poland is returning to the mainstream of Western Europe by joining the EU," says George Swirski, a director for Central Europe at Advent International Corp., the global private equity firm that has recently moved into the Polish market. "That's something that resonates in the Polish soul."

Shock Therapy It was the chance to rejoin the West that made the struggle against communism—and the painful sacrifices required to restructure the economy after its collapse—worthwhile. "Our standard of living fell, and unemployment rose," says Marlena Malecka, a Warsaw secretary who has been unemployed twice—once for 10 months and once for 6—since Balcerowicz launched a shock-therapy economic transformation program in 1990. "But we put up with it because we knew it was needed to bring us back to the West, where we belong."

Optimists hope Poland will become an economic and political powerhouse in the expanded EU, which will have 25 members as of May 1. Poland outperforms old-line Europe on many economic measures beyond its brisk growth rate. Its average labor costs, at $5.35 per hour, are less than a sixth of Germany's, giving it a huge edge in attracting manufacturing jobs. Productivity is expected to rise more than 3.7% this year, over twice the existing EU average. Jacob de Tusch-Lec of Merrill Lynch & Co. in London thinks taking in Poland and its fast-growing neighbors could radically change Western Europe. "So far, the focus has been on how the West will transform [the newcomers]," he says. "But maybe this is to miss the point."

Poland is likely to shake up EU politics, too. Some executives predict the Poles will bring fresh thinking and new ideas to Brussels that will liven up the staid European bureaucracy and shift the EU's center of gravity away from the Paris–Berlin axis. Although its government has yet to tackle its own budget problems, Poland, along with the other Central and Eastern European newcomers, is expected to support British-style, liberal economic policies at the EU level. "The European Commission will be confronted with a new way of thinking," says Michael Rogowski, president of the Federation of German Industry. And growing competition from low-cost but increasingly productive Polish manufacturers will ratchet up pressure on companies in the existing EU to restructure and cut costs. Polish companies were given an extra boost in January, when the government cut the corporation tax from 27% to 19%. "A new wind is blowing that will lead to more competition in Europe," Rogowski says.

Accommodating Poland in the EU club, though, won't be easy. Forty years of communism have generated a different set of policy priorities and a different mind-set. That's a key reason why the country is ardently pro-American, something that disturbs France and Germany. It is also prepared to fight hard to defend its interests. Last fall it refused to back the proposed European Constitution because it would have cut Poland's voting power in the EU Council, the most important decision-making authority in the EU. That, too, irked France and Germany, which have dominated policymaking. The big worry is that the enlargement experiment could end up a mess, characterized by slower, more rancorous decision making in Brussels and resentment and distrust between the existing and new members.

Just as Poland is joining the EU, its own political situation is in disarray. Miller is scheduled to resign on May 2, the day after Poland's accession, in a belated response to the March 27 decision by 21 members of Parliament to leave his Democratic Left Alliance and form a new party. For months analysts had been expecting the unpopular Miller, who has presided over rapidly rising unemployment and a widening budget deficit, to go. His Democratic Left Alliance, which rules in coalition with the Labor Union, has been weakened by allegations of corruption, accusations that it is mishandling the economy, and squabbles with its coalition partner and dissident party members. But Miller's departure will add to the political uncertainty. "Poland needs a stable government that will reform public finances, slash red tape, and make sure the transfers from Brussels are used to maximum benefit," says Richard Mbewe, chief economist at Warszawska Grupa Inwestycyjna, a foreign exchange trading company in Warsaw. "But I am not convinced it will get one." That could well prove to be one of Poland's biggest problems, since any new government that is formed will struggle to push through radical cuts in state spending and foster sustainable growth. One rising party, Samoobrona, even wants to reverse parts of the reform process and reexamine the sale of state companies to entrepreneurs and foreigners.

In the end, the results of enlargement will be measured primarily in economic terms. On one level, the Poles have done a remarkable job getting ready for entry to the EU. After slowing to a virtual standstill in 2001–02, the economy is growing faster than most pundits predicted, driven by the weak zloty and rapid rises in productivity. Exports have soared to new records as the value of the currency has fallen against the euro. Industrial production was up 18% year-to-year in February on the back of strong demand from abroad. At the same time, the structure of Polish exports has changed for the better. Coal, sulfur, and coke now account for just 4.5% of all exports, compared with about 18% in 1990. Machinery, cars, ships, and home appliance exports have grown strongly. The number of Polish-made Fiat, Opel, and Volkswagen cars sold in the

EU was 69% higher in January and February this year than in the same period of 2003. Some 57% of exports are produced by foreign-owned companies, which shows how investment from abroad is stimulating the economy.

Eager Beavers Many companies have dramatically boosted productivity in recent years. Five years ago, Polish workers produced just 40% as much as their EU counterparts. Now the figure is close to 50%. Makers of household appliances, furniture, auto supplies, and steel have improved international competitiveness. Take PKN Orlen, the country's largest energy company. Once a byword for inefficiency, it has been transformed by CEO Zbigniew Wrobel, who has streamlined the management structure, cut costs, and given employees individual performance targets. In 2002, PKN Orlen bought 495 gas stations in Germany and is now acquiring petrochemical company Czech Unipetrol.

Meanwhile, Poles are proving eager entrepreneurs. More than 1.5 million small and midsize companies have been formed since the collapse of communism. "Drive across the border into Poland, and the number of billboards advertising the products of small companies is really astonishing," says Dariusz Kociolek, CEO of Bolix, a thriving construction products company based in Zywiec, a town in the south of the country. "Give Polish entrepreneurs a chance, and they'll do O.K." Among the success stories are Air Polonia and Kross Bicycles. Founded in 1990, Kross is now the No. 2 bikemaker in Europe. Delphia Yachts exports more than 90% of its motorboats to the EU. Last year info-tech company ComArch boosted sales of software and systems 30%, to $65 million.

Joining the EU should give Poland's self-starters a big long-term boost. To be sure, the Polish economy is already fully integrated into the EU's, and it has been wide open to foreign competition in most sectors for years. But the few remaining tariff barriers—mostly in agriculture—will be swept away on May 1, giving Polish farmers unfettered access to the EU's single market. That could triple food exports, to $12 billion, over the next three years. At the same time, customs formalities will be abolished, making it far easier to transport goods to the existing EU. "It can take 10 hours and more to get across the German border, given all the queuing and paperwork," says trucker Dariusz Wojtyna, who regularly drives on the Katowice–Frankfurt route. "Now I'll just have to show my identity card—so I should be through in a few minutes." Free access to the single market could boost trade up to 4% a year, say economists.

Poland also will be entitled to a range of cash handouts from Brussels after May 1. According to the European Commission, the country will get between $14 billion and $16 billion by 2006 in farm subsidies, grants to encourage industrial restructuring, and other payouts. Analysts predict that transfers from Brussels could add as much as 1%

a year to GDP growth rates for the foreseeable future. Education will be one of the biggest beneficiaries of the structural funds. That's important because increased spending on education contributed to Spain's and Ireland's success in the EU.

On top of that, foreign investors are expected to pump more money into Poland once it finally joins the EU. In the past 10 years, Poland has attracted more foreign direct investment (FDI) than any other country in the region. But on a per capita basis, it is near the bottom of the league, with just $1,277 per inhabitant over the decade to 2002, compared with $1,888 in Hungary and $3,494 in the Czech Republic. And the country is increasingly vulnerable to competition from other countries, including China. It attracted $10.6 billion of FDI in 2000 but just $6.4 billion last year. British carmaker MG Rover, which is negotiating to buy the Daewoo-FSO auto plant just outside Warsaw, says it will go to China instead if it doesn't get the deal it wants.

This year should be better for foreign investment. Whirlpool Corp. has decided to invest $120 million in a new factory to make kitchen ranges in Wroclaw, an industrial city in the southwest. Italian white-goods producer Merloni Elettrodomestici and Spanish appliance maker Fagor also recently decided to invest in Poland. Government officials say FDI could reach $12 billion this year. Private equity houses, such as Advent International, which recently paid $40 million for Bolix, are looking for deals.

Foreign investors, though, increasingly balk at Poland's bureaucratic hassles. Companies must file tax returns every month, and decision making can be excruciatingly slow. Drawn-out negotiations with the government over the sale of steelmaker Polskie Huty to Anglo-Indian steel giant LNM Group may have been a key reason Poland lost a project with Korea's Hyundai Motor Co. in March. Poland hasn't won any of the three largest investments by carmakers in the East in the past three years. Hyundai and PSA Peugeot Citroën opted for Slovakia because of its low taxes and better infrastructure, and Toyota went for the Czech Republic. Foreign investors hope this will be a wake-up call. "This country has so much to offer, it was really criminal that they lost the car plants," says Mark Bardsley, CEO of Provident Polska, a subsidiary of British consumer credit company Provident.

Poland will rue the day it lost those plants. It needs all the jobs it can get. Despite rapid growth in the past two years, 20% of the workforce is unemployed because large companies keep laying off workers to improve competitiveness. That does wonders for productivity but boosts jobless rolls. Poland hopes new businesses will soak up the workers soon. But in the meantime, the Treasury is paying out billions a year in jobless and disability benefits.

Yet for every discouraging episode, there's another moment that gives Poland hope. Gillette Co. just decided to concentrate all its European manufacturing and distribution in Lodz: The low costs, high efficiencies, and great labor force were just too attractive to pass up. As it rejoins Europe, Poland has a fighting chance.

SOURCE: D. Fairlamb, "Poland and the EU," *BusinessWeek* (May 10, 2004), pp. 54–56.

Questions

1. How will Poland's economic expansion impact some of the traditional and advanced (e.g., Germany, France) European economies?

2. How have Poland's cultural, economic, human capital, and political–legal environments made it an attractive place for investment?

3. What do you think will be the major HR issues that a company like Gillette must deal with as they make major investments in the country?

Please see the video case at the end of the book that corresponds to this chapter: Jobs on the Move.

Notes

1. R. M. Kanter, "Transcending Business Boundaries: 12,000 World Managers View Change," *Harvard Business Review,* May–June 1991, pp. 151–64.

2. R. Norton, "Will a Global Slump Hurt the U.S.?" *Fortune* (February 22, 1993), pp. 63–64.

3. U.S. Department of Labor, "International Comparisons of Hourly Compensation Costs for Production Workers in Manufacturing, 1975–1999," Bureau of Labor Statistics news release, www.aoi.gov.

4. D. Kirkpatrick, "The Net Makes It All Easier—Including Exporting U.S. Jobs," *Fortune,* http://www.fortune.com/fortune/print/0,15935,450755,00.html (May 2003).

5. Towers Perrin, *Priorities for Competitive Advantage: A Worldwide Human Resource Study* (Valhalla, NY: Towers Perrin, 1991).

6. R. Schuler, "An Integrative Framework of Strategic International Human Resource Management," *Journal of Management* (1993), pp. 419–60.

7. L. Rubio, "The Rationale for NAFTA: Mexico's New 'Outward Looking' Strategy," *Business Economics* (1991), pp. 12–16.

8. H. Cooper, "Economic Impact of NAFTA: It's a Wash, Experts Say," *The Wall Street Journal,* interactive edition (June 17, 1997).

9. J. Mark, "Suzhou Factories Are Nearly Ready," *Asian Wall Street Journal* (August 14, 1995), p. 8.

10. R. Peiper, *Human Resource Management: An International Comparison* (Berlin: Walter de Gruyter, 1990).

11. V. Sathe, *Culture and Related Corporate Realities* (Homewood, IL: Richard D. Irwin, 1985).

12. M. Rokeach, *Beliefs, Attitudes, and Values* (San Francisco: Jossey-Bass, 1968).

13. L. Harrison, *Who Prospers? How Cultural Values Shape Economic and Political Success* (New York: Free Press, 1992).

14. N. Adler, *International Dimensions of Organizational Behavior,* 2nd ed. (Boston: PWS-Kent, 1991).

15. R. Yates, "Japanese Managers Say They're Adopting Some U.S. Ways," *Chicago Tribune* (February 29, 1992), p. B1.

16. G. Hofstede, "Dimensions of National Cultures in Fifty Countries and Three Regions," in *Expectations in Cross-Cultural Psychology,* eds. J. Deregowski, S. Dziurawiec, and R. C. Annis (Lisse, Netherlands: Swets and Zeitlinger, 1983).

17. G. Hofstede, "Cultural Constraints in Management Theories," *Academy of Management Executive* 7 (1993), pp. 81–90.

18. G. Hofstede, "The Cultural Relativity of Organizational Theories," *Journal of International Business Studies* 14 (1983), pp. 75–90.

19. G. Hofstede, "Cultural Constraints in Management Theories."

20. B. Gerhart and M. Fang, "National Culture and Human Resource Management: Assumptions and Evidence," *International Journal of Human Resource Management* (forthcoming).

21. S. Snell and J. Dean, "Integrated Manufacturing and Human Resource Management: A Human Capital Perspective," *Academy of Management Journal* 35 (1992), pp. 467–504.

22. W. Johnston and A. Packer, *Workforce 2000: Work and Workers for the Twenty-first Century* (Indianapolis, IN: Hudson Institute, 1988).

23. H. Meyer, "Human Resource Management in the German Democratic Republic: Problems of Availability and the Use of Manpower Potential in the Sphere of the High-Qualification Spectrum in a Retrospective View," in *Human Resource Management: An International Comparison,* ed. R. Peiper (Berlin: Walter de Gruyter, 1990).

24. P. Conrad and R. Peiper, "Human Resource Management in the Federal Republic of Germany," in ibid.

25. N. Adler and S. Bartholomew, "Managing Globally Competent People," *The Executive* 6 (1992), pp. 52–65.

26. B. O'Reilly, "Your New Global Workforce," *Fortune* (December 14, 1992), pp. 52–66.

27. A. Hoffman, "Are Technology Jobs Headed Offshore?" *Monster.com,* http://technology.monster.com/articles/offshore.

28. J. Ledvinka and V. Scardello, *Federal Employment Regulation in Human Resource Management* (Boston: PWS-Kent, 1991).

29. Conrad and Peiper, "Human Resource Management in the Federal Republic of Germany."

30. R. Solow, "Growth with Equity through Investment in Human Capital," The George Seltzer Distinguished Lecture, University of Minnesota.

31. M. Bloom, G. Milkovich, and A. Mitra, "Toward a Model of International Compensation and Rewards: Learning from How Managers Respond to Variations in Local Host Contexts," working paper 00-14 (Center for Advance Human Resource Studies, Cornell University: 2000).

32. R. Kopp, "International Human Resource Policies and Practices in Japanese, European, and United States Multinationals," *Human Resource Management* 33 (1994), pp. 581–99.

33. Adler, *International Dimensions of Organizational Behavior.*

34. S. Jackson and Associates, *Diversity in the Workplace: Human Resource Initiatives* (New York: The Guilford Press, 1991).

35. Adler and Bartholomew, "Managing Globally Competent People."

36. Ibid.

37. S. Dolianski, "Are Expats Getting Lost in the Translation?" *Workforce,* February 1997.

38. L. Copeland and L. Griggs, *Going International* (New York: Random House, 1985).

39. K. F. Misa and J. M. Fabriacatore, "Return on Investments of Overseas Personnel," *Financial Executive* 47 (April 1979), pp. 42–46.

40. N. Forster, "The Persistent Myth of High Expatriate Failure Rates: A Reappraisal," *International Journal of Human Resource Management* 8 (4) (1997), pp. 414–34.

41. M. Mendenhall, E. Dunbar, and G. R. Oddou, "Expatriate Selection, Training, and Career-Pathing: A Review and Critique," *Human Resource Management* 26 (1987), pp. 331–45.

42. M. Mendenhall and G. Oddou, "The Dimensions of Expatriate Acculturation," *Academy of Management Review* 10 (1985), pp. 39–47.

43. W. Arthur and W. Bennett, "The International Assignee: The Relative Importance of Factors Perceived to Contribute to Success," *Personnel Psychology* 48 (1995), pp. 99–114.

44. R. Tung, "Selecting and Training of Personnel for Overseas Assignments," *Columbia Journal of World Business* 16, no. 2 (1981), pp. 68–78.

45. Moran, Stahl, and Boyer, Inc., *International Human Resource Management* (Boulder, CO: Moran, Stahl, & Boyer, 1987).

46. P. Caligiuri, "The Big Five Personality Characteristics as Predictors of Expatriates' Desire to Terminate the Assignment and Supervisor Rated Performance," *Personnel Psychology* 53 (2000), pp. 67–88.

47. P. Caligiuri and R. Tung, "Comparing the Success of Male and Female Expatriates from a U.S.-based Multinational Company," *International Journal of Human Resource Management* 10(5) (1999), pp. 763–82.

48. L. Stroh, A. Varma, and S. Valy-Durbin, "Why Are Women Left at Home? Are They Unwilling to Go on International Assignments?" *Journal of World Business* 35(3) (2000), pp. 241–55.

49. A. Harzing, *Managing the Multinationals: An International Study of Control Mechanisms* (Cheltenham: Edward Elgar, 1999).

50. J. S. Black and M. Mendenhall, "Cross-Cultural Training Effectiveness: A Review and Theoretical Framework for Future Research," *Academy of Management Review* 15 (1990), pp. 113–36.

51. B. Fitzgerald-Turner, "Myths of Expatriate Life," *HRMagazine* 42, no. 6 (June 1997), pp. 65–74.

52. P. Dowling and R. Schuler, *International Dimensions of Human Resource Management* (Boston: PWS-Kent, 1990).

53. Adler, *International Dimensions of Organizational Behavior.*

54. Dowling and Schuler, *International Dimensions of Human Resource Management.*

55. R. Schuler and P. Dowling, *Survey of ASPA/I Members* (New York: Stern School of Business, New York University, 1988).

56. C. Solomon, "Repatriation: Up, Down, or Out?" *Personnel Journal* (1995), pp. 28–37.

57. "Workers Sent Overseas Have Adjustment Problems, a New Study Shows," *The Wall Street Journal* (June 19, 1984), p. 1.

58. J. S. Black, "Repatriation: A Comparison of Japanese and American Practices and Results," *Proceedings of the Eastern Academy of Management Bi-annual International Conference* (Hong Kong, 1989), pp. 45–49.

59. J. S. Black, "Coming Home: The Relationship of Expatriate Expectations with Repatriation Adjustment and Job Performance," *Human Relations* 45 (1992), pp. 177–92.

60. Adler, *International Dimensions of Organizational Behavior.*

61. Black, "Coming Home."

62. C. Solomon, "Repatriation: Up, Down, or Out?"

63. P. Evans, V. Pucik, and J. Barsoux, *The Global Challenge: International Human Resource Management* (New York: McGraw-Hill, 2002), p. 137.

16

Chapter

Strategically Managing the HRM Function

Objectives After reading this chapter, you should be able to:

1. Describe the roles that HRM plays in firms today and the categories of HRM activities.

2. Discuss how the HRM function can define its mission and market.

3. Explain the approaches to evaluating the effectiveness of HRM practices.

4. Describe the new structures for the HRM function.

5. Relate how process reengineering is used to review and redesign HRM practices.

6. Discuss the types of new technologies that can improve the efficiency and effectiveness of HRM.

7. Describe how outsourcing HRM activities can improve service delivery efficiency and effectiveness.

Enter the World of Business

Market-Driven HR at SYSCO

Hamburgers don't just deliver themselves, and SYSCO Corporation has made a surprisingly successful living by capitalizing on this fact. Founded in 1970 by John Baugh and eight other entrepreneurs, SYSCO has become North America's leading food service provider with approximately 400,000 customers, over $26 billion in sales, and a consistent #1 ranking within the industry on *Fortune*'s Most Admired list. SYSCO's customers range from Mom and Pop diners to large chains like Hilton Hotels and Wendy's International.

SYSCO's success has been driven by several factors. First, their operating principle of "Earned Autonomy" aims at building an entrepreneurial culture within each of their over 150 businesses. This principle means that as long as a business maintains successful performance, corporate headquarters will virtually let them run things however they see fit (within legal and ethical guidelines). They also encourage an entrepreneurial culture that keeps its operating companies close to the customers. They try to keep each business under 700 employees, so if a business becomes too large, they split it into two separate businesses. This results in SYSCO having a decentralized structure with small entrepreneurial business units serving local customers, providing both a sense of ownership for business presidents, and an opportunity for each unit to innovate with few corporate mandates.

Second, their army of marketing associates (MAs) differentiates them from competitors. These MAs are far more than salespersons. While they do take orders from customers, more importantly they act as consultants to help their customers succeed. They offer training in food handling techniques and inventory techniques, and they provide recipes and menu advice. These MAs provide the leading customer service within the industry, which clearly helps to fuel SYSCO's success.

Another component of its success is the company's SYSCO Brand product line. About 45,500 products are manufactured for SYSCO according to specifications that are developed and enforced by 180 Quality Assurance professionals.

Running an HR organization in a decentralized, entrepreneurial company presents a whole host of challenges, as Ken Carrig learned when he took over as corporate VP of HR in 1998. Ken wanted SYSCO's HR to provide services to employees and the leaders of the business units to help them improve their performance. But he felt corporate management couldn't force them on the local subsidiaries whose managers had been free to run their operations autonomously. Given that this autonomy of the business units had been a driver of SYSCO's success, HR had to find an alternative way to get things done.

Ken developed what he refers to as market-based HR. Under this HR operating model, each business unit uses only the corporate HR resources it is willing to actually pay for. So, if a business wants to conduct a climate survey, they can use the SYSCO corporate survey resources, or they can hire a consulting firm from outside to conduct the survey. This leads SYSCO's HR function to manage itself as a business. Carrig offers five guidelines for how this operating model for HR works.

1. Make HR an entrepreneurial business—view departments, managers, and employees as customers.
2. Allow for free choice—provide the services your customers want, rather than force them to accept what you think they need.
3. Data sells—focus on collecting the data that will help your customers succeed in their businesses.
4. Learn from winners—identify the units that are most successful and study what they do to discover what drives their success.
5. Demonstrate impact—collect the data that shows the bottom-line impact of your programs.

SYSCO's approach to HR presents a radically different model for the future roles and responsibilities of an HR function.

Source: Stoltz, R. "Ah, to be Strategic," *Human Resource Executive* (Nov. 2003), pp. 1, 20–30; Kiger, P., "HR Proves Its Value," *Workforce* (March 2002), pp. 28–33.

Introduction

Throughout this book we have emphasized how human resource management practices can help companies gain a competitive advantage. We identified specific practices related to managing the internal and external environment; designing work and measuring work outcomes; and acquiring, developing, and compensating human resources. We have also discussed the best of current research and practice to show how they may contribute to a company's competitive advantage.

As we said in Chapter 1, the role of the HRM function has been evolving over time. As we see in this chapter's opening story, it has now reached a crossroads. Although it began as a purely administrative function, most HR executives now see the function's major role as being much more strategic. However, this evolution has resulted in a misalignment between the skills and capabilities of members of the function and the new requirements placed on it. Virtually every HRM function in top companies is going through a transformation process to create a function that can play this new strategic role while successfully fulfilling its other roles. This transformation process is also going on globally (the "Competing through Globalization" box describes the different HR models that exist within the newly expanded European Union). Managing this process is the subject of this chapter. First we discuss the various activities of the HRM function. Then we examine how to develop a market- or customer-oriented HRM function. We then describe the current structure of most HRM functions. Finally, we explore measurement approaches for assessing the effectiveness of the function.

Activities of HRM

In order to understand the transformation going on in HRM, one must understand HRM activities in terms of their strategic value. One way of classifying these activities is depicted in Figure 16.1. Transactional activities (the day-to-day transactions

FIGURE 16.1

Categories of HRM Activities and Percentages of Time Spent on Them

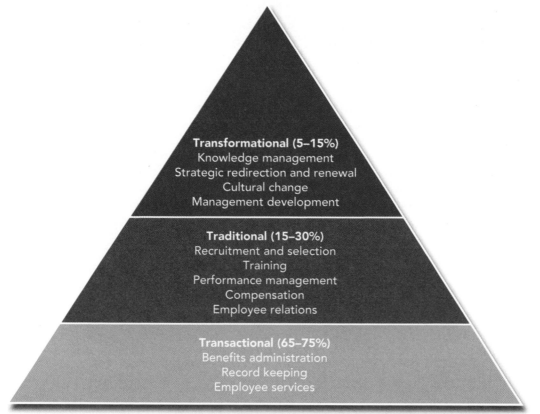

Transformational (5–15%)
Knowledge management
Strategic redirection and renewal
Cultural change
Management development

Traditional (15–30%)
Recruitment and selection
Training
Performance management
Compensation
Employee relations

Transactional (65–75%)
Benefits administration
Record keeping
Employee services

SOURCE: P. Wright, G. McMahan, S. Snell, and B. Gerhart, *Strategic Human Resource Management: Building Human Capital and Organizational Capability.* Technical report. Cornell University, 1998.

such as benefits administration, record keeping, and employee services) are low in their strategic value. Traditional activities such as performance management, training, recruiting, selection, compensation, and employee relations are the nuts and bolts of HRM. These activities have moderate strategic value because they often form the practices and systems to ensure strategy execution. Transformational activities create long-term capability and adaptability for the firm. These activities include knowledge management, management development, cultural change, and strategic redirection and renewal. Obviously, these activities comprise the greatest strategic value for the firm.

As we see in the figure, most HRM functions spend the vast majority of their time on transactional activities, with substantially less on traditional ones and very little on transformational activities. However, virtually all HRM functions, in order to add value to the firm, must increase their efforts in the traditional and transformational activities. To do this, however, requires that HR executives (1) develop a strategy for the HRM function, (2) assess the current effectiveness of the HRM function, and (3) redesign, reengineer, or outsource HRM processes to improve efficiency and effectiveness. These issues will be discussed in the following sections.

Human Resource Management in an Expanded European Union

The field of Human Resource Management continues to evolve on a global basis. In large part, the United States has led the way in HR innovations, but understanding how other parts of the world manage people and HR can be enlightening. In particular, the entrance into the EU of the 10 accession states as of May 2004 will result in even greater variety in HRM models.

In Europe, there has long been a considerable gap between the Anglo-Saxon and continental approaches to the way enterprises are organized and operated. Companies in the UK and Ireland have a significantly higher proportion of managers relative to other employees than companies in countries such as Germany, and particularly Italy. With the exception of Estonia and Latvia,

the accession states will display characteristics similar to the German/Italian model.

This emphasis on management positions has influenced the development of human resource management within the UK. If one considers the proportion of professionally qualified human resource (HR) staff compared to other employees in medium to large companies across Europe, the

RATIO OF MANAGEMENT TO OTHER EMPLOYEES				
UK & IRELAND	NETHERLANDS, BELGIUM & GREECE	OTHER ESTABLISHED EU STATES	ESTONIA & LATVIA	OTHER ACCESSION STATES
1:5	1:8	1:15	1:8	1:16

SOURCES: UNECE, ILO.

Strategic Management of the HRM Function

In light of the various roles and activities of the HRM function, we can easily see that it is highly unlikely that any function can (or should) effectively deliver on all roles and all activities. Although this is a laudable goal, resource constraints in terms of time, money, and head count require that the HR executive make strategic choices about where and how to allocate these resources for maximum value to the firm.

Chapter 2 explained the strategic management process that takes place at the organization level and discussed the role of HRM in this process. HRM has been seen as a strategic partner that has input into the formulation of the company's strategy and develops and aligns HRM programs to help implement the strategy. However, for the HRM function to become truly strategic in its orientation, it must view itself as a separate business entity and engage in strategic management in an effort to effectively serve the various internal customers.

In this respect, one recent trend within the field of HRM, consistent with the total quality management philosophy, is for the HR executive to take a customer-oriented approach to implementing the function. In other words, the strategic plan-

RATIO OF PROFESSIONAL HR STAFF TO OTHER EMPLOYEES HR/E (MEDIUM-LARGE COMPANIES ONLY)*					
UK	IRELAND	SWEDEN	POLAND (KOPEC)	OTHER EU15 STATES	ACCESSION STATES
1:127	1:189	1:402	1:166	1:2,790	1:5,105

SOURCES: Eurostat, EAPM, 2001 study by Dr. J. Kopec (Cracov University of Economics).

* Companies employing 50+ employees. EU15 states are the 15 member states of the European Union prior to accession on May 1, 2004.

UK has a ratio of just 1:127, while other (EU15) states (except for Ireland and Sweden) have an average ratio of 1:2,790. (In the United States, the numbers generally fall very close to 1:100.) In general, the larger the HR department and the more sophisticated its staff, the more HRM jobs can be expected to exist.

What the above figures suggest is that the ratio of HR/E is even higher in the accession states. However, the evidence from one study of HR management in Poland found a ratio of 1:166. This study suggests that one reason why the HR/E ratio appears to be so high in many accession and EU15 states is because, on the European continent, classification of HR professionals is confined to senior HR practitioners. Many HR staff, particularly in eastern Europe, perform only routine administrative functions and do not qualify as HR professionals.

How far HRM structures, methods, and processes progress in the accession states will greatly depend on the extent to which these economies receive investment from companies headquartered in the UK and North America. The established continental EU countries' progress toward modern and widespread HRM structures has been impaired by the existence of the codetermination power of works councils, the prevalence of collective bargaining at an industry level, and resistance to organizational innovation.

Particularly within the accession states, the recent sharp decline of unionization may make HRM's strong business orientation and emphasis upon increasing individual work commitment an attractive model to embrace, particularly as the new generation of managers rejects the collectivism of the former communist era.

SOURCE: Reprinted with permission of FedEE Services, Ltd.

ning process that takes place at the level of the business can also be performed with the HRM function. HR executives in more progressive U.S. companies have begun to view the HRM function as a strategic business unit and have tried to define that business in terms of their customer base, their customers' needs, and the technologies required to satisfy customers' needs (Figure 16.2). For example, Weyerhauser Corporation's human resources department identified 11 characteristics that would describe a quality human resource organization; these are presented in Table 16.1.

A customer orientation is one of the most important changes in the HRM function's attempts to become strategic. It entails first identifying customers. The most obvious example of HRM customers are the line managers who require HRM services. In addition, the strategic planning team is a customer in the sense that it requires the identification, analysis, and recommendations regarding people-oriented business problems. Employees are also HRM customers because the rewards they receive from the employment relationship are determined and/or administered by the HRM department.

In addition, the products of the HRM department must be identified. Line managers want to have high-quality employees committed to the organization. The strategic planning team requires information and recommendations for the planning

FIGURE 16.2

Customer-Oriented Perspective of the HRM Function

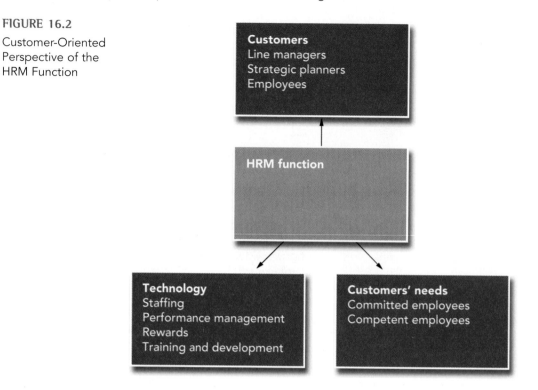

process as well as programs that support the strategic plan once it has been identified. Employees want compensation and benefit programs that are consistent, adequate, and equitable, and they want fair promotion decisions. At Southwest Airlines, the "People" department administers customer surveys to all clients as they leave the department to measure how well their needs have been satisfied.

Finally, the technologies through which HRM meets customer needs vary depending on the need being satisfied. Selection systems ensure that applicants selected for employment have the necessary knowledge, skills, and abilities to provide value to

TABLE 16.1

Characteristics of HRM Quality at Weyerhauser Corporation

- Human resources products and service are linked to customer requirements.
- Customer requirements are translated into internal service applications.
- Processes for producing products and services are documented with cost/value relationships understood.
- Reliable methods and standardized processes are in place.
- Waste and inefficiency are eliminated.
- Problem solving and decision making are based on facts and data.
- Critical success variables are tracked, displayed, and maintained.
- Human resources employees are trained and educated in total quality tools and principles.
- Human resource systems have been aligned to total quality implementation strategies.
- Human resource managers provide leadership and support to organizations on large-scale organizational change.
- Human resource professionals function as "strategic partners" in managing the business and implementing total quality principles.

the organization. Training and development systems meet the needs of both line managers and employees by giving employees development opportunities to ensure they are constantly increasing their human capital and, thus, providing increased value to the company. Performance management systems make clear to employees what is expected of them and assure line managers and strategic planners that employee behavior will be in line with the company's goals. Finally, reward systems similarly benefit all customers (line managers, strategic planners, and employees). These systems assure line managers that employees will use their skills for organizational benefit, and they provide strategic planners with ways to ensure that all employees are acting in ways that will support the strategic plan. Obviously, reward systems provide employees with an equitable return for their investment of skills and effort.

For example, Whirlpool Corporation's HR managers go through a formalized process of identifying their customer, the need/value they satisfy, and the technology used to satisfy the customer. As Whirlpool planned for start-up of a centralized service supercenter, the plan called for hiring between 100 and 150 employees to serve as call takers who receive service requests from Whirlpool appliance owners and set up service appointments from these calls. The HR manager in charge of developing a selection system for hiring these call takers identified the operations manager in charge of phone service as the HRM department's customer, the delivery of qualified phone call takers as the need satisfied, and the use of a structured interview and paper-and-pencil tests as the technologies employed. This customer service orientation may be the trend of the future. It provides a means for the HRM function to specifically identify who its customers are, what customers' needs are being met, and how well those needs are being met.

Building an HR Strategy
The Basic Process

How do HR functions build their HR strategies? Recent research has examined how HR functions go about the process of building their HR strategies that should support the business strategies. Conducting case studies on 20 different companies, Wright and colleagues describe the generic approach as somewhat consistent with the process for developing a business strategy.[1]

As depicted in Figure 16.3, the function first scans the environment to determine the trends or events that might have an impact on the organization (e.g., future talent shortage, increasing immigrant population, aging of the workforce). It then examines the strategic business issues or needs (e.g., is the company growing, expanding internationally, needing to develop new technologies?). For instance, Figure 16.4 displays IBM's major business strategy priorities. As can be seen in this example, a clear strategic priority is the attraction, motivation, and retention of talent.

FIGURE 16.3

Basic Process for HR Strategy

FIGURE 16.4

IBM Priorities and the On-Demand Era

IBM Strategic Priorities on Demand	
1. Delivering business value 2. Offering world class open infrastructure 3. Developing innovative leadership technology 4. Exploiting new profitable growth opportunities 5. Creating brand leadership and a superior customer experience 6. **Attracting, motivating, and retaining the best talent in our industry**	"An enterprise whose business processes—integrated end-to-end across the company and with key partners, suppliers, and customers—can respond with speed to any customer demand, market opportunity or external threat." —Sam Palmisano, *IBM Chairman and CEO*

From these issues, the HR strategy team needs to identify the specific people issues that will be critical to address in order for the business to succeed (a potential leadership vacuum, lack of technological expertise, lack of diversity, etc.). In light of all of this information, the HR strategy is developed which provides a detailed plan regarding the major priorities and the programs, policies, and processes that must be developed or executed. Finally, this HR strategy is communicated to the relevant parties, both internal and external to the function. Again, IBM's HR strategy is depicted in Figure 16.5, and shows how IBM seeks to differentiate itself in the labor market as well as the major priority areas that the HR strategy seeks to address.

Involving Line Executives

This generic process provides for the potential to involve line executives in a number of ways. Because the HR strategy seeks to address business issues, involving those in charge of running the business can increase the quality of information from which the HR strategy is created. This involvement can occur in a few ways. First, line ex-

FIGURE 16.5

IBM HR Strategy

ecutives could simply provide input, by either surveying or interviewing them regarding the business challenges and strategy. Second, they could be members of the team that actually develops the HR strategy. Third, once the strategy is developed, they could receive communications with the HR strategy information. Finally, they could have to formally approve the strategy, in essence "signing off" that the HR strategy fully supports the business strategy. The most progressive organizations use all four forms of involvement, asking a large group of executives for input, having one or two executives on the team, communicating the HR strategy broadly to executives, and having the senior executive team formally approve it.

Characterizing HR Strategies

As you can see in Figure 16.6, the variety of ways that HR strategies can be generated results in various levels of linkage with the business. In general, four categories of this relationship can be identified.

First, at the most elementary level, "HR-focused" HR functions' articulation of people outcomes stems more from an analysis of what their functions currently do than from an understanding of how those people outcomes relate to the larger business. Second, "people-linked" functions have clearly identified, articulated, and aligned their HR activities around people issues and outcomes, but not business issues and outcomes. Third, "business-linked" HR functions begin with an assessment of what HR is doing, then identify the major people outcomes they should focus on, and in a few cases, how those might translate into positive business outcomes. Finally, "business driven" functions have fully developed HR strategies which begin by identifying the major business needs and issues, consider how people fit in and what people outcomes are necessary, and then build HR systems focused on meeting those needs.

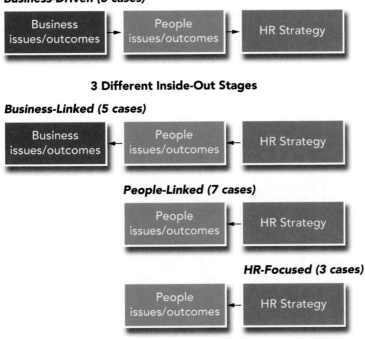

FIGURE 16.6

Approaches to Developing an HR Strategy

As can be seen by IBM's business and HR strategies in Figures 16.4 and 16.5, one of the major roles of the HR function is to enable the firm to attract and retain talent. Interestingly, recent research demonstrates that the ethical reputation of a firm may help or hinder such efforts. A survey of more than 800 MBAs from 11 leading North American and European schools found a substantial number were willing to forgo some financial benefits to work for an organization with a better reputation for corporate social responsibility and ethics. David B. Montgomery of Stanford and Catherine A. Ramus of the University of California at Santa Barbara explored whether a reputation for high ethical standards or caring about employees, environmental sustainability, and community stakeholders makes an organization more attractive to MBA candidates.

Their research showed that "intellectual challenge" topped the list as the most important attribute for MBAs in their job choice decision. In addition, the financial package was only 80 percent as important as intellectual challenge. However, most surprising was that "reputation for ethics" and "caring about employees" both rose to the top third of the list of 14 attributes, proving to be approximately 77 percent as important as "intellectual challenge."

Moreover, more than 97 percent of the MBAs in the sample said they were willing to sacrifice financial benefits to work for an organization with a better reputation for corporate social responsibility and ethics.

This research seems to suggest that ethics, social responsibility, and the concept of sustainability may increasingly lead to competitive advantage in labor markets. It seems that the greed, deceit, and fraud exhibited by business leaders at companies such as Enron, Global Crossing, and Tyco cannot lead to a sustainable organization.

SOURCE: http://www.gsb.stanford.edu/news/research/hr_mbajobchoice.shtml, 8/1/04.

The HR strategy must help address the issues that the business faces which will determine its success. As finding, attracting, and retaining talent has become a critical issue, virtually every HR function is addressing this as part of the HR strategy (as can be seen in IBM's HR strategy). The "Competing through Sustainability" box discusses a new development in the attraction of talent: MBAs' preference for working for companies with reputations for high ethics.

Measuring HRM Effectiveness

The strategic decision making process for the HRM function requires that decision makers have a good sense of the effectiveness of the current HRM function. This information provides the foundation for decisions regarding which processes, systems, and skills of HR employees need improvement. Often HRM functions that have been heavily involved in transactional activities for a long time tend to lack systems, processes, and skills for delivering state-of-the-art traditional activities and are thoroughly unable to contribute in the transformational arena. (The "Competing through Globalization" box illustrates how the role of HRM is being transformed in China.)

HRM's Evolving Role in China

The People's Republic of China (PRC) has become one of the most attractive business markets for foreign investors. Over the past 20 years, the PRC has registered an average annual growth rate of 9.8 percent and currently ranks seventh in the world in terms of economic strength. As the country becomes more open to foreign trade and investment, the role of HR managers has changed.

The "iron rice-bowl" concept, guaranteeing lifetime employment with an emphasis on managing employee needs through wages, housing, and medical and social insurance, used to be the dominant approach to employment. Under this concept, HRM sought to provide stable employment and maintain employees' standards of living through egalitarian reward structures. HRM also played a role in helping organizations achieve production goals assigned by the state. Managers sought to achieve these centrally dictated production goals without examining the wisdom of their actions. Absent competition, HRM was not concerned with increasing an organization's productivity, quality, or costs.

However, the recent economic transformation has similarly transformed the role of HR professionals in Chinese firms. There is now a greater focus on controlling the number and quality of employees based on business needs. Also, HRM seeks to increase the motivation level of employees through much greater use of pay incentives. In essence, HRM in China today must play the strategic partner role that we observe throughout the world.

This new role is problematic for a number of reasons. First, although China has an enormous population, there is still a tremendous lack of suitably qualified or skilled personnel. Second, the institutional system is so entrenched that it often is difficult to implement new policies and practices. For example, variable pay incentives are necessary and desired, but the old egalitarian culture makes them difficult to implement.

In any case, the PRC provides an incredibly rich case study in the transformation of both an economy and the HRM profession.

SOURCE: H. Mitsuhashi, H. Park, P. Wright, and R. Chua, "Line and HR Executives' Perceptions of HR Effectiveness in Firms in the People's Republic of China," *International Journal of Human Resource Management* 11(2) 2000, pp. 197–216.

Thus diagnosis of the effectiveness of the HRM function provides critical information for its strategic management.

In addition, having good measures of the function's effectiveness provides the following benefits:[2]

- *Marketing the function:* Evaluation is a sign to other managers that the HRM function really cares about the organization as a whole and is trying to support operations, production, marketing, and other functions of the company. Information regarding cost savings and benefits is useful to prove to internal customers that HRM practices contribute to the bottom line. Such information is also useful for gaining additional business for the HRM function.

- *Providing accountability:* Evaluation helps determine whether the HRM function is meeting its objectives and effectively using its budget.

Audit approach

Type of assessment of HRM effectiveness that involves review of customer satisfaction or key indicators (like turnover rate or average days to fill a position) related to an HRM functional area (such as recruiting or training).

Approaches for Evaluating Effectiveness

There are two commonly used approaches for evaluating the effectiveness of HRM practices: the audit approach and the analytic approach.

Audit Approach

The **audit approach** focuses on reviewing the various outcomes of the HRM functional areas. Both key indicators and customer satisfaction measures are typically collected. Table 16.2 lists examples of key indicators and customer satisfaction measures for staffing, equal employment opportunity, compensation, benefits, training, performance management, safety, labor relations, and succession planning. The development of electronic employee databases and information systems has made it much easier to collect, store, and analyze the functional key indicators (more on this later in the chapter) than in the past, when information was kept in file folders.

TABLE 16.2

Examples of Key Indicators and Customer Satisfaction Measures for HRM Functions

KEY INDICATORS	CUSTOMER SATISFACTION MEASURES
Staffing	
Average days taken to fill open requisitions	Anticipation of personnel needs
Ratio of acceptances to offers made	Timeliness of referring qualified workers to line
Ratio of minority/women applicants to representation in local labor market	supervisors
Per capita requirement costs	Treatment of applicants
Average years of experience/education of hires per job family	Skill in handling terminations
	Adaptability to changing labor market conditions
Equal employment opportunity	
Ratio of EEO grievances to employee population	Resolution of EEO grievances
Minority representation by EEO categories	Day-to-day assistance provided by personnel
Minority turnover rate	department in implementing affirmative action plan
	Aggressive recruitment to identify qualified women and minority applicants
Compensation	
Per capita (average) merit increases	Fairness of existing job evaluation system in
Ratio of recommendations for reclassification to number of employees	assigning grades and salaries
Percentage of overtime hours to straight time	Competitiveness in local labor market
Ratio of average salary offers to average salary in community	Relationship between pay and performance
	Employee satisfaction with pay
Benefits	
Average unemployment compensation payment (UCP)	Promptness in handling claims
Average workers' compensation payment (WCP)	Fairness and consistency in the application of benefit policies
Benefit cost per payroll dollar	Communication of benefits to employees
Percentage of sick leave to total pay	Assistance provided to line managers in reducing potential for unnecessary claims

continues

We previously discussed how HRM functions can become much more customer-oriented as part of the strategic management process. If, in fact, the function desires to be more customer-focused, then one important source of effectiveness data can be the customers. Just as firms often survey their customers to determine how effectively the customers feel they are being served, the HRM function can survey its internal customers.

TABLE 16.2 (concluded)

Examples of Key Indicators and Customer Satisfaction Measures for HRM Functions *concluded*

KEY INDICATORS	CUSTOMER SATISFACTION MEASURES
Training Percentage of employees participating in training programs per job family Percentage of employees receiving tuition refunds Training dollars per employee	Extent to which training programs meet the needs of employees and the company Communication to employees about available training opportunities Quality of introduction/orientation programs
Employee appraisal and development Distribution of performance appraisal ratings Appropriate psychometric properties of appraisal forms	Assistance in identifying management potential Organizational development activities provided by HRM department
Succession planning Ratio of promotions to number of employees Ratio of open requisitions filled internally to those filled externally	Extent to which promotions are made from within Assistance/counseling provided to employees in career planning
Safety Frequency/severity ratio of accidents Safety-related expenses per $1,000 of payroll Plant security losses per square foot (e.g., fires, burglaries)	Assistance to line managers in organizing safety programs Assistance to line managers in identifying potential safety hazards Assistance to line managers in providing a good working environment (lighting, cleanliness, heating, etc.)
Labor relations Ratio of grievances by pay plan to number of employees Frequency and duration of work stoppages Percentage of grievances settled	Assistance provided to line managers in handling grievances Efforts to promote a spirit of cooperation in plant Efforts to monitor the employee relations climate in plant
Overall effectiveness Ratio of personnel staff to employee population Turnover rate Absenteeism rate Ratio of per capita revenues to per capita cost Net income per employee	Accuracy and clarity of information provided to managers and employees Competence and expertise of staff Working relationship between organizations and HRM department

SOURCE: Reprinted with permission. Excerpts from Chapter 1.5, "Evaluating Human Resource Effectiveness," pp. 187–227, by Anne S. Tsui and Luis R. Gomez-Mejia, from *Human Resource Management: Evolving Roles and Responsibilities;* edited by Lee Dyer. Copyright © 1988 by The Bureau of National Affairs, Inc., Washington, DC 20037. To order BNA publications call toll free 1-800-960-1220.

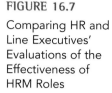

FIGURE 16.7

Comparing HR and Line Executives' Evaluations of the Effectiveness of HRM Roles

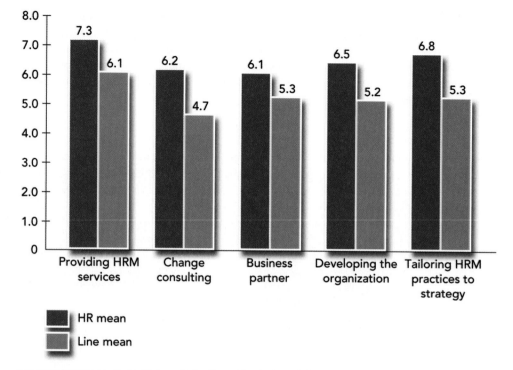

SOURCE: P. Wright, G. McMahan, S. Snell, and B. Gerhart, "Comparing Line and HR Executives' Perceptions of HR Effectiveness: Services, Roles, and Contributions." CAHRS (Center for Advanced Human Resource Studies) working paper 98-29, School of ILR, Cornell University, Ithaca, NY.

One important internal customer is the employees of the firm. Employees often have both direct contact with the HRM function (through activities such as benefits administration and payroll) and indirect contact with the function through their involvement in activities such as receiving performance appraisals, pay raises, and training programs. Many organizations such as AT&T, Motorola, and General Electric use their regular employee attitude survey as a way to assess the employees as users/customers of the HRM programs and practices.[3] However, the problem with assessing effectiveness only from the employees' perspective is that often they are responding not from the standpoint of the good of the firm, but, rather, from their own individual perspective. For example, employees notoriously and consistently express dissatisfaction with pay level (who doesn't want more money?), but to simply ratchet up pay across the board would put the firm at a serious labor cost disadvantage.

Thus, many firms have gone to surveys of top line executives as a better means of assessing the effectiveness of the HRM function. The top-level line executives can see how the systems and practices are impacting both employees and the overall effectiveness of the firm from a strategic standpoint. This can also be useful for determining how well HR employees' perceptions of their function's effectiveness align with the views of their line colleagues. For example, a study of 14 firms revealed that HR executives and line executives agreed on the relative effectiveness of HR's delivery of services such as staffing and training systems (that is, which were most and least effectively delivered) but not on the absolute level of effectiveness. As Figure 16.7 shows, HR executives' ratings of their effectiveness in different roles also diverged significantly from line executives'. In addition, line executives viewed HRM as being

FIGURE 16.8

Comparing HR and Line Executives' Evaluations of the Effectiveness of HRM Contributions

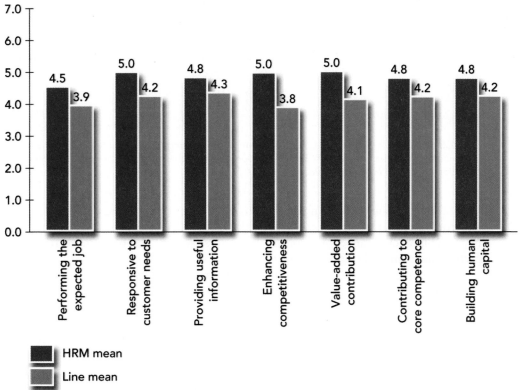

SOURCE: P. Wright, G. McMahan, S. Snell, and B. Gerhart, "Comparing Line and HR Executives' Perceptions of HR Effectiveness: Services, Roles, and Contributions." CAHRS (Center for Advanced Human Resource Studies) working paper 98-29, School of ILR, Cornell University, Ithaca, NY.

significantly less effective with regard to HRM's actual contributions to the firm's overall effectiveness, as we see in Figure 16.8.[4]

The Analytic Approach

The **analytic approach** focuses on either (1) determining whether the introduction of a program or practice (like a training program or a new compensation system) has the intended effect or (2) estimating the financial costs and benefits resulting from an HRM practice. For example, in Chapter 7 we discussed how companies can determine a training program's impact on learning, behavior, and results. Evaluating a training program is one strategy for determining whether the program works. Typically, in an overall evaluation of effectiveness, we are interested in determining the degree of change associated with the program.

The second strategy involves determining the dollar value of the training program, taking into account all the costs associated with the program. Using this strategy, we are not concerned with how much change occurred but rather with the dollar value (costs versus benefits) of the program. Table 16.3 lists the various types of cost–benefit analyses that are done. The human resource accounting approach attempts to

Analytic approach
Type of assessment of HRM effectiveness that involves determining the impact of, or the financial cost and benefits of, a program or practice.

TABLE 16.3

Types of Cost–Benefit Analysis

Human resource accounting
- Capitalization of salary
- Net present value of expected wage payments
- Returns on human assets and human investments

Utility analysis
- Turnover costs
- Absenteeism and sick leave costs
- Gains from selection programs
- Impact of positive employee attitudes
- Financial gains of training programs

SOURCE: Based on A. S. Tsui and L. R. Gomez-Mejia, "Evaluating HR Effectiveness," in *Human Resource Management: Evolving Roles and Responsibilities*, ed. L. Dyer (Washington, DC: Bureau of National Affairs, 1988), pp. 1–196.

place a dollar value on human resources as if they were physical resources (like plant and equipment) or financial resources (like cash). Utility analysis attempts to estimate the financial impact of employee behaviors (such as absenteeism, turnover, job performance, and substance abuse).

For example, wellness programs are a popular HRM program for reducing health care costs through reducing employees' risk of heart disease and cancer. One study evaluated four different types of wellness programs. Part of the evaluation involved determining the costs and benefits associated with the four programs over a three-year period.[5] A different type of wellness program was implemented at each site. Site A instituted a program involving raising employees' awareness of health risks (distributing news articles, blood pressure testing, health education classes). Site B set up a physical fitness facility for employees. Site C raised awareness of health risks and followed up with employees who had identified health risks. Site D provided health education and follow-up counseling and promoted physical competition and health-related events. Table 16.4 shows the effectiveness and cost-effectiveness of the Site C and Site D wellness models.

The analytic approach is more demanding than the audit approach because it requires the detailed use of statistics and finance. A good example of the level of sophistication that can be required for cost–benefit analysis is shown in Table 16.5. This table shows the types of information needed to determine the dollar value of a new selection test for entry-level computer programmers.

TABLE 16.4

Effectiveness and Cost-Effectiveness of Two Wellness Programs for Four Cardiovascular Disease Risk Factors

	SITE C	SITE D
Annual direct program costs, per employee per year	$30.96	$38.57
Percentage of cardiovascular disease risks[a] for which risk was moderately reduced or relapse prevented	48%	51%
Percentage of preceding entry per annual $1 spent per employee	1.55%	1.32%
Amount spent per 1% of risks reduced or relapse prevented	$.65	$.76

[a]High blood pressure, overweight, smoking, and lack of exercise.

SOURCE: J. C. Erfurt, A. Foote, and M. A. Heirich, "The Cost-Effectiveness of Worksite Wellness Programs," *Personnel Psychology* 45 (1992), p. 22.

Cost–benefit information		
Current employment	4,404	
Number separating	618	
Number selected	618	
Average tenure	9.69	years
Test information		
Number of applicants	1,236	
Testing cost per applicant	$10	
Total test cost	$12,360	
Average test score	.80	SD
Test validity	.76	
SD_y (per year)[a]	$10,413	
Computation		
Quantity	= Average tenure × Applicants selected	
	= 9.69 years × 618 applicants	
	= 5,988 person-years	
Quality	= Average test score × Test validity × SD_y	
	= .80 × .76 × $10,413	
	= $6,331 per year	
Utility	= (Quantity × Quality) – Costs	
	= (5,988 person-year × $6,331 per year) – $12,360	
	= $37.9 million	

TABLE 16.5

Example of Analysis Needed to Determine the Dollar Value of a Selection Test

[a]SD_y = Dollar value of one standard difference in job performance. Approximately 40% of average salary.
SOURCE: From J. W. Boudreau, "Utility Analysis," in *Human Resource Management: Evolving Roles and Responsibilities,* ed. L. Dyer (Washington, DC: Bureau of National Affairs, 1988), p. 150; F. L. Schmidt, J. E. Hunter, R. C. McKenzie, and T. W. Muldrow, "Impact of Valid Selection Procedures on Work-Force Productivity," *Journal of Applied Psychology* 64 (1979), pp. 609–26.

Improving HRM Effectiveness

Once a strategic direction has been established and HRM's effectiveness evaluated, leaders of the HRM function can explore how to improve its effectiveness in contributing to the firm's competitiveness. Returning briefly to Figure 16.1, which depicted the different activities of the HRM function, often the improvement focuses on two aspects of the pyramid. First, within each activity, HRM needs to improve both the efficiency and effectiveness in performing each of the activities. Second, often there is a push to eliminate as much of the transactional work as possible (and some of the traditional work) to free up time and resources to focus more on the higher–value-added transformational work. Redesign of the structure (reporting relationships) and processes (through outsourcing and information technology) enables the function to achieve these goals simultaneously. Figure 16.9 depicts this process.

Restructuring to Improve HRM Effectiveness

Traditional HRM functions were structured around the basic HRM subfunctions such as staffing, training, compensation, appraisal, and labor relations. Each of these areas had a director who reported to the VP of HRM, who often reported to a VP of finance and administration. However, for the HRM function to truly contribute strategically to firm effectiveness, the senior HR person must be part of the top management team

FIGURE 16.9

Improving HRM Effectiveness

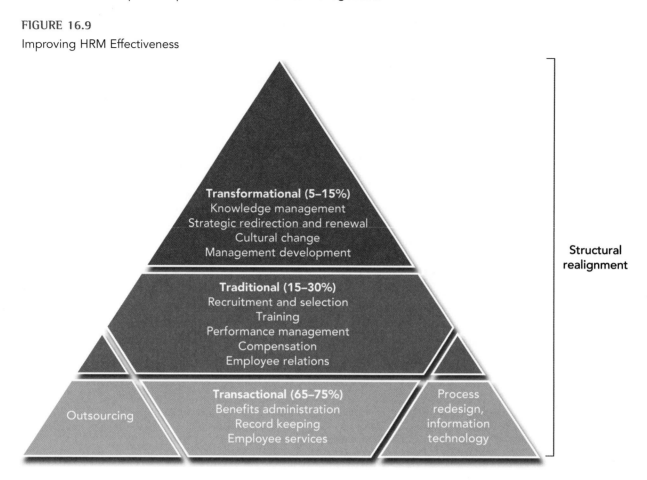

(reporting directly to the chief executive officer), and there must be a different structural arrangement within the function itself.

A recent generic structure for the HRM function is depicted in Figure 16.10. As we see, the HRM function effectively is divided into three divisions: the centers for expertise, the field generalists, and the service center.[6] The centers for expertise usually consist of the functional specialists in the traditional areas of HRM such as recruitment, selection, training, and compensation. These individuals ideally act as consultants in the development of state-of-the-art systems and processes for use in the organization. The field generalists consist of the HRM generalists who are assigned to a business unit within the firm. These individuals usually have dual reporting relationships to both the head of the line business and the head of HRM (although the line business tends to take priority). They ideally take responsibility for helping the line executives in their business strategically address people issues, and they ensure that the HRM systems enable the business to execute its strategy. Finally, the service center consists of individuals who ensure that the transactional activities are delivered throughout the organization. These service centers often leverage information technology to efficiently deliver employee services. For example, organizations such as Chevron have created call-in service centers where employees can dial a central number where service center employees are available to answer their questions and process their requests and transactions.

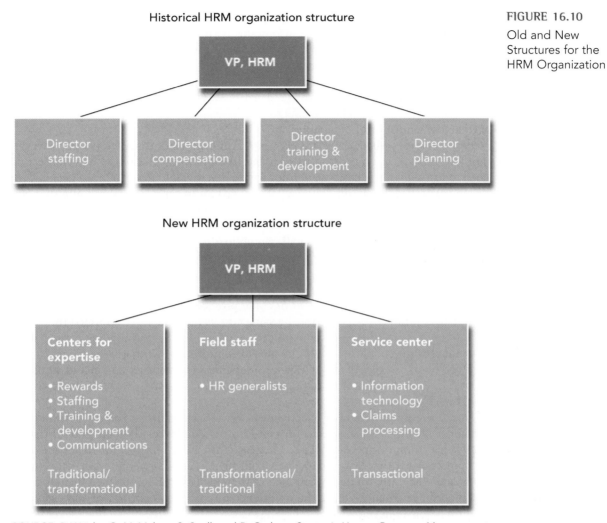

Historical HRM organization structure

New HRM organization structure

SOURCE: P. Wright, G. McMahan, S. Snell, and B. Gerhart, *Strategic Human Resource Management: Building Human Capital and Organizational Capability.* Technical report. Cornell University, 1998.

FIGURE 16.10
Old and New Structures for the HRM Organization

Such structural arrangements improve service delivery through specialization. Center for expertise employees can develop current functional skills without being distracted by transactional activities, and generalists can focus on learning the business environment without having to maintain expertise in functional specializations. Finally, service center employees can focus on efficient delivery of basic services across business units.

Outsourcing to Improve HRM Effectiveness

Restructuring the internal HRM function and redesigning the processes represent internal approaches to improving HRM effectiveness. However, increasingly HR executives are seeking to improve the effectiveness of the systems, processes, and services the function delivers through outsourcing. **Outsourcing** entails contracting with an outside vendor to provide a product or service to the firm, as opposed to producing the product using employees within the firm.

Outsourcing
An organization's use of an outside organization for a broad set of services.

Why would a firm outsource an HRM activity or service? Usually this is done for one of two reasons: Either the outsourcing partner can provide the service more cheaply than it would cost to do it internally, or the partner can provide it more effectively than it can be performed internally. Early on, firms resorted to outsourcing for efficiency reasons. Why would using an outsourced provider be more efficient than having internal employees provide a service? Usually it is because outsourced providers are specialists who are able to develop extensive expertise that can be leveraged across a number of companies.

For example, consider a relatively small firm that seeks to develop a pension system for employees. To provide this service to employees, the HRM function would need to learn all of the basics of pension law. Then it would need to hire a person with specific expertise in administering a pension system in terms of making sure that employee contributions are withheld and that the correct payouts are made to retired employees. Then the company would have to hire someone with expertise in investing pension funds. If the firm is small, requirements of the pension fund might not fill the time (80 hours per week) of these two new hires. Assume that it takes only 20 total hours a week for these people to do their jobs. The firm would be wasting 60 hours of employee time each week. However, a firm that specializes in providing pension administration services to multiple firms could provide the 20 hours of required time to that firm and three other firms for the same cost as had the firm performed this activity internally. Thus the specialist firm could charge the focal firm 50 percent of what it would cost the small firm to do the pensions internally. Of that 50 percent, 25 percent (20 hours) would go to paying direct salaries and the other 25 percent would be profit. Here the focal firm would save 50 percent of its expenses while the provider would make money.

Now consider the aspect of effectiveness. Because the outsourced provider works for a number of firms and specializes in pensions, its employees develop state-of-the-art knowledge of running pension plans. They can learn unique innovations from one company and transfer that learning to a new company. In addition, employees can be more easily and efficiently trained because all of them will be trained in the same processes and procedures. Finally, due to the experience in providing constant pension services, the firm is able to develop a capability to perform these services that could never be developed by two individuals working 25 percent of the time on these services.

What kind of services are being outsourced? Firms primarily outsource transactional activities and services of HRM such as pension and benefits administration as well as payroll. However, a number of traditional and some transformational activities have been outsourced as well. For example, in the 1990s, Compaq Computer outsourced a large portion of its staffing activities. The firm contracted with a company to conduct all of the interviewing of its hourly crew and some managerial employees. Compaq found that while the cost was higher than it might have been if the work had been done internally, it provided more flexibility to quickly and efficiently react (not having to lay off employees) if its hiring needs decreased.

Improving HRM Effectiveness through Process Redesign

In addition to structural arrangements, process redesign enables the HRM function to more efficiently and effectively deliver HRM services. Process redesign often uses information technology, but information technology applications are not a requirement. Thus we will discuss the general issue of process reengineering and then explore information technology applications that have aided HRM in process redesign.

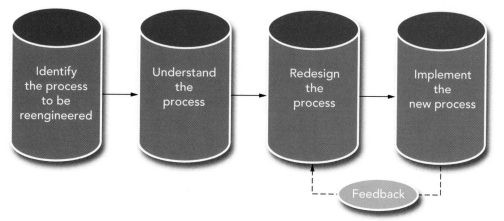

FIGURE 16.11
The Reengineering
Process

Reengineering is a complete review of critical work processes and redesign to make them more efficient and able to deliver higher quality. Reengineering is especially critical to ensuring that the benefits of new technology can be realized. Applying new technology to an inefficient process will not improve efficiency or effectiveness. Instead, it will increase product or service costs related to the introduction of the new technology.

Reengineering can be used to review the HRM department functions and processes, or it can be used to review specific HRM practices such as work design or the performance management system. The reengineering process involves the four steps shown in Figure 16.11: identify the process to be reengineered, understand the process, redesign the process, and implement the new process.[7]

Reengineering
Review and redesign of work processes to make them more efficient and improve the quality of the end product or service.

Identifying the Process

Managers who control the process or are responsible for functions within the process (sometimes called "process owners") should be identified and asked to be part of the reengineering team. Team members should include employees involved in the process (to provide expertise) and those outside the process, as well as internal or external customers who see the outcome of the process.

Understanding the Process

Several things need to be considered when evaluating a process:

- Can jobs be combined?
- Can employees be given more autonomy? Can decision making and control be built into the process through streamlining it?
- Are all the steps in the process necessary?
- Are data redundancy, unnecessary checks, and controls built into the process?
- How many special cases and exceptions have to be dealt with?
- Are the steps in the process arranged in their natural order?
- What is the desired outcome? Are all of the tasks necessary? What is the value of the process?

Various techniques are used to understand processes. *Data-flow diagrams* are useful to show the flow of data among departments. Figure 16.12 shows a data-flow diagram for payroll data and the steps in producing a paycheck. Information about the employee and department are sent to the general account. The payroll check is issued

FIGURE 16.12

A Data-Flow Diagram for Payroll Data

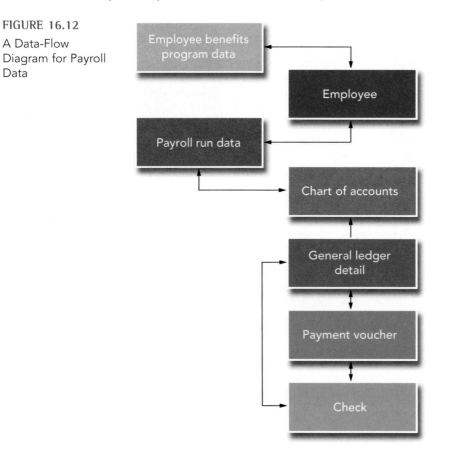

based on a payment voucher that is generated from the general accounting ledger. *Data-entity relationship diagrams* show the types of data used within a business function and the relationship among the different types of data. In *scenario analysis*, simulations of real-world issues are presented to data end users. The end users are asked to indicate how an information system could help address their particular situations and what data should be maintained to deal with those situations. *Surveys* and *focus groups* collect information about the data collected, used, and stored in a functional area, as well as information about time and information-processing requirements. Users may be asked to evaluate the importance, frequency, and criticality of automating specific tasks within a functional area. For example, how critical is it to have an applicant tracking system that maintains data on applicants' previous work experience? *Cost–benefit analyses* compare the costs of completing tasks with and without an automated system or software application. For example, the analysis should include the costs in terms of people, time, materials, and dollars; the anticipated costs of software and hardware; and labor, time, and material expenses.[8]

Redesigning the Process

During the redesign phase, the team develops models, tests them, chooses a prototype, and determines how to integrate the prototype into the organization.

Implementing the Process

The company tries out the process by testing it in a limited, controlled setting before expanding companywide. For example, J. M. Huber Corporation, a New Jersey–based conglomerate that has several operating divisions scattered throughout the United States, used reengineering to avoid installing new software onto inefficient processes.[9] HR staff began by documenting and studying the existing work flow and creating a strategy for improving efficiency. Top management, midlevel managers, and human resources staff worked together to identify the processes that they most wanted to improve. They determined that the most critical issue was to develop a client–server system that could access data more easily than the mainframe computer they were currently using. Also, the client–server system could eliminate many of the requisitions needed to get access to data, which slowed down work. The HRM department's efforts have streamlined record-keeping functions, eliminated redundant steps, and automated manual processes. The fully automated client–server system allows employees to sign up and change benefits information using an interactive voice-response system that is connected to the company's database. In addition, managers have easier access to employee's salary history, job descriptions, and other data. If an employee is eligible for a salary increase and the manager requests a change and it is approved, the system will process it (without entry by a clerical worker), and the changes will be seen on the employee's paycheck. Results of the reengineering effort are impressive. The redesigned processes have reduced the number of problems that HRM has to give to other departments by 42 percent, cut work steps by 26 percent, and eliminated 20 percent of the original work. Although the company is spending over $1 million to make the technology work, it estimates that the investment should pay for itself in five years.

Improving HRM Effectiveness through Using New Technologies—HRM Information Systems

Several new and emerging technologies can help improve the effectiveness of the HRM function. **New technologies** are current applications of knowledge, procedures, and equipment that have not been used previously. New technology usually involves automation—that is, replacing human labor with equipment, information processing, or some combination of the two.

In HRM, technology has already been used for three broad functions: transaction processing, reporting, and tracking; decision support systems; and expert systems.[10] **Transaction processing** refers to computations and calculations used to review and document HRM decisions and practices. This includes documenting relocation, training expenses, and course enrollments and filling out government reporting requirements (such as EEO-1 reports, which require companies to report information to the government regarding employees' race and gender by job category). **Decision support systems** are designed to help managers solve problems. They usually include a "what if" feature that allows users to see how outcomes change when assumptions or data change. These systems are useful, for example, for helping companies determine the number of new hires needed based on different turnover rates or the availability of employees with a certain skill in the labor market. **Expert systems** are computer systems incorporating the decision rules of people deemed to have expertise in a certain area. The system recommends actions that the user can take based on the information provided by the user. The recommended actions are those that a human

New technologies Current applications of knowledge, procedures, and equipment that have not been previously used. Usually involves replacing human labor with equipment, information processing, or some combination of the two.

Transaction processing Computations and calculations used to review and document HRM decisions and practices.

Decision support systems Problem-solving systems which usually include a "what-if" feature that allows users to see how outcomes change when assumptions or data change.

Expert systems Computer systems incorporating the decision rules of people recognized as experts in a certain area.

expert would take in a similar situation (such as a manager interviewing a job candidate). We discuss expert systems in more detail later in this chapter.

The newest technologies being applied to HRM include interactive voice technology, client–server architecture, relational databases, imaging, and development of specialized software. These technologies improve effectiveness through increasing access to information, improving communications, improving the speed with which HRM transactions and information can be gathered, and reducing the costs and making it easier to administer HRM functions such as recruiting, training, and performance management. Technology enables

- Employees to gain complete control over their training and benefits enrollments (more self-service).
- The creation of a paperless employment office.
- Streamlining the HRM department's work.
- Knowledge-based decision support technology, which allows employees and managers to access knowledge as needed.
- Employees and managers to select the type of media they want to use to send and receive information.
- Work to be completed at any time and place.
- Closer monitoring of employees' work.[11]

There is evidence that new technology is related to improvements in productivity. Improvements in productivity have been credited largely to downsizing, restructuring, and reengineering. But technology is also responsible because new technology has allowed companies to find leaner, more flexible ways of operating.[12] A study of companies in a variety of industries found that investments in computers provided a better return than investments in other kinds of capital.[13] Technology requires companies to have appropriately skilled and motivated people and streamlined work processes. In some cases technology is replacing human capital.[14] For example, Statewide, the regional telephone unit of Pacific Telesis Group, used to dispatch about 20,000 trucks a day to fix customers' lines. New technology has enabled the company to find broken lines using computer signals. As a result, now fewer truck dispatches (and fewer drivers) are necessary.

Interactive Voice Technology

Interactive voice technology uses a conventional personal computer to create an automated phone-response system. This technology is especially useful for benefits administration. For example, at Hannaford Brothers, a supermarket chain spread through the Northeastern United States, the HRM department installed an interactive voice-response system that allows employees to get information on their retirement accounts, stock purchases, and benefits plans by using the touchtone buttons on their phone.[15] Employees can also directly enroll in programs and speak to an HRM representative if they have questions. As a result of the technology, the company was able to reduce the size of the HRM staff and more quickly serve employees' benefits needs.

Network
A combination of desktop computers, computer terminals and mainframes or minicomputers that share access to databases and a method to transmit information throughout the system.

Networks and Client–Server Architecture

Traditionally, different computer systems (with separate databases) are used for payroll, recruiting, and other human resource management functions. A **network** is a combination of desktop computers, computer terminals, and mainframes or minicomputers that share access to databases and a means to transmit information throughout the system. A common form of network involves client–server architecture. **Client–server architecture** provides the means of consolidating data and applications into a single system (the client).[16] The data can be accessed by multiple users. Also, software applications can be stored on the server and "borrowed" by other users. Client–server architecture allows easier access to data, faster response time, and maximum use of the computing power of the personal computer.

For example, a pharmaceutical company with 50,000 employees worldwide has used client–server technology to create an employee information system that integrates data from six databases.[17] The available data include financial, operational, and human resource information. A manager at a European location can compare her plant's human resource costs with those for the entire company or a plant in Ohio, and at the same time senior management can use the same data to compare the productivity of the Ohio plant with a plant in Maine.

Relational Databases

Databases contain several data files (topics), which are made up of employee information (records) containing data fields. A data field is an element or type of information such as employee name, Social Security number, or job classification.

In a **relational database** information is stored in separate files, which look like tables. These files can be linked by common elements (fields) such as name, identification number, or location. This contrasts with the traditional file structure, in which all data associated with an employee was kept in one file. In the relational database shown in Figure 16.13, employees' personal information is located in one file and

Client–server architecture
Computer design that provides a method to consolidate data and applications into a single host system (the client).

Relational database
A database structure that stores information in separate files that can be linked by common elements.

FIGURE 16.13
Example of a Relational Database

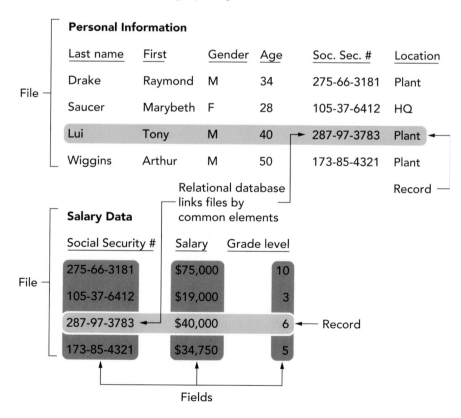

salary information in another, but both topics of information can be accessed via the employees' Social Security numbers.

Users of relational databases can file and retrieve information according to any field or multiple fields across different tables or databases. They provide an easy way to organize data. Also, the number of data fields that can be kept for any employee using a relational database is limitless. The ability to join or merge data from several different tables or to view only a subset of data is especially useful in human resource management. Databases that have been developed to track employee benefit costs, training courses, and compensation, for example, contain separate pieces of employee information that can be accessed and merged as desired by the user. Relational technology also allows databases to be established in several different locations. Users in one plant or division location can access data from any other company location. Consider an oil company. Human resources data—such as the names, salaries, and skills of employees working on an oil rig in the Gulf of Mexico—can be stored at company headquarters. Databases at the oil rig site itself might contain employee name, safety equipment issued, and appropriate skill certification. Headquarters and oil rig managers can access information on each database as needed.

Imaging

Imaging
A process for scanning documents, storing them electronically, and retrieving them.

Imaging refers to scanning documents, storing them electronically, and retrieving them.[18] Imaging is particularly useful because paper files take a large volume of space and are difficult to access. Imaging has been used in applicant tracking and in benefits management. Applicants' résumés can be scanned and stored in a database so they will be available for access at a later date. Some software applications (such as *Resumix*) allow the user to scan the résumé based on key items such as job history, education, or experience. At Warner-Lambert, the compensation and benefits department provides HR-related services for over 15,000 retirees.[19] Eight employees retire or die each month; approximately 100 employees terminate each month. This "exit" activity created a tremendous volume of paper for each employee, as well as requests for data from analysts in the department. It was very time-consuming and inefficient to locate the data and refile them. Using imaging, the compensation and benefits department was able to better serve its customers by reducing the time needed to locate a file or handle a phone inquiry from a retiree, providing the ability for sharing files among analysts simultaneously, eliminating the need to refile, and reducing the physical space needed to store the files.

Expert Systems

As we discussed earlier, expert systems are technologies that mimic a human expert. Expert systems have three elements:

- A knowledge base that contains facts, figures, and rules about a specific subject.
- A decision-making capability that draws conclusions from those facts and figures to solve problems and answer questions.
- A user interface that gathers and gives information to the person using the system.

The use of expert systems in HRM is relatively new. Some companies use expert systems to help employees decide how to allocate their money for benefits, help managers schedule the labor requirements for projects, and assist managers in conducting selection interviews. Pic 'n Pay stores (a chain of shoe stores) uses an expert system for the initial job interview. Candidates call a toll-free phone number. The candidates then respond to 100 questions, and the computer records the responses and scores them. At headquarters, a team of trained interviewers evaluates the responses and designs a list of follow-up questions, which are administered by the hiring manager. The expert system reduced employee turnover by 50 percent and reduced losses due to theft by 39 percent. Also, hiring of minorities has risen 8 percent, implying that decision biases may be less significant using the expert system.[20]

A large international food processor uses an expert system called *Performer*, designed to provide training and support to its plant operators. One of the problems the company was facing was determining why potato chips were being scorched in the fryer operation. An operator solved the problem using *Performer*. He selected the "troubleshooting" menu, then "product texture/flavor," then "off oil flavor." The program listed probable causes, beginning with high oxidation during frying. The operator chose that cause, and the system recommended adjusting the cooking line's oil flush, providing detailed steps for that procedure. Following those steps resolved the problem.[21]

Expert systems can deliver both high quality and lower costs. By using the decision processes of experts, the system enables many people to arrive at decisions that reflect the expert's knowledge. An expert system helps avoid the errors that can result from fatigue and decision biases. The efficiencies of an expert system can be realized if it can be operated by fewer employees or less skilled (and likely less costly) employees than the company would otherwise require.

Groupware

Groupware (electronic meeting software) is a software application that enables multiple users to track, share, and organize information and to work on the same document simultaneously.[22] A groupware system combines such elements as electronic mail, document management, and an electronic bulletin board. The most popular brand of groupware is *Lotus Notes*.

Companies have been using groupware to improve business processes such as sales and account management, to improve meeting effectiveness, and to identify and share knowledge in the organization. (See our earlier discussion of creating a learning organization in Chapter 7.) Monsanto uses *Lotus Notes* to link salespeople, account managers, and competitor-intelligence analysts.[23] The database contains updated news on competitors and customers, information from public news sources, salespeople's reports, an in-house directory of experts, and attendees' notes from conventions and conferences. Many companies are also creating their own "intranet," a private company network that competes with groupware programs such as *Lotus Notes*. Intranets are cheaper and simpler to use than groupware programs but pose potential security problems because of the difficulty of keeping people out of the network.[24]

Groupware
Software that enables multiple users to track, share, and organize information and to work on the same database or document simultaneously.

Software Applications for HRM
Improving HRM Effectiveness through New Technologies—E-HRM

Over the past 5–10 years, as HRM functions sought to play a more strategic role in their organizations, the first task was to eliminate transactional tasks in order to free up time to focus on traditional and transformational activities. Part of building a strategic HR function requires moving much of the transactional work away from

PeopleSoft and London Drugs: Partnering for Organizational Success

Founded in 1987 by Dave Duffield and Ken Morris, PeopleSoft offered one of the first human resources applications on a client–server platform instead of the traditional mainframe. The goal was to add needed flexibility to the application, thereby putting more power into the hands of users. Today, PeopleSoft owns more than 50 percent of the global human resources market, and both its customers and independent analysts consider PeopleSoft the market leader.

PeopleSoft has flourished during an economic period that has seen others in its industry struggling. "In the worst global environment in 30 years, PeopleSoft continued to thrive," says Conway in the company's annual report. This success has been driven by PeopleSoft 8, a new generation of pure Internet applications that enable organizations to move their business processes to the Internet. These processes can be extended directly to customers, suppliers, partners, and employees anywhere in the world, anytime. "The result," says Conway, "is a real-time enterprise with significantly lower costs and higher productivity."

London Drugs exemplifies how PeopleSoft's solutions can positively impact organizational performance. Retail is a fast-paced industry that operates on extremely low margins. Clint Mahlman, London Drugs' Vice President of HR and Distribution, states, "Because of the pace of the retail business, your employees need information that is extremely timely and quick to enable them to make business decisions faster, with deeper information than your competitors have. PeopleSoft operates with the integrity we've come to expect from our partners—they deliver, and their solutions enable us to be one step above our competitors and remain strong and number one in so many categories of our industry."

London Drugs has built a reputation that their employees have greater depth of knowledge than other retailers. In addition, PeopleSoft HRMS helps London Drugs maintain lower employee turnover than other Canadian retailers. Mahlman says, "We need our frontline people to get training in a very cost-effective, immediate way. PeopleSoft's Internet-based technologies are enabling us to meet needs like this far faster than we could before."

SOURCE: From W. Fodie, "People and Results: PeopleSoft's Technology and Features Gives Its Customers the Competitive Edge," *B.C. Business Magazine*, July 2003. Reprinted with permission.

being done by people so that the people can have time available to work on strategic activities. Consequently, the use of technology can both make HR more strategic and by doing so increase the value that HR adds to the business.[25] As indicated in Figure 16.9, outsourcing of many of these activities provided one mechanism for reducing this burden. However, more relevant today is the focus on the use of information technology to handle these tasks. Early on this was achieved by the development and implementation of information systems that were run by the HRM function but more recently have evolved into systems that allow employees to serve themselves. Thus, for example, employees can access the system and make their benefit enrollment, changes, or claims online. Clearly, technology has freed HRM functions from transactional activities to focus on more strategic actions. The "Competing through Tech-

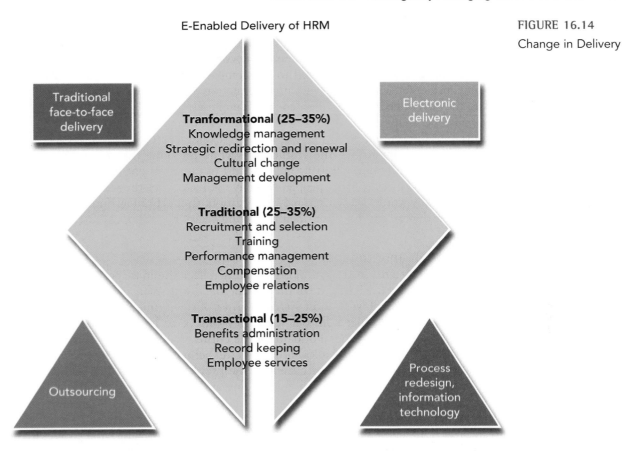

E-Enabled Delivery of HRM

FIGURE 16.14

Change in Delivery

nology" box describes how PeopleSoft, an HR software provider, has helped one company to be more effective.

However, the speed requirements of e-business force HRM functions to explore how to leverage technology for the delivery of traditional and transformational HRM activities. This does not imply that over time all of HRM will be executed over the Web, but that a number of HRM activities currently delivered via paper or face-to-face communications can be moved to the Web with no loss (and even gains) in effectiveness and efficiency. This is illustrated by Figure 16.14. We explore some examples next.

Recruitment and Selection

Traditional recruitment and selection processes have required considerable face-to-face communications with recruitment firms and potential employees, labor-intensive assessment devices, and significant monitoring of managerial decisions to ensure that hiring patterns and decisions do not run afoul of regulatory requirements. However, technology has transformed these processes.

For example, online recruiting accounted for one of every eight hires last year, according to k-force.com's poll of 300 U.S. companies. IBM employees now fill out forms on the Web to identify contract help they need, and that information is immediately sent to 14 temp agencies. Within an hour agencies respond with résumés for review, allowing IBM to cut hiring time from 10 days to 3 and save $3 million per year.

In addition, firms such as Q-Hire in Austin, Texas, provide online testing services. Applicants for positions at a firm are directed to a website where they complete an assessment device. Their scores are immediately compared to an ideal profile, and this profile comparison is communicated to the company screening manager. Firms can gather considerable amounts of relevant information about potential employees long before they ever need to set foot on company premises.

Finally, technology has enabled firms to monitor hiring processes to minimize the potential for discriminatory hiring decisions. For example, Home Depot was accused of forcing female applicants into cashier jobs while reserving the customer service jobs for males. While not admitting guilt, as part of their consent decree Home Depot uses technology to identify people who have skills for jobs they are not applying for based on key words in their résumés. In addition, the technology forces managers to interview diverse candidate sets before making decisions.

Compensation and Rewards

Compensation systems in organizations probably reflect the most pervasive form of bureaucracy within HRM. In spite of the critical role they play in attracting, motivating, and retaining employees, most systems consist of rigid, time-consuming, and ineffective processes. Managers fill out what they believe to be useless forms, ignore guidelines, and display a general disdain for the entire process.

Leveraging technology may allow firms to better achieve their compensation goals with considerably less effort. For example, one problem many merit or bonus pay plans face is that managers refuse to differentiate among performers, giving everyone similar pay increases. This allows them to spend less time thinking about how to manage (rate and review) performance as well as minimizes the potential conflict they might face. Thus employees do not see linkages between performance and pay, resulting in lower motivation among all employees and higher turnover among top performers (and possibly lower turnover among bottom performers). To minimize this, Cypress Semiconductors requires managers to distinguish between equity and merit and forces distributions with regard to both concepts.[26] For example, equity means that the top-ranked performer in any group of peers should make 50 percent more than the lowest-ranked performer, and people with comparable performance should receive comparable salaries. With regard to merit, there must be at least a 7 percent spread between the lowest and highest pay raises (if the lowest raise is 3 percent, then the highest must be at least 10 percent). If ratings and raises are input into a system, the firm can monitor and control the rating process to ensure that adequate differentiations are made consistent with the policy.

Training and Development

Exploring different vehicles for delivering training (PC, video, and the like) certainly is not a new concept. In addition, a number of firms have begun delivering training via the Web. Their experience suggests that some types of training can be done effectively via the Internet or an intranet, whereas others might not. For example, companies such as IBM and Dell both boast that they have developed Internet-based training for some parts of their workforce.

Interestingly, the challenge of speedy delivery of HRM services brings the concept of Internet-based training to the forefront. In today's competitive environment, firms compete to attract and retain both customers and talented employees. How well a firm develops and treats existing employees largely determines how well it achieves these outcomes. Yet the challenges of speed, project focus, and changing technology create environments that discourage managers from managing their people, resulting in a situation where employees may not feel respected or valued.

This presents a challenge to firms to provide both the incentive and the skills for managers to treat employees as assets rather than commodities. Consider how Internet-based training might facilitate this. Assume that you work for Widget.com, a fast-growing, fast-paced e-business. You arrive at work Monday morning, and your e-mail contains a high-priority message with either an attachment or a link to a URL. It is your Monday morning challenge from the CEO, and you know that the system will track whether you link and complete this challenge. When you link to it, you see a digital video of your CEO telling you how people are Widget.com's competitive advantage, and that when they don't feel valued, they leave. Thus his challenge to you is to make your employees feel valued today. To do so, you will in the next 10 minutes learn how to express appreciation to an employee. You receive six learning points; you observe a digitized video model performing the learning points; you review the learning points again and take a quiz. You then see the CEO giving you the final challenge: that in the next 15 minutes you are to take one of your employees aside and express your appreciation using the skill you just developed.

Notice the advantages of this process. First, it was not time-consuming like most three-day or one-week training programs. The entire process (training and demonstration with a real employee) took less than 30 minutes; you have developed a skill; and an employee now probably feels better about the organization. It communicated a real organizational value or necessary competency. It didn't require any travel expenses to a training facility. It did not overwhelm you with so much information that you would be lucky to remember 10 percent of what you were exposed to. Finally, it was a push, rather than pull, approach to training. The firm did not wait for you to realize you had a deficiency and then go search and sign up for training. It pushed the training to you.

Thus technology allows firms to deliver training and development for at least some skills or knowledge faster, more efficiently, and probably more effectively. It can quickly merge training, communication, and immediate response to strategic contingencies.

Finding and Keeping the Best Employees

Creating and nurturing a committed workforce presents a tremendous challenge to firms today. According to a recent survey conducted by Monster.com, 61 percent of Americans consider themselves overworked and 86 percent are not satisfied with their jobs. Such findings suggest that firms need to find ways to monitor commitment levels, identify potential obstacles to commitment, and respond quickly to eliminate those obstacles. In large part, attitude surveys have constituted the platform from which these activities were managed in the past.

Consider the traditional attitude survey. Surveys are administered to employees over a period of four to six weeks. The data are entered and analyzed, requiring another six to eight weeks. A group interprets the results to identify the major problem areas, and task forces are formed to develop recommendations; this process easily takes another four to six months. Finally, decisions must be made about implementing the task force recommendations. In the end, at best employees might see responses to their concerns 12 to 18 months after the survey—and then the survey administrators cannot understand why employees think that completing the survey is a waste of time.

Now consider how technology can shorten that cycle. E-pulse represents one attempt to create a platform for almost real-time attitude surveys. Developed by Theresa Welbourne at the University of Michigan, E-pulse is a scalable survey device administered online. Normally three questions are asked regarding how employees feel about work, but more questions can be added to get feedback on any specific issue. The survey goes out online, and when employees complete it, the data are immediately entered and analyzed. In essence, the part of the process that took four months in the past has been reduced to a day.

Next the firm can decide how it wants to use the information. For example, it could be broken down by business, site, or work unit, with the relevant information going to the leader of the chosen unit of analysis. In essence, a supervisor could receive almost immediate feedback about the attitudes of his or her work group, or a general manager about his or her business unit. The supervisor or manager can respond immediately, even if only to communicate that she or he realizes a problem exists and will take action soon.

One must recognize that although the technology provides for faster HRM, only a more systemic approach will ensure better and smarter HRM. For example, disseminating the information to the supervisors and managers may be faster, but unless those individuals possess good problem-solving and communication skills, they may either ignore the information or, worse yet, exacerbate the problem with inappropriate responses. As we noted with regard to training, this systemic approach requires knocking down traditional functional walls to deliver organizational solutions rather than functional programs. Thus the challenge is to get beyond viewing the technology as a panacea or even as a functional tool, but rather as a catalyst for transforming the HRM organization.

The Future for HR Professionals

The future for careers in the Human Resource profession seems brighter than ever. An increasing number of successful companies such as Microsoft have made the top HR job a member of the senior management team and a direct report to the Chief Executive Officer. CEOs recognize the importance of their workforce in driving competitive success. Firms need to seek the balance between attracting, motivating, and retaining the very best talent and keeping labor and administrative costs as low as possible. Finding such a balance requires HR leaders who have a deep knowledge of the business combined with a deep knowledge of HR issues, tools, processes, and technologies.

Such talented HR leaders are in high demand as evidenced by their compensation packages. For instance, Table 16.6 displays the compensation packages for the top paid HR professional at publicly traded companies. Heading this list is Dennis Donovan of Home Depot. When Bob Nardelli took over as the CEO at Home Depot, one of his first actions was to find the best HR leader he knew, and he chose Donovan, with whom he had worked at General Electric's Power Systems division. He knew that in order to drive the change necessary to align Home Depot's talented workforce he needed a professional HR organization led by a strong, business-oriented Senior VP of HR. Nardelli and Donovan have successfully transformed Home Depot into a successful retailing and services business that is the largest of its kind. Says Nardelli of his HR partner: "Dennis is a partner and a confidant. He's brought credibility and respect to a function that was in total disarray. His personal energy, his ability to energize others, and the professionalism by which he packages and gets acceptance of his ideas has been a credit to us in making this transformation."[28]

TABLE 16.6

Top-Paid HR Executives at Publicly Traded Companies

RANK	COMPANY NAME	NAME	TITLE	TOTAL COMPENSATION*	SALARY	BONUS	COMPANY ANNUAL REVENUES†
1	Home Depot Inc.	Dennis M. Donovan	exec. v.p., HR	$6,004,738	$579,808	$ 420,000	$58,247,000
2	Cigna Corp.	Donald M. Levinson	exec. v.p., HR & services	5,638,499	571,000	350,000	19,348,000
3	Capital One Financial Corp.	Dennis H. Liberson	exec. v.p., HR	4,330,152	345,000	500,035	4,180,766
4	Quantum Corp.	Jerald L. Maurer	exec., v.p., HR	4,293,733	461,105	84,443	1,087,792
5	Viacom Inc.	William A. Roskinsr.	v.p., HR & admin.	4,208,590	960,000	1,000,000	24,606,000
6	Continental Airlines Inc.	Michael H. Campbell	sr. v.p., HR and labor rel.	3,456,404	474,300	290,625	8,402,000
7	SPX Corp.	Robert B. Foreman	v.p., HR	3,421,821	400,000	711,678	5,045,800
8	ConAgra Foods Inc.	Owen C. Johnson	exec., v.p., HR & admin.	3,178,195	444,353	567,725	27,630,000
9	Bisys Group Inc.	Mark J. Rybarczyk	exec. v.p., HR	2,982,407	285,192	245,000	865,705
10	Textron Inc.	John D. Butler	exec. v.p., admin. & chief HR officer	2,844,226	460,000	350,000	10,658,000
11	Delta Air Lines Inc.	Robert L. Colman	exec. v.p., HR	2,780,705	440,000	542,850	13,305,000
12	Federated Department Stores Inc.	Thomas G. Cody	vice chair, legal, HR, internal audit & external affairs	2,509,820	730,000	388,500	15,435,000
13	Sara Lee Corp.	Lee A. Chaden	sr. v.p.	2,443,522	460,000	605,924	17,628,000
14	Symantec Corp.	Rebecca Ranninger	sr. v.p., HR	2,426,216	245,000	117,141	1,071,438
15	American Standard Cos. Inc.	Lawrence B. Costello	sr. v.p., HR	2,373,891	364,724	215,000	7,795,400
16	Toys "R" Us Inc.	Michael D'Ambrose	exec. v.p., HR	2,257,658	620,832	375,120	11,305,000
17	McDonald's Corp.	Stanley R. Stein	corp. exec. v.p., HR	2,173,262	520,000	299,844	15,406,000
18	Knight Ridder Inc.	Mary Jean Connors	sr. v.p., HR	2,156,069	535,000	326,203	2,841,594
19	Agco Corp.	Norman L. Boyd	sr. v.p., HR	1,918,154	252,888	128,720	2,922,700
20	Men's Wearhouse Inc.	Charles Bresler	exec. v.p., stores, mktg. & human development	1,914,530	330,000	40,000	1,295,049

* Total compensation is the sum of salary, bonus, total value of options granted, restricted stock, and LTIP payouts.

† Thousands of dollars.

SOURCE: From HR's Elite, *Human Resource Executive*, October 2, 2003, p. 54. Reprinted with permission of *Human Resource Executive*. Copyright © 2005. All rights reserved.

A Look Back

The chapter's opening story described SYSCO's market-driven HR operating model. How does this model play out in real life? It illustrates the analytical approach that HR functions require and highlights the analytical/quantitative skills and perspective that HR professionals need today.

Because SYSCO's HR function cannot impose programs on any business unit, they have to rely on persuasion to get things done. This requires (a) that HR understands the business well enough to be viewed as credible and (b) HR can demonstrate the value of what they offer. For instance, when Ken Carrig wanted to encourage business units to focus attention on employee climate as an important driver of success, he first went to the businesses with an offer to conduct a climate survey at a tremendously discounted cost. In the first year, about 54 percent of the business units paid a nominal fee to conduct the survey in their organizations. Ken and his team then statistically related the climate scores for each business with a number of performance measures such as workers' compensation costs, quality measures, customer satisfaction, and profits. Such data provided business leaders with the business case for building their employee climate. However, the question then came up: How? Ken's team studied the successful companies (those that had both high climate and high performance) and tried to learn how these companies managed their workforces. Out of these studies came ideas for reducing turnover among warehouse employees (resulting in a yearly cost savings of $15 million) and workers' compensation costs (in 2004 SYSCO's workers' compensation costs are at a level with what they were in 1999, when the company employed half as many workers).

Finally, he and his team created a knowledge management website to enable companies to benchmark themselves against their internal colleagues, and learn from them. Business leaders can track their performance on a number of operational, customer, financial, and human capital metrics and compare themselves to other units. If their performance is lacking on certain metrics, the system will help them identify the top performing companies on those metrics, provide information on the programs and policies that those superior companies use, and enable the user to contact the leaders at those companies to ask for help.

While SYSCO's market-driven approach is not readily transferable or even applicable to all companies, it does provide a set of basic principles that enable an HR function to more strategically manage itself as a business.

Questions

1. Do you think that SYSCO's approach to HR is a model for future HR functions? Why or why not?
2. In what ways does SYSCO's approach to HR model a business-driven approach?
3. How is SYSCO's approach to HR different from the approaches taken by HR functions that you have worked for or know of?

Summary

The roles required of the HRM function have changed as people have become recognized as a true source of competitive advantage. This has required a transformation of the HRM function from focusing solely on transactional activities to an increasing involvement in strategic activities. In fact, according to a recent study, 64 percent of HR executives said that their HRM function is in a process of transformation.[29] The strategic management of the HRM function will determine whether HRM will transform itself to a true strategic partner or simply be blown up.

In this chapter we have explored the various changing roles of the HRM function. HRM today must play roles as an administrative expert, employee advocate, change agent, and strategic partner. The function must also deliver transactional, traditional, and transformational services and activities to the firm, and it must be both effi-cient and effective. HR executives must strategically manage the HRM function just as the firm must be strategically managed. This requires that HRM develop measures of the function's performance through customer surveys and analytical methods. These measures can form the basis for planning ways to improve performance. HRM performance can increase through new structures for the function, through using reengineering and information technology, and through outsourcing.

Discussion Questions

1. Why have the roles and activities of the HRM function changed over the past 20 to 30 years? What has been driving this change? How effectively do you think HRM has responded?
2. How can the processes for strategic management discussed in Chapter 2 be transplanted to manage the HRM function?
3. Why do you think that few companies take the time to determine the effectiveness of HRM practices? Should a company be concerned about evaluating HRM practices? Why? What might people working in the HRM function gain by evaluating the function?
4. How might imaging technology be useful for recruitment? For training? For benefits administration? For performance management?
5. Employees in your company currently choose and enroll in benefits programs after reading communications brochures, completing enrollment forms, and sending them to their HR rep. A temporary staff has to be hired to process the large amount of paperwork that is generated. Enrollment forms need to be checked, sorted, batched, sent to data entry, keypunched, returned, and filed. The process is slow and prone to errors. How could you use process reengineering to make benefit enrollment more efficient and effective?
6. Some argue that outsourcing an activity is bad because the activity is no longer a means of distinguishing the firm from competitors. (All competitors can buy the same service from the same provider, so it cannot be a source of competitive advantage.) Is this true? If so, why would a firm outsource any activity?

Self-Assessment Exercise

How ethical are you? Read each of the following descriptions. For each, circle whether you believe the behavior described is ethical or unethical.

1. A company president found that a competitor had made an important scientific discovery that would sharply reduce the profits of his own company. The president hired a key employee of the competitor in an attempt to learn the details of the discovery.   Ethical   Unethical

2. To increase profits, a general manager used a production process that exceeded legal limits for environmental pollution.   Ethical   Unethical

3. Because of pressure from her brokerage firm, a stockbroker recommended a type of bond that she did not consider to be a good investment.   Ethical   Unethical

4. A small business received one-fourth of its revenues in the form of cash. On the company's income tax forms, the owner reported only one-half of the cash receipts.   Ethical   Unethical

5. A corporate executive promoted a loyal friend and competent manager to the position of divisional vice president in preference to a better qualified manager with whom she had no close ties.   Ethical   Unethical

6. An employer received applications for a supervisor's position from two equally qualified applicants. The employer hired the male applicant because he thought some employees might resent being supervised by a female.   Ethical   Unethical

7. An engineer discovered what he perceived to be a product design flaw that constituted a safety hazard. His company declined to correct the flaw. The engineer decided to keep quiet, rather than taking his complaint outside the company.   Ethical   Unethical

8. A comptroller selected a legal method of financial reporting that concealed some embarrassing financial facts. Otherwise, those facts would have been public knowledge.

Ethical
Unethical

9. A company paid a $350,000 "consulting" fee to an official of a foreign country. In return, the official promised to help the company obtain a contract that should produce a $10 million profit for the company.

Ethical
Unethical

10. A member of a corporation's board of directors learned that his company intended to announce a stock split and increase its dividend. On the basis of this favorable information, the director bought additional shares of the company's stock. Following the announcement of the information, he sold the stock at a gain.

Ethical
Unethical

Now score your results. How many actions did you judge to be unethical?

All of these actions are unethical. The more of the actions you judged to be unethical, the better your understanding of ethical business behavior.

SOURCE: Based on S. Morris et al., "A Test of Environmental, Situational, and Personal Influences on the Ethical Intentions of CEOs," *Business and Society* 34 (1995), pp. 119–47.

Manager's Hot Seat Exercise: Change: More Pain than Gain?

This Manager's Hot Seat case looks at the consequences organizations can experience when attempting to merge together. This transformational process can generate severe resistance to change within the remaining employees. New policies, procedures, and work methodologies can instill many feelings within these workers. Their feelings can run the gamut from fear to isolation to worthlessness.

The video depicts the vital role managers have during such times. It indicates how important effective communication is during these types of organizational changes. It also demonstrates how willingness to share information on what new changes employees can expect is paramount in ensuring a successful merger with the new organization.

Individual Activity
You have been a department supervisor at your place of employment for seven years. You have utilized every approach you could to do a "perfect" job for the employer because you simply value and love your job very much. Your current position provides you with much flexible time and leeway in making work-related decisions.

Prepare a brief report of how you would feel if your current employer informed you that in two days the company was being sold out to another organization—concluding the organization's five-month strategic plan. You had no

knowledge of this possibility! You are told your salary and position would remain the same, but you would have a new co-supervisor who is a key member of the new organization. This supervisor is to instruct you in the new organization's methodologies. You are told to "not worry" and that things *should* remain very similar to what you have been experiencing. However, the words do not ring true to your ears and you are filled with doubts and unanswered questions. Think about this dilemma before you begin to write! Be exact about the impact (both professionally and personally) this change would likely have on you.

Group Activity
Students should break into groups of four. Conduct an open group discussion, with each group member reading aloud the individual impacts such changes described above would create. Identify similar feelings that are found among the members, if any. Discuss how the company could have handled the situation more effectively. Discuss the importance of open communication lines. Identify how this uncertainty/insecurity could impact the new working environment. Describe organizational advantages of alleviating employee resistance to change. Identify ways the human resource department can assist employees' acceptance of and adaptability to the new culture.

Exercising Strategy: Transforming the Business and HR at Xerox

In the opening example of Chapter 1, we presented the story of Xerox, and how people have become a strategic asset. We also discussed some of the ways that HR influenced Xerox's turnaround. Having been through this book now, let us focus on the HR function at Xerox and explore more specifically how this function has contributed.

In 1958, Xerox launched the Xerox 914, the first automatic, plain-paper office copier. This product went on to

become the top-selling industrial product of all time. Xerox's successful xerography technology gave it a sustainable competitive advantage that endured for years. However, all good things must come to an end, and in Xerox's case, that end was the late 1990s. By 2000, Xerox experienced its biggest slide in history, and the consensus among analysts within the industry was that Xerox was working with "an unsustainable business model," meaning unless things changed drastically, Xerox would soon cease to exist. In 2000 Xerox had $17.1 billion in debt, with only $154 million in cash on hand. By 2001, Xerox's stock, which had peaked at $63, fell to about $4—a loss of 90 percent of its market capitalization. And as if that was not enough, it also faced an accounting investigation by the Securities and Exchange Commission for how it accounted for its customer leases on copiers.

Enter new VP of HR Pat Nazemetz in 1999 and new CEO Anne Mulcahy in 2000 to try to right a sinking ship. Mulcahy put the company on a starvation diet. This entailed selling major operations in China and Hong Kong, reducing global headcount to 61,100 from 91,500 through selloffs, early retirements, and layoffs, and implementing drastic cost controls. While Mulcahy's strategy has brought Xerox back to life (2003 saw Xerox triple its net income to $360 million) as an organization, the HR function had to drive the change in the business while simultaneously transforming the function.

While many HR functions look to outsource, Xerox transformed its HR function largely internally. According to Nazemetz, outsourcing providers say " 'Let us in, let us take over your HR function and we can take 10 percent to 30 percent out of your cost base.' We began trimming down, finding synergies and opportunities to get more efficient. We found the savings ourselves."

The largest single savings came from consolidating and expanding the HR Service Center. The Center began with purely transactional work (e.g., address changes), then added Web-based processes to handle routine work. The Center now conducts research and analysis to HR operations and handles employee-relations issues. This has enabled HR to reduce headcount without reducing levels of service.

Also, as with any organization that has shed 30 percent of its workforce, employee morale was and continues to be an issue. Even before the fall, HR had been taking the pulse of employees through their "hearts and minds" surveys. This intranet-based survey taps into a number of employee attitudes and seeks to identify the problem areas for HR and line executives to focus on. Employees have noted concerns with items like "Company supports risk-taking," "Company considers impact on employees," "Senior-management behavior is consistent with words," and "Trust level is high."

"People often ask me how Xerox has found success" says Mulcahy. "My answer is that you have to have a strategy and a plan, but [more importantly], what you really need is excellence of execution, and that starts and ends with a talented, motivated group of people aligned around a common set of goals. Our HR people came through with a series of alignment workshops and retention incentives just when we needed them [to] make Xerox the stronger, better company it is today."

Questions

1. After having gone through the massive downsizing, morale obviously has presented challenges. While Xerox employees seem to understand the need for change (minds), they may not emotionally embrace it (hearts). How can Xerox gain both "hearts" and "minds"?

2. Xerox's HR function focuses on three initiatives: (*a*) employee value proposition (what can employees expect from the company, and what can the company expect from employees?), (*b*) performance culture (how can the company develop a culture that encourage continuous improvement and high performance from all employees?), and (*c*) "three exceptional candidates" (how can HR deliver a pipeline of three-deep bench talent for every position within the organization?). From everything you have learned, how might Xerox address each of these issues?

Managing People: From the Pages of *BusinessWeek*

BusinessWeek ## Gap: Missing That Ol' Mickey Magic

Bad Fashion Calls and an Exodus of Execs Have Mickey Drexler's Retail Empire Hurting

For most of us, polo shirts peaked in popularity back in the mid-1990s. But somehow, fashion guru Millard S. "Mickey" Drexler became captivated by them last year. The chief executive of Gap Inc. insisted that his Gap-brand stores carry deep inventories in an unusually wide palette of colors. Gap merchandising managers, unable to dissuade him from the idea, produced data suggesting that three or four colors account for the vast majority of sales. But Drexler was adamant, saying he didn't want to miss a sale to an XXL customer who wanted the shirt in purple. While Gap defends the plan as having "brought fashion to a basic item," the offbeat colors bombed. Stores wound up with mounds of marked-down polo shirts.

Call it another losing bet for Mickey Drexler. Long hailed as the merchant king whose inspired wager on khaki pants ignited a huge growth spurt in the late 1990s, Drexler recently has been on a ruinous losing streak. Gap's once-reliable growth engine has seized up: sales at stores open at least a year plummeted by 17 percent in both August and September. As Drexler acknowledges, each of the company's three core brands—Gap, Banana Republic, and Old Navy—has come untethered from the tight rapport with consumers that accounted for its earlier prosperity. Aggravating those tensions are the CEO's dogged insistence on adding new stores while trying to fix the fundamentals, plus management turnover, in particular last year's exodus of some seasoned executives who knew when to rein in Drexler's impulses.

Now, many analysts and investors, who long trusted that Drexler, 57, would once again pull a rabbit out of his hat as he did during a downturn in the mid-1990s, fear that he has lost his magic. Even in a tough retail environment, Gap's declining same-store sales are worse than those of its peers, having fallen 11 percent so far this year after declining 5 percent in 2000. In contrast, Abercrombie & Fitch Co.'s are down 7 percent, while American Eagle Outfitters Inc.'s are up 4.4 percent. Emme P. Kozloff, an analyst at Sanford C. Bernstein & Co., expects Gap to lose $216.6 million in the third quarter, including a charge of $140 million to $150 million related to an adjustment in tax rates. That follows five consecutive quarters of declining profits. Says Kozloff, "The Street has relied way too much on the 'Mickey will fix it' idea. It's amazing that people give him the benefit of the doubt." Increasingly, however, they don't: Gap's shares are trading around $14, down from $35 in May and slightly more than one-quarter of their high in February 2000.

While some observers figure the nation's more sober mood could spur a shift from rhinestone-encrusted jeans and other novelties to more tried-and-true styles, Gap won't necessarily benefit. Its customers have been fleeing to discounters, such as Kohl's and Target, and youth-oriented chains, such as American Eagle, that offer similar goods. "Somewhere along the line, Gap just lost it," says New York retail consultant Wendy Liebmann.

Drexler scoffs at that and refuses to concede that he doesn't get it anymore. "I'm absolutely still in touch, talking to customers every day, looking at product every day, involved in the creative processes," he says. And so far, Gap board members and the company's founding Fisher family continue to express full support. "I don't know of a merchant better than Mickey," says director Adrian D. P. Bellamy, chairman of Gucci Group. "He's going through a difficult time, but I believe Mickey will lead the company to better days ahead." Board member and Apple Computer Inc. CEO Steven P. Jobs insists there's no talk of replacing Drexler: "The question's not even in the ballpark."

But talk to some of the legions of executives who have left Gap over the past couple of years and you get a different assessment. *BusinessWeek* spoke to 10 former executives, none of whom would be identified, who painted a disturbing picture of a manager whose short attention span and impulsive flip-flopping has cost the company dearly in both dollars and strategic detours. Drexler's erratic style arguably didn't matter so much during the flush times, when Gap could afford the inefficiency and waste

that sudden changes of heart create. Besides, his guesses were more often right than wrong. Old Navy, launched in 1994, soared to $1 billion in sales in only five years on the strength of low-cost, whimsical fashions aimed at teens and their parents.

Former execs say Drexler still insists, though, on running the chain in a hands-on style and relying to an alarming degree on gut decisions. Critics contend that the company "is too big to be run by an entrepreneurial, possessed genius," as one alumnus puts it. It hasn't been unusual for Drexler to approve, say, gingham-check skirts for the Gap chain only to cool on them once they arrive from the factory, says a former manager. The skirts were shipped to Gap's outlet stores, forcing the regular stores to overemphasize core denim styles to fill the void. "When you see the denim stretched out in the store and think it sure looks kind of basic, it means Mickey fell out of love with something," the exec says. . . . "He'll pull the plug on things," says the former exec. "It's part of his emotional style." Gap dismisses such complaints, saying such changes are "part of the normal give and take of the business."

Concrete Floors?   Some of the flip-flops have strained relations not just among Drexler's staff but also with external partners whose goodwill Gap needs to cultivate. Drexler created an internal uproar last summer when he greenlighted a change in design for new Gap stores without making sure that company real estate specialists assigned to negotiate with mall developers had been informed. The real estate team then had to go back to developers to persuade them to accept the new design, which uses concrete floors and open ceilings rather than the maple floors and finished ceilings that had been promised. . . .

Of course, creative types often have disruptive personalities. Board member Jobs, no stranger to an impulsive management style, defends Drexler—who sits on Apple's board—on those grounds. "I think Mickey Drexler is a creative person," Jobs says. "As a creative person, he's not a robot—he's a human being with moods. When he sees something he doesn't like, he says so." Drexler sees that as a requirement in an ever-changing industry. "I do like to introduce newness at the edges of the business all the time," he says. "That might be read as mercurial or inconsistent, but you can't get the new ideas without challenging current ideas."

To be sure, some of Drexler's staff find his style motivating. "Creative people really like working with him because he's emotional, passionate," says Amy Schoening, senior vice president and chief marketing officer at Gap. She recalls Drexler's insistence two years ago that Banana Republic cast some older people in its catalog, over the objections of Schoening and her staff. Now, she concedes the "inclusive" move generated goodwill among those older customers. Dennis Connors, who left his post as Gap's chief information officer in 1999, adds, "People who blame Mickey, they have to grow up. It's a fast-paced company. The cycle times for fashion are getting shorter and shorter."

Reaching Out Problem is, in the past, there were plenty of veteran managers and staffers around who could talk Drexler out of going too far out on a limb. Today many of those veterans have left the company. Of the 23 corporate and divisional officers named in Gap's 1999 annual report, 8 have departed for various reasons, including 4 of the 5 officers in the Gap division. True, Drexler gets good marks for some of his replacements. That's particularly the case with nine-year board member John M. Lillie, who was put on the payroll in January as vice chairman and assigned to such crucial matters as manufacturing and distribution systems and cost-cutting, none of them Drexler's forte. . . .

Still, it may take a while for the new execs to decode Drexler—to "lip-read" him, as company insiders say. An edict to order 50,000 more shirts might be meant literally, or it could just be a metaphor for taking risks. "You have to figure out when he's serious and when he's emotionally going off," explains a former Gap exec. Meanwhile, staffers often end up playing guessing games in which they debate what they think the CEO wants, says another former manager. And with some of the newcomers arriving from very different corporate cultures, the learning curve may be steep. "They all could potentially have what it takes to run their businesses, but do they have experience in their positions? No," says Karen Hiatt, an analyst at Gap shareholder Dresdner RCM Global Investors.

With all three chains facing big problems, there's no time to waste. . . . The biggest problem, though, is at the core Gap chain, which in its peak years appealed to everyone from teens to baby boomers with its huge selection of khakis and wearable tops. Drexler took a serious wrong turn in 1999, pushing Gap into fashions that were too young-looking for its clientele. Today, he has gotten rid of the oodles of pink capri pants and cargo pants in favor of items with broader appeal that he hopes reflect "casual style." But that emphasis still seems to span irreconcilable genres. Earlier this year, Drexler declared Gap's target market to be 20- to 30-year-olds who crave fashion. So for the fall season, he ditched much of Gap's basic-style merchandise and took a stab at offering trendier, more cutting-edge fashions, such as belted sweaters and super-dark denim jeans and handbags. That's a risky move that has Gap vying in apparel's most treacherous segment against more agile competitors, such as American Eagle, which can revamp its merchandise mix in half the time Gap needs to respond to shifting tastes. Gap's plummeting same-store sales this fall suggest that Drexler is off-base again.

With Lillie in place, Gap has finally committed to realistic cost-cutting. One of Lillie's more dramatic moves was a first-ever layoff of 1,040 employees in July. Yet Drexler continued to increase his store count by over 20 percent in both 1999 and 2000. He has backed off a bit on the pace of expansion—from 10 percent for next year, to 5 percent to 7 percent—but some analysts wonder why he's expanding at all. Drexler insists there's still opportunity to be tapped but admits he's evaluating 2002 leases that haven't already been signed.

Drexler's loyal supporters on the board say he's merely executing the strategy they set. "We all agreed to put the foot on the accelerator" for the massive expansion, says director Bellamy. But with Gap heading for what looks like a wreck of a year, more investors wonder if Drexler has both hands on the wheel.

SOURCE: *BusinessWeek Online* (November 9, 2001).

Questions

1. What are some of the HRM issues inherent in Gap's recent problems?
2. How would an effective strategic HRM function contribute to putting Gap back on track?

Notes

1. P. Wright, S. Snell, and P. Jacobsen, "Current Approaches to HR Strategies: Inside-Out vs. Outside-In," *Human Resource Planning* (in press).
2. A. S. Tsui and L. R. Gomez-Mejia, "Evaluating HR Effectiveness," in *Human Resource Management: Evolving Roles and Responsibilities*, ed. L. Dyer (Washington, DC: Bureau of National Affairs, 1988), pp. 1-187–1-227.
3. D. Ulrich, "Measuring Human Resources: An Overview of Practice and a Prescription for Results," *Human Resource Management* 36, no. 3 (1997), pp. 303–20.
4. P. Wright, G. McMahan, S. Snell, and B. Gerhart, "Comparing Line and HR Executives' Perceptions of HR Effectiveness: Services, Roles, and Contributions," CAHRS (Center for Advanced Human Resource Studies) working paper 98-29, School of ILR, Cornell University, Ithaca, NY.
5. J. C. Erfurt, A. Foote, and M. A. Heirich, "The Cost-Effectiveness of Worksite Wellness Programs," *Personnel Psychology* 15 (1992), p. 22.
6. P. Wright, G. McMahan, S. Snell, and B. Gerhart, *Strategic HRM: Building Human Capital and Organizational Capability*, Technical report. Cornell University, Ithaca, NY, 1998.
7. T. B. Kinni, "A Reengineering Primer," *Quality Digest*, January 1994, pp. 26–30; "Reengineering Is Helping Health of Hospitals and Its Patients," *Total Quality Newsletter*, February 1994, p. 5; R. Recardo, "Process Reengineering in a Finance Division," *Journal for Quality and Participation*, June 1994, pp. 70–73.

8. L. Quillen, "Human Resource Computerization: A Dollar and Cents Approach," *Personnel Journal*, July 1989, pp. 74–77.

9. S. Greengard, "New Technology Is HR's Route to Reengineering," *Personnel Journal*, July 1994, pp. 32c–32o.

10. R. Broderick and J. W. Boudreau, "Human Resource Management, Information Technology, and the Competitive Edge," *Academy of Management Executive* 6 (1992), pp. 7–17.

11. S. E. O'Connell, "New Technologies Bring New Tools, New Rules," *HRMagazine*, December 1995, pp. 43–48; S. F. O'Connell, "The Virtual Workplace Moves at Warp Speed," *HRMagazine*, March 1996, pp. 51–57.

12. E. Brynjolfsson and L. Hitt, "The Productivity Paradox of Information Technology," *Communications of the ACM*, December 1993, pp. 66–77.

13. "Seven Critical Success Factors for Using Information Technology," *Total Quality Newsletter*, February 1994, p. 6.

14. J. E. Rigdon, "Technological Gains Are Cutting Costs in Jobs and Services," *The Wall Street Journal* (February 24, 1995), pp. A1, A5, A6.

15. S. Greengard, "How Technology Is Advancing HR," *Personnel Journal*, September 1993, pp. 80–90.

16. T. L. Hunter, "How Client/Server Is Reshaping the HRIS," *Personnel Journal*, July 1992, pp. 38–46; B. Busbin, "The Hidden Costs of Client/Server," *The Review*, August–September 1995, pp. 21–24.

17. D. Drechsel, "Principles for Client/Server Success," *The Review*, August–September 1995, pp. 26–29.

18. A. L. Lederer, "Emerging Technology and the Buy–Wait Dilemma: Sorting Fact from Fantasy," *The Review*, June–July 1993, pp. 16–19.

19. D. L. Fowler, "Imaging in HR: A Case Study," *The Review*, October–November 1994, pp. 29–33.

20. "Dial a Job Interview," *Chain Store Age Executive*, July 1994, pp. 35–36.

21. P. A. Galagan, "Think Performance: A Conversation with Gloria Gery," *Training and Development*, March 1994, pp. 47–51.

22. J. Clark and R. Koonce, "Meetings Go High-Tech," *Training and Development*, November 1995, pp. 32–38; A. M. Townsend, M. E. Whitman, and A. R. Hendrickson, "Computer Support Adds Power to Group Processes," *HRMagazine*, September 1995, pp. 87–91.

23. T. A. Stewart, "Getting Real about Brainpower," *Fortune* (November 27), 1994, pp. 201–3.

24. B. Ziegler, "Internet Software Poses Big Threat to Notes, IBM's Stake in Lotus," *The Wall Street Journal* (November 7, 1995), pp. A1, A8.

25. S. Shrivastava and J. Shaw, "Liberating HR through Technology," *Human Resource Management* 42(3) (2003), pp. 201–17.

26. C. O'Reilly and P. Caldwell, *Cypress Semiconductor (A): Vision, Values, and Killer Software* (Stanford University Case Study, HR-8A, 1998).

27. "61 Percent of Americans Consider Themselves Overworked and 86 Percent Are Not Satisfied with Their Job, According to Monster's 2004 Work/Life Balance Survey," *Business Wire* (August 3, 2004).

28. A. McIlvane, "Retooling HR," *HR Executive* (October 2, 2003), pp. 1, 18–26.

29. S. Csoka and B. Hackett, *Transforming the HR Function for Global Business Success*, Report 1209-19RR, New York: The Conference Board, 1998.

When you were a child you were probably asked that age-old question, "What do you want to be when you grow up?" Your response might have been a movie star, professional athlete, or even President of the United States. Today, as you face the challenge of college, you may still dream of those glamour jobs even though they seem a bit more remote than they did as a youngster. As a college student, you realize it's time to start taking that question more seriously. A goal of this video series and your textbook is to help you answer this longstanding question.

Christopher Jones of HotJobs.com says that a career is really a patchwork of jobs. Today, college graduates are likely to experience many different jobs that may lead to several different careers. This is a major change from your grandparents' days when a person generally stayed with a particular job or company for their entire work career. Because of such changes, each video in this series asks the businesspeople interviewed two specific questions:

1. How did you get to where you are today?
2. What advice do you have for college students?

This opening video reveals the answers of the businesspeople you will meet in the later videos. For example, Christopher Jones suggests diligence and the ability to accept rejection as needed traits in finding the right career. Garrett Boone, cofounder of The Container Store, is a true believer in passion and patience. He stresses a very long-term perspective in searching for the right career. He also advises job seekers that attention to detail is critical in the competitive job market of the 21st century. Matt Hoffman of Hoffman Sports Association and Todd McFarlane of the McFarlane companies are two entrepreneurs you will meet in the videos who personify these characteristics.

There is no better time to learn to act like a businessperson than the present. Learning the positive business behaviors suggested in the videos will go a long way in preparing you for your career search. For example, practicing good "netiquette" will help you send an e-mail to recruiters that may get answered. Posting a résumé that is carefully constructed and proofread may get employers to come to you. Your résumé, remember, is really your calling card. Networking, both online and offline, is also an effective way of finding the right job. Companies such as HotJobs.com strongly encourage networking and offer assistance to job seekers and employers looking to find the right match.

Success in your career is often related to the satisfaction and enjoyment you get from your job. Elizabeth Bryant from Southwest Airlines and Sharon Larking of Abbott Laboratories attest to this fact in videos profiling their companies. Being prepared to change jobs and careers also helps keep you fresh and enthusiastic. Scott Ross of Digital Domain left a secure job to follow his dream. As you move on the path toward determining your career, perhaps the best advice to follow was offered over 2,500 years ago by the Chinese philosopher Confucius who said, "Choose a job you love, and you will never have to work a day in your life." Enjoy the video series and good career hunting!

THINKING IT OVER

1. Discuss the impact the Internet has had on job seekers just like you.
2. Have you ever utilized a resource such as HotJobs.com to post your résumé? Explain why or why not.
3. How have companies such as HotJobs.com affected the way in which companies are able to better manage their human resources?
4. Discuss how organizations that possess an effective human resource management department can be of benefit to you and your career path.

JetBlue Airways Founder and CEO David Neeleman Discusses the Launching of His New Airline

No one can say that being in the airline industry today is anything but tough. This industry has undergone vast changes since the September 11 tragedy occurred. Many airlines simply did not withstand these changes and either wound up filing for bankruptcy or closing their operations entirely.

However, JetBlue is determined to go forward in this struggling industry. Founded by David Neeleman, who is also the company's chief executive officer, this airline is preparing to meet its future challenges head on. David has been associated with three other airlines throughout his career. He is extremely optimistic about the potential for this, his latest endeavor—JetBlue.

Neeleman states that a lot of capital—about $130 million—has been raised to help get the airline off the ground. No pun intended! Eighty-two new planes have been purchased with plans for a new plane to be added to the fleet every five weeks for the first several years. The company's low fares and extra passenger comforts, like wider leather seats and live Direct TV in flight, are certain to help take JetBlue to the top.

JetBlue's airfares are set to range from $79 to $159. The airline will start out flying to and from Buffalo and Fort Lauderdale from New York and will reach 30 cities within the next three years. While he states that all the amenities offered by the airline are nice, Neeleman believes that the people associated with the company are what will seal its success within the industry.

THINKING IT OVER

1. Discuss how David Neeleman is planning to implement his strategic plan for JetBlue.
2. Discuss the strategic value Neeleman is placing on his employees. Do you agree with him? Explain why or why not.
3. Identify the difference between strategy formulation and strategy implementation. Discuss your personal point of view on the effectiveness of David Neeleman's approach to these two vital aspects.

Let's say you have a wonderful job in your local manufacturing plant. It provides an excellent salary, outstanding benefits, and plenty of vacation time, which you have let build up over the years. You feel like you are sitting on top of the world right now. The children are almost through college and the house is nearly paid for—all thanks to your great job. You have provided the company with years of loyal and dedicated service and truly believe your employer appreciates your work contributions. You believe the job will last until you can retire from the company with a nice pension that will carry you comfortably through the later years. Well, guess what? Things are probably not going to turn out like you had planned. Just like so many other manufacturing workers, you may have to face the fact that reality might just take a big bite out of your dream.

Approximately 2.5 million jobs have been lost since the most recent recession began in March 2001. Two million of the jobs lost have been within the manufacturing industry—mostly blue-collar workers. Ed Landry is one of the many casualties of this recession. At age 62, Ed has recently begun a retraining program in order to acquire new skills for a different job. He had been with his employer since returning from military service in Vietnam. His world changed forever when his employer informed him the company would now be buying their products from China. Louis De Claybrook is just one more casualty of the changing times we are all experiencing. Sadly, Louis is having a very hard time securing another job—he can't even seem to land a supermarket bagger's job. Dan Methot, a former aircraft

engine builder at Pratt and Whitney, doesn't really have a new game plan for finding future employment yet. Dan says, "Nothing I can do about it. I'll go with the flow and start over again. It seems to be the American way now." Indeed, it does seem that the job loss experienced in manufacturing has definitely become the newest American way.

Economist Nicholas Perna coined the phrase "jobless recovery" during the recovery period from the last recession in the 90s. This phrase appears to fit quite well with the recession taking place now. The global migration of labor in search of jobs and capital's search for the cheapest labor market as well as other forces that have been building over the years are considered predominate reasons for the current job loss felt by the manufacturing segment of American industry. No one knows where factory work is headed next, but experts don't believe it is back to the United States. The high cost of American labor, the fact that products can be purchased cheaper abroad, and the increasing expense of buying American-made products all point to the blatant fact that manufacturing in America is never going to go back to the way it was.

On the flip side of this coin, while millions of manufacturing jobs have been lost, millions have survived. This is attributed to the American firms which envisioned where things were heading and modified their processes to become more productive. These firms quickly adopted methods to get more output from each hour of labor. Nicholas Perna comments on this as an effective strategy that unfortunately provides no room for job growth in the future.

While economists say that in the long run high productivity is the greatest thing since the invention of the wheel, the end result of this high productivity is actually "creative destruction." The problem with creative destruction is that people have to make the transition from what they used to do to doing the next big thing. Many unemployed workers have become so discouraged by the length of their jobless stints and the problems encountered in attempting to make the necessary transitions, they have dropped out of the labor force entirely.

The creation of new industries and thus new jobs is looked at by some experts as being the saving grace to this whole scenario. However, updated skills will be needed by workers in order to be competitive in the labor market of the future. Jobless recovery? Creative destruction? Where are they leading our nation and just exactly where do they leave us now?

THINKING IT OVER

1. Discuss how you perceive the trend of "creative destruction" will affect the way tomorrow's companies will plan for their human resource needs.

2. Discuss how today's jobless recovery may impact the labor supply and demand of the future.

3. Express your personal opinion on the so-called jobless recovery of today. Discuss how this can affect your own future career moves.

4. Discuss the advantages companies may gain from creative destruction. How will this impact the way these companies strategically plan for future human resources?

Diversity in Hiring

Most jobs start with an interview, whether it's conducted in person, by phone, or even online. Interpersonal dynamics can affect those interviews, so a human resource manager who is looking to develop a diverse workforce to meet company needs must be able to ask the right questions of a candidate and listen to the answers in an objective, controlled manner. The ultimate goal is to evaluate the candidate fairly and accurately so that he or she fits well with job requirements. As you'll see in the video, two managers for the Beck 'n' Call company are interviewing two job applicants, and how they conduct the interviews and evaluate the applicants will affect both the organization and the individuals—in the composition of the company's workforce and the way those employees later develop in their positions. Both racial and gender issues enter into play in this scenario.

The U.S. workforce is becoming increasingly diverse. Experts estimate that by 2006 the American workforce will be 72 percent Caucasian, 11 percent African American, 12 percent Hispanic, and 5 percent Asian and other ethnic or cultural groups. Companies that want to grow and remain competitive need to utilize the talents, experience, and knowledge of workers from different backgrounds and cultures. If they do not, they may miss a golden opportunity to reach a larger customer base. The customer base for Beck 'n' Call is growing more and more diverse, with African American and Hispanic communities increasing in population where Beck 'n' Call is located. So it makes sense to recruit, develop, and retain employees who can relate to this broadening customer base and meet their needs in specific ways.

Managers at all companies, whether product or service oriented, can reap the rewards of diversity for their organizations if they practice *ethnorelativism*—the belief that groups and subcultures are inherently equal. The first step toward this belief may be consciously recognizing their own tendencies toward ethnocentrism—the belief that their own cultures are superior. Once a person recognizes and acknowledges his or her own attitudes and stereotypical beliefs, he or she can open up to new ideas and begin to change. For instance, conducting a structured employment interview with questions that are standardized and focused on accomplishing defined goals will help promote ethnorelativism as opposed to ethnocentrism. In addition, the interview should contain questions that allow the job applicant to respond and demonstrate his or her competencies in ways that are job related, not personal. Hunches and gut feelings should play a tiny part in such an interview, because once a job applicant becomes an employee, it's the concrete evidence of performance that counts, not whether the interviewer and employer went to the same college or like the same sports teams.

After employees are hired, it is important to give them opportunities to develop their skills and advance. This practice not only enhances the employee–employer relationship but also boosts overall productivity of the company. Managers must also be aware of the possibility of a "glass ceiling," an invisible barrier that separates female employees or those of different cultural or ethnic backgrounds from top levels of the organization. One way to guard against barriers to advancement is to examine workforce composition and statistics. Do certain groups of employees top out at middle management positions? Is there a cluster of women and minorities near the bottom of the employment ladder? Is upper management made up entirely of Caucasian males? If so, why? Do all employees receive equal training and opportunities for advancement, or do some receive preferential treatment, even if it isn't obvious? Some studies indicate that companies may also have "glass walls," which are invisible barriers to important lateral moves within the company. These barriers are just as important as the glass ceiling because a glass wall can prevent an employee from receiving training or experience in certain areas that would enable him or her to move up eventually. Studies confirm the existence of the glass ceiling and glass walls; one showed recently that 97 percent of the top U.S. managers are Caucasian and 95 percent of them are male. Limiting career advancement for certain groups undermines morale at a company and reduces productivity and competitiveness. If employees believe that no matter how well they perform they will never advance, they will not try their hardest for the organization. Because a company's most important asset is its employees, it makes sense to be sure they have the opportunities to perform at the highest possible level of creativity and productivity.

A firm like Beck 'n' Call can do plenty to develop its workforce to its fullest potential: if the company hires one of the candidates in the videotaped interview, it can assign a mentor to the new hire to help her learn the ropes and identify ways to further her career within the organization. It can also offer specific training and opportunities for general education. It can make sure that its approach to assessment is fair and accurate, and it can introduce benchmarking to help the employee mark her own progress. Down the road, it could consider ways to enlarge her job. Of course, the company must review its organizational culture to be sure no glass ceiling or glass wall exists.

Thus an interview is much more important than a casual conversation about a job. It is the first step toward shaping an organization's future workforce. If it is conducted well, both parties win.

THINKING IT OVER

1. Evaluate the interviewers in terms of their interviewing techniques and follow-up. Did the managers conduct the interviews with unfair or discriminating practices? Did they evaluate the best person for the job fairly and accurately? What could or should they have done differently?

2. Imagine that you were interviewing either of these candidates. How would you conduct your interview? Write four or five questions that you think should be asked to find the best applicant. Which candidate do you think you would hire, and why? (Be sure to think about long-term implications for both the employee and the organization.)

3. Think of your own experience in job interviews. Based on what you now know about interviewing, in what ways might you be able to improve your own techniques for participating in an interview as a job applicant?

SOURCE: Bureau of Labor Statistics, "BLS Releases New 1996–2006 Employment Projections," www.bls.gov/new.release/ecopro.nws.htm; S. Nelton, "Nurturing Diversity," *Nation's Business*, June 1995, pp. 25–27.

Reality on Request— Digital Domain

As Chairman and CEO of Digital Domain in Venice, California, Scott Ross runs one of the largest digital production studios in the world. His studio won an Academy Award for doing the simulation of the sinking of the *Titanic* in the movie of that name. The studio also created the digital waves that wiped out the horsemen in *Lord of the Rings*.

Operations management is unique at Digital Domain because no two projects are ever the same. One day they may be making a digital cow (*O Brother*), on another a digital spaceship (*Apollo 13*), on still another, digital waves (*Titanic*). Digital Domain is both a production and service provider. How so? In addition to producing digital scenes for movies, the company advises movie producers as to what is possible to do digitally. Still, certain activities such as facility location and facility layout are common to both service organizations and production firms.

Since many movies are made in Los Angeles, it's important for Digital Domain to be close to the city. Actors are often chosen from that area, as are workers and specialists at Digital. The company's most important resource is its workers. Thus facilities layout is designed to make the jobs of workers easier, yet efficient. For example, there's a combination conference room and cafeteria. Given the company's passion for *quality*, everything is designed to be clean and logical. Facility layout assists workers in developing the highest quality product possible, given time and money constraints.

Materials requirement planning (MRP) is a computer-based operations management system that uses sales forecasts to make needed parts and materials available at the right time and place. Since Digital's primary resource is people, the company lists 54 key disciplines in its database so it's easy to find the right person for the right job. For example, a project may come up on Wednesday that demands having resources available the next Monday. People have to be contacted and hired *just in time* to keep the project on time and within budget.

The company does much of its purchasing on the Internet. It also uses *flexible manufacturing*. To keep costs down, Digital uses *lean manufacturing*, the production of goods using less of everything: less human effort, less manufacturing space, less investment in tools, and less engineering time for a given project. To keep costs down, the company does a lot of pre-visualizing—simulating projects to determine the best way to proceed.

Of course, *mass customization* is basically what Digital Domain is all about—creating new and different scenes that can't be duplicated. Once the company learns to create artificial waves or some other image, it is easier to duplicate a similar image next time. Since film is very expensive, many ideas are created using pen and pencil first. From such "primitive" tools, the company goes on to use *computer-aided design*.

Making movies is expensive. Everything needs to be done as planned. Scott Ross knows it's *show business*, but the accent is on *business* and making a profit. For this reason, Digital uses PERT charts to follow projects and to determine what series of steps is critical to getting things out on time. The studio also uses computerized GANTT charts to follow goods in process. Getting things done right and on time is the hallmark at Digital Domain.

THINKING IT OVER

1. Discuss how Digital's method of categorizing candidates streamlines its selection process.

2. Discuss your personal opinion of Digital's candidate selection process. Explain why you like it or why you don't. Discuss how this method would impact you, if you were a candidate at this company.

3. Does employment with a company like Digital interest you? Discuss why or why not.

4. The video points out the importance of quality production to Digital. How does its selection methodology support this?

Doing Unto Others—Abbott Laboratories

Why should a company establish ethical standards? For Abbott Laboratories, the answer is: "Because it is the right thing to do." It's also important for business reasons because a pharmaceutical company needs to establish trust with all its stakeholders: employees, customers, regulators, shareholders, and so on.

Abbott has been in business for over a hundred years. It now employs some 70,000 people around the world and operates in 130 countries. The company makes and distributes pharmaceuticals, medical devices, and nutritional aids. You can imagine the challenge the company has in meeting the legal, moral, and ethical codes of so many different countries. This is especially true in the pharmaceutical industry that is plagued by many ethical issues, like kickbacks, overpricing, and unethical promotions. Only an effort by top management is enough to address such major issues.

Abbott has had a compliance-based ethics code for many years. But it's one thing to talk about establishing a strong ethics program; it is quite another to implement one. That's why the company appointed Charlie Brock as Abbott's Chief Ethics and Compliance Officer. Each division has an ethics staff and Brock is the coordinator of them all.

One of Brock's first steps in implementing Abbott's ethics program was to let everyone in the company know what the firm's ethical standards are. But the company did not stop with employees; suppliers, distributors, and customers also needed to know that Abbott has such standards and intends to apply them rigorously. That meant establishing a program based on specific standards that are communicated clearly and are enforced with penalties for noncompliance. Abbott uses the latest in technology to train employees in ethical standards. Interactive software developed by California-based company LRN presents difficult ethical cases and teaches employees what to do when hard ethical issues arise.

Abbott goes beyond just compliance-based ethics to integrity-based ethics. That is, it has a broad program of "global citizenship" that covers everything from how the company reports information to stockholders to how it treats its employees, from how it manufactures goods to how it tries to minimize environmental effects. The company has been very generous to many nonprofit groups, but takes special pride in its efforts to conquer AIDS in the world, including developing products to treat and maybe cure the disease. This effort also means teaching people in developing countries how to test for HIV in order to prevent spreading AIDS to their children. All told, Abbott will spend over $100 million on such efforts over the next five years. That includes building partnerships with other firms to make a difference in the world.

Abbott is truly a company to be admired for its corporate citizenship and its active involvement in self-regulation. Not only has the company established an ethics office and set clear ethics codes, it vigorously applies those codes. Its community outreach, including a strong commitment to ending the AIDS crisis, sets a model for other companies to benchmark. Most important, the company does it all for the right reason. It is the morally right thing to do!

THINKING IT OVER

1. Do you believe Abbott's employee training contributes to its high ethical standards? Explain.
2. In your opinion, how does a company, facing such diversity in its working environments and employees, benefit from providing extensive training to the myriad of workers?
3. Discuss how ethical business behavior creates a competitive advantage for organizations like Abbott.

Patagonia Nurtures the Environment—and Employees

There are very few companies that exist and grow in the retail business with the primary goal of funding environmental programs. Patagonia is one of those exceptions. Its culture, including everything from daily business decisions to employee hiring, is based upon Patagonia's commitment to its environmental, moral, ethical, and philosophical causes. Thus, many workers with similar work and personal life values join the company in an effort to further these socially responsible efforts.

This strong inspiration is evident through the company at all levels and began early on. As the company evolved, its owners asked employees to help draft a statement of purpose and core values. The "Statement of Purpose" reads: "Patagonia exists to use business to inspire and implement solutions to the environmental crisis." Employees on product line teams have business-environmental goals, for example, to reduce the environmental impact of their products. As you can imagine, the organization walks a precarious line between social responsibility and profits.

The company's twofold focus on quality and environmental issues has propelled Patagonia toward innovation. The revolutionary products developed and offered in outdoor gear have earned Patagonia a loyal customer base. In addition, building clothes that last longer and work better has supported its environmental efforts.

So how does the company ensure that employees adopt and maintain the same attitude and passion for its environmental programs? Maybe it is because Patagonia devotes one full morning of its three-day new-hire orientation to a voluntary surfing lesson. Or there is the conference that teaches organizational and marketing skills to grass-roots environmental activists, which some Patagonia employees attend. In addition, a civil disobedience training course is available to anyone interested; and the company even posts bail for workers who utilize that training in actions consistent with Patagonia's core values! Employees may also apply to take up to two months' sabbatical to work as full-time volunteers for nonprofit environmental groups; or receive a $2000 reimbursement from the company for purchasing a hybrid electric vehicle.

Many employees join Patagonia and bring their own enthusiasm, however. To quote the company website: "Our product-tester spends days in the back and front country of Colorado beating up new gear. One of our retail stores is managed by a world-class surfer . . . an employee in Reno lobbies state and federal officials on behalf of the environment . . . the fellow who answers the phone is an 11-time world champion frisbee player." Most of Patagonia's employees come to the company with their own extracurricular hobbies and interests; and combining those lifestyles and values enhances the company's culture.

After being named one of America's top companies to work for by *Fortune* for many years, Patagonia's reputation is such that it has to spend very little on recruiting. Between its formal environmental program and the steady labor pool of like-minded workers, employee motivation is all but inevitable.

THINKING IT OVER

1. What are some of the programs or benefits that Patagonia provides its employees that may motivate them? Which ones would be effective motivators for you?

2. Discuss the advantages a company may gain from offering sabbaticals and similar options. Why may some companies be reluctant to participate in such practices?

3. As an employee, which is more important to you, your pay or other benefits? Why? Do you think this might change as you grow older and progress in your career?

Hey ladies! It's time to pack the lunch bucket, grab your tool belt and hardhat, and head for work. Today's job is to finish installing the plumbing lines at the Bensons' new million-dollar home on Elm Street. Sound different to you? Well, it is! Times in the workplace have definitely changed from those of your grandpa and grandma.

Over 63 million people are in the American workforce. More than 3 million of these are women who now hold jobs that were previously known to be "man's work." The women in the workforce of today are no longer only secretaries or nurses—you know, the "softer forms of work." They are getting jobs as construction workers, forklift operators, builders, and machinists. Quite a difference from the old days.

Women are relishing these workforce changes. They attribute having unfulfilled needs—like pensions and nice benefits—to be the prominent reasons why these changes have been necessary. Today's woman now believes in her own value and what she is able to accomplish.

Catherine Simpson, owner of Catherine's Automotive Repair & Service, is proud to display her name on the business sign. She believes that her gender actually makes customers more trusting of the services her company provides them. She looks at it as a type of marketing gimmick and is finding it is helping her achieve success in this predominantly male industry.

Unfortunately, this workforce transition is not an easy one to accomplish. As *Tradeswomen Now & Tomorrow*'s Lauren Sugarman states, "We have often joked that we get work in public jobs, you know, where there's public commitment to having diversity and equal opportunity, but we can't get hired on private jobs. We need that to change so that women can work consistently."

Women are gaining ground in the "man-only world." They should be very proud of their accomplishments today and get themselves ready to accept an even bigger slice of the workforce pie tomorrow. Women, remember that today there are fewer boundaries than ever before. You can achieve anything you want to achieve. The right attitude and aptitude is all you need. The workplace is no longer a predominately male entity. Step up and claim your spot doing whatever type of work brings you the most satisfaction!

THINKING IT OVER

1. Discuss how organizations can assist their female workers in achieving positions that were previously held almost exclusively by male workers.

2. Discuss what organizations can do to remove the "glass ceiling." Discuss how this would impact female employees, male employees, and the organization as a whole.

3. Discuss your personal point of view on women working at jobs that were once known to be held almost exclusively by men, like heavy equipment operators or construction workers. If you are a male, would you feel comfortable working in a safety-sensitive job with a woman teammate? Why or why not? If you are a female, what problems do you foresee in trying for a construction worker's job? How would you handle this? Explain.

Working for the Best: The Container Store

Looking for a company where motivational techniques are effectively applied? Look no further than The Container Store, which was voted "the best company to work for in America" twice and was second two other times. That record demands attention and copying, if possible.

What's the secret to hiring highly motivated people who feel their company is America's best? First, you need good products. Employees are motivated when they know that the products they sell are helpful to consumers and top quality. Second, you have to empower workers to do what they can to exceed customer expectations, even if that means having them go out in the parking lot to give a customer a driving lesson.

One of the cornerstones at The Container Store is: Hire Great People. Management believes that one great person is worth three good people. They cite famed home-run hitter Babe Ruth, who hit 56 home runs in one year; the second-best home-run hitter hit only 13. A great player may be worth over four times what a good player is worth. The challenge is to find and keep great workers. The Container Store often does that by hiring part-time people and then motivating the best of them to stay.

Workers must be taught to provide astonishing levels of customer service. One such case is the worker in Houston who loaned her car to a stranded customer. How do you encourage such outstanding service? Management at The Container Store knows motivational principles. They know, for example, that Frederick Taylor looked at workers as if they were machines to be programmed, and that such a style is no longer effective in most organizations. They also know that Elton Mayo introduced a more human-based form of motivation.

It's clear that the store uses Maslow's needs hierarchy. Wages paid are above the industry standard meeting the physiological needs of workers. Safety needs "(the need to feel secure at work and at home)" are met by tolerating mistakes and urging employees to do what's necessary to please customers. Employees also feel secure because the store emphasizes proper values, including integrity, honesty, and open communications. Good employees are recognized for their contribution and the social atmosphere is one of "family." It's clear The Container Store uses McGregor's "theory Y" concepts.

Herzberg claims that a good job environment is not a motivator; it is considered a hygiene factor (i.e., it doesn't motivate workers if it is present, but causes dissatisfaction if missing). Container Store employees place a high importance on the job environment, including the quality of their co-workers. This implies that people like to work with others who are equally motivated and responsible. This also fits into Maslow's social needs.

The Container Store focuses on job enrichment. Employees are trained to do a variety of jobs that help prepare them to become managers when openings are available. The store uses daily coaching so employees can understand and implement management by objectives. The store also uses open communication to stress that good work will be rewarded. That includes peer-to-peer communication where everyone helps everyone else to do the best job possible.

In short, The Container Store uses a humanistic approach coupled with empowerment, strong values, cross training, and open communication to motivate employees to the point where they will continue to be one of the best companies to work for in America.

THINKING IT OVER

1. Discuss how employees' achievements can be recognized through an organization's monetary compensation system. Does this always provide motivation for employees? Explain.
2. Discuss what factors have provided motivation for you to do your best work. Discuss what factors have discouraged you from doing your best.
3. Discuss how the pay and motivational strategy in effect at the Container Store supports its overall organizational strategy.

Jeff Chambers is vice president of human resources at SAS, the world's largest privately owned software company. At such a company, employees are the most important asset because the company can't produce any software or provide any service without good, quality people. Part of Jeff's job is to find and keep such employees. Finding people who want to work at SAS isn't difficult; there are about 93,000 applicants for 500 jobs. The challenge is to screen those people to find those who fit best.

The company assesses future labor requirements, prepares job analyses to see what various jobs entail, and then tries to find employees within the firm to meet those future needs. If they are not available, the company must search outside the firm to find the best people. Its strategic plan calls for interviewing, testing, and evaluating prospects. Spending more time in the hiring process means spending less time later trying to replace workers who were not a good fit in the firm.

In the future, there will be a great demand for skilled workers; thus, employee retention is critical at SAS. Evidence of how successfully the company retains people is the fact that turnover each year is about 4 percent, way below the industry average. One way to keep employees is to promote from within, and that means training people to move up within the organization. Such training includes in-house classes, online training, internships, and apprenticeships. Of course, managers get management training to keep them up to date and more qualified for promotion.

Keeping employees means more than providing them with a satisfying job and a good chance for promotion. It also means providing fringe benefits that employees want and need. That includes health care, day care, and an in-house recreation center. Medical insurance carries over to retired workers as well. SAS tries to accommodate the needs of individual workers as much as possible. If someone needs to take off early, he or she can. Employees can work from home (telecommuting) if they prefer. The company also has job sharing and flextime.

At a company like SAS, the performance evaluations are very important. That's why the company doesn't use a simple form like so many others do. Instead, the company works closely with each employee to make sure the person understands the goals of the firm and how she or he fits into those goals.

SAS has a great relationship with its customers. The company spends 25 percent of its bottom line on research and development. Its quality products result in customer retention rates in the 98 percent range. The company treats its employees with the same care that it treats its customers. Because employees are so happy and turnover is so low, the company has more funds to invest in R&D and more happy customers. All this leads to more business and therefore the need to hire even more people.

THINKING IT OVER

1. SAS is dedicated to providing its employees with what brings them the most employment satisfaction. Discuss the impact the employee benefits package offered by the company has on the entire organization.

2. After viewing the video, does employment with an organization like SAS appeal to you? Explain why or why not. Would you find a working environment like SAS to be challenging? Rewarding? Explain.

3. Discuss the effects that concentrated and well-structured benefits management produce on organizational costs and the quality of the workforce.

4. How important are receiving benefits at work to you? Would you be willing to sacrifice certain benefits, such as health insurance, for increased pay?

LUV in the Workplace: Southwest Airlines

You feel the difference the first time you fly Southwest Airlines (stock symbol: LUV). Employees are friendly and funny. They joke with passengers, but are helpful whenever needed. That's not always the case with airlines these days, especially since September 11, 2001, and the extra security and fall-off in airline revenues. Southwest is the only consistently profitable major airline.

Other carriers try to imitate Southwest, with some success, but Southwest still leads the way. It has the best service record for baggage handling, the least customer complaints, the best safety record, the lowest workforce turnover, and the best labor relations. The latter is somewhat surprising because the airline's workforce is 85 percent unionized. Nonetheless, Southwest continues to outshine other companies in the industry for some reason. Why? The video offers several explanations, but perhaps the most important is that Southwest focuses as much on pleasing its workers as it does on pleasing its customers.

The relationship between management and workers, historically, has not always been so pleasing. That's the reason there are unions in the United States. Unions fought for improvements in the minimum wage, overtime pay, workers' compensation, severance pay, job safety, and child labor laws. Workers today often forget the debt they owe unions for making such improvements in working conditions.

Today, labor contracts include the terms and conditions under which labor and management will function over a set period of time. If an employee has a grievance, he or she can go to a union representative to have it settled. If settlement is not forthcoming, a formal grievance process is in place to reach a satisfactory conclusion.

Such procedures seem straightforward and mutually satisfying. The truth is, however, that labor and management often fail to reach a labor contract. In such cases, union workers may resort to a strike—that is, a work stoppage. They may also picket or call for a boycott of a company and its products. Management may lock employees out of their jobs or hire temporary workers (called scabs) to replace union workers while they are on strike. In short, tensions can develop between both sides that become quite heated. In these cases a mediator may be brought in to make suggestions as to a fair and equitable solution. An arbitrator can also be used; both sides are bound by the arbitrator's ruling.

How has Southwest avoided such labor problems? Southwest begins its close cooperation with employees by bringing them to its University for People. The New Hire Training Course gives them a history of Southwest and the importance of employees to that history. The training looks at failed airlines of the past that at one time were large, effective, and profitable. Employees today are less concerned about wage increases and work conditions and are more concerned about employee benefits and job security, the latter being especially important in the airline industry. That does not mean, however, that Southwest does not pay well or provide great benefits. Benefits include child-care and elder-care referrals, a counseling service, and a catastrophe fund for those who get caught in dire emergencies.

The airline "hires for attitude and trains for skill." Skills can be learned and Southwest helps people attain their goals. Many employees even bring their spouses to work for the firm as well. A good company with good employees is a winner today, even in highly competitive and hard-to-make-money industries like the airlines.

THINKING IT OVER

1. Discuss how the labor–management relations maintained by Southwest have provided a significant benefit to the organization.

2. Describe why you would or would not like to work for an organization such as Southwest. Identify the primary reason associated with your choice.

3. Labor–management relations have a history of being adversarial. Discuss methods used by Southwest to diminish this adversarial relationship. Have these methods proven to be beneficial to the organization? To the employees? Explain.

Jobs on the Move

Think your high-paying position at work is safe? Well, you might just want to guess again! Judy Adelstein thought hers was safe. As an experienced assistant vice president for a major New York bank, she wasn't too worried about losing her job. However, a brief moment in her employer's office changed her mind—forever. She found out the hard way just what the new business practice of "outsourcing" could do to a career path.

Judy's husband Scott also found out the hard way how fast career paths can be changed. After 26 years of service, a medical condition forced him to change jobs in his field. However, sending out 350 job applications did not get him employed by anybody. He too attributes his inability to secure a new job to outsourcing. The "offshoring" of American service jobs is decidedly wreaking havoc on the lives of people like Judy and Scott, who have excellent qualifications but few if any job prospects.

The outsourcing trend for service industries has become a very real problem for the employees of these companies. This trend has broadened from call centers to higher-level work. Nothing is currently safe from it. All types of high-skill jobs are now heading for low-wage countries—at a pay scale that is about one-tenth the rate in America.

IBM defends its decision to outsource by stating, "Our competitors are doing it and we have to do it too." The chance to save money is extremely tempting to organizations.

For instance, transcribing audiotapes can be done in India for about $6 per hour of tape. This is compared to paying $100 or more in the United States. The appeal offshoring has to organizations is obvious. Even the medical profession is looking to outsource transcription needs to India in order to save substantial sums of money.

The website elance.com is striking evidence for the growth of the offshoring of jobs. This site allows employers to post a job opening and the workers of the world can bid for it. Sergey Rud of AI Studio claims, "Elance is a god for the outsourcing industry, just like eBay is for auctions." This is concurred in by management consultant John McCarthy. McCarthy has spent much time researching this new outsourcing trend.

McCarthy predicts this trend will do nothing but increase in the future. He claims it should be expected that 3.3 million jobs will be going offshore within the next 10 years. This is frightening to those workers who have to depend on their American jobs to survive financially. Scott Adelstein comments that American pride just does not exist at corporations anymore. His wife Judy feels that corporate greed must be tempered with a little bit of conscience to keep from selling everyone down the river.

While there are benefits to outsourcing, such as increasing the service economy within the United States through other nations' citizens who can now afford to come to America, the downside is still bleak

for the U.S. service industry overall. This is especially true for those currently employed within the industry.

According to John McCarthy, the outsourcing trend simply indicates that nothing can be taken for granted in regard to employment. The age of full employment is gone and perhaps gone forever. American workers must prepare themselves to be competitive in the labor market. This must include upgrading skills and preparation for the transition to new opportunities. Even by doing this, American service workers may still have a hard road to travel in the future.

THINKING IT OVER

1. Give your personal opinion of outsourcing. How do you perceive it has or will impact you personally? Do you agree with the reference to tempering corporate greed made in the video? Explain.

2. Discuss how the outsourcing trend affects the manner in which organizations currently manage human resources. Discuss how this trend will affect future HR management.

3. Let's say you own a large service company that employs 1,000 people. You can save millions of dollars per year by outsourcing work to India. However, 500 jobs would be sacrificed here at home. Many of these workers have been with your company since you started it. Explain why you would outsource the work. Explain why you would not outsource the work.

Glossary

Acceptability The extent to which a performance measure is deemed to be satisfactory or adequate by those who use it.

Action learning Teams work on an actual business problem, commit to an action plan, and are accountable for carrying out the plan.

Action plan Document summarizing what the trainee and manager will do to ensure that training transfers to the job.

Action steps The part of a written affirmative plan that specifies what an employer plans to do to reduce underutilization of protected groups.

Adventure learning Learning focused on the development of teamwork and leadership skills by using structured outdoor activities.

Agency shop A union security provision that requires an employee to pay union membership dues but not to join the union.

Agent In agency theory, a person (e.g., a manager) who is expected to act on behalf of a principal (e.g., an owner).

Alternative dispute resolution (ADR) A method of resolving disputes that does not rely on the legal system. Often proceeds through the four stages of open door policy, peer review, mediation, and arbitration.

Alternative work arrangements Independent contractors, on-call workers, temporary workers, and contract company workers who are not employed full-time by the company.

Americans with Disabilities Act (ADA) A 1990 act prohibiting individuals with disabilities from being discriminated against in the workplace.

Analytic approach Type of assessment of HRM effectiveness that involves determining the impact of, or the financial costs and benefits of, a program or practice.

Anticipatory socialization Socialization that occurs before an individual joins a company. Includes expectations about the company, job, working conditions, and interpersonal relationships.

Appraisal politics A situation in which evaluators purposefully distort a rating to achieve personal or company goals.

Apprenticeship A work-study training method with both on-the-job and classroom training.

Arbitration A procedure for resolving collective bargaining impasses by which an arbitrator chooses a solution to the dispute.

Assessment Collecting information and providing feedback to employees about their behavior, communication style, or skills.

Assessment center A process in which multiple raters evaluate employees' performance on a number of exercises.

Associate union membership A form of union membership by which the union receives dues in exchange for services (e.g., health insurance, credit cards) but does not provide representation in collective bargaining.

Attitude awareness and change program Program focusing on increasing employees' awareness of differences in cultural and ethnic backgrounds, physical characteristics, and personal characteristics that influence behavior toward others.

Attitudinal structuring The aspect of the labor–management negotiation process that refers to the relationship and level of trust between the negotiators.

Audiovisual instruction Includes overheads, slides, and video.

Audit approach Type of assessment of HRM effectiveness that involves review of customer satisfaction or key indicators (e.g., turnover rate, average days to fill a position) related to an HRM functional area (e.g., recruiting, training).

Balanced scorecard A means of performance measurement that gives managers a chance to look at their company from the perspectives of internal and external customers, employees, and shareholders.

Basic skills   Reading, writing, and communication skills needed to understand the content of a training program.

Behavior-based program   A program focusing on changing the organizational policies and individual behaviors that inhibit employees' personal growth and productivity.

Benchmarking   Comparing an organization's practices against those of the competition.

Benchmarks©   An instrument designed to measure the factors that are important to managerial success.

Bona fide occupational qualification (BFOQ)   A job qualification based on race, sex, religion, and so on that an employer asserts is a necessary qualification for the job.

Career management system   A system to retain and motivate employees by identifying and meeting their development needs (also called *development planning system*).

Career support   Coaching, protection, sponsorship, and providing challenging assignments, exposure, and visibility.

Cash balance plan   Retirement plan in which the employer sets up an individual account for each employee and contributes a percentage of the employee's salary; the account earns interest at a predetermined rate.

Centralization   Degree to which decision-making authority resides at the top of the organizational chart.

Checkoff provision   A union contract provision that requires an employer to deduct union dues from employees' paychecks.

Client–server architecture   Computer design that provides a method to consolidate data and applications into a single host system (the client).

Climate for transfer   Trainees' perceptions of characteristics of the work environment (social support and situational constraints) that can either facilitate or inhibit use of trained skills or behavior.

Closed shop   A union security provision requiring a person to be a union member before being hired. Illegal under NLRA.

Coach   A peer or manager who works with an employee to motivate her, help her develop skills, and provide reinforcement and feedback.

Cognitive ability   Includes three dimensions: verbal comprehension, quantitative ability, and reasoning ability.

Cognitive ability tests   Tests that include three dimensions: verbal comprehension, quantitative ability, and reasoning ability.

Communities of practice   Groups of employees who work together, learn from each other, and develop a common understanding of how to get work accomplished.

Compa-ratio   An index of the correspondence between actual and intended pay.

Compensable factors   The characteristics of jobs that an organization values and chooses to pay for.

Competitiveness   A company's ability to maintain and gain market share in its industry.

Concentration strategy   A strategy focusing on increasing market share, reducing costs, or creating and maintaining a market niche for products and services.

Concurrent validation   A criterion-related validity study in which a test is administered to all the people currently in a job and then incumbents' scores are correlated with existing measures of their performance on the job.

Consequences   The incentives that employees receive for performing well.

Consolidated Omnibus Budget Reconciliation Act (COBRA)   The 1985 act that requires employers to permit employees to extend their health insurance coverage at group rates for up to 36 months following a qualifying event, such as a layoff.

Content validation   A test validation strategy performed by demonstrating that the items, questions, or problems posed by a test are a representative sample of the kinds of situations or problems that occur on the job.

Continuous learning   A learning system that requires employees to understand the entire work process and expects them to acquire new skills, apply them on the job, and share what they have learned with other employees.

Coordination training   Training a team in how to share information and decision-making responsibilities to maximize team performance.

Corporate campaigns   Union activities designed to exert public, financial, or political pressure on employers during the union-organizing process.

Cost–benefit analysis   The process of determining the economic benefits of a training program using accounting methods.

Criterion-related validity   A method of establishing the validity of a personnel selection method by showing a substantial correlation between test scores and job performance scores.

Cross-cultural preparation   The process of educating employees (and their families) who are given an assignment in a foreign country.

Cross-training   Training in which team members understand and practice each other's skills so that members are prepared to step in and take another member's place should he or she temporarily or permanently leave the team.

Cultural immersion A behavior-based diversity program that sends employees into communities where they interact with persons from different cultures, races, and nationalities.

Decision support systems Problem-solving systems that usually include a "what-if" feature that allows users to see how outcomes change when assumptions or data change.

Delayering Reducing the number of job levels within an organization.

Departmentalization Degree to which work units are grouped based on functional similarity or similarity of workflow.

Development The acquisition of knowledge, skills, and behaviors that improve an employee's ability to meet changes in job requirements and in client and customer demands.

Direct applicants People who apply for a job vacancy without prompting from the organization.

Disparate impact A theory of discrimination based on facially neutral employment practices that disproportionately exclude a protected group from employment opportunities.

Disparate treatment A theory of discrimination based on different treatment given to individuals because of their race, color, religion, sex, national origin, age, or disability status.

Distributive bargaining The part of the labor–management negotiation process that focuses on dividing a fixed economic "pie."

Diversity training Training designed to change employee attitudes about diversity and/or develop skills needed to work with a diverse workforce.

Downsizing The planned elimination of large numbers of personnel, designed to enhance organizational effectiveness.

Downward move A job change involving a reduction in an employee's level of responsibility and authority.

Due process policies Policies by which a company formally lays out the steps an employee can take to appeal a termination decision.

Duty of fair representation The National Labor Relations Act requirement that all bargaining unit members have equal access to and representation by the union.

Efficiency wage theory A theory stating that wage influences worker productivity.

E-learning Instruction and delivery of training by computers through the Internet or company intranet.

Electronic business (e-business) Any business that a company conducts electronically.

Electronic human resource management (e-HRM) The processing and transmission of digitized information used in HRM.

Electronic performance support systems (EPSS) Computer applications that can provide (as requested) skills training, information access, and expert advice.

Employee assistance programs (EAPs) Employer programs that attempt to ameliorate problems encountered by workers who are drug dependent, alcoholic, or psychologically troubled.

Employee Retirement Income Security Act (ERISA) The 1974 act that increased the fiduciary responsibilities of pension plan trustees, established vesting rights and portability provisions, and established the Pension Benefit Guaranty Corporation (PBGC).

Employee stock ownership plan (ESOP) An employee ownership plan that provides employers certain tax and financial advantages when stock is granted to employees.

Employment-at-will doctrine The doctrine that, in the absence of a specific contract, either an employer or employee could sever the employment relationship at any time.

Employment-at-will policies Policies which state that either an employer or employee can terminate the employment relationship at any time, regardless of cause.

Empowering Giving employees the responsibility and authority to make decisions.

Encounter phase The phase that occurs when an employee begins a new job.

Equal employment opportunity (EEO) The government's attempt to ensure that all individuals have an equal opportunity for employment, regardless of race, color, religion, sex, age, disability, or national origin.

Equal Employment Opportunity Commission (EEOC) The government commission established to ensure that all individuals have an equal opportunity for employment, regardless of race, color, religion, sex, age, disability, or national origin.

Ergonomics The interface between individuals' physiological characteristics and the physical work environment.

Exempt Employees who are not covered by the Fair Labor Standards Act. Exempt employees are not eligible for overtime pay.

Expatriate Employee sent by his or her company to manage operations in a different country.

Expectancy theory The theory that says motivation is a function of valence, instrumentality, and expectancy.

Expert systems Computer systems incorporating the decision rules of people recognized as experts in a certain area.

External analysis Examining the organization's operating environment to identify strategic opportunities and threats.

External growth strategy An emphasis on acquiring vendors and suppliers or buying businesses that allow a company to expand into new markets.

External labor market Persons outside the firm who are actively seeking employment.

Externship When a company allows an employee to take a full-time operational role at another company.

Fact finder A person who reports on the reasons for a labor–management dispute, the views and arguments of both sides, and a nonbinding recommendation for settling the dispute.

Fair Labor Standards Act (FLSA) The 1938 law that established the minimum wage and overtime pay.

Family and Medical Leave Act The 1993 act that requires employers with 50 or more employees to provide up to 12 weeks of unpaid leave after childbirth or adoption; to care for a seriously ill child, spouse, or parent; or for an employee's own serious illness.

Feedback Information that employees receive while they are performing concerning how well they are meeting objectives.

Financial Accounting Statement (FAS) 106 The rule issued by the Financial Accounting Standards Board in 1993 requiring companies to fund benefits provided after retirement on an accrual rather than a pay-as-you-go basis and to enter these future cost obligations on their financial statements.

Formal education programs Employee development programs, including short courses offered by consultants or universities, executive MBA programs, and university programs.

Four-fifths rule A rule that states that an employment test has disparate impact if the hiring rate for a minority group is less than four-fifths, or 80 percent, of the hiring rate for the majority group.

Frame of reference A standard point that serves as a comparison for other points and thus provides meaning.

Gainsharing A form of group compensation based on group or plant performance (rather than organizationwide profits) that does not become part of the employee's base salary.

General duty clause The provision of the Occupational Safety and Health Act that states an employer has an overall obligation to furnish employees with a place of employment free from recognized hazards.

Generalizability The degree to which the validity of a selection method established in one context extends to other contexts.

Glass ceiling A barrier to advancement to higher-level jobs in the company that adversely affects women and minorities. The barrier may be due to lack of access to training programs, development experiences, or relationships (e.g., mentoring).

Goals What an organization hopes to achieve in the medium- to long-term future.

Goals and timetables The part of a written affirmative action plan that specifies the percentage of women and minorities that an employer seeks to have in each job group and the date by which that percentage is to be attained.

Group-building methods Training methods that help trainees share ideas and experiences, build group identity, understand the dynamics of interpersonal relationships, and get to know their own strengths and weaknesses and those of their coworkers.

Group mentoring program A program pairing a successful senior employee with a group of four to six less experienced protégés.

Groupware Software application that enables multiple users to track, share, and organize information and to work on the same database or document simultaneously.

Hands-on methods Training methods that require the trainee to be actively involved in learning.

Health maintenance organization (HMO) A health care plan that provides benefits on a prepaid basis for employees who are required to use only HMO medical service providers.

High-leverage training Training practice that links training to strategic business goals, has top management support, relies on an instructional design model, and is benchmarked to programs in other organizations.

High-performance work systems Work systems that maximize the fit between employees and technology.

High-potential employees Employees the company believes are capable of being successful in high-level management positions.

Host country The country in which the parent-country organization seeks to locate or has already located a facility.

Host-country nationals (HCNs) Employees born and raised in a host, not parent, country.

Human resource information system (HRIS) A system used to acquire, store, manipulate, analyze, retrieve, and distribute information related to human resources.

Human resource management (HRM) The policies, practices, and systems that influence employees' behavior, attitudes, and performances.

Human resource recruitment The practice or activity carried on by the organization with the primary purpose of identifying and attracting potential employees.

Imaging A process for scanning documents, storing them electronically, and retrieving them.

In-basket A simulation of the administrative tasks of a manager's job.

Individualism–collectivism One of Hofstede's cultural dimensions; describes the strength of the relation between an individual and other individuals in a society.

Input Instructions that tell the employee what, how, and when to perform; also the support they are given to help them perform.

Integrative bargaining The part of the labor–management negotiation process that seeks solutions beneficial to both sides.

Intellectual capital Creativity, productivity, and service provided by employees.

Interactional justice A concept of justice referring to the interpersonal nature of how the outcomes were implemented.

Internal analysis The process of examining an organization's strengths and weaknesses.

Internal growth strategy A focus on new market and product development, innovation, and joint ventures.

Internal labor force Labor force of current employees.

Interview Employees are questioned about their work and personal experiences, skills, and career plans.

Intraorganizational bargaining The part of the labor–management negotiation process that focuses on the conflicting objectives of factions within labor and management.

Involuntary turnover Turnover initiated by the organization (often among people who would prefer to stay).

ISO 9000:2000 A series of quality assurance standards developed by the International Organization for Standardization in Switzerland and adopted worldwide.

Job analysis The process of getting detailed information about jobs.

Job description A list of the tasks, duties, and responsibilities that a job entails.

Job design The process of defining the way work will be performed and the tasks that will be required in a given job.

Job enlargement Adding challenges or new responsibilities to an employee's current job.

Job enrichment Ways to add complexity and meaningfulness to a person's work.

Job evaluation An administrative procedure used to measure internal job worth.

Job experience The relationships, problems, demands, tasks, and other features that employees face in their jobs.

Job hazard analysis technique A breakdown of each job into basic elements, each of which is rated for its potential for harm or injury.

Job involvement The degree to which people identify themselves with their jobs.

Job redesign The process of changing the tasks or the way work is performed in an existing job.

Job rotation The process of systematically moving a single individual from one job to another over the course of time. The job assignments may be in various functional areas of the company or movement may be between jobs in a single functional area or department.

Job satisfaction A pleasurable feeling that results from the perception that one's job fulfills or allows for the fulfillment of one's important job values.

Job specification A list of the knowledge, skills, abilities, and other characteristics (KSAOs) that an individual must have to perform a job.

Job structure The relative pay of jobs in an organization.

Key jobs Benchmark jobs, used in pay surveys, that have relatively stable content and are common to many organizations.

Knowledge workers Employees who own the intellectual means of producing a product or service.

Leaderless group discussion Process in which a team of five to seven employees solve an assigned problem together within a certain time period.

Leading indicator An objective measure that accurately predicts future labor demand.

Learner control Ability of trainees to actively learn through self-pacing, exercises, links to other materials, and conversations with other trainees and experts.

Learning organization An organization whose employees are continuously attempting to learn new things and apply what they have learned to improve product or service quality.

Long-term–short-term orientation One of Hofstede's cultural dimensions; describes how a culture balances immediate benefits with future rewards.

Maintenance of membership Union rules requiring members to remain members for a certain period of time (e.g., the length of the union contract).

Malcolm Baldrige National Quality Award An award established in 1987 to promote quality awareness, to recognize quality achievements of U.S. companies, and to publicize successful quality strategies.

Managing diversity The process of creating an environment that allows all employees to contribute to organizational goals and experience personal growth.

Marginal employee An employee performing at a barely acceptable level because of lack of ability and/or motivation to perform well, not poor work conditions.

Marginal tax rate The percentage of an additional dollar of earnings that goes to taxes.

Masculinity–femininity dimension One of Hofstede's cultural dimensions; describes the division of roles between the sexes within a society.

Mediation A procedure for resolving collective bargaining impasses by which a mediator with no formal authority acts as a facilitator and go-between in the negotiations.

Mentor An experienced, productive senior employee who helps develop a less experienced employee.

Merit increase grid A grid that combines an employee's performance rating with his or her position in a pay range to determine the size and frequency of his or her pay increases.

Minimum wage The lowest amount that employers are legally allowed to pay; the 1990 amendment of the Fair Labor Standards Act permits a subminimum wage to workers under the age of 20 for a period of up to 90 days.

Motivation to learn The desire of the trainee to learn the content of a training program.

Myers-Briggs Type Indicator (MBTI) A psychological test used for team building and leadership development that identifies employees' preferences for energy, information gathering, decision making, and lifestyle.

Needs assessment The process used to determine if training is necessary.

Negative affectivity A dispositional dimension that reflects pervasive individual differences in satisfaction with any and all aspects of life.

Network A combination of desktop computers, computer terminals, and mainframes or minicomputers that share access to databases and a method to transmit information throughout the system.

New technologies Current applications of knowledge, procedures, and equipment that have not been previously used. Usually involves replacing human labor with equipment, information processing, or some combination of the two.

Nonkey jobs Jobs that are unique to organizations and that cannot be directly valued or compared through the use of market surveys.

Objective The purpose and expected outcome of training activities.

Occupational Safety and Health Act (OSHA) The 1970 law that authorizes the federal government to establish and enforce occupational safety and health standards for all places of employment engaging in interstate commerce.

Offshoring A special case of outsourcing where the jobs that move actually leave one country and go to another.

Opportunity to perform The trainee is provided with or actively seeks experience using newly learned knowledge skills, or behavior.

Organizational analysis A process for determining the business appropriateness of training.

Organizational commitment The degree to which an employee identifies with the organization and is willing to put forth effort on its behalf.

Organizational socialization The process by which new employees are transformed into effective members of a company.

Outcome fairness The judgment that people make with respect to the outcomes received relative to the outcomes received by other people with whom they identity.

Outplacement counseling Counseling to help displaced employees manage the transition from one job to another.

Output A job's performance standards.

Outsourcing An organization's use of an outside organization for a broad set of services.

Overlearning The continuation of practice even after trainees have been able to perform the objective several times.

Parent country The country in which a company's corporate headquarters is located.

Parent-country nationals (PCNs) Employees who were born and live in a parent country.

Pay grades Jobs of similar worth or content grouped together for pay administration purposes.

Pay level The average pay, including wages, salaries, and bonuses, of jobs in an organization.

Pay policy line A mathematical expression that describes the relationship between a job's pay and its job evaluation points.

Pay structure The relative pay of different jobs (job structure) and how much they are paid (pay level).

Pension Benefit Guaranty Corporation (PBGC) The agency that guarantees to pay employees a basic retirement benefit in the event that financial difficulties force a company to terminate or reduce employee pension benefits.

Performance appraisal The process through which an organization gets information on how well an employee is doing his or her job.

Performance feedback The process of providing employees information regarding their performance effectiveness.

Performance management The means through which managers ensure that employees' activities and outputs are congruent with the organization's goals.

Performance planning and evaluation (PPE) system Any system that seeks to tie the formal performance appraisal process to the company's strategies by specifying at the beginning of the evaluation period the types and level of performance that must be accomplished in order to achieve the strategy.

Person analysis A process for determining whether employees need training, who needs training, and whether employees are ready for training.

Person characteristics An employee's knowledge, skills, abilities, and attitudes.

Power distance One of Hofstede's cultural dimensions; concerns how a culture deals with hierarchical power relationships—particularly the unequal distribution of power.

Practice Having the employee demonstrate what he or she has learned in training.

Predictive validation A criterion-related validity study that seeks to establish an empirical relationship between applicants' test scores and their eventual performance on the job.

Preferred provider organization (PPO) A group of health care providers who contract with employers, insurance companies, and so forth to provide health care at a reduced fee.

Presentation methods Training methods in which trainees are passive recipients of information.

Principal In agency theory, a person (e.g., the owner) who seeks to direct another person's behavior.

Procedural justice A concept of justice focusing on the methods used to determine the outcomes received.

Profit sharing A compensation plan in which payments are based on a measure of organization performance (profits) and do not become part of the employees' base salary.

Progression of withdrawal Theory that dissatisfied individuals enact a set of behaviors to avoid the work situation.

Promotions Advances into positions with greater challenge, more responsibility, and more authority than the employee's previous job.

Protean career A career that is frequently changing due to both changes in the person's interests, abilities, and values and changes in the work environment.

Psychological contract Expectations of employee contributions and what the company will provide in return.

Psychological success The feeling of pride and accomplishment that comes from achieving life goals.

Psychosocial support Serving as a friend and role model, providing positive regard and acceptance, and creating an outlet for a protégé to talk about anxieties and fears.

Quantitative ability Concerns the speed and accuracy with which one can solve arithmetic problems of all kinds.

Range spread The distance between the minimum and maximum amounts in a pay grade.

Rate ranges Different employees in the same job may have different pay rates.

Readability The difficulty level of written materials.

Realistic job preview Provides accurate information about the attractive and unattractive aspects of a job, working conditions, company, and location to ensure that potential employees develop appropriate expectations.

Reasonable accommodation Making facilities readily accessible to and usable by individuals with disabilities.

Reasoning ability Refers to a person's capacity to invent solutions to many diverse problems.

Recruitment The process of seeking applicants for potential employment.

Reengineering Review and redesign of work processes to make them more efficient and improve the quality of the end product or service.

Referrals People who are prompted to apply for a job by someone within the organization.

Relational database A database structure that stores information in separate files that can be linked by common elements.

Reliability The consistency of a performance measure; the degree to which a performance measure is free from random error.

Repatriation The preparation of expatriates for return to the parent company and country from a foreign assignment.

Repurposing Directly translating instructor-led training online.

Request for proposal (RFP) A document that outlines for potential vendors and consultants the type of service the company is seeking, references needed, number of employees who should be trained, project funding, the follow-up process, expected completion date, and the date when proposals must be received by the company.

Results Measurements used to determine a training program's payoff for a company.

Right-to-work laws State laws that make union shops, maintenance of membership, and agency shops illegal.

Role What an organization expects from an employee in terms of what to do and how to do it.

Role ambiguity Uncertainty about what an organization expects from an employee in terms of what to do and how to do it.

Role analysis technique A method that enables a role occupant and other members of the role occupant's role set to specify and examine their expectations for the role occupant.

Role behaviors Behaviors that are required of an individual in his or her role as a job holder in a social work environment.

Role conflict Recognition of incompatible or contradictory demands by the person occupying the role.

Role overload A state in which too many expectations or demands are placed on a person.

Role play A participant taking the part or role of a manager or other employee.

Sabbatical A leave of absence from the company to renew or develop skills.

Safety awareness programs Employer programs that attempt to instill symbolic and substantive changes in the organization's emphasis on safety.

Sarbanes-Oxley Act of 2002 A congressional act passed in response to illegal and unethical behavior by managers and executives. The Act sets stricter rules for business, especially accounting practices including requiring more open and consistent disclosure of financial data, CEO's assurance that the data is completely accurate, and provisions that affect the employee–employer relationship (e.g., development of a code of conduct for senior financial officers).

School-to-work Programs including basic skills training and joint training ventures with universities, community colleges, and high schools.

Selection The process by which an organization attempts to identify applicants with the necessary knowledge, skills, abilities, and other characteristics that will help it achieve its goals.

Self-directed learning A program in which employees take responsibility for all aspects of learning.

Self-efficacy The employees' belief that they can successfully learn the content of a training program.

Self-service Giving employees online access to human resources information.

Settling-in phase Phase of socialization that occurs when employees are comfortable with job demands and social relationships.

Simulation A training method that represents a real-life situation, allowing trainees to see the outcomes of their decisions in an artificial environment.

Situational interview An interview procedure where applicants are confronted with specific issues, questions, or problems that are likely to arise on the job.

Six Sigma process System of measuring, analyzing, improving, and controlling processes once they meet quality standards.

Skill-based pay Pay based on the skills employees acquire and are capable of using.

Specificity The extent to which a performance measure gives detailed guidance to employees about what is expected of them and how they can meet these expectations.

Stakeholders The various interest groups who have relationships with, and consequently, whose interests are tied to the organization (e.g., employees, suppliers, customers, shareholders, community).

Standard deviation rule A rule used to analyze employment tests to determine disparate impact; it uses the difference between the expected representation for minority groups and the actual representation to determine whether the difference between the two is greater than would occur by chance.

Stock options An employee ownership plan that gives employees the opportunity to buy the company's stock at a previously fixed price.

Strategic choice The organization's strategy; the ways an organization will attempt to fulfill its mission and achieve its long-term goals.

Strategic congruence The extent to which the performance management system elicits job performance that is consistent with the organization's strategy, goals, and culture.

Strategic human resource management (SHRM) A pattern of planned human resource deployments and activities intended to enable an organization to achieve its goals.

Strategy formulation The process of deciding on a strategic direction by defining a company's mission and goals, its external opportunities and threats, and its internal strengths and weaknesses.

Strategy implementation The process of devising structures and allocating resources to enact the strategy a company has chosen.

Summary plan description A reporting requirement of the Employee Retirement Income Security Act (ERISA) that obligates employers to describe the plan's funding, eligibility requirements, risks, and so forth within 90 days after an employee has entered the plan.

Support network Trainees who meet to discuss their progress in using learned capabilities on the job.

Sustainability The ability of a company to survive in a dynamic competitive environment. Based on an approach to organizational decision making that considers the long term impact of strategies on stakeholders (e.g., employees, shareholders, suppliers, community).

Taft-Hartley Act The 1947 act that outlawed unfair union labor practices.

Task analysis The process of identifying the tasks, knowledge, skills, and behaviors that need to be emphasized in training.

Team leader training Training of the team manager or facilitator.

Technic of operations review (TOR) Method of determining safety problems via an analysis of past accidents.

Third country A country other than a host or parent country.

Third-country nationals (TCNs) Employees born in a country other than a parent or host country.

360-degree appraisal (feedback systems) A performance appraisal process for managers that includes evaluations from a wide range of persons who interact with the manager. The process includes self-evaluations as well as evaluations from the manager's boss, subordinates, peers, and customers.

Total quality management (TQM) A cooperative form of doing business that relies on the talents and capabilities of both labor and management to continually improve quality and productivity.

Training A planned effort to facilitate the learning of job-related knowledge, skills, and behavior by employees.

Training administration Coordinating activities before, during, and after a training program.

Training design process A systematic approach for developing training programs.

Training outcomes A way to evaluate the effectiveness of a training program based on cognitive, skill-based, affective, and results outcomes.

Transaction processing Computations and calculations used to review and document HRM decisions and practices.

Transfer The movement of an employee to a different job assignment in a different area of the company.

Transfer of training The use of knowledge, skills, and behaviors learned in training on the job.

Transitional matrix Matrix showing the proportion or number of employees in different job categories at different times.

Transnational process The extent to which a company's planning and decision-making processes include representatives and ideas from a variety of cultures.

Transnational representation Reflects the multinational composition of a company's managers.

Transnational scope A company's ability to make HRM decisions from an international perspective.

Uncertainty avoidance One of Hofstede's cultural dimensions; describes how cultures seek to deal with an unpredictable future.

Union shop A union security provision that requires a person to join the union within a certain amount of time after being hired.

Upward feedback A performance appraisal process for managers that includes subordinates' evaluations.

Utility The degree to which the information provided by selection methods enhances the effectiveness of selecting personnel in real organizations.

Utilization analysis A comparison of the race, sex, and ethnic composition of an employer's workforce with that of the available labor supply.

Validity The extent to which a performance measure assesses all the relevant—and only the relevant—aspects of job performance.

Verbal comprehension Refers to a person's capacity to understand and use written and spoken language.

Virtual reality Computer-based technology that provides trainees with a three-dimensional learning experience. Trainees operate in a simulated environment that responds to their behaviors and reactions.

Virtual teams Teams that are separated by time, geographic distance, culture and/or organizational boundaries and rely exclusively on technology for interaction between team members.

Voicing A formal opportunity to complain about one's work situation.

Voluntary turnover Turnover initiated by employees (often whom the company would prefer to keep).

Whistle-blowing Making grievances public by going to the media or government.

Workforce utilization review A comparison of the proportion of workers in protected subgroups with the proportion that each subgroup represents in the relevant labor market.

World Wide Web Service on the Internet that provides browser software allowing the user to explore the items (home pages) on the Web.

Photo Credits

Name and Company Index

Subject Index